THE COMPLETE ON-BOARD

CELESTIAL
NAVIGATOR

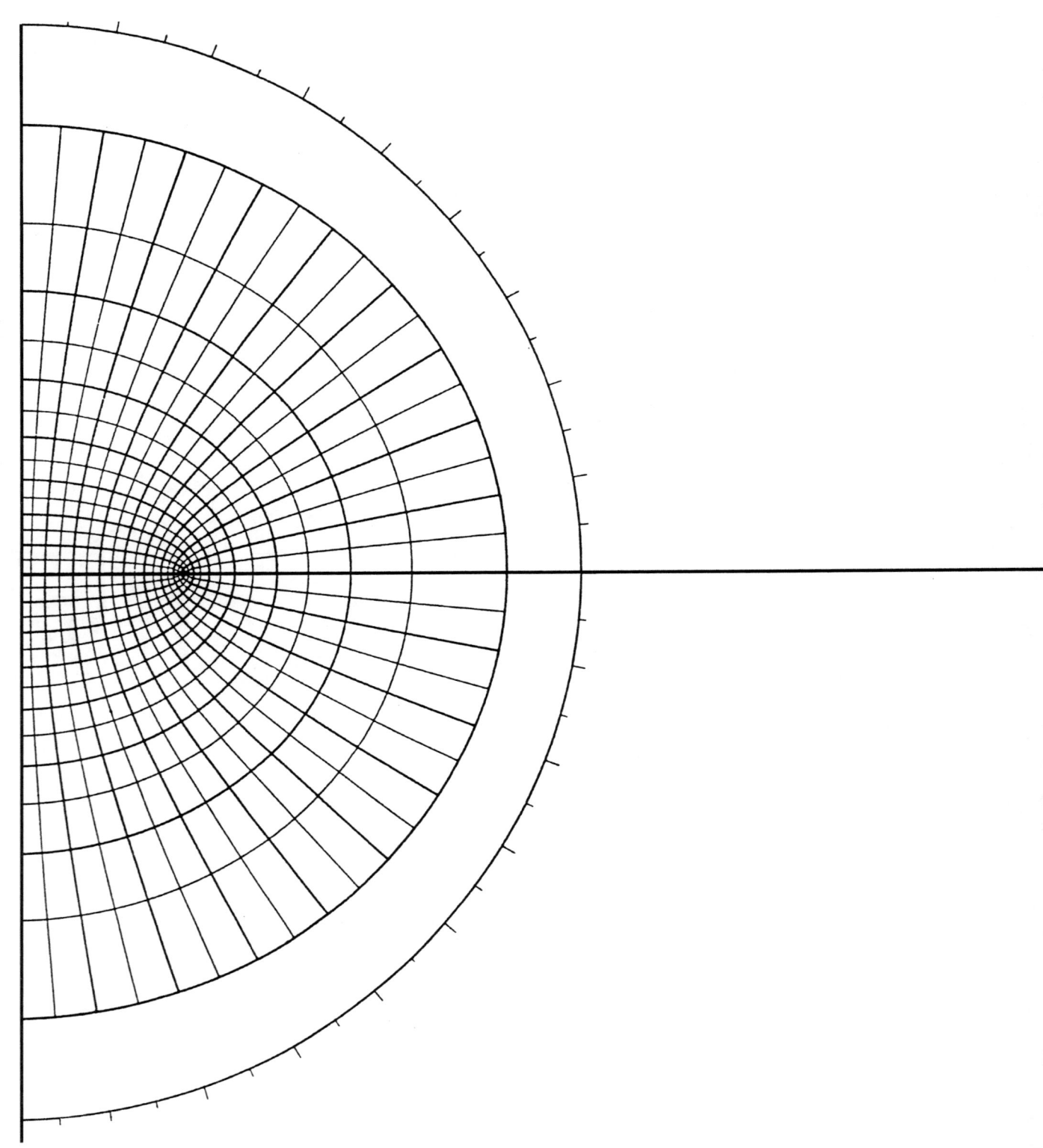

THE COMPLETE ON-BOARD

CELESTIAL
NAVIGATOR

George G. Bennett

CAMDEN, MAINE ◆ NEW YORK ◆ SAN FRANCISCO ◆ WASHINGTON, D.C.
AUCKLAND ◆ BOGOTÁ ◆ CARACAS ◆ LISBON ◆ LONDON ◆ MADRID
MEXICO CITY ◆ MILAN ◆ MONTRÉAL ◆ NEW DELHI ◆ SAN JUAN
SINGAPORE ◆ SYDNEY ◆ TOKYO ◆ TORONTO

International Marine
A Division of The McGraw-Hill Companies

10 9 8 7 6 5 4 3 2 1

Library of Congress Cataloging-in-Publication Data
Bennett, George G., 1926-
        The complete on-board celestial navigator / George G. Bennett.
            p.   cm.
        Includes index.
        ISBN 0-07-007110-1
        1. Nautical astronomy—Handbooks, manuals, etc.   2. Navigation—
Handbooks, manuals, etc.   I. Title.
        VK555.B45   1998
        527—dc21   98-44327
                                                        CIP

Questions regarding the content of this book should be addressed to:

International Marine
P.O. Box 220
Camden, ME 04843
Visit us at www.internationalmarine.com

Questions regarding the ordering of this book should be addressed to:

The McGraw-Hill Companies
Customer Service Department
P.O. Box 547
Blacklick, OH 43004
Retail customers: 1-800-262-4729
Bookstores: 1-800-722-4726

This book is printed on 60-lb QP Offset B/W Smooth.
Printed by Quebecor Printing, Dubuque, Iowa
Design by Shannon Thomas
Production by Shannon Thomas and Dan Kirchoff
Edited by Jonathan Eaton, Captain Bill Brogdon

Glossary of navigational stars on pages 170 to 172 courtesy of *Ocean Navigator*.
Used by permission.

CONTENTS

HOW TO WORK A SIGHT—
An Overview

The Note Numbers refer also to the Line Numbers on the Sight Reduction Form (see page 168). You will find it more efficient if for most of the work, you proceed across the Sight Reduction Form rather than work column by column. In order to keep interpolation errors to a minimum many of the tables are arranged in critical form. If you find your data entry coincides with a tabulated value then take the upper (up the page) value of the correction.

1 Indicate the day of the week as an additional check on the date.

2 The name of the body as identified.

3 It is preferable to use a digital rather than an analogue watch; there is less chance of making a reading mistake.

4 Determine the watch correction by comparing the watch with another timepiece whose error is known or with a Radio Time Signal, e.g., WWV(Colorado) & WWV(H) (Hawaii) USA, MSF England, ZUO South Africa, JJY Japan & VNG Australia.

5 Standard Time or Zone Time, i.e., time referred to a given Time Zone.

6 Time Zones, with a few exceptions, are an integral number of hours.

7 The date of this GMT will change from that given in line 1 under the following circumstances,

   1 In eastern Time Zones if the Time Zone is greater than the Standard Time, add 24 hours to the Standard Time on line 5 and then proceed. The date changes to the previous day.

   2 In western Time Zones if after the addition of the Time Zone, the GMT is greater than 24 hours, subtract 24 hours from the GMT. The date changes to the next day.

8 **ALL BODIES.** Convert all GMTs from Time to Arc using the table on page 176.

9 **STARS.** From pages 26 to 35 (1) look up the GHA of Aries at 0hrs/GMT for the given date and add the Aries Correction given at the side and (2) record the tabulated values of SHA and Declination on lines 10 and 15 respectively.

   SUN and PLANETS. From pages 36 to 65 look up the GHA and Declination for the given date and note the changes v and d. From the interpolation tables on pages 66 and 67 determine the proportional parts of v and d and correct the tabulated values of

GHA and Declination. Alternatively look up the interpolation factor F on page 166 and multiply this by v and d to determine the proportional parts, etc. Note that the change in Declination d is not signed so be careful how you apply the correction. Record the corrected values of GHA and Declination on lines 9 and 15 respectively.

   MOON. For the Moon the process is identical to that for the Sun and Planets except that the tabulated values of (GHA-GMT) and Declination on pages 68 to 97 are given at every 6 hours of GMT. The interpolation tables are on pages 98 to 100. The factor F on page 166 now covers a period of 6 hours. Record the value of Horizontal Parallax (HP, given daily) for use on line 23.

10 See note 9.

11 Add lines 8, 9 and 10 together (do not subtract 360° if the sum exceeds 360°) to obtain the GHA of the body.

12 Enter the DR value of Longitude and heed the sign convention shown in the notes in the left-hand margin.

DATA FOR SIGHT REDUCTION

13 Add or subtract the DR Longitude to obtain the LHA of the body. You may have to add 360° to the GHA to effect the subtraction or subtract 360° from the LHA if it is greater than 360°.

14 Enter the DR value of Latitude.

15 See note 9.

16 See under "Sight Reduction" below.

17 Form the difference, Latitude~Declination (L twiddle D). If the Latitude and Declination have the same name (i.e., both North or both South), take their difference, otherwise take their sum. This quantity has no sign.

SIGHT REDUCTION

13, 14, 15, and 17. Extract the appropriate tabulated quantities under the headings LHA, LAT, DEC, and L~D in the Sight Reduction tables on pages 132 to 151. Note when using these tables, use the minutes column on the left side when entering from the top of the page, but when entering from the bottom use the minutes column on the right-hand side.

16 Add the tabulated quantities on lines 13, 14, and 15. Re-enter the tables and find a value of SUM as near as possible to that sum and write down the tabulated value next to it under the heading RES (Result). Do not attempt to interpolate the tables.

18 Add the values in lines 16 and 17 and look up this sum in the tables from the bottom under the heading ALT (Computed Altitude). Your point of entry in the tables for this quantity is simplified because you know the value of the observed altitude.

ALTITUDE CORRECTIONS AND AZIMUTH

19 Record the observed sextant altitude reading.

20 For the Dip Correction note the height of eye (meters or feet). For convenience the correction, always negative, has been tabulated for the stars on pages 27 to 35, for the Sun and Planets on page 66, and for the Moon on pages 101 and 102.

21 Record the sextant (Index) correction noting its sign: negative if read on the arc or positive if off the arc.

22 The corrections on lines 20 and 21 are combined and applied to the sextant altitude. The result is the apparent altitude.

23 A single altitude correction for the Stars is given on pages 27 to 35, for the Sun or Planets on page 66 and for the Moon on pages 101 and 102.

24 The observed altitude is obtained after the above correction is applied to the apparent altitude from line 22.

25 The Intercept is the difference between the Observed Altitude (line 24) and the Computed Altitude (line 18). A useful mnemonic is GOAT, meaning (G)reater (O)bserved (A)ltitude (T)oward. If the reverse is true then the Intercept is said to be (A)way.

26 Azimuth, to the nearest few degrees, is more than adequate for plotting lines of position from the DR position and can be obtained from one of the following sources:

   1 Azimuths found from the Azimuth tables on pages 152 to 155 with explanation in Section 7.2.

   2 Azimuths obtained from the Prediction and Identification tables on pages 104 to 129 with explanation in Section 5.1.

   3 Azimuths found from the Weir diagrams on pages 156 to 159 with explanation in Section 7.2.

   4 Near to the time of observation, bearings taken with a magnetic compass, corrected for compass error.

1 INTRODUCTION

This book provides, in a compact form, all the essential instructions, almanac data, and tables for finding the latitude and longitude of a ship by celestial navigation and also the means for making a compass check, for a five-year period. Many numerical examples that illustrate the use of its methods and tables are provided as well. This is especially helpful for the navigator who uses celestial methods infrequently.

The difference between this and most other standard works on this subject is that it is entirely self-contained and yet remarkably compact. With the information supplied here, the navigator is independent of any other individual or agency. No longer will it be necessary to purchase separately a book on astronomical navigation, a nautical almanac, a set of tables for reducing sights, and a star and planet identifier.

This has been achieved in part by reducing the accuracy of the almanac data from one-tenth of a minute to one minute of arc. This reduction can be readily tolerated when one considers that now and in the future, astronomical methods will not be the basis for navigation; satellite systems will be the navigator's mainstay for position fixing. The prudent navigator, however, will not rely entirely on satellite systems and electronic devices, which may not be always available, but will choose as well independent methods such as are described here.

The skills required by the celestial navigator can be divided broadly into three areas:

1 An ability to make reliable instrumental observations.
2 An understanding of how astronomical coordinates and other data can be extracted from the almanac section.
3 A proficiency in combining astronomical and terrestrial coordinates with sextant and compass observations to derive data for position fixing and azimuth (true bearing).

2 SCOPE AND CONTENTS

The *Complete On-Board Celestial Navigator* contains the following:

1 Explanations of the equipment used and practical methods for predicting, observing, calculating, and plotting celestial observations.
2 The coordinates of the Sun, Moon, navigational planets and 58 selected stars, and other astronomical data useful for navigation for five years.
3 Tables for interpolating the above coordinates and for correcting sextant observations.
4 Tables and graphs for sight reduction that will enable a navigator to fix position by the Marcq St. Hilaire method and to find the azimuth of any of the principal celestial bodies.
5 Tables for predicting the position in the sky of the Sun, Moon, planets, and 58 stars from which an optimum observing routine can be compiled. These tables can be used in reverse to identify bodies that, in difficult observing conditions, may not have been located or were mistakenly identified.
6 Examples of calculation and plotting that illustrate the use of the almanac and tables.

To keep the interpolation of data and the application of corrections simple and accurate, critical tables have been widely used. This has the advantage that no errors greater than half a unit in the value of the

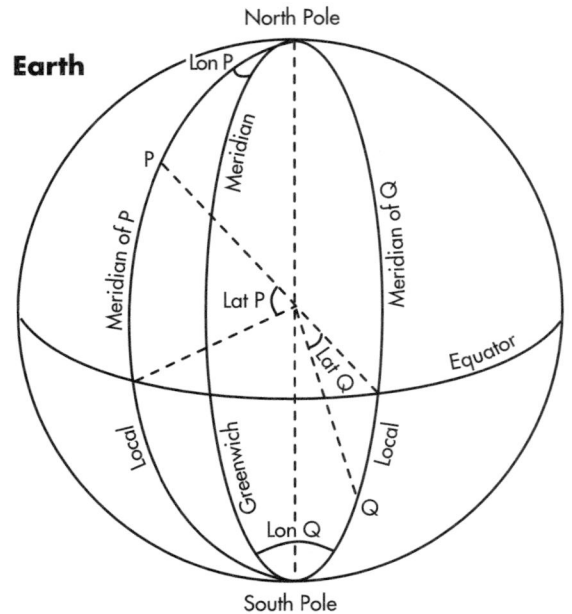

quantity extracted can be incurred, and the average error will be a quarter of a unit. If when entering such a table one finds the point of entry is the same as that given in the table, the upper (that is, moving up the page) value of the two possible data values is chosen.

Before studying celestial navigation, the reader must be conversant with such basic navigational quantities as latitude, longitude, azimuth, etc., and be able to plot the passage of a vessel and fix its position in a coastal situation.

The figure at left shows the position (latitude and longitude) of two points, P and Q, on the surface of the Earth, considered to be spherical. Latitude is measured north or south (0°–90°) from the equator, and longitude east or west (0°–180°) from the Greenwich meridian. P has a north latitude and west longitude, while Q has a south latitude and an east longitude.

3 EQUIPMENT

In addition to this book and basic navigation equipment such as charts, plotting aids, and a hand-bearing compass, the navigator should possess a sextant, a timepiece, and a shortwave radio receiver.

3.1 Sextant

If you have a choice when buying a sextant, then a metal one should be preferred over plastic. Plastic sextants are not as robust as the metal types and can deform and develop errors if allowed to heat up. Secondhand sextants should be checked by an instrument technician before purchase. Large sextants, although they look magnificent, may not be ideal on a small craft. Observations in rough weather with the navigator standing on a heaving deck clinging to a stay are best made with a light sextant. Beginners will also find that observations without a telescope (the telescope may become misted over with salt spray) with both eyes open will give surprisingly good results. Practice using this technique—it is well worthwhile. The unaided human eye is capable of very accurate observations.

The sextant is one of the most delicate pieces of equipment on a vessel and should be treated with utmost care. Before stowing the sextant in its box, wash salt spray off with freshwater and carefully dry the instrument. If the sextant will not be used in the near future, remove the lighting batteries to prevent corrosion. Periodically check it for adjustment, especially if it may have been subjected to rough handling. Sextants vary slightly in their arrangement of adjusting screws, and if the handbook for the instrument is

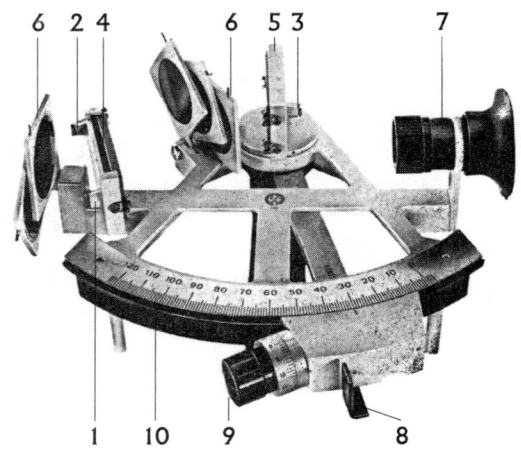

Adjusting screws for 1) index error, 2) side error, 3) perpendicularity error, 4) horizon glass, 5) index mirror, 6) shades, 7) telescope, 8) clamp, 9) micrometer drum, 10) graduated arc.

missing, try to obtain a copy from the manufacturer.

The following errors are listed in the order in which they should be corrected.

Perpendicularity Error

When in adjustment, the index mirror—the mirror that rotates at the center of the instrument—should be perpendicular to the plane of the sextant. To check this, set the instrument to read near the middle of the graduated arc (about 60°). Then look along the edge of the index mirror so you can see both the direct and reflected images of the graduated arc. These images should coincide. If not, then use the adjusting screw(s) on the back of the mirror to perfect coincidence.

Side Error

When in adjustment, the horizon glass should be perpendicular to the plane of the sextant. For this test, select and sight a well-defined distant object; a star is ideal for this purpose. The direct and reflected images of the object should pass over one another as you move the sextant setting across the zero of the graduated arc. If they appear side by side, then use the adjusting screw(s), usually farthest from the graduated arc, on the horizon glass to correct the error.

Index Error

Before observations, and preferably afterward as well, the sextant should be checked for index error. To do this, set the sextant reading to approximately zero, aim at the sea horizon or at a clear horizontal line a mile or so distant, and bring the direct and reflected images into coincidence by operating the micrometer drum, which acts as a slow-motion screw.

If the sextant reading is not zero, this amount is the index error. Provided it is not more than a few minutes of arc, do not attempt to adjust it. If the reading is greater than zero (on the arc), then subtract this amount from all subsequent readings. If the reading is below zero (off the arc), then add this amount.

To correct for a large index error, set the reading to zero and use the adjusting screw at the rear of the horizon glass (fixed mirror) close to the graduated arc to make the two images coincide as nearly as possible.

Each of the above tests and adjustments is designed to be independent of the others. Unavoidable errors do arise and therefore it must be stressed that if any of the above adjustments are made, it is imperative that *all* be checked before one attempts any observations.

3.2   Clocks

An accuracy of about a minute is usually sufficient for routine timekeeping on a vessel. However, for celestial observations this accuracy is increased to a second or so (an error of one second of time will lead to an error of a quarter of a mile in longitude at the equator, less as the latitude increases).

Gone are the days when it was necessary to maintain accurate time using an expensive chronometer. A budget-priced digital watch is adequate. A digital timepiece,

rather than an analogue type with hour, minute, and second hands, is preferred for timing observations. When timing with the latter, the incorrect minute may be inadvertently recorded when the time is near the whole minute.

The worth of a clock is not necessarily its ability to keep time exactly but that the time it keeps can be predicted accurately over many days, provided that it has been subjected to reasonable changes in temperature and motion. If over a test period the clock gains or loses at a steady rate, then it is a simple matter to find a reliable clock correction some days after the last clock correction has been made. Clocks that perform erratically should be rejected. Note that it costs little, and it is a good safeguard, to have two or more clocks on a vessel.

To test a clock's performance, it should be compared with another timepiece of known accuracy or against a radio time signal. The latter method is convenient because continuous time signals are broadcast from many countries. Perhaps the best known are the signals that originate from WWV (Fort Collins) and WWV(H) (Hawaii) on 2.5, 5, 10, 15, and 20 (Fort Collins only) MHz in the USA. Provided ionospheric conditions are not abnormal and depending on the time of day, the signals can be heard throughout the world.

Although it will be necessary to find the Greenwich mean time (GMT or UTC or Zulu) of celestial observations, it is not necessary that the clock keep GMT. If the clock is set to keep standard time (zone time), it is a simple matter to add or subtract the time zone, usually expressed in hours, to obtain GMT. (There are a few exceptions to whole hours of half and quarter hours.) There is a danger if time is kept in GMT, without a date display, that the date may be confused, but when working with standard time the date is known without ambiguity because the appearance of the day (daylight and night) correspond approximately with the clock reading; for example, if the clock reading is about 12 hours and it is daylight, then it is near noon on the date for this day—a fact that would not necessarily be obvious if the clock were keeping GMT. A change of date occurs if, when applying the time zone to obtain GMT, one passes through midnight into the next or previous day. To avoid these problems, some navigators therefore prefer to carry a digital watch set to GMT that also shows the Greenwich date.

4   ALMANAC DATA

The astronomical coordinates of celestial bodies at their times of observation will need to be extracted from the almanac data for the various calculations described in later sections of this book.

Astronomical coordinates can be depicted on the

surface of an imaginary sphere of infinite radius, called the celestial sphere, which has the Earth for its center. The positions of the stars are given by declination and sidereal hour angle (SHA), being the celestial counterparts of latitude and longitude respectively.

Declinations are measured (0°–90°) north or south from the celestial equator. SHAs are measured (0°–360°) not from a terrestrial meridian containing Greenwich but west from a celestial meridian containing "the first point of Aries," often denoted by the zodiacal symbol ♈.

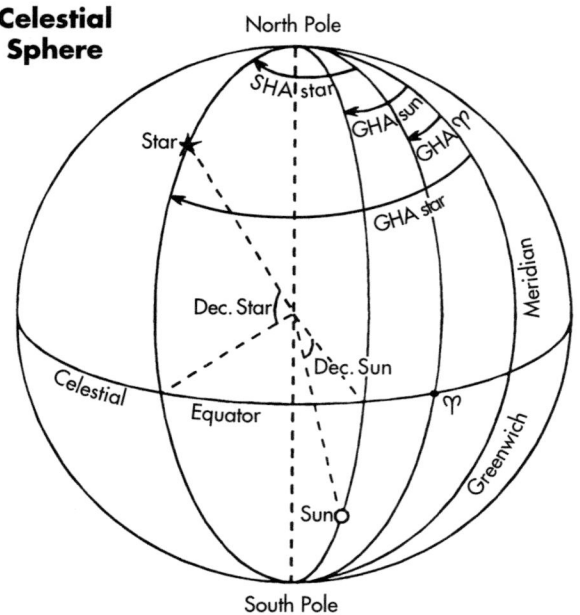

Celestial Sphere

The figure above, in contrast to that on page 8, which may be considered as static with respect to the Earth, can be thought of as dynamic. Apart from the stationary Greenwich meridian, the rest of the above figure can be imagined as rotating from east to west around an axis (dotted line) through the north and south celestial poles. A complete rotation of 360° is the same as 24 hours, i.e., 15° = 1 hour.

The Greenwich hour angle (GHA) is a measure of how far a celestial body has progressed since it passed the meridian of Greenwich. For a star the GHA is found by adding its SHA to the GHA of Aries, a quantity tabulated throughout the year. The declination of stars can be assumed constant.

Unlike stars, which maintain their relative positions on the celestial sphere, the Sun, Moon, and planets appear to move, sometimes in an irregular way, through the patterns (constellations)* of stars, and are therefore assigned individual coordinates of GHA and declination.

(*For convenience in identification, constellations have been named from their appearance. In some cases there is some justification for the name—e.g., the Scorpion, the

Southern Cross—but in many others the name bears only a fanciful relationship to the constellation's appearance.)

4.1 Stars and Aries

The GHA of Aries, and the SHA, declination, and magnitude** of 57 bright stars and Polaris are tabulated for each year on pages 26 to 35. The stars are listed in both alphabetical order and in reverse order of SHA. No interpolation is required to extract the data.

(**"Magnitude" is an indicator of the brightness of a celestial body. In order that the magnitudes of bright and dim bodies can be represented by small numbers, a logarithmic scale for magnitudes has been chosen. The brighter the body, the lower the magnitude number. The brightest stars are said to be of the first magnitude. We can just see a star of the sixth magnitude with the naked eye. Bright bodies may even have a negative value, e.g., Sirius m = −1.6, or show a variable magnitude, e.g., Betelgeuse m = 0.1 to 1.2.)

To find the GHA of Aries at any instant of GMT, convert the GMT from time to arc using the table on page 176. To this add the GHA of Aries tabulated at GMT0hrs on the given Greenwich date, together with the Aries correction found at the side of the table. Then

GHA Aries = GMT(arc) + GHA Aries at GMT0hrs + Aries Corrn.

The GHA of a star is the sum of the GHA Aries as found above and the SHA—

GHA star = GHA Aries + SHA

The declination of a star is the value tabulated.

4.2 Sun and Planets

The GHA and declination of the Sun, Venus, Mars, Jupiter, and Saturn are tabulated at GMT0hrs for every day of the year on pages 36 to 65. Each page lists two months of data. The magnitudes of the planets are quoted for the middle of the month. The daily differences at GMT0hrs of GHA, (v) and declination (d), are also listed. The difference (v) is given a sign to show the direction of change, but the difference (d) is unsigned because declination is marked N or S. Therefore, when interpolating declination the user must note the direction of change.

To find the GHA at any instant of GMT:

1   Convert the GMT from time to arc using the table on page 176.

2 Extract the listed GHA at GMT0hrs and (v) of the body on the date.

3 Using the given value of GMT and (v), look up the correction to GHA at GMT0hrs in the interpolation tables on pages 66 and 67. If (v) is greater than 60', the correction is found by adding the correction for hours to that for minutes in the table. The required GHA is:

GHA Sun/planet = GMT(arc) + GHA at GMT0hrs + (v) Corrn.

To find the declination at the same instant of GMT, use the same technique as described before, but use (d) instead of (v). The required value of declination is:

Declination Sun/planet = Declination at GMT0hrs ± (d) Corrn.

4.3   Moon

The GHA-GMT and declination of the Moon are tabulated at every six hours of GMT for every day of the year on pages 68 to 97. Each page lists two months of data. The horizontal parallax (HP), see explanation in Sections 6.4 and 6.5, is given daily. The times of the phases of the Moon (new, first quarter, full, and last quarter) are summarized at the end of each month. The process of interpolation using the differences of (GHA-GMT) (v) and declination (d) is similar to that used for the Sun and planets except that the data is given at every six hours of GMT. To find the GHA at any instant of GMT:

1 Convert the GMT from time to arc using the table on page 176.

2 Extract the listed (GHA-GMT) at the nearest preceding six hours of GMT(0/6/12/18)hrs and (v) on the date.

3 Using the values of GMT and (v), look up the correction to (GHA-GMT) at GMT(0/6/12/18)hrs in the interpolation tables on pages 99 and 100. The correction is found by adding the correction for hours to that for minutes. The required GHA is then:

GHA Moon = GMT(arc) + (GHA-GMT) at GMT(0/6/12/18)hrs + (v) Corrn.

To find the declination at the same instant of GMT, use the same technique as described before, but use (d) instead of (v) and the interpolation table on page 98.

The required value of declination is:

Declination Moon = Declination at GMT(0/6/12/18)hrs ± (d) Corrn.

4.4   Summary

From the preceding text it becomes clear that the process of finding the GHA of Aries, stars, Sun, planets, and Moon is very similar. The GMT is converted from time to arc, then the tabulated value of the GHA at GMT0hrs for Aries, Sun, and planets—or at a multiple of six hours for the Moon—is extracted and an interpolation correction applied. The sum of these components is then taken. For stars, the GHA is found by adding the SHA. For declination, all that is required is an interpolation correction to be applied to the tabulated declination, except for stars, which do not need interpolation. In later sections we will often be required to find the local hour angle (LHA) of the body, which is a measure of how far the body has progressed since it passed the observer's meridian (north – south). This can be done by applying the longitude (usually the DR value) to the GHA. The following examples illustrate the complete procedure for all bodies:

EXAMPLES

Find the LHAs and declinations for Arcturus, Sun, Moon, and planets in DR latitude N33°50', longitude W072°15' at standard time 4h 40m (time zone W5h) on 26 April 1999.

ARIES		
Standard time	4h	40m
Time zone (+W, −E)	W5	
GMT(time)	9	40
GMT(arc)	145°	00'
GHA Aries at GMT0hrs + Corr.	213	57
GHA Aries	358	57
Longitude (−W, +E)	W072	15
LHA Aries	286	42

STARS		
GHA Aries (see above)	358°	57'
SHA Arcturus	146	05
GHA Arcturus (subtract 360°)	145	02
Longitude (−W, +E)	W072	15
LHA Arcturus	72	47
Declination (Arcturus)	N19°	11'

SUN, MOON, AND PLANETS						
Body	Sun	(v)	Venus	(v)	Mars	(v)
GMT(arc)	145°00'		145°00'		145°00'	
GHA*	180 31	+2'	139 24	−16'	1 43	+82'
Corrn.	+1		−7		+33	
GHA	325 32		284 17		147 16	
Long**	W072 15		W072 15		W072 15	
LHA	253 17		212 02		75 01	
		(d)		(d)		(d)
Dec.*	N13°18'	+19'	N24°42'	+10'	S11°30'	−5'
Corrn.	+8		+4		−2	
Dec.	N13 26		N24 46		S11 28	
Body	Jupiter	(v)	Saturn	(v)	Moon	(v)
GMT(arc)	145°00'		145°00'		145°00'	
GHA*	197 27	+46'	178 35	+52'	45 05	−164'
Corrn.	+18		+21		−1 40	(−100)
GHA	342 45		323 56		188 25	
Long**	W072 15		W072 15		W072 15	
LHA	270 30		251 41		116 10	
		(d)		(d)		(d)
Dec.*	N5°40'	+6'	N11°39'	+2'	N7°23'	−60'
Corrn.	+3		+1		−37	
Dec.	N5 43		N11 40		N6 46	

*   *Listed values for the Sun and planets at GMT0hrs on the date or for Moon listed values at nearest preceding GMT6hrs on date.*
**   *−W, +E*

4.5   Alternative Interpolation Method

If a simple four-function calculator is available, the following interpolation technique may be used instead of the method previously described. A table for this is on page 166. The technique is as follows:

1   Look up in the table the value of a factor (F) that corresponds to the given value of GMT. For the Moon, use GMT minus the multiple of six hours chosen for extracting the Moon's coordinates. There is no need to interpolate F.

2   Multiply (v) and (d) by F to obtain the desired corrections.

This method is slightly more accurate than that previously described. It is suggested that both methods be tried and the one more suited to the user's needs be adopted.

From the following table, a comparison can be made of the interpolation corrections found using this and the previous method.

GMT 9h 40m CORRN. = F × (v) or (d)					
	F	(v)	Corrn.	(d)	Corrn.
Sun	0.41	+2'	+1'	+19'	+8'
Venus	0.41	−16	−7	+10	+4
Mars	0.41	+82	+34	−5	−2
Jupiter	0.41	+46	+19	+6	+2
Saturn	0.41	+52	+21	+2	+1
Moon	0.611	−164	−100	−60	−37

5 PLANNING AND OBSERVATIONS

5.1   Planning

An observation is a timed sextant altitude taken to a celestial body. The simplest of such observations are those made during the daylight hours when there are few restrictions on the visibility of the horizon and the identification of celestial bodies. However, observations at these times will generally be confined to the Sun and, for half of the month, the Moon. With such a small choice of bodies, the navigational information that results, although valuable, will be limited. Nevertheless, the prudent navigator will, weather permitting, take observations throughout the day. Even though they may not be processed, they will form a valuable store of potentially useful information.

To take advantage of a wider choice of bodies will require some planning, and therefore—before making any celestial observations—it is advisable to check on what bodies can be seen. This may be done conveniently using the prediction and identification tables on pages 104 to 129, which give the altitudes and azimuths of 58 stars between the latitudes of N60° and S60° at 10° intervals for every 10° of LHA of Aries. A separate tabulation for use with the Sun, Moon, and planets is given at the bottom of each page, covering declinations N30° to S30° at 5° intervals.

To locate all the bodies that can be seen at a given instant of time, find the LHA of Aries and the LHA and declination of the Sun, Moon, and planets for the time of observation. If observations are planned for the time of civil twilight—that is, when stars, planets, and the horizon are visible (see Section 5.5)—you may wish to design an observation routine that optimizes the use of the restricted time available.

An example of the calculations involved is shown in detail in Section 4 and is summarized as follows:

Body	LHA	Declination
Aries	286° 42′	
Sun	253 17	N13° 26′
Moon	116 10	N6 46
Venus	212 02	N24 46
Mars	75 01	S11 28
Jupiter	270 30	N5 43
Saturn	251 41	N11 40

Turn now to page 111 of the prediction and identification tables for latitude N30° (nearest 10°), and in the column for LHA of Aries equal to 290° (nearest 10°) are listed the altitudes and azimuths to the nearest degree of those stars that are above the horizon at this time. The altitude is printed first, followed by a space and then the azimuth—a three-figure number in bold type. If a body is below the horizon, "# ###" will be shown, indicating that the body is not visible. The altitudes and azimuths of the Sun, Moon, and planets are found from the tables at the bottom of each page. Enter the table on the left with the value of declination (nearest 5°) and from the top with the LHA of the body (nearest 10°). The results of that search are as follows:

Body	LHA	Declination	Altitude	Azimuth
Sun	250°	N15°	#	###
Moon	120	N5	#	###
Venus	210	N25	#	###
Mars	80	S10	4°	256°
Jupiter	270	N5	2	086
Saturn	250	N10	#	###

In summary there are 27 stars and two planets available for observation. As will be discussed later, however, many of the bodies may not be selected for observation because of other restrictions that the observer may wish to impose.

In the first instance, bodies should be selected that are not at very low or high altitudes. At low alti-

tudes the brightness of stars and planets is diminished because the light has to pass through more atmosphere than with those sights taken at high altitudes; there is a loss of about two magnitudes between the zenith and the horizon. In addition, because the light rays pass close to the sea's surface, the refraction correction (bending of the light path) is large and may be adversely affected by abnormal atmospheric conditions. At high altitudes, although the refraction correction (zero in the zenith) is small and of greater certainty, it will be difficult to estimate when the body and horizon are in proper coincidence. Bringing a body down to the horizon with the sextant can be a difficult operation.

From the bodies that satisfy the altitude restrictions, select those that will give a good fix. One observation to each of two bodies, not in line but preferably close to 90° apart in azimuth, will be the minimum requirement to obtain a fix. If time and opportunity permit, observations to a number of bodies are desirable to provide not only a check on the observations and calculations but an assessment of the quality of the observed position.

It is good practice also to select the bodies that are well distributed in azimuth because even if there is, say, a constant error in altitude—for example, a poor determination of the sextant index correction—the selected position should lie within the figure formed by the intersecting lines of position (see Section 7.3). For three well-spaced lines not intersecting at a point, the figure is called a "cocked hat."

5.2   Sextant Observations

Observations to celestial bodies with a sextant are not difficult. However, good results can be achieved only if the observer has acquired skill and confidence in handling the instrument. Before attempting observations on the Sun, a suitable shade should be swung in front of the index mirror to guard against permanently damaging the eyes. Also, if there is glare on the sea, or the horizon is not sharp, a light shade in front of the horizon glass may be of assistance. The following guidelines may be helpful:

1   Face the body to be observed and with the sextant set roughly on zero, sight the body in the index mirror. Unclamp and slowly bring this reflected image of the body down to the horizon while moving the index arm along the graduated scale. Clamp gently and then tilt the sextant from side to side like a pendulum and watch the body make an arc near the

horizon; the lowest point of the arc is where the altitude is measured. Perfect the coincidence by operating the slow-motion screw until the body appears to touch the horizon. Call out "time" to the recorder or, if operating single-handed, start counting seconds until you can note a time on the watch. The watch reading minus the seconds count is the time of observation. Read the degrees on the main scale and add the reading from the micrometer drum, which is graduated from 0 to 60 minutes.

This technique is suitable for stars and planets, but with the Sun or Moon the contact of the body with the horizon is made with either the upper or lower limbs (edges). The following figure shows the appearance in the field of view of the path of the Sun's lower limb and a star as they touch the horizon at the time of observation.

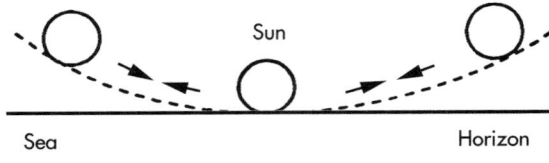

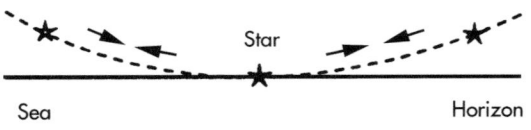

2   If it is difficult to bring a dim body down to the horizon, the following technique may be employed. Turn the sextant upside down, and with the sextant set roughly on zero, point to the body. Bring the horizon up to the body by sliding the index arm along the graduated scale, then clamp and reverse the sextant. The body can now be relocated on the horizon below the body.

3   When the weather is fine, take observa-tions from as high a vantage point as possible.

4   In fog or mist it may be necessary to find a low observation point in order to see the horizon clearly.

5   When there is broken cloud, the body may appear only fleetingly; under these circumstances the navigator should pre-pare a list of altitudes for setting the sex-tant and compass bearings to locate the bodies. The prediction and identification tables are invaluable for this purpose. As a precaution, if you are uncertain of the identity of any body, take a compass bear-ing to help in later identification.

6   When the vessel is rolling and pitching heavily, it is best to take observations amidships to limit the motion of the observer and the variability of the height of eye.

7   Get into the habit of making observations as early as possible at evening twilight and as late as possible at morning twilight, when the horizon will have its best defini-tion. At morning twilight, however, it is all too easy to wait too long and see the stars disappear as you try to observe their altitudes.

5.3   Identification

Situations will sometimes arise when observations have been made to the wrong body or, because of partial cloud cover, the identity of the observed body is in doubt. For example, a few fleeting observations between clouds may be all that is possible in inclement weather, but nevertheless a good position fix may be possible. If there is a doubt about the body's identity at the time of observation, it is a sensible precaution to note the brightness and, if possible, take a compass bearing to the body. Even a rough direction may be of considerable value in deciding which body has been observed. The process of identification can best be illustrated with an example:

EXAMPLE

Identify a body that has been observed at an alti-tude of 33° 15′ with a magnetic bearing of 225° (mag-netic variation W10°) in the circumstances given in Section 4.

When we examine the prediction and identification tables we find that seven bodies have altitudes within a few degrees of the observed altitude as follows:

Body	Altitude	Azimuth
Alpheratz	28°	071°
Schedar	30	039
Polaris	30	001
Kochab	35	342
Sabik	35	219
Nunki	33	187
Markab	37	093

There is only one body, Sabik, which has an azimuth (219°) that is close to the observed value, i.e., 215° (225°–10°).

5.4 Observation Methods

There are two approaches to making observations: Either (a) make a single observation on a large number of bodies, or (b) make multiple observations on each of a few bodies. It is also possible to make observations combining both techniques. For (a) there is an advantage in that many lines of position (see Section 7.3) result from the calculations. These should all intersect closely together. If one or more lines cannot be plotted or is markedly distant from this network of lines, we should suspect that a mistake has been made in the observation or calculation, or the incorrect body has been observed. In the latter situation an examination of the prediction and identification tables as described in Section 5.3 may assist in identifying the correct body.

If calculations are not being made on a programmable calculator or computer but by tables, then observing a large number of bodies will lead to the burden of a large number of sight reductions. For (b), multiple observations to a few bodies can be made quickly because the sextant does not have to be reset from one observation to the next on the same body. The large number of calculations can be avoided in (b) if one observation that best represents the whole series of observations on that body is selected.

First, one should notice that if the body lies to the east of the meridian, altitudes will increase with time, and decrease with time to the west. When a body is close to the meridian (north or south), altitudes change slowly with time.

It is best to make a more detailed examination of the multiple observation data so that possible mistakes can be excluded and an assessment made of the quality of the data. This may be done without any extra calculation as follows. Take a piece of prepared squared paper, a sample of which is given on page 167, mark off convenient vertical and horizontal scales for altitude and time, and plot each observation point (see the example on page 103). If the observations are error free, the observation points will follow a steady slope or trend (change of altitude with time). This slope can be found, using the diagram on page 161, where we see that approximate values of latitude and azimuth are required for its evaluation. The azimuth is usually known from a prediction or compass bearing or can be obtained from the prediction and identification tables. Now construct a line anywhere on the paper corresponding to this slope (dotted line)—positive upward, negative downward. Then draw a line parallel to it that best fits the observation points (full line). In the example given, it appears that the first observation deviates markedly from the general trend of the remaining observations, and for this reason it has been excluded. The navigator may have noted at the time that the observation was uncharacteristically poor or a mistake could have been made in reading the sextant or recording the time.

The best single representative observation is the mean of all the accepted observations, which can be found by taking the average of the times and the altitudes. Taking averages can be a source of arithmetical mistake, which can be avoided by taking instead a point on this line of best fit. *Any convenient point* will do, and this best estimate can be used in the calculations.

This technique should be used only if the time interval between the first and last observation is small, i.e., not greater than five minutes; otherwise, the observation points may follow a discernible curve instead of a straight line. The departure from a straight line (curvature) is at a maximum for bodies near the meridian (north–south) and a minimum near the prime vertical (east–west).

5.5 Sunrise, Sunset, and Twilight

A knowledge of the times of the rising and setting of the Sun is not only helpful for gauging the hours of darkness and light but also useful when determining azimuth by the method of amplitudes (see Section 8). At the beginning of morning and the end of evening civil twilight, the Sun's center is 6° below the horizon, and in good conditions the bright stars and the horizon are visible. These are ideal times for making observations with a sextant, and they extend for some time between the beginning of morning twilight and sunrise and between sunset and the end of evening twilight. Note that in equatorial latitudes this period is short but becomes quite long in high latitudes. The graphs on pages 130 and 131 give the LAT (local apparent time)—the local time kept by the apparent or real Sun—of sunrise, sunset, and twilight referred to the meridian of the observer. An additional graph gives the correction (the equation of time with the sign reversed) to LAT to obtain LMT (local mean time)—the local time kept by the mean Sun: a fictitious body. If it were possible to view the apparent (real) and the mean Sun in the sky, we would see the mean Sun traveling at a constant rate along the celestial equator and the apparent Sun sometimes ahead or behind the mean Sun. The apparent Sun would be removed from the equator by a distance equal to its declination.

The following examples illustrate the use of these tables in finding the times of sunrise or sunset and the beginning or end of civil twilight:

EXAMPLE

Find the standard time (time zone W2h) of sunrise on 18 August 1999, in latitude N48° 40', longitude W033° 30' (W2h 14m, page 176).

LAT of sunrise (page 130)	4h	50m
Correction (same page)		+4
LMT of sunrise	4	54
Longitude (+ W, −E)	W2	14
GMT	7	08
Time zone (−W , +E)	W2	
Standard time of sunrise	5	08

EXAMPLE

Find the standard time (time zone E12h) of the end of evening civil twilight on 25 January 1999, in latitude

S34° 20', longitude E170° 45' (E11h 23m, page 176).

LAT of civil twilight (page 131)	19h	25m
Correction (same page)		+12
LMT of Civil Twilight	19	37
Longitude (+ W, −E)	E11	23
GMT	8	14
Time zone (−W , +E)	E12	
Standard time of civil twilight	20	14

Special Cases of Rising and Setting

In high latitudes and at certain times of the year, it may not be possible to find a point of interpolation in the diagrams on pages 130 and 131. These special situations are categorized as follows:

1. The Sun will remain continuously above the horizon if the latitude and declination are of the same name—that is, both north or both south—and their sum is greater than 89° 10'.
2. The Sun will remain continuously below the horizon if the latitude and declination are of opposite names and their sum is greater than 90° 50'.
3. Civil twilight will last all night if the latitude and declination are of the same name and their sum is greater than 84°.

6 SEXTANT ALTITUDE CORRECTIONS

Corrections must be applied to observed sextant altitudes in the correct sequence. If a number of bodies have been observed, time will be saved if each correction is applied to all bodies in turn rather than treating each body separately, that is, work across the form sheet (see page 168). All of the altitude correction tables are set out in the form of critical tables. The complete process of correcting observed altitudes to obtain the true altitude is usually described as "clearing the altitude."

6.1 Dip Correction

The visible sea horizon lies slightly below a horizontal plane stretching out from the observer. Therefore, sextant altitude observations made using the sea horizon as a reference are too large and need to be corrected. The size of this correction, called dip, is always negative and depends upon how high the observer is above the sea surface (height of eye). For convenience, tables of dip for heights of eye in meters and feet are included throughout this book.

6.2 Index Correction

This is also known as sextant correction. The correction should be determined preferably before and after observations have been completed (see "Index Error," p. 9). It should be added to the sextant altitude if it is "off the arc" and subtracted if "on the arc." It is immaterial in which order the dip and sextant corrections are made to the sextant altitude, but they must be applied before further corrections are made. The altitude corrected for dip and sextant correction is called the apparent altitude.

6.3 Star and Planet Corrections

Light coming from a celestial body toward an observer on the Earth travels in a straight line through the vacuum of outer space until it meets the Earth's atmosphere. Unless this light comes from directly overhead, upon entering the Earth's atmosphere the light bends in a vertical plane containing the observer and the body. The amount of bending, called astronomical refraction, reaches a maximum of about 34' near the horizon but reduces to about 10' at about 5° altitude and to zero in the zenith. Tables of astronomical refraction correction are given in many places throughout this work with the apparent altitude as argument. The correction is always negative.

6.4 Sun Correction

When the Sun and Moon are observed, it is not possible to make an accurate pointing on the center of the body, which is where the astronomical coordinates are referred. Instead, observations are made to the edges (limbs) of the body. Reducing an observation made to the upper or lower limb will require a correction equal to the radius (semidiameter, or s.d.) of the body.

In addition, another phenomenon called parallax in altitude, or just parallax, must be compensated for. This correction arises because of the simplifying assumption made in astronomical calculations that all celestial bodies lie at an infinite distance from the Earth. Allowance for this, for bodies other than stars, can be made by applying a correction, always positive, to the measured altitude. This parallax correction is extremely small for the Sun and planets but for the Moon it can be in excess of one degree. On page 66 is a table for correcting observations made to either the upper or lower limb of the Sun. This correction, using apparent altitude as argument, allows for refraction, parallax, and semidiameter and may be either positive or negative.

6.5 Moon Correction

These tables on pages 101 and 102 incorporate the same components as that for the Sun except that it is necessary to allow for the variable distance of the Moon from the Earth. The measure of this distance is horizontal parallax (HP), which is tabulated for every day of the year.

Because the Moon correction can have identical values for two different altitudes, the argument may be entered from either side of the columns of tabulated correction. It is also apparent from the tables that the correction is sensitive to altitude changes at low altitudes, and therefore the altitude argument is given in degrees and minutes up to about 10° or so when the correction reaches a maximum. Between about 10° and 20° the correction remains almost constant. At higher altitudes, the altitude argument is given only in degrees. The correction may be either positive or negative.

6.6 Summary

The process of applying the dip and sextant correction is common to all bodies. Only one further correction to altitude is necessary to complete the process. This is obtained directly from the tables appropriate to the body.

The following examples illustrate the procedures in a variety of situations:

EXAMPLES

Body	Sextant Altitude	H. of E.	Dip	Sextant Corrn.	Apparent Altitude
Star	18° 43'	5.1m	−4'	+3'	18° 42'
Sun	25 17	15ft	−4	−4	25 09
Planet	36 07	18.1m	−7	−8	35 52
Moon	8 54	6ft	−2	−2	8 50

Body	Apparent Altitude	Altitude Corrn.	Observed Altitude
Star	18° 42'	−3'	18° 39'
Sun (LL)	25 09	+14	25 23
Planet	35 52	−1	35 51
Moon LL*	8 50	+67	9 57
* HP = 58'			

7 The Marcq St. Hilaire Method

This method has been universally accepted as the simplest and most practical technique for position fixing. A line of position (LOP) for each observed body can be drawn on the chart using an "intercept" and "azimuth." The intercept is the difference between the corrected observed sextant altitude, and the altitude obtained from calculation, using the celestial coordinates of the body and the best known position, usually the DR, of the observer. The intercept is marked off from the DR position in a direction (calculated azimuth) toward or away from the body. The LOP is drawn from this point at right angles to this direction. The position of the vessel is somewhere along the LOP. Obviously two or more LOPs, which give a reasonable intersection, will resolve that uncertainty. The data required for this process, called sight reduction, are as follows:

1   The LHA obtained from the GHA of the body as described in Section 4, using the DR longitude.

LHA = GHA ± DR longitude (+east, −west)

2   The DR latitude.
3   The declination of the body as described in Section 4.

7.1   Intercept

From the LHA, DR latitude, and declination, an altitude is calculated. The observed altitude is obtained from the sextant altitude after those corrections described in Section 6 have been applied. The intercept is found from the difference "observed minus calculated altitude," expressed in minutes of arc (nautical miles).

The sight reduction tables on pages 132 to 151 are designed to provide the navigator with a simple, universal method of calculating the altitude, using a minimum number of steps. There are no decimal points, only one rule for the manipulation of data, no interpolation, and no special cases in which certain combinations of data lead to poor or even indeterminate solutions, as may happen with some other methods. Because we can work with a DR position, plotting is simpler, and for most situations the intercepts are short. If a chosen position is adopted—that is, latitude is taken to the nearest whole degree and LHA rounded off to the nearest whole degree—the intercepts are often long. Sometimes it is not known until after plotting that a mistake may have been made in the sight reduction procedure.

The process of sight reduction, listed below, is best followed on a form sheet (see page 168), which can be followed in conjunction with the information in "How to Work a Sight—An Overview," page 6.

Step 1   Write down the values of the LHA, latitude, and declination. Form the difference between latitude and declination, L ~ D (called "L twiddle D"), where "twiddle" (~) means that if the latitude and declination have the same name, take their difference; but if they have opposite names, take their sum. Unlike most other sight

reduction tables, this table requires only this one special rule.

Step 2   Extract the appropriate quantities under the headings LHA (local hour angle), LAT (latitude), DEC (declination), and L ~ D from the sight reduction tables. Like standard trignometrical tables, these tables are arranged to use the minutes column on the left-hand side when entering from the top of the page, but when entering from the bottom use the minutes column on the right-hand side.

Step 3   Add the tabulated quantities for LHA, LAT, and DEC. This is labeled SUM. Reenter the tables and find under the heading SUM a value as near as possible to it. Write down the tabulated value next to it under the heading RES (Result). Do not attempt to interpolate the tables.

Step 4   Add the value of RES found from the tables to the tabulated value for L ~ D previously extracted and look up this sum in the tables from the bottom under the heading ALT. The search for this place in the tables is simplified because the value you seek is close to that tabulated for the sextant or observed altitude.

EXAMPLE

LHA	356° 12′	38554		
LAT	N48 31	2331		
DEC	S21 39	414		
		SUM 41299	RES	136
LAT ~ DEC	70 10			66071
ALT	19 45			66207

The intercept is the difference between the above calculated altitude "Hc" and the observed altitude "Ho."

7.2   Azimuth

To construct LOPs, plotting the azimuth of celestial bodies is required. Provided the DR position is not too far removed from the true position, the intercepts will be short. Therefore the required azimuth accuracy will not be very high; a few degrees should be sufficient for most work. It is best to be familiar with one of the methods described under "Azimuth Tables," on page 19, and "Weir Diagrams," on page 20.

If only an approximate azimuth is needed, two other techniques are available:

1 Close to the time of observation, take compass bearings to the various bodies. After correcting for compass error (magnetic variation and deviation), true bearings may be found. The reverse process of finding the compass error from an observed compass bearing and a calculated azimuth is also possible using one of the methods described under "Azimuth Tables," on page 19, and "Weir Diagrams," on page 20, and in Sections 8 and 9.1. The accuracy of azimuth derived from a compass bearing is only as good as the error of observation combined with the uncertainty of the compass error (magnetic deviation and variation).

2 Azimuths can be found directly from the prediction and identification tables on pages 104 to 129. Details of the way in which these tables can be used will be found in Section 5.1. The accuracy of azimuths found by this method may not be very high because we have chosen a latitude and LHA to the nearest 10° in order to enter the tables.

Azimuth Tables

This method of finding the solution of azimuth (see pages 152 to 155), involves one table with different points of entry. No interpolation is required, and it is one of the simplest techniques for finding azimuth with an accuracy of one or two degrees.

Step 1 Enter the table at the top with the declination (ignore the N or S) and from the side with the value of LHA. Record the tabulated value (X).

Step 2 Enter the table again at the top with the altitude and find in the vertical column a value that most nearly corresponds to that of (X), found in Step 1. On the same line but on the side opposite that used in Step 1, record the two values of azimuth.

In most cases, it will be obvious which of the two values is correct, e.g., from prediction or a compass bearing (see Section 7.2). If you are not sure which of the two values of azimuth to select, mainly because the body is near to the east–west line (prime vertical), proceed as follows:

Step 3 (a) If the declination has the opposite name of the latitude, then the body lies in the southern sky in north latitudes, and in the northern sky in south latitudes. (b) If the declination has the same name (north or south—N or S) as the latitude and is greater than the latitude, then in northern latitudes the body lies in the northern sky and in southern latitudes in the southern sky.

If the ambiguity has not been resolved in the previous steps—that is, the declination has the same name as the latitude but is numerically smaller—then proceed as follows:

Step 4 Enter the table from the bottom with the declination and note the value immediately over the point of entry (Y). Enter the table again from the left-hand side with the latitude and find on the same line a value that most nearly corresponds to that of (Y). At the bottom of this column, read off the value of altitude, which is the prime vertical altitude—the altitude when the body lies directly east or west of the observer. A comparison between the values of the observed and prime vertical altitudes will resolve the ambiguity of whether the body lies to the north or south of the prime vertical. A simple summary of the situation in steps 3 and

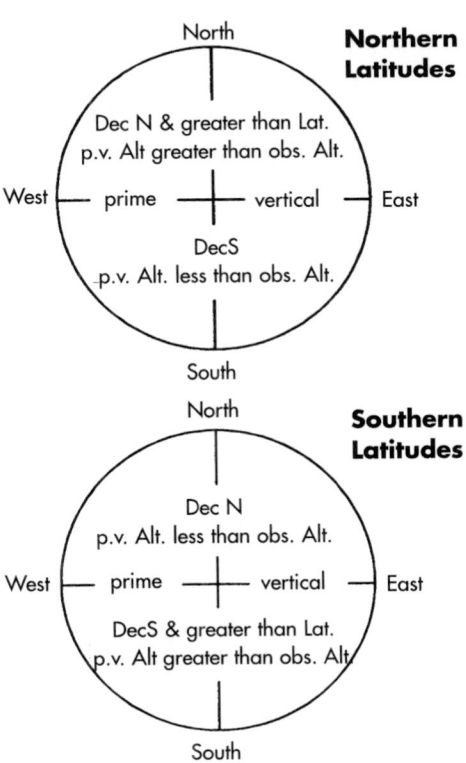

4 above is given in the diagrams above:

Choose the latitude, north or south, that corresponds to your situation. Compare the declination or prime vertical altitude with those given in the diagram to decide whether the body lies in the northern or southern azimuth quadrants.

EXAMPLE

Dec.	LHA	X	Alt. (Obs.)	Lat.	Y	Alt. (P.V.)	Az.
S18°	325°	545	23°	N41°			144°
N63	123	380	20	N37			336
N15	284	936	19	N27	259	35°	082
N23	62	812	34	N59	390	27	259
N16	301	823	4	S53			056
S54	109	555	24	S42			217
S17	88	955	11	S36	292	30	257
S8	345	256	60	S35	139	14	031

Weir Diagrams

The accuracy of this method is superior to that of those previously described. The original Weir diagram as used by the British Navy (Admiralty Chart No. 5000) has been redrawn on pages 156 to 159 so that it is not necessary to distinguish between colors and double graduated scales that were required in the original diagram to discriminate between north and south celestial and terrestrial hemispheres—a fruitful source of error. Each diagram consists of a series of ovals (ellipses) that correspond to latitude and a series of radiating curves (hyperbolas) that correspond to the LHA of the body. The steps are as follows:

1   Select one of the diagrams appropriate to the latitude, north or south and LHA, east or west.
2   Mark a point on the vertical line (meridian) corresponding to the declination (north or south) of the body. Point X.
3   Locate a position on the LHA scale corresponding to the LHA of the body and follow this inward until it first cuts the required latitude ellipse. Point Y.

The direction of the line X–Y is the azimuth of the body, which may be measured either by

(a) placing a protractor, oriented with respect to the vertical line, with the center on point X and reading off the azimuth on the protractor scale, or

(b) transferring the direction X–Y to the center of the diagram with a parallel ruler and reading off the azimuth on the outer azimuth scale.

For practice with this method use the examples given under "Azimuth Tables," this page, and those on the diagrams.

7.3   The Position Fix

Every timed altitude observation, be it a single observation or the representative of a set of observations on a body, will give an LOP. This LOP may be constructed on the chart from the intercept—which is the difference between the observed and computed altitudes—and the azimuth of the body. The position of the observer would lie somewhere along this line. It is obvious that if we have made observations to two bodies at different azimuths, the intersection of the two LOPs would give a position for the observer. Observations to more than two bodies are desirable because they will not only provide a check on the observations and calculations but also allow an assessment of the quality of the observed position.

If we would rather not clutter up the chart with a lot of construction lines, we can draw the LOPs and so forth on a plotting sheet (see page 169), and transfer the resulting position to the chart. In either case, the principles for plotting are the same. Proceed as follows:

1   Mark a point on the chart, or adopt the center of the protractor scale on the plotting sheet, corresponding to the DR position and draw radial lines (azimuth lines) from this point corresponding to the azimuths of the bodies.
2   Using the scale of latitude on the side of the chart, or on the central vertical line of the plotting sheet, mark off the intercepts along the azimuth lines, toward or away from the bodies. (One minute of altitude equals 1 minute of latitude equals 1 nautical mile.) Intercepts are said to be "toward" if the observed altitude is greater than the calculated altitude and "away" if otherwise. If the intercept is "away," then the azimuth line must be produced backward from the DR position to mark off the intercept.
3   Draw lines, LOPs, at right angles to the azimuth lines—through these points—

which were marked off in step 2. These lines should be made heavy, to distinguish them from the azimuth lines with arrowheads at the ends of the lines and the name of the body written against them.

4 If more than two bodies have been observed and the resulting LOPs do not intersect at a point but crisscross closely together, we must select a point that best fits this configuration. In so doing, try to keep the selected point as close as possible to all LOPs. Some simple configurations are shown as follows:

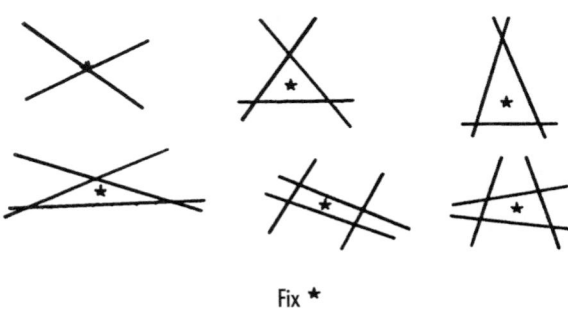

Fix ★

5 Finally, read the latitude and longitude of the selected point. If using a plotting sheet, be sure to use the central vertical scale for changes in latitude; for changes in longitude, use the longitude scale selected for the DR latitude at the bottom right-hand corner of the sheet.

There have been many suggestions as to where this point of fix lies but—provided systematic errors are not suspected—the most probable position lies such that the sum of the squares of the distances (errors or residuals) from this point to each LOP is a minimum. We are applying the "principle of least squares," a universally accepted method of dealing with redundant data. Taking the average, or mean, of a set of numbers is a good illus-

tration of this; for example, the average of 6, 7, 9, and 6 is 7 (sum divided by four); the differences, without regard to sign, from the average and the individual numbers are 1, 0, 2, and 1, and the sum of the squares of these differences is 6. You will find that there is no number, other than 7, that will give a smaller sum of squares of differences. To become familiar with the technique of least squares, set yourself some examples of plots of LOPs at a large scale. Select the point of fix, measure off the distances (errors), and form the sum of their squares. Move the point of fix to another position and compare the new sum of squares with the previous value. After a little practice, you will be able to choose the optimum point without taking any measurement. This process of selecting the point of fix could be called "eyeball least squares."

EXAMPLE OF A POSITION FIX

Timed sextant altitude observations were made to four bodies on the morning of 30 May 1999. Determine the vessel's position using the following additional data: DR position N10° 30', W135° 50'; watch correction 15s fast; time zone W9h; height of eye 2.0m; and index correction 5' off the arc.

Body	Watch Time			Sextant Altitude	
Vega	5h	15m	35s	39°	57'
Fomalhaut	5	16	20	45	50
Jupiter	5	17	18	33	56
Moon UL	5	18	52	9	10
Fix: latitude N10° 51', longitude W135° 31'					

See pages 162 and 163 for full details of extracting almanac data, altitude corrections, sight reduction, and plotting.

8 AMPLITUDES

One of the simplest and most practical ways of checking a compass is to observe the Sun or Moon when near rising or setting. At these times their azimuths do not change very rapidly, especially in low to medium latitudes. This form of solution assumes that the altitude of the body at rising or setting is zero, which

could only be the case if the observer's eye were situated at sea level and the Earth had no atmosphere. To observe the altitude close to zero, the Sun should be observed when the lower limb lies about a semidiameter above the horizon, and the Moon when the upper limb touches the horizon—at the time of appearing and disappearing. The accuracy of this method is similar to that described under "Azimuth Tables," on page 19.

Given the latitude and the declination of the body, the amplitude (horizontal angle from the east or west points) can be derived from a formula or obtained from special tables. The azimuth tables on pages 152 to 155, although not intended for this purpose, can be used to derive amplitudes conveniently as follows:

Step 1 Enter the table at the bottom with the declination (N or S) and note the value immediately over the point of entry (P).

Step 2 Enter the table at the top with the latitude (ignore the N or S) and find in the vertical column where a value occurs that most nearly corresponds to (P) found in step 1. On the same line on the left-hand side, read off the amplitude on the latitude scale. Azimuth is given as follows:

At Rise
Azimuth = 090° ± amplitude
+ for south declinations, −for north declinations
At Set
Azimuth = 270° ± amplitude
+ for north declinations, −for south declinations

EXAMPLE
At rise.
Declination N19°, latitude N29°.
From the table P = 325 and Amplitude = 22°.
Azimuth = 90°−22° = 068°

9 POLARIS

The proximity of Polaris (the "pole star," α Ursae Minoris, magnitude 2.1) to the north celestial pole makes it a good object for determining azimuth and latitude even though the observer's position and the time of observation may not be known very accurately. First calculate the LHA of Aries using the procedure in Section 4.4.

9.1 Azimuth

With the above value of LHA of Aries and an approximate latitude, the azimuth of Polaris may be read directly from the table on page 160.

EXAMPLE

Find the azimuth of Polaris and the latitude from a sextant altitude observation of 38° 05′ made on 12 April 1999, at standard time 4h 51m (time zone W5h). DR latitude N38° 20′, longitude W072° 20′, height of eye 9.0m, and index correction 5′ on the arc.

Standard time	4h 51m
Time zone (+W, −E)	W5
GMT (time)	9 51
GMT (arc)	147° 45′
GHA Aries at GMT0hrs + Corrn.	200 09
GHA Aries	347 54
DR longitude (+E, −W)	W072 20
LHA Aries	275 34
Azimuth from table (page 160)	000° .8

9.2 Latitude

The sextant altitude given in Section 9.1 is corrected for index error, dip, and refraction, using the tables on page 160. Using the LHA of Aries, read off on the same page the altitude correction that when added to or subtracted from the apparent altitude will give the latitude of the observer.

Sextant altitude	38°	05′
Dip		−5
Index correction		−5
Apparent altitude	37	55
Refraction		−1
Observed altitude	37	54
Altitude correction (page 160)		+24
Latitude	N38	18

10 Sun Observations

10.1 Running Fixes

The Sun is a most useful body for celestial navigation, being bright and available for observation throughout most of the day. Methods of calculating the azimuth of the Sun are given in Section 7.2.

If a body such as the Sun or Moon is observed on a number of occasions during the day, an LOP can be drawn from each DR position where those observations were taken. When at least two or more of these LOPs are combined, the position of the vessel can then be determined by either (a) plotting the LOPs at any selected DR position on the vessel's run or (b), as in coastal navigation, advancing previous LOPs by the course and distance run between the times of observation and fix. The result is called a running fix. LOPs not plotted at the DR position from which they were calculated are called double sights, transferred sights, or simply transfers. To distinguish them from normal sights, the LOPs are usually marked with a double arrowhead on each end.

EXAMPLE

The following observations were taken to the lower limb of the Sun in the forenoon, near noon, and afternoon of 15 July 1999. Determine the vessel's position at watch time 16h 50m (time zone E10h). The watch was 1m 10s slow, the height of eye 12ft, and the index correction 2′ on the arc.

DR Position			
Latitude	Longitude	Watch Time	Sext. Alt.
S33° 15′	E155° 24′	8h 08m 30s	14° 34′
S33 04	E155 41	12 14 47	34 30
S32 52	E156 03	15 57 14	8 11
S32 40	E156 25	16 50	
Fix: latitude S32° 48′, longitude E156° 04′			

See pages 164 and 165 for details of sight reduction and plotting.

The accuracy of these "running" fixes is dependent on the reliability of the estimates of the vessel's run (courses and distances) between the celestial observations. The method is flexible in that there are no special times when observations need to be made, and the point selected along the vessel's run for the plotting is irrelevant. Inclement weather or some other circumstance may prevent observation at a specific time, such as "noon" (see Section 10.2), and therefore the navi-

gator should be circumspect about relying on making such observations. A plot of an LOP near the middle of the day is just as valuable as a "noon" sight, described in the next section.

10.2 Meridian Observations

The Sun will cross the observer's meridian (north–south line) twice each day, at upper and lower transit. The Sun at lower transit can be observed only at certain times of the year inside the Arctic or Antarctic Circles: an unusually high latitude for shipping. If the altitude of the Sun is observed as it makes its upper transit, it will be noticed that altitudes slowly increase to a maximum and then decrease. At the highest altitude, the Sun is said to be making its upper meridian passage at a time called local apparent noon (LAN). This will not occur at "12 hours" but will depend on the time of the year and the vessel's position with respect to the standard meridian adopted for timekeeping; see the following example.

If the longitude is known with reasonable certainty and the altitude is not too high, a compass bearing at upper transit will provide a useful compass check. The time of meridian passage can be calculated as follows:

EXAMPLE

Find the standard time (time zone W10h) of the meridian passage of the Sun on 24 September 1999, in longitude W149° 46′ (W9h 59m).

The LMT (local mean time) of the meridian passage of the Sun is 12h ± the correction found on pages 130 or 131.

LAT of meridian passage	12h	00m
Correction (pages 130 or 131)		−8
LMT of meridian passage	11	52
Longitude (+ W, −E)	W 9	59
GMT	21	51
Time zone (−W , +E)	W10	
Standard time	11	51

See Section 5.5 for a discussion of the meanings of LAT and LMT.

Historically the "noon sight" is deeply entrenched in maritime lore, its main attraction being the simple relationship that exists between the Sun's altitude and declination, and the observer's latitude. The method can best be illustrated with an example.

EXAMPLE

A navigator in DR position S55°, E155° observed the Sun (LL) toward the north at its meridian passage on 24 September 1999. Find the latitude if the sextant altitude was 35° 18′, height of eye 2.5m, and index correction 2′ on the arc.

Step 1 Clear (correct) the altitude and calculate the zenith distance, which is 90° minus the altitude (that is, an angle measured in a vertical plane from the zenith downward to the body).

Sextant altitude	35° 18′
Dip (2.5m)	−3
Index correction	−2
Apparent altitude	35 13
Altitude correction (page 66)	+15
Observed altitude	35 28
Zenith distance	54 32

Step 2 Calculate the declination.

The approximate GMT of observation is

180° ± longitude (+W, −E) = 180°−155°
= 25°
= 1h 40m (time)

Declination at GMT 0hrs 24th September	S0° 12′
Correction (d =+23′)	+2
Declination	S0 14

Step 3 The latitude is calculated from the numerical sum of, or difference between, the zenith distance and the declination using the following table:

Declination	Direction of Observation	
	North	South
North	Difference	Sum
South	Sum	Difference

The Sun was observed to the north and the declination was south, therefore the latitude is found from the sum of the zenith distance and the declination:

54° 32′ + 0°14′ = 54° 46′

Therefore the latitude was S54° 46′.

The navigator will find it convenient to make copies of some of the more frequently used forms and tables, e.g., pages 6, 161, 166, 167, 168, 169, 176. In particular a back-to-back copy of pages 6 and 176, covered in clear plastic film, will make an excellent bookmark.

TABLES, EXAMPLES, AND FORMS

GHA ARIES AT GMT 0hrs 1999

Day	JANUARY	FEBRUARY	MARCH	APRIL	MAY	JUNE	Day
1	FRI 100°12'	MON 130°46'	MON 158°21'	THU 188°55'	SAT 218°29'	TUE 249°02'	1
2	SAT 101 11	TUE 131 45	TUE 159 21	FRI 189 54	SUN 219 28	WED 250 01	2
3	SUN 102 11	WED 132 44	WED 160 20	SAT 190 53	MON 220 27	THU 251 00	3
4	MON 103 10	THU 133 43	THU 161 19	SUN 191 52	TUE 221 26	FRI 252 00	4
5	TUE 104 09	FRI 134 42	FRI 162 18	MON 192 51	WED 222 25	SAT 252 59	5
6	WED 105 08	SAT 135 41	SAT 163 17	TUE 193 50	THU 223 25	SUN 253 58	6
7	THU 106 07	SUN 136 40	SUN 164 16	WED 194 50	FRI 224 24	MON 254 57	7
8	FRI 107 06	MON 137 40	MON 165 15	THU 195 49	SAT 225 23	TUE 255 56	8
9	SAT 108 05	TUE 138 39	TUE 166 15	FRI 196 48	SUN 226 22	WED 256 55	9
10	SUN 109 04	WED 139 38	WED 167 14	SAT 197 47	MON 227 21	THU 257 54	10
11	MON 110 04	THU 140 37	THU 168 13	SUN 198 46	TUE 228 20	FRI 258 54	11
12	TUE 111 03	FRI 141 36	FRI 169 12	MON 199 45	WED 229 19	SAT 259 53	12
13	WED 112 02	SAT 142 35	SAT 170 11	TUE 200 44	THU 230 19	SUN 260 52	13
14	THU 113 01	SUN 143 34	SUN 171 10	WED 201 43	FRI 231 18	MON 261 51	14
15	FRI 114 00	MON 144 33	MON 172 09	THU 202 43	SAT 232 17	TUE 262 50	15
16	SAT 114 59	TUE 145 33	TUE 173 08	FRI 203 42	SUN 233 16	WED 263 49	16
17	SUN 115 58	WED 146 32	WED 174 08	SAT 204 41	MON 234 15	THU 264 48	17
18	MON 116 58	THU 147 31	THU 175 07	SUN 205 40	TUE 235 14	FRI 265 48	18
19	TUE 117 57	FRI 148 30	FRI 176 06	MON 206 39	WED 236 13	SAT 266 47	19
20	WED 118 56	SAT 149 29	SAT 177 05	TUE 207 38	THU 237 12	SUN 267 46	20
21	THU 119 55	SUN 150 28	SUN 178 04	WED 208 37	FRI 238 12	MON 268 45	21
22	FRI 120 54	MON 151 27	MON 179 03	THU 209 37	SAT 239 11	TUE 269 44	22
23	SAT 121 53	TUE 152 27	TUE 180 02	FRI 210 36	SUN 240 10	WED 270 43	23
24	SUN 122 52	WED 153 26	WED 181 02	SAT 211 35	MON 241 09	THU 271 42	24
25	MON 123 52	THU 154 25	THU 182 01	SUN 212 34	TUE 242 08	FRI 272 41	25
26	TUE 124 51	FRI 155 24	FRI 183 00	MON 213 33	WED 243 07	SAT 273 41	26
27	WED 125 50	SAT 156 23	SAT 183 59	TUE 214 32	THU 244 06	SUN 274 40	27
28	THU 126 49	SUN 157 22	SUN 184 58	WED 215 31	FRI 245 06	MON 275 39	28
29	FRI 127 48		MON 185 57	THU 216 31	SAT 246 05	TUE 276 38	29
30	SAT 128 47		TUE 186 56	FRI 217 30	SUN 247 04	WED 277 37	30
31	SUN 129 46		WED 187 56		MON 248 03		31

Day	JULY	AUGUST	SEPTEMBER	OCTOBER	NOVEMBER	DECEMBER	Day
1	THU 278°36'	SUN 309°10'	WED 339°43'	FRI 9°17'	MON 39°50'	WED 69°25'	1
2	FRI 279 35	MON 310 09	THU 340 42	SAT 10 16	TUE 40 49	THU 70 24	2
3	SAT 280 35	TUE 311 08	FRI 341 41	SUN 11 15	WED 41 49	FRI 71 23	3
4	SUN 281 34	WED 312 07	SAT 342 40	MON 12 14	THU 42 48	SAT 72 22	4
5	MON 282 33	THU 313 06	SUN 343 39	TUE 13 14	FRI 43 47	SUN 73 21	5
6	TUE 283 32	FRI 314 05	MON 344 39	WED 14 13	SAT 44 46	MON 74 20	6
7	WED 284 31	SAT 315 04	TUE 345 38	THU 15 12	SUN 45 45	TUE 75 19	7
8	THU 285 30	SUN 316 04	WED 346 37	FRI 16 11	MON 46 44	WED 76 18	8
9	FRI 286 29	MON 317 03	THU 347 36	SAT 17 10	TUE 47 43	THU 77 18	9
10	SAT 287 29	TUE 318 02	FRI 348 35	SUN 18 09	WED 48 43	FRI 78 17	10
11	SUN 288 28	WED 319 01	SAT 349 34	MON 19 08	THU 49 42	SAT 79 16	11
12	MON 289 27	THU 320 00	SUN 350 33	TUE 20 08	FRI 50 41	SUN 80 15	12
13	TUE 290 26	FRI 320 59	MON 351 33	WED 21 07	SAT 51 40	MON 81 14	13
14	WED 291 25	SAT 321 58	TUE 352 32	THU 22 06	SUN 52 39	TUE 82 13	14
15	THU 292 24	SUN 322 58	WED 353 31	FRI 23 05	MON 53 38	WED 83 12	15
16	FRI 293 23	MON 323 57	THU 354 30	SAT 24 04	TUE 54 37	THU 84 12	16
17	SAT 294 23	TUE 324 56	FRI 355 29	SUN 25 03	WED 55 37	FRI 85 11	17
18	SUN 295 22	WED 325 55	SAT 356 28	MON 26 02	THU 56 36	SAT 86 10	18
19	MON 296 21	THU 326 54	SUN 357 27	TUE 27 02	FRI 57 35	SUN 87 09	19
20	TUE 297 20	FRI 327 53	MON 358 27	WED 28 01	SAT 58 34	MON 88 08	20
21	WED 298 19	SAT 328 52	TUE 359 26	THU 29 00	SUN 59 33	TUE 89 07	21
22	THU 299 18	SUN 329 52	WED 0 25	FRI 29 59	MON 60 32	WED 90 06	22
23	FRI 300 17	MON 330 51	THU 1 24	SAT 30 58	TUE 61 31	THU 91 06	23
24	SAT 301 17	TUE 331 50	FRI 2 23	SUN 31 57	WED 62 31	FRI 92 05	24
25	SUN 302 16	WED 332 49	SAT 3 22	MON 32 56	THU 63 30	SAT 93 04	25
26	MON 303 15	THU 333 48	SUN 4 21	TUE 33 56	FRI 64 29	SUN 94 03	26
27	TUE 304 14	FRI 334 47	MON 5 21	WED 34 55	SAT 65 28	MON 95 02	27
28	WED 305 13	SAT 335 46	TUE 6 20	THU 35 54	SUN 66 27	TUE 96 01	28
29	THU 306 12	SUN 336 46	WED 7 19	FRI 36 53	MON 67 26	WED 97 00	29
30	FRI 307 11	MON 337 45	THU 8 18	SAT 37 52	TUE 68 25	THU 98 00	30
31	SAT 308 10	TUE 338 44		SUN 38 51		FRI 98 59	31

ARIES Corrn

GMT h m	Corrn
0 12	0'
0 12	+1
0 36	+2
1 00	+3
1 25	+4
1 49	+5
2 13	+6
2 38	+7
3 02	+8
3 26	+9
3 51	+10
4 15	+11
4 40	+12
5 04	+13
5 28	+14
5 53	+15
6 17	+16
6 41	+17
7 06	+18
7 30	+19
7 54	+20
8 19	+21
8 43	+22
9 07	+23
9 32	+24
9 56	+25
10 20	+26
10 45	+27
11 09	+28
11 33	+29
11 58	+30
12 22	+31
12 47	+32
13 11	+33
13 35	+34
14 00	+35
14 24	+36
14 48	+37
15 13	+38
15 37	+39
16 01	+40
16 26	+41
16 50	+42
17 14	+43
17 39	+44
18 03	+45
18 27	+46
18 52	+47
19 16	+48
19 40	+49
20 05	+50
20 29	+51
20 53	+52
21 18	+53
21 42	+54
22 07	+55
22 31	+56
22 55	+57
23 20	+58
23 44	+59
24 00	

INDEX OF BRIGHT STARS 1999

NAME	No	Mag.	SHA	DEC	NAME	No	Mag	SHA	DEC
Acamar	1	3.1	315°27'	S40°18'	Alpheratz	12	2.2	357°55'	N29°05'
Achernar	2	0.6	335 35	S57 14	Ankaa	14	2.4	353 26	S42 18
Acrux	3	1.1	173 21	S63 06	Schedah	52	2.5	349 53	N56 32
Adhara	4	1.6	255 21	S28 58	Diphda	25	2.2	349 07	S17 59
Aldebaran	5	1.1	291 02	N16 30	Achernar	2	0.6	335 35	S57 14
Alioth	6	1.7	166 30	N55 58	Hamal	34	2.2	328 13	N23 27
Alkaid	7	1.9	153 07	N49 19	Polaris	44	2.1	322 21	N89 15
Al Na'ir	8	2.2	27 57	S46 58	Acamar	1	3.1	315 27	S40 18
Alnilam	9	1.8	275 58	S 1 12	Menkar	38	2.8	314 27	N 4 05
Alphard	10	2.2	218 07	S 8 39	Mirfak	41	1.9	308 56	N49 51
Alphecca	11	2.3	126 20	N26 43	Aldebaran	5	1.1	291 02	N16 30
Alpheratz	12	2.2	357 55	N29 05	Rigel	49	0.3	281 23	S 8 12
Altair	13	0.9	62 18	N 8 52	Capella	22	0.2	280 51	N46 00
Ankaa	14	2.4	353 26	S42 18	Bellatrix	19	1.7	278 44	N 6 21
Antares	15	1.2	112 39	S26 26	Elnath	27	1.8	278 27	N28 36
Arcturus	16	0.2	146 05	N19 11	Alnilam	9	1.8	276 09	S 1 13
Atria	17	1.9	107 50	S69 02	Betelgeuse	20	Var*	271 13	N 7 24
Avior	18	1.7	234 23	S59 31	Canopus	21	-0.9	264 02	S52 42
Bellatrix	19	1.7	278 44	N 6 21	Sirius	54	-1.6	258 44	S16 43
Betelgeuse	20	Var*	271 13	N 7 24	Adhara	4	1.6	255 21	S28 58
Canopus	21	-0.9	264 02	S52 42	Procyon	46	0.5	245 11	N 5 14
Capella	22	0.2	280 51	N46 00	Pollux	45	1.2	243 41	N28 02
Deneb	23	1.3	49 38	N45 17	Avior	18	1.7	234 23	S59 31
Denebola	24	2.2	182 45	N14 35	Suhail	56	2.2	223 01	S43 26
Diphda	25	2.2	349 07	S17 59	Miaplacidus	40	1.8	221 43	S69 43
Dubhe	26	2.0	194 05	N61 46	Alphard	10	2.2	218 07	S 8 39
Elnath	27	1.8	278 27	N28 36	Regulus	48	1.3	207 55	N11 58
Eltanin	28	2.4	90 51	N51 30	Dubhe	26	2.0	194 05	N61 46
Enif	29	2.5	33 58	N 9 52	Denebola	24	2.2	182 45	N14 35
Fomalhaut	30	1.3	15 36	S29 37	Gienah	32	2.8	176 03	S17 32
Gacrux	31	1.6	172 13	S57 07	Acrux	3	1.1	173 21	S63 06
Gienah	32	2.8	176 03	S17 32	Gacrux	31	1.6	172 13	S57 07
Hadar	33	0.9	149 03	S60 22	Alioth	6	1.7	166 30	N55 58
Hamal	34	2.2	328 13	N23 27	Spica	55	1.2	158 43	S11 09
Kaus Australis	35	2.0	83 58	S34 23	Alkaid	7	1.9	153 07	N49 19
Kochab	36	2.2	137 19	N74 10	Hadar	33	0.9	149 03	S60 22
Markab	37	2.6	13 49	N15 12	Menkent	39	2.3	148 20	S36 22
Menkar	38	2.8	314 27	N 4 05	Arcturus	16	0.2	146 05	N19 11
Menkent	39	2.3	148 20	S36 22	Rigil Kentaurus	50	0.1	140 06	S60 50
Miaplacidus	40	1.8	221 43	S69 43	Zubenelgenubi	58	2.9	137 17	S16 02
Mirfak	41	1.9	308 56	N49 51	Kochab	36	2.2	137 19	N74 10
Nunki	42	2.1	76 11	S26 18	Alphecca	11	2.3	126 20	N26 43
Peacock	43	2.1	53 36	S56 44	Antares	15	1.2	112 39	S26 26
Polaris	44	2.1	322 21	N89 15	Atria	17	1.9	107 50	S69 02
Pollux	45	1.2	243 41	N28 02	Sabik	51	2.6	102 25	S15 43
Procyon	46	0.5	245 11	N 5 14	Shaula	53	1.7	96 36	S37 06
Rasalhague	47	2.1	96 16	N12 34	Rasalhague	47	2.1	96 16	N12 34
Regulus	48	1.3	207 55	N11 58	Eltanin	28	2.4	90 51	N51 30
Rigel	49	0.3	281 23	S 8 12	Kaus Australis	35	2.0	83 58	S34 23
Rigil Kentaurus	50	0.1	140 06	S60 50	Vega	57	0.1	80 46	N38 47
Sabik	51	2.6	102 25	S15 43	Nunki	42	2.1	76 11	S26 18
Schedar	52	2.5	349 53	N56 32	Altair	13	0.9	62 18	N 8 52
Shaula	53	1.7	96 36	S37 06	Peacock	43	2.1	53 36	S56 44
Sirius	54	-1.6	258 44	S16 43	Deneb	23	1.3	49 38	N45 17
Spica	55	1.2	158 43	S11 09	Enif	29	2.5	34 01	N 9 51
Suhail	56	2.2	223 01	S43 26	Al Na'ir	8	2.2	27 57	S46 58
Vega	57	0.1	80 46	N38 47	Fomalhaut	30	1.3	15 36	S29 37
Zubenelgenubi	58	2.9	137 17	S16 02	Markab	37	2.6	13 49	N15 12

* 0.1 - 1.2

DIP Corrn

Corrn		
m	0'	ft
0.0		0
0.7	-1	2
2.0	-2	6
3.9	-3	13
6.5	-4	21
9.7	-5	32
13.6	-6	44
18.1	-7	59
23.3	-8	76
29.1	-9	95
	-10	

STARS REFN Corrn

Alt	Corrn
0° 05'	-34'
0 10	-33
0 15	-32
0 20	-31
0 26	-30
0 32	-29
0 38	-28
0 45	-27
0 52	-26
0 59	-25
1 07	-24
1 16	-23
1 25	-22
1 35	-21
1 46	-20
1 58	-19
2 11	-18
2 25	-17
2 41	-16
2 58	-15
3 18	-14
3 41	-13
4 07	-12
4 38	-11
5 14	-10
5 59	-9
6 54	-8
8 06	-7
9 41	-6
11 56	-5
15 21	-4
21 10	-3
32 54	-2
62 22	-1
	0

GHA ARIES AT GMT 0hrs 2000

Day	JANUARY	FEBRUARY	MARCH	APRIL	MAY	JUNE	Day
1	SAT 99°58'	TUE 130°31'	WED 159°06'	SAT 189°39'	MON 219°14'	THU 249°47'	1
2	SUN 100 57	WED 131 30	THU 160 05	SUN 190 39	TUE 220 13	FRI 250 46	2
3	MON 101 56	THU 132 29	FRI 161 04	MON 191 38	WED 221 12	SAT 251 45	3
4	TUE 102 55	FRI 133 29	SAT 162 04	TUE 192 37	THU 222 11	SUN 252 44	4
5	WED 103 54	SAT 134 28	SUN 163 03	WED 193 36	FRI 223 10	MON 253 43	5
6	THU 104 54	SUN 135 27	MON 164 02	THU 194 35	SAT 224 09	TUE 254 43	6
7	FRI 105 53	MON 136 26	TUE 165 01	FRI 195 34	SUN 225 08	WED 255 42	7
8	SAT 106 52	TUE 137 25	WED 166 00	SAT 196 33	MON 226 08	THU 256 41	8
9	SUN 107 51	WED 138 24	THU 166 59	SUN 197 33	TUE 227 07	FRI 257 40	9
10	MON 108 50	THU 139 23	FRI 167 58	MON 198 32	WED 228 06	SAT 258 39	10
11	TUE 109 49	FRI 140 23	SAT 168 58	TUE 199 31	THU 229 05	SUN 259 38	11
12	WED 110 48	SAT 141 22	SUN 169 57	WED 200 30	FRI 230 04	MON 260 37	12
13	THU 111 48	SUN 142 21	MON 170 56	THU 201 29	SAT 231 03	TUE 261 37	13
14	FRI 112 47	MON 143 20	TUE 171 55	FRI 202 28	SUN 232 02	WED 262 36	14
15	SAT 113 46	TUE 144 19	WED 172 54	SAT 203 27	MON 233 02	THU 263 35	15
16	SUN 114 45	WED 145 18	THU 173 53	SUN 204 27	TUE 234 01	FRI 264 34	16
17	MON 115 44	THU 146 17	FRI 174 52	MON 205 26	WED 235 00	SAT 265 33	17
18	TUE 116 43	FRI 147 17	SAT 175 52	TUE 206 25	THU 235 59	SUN 266 32	18
19	WED 117 42	SAT 148 16	SUN 176 51	WED 207 24	FRI 236 58	MON 267 31	19
20	THU 118 41	SUN 149 15	MON 177 50	THU 208 23	SAT 237 57	TUE 268 31	20
21	FRI 119 41	MON 150 14	TUE 178 49	FRI 209 22	SUN 238 56	WED 269 30	21
22	SAT 120 40	TUE 151 13	WED 179 48	SAT 210 21	MON 239 56	THU 270 29	22
23	SUN 121 39	WED 152 12	THU 180 47	SUN 211 20	TUE 240 55	FRI 271 28	23
24	MON 122 38	THU 153 11	FRI 181 46	MON 212 20	WED 241 54	SAT 272 27	24
25	TUE 123 37	FRI 154 10	SAT 182 45	TUE 213 19	THU 242 53	SUN 273 26	25
26	WED 124 36	SAT 155 10	SUN 183 45	WED 214 18	FRI 243 52	MON 274 25	26
27	THU 125 35	SUN 156 09	MON 184 44	THU 215 17	SAT 244 51	TUE 275 25	27
28	FRI 126 35	MON 157 08	TUE 185 43	FRI 216 16	SUN 245 50	WED 276 24	28
29	SAT 127 34	TUE 158 07	WED 186 42	SAT 217 15	MON 246 49	THU 277 23	29
30	SUN 128 33		THU 187 41	SUN 218 14	TUE 247 49	FRI 278 22	30
31	MON 129 32		FRI 188 40		WED 248 48		31

Day	JULY	AUGUST	SEPTEMBER	OCTOBER	NOVEMBER	DECEMBER	Day
1	SAT 279°21'	TUE 309°54'	FRI 340°28'	SUN 10°02'	WED 40°35'	FRI 70°09'	1
2	SUN 280 20	WED 310 54	SAT 341 27	MON 11 01	THU 41 34	SAT 71 08	2
3	MON 281 19	THU 311 53	SUN 342 26	TUE 12 00	FRI 42 33	SUN 72 08	3
4	TUE 282 19	FRI 312 52	MON 343 25	WED 12 59	SAT 43 33	MON 73 07	4
5	WED 283 18	SAT 313 51	TUE 344 24	THU 13 58	SUN 44 32	TUE 74 06	5
6	THU 284 17	SUN 314 50	WED 345 23	FRI 14 58	MON 45 31	WED 75 05	6
7	FRI 285 16	MON 315 49	THU 346 23	SAT 15 57	TUE 46 30	THU 76 04	7
8	SAT 286 15	TUE 316 48	FRI 347 22	SUN 16 56	WED 47 29	FRI 77 03	8
9	SUN 287 14	WED 317 48	SAT 348 21	MON 17 55	THU 48 28	SAT 78 02	9
10	MON 288 13	THU 318 47	SUN 349 20	TUE 18 54	FRI 49 27	SUN 79 02	10
11	TUE 289 12	FRI 319 46	MON 350 19	WED 19 53	SAT 50 27	MON 80 01	11
12	WED 290 12	SAT 320 45	TUE 351 18	THU 20 52	SUN 51 26	TUE 81 00	12
13	THU 291 11	SUN 321 44	WED 352 17	FRI 21 51	MON 52 25	WED 81 59	13
14	FRI 292 10	MON 322 43	THU 353 16	SAT 22 51	TUE 53 24	THU 82 58	14
15	SAT 293 09	TUE 323 42	FRI 354 16	SUN 23 50	WED 54 23	FRI 83 57	15
16	SUN 294 08	WED 324 41	SAT 355 15	MON 24 49	THU 55 22	SAT 84 56	16
17	MON 295 07	THU 325 41	SUN 356 14	TUE 25 48	FRI 56 21	SUN 85 56	17
18	TUE 296 06	FRI 326 40	MON 357 13	WED 26 47	SAT 57 20	MON 86 55	18
19	WED 297 06	SAT 327 39	TUE 358 12	THU 27 46	SUN 58 20	TUE 87 54	19
20	THU 298 05	SUN 328 38	WED 359 11	FRI 28 45	MON 59 19	WED 88 53	20
21	FRI 299 04	MON 329 37	THU 0 10	SAT 29 45	TUE 60 18	THU 89 52	21
22	SAT 300 03	TUE 330 36	FRI 1 10	SUN 30 44	WED 61 17	FRI 90 51	22
23	SUN 301 02	WED 331 35	SAT 2 09	MON 31 43	THU 62 16	SAT 91 50	23
24	MON 302 01	THU 332 35	SUN 3 08	TUE 32 42	FRI 63 15	SUN 92 50	24
25	TUE 303 00	FRI 333 34	MON 4 07	WED 33 41	SAT 64 14	MON 93 49	25
26	WED 304 00	SAT 334 33	TUE 5 06	THU 34 40	SUN 65 14	TUE 94 48	26
27	THU 304 59	SUN 335 32	WED 6 05	FRI 35 39	MON 66 13	WED 95 47	27
28	FRI 305 58	MON 336 31	THU 7 04	SAT 36 39	TUE 67 12	THU 96 46	28
29	SAT 306 57	TUE 337 30	FRI 8 04	SUN 37 38	WED 68 11	FRI 97 45	29
30	SUN 307 56	WED 338 29	SAT 9 03	MON 38 37	THU 69 10	SAT 98 44	30
31	MON 308 55	THU 339 29		TUE 39 36		SUN 99 43	31

ARIES Corrn

GMT	Corrn
h m	0'
0 12	+1
0 36	+2
1 00	+3
1 25	+4
1 49	+5
2 13	+6
2 38	+7
3 02	+8
3 26	+9
3 51	+10
4 15	+11
4 40	+12
5 04	+13
5 28	+14
5 53	+15
6 17	+16
6 41	+17
7 06	+18
7 30	+19
7 54	+20
8 19	+21
8 43	+22
9 07	+23
9 32	+24
9 56	+25
10 20	+26
10 45	+27
11 09	+28
11 33	+29
11 58	+30
12 22	+31
12 47	+32
13 11	+33
13 35	+34
14 00	+35
14 24	+36
14 48	+37
15 13	+38
15 37	+39
16 01	+40
16 26	+41
16 50	+42
17 14	+43
17 39	+44
18 03	+45
18 27	+46
18 52	+47
19 16	+48
19 40	+49
20 05	+50
20 29	+51
20 53	+52
21 18	+53
21 42	+54
22 07	+55
22 31	+56
22 55	+57
23 20	+58
23 44	+59
24 00	

INDEX OF BRIGHT STARS 2000

NAME	No	Mag.	SHA	DEC	NAME	No	Mag	SHA	DEC
Acamar	1	3.1	315°26'	S40°18'	Alpheratz	12	2.2	357°54'	N29°05'
Achernar	2	0.6	335 34	S57 14	Ankaa	14	2.4	353 26	S42 18
Acrux	3	1.1	173 21	S63 06	Schedah	52	2.5	349 52	N56 32
Adhara	4	1.6	255 21	S28 58	Diphda	25	2.2	349 06	S17 59
Aldebaran	5	1.1	291 01	N16 30	Achernar	2	0.6	335 34	S57 14
Alioth	6	1.7	166 30	N55 58	Hamal	34	2.2	328 12	N23 28
Alkaid	7	1.9	153 07	N49 19	Polaris	44	2.1	322 08	N89 16
Al Na'ir	8	2.2	27 56	S46 57	Acamar	1	3.1	315 26	S40 18
Alnilam	9	1.8	275 57	S 1 12	Menkar	38	2.8	314 26	N 4 05
Alphard	10	2.2	218 06	S 8 40	Mirfak	41	1.9	308 55	N49 52
Alphecca	11	2.3	126 19	N26 43	Aldebaran	5	1.1	291 01	N16 30
Alpheratz	12	2.2	357 54	N29 05	Rigel	49	0.3	281 22	S 8 12
Altair	13	0.9	62 18	N 8 52	Capella	22	0.2	280 50	N46 00
Ankaa	14	2.4	353 26	S42 18	Bellatrix	19	1.7	278 43	N 6 21
Antares	15	1.2	112 38	S26 26	Elnath	27	1.8	278 26	N28 36
Arcturus	16	0.2	146 05	N19 11	Alnilam	9	1.8	276 08	S 1 13
Atria	17	1.9	107 49	S69 02	Betelgeuse	20	Var*	271 13	N 7 24
Avior	18	1.7	234 23	S59 31	Canopus	21	-0.9	264 01	S52 42
Bellatrix	19	1.7	278 43	N 6 21	Sirius	54	-1.6	258 43	S16 43
Betelgeuse	20	Var*	271 13	N 7 24	Adhara	4	1.6	255 21	S28 58
Canopus	21	-0.9	264 01	S52 42	Procyon	46	0.5	245 11	N 5 13
Capella	22	0.2	280 50	N46 00	Pollux	45	1.2	243 40	N28 02
Deneb	23	1.3	49 38	N45 17	Avior	18	1.7	234 23	S59 31
Denebola	24	2.2	182 44	N14 34	Suhail	56	2.2	223 00	S43 26
Diphda	25	2.2	349 06	S17 59	Miaplacidus	40	1.8	221 43	S69 43
Dubhe	26	2.0	194 04	N61 45	Alphard	10	2.2	218 06	S 8 40
Elnath	27	1.8	278 26	N28 36	Regulus	48	1.3	207 55	N11 58
Eltanin	28	2.4	90 50	N51 29	Dubhe	26	2.0	194 04	N61 45
Enif	29	2.5	33 57	N 9 53	Denebola	24	2.2	182 44	N14 34
Fomalhaut	30	1.3	15 35	S29 37	Gienah	32	2.8	176 03	S17 33
Gacrux	31	1.6	172 12	S57 07	Acrux	3	1.1	173 21	S63 06
Gienah	32	2.8	176 03	S17 33	Gacrux	31	1.6	172 12	S57 07
Hadar	33	0.9	149 02	S60 23	Alioth	6	1.7	166 30	N55 58
Hamal	34	2.2	328 12	N23 28	Spica	55	1.2	158 42	S11 10
Kaus Australis	35	2.0	83 57	S34 23	Alkaid	7	1.9	153 07	N49 19
Kochab	36	2.2	137 19	N74 10	Hadar	33	0.9	149 02	S60 23
Markab	37	2.6	13 48	N15 12	Menkent	39	2.3	148 19	S36 22
Menkar	38	2.8	314 26	N 4 05	Arcturus	16	0.2	146 05	N19 11
Menkent	39	2.3	148 19	S36 22	Rigil Kentaurus	50	0.1	140 05	S60 50
Miaplacidus	40	1.8	221 43	S69 43	Zubenelgenubi	58	2.9	137 16	S16 03
Mirfak	41	1.9	308 55	N49 52	Kochab	36	2.2	137 19	N74 10
Nunki	42	2.1	76 10	S26 18	Alphecca	11	2.3	126 19	N26 43
Peacock	43	2.1	53 35	S56 44	Antares	15	1.2	112 38	S26 26
Polaris	44	2.1	322 08	N89 16	Atria	17	1.9	107 49	S69 02
Pollux	45	1.2	243 40	N28 02	Sabik	51	2.6	102 24	S15 43
Procyon	46	0.5	245 11	N 5 13	Shaula	53	1.7	96 35	S37 06
Rasalhague	47	2.1	96 16	N12 34	Rasalhague	47	2.1	96 16	N12 34
Regulus	48	1.3	207 55	N11 58	Eltanin	28	2.4	90 50	N51 29
Rigel	49	0.3	281 22	S 8 12	Kaus Australis	35	2.0	83 57	S34 23
Rigil Kentaurus	50	0.1	140 05	S60 50	Vega	57	0.1	80 45	N38 47
Sabik	51	2.6	102 24	S15 43	Nunki	42	2.1	76 10	S26 18
Schedar	52	2.5	349 52	N56 32	Altair	13	0.9	62 18	N 8 52
Shaula	53	1.7	96 35	S37 06	Peacock	43	2.1	53 35	S56 44
Sirius	54	-1.6	258 43	S16 43	Deneb	23	1.3	49 38	N45 17
Spica	55	1.2	158 42	S11 10	Enif	29	2.5	34 01	N 9 51
Suhail	56	2.2	223 00	S43 26	Al Na'ir	8	2.2	27 56	S46 57
Vega	57	0.1	80 45	N38 47	Fomalhaut	30	1.3	15 35	S29 37
Zubenelgenubi	58	2.9	137 16	S16 03	Markab	37	2.6	13 48	N15 12

* 0.1 - 1.2

DIP Corrn

m	Corrn	ft
0.0	0'	0
0.7	-1	2
2.0	-2	6
3.9	-3	13
6.5	-4	21
9.7	-5	32
13.6	-6	44
18.1	-7	59
23.3	-8	76
29.1	-9	95
	-10	

STARS REFN Corrn

Alt	Corrn
0° 05'	-34'
0 10	-33
0 15	-32
0 20	-31
0 26	-30
0 32	-29
0 38	-28
0 45	-27
0 52	-26
0 59	-25
1 07	-24
1 16	-23
1 25	-22
1 35	-21
1 46	-20
1 58	-19
2 11	-18
2 25	-17
2 41	-16
2 58	-15
3 18	-14
3 41	-13
4 07	-12
4 38	-11
5 14	-10
5 59	-9
6 54	-8
8 06	-7
9 41	-6
11 56	-5
15 21	-4
21 10	-3
32 54	-2
62 22	-1
	0

GHA ARIES AT GMT 0hrs 2001

Day	JANUARY	FEBRUARY	MARCH	APRIL	MAY	JUNE	Day
1	MON 100°43'	THU 131°16'	THU 158°52'	SUN 189°25'	TUE 218°59'	FRI 249°33'	1
2	TUE 101 42	FRI 132 15	FRI 159 51	MON 190 24	WED 219 58	SAT 250 32	2
3	WED 102 41	SAT 133 14	SAT 160 50	TUE 191 23	THU 220 58	SUN 251 31	3
4	THU 103 40	SUN 134 13	SUN 161 49	WED 192 23	FRI 221 57	MON 252 30	4
5	FRI 104 39	MON 135 12	MON 162 48	THU 193 22	SAT 222 56	TUE 253 29	5
6	SAT 105 38	TUE 136 12	TUE 163 48	FRI 194 21	SUN 223 55	WED 254 28	6
7	SUN 106 37	WED 137 11	WED 164 47	SAT 195 20	MON 224 54	THU 255 27	7
8	MON 107 37	THU 138 10	THU 165 46	SUN 196 19	TUE 225 53	FRI 256 27	8
9	TUE 108 36	FRI 139 09	FRI 166 45	MON 197 18	WED 226 52	SAT 257 26	9
10	WED 109 35	SAT 140 08	SAT 167 44	TUE 198 17	THU 227 51	SUN 258 25	10
11	THU 110 34	SUN 141 07	SUN 168 43	WED 199 16	FRI 228 51	MON 259 24	11
12	FRI 111 33	MON 142 06	MON 169 42	THU 200 16	SAT 229 50	TUE 260 23	12
13	SAT 112 32	TUE 143 06	TUE 170 41	FRI 201 15	SUN 230 49	WED 261 22	13
14	SUN 113 31	WED 144 05	WED 171 41	SAT 202 14	MON 231 48	THU 262 21	14
15	MON 114 31	THU 145 04	THU 172 40	SUN 203 13	TUE 232 47	FRI 263 21	15
16	TUE 115 30	FRI 146 03	FRI 173 39	MON 204 12	WED 233 46	SAT 264 20	16
17	WED 116 29	SAT 147 02	SAT 174 38	TUE 205 11	THU 234 45	SUN 265 19	17
18	THU 117 28	SUN 148 01	SUN 175 37	WED 206 10	FRI 235 45	MON 266 18	18
19	FRI 118 27	MON 149 00	MON 176 36	THU 207 10	SAT 236 44	TUE 267 17	19
20	SAT 119 26	TUE 150 00	TUE 177 35	FRI 208 09	SUN 237 43	WED 268 16	20
21	SUN 120 25	WED 150 59	WED 178 35	SAT 209 08	MON 238 42	THU 269 15	21
22	MON 121 25	THU 151 58	THU 179 34	SUN 210 07	TUE 239 41	FRI 270 14	22
23	TUE 122 24	FRI 152 57	FRI 180 33	MON 211 06	WED 240 40	SAT 271 14	23
24	WED 123 23	SAT 153 56	SAT 181 32	TUE 212 05	THU 241 39	SUN 272 13	24
25	THU 124 22	SUN 154 55	SUN 182 31	WED 213 04	FRI 242 39	MON 273 12	25
26	FRI 125 21	MON 155 54	MON 183 30	THU 214 04	SAT 243 38	TUE 274 11	26
27	SAT 126 20	TUE 156 54	TUE 184 29	FRI 215 03	SUN 244 37	WED 275 10	27
28	SUN 127 19	WED 157 53	WED 185 29	SAT 216 02	MON 245 36	THU 276 09	28
29	MON 128 19		THU 186 28	SUN 217 01	TUE 246 35	FRI 277 08	29
30	TUE 129 18		FRI 187 27	MON 218 00	WED 247 34	SAT 278 08	30
31	WED 130 17		SAT 188 26		THU 248 33		31

Day	JULY	AUGUST	SEPTEMBER	OCTOBER	NOVEMBER	DECEMBER	Day
1	SUN 279°07'	WED 309°40'	SAT 340°13'	MON 9°47'	THU 40°21'	SAT 69°55'	1
2	MON 280 06	THU 310 39	SUN 341 12	TUE 10 47	FRI 41 20	SUN 70 54	2
3	TUE 281 05	FRI 311 38	MON 342 12	WED 11 46	SAT 42 19	MON 71 53	3
4	WED 282 04	SAT 312 37	TUE 343 11	THU 12 45	SUN 43 18	TUE 72 52	4
5	THU 283 03	SUN 313 37	WED 344 10	FRI 13 44	MON 44 17	WED 73 52	5
6	FRI 284 02	MON 314 36	THU 345 09	SAT 14 43	TUE 45 16	THU 74 51	6
7	SAT 285 02	TUE 315 35	FRI 346 08	SUN 15 42	WED 46 16	FRI 75 50	7
8	SUN 286 01	WED 316 34	SAT 347 07	MON 16 41	THU 47 15	SAT 76 49	8
9	MON 287 00	THU 317 33	SUN 348 06	TUE 17 41	FRI 48 14	SUN 77 48	9
10	TUE 287 59	FRI 318 32	MON 349 06	WED 18 40	SAT 49 13	MON 78 47	10
11	WED 288 58	SAT 319 31	TUE 350 05	THU 19 39	SUN 50 12	TUE 79 46	11
12	THU 289 57	SUN 320 31	WED 351 04	FRI 20 38	MON 51 11	WED 80 45	12
13	FRI 290 56	MON 321 30	THU 352 03	SAT 21 37	TUE 52 10	THU 81 45	13
14	SAT 291 56	TUE 322 29	FRI 353 02	SUN 22 36	WED 53 10	FRI 82 44	14
15	SUN 292 55	WED 323 28	SAT 354 01	MON 23 35	THU 54 09	SAT 83 43	15
16	MON 293 54	THU 324 27	SUN 355 00	TUE 24 35	FRI 55 08	SUN 84 42	16
17	TUE 294 53	FRI 325 26	MON 356 00	WED 25 34	SAT 56 07	MON 85 41	17
18	WED 295 52	SAT 326 25	TUE 356 59	THU 26 33	SUN 57 06	TUE 86 40	18
19	THU 296 51	SUN 327 25	WED 357 58	FRI 27 32	MON 58 05	WED 87 39	19
20	FRI 297 50	MON 328 24	THU 358 57	SAT 28 31	TUE 59 04	THU 88 39	20
21	SAT 298 50	TUE 329 23	FRI 359 56	SUN 29 30	WED 60 04	FRI 89 38	21
22	SUN 299 49	WED 330 22	SAT 0 55	MON 30 29	THU 61 03	SAT 90 37	22
23	MON 300 48	THU 331 21	SUN 1 54	TUE 31 29	FRI 62 02	SUN 91 36	23
24	TUE 301 47	FRI 332 20	MON 2 54	WED 32 28	SAT 63 01	MON 92 35	24
25	WED 302 46	SAT 333 19	TUE 3 53	THU 33 27	SUN 64 00	TUE 93 34	25
26	THU 303 45	SUN 334 19	WED 4 52	FRI 34 26	MON 64 59	WED 94 33	26
27	FRI 304 44	MON 335 18	THU 5 51	SAT 35 25	TUE 65 58	THU 95 33	27
28	SAT 305 43	TUE 336 17	FRI 6 50	SUN 36 24	WED 66 58	FRI 96 32	28
29	SUN 306 43	WED 337 16	SAT 7 49	MON 37 23	THU 67 57	SAT 97 31	29
30	MON 307 42	THU 338 15	SUN 8 48	TUE 38 23	FRI 68 56	SUN 98 30	30
31	TUE 308 41	FRI 339 14		WED 39 22		MON 99 29	31

ARIES Corrn

GMT h m	Corrn 0'
0 12	+1
0 36	+2
1 00	+3
1 25	+4
1 49	+5
2 13	+6
2 38	+7
3 02	+8
3 26	+9
3 51	+10
4 15	+11
4 40	+12
5 04	+13
5 28	+14
5 53	+15
6 17	+16
6 41	+17
7 06	+18
7 30	+19
7 54	+20
8 19	+21
8 43	+22
9 07	+23
9 32	+24
9 56	+25
10 20	+26
10 45	+27
11 09	+28
11 33	+29
11 58	+30
12 22	+31
12 47	+32
13 11	+33
13 35	+34
14 00	+35
14 24	+36
14 48	+37
15 13	+38
15 37	+39
16 01	+40
16 26	+41
16 50	+42
17 14	+43
17 39	+44
18 03	+45
18 27	+46
18 52	+47
19 16	+48
19 40	+49
20 05	+50
20 29	+51
20 53	+52
21 18	+53
21 42	+54
22 07	+55
22 31	+56
22 55	+57
23 20	+58
23 44	+59
24 00	

INDEX OF BRIGHT STARS 2001

NAME	No	Mag.	SHA	DEC		NAME	No	Mag	SHA	DEC
Acamar	1	3.1	315°26'	S40°18'		Alpheratz	12	2.2	357°53'	N29°06'
Achernar	2	0.6	335 34	S57 14		Ankaa	14	2.4	353 25	S42 18
Acrux	3	1.1	173 20	S63 07		Schedah	52	2.5	349 51	N56 32
Adhara	4	1.6	255 20	S28 58		Diphda	25	2.2	349 05	S17 59
Aldebaran	5	1.1	291 01	N16 31		Achernar	2	0.6	335 34	S57 14
Alioth	6	1.7	166 29	N55 58		Hamal	34	2.2	328 12	N23 28
Alkaid	7	1.9	153 06	N49 19		Polaris	44	2.1	321 55	N89 16
Al Na'ir	8	2.2	27 55	S46 57		Acamar	1	3.1	315 26	S40 18
Alnilam	9	1.8	275 56	S 1 12		Menkar	38	2.8	314 25	N 4 06
Alphard	10	2.2	218 06	S 8 40		Mirfak	41	1.9	308 54	N49 52
Alphecca	11	2.3	126 19	N26 43		Aldebaran	5	1.1	291 01	N16 31
Alpheratz	12	2.2	357 53	N29 06		Rigel	49	0.3	281 21	S 8 12
Altair	13	0.9	62 17	N 8 52		Capella	22	0.2	280 49	N46 00
Ankaa	14	2.4	353 25	S42 18		Bellatrix	19	1.7	278 42	N 6 21
Antares	15	1.2	112 37	S26 26		Elnath	27	1.8	278 25	N28 36
Arcturus	16	0.2	146 04	N19 11		Alnilam	9	1.8	276 07	S 1 13
Atria	17	1.9	107 47	S69 02		Betelgeuse	20	Var*	271 12	N 7 24
Avior	18	1.7	234 23	S59 31		Canopus	21	-0.9	264 01	S52 42
Bellatrix	19	1.7	278 42	N 6 21		Sirius	54	-1.6	258 42	S16 43
Betelgeuse	20	Var*	271 12	N 7 24		Adhara	4	1.6	255 20	S28 58
Canopus	21	-0.9	264 01	S52 42		Procyon	46	0.5	245 10	N 5 13
Capella	22	0.2	280 49	N46 00		Pollux	45	1.2	243 40	N28 01
Deneb	23	1.3	49 38	N45 17		Avior	18	1.7	234 23	S59 31
Denebola	24	2.2	182 43	N14 34		Suhail	56	2.2	223 00	S43 26
Diphda	25	2.2	349 05	S17 59		Miaplacidus	40	1.8	221 43	S69 44
Dubhe	26	2.0	194 03	N61 45		Alphard	10	2.2	218 06	S 8 40
Elnath	27	1.8	278 25	N28 36		Regulus	48	1.3	207 54	N11 58
Eltanin	28	2.4	90 50	N51 29		Dubhe	26	2.0	194 03	N61 45
Enif	29	2.5	33 56	N 9 53		Denebola	24	2.2	182 43	N14 34
Fomalhaut	30	1.3	15 34	S29 37		Gienah	32	2.8	176 02	S17 33
Gacrux	31	1.6	172 12	S57 07		Acrux	3	1.1	173 20	S63 07
Gienah	32	2.8	176 02	S17 33		Gacrux	31	1.6	172 12	S57 07
Hadar	33	0.9	149 01	S60 23		Alioth	6	1.7	166 29	N55 58
Hamal	34	2.2	328 12	N23 28		Spica	55	1.2	158 41	S11 10
Kaus Australis	35	2.0	83 56	S34 23		Alkaid	7	1.9	153 06	N49 19
Kochab	36	2.2	137 19	N74 09		Hadar	33	0.9	149 01	S60 23
Markab	37	2.6	13 48	N15 13		Menkent	39	2.3	148 19	S36 23
Menkar	38	2.8	314 25	N 4 06		Arcturus	16	0.2	146 04	N19 11
Menkent	39	2.3	148 19	S36 23		Rigil Kentaurus	50	0.1	140 04	S60 51
Miaplacidus	40	1.8	221 43	S69 44		Zubenelgenubi	58	2.9	137 16	S16 03
Mirfak	41	1.9	308 54	N49 52		Kochab	36	2.2	137 19	N74 09
Nunki	42	2.1	76 10	S26 18		Alphecca	11	2.3	126 19	N26 43
Peacock	43	2.1	53 33	S56 44		Antares	15	1.2	112 37	S26 26
Polaris	44	2.1	321 55	N89 16		Atria	17	1.9	107 47	S69 02
Pollux	45	1.2	243 40	N28 01		Sabik	51	2.6	102 23	S15 44
Procyon	46	0.5	245 10	N 5 13		Shaula	53	1.7	96 34	S37 06
Rasalhague	47	2.1	96 15	N12 34		Rasalhague	47	2.1	96 15	N12 34
Regulus	48	1.3	207 54	N11 58		Eltanin	28	2.4	90 50	N51 29
Rigel	49	0.3	281 21	S 8 12		Kaus Australis	35	2.0	83 56	S34 23
Rigil Kentaurus	50	0.1	140 04	S60 51		Vega	57	0.1	80 45	N38 47
Sabik	51	2.6	102 23	S15 44		Nunki	42	2.1	76 10	S26 18
Schedar	52	2.5	349 51	N56 32		Altair	13	0.9	62 17	N 8 52
Shaula	53	1.7	96 34	S37 06		Peacock	43	2.1	53 33	S56 44
Sirius	54	-1.6	258 42	S16 43		Deneb	23	1.3	49 38	N45 17
Spica	55	1.2	158 41	S11 10		Enif	29	2.5	34 00	N 9 51
Suhail	56	2.2	223 00	S43 26		Al Na'ir	8	2.2	27 55	S46 57
Vega	57	0.1	80 45	N38 47		Fomalhaut	30	1.3	15 34	S29 37
Zubenelgenubi	58	2.9	137 16	S16 03		Markab	37	2.6	13 48	N15 13

* 0.1 - 1.2

DIP Corrn

Corrn		
m		ft
0.0	0'	0
0.7	-1	2
2.0	-2	6
3.9	-3	13
6.5	-4	21
9.7	-5	32
13.6	-6	44
18.1	-7	59
23.3	-8	76
29.1	-9	95
	-10	

STARS REFN Corrn

Alt	Corrn
0° 05'	-34'
0 10	-33
0 15	-32
0 20	-31
0 26	-30
0 32	-29
0 38	-28
0 45	-27
0 52	-26
0 59	-25
1 07	-24
1 16	-23
1 25	-22
1 35	-21
1 46	-20
1 58	-19
2 11	-18
2 25	-17
2 41	-16
2 58	-15
3 18	-14
3 41	-13
4 07	-12
4 38	-11
5 14	-10
5 59	-9
6 54	-8
8 06	-7
9 41	-6
11 56	-5
15 21	-4
21 10	-3
32 54	-2
62 22	-1
	0

GHA ARIES AT GMT 0hrs 2002

Day	JANUARY	FEBRUARY	MARCH	APRIL	MAY	JUNE	Day
1	TUE 100°28'	FRI 131°02'	FRI 158°37'	MON 189°11'	WED 218°45'	SAT 249°18'	1
2	WED 101 27	SAT 132 01	SAT 159 37	TUE 190 10	THU 219 44	SUN 250 17	2
3	THU 102 27	SUN 133 00	SUN 160 36	WED 191 09	FRI 220 43	MON 251 17	3
4	FRI 103 26	MON 133 59	MON 161 35	THU 192 08	SAT 221 42	TUE 252 16	4
5	SAT 104 25	TUE 134 58	TUE 162 34	FRI 193 07	SUN 222 41	WED 253 15	5
6	SUN 105 24	WED 135 57	WED 163 33	SAT 194 06	MON 223 41	THU 254 14	6
7	MON 106 23	THU 136 56	THU 164 32	SUN 195 06	TUE 224 40	FRI 255 13	7
8	TUE 107 22	FRI 137 56	FRI 165 31	MON 196 05	WED 225 39	SAT 256 12	8
9	WED 108 21	SAT 138 55	SAT 166 31	TUE 197 04	THU 226 38	SUN 257 11	9
10	THU 109 21	SUN 139 54	SUN 167 30	WED 198 03	FRI 227 37	MON 258 10	10
11	FRI 110 20	MON 140 53	MON 168 29	THU 199 02	SAT 228 36	TUE 259 10	11
12	SAT 111 19	TUE 141 52	TUE 169 28	FRI 200 01	SUN 229 35	WED 260 09	12
13	SUN 112 18	WED 142 51	WED 170 27	SAT 201 00	MON 230 35	THU 261 08	13
14	MON 113 17	THU 143 50	THU 171 26	SUN 202 00	TUE 231 34	FRI 262 07	14
15	TUE 114 16	FRI 144 50	FRI 172 25	MON 202 59	WED 232 33	SAT 263 06	15
16	WED 115 15	SAT 145 49	SAT 173 25	TUE 203 58	THU 233 32	SUN 264 05	16
17	THU 116 15	SUN 146 48	SUN 174 24	WED 204 57	FRI 234 31	MON 265 04	17
18	FRI 117 14	MON 147 47	MON 175 23	THU 205 56	SAT 235 30	TUE 266 04	18
19	SAT 118 13	TUE 148 46	TUE 176 22	FRI 206 55	SUN 236 29	WED 267 03	19
20	SUN 119 12	WED 149 45	WED 177 21	SAT 207 54	MON 237 29	THU 268 02	20
21	MON 120 11	THU 150 44	THU 178 20	SUN 208 54	TUE 238 28	FRI 269 01	21
22	TUE 121 10	FRI 151 44	FRI 179 19	MON 209 53	WED 239 27	SAT 270 00	22
23	WED 122 09	SAT 152 43	SAT 180 19	TUE 210 52	THU 240 26	SUN 270 59	23
24	THU 123 08	SUN 153 42	SUN 181 18	WED 211 51	FRI 241 25	MON 271 58	24
25	FRI 124 08	MON 154 41	MON 182 17	THU 212 50	SAT 242 24	TUE 272 58	25
26	SAT 125 07	TUE 155 40	TUE 183 16	FRI 213 49	SUN 243 23	WED 273 57	26
27	SUN 126 06	WED 156 39	WED 184 15	SAT 214 48	MON 244 23	THU 274 56	27
28	MON 127 05	THU 157 38	THU 185 14	SUN 215 48	TUE 245 22	FRI 275 55	28
29	TUE 128 04		FRI 186 13	MON 216 47	WED 246 21	SAT 276 54	29
30	WED 129 03		SAT 187 12	TUE 217 46	THU 247 20	SUN 277 53	30
31	THU 130 02		SUN 188 12		FRI 248 19		31

Day	JULY	AUGUST	SEPTEMBER	OCTOBER	NOVEMBER	DECEMBER	Day
1	MON 278°52'	THU 309°26'	SUN 339°59'	TUE 9°33'	FRI 40°06'	SUN 69°41'	1
2	TUE 279 52	FRI 310 25	MON 340 58	WED 10 32	SAT 41 06	MON 70 40	2
3	WED 280 51	SAT 311 24	TUE 341 57	THU 11 31	SUN 42 05	TUE 71 39	3
4	THU 281 50	SUN 312 23	WED 342 56	FRI 12 31	MON 43 04	WED 72 38	4
5	FRI 282 49	MON 313 22	THU 343 56	SAT 13 30	TUE 44 03	THU 73 37	5
6	SAT 283 48	TUE 314 21	FRI 344 55	SUN 14 29	WED 45 02	FRI 74 36	6
7	SUN 284 47	WED 315 21	SAT 345 54	MON 15 28	THU 46 01	SAT 75 35	7
8	MON 285 46	THU 316 20	SUN 346 53	TUE 16 27	FRI 47 00	SUN 76 35	8
9	TUE 286 46	FRI 317 19	MON 347 52	WED 17 26	SAT 48 00	MON 77 34	9
10	WED 287 45	SAT 318 18	TUE 348 51	THU 18 25	SUN 48 59	TUE 78 33	10
11	THU 288 44	SUN 319 17	WED 349 50	FRI 19 25	MON 49 58	WED 79 32	11
12	FRI 289 43	MON 320 16	THU 350 50	SAT 20 24	TUE 50 57	THU 80 31	12
13	SAT 290 42	TUE 321 15	FRI 351 49	SUN 21 23	WED 51 56	FRI 81 30	13
14	SUN 291 41	WED 322 15	SAT 352 48	MON 22 22	THU 52 55	SAT 82 29	14
15	MON 292 40	THU 323 14	SUN 353 47	TUE 23 21	FRI 53 54	SUN 83 29	15
16	TUE 293 40	FRI 324 13	MON 354 46	WED 24 20	SAT 54 54	MON 84 28	16
17	WED 294 39	SAT 325 12	TUE 355 45	THU 25 19	SUN 55 53	TUE 85 27	17
18	THU 295 38	SUN 326 11	WED 356 44	FRI 26 19	MON 56 52	WED 86 26	18
19	FRI 296 37	MON 327 10	THU 357 44	SAT 27 18	TUE 57 51	THU 87 25	19
20	SAT 297 36	TUE 328 09	FRI 358 43	SUN 28 17	WED 58 50	FRI 88 24	20
21	SUN 298 35	WED 329 09	SAT 359 42	MON 29 16	THU 59 49	SAT 89 23	21
22	MON 299 34	THU 330 08	SUN 0 41	TUE 30 15	FRI 60 48	SUN 90 23	22
23	TUE 300 33	FRI 331 07	MON 1 40	WED 31 14	SAT 61 48	MON 91 22	23
24	WED 301 33	SAT 332 06	TUE 2 39	THU 32 13	SUN 62 47	TUE 92 21	24
25	THU 302 32	SUN 333 05	WED 3 38	FRI 33 13	MON 63 46	WED 93 20	25
26	FRI 303 31	MON 334 04	THU 4 37	SAT 34 12	TUE 64 45	THU 94 19	26
27	SAT 304 30	TUE 335 03	FRI 5 37	SUN 35 11	WED 65 44	FRI 95 18	27
28	SUN 305 29	WED 336 02	SAT 6 36	MON 36 10	THU 66 43	SAT 96 17	28
29	MON 306 28	THU 337 02	SUN 7 35	TUE 37 09	FRI 67 42	SUN 97 17	29
30	TUE 307 27	FRI 338 01	MON 8 34	WED 38 08	SAT 68 42	MON 98 16	30
31	WED 308 27	SAT 339 00		THU 39 07		TUE 99 15	31

ARIES Corrn

GMT Corrn	
h m	0'
0 12	+1
0 36	+2
1 00	+3
1 25	+4
1 49	+5
2 13	+6
2 38	+7
3 02	+8
3 26	+9
3 51	+10
4 15	+11
4 40	+12
5 04	+13
5 28	+14
5 53	+15
6 17	+16
6 41	+17
7 06	+18
7 30	+19
7 54	+20
8 19	+21
8 43	+22
9 07	+23
9 32	+24
9 56	+25
10 20	+26
10 45	+27
11 09	+28
11 33	+29
11 58	+30
12 22	+31
12 47	+32
13 11	+33
13 35	+34
14 00	+35
14 24	+36
14 48	+37
15 13	+38
15 37	+39
16 01	+40
16 26	+41
16 50	+42
17 14	+43
17 39	+44
18 03	+45
18 27	+46
18 52	+47
19 16	+48
19 40	+49
20 05	+50
20 29	+51
20 53	+52
21 18	+53
21 42	+54
22 07	+55
22 31	+56
22 55	+57
23 20	+58
23 44	+59
24 00	

INDEX OF BRIGHT STARS 2002

NAME	No.	Mag.	SHA	DEC	NAME	No.	Mag.	SHA	DEC
Acamar	1	3.1	315°25'	S40°18'	Alpheratz	12	2.2	357°52'	N29°06'
Achernar	2	0.6	335 33	S57 13	Ankaa	14	2.4	353 24	S42 17
Acrux	3	1.1	173 19	S63 07	Schedah	52	2.5	349 51	N56 33
Adhara	4	1.6	255 20	S28 58	Diphda	25	2.2	349 05	S17 58
Aldebaran	5	1.1	291 00	N16 31	Achernar	2	0.6	335 33	S57 13
Alioth	6	1.7	166 28	N55 57	Hamal	34	2.2	328 11	N23 28
Alkaid	7	1.9	153 05	N49 18	Polaris	44	2.1	321 41	N89 16
Al Na'ir	8	2.2	27 54	S46 57	Acamar	1	3.1	315 25	S40 18
Alnilam	9	1.8	275 55	S 1 12	Menkar	38	2.8	314 24	N 4 06
Alphard	10	2.2	218 05	S 8 40	Mirfak	41	1.9	308 53	N49 52
Alphecca	11	2.3	126 18	N26 43	Aldebaran	5	1.1	291 00	N16 31
Alpheratz	12	2.2	357 52	N29 06	Rigel	49	0.3	281 21	S 8 12
Altair	13	0.9	62 16	N 8 52	Capella	22	0.2	280 48	N46 00
Ankaa	14	2.4	353 24	S42 17	Bellatrix	19	1.7	278 42	N 6 21
Antares	15	1.2	112 37	S26 26	Elnath	27	1.8	278 24	N28 37
Arcturus	16	0.2	146 03	N19 10	Alnilam	9	1.8	276 06	S 1 12
Atria	17	1.9	107 46	S69 02	Betelgeuse	20	Var*	271 11	N 7 24
Avior	18	1.7	234 22	S59 31	Canopus	21	-0.9	264 01	S52 42
Bellatrix	19	1.7	278 42	N 6 21	Sirius	54	-1.6	258 42	S16 43
Betelgeuse	20	Var*	271 11	N 7 24	Adhara	4	1.6	255 20	S28 58
Canopus	21	-0.9	264 01	S52 42	Procyon	46	0.5	245 09	N 5 13
Capella	22	0.2	280 48	N46 00	Pollux	45	1.2	243 39	N28 01
Deneb	23	1.3	49 37	N45 17	Avior	18	1.7	234 22	S59 31
Denebola	24	2.2	182 43	N14 34	Suhail	56	2.2	222 59	S43 27
Diphda	25	2.2	349 05	S17 58	Miaplacidus	40	1.8	221 42	S69 44
Dubhe	26	2.0	194 02	N61 45	Alphard	10	2.2	218 05	S 8 40
Elnath	27	1.8	278 24	N28 37	Regulus	48	1.3	207 53	N11 57
Eltanin	28	2.4	90 50	N51 29	Dubhe	26	2.0	194 02	N61 45
Enif	29	2.5	33 55	N 9 53	Denebola	24	2.2	182 43	N14 34
Fomalhaut	30	1.3	15 33	S29 36	Gienah	32	2.8	176 01	S17 33
Gacrux	31	1.6	172 11	S57 08	Acrux	3	1.1	173 19	S63 07
Gienah	32	2.8	176 01	S17 33	Gacrux	31	1.6	172 11	S57 08
Hadar	33	0.9	149 00	S60 23	Alioth	6	1.7	166 28	N55 57
Hamal	34	2.2	328 11	N23 28	Spica	55	1.2	158 40	S11 10
Kaus Australis	35	2.0	83 55	S34 23	Alkaid	7	1.9	153 05	N49 18
Kochab	36	2.2	137 19	N74 09	Hadar	33	0.9	149 00	S60 23
Markab	37	2.6	13 47	N15 13	Menkent	39	2.3	148 18	S36 23
Menkar	38	2.8	314 24	N 4 06	Arcturus	16	0.2	146 03	N19 10
Menkent	39	2.3	148 18	S36 23	Rigil Kentaurus	50	0.1	140 03	S60 51
Miaplacidus	40	1.8	221 42	S69 44	Zubenelgenubi	58	2.9	137 15	S16 03
Mirfak	41	1.9	308 53	N49 52	Kochab	36	2.2	137 19	N74 09
Nunki	42	2.1	76 09	S26 18	Alphecca	11	2.3	126 18	N26 43
Peacock	43	2.1	53 32	S56 44	Antares	15	1.2	112 37	S26 26
Polaris	44	2.1	321 41	N89 16	Atria	17	1.9	107 46	S69 02
Pollux	45	1.2	243 39	N28 01	Sabik	51	2.6	102 22	S15 44
Procyon	46	0.5	245 09	N 5 13	Shaula	53	1.7	96 33	S37 06
Rasalhague	47	2.1	96 14	N12 34	Rasalhague	47	2.1	96 14	N12 34
Regulus	48	1.3	207 53	N11 57	Eltanin	28	2.4	90 50	N51 29
Rigel	49	0.3	281 21	S 8 12	Kaus Australis	35	2.0	83 55	S34 23
Rigil Kentaurus	50	0.1	140 03	S60 51	Vega	57	0.1	80 44	N38 47
Sabik	51	2.6	102 22	S15 44	Nunki	42	2.1	76 09	S26 18
Schedar	52	2.5	349 51	N56 33	Altair	13	0.9	62 16	N 8 52
Shaula	53	1.7	96 33	S37 06	Peacock	43	2.1	53 32	S56 44
Sirius	54	-1.6	258 42	S16 43	Deneb	23	1.3	49 37	N45 17
Spica	55	1.2	158 40	S11 10	Enif	29	2.5	33 55	N 9 52
Suhail	56	2.2	222 59	S43 27	Al Na'ir	8	2.2	27 54	S46 57
Vega	57	0.1	80 44	N38 47	Fomalhaut	30	1.3	15 33	S29 36
Zubenelgenubi	58	2.9	137 15	S16 03	Markab	37	2.6	13 47	N15 13

* 0.1 - 1.2

DIP Corr'n

Corr'n		
m	0'	ft
0.0	0'	0
0.7	-1	2
2.0	-2	6
3.9	-3	13
6.5	-4	21
9.7	-5	32
13.6	-6	44
18.1	-7	59
23.3	-8	76
29.1	-9	95
	-10	

STARS REFN Corr'n

Alt	Corr'n
0° 05'	-34'
0 10	-33
0 15	-32
0 20	-31
0 26	-30
0 32	-29
0 38	-28
0 45	-27
0 52	-26
0 59	-25
1 07	-24
1 16	-23
1 25	-22
1 35	-21
1 46	-20
1 58	-19
2 11	-18
2 25	-17
2 41	-16
2 58	-15
3 18	-14
3 41	-13
4 07	-12
4 38	-11
5 14	-10
5 59	-9
6 54	-8
8 06	-7
9 41	-6
11 56	-5
15 21	-4
21 10	-3
32 54	-2
62 22	-1
	0

GHA ARIES AT GMT 0hrs 2003

Day	JANUARY	FEBRUARY	MARCH	APRIL	MAY	JUNE	Day
1	WED 100°14'	SAT 130°47'	SAT 158°23'	TUE 188°56'	THU 218°31'	SUN 249°04'	1
2	THU 101 13	SUN 131 46	SUN 159 22	WED 189 56	FRI 219 30	MON 250 03	2
3	FRI 102 12	MON 132 46	MON 160 21	THU 190 55	SAT 220 29	TUE 251 02	3
4	SAT 103 11	TUE 133 45	TUE 161 21	FRI 191 54	SUN 221 28	WED 252 01	4
5	SUN 104 11	WED 134 44	WED 162 20	SAT 192 53	MON 222 27	THU 253 01	5
6	MON 105 10	THU 135 43	THU 163 19	SUN 193 52	TUE 223 26	FRI 254 00	6
7	TUE 106 09	FRI 136 42	FRI 164 18	MON 194 51	WED 224 25	SAT 254 59	7
8	WED 107 08	SAT 137 41	SAT 165 17	TUE 195 50	THU 225 25	SUN 255 58	8
9	THU 108 07	SUN 138 40	SUN 166 16	WED 196 50	FRI 226 24	MON 256 57	9
10	FRI 109 06	MON 139 40	MON 167 15	THU 197 49	SAT 227 23	TUE 257 56	10
11	SAT 110 05	TUE 140 39	TUE 168 15	FRI 198 48	SUN 228 22	WED 258 55	11
12	SUN 111 05	WED 141 38	WED 169 14	SAT 199 47	MON 229 21	THU 259 54	12
13	MON 112 04	THU 142 37	THU 170 13	SUN 200 46	TUE 230 20	FRI 260 54	13
14	TUE 113 03	FRI 143 36	FRI 171 12	MON 201 45	WED 231 19	SAT 261 53	14
15	WED 114 02	SAT 144 35	SAT 172 11	TUE 202 44	THU 232 19	SUN 262 52	15
16	THU 115 01	SUN 145 34	SUN 173 10	WED 203 44	FRI 233 18	MON 263 51	16
17	FRI 116 00	MON 146 34	MON 174 09	THU 204 43	SAT 234 17	TUE 264 50	17
18	SAT 116 59	TUE 147 33	TUE 175 09	FRI 205 42	SUN 235 16	WED 265 49	18
19	SUN 117 58	WED 148 32	WED 176 08	SAT 206 41	MON 236 15	THU 266 48	19
20	MON 118 58	THU 149 31	THU 177 07	SUN 207 40	TUE 237 14	FRI 267 48	20
21	TUE 119 57	FRI 150 30	FRI 178 06	MON 208 39	WED 238 13	SAT 268 47	21
22	WED 120 56	SAT 151 29	SAT 179 05	TUE 209 38	THU 239 13	SUN 269 46	22
23	THU 121 55	SUN 152 28	SUN 180 04	WED 210 38	FRI 240 12	MON 270 45	23
24	FRI 122 54	MON 153 27	MON 181 03	THU 211 37	SAT 241 11	TUE 271 44	24
25	SAT 123 53	TUE 154 27	TUE 182 03	FRI 212 36	SUN 242 10	WED 272 43	25
26	SUN 124 52	WED 155 26	WED 183 02	SAT 213 35	MON 243 09	THU 273 42	26
27	MON 125 52	THU 156 25	THU 184 01	SUN 214 34	TUE 244 08	FRI 274 42	27
28	TUE 126 51	FRI 157 24	FRI 185 00	MON 215 33	WED 245 07	SAT 275 41	28
29	WED 127 50		SAT 185 59	TUE 216 32	THU 246 07	SUN 276 40	29
30	THU 128 49		SUN 186 58	WED 217 31	FRI 247 06	MON 277 39	30
31	FRI 129 48		MON 187 57		SAT 248 05		31

Day	JULY	AUGUST	SEPTEMBER	OCTOBER	NOVEMBER	DECEMBER	Day
1	TUE 278°38'	FRI 309°11'	MON 339°45'	WED 9°19'	SAT 39°52'	MON 69°26'	1
2	WED 279 37	SAT 310 11	TUE 340 44	THU 10 18	SUN 40 51	TUE 70 26	2
3	THU 280 36	SUN 311 10	WED 341 43	FRI 11 17	MON 41 50	WED 71 25	3
4	FRI 281 36	MON 312 09	THU 342 42	SAT 12 16	TUE 42 50	THU 72 24	4
5	SAT 282 35	TUE 313 08	FRI 343 41	SUN 13 15	WED 43 49	FRI 73 23	5
6	SUN 283 34	WED 314 07	SAT 344 40	MON 14 15	THU 44 48	SAT 74 22	6
7	MON 284 33	THU 315 06	SUN 345 40	TUE 15 14	FRI 45 47	SUN 75 21	7
8	TUE 285 32	FRI 316 05	MON 346 39	WED 16 13	SAT 46 46	MON 76 20	8
9	WED 286 31	SAT 317 05	TUE 347 38	THU 17 12	SUN 47 45	TUE 77 19	9
10	THU 287 30	SUN 318 04	WED 348 37	FRI 18 11	MON 48 44	WED 78 19	10
11	FRI 288 30	MON 319 03	THU 349 36	SAT 19 10	TUE 49 44	THU 79 18	11
12	SAT 289 29	TUE 320 02	FRI 350 35	SUN 20 09	WED 50 43	FRI 80 17	12
13	SUN 290 28	WED 321 01	SAT 351 34	MON 21 09	THU 51 42	SAT 81 16	13
14	MON 291 27	THU 322 00	SUN 352 34	TUE 22 08	FRI 52 41	SUN 82 15	14
15	TUE 292 26	FRI 322 59	MON 353 33	WED 23 07	SAT 53 40	MON 83 14	15
16	WED 293 25	SAT 323 59	TUE 354 32	THU 24 06	SUN 54 39	TUE 84 13	16
17	THU 294 24	SUN 324 58	WED 355 31	FRI 25 05	MON 55 38	WED 85 13	17
18	FRI 295 24	MON 325 57	THU 356 30	SAT 26 04	TUE 56 38	THU 86 12	18
19	SAT 296 23	TUE 326 56	FRI 357 29	SUN 27 03	WED 57 37	FRI 87 11	19
20	SUN 297 22	WED 327 55	SAT 358 28	MON 28 03	THU 58 36	SAT 88 10	20
21	MON 298 21	THU 328 54	SUN 359 28	TUE 29 02	FRI 59 35	SUN 89 09	21
22	TUE 299 20	FRI 329 53	MON 0 27	WED 30 01	SAT 60 34	MON 90 08	22
23	WED 300 19	SAT 330 53	TUE 1 26	THU 31 00	SUN 61 33	TUE 91 07	23
24	THU 301 18	SUN 331 52	WED 2 25	FRI 31 59	MON 62 32	WED 92 07	24
25	FRI 302 17	MON 332 51	THU 3 24	SAT 32 58	TUE 63 32	THU 93 06	25
26	SAT 303 17	TUE 333 50	FRI 4 23	SUN 33 57	WED 64 31	FRI 94 05	26
27	SUN 304 16	WED 334 49	SAT 5 22	MON 34 57	THU 65 30	SAT 95 04	27
28	MON 305 15	THU 335 48	SUN 6 21	TUE 35 56	FRI 66 29	SUN 96 03	28
29	TUE 306 14	FRI 336 47	MON 7 21	WED 36 55	SAT 67 28	MON 97 02	29
30	WED 307 13	SAT 337 46	TUE 8 20	THU 37 54	SUN 68 27	TUE 98 01	30
31	THU 308 12	SUN 338 46		FRI 38 53		WED 99 01	31

ARIES Corrn

GMT Corrn	
h m	0'
0 12	+1
0 36	+2
1 00	+3
1 25	+4
1 49	+5
2 13	+6
2 38	+7
3 02	+8
3 26	+9
3 51	+10
4 15	+11
4 40	+12
5 04	+13
5 28	+14
5 53	+15
6 17	+16
6 41	+17
7 06	+18
7 30	+19
7 54	+20
8 19	+21
8 43	+22
9 07	+23
9 32	+24
9 56	+25
10 20	+26
10 45	+27
11 09	+28
11 33	+29
11 58	+30
12 22	+31
12 47	+32
13 11	+33
13 35	+34
14 00	+35
14 24	+36
14 48	+37
15 13	+38
15 37	+39
16 01	+40
16 26	+41
16 50	+42
17 14	+43
17 39	+44
18 03	+45
18 27	+46
18 52	+47
19 16	+48
19 40	+49
20 05	+50
20 29	+51
20 53	+52
21 18	+53
21 42	+54
22 07	+55
22 31	+56
22 55	+57
23 20	+58
23 44	+59
24 00	

INDEX OF BRIGHT STARS 2003

NAME	No	Mag.	SHA	DEC	NAME	No	Mag	SHA	DEC
Acamar	1	3.1	315°24'	S40°17'	Alpheratz	12	2.2	357°52'	N29°06'
Achernar	2	0.6	335 33	S57 13	Ankaa	14	2.4	353 23	S42 17
Acrux	3	1.1	173 18	S63 07	Schedah	52	2.5	349 50	N56 33
Adhara	4	1.6	255 19	S28 59	Diphda	25	2.2	349 04	S17 58
Aldebaran	5	1.1	290 59	N16 31	Achernar	2	0.6	335 33	S57 13
Alioth	6	1.7	166 27	N55 57	Hamal	34	2.2	328 10	N23 29
Alkaid	7	1.9	153 05	N49 18	Polaris	44	2.1	321 26	N89 16
Al Na'ir	8	2.2	27 53	S46 57	Acamar	1	3.1	315 24	S40 17
Alnilam	9	1.8	275 55	S 1 12	Menkar	38	2.8	314 24	N 4 06
Alphard	10	2.2	218 04	S 8 40	Mirfak	41	1.9	308 52	N49 52
Alphecca	11	2.3	126 17	N26 42	Aldebaran	5	1.1	290 59	N16 31
Alpheratz	12	2.2	357 52	N29 06	Rigel	49	0.3	281 20	S 8 12
Altair	13	0.9	62 16	N 8 53	Capella	22	0.2	280 47	N46 00
Ankaa	14	2.4	353 23	S42 17	Bellatrix	19	1.7	278 41	N 6 21
Antares	15	1.2	112 36	S26 26	Elnath	27	1.8	278 23	N28 37
Arcturus	16	0.2	146 03	N19 10	Alnilam	9	1.8	276 05	S 1 12
Atria	17	1.9	107 44	S69 02	Betelgeuse	20	Var*	271 10	N 7 25
Avior	18	1.7	234 22	S59 31	Canopus	21	-0.9	264 00	S52 42
Bellatrix	19	1.7	278 41	N 6 21	Sirius	54	-1.6	258 41	S16 43
Betelgeuse	20	Var*	271 10	N 7 25	Adhara	4	1.6	255 19	S28 59
Canopus	21	-0.9	264 00	S52 42	Procyon	46	0.5	245 08	N 5 13
Capella	22	0.2	280 47	N46 00	Pollux	45	1.2	243 38	N28 01
Deneb	23	1.3	49 37	N45 17	Avior	18	1.7	234 22	S59 31
Denebola	24	2.2	182 42	N14 33	Suhail	56	2.2	222 59	S43 27
Diphda	25	2.2	349 04	S17 58	Miaplacidus	40	1.8	221 42	S69 44
Dubhe	26	2.0	194 01	N61 44	Alphard	10	2.2	218 04	S 8 40
Elnath	27	1.8	278 23	N28 37	Regulus	48	1.3	207 52	N11 57
Eltanin	28	2.4	90 49	N51 29	Dubhe	26	2.0	194 01	N61 44
Enif	29	2.5	33 55	N 9 53	Denebola	24	2.2	182 42	N14 33
Fomalhaut	30	1.3	15 32	S29 36	Gienah	32	2.8	176 00	S17 34
Gacrux	31	1.6	172 10	S57 08	Acrux	3	1.1	173 18	S63 07
Gienah	32	2.8	176 00	S17 34	Gacrux	31	1.6	172 10	S57 08
Hadar	33	0.9	148 59	S60 24	Alioth	6	1.7	166 27	N55 57
Hamal	34	2.2	328 10	N23 29	Spica	55	1.2	158 40	S11 11
Kaus Australis	35	2.0	83 54	S34 23	Alkaid	7	1.9	153 05	N49 18
Kochab	36	2.2	137 19	N74 09	Hadar	33	0.9	148 59	S60 24
Markab	37	2.6	13 46	N15 13	Menkent	39	2.3	148 17	S36 23
Menkar	38	2.8	314 24	N 4 06	Arcturus	16	0.2	146 03	N19 10
Menkent	39	2.3	148 17	S36 23	Rigil Kentaurus	50	0.1	140 02	S60 51
Miaplacidus	40	1.8	221 42	S69 44	Zubenelgenubi	58	2.9	137 14	S16 03
Mirfak	41	1.9	308 52	N49 52	Kochab	36	2.2	137 19	N74 09
Nunki	42	2.1	76 08	S26 18	Alphecca	11	2.3	126 17	N26 42
Peacock	43	2.1	53 31	S56 43	Antares	15	1.2	112 36	S26 26
Polaris	44	2.1	321 26	N89 16	Atria	17	1.9	107 44	S69 02
Pollux	45	1.2	243 38	N28 01	Sabik	51	2.6	102 21	S15 44
Procyon	46	0.5	245 08	N 5 13	Shaula	53	1.7	96 32	S37 06
Rasalhague	47	2.1	96 13	N12 33	Rasalhague	47	2.1	96 13	N12 33
Regulus	48	1.3	207 52	N11 57	Eltanin	28	2.4	90 49	N51 29
Rigel	49	0.3	281 20	S 8 12	Kaus Australis	35	2.0	83 54	S34 23
Rigil Kentaurus	50	0.1	140 02	S60 51	Vega	57	0.1	80 44	N38 47
Sabik	51	2.6	102 21	S15 44	Nunki	42	2.1	76 08	S26 18
Schedar	52	2.5	349 50	N56 33	Altair	13	0.9	62 16	N 8 53
Shaula	53	1.7	96 32	S37 06	Peacock	43	2.1	53 31	S56 43
Sirius	54	-1.6	258 41	S16 43	Deneb	23	1.3	49 37	N45 17
Spica	55	1.2	158 40	S11 11	Enif	29	2.5	33 58	N 9 52
Suhail	56	2.2	222 59	S43 27	Al Na'ir	8	2.2	27 53	S46 57
Vega	57	0.1	80 44	N38 47	Fomalhaut	30	1.3	15 32	S29 36
Zubenelgenubi	58	2.9	137 14	S16 03	Markab	37	2.6	13 46	N15 13

* 0.1 - 1.2

DIP Corrn

Corrn		
m	0'	ft
0.0	0'	0
0.7	-1	2
2.0	-2	6
3.9	-3	13
6.5	-4	21
9.7	-5	32
13.6	-6	44
18.1	-7	59
23.3	-8	76
29.1	-9	95
	-10	

STARS REFN Corrn

Alt	Corrn
0° 05'	-34'
0 10	-33
0 15	-32
0 20	-31
0 26	-30
0 32	-29
0 38	-28
0 45	-27
0 52	-26
0 59	-25
1 07	-24
1 16	-23
1 25	-22
1 35	-21
1 46	-20
1 58	-19
2 11	-18
2 25	-17
2 41	-16
2 58	-15
3 18	-14
3 41	-13
4 07	-12
4 38	-11
5 14	-10
5 59	-9
6 54	-8
8 06	-7
9 41	-6
11 56	-5
15 21	-4
21 10	-3
32 54	-2
62 22	-1
	0

SUN & PLANETS AT GMT 0hrs JANUARY 1999

Day	SUN SD 16' GHA	v	Dec	d	VENUS Mag. -3.9 GHA	v	Dec	d	MARS Mag. +0.8 GHA	v	Dec	d	JUPITER Mag. -2.2 GHA	v	Dec	d	SATURN Mag. +0.5 GHA	v	Dec	d	Day
1 FRI	179° 13'	-7	S23° 03'	5	162° 36'	-21	S22° 21'	13	262° 31'	32	S 5° 27'	11	107° 07'	51	S 4° 20'	4	74° 26'	59	N 7° 57'	0	FRI 1
2 SAT	179 06	-7	S22 58	5	162 15	-21	S22 08	14	263 03	32	S 5 38	11	107 58	51	S 4 16	3	75 25	59	N 7 57	0	SAT 2
3 SUN	178 59	-7	S22 53	6	161 54	-20	S21 54	14	263 35	31	S 5 49	10	108 49	51	S 4 13	4	76 24	59	N 7 57	1	SUN 3
4 MON	178 52	-7	S22 47	6	161 34	-20	S21 40	14	264 06	32	S 5 59	11	109 40	51	S 4 09	4	77 23	58	N 7 58	0	MON 4
5 TUE	178 45	-7	S22 41	7	161 14	-20	S21 26	16	264 38	32	S 6 10	10	110 31	50	S 4 05	4	78 21	59	N 7 58	1	TUE 5
6 WED	178 38	-6	S22 34	7	160 54	-19	S21 10	16	265 10	32	S 6 20	11	111 21	51	S 4 01	4	79 20	58	N 7 59	0	WED 6
7 THU	178 32	-7	S22 27	7	160 35	-20	S20 54	17	265 42	32	S 6 31	10	112 12	50	S 3 57	4	80 18	59	N 7 59	1	THU 7
8 FRI	178 25	-6	S22 20	8	160 15	-19	S20 37	17	266 14	33	S 6 41	10	113 02	50	S 3 53	4	81 17	58	N 8 00	1	FRI 8
9 SAT	178 19	-6	S22 12	9	159 56	-18	S20 20	18	266 47	32	S 6 51	10	113 52	50	S 3 49	4	82 15	58	N 8 01	0	SAT 9
10 SUN	178 13	-7	S22 03	9	159 38	-18	S20 02	18	267 19	33	S 7 01	10	114 42	50	S 3 45	4	83 13	58	N 8 01	1	SUN 10
11 MON	178 06	-6	S21 54	9	159 20	-18	S19 44	19	267 52	33	S 7 11	10	115 32	50	S 3 41	4	84 11	58	N 8 02	0	MON 11
12 TUE	178 00	-5	S21 45	10	159 02	-18	S19 25	19	268 25	33	S 7 21	10	116 22	50	S 3 37	4	85 09	58	N 8 03	1	TUE 12
13 WED	177 55	-6	S21 35	10	158 44	-17	S19 05	20	268 58	33	S 7 31	10	117 12	49	S 3 33	5	86 07	57	N 8 04	1	WED 13
14 THU	177 49	-5	S21 25	11	158 27	-17	S18 45	20	269 31	33	S 7 41	9	118 01	50	S 3 28	4	87 04	58	N 8 05	1	THU 14
15 FRI	177 44	-6	S21 14	10	158 10	-17	S18 25	22	270 04	34	S 7 50	10	118 51	49	S 3 24	4	88 02	58	N 8 06	0	FRI 15
16 SAT	177 38	-5	S21 04	12	157 53	-16	S18 03	21	270 38	34	S 8 00	9	119 40	50	S 3 20	5	89 00	57	N 8 06	1	SAT 16
17 SUN	177 33	-5	S20 52	12	157 37	-16	S17 42	22	271 12	34	S 8 09	10	120 30	49	S 3 15	4	89 57	57	N 8 07	1	SUN 17
18 MON	177 28	-5	S20 40	12	157 21	-16	S17 20	23	271 46	34	S 8 19	9	121 19	49	S 3 11	5	90 54	57	N 8 08	2	MON 18
19 TUE	177 23	-4	S20 28	12	157 05	-15	S16 57	23	272 20	34	S 8 28	9	122 08	49	S 3 06	4	91 51	57	N 8 10	1	TUE 19
20 WED	177 19	-5	S20 16	13	156 50	-15	S16 34	24	272 54	34	S 8 37	9	122 57	49	S 3 02	5	92 48	57	N 8 11	1	WED 20
21 THU	177 14	-4	S20 03	14	156 35	-15	S16 10	24	273 28	35	S 8 46	8	123 46	49	S 2 57	5	93 45	57	N 8 12	1	THU 21
22 FRI	177 10	-4	S19 49	13	156 20	-14	S15 46	24	274 03	35	S 8 54	9	124 35	49	S 2 52	4	94 42	57	N 8 13	1	FRI 22
23 SAT	177 06	-4	S19 36	14	156 06	-14	S15 22	25	274 38	35	S 9 03	9	125 24	48	S 2 48	5	95 39	57	N 8 14	1	SAT 23
24 SUN	177 02	-4	S19 22	15	155 52	-14	S14 57	25	275 13	35	S 9 12	9	126 12	49	S 2 43	5	96 36	56	N 8 15	2	SUN 24
25 MON	176 58	-3	S19 07	14	155 38	-14	S14 32	26	275 48	36	S 9 20	9	127 01	48	S 2 38	4	97 32	57	N 8 17	1	MON 25
26 TUE	176 55	-4	S18 53	15	155 24	-13	S14 06	26	276 24	36	S 9 29	8	127 49	49	S 2 34	5	98 29	56	N 8 18	1	TUE 26
27 WED	176 51	-3	S18 38	16	155 11	-12	S13 40	26	277 00	36	S 9 37	8	128 38	48	S 2 29	5	99 25	57	N 8 19	2	WED 27
28 THU	176 48	-2	S18 22	16	154 59	-13	S13 14	27	277 36	36	S 9 45	8	129 26	49	S 2 24	5	100 22	56	N 8 21	1	THU 28
29 FRI	176 46	-3	S18 06	16	154 46	-12	S12 47	27	278 12	37	S 9 53	8	130 14	49	S 2 19	5	101 18	56	N 8 22	1	FRI 29
30 SAT	176 43	-3	S17 50	16	154 34	-12	S12 20	28	278 49	36	S10 01	7	131 03	48	S 2 14	5	102 14	56	N 8 23	2	SAT 30
31 SUN	176 40	-2	S17 34	17	154 22	-12	S11 52	27	279 25	37	S10 08	8	131 51	48	S 2 09	5	103 10	56	N 8 25	1	SUN 31
32 MON	176 38		S17 17		154 10		S11 25		280 02		S10 16		132 39		S 2 04		104 06		N 8 26		MON 32

SUN & PLANETS AT GMT 0hrs FEBRUARY 1999

Day	SUN SD 16' GHA	v	Dec	d	VENUS Mag. -3.9 GHA	v	Dec	d	MARS Mag. +0.2 GHA	v	Dec	d	JUPITER Mag. -2.1 GHA	v	Dec	d	SATURN Mag. +0.5 GHA	v	Dec	d	Day
1 MON	176° 38'	-2	S17° 17'	17	154° 10'	-11	S11° 25'	28	280° 02'	38	S10° 16'	8	132° 39'	48	S 2° 04'	5	104° 06'	56	N 8° 26'	2	MON 1
2 TUE	176 36	-2	S17 00	17	153 59	-11	S10 57	29	280 40	37	S10 24	7	133 27	47	S 1 59	5	105 02	55	N 8 28	1	TUE 2
3 WED	176 34	-1	S16 43	18	153 48	-11	S10 28	28	281 17	38	S10 31	7	134 14	48	S 1 54	5	105 57	56	N 8 29	2	WED 3
4 THU	176 33	-2	S16 25	18	153 37	-11	S10 00	29	281 55	38	S10 38	7	135 02	48	S 1 49	5	106 53	56	N 8 31	2	THU 4
5 FRI	176 31	-1	S16 07	18	153 26	-10	S 9 31	29	282 33	38	S10 45	7	135 50	47	S 1 44	5	107 49	55	N 8 33	1	FRI 5
6 SAT	176 30	-1	S15 49	18	153 16	-10	S 9 02	29	283 11	39	S10 52	7	136 37	48	S 1 39	5	108 44	56	N 8 34	2	SAT 6
7 SUN	176 29	-1	S15 31	19	153 06	-10	S 8 33	30	283 50	39	S10 59	7	137 25	48	S 1 34	5	109 40	55	N 8 36	2	SUN 7
8 MON	176 28	0	S15 12	19	152 56	-10	S 8 03	30	284 29	39	S11 06	6	138 13	47	S 1 29	5	110 35	55	N 8 38	1	MON 8
9 TUE	176 28	-1	S14 53	19	152 46	-10	S 7 33	30	285 08	40	S11 12	6	139 00	47	S 1 23	5	111 30	55	N 8 39	2	TUE 9
10 WED	176 27	0	S14 34	20	152 36	-9	S 7 03	30	285 48	40	S11 19	6	139 47	48	S 1 18	5	112 25	55	N 8 41	2	WED 10
11 THU	176 27	0	S14 14	19	152 27	-9	S 6 33	30	286 28	40	S11 25	6	140 35	47	S 1 13	5	113 20	55	N 8 43	2	THU 11
12 FRI	176 27	0	S13 55	20	152 18	-9	S 6 03	31	287 08	41	S11 31	6	141 22	47	S 1 08	6	114 15	55	N 8 45	2	FRI 12
13 SAT	176 27	0	S13 35	20	152 09	-9	S 5 32	30	287 49	41	S11 37	6	142 09	47	S 1 02	5	115 10	55	N 8 47	1	SAT 13
14 SUN	176 27	1	S13 15	21	152 00	-9	S 5 02	31	288 30	42	S11 43	6	142 56	47	S 0 57	5	116 05	55	N 8 48	2	SUN 14
15 MON	176 28	0	S12 54	20	151 51	-8	S 4 31	31	289 12	42	S11 49	5	143 43	47	S 0 52	6	117 00	54	N 8 50	2	MON 15
16 TUE	176 28	1	S12 34	21	151 43	-9	S 4 00	31	289 54	42	S11 54	6	144 30	47	S 0 46	5	117 54	55	N 8 52	2	TUE 16
17 WED	176 29	1	S12 13	21	151 34	-8	S 3 29	31	290 36	42	S12 00	5	145 17	47	S 0 41	6	118 49	55	N 8 54	2	WED 17
18 THU	176 30	1	S11 52	21	151 26	-8	S 2 58	31	291 18	44	S12 05	5	146 04	47	S 0 36	5	119 44	54	N 8 56	2	THU 18
19 FRI	176 31	2	S11 31	22	151 18	-9	S 2 27	31	292 02	43	S12 10	5	146 51	47	S 0 30	5	120 38	54	N 8 58	2	FRI 19
20 SAT	176 33	1	S11 09	21	151 09	-8	S 1 56	31	292 45	44	S12 15	5	147 38	46	S 0 25	6	121 32	55	N 9 00	2	SAT 20
21 SUN	176 34	2	S10 48	22	151 01	-8	S 1 25	32	293 29	44	S12 20	4	148 24	47	S 0 19	6	122 27	54	N 9 02	2	SUN 21
22 MON	176 36	2	S10 26	22	150 53	-7	S 0 53	31	294 13	45	S12 24	5	149 11	47	S 0 14	6	123 21	54	N 9 04	2	MON 22
23 TUE	176 38	2	S10 04	22	150 46	-8	S 0 22	13	294 58	45	S12 29	4	149 58	46	S 0 08	5	124 15	54	N 9 06	2	TUE 23
24 WED	176 40	2	S 9 42	22	150 38	-8	N 0 09	32	295 43	46	S12 33	4	150 44	47	S 0 03	0	125 09	54	N 9 08	3	WED 24
25 THU	176 42	2	S 9 20	22	150 30	-8	N 0 41	31	296 29	47	S12 37	4	151 31	46	N 0 03	5	126 03	54	N 9 11	2	THU 25
26 FRI	176 44	3	S 8 58	23	150 22	-7	N 1 12	31	297 16	46	S12 41	4	152 17	47	N 0 08	6	126 57	54	N 9 13	2	FRI 26
27 SAT	176 47	3	S 8 35	22	150 15	-8	N 1 43	32	298 02	48	S12 45	4	153 04	46	N 0 14	6	127 51	54	N 9 15	2	SAT 27
28 SUN	176 50	2	S 8 13	23	150 07	-8	N 2 15	31	298 50	47	S12 49	4	153 50	47	N 0 20	5	128 45	53	N 9 17	2	SUN 28
29 MON	176 52		S 7 50		149 59		N 2 46		299 37		S12 53		154 37		N 0 25		129 38		N 9 19		MON 29

SUN & PLANETS AT GMT 0hrs MARCH 1999

Day	SUN SD 16' GHA	v	Dec	d	VENUS Mag. -4.0 GHA	v	Dec	d	MARS Mag. -0.5 GHA	v	Dec	d	JUPITER Mag. -2.1 GHA	v	Dec	d	SATURN Mag. +0.5 GHA	v	Dec	d	Day
1 MON	176° 52'	3'	S 7° 50'	22'	149° 59'	-7'	N 2° 46'	31'	299° 37'	49'	S12° 53'	3'	154° 37'	46'	N 0° 25'	6'	129° 38'	54'	N 9° 19'	3'	MON 1
2 TUE	176 55	3	S 7 28	23	149 52	-8	N 3 17	31	300 26	48	S12 56	3	155 23	46	N 0 31	5	130 32	53	N 9 22	2	TUE 2
3 WED	176 58	3	S 7 05	23	149 44	-8	N 3 48	31	301 14	50	S12 59	3	156 09	47	N 0 36	6	131 25	54	N 9 24	2	WED 3
4 THU	177 01	4	S 6 42	23	149 36	-7	N 4 19	31	302 04	50	S13 02	3	156 56	46	N 0 42	6	132 19	53	N 9 26	2	THU 4
5 FRI	177 05	3	S 6 19	24	149 29	-8	N 4 50	31	302 54	50	S13 05	3	157 42	46	N 0 48	5	133 12	54	N 9 28	3	FRI 5
6 SAT	177 08	4	S 5 55	23	149 21	-8	N 5 21	31	303 44	52	S13 08	2	158 28	46	N 0 53	6	134 06	53	N 9 31	2	SAT 6
7 SUN	177 12	4	S 5 32	23	149 13	-8	N 5 52	31	304 36	51	S13 10	2	159 14	46	N 0 59	6	134 59	54	N 9 33	2	SUN 7
8 MON	177 15	4	S 5 09	23	149 05	-8	N 6 23	30	305 27	53	S13 13	2	160 00	47	N 1 05	5	135 53	53	N 9 35	3	MON 8
9 TUE	177 19	4	S 4 46	24	148 57	-8	N 6 53	30	306 20	53	S13 15	2	160 47	46	N 1 10	6	136 46	53	N 9 38	2	TUE 9
10 WED	177 23	3	S 4 22	23	148 49	-8	N 7 23	31	307 13	53	S13 17	2	161 33	46	N 1 16	6	137 39	53	N 9 40	2	WED 10
11 THU	177 26	4	S 3 59	24	148 41	-8	N 7 54	30	308 06	55	S13 19	2	162 19	46	N 1 22	5	138 32	53	N 9 42	3	THU 11
12 FRI	177 30	4	S 3 35	24	148 33	-8	N 8 24	29	309 01	55	S13 21	1	163 05	46	N 1 27	6	139 25	53	N 9 45	2	FRI 12
13 SAT	177 34	4	S 3 11	23	148 25	-9	N 8 53	30	309 56	55	S13 22	1	163 51	46	N 1 33	6	140 18	53	N 9 47	2	SAT 13
14 SUN	177 38	4	S 2 48	24	148 16	-8	N 9 23	29	310 51	57	S13 23	1	164 37	46	N 1 39	5	141 11	53	N 9 49	3	SUN 14
15 MON	177 42	5	S 2 24	24	148 08	-9	N 9 52	30	311 48	57	S13 25	0	165 23	46	N 1 44	6	142 04	53	N 9 52	2	MON 15
16 TUE	177 47	4	S 2 00	23	147 59	-9	N10 22	29	312 45	57	S13 25	1	166 09	46	N 1 50	5	142 57	53	N 9 54	3	TUE 16
17 WED	177 51	4	S 1 37	24	147 50	-9	N10 51	28	313 42	59	S13 26	1	166 55	46	N 1 56	6	143 50	53	N 9 57	2	WED 17
18 THU	177 55	4	S 1 13	24	147 41	-9	N11 19	29	314 41	59	S13 27	0	167 41	45	N 2 02	5	144 43	52	N 9 59	3	THU 18
19 FRI	177 59	5	S 0 49	24	147 32	-9	N11 48	28	315 40	60	S13 27	0	168 26	46	N 2 07	6	145 35	53	N10 02	2	FRI 19
20 SAT	178 04	4	S 0 25	23	147 23	-9	N12 16	28	316 40	61	S13 27	0	169 12	46	N 2 13	6	146 28	53	N10 04	3	SAT 20
21 SUN	178 08	5	S 0 02	20	147 14	-10	N12 44	27	317 41	61	S13 27	0	169 58	46	N 2 19	6	147 21	52	N10 07	3	SUN 21
22 MON	178 13	4	N 0 22	24	147 04	-10	N13 11	28	318 42	62	S13 27	0	170 44	46	N 2 25	5	148 13	53	N10 09	3	MON 22
23 TUE	178 17	5	N 0 46	23	146 54	-10	N13 39	27	319 44	63	S13 27	1	171 30	46	N 2 30	6	149 06	52	N10 12	2	TUE 23
24 WED	178 22	4	N 1 09	24	146 44	-10	N14 06	26	320 47	64	S13 26	1	172 16	45	N 2 36	6	149 58	53	N10 14	3	WED 24
25 THU	178 26	5	N 1 33	24	146 34	-10	N14 32	27	321 51	64	S13 25	0	173 01	46	N 2 42	5	150 51	52	N10 17	2	THU 25
26 FRI	178 31	4	N 1 57	23	146 24	-11	N14 59	25	322 55	66	S13 25	1	173 47	46	N 2 47	6	151 43	52	N10 19	3	FRI 26
27 SAT	178 35	5	N 2 20	24	146 13	-11	N15 24	26	324 01	66	S13 23	1	174 33	46	N 2 53	6	152 35	53	N10 22	2	SAT 27
28 SUN	178 40	5	N 2 44	23	146 02	-11	N15 50	25	325 07	66	S13 22	1	175 19	46	N 2 59	5	153 28	52	N10 24	3	SUN 28
29 MON	178 44	5	N 3 07	23	145 51	-11	N16 15	25	326 13	68	S13 21	2	176 05	45	N 3 04	6	154 20	52	N10 27	2	MON 29
30 TUE	178 49	4	N 3 30	24	145 40	-11	N16 40	24	327 21	68	S13 19	2	176 50	46	N 3 10	6	155 12	53	N10 29	3	TUE 30
31 WED	178 53	5	N 3 54	23	145 29	-12	N17 04	24	328 29	69	S13 17	2	177 36	46	N 3 16	6	156 05	52	N10 32	2	WED 31
32 THU	178 58		N 4 17		145 17		N17 28		329 38		S13 15		178 22		N 3 22		156 57		N10 34		THU 32

SUN & PLANETS AT GMT 0hrs APRIL 1999

Day	SUN SD 16' GHA	v	Dec	d	VENUS Mag. -4.1 GHA	v	Dec	d	MARS Mag. -1.5 GHA	v	Dec	d	JUPITER Mag. -2.0 GHA	v	Dec	d	SATURN Mag. +0.4 GHA	v	Dec	d	Day
1 THU	178° 58'	4'	N 4° 17'	23'	145° 17'	-12'	N17° 28'	24'	329° 38'	70'	S13° 15'	3'	178° 22'	46'	N 3° 22'	5'	156° 57'	52'	N10° 34'	3'	THU 1
2 FRI	179 02	5	N 4 40	23	145 05	-12	N17 52	23	330 48	70	S13 12	3	179 08	45	N 3 27	6	157 49	52	N10 37	3	FRI 2
3 SAT	179 07	4	N 5 03	23	144 53	-12	N18 15	23	331 58	72	S13 10	3	179 53	46	N 3 33	6	158 41	52	N10 40	2	SAT 3
4 SUN	179 11	5	N 5 26	23	144 41	-12	N18 38	22	333 10	71	S13 07	3	180 39	46	N 3 39	5	159 33	53	N10 42	3	SUN 4
5 MON	179 16	4	N 5 49	23	144 29	-13	N19 00	22	334 21	73	S13 04	3	181 25	46	N 3 44	6	160 26	52	N10 45	2	MON 5
6 TUE	179 20	4	N 6 12	23	144 16	-13	N19 22	21	335 34	74	S13 01	3	182 11	45	N 3 50	6	161 18	52	N10 47	3	TUE 6
7 WED	179 24	5	N 6 35	22	144 03	-13	N19 43	21	336 48	74	S12 58	3	182 56	46	N 3 56	5	162 10	52	N10 50	2	WED 7
8 THU	179 29	4	N 6 57	23	143 50	-13	N20 04	20	338 02	74	S12 55	4	183 42	46	N 4 01	6	163 02	52	N10 52	3	THU 8
9 FRI	179 33	4	N 7 20	22	143 37	-14	N20 24	20	339 16	76	S12 51	4	184 28	46	N 4 07	5	163 54	52	N10 55	3	FRI 9
10 SAT	179 37	4	N 7 42	22	143 23	-13	N20 44	19	340 32	76	S12 48	4	185 14	45	N 4 12	6	164 46	52	N10 58	2	SAT 10
11 SUN	179 41	4	N 8 04	22	143 10	-14	N21 03	18	341 48	76	S12 44	4	185 59	46	N 4 18	5	165 38	52	N11 00	3	SUN 11
12 MON	179 45	4	N 8 26	22	142 56	-14	N21 21	19	343 04	78	S12 40	5	186 45	46	N 4 24	5	166 30	51	N11 03	2	MON 12
13 TUE	179 49	4	N 8 48	22	142 42	-15	N21 40	17	344 22	78	S12 35	4	187 31	46	N 4 29	6	167 21	52	N11 05	3	TUE 13
14 WED	179 52	4	N 9 10	22	142 27	-14	N21 57	17	345 40	78	S12 31	5	188 17	45	N 4 35	5	168 13	52	N11 08	2	WED 14
15 THU	179 56	4	N 9 32	21	142 13	-15	N22 14	17	346 58	79	S12 26	4	189 02	46	N 4 40	6	169 05	52	N11 10	3	THU 15
16 FRI	180 00	3	N 9 53	21	141 58	-15	N22 31	16	348 17	79	S12 22	5	189 48	45	N 4 46	5	169 57	52	N11 13	3	FRI 16
17 SAT	180 03	4	N10 14	22	141 43	-15	N22 47	15	349 36	80	S12 17	5	190 34	46	N 4 51	6	170 49	52	N11 16	2	SAT 17
18 SUN	180 07	3	N10 36	20	141 28	-15	N23 02	14	350 56	80	S12 12	5	191 20	46	N 4 57	5	171 41	51	N11 18	3	SUN 18
19 MON	180 10	3	N10 56	21	141 13	-15	N23 16	15	352 16	80	S12 07	5	192 06	46	N 5 02	6	172 33	51	N11 21	2	MON 19
20 TUE	180 13	4	N11 17	21	140 58	-16	N23 31	13	353 36	81	S12 02	5	192 52	46	N 5 08	5	173 24	52	N11 23	3	TUE 20
21 WED	180 17	3	N11 38	20	140 42	-15	N23 44	13	354 57	81	S11 57	5	193 38	45	N 5 13	6	174 16	52	N11 26	2	WED 21
22 THU	180 20	3	N11 58	21	140 27	-16	N23 57	12	356 18	81	S11 52	6	194 23	46	N 5 19	5	175 08	52	N11 28	3	THU 22
23 FRI	180 23	2	N12 19	20	140 11	-16	N24 09	12	357 39	81	S11 46	5	195 09	46	N 5 24	6	176 00	51	N11 31	2	FRI 23
24 SAT	180 25	3	N12 39	19	139 55	-15	N24 21	11	359 00	81	S11 41	5	195 55	46	N 5 30	5	176 51	52	N11 33	3	SAT 24
25 SUN	180 28	3	N12 58	20	139 40	-16	N24 32	10	0 21	82	S11 36	6	196 41	46	N 5 35	5	177 43	52	N11 36	3	SUN 25
26 MON	180 31	2	N13 18	19	139 24	-16	N24 42	10	1 43	82	S11 30	5	197 27	46	N 5 40	6	178 35	52	N11 39	2	MON 26
27 TUE	180 33	3	N13 37	19	139 08	-16	N24 52	9	3 05	81	S11 25	5	198 13	46	N 5 51	6	179 27	51	N11 41	3	TUE 27
28 WED	180 36	2	N13 56	19	138 52	-16	N25 01	8	4 26	82	S11 20	6	198 59	46	N 5 51	6	180 18	52	N11 44	2	WED 28
29 THU	180 38	2	N14 15	19	138 36	-16	N25 09	8	5 48	81	S11 14	5	199 45	47	N 5 56	6	181 10	52	N11 46	3	THU 29
30 FRI	180 40	2	N14 34	18	138 20	-16	N25 17	7	7 09	81	S11 09	5	200 32	46	N 6 02	5	182 02	52	N11 49	2	FRI 30
31 SAT	180 42		N14 52		138 04		N25 24		8 30		S11 04		201 18		N 6 07		182 54		N11 51		SAT 31

SUN & PLANETS AT GMT 0hrs MAY 1999

Day	SUN SD 16' GHA	v	Dec	d	VENUS Mag. -4.3 GHA	v	Dec	d	MARS Mag. -1.4 GHA	v	Dec	d	JUPITER Mag. -2.1 GHA	v	Dec	d	SATURN Mag. +0.3 GHA	v	Dec	d	Day
1 SAT	180°42'	2'	N14°52'	19'	138°04'	-16	N25°24'	6'	8°30'	81	S11°04'	6'	201°18'	46	N 6°07'	5'	182°54'	51	N11°51'	3'	SAT 1
2 SUN	180 44	2	N15 11	18	137 48	-16	N25 30	6	9 51	81	S10 58	5	202 04	46	N 6 12	5	183 45	52	N11 54	2	SUN 2
3 MON	180 46	1	N15 29	17	137 32	-16	N25 36	5	11 12	81	S10 53	5	202 50	46	N 6 17	5	184 37	52	N11 56	2	MON 3
4 TUE	180 47	2	N15 46	18	137 16	-16	N25 41	4	12 33	80	S10 48	5	203 36	46	N 6 22	6	185 29	52	N11 58	3	TUE 4
5 WED	180 49	1	N16 04	17	137 00	-15	N25 45	4	13 53	80	S10 43	5	204 22	47	N 6 28	5	186 21	51	N12 01	2	WED 5
6 THU	180 50	1	N16 21	17	136 45	-16	N25 49	3	15 13	80	S10 38	4	205 09	46	N 6 33	5	187 12	52	N12 03	3	THU 6
7 FRI	180 51	1	N16 38	16	136 29	-15	N25 52	2	16 33	79	S10 34	4	205 55	47	N 6 38	5	188 04	52	N12 06	2	FRI 7
8 SAT	180 52	1	N16 54	17	136 14	-15	N25 54	2	17 52	79	S10 29	4	206 41	47	N 6 43	5	188 56	52	N12 08	3	SAT 8
9 SUN	180 53	1	N17 11	16	135 59	-16	N25 56	1	19 11	78	S10 25	5	207 28	46	N 6 48	5	189 48	51	N12 11	2	SUN 9
10 MON	180 54	0	N17 27	15	135 43	-15	N25 57	0	20 29	78	S10 20	4	208 14	47	N 6 53	5	190 39	52	N12 13	3	MON 10
11 TUE	180 54	1	N17 42	16	135 28	-14	N25 57	0	21 47	77	S10 16	4	209 01	46	N 6 58	5	191 31	52	N12 16	2	TUE 11
12 WED	180 55	0	N17 58	15	135 14	-15	N25 57	1	23 04	77	S10 12	4	209 47	47	N 7 03	5	192 23	52	N12 18	2	WED 12
13 THU	180 55	0	N18 13	15	134 59	-14	N25 56	1	24 21	76	S10 08	3	210 34	46	N 7 08	5	193 15	52	N12 20	2	THU 13
14 FRI	180 55	0	N18 28	14	134 45	-14	N25 55	3	25 37	76	S10 05	3	211 20	47	N 7 13	5	194 07	51	N12 23	2	FRI 14
15 SAT	180 55	0	N18 42	15	134 31	-14	N25 52	3	26 53	75	S10 02	2	212 07	47	N 7 18	5	194 58	52	N12 25	2	SAT 15
16 SUN	180 55	0	N18 57	14	134 17	-13	N25 49	3	28 08	74	S 9 58	2	212 54	46	N 7 23	5	195 50	52	N12 27	3	SUN 16
17 MON	180 55	-1	N19 11	13	134 04	-13	N25 46	4	29 22	73	S 9 56	3	213 40	47	N 7 28	5	196 42	52	N12 30	2	MON 17
18 TUE	180 54	0	N19 24	13	133 51	-13	N25 42	5	30 35	73	S 9 53	3	214 27	47	N 7 33	4	197 34	52	N12 32	2	TUE 18
19 WED	180 54	-1	N19 37	13	133 38	-12	N25 37	6	31 48	72	S 9 50	2	215 14	47	N 7 37	5	198 26	52	N12 34	2	WED 19
20 THU	180 53	-1	N19 50	13	133 26	-12	N25 31	6	33 00	71	S 9 48	2	216 01	47	N 7 42	5	199 18	52	N12 37	2	THU 20
21 FRI	180 52	-1	N20 03	12	133 14	-12	N25 25	6	34 11	70	S 9 46	1	216 48	47	N 7 47	4	200 10	52	N12 39	2	FRI 21
22 SAT	180 51	-1	N20 15	12	133 02	-11	N25 19	8	35 22	70	S 9 45	2	217 35	47	N 7 51	5	201 02	52	N12 41	2	SAT 22
23 SUN	180 50	-1	N20 27	11	132 51	-11	N25 11	7	36 32	69	S 9 43	1	218 22	47	N 7 56	5	201 54	52	N12 43	2	SUN 23
24 MON	180 49	-1	N20 38	12	132 40	-11	N25 04	9	37 41	68	S 9 42	1	219 09	47	N 8 01	4	202 46	52	N12 46	2	MON 24
25 TUE	180 48	-2	N20 50	10	132 29	-9	N24 55	9	38 49	67	S 9 41	0	219 56	47	N 8 05	5	203 38	52	N12 48	2	TUE 25
26 WED	180 46	-1	N21 00	11	132 20	-10	N24 46	9	39 56	67	S 9 41	1	220 43	47	N 8 10	5	204 30	52	N12 50	2	WED 26
27 THU	180 45	-2	N21 11	10	132 10	-9	N24 37	10	41 03	66	S 9 40	1	221 30	48	N 8 14	5	205 22	52	N12 52	2	THU 27
28 FRI	180 43	-2	N21 21	10	132 01	-8	N24 27	11	42 09	65	S 9 40	0	222 18	47	N 8 19	4	206 14	52	N12 54	2	FRI 28
29 SAT	180 41	-2	N21 31	9	131 53	-8	N24 16	11	43 14	64	S 9 40	1	223 05	47	N 8 23	5	207 06	52	N12 56	3	SAT 29
30 SUN	180 39	-2	N21 40	9	131 45	-7	N24 05	12	44 18	64	S 9 41	1	223 52	48	N 8 28	4	207 58	52	N12 59	2	SUN 30
31 MON	180 37	-2	N21 49	9	131 38	-7	N23 53	12	45 22	63	S 9 42	0	224 40	48	N 8 32	5	208 50	53	N13 01	2	MON 31
32 TUE	180 35		N21 58		131 31		N23 41		46 25		S 9 42		225 28		N 8 37		209 43		N13 03		TUE 32

SUN & PLANETS AT GMT 0hrs JUNE 1999

Day	SUN SD 16' GHA	v	Dec	d	VENUS Mag. -4.4 GHA	v	Dec	d	MARS Mag. -0.8 GHA	v	Dec	d	JUPITER Mag. -2.2 GHA	v	Dec	d	SATURN Mag. +0.4 GHA	v	Dec	d	Day
1 TUE	180°35'	-2'	N21°58'	8'	131°31'	-6'	N23°41'	13'	46°25'	62	S 9°42'	2'	225°28'	47	N 8°37'	4'	209°43'	52	N13°03'	2'	TUE 1
2 WED	180 33	-3	N22 06	8	131 25	-6	N23 28	13	47 27	61	S 9 44	1	226 16	48	N 8 41	4	210 35	52	N13 05	2	WED 2
3 THU	180 30	-2	N22 14	7	131 19	-5	N23 15	14	48 28	60	S 9 45	2	227 03	47	N 8 45	4	211 27	53	N13 07	2	THU 3
4 FRI	180 28	-3	N22 21	7	131 14	-4	N23 01	14	49 28	60	S 9 47	2	227 51	47	N 8 49	5	212 20	52	N13 09	2	FRI 4
5 SAT	180 25	-2	N22 28	7	131 10	-4	N22 47	14	50 28	59	S 9 49	2	228 38	48	N 8 54	4	213 12	52	N13 11	2	SAT 5
6 SUN	180 23	-3	N22 35	6	131 06	-3	N22 33	15	51 27	58	S 9 51	3	229 26	48	N 8 58	4	214 04	53	N13 13	2	SUN 6
7 MON	180 20	-3	N22 41	6	131 03	-3	N22 18	16	52 25	58	S 9 54	3	230 14	48	N 9 02	4	214 57	52	N13 15	2	MON 7
8 TUE	180 17	-3	N22 47	5	131 00	-1	N22 02	15	53 23	57	S 9 57	3	231 02	49	N 9 06	4	215 49	53	N13 17	2	TUE 8
9 WED	180 14	-2	N22 52	5	130 59	-2	N21 47	17	54 20	56	S10 00	3	231 51	48	N 9 10	4	216 42	53	N13 19	2	WED 9
10 THU	180 12	-3	N22 57	5	130 57	0	N21 30	16	55 16	55	S10 03	3	232 39	48	N 9 14	4	217 34	53	N13 21	2	THU 10
11 FRI	180 09	-4	N23 03	4	130 57	0	N21 14	16	56 11	55	S10 06	4	233 27	48	N 9 18	4	218 27	53	N13 23	2	FRI 11
12 SAT	180 05	-3	N23 06	4	130 57	1	N20 57	17	57 06	54	S10 10	4	234 15	49	N 9 22	4	219 20	52	N13 25	2	SAT 12
13 SUN	180 02	-3	N23 10	4	130 58	2	N20 40	18	58 00	53	S10 14	4	235 04	48	N 9 26	4	220 12	53	N13 27	1	SUN 13
14 MON	179 59	-3	N23 14	3	131 00	2	N20 22	18	58 53	52	S10 18	5	235 52	49	N 9 30	4	221 05	53	N13 28	2	MON 14
15 TUE	179 56	-3	N23 17	2	131 02	3	N20 04	18	59 45	52	S10 23	5	236 41	49	N 9 34	4	221 58	53	N13 30	2	TUE 15
16 WED	179 53	-3	N23 19	2	131 05	4	N19 46	19	60 37	51	S10 28	5	237 30	49	N 9 37	4	222 51	52	N13 32	2	WED 16
17 THU	179 50	-4	N23 21	2	131 09	5	N19 27	19	61 28	51	S10 32	6	238 19	49	N 9 41	4	223 43	53	N13 34	2	THU 17
18 FRI	179 46	-3	N23 23	2	131 14	6	N19 08	19	62 19	50	S10 38	6	239 08	49	N 9 45	4	224 36	53	N13 36	1	FRI 18
19 SAT	179 43	-3	N23 25	1	131 20	6	N18 49	19	63 09	49	S10 43	5	239 57	49	N 9 48	4	225 29	53	N13 37	2	SAT 19
20 SUN	179 40	-3	N23 26	0	131 26	7	N18 30	20	63 59	49	S10 48	5	240 46	49	N 9 52	4	226 22	53	N13 39	2	SUN 20
21 MON	179 37	-4	N23 26	0	131 33	8	N18 10	20	64 47	48	S10 54	6	241 35	49	N 9 56	3	227 15	53	N13 41	2	MON 21
22 TUE	179 33	-3	N23 26	0	131 41	9	N17 50	20	65 35	47	S11 00	6	242 24	49	N 9 59	3	228 08	54	N13 43	1	TUE 22
23 WED	179 30	-3	N23 26	1	131 50	10	N17 30	20	66 22	47	S11 06	7	243 13	50	N10 02	4	229 02	53	N13 44	2	WED 23
24 THU	179 27	-3	N23 25	1	132 00	11	N17 10	20	67 09	46	S11 13	6	244 03	50	N10 06	3	229 55	53	N13 46	1	THU 24
25 FRI	179 24	-4	N23 24	1	132 11	12	N16 50	21	67 55	45	S11 19	7	244 53	50	N10 09	3	230 48	54	N13 47	2	FRI 25
26 SAT	179 20	-3	N23 23	2	132 23	13	N16 29	20	68 40	45	S11 26	7	245 42	50	N10 13	4	231 42	53	N13 49	2	SAT 26
27 SUN	179 17	-3	N23 21	3	132 36	13	N16 09	21	69 25	45	S11 32	7	246 32	50	N10 16	3	232 35	53	N13 51	1	SUN 27
28 MON	179 14	-3	N23 18	2	132 49	15	N15 48	21	70 10	44	S11 39	8	247 22	50	N10 19	3	233 28	53	N13 52	2	MON 28
29 TUE	179 11	-3	N23 16	4	133 04	16	N15 27	21	70 54	43	S11 47	7	248 12	50	N10 22	3	234 22	53	N13 54	1	TUE 29
30 WED	179 08	-3	N23 12	3	133 20	16	N15 06	21	71 37	43	S11 54	7	249 02	50	N10 25	3	235 16	53	N13 55	2	WED 30
31 THU	179 05		N23 09		133 36		N14 45		72 20		S12 01		249 52		N10 28		236 09		N13 57		THU 31

SUN & PLANETS AT GMT 0hrs JULY 1999

Day	SUN SD 16' GHA	v	Dec	d	VENUS Mag. -4.5 GHA	v	Dec	d	MARS Mag. -0.2 GHA	v	Dec	d	JUPITER Mag. -2.4 GHA	v	Dec	d	SATURN Mag. +0.3 GHA	v	Dec	d	Day
1 THU	179° 05'	-3'	N23° 09'	4'	133° 36'	18'	N14° 45'	21'	72° 20'	43'	S12° 01'	8'	249° 52'	51'	N10° 28'	3'	236° 09'	54'	N13° 57'	1'	THU 1
2 FRI	179 02	-3	N23 05	4	133 54	19	N14 24	21	73 03	41	S12 09	8	250 43	50	N10 31	3	237 03	54	N13 58	1	FRI 2
3 SAT	178 59	-2	N23 01	5	134 13	20	N14 03	21	73 44	42	S12 17	8	251 33	51	N10 34	3	237 57	54	N13 59	2	SAT 3
4 SUN	178 57	-3	N22 56	5	134 33	21	N13 42	21	74 26	41	S12 25	8	252 24	50	N10 37	3	238 51	53	N14 01	1	SUN 4
5 MON	178 54	-3	N22 51	6	134 54	23	N13 21	21	75 07	40	S12 33	8	253 14	51	N10 40	3	239 44	54	N14 02	2	MON 5
6 TUE	178 51	-2	N22 45	6	135 17	23	N13 00	21	75 47	40	S12 41	8	254 05	51	N10 43	3	240 38	54	N14 04	1	TUE 6
7 WED	178 49	-3	N22 39	6	135 40	25	N12 39	21	76 27	39	S12 49	8	254 56	51	N10 46	3	241 32	55	N14 05	1	WED 7
8 THU	178 46	-2	N22 33	7	136 05	26	N12 18	21	77 06	39	S12 58	8	255 47	51	N10 49	3	242 27	54	N14 06	1	THU 8
9 FRI	178 44	-2	N22 26	7	136 31	27	N11 57	21	77 45	39	S13 06	9	256 38	52	N10 51	3	243 21	54	N14 07	2	FRI 9
10 SAT	178 42	-2	N22 19	8	136 58	29	N11 36	21	78 24	38	S13 15	8	257 30	51	N10 54	3	244 15	54	N14 09	1	SAT 10
11 SUN	178 40	-2	N22 11	8	137 27	30	N11 15	20	79 02	37	S13 23	9	258 21	52	N10 56	3	245 09	55	N14 10	1	SUN 11
12 MON	178 38	-2	N22 03	8	137 57	31	N10 55	20	79 39	37	S13 32	9	259 13	51	N10 59	2	246 04	54	N14 11	1	MON 12
13 TUE	178 36	-2	N21 55	8	138 28	33	N10 35	20	80 16	37	S13 41	9	260 04	52	N11 01	3	246 58	55	N14 12	1	TUE 13
14 WED	178 34	-2	N21 47	9	139 01	35	N10 15	20	80 53	36	S13 50	9	260 56	52	N11 04	2	247 53	54	N14 13	2	WED 14
15 THU	178 32	-1	N21 38	10	139 36	36	N 9 55	20	81 29	36	S13 59	9	261 48	52	N11 06	2	248 47	55	N14 15	1	THU 15
16 FRI	178 31	-1	N21 28	10	140 12	37	N 9 35	19	82 05	35	S14 08	10	262 40	53	N11 08	3	249 42	55	N14 16	1	FRI 16
17 SAT	178 29	-1	N21 18	10	140 49	40	N 9 16	19	82 40	35	S14 18	9	263 33	52	N11 11	2	250 37	55	N14 17	1	SAT 17
18 SUN	178 28	-1	N21 08	10	141 29	41	N 8 57	19	83 15	35	S14 27	10	264 25	53	N11 13	2	251 32	55	N14 18	1	SUN 18
19 MON	178 27	-1	N20 58	11	142 10	42	N 8 38	18	83 50	34	S14 37	9	265 18	52	N11 15	2	252 27	55	N14 19	1	MON 19
20 TUE	178 26	-1	N20 47	11	142 52	45	N 8 20	18	84 24	34	S14 46	10	266 10	53	N11 17	2	253 22	55	N14 20	1	TUE 20
21 WED	178 25	-1	N20 36	12	143 37	46	N 8 02	17	84 58	33	S14 56	9	267 03	53	N11 19	2	254 17	55	N14 21	1	WED 21
22 THU	178 24	-1	N20 24	12	144 23	49	N 7 45	17	85 31	33	S15 05	10	267 56	53	N11 21	2	255 12	55	N14 22	1	THU 22
23 FRI	178 23	0	N20 12	12	145 12	50	N 7 28	17	86 04	33	S15 15	10	268 49	53	N11 23	2	256 07	56	N14 23	0	FRI 23
24 SAT	178 23	0	N20 00	12	146 02	52	N 7 11	16	86 37	32	S15 25	9	269 42	54	N11 25	1	257 03	55	N14 23	1	SAT 24
25 SUN	178 23	-1	N19 48	13	146 54	54	N 6 55	15	87 09	32	S15 34	10	270 36	54	N11 26	2	257 58	56	N14 24	1	SUN 25
26 MON	178 22	0	N19 35	13	147 48	56	N 6 40	15	87 41	31	S15 44	10	271 30	53	N11 28	2	258 54	55	N14 25	1	MON 26
27 TUE	178 22	1	N19 22	14	148 44	59	N 6 25	14	88 12	31	S15 54	10	272 23	54	N11 30	2	259 49	56	N14 26	1	TUE 27
28 WED	178 23	0	N19 08	14	149 43	60	N 6 11	14	88 43	31	S16 04	10	273 17	54	N11 31	2	260 45	56	N14 27	0	WED 28
29 THU	178 23	0	N18 54	14	150 43	63	N 5 57	12	89 14	31	S16 14	10	274 11	54	N11 33	2	261 41	56	N14 27	1	THU 29
30 FRI	178 23	1	N18 40	14	151 46	65	N 5 45	12	89 45	30	S16 24	10	275 05	55	N11 34	2	262 37	56	N14 28	1	FRI 30
31 SAT	178 24	1	N18 26	15	152 51	67	N 5 33	11	90 15	29	S16 34	10	276 00	54	N11 36	1	263 33	56	N14 29	0	SAT 31
32 SUN	178 25		N18 11		153 58		N 5 22		90 44		S16 44		276 54		N11 37		264 29		N14 29		SUN 32

SUN & PLANETS AT GMT 0hrs AUGUST 1999

Day	SUN SD 16' GHA	v	Dec	d	VENUS Mag. -4.0 GHA	v	Dec	d	MARS Mag. +0.2 GHA	v	Dec	d	JUPITER Mag. -2.6 GHA	v	Dec	d	SATURN Mag. +0.2 GHA	v	Dec	d	Day
1 SUN	178° 25'	1'	N18° 11'	15'	153° 58'	70'	N 5° 22'	11'	90° 44'	30'	S16° 44'	10'	276° 54'	55'	N11° 37'	2'	264° 29'	56'	N14° 29'	1'	SUN 1
2 MON	178 26	1	N17 56	16	155 08	71	N 5 11	9	91 14	29	S16 54	10	277 49	55	N11 39	1	265 25	56	N14 30	0	MON 2
3 TUE	178 27	1	N17 40	15	156 19	74	N 5 02	9	91 43	29	S17 04	10	278 44	55	N11 40	1	266 21	57	N14 31	0	TUE 3
4 WED	178 28	1	N17 25	16	157 33	76	N 4 53	8	92 12	28	S17 14	10	279 39	55	N11 41	1	267 18	56	N14 31	1	WED 4
5 THU	178 29	2	N17 09	16	158 49	78	N 4 45	6	92 40	28	S17 24	10	280 34	56	N11 42	1	268 14	57	N14 32	0	THU 5
6 FRI	178 31	1	N16 53	17	160 07	80	N 4 39	6	93 08	28	S17 34	10	281 30	55	N11 43	1	269 11	56	N14 32	1	FRI 6
7 SAT	178 32	2	N16 36	16	161 27	82	N 4 33	5	93 36	27	S17 44	10	282 25	56	N11 44	1	270 07	57	N14 33	0	SAT 7
8 SUN	178 34	2	N16 20	17	162 49	84	N 4 28	4	94 03	27	S17 54	10	283 21	56	N11 45	1	271 04	57	N14 33	0	SUN 8
9 MON	178 36	2	N16 03	18	164 13	86	N 4 24	3	94 30	27	S18 04	10	284 17	56	N11 46	1	272 01	57	N14 33	1	MON 9
10 TUE	178 38	2	N15 45	17	165 39	87	N 4 21	1	94 57	26	S18 14	9	285 13	57	N11 47	0	272 58	57	N14 34	0	TUE 10
11 WED	178 40	3	N15 28	18	167 06	90	N 4 20	1	95 23	26	S18 23	10	286 10	56	N11 47	1	273 55	57	N14 34	1	WED 11
12 THU	178 43	2	N15 10	18	168 36	90	N 4 19	0	95 49	26	S18 33	10	287 06	57	N11 48	1	274 52	57	N14 35	0	THU 12
13 FRI	178 45	3	N14 52	18	170 06	92	N 4 19	2	96 15	26	S18 43	10	288 03	57	N11 49	0	275 49	58	N14 35	0	FRI 13
14 SAT	178 48	2	N14 34	19	171 38	93	N 4 21	2	96 41	25	S18 53	10	289 00	57	N11 49	1	276 47	57	N14 35	0	SAT 14
15 SUN	178 50	3	N14 15	18	173 11	94	N 4 23	3	97 06	25	S19 03	10	289 57	57	N11 50	0	277 44	58	N14 35	1	SUN 15
16 MON	178 53	3	N13 57	19	174 45	95	N 4 26	5	97 31	24	S19 13	9	290 54	57	N11 50	0	278 42	57	N14 36	0	MON 16
17 TUE	178 56	4	N13 38	19	176 20	95	N 4 31	5	97 55	25	S19 22	10	291 51	58	N11 51	0	279 39	58	N14 36	0	TUE 17
18 WED	179 00	3	N13 19	20	177 55	96	N 4 36	6	98 20	24	S19 32	9	292 49	58	N11 51	0	280 37	58	N14 36	0	WED 18
19 THU	179 03	3	N12 59	19	179 31	95	N 4 42	7	98 44	23	S19 41	10	293 47	58	N11 51	0	281 35	58	N14 36	0	THU 19
20 FRI	179 06	4	N12 40	20	181 06	96	N 4 49	8	99 07	24	S19 51	9	294 45	58	N11 51	0	282 33	58	N14 36	0	FRI 20
21 SAT	179 10	4	N12 20	20	182 42	95	N 4 57	8	99 31	23	S20 00	10	295 43	58	N11 51	0	283 31	58	N14 36	0	SAT 21
22 SUN	179 14	3	N12 00	20	184 17	95	N 5 05	9	99 54	22	S20 10	9	296 41	59	N11 51	0	284 29	58	N14 36	0	SUN 22
23 MON	179 17	4	N11 40	20	185 52	94	N 5 14	9	100 16	23	S20 19	9	297 40	59	N11 51	0	285 27	59	N14 36	0	MON 23
24 TUE	179 21	4	N11 20	21	187 26	93	N 5 24	10	100 39	22	S20 28	10	298 39	59	N11 51	0	286 26	58	N14 36	0	TUE 24
25 WED	179 25	4	N10 59	20	188 59	92	N 5 34	10	101 01	22	S20 38	9	299 38	59	N11 51	0	287 24	59	N14 36	0	WED 25
26 THU	179 29	5	N10 39	21	190 31	90	N 5 44	11	101 23	22	S20 47	9	300 37	59	N11 51	1	288 23	59	N14 36	0	THU 26
27 FRI	179 34	4	N10 18	21	192 01	89	N 5 55	11	101 45	21	S20 56	9	301 36	60	N11 50	0	289 22	59	N14 36	0	FRI 27
28 SAT	179 38	4	N 9 57	21	193 30	87	N 6 06	12	102 06	21	S21 05	8	302 36	59	N11 50	0	290 20	59	N14 36	0	SAT 28
29 SUN	179 42	5	N 9 36	22	194 57	86	N 6 18	11	102 27	21	S21 13	9	303 35	60	N11 50	1	291 19	59	N14 36	1	SUN 29
30 MON	179 47	4	N 9 14	21	196 23	83	N 6 29	12	102 48	21	S21 22	9	304 35	60	N11 49	1	292 18	59	N14 35	0	MON 30
31 TUE	179 51	5	N 8 53	22	197 46	81	N 6 41	12	103 09	20	S21 31	8	305 35	61	N11 48	0	293 17	60	N14 35	0	TUE 31
32 WED	179 56		N 8 31		199 07		N 6 53		103 29		S21 39		306 36		N11 48		294 17		N14 35		WED 32

SUN & PLANETS AT GMT 0hrs SEPTEMBER 1999

Day	SUN SD 16' GHA	v	Dec	d	VENUS Mag. -4.5 GHA	v	Dec	d	MARS Mag. +0.4 GHA	v	Dec	d	JUPITER Mag. -2.8 GHA	v	Dec	d	SATURN Mag. +0.1 GHA	v	Dec	d	Day
1 WED	179°56'	5'	N 8°31'	21'	199°07'	79'	N 6°53'	11'	103°29'	20'	S21°39'	9'	306°36'	60'	N11°48'	1'	294°17'	59'	N14°35'	0'	WED 1
2 THU	180 01	5	N 8 10	22	200 26	77	N 7 04	12	103 49	20	S21 48	8	307 36	61	N11 47	1	295 16	59	N14 35	1	THU 2
3 FRI	180 06	5	N 7 48	22	201 43	74	N 7 16	11	104 09	20	S21 56	8	308 37	61	N11 46	0	296 15	60	N14 34	0	FRI 3
4 SAT	180 11	4	N 7 26	22	202 57	72	N 7 27	11	104 29	19	S22 04	8	309 38	61	N11 46	1	297 15	60	N14 34	0	SAT 4
5 SUN	180 15	5	N 7 04	23	204 09	70	N 7 38	11	104 48	19	S22 12	8	310 39	61	N11 45	1	298 15	59	N14 34	1	SUN 5
6 MON	180 20	5	N 6 41	22	205 19	67	N 7 49	10	105 07	19	S22 20	8	311 40	61	N11 44	1	299 14	60	N14 33	0	MON 6
7 TUE	180 25	6	N 6 19	22	206 26	64	N 7 59	11	105 26	19	S22 28	7	312 41	62	N11 43	1	300 14	60	N14 33	1	TUE 7
8 WED	180 31	5	N 5 57	23	207 30	63	N 8 10	9	105 45	18	S22 35	8	313 43	62	N11 42	2	301 14	60	N14 32	0	WED 8
9 THU	180 36	5	N 5 34	23	208 33	60	N 8 19	10	106 03	18	S22 43	7	314 45	62	N11 40	2	302 14	60	N14 32	1	THU 9
10 FRI	180 41	5	N 5 11	22	209 33	57	N 8 29	9	106 21	18	S22 50	7	315 47	62	N11 39	1	303 14	61	N14 31	0	FRI 10
11 SAT	180 46	5	N 4 49	23	210 30	56	N 8 38	8	106 39	17	S22 57	7	316 49	62	N11 38	1	304 15	60	N14 31	1	SAT 11
12 SUN	180 51	6	N 4 26	23	211 26	53	N 8 46	8	106 56	18	S23 04	7	317 51	63	N11 37	2	305 15	61	N14 30	1	SUN 12
13 MON	180 57	5	N 4 03	23	212 19	50	N 8 54	7	107 14	17	S23 11	7	318 54	63	N11 35	1	306 16	60	N14 29	0	MON 13
14 TUE	181 02	5	N 3 40	23	213 09	49	N 9 01	7	107 31	17	S23 18	7	319 57	63	N11 34	2	307 16	61	N14 29	1	TUE 14
15 WED	181 07	6	N 3 17	23	213 58	46	N 9 08	6	107 48	16	S23 25	6	321 00	63	N11 32	1	308 17	61	N14 28	0	WED 15
16 THU	181 13	5	N 2 54	23	214 44	45	N 9 14	6	108 04	17	S23 31	6	322 03	63	N11 31	1	309 18	61	N14 28	1	THU 16
17 FRI	181 18	5	N 2 31	23	215 29	42	N 9 20	5	108 21	16	S23 37	6	323 06	63	N11 29	2	310 19	61	N14 27	1	FRI 17
18 SAT	181 23	6	N 2 08	24	216 11	41	N 9 25	5	108 37	16	S23 43	6	324 09	64	N11 27	1	311 20	61	N14 26	1	SAT 18
19 SUN	181 29	5	N 1 44	23	216 52	38	N 9 30	4	108 53	16	S23 49	6	325 13	64	N11 26	2	312 21	61	N14 25	0	SUN 19
20 MON	181 34	5	N 1 21	23	217 30	37	N 9 34	3	109 09	15	S23 55	6	326 17	64	N11 24	2	313 22	61	N14 25	1	MON 20
21 TUE	181 39	6	N 0 58	23	218 07	35	N 9 37	3	109 24	15	S24 01	5	327 21	64	N11 22	2	314 23	61	N14 24	1	TUE 21
22 WED	181 45	5	N 0 35	24	218 42	33	N 9 40	2	109 39	16	S24 06	5	328 25	64	N11 20	2	315 24	62	N14 23	1	WED 22
23 THU	181 50	5	N 0 11	1	219 15	32	N 9 42	2	109 55	14	S24 11	5	329 29	64	N11 18	2	316 26	61	N14 22	1	THU 23
24 FRI	181 55	6	S 0 12	23	219 47	29	N 9 44	1	110 09	15	S24 16	5	330 33	65	N11 16	2	317 27	62	N14 21	1	FRI 24
25 SAT	182 00	6	S 0 35	24	220 16	29	N 9 45	0	110 24	15	S24 21	5	331 38	65	N11 14	2	318 29	62	N14 20	1	SAT 25
26 SUN	182 06	5	S 0 59	23	220 45	27	N 9 45	0	110 39	14	S24 26	4	332 43	64	N11 12	2	319 31	62	N14 19	1	SUN 26
27 MON	182 11	5	S 1 22	24	221 12	25	N 9 45	1	110 53	14	S24 30	4	333 47	65	N11 10	2	320 33	62	N14 18	1	MON 27
28 TUE	182 16	5	S 1 46	23	221 37	25	N 9 44	2	111 07	14	S24 34	4	334 52	66	N11 08	3	321 35	62	N14 17	1	TUE 28
29 WED	182 21	5	S 2 09	23	222 02	23	N 9 42	2	111 21	14	S24 38	4	335 58	65	N11 05	2	322 37	62	N14 16	1	WED 29
30 THU	182 26	5	S 2 32	24	222 25	21	N 9 40	2	111 35	14	S24 42	4	337 03	65	N11 03	2	323 39	62	N14 15	1	THU 30
31 FRI	182 31		S 2 56		222 46		N 9 38		111 49		S24 46		338 08		N11 01		324 41		N14 14		FRI 31

SUN & PLANETS AT GMT 0hrs OCTOBER 1999

Day	SUN SD 16' GHA	v	Dec	d	VENUS Mag. -4.6 GHA	v	Dec	d	MARS Mag. +0.6 GHA	v	Dec	d	JUPITER Mag. -2.9 GHA	v	Dec	d	SATURN Mag. -0.1 GHA	v	Dec	d	Day
1 FRI	182°31'	5'	S 2°56'	23'	222°46'	21'	N 9°38'	4'	111°49'	13'	S24°46'	3'	338°08'	66'	N11°01'	3'	324°41'	62'	N14°14'	1'	FRI 1
2 SAT	182 36	5	S 3 19	23	223 07	19	N 9 34	4	112 02	14	S24 49	3	339 14	65	N10 58	2	325 43	63	N14 12	1	SAT 2
3 SUN	182 41	4	S 3 42	23	223 26	18	N 9 30	4	112 16	13	S24 52	3	340 19	66	N10 56	2	326 46	62	N14 12	1	SUN 3
4 MON	182 45	5	S 4 05	23	223 44	17	N 9 26	6	112 29	13	S24 55	3	341 25	66	N10 54	3	327 48	63	N14 11	1	MON 4
5 TUE	182 50	4	S 4 28	23	224 01	16	N 9 20	5	112 42	13	S24 58	2	342 31	66	N10 51	2	328 51	62	N14 10	1	TUE 5
6 WED	182 54	5	S 4 51	24	224 17	16	N 9 15	7	112 55	12	S25 00	3	343 37	66	N10 49	3	329 53	63	N14 09	1	WED 6
7 THU	182 59	4	S 5 15	23	224 33	14	N 9 08	7	113 07	13	S25 03	2	344 43	66	N10 46	2	330 56	63	N14 08	1	THU 7
8 FRI	183 03	4	S 5 38	22	224 47	13	N 9 01	7	113 20	12	S25 05	1	345 49	66	N10 44	3	331 59	62	N14 07	2	FRI 8
9 SAT	183 07	4	S 6 00	23	225 00	13	N 8 54	8	113 32	12	S25 06	2	346 55	66	N10 41	3	333 01	63	N14 05	1	SAT 9
10 SUN	183 11	4	S 6 23	23	225 13	12	N 8 46	9	113 44	12	S25 08	1	348 01	67	N10 38	3	334 04	63	N14 04	1	SUN 10
11 MON	183 15	4	S 6 46	23	225 25	11	N 8 37	9	113 56	12	S25 09	1	349 08	66	N10 36	3	335 07	63	N14 03	1	MON 11
12 TUE	183 19	4	S 7 09	22	225 36	10	N 8 28	10	114 08	12	S25 10	1	350 14	67	N10 33	3	336 10	63	N14 02	2	TUE 12
13 WED	183 23	4	S 7 31	23	225 46	10	N 8 18	10	114 20	12	S25 11	1	351 21	66	N10 30	2	337 13	63	N14 00	1	WED 13
14 THU	183 27	3	S 7 54	22	225 56	9	N 8 08	11	114 32	12	S25 12	0	352 27	67	N10 28	3	338 16	64	N13 59	1	THU 14
15 FRI	183 30	4	S 8 16	22	226 05	9	N 7 57	12	114 44	11	S25 12	0	353 34	67	N10 25	3	339 20	63	N13 58	1	FRI 15
16 SAT	183 34	3	S 8 38	22	226 14	7	N 7 45	11	114 55	11	S25 12	0	354 41	67	N10 22	3	340 23	63	N13 57	2	SAT 16
17 SUN	183 37	3	S 9 00	22	226 21	8	N 7 34	13	115 06	12	S25 12	1	355 48	66	N10 19	3	341 26	64	N13 55	1	SUN 17
18 MON	183 40	3	S 9 22	22	226 29	6	N 7 21	13	115 18	11	S25 11	1	356 54	67	N10 16	2	342 30	63	N13 54	1	MON 18
19 TUE	183 43	3	S 9 44	22	226 35	7	N 7 08	13	115 29	11	S25 11	1	358 01	67	N10 14	3	343 33	63	N13 53	2	TUE 19
20 WED	183 46	2	S10 06	21	226 42	5	N 6 55	14	115 40	11	S25 10	1	359 08	67	N10 11	3	344 36	64	N13 51	1	WED 20
21 THU	183 48	3	S10 27	22	226 47	6	N 6 41	14	115 51	11	S25 09	1	0 15	67	N10 08	3	345 40	64	N13 50	1	THU 21
22 FRI	183 51	2	S10 49	21	226 53	4	N 6 27	15	116 02	11	S25 08	2	1 22	67	N10 05	3	346 44	63	N13 49	2	FRI 22
23 SAT	183 53	2	S11 10	21	226 57	5	N 6 12	15	116 13	11	S25 06	2	2 29	67	N10 03	3	347 47	64	N13 47	1	SAT 23
24 SUN	183 55	2	S11 31	21	227 02	4	N 5 57	16	116 24	11	S25 04	2	3 36	66	N10 00	3	348 51	64	N13 46	1	SUN 24
25 MON	183 57	2	S11 52	21	227 06	3	N 5 41	16	116 35	10	S25 02	2	4 42	67	N 9 57	3	349 54	64	N13 43	2	MON 25
26 TUE	183 59	2	S12 13	20	227 09	3	N 5 25	16	116 45	11	S25 00	3	5 49	67	N 9 54	3	350 58	64	N13 43	1	TUE 26
27 WED	184 01	1	S12 33	20	227 12	3	N 5 09	17	116 56	10	S24 57	3	6 56	67	N 9 51	2	352 02	64	N13 42	2	WED 27
28 THU	184 02	1	S12 53	21	227 15	3	N 4 52	18	117 06	11	S24 54	3	8 03	67	N 9 49	3	353 06	63	N13 40	1	THU 28
29 FRI	184 03	1	S13 14	19	227 18	2	N 4 34	17	117 17	11	S24 51	3	9 10	67	N 9 46	3	354 09	64	N13 39	1	FRI 29
30 SAT	184 04	1	S13 33	20	227 20	1	N 4 17	19	117 28	10	S24 48	4	10 17	66	N 9 43	3	355 13	64	N13 38	2	SAT 30
31 SUN	184 05	1	S13 53	20	227 21	2	N 3 58	18	117 38	10	S24 44	4	11 23	67	N 9 40	2	356 17	64	N13 36	1	SUN 31
32 MON	184 06		S14 13		227 23		N 3 40		117 48		S24 40		12 30		N 9 38		357 21		N13 35		MON 32

SUN & PLANETS AT GMT 0hrs NOVEMBER 1999

Day	SUN SD 16' GHA	v	Dec	d	VENUS Mag. -4.4 GHA	v	Dec	d	MARS Mag. +0.8 GHA	v	Dec	d	JUPITER Mag. -2.9 GHA	v	Dec	d	SATURN Mag. -0.2 GHA	v	Dec	d	Day
1 MON	184° 06'	0'	S14° 13'	19'	227° 23'	1'	N 3° 40'	19'	117° 48'	11	S24° 40'	4'	12° 30'	67'	N 9° 38'	3'	357° 21'	64'	N13° 35'	2'	MON 1
2 TUE	184 06	1	S14 32	19	227 24	1	N 3 21	19	117 59	10	S24 36	5	13 37	66	N 9 35	2	358 25	64	N13 33	1	TUE 2
3 WED	184 07	0	S14 51	19	227 25	0	N 3 02	20	118 09	11	S24 31	4	14 43	67	N 9 32	2	359 29	64	N13 32	1	WED 3
4 THU	184 07	-1	S15 10	18	227 25	0	N 2 42	19	118 20	10	S24 27	5	15 50	66	N 9 30	3	0 33	63	N13 31	2	THU 4
5 FRI	184 06	0	S15 28	19	227 25	0	N 2 23	21	118 30	10	S24 22	6	16 56	67	N 9 27	2	1 36	64	N13 29	1	FRI 5
6 SAT	184 06	-1	S15 47	18	227 25	0	N 2 02	20	118 40	11	S24 16	5	18 03	66	N 9 25	3	2 40	64	N13 28	2	SAT 6
7 SUN	184 05	0	S16 05	17	227 25	-1	N 1 42	21	118 51	10	S24 11	6	19 09	66	N 9 22	2	3 44	64	N13 26	1	SUN 7
8 MON	184 05	0	S16 22	18	227 24	0	N 1 21	21	119 01	10	S24 05	6	20 15	67	N 9 20	3	4 48	64	N13 25	1	MON 8
9 TUE	184 04	-2	S16 40	17	227 24	-1	N 1 00	21	119 11	11	S23 59	6	21 22	66	N 9 17	2	5 52	64	N13 24	2	TUE 9
10 WED	184 02	-1	S16 57	17	227 23	-2	N 0 39	21	119 22	10	S23 53	7	22 28	66	N 9 15	3	6 56	64	N13 22	1	WED 10
11 THU	184 01	-2	S17 14	17	227 21	-1	N 0 18	14	119 32	10	S23 46	7	23 34	65	N 9 12	2	8 00	64	N13 21	2	THU 11
12 FRI	183 59	-2	S17 31	16	227 20	-2	S 0 04	22	119 42	11	S23 39	7	24 39	66	N 9 10	2	9 04	64	N13 19	1	FRI 12
13 SAT	183 57	-2	S17 47	16	227 18	-2	S 0 26	22	119 53	10	S23 32	7	25 45	66	N 9 08	3	10 08	64	N13 18	1	SAT 13
14 SUN	183 55	-2	S18 03	16	227 16	-2	S 0 48	23	120 03	11	S23 25	7	26 51	66	N 9 05	2	11 12	63	N13 17	2	SUN 14
15 MON	183 53	-2	S18 19	15	227 14	-3	S 1 11	22	120 14	10	S23 18	8	27 56	66	N 9 03	2	12 15	64	N13 15	1	MON 15
16 TUE	183 51	-3	S18 34	15	227 11	-2	S 1 33	23	120 24	11	S23 10	8	29 02	65	N 9 01	2	13 19	64	N13 14	1	TUE 16
17 WED	183 48	-3	S18 49	15	227 09	-3	S 1 56	23	120 35	10	S23 02	9	30 07	65	N 8 59	2	14 23	64	N13 13	2	WED 17
18 THU	183 45	-3	S19 04	14	227 06	-3	S 2 19	23	120 45	11	S22 53	8	31 12	65	N 8 57	2	15 27	63	N13 11	1	THU 18
19 FRI	183 42	-3	S19 18	14	227 03	-4	S 2 42	23	120 56	10	S22 45	9	32 17	65	N 8 55	2	16 30	64	N13 10	1	FRI 19
20 SAT	183 39	-4	S19 32	14	226 59	-3	S 3 05	23	121 06	11	S22 36	9	33 22	65	N 8 53	2	17 34	64	N13 09	1	SAT 20
21 SUN	183 35	-3	S19 46	13	226 56	-4	S 3 28	23	121 17	11	S22 27	9	34 27	64	N 8 51	2	18 38	63	N13 08	2	SUN 21
22 MON	183 32	-4	S19 59	13	226 52	-4	S 3 51	24	121 28	11	S22 18	10	35 31	65	N 8 49	1	19 41	64	N13 06	1	MON 22
23 TUE	183 28	-4	S20 12	12	226 48	-4	S 4 15	23	121 39	11	S22 08	9	36 36	64	N 8 48	2	20 45	63	N13 05	1	TUE 23
24 WED	183 24	-5	S20 24	13	226 44	-5	S 4 38	24	121 50	11	S21 59	10	37 40	64	N 8 46	2	21 49	63	N13 04	1	WED 24
25 THU	183 19	-5	S20 37	11	226 39	-4	S 5 02	24	122 01	11	S21 49	11	38 44	64	N 8 44	1	22 52	64	N13 03	1	THU 25
26 FRI	183 15	-5	S20 48	12	226 35	-5	S 5 26	23	122 12	11	S21 38	10	39 48	64	N 8 43	2	23 56	63	N13 02	2	FRI 26
27 SAT	183 10	-5	S21 00	11	226 30	-6	S 5 49	24	122 23	11	S21 28	11	40 52	63	N 8 41	2	24 59	63	N13 00	1	SAT 27
28 SUN	183 05	-5	S21 11	11	226 24	-5	S 6 13	24	122 34	11	S21 17	10	41 55	63	N 8 40	2	26 02	64	N12 59	1	SUN 28
29 MON	183 00	-5	S21 22	10	226 19	-6	S 6 37	23	122 45	12	S21 07	12	42 59	63	N 8 38	1	27 06	63	N12 58	1	MON 29
30 TUE	182 55	-5	S21 32	10	226 13	-6	S 7 00	24	122 57	11	S20 55	11	44 02	63	N 8 37	1	28 09	63	N12 57	1	TUE 30
31 WED	182 50		S21 42		226 07		S 7 24		123 08		S20 44		45 05		N 8 36		29 12		N12 56		WED 31

SUN & PLANETS AT GMT 0hrs DECEMBER 1999

Day	SUN SD 16' GHA	v	Dec	d	VENUS Mag. -4.2 GHA	v	Dec	d	MARS Mag. +1.0 GHA	v	Dec	d	JUPITER Mag. -2.7 GHA	v	Dec	d	SATURN Mag. +0.0 GHA	v	Dec	d	Day
1 WED	182° 50'	-6'	S21° 42'	9'	226° 07'	-6'	S 7° 24'	24'	123° 08'	12	S20° 44'	11'	45° 05'	63'	N 8° 36'	1'	29° 12'	63'	N12° 56'	1'	WED 1
2 THU	182 44	-6	S21 51	9	226 01	-7	S 7 48	24	123 20	11	S20 33	12	46 08	63	N 8 35	1	30 15	63	N12 55	1	THU 2
3 FRI	182 38	-6	S22 00	9	225 54	-6	S 8 12	23	123 31	12	S20 21	12	47 11	62	N 8 34	1	31 18	63	N12 54	1	FRI 3
4 SAT	182 32	-6	S22 09	8	225 48	-7	S 8 35	24	123 43	12	S20 09	12	48 13	63	N 8 33	1	32 21	63	N12 53	1	SAT 4
5 SUN	182 26	-6	S22 17	7	225 41	-8	S 8 59	23	123 55	11	S19 57	13	49 16	62	N 8 32	1	33 24	63	N12 52	1	SUN 5
6 MON	182 20	-6	S22 24	7	225 33	-8	S 9 22	24	124 06	12	S19 44	12	50 18	62	N 8 31	1	34 27	63	N12 51	1	MON 6
7 TUE	182 14	-7	S22 32	6	225 26	-8	S 9 46	23	124 18	12	S19 32	13	51 20	62	N 8 30	1	35 30	62	N12 50	1	TUE 7
8 WED	182 07	-6	S22 38	7	225 18	-8	S10 09	23	124 30	12	S19 19	13	52 22	61	N 8 29	0	36 32	63	N12 49	1	WED 8
9 THU	182 01	-7	S22 45	6	225 10	-9	S10 32	23	124 42	13	S19 06	13	53 23	62	N 8 29	1	37 35	63	N12 48	1	THU 9
10 FRI	181 54	-7	S22 51	5	225 01	-8	S10 55	23	124 55	12	S18 53	14	54 25	61	N 8 28	0	38 38	62	N12 47	0	FRI 10
11 SAT	181 47	-7	S22 56	5	224 53	-9	S11 18	23	125 07	12	S18 39	13	55 26	61	N 8 28	1	39 40	63	N12 47	1	SAT 11
12 SUN	181 40	-6	S23 01	5	224 44	-9	S11 41	22	125 19	13	S18 26	14	56 27	61	N 8 27	0	40 43	62	N12 46	1	SUN 12
13 MON	181 34	-8	S23 06	4	224 35	-10	S12 03	22	125 32	12	S18 12	14	57 28	61	N 8 27	0	41 45	62	N12 45	1	MON 13
14 TUE	181 26	-7	S23 10	4	224 25	-10	S12 25	22	125 44	13	S17 58	14	58 29	60	N 8 27	0	42 47	62	N12 44	0	TUE 14
15 WED	181 19	-7	S23 14	3	224 15	-10	S12 47	22	125 57	13	S17 44	14	59 29	60	N 8 27	1	43 49	62	N12 44	1	WED 15
16 THU	181 12	-7	S23 17	3	224 05	-10	S13 09	22	126 10	13	S17 30	15	60 29	60	N 8 26	0	44 51	62	N12 43	1	THU 16
17 FRI	181 05	-7	S23 20	2	223 55	-11	S13 31	21	126 23	13	S17 15	15	61 29	60	N 8 26	0	45 53	62	N12 42	0	FRI 17
18 SAT	180 58	-8	S23 22	2	223 44	-11	S13 52	22	126 36	13	S17 00	14	62 29	60	N 8 26	1	46 55	62	N12 42	1	SAT 18
19 SUN	180 50	-7	S23 24	1	223 33	-11	S14 14	20	126 49	13	S16 46	15	63 29	59	N 8 27	0	47 57	62	N12 41	0	SUN 19
20 MON	180 43	-8	S23 25	1	223 22	-12	S14 34	21	127 02	14	S16 31	15	64 28	60	N 8 27	0	48 59	61	N12 40	1	MON 20
21 TUE	180 35	-7	S23 26	0	223 10	-12	S14 55	20	127 16	13	S16 16	16	65 28	59	N 8 27	0	50 00	62	N12 40	0	TUE 21
22 WED	180 28	-7	S23 26	0	222 58	-12	S15 15	20	127 29	14	S16 00	15	66 27	59	N 8 28	0	51 02	61	N12 40	1	WED 22
23 THU	180 21	-8	S23 26	0	222 46	-13	S15 35	20	127 43	13	S15 45	16	67 26	58	N 8 28	0	52 03	61	N12 39	0	THU 23
24 FRI	180 13	-7	S23 26	1	222 33	-13	S15 55	19	127 56	14	S15 29	16	68 24	59	N 8 28	1	53 04	62	N12 39	1	FRI 24
25 SAT	180 06	-8	S23 25	2	222 20	-13	S16 14	19	128 10	14	S15 13	15	69 23	58	N 8 29	1	54 06	61	N12 38	0	SAT 25
26 SUN	179 58	-7	S23 23	2	222 07	-13	S16 33	19	128 24	14	S14 58	16	70 21	58	N 8 30	1	55 07	61	N12 38	0	SUN 26
27 MON	179 51	-8	S23 21	2	221 54	-14	S16 52	18	128 38	14	S14 42	17	71 19	58	N 8 30	1	56 08	61	N12 37	1	MON 27
28 TUE	179 43	-7	S23 19	3	221 40	-14	S17 10	18	128 52	14	S14 25	16	72 17	58	N 8 31	1	57 09	61	N12 37	0	TUE 28
29 WED	179 36	-7	S23 16	4	221 26	-15	S17 28	17	129 06	14	S14 09	16	73 15	57	N 8 32	1	58 10	60	N12 37	0	WED 29
30 THU	179 29	-7	S23 12	3	221 11	-15	S17 45	17	129 20	15	S13 53	17	74 12	58	N 8 33	1	59 10	61	N12 37	0	THU 30
31 FRI	179 22	-8	S23 09	5	220 56	-15	S18 02	17	129 35	14	S13 36	17	75 10	57	N 8 34	1	60 11	60	N12 37	0	FRI 31
32 SAT	179 14		S23 04		220 41		S18 19		129 49		S13 19		76 07		N 8 35		61 11		N12 37		SAT 32

SUN & PLANETS AT GMT 0hrs JANUARY 2000

Day	SUN SD 16' GHA	v	Dec	d	VENUS Mag. -4.1 GHA	v	Dec	d	MARS Mag. +1.1 GHA	v	Dec	d	JUPITER Mag. -2.4 GHA	v	Dec	d	SATURN Mag. +0.2 GHA	v	Dec	d	Day
1 SAT	179° 14'	-7'	S23° 04'	4'	220° 41'	-15'	S18° 19'	16'	129° 49'	15'	S13° 19'	16'	76° 07'	57'	N 8° 35'	1'	61° 11'	61'	N12° 37'	0'	SAT 1
2 SUN	179 07	-7	S23 00	6	220 26	-16	S18 35	16	130 04	14	S13 03	17	77 04	57	N 8 36	2	62 12	60	N12 37	0	SUN 2
3 MON	179 00	-7	S22 54	5	220 10	-16	S18 51	15	130 18	15	S12 46	17	78 01	56	N 8 38	1	63 12	60	N12 37	0	MON 3
4 TUE	178 53	-7	S22 49	6	219 54	-16	S19 06	15	130 33	15	S12 29	18	78 57	57	N 8 39	1	64 12	60	N12 37	0	TUE 4
5 WED	178 46	-6	S22 43	7	219 38	-17	S19 21	14	130 48	15	S12 11	17	79 54	56	N 8 40	2	65 12	60	N12 37	0	WED 5
6 THU	178 40	-7	S22 36	7	219 21	-16	S19 35	14	131 03	15	S11 54	17	80 50	56	N 8 42	1	66 12	60	N12 37	0	THU 6
7 FRI	178 33	-7	S22 29	8	219 05	-17	S19 49	13	131 18	15	S11 37	18	81 46	56	N 8 43	2	67 12	60	N12 37	0	FRI 7
8 SAT	178 26	-6	S22 21	7	218 48	-18	S20 02	12	131 33	15	S11 19	17	82 42	55	N 8 45	2	68 12	60	N12 37	0	SAT 8
9 SUN	178 20	-6	S22 14	9	218 30	-17	S20 14	13	131 48	16	S11 02	18	83 37	56	N 8 47	1	69 12	59	N12 37	0	SUN 9
10 MON	178 14	-7	S22 05	9	218 13	-18	S20 27	11	132 04	15	S10 44	18	84 33	55	N 8 48	2	70 11	59	N12 37	0	MON 10
11 TUE	178 07	-6	S21 56	9	217 55	-18	S20 38	11	132 19	16	S10 26	18	85 28	55	N 8 50	2	71 10	60	N12 37	1	TUE 11
12 WED	178 01	-5	S21 47	9	217 37	-19	S20 49	11	132 35	15	S10 08	18	86 23	55	N 8 52	2	72 10	59	N12 38	0	WED 12
13 THU	177 56	-6	S21 38	10	217 18	-18	S21 00	10	132 50	16	S 9 50	18	87 18	55	N 8 54	2	73 09	59	N12 38	0	THU 13
14 FRI	177 50	-6	S21 28	11	217 00	-19	S21 10	10	133 06	16	S 9 32	18	88 13	54	N 8 56	2	74 08	59	N12 38	1	FRI 14
15 SAT	177 44	-5	S21 17	11	216 41	-19	S21 19	9	133 22	15	S 9 14	18	89 07	55	N 8 58	2	75 07	59	N12 38	0	SAT 15
16 SUN	177 39	-5	S21 06	11	216 22	-19	S21 28	8	133 37	16	S 8 56	18	90 02	54	N 9 00	2	76 06	59	N12 39	0	SUN 16
17 MON	177 34	-5	S20 55	12	216 03	-20	S21 36	7	133 53	16	S 8 38	18	90 56	54	N 9 02	3	77 05	58	N12 39	1	MON 17
18 TUE	177 29	-5	S20 43	12	215 43	-19	S21 43	7	134 09	17	S 8 20	19	91 50	54	N 9 05	2	78 03	59	N12 40	0	TUE 18
19 WED	177 24	-5	S20 31	12	215 24	-20	S21 50	6	134 26	16	S 8 01	18	92 44	53	N 9 07	2	79 02	58	N12 40	1	WED 19
20 THU	177 19	-4	S20 19	13	215 04	-20	S21 56	6	134 42	16	S 7 43	19	93 37	54	N 9 09	3	80 00	59	N12 41	0	THU 20
21 FRI	177 15	-4	S20 06	13	214 44	-20	S22 02	5	134 58	16	S 7 24	18	94 31	53	N 9 12	2	80 59	58	N12 41	1	FRI 21
22 SAT	177 11	-4	S19 53	14	214 24	-20	S22 07	4	135 14	17	S 7 06	19	95 24	54	N 9 14	3	81 57	58	N12 42	1	SAT 22
23 SUN	177 07	-4	S19 39	14	214 04	-20	S22 11	4	135 31	16	S 6 47	18	96 18	53	N 9 17	2	82 55	58	N12 43	1	SUN 23
24 MON	177 03	-4	S19 25	14	213 44	-21	S22 15	3	135 47	17	S 6 29	19	97 11	53	N 9 19	3	83 53	58	N12 43	1	MON 24
25 TUE	176 59	-4	S19 11	15	213 23	-20	S22 18	3	136 04	16	S 6 10	19	98 04	52	N 9 22	3	84 51	58	N12 44	1	TUE 25
26 WED	176 55	-3	S18 56	15	213 03	-21	S22 21	2	136 20	17	S 5 51	18	98 56	53	N 9 25	3	85 49	57	N12 45	1	WED 26
27 THU	176 52	-3	S18 41	15	212 42	-20	S22 23	1	136 37	17	S 5 33	19	99 49	52	N 9 28	2	86 46	58	N12 46	0	THU 27
28 FRI	176 49	-3	S18 26	16	212 22	-21	S22 24	1	136 54	17	S 5 14	19	100 41	53	N 9 30	3	87 44	57	N12 46	1	FRI 28
29 SAT	176 46	-3	S18 10	16	212 01	-20	S22 24	0	137 11	16	S 4 55	19	101 34	52	N 9 33	3	88 41	58	N12 47	1	SAT 29
30 SUN	176 43	-2	S17 54	16	211 41	-21	S22 24	1	137 27	17	S 4 36	19	102 26	52	N 9 36	3	89 39	57	N12 48	1	SUN 30
31 MON	176 41	-2	S17 38	17	211 20	-21	S22 23	1	137 44	17	S 4 17	19	103 18	52	N 9 39	3	90 36	57	N12 49	1	MON 31
32 TUE	176 39		S17 21		210 59		S22 22		138 01		S 3 58		104 10		N 9 42		91 33		N12 50		TUE 32

SUN & PLANETS AT GMT 0hrs FEBRUARY 2000

Day	SUN SD 16' GHA	v	Dec	d	VENUS Mag. -4.0 GHA	v	Dec	d	MARS Mag. +1.2 GHA	v	Dec	d	JUPITER Mag. -2.2 GHA	v	Dec	d	SATURN Mag. +0.3 GHA	v	Dec	d	Day
1 TUE	176° 39'	-3'	S17° 21'	17'	210° 59'	-21'	S22° 22'	3'	138° 01'	17'	S 3° 58'	19'	104° 10'	51'	N 9° 42'	3'	91° 33'	57'	N12° 50'	1'	TUE 1
2 WED	176 36	-1	S17 04	17	210 38	-20	S22 19	2	138 18	17	S 3 39	19	105 01	52	N 9 45	3	92 30	57	N12 51	1	WED 2
3 THU	176 35	-2	S16 47	18	210 18	-21	S22 17	4	138 35	17	S 3 20	18	105 53	51	N 9 48	3	93 27	57	N12 52	1	THU 3
4 FRI	176 33	-2	S16 29	17	209 57	-20	S22 13	4	138 52	18	S 3 02	19	106 44	52	N 9 52	3	94 24	57	N12 53	1	FRI 4
5 SAT	176 31	-1	S16 12	18	209 37	-21	S22 09	5	139 10	17	S 2 43	19	107 36	51	N 9 55	3	95 21	56	N12 54	1	SAT 5
6 SUN	176 30	-1	S15 54	19	209 16	-20	S22 04	6	139 27	17	S 2 24	19	108 27	51	N 9 58	3	96 17	57	N12 55	1	SUN 6
7 MON	176 29	-1	S15 35	18	208 56	-21	S21 58	6	139 44	17	S 2 05	19	109 18	51	N10 01	3	97 14	56	N12 56	1	MON 7
8 TUE	176 28	-1	S15 17	19	208 35	-20	S21 52	7	140 01	18	S 1 46	19	110 09	50	N10 05	3	98 10	57	N12 57	2	TUE 8
9 WED	176 27	0	S14 58	20	208 15	-20	S21 45	7	140 19	17	S 1 27	19	110 59	51	N10 08	3	99 07	56	N12 59	1	WED 9
10 THU	176 27	-1	S14 38	19	207 55	-20	S21 38	8	140 36	17	S 1 08	19	111 50	50	N10 11	3	100 03	56	N13 00	1	THU 10
11 FRI	176 26	0	S14 19	20	207 35	-20	S21 30	9	140 53	18	S 0 49	19	112 40	51	N10 15	3	100 59	56	N13 01	1	FRI 11
12 SAT	176 26	0	S13 59	19	207 15	-19	S21 21	9	141 11	17	S 0 30	19	113 31	50	N10 18	4	101 55	56	N13 02	2	SAT 12
13 SUN	176 26	1	S13 40	21	206 56	-20	S21 12	10	141 28	18	S 0 11	3	114 21	50	N10 22	4	102 51	56	N13 04	1	SUN 13
14 MON	176 27	0	S13 19	20	206 36	-19	S21 02	11	141 46	17	N 0 08	19	115 11	50	N10 26	3	103 47	55	N13 05	1	MON 14
15 TUE	176 27	1	S12 59	20	206 17	-19	S20 51	11	142 03	18	N 0 27	19	116 01	50	N10 29	4	104 42	56	N13 06	2	TUE 15
16 WED	176 28	1	S12 39	21	205 58	-19	S20 40	12	142 21	18	N 0 46	18	116 51	49	N10 33	4	105 38	56	N13 08	1	WED 16
17 THU	176 29	1	S12 18	21	205 39	-19	S20 28	12	142 39	17	N 1 04	19	117 40	50	N10 37	3	106 34	55	N13 09	2	THU 17
18 FRI	176 30	1	S11 57	21	205 20	-19	S20 16	13	142 56	18	N 1 23	19	118 30	50	N10 40	4	107 29	55	N13 11	1	FRI 18
19 SAT	176 31	1	S11 36	21	205 01	-18	S20 03	14	143 14	17	N 1 42	19	119 20	49	N10 44	4	108 24	56	N13 12	2	SAT 19
20 SUN	176 32	2	S11 15	22	204 43	-18	S19 49	14	143 31	18	N 2 01	18	120 09	49	N10 48	4	109 20	55	N13 14	1	SUN 20
21 MON	176 34	2	S10 53	21	204 25	-18	S19 35	15	143 49	18	N 2 19	19	120 58	49	N10 52	4	110 15	55	N13 15	2	MON 21
22 TUE	176 36	1	S10 31	21	204 07	-18	S19 20	15	144 07	18	N 2 38	17	121 47	49	N10 55	3	111 10	55	N13 17	1	TUE 22
23 WED	176 37	2	S10 10	22	203 49	-17	S19 05	16	144 24	18	N 2 57	18	122 36	49	N10 59	4	112 05	55	N13 18	2	WED 23
24 THU	176 39	3	S 9 48	22	203 32	-17	S18 49	17	144 42	18	N 3 15	19	123 25	49	N11 03	4	113 00	55	N13 20	1	THU 24
25 FRI	176 42	2	S 9 26	23	203 15	-17	S18 32	17	145 00	18	N 3 34	18	124 14	49	N11 07	4	113 55	55	N13 21	2	FRI 25
26 SAT	176 44	2	S 9 03	22	202 58	-17	S18 15	17	145 18	17	N 3 52	19	125 03	49	N11 11	4	114 50	54	N13 23	2	SAT 26
27 SUN	176 46	2	S 8 41	23	202 41	-16	S17 58	18	145 35	18	N 4 11	18	125 52	48	N11 15	4	115 44	55	N13 25	1	SUN 27
28 MON	176 49	3	S 8 18	22	202 25	-16	S17 40	19	145 53	18	N 4 29	18	126 40	49	N11 19	4	116 39	54	N13 26	2	MON 28
29 TUE	176 52	3	S 7 56	23	202 09	-16	S17 21	19	146 11	17	N 4 47	18	127 29	48	N11 23	4	117 33	55	N13 28	2	TUE 29
30 WED	176 55		S 7 33		201 53		S17 02		146 28		N 5 05		128 17		N11 27		118 28		N13 30		WED 30

SUN & PLANETS AT GMT 0hrs MARCH 2000

Day	SUN SD 16' GHA	v	Dec	d	VENUS Mag. -3.9 GHA	v	Dec	d	MARS Mag. +1.4 GHA	v	Dec	d	JUPITER Mag. -2.1 GHA	v	Dec	d	SATURN Mag. +0.3 GHA	v	Dec	d	Day
1 WED	176° 55'	2'	S 7° 33'	23'	201° 53'	-16'	S17° 02'	19'	146° 28'	18'	N 5° 05'	19'	128° 17'	48'	N11° 27'	4'	118° 28'	54'	N13° 30'	1'	WED 1
2 THU	176 57	4	S 7 10	23	201 37	-15	S16 43	20	146 46	18	N 5 24	18	129 05	48	N11 31	5	119 22	54	N13 31	2	THU 2
3 FRI	177 01	3	S 6 47	23	201 22	-16	S16 23	21	147 04	18	N 5 42	18	129 53	48	N11 36	4	120 16	55	N13 33	2	FRI 3
4 SAT	177 04	3	S 6 24	23	201 06	-14	S16 02	21	147 22	17	N 6 00	18	130 41	48	N11 40	4	121 11	54	N13 35	2	SAT 4
5 SUN	177 07	3	S 6 01	23	200 52	-15	S15 41	21	147 39	18	N 6 18	18	131 29	48	N11 44	4	122 05	54	N13 37	1	SUN 5
6 MON	177 10	4	S 5 38	24	200 37	-14	S15 20	22	147 57	18	N 6 36	17	132 17	48	N11 48	4	122 59	54	N13 38	2	MON 6
7 TUE	177 14	4	S 5 14	23	200 23	-14	S14 58	22	148 15	17	N 6 53	18	133 05	47	N11 52	4	123 53	54	N13 40	2	TUE 7
8 WED	177 18	4	S 4 51	23	200 09	-14	S14 36	23	148 32	18	N 7 11	18	133 52	48	N11 56	5	124 47	53	N13 42	2	WED 8
9 THU	177 21	4	S 4 28	24	199 55	-14	S14 13	23	148 50	17	N 7 29	17	134 40	48	N12 01	4	125 40	54	N13 44	2	THU 9
10 FRI	177 25	4	S 4 04	23	199 41	-13	S13 50	23	149 07	18	N 7 46	18	135 28	47	N12 05	4	126 34	54	N13 46	2	FRI 10
11 SAT	177 29	4	S 3 41	24	199 28	-13	S13 27	24	149 25	18	N 8 04	17	136 15	47	N12 09	4	127 28	53	N13 48	2	SAT 11
12 SUN	177 33	4	S 3 17	24	199 15	-13	S13 03	24	149 43	17	N 8 21	17	137 02	47	N12 13	5	128 21	54	N13 50	1	SUN 12
13 MON	177 37	4	S 2 53	23	199 02	-12	S12 39	24	150 00	18	N 8 38	18	137 50	47	N12 18	4	129 15	53	N13 51	2	MON 13
14 TUE	177 41	4	S 2 30	24	198 50	-13	S12 15	25	150 18	17	N 8 56	17	138 37	47	N12 22	4	130 08	54	N13 53	2	TUE 14
15 WED	177 45	5	S 2 06	24	198 37	-12	S11 50	25	150 35	18	N 9 13	17	139 24	47	N12 26	5	131 02	53	N13 55	2	WED 15
16 THU	177 50	4	S 1 42	23	198 25	-12	S11 25	25	150 53	17	N 9 30	17	140 11	47	N12 31	4	131 55	53	N13 57	2	THU 16
17 FRI	177 54	4	S 1 19	24	198 13	-11	S11 00	26	151 10	18	N 9 47	16	140 58	47	N12 35	4	132 48	53	N13 59	2	FRI 17
18 SAT	177 58	5	S 0 55	24	198 02	-12	S10 34	26	151 28	17	N10 03	17	141 45	47	N12 39	5	133 41	54	N14 01	2	SAT 18
19 SUN	178 03	4	S 0 31	24	197 50	-11	S10 08	26	151 45	17	N10 20	17	142 32	46	N12 44	4	134 35	53	N14 03	2	SUN 19
20 MON	178 07	5	S 0 07	9	197 39	-11	S 9 42	27	152 02	18	N10 37	16	143 18	47	N12 48	4	135 28	53	N14 05	2	MON 20
21 TUE	178 12	4	N 0 16	24	197 28	-11	S 9 15	26	152 20	17	N10 53	16	144 05	46	N12 52	5	136 21	53	N14 07	2	TUE 21
22 WED	178 16	5	N 0 40	24	197 17	-10	S 8 49	27	152 37	17	N11 09	17	144 52	46	N12 57	4	137 14	53	N14 09	2	WED 22
23 THU	178 21	4	N 1 04	23	197 07	-11	S 8 22	28	152 54	18	N11 26	16	145 38	47	N13 01	5	138 07	52	N14 11	2	THU 23
24 FRI	178 25	5	N 1 27	24	196 56	-10	S 7 54	27	153 12	17	N11 42	16	146 25	46	N13 06	4	138 59	53	N14 13	3	FRI 24
25 SAT	178 30	4	N 1 51	23	196 46	-10	S 7 27	28	153 29	17	N11 58	16	147 11	47	N13 10	4	139 52	53	N14 16	2	SAT 25
26 SUN	178 34	5	N 2 14	24	196 36	-10	S 6 59	28	153 46	17	N12 14	15	147 58	46	N13 14	5	140 45	53	N14 18	2	SUN 26
27 MON	178 39	4	N 2 38	23	196 26	-10	S 6 31	28	154 03	17	N12 29	16	148 44	46	N13 19	4	141 38	52	N14 20	2	MON 27
28 TUE	178 43	5	N 3 01	24	196 16	-10	S 6 03	28	154 20	17	N12 45	15	149 30	46	N13 23	5	142 30	53	N14 22	2	TUE 28
29 WED	178 48	4	N 3 25	23	196 06	-10	S 5 35	28	154 37	17	N13 00	16	150 16	46	N13 28	4	143 23	52	N14 24	2	WED 29
30 THU	178 52	5	N 3 48	23	195 56	-9	S 5 07	29	154 54	17	N13 16	15	151 02	46	N13 32	4	144 15	53	N14 26	2	THU 30
31 FRI	178 57	4	N 4 11	23	195 47	-9	S 4 38	28	155 11	17	N13 31	15	151 48	46	N13 36	5	145 08	52	N14 28	2	FRI 31
32 SAT	179 01		N 4 34		195 38		S 4 10		155 28		N13 46		152 34		N13 41		146 00		N14 30		SAT 32

SUN & PLANETS AT GMT 0hrs APRIL 2000

Day	SUN SD 16' GHA	v	Dec	d	VENUS Mag. -3.8 GHA	v	Dec	d	MARS Mag. +1.5 GHA	v	Dec	d	JUPITER Mag. -2.0 GHA	v	Dec	d	SATURN Mag. +0.3 GHA	v	Dec	d	Day
1 SAT	179° 01'	5'	N 4° 34'	24'	195° 38'	-10'	S 4° 10'	29'	155° 28'	17'	N13° 46'	15'	152° 34'	46'	N13° 41'	4'	146° 00'	53'	N14° 30'	2'	SAT 1
2 SUN	179 06	4	N 4 58	23	195 28	-9	S 3 41	29	155 45	17	N14 01	15	153 20	46	N13 45	5	146 53	52	N14 32	2	SUN 2
3 MON	179 10	5	N 5 21	23	195 19	-9	S 3 12	29	156 02	17	N14 16	15	154 06	46	N13 50	4	147 45	52	N14 34	3	MON 3
4 TUE	179 15	4	N 5 44	22	195 10	-9	S 2 43	29	156 19	16	N14 31	14	154 52	46	N13 54	4	148 37	52	N14 37	2	TUE 4
5 WED	179 19	4	N 6 06	23	195 01	-9	S 2 14	29	156 35	17	N14 45	14	155 38	46	N13 58	5	149 29	53	N14 39	2	WED 5
6 THU	179 23	4	N 6 29	23	194 52	-9	S 1 45	29	156 52	17	N14 59	15	156 24	45	N14 03	4	150 22	52	N14 41	2	THU 6
7 FRI	179 27	5	N 6 52	22	194 43	-9	S 1 16	29	157 09	16	N15 14	14	157 09	46	N14 07	5	151 14	52	N14 43	2	FRI 7
8 SAT	179 32	4	N 7 14	22	194 34	-9	S 0 47	30	157 25	17	N15 28	14	157 55	46	N14 12	4	152 06	52	N14 45	2	SAT 8
9 SUN	179 36	4	N 7 37	22	194 25	-8	S 0 17	5	157 42	16	N15 42	13	158 41	45	N14 16	4	152 58	52	N14 47	3	SUN 9
10 MON	179 40	4	N 7 59	22	194 17	-9	N 0 12	29	157 58	17	N15 55	14	159 26	46	N14 20	5	153 50	52	N14 50	2	MON 10
11 TUE	179 44	4	N 8 21	22	194 08	-9	N 0 41	30	158 15	16	N16 09	13	160 12	45	N14 25	4	154 42	52	N14 52	2	TUE 11
12 WED	179 48	3	N 8 43	22	193 59	-9	N 1 11	29	158 31	16	N16 22	14	160 57	46	N14 29	5	155 34	52	N14 54	2	WED 12
13 THU	179 51	4	N 9 05	21	193 50	-9	N 1 40	29	158 47	17	N16 36	13	161 43	45	N14 34	4	156 26	52	N14 56	2	THU 13
14 FRI	179 55	4	N 9 26	22	193 41	-8	N 2 09	29	159 04	16	N16 49	13	162 28	46	N14 38	4	157 18	52	N14 58	2	FRI 14
15 SAT	179 59	4	N 9 48	21	193 33	-9	N 2 38	30	159 20	16	N17 02	13	163 14	45	N14 42	5	158 10	52	N15 00	3	SAT 15
16 SUN	180 03	3	N10 09	21	193 24	-9	N 3 08	29	159 36	16	N17 15	12	163 59	45	N14 47	4	159 02	51	N15 03	2	SUN 16
17 MON	180 06	3	N10 30	21	193 15	-9	N 3 37	29	159 52	16	N17 27	13	164 44	46	N14 51	4	159 53	52	N15 05	2	MON 17
18 TUE	180 09	3	N10 51	21	193 06	-9	N 4 06	29	160 08	16	N17 40	12	165 30	45	N14 55	5	160 45	52	N15 07	2	TUE 18
19 WED	180 13	3	N11 12	21	192 57	-9	N 4 35	29	160 24	16	N17 52	12	166 15	45	N15 00	4	161 37	52	N15 09	2	WED 19
20 THU	180 16	3	N11 33	20	192 48	-10	N 5 04	29	160 40	16	N18 04	12	167 00	45	N15 04	4	162 29	51	N15 11	2	THU 20
21 FRI	180 19	3	N11 53	21	192 38	-9	N 5 33	28	160 56	16	N18 16	12	167 45	45	N15 08	5	163 20	52	N15 13	3	FRI 21
22 SAT	180 22	3	N12 14	20	192 29	-9	N 6 01	29	161 12	16	N18 28	12	168 30	46	N15 13	4	164 12	52	N15 15	2	SAT 22
23 SUN	180 25	3	N12 34	19	192 20	-10	N 6 30	28	161 28	16	N18 40	11	169 16	45	N15 17	4	165 04	51	N15 18	2	SUN 23
24 MON	180 28	2	N12 53	20	192 10	-10	N 6 58	29	161 44	16	N18 51	11	170 01	45	N15 21	4	165 55	52	N15 20	2	MON 24
25 TUE	180 30	3	N13 13	20	192 00	-9	N 7 27	28	162 00	15	N19 02	11	170 46	45	N15 25	5	166 47	51	N15 22	2	TUE 25
26 WED	180 33	2	N13 33	19	191 51	-10	N 7 55	28	162 15	16	N19 13	11	171 31	45	N15 30	4	167 38	52	N15 24	2	WED 26
27 THU	180 35	3	N13 52	19	191 41	-10	N 8 23	28	162 31	15	N19 24	11	172 16	45	N15 34	4	168 30	51	N15 26	3	THU 27
28 FRI	180 38	2	N14 11	18	191 31	-11	N 8 51	27	162 46	16	N19 35	10	173 01	45	N15 38	4	169 22	51	N15 28	2	FRI 28
29 SAT	180 40	2	N14 29	19	191 20	-11	N 9 18	28	163 02	15	N19 45	11	173 46	45	N15 42	4	170 13	52	N15 31	2	SAT 29
30 SUN	180 42	2	N14 48	18	191 10	-11	N 9 46	27	163 17	16	N19 56	10	174 31	45	N15 46	5	171 05	51	N15 33	2	SUN 30
31 MON	180 44		N15 06		190 59		N10 13		163 33		N20 06		175 16		N15 51		171 56		N15 35		MON 31

SUN & PLANETS AT GMT 0hrs MAY 2000

Day	SUN SD 16'				VENUS Mag. -3.9				MARS Mag. +1.5				JUPITER Mag. -2.0				SATURN Mag. +0.2				Day
	GHA	v	Dec	d	GHA	v	Dec	d	GHA	v	Dec	d	GHA	v	Dec	d	GHA	v	Dec	d	
1 MON	180° 44'	1'	N15° 06'	18'	190° 59'	-10'	N10° 13'	27'	163° 33'	15'	N20° 06'	10'	175° 16'	45'	N15° 51'	4'	171° 56'	52'	N15° 35'	2'	MON 1
2 TUE	180 45	2	N15 24	18	190 49	-11	N10 40	26	163 48	16	N20 16	10	176 01	45	N15 55	4	172 48	51	N15 37	2	TUE 2
3 WED	180 47	1	N15 42	17	190 38	-12	N11 06	27	164 04	15	N20 26	9	176 46	45	N15 59	4	173 39	52	N15 39	2	WED 3
4 THU	180 48	2	N15 59	18	190 26	-11	N11 33	26	164 19	15	N20 35	9	177 31	45	N16 03	4	174 31	51	N15 41	2	THU 4
5 FRI	180 50	1	N16 17	17	190 15	-12	N11 59	26	164 34	15	N20 44	10	178 16	44	N16 07	4	175 22	51	N15 43	3	FRI 5
6 SAT	180 51	1	N16 34	16	190 03	-12	N12 25	25	164 49	16	N20 54	9	179 00	45	N16 11	4	176 13	52	N15 46	2	SAT 6
7 SUN	180 52	1	N16 50	17	189 51	-12	N12 50	25	165 05	15	N21 03	8	179 45	45	N16 15	4	177 05	51	N15 48	2	SUN 7
8 MON	180 53	1	N17 07	16	189 39	-12	N13 16	25	165 20	15	N21 11	9	180 30	45	N16 19	4	177 56	52	N15 50	2	MON 8
9 TUE	180 54	0	N17 23	16	189 27	-12	N13 41	24	165 35	15	N21 20	8	181 15	45	N16 23	4	178 48	51	N15 52	2	TUE 9
10 WED	180 54	1	N17 39	15	189 15	-13	N14 05	25	165 50	15	N21 28	9	182 00	45	N16 27	4	179 39	51	N15 54	2	WED 10
11 THU	180 55	0	N17 54	15	189 02	-13	N14 30	24	166 05	15	N21 37	7	182 45	45	N16 31	4	180 30	52	N15 56	2	THU 11
12 FRI	180 55	0	N18 09	15	188 49	-14	N14 54	23	166 20	15	N21 44	8	183 30	44	N16 35	4	181 22	51	N15 58	2	FRI 12
13 SAT	180 55	0	N18 24	15	188 35	-13	N15 17	23	166 35	15	N21 52	8	184 14	45	N16 39	4	182 13	52	N16 00	2	SAT 13
14 SUN	180 55	0	N18 39	14	188 22	-14	N15 40	23	166 50	15	N22 00	7	184 59	45	N16 43	4	183 05	51	N16 02	2	SUN 14
15 MON	180 55	0	N18 53	14	188 08	-14	N16 03	23	167 05	15	N22 07	7	185 44	45	N16 47	4	183 56	51	N16 04	2	MON 15
16 TUE	180 55	0	N19 07	14	187 54	-14	N16 26	22	167 20	15	N22 14	7	186 29	45	N16 51	4	184 47	52	N16 06	2	TUE 16
17 WED	180 55	-1	N19 21	13	187 40	-15	N16 48	21	167 35	14	N22 21	7	187 14	45	N16 55	4	185 39	51	N16 08	2	WED 17
18 THU	180 54	-1	N19 34	13	187 25	-15	N17 09	21	167 49	15	N22 28	7	187 59	44	N16 59	3	186 30	52	N16 10	2	THU 18
19 FRI	180 53	0	N19 47	13	187 10	-15	N17 30	21	168 04	15	N22 35	6	188 43	45	N17 02	4	187 22	51	N16 12	2	FRI 19
20 SAT	180 53	-1	N20 00	12	186 55	-16	N17 51	20	168 19	15	N22 41	6	189 28	45	N17 06	4	188 13	51	N16 14	2	SAT 20
21 SUN	180 52	-1	N20 12	12	186 39	-15	N18 11	20	168 34	15	N22 47	6	190 13	45	N17 10	4	189 04	52	N16 16	2	SUN 21
22 MON	180 51	-1	N20 24	12	186 24	-16	N18 31	19	168 49	14	N22 53	6	190 58	45	N17 14	3	189 56	51	N16 18	2	MON 22
23 TUE	180 50	-2	N20 36	11	186 08	-17	N18 50	19	169 03	15	N22 59	5	191 43	45	N17 17	4	190 47	52	N16 20	2	TUE 23
24 WED	180 48	-1	N20 47	11	185 51	-16	N19 09	18	169 18	15	N23 04	6	192 28	45	N17 21	4	191 39	51	N16 22	2	WED 24
25 THU	180 47	-2	N20 58	10	185 35	-17	N19 27	18	169 33	15	N23 10	5	193 13	44	N17 25	3	192 30	52	N16 24	2	THU 25
26 FRI	180 45	-1	N21 08	11	185 18	-17	N19 45	17	169 48	14	N23 15	5	193 57	45	N17 28	4	193 22	51	N16 26	2	FRI 26
27 SAT	180 44	-2	N21 19	9	185 01	-18	N20 02	17	170 02	15	N23 20	4	194 42	45	N17 32	4	194 13	52	N16 28	2	SAT 27
28 SUN	180 42	-2	N21 28	10	184 43	-17	N20 19	16	170 17	15	N23 24	5	195 27	45	N17 36	3	195 05	51	N16 30	2	SUN 28
29 MON	180 40	-2	N21 38	9	184 26	-18	N20 35	16	170 32	15	N23 29	4	196 12	45	N17 39	4	195 56	52	N16 32	2	MON 29
30 TUE	180 38	-2	N21 47	9	184 08	-18	N20 51	14	170 46	15	N23 33	4	196 57	45	N17 43	3	196 48	51	N16 34	2	TUE 30
31 WED	180 36	-3	N21 56	8	183 50	-19	N21 05	15	171 01	15	N23 37	4	197 42	45	N17 46	4	197 39	52	N16 36	1	WED 31
32 THU	180 33		N22 04		183 31		N21 20		171 16		N23 41		198 27		N17 50		198 31		N16 37		THU 32

SUN & PLANETS AT GMT 0hrs JUNE 2000

Day	SUN SD 16'				VENUS Mag. -3.9				MARS Mag. +1.6				JUPITER Mag. -2.0				SATURN Mag. +0.2				Day
	GHA	v	Dec	d	GHA	v	Dec	d	GHA	v	Dec	d	GHA	v	Dec	d	GHA	v	Dec	d	
1 THU	180° 33'	-2'	N22° 04'	8'	183° 31'	-19'	N21° 20'	14'	171° 16'	14'	N23° 41'	3'	198° 27'	45'	N17° 50'	3'	198° 31'	51'	N16° 37'	2'	THU 1
2 FRI	180 31	-2	N22 12	7	183 12	-19	N21 34	13	171 30	15	N23 44	3	199 12	45	N17 53	3	199 22	51	N16 39	2	FRI 2
3 SAT	180 29	-3	N22 19	7	182 53	-19	N21 47	13	171 45	15	N23 48	3	199 57	45	N17 57	3	200 14	51	N16 41	2	SAT 3
4 SUN	180 26	-3	N22 26	7	182 34	-19	N22 00	11	172 00	14	N23 51	3	200 42	45	N18 00	4	201 05	52	N16 43	2	SUN 4
5 MON	180 23	-2	N22 33	7	182 15	-20	N22 11	12	172 14	15	N23 54	3	201 27	45	N18 04	3	201 57	52	N16 45	2	MON 5
6 TUE	180 21	-3	N22 40	6	181 55	-20	N22 23	10	172 29	15	N23 57	2	202 12	45	N18 07	3	202 49	51	N16 47	1	TUE 6
7 WED	180 18	-3	N22 46	5	181 35	-20	N22 34	10	172 44	14	N23 59	2	202 57	46	N18 10	4	203 40	52	N16 48	2	WED 7
8 THU	180 15	-3	N22 51	5	181 15	-20	N22 44	9	172 58	15	N24 01	3	203 43	45	N18 14	3	204 32	52	N16 50	2	THU 8
9 FRI	180 12	-3	N22 56	5	180 55	-20	N22 53	9	173 13	15	N24 04	1	204 28	45	N18 17	3	205 24	52	N16 52	2	FRI 9
10 SAT	180 09	-3	N23 01	4	180 35	-21	N23 02	8	173 28	15	N24 05	2	205 13	45	N18 20	3	206 16	51	N16 54	1	SAT 10
11 SUN	180 06	-3	N23 05	4	180 14	-21	N23 10	7	173 43	15	N24 07	2	205 58	46	N18 23	3	207 07	52	N16 55	2	SUN 11
12 MON	180 03	-3	N23 09	4	179 53	-20	N23 17	7	173 58	14	N24 09	1	206 44	45	N18 26	4	207 59	52	N16 57	2	MON 12
13 TUE	180 00	-3	N23 13	3	179 33	-21	N23 24	6	174 12	15	N24 10	1	207 29	45	N18 30	3	208 51	52	N16 59	1	TUE 13
14 WED	179 57	-3	N23 16	3	179 12	-21	N23 30	6	174 27	15	N24 11	1	208 14	46	N18 33	3	209 43	52	N17 00	2	WED 14
15 THU	179 54	-3	N23 19	2	178 51	-22	N23 36	4	174 42	15	N24 12	0	209 00	45	N18 36	3	210 35	52	N17 02	2	THU 15
16 FRI	179 51	-4	N23 21	2	178 29	-21	N23 40	4	174 57	15	N24 12	1	209 45	45	N18 39	3	211 27	52	N17 04	1	FRI 16
17 SAT	179 47	-3	N23 23	1	178 08	-21	N23 44	4	175 12	15	N24 13	0	210 30	46	N18 42	3	212 19	52	N17 05	2	SAT 17
18 SUN	179 44	-3	N23 24	1	177 47	-22	N23 48	2	175 27	15	N24 13	0	211 16	46	N18 45	3	213 11	52	N17 07	1	SUN 18
19 MON	179 41	-3	N23 25	1	177 25	-21	N23 50	2	175 42	15	N24 13	0	212 02	45	N18 48	3	214 03	52	N17 08	2	MON 19
20 TUE	179 38	-4	N23 26	0	177 04	-22	N23 52	1	175 57	15	N24 13	1	212 47	46	N18 51	3	214 55	52	N17 10	1	TUE 20
21 WED	179 34	-3	N23 26	0	176 42	-21	N23 53	1	176 12	15	N24 12	0	213 33	45	N18 54	3	215 47	53	N17 11	2	WED 21
22 THU	179 31	-3	N23 26	0	176 21	-21	N23 54	1	176 28	15	N24 12	1	214 18	46	N18 57	3	216 39	53	N17 13	2	THU 22
23 FRI	179 28	-3	N23 26	1	175 59	-21	N23 53	1	176 43	15	N24 11	1	215 04	46	N19 00	3	217 32	52	N17 15	1	FRI 23
24 SAT	179 25	-3	N23 25	2	175 38	-22	N23 52	1	176 58	15	N24 10	1	215 50	46	N19 03	2	218 24	52	N17 16	2	SAT 24
25 SUN	179 22	-4	N23 23	2	175 16	-21	N23 51	3	177 13	16	N24 09	2	216 36	46	N19 05	3	219 16	53	N17 18	1	SUN 25
26 MON	179 18	-3	N23 21	2	174 55	-22	N23 48	3	177 29	15	N24 07	1	217 22	46	N19 08	3	220 09	52	N17 19	1	MON 26
27 TUE	179 15	-3	N23 19	3	174 33	-21	N23 45	3	177 44	16	N24 06	2	218 08	46	N19 11	3	221 01	52	N17 20	2	TUE 27
28 WED	179 12	-3	N23 16	3	174 12	-21	N23 42	4	178 00	15	N24 04	2	218 54	46	N19 14	2	221 53	53	N17 22	1	WED 28
29 THU	179 09	-3	N23 13	3	173 51	-21	N23 37	5	178 15	16	N24 02	2	219 40	46	N19 16	3	222 46	53	N17 23	2	THU 29
30 FRI	179 06	-3	N23 10	4	173 30	-21	N23 32	6	178 31	16	N24 00	3	220 26	46	N19 19	3	223 39	52	N17 25	1	FRI 30
31 SAT	179 03		N23 06		173 09		N23 26		178 47		N23 57		221 12		N19 22		224 31		N17 26		SAT 31

44

SUN & PLANETS AT GMT 0hrs JULY 2000

Day	SUN SD 16' GHA	v	Dec	d	VENUS Mag. -3.9 GHA	v	Dec	d	MARS Mag. +1.6 GHA	v	Dec	d	JUPITER Mag. -2.1 GHA	v	Dec	d	SATURN Mag. +0.2 GHA	v	Dec	d	Day
1 SAT	179° 03'	-3'	N23° 06'	4'	173° 09'	-21'	N23° 26'	6'	178° 47'	15'	N23° 57'	2'	221° 12'	46'	N19° 22'	2'	224° 31'	53'	N17° 26'	1'	SAT 1
2 SUN	179 00	-3	N23 02	5	172 48	-21	N23 20	8	179 02	16	N23 55	3	221 58	46	N19 24	3	225 24	52	N17 27	2	SUN 2
3 MON	178 57	-2	N22 57	5	172 27	-21	N23 12	8	179 18	16	N23 52	3	222 44	47	N19 27	2	226 16	53	N17 29	1	MON 3
4 TUE	178 55	-3	N22 52	5	172 06	-20	N23 04	8	179 34	16	N23 49	4	223 31	46	N19 29	3	227 09	53	N17 30	1	TUE 4
5 WED	178 52	-3	N22 47	6	171 46	-20	N22 56	10	179 50	16	N23 45	3	224 17	47	N19 32	2	228 02	53	N17 31	2	WED 5
6 THU	178 49	-2	N22 41	7	171 26	-20	N22 46	10	180 06	16	N23 42	4	225 04	46	N19 34	3	228 55	53	N17 33	1	THU 6
7 FRI	178 47	-2	N22 34	6	171 06	-20	N22 36	10	180 22	16	N23 38	3	225 50	47	N19 37	2	229 48	53	N17 34	1	FRI 7
8 SAT	178 45	-3	N22 28	7	170 46	-20	N22 26	11	180 38	16	N23 35	4	226 37	46	N19 39	2	230 41	53	N17 35	1	SAT 8
9 SUN	178 42	-2	N22 21	8	170 26	-19	N22 15	12	180 54	17	N23 31	4	227 23	47	N19 41	3	231 34	53	N17 36	2	SUN 9
10 MON	178 40	-2	N22 13	8	170 07	-20	N22 03	13	181 11	16	N23 27	5	228 10	47	N19 44	2	232 27	53	N17 38	1	MON 10
11 TUE	178 38	-2	N22 05	8	169 47	-19	N21 50	13	181 27	17	N23 22	4	228 57	47	N19 46	2	233 20	53	N17 39	1	TUE 11
12 WED	178 36	-2	N21 57	8	169 28	-18	N21 37	14	181 44	16	N23 18	5	229 44	47	N19 48	3	234 13	54	N17 40	1	WED 12
13 THU	178 34	-1	N21 49	9	169 10	-19	N21 23	14	182 00	17	N23 13	5	230 31	47	N19 51	2	235 07	53	N17 41	1	THU 13
14 FRI	178 33	-2	N21 40	10	168 51	-18	N21 09	15	182 17	17	N23 08	5	231 18	47	N19 53	2	236 00	54	N17 42	1	FRI 14
15 SAT	178 31	-1	N21 30	9	168 33	-18	N20 54	16	182 34	16	N23 03	5	232 05	48	N19 55	2	236 54	53	N17 43	1	SAT 15
16 SUN	178 30	-2	N21 21	10	168 15	-18	N20 38	16	182 50	17	N22 58	6	232 53	47	N19 57	2	237 47	54	N17 44	1	SUN 16
17 MON	178 28	-1	N21 11	11	167 57	-17	N20 22	17	183 07	17	N22 52	5	233 40	47	N19 59	2	238 41	53	N17 45	2	MON 17
18 TUE	178 27	-1	N21 00	10	167 40	-17	N20 05	17	183 24	17	N22 47	6	234 27	48	N20 01	2	239 34	54	N17 47	1	TUE 18
19 WED	178 26	-1	N20 50	11	167 23	-17	N19 48	18	183 41	18	N22 41	6	235 15	48	N20 03	2	240 28	54	N17 48	1	WED 19
20 THU	178 25	-1	N20 39	12	167 06	-17	N19 30	19	183 59	17	N22 35	6	236 03	47	N20 05	2	241 22	54	N17 49	1	THU 20
21 FRI	178 24	0	N20 27	12	166 49	-16	N19 11	19	184 16	17	N22 29	7	236 50	48	N20 07	2	242 16	53	N17 50	1	FRI 21
22 SAT	178 24	-1	N20 15	12	166 33	-16	N18 52	19	184 33	18	N22 22	6	237 38	48	N20 09	2	243 09	54	N17 51	0	SAT 22
23 SUN	178 23	0	N20 03	12	166 17	-15	N18 33	20	184 51	17	N22 16	7	238 26	48	N20 11	2	244 03	55	N17 51	1	SUN 23
24 MON	178 23	0	N19 51	13	166 02	-16	N18 13	21	185 08	18	N22 09	7	239 14	48	N20 13	2	244 58	54	N17 52	1	MON 24
25 TUE	178 23	0	N19 38	13	165 46	-15	N17 52	21	185 26	17	N22 02	7	240 02	48	N20 15	2	245 52	54	N17 53	1	TUE 25
26 WED	178 23	0	N19 25	14	165 31	-15	N17 31	22	185 43	18	N21 55	7	240 50	48	N20 17	2	246 46	54	N17 54	1	WED 26
27 THU	178 23	0	N19 11	13	165 16	-14	N17 09	22	186 01	18	N21 48	7	241 38	49	N20 19	1	247 40	55	N17 55	1	THU 27
28 FRI	178 23	0	N18 58	14	165 02	-14	N16 47	22	186 19	18	N21 41	7	242 27	48	N20 20	2	248 35	54	N17 56	1	FRI 28
29 SAT	178 23	1	N18 44	15	164 48	-14	N16 25	23	186 37	18	N21 34	8	243 15	49	N20 22	2	249 29	55	N17 57	0	SAT 29
30 SUN	178 24	1	N18 29	14	164 34	-14	N16 02	23	186 55	19	N21 26	8	244 04	49	N20 24	2	250 24	54	N17 57	1	SUN 30
31 MON	178 25	0	N18 15	15	164 20	-13	N15 39	24	187 14	18	N21 18	8	244 53	49	N20 26	1	251 18	55	N17 58	1	MON 31
32 TUE	178 25		N18 00		164 07		N15 15		187 32		N21 10		245 42		N20 27		252 13		N17 59		TUE 32

SUN & PLANETS AT GMT 0hrs AUGUST 2000

Day	SUN SD 16' GHA	v	Dec	d	VENUS Mag. -3.9 GHA	v	Dec	d	MARS Mag. +1.8 GHA	v	Dec	d	JUPITER Mag. -2.3 GHA	v	Dec	d	SATURN Mag. +0.2 GHA	v	Dec	d	Day
1 TUE	178° 25'	1'	N18° 00'	16'	164° 07'	-13'	N15° 15'	24'	187° 32'	18'	N21° 10'	8'	245° 42'	49'	N20° 27'	2'	252° 13'	55'	N17° 59'	1'	TUE 1
2 WED	178 26	1	N17 44	15	163 54	-13	N14 51	25	187 50	19	N21 02	8	246 31	49	N20 29	1	253 08	55	N18 00	0	WED 2
3 THU	178 27	2	N17 29	16	163 41	-12	N14 26	25	188 09	18	N20 54	8	247 20	49	N20 30	2	254 03	55	N18 00	1	THU 3
4 FRI	178 29	1	N17 13	16	163 29	-13	N14 01	25	188 27	19	N20 46	9	248 09	49	N20 32	2	254 58	55	N18 01	1	FRI 4
5 SAT	178 30	2	N16 57	17	163 16	-12	N13 36	26	188 46	19	N20 37	9	248 58	50	N20 34	1	255 53	55	N18 02	0	SAT 5
6 SUN	178 32	2	N16 40	16	163 04	-11	N13 10	26	189 05	19	N20 28	8	249 48	49	N20 35	2	256 48	55	N18 02	1	SUN 6
7 MON	178 34	2	N16 24	17	162 53	-12	N12 44	26	189 24	19	N20 20	9	250 37	50	N20 37	1	257 43	56	N18 03	1	MON 7
8 TUE	178 35	2	N16 07	17	162 41	-11	N12 18	27	189 43	19	N20 11	9	251 27	50	N20 38	2	258 39	55	N18 04	0	TUE 8
9 WED	178 37	3	N15 50	18	162 30	-11	N11 51	27	190 02	19	N20 02	10	252 17	50	N20 39	2	259 34	55	N18 04	1	WED 9
10 THU	178 40	2	N15 32	18	162 19	-10	N11 24	27	190 21	19	N19 52	9	253 07	50	N20 41	1	260 29	56	N18 05	0	THU 10
11 FRI	178 42	2	N15 14	17	162 09	-11	N10 57	28	190 40	20	N19 43	10	253 57	50	N20 42	1	261 25	56	N18 05	1	FRI 11
12 SAT	178 44	3	N14 57	19	161 58	-10	N10 29	28	191 00	19	N19 33	9	254 47	50	N20 43	2	262 21	56	N18 06	0	SAT 12
13 SUN	178 47	3	N14 38	18	161 48	-10	N10 01	28	191 19	20	N19 24	10	255 37	51	N20 45	1	263 17	56	N18 06	1	SUN 13
14 MON	178 50	3	N14 20	19	161 38	-10	N 9 33	28	191 39	20	N19 14	10	256 28	51	N20 46	1	264 13	56	N18 07	0	MON 14
15 TUE	178 53	3	N14 01	19	161 28	-10	N 9 05	29	191 59	20	N19 04	10	257 18	51	N20 47	1	265 09	56	N18 07	1	TUE 15
16 WED	178 56	3	N13 42	19	161 18	-9	N 8 36	29	192 19	20	N18 54	10	258 09	51	N20 48	2	266 05	56	N18 08	0	WED 16
17 THU	178 59	3	N13 23	19	161 09	-9	N 8 07	29	192 39	20	N18 44	11	259 00	51	N20 49	2	267 01	56	N18 08	1	THU 17
18 FRI	179 02	4	N13 04	19	161 00	-9	N 7 38	29	192 59	20	N18 34	11	259 51	52	N20 51	1	267 57	57	N18 09	0	FRI 18
19 SAT	179 06	3	N12 45	20	160 51	-9	N 7 09	29	193 19	20	N18 23	10	260 43	51	N20 52	1	268 54	57	N18 09	0	SAT 19
20 SUN	179 09	4	N12 25	20	160 42	-9	N 6 40	30	193 39	20	N18 13	11	261 34	51	N20 53	1	269 50	57	N18 09	1	SUN 20
21 MON	179 13	4	N12 05	20	160 33	-9	N 6 10	30	193 59	21	N18 02	11	262 25	52	N20 54	1	270 47	56	N18 10	0	MON 21
22 TUE	179 17	4	N11 45	20	160 24	-8	N 5 40	30	194 20	20	N17 51	10	263 17	52	N20 55	1	271 43	57	N18 10	0	TUE 22
23 WED	179 21	3	N11 25	21	160 16	-8	N 5 10	30	194 40	21	N17 41	11	264 09	52	N20 56	1	272 40	57	N18 10	0	WED 23
24 THU	179 24	5	N11 04	20	160 08	-9	N 4 40	30	195 01	20	N17 30	12	265 01	52	N20 57	1	273 37	57	N18 10	1	THU 24
25 FRI	179 29	4	N10 44	21	159 59	-8	N 4 10	31	195 21	21	N17 18	11	265 53	52	N20 58	1	274 34	57	N18 11	0	FRI 25
26 SAT	179 33	4	N10 23	21	159 51	-8	N 3 39	30	195 42	21	N17 07	11	266 45	53	N20 59	0	275 31	57	N18 11	0	SAT 26
27 SUN	179 37	4	N10 02	21	159 43	-8	N 3 09	31	196 03	21	N16 56	11	267 38	53	N21 00	1	276 28	58	N18 11	0	SUN 27
28 MON	179 41	4	N 9 41	21	159 35	-8	N 2 38	30	196 24	21	N16 45	12	268 31	52	N21 00	1	277 26	57	N18 11	0	MON 28
29 TUE	179 46	4	N 9 20	22	159 27	-8	N 2 08	31	196 45	21	N16 33	12	269 23	53	N21 01	1	278 23	58	N18 11	0	TUE 29
30 WED	179 50	5	N 8 58	21	159 19	-7	N 1 37	31	197 06	22	N16 21	11	270 16	54	N21 02	1	279 21	57	N18 11	1	WED 30
31 THU	179 55	5	N 8 37	22	159 12	-8	N 1 06	31	197 28	21	N16 10	12	271 10	53	N21 03	0	280 18	58	N18 12	0	THU 31
32 FRI	180 00		N 8 15		159 04		N 0 35		197 49		N15 58		272 03		N21 03		281 16		N18 12		FRI 32

45

SUN & PLANETS AT GMT 0hrs SEPTEMBER 2000

Day	SUN SD 16' GHA	v	Dec	d	VENUS Mag. -3.9 GHA	v	Dec	d	MARS Mag. +1.8 GHA	v	Dec	d	JUPITER Mag. -2.5 GHA	v	Dec	d	SATURN Mag. +0.0 GHA	v	Dec	d	Day
1 FRI	180° 00'	4'	N 8° 15'	22'	159° 04'	-8'	N 0° 35'	31'	197° 49'	21'	N15° 58'	12'	272° 03'	53'	N21° 03'	1'	281° 16'	58'	N18° 12'	0'	FRI 1
2 SAT	180 04	5	N 7 53	22	158 56	-8	N 0 04	22	198 10	22	N15 46	12	272 56	54	N21 04	0	282 14	58	N18 12	0	SAT 2
3 SUN	180 09	5	N 7 31	22	158 48	-7	S 0 26	31	198 32	22	N15 34	12	273 50	54	N21 05	0	283 12	58	N18 12	0	SUN 3
4 MON	180 14	5	N 7 09	22	158 41	-8	S 0 57	31	198 54	21	N15 22	12	274 44	54	N21 05	1	284 10	58	N18 12	0	MON 4
5 TUE	180 19	5	N 6 47	23	158 33	-8	S 1 28	31	199 15	22	N15 10	13	275 38	54	N21 06	1	285 08	59	N18 12	0	TUE 5
6 WED	180 24	5	N 6 24	22	158 25	-7	S 1 59	31	199 37	22	N14 57	12	276 32	55	N21 07	0	286 07	58	N18 12	0	WED 6
7 THU	180 29	5	N 6 02	22	158 18	-8	S 2 30	31	199 59	22	N14 45	13	277 27	54	N21 07	1	287 05	59	N18 12	0	THU 7
8 FRI	180 34	6	N 5 40	23	158 10	-8	S 3 01	31	200 21	22	N14 32	12	278 21	55	N21 08	0	288 04	58	N18 12	0	FRI 8
9 SAT	180 40	5	N 5 17	23	158 02	-8	S 3 32	30	200 43	22	N14 20	13	279 16	55	N21 08	1	289 02	59	N18 12	1	SAT 9
10 SUN	180 45	5	N 4 54	23	157 54	-8	S 4 02	31	201 05	23	N14 07	12	280 11	55	N21 09	0	290 01	59	N18 11	0	SUN 10
11 MON	180 50	5	N 4 31	22	157 46	-8	S 4 33	31	201 28	22	N13 55	13	281 06	56	N21 09	0	291 00	59	N18 11	0	MON 11
12 TUE	180 55	6	N 4 09	23	157 38	-8	S 5 04	30	201 50	22	N13 42	13	282 02	55	N21 09	0	291 59	59	N18 11	0	TUE 12
13 WED	181 01	5	N 3 46	23	157 30	-8	S 5 34	30	202 12	23	N13 29	13	282 57	56	N21 10	0	292 58	59	N18 11	0	WED 13
14 THU	181 06	5	N 3 23	23	157 22	-8	S 6 05	30	202 35	23	N13 16	13	283 53	56	N21 10	1	293 57	60	N18 11	0	THU 14
15 FRI	181 11	6	N 3 00	23	157 14	-8	S 6 35	30	202 58	22	N13 03	13	284 49	56	N21 11	0	294 57	59	N18 11	1	FRI 15
16 SAT	181 17	5	N 2 37	24	157 06	-9	S 7 05	30	203 20	23	N12 50	13	285 45	57	N21 11	0	295 56	60	N18 10	0	SAT 16
17 SUN	181 22	6	N 2 13	23	156 57	-8	S 7 35	30	203 43	23	N12 37	14	286 42	56	N21 11	0	296 56	59	N18 10	0	SUN 17
18 MON	181 28	5	N 1 50	23	156 49	-9	S 8 05	30	204 06	23	N12 23	13	287 38	57	N21 11	1	297 55	60	N18 10	1	MON 18
19 TUE	181 33	5	N 1 27	23	156 40	-9	S 8 35	29	204 29	23	N12 10	13	288 35	57	N21 12	0	298 55	60	N18 09	0	TUE 19
20 WED	181 38	6	N 1 04	24	156 31	-9	S 9 04	29	204 52	23	N11 57	14	289 32	57	N21 12	0	299 55	60	N18 09	0	WED 20
21 THU	181 44	5	N 0 40	23	156 22	-9	S 9 33	29	205 15	23	N11 43	13	290 29	58	N21 12	0	300 55	60	N18 09	1	THU 21
22 FRI	181 49	5	N 0 17	11	156 13	-10	S10 02	29	205 38	23	N11 30	14	291 27	57	N21 12	0	301 55	60	N18 08	0	FRI 22
23 SAT	181 54	5	S 0 06	24	156 03	-10	S10 31	29	206 01	23	N11 16	13	292 24	58	N21 12	0	302 55	61	N18 08	0	SAT 23
24 SUN	181 59	6	S 0 30	23	155 53	-9	S11 00	28	206 24	24	N11 03	14	293 22	58	N21 12	0	303 56	60	N18 08	1	SUN 24
25 MON	182 05	5	S 0 53	23	155 44	-10	S11 28	29	206 48	23	N10 49	14	294 20	59	N21 12	1	304 56	60	N18 07	0	MON 25
26 TUE	182 10	5	S 1 16	24	155 34	-11	S11 57	27	207 11	23	N10 35	14	295 19	58	N21 13	0	305 56	61	N18 07	1	TUE 26
27 WED	182 15	5	S 1 40	23	155 23	-10	S12 24	28	207 34	24	N10 21	14	296 17	59	N21 13	0	306 57	61	N18 06	0	WED 27
28 THU	182 20	5	S 2 03	24	155 13	-11	S12 52	27	207 58	24	N10 07	13	297 16	59	N21 13	1	307 58	61	N18 06	1	THU 28
29 FRI	182 25	5	S 2 27	23	155 02	-11	S13 19	27	208 22	23	N 9 54	14	298 15	59	N21 12	0	308 59	61	N18 05	0	FRI 29
30 SAT	182 30	5	S 2 50	23	154 51	-11	S13 46	27	208 45	24	N 9 40	14	299 14	59	N21 12	0	310 00	61	N18 05	1	SAT 30
31 SUN	182 35		S 3 13		154 40		S14 13		209 09		N 9 26		300 13		N21 12		311 01		N18 04		SUN 31

SUN & PLANETS AT GMT 0hrs OCTOBER 2000

Day	SUN SD 16' GHA	v	Dec	d	VENUS Mag. -4.0 GHA	v	Dec	d	MARS Mag. +1.8 GHA	v	Dec	d	JUPITER Mag. -2.7 GHA	v	Dec	d	SATURN Mag. -0.2 GHA	v	Dec	d	Day
1 SUN	182° 35'	4'	S 3° 13'	23'	154° 40'	-12'	S14° 13'	27'	209° 09'	24'	N 9° 26'	14'	300° 13'	60'	N21° 12'	0'	311° 01'	61'	N18° 04'	0'	SUN 1
2 MON	182 39	5	S 3 36	24	154 28	-11	S14 40	26	209 33	24	N 9 12	14	301 13	59	N21 12	0	312 02	61	N18 04	1	MON 2
3 TUE	182 44	5	S 4 00	23	154 17	-12	S15 06	25	209 57	23	N 8 58	15	302 12	60	N21 12	0	313 03	62	N18 03	1	TUE 3
4 WED	182 49	4	S 4 23	23	154 05	-13	S15 31	26	210 20	24	N 8 43	14	303 12	61	N21 12	0	314 05	61	N18 02	0	WED 4
5 THU	182 53	5	S 4 46	23	153 52	-12	S15 57	24	210 44	24	N 8 29	14	304 13	60	N21 12	1	315 06	62	N18 02	1	THU 5
6 FRI	182 58	4	S 5 09	23	153 40	-13	S16 21	25	211 08	24	N 8 15	14	305 13	61	N21 11	0	316 08	61	N18 01	0	FRI 6
7 SAT	183 02	4	S 5 32	23	153 27	-13	S16 46	24	211 32	25	N 8 01	14	306 14	60	N21 11	0	317 09	62	N18 01	1	SAT 7
8 SUN	183 06	5	S 5 55	23	153 14	-13	S17 10	24	211 57	24	N 7 47	15	307 14	61	N21 11	0	318 11	62	N18 00	1	SUN 8
9 MON	183 11	4	S 6 18	22	153 01	-14	S17 34	23	212 21	24	N 7 32	14	308 15	62	N21 11	1	319 13	62	N17 59	1	MON 9
10 TUE	183 15	4	S 6 40	23	152 47	-14	S17 57	23	212 45	24	N 7 18	15	309 17	61	N21 10	0	320 15	62	N17 58	0	TUE 10
11 WED	183 19	3	S 7 03	23	152 33	-14	S18 20	22	213 09	25	N 7 03	14	310 18	62	N21 10	0	321 17	62	N17 58	1	WED 11
12 THU	183 22	4	S 7 26	22	152 19	-15	S18 42	22	213 34	24	N 6 49	14	311 20	62	N21 10	1	322 19	63	N17 57	1	THU 12
13 FRI	183 26	4	S 7 48	22	152 04	-15	S19 04	22	213 58	25	N 6 35	15	312 22	62	N21 09	0	323 22	62	N17 56	1	FRI 13
14 SAT	183 30	3	S 8 10	23	151 49	-15	S19 26	21	214 23	24	N 6 20	14	313 24	62	N21 09	1	324 24	62	N17 55	0	SAT 14
15 SUN	183 33	3	S 8 33	22	151 34	-15	S19 47	20	214 47	25	N 6 06	15	314 26	63	N21 08	0	325 26	63	N17 55	1	SUN 15
16 MON	183 36	3	S 8 55	22	151 19	-16	S20 07	20	215 12	24	N 5 51	14	315 29	62	N21 08	1	326 29	62	N17 54	1	MON 16
17 TUE	183 39	3	S 9 17	22	151 03	-16	S20 27	19	215 36	25	N 5 37	15	316 31	63	N21 07	0	327 31	63	N17 53	1	TUE 17
18 WED	183 42	3	S 9 39	22	150 47	-16	S20 46	19	216 01	24	N 5 22	15	317 34	63	N21 07	1	328 34	63	N17 52	1	WED 18
19 THU	183 45	3	S10 00	22	150 31	-17	S21 05	18	216 25	25	N 5 07	14	318 37	64	N21 06	0	329 37	63	N17 51	0	THU 19
20 FRI	183 48	2	S10 22	21	150 14	-16	S21 23	18	216 50	25	N 4 53	15	319 41	63	N21 06	1	330 40	63	N17 51	1	FRI 20
21 SAT	183 50	3	S10 43	22	149 58	-18	S21 41	17	217 15	25	N 4 38	14	320 44	64	N21 05	1	331 43	63	N17 50	1	SAT 21
22 SUN	183 53	2	S11 05	21	149 40	-17	S21 58	17	217 40	24	N 4 24	15	321 48	64	N21 04	0	332 46	63	N17 49	1	SUN 22
23 MON	183 55	2	S11 26	21	149 23	-18	S22 15	16	218 04	25	N 4 09	14	322 52	64	N21 04	1	333 49	63	N17 48	1	MON 23
24 TUE	183 57	2	S11 47	21	149 05	-18	S22 31	15	218 29	25	N 3 54	14	323 56	64	N21 03	1	334 52	63	N17 47	1	TUE 24
25 WED	183 59	1	S12 08	20	148 47	-18	S22 46	15	218 54	25	N 3 40	15	325 00	65	N21 02	0	335 55	63	N17 46	1	WED 25
26 THU	184 00	2	S12 28	20	148 29	-18	S23 01	14	219 19	25	N 3 25	15	326 05	64	N21 02	1	336 58	64	N17 45	1	THU 26
27 FRI	184 02	1	S12 48	21	148 11	-19	S23 15	13	219 44	25	N 3 10	14	327 09	65	N21 01	1	338 02	63	N17 44	1	FRI 27
28 SAT	184 03	1	S13 09	20	147 52	-19	S23 28	13	220 09	25	N 2 56	15	328 14	65	N21 00	1	339 05	64	N17 43	1	SAT 28
29 SUN	184 04	1	S13 29	19	147 33	-19	S23 41	12	220 34	25	N 2 41	14	329 19	65	N20 59	1	340 09	64	N17 42	1	SUN 29
30 MON	184 05	1	S13 48	20	147 14	-19	S23 53	11	220 59	25	N 2 26	15	330 24	66	N20 58	1	341 12	64	N17 41	1	MON 30
31 TUE	184 06	0	S14 08	19	146 55	-20	S24 04	11	221 24	25	N 2 12	15	331 30	65	N20 57	0	342 16	63	N17 40	1	TUE 31
32 WED	184 06		S14 27		146 35		S24 15		221 49		N 1 57		332 35		N20 57		343 19		N17 39		WED 32

SUN & PLANETS AT GMT 0hrs NOVEMBER 2000

Day	SUN SD 16' GHA	v	Dec	d	VENUS Mag. -4.1 GHA	v	Dec	d	MARS Mag. +1.7 GHA	v	Dec	d	JUPITER Mag. -2.8 GHA	v	Dec	d	SATURN Mag. -0.3 GHA	v	Dec	d	Day
1 WED	184° 06'	0'	S14° 27'	19'	146° 35'	-19'	S24° 15'	10'	221° 49'	25'	N 1° 57'	15'	332° 35'	66'	N20° 57'	1'	343° 19'	64'	N17° 39'	1'	WED 1
2 THU	184 06	1	S14 46	19	146 16	-20	S24 25	10	222 14	25	N 1 42	14	333 41	65	N20 56	1	344 23	64	N17 38	1	THU 2
3 FRI	184 07	-1	S15 05	19	145 56	-20	S24 35	8	222 39	25	N 1 28	15	334 46	66	N20 55	1	345 27	64	N17 37	1	FRI 3
4 SAT	184 06	0	S15 24	18	145 36	-20	S24 43	8	223 04	26	N 1 13	15	335 52	66	N20 54	1	346 31	63	N17 36	1	SAT 4
5 SUN	184 06	0	S15 42	18	145 16	-21	S24 51	8	223 30	25	N 0 58	14	336 58	67	N20 53	1	347 34	64	N17 35	1	SUN 5
6 MON	184 06	-1	S16 00	18	144 55	-20	S24 59	6	223 55	25	N 0 44	15	338 05	66	N20 52	1	348 38	64	N17 34	1	MON 6
7 TUE	184 05	-1	S16 18	18	144 35	-20	S25 05	6	224 20	25	N 0 29	15	339 11	66	N20 51	1	349 42	64	N17 33	1	TUE 7
8 WED	184 04	-1	S16 36	17	144 15	-21	S25 11	5	224 45	26	N 0 14	14	340 17	67	N20 50	1	350 46	64	N17 32	1	WED 8
9 THU	184 03	-2	S16 53	17	143 54	-20	S25 16	5	225 11	25	S 0 00	15	341 24	67	N20 49	1	351 50	64	N17 31	1	THU 9
10 FRI	184 01	-1	S17 10	17	143 34	-21	S25 21	3	225 36	25	S 0 15	15	342 31	67	N20 48	1	352 54	64	N17 30	1	FRI 10
11 SAT	184 00	-2	S17 27	16	143 13	-20	S25 24	3	226 01	26	S 0 30	14	343 38	66	N20 47	1	353 58	64	N17 29	1	SAT 11
12 SUN	183 58	-2	S17 43	16	142 53	-21	S25 27	2	226 27	25	S 0 44	15	344 44	67	N20 46	2	355 02	64	N17 28	1	SUN 12
13 MON	183 56	-2	S17 59	16	142 32	-21	S25 29	2	226 52	25	S 0 59	14	345 51	68	N20 44	1	356 06	64	N17 27	1	MON 13
14 TUE	183 54	-2	S18 15	15	142 11	-20	S25 31	1	227 17	26	S 1 13	15	346 59	67	N20 43	1	357 10	64	N17 26	1	TUE 14
15 WED	183 52	-3	S18 30	15	141 51	-21	S25 32	0	227 43	25	S 1 28	14	348 06	67	N20 42	1	358 14	65	N17 25	1	WED 15
16 THU	183 49	-3	S18 45	15	141 30	-20	S25 32	1	228 08	25	S 1 42	15	349 13	67	N20 41	1	359 19	64	N17 24	1	THU 16
17 FRI	183 46	-3	S19 00	15	141 10	-20	S25 31	2	228 33	26	S 1 57	14	350 20	68	N20 40	1	0 23	64	N17 23	1	FRI 17
18 SAT	183 43	-3	S19 15	14	140 50	-21	S25 29	2	228 59	25	S 2 11	15	351 28	67	N20 39	2	1 27	64	N17 22	1	SAT 18
19 SUN	183 40	-4	S19 29	13	140 29	-20	S25 27	3	229 24	26	S 2 26	14	352 35	68	N20 37	1	2 31	64	N17 21	1	SUN 19
20 MON	183 36	-3	S19 42	14	140 09	-20	S25 24	3	229 50	25	S 2 40	14	353 43	67	N20 36	1	3 35	64	N17 20	1	MON 20
21 TUE	183 33	-4	S19 56	13	139 49	-19	S25 21	5	230 15	25	S 2 54	15	354 50	68	N20 35	1	4 39	64	N17 19	1	TUE 21
22 WED	183 29	-4	S20 09	12	139 30	-20	S25 16	5	230 40	26	S 3 09	14	355 58	68	N20 34	2	5 43	65	N17 18	1	WED 22
23 THU	183 25	-5	S20 21	12	139 10	-20	S25 11	6	231 06	25	S 3 23	14	357 06	67	N20 32	1	6 48	64	N17 17	1	THU 23
24 FRI	183 20	-4	S20 34	12	138 50	-19	S25 05	6	231 31	26	S 3 37	14	358 14	67	N20 31	1	7 52	64	N17 16	1	FRI 24
25 SAT	183 16	-5	S20 46	11	138 31	-19	S24 59	8	231 57	25	S 3 51	15	359 21	68	N20 30	1	8 56	64	N17 15	1	SAT 25
26 SUN	183 11	-5	S20 57	11	138 12	-19	S24 51	7	232 22	26	S 4 06	14	0 29	68	N20 29	2	10 00	64	N17 14	1	SUN 26
27 MON	183 06	-5	S21 08	11	137 53	-18	S24 44	9	232 48	25	S 4 20	14	1 37	68	N20 27	1	11 04	64	N17 13	1	MON 27
28 TUE	183 01	-5	S21 19	10	137 35	-18	S24 35	10	233 13	25	S 4 34	14	2 45	67	N20 26	1	12 08	64	N17 12	1	TUE 28
29 WED	182 56	-5	S21 29	10	137 17	-18	S24 25	10	233 38	26	S 4 48	14	3 52	68	N20 25	1	13 12	64	N17 11	1	WED 29
30 THU	182 51	-6	S21 39	10	136 59	-18	S24 15	10	234 04	25	S 5 02	14	5 00	68	N20 24	2	14 16	64	N17 10	1	THU 30
31 FRI	182 45		S21 49		136 41		S24 05		234 29		S 5 16		6 08		N20 22		15 20		N17 09		FRI 31

SUN & PLANETS AT GMT 0hrs DECEMBER 2000

Day	SUN SD 16' GHA	v	Dec	d	VENUS Mag. -4.3 GHA	v	Dec	d	MARS Mag. +1.5 GHA	v	Dec	d	JUPITER Mag. -2.8 GHA	v	Dec	d	SATURN Mag. -0.2 GHA	v	Dec	d	Day
1 FRI	182° 45'	-5'	S21° 49'	9'	136° 41'	-17'	S24° 05'	12'	234° 29'	26'	S 5° 16'	14'	6° 08'	68'	N20° 22'	1'	15° 20'	64'	N17° 09'	1'	FRI 1
2 SAT	182 40	-6	S21 58	9	136 24	-17	S23 53	12	234 55	25	S 5 30	14	7 16	67	N20 21	1	16 24	64	N17 08	1	SAT 2
3 SUN	182 34	-6	S22 07	8	136 07	-17	S23 41	12	235 20	26	S 5 44	13	8 23	68	N20 20	2	17 28	64	N17 07	1	SUN 3
4 MON	182 28	-6	S22 15	8	135 50	-16	S23 29	14	235 46	25	S 5 57	14	9 31	68	N20 18	1	18 32	64	N17 06	1	MON 4
5 TUE	182 22	-7	S22 23	7	135 34	-16	S23 15	14	236 11	26	S 6 11	14	10 39	67	N20 17	1	19 36	63	N17 05	1	TUE 5
6 WED	182 15	-6	S22 30	7	135 18	-16	S23 01	14	236 37	26	S 6 25	14	11 46	67	N20 16	1	20 39	64	N17 04	1	WED 6
7 THU	182 09	-6	S22 37	6	135 02	-15	S22 47	15	237 02	26	S 6 39	13	12 54	67	N20 15	2	21 43	64	N17 03	1	THU 7
8 FRI	182 03	-7	S22 43	6	134 47	-14	S22 32	16	237 28	25	S 6 52	14	14 01	67	N20 13	1	22 47	64	N17 02	0	FRI 8
9 SAT	181 56	-7	S22 49	6	134 33	-15	S22 16	17	237 53	26	S 7 06	13	15 08	68	N20 12	1	23 51	63	N17 02	1	SAT 9
10 SUN	181 49	-7	S22 55	5	134 18	-14	S21 59	16	238 19	25	S 7 19	14	16 16	67	N20 11	1	24 54	64	N17 01	1	SUN 10
11 MON	181 42	-7	S23 00	5	134 04	-13	S21 43	18	238 44	25	S 7 33	13	17 23	67	N20 10	2	25 58	63	N17 00	1	MON 11
12 TUE	181 35	-7	S23 05	4	133 51	-13	S21 25	18	239 09	26	S 7 46	13	18 30	67	N20 08	1	27 01	64	N16 59	1	TUE 12
13 WED	181 28	-7	S23 09	4	133 38	-13	S21 07	19	239 35	25	S 7 59	14	19 37	67	N20 07	1	28 05	63	N16 58	1	WED 13
14 THU	181 21	-7	S23 13	3	133 25	-12	S20 48	19	240 00	26	S 8 13	13	20 44	67	N20 06	1	29 08	63	N16 57	0	THU 14
15 FRI	181 14	-7	S23 16	3	133 13	-11	S20 29	19	240 26	25	S 8 26	13	21 51	66	N20 05	1	30 11	63	N16 57	1	FRI 15
16 SAT	181 07	-7	S23 19	2	133 02	-12	S20 10	20	240 51	26	S 8 39	13	22 58	66	N20 04	1	31 14	64	N16 56	1	SAT 16
17 SUN	181 00	-8	S23 21	2	132 50	-10	S19 50	21	241 17	25	S 8 52	13	24 04	67	N20 03	2	32 18	63	N16 55	0	SUN 17
18 MON	180 52	-7	S23 23	2	132 40	-11	S19 29	21	241 42	25	S 9 05	13	25 11	66	N20 01	1	33 21	63	N16 55	1	MON 18
19 TUE	180 45	-8	S23 25	1	132 29	-9	S19 08	22	242 07	26	S 9 18	13	26 17	66	N20 00	1	34 24	63	N16 54	1	TUE 19
20 WED	180 37	-7	S23 26	0	132 20	-10	S18 46	22	242 33	25	S 9 31	13	27 23	66	N19 59	1	35 27	63	N16 53	0	WED 20
21 THU	180 30	-8	S23 26	0	132 10	-9	S18 24	22	242 58	25	S 9 43	13	28 29	66	N19 58	1	36 30	62	N16 53	1	THU 21
22 FRI	180 22	-7	S23 26	0	132 01	-8	S18 02	23	243 24	25	S 9 56	13	29 35	66	N19 57	1	37 32	63	N16 52	1	FRI 22
23 SAT	180 15	-7	S23 26	1	131 53	-8	S17 39	23	243 49	25	S10 09	12	30 41	66	N19 56	1	38 35	62	N16 51	0	SAT 23
24 SUN	180 08	-8	S23 25	1	131 45	-7	S17 16	24	244 14	26	S10 21	13	31 47	65	N19 55	1	39 38	62	N16 51	1	SUN 24
25 MON	180 00	-7	S23 24	2	131 38	-7	S16 52	24	244 40	25	S10 34	12	32 52	66	N19 54	1	40 40	63	N16 50	0	MON 25
26 TUE	179 53	-8	S23 22	3	131 31	-7	S16 28	24	245 05	26	S10 46	13	33 58	65	N19 53	1	41 43	62	N16 50	1	TUE 26
27 WED	179 45	-8	S23 19	2	131 24	-6	S16 04	25	245 31	25	S10 59	12	35 03	65	N19 52	0	42 45	62	N16 49	1	WED 27
28 THU	179 38	-8	S23 17	3	131 18	-5	S15 39	25	245 56	25	S11 11	12	36 08	65	N19 52	1	43 47	62	N16 49	1	THU 28
29 FRI	179 30	-7	S23 13	3	131 13	-5	S15 14	25	246 21	26	S11 23	12	37 13	64	N19 51	1	44 49	62	N16 48	0	FRI 29
30 SAT	179 23	-7	S23 10	5	131 08	-4	S14 49	26	246 47	25	S11 35	12	38 17	65	N19 50	1	45 51	62	N16 48	1	SAT 30
31 SUN	179 16	-7	S23 05	4	131 04	-4	S14 23	26	247 12	25	S11 47	12	39 22	64	N19 49	1	46 53	62	N16 47	0	SUN 31
32 MON	179 09		S23 01		131 00		S13 57		247 37		S11 59		40 26		N19 48		47 55		N16 47		MON 32

SUN & PLANETS AT GMT 0hrs JANUARY 2001

Day	SUN SD 16' GHA v	Dec d	VENUS Mag. -4.5 GHA v	Dec d	MARS Mag. +1.2 GHA v	Dec d	JUPITER Mag. -2.6 GHA v	Dec d	SATURN Mag. -0.0 GHA v	Dec d	Day
1 MON	179° 09' -7'	S23° 01' 5'	131° 00' -4'	S13° 57' 27'	247° 37' 26'	S11° 59' 12'	40° 26' 64'	N19° 48' 0'	47° 55' 62'	N16° 47' 1'	MON 1
2 TUE	179 02 -7	S22 56 6	130 56 -3	S13 30 26	248 03 25	S12 11 11	41 30 64	N19 48 1	48 57 62	N16 46 0	TUE 2
3 WED	178 55 -7	S22 50 6	130 53 -2	S13 04 27	248 28 26	S12 22 12	42 34 64	N19 47 1	49 59 61	N16 46 0	WED 3
4 THU	178 48 -7	S22 44 6	130 51 -2	S12 37 27	248 54 25	S12 34 12	43 38 63	N19 46 0	51 00 62	N16 46 0	THU 4
5 FRI	178 41 -7	S22 38 7	130 49 -2	S12 10 27	249 19 25	S12 46 11	44 41 64	N19 46 1	52 02 61	N16 46 1	FRI 5
6 SAT	178 34 -6	S22 31 8	130 47 0	S11 43 28	249 44 25	S12 57 11	45 45 63	N19 45 0	53 03 61	N16 45 0	SAT 6
7 SUN	178 28 -6	S22 23 7	130 47 -1	S11 15 28	250 10 25	S13 08 12	46 48 63	N19 45 1	54 04 62	N16 45 0	SUN 7
8 MON	178 22 -7	S22 16 9	130 46 0	S10 47 28	250 35 26	S13 20 11	47 51 63	N19 44 0	55 06 61	N16 45 0	MON 8
9 TUE	178 15 -6	S22 07 8	130 46 1	S10 19 28	251 01 25	S13 31 11	48 54 62	N19 44 1	56 07 61	N16 45 1	TUE 9
10 WED	178 09 -6	S21 59 9	130 47 1	S 9 51 28	251 26 25	S13 42 11	49 56 63	N19 43 0	57 08 60	N16 44 0	WED 10
11 THU	178 03 -6	S21 50 10	130 48 2	S 9 23 28	251 51 26	S13 53 11	50 59 61	N19 43 0	58 08 61	N16 44 0	THU 11
12 FRI	177 57 . -5	S21 40 10	130 50 2	S 8 55 29	252 17 25	S14 04 10	52 01 61	N19 43 0	59 09 61	N16 44 0	FRI 12
13 SAT	177 52 -6	S21 30 10	130 52 2	S 8 26 28	252 42 26	S14 14 11	53 03 61	N19 42 0	60 10 60	N16 44 0	SAT 13
14 SUN	177 46 -5	S21 20 11	130 54 4	S 7 58 29	253 08 25	S14 25 11	54 04 62	N19 42 0	61 10 61	N16 44 0	SUN 14
15 MON	177 41 -6	S21 09 11	130 58 3	S 7 29 29	253 33 25	S14 36 10	55 06 61	N19 42 0	62 11 60	N16 44 0	MON 15
16 TUE	177 35 -5	S20 58 12	131 01 5	S 7 00 29	253 58 26	S14 46 11	56 07 61	N19 42 0	63 11 60	N16 44 0	TUE 16
17 WED	177 30 -5	S20 46 12	131 06 4	S 6 31 29	254 24 25	S14 57 10	57 08 61	N19 42 0	64 11 60	N16 44 0	WED 17
18 THU	177 25 -4	S20 34 12	131 10 6	S 6 02 29	254 49 26	S15 07 10	58 09 61	N19 42 0	65 11 60	N16 44 0	THU 18
19 FRI	177 21 -5	S20 22 13	131 16 6	S 5 33 29	255 15 25	S15 17 10	59 10 60	N19 42 0	66 11 60	N16 44 0	FRI 19
20 SAT	177 16 -4	S20 09 13	131 22 6	S 5 04 29	255 40 26	S15 27 10	60 10 61	N19 42 0	67 11 60	N16 44 1	SAT 20
21 SUN	177 12 -4	S19 56 13	131 28 7	S 4 35 29	256 06 25	S15 37 10	61 11 60	N19 42 0	68 11 59	N16 45 0	SUN 21
22 MON	177 08 -4	S19 43 14	131 35 8	S 4 06 29	256 31 26	S15 47 10	62 11 59	N19 42 0	69 10 60	N16 45 0	MON 22
23 TUE	177 04 -4	S19 29 15	131 43 8	S 3 37 29	256 57 25	S15 57 9	63 10 60	N19 42 0	70 10 59	N16 45 0	TUE 23
24 WED	177 00 -4	S19 14 14	131 51 8	S 3 08 29	257 22 26	S16 06 10	64 10 59	N19 42 0	71 09 60	N16 45 0	WED 24
25 THU	176 56 -3	S19 00 15	131 59 10	S 2 39 29	257 48 26	S16 16 9	65 09 60	N19 42 1	72 09 59	N16 45 1	THU 25
26 FRI	176 53 -3	S18 45 15	132 09 9	S 2 10 29	258 14 25	S16 25 10	66 09 58	N19 42 1	73 08 59	N16 46 0	FRI 26
27 SAT	176 50 -3	S18 30 16	132 18 11	S 1 41 29	258 39 26	S16 35 9	67 07 59	N19 43 0	74 07 59	N16 46 0	SAT 27
28 SUN	176 47 -3	S18 14 16	132 29 11	S 1 12 29	259 05 26	S16 44 9	68 06 59	N19 43 0	75 06 59	N16 46 1	SUN 28
29 MON	176 44 -3	S17 58 16	132 40 12	S 0 43 28	259 31 26	S16 53 9	69 05 58	N19 43 1	76 05 58	N16 47 0	MON 29
30 TUE	176 41 -2	S17 42 17	132 52 12	S 0 15 1	259 57 25	S17 02 9	70 03 58	N19 44 1	77 03 59	N16 47 1	TUE 30
31 WED	176 39 -2	S17 25 17	133 04 13	N 0 14 28	260 22 26	S17 11 9	71 01 58	N19 44 1	78 02 58	N16 48 0	WED 31
32 THU	176 37	S17 08	133 17	N 0 42	260 48	S17 20	71 59	N19 45	79 00	N16 48	THU 32

SUN & PLANETS AT GMT 0hrs FEBRUARY 2001

Day	SUN SD 16' GHA v	Dec d	VENUS Mag. -4.7 GHA v	Dec d	MARS Mag. +0.8 GHA v	Dec d	JUPITER Mag. -2.4 GHA v	Dec d	SATURN Mag. +0.1 GHA v	Dec d	Day
1 THU	176° 37' -2'	S17° 08' 17'	133° 17' 14'	N 0° 42' 29'	260° 48' 26'	S17° 20' 8'	71° 59' 58'	N19° 45' 0'	79° 00' 59'	N16° 48' 1'	THU 1
2 FRI	176 35 -2	S16 51 17	133 31 15	N 1 11 28	261 14 26	S17 28 9	72 57 57	N19 45 1	79 59 58	N16 49 0	FRI 2
3 SAT	176 33 -1	S16 34 18	133 46 15	N 1 39 28	261 40 26	S17 37 8	73 54 57	N19 46 1	80 57 58	N16 49 1	SAT 3
4 SUN	176 32 -2	S16 16 18	134 01 16	N 2 07 27	262 06 26	S17 45 9	74 51 57	N19 47 0	81 55 58	N16 50 0	SUN 4
5 MON	176 30 -1	S15 58 18	134 17 17	N 2 34 28	262 32 26	S17 54 8	75 48 57	N19 47 1	82 53 58	N16 50 1	MON 5
6 TUE	176 29 -1	S15 40 19	134 34 18	N 3 02 27	262 58 26	S18 02 8	76 45 57	N19 48 1	83 51 58	N16 51 0	TUE 6
7 WED	176 28 0	S15 21 19	134 52 18	N 3 29 27	263 24 27	S18 10 8	77 42 56	N19 49 0	84 49 57	N16 51 1	WED 7
8 THU	176 28 -1	S15 02 19	135 10 19	N 3 56 27	263 51 26	S18 18 8	78 38 57	N19 49 1	85 46 57	N16 52 1	THU 8
9 FRI	176 27 0	S14 43 19	135 29 21	N 4 23 26	264 17 26	S18 26 8	79 35 56	N19 50 1	86 44 57	N16 53 0	FRI 9
10 SAT	176 27 0	S14 24 20	135 50 21	N 4 49 26	264 43 27	S18 34 7	80 31 55	N19 51 1	87 41 58	N16 53 1	SAT 10
11 SUN	176 27 0	S14 04 20	136 11 22	N 5 15 26	265 10 26	S18 41 8	81 26 56	N19 52 1	88 39 57	N16 54 1	SUN 11
12 MON	176 27 0	S13 44 20	136 33 23	N 5 41 26	265 36 26	S18 49 7	82 22 55	N19 53 1	89 36 57	N16 55 1	MON 12
13 TUE	176 27 0	S13 24 20	136 56 24	N 6 07 25	266 03 26	S18 56 7	83 17 56	N19 54 1	90 33 57	N16 56 0	TUE 13
14 WED	176 27 0	S13 04 20	137 20 24	N 6 32 24	266 29 27	S19 03 7	84 13 55	N19 55 1	91 30 57	N16 56 1	WED 14
15 THU	176 28 1	S12 44 21	137 46 26	N 6 56 25	266 56 27	S19 11 7	85 08 55	N19 56 1	92 27 57	N16 57 1	THU 15
16 FRI	176 29 1	S12 23 21	138 12 28	N 7 21 24	267 23 26	S19 18 7	86 03 54	N19 57 1	93 24 56	N16 58 1	FRI 16
17 SAT	176 30 1	S12 02 21	138 40 28	N 7 45 23	267 50 26	S19 25 6	86 57 55	N19 58 1	94 20 57	N16 59 1	SAT 17
18 SUN	176 31 1	S11 41 21	139 08 30	N 8 08 23	268 16 28	S19 31 7	87 52 54	N19 59 1	95 17 57	N17 00 1	SUN 18
19 MON	176 32 2	S11 20 22	139 38 31	N 8 31 22	268 44 27	S19 38 7	88 46 54	N20 00 1	96 14 56	N17 01 1	MON 19
20 TUE	176 34 1	S10 58 21	140 09 33	N 8 53 22	269 11 27	S19 45 6	89 40 54	N20 01 2	97 10 56	N17 02 1	TUE 20
21 WED	176 35 2	S10 37 22	140 42 34	N 9 15 22	269 38 28	S19 51 7	90 34 54	N20 03 1	98 06 56	N17 03 1	WED 21
22 THU	176 37 1	S10 15 22	141 16 35	N 9 37 21	270 05 28	S19 58 6	91 28 53	N20 04 1	99 02 56	N17 04 1	THU 22
23 FRI	176 39 2	S 9 53 22	141 51 37	N 9 58 20	270 33 27	S20 04 6	92 21 53	N20 05 2	99 58 56	N17 05 1	FRI 23
24 SAT	176 41 2	S 9 31 22	142 28 39	N10 18 19	271 00 28	S20 10 6	93 14 54	N20 07 1	100 54 56	N17 06 1	SAT 24
25 SUN	176 43 3	S 9 09 23	143 07 40	N10 37 19	271 28 28	S20 16 6	94 08 53	N20 08 2	101 50 56	N17 07 1	SUN 25
26 MON	176 46 2	S 8 46 22	143 47 41	N10 56 18	271 56 28	S20 22 6	95 01 52	N20 09 2	102 46 56	N17 08 1	MON 26
27 TUE	176 48 3	S 8 24 23	144 28 44	N11 14 18	272 24 28	S20 28 6	95 53 53	N20 11 1	103 42 55	N17 09 1	TUE 27
28 WED	176 51 3	S 8 01 22	145 12 45	N11 32 16	272 52 28	S20 34 6	96 46 53	N20 12 1	104 37 56	N17 10 1	WED 28
29 THU	176 54	S 7 39	145 57	N11 48	273 20	S20 39	97 39	N20 13	105 33	N17 11	THU 29

SUN & PLANETS AT GMT 0hrs MARCH 2001

Day	SUN SD 16' GHA	v	Dec	d	VENUS Mag. -4.4 GHA	v	Dec	d	MARS Mag. +0.2 GHA	v	Dec	d	JUPITER Mag. -2.2 GHA	v	Dec	d	SATURN Mag. +0.2 GHA	v	Dec	d	Day
1 THU	176° 54'	3'	S 7° 39'	23'	145° 57'	47'	N11° 48'	16'	273° 20'	28'	S20° 39'	6'	97° 39'	52'	N20° 13'	2'	105° 33'	55'	N17° 11'	1'	THU 1
2 FRI	176 57	3	S 7 16	23	146 44	49	N12 04	15	273 48	29	S20 45	5	98 31	52	N20 15	1	106 28	55	N17 12	2	FRI 2
3 SAT	177 00	3	S 6 53	23	147 33	51	N12 19	14	274 17	29	S20 50	5	99 23	52	N20 16	1	107 23	55	N17 13	1	SAT 3
4 SUN	177 03	3	S 6 30	23	148 24	53	N12 33	13	274 46	28	S20 56	5	100 15	52	N20 18	1	108 18	55	N17 15	1	SUN 4
5 MON	177 06	4	S 6 07	24	149 17	55	N12 46	12	275 14	29	S21 01	5	101 07	51	N20 19	2	109 13	55	N17 16	1	MON 5
6 TUE	177 10	3	S 5 43	23	150 12	57	N12 58	11	275 43	30	S21 06	5	101 58	52	N20 21	2	110 08	55	N17 17	1	TUE 6
7 WED	177 13	4	S 5 20	23	151 09	59	N13 09	10	276 13	29	S21 11	5	102 50	51	N20 23	1	111 03	55	N17 18	2	WED 7
8 THU	177 17	4	S 4 57	24	152 08	62	N13 19	9	276 42	29	S21 16	5	103 41	51	N20 24	2	111 58	55	N17 20	1	THU 8
9 FRI	177 21	3	S 4 33	23	153 10	63	N13 28	7	277 11	30	S21 21	4	104 32	51	N20 26	2	112 53	54	N17 21	1	FRI 9
10 SAT	177 24	4	S 4 10	24	154 13	66	N13 35	6	277 41	30	S21 25	5	105 23	51	N20 27	2	113 47	55	N17 22	2	SAT 10
11 SUN	177 28	3	S 3 46	23	155 19	68	N13 41	5	278 11	30	S21 30	5	106 14	51	N20 29	2	114 42	54	N17 24	1	SUN 11
12 MON	177 32	4	S 3 23	24	156 27	71	N13 46	4	278 41	30	S21 35	4	107 05	51	N20 31	1	115 36	55	N17 25	1	MON 12
13 TUE	177 36	4	S 2 59	23	157 38	72	N13 50	2	279 11	31	S21 39	4	107 56	50	N20 32	2	116 31	54	N17 26	2	TUE 13
14 WED	177 40	5	S 2 36	24	158 50	75	N13 52	1	279 42	30	S21 43	5	108 46	50	N20 34	2	117 25	54	N17 28	1	WED 14
15 THU	177 45	4	S 2 12	24	160 05	76	N13 53	1	280 12	31	S21 48	4	109 36	50	N20 36	2	118 19	54	N17 29	1	THU 15
16 FRI	177 49	4	S 1 48	23	161 21	79	N13 52	2	280 43	31	S21 52	4	110 26	50	N20 38	2	119 13	54	N17 30	2	FRI 16
17 SAT	177 53	5	S 1 25	24	162 40	81	N13 50	4	281 14	31	S21 56	4	111 16	50	N20 39	2	120 07	54	N17 32	1	SAT 17
18 SUN	177 58	4	S 1 01	24	164 01	82	N13 46	5	281 45	32	S22 00	4	112 06	50	N20 41	2	121 01	54	N17 33	1	SUN 18
19 MON	178 02	4	S 0 37	24	165 23	84	N13 41	6	282 17	32	S22 04	4	112 56	50	N20 43	2	121 55	54	N17 34	2	MON 19
20 TUE	178 06	5	S 0 13	3	166 47	86	N13 35	8	282 49	32	S22 08	3	113 46	49	N20 45	1	122 49	53	N17 36	1	TUE 20
21 WED	178 11	4	N 0 10	24	168 13	87	N13 27	10	283 21	32	S22 11	4	114 35	49	N20 46	2	123 42	54	N17 37	2	WED 21
22 THU	178 15	4	N 0 34	24	169 40	89	N13 17	11	283 53	33	S22 15	4	115 24	50	N20 48	2	124 36	54	N17 39	1	THU 22
23 FRI	178 20	4	N 0 58	23	171 09	89	N13 06	13	284 26	33	S22 19	3	116 14	49	N20 50	2	125 30	53	N17 40	2	FRI 23
24 SAT	178 24	5	N 1 21	24	172 38	91	N12 53	14	284 59	33	S22 22	4	117 03	49	N20 52	2	126 23	54	N17 42	1	SAT 24
25 SUN	178 29	4	N 1 45	24	174 09	91	N12 39	15	285 32	33	S22 26	3	117 52	48	N20 54	2	127 17	53	N17 43	2	SUN 25
26 MON	178 33	5	N 2 09	23	175 40	92	N12 24	17	286 05	34	S22 29	3	118 40	49	N20 56	1	128 10	53	N17 45	1	MON 26
27 TUE	178 38	4	N 2 32	24	177 12	92	N12 07	17	286 39	34	S22 32	3	119 29	49	N20 57	2	129 03	53	N17 46	2	TUE 27
28 WED	178 42	5	N 2 56	23	178 44	92	N11 50	19	287 13	35	S22 36	3	120 18	48	N20 59	2	129 56	53	N17 48	1	WED 28
29 THU	178 47	4	N 3 19	23	180 16	91	N11 31	20	287 48	34	S22 39	3	121 06	48	N21 01	2	130 49	53	N17 49	2	THU 29
30 FRI	178 51	5	N 3 42	24	181 47	92	N11 11	20	288 22	35	S22 42	3	121 54	49	N21 03	2	131 42	53	N17 51	1	FRI 30
31 SAT	178 56	4	N 4 06	23	183 19	91	N10 51	21	288 57	36	S22 45	3	122 43	48	N21 05	2	132 35	53	N17 52	2	SAT 31
32 SUN	179 00		N 4 29		184 50		N10 30		289 33		S22 48		123 31		N21 07		133 28		N17 54		SUN 32

SUN & PLANETS AT GMT 0hrs APRIL 2001

Day	SUN SD 16' GHA	v	Dec	d	VENUS Mag. -4.3 GHA	v	Dec	d	MARS Mag. -0.6 GHA	v	Dec	d	JUPITER Mag. -2.0 GHA	v	Dec	d	SATURN Mag. +0.2 GHA	v	Dec	d	Day
1 SUN	179° 00'	5'	N 4° 29'	23'	184° 50'	90'	N10° 30'	22'	289° 33'	36'	S22° 48'	3'	123° 31'	48'	N21° 07'	2'	133° 28'	53'	N17° 54'	2'	SUN 1
2 MON	179 05	4	N 4 52	23	186 20	89	N10 08	22	290 09	36	S22 51	3	124 19	48	N21 09	2	134 21	53	N17 56	1	MON 2
3 TUE	179 09	5	N 5 15	23	187 49	88	N 9 46	23	290 45	36	S22 54	3	125 07	47	N21 11	1	135 14	53	N17 57	2	TUE 3
4 WED	179 14	5	N 5 38	23	189 17	86	N 9 23	22	291 21	37	S22 57	3	125 54	48	N21 12	2	136 07	52	N17 59	1	WED 4
5 THU	179 18	4	N 6 01	23	190 43	85	N 9 01	23	291 58	37	S23 00	2	126 42	48	N21 14	2	136 59	53	N18 00	2	THU 5
6 FRI	179 22	5	N 6 24	22	192 08	84	N 8 38	23	292 35	38	S23 02	3	127 30	47	N21 16	2	137 52	53	N18 02	1	FRI 6
7 SAT	179 27	4	N 6 46	22	193 32	81	N 8 15	22	293 13	38	S23 05	3	128 17	48	N21 18	2	138 45	52	N18 03	2	SAT 7
8 SUN	179 31	4	N 7 09	22	194 53	80	N 7 53	22	293 51	39	S23 08	3	129 05	47	N21 20	2	139 37	52	N18 05	2	SUN 8
9 MON	179 35	4	N 7 31	22	196 13	77	N 7 31	22	294 30	38	S23 11	2	129 52	47	N21 22	2	140 29	53	N18 07	1	MON 9
10 TUE	179 39	4	N 7 53	22	197 30	76	N 7 09	21	295 08	40	S23 13	3	130 39	47	N21 24	1	141 22	52	N18 08	2	TUE 10
11 WED	179 43	4	N 8 15	22	198 46	73	N 6 48	21	295 48	40	S23 16	3	131 26	47	N21 25	2	142 14	52	N18 10	2	WED 11
12 THU	179 47	4	N 8 37	22	199 59	71	N 6 27	20	296 28	40	S23 19	2	132 13	47	N21 27	2	143 06	53	N18 11	2	THU 12
13 FRI	179 51	4	N 8 59	22	201 10	69	N 6 07	19	297 08	41	S23 21	3	133 00	47	N21 29	2	143 59	52	N18 13	2	FRI 13
14 SAT	179 55	3	N 9 21	22	202 19	66	N 5 48	18	297 49	41	S23 24	2	133 47	47	N21 31	2	144 51	52	N18 15	1	SAT 14
15 SUN	179 58	4	N 9 43	21	203 25	64	N 5 30	17	298 30	41	S23 26	3	134 34	46	N21 33	2	145 43	52	N18 16	2	SUN 15
16 MON	180 02	4	N10 04	21	204 29	62	N 5 13	16	299 11	41	S23 29	3	135 20	47	N21 35	2	146 35	52	N18 18	2	MON 16
17 TUE	180 06	3	N10 25	21	205 31	59	N 4 57	16	299 54	42	S23 32	2	136 07	46	N21 37	1	147 27	52	N18 20	1	TUE 17
18 WED	180 09	4	N10 46	21	206 30	58	N 4 41	14	300 36	44	S23 34	3	136 53	47	N21 38	2	148 19	52	N18 21	2	WED 18
19 THU	180 12	4	N11 07	21	207 28	55	N 4 27	13	301 20	44	S23 37	2	137 40	46	N21 40	2	149 11	52	N18 23	1	THU 19
20 FRI	180 16	3	N11 28	21	208 23	53	N 4 14	12	302 04	44	S23 39	3	138 26	46	N21 42	2	150 03	52	N18 24	2	FRI 20
21 SAT	180 19	3	N11 48	21	209 16	51	N 4 02	11	302 48	45	S23 42	3	139 12	46	N21 44	2	150 55	51	N18 26	2	SAT 21
22 SUN	180 22	3	N12 09	20	210 07	49	N 3 51	10	303 33	46	S23 45	2	139 58	46	N21 46	1	151 46	52	N18 28	1	SUN 22
23 MON	180 25	2	N12 29	20	210 56	47	N 3 41	9	304 19	46	S23 47	3	140 44	46	N21 47	2	152 38	52	N18 29	2	MON 23
24 TUE	180 27	3	N12 49	19	211 43	45	N 3 32	8	305 05	47	S23 50	3	141 30	46	N21 49	2	153 30	52	N18 31	2	TUE 24
25 WED	180 30	2	N13 08	20	212 28	43	N 3 24	7	305 52	47	S23 53	2	142 16	46	N21 51	2	154 22	51	N18 33	1	WED 25
26 THU	180 32	3	N13 28	19	213 11	42	N 3 17	6	306 39	48	S23 55	3	143 02	46	N21 52	2	155 13	52	N18 34	2	THU 26
27 FRI	180 35	2	N13 47	19	213 53	39	N 3 11	5	307 27	49	S23 58	3	143 48	46	N21 54	1	156 05	51	N18 36	2	FRI 27
28 SAT	180 37	2	N14 06	19	214 32	38	N 3 06	4	308 16	49	S24 01	2	144 34	45	N21 56	2	156 56	52	N18 38	1	SAT 28
29 SUN	180 39	2	N14 25	18	215 10	37	N 3 02	3	309 05	50	S24 03	3	145 19	46	N21 58	2	157 48	51	N18 39	2	SUN 29
30 MON	180 41	2	N14 43	19	215 47	35	N 2 59	1	309 55	51	S24 06	3	146 05	45	N22 00	1	158 39	52	N18 41	1	MON 30
31 TUE	180 43		N15 02		216 22		N 2 58		310 46		S24 09		146 50		N22 01		159 31		N18 42		TUE 31

SUN & PLANETS AT GMT 0hrs MAY 2001

Day	SUN SD 16' GHA	v	Dec	d	VENUS Mag. -4.5 GHA	v	Dec	d	MARS Mag. -1.5 GHA	v	Dec	d	JUPITER Mag. -2.0 GHA	v	Dec	d	SATURN Mag. +0.1 GHA	v	Dec	d	Day
1 TUE	180°43'	2'	N15°02'	18'	216°22'	33'	N 2°58'	1'	310°46'	52'	S24°09'	3'	146°50'	46'	N22°01'	2'	159°31'	51'	N18°42'	2'	TUE 1
2 WED	180 45	2	N15 20	18	216 55	32	N 2 57	1	311 38	52	S24 12	3	147 36	45	N22 03	2	160 22	52	N18 44	2	WED 2
3 THU	180 47	1	N15 38	17	217 27	30	N 2 56	1	312 30	53	S24 15	3	148 21	45	N22 05	1	161 14	51	N18 46	1	THU 3
4 FRI	180 48	2	N15 55	17	217 57	30	N 2 57	2	313 23	53	S24 18	3	149 06	46	N22 06	2	162 05	52	N18 47	2	FRI 4
5 SAT	180 50	1	N16 12	18	218 27	27	N 2 59	3	314 16	55	S24 21	3	149 52	45	N22 08	2	162 57	51	N18 49	2	SAT 5
6 SUN	180 51	1	N16 30	16	218 54	27	N 3 02	3	315 11	55	S24 24	3	150 37	45	N22 10	1	163 48	51	N18 51	1	SUN 6
7 MON	180 52	1	N16 46	17	219 21	25	N 3 05	4	316 06	55	S24 27	3	151 22	45	N22 11	2	164 39	51	N18 52	2	MON 7
8 TUE	180 53	1	N17 03	16	219 46	25	N 3 09	5	317 01	57	S24 30	3	152 07	45	N22 13	1	165 30	52	N18 54	1	TUE 8
9 WED	180 54	0	N17 19	16	220 11	23	N 3 14	6	317 58	58	S24 33	3	152 52	45	N22 14	2	166 22	51	N18 55	2	WED 9
10 THU	180 54	1	N17 35	15	220 34	22	N 3 20	6	318 56	58	S24 36	3	153 37	45	N22 16	1	167 13	51	N18 57	1	THU 10
11 FRI	180 55	0	N17 50	16	220 56	21	N 3 26	7	319 54	59	S24 39	4	154 22	45	N22 17	2	168 04	51	N18 58	2	FRI 11
12 SAT	180 55	1	N18 06	15	221 17	20	N 3 33	8	320 53	60	S24 43	3	155 07	45	N22 19	1	168 55	52	N19 00	2	SAT 12
13 SUN	180 56	0	N18 21	14	221 37	20	N 3 41	8	321 53	60	S24 46	3	155 52	45	N22 20	1	169 47	51	N19 02	1	SUN 13
14 MON	180 56	0	N18 35	15	221 57	18	N 3 49	9	322 53	62	S24 49	4	156 37	45	N22 22	1	170 38	51	N19 03	2	MON 14
15 TUE	180 56	-1	N18 50	14	222 15	17	N 3 58	10	323 55	62	S24 53	3	157 22	45	N22 23	2	171 29	51	N19 05	1	TUE 15
16 WED	180 55	0	N19 04	13	222 32	17	N 4 08	10	324 57	63	S24 56	4	158 07	44	N22 25	1	172 20	51	N19 06	2	WED 16
17 THU	180 55	0	N19 17	14	222 49	16	N 4 18	11	326 00	64	S25 00	3	158 51	45	N22 26	1	173 11	51	N19 08	1	THU 17
18 FRI	180 55	-1	N19 31	13	223 05	15	N 4 29	11	327 04	65	S25 03	4	159 36	45	N22 28	1	174 02	51	N19 09	2	FRI 18
19 SAT	180 54	-1	N19 44	13	223 20	14	N 4 40	12	328 09	66	S25 07	3	160 21	44	N22 29	1	174 53	52	N19 11	1	SAT 19
20 SUN	180 53	-1	N19 57	12	223 34	14	N 4 52	12	329 15	67	S25 10	4	161 05	45	N22 30	2	175 45	51	N19 12	2	SUN 20
21 MON	180 52	-1	N20 09	12	223 48	13	N 5 04	12	330 22	67	S25 14	3	161 50	44	N22 32	1	176 36	51	N19 14	1	MON 21
22 TUE	180 51	-1	N20 21	12	224 01	12	N 5 16	14	331 29	68	S25 17	4	162 34	45	N22 33	1	177 27	51	N19 15	2	TUE 22
23 WED	180 50	-1	N20 33	11	224 13	12	N 5 30	13	332 37	70	S25 21	4	163 19	44	N22 34	2	178 18	51	N19 17	1	WED 23
24 THU	180 49	-2	N20 44	11	224 25	11	N 5 43	14	333 47	69	S25 25	3	164 03	45	N22 36	1	179 09	51	N19 18	2	THU 24
25 FRI	180 47	-1	N20 55	11	224 36	10	N 5 57	14	334 56	71	S25 25	4	164 48	45	N22 37	1	180 00	51	N19 20	1	FRI 25
26 SAT	180 46	-2	N21 06	10	224 46	10	N 6 11	15	336 07	72	S25 32	4	165 32	44	N22 38	1	180 51	51	N19 21	2	SAT 26
27 SUN	180 44	-2	N21 16	10	224 56	9	N 6 26	15	337 19	72	S25 36	3	166 16	45	N22 39	2	181 42	51	N19 22	1	SUN 27
28 MON	180 42	-2	N21 26	10	225 05	9	N 6 41	15	338 31	73	S25 39	4	167 01	44	N22 41	1	182 33	51	N19 24	2	MON 28
29 TUE	180 40	-2	N21 36	9	225 14	8	N 6 56	15	339 44	74	S25 43	3	167 45	44	N22 42	1	183 24	51	N19 26	1	TUE 29
30 WED	180 38	-2	N21 45	9	225 22	8	N 7 11	16	340 58	74	S25 46	4	168 29	45	N22 43	1	184 15	51	N19 27	2	WED 30
31 THU	180 36	-2	N21 54	8	225 30	7	N 7 27	16	342 12	76	S25 50	3	169 14	44	N22 44	1	185 06	51	N19 29	1	THU 31
32 FRI	180 34		N22 02		225 37		N 7 43		343 28		S25 53		169 58		N22 45		185 57		N19 30		FRI 32

SUN & PLANETS AT GMT 0hrs JUNE 2001

Day	SUN SD 16' GHA	v	Dec	d	VENUS Mag. -4.4 GHA	v	Dec	d	MARS Mag. -2.4 GHA	v	Dec	d	JUPITER Mag. -1.9 GHA	v	Dec	d	SATURN Mag. +0.1 GHA	v	Dec	d	Day
1 FRI	180°34'	-2'	N22°02'	8'	225°37'	7'	N 7°43'	16'	343°28'	75'	S25°53'	4'	169°58'	44'	N22°45'	1'	185°57'	51'	N19°30'	1'	FRI 1
2 SAT	180 32	-3	N22 10	8	225 44	6	N 7 59	17	344 43	77	S25 57	3	170 42	44	N22 46	1	186 48	51	N19 31	2	SAT 2
3 SUN	180 29	-2	N22 18	7	225 50	6	N 8 16	17	346 00	77	S26 00	3	171 26	45	N22 47	1	187 39	51	N19 33	1	SUN 3
4 MON	180 27	-3	N22 25	7	225 56	5	N 8 33	17	347 17	77	S26 03	3	172 11	44	N22 48	1	188 30	51	N19 34	2	MON 4
5 TUE	180 24	-2	N22 32	6	226 01	5	N 8 50	17	348 34	79	S26 06	4	172 55	44	N22 49	1	189 21	52	N19 36	1	TUE 5
6 WED	180 22	-3	N22 38	6	226 06	4	N 9 07	17	349 53	78	S26 10	3	173 39	44	N22 50	1	190 13	51	N19 37	1	WED 6
7 THU	180 19	-3	N22 44	6	226 10	4	N 9 24	17	351 11	79	S26 13	3	174 23	44	N22 51	1	191 04	51	N19 38	2	THU 7
8 FRI	180 16	-3	N22 50	5	226 14	4	N 9 41	17	352 30	80	S26 16	2	175 07	44	N22 52	1	191 55	51	N19 40	1	FRI 8
9 SAT	180 13	-3	N22 55	5	226 18	3	N 9 58	18	353 50	80	S26 18	3	175 51	45	N22 53	1	192 46	51	N19 41	1	SAT 9
10 SUN	180 10	-3	N23 00	4	226 21	2	N10 16	18	355 10	80	S26 21	3	176 36	44	N22 54	1	193 37	51	N19 42	2	SUN 10
11 MON	180 07	-3	N23 04	4	226 23	2	N10 34	17	356 30	80	S26 24	2	177 20	44	N22 55	1	194 28	51	N19 44	1	MON 11
12 TUE	180 04	-3	N23 08	4	226 25	2	N10 51	18	357 50	81	S26 26	3	178 04	44	N22 57	0	195 19	52	N19 45	1	TUE 12
13 WED	180 01	-3	N23 12	3	226 27	1	N11 09	18	359 11	81	S26 29	2	178 48	44	N22 57	1	196 11	51	N19 46	2	WED 13
14 THU	179 58	-3	N23 15	3	226 28	1	N11 27	18	0 32	81	S26 31	2	179 32	44	N22 57	1	197 02	51	N19 48	1	THU 14
15 FRI	179 55	-3	N23 18	2	226 29	0	N11 45	17	1 53	81	S26 33	2	180 16	44	N22 58	1	197 53	51	N19 49	1	FRI 15
16 SAT	179 52	-4	N23 20	2	226 29	0	N12 02	18	3 14	81	S26 35	2	181 00	44	N22 59	1	198 44	51	N19 50	1	SAT 16
17 SUN	179 48	-3	N23 22	2	226 29	0	N12 20	18	4 35	81	S26 37	2	181 44	45	N23 00	0	199 35	52	N19 51	1	SUN 17
18 MON	179 45	-3	N23 24	1	226 29	-1	N12 38	18	5 56	81	S26 39	2	182 29	44	N23 00	1	200 27	51	N19 53	1	MON 18
19 TUE	179 42	-3	N23 25	1	226 28	-1	N12 56	18	7 17	81	S26 41	1	183 13	44	N23 01	1	201 18	51	N19 54	1	TUE 19
20 WED	179 39	-4	N23 26	0	226 27	-1	N13 13	18	8 38	81	S26 42	1	183 57	44	N23 02	0	202 09	52	N19 55	1	WED 20
21 THU	179 35	-3	N23 26	0	226 26	-2	N13 31	17	9 59	80	S26 43	2	184 41	44	N23 02	1	203 01	51	N19 56	1	THU 21
22 FRI	179 32	-3	N23 26	0	226 24	-3	N13 48	18	11 19	81	S26 45	1	185 25	44	N23 03	0	203 52	51	N19 57	1	FRI 22
23 SAT	179 29	-4	N23 26	1	226 21	-2	N14 06	17	12 40	79	S26 46	1	186 09	44	N23 03	1	204 43	52	N19 58	2	SAT 23
24 SUN	179 25	-3	N23 25	1	226 19	-3	N14 23	17	13 59	80	S26 47	1	186 53	45	N23 04	1	205 35	51	N20 00	1	SUN 24
25 MON	179 22	-3	N23 24	2	226 16	-4	N14 40	17	15 19	79	S26 48	0	187 38	44	N23 05	0	206 26	52	N20 01	1	MON 25
26 TUE	179 19	-3	N23 22	2	226 12	-4	N14 57	17	16 38	78	S26 48	1	188 22	44	N23 05	0	207 18	51	N20 02	1	TUE 26
27 WED	179 16	-3	N23 20	3	226 08	-4	N15 14	17	17 56	78	S26 49	1	189 06	44	N23 05	1	208 09	52	N20 03	1	WED 27
28 THU	179 13	-3	N23 17	3	226 04	-4	N15 31	16	19 14	77	S26 50	0	189 50	45	N23 06	0	209 01	51	N20 04	1	THU 28
29 FRI	179 10	-3	N23 14	3	226 00	-5	N15 47	16	20 31	77	S26 50	1	190 35	44	N23 06	1	209 52	52	N20 05	1	FRI 29
30 SAT	179 07	-3	N23 11	4	225 55	-6	N16 03	16	21 48	76	S26 51	0	191 19	44	N23 07	0	210 44	52	N20 06	1	SAT 30
31 SUN	179 04		N23 07		225 49		N16 19		23 04		S26 51		192 03		N23 07		211 36		N20 07		SUN 31

SUN & PLANETS AT GMT 0hrs JULY 2001

Day	SUN SD 16' GHA	v	Dec	d	VENUS Mag. -4.2 GHA	v	Dec	d	MARS Mag. -1.9 GHA	v	Dec	d	JUPITER Mag. -1.9 GHA	v	Dec	d	SATURN Mag. +0.2 GHA	v	Dec	d	Day
1 SUN	179° 04'	-3'	N23° 07'	4'	225° 49'	-5'	N16° 19'	16'	23° 04'	75'	S26° 51'	0'	192° 03'	44'	N23° 07'	0'	211° 36'	51'	N20° 07'	1'	SUN 1
2 MON	179 01	-3	N23 03	5	225 44	-6	N16 35	16	24 19	75	S26 51	0	192 47	45	N23 07	1	212 27	52	N20 08	1	MON 2
3 TUE	178 58	-3	N22 58	5	225 38	-7	N16 51	15	25 34	74	S26 51	0	193 32	44	N23 08	0	213 19	52	N20 09	1	TUE 3
4 WED	178 55	-2	N22 53	5	225 31	-7	N17 06	15	26 48	73	S26 51	1	194 16	44	N23 08	0	214 11	52	N20 10	1	WED 4
5 THU	178 53	-3	N22 48	6	225 24	-7	N17 21	15	28 01	72	S26 52	0	195 00	45	N23 08	1	215 03	52	N20 11	1	THU 5
6 FRI	178 50	-2	N22 42	6	225 17	-7	N17 36	15	29 13	72	S26 52	0	195 45	45	N23 08	0	215 55	52	N20 12	1	FRI 6
7 SAT	178 48	-3	N22 36	7	225 10	-8	N17 51	14	30 25	70	S26 52	1	196 29	45	N23 09	0	216 47	52	N20 13	1	SAT 7
8 SUN	178 45	-2	N22 29	6	225 02	-9	N18 05	14	31 35	70	S26 51	0	197 14	44	N23 09	0	217 39	52	N20 14	1	SUN 8
9 MON	178 43	-2	N22 23	8	224 53	-8	N18 19	13	32 45	69	S26 51	0	197 58	45	N23 09	0	218 31	52	N20 15	1	MON 9
10 TUE	178 41	-2	N22 15	8	224 45	-9	N18 32	13	33 54	68	S26 51	0	198 43	44	N23 09	1	219 23	52	N20 16	1	TUE 10
11 WED	178 39	-2	N22 07	8	224 36	-9	N18 45	13	35 02	67	S26 51	0	199 27	45	N23 10	0	220 15	52	N20 17	1	WED 11
12 THU	178 37	-2	N21 59	8	224 27	-10	N18 58	13	36 09	66	S26 51	0	200 12	45	N23 10	0	221 07	52	N20 18	1	THU 12
13 FRI	178 35	-2	N21 51	9	224 17	-10	N19 11	12	37 15	65	S26 51	0	200 56	45	N23 10	0	221 59	52	N20 19	1	FRI 13
14 SAT	178 33	-1	N21 42	9	224 07	-10	N19 23	12	38 20	64	S26 51	0	201 41	45	N23 10	0	222 51	53	N20 20	1	SAT 14
15 SUN	178 32	-2	N21 33	10	223 57	-11	N19 35	11	39 24	64	S26 51	0	202 26	45	N23 10	0	223 44	52	N20 21	1	SUN 15
16 MON	178 30	-1	N21 23	10	223 46	-11	N19 46	11	40 28	62	S26 51	1	203 11	44	N23 10	0	224 36	52	N20 22	0	MON 16
17 TUE	178 29	-2	N21 13	10	223 35	-11	N19 57	10	41 30	62	S26 50	0	203 55	45	N23 10	0	225 28	53	N20 22	1	TUE 17
18 WED	178 27	-1	N21 03	11	223 24	-12	N20 07	10	42 32	60	S26 50	0	204 40	45	N23 10	0	226 21	52	N20 23	1	WED 18
19 THU	178 26	-1	N20 52	11	223 12	-12	N20 17	10	43 32	60	S26 50	0	205 25	45	N23 10	0	227 13	53	N20 24	1	THU 19
20 FRI	178 25	-1	N20 41	11	223 00	-12	N20 27	9	44 32	58	S26 50	0	206 10	45	N23 10	0	228 06	53	N20 25	1	FRI 20
21 SAT	178 24	0	N20 30	12	222 48	-12	N20 36	9	45 30	58	S26 50	0	206 55	45	N23 10	1	228 59	52	N20 26	0	SAT 21
22 SUN	178 24	-1	N20 18	12	222 36	-13	N20 45	8	46 28	57	S26 50	0	207 40	45	N23 10	0	229 51	53	N20 26	1	SUN 22
23 MON	178 23	0	N20 06	12	222 23	-13	N20 53	8	47 25	56	S26 50	0	208 25	45	N23 09	0	230 44	53	N20 27	1	MON 23
24 TUE	178 23	-1	N19 54	13	222 10	-13	N21 01	7	48 21	54	S26 50	1	209 10	45	N23 09	0	231 37	53	N20 28	1	TUE 24
25 WED	178 22	0	N19 41	13	221 57	-14	N21 08	7	49 15	54	S26 51	0	209 55	45	N23 09	0	232 30	53	N20 29	0	WED 25
26 THU	178 22	0	N19 28	13	221 43	-13	N21 15	6	50 09	53	S26 51	0	210 40	46	N23 09	0	233 23	53	N20 29	1	THU 26
27 FRI	178 22	1	N19 15	14	221 30	-14	N21 21	6	51 02	52	S26 51	0	211 26	45	N23 09	0	234 16	53	N20 30	1	FRI 27
28 SAT	178 23	0	N19 01	14	221 16	-15	N21 27	5	51 54	52	S26 51	0	212 11	45	N23 09	1	235 09	53	N20 31	0	SAT 28
29 SUN	178 23	0	N18 47	14	221 01	-14	N21 32	5	52 46	50	S26 51	0	212 56	46	N23 08	0	236 02	53	N20 31	1	SUN 29
30 MON	178 23	1	N18 33	15	220 47	-14	N21 37	4	53 36	49	S26 52	0	213 42	45	N23 08	0	236 55	53	N20 32	1	MON 30
31 TUE	178 24	1	N18 18	15	220 33	-15	N21 41	4	54 25	49	S26 52	0	214 27	46	N23 08	1	237 48	54	N20 33	0	TUE 31
32 WED	178 25		N18 03		220 18		N21 45		55 14		S26 52		215 13		N23 07		238 42		N20 33		WED 32

SUN & PLANETS AT GMT 0hrs AUGUST 2001

Day	SUN SD 16' GHA	v	Dec	d	VENUS Mag. -4.1 GHA	v	Dec	d	MARS Mag. -1.2 GHA	v	Dec	d	JUPITER Mag. -2.0 GHA	v	Dec	d	SATURN Mag. +0.1 GHA	v	Dec	d	Day
1 WED	178° 25'	1'	N18° 03'	15'	220° 18'	-15'	N21° 45'	3'	55° 14'	48'	S26° 52'	1'	215° 13'	45'	N23° 07'	0'	238° 42'	53'	N20° 33'	1'	WED 1
2 THU	178 26	1	N17 48	16	220 03	-15	N21 48	2	56 02	47	S26 53	0	215 58	46	N23 07	0	239 35	54	N20 34	0	THU 2
3 FRI	178 27	1	N17 32	15	219 48	-16	N21 50	2	56 49	46	S26 53	1	216 44	46	N23 07	1	240 29	53	N20 34	1	FRI 3
4 SAT	178 28	2	N17 17	16	219 32	-15	N21 52	1	57 35	45	S26 54	0	217 30	46	N23 06	0	241 22	54	N20 35	1	SAT 4
5 SUN	178 30	1	N17 01	17	219 17	-16	N21 53	1	58 20	44	S26 54	1	218 16	46	N23 06	0	242 16	54	N20 36	0	SUN 5
6 MON	178 31	2	N16 44	16	219 01	-15	N21 54	0	59 04	44	S26 55	0	219 02	46	N23 06	1	243 10	54	N20 36	1	MON 6
7 TUE	178 33	2	N16 28	17	218 46	-16	N21 54	1	59 48	43	S26 55	1	219 48	46	N23 05	0	244 04	54	N20 37	0	TUE 7
8 WED	178 35	2	N16 11	17	218 30	-16	N21 54	1	60 31	42	S26 56	0	220 34	46	N23 05	1	244 58	54	N20 37	1	WED 8
9 THU	178 37	2	N15 54	18	218 14	-16	N21 53	1	61 13	42	S26 56	1	221 20	46	N23 04	0	245 52	54	N20 38	0	THU 9
10 FRI	178 39	2	N15 36	17	217 58	-16	N21 52	3	61 55	41	S26 57	0	222 06	46	N23 04	0	246 46	54	N20 38	1	FRI 10
11 SAT	178 41	3	N15 19	18	217 42	-16	N21 49	2	62 36	40	S26 57	1	222 52	47	N23 04	1	247 40	54	N20 39	0	SAT 11
12 SUN	178 44	2	N15 01	18	217 26	-17	N21 47	4	63 16	39	S26 58	0	223 39	46	N23 03	0	248 34	54	N20 39	1	SUN 12
13 MON	178 46	3	N14 43	19	217 09	-16	N21 43	4	63 55	39	S26 58	1	224 25	47	N23 03	0	249 28	55	N20 40	0	MON 13
14 TUE	178 49	3	N14 24	18	216 53	-16	N21 39	4	64 34	38	S26 58	1	225 12	47	N23 02	0	250 23	54	N20 40	1	TUE 14
15 WED	178 52	3	N14 06	19	216 37	-16	N21 35	5	65 12	37	S26 59	0	225 58	47	N23 02	1	251 17	55	N20 41	0	WED 15
16 THU	178 55	3	N13 47	19	216 21	-17	N21 30	6	65 49	37	S26 59	1	226 45	47	N23 01	1	252 12	55	N20 41	1	THU 16
17 FRI	178 58	3	N13 28	19	216 04	-16	N21 24	6	66 26	36	S27 00	0	227 32	47	N23 00	0	253 07	54	N20 41	1	FRI 17
18 SAT	179 01	4	N13 09	20	215 48	-16	N21 18	7	67 02	36	S27 00	0	228 19	46	N23 00	1	254 01	55	N20 42	0	SAT 18
19 SUN	179 05	3	N12 49	19	215 32	-17	N21 11	7	67 38	34	S27 00	1	229 05	48	N22 59	0	254 56	55	N20 42	0	SUN 19
20 MON	179 08	4	N12 30	20	215 15	-16	N21 04	8	68 12	35	S27 01	0	229 53	47	N22 59	1	255 51	55	N20 42	1	MON 20
21 TUE	179 12	3	N12 10	20	214 59	-16	N20 56	9	68 47	33	S27 01	0	230 40	47	N22 58	0	256 46	55	N20 43	0	TUE 21
22 WED	179 15	4	N11 50	20	214 43	-16	N20 47	9	69 20	33	S27 01	1	231 27	47	N22 58	1	257 41	56	N20 43	0	WED 22
23 THU	179 19	4	N11 30	21	214 27	-16	N20 38	10	69 53	33	S27 01	1	232 14	48	N22 57	0	258 37	55	N20 43	1	THU 23
24 FRI	179 23	4	N11 09	20	214 11	-16	N20 28	10	70 26	31	S27 02	0	233 02	47	N22 56	0	259 32	55	N20 44	0	FRI 24
25 SAT	179 27	4	N10 49	21	213 55	-16	N20 18	11	70 57	31	S27 02	0	233 49	48	N22 56	1	260 27	56	N20 44	0	SAT 25
26 SUN	179 31	5	N10 28	21	213 39	-16	N20 07	12	71 29	31	S27 02	0	234 37	48	N22 55	0	261 23	55	N20 44	1	SUN 26
27 MON	179 36	4	N10 07	21	213 23	-15	N19 55	12	72 00	30	S27 01	0	235 25	48	N22 54	1	262 18	56	N20 45	0	MON 27
28 TUE	179 40	4	N 9 46	21	213 08	-16	N19 43	13	72 30	30	S27 01	0	236 13	48	N22 54	0	263 14	56	N20 45	0	TUE 28
29 WED	179 44	5	N 9 25	22	212 52	-15	N19 30	13	73 00	29	S27 01	0	237 01	48	N22 53	0	264 10	56	N20 45	0	WED 29
30 THU	179 49	4	N 9 03	21	212 37	-16	N19 17	14	73 29	29	S27 01	1	237 49	48	N22 53	1	265 06	56	N20 45	1	THU 30
31 FRI	179 53	5	N 8 42	21	212 21	-15	N19 03	14	73 58	28	S27 00	0	238 37	48	N22 52	1	266 02	56	N20 46	0	FRI 31
32 SAT	179 58		N 8 20		212 06		N18 49		74 26		S27 00		239 25		N22 51		266 58		N20 46		SAT 32

SUN & PLANETS AT GMT 0hrs SEPTEMBER 2001

Day	SUN SD 16' GHA	v	Dec	d	VENUS Mag. -4.0 GHA	v	Dec	d	MARS Mag. -0.6 GHA	v	Dec	d	JUPITER Mag. -2.1 GHA	v	Dec	d	SATURN Mag. +0.0 GHA	v	Dec	d	Day
1 SAT	179° 58'	5'	N 8° 20'	22'	212° 06'	-15'	N18° 49'	15'	74° 26'	28'	S27° 00'	1'	239° 25'	49'	N22° 51'	0'	266° 58'	56'	N20° 46'	0'	SAT 1
2 SUN	180 03	5	N 7 58	22	211 51	-15	N18 34	15	74 54	28	S26 59	0	240 14	48	N22 51	1	267 54	57	N20 46	0	SUN 2
3 MON	180 08	5	N 7 36	22	211 36	-14	N18 19	16	75 22	27	S26 59	1	241 02	49	N22 50	1	268 51	56	N20 46	0	MON 3
4 TUE	180 13	5	N 7 14	22	211 22	-15	N18 03	16	75 49	26	S26 58	1	241 51	49	N22 49	0	269 47	57	N20 46	0	TUE 4
5 WED	180 18	5	N 6 52	22	211 07	-14	N17 47	17	76 15	26	S26 57	1	242 40	48	N22 49	1	270 44	56	N20 46	1	WED 5
6 THU	180 23	5	N 6 30	23	210 53	-14	N17 30	18	76 41	26	S26 56	1	243 28	49	N22 48	1	271 40	57	N20 47	0	THU 6
7 FRI	180 28	5	N 6 07	22	210 39	-15	N17 12	17	77 07	26	S26 55	2	244 17	50	N22 47	0	272 37	57	N20 47	0	FRI 7
8 SAT	180 33	5	N 5 45	23	210 24	-13	N16 55	19	77 33	25	S26 53	1	245 07	49	N22 47	1	273 34	57	N20 47	0	SAT 8
9 SUN	180 38	5	N 5 22	22	210 11	-14	N16 36	19	77 58	25	S26 52	1	245 56	49	N22 46	0	274 31	57	N20 47	0	SUN 9
10 MON	180 43	6	N 5 00	23	209 57	-14	N16 17	19	78 22	25	S26 51	2	246 45	50	N22 45	0	275 28	57	N20 47	0	MON 10
11 TUE	180 49	5	N 4 37	23	209 43	-13	N15 58	20	78 47	23	S26 49	2	247 35	50	N22 44	0	276 25	58	N20 47	0	TUE 11
12 WED	180 54	5	N 4 14	23	209 30	-13	N15 38	20	79 10	24	S26 47	2	248 25	49	N22 44	1	277 23	57	N20 47	0	WED 12
13 THU	180 59	6	N 3 51	23	209 17	-13	N15 18	21	79 34	23	S26 45	2	249 14	50	N22 43	1	278 20	58	N20 47	0	THU 13
14 FRI	181 05	5	N 3 28	23	209 04	-13	N14 57	21	79 57	23	S26 43	2	250 04	50	N22 42	0	279 18	57	N20 47	0	FRI 14
15 SAT	181 10	5	N 3 05	23	208 51	-13	N14 36	21	80 20	23	S26 41	3	250 54	51	N22 42	1	280 15	58	N20 47	0	SAT 15
16 SUN	181 15	6	N 2 42	23	208 38	-12	N14 15	22	80 43	22	S26 38	2	251 45	50	N22 41	1	281 13	58	N20 47	0	SUN 16
17 MON	181 21	5	N 2 19	23	208 26	-13	N13 53	22	81 05	22	S26 36	3	252 35	51	N22 40	0	282 11	58	N20 47	0	MON 17
18 TUE	181 26	5	N 1 56	24	208 13	-12	N13 31	23	81 27	22	S26 33	3	253 26	51	N22 40	1	283 09	58	N20 47	0	TUE 18
19 WED	181 31	6	N 1 32	23	208 01	-12	N13 08	23	81 49	21	S26 30	3	254 16	51	N22 39	1	284 07	59	N20 47	0	WED 19
20 THU	181 37	5	N 1 09	23	207 49	-12	N12 45	24	82 10	21	S26 27	3	255 07	51	N22 38	0	285 06	58	N20 47	0	THU 20
21 FRI	181 42	5	N 0 46	24	207 37	-11	N12 21	23	82 31	21	S26 24	3	255 58	51	N22 38	1	286 04	58	N20 47	0	FRI 21
22 SAT	181 47	5	N 0 22	21	207 26	-12	N11 58	25	82 52	21	S26 21	4	256 49	51	N22 37	0	287 02	59	N20 47	0	SAT 22
23 SUN	181 52	6	S 0 01	23	207 14	-11	N11 33	24	83 13	20	S26 17	3	257 40	52	N22 37	1	288 01	59	N20 47	0	SUN 23
24 MON	181 58	5	S 0 24	24	207 03	-11	N11 09	25	83 33	20	S26 14	4	258 32	51	N22 36	1	289 00	59	N20 47	0	MON 24
25 TUE	182 03	5	S 0 48	23	206 52	-11	N10 44	25	83 53	20	S26 10	4	259 23	52	N22 35	0	289 59	58	N20 47	0	TUE 25
26 WED	182 08	5	S 1 11	23	206 41	-11	N10 19	25	84 13	19	S26 06	4	260 15	52	N22 35	1	290 57	60	N20 47	0	WED 26
27 THU	182 13	5	S 1 34	24	206 30	-11	N 9 54	26	84 32	19	S26 02	4	261 07	52	N22 34	0	291 57	59	N20 46	0	THU 27
28 FRI	182 18	5	S 1 58	23	206 19	-10	N 9 28	26	84 52	19	S25 57	4	261 59	52	N22 34	1	292 56	59	N20 46	0	FRI 28
29 SAT	182 23	5	S 2 21	23	206 09	-11	N 9 02	26	85 11	19	S25 53	5	262 51	53	N22 33	1	293 55	59	N20 46	0	SAT 29
30 SUN	182 28	5	S 2 44	24	205 58	-10	N 8 36	27	85 30	19	S25 48	5	263 44	52	N22 32	0	294 54	60	N20 46	0	SUN 30
31 MON	182 33		S 3 08		205 48		N 8 09		85 49		S25 43		264 36		N22 32		295 54		N20 46		MON 31

SUN & PLANETS AT GMT 0hrs OCTOBER 2001

Day	SUN SD 16' GHA	v	Dec	d	VENUS Mag. -3.9 GHA	v	Dec	d	MARS Mag. -0.2 GHA	v	Dec	d	JUPITER Mag. -2.3 GHA	v	Dec	d	SATURN Mag. -0.1 GHA	v	Dec	d	Day
1 MON	182° 33'	5'	S 3° 08'	23'	205° 48'	-10'	N 8° 09'	27'	85° 49'	19'	S25° 43'	5'	264° 36'	53'	N22° 32'	1'	295° 54'	60'	N20° 46'	0'	MON 1
2 TUE	182 38	5	S 3 31	23	205 38	-10	N 7 42	27	86 08	18	S25 38	5	265 29	53	N22 31	1	296 54	59	N20 46	0	TUE 2
3 WED	182 43	4	S 3 54	23	205 28	-10	N 7 15	27	86 26	18	S25 33	6	266 22	53	N22 31	1	297 53	60	N20 46	1	WED 3
4 THU	182 47	5	S 4 17	23	205 18	-10	N 6 48	27	86 44	19	S25 27	6	267 15	54	N22 30	0	298 53	60	N20 45	0	THU 4
5 FRI	182 52	5	S 4 40	23	205 08	-10	N 6 21	28	87 03	18	S25 21	6	268 09	53	N22 30	1	299 53	60	N20 45	0	FRI 5
6 SAT	182 57	4	S 5 03	23	204 58	-10	N 5 53	28	87 21	17	S25 15	6	269 02	54	N22 29	0	300 53	61	N20 45	0	SAT 6
7 SUN	183 01	4	S 5 26	23	204 48	-9	N 5 25	28	87 38	18	S25 09	6	269 56	54	N22 29	1	301 54	60	N20 45	0	SUN 7
8 MON	183 05	4	S 5 49	23	204 39	-10	N 4 57	28	87 56	18	S25 03	6	270 50	54	N22 28	0	302 54	60	N20 45	1	MON 8
9 TUE	183 09	4	S 6 12	23	204 29	-9	N 4 29	28	88 14	17	S24 57	7	271 44	54	N22 28	0	303 54	61	N20 44	0	TUE 9
10 WED	183 13	4	S 6 35	23	204 20	-10	N 4 01	29	88 31	18	S24 50	7	272 38	54	N22 28	1	304 55	61	N20 44	0	WED 10
11 THU	183 17	4	S 6 58	22	204 10	-9	N 3 32	28	88 49	17	S24 43	7	273 32	55	N22 27	0	305 56	60	N20 44	0	THU 11
12 FRI	183 21	4	S 7 20	23	204 01	-10	N 3 04	29	89 06	17	S24 36	7	274 27	54	N22 27	1	306 56	61	N20 44	1	FRI 12
13 SAT	183 25	4	S 7 43	22	203 51	-9	N 2 35	29	89 23	17	S24 29	8	275 21	55	N22 26	0	307 57	61	N20 43	0	SAT 13
14 SUN	183 29	3	S 8 05	22	203 42	-9	N 2 06	29	89 40	17	S24 21	8	276 16	56	N22 26	0	308 58	61	N20 43	0	SUN 14
15 MON	183 32	3	S 8 27	23	203 33	-10	N 1 37	29	89 57	17	S24 13	8	277 12	55	N22 26	1	309 59	62	N20 42	1	MON 15
16 TUE	183 35	3	S 8 50	22	203 23	-9	N 1 08	29	90 14	17	S24 06	9	278 07	56	N22 25	0	311 01	61	N20 42	0	TUE 16
17 WED	183 38	3	S 9 12	22	203 14	-9	N 0 39	29	90 31	16	S23 57	8	279 03	55	N22 25	0	312 02	62	N20 42	0	WED 17
18 THU	183 41	3	S 9 34	21	203 05	-10	N 0 10	9	90 47	17	S23 49	8	279 58	56	N22 25	0	313 04	61	N20 42	1	THU 18
19 FRI	183 44	3	S 9 55	22	202 55	-9	S 0 19	30	91 04	17	S23 41	9	280 54	56	N22 25	1	314 05	62	N20 41	0	FRI 19
20 SAT	183 47	2	S10 17	21	202 46	-10	S 0 49	29	91 21	16	S23 32	9	281 50	57	N22 24	0	315 07	62	N20 41	0	SAT 20
21 SUN	183 49	3	S10 38	22	202 36	-9	S 1 18	29	91 37	16	S23 23	9	282 47	56	N22 24	0	316 09	61	N20 41	1	SUN 21
22 MON	183 52	2	S11 00	21	202 27	-10	S 1 47	29	91 53	17	S23 14	9	283 43	57	N22 24	0	317 10	62	N20 40	0	MON 22
23 TUE	183 54	2	S11 21	21	202 17	-9	S 2 16	30	92 10	16	S23 05	10	284 40	57	N22 24	1	318 12	63	N20 40	0	TUE 23
24 WED	183 56	2	S11 42	21	202 08	-10	S 2 46	29	92 26	16	S22 55	9	285 37	57	N22 24	0	319 14	63	N20 39	0	WED 24
25 THU	183 58	2	S12 03	20	201 58	-10	S 3 15	29	92 42	17	S22 46	10	286 34	58	N22 24	0	320 17	62	N20 39	0	THU 25
26 FRI	184 00	1	S12 23	21	201 48	-10	S 3 44	29	92 59	16	S22 36	10	287 32	57	N22 24	1	321 19	62	N20 39	1	FRI 26
27 SAT	184 01	1	S12 44	20	201 38	-10	S 4 13	29	93 15	16	S22 26	11	288 29	58	N22 24	1	322 21	63	N20 38	0	SAT 27
28 SUN	184 02	2	S13 04	20	201 28	-10	S 4 42	29	93 31	16	S22 15	10	289 27	58	N22 23	0	323 24	62	N20 38	1	SUN 28
29 MON	184 04	1	S13 24	20	201 18	-10	S 5 11	29	93 47	17	S22 05	11	290 25	58	N22 23	0	324 26	63	N20 37	0	MON 29
30 TUE	184 05	0	S13 44	19	201 08	-10	S 5 40	29	94 04	16	S21 54	10	291 23	59	N22 23	0	325 29	63	N20 37	0	TUE 30
31 WED	184 05	1	S14 03	20	200 58	-11	S 6 09	28	94 20	16	S21 44	11	292 22	58	N22 23	1	326 32	63	N20 36	1	WED 31
32 THU	184 06		S14 23		200 47		S 6 37		94 36		S21 33		293 20		N22 24		327 35		N20 36		THU 32

SUN & PLANETS AT GMT 0hrs NOVEMBER 2001

Day	SUN SD 16' GHA	v	Dec	d	VENUS Mag. -3.9 GHA	v	Dec	d	MARS Mag. +0.2 GHA	v	Dec	d	JUPITER Mag. -2.5 GHA	v	Dec	d	SATURN Mag. -0.3 GHA	v	Dec	d	Day
1 THU	184°06'	0'	S14°23'	19'	200°47'	-10'	S 6°37'	29'	94°36'	16'	S21°33'	12'	293°20'	59'	N22°24'	0'	327°35'	62'	N20°36'	1'	THU 1
2 FRI	184 06	0	S14 42	19	200 37	-11	S 7 06	28	94 52	16	S21 21	11	294 19	59	N22 24	0	328 37	63	N20 35	0	FRI 2
3 SAT	184 06	0	S15 01	18	200 26	-11	S 7 34	28	95 08	17	S21 10	12	295 18	60	N22 24	0	329 40	63	N20 35	1	SAT 3
4 SUN	184 06	0	S15 19	19	200 15	-11	S 8 02	29	95 25	16	S20 58	11	296 18	59	N22 24	0	330 43	64	N20 34	0	SUN 4
5 MON	184 06	0	S15 38	18	200 04	-11	S 8 31	27	95 41	16	S20 47	12	297 17	60	N22 24	0	331 47	63	N20 34	1	MON 5
6 TUE	184 06	-1	S15 56	18	199 53	-12	S 8 58	28	95 57	16	S20 35	12	298 17	60	N22 24	0	332 50	63	N20 33	0	TUE 6
7 WED	184 05	-1	S16 14	17	199 41	-12	S 9 26	28	96 13	16	S20 23	13	299 17	60	N22 24	1	333 53	64	N20 33	1	WED 7
8 THU	184 04	-1	S16 31	18	199 29	-11	S 9 54	27	96 29	17	S20 10	12	300 17	61	N22 25	0	334 57	63	N20 32	0	THU 8
9 FRI	184 03	-1	S16 49	17	199 18	-13	S10 21	27	96 46	16	S19 58	13	301 18	60	N22 25	0	336 00	63	N20 32	1	FRI 9
10 SAT	184 02	-2	S17 06	17	199 05	-12	S10 48	27	97 02	16	S19 45	13	302 18	61	N22 25	0	337 03	64	N20 31	0	SAT 10
11 SUN	184 00	-1	S17 23	16	198 53	-13	S11 15	26	97 18	17	S19 32	13	303 19	61	N22 25	1	338 07	64	N20 31	1	SUN 11
12 MON	183 59	-2	S17 39	16	198 40	-13	S11 41	26	97 35	16	S19 19	13	304 20	61	N22 26	0	339 11	63	N20 30	0	MON 12
13 TUE	183 57	-3	S17 55	16	198 27	-13	S12 07	26	97 51	17	S19 06	13	305 21	62	N22 26	0	340 14	64	N20 30	1	TUE 13
14 WED	183 54	-2	S18 11	16	198 14	-13	S12 33	26	98 08	16	S18 53	13	306 23	61	N22 26	1	341 18	64	N20 29	0	WED 14
15 THU	183 52	-3	S18 27	15	198 01	-14	S12 59	25	98 24	16	S18 40	14	307 24	62	N22 27	0	342 22	64	N20 29	1	THU 15
16 FRI	183 49	-2	S18 42	15	197 47	-14	S13 24	25	98 40	17	S18 26	14	308 26	62	N22 27	1	343 26	64	N20 28	0	FRI 16
17 SAT	183 47	-3	S18 57	14	197 33	-14	S13 49	25	98 57	17	S18 12	14	309 28	63	N22 28	0	344 30	64	N20 28	1	SAT 17
18 SUN	183 44	-4	S19 11	14	197 19	-14	S14 14	24	99 14	17	S17 58	14	310 31	62	N22 28	1	345 34	64	N20 27	1	SUN 18
19 MON	183 40	-3	S19 25	14	197 05	-15	S14 38	24	99 30	17	S17 44	14	311 33	63	N22 29	0	346 38	64	N20 26	0	MON 19
20 TUE	183 37	-4	S19 39	14	196 50	-15	S15 02	24	99 47	16	S17 30	15	312 36	63	N22 29	1	347 42	64	N20 26	1	TUE 20
21 WED	183 33	-4	S19 53	13	196 35	-15	S15 26	23	100 03	17	S17 15	14	313 39	63	N22 30	0	348 46	64	N20 25	0	WED 21
22 THU	183 29	-4	S20 06	13	196 20	-16	S15 49	23	100 20	17	S17 01	15	314 42	63	N22 30	1	349 50	64	N20 25	1	THU 22
23 FRI	183 25	-4	S20 19	12	196 04	-16	S16 12	22	100 37	17	S16 46	15	315 45	64	N22 31	0	350 54	64	N20 24	0	FRI 23
24 SAT	183 21	-4	S20 31	12	195 48	-16	S16 34	22	100 54	17	S16 31	15	316 49	64	N22 31	1	351 58	65	N20 24	1	SAT 24
25 SUN	183 17	-5	S20 43	12	195 32	-16	S16 56	22	101 11	17	S16 16	15	317 53	63	N22 32	0	353 03	64	N20 23	1	SUN 25
26 MON	183 12	-5	S20 55	11	195 16	-17	S17 17	21	101 28	17	S16 01	15	318 56	65	N22 32	1	354 07	64	N20 22	0	MON 26
27 TUE	183 07	-4	S21 06	11	194 59	-17	S17 39	20	101 45	17	S15 46	15	320 01	64	N22 33	1	355 11	65	N20 22	1	TUE 27
28 WED	183 03	-6	S21 17	10	194 42	-17	S17 59	20	102 02	17	S15 31	16	321 05	64	N22 34	0	356 16	64	N20 21	0	WED 28
29 THU	182 57	-5	S21 27	10	194 25	-18	S18 19	20	102 19	17	S15 15	16	322 09	65	N22 34	1	357 20	64	N20 21	1	THU 29
30 FRI	182 52	-5	S21 37	10	194 07	-18	S18 39	19	102 36	17	S14 59	15	323 14	65	N22 35	1	358 24	65	N20 20	1	FRI 30
31 SAT	182 47		S21 47		193 49		S18 58		102 53		S14 44		324 19		N22 36		359 29		N20 19		SAT 31

SUN & PLANETS AT GMT 0hrs DECEMBER 2001

Day	SUN SD 16' GHA	v	Dec	d	VENUS Mag. -3.9 GHA	v	Dec	d	MARS Mag. +0.6 GHA	v	Dec	d	JUPITER Mag. -2.7 GHA	v	Dec	d	SATURN Mag. -0.4 GHA	v	Dec	d	Day
1 SAT	182°47'	-6'	S21°47'	9'	193°49'	-18'	S18°58'	18'	102°53'	18'	S14°44'	16'	324°19'	65'	N22°36'	0'	359°29'	64'	N20°19'	0'	SAT 1
2 SUN	182 41	-6	S21 56	9	193 31	-19	S19 16	18	103 11	17	S14 28	16	325 24	65	N22 36	1	0 33	64	N20 19	1	SUN 2
3 MON	182 35	-6	S22 05	8	193 12	-19	S19 34	18	103 28	17	S14 12	16	326 29	65	N22 37	1	1 37	65	N20 18	0	MON 3
4 TUE	182 29	-6	S22 13	8	192 53	-19	S19 52	17	103 45	18	S13 56	16	327 34	66	N22 38	1	2 42	64	N20 18	1	TUE 4
5 WED	182 23	-6	S22 21	7	192 34	-19	S20 09	16	104 03	17	S13 40	17	328 40	65	N22 39	0	3 46	64	N20 17	0	WED 5
6 THU	182 17	-6	S22 28	7	192 15	-20	S20 25	16	104 20	18	S13 23	16	329 45	66	N22 39	1	4 50	65	N20 17	1	THU 6
7 FRI	182 11	-7	S22 35	7	191 55	-20	S20 41	15	104 38	18	S13 07	17	330 51	66	N22 40	1	5 55	64	N20 16	1	FRI 7
8 SAT	182 04	-6	S22 42	6	191 35	-20	S20 56	14	104 56	18	S12 50	16	331 57	66	N22 41	1	6 59	64	N20 15	0	SAT 8
9 SUN	181 58	-7	S22 48	6	191 15	-21	S21 10	14	105 13	18	S12 34	17	333 03	67	N22 42	1	8 03	65	N20 15	1	SUN 9
10 MON	181 51	-7	S22 54	5	190 54	-20	S21 24	14	105 31	18	S12 17	17	334 10	66	N22 43	0	9 08	64	N20 14	0	MON 10
11 TUE	181 44	-7	S22 59	5	190 34	-21	S21 38	12	105 49	18	S12 00	17	335 16	67	N22 43	1	10 12	64	N20 14	1	TUE 11
12 WED	181 37	-7	S23 04	4	190 13	-22	S21 50	12	106 07	18	S11 43	17	336 23	66	N22 44	1	11 16	64	N20 13	0	WED 12
13 THU	181 30	-7	S23 08	4	189 51	-21	S22 02	12	106 25	18	S11 26	17	337 29	67	N22 46	1	12 20	65	N20 13	1	THU 13
14 FRI	181 23	-7	S23 12	3	189 30	-22	S22 14	10	106 43	18	S11 09	17	338 36	67	N22 46	1	13 25	64	N20 12	1	FRI 14
15 SAT	181 16	-7	S23 15	3	189 08	-22	S22 24	10	107 01	18	S10 52	17	339 43	67	N22 47	1	14 29	64	N20 12	1	SAT 15
16 SUN	181 09	-8	S23 18	3	188 46	-22	S22 34	10	107 19	18	S10 35	18	340 50	67	N22 48	0	15 33	64	N20 11	1	SUN 16
17 MON	181 01	-7	S23 21	2	188 24	-22	S22 44	8	107 37	19	S10 17	17	341 57	67	N22 48	1	16 37	64	N20 10	0	MON 17
18 TUE	180 54	-8	S23 23	1	188 02	-23	S22 52	8	107 56	18	S10 00	18	343 04	68	N22 49	1	17 41	64	N20 10	1	TUE 18
19 WED	180 46	-7	S23 24	2	187 39	-22	S23 00	8	108 14	18	S 9 42	17	344 12	67	N22 50	1	18 45	64	N20 09	0	WED 19
20 THU	180 39	-7	S23 26	0	187 17	-23	S23 08	6	108 32	19	S 9 25	18	345 19	68	N22 51	1	19 49	64	N20 09	1	THU 20
21 FRI	180 32	-8	S23 26	0	186 54	-23	S23 14	6	108 51	18	S 9 07	18	346 27	67	N22 52	1	20 53	64	N20 08	0	FRI 21
22 SAT	180 24	-7	S23 26	0	186 31	-23	S23 20	5	109 09	19	S 8 49	17	347 34	67	N22 53	0	21 57	64	N20 08	1	SAT 22
23 SUN	180 17	-7	S23 26	1	186 08	-23	S23 25	3	109 27	19	S 8 32	18	348 42	67	N22 53	1	23 01	64	N20 07	0	SUN 23
24 MON	180 09	-7	S23 25	1	185 45	-23	S23 30	3	109 46	19	S 8 14	18	349 49	68	N22 54	1	24 05	63	N20 07	0	MON 24
25 TUE	180 02	-8	S23 24	2	185 22	-23	S23 33	3	110 05	18	S 7 56	18	350 57	68	N22 55	1	25 08	64	N20 07	1	TUE 25
26 WED	179 54	-7	S23 22	2	184 59	-24	S23 36	3	110 23	19	S 7 38	18	352 05	68	N22 56	1	26 12	63	N20 06	0	WED 26
27 THU	179 47	-7	S23 20	3	184 35	-23	S23 39	1	110 42	19	S 7 20	18	353 13	68	N22 57	1	27 15	64	N20 06	1	THU 27
28 FRI	179 40	-8	S23 17	3	184 12	-23	S23 40	1	111 01	18	S 7 02	18	354 21	67	N22 58	0	28 19	64	N20 05	0	FRI 28
29 SAT	179 32	-7	S23 14	3	183 49	-23	S23 41	0	111 19	19	S 6 44	18	355 28	68	N22 58	1	29 22	64	N20 05	1	SAT 29
30 SUN	179 25	-7	S23 11	4	183 25	-23	S23 41	1	111 38	19	S 6 26	18	356 36	68	N22 59	1	30 26	63	N20 04	0	SUN 30
31 MON	179 18	-7	S23 07	5	183 02	-23	S23 40	1	111 57	19	S 6 08	18	357 44	68	N23 00	1	31 29	63	N20 04	0	MON 31
32 TUE	179 11		S23 02		182 39		S23 39		112 16		S 5 50		358 52		N23 01		32 32		N20 04		TUE 32

SUN & PLANETS AT GMT 0hrs JANUARY 2002

Day	SUN SD 16' GHA	v	Dec	d	VENUS Mag. -3.9 GHA	v	Dec	d	MARS Mag. +0.9 GHA	v	Dec	d	JUPITER Mag. -2.7 GHA	v	Dec	d	SATURN Mag. -0.2 GHA	v	Dec	d	Day
1 TUE	179° 11'	-7'	S23° 02'	5'	182° 39'	-24'	S23° 39'	2'	112° 16'	19'	S 5° 50'	19'	358° 52'	68'	N23° 01'	1'	32° 32'	64'	N20° 04'	1'	TUE 1
2 WED	179 04	-7	S22 57	5	182 15	-23	S23 37	3	112 35	19	S 5 31	18	0 00	68	N23 02	0	33 36	63	N20 03	0	WED 2
3 THU	178 57	-7	S22 52	6	181 52	-23	S23 34	4	112 54	19	S 5 13	18	1 08	68	N23 02	1	34 39	63	N20 03	0	THU 3
4 FRI	178 50	-7	S22 46	7	181 29	-23	S23 30	4	113 13	19	S 4 55	18	2 16	68	N23 03	1	35 42	63	N20 03	1	FRI 4
5 SAT	178 43	-7	S22 39	7	181 06	-23	S23 26	5	113 32	19	S 4 37	19	3 24	68	N23 04	1	36 45	62	N20 02	0	SAT 5
6 SUN	178 36	-6	S22 32	7	180 43	-23	S23 21	6	113 51	20	S 4 18	18	4 32	68	N23 05	0	37 47	63	N20 02	0	SUN 6
7 MON	178 30	-7	S22 25	7	180 20	-22	S23 15	7	114 11	19	S 4 00	18	5 40	67	N23 05	1	38 50	63	N20 02	1	MON 7
8 TUE	178 23	-6	S22 18	9	179 58	-23	S23 08	7	114 30	19	S 3 42	19	6 47	68	N23 06	1	39 53	62	N20 01	0	TUE 8
9 WED	178 17	-6	S22 09	8	179 35	-22	S23 01	8	114 49	19	S 3 23	18	7 55	68	N23 07	1	40 55	63	N20 01	0	WED 9
10 THU	178 11	-6	S22 01	9	179 13	-23	S22 53	8	115 08	19	S 3 05	19	9 03	68	N23 08	0	41 58	62	N20 01	1	THU 10
11 FRI	178 05	-6	S21 52	10	178 50	-22	S22 45	10	115 27	20	S 2 46	18	10 11	67	N23 08	1	43 00	62	N20 00	0	FRI 11
12 SAT	177 59	-6	S21 42	9	178 28	-22	S22 35	10	115 47	19	S 2 28	18	11 18	68	N23 09	1	44 02	63	N20 00	0	SAT 12
13 SUN	177 53	-6	S21 33	11	178 06	-21	S22 25	11	116 06	19	S 2 10	19	12 26	67	N23 10	1	45 05	62	N20 00	0	SUN 13
14 MON	177 47	-5	S21 22	10	177 45	-22	S22 14	11	116 25	20	S 1 51	18	13 33	67	N23 10	1	46 07	62	N20 00	0	MON 14
15 TUE	177 42	-5	S21 12	11	177 23	-21	S22 03	12	116 45	19	S 1 33	19	14 40	68	N23 11	0	47 09	61	N20 00	1	TUE 15
16 WED	177 37	-6	S21 01	12	177 02	-21	S21 51	13	117 04	20	S 1 14	18	15 48	67	N23 12	1	48 10	62	N19 59	0	WED 16
17 THU	177 31	-5	S20 49	12	176 41	-21	S21 38	13	117 24	19	S 0 56	18	16 55	67	N23 12	1	49 12	62	N19 59	0	THU 17
18 FRI	177 26	-4	S20 37	12	176 20	-20	S21 25	14	117 43	19	S 0 38	19	18 02	67	N23 13	0	50 14	61	N19 59	0	FRI 18
19 SAT	177 22	-5	S20 25	13	176 00	-20	S21 11	15	118 02	20	S 0 19	18	19 09	67	N23 13	1	51 15	62	N19 59	0	SAT 19
20 SUN	177 17	-4	S20 12	13	175 40	-20	S20 56	15	118 22	19	S 0 01	16	20 16	66	N23 14	1	52 17	61	N19 59	0	SUN 20
21 MON	177 13	-4	S19 59	13	175 20	-20	S20 41	16	118 41	20	N 0 17	19	21 22	67	N23 15	0	53 18	61	N19 59	0	MON 21
22 TUE	177 09	-4	S19 46	14	175 00	-19	S20 25	15	119 01	19	N 0 36	18	22 29	67	N23 15	1	54 19	62	N19 59	0	TUE 22
23 WED	177 05	-4	S19 32	14	174 41	-19	S20 09	17	119 20	20	N 0 54	18	23 36	66	N23 16	0	55 21	61	N19 59	0	WED 23
24 THU	177 01	-4	S19 18	15	174 22	-19	S19 52	18	119 40	19	N 1 12	19	24 42	66	N23 16	1	56 22	60	N19 59	0	THU 24
25 FRI	176 57	-3	S19 03	14	174 03	-18	S19 34	18	119 59	20	N 1 31	18	25 48	66	N23 17	0	57 22	61	N19 59	0	FRI 25
26 SAT	176 54	-3	S18 49	16	173 45	-18	S19 16	19	120 19	19	N 1 49	18	26 54	66	N23 17	1	58 23	61	N19 59	0	SAT 26
27 SUN	176 51	-3	S18 33	15	173 27	-18	S18 57	19	120 38	20	N 2 07	18	28 00	65	N23 18	0	59 24	60	N19 59	0	SUN 27
28 MON	176 48	-3	S18 18	16	173 09	-17	S18 38	20	120 58	19	N 2 25	18	29 06	65	N23 18	1	60 24	61	N19 59	0	MON 28
29 TUE	176 45	-3	S18 02	16	172 52	-18	S18 18	21	121 17	20	N 2 43	18	30 11	65	N23 19	0	61 25	60	N19 59	0	TUE 29
30 WED	176 42	-2	S17 46	17	172 34	-16	S17 57	20	121 37	19	N 3 01	18	31 17	65	N23 19	1	62 25	60	N19 59	0	WED 30
31 THU	176 40	-2	S17 29	16	172 18	-17	S17 37	22	121 56	20	N 3 19	18	32 22	65	N23 19	1	63 25	60	N19 59	0	THU 31
32 FRI	176 38		S17 13		172 01		S17 15		122 16		N 3 37		33 27		N23 20		64 25		N19 59		FRI 32

SUN & PLANETS AT GMT 0hrs FEBRUARY 2002

Day	SUN SD 16' GHA	v	Dec	d	VENUS Mag. -3.9 GHA	v	Dec	d	MARS Mag. +1.2 GHA	v	Dec	d	JUPITER Mag. -2.5 GHA	v	Dec	d	SATURN Mag. -0.0 GHA	v	Dec	d	Day
1 FRI	176° 38'	-2'	S17° 13'	17'	172° 01'	-16'	S17° 15'	22'	122° 16'	19'	N 3° 37'	18'	33° 27'	65'	N23° 20'	0'	64° 25'	60'	N19° 59'	0'	FRI 1
2 SAT	176 36	-2	S16 56	18	171 45	-16	S16 53	22	122 35	20	N 3 55	18	34 32	65	N23 20	0	65 25	60	N19 59	0	SAT 2
3 SUN	176 34	-2	S16 38	18	171 29	-16	S16 31	23	122 55	19	N 4 13	18	35 37	64	N23 21	0	66 25	60	N19 59	1	SUN 3
4 MON	176 32	-1	S16 20	18	171 13	-15	S16 08	23	123 14	20	N 4 31	18	36 41	65	N23 21	0	67 25	60	N20 00	0	MON 4
5 TUE	176 31	-1	S16 02	18	170 58	-15	S15 45	24	123 34	19	N 4 49	17	37 46	64	N23 21	1	68 25	59	N20 00	0	TUE 5
6 WED	176 30	-1	S15 44	18	170 43	-15	S15 21	24	123 53	20	N 5 06	18	38 50	64	N23 22	0	69 24	59	N20 00	0	WED 6
7 THU	176 29	-1	S15 26	19	170 28	-14	S14 57	24	124 13	19	N 5 24	18	39 54	64	N23 22	0	70 23	60	N20 00	1	THU 7
8 FRI	176 28	-1	S15 07	19	170 14	-14	S14 33	25	124 32	19	N 5 42	17	40 58	63	N23 22	1	71 23	59	N20 01	0	FRI 8
9 SAT	176 27	0	S14 48	19	170 00	-14	S14 08	26	124 51	20	N 5 59	18	42 01	64	N23 23	0	72 22	59	N20 01	0	SAT 9
10 SUN	176 27	0	S14 29	20	169 46	-13	S13 42	25	125 11	19	N 6 17	17	43 05	63	N23 23	0	73 21	59	N20 01	0	SUN 10
11 MON	176 27	0	S14 09	20	169 33	-14	S13 17	26	125 30	20	N 6 34	17	44 08	63	N23 23	1	74 20	59	N20 01	1	MON 11
12 TUE	176 27	0	S13 49	20	169 19	-13	S12 51	27	125 50	19	N 6 51	18	45 11	63	N23 24	0	75 19	58	N20 02	0	TUE 12
13 WED	176 27	0	S13 29	20	169 06	-12	S12 24	26	126 09	19	N 7 09	17	46 14	62	N23 24	0	76 17	59	N20 02	0	WED 13
14 THU	176 27	1	S13 09	20	168 54	-13	S11 58	27	126 28	19	N 7 26	17	47 16	63	N23 24	0	77 16	58	N20 02	1	THU 14
15 FRI	176 28	0	S12 49	21	168 41	-12	S11 31	28	126 47	20	N 7 43	17	48 19	62	N23 24	1	78 14	58	N20 03	0	FRI 15
16 SAT	176 28	1	S12 28	21	168 29	-12	S11 03	27	127 07	19	N 8 00	17	49 21	62	N23 25	0	79 12	59	N20 03	1	SAT 16
17 SUN	176 29	1	S12 07	21	168 17	-12	S10 36	28	127 26	19	N 8 17	17	50 23	62	N23 25	0	80 11	58	N20 04	0	SUN 17
18 MON	176 30	2	S11 46	21	168 05	-11	S10 08	28	127 45	19	N 8 34	17	51 25	61	N23 25	0	81 09	58	N20 04	0	MON 18
19 TUE	176 32	1	S11 25	21	167 54	-11	S 9 40	29	128 04	19	N 8 51	16	52 26	61	N23 25	0	82 07	57	N20 04	1	TUE 19
20 WED	176 33	2	S11 04	22	167 43	-11	S 9 11	29	128 23	19	N 9 07	17	53 27	62	N23 25	1	83 04	58	N20 05	0	WED 20
21 THU	176 35	1	S10 42	22	167 32	-11	S 8 42	28	128 42	20	N 9 24	16	54 29	60	N23 26	0	84 02	58	N20 05	1	THU 21
22 FRI	176 36	3	S10 20	22	167 21	-11	S 8 14	30	129 02	19	N 9 40	17	55 29	61	N23 26	0	85 00	57	N20 06	0	FRI 22
23 SAT	176 38	2	S 9 58	22	167 10	-10	S 7 44	29	129 21	19	N 9 57	16	56 30	61	N23 26	0	85 57	58	N20 06	1	SAT 23
24 SUN	176 41	2	S 9 36	22	167 00	-11	S 7 15	29	129 40	18	N10 13	16	57 31	60	N23 26	0	86 55	57	N20 07	0	SUN 24
25 MON	176 43	2	S 9 14	22	166 49	-10	S 6 46	30	129 58	19	N10 29	16	58 31	60	N23 26	0	87 52	57	N20 07	1	MON 25
26 TUE	176 45	3	S 8 52	23	166 39	-10	S 6 16	30	130 17	19	N10 45	16	59 31	60	N23 26	1	88 49	57	N20 08	1	TUE 26
27 WED	176 48	2	S 8 29	22	166 29	-9	S 5 46	30	130 36	19	N11 01	16	60 31	59	N23 27	0	89 46	57	N20 09	0	WED 27
28 THU	176 50	3	S 8 07	23	166 20	-10	S 5 16	30	130 55	19	N11 17	16	61 30	60	N23 27	0	90 43	57	N20 09	1	THU 28
29 FRI	176 53		S 7 44		166 10		S 4 46		131 14		N11 33		62 30		N23 27		91 40		N20 10		FRI 29

SUN & PLANETS AT GMT 0hrs MARCH 2002

Day	SUN SD 16' GHA	v	Dec	d	VENUS Mag. -3.9 GHA	v	Dec	d	MARS Mag. +1.4 GHA	v	Dec	d	JUPITER Mag. -2.3 GHA	v	Dec	d	SATURN Mag. +0.1 GHA	v	Dec	d	Day
1 FRI	176° 53'	3'	S 7° 44'	23'	166° 10'	-9'	S 4° 46'	30'	131° 14'	19'	N11° 33'	16'	62° 30'	59'	N23° 27'	0'	91° 40'	56'	N20° 10'	0'	FRI 1
2 SAT	176 56	3	S 7 21	23	166 01	-10	S 4 16	31	131 33	18	N11 49	15	63 29	59	N23 27	0	92 36	57	N20 10	1	SAT 2
3 SUN	176 59	3	S 6 58	23	165 51	-9	S 3 45	30	131 51	19	N12 04	16	64 28	58	N23 27	0	93 33	56	N20 11	1	SUN 3
4 MON	177 02	4	S 6 35	23	165 42	-9	S 3 15	31	132 10	19	N12 20	15	65 26	59	N23 27	0	94 29	57	N20 12	0	MON 4
5 TUE	177 06	4	S 6 12	23	165 33	-9	S 2 44	30	132 29	18	N12 35	15	66 25	58	N23 27	0	95 26	56	N20 12	1	TUE 5
6 WED	177 09	4	S 5 49	23	165 24	-9	S 2 14	31	132 47	19	N12 50	15	67 23	58	N23 27	0	96 22	56	N20 13	1	WED 6
7 THU	177 13	3	S 5 26	23	165 15	-9	S 1 43	31	133 06	18	N13 05	15	68 21	58	N23 27	0	97 18	56	N20 14	0	THU 7
8 FRI	177 16	4	S 5 03	24	165 06	-9	S 1 12	31	133 24	19	N13 20	15	69 19	58	N23 27	0	98 14	56	N20 14	1	FRI 8
9 SAT	177 20	4	S 4 39	23	164 57	-9	S 0 41	30	133 43	18	N13 35	15	70 17	57	N23 27	0	99 10	56	N20 15	1	SAT 9
10 SUN	177 24	3	S 4 16	24	164 48	-9	S 0 11	9	134 01	18	N13 50	15	71 14	58	N23 27	0	100 06	55	N20 16	1	SUN 10
11 MON	177 27	4	S 3 52	23	164 39	-9	N 0 20	31	134 19	19	N14 05	14	72 12	57	N23 27	0	101 01	56	N20 17	0	MON 11
12 TUE	177 31	4	S 3 29	24	164 30	-8	N 0 51	31	134 38	18	N14 19	14	73 09	56	N23 27	0	101 57	56	N20 17	1	TUE 12
13 WED	177 35	4	S 3 05	24	164 22	-9	N 1 22	31	134 56	18	N14 33	15	74 05	57	N23 27	0	102 53	55	N20 18	1	WED 13
14 THU	177 39	5	S 2 41	23	164 13	-9	N 1 53	31	135 14	18	N14 48	14	75 02	57	N23 27	0	103 48	55	N20 19	1	THU 14
15 FRI	177 44	4	S 2 18	24	164 04	-9	N 2 24	30	135 32	18	N15 02	14	75 59	56	N23 27	0	104 43	55	N20 20	0	FRI 15
16 SAT	177 48	4	S 1 54	24	163 55	-9	N 2 54	31	135 50	18	N15 16	13	76 55	56	N23 27	0	105 38	56	N20 20	1	SAT 16
17 SUN	177 52	4	S 1 30	24	163 46	-9	N 3 25	31	136 08	18	N15 29	14	77 51	56	N23 27	0	106 34	55	N20 21	1	SUN 17
18 MON	177 56	5	S 1 06	23	163 37	-8	N 3 56	30	136 26	18	N15 43	14	78 47	55	N23 27	0	107 29	54	N20 22	1	MON 18
19 TUE	178 01	4	S 0 43	24	163 29	-9	N 4 26	31	136 44	18	N15 57	13	79 42	56	N23 27	0	108 23	55	N20 23	1	TUE 19
20 WED	178 05	4	S 0 19	14	163 20	-10	N 4 57	30	137 02	17	N16 10	13	80 38	55	N23 27	0	109 18	55	N20 24	1	WED 20
21 THU	178 09	5	N 0 05	24	163 10	-9	N 5 27	30	137 19	18	N16 23	13	81 33	55	N23 27	0	110 13	55	N20 25	0	THU 21
22 FRI	178 14	4	N 0 28	24	163 01	-9	N 5 57	30	137 37	18	N16 36	13	82 28	55	N23 27	0	111 08	54	N20 25	1	FRI 22
23 SAT	178 18	5	N 0 52	24	162 52	-9	N 6 27	30	137 55	17	N16 49	13	83 23	54	N23 27	0	112 02	54	N20 26	1	SAT 23
24 SUN	178 23	5	N 1 16	23	162 43	-10	N 6 57	30	138 12	18	N17 02	13	84 17	55	N23 27	0	112 56	55	N20 27	1	SUN 24
25 MON	178 28	4	N 1 39	24	162 33	-9	N 7 27	30	138 30	17	N17 15	12	85 12	54	N23 27	1	113 51	54	N20 28	1	MON 25
26 TUE	178 32	5	N 2 03	23	162 24	-10	N 7 57	29	138 47	18	N17 27	12	86 06	54	N23 27	0	114 45	54	N20 29	1	TUE 26
27 WED	178 37	4	N 2 26	24	162 14	-10	N 8 26	30	139 05	17	N17 39	13	87 00	54	N23 26	0	115 39	54	N20 30	1	WED 27
28 THU	178 41	5	N 2 50	23	162 04	-10	N 8 56	29	139 22	17	N17 52	12	87 54	54	N23 26	0	116 33	54	N20 31	1	THU 28
29 FRI	178 46	4	N 3 13	24	161 54	-10	N 9 25	28	139 39	18	N18 04	11	88 48	53	N23 26	0	117 27	54	N20 32	1	FRI 29
30 SAT	178 50	5	N 3 37	23	161 44	-10	N 9 53	29	139 57	17	N18 15	12	89 41	53	N23 26	0	118 21	54	N20 33	1	SAT 30
31 SUN	178 55	4	N 4 00	23	161 34	-10	N10 22	28	140 14	17	N18 27	12	90 34	54	N23 26	1	119 15	54	N20 34	0	SUN 31
32 MON	178 59		N 4 23		161 24		N10 50		140 31		N18 39		91 28		N23 25		120 09		N20 34		MON 32

SUN & PLANETS AT GMT 0hrs APRIL 2002

Day	SUN SD 16' GHA	v	Dec	d	VENUS Mag. -3.9 GHA	v	Dec	d	MARS Mag. +1.6 GHA	v	Dec	d	JUPITER Mag. -2.1 GHA	v	Dec	d	SATURN Mag. +0.1 GHA	v	Dec	d	Day
1 MON	178° 59'	5'	N 4° 23'	23'	161° 24'	-11'	N10° 50'	29'	140° 31'	17'	N18° 39'	11'	91° 28'	53'	N23° 25'	0'	120° 09'	53'	N20° 34'	1'	MON 1
2 TUE	179 04	4	N 4 46	23	161 13	-11	N11 19	27	140 48	17	N18 50	11	92 21	52	N23 25	0	121 02	54	N20 35	1	TUE 2
3 WED	179 08	5	N 5 09	23	161 02	-11	N11 46	28	141 05	17	N19 01	11	93 13	53	N23 25	0	121 56	53	N20 36	1	WED 3
4 THU	179 13	4	N 5 32	23	160 51	-11	N12 14	27	141 22	17	N19 12	11	94 06	53	N23 25	1	122 49	54	N20 37	1	THU 4
5 FRI	179 17	4	N 5 55	23	160 40	-11	N12 41	27	141 39	17	N19 23	10	94 59	52	N23 24	0	123 43	53	N20 38	1	FRI 5
6 SAT	179 21	5	N 6 18	23	160 29	-12	N13 08	27	141 56	17	N19 33	11	95 51	52	N23 24	0	124 36	53	N20 39	1	SAT 6
7 SUN	179 26	4	N 6 41	22	160 17	-12	N13 35	26	142 13	16	N19 44	10	96 43	52	N23 24	0	125 29	54	N20 40	1	SUN 7
8 MON	179 30	4	N 7 03	23	160 05	-12	N14 01	26	142 29	17	N19 54	10	97 35	52	N23 24	1	126 23	53	N20 41	1	MON 8
9 TUE	179 34	4	N 7 26	22	159 53	-12	N14 27	26	142 46	17	N20 04	10	98 27	52	N23 23	0	127 16	53	N20 42	1	TUE 9
10 WED	179 38	4	N 7 48	22	159 41	-13	N14 53	25	143 03	16	N20 14	10	99 19	51	N23 23	0	128 09	53	N20 43	1	WED 10
11 THU	179 42	4	N 8 10	22	159 28	-13	N15 18	25	143 19	17	N20 24	10	100 10	51	N23 23	0	129 02	53	N20 44	1	THU 11
12 FRI	179 46	4	N 8 32	22	159 15	-13	N15 43	24	143 36	16	N20 32	9	101 01	52	N23 22	0	129 55	52	N20 45	1	FRI 12
13 SAT	179 50	4	N 8 54	22	159 02	-13	N16 07	23	143 52	16	N20 43	9	101 53	51	N23 22	1	130 47	53	N20 46	1	SAT 13
14 SUN	179 54	3	N 9 16	21	158 49	-14	N16 32	23	144 09	16	N20 52	9	102 44	51	N23 21	0	131 40	53	N20 47	1	SUN 14
15 MON	179 57	4	N 9 37	22	158 35	-14	N16 55	24	144 25	16	N21 01	9	103 35	50	N23 21	0	132 33	52	N20 48	1	MON 15
16 TUE	180 01	4	N 9 59	21	158 21	-14	N17 19	22	144 41	17	N21 10	9	104 25	51	N23 21	1	133 25	53	N20 49	1	TUE 16
17 WED	180 05	3	N10 20	21	158 07	-14	N17 41	23	144 58	16	N21 19	8	105 16	50	N23 20	0	134 18	52	N20 50	1	WED 17
18 THU	180 08	3	N10 41	21	157 53	-15	N18 04	22	145 14	16	N21 27	9	106 06	51	N23 19	0	135 10	53	N20 51	1	THU 18
19 FRI	180 11	4	N11 02	21	157 38	-15	N18 26	21	145 30	16	N21 36	8	106 57	50	N23 19	1	136 03	52	N20 52	1	FRI 19
20 SAT	180 15	3	N11 23	20	157 23	-15	N18 47	21	145 46	16	N21 44	8	107 47	50	N23 19	0	136 55	53	N20 53	1	SAT 20
21 SUN	180 18	3	N11 43	21	157 08	-16	N19 08	20	146 02	16	N21 52	8	108 37	50	N23 18	0	137 48	52	N20 54	1	SUN 21
22 MON	180 21	3	N12 04	20	156 52	-15	N19 28	20	146 18	16	N22 00	7	109 27	50	N23 18	1	138 40	52	N20 55	1	MON 22
23 TUE	180 24	3	N12 24	20	156 37	-16	N19 48	20	146 34	16	N22 07	7	110 17	50	N23 17	0	139 32	52	N20 56	1	TUE 23
24 WED	180 27	2	N12 44	20	156 21	-17	N20 08	19	146 50	16	N22 14	8	111 07	49	N23 17	1	140 24	52	N20 57	1	WED 24
25 THU	180 29	3	N13 04	19	156 04	-16	N20 27	18	147 06	16	N22 22	7	111 56	50	N23 16	0	141 16	52	N20 58	1	THU 25
26 FRI	180 32	2	N13 23	19	155 48	-17	N20 45	18	147 22	16	N22 29	6	112 46	49	N23 15	0	142 08	52	N20 59	1	FRI 26
27 SAT	180 34	3	N13 42	19	155 31	-17	N21 03	17	147 38	16	N22 35	7	113 35	49	N23 15	1	143 00	52	N21 00	1	SAT 27
28 SUN	180 37	2	N14 02	18	155 14	-17	N21 20	16	147 54	16	N22 42	6	114 24	49	N23 14	1	143 52	52	N21 01	1	SUN 28
29 MON	180 39	2	N14 20	19	154 57	-18	N21 36	16	148 10	16	N22 48	6	115 13	49	N23 13	0	144 44	52	N21 02	1	MON 29
30 TUE	180 41	2	N14 39	18	154 39	-17	N21 52	16	148 26	15	N22 54	6	116 02	49	N23 13	1	145 36	52	N21 03	1	TUE 30
31 WED	180 43		N14 57		154 22		N22 08		148 41		N23 00		116 51		N23 12		146 28		N21 04		WED 31

SUN & PLANETS AT GMT 0hrs MAY 2002

Day	SUN SD 16' GHA	v	Dec	d	VENUS Mag. -4.0 GHA	v	Dec	d	MARS Mag. +1.7 GHA	v	Dec	d	JUPITER Mag. -1.9 GHA	v	Dec	d	SATURN Mag. +0.1 GHA	v	Dec	d	Day
1 WED	180° 43'	2	N14° 57'	18	154° 22'	-18	N22° 08'	15	148° 41'	16	N23° 00'	6	116° 51'	49	N23° 12'	1	146° 28'	51	N21° 04'	1	WED 1
2 THU	180 45	2	N15 15	18	154 04	-18	N22 23	14	148 57	16	N23 06	6	117 40	48	N23 11	0	147 19	52	N21 05	1	THU 2
3 FRI	180 47	1	N15 33	18	153 46	-19	N22 37	13	149 13	16	N23 12	5	118 28	49	N23 11	1	148 11	52	N21 06	1	FRI 3
4 SAT	180 48	1	N15 51	17	153 27	-18	N22 50	13	149 29	15	N23 17	5	119 17	48	N23 10	1	149 03	51	N21 07	1	SAT 4
5 SUN	180 49	2	N16 08	17	153 09	-19	N23 03	13	149 44	16	N23 22	5	120 05	48	N23 09	1	149 54	52	N21 08	1	SUN 5
6 MON	180 51	1	N16 25	17	152 50	-19	N23 16	11	150 00	16	N23 27	5	120 53	49	N23 08	1	150 46	51	N21 09	1	MON 6
7 TUE	180 52	1	N16 42	17	152 31	-19	N23 27	11	150 16	15	N23 32	4	121 42	48	N23 07	0	151 37	52	N21 10	1	TUE 7
8 WED	180 53	1	N16 59	16	152 12	-20	N23 38	11	150 31	16	N23 36	5	122 30	48	N23 07	1	152 29	51	N21 11	1	WED 8
9 THU	180 54	0	N17 15	16	151 52	-19	N23 49	9	150 47	15	N23 41	4	123 18	48	N23 06	1	153 20	52	N21 12	1	THU 9
10 FRI	180 54	1	N17 31	16	151 33	-20	N23 58	9	151 02	16	N23 45	4	124 06	47	N23 05	1	154 12	51	N21 13	1	FRI 10
11 SAT	180 55	0	N17 47	15	151 13	-20	N24 07	9	151 18	15	N23 49	4	124 53	48	N23 04	1	155 03	51	N21 14	1	SAT 11
12 SUN	180 55	0	N18 02	15	150 53	-19	N24 16	7	151 33	16	N23 53	3	125 41	48	N23 03	1	155 54	51	N21 15	1	SUN 12
13 MON	180 55	0	N18 17	15	150 34	-20	N24 23	7	151 49	16	N23 56	3	126 29	47	N23 02	1	156 45	52	N21 16	1	MON 13
14 TUE	180 56	-1	N18 32	14	150 14	-20	N24 30	6	152 05	15	N24 00	3	127 16	48	N23 01	1	157 37	51	N21 17	1	TUE 14
15 WED	180 55	0	N18 46	14	149 54	-20	N24 36	6	152 20	16	N24 03	3	128 04	47	N23 00	1	158 28	51	N21 18	1	WED 15
16 THU	180 55	0	N19 00	14	149 34	-21	N24 42	5	152 36	15	N24 06	2	128 51	47	N22 59	1	159 19	51	N21 19	0	THU 16
17 FRI	180 55	0	N19 14	14	149 13	-20	N24 47	4	152 51	16	N24 08	3	129 38	47	N22 58	1	160 10	51	N21 19	1	FRI 17
18 SAT	180 55	-1	N19 28	13	148 53	-20	N24 51	3	153 07	15	N24 11	2	130 25	47	N22 57	1	161 01	51	N21 20	1	SAT 18
19 SUN	180 54	-1	N19 41	13	148 33	-20	N24 54	3	153 22	16	N24 13	2	131 12	47	N22 56	1	161 52	52	N21 21	1	SUN 19
20 MON	180 53	-1	N19 54	12	148 13	-20	N24 57	2	153 38	15	N24 15	2	131 59	47	N22 55	1	162 44	51	N21 22	1	MON 20
21 TUE	180 52	-1	N20 06	12	147 53	-21	N24 59	1	153 53	15	N24 17	2	132 46	47	N22 54	2	163 35	51	N21 23	1	TUE 21
22 WED	180 51	-1	N20 18	12	147 32	-20	N25 00	1	154 09	16	N24 19	1	133 33	47	N22 52	1	164 26	51	N21 24	1	WED 22
23 THU	180 50	-1	N20 30	12	147 12	-20	N25 01	0	154 25	15	N24 20	2	134 20	47	N22 51	1	165 17	51	N21 25	1	THU 23
24 FRI	180 49	-1	N20 42	11	146 52	-20	N25 01	1	154 40	16	N24 22	1	135 07	46	N22 50	1	166 08	51	N21 26	1	FRI 24
25 SAT	180 48	-2	N20 53	10	146 32	-20	N25 00	2	154 56	16	N24 23	1	135 53	47	N22 49	2	166 59	50	N21 27	0	SAT 25
26 SUN	180 46	-1	N21 03	11	146 12	-19	N24 58	2	155 12	15	N24 24	0	136 40	46	N22 48	2	167 49	51	N21 27	1	SUN 26
27 MON	180 45	-2	N21 14	10	145 53	-20	N24 56	3	155 27	16	N24 24	1	137 26	47	N22 46	2	168 40	51	N21 28	1	MON 27
28 TUE	180 43	-2	N21 24	9	145 33	-20	N24 53	4	155 43	16	N24 25	0	138 13	46	N22 45	1	169 31	51	N21 29	1	TUE 28
29 WED	180 41	-2	N21 33	10	145 13	-19	N24 49	4	155 59	15	N24 25	0	138 59	47	N22 44	2	170 22	51	N21 30	1	WED 29
30 THU	180 39	-2	N21 43	8	144 54	-19	N24 45	5	156 14	16	N24 25	0	139 46	46	N22 42	1	171 13	51	N21 31	1	THU 30
31 FRI	180 37	-2	N21 51	9	144 35	-19	N24 40	6	156 30	16	N24 25	0	140 32	46	N22 41	2	172 04	51	N21 32	0	FRI 31
32 SAT	180 35		N22 00		144 16		N24 34		156 46		N24 25		141 18		N22 39		172 55		N21 32		SAT 32

SUN & PLANETS AT GMT 0hrs JUNE 2002

Day	SUN SD 16' GHA	v	Dec	d	VENUS Mag. -4.1 GHA	v	Dec	d	MARS Mag. +1.7 GHA	v	Dec	d	JUPITER Mag. -1.8 GHA	v	Dec	d	SATURN Mag. +0.0 GHA	v	Dec	d	Day
1 SAT	180° 35'	-2	N22° 00'	8	144° 16'	-19	N24° 34'	7	156° 46'	16	N24° 25'	1	141° 18'	46	N22° 39'	1	172° 55'	51	N21° 32'	1	SAT 1
2 SUN	180 33	-3	N22 08	8	143 57	-19	N24 27	7	157 02	16	N24 24	1	142 04	46	N22 38	1	173 46	50	N21 33	1	SUN 2
3 MON	180 30	-2	N22 16	7	143 38	-18	N24 20	8	157 18	16	N24 23	1	142 50	46	N22 37	2	174 36	51	N21 34	1	MON 3
4 TUE	180 28	-3	N22 23	7	143 20	-18	N24 12	8	157 34	16	N24 22	1	143 36	46	N22 35	1	175 27	51	N21 35	1	TUE 4
5 WED	180 25	-3	N22 30	7	143 02	-18	N24 04	9	157 50	16	N24 21	1	144 22	46	N22 34	2	176 18	51	N21 36	0	WED 5
6 THU	180 22	-2	N22 37	6	142 44	-18	N23 55	10	158 06	16	N24 20	2	145 08	46	N22 32	1	177 09	51	N21 36	1	THU 6
7 FRI	180 20	-3	N22 43	6	142 26	-17	N23 45	11	158 22	16	N24 18	1	145 54	46	N22 31	2	178 00	50	N21 37	1	FRI 7
8 SAT	180 17	-3	N22 49	5	142 09	-17	N23 34	11	158 38	16	N24 17	2	146 40	46	N22 29	2	178 50	51	N21 38	1	SAT 8
9 SUN	180 14	-3	N22 54	5	141 52	-17	N23 23	12	158 54	16	N24 15	2	147 26	45	N22 27	1	179 41	51	N21 39	0	SUN 9
10 MON	180 11	-3	N22 59	4	141 35	-16	N23 11	12	159 10	16	N24 13	3	148 11	46	N22 26	2	180 32	51	N21 39	1	MON 10
11 TUE	180 08	-3	N23 03	5	141 19	-16	N22 59	13	159 26	17	N24 10	2	148 57	46	N22 24	1	181 23	51	N21 40	1	TUE 11
12 WED	180 05	-3	N23 08	3	141 03	-16	N22 46	14	159 43	16	N24 08	3	149 43	45	N22 23	2	182 14	50	N21 41	1	WED 12
13 THU	180 02	-3	N23 11	4	140 47	-16	N22 32	14	159 59	17	N24 05	3	150 28	46	N22 21	2	183 04	51	N21 42	0	THU 13
14 FRI	179 59	-4	N23 15	3	140 31	-15	N22 18	15	160 16	16	N24 02	3	151 14	45	N22 19	2	183 55	51	N21 42	1	FRI 14
15 SAT	179 55	-3	N23 17	3	140 16	-14	N22 03	15	160 32	16	N23 59	4	151 59	46	N22 17	1	184 46	51	N21 43	1	SAT 15
16 SUN	179 52	-3	N23 20	2	140 02	-15	N21 48	16	160 48	17	N23 56	4	152 45	45	N22 16	2	185 37	51	N21 44	0	SUN 16
17 MON	179 49	-3	N23 22	2	139 47	-14	N21 32	17	161 05	17	N23 52	3	153 30	46	N22 14	2	186 28	50	N21 44	1	MON 17
18 TUE	179 46	-4	N23 24	1	139 33	-14	N21 15	17	161 22	16	N23 49	4	154 16	45	N22 12	2	187 18	51	N21 45	1	TUE 18
19 WED	179 42	-3	N23 25	1	139 19	-13	N20 58	17	161 38	17	N23 45	4	155 01	45	N22 10	2	188 09	51	N21 46	0	WED 19
20 THU	179 39	-3	N23 26	0	139 06	-13	N20 41	19	161 55	17	N23 41	4	155 46	46	N22 08	2	189 00	51	N21 46	1	THU 20
21 FRI	179 36	-3	N23 26	0	138 53	-12	N20 22	18	162 12	17	N23 37	5	156 32	45	N22 06	1	189 51	51	N21 47	1	FRI 21
22 SAT	179 33	-4	N23 26	1	138 41	-12	N20 04	19	162 29	17	N23 32	4	157 17	45	N22 05	2	190 42	51	N21 48	1	SAT 22
23 SUN	179 29	-3	N23 26	1	138 29	-12	N19 45	20	162 46	17	N23 28	5	158 02	45	N22 03	2	191 33	50	N21 48	0	SUN 23
24 MON	179 26	-3	N23 25	1	138 17	-11	N19 25	20	163 03	17	N23 23	5	158 47	46	N22 01	2	192 23	51	N21 49	1	MON 24
25 TUE	179 23	-3	N23 24	2	138 06	-11	N19 05	21	163 20	17	N23 18	5	159 33	45	N21 59	2	193 14	51	N21 49	0	TUE 25
26 WED	179 20	-3	N23 22	2	137 55	-11	N18 44	21	163 37	18	N23 13	6	160 18	45	N21 57	2	194 05	51	N21 50	1	WED 26
27 THU	179 17	-3	N23 20	2	137 44	-10	N18 23	21	163 55	17	N23 07	5	161 03	45	N21 55	2	194 56	51	N21 51	0	THU 27
28 FRI	179 14	-3	N23 18	3	137 34	-9	N18 02	22	164 12	17	N23 02	6	161 48	45	N21 53	2	195 47	51	N21 51	1	FRI 28
29 SAT	179 11	-3	N23 15	3	137 25	-10	N17 40	22	164 29	18	N22 56	5	162 33	45	N21 51	3	196 38	51	N21 52	1	SAT 29
30 SUN	179 08	-3	N23 12	4	137 15	-9	N17 18	23	164 47	18	N22 51	6	163 18	45	N21 48	2	197 29	51	N21 52	1	SUN 30
31 MON	179 05		N23 08		137 06		N16 55		165 05		N22 45		164 03		N21 46		198 20		N21 53		MON 31

SUN & PLANETS AT GMT 0hrs JULY 2002

Day	SUN SD 16' GHA	v	Dec	d	VENUS Mag. -4.2 GHA	v	Dec	d	MARS Mag. +1.8 GHA	v	Dec	d	JUPITER Mag. -1.8 GHA	v	Dec	d	SATURN Mag. +0.1 GHA	v	Dec	d	Day
1 MON	179°05'	-3'	N23°08'	4'	137°06'	-8'	N16°55'	23'	165°05'	17'	N22°45'	7'	164°03'	46'	N21°46'	2'	198°20'	51'	N21°53'	0'	MON 1
2 TUE	179 02	-3	N23 04	5	136 58	-8	N16 32	24	165 22	18	N22 38	6	164 49	45	N21 44	2	199 11	51	N21 53	1	TUE 2
3 WED	178 59	-3	N22 59	5	136 50	-8	N16 08	24	165 40	18	N22 32	6	165 34	45	N21 42	2	200 02	51	N21 54	0	WED 3
4 THU	178 56	-3	N22 55	6	136 42	-7	N15 44	24	165 58	18	N22 26	7	166 19	45	N21 40	2	200 53	51	N21 54	1	THU 4
5 FRI	178 53	-2	N22 49	5	136 35	-7	N15 20	24	166 16	18	N22 19	7	167 04	45	N21 38	3	201 44	51	N21 55	0	FRI 5
6 SAT	178 51	-3	N22 44	6	136 28	-7	N14 56	25	166 34	18	N22 12	7	167 49	45	N21 35	2	202 35	52	N21 55	1	SAT 6
7 SUN	178 48	-2	N22 38	7	136 21	-6	N14 31	26	166 52	18	N22 05	7	168 34	45	N21 33	2	203 27	51	N21 56	0	SUN 7
8 MON	178 46	-2	N22 31	7	136 15	-6	N14 05	25	167 10	18	N21 58	7	169 19	45	N21 31	2	204 18	51	N21 56	1	MON 8
9 TUE	178 44	-3	N22 24	7	136 09	-5	N13 40	26	167 28	19	N21 51	8	170 04	45	N21 29	3	205 09	51	N21 57	0	TUE 9
10 WED	178 41	-2	N22 17	8	136 04	-5	N13 14	26	167 47	18	N21 43	8	170 49	45	N21 26	2	206 00	52	N21 57	1	WED 10
11 THU	178 39	-2	N22 09	8	135 59	-5	N12 48	27	168 05	18	N21 35	7	171 34	45	N21 24	2	206 52	51	N21 58	0	THU 11
12 FRI	178 37	-2	N22 01	8	135 54	-4	N12 21	26	168 23	19	N21 28	8	172 19	45	N21 22	3	207 43	51	N21 58	0	FRI 12
13 SAT	178 35	-2	N21 53	9	135 50	-4	N11 55	27	168 42	19	N21 20	8	173 04	45	N21 19	2	208 34	52	N21 58	1	SAT 13
14 SUN	178 33	-1	N21 44	9	135 46	-4	N11 28	28	169 01	18	N21 12	9	173 49	45	N21 17	3	209 26	51	N21 59	0	SUN 14
15 MON	178 32	-2	N21 35	9	135 42	-3	N11 00	27	169 19	19	N21 03	9	174 34	45	N21 14	2	210 17	51	N21 59	1	MON 15
16 TUE	178 30	-1	N21 26	10	135 39	-3	N10 33	28	169 38	19	N20 55	9	175 19	45	N21 12	3	211 08	52	N22 00	0	TUE 16
17 WED	178 29	-1	N21 16	10	135 36	-2	N10 05	28	169 57	19	N20 46	8	176 04	45	N21 09	2	212 00	52	N22 00	0	WED 17
18 THU	178 28	-2	N21 06	11	135 34	-3	N 9 37	28	170 16	19	N20 38	9	176 49	45	N21 07	2	212 52	51	N22 00	1	THU 18
19 FRI	178 26	-1	N20 55	11	135 31	-1	N 9 09	28	170 35	20	N20 29	9	177 34	45	N21 05	3	213 43	52	N22 01	0	FRI 19
20 SAT	178 25	0	N20 44	11	135 30	-2	N 8 41	28	170 55	19	N20 20	9	178 19	45	N21 02	3	214 35	51	N22 01	0	SAT 20
21 SUN	178 25	-1	N20 33	12	135 28	-1	N 8 13	29	171 14	19	N20 11	10	179 04	45	N20 59	2	215 26	52	N22 01	1	SUN 21
22 MON	178 24	-1	N20 21	12	135 27	-1	N 7 44	29	171 33	20	N20 01	9	179 49	45	N20 57	3	216 18	52	N22 02	0	MON 22
23 TUE	178 23	0	N20 09	12	135 26	-1	N 7 15	29	171 53	19	N19 52	9	180 34	45	N20 54	2	217 10	52	N22 02	0	TUE 23
24 WED	178 23	0	N19 57	13	135 25	0	N 6 46	29	172 12	20	N19 43	10	181 19	45	N20 52	3	218 02	52	N22 02	1	WED 24
25 THU	178 23	-1	N19 44	13	135 25	1	N 6 17	29	172 32	20	N19 33	10	182 04	45	N20 49	2	218 54	52	N22 03	0	THU 25
26 FRI	178 22	1	N19 31	13	135 25	1	N 5 48	29	172 52	20	N19 23	10	182 49	45	N20 47	3	219 46	52	N22 03	0	FRI 26
27 SAT	178 23	0	N19 18	14	135 26	0	N 5 19	29	173 12	20	N19 13	10	183 34	46	N20 44	3	220 38	52	N22 03	0	SAT 27
28 SUN	178 23	0	N19 04	14	135 26	1	N 4 50	30	173 32	20	N19 03	10	184 20	45	N20 41	2	221 30	52	N22 03	1	SUN 28
29 MON	178 23	0	N18 50	14	135 27	2	N 4 20	29	173 52	20	N18 53	11	185 05	45	N20 39	3	222 22	52	N22 04	0	MON 29
30 TUE	178 23	0	N18 36	14	135 29	1	N 3 51	30	174 12	20	N18 42	10	185 50	45	N20 36	3	223 14	52	N22 04	0	TUE 30
31 WED	178 24	1	N18 22	15	135 30	2	N 3 21	29	174 32	20	N18 32	11	186 35	45	N20 33	2	224 06	52	N22 04	0	WED 31
32 THU	178 25		N18 07		135 32		N 2 52		174 52		N18 21		187 20		N20 31		224 58		N22 04		THU 32

SUN & PLANETS AT GMT 0hrs AUGUST 2002

Day	SUN SD 16' GHA	v	Dec	d	VENUS Mag. -4.4 GHA	v	Dec	d	MARS Mag. +1.7 GHA	v	Dec	d	JUPITER Mag. -1.8 GHA	v	Dec	d	SATURN Mag. +0.1 GHA	v	Dec	d	Day
1 THU	178°25'	1'	N18°07'	15'	135°32'	2'	N 2°52'	30'	174°52'	20'	N18°21'	10'	187°20'	46'	N20°31'	3'	224°58'	53'	N22°04'	1'	THU 1
2 FRI	178 26	1	N17 52	16	135 34	3	N 2 22	30	175 13	20	N18 11	11	188 06	45	N20 28	3	225 51	52	N22 05	0	FRI 2
3 SAT	178 27	1	N17 36	15	135 37	3	N 1 52	30	175 33	21	N18 00	11	188 51	45	N20 25	3	226 43	52	N22 05	0	SAT 3
4 SUN	178 28	1	N17 21	16	135 40	3	N 1 22	29	175 54	20	N17 49	11	189 36	45	N20 22	2	227 35	53	N22 05	0	SUN 4
5 MON	178 29	2	N17 05	17	135 43	3	N 0 53	30	176 14	21	N17 38	11	190 21	46	N20 20	3	228 28	52	N22 05	0	MON 5
6 TUE	178 31	2	N16 48	16	135 46	3	N 0 23	16	176 35	21	N17 27	12	191 07	45	N20 17	3	229 20	53	N22 05	1	TUE 6
7 WED	178 33	2	N16 32	17	135 49	4	S 0 07	30	176 56	21	N17 15	11	191 52	46	N20 14	3	230 13	53	N22 06	0	WED 7
8 THU	178 34	2	N16 15	17	135 53	4	S 0 37	29	177 17	21	N17 04	12	192 38	45	N20 11	3	231 06	53	N22 06	0	THU 8
9 FRI	178 36	2	N15 58	17	135 57	5	S 1 06	30	177 38	21	N16 52	11	193 23	45	N20 08	2	231 58	53	N22 06	0	FRI 9
10 SAT	178 38	3	N15 41	18	136 02	4	S 1 36	30	177 59	21	N16 41	12	194 08	46	N20 06	3	232 51	53	N22 06	0	SAT 10
11 SUN	178 41	2	N15 23	18	136 06	5	S 2 06	29	178 20	21	N16 29	12	194 54	45	N20 03	3	233 44	53	N22 06	0	SUN 11
12 MON	178 43	3	N15 05	18	136 11	5	S 2 35	30	178 41	22	N16 17	12	195 39	46	N20 00	3	234 37	53	N22 06	1	MON 12
13 TUE	178 46	2	N14 47	18	136 16	6	S 3 05	29	179 03	21	N16 05	12	196 25	46	N19 57	3	235 30	53	N22 07	0	TUE 13
14 WED	178 48	3	N14 29	19	136 22	6	S 3 34	29	179 24	21	N15 53	12	197 11	46	N19 54	3	236 23	53	N22 07	0	WED 14
15 THU	178 51	3	N14 10	18	136 27	6	S 4 03	30	179 45	22	N15 41	12	197 56	46	N19 51	3	237 16	54	N22 07	0	THU 15
16 FRI	178 54	3	N13 52	19	136 33	7	S 4 33	29	180 07	22	N15 29	13	198 42	46	N19 48	3	238 10	53	N22 07	0	FRI 16
17 SAT	178 57	3	N13 33	20	136 40	6	S 5 02	29	180 29	21	N15 16	12	199 28	46	N19 45	2	239 03	54	N22 07	0	SAT 17
18 SUN	179 00	4	N13 13	19	136 46	7	S 5 31	29	180 50	22	N15 04	13	200 14	45	N19 43	3	239 56	54	N22 07	0	SUN 18
19 MON	179 04	3	N12 54	20	136 53	7	S 6 00	28	181 12	22	N14 51	12	200 59	46	N19 40	3	240 50	53	N22 07	0	MON 19
20 TUE	179 07	4	N12 34	19	137 00	8	S 6 28	29	181 34	22	N14 39	13	201 45	46	N19 37	3	241 43	54	N22 07	1	TUE 20
21 WED	179 11	3	N12 15	20	137 08	7	S 6 57	28	181 56	22	N14 26	13	202 31	46	N19 34	3	242 37	54	N22 08	0	WED 21
22 THU	179 14	4	N11 55	21	137 15	9	S 7 25	29	182 18	22	N14 13	13	203 17	46	N19 31	3	243 31	54	N22 08	0	THU 22
23 FRI	179 18	4	N11 34	20	137 24	8	S 7 54	29	182 40	22	N14 00	13	204 03	46	N19 28	3	244 25	54	N22 08	0	FRI 23
24 SAT	179 22	4	N11 14	20	137 32	9	S 8 22	28	183 02	22	N13 47	13	204 49	46	N19 25	3	245 19	54	N22 08	0	SAT 24
25 SUN	179 26	4	N10 54	21	137 41	9	S 8 50	27	183 24	23	N13 34	13	205 35	47	N19 22	3	246 13	54	N22 08	0	SUN 25
26 MON	179 30	5	N10 33	21	137 50	9	S 9 17	28	183 47	22	N13 21	13	206 22	46	N19 19	3	247 07	54	N22 08	0	MON 26
27 TUE	179 35	4	N10 12	21	137 59	10	S 9 45	27	184 09	22	N13 08	14	207 08	46	N19 16	3	248 01	54	N22 08	0	TUE 27
28 WED	179 39	4	N 9 51	21	138 09	10	S10 12	27	184 31	23	N12 54	13	207 54	46	N19 13	3	248 55	55	N22 08	0	WED 28
29 THU	179 43	5	N 9 30	22	138 19	11	S10 39	27	184 54	22	N12 41	14	208 40	47	N19 10	3	249 49	55	N22 08	0	THU 29
30 FRI	179 48	5	N 9 08	21	138 30	11	S11 06	26	185 16	23	N12 27	13	209 27	46	N19 07	3	250 44	54	N22 08	0	FRI 30
31 SAT	179 53	4	N 8 47	22	138 41	11	S11 32	27	185 39	23	N12 14	14	210 13	47	N19 04	3	251 38	55	N22 08	0	SAT 31
32 SUN	179 57		N 8 25		138 52		S11 59		186 02		N12 00		211 00		N19 01		252 33		N22 08		SUN 32

SUN & PLANETS AT GMT 0hrs SEPTEMBER 2002

Day	GHA	v	Dec	d	GHA	v	Dec	d	GHA	v	Dec	d	GHA	v	Dec	d	GHA	v	Dec	d	Day
	SUN SD 16'				VENUS Mag. -4.6				MARS Mag. +1.8				JUPITER Mag. -1.9				SATURN Mag. +0.1				
1 SUN	179° 57'	5'	N 8 25'	21'	138° 52'	12'	S11 59'	26'	186° 02'	22'	N12 00'	13'	211° 00'	46'	N19° 01'	2'	252° 33'	55'	N22° 08'	0'	SUN 1
2 MON	180 02	5	N 8 04	22	139 04	12	S12 25	25	186 24	23	N11 47	14	211 46	47	N18 59	3	253 28	54	N22 08	0	MON 2
3 TUE	180 07	5	N 7 42	22	139 16	13	S12 50	26	186 47	23	N11 33	14	212 33	47	N18 56	3	254 22	55	N22 08	0	TUE 3
4 WED	180 12	5	N 7 20	23	139 29	13	S13 16	25	187 10	23	N11 19	14	213 20	46	N18 53	3	255 17	55	N22 08	0	WED 4
5 THU	180 17	5	N 6 57	22	139 42	14	S13 41	25	187 33	23	N11 05	14	214 06	47	N18 50	3	256 12	55	N22 08	0	THU 5
6 FRI	180 22	5	N 6 35	22	139 56	14	S14 06	24	187 56	23	N10 51	14	214 53	47	N18 47	3	257 07	56	N22 08	0	FRI 6
7 SAT	180 27	5	N 6 13	23	140 10	15	S14 30	24	188 19	23	N10 37	14	215 40	47	N18 44	3	258 03	55	N22 08	0	SAT 7
8 SUN	180 32	5	N 5 50	22	140 25	16	S14 54	24	188 42	23	N10 23	14	216 27	47	N18 41	3	258 58	55	N22 08	0	SUN 8
9 MON	180 37	5	N 5 28	23	140 41	16	S15 18	23	189 05	23	N10 09	15	217 14	47	N18 38	3	259 53	56	N22 08	0	MON 9
10 TUE	180 42	5	N 5 05	23	140 57	16	S15 41	23	189 28	24	N 9 54	14	218 01	47	N18 35	3	260 49	55	N22 08	0	TUE 10
11 WED	180 47	5	N 4 42	22	141 13	18	S16 04	23	189 52	23	N 9 40	14	218 48	48	N18 32	3	261 44	56	N22 08	0	WED 11
12 THU	180 52	6	N 4 20	23	141 31	18	S16 27	22	190 15	24	N 9 26	15	219 36	47	N18 29	3	262 40	56	N22 08	0	THU 12
13 FRI	180 58	5	N 3 57	23	141 49	19	S16 49	22	190 38	24	N 9 11	14	220 23	47	N18 26	3	263 36	56	N22 08	0	FRI 13
14 SAT	181 03	5	N 3 34	23	142 08	19	S17 11	21	191 02	23	N 8 57	15	221 10	48	N18 23	3	264 32	56	N22 08	0	SAT 14
15 SUN	181 08	6	N 3 11	23	142 27	21	S17 32	21	191 25	23	N 8 42	14	221 58	48	N18 20	2	265 28	56	N22 08	0	SUN 15
16 MON	181 14	5	N 2 48	24	142 48	21	S17 53	21	191 48	24	N 8 28	15	222 46	47	N18 18	3	266 24	56	N22 08	0	MON 16
17 TUE	181 19	5	N 2 24	23	143 09	23	S18 14	20	192 12	24	N 8 13	14	223 33	48	N18 15	3	267 20	57	N22 08	0	TUE 17
18 WED	181 24	6	N 2 01	23	143 32	23	S18 34	19	192 36	23	N 7 59	15	224 21	48	N18 12	3	268 16	57	N22 08	0	WED 18
19 THU	181 30	5	N 1 38	23	143 55	24	S18 53	19	192 59	24	N 7 44	15	225 09	48	N18 09	3	269 13	56	N22 08	0	THU 19
20 FRI	181 35	6	N 1 15	24	144 19	26	S19 12	19	193 23	23	N 7 29	15	225 57	48	N18 06	3	270 09	57	N22 08	0	FRI 20
21 SAT	181 41	5	N 0 51	23	144 45	26	S19 31	18	193 46	24	N 7 14	14	226 45	48	N18 03	2	271 06	57	N22 08	0	SAT 21
22 SUN	181 46	5	N 0 28	23	145 11	28	S19 49	17	194 10	24	N 7 00	15	227 33	48	N18 01	3	272 03	57	N22 08	0	SUN 22
23 MON	181 51	5	N 0 05	14	145 39	29	S20 06	17	194 34	24	N 6 45	15	228 21	48	N17 58	3	273 00	57	N22 08	0	MON 23
24 TUE	181 56	6	S 0 19	23	146 08	30	S20 23	16	194 58	23	N 6 30	15	229 09	48	N17 55	3	273 57	57	N22 08	0	TUE 24
25 WED	182 02	5	S 0 42	23	146 38	32	S20 39	16	195 21	24	N 6 15	15	229 58	48	N17 52	2	274 54	57	N22 08	0	WED 25
26 THU	182 07	5	S 1 05	24	147 10	33	S20 55	15	195 45	24	N 6 00	15	230 46	49	N17 49	3	275 51	58	N22 08	0	THU 26
27 FRI	182 12	5	S 1 29	23	147 43	35	S21 10	14	196 09	24	N 5 45	15	231 35	48	N17 47	3	276 49	57	N22 08	0	FRI 27
28 SAT	182 17	5	S 1 52	23	148 18	36	S21 24	14	196 33	24	N 5 30	15	232 23	49	N17 44	3	277 46	58	N22 08	0	SAT 28
29 SUN	182 22	5	S 2 15	24	148 54	37	S21 38	12	196 57	24	N 5 15	15	233 12	49	N17 41	3	278 44	57	N22 08	1	SUN 29
30 MON	182 27	5	S 2 39	23	149 31	40	S21 50	12	197 21	24	N 5 00	16	234 01	49	N17 39	3	279 41	58	N22 07	0	MON 30
31 TUE	182 32		S 3 02		150 11		S22 02		197 45		N 4 44		234 50		N17 36		280 39		N22 07		TUE 31

SUN & PLANETS AT GMT 0hrs OCTOBER 2002

Day	GHA	v	Dec	d	GHA	v	Dec	d	GHA	v	Dec	d	GHA	v	Dec	d	GHA	v	Dec	d	Day
	SUN SD 16'				VENUS Mag. -4.4				MARS Mag. +1.8				JUPITER Mag. -2.0				SATURN Mag. -0.1				
1 TUE	182° 32'	5'	S 3 02'	23'	150° 11'	41'	S22° 02'	12'	197° 45'	24'	N 4 44'	15'	234° 50'	49'	N17° 36'	3'	280° 39'	58'	N22° 07'	0'	TUE 1
2 WED	182 37	5	S 3 25	23	150 52	43	S22 14	10	198 09	24	N 4 29	15	235 39	49	N17 33	2	281 37	58	N22 07	0	WED 2
3 THU	182 42	5	S 3 48	24	151 35	45	S22 24	10	198 33	24	N 4 14	15	236 28	49	N17 31	3	282 35	58	N22 07	0	THU 3
4 FRI	182 46	5	S 4 12	23	152 20	46	S22 34	9	198 57	24	N 3 59	15	237 17	50	N17 28	3	283 33	59	N22 07	0	FRI 4
5 SAT	182 51	4	S 4 35	23	153 06	49	S22 43	8	199 21	24	N 3 44	16	238 07	49	N17 25	2	284 32	58	N22 07	0	SAT 5
6 SUN	182 55	5	S 4 58	23	153 55	51	S22 51	7	199 45	24	N 3 28	15	238 56	50	N17 23	3	285 30	59	N22 07	0	SUN 6
7 MON	183 00	4	S 5 21	23	154 46	52	S22 58	6	200 09	24	N 3 13	15	239 46	50	N17 20	2	286 29	58	N22 07	0	MON 7
8 TUE	183 04	4	S 5 44	23	155 38	55	S23 04	5	200 33	24	N 2 58	15	240 36	50	N17 18	3	287 27	59	N22 07	0	TUE 8
9 WED	183 08	4	S 6 07	23	156 33	58	S23 09	4	200 57	24	N 2 43	16	241 26	49	N17 15	2	288 26	59	N22 07	0	WED 9
10 THU	183 12	4	S 6 30	22	157 31	59	S23 13	3	201 21	24	N 2 27	15	242 15	51	N17 13	3	289 25	59	N22 07	0	THU 10
11 FRI	183 16	4	S 6 52	23	158 30	62	S23 16	2	201 45	24	N 2 12	15	243 06	50	N17 11	3	290 24	59	N22 07	0	FRI 11
12 SAT	183 20	4	S 7 15	22	159 32	64	S23 18	0	202 09	24	N 1 57	16	243 56	50	N17 08	2	291 23	59	N22 07	0	SAT 12
13 SUN	183 24	4	S 7 37	23	160 36	66	S23 18	1	202 33	24	N 1 41	15	244 46	51	N17 06	2	292 22	60	N22 07	0	SUN 13
14 MON	183 28	3	S 8 00	22	161 42	69	S23 17	1	202 57	24	N 1 26	16	245 37	50	N17 04	3	293 22	59	N22 07	0	MON 14
15 TUE	183 31	3	S 8 22	22	162 51	71	S23 16	4	203 21	24	N 1 10	15	246 27	51	N17 01	2	294 21	60	N22 07	0	TUE 15
16 WED	183 34	4	S 8 44	22	164 02	73	S23 12	4	203 45	25	N 0 55	16	247 18	51	N16 59	2	295 21	59	N22 07	0	WED 16
17 THU	183 38	3	S 9 06	22	165 15	75	S23 08	6	204 10	24	N 0 40	16	248 09	51	N16 57	3	296 20	60	N22 07	1	THU 17
18 FRI	183 41	3	S 9 28	22	166 30	78	S23 02	8	204 34	24	N 0 24	15	249 00	51	N16 55	3	297 20	60	N22 06	0	FRI 18
19 SAT	183 44	2	S 9 50	22	167 48	80	S22 54	8	204 58	24	N 0 09	3	249 51	51	N16 52	2	298 20	60	N22 06	0	SAT 19
20 SUN	183 46	3	S10 12	21	169 08	81	S22 46	11	205 22	24	S 0 06	16	250 42	51	N16 50	2	299 20	61	N22 06	0	SUN 20
21 MON	183 49	2	S10 33	22	170 29	84	S22 35	11	205 46	24	S 0 22	15	251 33	52	N16 48	2	300 21	60	N22 06	0	MON 21
22 TUE	183 51	3	S10 55	21	171 53	85	S22 24	13	206 10	24	S 0 37	15	252 25	52	N16 46	2	301 21	60	N22 06	0	TUE 22
23 WED	183 54	2	S11 16	21	173 18	87	S22 11	15	206 34	24	S 0 52	16	253 17	51	N16 44	2	302 21	61	N22 06	0	WED 23
24 THU	183 56	2	S11 37	21	174 45	87	S21 56	15	206 58	24	S 1 08	15	254 08	52	N16 42	2	303 22	61	N22 06	0	THU 24
25 FRI	183 58	1	S11 58	20	176 12	90	S21 41	17	207 22	24	S 1 23	15	255 00	52	N16 40	2	304 23	60	N22 06	0	FRI 25
26 SAT	183 59	2	S12 18	21	177 42	90	S21 24	19	207 46	24	S 1 38	16	255 52	53	N16 38	2	305 23	61	N22 06	0	SAT 26
27 SUN	184 01	1	S12 39	20	179 12	90	S21 05	19	208 10	24	S 1 54	15	256 45	52	N16 36	2	306 24	61	N22 06	0	SUN 27
28 MON	184 02	2	S12 59	20	180 42	91	S20 46	21	208 34	24	S 2 09	15	257 37	52	N16 34	1	307 25	61	N22 06	0	MON 28
29 TUE	184 04	1	S13 19	20	182 13	92	S20 25	21	208 58	24	S 2 24	16	258 29	53	N16 33	2	308 26	62	N22 06	0	TUE 29
30 WED	184 05	0	S13 39	20	183 45	91	S20 04	22	209 22	24	S 2 40	15	259 22	53	N16 31	2	309 28	61	N22 06	0	WED 30
31 THU	184 05	1	S13 59	19	185 16	91	S19 42	23	209 46	24	S 2 55	15	260 15	53	N16 29	1	310 29	62	N22 06	0	THU 31
32 FRI	184 06		S14 18		186 47		S19 19		210 10		S 3 10		261 08		N16 28		311 31		N22 06		FRI 32

SUN & PLANETS AT GMT 0hrs NOVEMBER 2002

Day	SUN SD 16' GHA	v	Dec	d	VENUS Mag. -4.4 GHA	v	Dec	d	MARS Mag. +1.8 GHA	v	Dec	d	JUPITER Mag. -2.2 GHA	v	Dec	d	SATURN Mag. -0.3 GHA	v	Dec	d	Day
1 FRI	184° 06'	0'	S14° 18'	19'	186° 47'	91'	S19° 19'	24'	210° 10'	24'	S 3° 10'	15'	261° 08'	53'	N16° 28'	2'	311° 31'	61'	N22° 06'	0'	FRI	1
2 SAT	184 06	0	S14 37	19	188 18	90	S18 55	24	210 34	23	S 3 25	16	262 01	53	N16 26	2	312 32	62	N22 06	0	SAT	2
3 SUN	184 06	0	S14 56	19	189 48	89	S18 31	24	210 57	24	S 3 41	15	262 54	54	N16 24	1	313 34	62	N22 06	0	SUN	3
4 MON	184 06	0	S15 15	18	191 17	89	S18 07	25	211 21	24	S 3 56	15	263 48	53	N16 23	2	314 36	61	N22 06	0	MON	4
5 TUE	184 06	0	S15 33	19	192 46	87	S17 42	25	211 45	24	S 4 11	15	264 41	54	N16 21	1	315 37	63	N22 06	1	TUE	5
6 WED	184 06	-1	S15 52	18	194 13	85	S17 17	24	212 09	23	S 4 26	15	265 35	54	N16 20	1	316 40	62	N22 05	0	WED	6
7 THU	184 05	-1	S16 10	17	195 38	84	S16 53	25	212 32	24	S 4 41	15	266 29	54	N16 19	2	317 42	62	N22 05	0	THU	7
8 FRI	184 04	-1	S16 27	18	197 02	83	S16 28	24	212 56	24	S 4 56	15	267 23	54	N16 17	1	318 44	62	N22 05	0	FRI	8
9 SAT	184 03	-1	S16 45	17	198 25	80	S16 04	24	213 20	23	S 5 11	15	268 17	55	N16 16	1	319 46	63	N22 05	0	SAT	9
10 SUN	184 02	-2	S17 02	17	199 45	79	S15 40	23	213 43	24	S 5 26	15	269 12	55	N16 15	1	320 49	62	N22 05	0	SUN	10
11 MON	184 00	-1	S17 19	16	201 04	76	S15 17	23	214 07	24	S 5 41	15	270 07	54	N16 14	1	321 51	63	N22 05	0	MON	11
12 TUE	183 59	-2	S17 35	16	202 20	75	S14 54	22	214 31	23	S 5 56	15	271 01	55	N16 13	1	322 54	62	N22 05	0	TUE	12
13 WED	183 57	-2	S17 51	16	203 35	72	S14 32	20	214 54	23	S 6 11	15	271 56	55	N16 12	1	323 56	63	N22 05	0	WED	13
14 THU	183 55	-2	S18 07	16	204 47	69	S14 12	21	215 18	23	S 6 26	14	272 51	56	N16 11	1	324 59	63	N22 05	0	THU	14
15 FRI	183 53	-3	S18 23	15	205 56	68	S13 51	19	215 41	23	S 6 40	15	273 47	55	N16 10	1	326 02	63	N22 05	0	FRI	15
16 SAT	183 50	-3	S18 38	15	207 04	65	S13 32	18	216 04	24	S 6 55	15	274 42	56	N16 09	1	327 05	63	N22 05	0	SAT	16
17 SUN	183 47	-3	S18 53	15	208 09	63	S13 14	16	216 28	23	S 7 10	15	275 38	56	N16 08	1	328 08	63	N22 05	0	SUN	17
18 MON	183 44	-3	S19 08	14	209 12	61	S12 58	16	216 51	23	S 7 25	14	276 34	56	N16 07	1	329 11	63	N22 05	0	MON	18
19 TUE	183 41	-3	S19 22	14	210 13	58	S12 42	15	217 14	23	S 7 39	15	277 30	56	N16 06	0	330 14	64	N22 05	0	TUE	19
20 WED	183 38	-4	S19 36	13	211 11	57	S12 27	13	217 37	24	S 7 54	14	278 26	56	N16 06	1	331 18	63	N22 05	0	WED	20
21 THU	183 34	-3	S19 49	14	212 08	53	S12 14	13	218 01	23	S 8 08	15	279 22	57	N16 05	1	332 21	64	N22 05	0	THU	21
22 FRI	183 31	-4	S20 03	12	213 01	52	S12 01	11	218 24	23	S 8 23	14	280 19	57	N16 04	0	333 25	63	N22 05	0	FRI	22
23 SAT	183 27	-4	S20 15	13	213 53	50	S11 50	10	218 47	23	S 8 37	14	281 16	57	N16 04	1	334 28	63	N22 05	0	SAT	23
24 SUN	183 23	-5	S20 28	12	214 43	47	S11 40	8	219 10	23	S 8 51	15	282 13	57	N16 03	0	335 32	63	N22 05	1	SUN	24
25 MON	183 18	-4	S20 40	12	215 30	46	S11 32	8	219 33	23	S 9 06	14	283 10	57	N16 03	0	336 35	64	N22 04	0	MON	25
26 TUE	183 14	-5	S20 52	11	216 16	43	S11 24	6	219 56	22	S 9 20	14	284 07	58	N16 03	1	337 39	64	N22 04	0	TUE	26
27 WED	183 09	-5	S21 03	11	216 59	42	S11 18	6	220 18	23	S 9 34	14	285 05	57	N16 02	0	338 43	64	N22 04	0	WED	27
28 THU	183 04	-5	S21 14	10	217 41	40	S11 12	4	220 41	23	S 9 48	14	286 02	58	N16 02	0	339 47	64	N22 04	0	THU	28
29 FRI	182 59	-5	S21 24	11	218 21	37	S11 08	3	221 04	22	S10 02	14	287 00	58	N16 02	0	340 51	64	N22 04	0	FRI	29
30 SAT	182 54	-6	S21 35	9	218 58	37	S11 05	2	221 26	23	S10 16	14	287 58	59	N16 02	0	341 55	64	N22 04	0	SAT	30
31 SUN	182 48		S21 44		219 35		S11 03		221 49		S10 30		288 57		N16 02		342 59		N22 04		SUN	31

SUN & PLANETS AT GMT 0hrs DECEMBER 2002

Day	SUN SD 16' GHA	v	Dec	d	VENUS Mag. -4.7 GHA	v	Dec	d	MARS Mag. +1.6 GHA	v	Dec	d	JUPITER Mag. -2.4 GHA	v	Dec	d	SATURN Mag. -0.5 GHA	v	Dec	d	Day
1 SUN	182° 48'	-5'	S21° 44'	10'	219° 35'	34'	S11° 03'	2'	221° 49'	23'	S10° 30'	14'	288° 57'	58'	N16° 02'	0'	342° 59'	64'	N22° 04'	0'	SUN	1
2 MON	182 43	-6	S21 54	8	220 09	33	S11 01	0	222 12	22	S10 44	14	289 55	59	N16 02	0	344 03	64	N22 04	0	MON	2
3 TUE	182 37	-6	S22 02	9	220 42	31	S11 01	1	222 34	22	S10 58	13	290 54	59	N16 02	0	345 07	64	N22 04	0	TUE	3
4 WED	182 31	-6	S22 11	8	221 13	30	S11 02	1	222 56	23	S11 11	14	291 53	59	N16 02	0	346 11	64	N22 04	0	WED	4
5 THU	182 25	-6	S22 19	8	221 43	28	S11 03	3	223 19	22	S11 25	13	292 52	59	N16 02	1	347 15	64	N22 04	0	THU	5
6 FRI	182 19	-7	S22 27	7	222 11	27	S11 06	3	223 41	22	S11 38	14	293 51	59	N16 03	0	348 19	65	N22 04	0	FRI	6
7 SAT	182 12	-7	S22 34	6	222 38	26	S11 09	4	224 03	22	S11 52	13	294 50	60	N16 03	0	349 24	64	N22 04	0	SAT	7
8 SUN	182 06	-7	S22 40	5	223 04	24	S11 13	4	224 25	22	S12 05	14	295 50	60	N16 04	0	350 28	64	N22 04	0	SUN	8
9 MON	181 59	-7	S22 47	5	223 28	23	S11 18	5	224 47	22	S12 19	13	296 50	60	N16 04	0	351 32	65	N22 04	0	MON	9
10 TUE	181 52	-6	S22 52	6	223 51	21	S11 23	6	225 09	22	S12 32	13	297 50	60	N16 04	1	352 37	64	N22 04	1	TUE	10
11 WED	181 46	-7	S22 58	5	224 12	21	S11 29	7	225 31	22	S12 45	13	298 50	61	N16 05	0	353 41	65	N22 03	0	WED	11
12 THU	181 39	-7	S23 03	4	224 33	19	S11 36	7	225 53	22	S12 58	13	299 51	60	N16 06	0	354 46	64	N22 03	0	THU	12
13 FRI	181 32	-7	S23 07	4	224 52	19	S11 43	8	226 15	22	S13 11	13	300 51	61	N16 06	1	355 50	65	N22 03	0	FRI	13
14 SAT	181 25	-8	S23 11	4	225 11	17	S11 51	8	226 37	22	S13 24	13	301 52	61	N16 07	1	356 55	64	N22 03	0	SAT	14
15 SUN	181 17	-7	S23 15	3	225 28	16	S11 59	9	226 59	21	S13 37	12	302 53	61	N16 08	1	357 59	65	N22 03	0	SUN	15
16 MON	181 10	-7	S23 18	2	225 44	15	S12 08	10	227 20	22	S13 49	13	303 54	62	N16 09	1	359 03	65	N22 03	0	MON	16
17 TUE	181 03	-7	S23 20	1	225 59	14	S12 18	9	227 42	21	S14 02	12	304 56	61	N16 10	1	0 08	64	N22 03	0	TUE	17
18 WED	180 56	-8	S23 23	1	226 13	13	S12 27	11	228 03	21	S14 14	13	305 57	62	N16 11	1	1 12	65	N22 03	0	WED	18
19 THU	180 48	-7	S23 24	1	226 26	13	S12 38	10	228 24	22	S14 27	12	306 59	62	N16 12	1	2 17	64	N22 03	0	THU	19
20 FRI	180 41	-7	S23 25	1	226 39	11	S12 48	11	228 46	21	S14 39	12	308 01	62	N16 13	1	3 21	65	N22 03	0	FRI	20
21 SAT	180 34	-8	S23 26	0	226 50	10	S12 59	12	229 07	21	S14 51	12	309 03	62	N16 14	1	4 26	64	N22 03	0	SAT	21
22 SUN	180 26	-7	S23 26	0	227 00	10	S13 11	11	229 28	21	S15 03	12	310 05	63	N16 15	2	5 30	65	N22 03	0	SUN	22
23 MON	180 19	-8	S23 26	0	227 10	9	S13 22	12	229 49	21	S15 15	12	311 08	63	N16 17	1	6 35	64	N22 03	0	MON	23
24 TUE	180 11	-7	S23 26	0	227 19	8	S13 34	12	230 10	21	S15 27	12	312 11	63	N16 18	1	7 39	65	N22 03	0	TUE	24
25 WED	180 04	-8	S23 24	1	227 27	7	S13 46	12	230 31	21	S15 39	11	313 14	63	N16 19	2	8 44	64	N22 03	0	WED	25
26 THU	179 56	-7	S23 23	2	227 34	6	S13 58	13	230 52	21	S15 50	12	314 17	63	N16 21	1	9 48	64	N22 03	1	THU	26
27 FRI	179 49	-7	S23 21	3	227 40	6	S14 11	12	231 13	20	S16 02	11	315 20	63	N16 22	2	10 52	65	N22 02	0	FRI	27
28 SAT	179 42	-8	S23 18	3	227 46	5	S14 23	13	231 33	21	S16 13	12	316 23	64	N16 24	1	11 57	64	N22 02	0	SAT	28
29 SUN	179 34	-7	S23 15	3	227 51	4	S14 36	13	231 54	21	S16 25	11	317 27	64	N16 25	2	13 01	64	N22 02	0	SUN	29
30 MON	179 27	-7	S23 12	4	227 55	4	S14 49	13	232 15	20	S16 36	11	318 31	64	N16 27	2	14 05	64	N22 02	0	MON	30
31 TUE	179 20	-8	S23 08	5	227 59	2	S15 02	13	232 35	20	S16 47	11	319 35	64	N16 29	1	15 09	65	N22 02	0	TUE	31
32 WED	179 12		S23 03		228 01		S15 15		232 55		S16 58		320 39		N16 31		16 14		N22 02		WED	32

SUN & PLANETS AT GMT 0hrs JANUARY 2003

	SUN SD 16'				VENUS Mag. -4.5				MARS Mag. +1.4				JUPITER Mag. -2.6				SATURN Mag. -0.3				
Day	GHA	v	Dec	d	GHA	v	Dec	d	GHA	v	Dec	d	GHA	v	Dec	d	GHA	v	Dec	d	Day
1 WED	179° 12'	-7'	S23° 03'	5'	228° 01'	3'	S15° 15'	13'	232° 55'	21'	S16° 58'	11'	320° 39'	64'	N16° 31'	1'	16° 14'	64'	N22° 02'	0'	WED 1
2 THU	179 05	-7	S22 58	5	228 04	1	S15 28	13	233 16	20	S17 09	10	321 43	64	N16 32	2	17 18	64	N22 02	0	THU 2
3 FRI	178 58	-7	S22 53	6	228 05	1	S15 41	13	233 36	20	S17 19	11	322 47	65	N16 34	2	18 22	64	N22 02	0	FRI 3
4 SAT	178 51	-7	S22 47	6	228 06	0	S15 54	13	233 56	20	S17 30	11	323 52	65	N16 36	2	19 26	64	N22 02	0	SAT 4
5 SUN	178 44	-6	S22 41	7	228 06	0	S16 07	13	234 16	20	S17 41	10	324 57	65	N16 38	2	20 30	64	N22 02	0	SUN 5
6 MON	178 38	-7	S22 34	7	228 06	-1	S16 20	13	234 36	20	S17 51	10	326 02	65	N16 40	2	21 34	64	N22 02	0	MON 6
7 TUE	178 31	-6	S22 27	8	228 05	-1	S16 33	13	234 56	20	S18 01	10	327 07	65	N16 42	2	22 38	64	N22 02	0	TUE 7
8 WED	178 25	-7	S22 19	8	228 04	-2	S16 46	12	235 16	20	S18 11	10	328 12	65	N16 44	2	23 42	63	N22 02	0	WED 8
9 THU	178 18	-6	S22 11	8	228 02	-3	S16 58	13	235 36	19	S18 21	10	329 17	66	N16 46	2	24 45	64	N22 02	0	THU 9
10 FRI	178 12	-6	S22 03	9	227 59	-3	S17 11	12	235 55	20	S18 31	10	330 23	65	N16 48	2	25 49	64	N22 02	0	FRI 10
11 SAT	178 06	-6	S21 54	9	227 56	-4	S17 23	12	236 15	19	S18 41	9	331 28	66	N16 50	2	26 53	63	N22 02	0	SAT 11
12 SUN	178 00	-6	S21 45	10	227 52	-4	S17 35	12	236 34	20	S18 50	10	332 34	66	N16 52	3	27 56	64	N22 02	0	SUN 12
13 MON	177 54	-5	S21 35	10	227 48	-5	S17 47	12	236 54	19	S19 00	9	333 40	66	N16 55	2	29 00	63	N22 02	0	MON 13
14 TUE	177 49	-6	S21 25	11	227 43	-5	S17 59	12	237 13	20	S19 09	9	334 46	66	N16 57	2	30 03	63	N22 02	0	TUE 14
15 WED	177 43	-5	S21 14	11	227 38	-6	S18 11	11	237 33	19	S19 18	9	335 52	66	N16 59	2	31 06	64	N22 02	0	WED 15
16 THU	177 38	-5	S21 03	11	227 32	-6	S18 22	11	237 52	19	S19 27	9	336 58	66	N17 01	3	32 10	63	N22 02	0	THU 16
17 FRI	177 33	-5	S20 52	12	227 26	-6	S18 33	11	238 11	19	S19 36	8	338 04	67	N17 04	2	33 13	63	N22 02	0	FRI 17
18 SAT	177 28	-5	S20 40	12	227 20	-7	S18 44	10	238 30	19	S19 44	9	339 11	66	N17 06	2	34 16	63	N22 02	0	SAT 18
19 SUN	177 23	-5	S20 28	13	227 13	-8	S18 54	11	238 49	19	S19 53	8	340 17	67	N17 08	3	35 19	63	N22 02	0	SUN 19
20 MON	177 18	-4	S20 15	13	227 05	-8	S19 05	10	239 08	19	S20 01	9	341 23	67	N17 11	2	36 22	63	N22 02	0	MON 20
21 TUE	177 14	-4	S20 02	13	226 57	-9	S19 15	9	239 27	19	S20 10	8	342 30	67	N17 13	2	37 25	62	N22 02	0	TUE 21
22 WED	177 10	-4	S19 49	14	226 48	-8	S19 24	9	239 46	19	S20 18	8	343 37	67	N17 15	3	38 27	63	N22 02	0	WED 22
23 THU	177 06	-4	S19 35	14	226 40	-10	S19 33	9	240 05	18	S20 26	8	344 44	66	N17 18	2	39 30	63	N22 02	0	THU 23
24 FRI	177 02	-4	S19 21	14	226 30	-9	S19 42	9	240 23	19	S20 34	7	345 50	67	N17 20	2	40 33	62	N22 02	0	FRI 24
25 SAT	176 58	-3	S19 07	15	226 21	-10	S19 51	8	240 42	19	S20 41	8	346 57	67	N17 22	3	41 35	62	N22 02	0	SAT 25
26 SUN	176 55	-4	S18 52	15	226 11	-11	S19 59	7	241 01	18	S20 49	7	348 04	67	N17 25	2	42 37	63	N22 02	0	SUN 26
27 MON	176 51	-3	S18 37	15	226 00	-11	S20 06	8	241 19	19	S20 56	7	349 11	67	N17 27	3	43 40	62	N22 02	0	MON 27
28 TUE	176 48	-3	S18 22	16	225 49	-11	S20 14	6	241 38	18	S21 03	7	350 18	67	N17 30	2	44 42	62	N22 02	0	TUE 28
29 WED	176 45	-2	S18 06	16	225 38	-11	S20 20	7	241 56	18	S21 10	7	351 25	67	N17 32	2	45 44	62	N22 02	0	WED 29
30 THU	176 43	-3	S17 50	17	225 27	-12	S20 27	6	242 14	19	S21 17	7	352 32	67	N17 34	3	46 46	62	N22 02	0	THU 30
31 FRI	176 40	-2	S17 33	16	225 15	-12	S20 33	5	242 33	18	S21 24	6	353 39	68	N17 37	2	47 48	61	N22 02	0	FRI 31
32 SAT	176 38		S17 17		225 03		S20 38		242 51		S21 30		354 47		N17 39		48 49		N22 02		SAT 32

SUN & PLANETS AT GMT 0hrs FEBRUARY 2003

	SUN SD 16'				VENUS Mag. -4.3				MARS Mag. +1.1				JUPITER Mag. -2.6				SATURN Mag. -0.1				
Day	GHA	v	Dec	d	GHA	v	Dec	d	GHA	v	Dec	d	GHA	v	Dec	d	GHA	v	Dec	d	Day
1 SAT	176° 38'	-2'	S17° 17'	17'	225° 03'	-12'	S20° 38'	5'	242° 51'	18'	S21° 30'	7'	354° 47'	67'	N17° 39'	3'	48° 49'	62'	N22° 02'	0'	SAT 1
2 SUN	176 36	-2	S17 00	17	224 51	-13	S20 43	4	243 09	18	S21 37	6	355 54	67	N17 42	2	49 51	61	N22 02	0	SUN 2
3 MON	176 34	-2	S16 42	17	224 38	-13	S20 47	4	243 27	18	S21 43	6	357 01	67	N17 44	2	50 52	62	N22 02	0	MON 3
4 TUE	176 32	-1	S16 25	18	224 25	-13	S20 51	4	243 45	18	S21 49	6	358 08	67	N17 46	3	51 54	61	N22 02	0	TUE 4
5 WED	176 31	-1	S16 07	18	224 12	-14	S20 55	3	244 03	18	S21 55	6	359 15	67	N17 49	2	52 55	61	N22 02	1	WED 5
6 THU	176 30	-1	S15 49	19	223 58	-13	S20 58	2	244 21	18	S22 01	5	0 22	68	N17 51	3	53 56	61	N22 03	0	THU 6
7 FRI	176 29	-1	S15 30	19	223 45	-14	S21 00	2	244 39	18	S22 06	5	1 30	67	N17 54	2	54 57	61	N22 03	0	FRI 7
8 SAT	176 28	-1	S15 11	19	223 31	-14	S21 02	2	244 57	18	S22 12	5	2 37	67	N17 56	2	55 58	61	N22 03	0	SAT 8
9 SUN	176 27	0	S14 52	19	223 17	-14	S21 04	0	245 15	18	S22 17	5	3 44	67	N17 58	2	56 59	61	N22 03	0	SUN 9
10 MON	176 27	-1	S14 33	19	223 03	-15	S21 04	1	245 33	17	S22 22	5	4 51	67	N18 00	3	58 00	60	N22 03	0	MON 10
11 TUE	176 26	0	S14 14	20	222 48	-14	S21 05	0	245 50	18	S22 27	5	5 58	67	N18 03	2	59 00	61	N22 03	0	TUE 11
12 WED	176 26	1	S13 54	20	222 34	-15	S21 05	1	246 08	18	S22 32	4	7 05	67	N18 05	2	60 01	60	N22 03	0	WED 12
13 THU	176 27	0	S13 34	20	222 19	-14	S21 04	2	246 26	17	S22 36	5	8 12	66	N18 07	2	61 01	60	N22 03	1	THU 13
14 FRI	176 27	0	S13 14	20	222 05	-15	S21 02	2	246 43	18	S22 41	4	9 18	67	N18 09	3	62 01	60	N22 04	0	FRI 14
15 SAT	176 27	1	S12 54	21	221 50	-15	S21 00	2	247 01	18	S22 45	4	10 25	67	N18 12	2	63 01	60	N22 04	0	SAT 15
16 SUN	176 28	1	S12 33	21	221 35	-15	S20 58	3	247 19	17	S22 49	4	11 32	66	N18 14	2	64 01	60	N22 04	0	SUN 16
17 MON	176 29	1	S12 12	21	221 20	-15	S20 55	4	247 36	18	S22 53	3	12 38	67	N18 16	2	65 01	60	N22 04	0	MON 17
18 TUE	176 30	1	S11 51	21	221 05	-16	S20 51	4	247 54	17	S22 56	4	13 45	66	N18 18	2	66 01	60	N22 04	0	TUE 18
19 WED	176 31	1	S11 30	21	220 49	-15	S20 47	5	248 11	18	S23 00	3	14 51	67	N18 20	2	67 01	59	N22 04	1	WED 19
20 THU	176 33	1	S11 09	22	220 34	-15	S20 42	5	248 29	17	S23 03	4	15 58	66	N18 22	2	68 00	59	N22 05	0	THU 20
21 FRI	176 34	2	S10 47	21	220 19	-15	S20 37	6	248 46	18	S23 07	3	17 04	66	N18 24	2	68 59	60	N22 05	0	FRI 21
22 SAT	176 36	2	S10 26	22	220 04	-16	S20 31	6	249 04	17	S23 10	2	18 10	66	N18 26	2	69 59	59	N22 05	0	SAT 22
23 SUN	176 38	2	S10 04	22	219 48	-15	S20 25	7	249 21	18	S23 12	3	19 16	66	N18 28	2	70 58	59	N22 05	1	SUN 23
24 MON	176 40	2	S 9 42	22	219 33	-15	S20 18	8	249 39	17	S23 15	3	20 22	66	N18 30	1	71 57	59	N22 06	0	MON 24
25 TUE	176 42	3	S 9 20	23	219 18	-16	S20 10	8	249 56	17	S23 18	2	21 28	66	N18 31	2	72 56	58	N22 06	0	TUE 25
26 WED	176 45	2	S 8 57	22	219 02	-15	S20 02	9	250 13	18	S23 20	2	22 34	65	N18 33	2	73 54	59	N22 06	0	WED 26
27 THU	176 47	3	S 8 35	23	218 47	-15	S19 53	9	250 31	17	S23 22	2	23 39	66	N18 35	2	74 53	59	N22 06	0	THU 27
28 FRI	176 50	2	S 8 12	22	218 32	-15	S19 44	10	250 48	17	S23 24	2	24 45	65	N18 37	1	75 52	58	N22 06	1	FRI 28
29 SAT	176 52		S 7 50		218 17		S19 34		251 05		S23 26		25 50		N18 38		76 50		N22 07		SAT 29

SUN & PLANETS AT GMT 0hrs MARCH 2003

Day	SUN SD 16' GHA	v	Dec	d	VENUS Mag. -4.1 GHA	v	Dec	d	MARS Mag. +0.8 GHA	v	Dec	d	JUPITER Mag. -2.4 GHA	v	Dec	d	SATURN Mag. +0.0 GHA	v	Dec	d	Day
1 SAT	176° 52'	3'	S 7° 50'	23'	218° 17'	-15'	S19° 34'	10'	251° 05'	18'	S23° 26'	1'	25° 50'	65'	N18° 38'	2'	76° 50'	58'	N22° 07'	0'	SAT 1
2 SUN	176 55	3	S 7 27	23	218 02	-15	S19 24	11	251 23	17	S23 27	2	26 55	65	N18 40	1	77 48	58	N22 07	0	SUN 2
3 MON	176 58	3	S 7 04	23	217 47	-15	S19 13	12	251 40	18	S23 29	1	28 00	65	N18 41	2	78 46	58	N22 07	1	MON 3
4 TUE	177 01	4	S 6 41	23	217 32	-14	S19 01	12	251 58	17	S23 30	1	29 05	65	N18 43	1	79 44	58	N22 08	0	TUE 4
5 WED	177 05	3	S 6 18	23	217 18	-15	S18 49	13	252 15	17	S23 31	1	30 10	65	N18 44	2	80 42	58	N22 08	0	WED 5
6 THU	177 08	3	S 5 55	24	217 03	-14	S18 36	13	252 32	18	S23 32	1	31 15	64	N18 46	1	81 40	58	N22 08	0	THU 6
7 FRI	177 11	4	S 5 31	23	216 49	-15	S18 23	13	252 50	17	S23 33	1	32 19	64	N18 47	2	82 38	57	N22 08	1	FRI 7
8 SAT	177 15	3	S 5 08	23	216 34	-14	S18 10	15	253 07	18	S23 34	0	33 23	65	N18 49	1	83 35	58	N22 09	0	SAT 8
9 SUN	177 18	4	S 4 45	24	216 20	-14	S17 55	14	253 25	17	S23 34	0	34 28	63	N18 50	1	84 33	57	N22 09	0	SUN 9
10 MON	177 22	4	S 4 21	23	216 06	-14	S17 41	15	253 42	18	S23 34	0	35 31	64	N18 51	1	85 30	57	N22 09	1	MON 10
11 TUE	177 26	4	S 3 58	24	215 52	-13	S17 26	16	254 00	18	S23 34	0	36 35	64	N18 52	1	86 27	57	N22 10	0	TUE 11
12 WED	177 30	4	S 3 34	23	215 39	-14	S17 10	16	254 18	17	S23 34	0	37 39	63	N18 53	1	87 24	57	N22 10	0	WED 12
13 THU	177 34	4	S 3 11	24	215 25	-13	S16 54	17	254 35	18	S23 34	0	38 42	64	N18 54	2	88 21	57	N22 10	1	THU 13
14 FRI	177 38	4	S 2 47	24	215 12	-13	S16 37	17	254 53	17	S23 34	1	39 46	63	N18 56	1	89 18	57	N22 11	0	FRI 14
15 SAT	177 42	4	S 2 23	23	214 59	-13	S16 20	17	255 10	18	S23 33	1	40 49	63	N18 57	0	90 15	57	N22 11	0	SAT 15
16 SUN	177 46	5	S 2 00	24	214 46	-13	S16 03	19	255 28	18	S23 32	1	41 52	62	N18 57	1	91 12	56	N22 11	1	SUN 16
17 MON	177 51	4	S 1 36	24	214 33	-13	S15 44	18	255 46	18	S23 31	1	42 54	63	N18 58	1	92 08	57	N22 12	0	MON 17
18 TUE	177 55	4	S 1 12	24	214 20	-12	S15 26	19	256 04	17	S23 30	1	43 57	62	N18 59	1	93 05	56	N22 12	0	TUE 18
19 WED	177 59	5	S 0 48	23	214 08	-13	S15 07	19	256 21	18	S23 29	1	44 59	62	N19 00	1	94 01	56	N22 12	1	WED 19
20 THU	178 04	4	S 0 25	24	213 55	-12	S14 48	20	256 39	18	S23 28	2	46 01	62	N19 01	0	94 57	56	N22 13	0	THU 20
21 FRI	178 08	5	S 0 01	22	213 43	-12	S14 28	20	256 57	18	S23 26	2	47 03	62	N19 01	1	95 53	56	N22 13	0	FRI 21
22 SAT	178 13	4	N 0 23	23	213 31	-11	S14 08	21	257 15	18	S23 24	2	48 05	62	N19 02	1	96 49	56	N22 13	1	SAT 22
23 SUN	178 17	5	N 0 46	24	213 20	-12	S13 47	21	257 33	18	S23 22	2	49 07	61	N19 03	0	97 45	56	N22 14	0	SUN 23
24 MON	178 22	4	N 1 10	24	213 08	-11	S13 26	21	257 51	18	S23 20	2	50 08	61	N19 03	1	98 41	55	N22 14	0	MON 24
25 TUE	178 26	5	N 1 34	23	212 57	-11	S13 05	22	258 09	18	S23 18	2	51 09	61	N19 04	0	99 36	56	N22 14	1	TUE 25
26 WED	178 31	4	N 1 57	24	212 46	-11	S12 43	22	258 27	19	S23 16	3	52 10	61	N19 04	0	100 32	55	N22 15	0	WED 26
27 THU	178 35	5	N 2 21	23	212 35	-12	S12 21	22	258 46	18	S23 13	2	53 11	61	N19 04	1	101 27	55	N22 15	1	THU 27
28 FRI	178 40	4	N 2 44	24	212 24	-11	S11 59	23	259 04	18	S23 11	3	54 12	60	N19 05	0	102 22	56	N22 16	0	FRI 28
29 SAT	178 44	5	N 3 08	23	212 13	-10	S11 36	23	259 22	19	S23 08	3	55 12	61	N19 05	0	103 18	55	N22 16	0	SAT 29
30 SUN	178 49	4	N 3 31	23	212 03	-11	S11 13	24	259 41	18	S23 05	3	56 13	60	N19 05	0	104 13	55	N22 16	1	SUN 30
31 MON	178 53	5	N 3 54	24	211 52	-10	S10 49	23	259 59	19	S23 02	4	57 13	60	N19 05	1	105 08	55	N22 17	0	MON 31
32 TUE	178 58		N 4 18		211 42		S10 26		260 18		S22 58		58 13		N19 06		106 03		N22 17		TUE 32

SUN & PLANETS AT GMT 0hrs APRIL 2003

Day	SUN SD 16' GHA	v	Dec	d	VENUS Mag. -4.0 GHA	v	Dec	d	MARS Mag. +0.3 GHA	v	Dec	d	JUPITER Mag. -2.2 GHA	v	Dec	d	SATURN Mag. +0.1 GHA	v	Dec	d	Day
1 TUE	178° 58'	4'	N 4° 18'	23'	211° 42'	-10'	S10° 26'	25'	260° 18'	19'	S22° 58'	3'	58° 13'	59'	N19° 06'	0'	106° 03'	55'	N22° 17'	0'	TUE 1
2 WED	179 02	5	N 4 41	23	211 32	-9	S10 01	24	260 37	18	S22 55	4	59 12	60	N19 06	0	106 58	54	N22 17	1	WED 2
3 THU	179 07	4	N 5 04	23	211 23	-10	S 9 37	24	260 55	19	S22 51	3	60 12	59	N19 06	0	107 52	55	N22 18	0	THU 3
4 FRI	179 11	5	N 5 27	23	211 13	-9	S 9 13	25	261 14	19	S22 48	4	61 11	59	N19 06	0	108 47	54	N22 18	1	FRI 4
5 SAT	179 16	4	N 5 50	23	211 04	-10	S 8 48	25	261 33	19	S22 44	4	62 10	59	N19 06	1	109 41	55	N22 19	0	SAT 5
6 SUN	179 20	4	N 6 13	22	210 54	-9	S 8 23	26	261 52	19	S22 40	4	63 09	59	N19 05	0	110 36	54	N22 19	0	SUN 6
7 MON	179 24	4	N 6 35	23	210 45	-9	S 7 57	26	262 11	20	S22 36	4	64 08	58	N19 05	0	111 30	54	N22 20	0	MON 7
8 TUE	179 28	4	N 6 58	22	210 36	-9	S 7 32	26	262 31	19	S22 32	5	65 06	58	N19 05	0	112 24	55	N22 20	0	TUE 8
9 WED	179 32	5	N 7 20	23	210 27	-9	S 7 06	26	262 50	19	S22 27	4	66 04	59	N19 05	1	113 19	54	N22 20	1	WED 9
10 THU	179 37	4	N 7 43	22	210 18	-8	S 6 40	26	263 09	20	S22 23	5	67 03	57	N19 04	0	114 13	54	N22 21	0	THU 10
11 FRI	179 41	4	N 8 05	22	210 10	-9	S 6 14	27	263 29	19	S22 18	5	68 00	58	N19 04	0	115 07	53	N22 21	0	FRI 11
12 SAT	179 45	4	N 8 27	22	210 01	-8	S 5 47	26	263 48	20	S22 13	5	68 58	58	N19 04	1	116 00	54	N22 21	1	SAT 12
13 SUN	179 49	3	N 8 49	22	209 53	-9	S 5 21	27	264 08	20	S22 08	5	69 56	57	N19 03	0	116 54	54	N22 22	0	SUN 13
14 MON	179 52	4	N 9 11	21	209 44	-8	S 4 54	27	264 28	20	S22 03	5	70 53	57	N19 03	1	117 48	53	N22 22	0	MON 14
15 TUE	179 56	4	N 9 32	22	209 36	-8	S 4 27	27	264 48	20	S21 58	5	71 50	57	N19 02	1	118 42	53	N22 22	1	TUE 15
16 WED	180 00	3	N 9 54	21	209 28	-8	S 4 00	27	265 08	20	S21 53	5	72 47	57	N19 01	0	119 35	54	N22 23	0	WED 16
17 THU	180 03	4	N10 15	21	209 20	-8	S 3 33	28	265 28	20	S21 48	6	73 44	57	N19 01	1	120 29	53	N22 23	1	THU 17
18 FRI	180 07	3	N10 36	21	209 12	-8	S 3 05	27	265 48	21	S21 42	5	74 41	56	N19 00	1	121 22	53	N22 24	0	FRI 18
19 SAT	180 10	4	N10 57	21	209 04	-8	S 2 38	28	266 09	20	S21 37	6	75 37	56	N18 59	0	122 15	54	N22 24	0	SAT 19
20 SUN	180 14	3	N11 18	21	208 56	-8	S 2 10	27	266 29	21	S21 31	6	76 33	56	N18 59	1	123 09	53	N22 24	1	SUN 20
21 MON	180 17	3	N11 39	20	208 48	-8	S 1 43	28	266 50	21	S21 25	6	77 29	56	N18 58	1	124 02	53	N22 25	0	MON 21
22 TUE	180 20	3	N11 59	20	208 40	-8	S 1 15	28	267 11	21	S21 19	6	78 25	56	N18 57	1	124 55	53	N22 25	0	TUE 22
23 WED	180 23	3	N12 19	20	208 32	-7	S 0 47	28	267 32	21	S21 13	6	79 21	55	N18 56	1	125 48	53	N22 25	1	WED 23
24 THU	180 26	2	N12 39	20	208 25	-8	S 0 19	11	267 53	21	S21 07	6	80 17	55	N18 55	1	126 41	53	N22 26	0	THU 24
25 FRI	180 28	3	N12 59	20	208 17	-8	N 0 08	28	268 14	21	S21 01	6	81 12	55	N18 54	1	127 34	52	N22 26	1	FRI 25
26 SAT	180 31	2	N13 19	19	208 09	-8	N 0 36	28	268 35	22	S20 55	6	82 07	55	N18 53	1	128 26	53	N22 27	0	SAT 26
27 SUN	180 33	3	N13 38	19	208 01	-8	N 1 04	28	268 57	21	S20 49	7	83 02	55	N18 52	2	129 19	53	N22 27	0	SUN 27
28 MON	180 36	2	N13 57	19	207 53	-7	N 1 32	28	269 18	22	S20 42	6	83 57	55	N18 50	1	130 12	52	N22 27	1	MON 28
29 TUE	180 38	2	N14 16	19	207 46	-8	N 2 00	28	269 40	22	S20 36	7	84 52	54	N18 49	1	131 04	53	N22 28	0	TUE 29
30 WED	180 40	2	N14 35	18	207 38	-8	N 2 28	28	270 02	22	S20 29	7	85 46	55	N18 48	1	131 57	52	N22 28	0	WED 30
31 THU	180 42		N14 53		207 30		N 2 56		270 24		S20 22		86 41		N18 47		132 49		N22 28		THU 31

SUN & PLANETS AT GMT 0hrs MAY 2003

Day	SUN SD 16' GHA	v	Dec	d	VENUS Mag. -3.9 GHA	v	Dec	d	MARS Mag. -0.3 GHA	v	Dec	d	JUPITER Mag. -2.0 GHA	v	Dec	d	SATURN Mag. +0.1 GHA	v	Dec	d	Day
1 THU	180° 42'	2'	N14° 53'	18'	207° 30'	-8'	N 2° 56'	28'	270° 24'	22'	S20° 22'	7'	86° 41'	54'	N18° 47'	2'	132° 49'	53'	N22° 28'	1'	THU 1
2 FRI	180 44	2	N15 11	18	207 22	-8	N 3 24	28	270 46	23	S20 15	6	87 35	54	N18 45	1	133 42	52	N22 29	0	FRI 2
3 SAT	180 46	1	N15 29	18	207 14	-8	N 3 52	28	271 09	22	S20 09	7	88 29	54	N18 44	2	134 34	52	N22 29	0	SAT 3
4 SUN	180 47	2	N15 47	17	207 06	-9	N 4 20	27	271 31	23	S20 02	7	89 23	54	N18 42	1	135 26	52	N22 29	1	SUN 4
5 MON	180 49	1	N16 04	17	206 57	-8	N 4 47	28	271 54	23	S19 55	7	90 17	53	N18 41	2	136 18	52	N22 30	0	MON 5
6 TUE	180 50	1	N16 21	17	206 49	-8	N 5 15	28	272 17	23	S19 48	7	91 10	53	N18 39	1	137 10	53	N22 30	0	TUE 6
7 WED	180 51	1	N16 38	17	206 41	-9	N 5 43	27	272 40	23	S19 41	7	92 04	53	N18 38	2	138 03	52	N22 30	1	WED 7
8 THU	180 52	1	N16 55	16	206 32	-8	N 6 10	27	273 03	23	S19 34	8	92 57	53	N18 36	1	138 55	52	N22 31	0	THU 8
9 FRI	180 53	1	N17 11	16	206 24	-9	N 6 37	28	273 26	24	S19 26	7	93 50	53	N18 35	2	139 47	51	N22 31	0	FRI 9
10 SAT	180 54	0	N17 27	16	206 15	-9	N 7 05	27	273 50	24	S19 19	7	94 43	53	N18 33	2	140 38	52	N22 31	0	SAT 10
11 SUN	180 54	1	N17 43	16	206 06	-9	N 7 32	27	274 14	23	S19 12	7	95 36	52	N18 31	2	141 30	52	N22 31	1	SUN 11
12 MON	180 55	0	N17 59	15	205 57	-9	N 7 59	26	274 37	25	S19 05	8	96 28	53	N18 29	2	142 22	52	N22 32	0	MON 12
13 TUE	180 55	0	N18 14	15	205 48	-9	N 8 25	27	275 02	24	S18 57	7	97 21	52	N18 27	1	143 14	52	N22 32	0	TUE 13
14 WED	180 55	0	N18 28	15	205 39	-10	N 8 52	27	275 26	24	S18 50	7	98 13	53	N18 26	2	144 06	51	N22 32	0	WED 14
15 THU	180 55	0	N18 43	14	205 29	-10	N 9 19	26	275 50	25	S18 43	8	99 06	52	N18 24	2	144 57	52	N22 32	1	THU 15
16 FRI	180 55	0	N18 57	14	205 19	-9	N 9 45	26	276 15	25	S18 35	7	99 58	52	N18 22	2	145 49	51	N22 33	0	FRI 16
17 SAT	180 55	-1	N19 11	14	205 10	-10	N10 11	26	276 40	25	S18 28	8	100 50	52	N18 20	2	146 40	52	N22 33	0	SAT 17
18 SUN	180 54	0	N19 25	13	205 00	-11	N10 37	25	277 05	25	S18 20	7	101 42	51	N18 18	2	147 32	51	N22 33	0	SUN 18
19 MON	180 54	-1	N19 38	13	204 49	-10	N11 02	26	277 30	25	S18 13	8	102 33	52	N18 16	2	148 23	51	N22 33	1	MON 19
20 TUE	180 53	-1	N19 51	12	204 39	-11	N11 28	25	277 55	26	S18 05	7	103 25	51	N18 14	3	149 15	51	N22 34	0	TUE 20
21 WED	180 52	-1	N20 03	13	204 28	-10	N11 53	25	278 21	26	S17 58	8	104 16	52	N18 11	2	150 06	52	N22 34	0	WED 21
22 THU	180 51	0	N20 16	11	204 18	-12	N12 18	24	278 47	26	S17 50	8	105 08	51	N18 09	2	150 58	51	N22 34	0	THU 22
23 FRI	180 50	-1	N20 27	12	204 06	-11	N12 42	24	279 13	26	S17 42	7	105 59	51	N18 07	2	151 49	51	N22 34	1	FRI 23
24 SAT	180 49	-1	N20 39	11	203 55	-11	N13 06	24	279 39	27	S17 35	8	106 50	51	N18 05	3	152 40	51	N22 35	0	SAT 24
25 SUN	180 48	-2	N20 50	11	203 44	-12	N13 30	24	280 06	27	S17 27	7	107 41	51	N18 02	2	153 31	52	N22 35	0	SUN 25
26 MON	180 46	-1	N21 01	10	203 32	-12	N13 54	24	280 33	27	S17 20	8	108 32	51	N18 00	2	154 23	51	N22 35	0	MON 26
27 TUE	180 45	-2	N21 11	10	203 20	-12	N14 18	23	281 00	27	S17 12	7	109 23	50	N17 58	3	155 14	51	N22 35	0	TUE 27
28 WED	180 43	-2	N21 21	10	203 08	-13	N14 41	22	281 27	27	S17 05	7	110 13	51	N17 55	2	156 05	51	N22 35	0	WED 28
29 THU	180 41	-2	N21 31	9	202 55	-13	N15 03	23	281 54	28	S16 58	8	111 04	50	N17 53	3	156 56	51	N22 35	1	THU 29
30 FRI	180 39	-2	N21 40	9	202 42	-13	N15 26	22	282 22	28	S16 50	7	111 54	51	N17 50	2	157 47	51	N22 36	0	FRI 30
31 SAT	180 37	-2	N21 49	9	202 29	-13	N15 48	21	282 50	28	S16 43	8	112 45	50	N17 48	3	158 38	51	N22 36	0	SAT 31
32 SUN	180 35		N21 58		202 16		N16 09		283 18		S16 35		113 35		N17 45		159 29		N22 36		SUN 32

SUN & PLANETS AT GMT 0hrs JUNE 2003

Day	SUN SD 16' GHA	v	Dec	d	VENUS Mag. -3.9 GHA	v	Dec	d	MARS Mag. -1.0 GHA	v	Dec	d	JUPITER Mag. -1.9 GHA	v	Dec	d	SATURN Mag. +0.0 GHA	v	Dec	d	Day
1 SUN	180° 35'	-2'	N21° 58'	8'	202° 16'	-14'	N16° 09'	21'	283° 18'	29'	S16° 35'	7'	113° 35'	50'	N17° 45'	3'	159° 29'	51'	N22° 36'	0'	SUN 1
2 MON	180 33	-3	N22 06	7	202 02	-14	N16 30	21	283 47	29	S16 28	7	114 25	50	N17 43	3	160 20	51	N22 36	0	MON 2
3 TUE	180 30	-2	N22 14	7	201 48	-14	N16 51	21	284 16	29	S16 21	7	115 15	50	N17 40	3	161 11	51	N22 36	0	TUE 3
4 WED	180 28	-3	N22 21	8	201 34	-14	N17 12	20	284 45	29	S16 14	7	116 05	50	N17 37	2	162 02	51	N22 36	0	WED 4
5 THU	180 25	-2	N22 29	6	201 20	-15	N17 32	19	285 14	30	S16 07	8	116 55	49	N17 35	3	162 53	51	N22 36	0	THU 5
6 FRI	180 23	-3	N22 35	6	201 05	-15	N17 51	19	285 44	30	S15 59	7	117 44	50	N17 32	3	163 44	51	N22 36	0	FRI 6
7 SAT	180 20	-3	N22 41	6	200 50	-15	N18 10	19	286 14	30	S15 52	6	118 34	49	N17 29	3	164 35	50	N22 37	1	SAT 7
8 SUN	180 17	-3	N22 47	6	200 35	-15	N18 29	18	286 44	31	S15 46	7	119 23	50	N17 26	2	165 25	51	N22 37	0	SUN 8
9 MON	180 14	-3	N22 53	5	200 20	-16	N18 47	18	287 15	30	S15 39	7	120 13	49	N17 24	3	166 16	51	N22 37	0	MON 9
10 TUE	180 11	-3	N22 58	4	200 04	-16	N19 05	17	287 45	32	S15 32	7	121 02	49	N17 21	3	167 07	51	N22 37	0	TUE 10
11 WED	180 08	-3	N23 02	5	199 48	-17	N19 22	16	288 17	31	S15 25	6	121 51	50	N17 18	3	167 58	51	N22 37	0	WED 11
12 THU	180 05	-3	N23 07	3	199 31	-16	N19 38	16	288 48	32	S15 19	7	122 41	49	N17 15	3	168 49	50	N22 37	0	THU 12
13 FRI	180 02	-3	N23 10	4	199 15	-17	N19 54	16	289 20	32	S15 12	6	123 30	49	N17 12	3	169 39	51	N22 37	0	FRI 13
14 SAT	179 59	-3	N23 14	3	198 58	-17	N20 10	15	289 52	33	S15 06	7	124 19	49	N17 09	3	170 30	51	N22 37	0	SAT 14
15 SUN	179 56	-3	N23 17	2	198 41	-18	N20 25	15	290 25	32	S14 59	6	125 08	48	N17 06	3	171 21	51	N22 37	0	SUN 15
16 MON	179 53	-3	N23 19	3	198 23	-17	N20 40	14	290 57	34	S14 53	6	125 56	49	N17 03	3	172 12	50	N22 37	0	MON 16
17 TUE	179 50	-4	N23 22	1	198 06	-18	N20 54	13	291 31	33	S14 47	6	126 45	49	N17 00	4	173 02	51	N22 37	0	TUE 17
18 WED	179 46	-3	N23 23	2	197 48	-18	N21 07	13	292 04	34	S14 41	6	127 34	48	N16 56	3	173 53	51	N22 37	0	WED 18
19 THU	179 43	-3	N23 25	1	197 30	-19	N21 20	12	292 38	34	S14 35	6	128 22	49	N16 53	3	174 44	51	N22 37	0	THU 19
20 FRI	179 40	-3	N23 26	0	197 11	-18	N21 32	12	293 12	35	S14 29	5	129 11	48	N16 50	3	175 35	50	N22 37	0	FRI 20
21 SAT	179 37	-4	N23 26	0	196 53	-19	N21 44	11	293 47	35	S14 24	6	129 59	49	N16 47	3	176 25	51	N22 37	0	SAT 21
22 SUN	179 33	-3	N23 26	0	196 34	-19	N21 55	10	294 22	35	S14 18	5	130 48	48	N16 44	3	177 16	51	N22 37	0	SUN 22
23 MON	179 30	-3	N23 26	1	196 15	-19	N22 05	10	294 57	36	S14 13	5	131 36	48	N16 40	3	178 07	51	N22 37	0	MON 23
24 TUE	179 27	-3	N23 25	1	195 56	-20	N22 15	9	295 33	37	S14 08	5	132 24	48	N16 37	3	178 57	51	N22 37	0	TUE 24
25 WED	179 24	-4	N23 24	1	195 36	-19	N22 24	9	296 10	36	S14 03	5	133 12	48	N16 34	4	179 48	50	N22 37	1	WED 25
26 THU	179 20	-3	N23 23	2	195 17	-20	N22 33	8	296 46	38	S13 58	5	134 00	48	N16 30	3	180 39	50	N22 36	0	THU 26
27 FRI	179 17	-3	N23 21	3	194 57	-20	N22 41	7	297 24	37	S13 53	4	134 48	48	N16 27	3	181 29	51	N22 36	0	FRI 27
28 SAT	179 14	-3	N23 18	2	194 37	-20	N22 48	7	298 01	39	S13 49	5	135 36	48	N16 23	3	182 20	51	N22 36	0	SAT 28
29 SUN	179 11	-3	N23 16	3	194 17	-21	N22 55	6	298 40	38	S13 44	4	136 24	48	N16 20	3	183 11	50	N22 36	0	SUN 29
30 MON	179 08	-3	N23 13	4	193 56	-20	N23 01	5	299 18	39	S13 40	4	137 12	48	N16 16	3	184 01	51	N22 36	0	MON 30
31 TUE	179 05		N23 09		193 36		N23 06		299 57		S13 36		138 00		N16 13		184 52		N22 36		TUE 31

SUN & PLANETS AT GMT 0hrs JULY 2003

Day	SUN SD 16' GHA	v	Dec	d	VENUS Mag. -3.9 GHA	v	Dec	d	MARS Mag. -1.8 GHA	v	Dec	d	JUPITER Mag. -1.8 GHA	v	Dec	d	SATURN Mag. +0.1 GHA	v	Dec	d	Day
1 TUE	179° 05'	-3'	N23° 09'	4'	193° 36'	-21'	N23° 06'	5'	299° 57'	40'	S13° 36'	3'	138° 00'	48'	N16° 13'	4'	184° 52'	51'	N22° 36'	0'	TUE 1
2 WED	179 02	-3	N23 05	4	193 15	-20	N23 11	4	300 37	40	S13 33	4	138 48	47	N16 09	3	185 43	51	N22 36	0	WED 2
3 THU	178 59	-3	N23 01	5	192 55	-21	N23 15	3	301 17	41	S13 29	3	139 35	48	N16 06	4	186 34	50	N22 36	1	THU 3
4 FRI	178 56	-2	N22 56	5	192 34	-21	N23 18	3	301 58	41	S13 26	3	140 23	48	N16 02	3	187 24	51	N22 35	0	FRI 4
5 SAT	178 54	-3	N22 51	6	192 13	-21	N23 21	2	302 39	42	S13 23	3	141 11	47	N15 59	4	188 15	51	N22 35	0	SAT 5
6 SUN	178 51	-2	N22 45	6	191 52	-20	N23 23	1	303 21	42	S13 20	3	141 58	48	N15 55	4	189 06	51	N22 35	0	SUN 6
7 MON	178 49	-3	N22 39	6	191 32	-21	N23 24	0	304 03	43	S13 17	3	142 46	47	N15 51	4	189 57	50	N22 35	0	MON 7
8 TUE	178 46	-2	N22 33	6	191 11	-21	N23 24	0	304 46	43	S13 14	2	143 33	47	N15 47	3	190 47	51	N22 35	0	TUE 8
9 WED	178 44	-2	N22 26	7	190 50	-21	N23 24	1	305 29	44	S13 12	2	144 20	48	N15 44	4	191 38	51	N22 35	1	WED 9
10 THU	178 42	-3	N22 19	8	190 29	-21	N23 23	1	306 13	45	S13 10	2	145 08	47	N15 40	4	192 29	51	N22 34	0	THU 10
11 FRI	178 39	-2	N22 11	8	190 08	-21	N23 22	2	306 58	45	S13 08	1	145 55	47	N15 36	4	193 20	51	N22 34	0	FRI 11
12 SAT	178 37	-1	N22 03	8	189 47	-21	N23 20	3	307 43	46	S13 07	2	146 42	47	N15 32	3	194 11	50	N22 34	0	SAT 12
13 SUN	178 36	-2	N21 55	9	189 26	-21	N23 17	4	308 29	46	S13 05	1	147 29	48	N15 28	3	195 01	51	N22 34	0	SUN 13
14 MON	178 34	-2	N21 46	9	189 05	-21	N23 13	4	309 15	47	S13 04	1	148 17	47	N15 25	4	195 52	51	N22 34	1	MON 14
15 TUE	178 32	-1	N21 37	9	188 44	-20	N23 09	5	310 03	47	S13 03	1	149 04	47	N15 21	4	196 43	51	N22 33	0	TUE 15
16 WED	178 31	-1	N21 28	10	188 24	-21	N23 04	5	310 50	49	S13 03	1	149 51	47	N15 17	4	197 34	51	N22 33	0	WED 16
17 THU	178 29	-1	N21 18	10	188 03	-21	N22 59	7	311 39	49	S13 02	0	150 38	47	N15 13	4	198 25	51	N22 33	0	THU 17
18 FRI	178 28	-1	N21 08	10	187 42	-20	N22 52	7	312 28	49	S13 02	0	151 25	47	N15 09	4	199 16	51	N22 33	1	FRI 18
19 SAT	178 27	-1	N20 58	11	187 22	-20	N22 45	7	313 17	51	S13 02	1	152 12	47	N15 05	4	200 07	51	N22 32	0	SAT 19
20 SUN	178 26	-1	N20 47	11	187 02	-20	N22 38	9	314 08	51	S13 03	0	152 59	47	N15 01	4	200 58	51	N22 32	0	SUN 20
21 MON	178 25	-1	N20 36	12	186 42	-21	N22 29	9	314 59	52	S13 03	1	153 46	47	N14 57	4	201 49	51	N22 32	1	MON 21
22 TUE	178 24	-1	N20 24	12	186 21	-19	N22 20	9	315 51	53	S13 04	1	154 33	47	N14 53	4	202 40	52	N22 31	0	TUE 22
23 WED	178 23	0	N20 12	12	186 02	-20	N22 11	11	316 44	53	S13 05	2	155 20	46	N14 49	4	203 32	51	N22 31	0	WED 23
24 THU	178 23	0	N20 00	13	185 42	-20	N22 00	10	317 37	54	S13 07	2	156 06	47	N14 45	4	204 23	51	N22 31	0	THU 24
25 FRI	178 23	-1	N19 47	13	185 22	-19	N21 50	12	318 31	55	S13 09	2	156 53	47	N14 41	5	205 14	51	N22 31	1	FRI 25
26 SAT	178 22	0	N19 34	13	185 03	-19	N21 38	12	319 26	56	S13 11	2	157 40	47	N14 37	5	206 05	51	N22 30	0	SAT 26
27 SUN	178 22	1	N19 21	13	184 44	-19	N21 26	13	320 22	56	S13 13	2	158 27	46	N14 32	4	206 56	52	N22 30	0	SUN 27
28 MON	178 23	0	N19 08	14	184 25	-19	N21 13	13	321 18	58	S13 15	3	159 13	47	N14 28	4	207 48	51	N22 30	1	MON 28
29 TUE	178 23	0	N18 54	14	184 06	-18	N21 00	14	322 16	58	S13 18	3	160 00	47	N14 24	4	208 39	51	N22 29	0	TUE 29
30 WED	178 23	1	N18 40	15	183 48	-19	N20 46	15	323 14	59	S13 21	3	160 47	47	N14 20	4	209 30	51	N22 29	0	WED 30
31 THU	178 24	0	N18 25	15	183 29	-18	N20 31	15	324 12	60	S13 24	4	161 34	46	N14 16	5	210 22	51	N22 29	1	THU 31
32 FRI	178 24		N18 10		183 11		N20 16		325 12		S13 28		162 20		N14 11		211 13		N22 28		FRI 32

SUN & PLANETS AT GMT 0hrs AUGUST 2003

Day	SUN SD 16' GHA	v	Dec	d	VENUS Mag. -3.9 GHA	v	Dec	d	MARS Mag. -2.7 GHA	v	Dec	d	JUPITER Mag. -1.7 GHA	v	Dec	d	SATURN Mag. +0.1 GHA	v	Dec	d	Day
1 FRI	178° 24'	1'	N18° 10'	15'	183° 11'	-17'	N20° 16'	16'	325° 12'	60'	S13° 28'	3'	162° 20'	47'	N14° 11'	4'	211° 13'	52'	N22° 28'	0'	FRI 1
2 SAT	178 25	1	N17 55	15	182 54	-18	N20 00	17	326 12	62	S13 31	4	163 07	46	N14 07	4	212 05	51	N22 28	0	SAT 2
3 SUN	178 26	1	N17 40	16	182 36	-17	N19 43	16	327 14	61	S13 35	4	163 53	47	N14 03	4	212 56	52	N22 28	1	SUN 3
4 MON	178 28	1	N17 24	16	182 19	-17	N19 27	18	328 15	63	S13 39	4	164 40	47	N13 59	5	213 48	52	N22 27	0	MON 4
5 TUE	178 29	1	N17 08	16	182 02	-17	N19 09	18	329 18	64	S13 43	5	165 27	46	N13 54	4	214 40	51	N22 27	1	TUE 5
6 WED	178 30	2	N16 52	16	181 45	-17	N18 51	19	330 22	64	S13 48	4	166 13	47	N13 50	4	215 31	52	N22 26	0	WED 6
7 THU	178 32	2	N16 36	17	181 28	-16	N18 32	19	331 26	65	S13 53	4	167 00	46	N13 46	5	216 23	52	N22 26	0	THU 7
8 FRI	178 34	2	N16 19	17	181 12	-16	N18 13	19	332 31	65	S13 57	5	167 46	47	N13 41	4	217 15	52	N22 25	0	FRI 8
9 SAT	178 36	2	N16 02	17	180 56	-15	N17 54	20	333 36	67	S14 02	5	168 33	47	N13 37	4	218 07	52	N22 25	0	SAT 9
10 SUN	178 38	2	N15 45	18	180 41	-16	N17 34	21	334 43	67	S14 07	6	169 20	46	N13 33	5	218 59	52	N22 25	0	SUN 10
11 MON	178 40	2	N15 27	17	180 25	-15	N17 13	21	335 50	68	S14 13	5	170 06	47	N13 28	4	219 51	52	N22 25	1	MON 11
12 TUE	178 42	2	N15 10	18	180 10	-15	N16 52	22	336 58	68	S14 18	5	170 53	46	N13 24	5	220 43	52	N22 24	0	TUE 12
13 WED	178 45	3	N14 52	19	179 55	-15	N16 30	22	338 06	69	S14 23	6	171 39	47	N13 19	4	221 35	52	N22 24	1	WED 13
14 THU	178 48	3	N14 33	18	179 40	-14	N16 08	22	339 15	70	S14 29	5	172 26	46	N13 15	5	222 27	52	N22 23	0	THU 14
15 FRI	178 51	2	N14 15	19	179 26	-14	N15 46	23	340 25	70	S14 34	6	173 12	47	N13 10	4	223 19	52	N22 23	0	FRI 15
16 SAT	178 53	4	N13 56	19	179 12	-14	N15 23	23	341 35	71	S14 40	6	173 59	46	N13 06	4	224 11	53	N22 22	1	SAT 16
17 SUN	178 57	3	N13 37	19	178 58	-13	N15 00	24	342 46	71	S14 46	6	174 45	47	N13 02	5	225 04	52	N22 22	0	SUN 17
18 MON	179 00	3	N13 18	19	178 45	-14	N14 36	24	343 57	72	S14 52	5	175 32	46	N12 57	4	225 56	52	N22 22	1	MON 18
19 TUE	179 03	3	N12 59	20	178 31	-13	N14 12	25	345 09	73	S14 57	6	176 18	47	N12 53	4	226 48	53	N22 21	0	TUE 19
20 WED	179 06	4	N12 39	19	178 18	-12	N13 47	25	346 22	73	S15 03	6	177 05	46	N12 48	4	227 41	52	N22 21	0	WED 20
21 THU	179 10	4	N12 20	20	178 06	-13	N13 22	25	347 35	73	S15 09	5	177 51	47	N12 44	5	228 33	53	N22 21	1	THU 21
22 FRI	179 14	3	N12 00	21	177 53	-12	N12 57	26	348 48	74	S15 14	5	178 38	46	N12 39	4	229 26	53	N22 20	0	FRI 22
23 SAT	179 17	4	N11 39	20	177 41	-12	N12 31	26	350 02	74	S15 20	5	179 24	47	N12 35	5	230 19	52	N22 20	1	SAT 23
24 SUN	179 21	4	N11 19	20	177 29	-12	N12 05	26	351 16	74	S15 25	5	180 11	47	N12 30	4	231 11	53	N22 19	0	SUN 24
25 MON	179 25	4	N10 59	21	177 17	-12	N11 39	26	352 30	74	S15 30	6	180 58	46	N12 26	5	232 04	53	N22 19	0	MON 25
26 TUE	179 29	5	N10 38	21	177 05	-11	N11 13	27	353 44	75	S15 36	5	181 44	47	N12 21	5	232 57	53	N22 19	1	TUE 26
27 WED	179 34	4	N10 17	21	176 54	-12	N10 46	28	354 59	75	S15 41	5	182 31	46	N12 16	4	233 50	53	N22 18	0	WED 27
28 THU	179 38	4	N 9 56	21	176 42	-11	N10 18	27	356 14	75	S15 46	4	183 17	47	N12 12	5	234 43	53	N22 18	1	THU 28
29 FRI	179 42	5	N 9 35	21	176 31	-11	N 9 51	28	357 29	75	S15 50	5	184 04	47	N12 07	4	235 36	53	N22 17	0	FRI 29
30 SAT	179 47	4	N 9 14	22	176 20	-10	N 9 23	28	358 44	75	S15 55	4	184 51	46	N12 03	5	236 29	54	N22 17	0	SAT 30
31 SUN	179 51	5	N 8 52	21	176 10	-11	N 8 55	28	359 59	75	S15 59	4	185 37	47	N11 58	5	237 23	53	N22 17	1	SUN 31
32 MON	179 56		N 8 31		175 59		N 8 27		1 14		S16 03		186 24		N11 54		238 16		N22 16		MON 32

SUN & PLANETS AT GMT 0hrs SEPTEMBER 2003

Day	SUN SD 16' GHA	v	Dec	d	VENUS Mag. -3.9 GHA	v	Dec	d	MARS Mag. -2.6 GHA	v	Dec	d	JUPITER Mag. -1.7 GHA	v	Dec	d	SATURN Mag. +0.1 GHA	v	Dec	d	Day
1 MON	179° 56'	5'	N 8° 31'	22'	175° 59'	-10'	N 8° 27'	29'	1° 14'	75'	S16° 03'	4'	186° 24'	47'	N11° 54'	5'	238° 16'	53'	N22° 16'	0'	MON 1
2 TUE	180 01	4	N 8 09	22	175 49	-10	N 7 58	28	2 29	75	S16 07	3	187 11	46	N11 49	4	239 09	54	N22 16	1	TUE 2
3 WED	180 05	5	N 7 47	22	175 39	-10	N 7 30	29	3 44	75	S16 10	3	187 57	47	N11 45	5	240 03	54	N22 15	0	WED 3
4 THU	180 10	5	N 7 25	22	175 29	-10	N 7 01	29	4 59	74	S16 14	3	188 44	47	N11 40	5	240 57	53	N22 15	0	THU 4
5 FRI	180 15	5	N 7 03	22	175 19	-10	N 6 32	30	6 13	74	S16 17	2	189 31	46	N11 35	4	241 50	54	N22 15	1	FRI 5
6 SAT	180 20	5	N 6 41	23	175 09	-9	N 6 02	29	7 27	74	S16 19	3	190 17	47	N11 31	5	242 44	54	N22 14	0	SAT 6
7 SUN	180 25	5	N 6 18	22	175 00	-10	N 5 33	30	8 41	73	S16 22	2	191 04	47	N11 26	4	243 38	54	N22 14	1	SUN 7
8 MON	180 30	6	N 5 56	23	174 50	-9	N 5 03	30	9 54	74	S16 24	1	191 51	47	N11 22	5	244 32	54	N22 13	0	MON 8
9 TUE	180 36	5	N 5 33	22	174 41	-9	N 4 33	29	11 08	72	S16 25	2	192 38	47	N11 17	4	245 26	54	N22 13	1	TUE 9
10 WED	180 41	5	N 5 11	23	174 32	-9	N 4 04	31	12 20	72	S16 27	1	193 25	47	N11 13	5	246 20	54	N22 12	0	WED 10
11 THU	180 46	5	N 4 48	23	174 23	-10	N 3 33	30	13 32	72	S16 28	0	194 12	46	N11 08	4	247 14	54	N22 12	0	THU 11
12 FRI	180 51	6	N 4 25	23	174 13	-9	N 3 03	30	14 44	71	S16 28	1	194 58	47	N11 03	4	248 08	55	N22 12	0	FRI 12
13 SAT	180 57	5	N 4 02	23	174 04	-9	N 2 33	30	15 55	71	S16 29	0	195 45	47	N10 59	5	249 03	54	N22 12	1	SAT 13
14 SUN	181 02	5	N 3 39	23	173 55	-9	N 2 03	31	17 06	70	S16 29	0	196 32	47	N10 54	4	249 57	55	N22 11	0	SUN 14
15 MON	181 07	6	N 3 16	23	173 46	-8	N 1 32	30	18 16	69	S16 29	1	197 19	47	N10 50	5	250 52	54	N22 11	1	MON 15
16 TUE	181 13	5	N 2 53	23	173 38	-9	N 1 02	31	19 25	69	S16 28	1	198 06	47	N10 45	4	251 46	55	N22 10	0	TUE 16
17 WED	181 18	5	N 2 30	23	173 29	-9	N 0 31	31	20 34	68	S16 27	1	198 53	47	N10 41	5	252 41	55	N22 10	0	WED 17
18 THU	181 23	6	N 2 07	23	173 20	-9	N 0 01	29	21 42	67	S16 26	2	199 40	48	N10 36	4	253 36	55	N22 10	1	THU 18
19 FRI	181 29	5	N 1 44	24	173 11	-9	S 0 30	30	22 49	67	S16 24	2	200 28	47	N10 32	5	254 31	55	N22 09	0	FRI 19
20 SAT	181 34	5	N 1 20	23	173 02	-9	S 1 00	31	23 56	66	S16 22	2	201 15	47	N10 27	4	255 26	55	N22 09	0	SAT 20
21 SUN	181 39	6	N 0 57	23	172 53	-9	S 1 31	31	25 02	66	S16 20	2	202 02	47	N10 23	5	256 21	55	N22 09	1	SUN 21
22 MON	181 45	5	N 0 34	24	172 44	-9	S 2 02	30	26 08	64	S16 18	3	202 49	47	N10 18	4	257 16	55	N22 08	0	MON 22
23 TUE	181 50	5	N 0 10	3	172 35	-9	S 2 32	31	27 12	63	S16 15	4	203 36	48	N10 14	5	258 11	56	N22 08	0	TUE 23
24 WED	181 55	6	S 0 13	24	172 26	-9	S 3 03	30	28 16	63	S16 11	3	204 24	47	N10 09	4	259 07	55	N22 08	0	WED 24
25 THU	182 01	5	S 0 36	24	172 17	-9	S 3 33	31	29 19	62	S16 08	4	205 11	48	N10 05	5	260 02	56	N22 08	1	THU 25
26 FRI	182 06	5	S 1 00	23	172 08	-9	S 4 04	30	30 21	62	S16 04	4	205 59	47	N10 00	4	260 58	56	N22 07	0	FRI 26
27 SAT	182 11	5	S 1 23	23	171 59	-9	S 4 34	30	31 23	61	S16 00	5	206 46	48	N 9 56	5	261 54	56	N22 07	0	SAT 27
28 SUN	182 16	5	S 1 46	24	171 50	-10	S 5 04	30	32 24	60	S15 55	5	207 34	47	N 9 51	4	262 50	56	N22 07	1	SUN 28
29 MON	182 21	5	S 2 10	23	171 40	-9	S 5 34	30	33 24	59	S15 50	5	208 21	48	N 9 47	5	263 46	56	N22 06	0	MON 29
30 TUE	182 26	5	S 2 33	23	171 31	-10	S 6 04	30	34 23	58	S15 45	5	209 09	47	N 9 42	4	264 42	56	N22 06	0	TUE 30
31 WED	182 31		S 2 56		171 21		S 6 34		35 21		S15 40		209 56		N 9 38		265 38		N22 06		WED 31

SUN & PLANETS AT GMT 0hrs OCTOBER 2003

Day	SUN SD 16' GHA	v	Dec	d	VENUS Mag. -3.9 GHA	v	Dec	d	MARS Mag. -1.7 GHA	v	Dec	d	JUPITER Mag. -1.8 GHA	v	Dec	d	SATURN Mag. +0.0 GHA	v	Dec	d	Day
1 WED	182° 31'	5'	S 2° 56'	24'	171° 21'	-10'	S 6° 34'	30'	35° 21'	58'	S15° 40'	6'	209° 56'	48'	N 9° 38'	4'	265° 38'	56'	N22° 06'	0'	WED 1
2 THU	182 36	4	S 3 20	23	171 11	-10	S 7 04	30	36 19	57	S15 34	6	210 44	48	N 9 34	5	266 34	56	N22 06	1	THU 2
3 FRI	182 40	5	S 3 43	23	171 01	-10	S 7 34	29	37 16	56	S15 28	6	211 32	48	N 9 29	4	267 30	57	N22 05	0	FRI 3
4 SAT	182 45	5	S 4 06	23	170 51	-10	S 8 03	30	38 12	55	S15 22	6	212 20	47	N 9 25	4	268 27	57	N22 05	0	SAT 4
5 SUN	182 50	4	S 4 29	23	170 41	-11	S 8 33	29	39 07	55	S15 16	7	213 07	48	N 9 21	5	269 24	56	N22 05	0	SUN 5
6 MON	182 54	5	S 4 52	23	170 30	-10	S 9 02	29	40 02	54	S15 09	7	213 55	48	N 9 16	4	270 20	57	N22 05	0	MON 6
7 TUE	182 59	4	S 5 15	23	170 20	-11	S 9 31	29	40 56	53	S15 02	7	214 43	48	N 9 12	4	271 17	57	N22 05	1	TUE 7
8 WED	183 03	4	S 5 38	23	170 09	-11	S 9 59	29	41 49	52	S14 55	7	215 31	49	N 9 08	5	272 14	57	N22 04	0	WED 8
9 THU	183 07	5	S 6 01	23	169 58	-11	S10 28	28	42 41	52	S14 47	7	216 20	48	N 9 03	4	273 11	57	N22 04	0	THU 9
10 FRI	183 12	4	S 6 24	23	169 47	-12	S10 56	28	43 33	51	S14 40	8	217 08	48	N 8 59	4	274 08	58	N22 04	0	FRI 10
11 SAT	183 16	3	S 6 47	22	169 35	-11	S11 24	28	44 24	51	S14 32	9	217 56	48	N 8 55	5	275 06	57	N22 04	0	SAT 11
12 SUN	183 19	4	S 7 09	23	169 24	-12	S11 52	27	45 15	49	S14 23	8	218 44	49	N 8 51	5	276 03	58	N22 04	0	SUN 12
13 MON	183 23	4	S 7 32	22	169 12	-12	S12 19	27	46 04	49	S14 15	9	219 33	48	N 8 46	4	277 01	57	N22 04	0	MON 13
14 TUE	183 27	3	S 7 54	23	169 00	-13	S12 46	27	46 53	49	S14 06	9	220 21	48	N 8 42	4	277 58	58	N22 04	1	TUE 14
15 WED	183 30	4	S 8 17	22	168 47	-12	S13 13	27	47 42	48	S13 58	9	221 09	49	N 8 38	4	278 56	58	N22 03	0	WED 15
16 THU	183 34	3	S 8 39	22	168 35	-13	S13 40	26	48 30	47	S13 49	10	221 58	49	N 8 34	4	279 54	58	N22 03	0	THU 16
17 FRI	183 37	3	S 9 01	22	168 22	-13	S14 06	26	49 17	46	S13 39	9	222 47	48	N 8 30	4	280 52	58	N22 03	0	FRI 17
18 SAT	183 40	3	S 9 23	22	168 09	-14	S14 32	25	50 03	46	S13 30	10	223 35	49	N 8 26	4	281 50	58	N22 03	0	SAT 18
19 SUN	183 43	3	S 9 45	21	167 55	-13	S14 57	26	50 49	46	S13 20	9	224 24	49	N 8 22	4	282 48	59	N22 03	0	SUN 19
20 MON	183 46	2	S10 06	22	167 42	-14	S15 23	24	51 35	45	S13 11	10	225 13	49	N 8 18	4	283 47	58	N22 03	0	MON 20
21 TUE	183 48	3	S10 28	21	167 28	-15	S15 47	25	52 20	44	S13 01	10	226 02	49	N 8 14	4	284 45	59	N22 03	0	TUE 21
22 WED	183 51	2	S10 49	22	167 13	-14	S16 12	24	53 04	44	S12 51	11	226 51	49	N 8 10	4	285 44	58	N22 03	0	WED 22
23 THU	183 53	2	S11 11	21	166 59	-15	S16 36	23	53 48	43	S12 40	11	227 40	49	N 8 06	4	286 42	59	N22 03	0	THU 23
24 FRI	183 55	2	S11 32	21	166 44	-15	S16 59	23	54 31	42	S12 30	11	228 29	49	N 8 02	4	287 41	59	N22 03	0	FRI 24
25 SAT	183 57	2	S11 53	20	166 29	-16	S17 22	23	55 13	43	S12 19	11	229 18	50	N 7 58	4	288 40	59	N22 03	0	SAT 25
26 SUN	183 59	2	S12 13	21	166 13	-16	S17 45	22	55 56	41	S12 08	11	230 08	49	N 7 54	3	289 39	59	N22 03	0	SUN 26
27 MON	184 01	1	S12 34	20	165 57	-16	S18 07	22	56 37	41	S11 57	11	230 57	50	N 7 51	4	290 38	60	N22 03	0	MON 27
28 TUE	184 02	1	S12 54	20	165 41	-16	S18 29	21	57 18	41	S11 46	11	231 47	49	N 7 47	4	291 38	59	N22 03	0	TUE 28
29 WED	184 03	1	S13 14	20	165 25	-17	S18 50	21	57 59	40	S11 35	12	232 36	50	N 7 43	4	292 37	60	N22 03	0	WED 29
30 THU	184 04	1	S13 34	20	165 08	-17	S19 11	20	58 39	40	S11 23	11	233 26	50	N 7 39	3	293 37	59	N22 03	0	THU 30
31 FRI	184 05	1	S13 54	19	164 51	-18	S19 31	20	59 19	39	S11 12	12	234 16	49	N 7 36	3	294 36	60	N22 03	0	FRI 31
32 SAT	184 06		S14 13		164 33		S19 51		59 58		S11 00		235 05		N 7 32		295 36		N22 03		SAT 32

SUN & PLANETS AT GMT 0hrs NOVEMBER 2003

Day	SUN SD 16'				VENUS Mag. -3.9				MARS Mag. -0.8				JUPITER Mag. -1.9				SATURN Mag. -0.1				Day
	GHA	v	Dec	d	GHA	v	Dec	d	GHA	v	Dec	d	GHA	v	Dec	d	GHA	v	Dec	d	
1 SAT	184°06'	0'	S14°13'	20'	164°33'	-17'	S19°51'	19'	59°58'	39'	S11°00'	12'	235°05'	50'	N 7°32'	3'	295°36'	60'	N22°03'	0'	SAT 1
2 SUN	184 06	0	S14 33	19	164 16	-18	S20 10	19	60 37	39	S10 48	12	235 55	50	N 7 29	4	296 36	60	N22 03	0	SUN 2
3 MON	184 06	0	S14 52	18	163 58	-18	S20 29	18	61 16	38	S10 36	12	236 45	51	N 7 25	4	297 36	60	N22 03	1	MON 3
4 TUE	184 06	0	S15 10	19	163 40	-19	S20 47	17	61 54	37	S10 24	12	237 36	50	N 7 22	4	298 36	61	N22 04	0	TUE 4
5 WED	184 06	0	S15 29	18	163 21	-19	S21 04	17	62 31	38	S10 12	13	238 26	50	N 7 18	3	299 37	60	N22 04	0	WED 5
6 THU	184 06	-1	S15 47	18	163 02	-19	S21 21	16	63 09	37	S 9 59	12	239 16	51	N 7 15	4	300 37	61	N22 04	0	THU 6
7 FRI	184 05	0	S16 05	18	162 43	-19	S21 37	16	63 46	36	S 9 47	13	240 07	50	N 7 11	3	301 38	60	N22 04	0	FRI 7
8 SAT	184 05	-1	S16 23	17	162 24	-20	S21 53	15	64 22	36	S 9 34	13	240 57	51	N 7 08	3	302 38	61	N22 04	0	SAT 8
9 SUN	184 04	-2	S16 40	18	162 04	-20	S22 08	14	64 58	36	S 9 21	13	241 48	51	N 7 05	4	303 39	61	N22 04	1	SUN 9
10 MON	184 02	-1	S16 58	17	161 44	-20	S22 22	14	65 34	36	S 9 08	13	242 39	50	N 7 01	3	304 40	61	N22 05	0	MON 10
11 TUE	184 01	-2	S17 15	16	161 24	-21	S22 36	13	66 10	35	S 8 55	13	243 29	51	N 6 58	3	305 41	61	N22 05	0	TUE 11
12 WED	183 59	-1	S17 31	16	161 03	-21	S22 49	13	66 45	35	S 8 42	13	244 20	51	N 6 55	3	306 42	61	N22 05	0	WED 12
13 THU	183 58	-2	S17 47	16	160 42	-20	S23 02	11	67 20	35	S 8 29	13	245 11	52	N 6 52	3	307 43	61	N22 05	0	THU 13
14 FRI	183 56	-3	S18 03	16	160 22	-22	S23 13	12	67 55	34	S 8 16	14	246 03	51	N 6 49	3	308 44	62	N22 05	1	FRI 14
15 SAT	183 53	-2	S18 19	15	160 00	-21	S23 25	10	68 29	34	S 8 02	13	246 54	51	N 6 46	3	309 46	61	N22 06	0	SAT 15
16 SUN	183 51	-3	S18 34	15	159 39	-22	S23 35	10	69 03	34	S 7 49	14	247 45	52	N 6 43	3	310 47	62	N22 06	0	SUN 16
17 MON	183 48	-3	S18 49	15	159 17	-21	S23 45	9	69 37	34	S 7 35	14	248 37	52	N 6 40	3	311 49	62	N22 06	0	MON 17
18 TUE	183 45	-3	S19 04	15	158 56	-22	S23 54	9	70 11	33	S 7 21	13	249 29	51	N 6 37	3	312 51	62	N22 06	1	TUE 18
19 WED	183 42	-3	S19 19	14	158 34	-22	S24 02	8	70 44	33	S 7 08	14	250 20	52	N 6 34	3	313 53	61	N22 07	0	WED 19
20 THU	183 39	-4	S19 33	13	158 12	-23	S24 10	7	71 17	33	S 6 54	14	251 12	52	N 6 31	2	314 54	63	N22 07	0	THU 20
21 FRI	183 35	-3	S19 46	13	157 49	-22	S24 17	6	71 50	32	S 6 40	14	252 04	53	N 6 29	3	315 57	62	N22 07	1	FRI 21
22 SAT	183 32	-4	S19 59	13	157 27	-23	S24 23	5	72 22	32	S 6 26	15	252 57	52	N 6 26	3	316 59	62	N22 08	0	SAT 22
23 SUN	183 28	-4	S20 12	13	157 04	-22	S24 28	5	72 54	32	S 6 11	14	253 49	52	N 6 23	2	318 01	62	N22 08	0	SUN 23
24 MON	183 24	-5	S20 25	12	156 42	-23	S24 33	4	73 26	32	S 5 57	14	254 41	53	N 6 21	3	319 03	63	N22 08	1	MON 24
25 TUE	183 19	-4	S20 37	12	156 19	-23	S24 37	3	73 58	31	S 5 43	15	255 34	52	N 6 18	2	320 06	62	N22 09	0	TUE 25
26 WED	183 15	-5	S20 49	11	155 56	-23	S24 40	2	74 30	31	S 5 28	15	256 26	53	N 6 16	3	321 08	63	N22 09	0	WED 26
27 THU	183 10	-5	S21 00	11	155 33	-22	S24 42	2	75 01	31	S 5 14	15	257 19	53	N 6 13	2	322 11	63	N22 09	1	THU 27
28 FRI	183 05	-5	S21 11	11	155 11	-23	S24 44	1	75 32	31	S 4 59	14	258 12	53	N 6 11	2	323 14	63	N22 10	0	FRI 28
29 SAT	183 00	-5	S21 22	10	154 48	-23	S24 45	0	76 03	31	S 4 45	15	259 05	54	N 6 09	3	324 17	63	N22 10	0	SAT 29
30 SUN	182 55	-6	S21 32	10	154 25	-23	S24 45	0	76 34	30	S 4 30	15	259 59	53	N 6 06	2	325 20	63	N22 10	1	SUN 30
31 MON	182 49		S21 42		154 02		S24 45		77 04		S 4 15		260 52		N 6 04		326 23		N22 11		MON 31

SUN & PLANETS AT GMT 0hrs DECEMBER 2003

Day	SUN SD 16'				VENUS Mag. -4.0				MARS Mag. -0.1				JUPITER Mag. -2.1				SATURN Mag. -0.4				Day
	GHA	v	Dec	d	GHA	v	Dec	d	GHA	v	Dec	d	GHA	v	Dec	d	GHA	v	Dec	d	
1 MON	182°49'	-5'	S21°42'	9'	154°02'	-23'	S24°45'	2'	77°04'	31'	S 4°15'	15'	260°52'	53'	N 6°04'	2'	326°23'	63'	N22°11'	0'	MON 1
2 TUE	182 44	-6	S21 51	9	153 39	-23	S24 43	2	77 35	30	S 4 00	14	261 45	54	N 6 02	2	327 26	63	N22 11	0	TUE 2
3 WED	182 38	-6	S22 00	9	153 16	-22	S24 41	3	78 05	30	S 3 46	15	262 39	54	N 6 00	2	328 29	63	N22 11	1	WED 3
4 THU	182 32	-6	S22 09	8	152 54	-23	S24 38	3	78 35	30	S 3 31	15	263 33	54	N 5 58	2	329 32	64	N22 12	0	THU 4
5 FRI	182 26	-6	S22 17	8	152 31	-22	S24 35	5	79 05	29	S 3 16	15	264 27	54	N 5 56	2	330 36	63	N22 12	1	FRI 5
6 SAT	182 20	-6	S22 25	7	152 09	-23	S24 30	5	79 34	30	S 3 01	15	265 21	54	N 5 54	1	331 39	63	N22 13	0	SAT 6
7 SUN	182 14	-7	S22 32	7	151 46	-22	S24 24	5	80 04	29	S 2 46	16	266 15	55	N 5 53	2	332 42	64	N22 13	1	SUN 7
8 MON	182 07	-6	S22 39	6	151 24	-22	S24 20	7	80 33	29	S 2 30	15	267 10	54	N 5 51	2	333 46	64	N22 14	0	MON 8
9 TUE	182 01	-7	S22 45	6	151 02	-22	S24 13	7	81 02	29	S 2 15	15	268 04	55	N 5 49	1	334 50	63	N22 14	0	TUE 9
10 WED	181 54	-7	S22 51	6	150 40	-21	S24 06	8	81 31	29	S 2 00	15	268 59	55	N 5 48	1	335 53	64	N22 14	1	WED 10
11 THU	181 47	-6	S22 57	5	150 19	-22	S23 58	9	82 00	29	S 1 45	16	269 54	55	N 5 46	1	336 57	64	N22 15	0	THU 11
12 FRI	181 41	-7	S23 02	4	149 57	-21	S23 49	9	82 29	29	S 1 29	15	270 49	55	N 5 45	2	338 01	64	N22 15	1	FRI 12
13 SAT	181 34	-7	S23 06	4	149 36	-21	S23 40	11	82 58	28	S 1 14	15	271 44	55	N 5 43	1	339 05	64	N22 16	0	SAT 13
14 SUN	181 27	-8	S23 10	4	149 15	-21	S23 29	10	83 26	28	S 0 59	16	272 39	56	N 5 42	1	340 09	64	N22 16	1	SUN 14
15 MON	181 19	-7	S23 14	3	148 54	-21	S23 19	12	83 54	28	S 0 43	15	273 35	55	N 5 41	1	341 13	64	N22 17	0	MON 15
16 TUE	181 12	-7	S23 17	3	148 33	-20	S23 07	12	84 22	28	S 0 28	16	274 30	56	N 5 39	1	342 17	64	N22 17	1	TUE 16
17 WED	181 05	-7	S23 20	2	148 13	-20	S22 55	13	84 50	28	S 0 12	9	275 26	56	N 5 38	1	343 21	64	N22 18	0	WED 17
18 THU	180 58	-8	S23 22	2	147 53	-20	S22 42	14	85 18	28	N 0 03	16	276 22	56	N 5 37	1	344 25	64	N22 18	0	THU 18
19 FRI	180 50	-7	S23 24	1	147 33	-19	S22 28	14	85 46	28	N 0 19	15	277 18	57	N 5 36	1	345 29	65	N22 18	1	FRI 19
20 SAT	180 43	-8	S23 25	1	147 14	-19	S22 14	15	86 14	27	N 0 34	16	278 15	56	N 5 35	0	346 34	64	N22 19	0	SAT 20
21 SUN	180 35	-7	S23 26	1	146 55	-19	S21 59	15	86 41	28	N 0 50	15	279 11	57	N 5 35	1	347 38	64	N22 19	1	SUN 21
22 MON	180 28	-8	S23 26	0	146 36	-19	S21 44	16	87 09	27	N 1 05	16	280 08	57	N 5 34	1	348 42	64	N22 20	0	MON 22
23 TUE	180 20	-7	S23 26	0	146 17	-18	S21 28	17	87 36	27	N 1 21	16	281 05	57	N 5 33	0	349 46	65	N22 20	1	TUE 23
24 WED	180 13	-8	S23 26	1	145 59	-18	S21 11	17	88 03	27	N 1 36	16	282 02	57	N 5 33	0	350 51	64	N22 21	0	WED 24
25 THU	180 05	-7	S23 25	2	145 41	-17	S20 54	18	88 30	27	N 1 52	16	282 59	57	N 5 32	0	351 55	65	N22 21	1	THU 25
26 FRI	179 58	-7	S23 23	2	145 24	-18	S20 36	19	88 57	27	N 2 08	15	283 56	58	N 5 32	1	353 00	64	N22 22	0	FRI 26
27 SAT	179 51	-8	S23 21	2	145 06	-17	S20 17	19	89 24	26	N 2 23	16	284 54	57	N 5 31	0	354 04	65	N22 22	1	SAT 27
28 SUN	179 43	-7	S23 19	3	144 49	-16	S19 58	20	89 50	27	N 2 39	15	285 51	58	N 5 31	0	355 09	64	N22 23	0	SUN 28
29 MON	179 36	-8	S23 16	4	144 33	-16	S19 38	20	90 17	26	N 2 54	16	286 49	58	N 5 31	0	356 13	64	N22 23	1	MON 29
30 TUE	179 28	-7	S23 12	3	144 17	-16	S19 18	21	90 43	27	N 3 10	16	287 47	58	N 5 31	0	357 17	65	N22 24	0	TUE 30
31 WED	179 21	-7	S23 09	5	144 01	-15	S18 57	21	91 10	26	N 3 26	15	288 45	59	N 5 30	0	358 22	64	N22 24	1	WED 31
32 THU	179 14		S23 04		143 46		S18 36		91 36		N 3 41		289 44		N 5 30		359 26		N22 25		THU 32

SUN AND PLANET INTERPOLATION AND CORRECTIONS

DIP Corrn

m	Corrn	ft
0.0	0'	0
0.7	-1	2
2.0	-2	6
3.9	-3	13
6.5	-4	21
9.7	-5	32
13.6	-6	44
18.1	-7	59
23.3	-8	76
29.1	-9	95
	-10	

SUN Correction

LL Alt	Corrn	UL Alt	Corrn
0° 03'	-18'	0° 04'	-50'
0 08	-17	0 08	-49
0 13	-16	0 14	-48
0 19	-15	0 19	-47
0 24	-14	0 24	-46
0 30	-13	0 30	-45
0 36	-12	0 36	-44
0 43	-11	0 43	-43
0 50	-10	0 50	-44
0 57	-9	0 57	-41
1 05	-8	1 05	-40
1 13	-7	1 13	-39
1 22	-6	1 23	-38
1 32	-5	1 32	-37
1 42	-4	1 43	-36
1 54	-3	1 54	-35
2 07	-2	2 07	-34
2 21	-1	2 21	-33
2 36	0	2 37	-32
2 53	+1	2 54	-31
3 13	+2	3 14	-30
3 36	+3	3 37	-29
4 02	+4	4 03	-28
4 32	+5	4 33	-27
5 08	+6	5 10	-26
5 52	+7	5 54	-25
6 46	+8	6 49	-24
7 56	+9	7 59	-23
9 29	+10	9 33	-22
11 39	+11	11 45	-21
14 54	+12	15 04	-20
20 20	+13	20 38	-19
31 06	+14	31 45	-18
59 11	+15	61 05	-17
	+16		-16

PLANET REFN Corrn

Alt	Corrn
0° 05'	-34'
0 10	-33
0 15	-32
0 20	-31
0 26	-30
0 32	-29
0 38	-28
0 45	-27
0 52	-26
0 59	-25
1 07	-24
1 16	-23
1 25	-22
1 35	-21
1 46	-20
1 58	-19
2 11	-18
2 25	-17
2 41	-16
2 58	-15
3 18	-14
3 41	-13
4 07	-12
4 38	-11
5 14	-10
5 59	-9
6 54	-8
8 06	-7
9 41	-6
11 56	-5
15 21	-4
21 10	-3
32 54	-2
62 22	-1
	0

SUN AND PLANET INTERPOLATION

v/d 0' to 60'

GMT HOURS

v/d	00	01	02	03	04	05	06	07	08	09	10	11	12	13	14	15	16	17	18	19	20	21	22	23	24
00	0	0	0	0	0	0	0	0	0	0	0	0	0	0	0	0	0	0	0	0	0	0	0	0	0
01	0	0	0	0	0	0	0	0	0	0	0	0	1	1	1	1	1	1	1	1	1	1	1	1	1
02	0	0	0	0	0	0	1	1	1	1	1	1	1	1	1	1	1	1	2	2	2	2	2	2	2
03	0	0	0	0	1	1	1	1	1	1	1	1	2	2	2	2	2	2	2	2	3	3	3	3	3
04	0	0	0	1	1	1	1	1	1	2	2	2	2	2	2	3	3	3	3	3	3	4	4	4	4
05	0	0	0	1	1	1	1	1	2	2	2	2	3	3	3	3	3	4	4	4	4	4	5	5	5
06	0	0	1	1	1	1	2	2	2	2	3	3	3	3	4	4	4	4	5	5	5	5	6	6	6
07	0	0	1	1	1	1	2	2	2	3	3	3	4	4	4	4	5	5	5	6	6	6	6	7	7
08	0	0	1	1	1	2	2	2	3	3	3	4	4	4	5	5	5	6	6	6	7	7	7	8	8
09	0	0	1	1	2	2	2	3	3	3	4	4	5	5	5	6	6	6	7	7	8	8	8	9	9
10	0	0	1	1	2	2	3	3	3	4	4	5	5	5	6	6	7	7	8	8	8	9	9	10	10
11	0	0	1	1	2	2	3	3	4	4	5	5	6	6	6	7	7	8	8	9	9	10	10	11	11
12	0	1	1	2	2	3	3	4	4	5	5	6	6	7	7	8	8	9	9	10	10	11	11	12	12
13	0	1	1	2	2	3	3	4	4	5	5	6	7	7	8	8	9	9	10	10	11	11	12	12	13
14	0	1	1	2	2	3	4	4	5	5	6	6	7	8	8	9	9	10	11	11	12	12	13	13	14
15	0	1	1	2	3	3	4	4	5	6	6	7	8	8	9	9	10	11	11	12	13	13	14	14	15
16	0	1	1	2	3	3	4	5	5	6	7	7	8	9	9	10	11	11	12	13	13	14	15	15	16
17	0	1	1	2	3	4	4	5	6	6	7	8	9	9	10	11	11	12	13	13	14	15	16	16	17
18	0	1	2	2	3	4	5	5	6	7	8	8	9	10	11	11	12	13	14	14	15	16	17	17	18
19	0	1	2	2	3	4	5	6	6	7	8	9	10	10	11	12	13	13	14	15	16	17	17	18	19
20	0	1	2	3	3	4	5	6	7	8	8	9	10	11	12	13	13	14	15	16	17	18	18	19	20
21	0	1	2	3	4	4	5	6	7	8	9	10	11	11	12	13	14	15	16	17	18	18	19	20	21
22	0	1	2	3	4	5	6	6	7	8	9	10	11	12	13	14	15	16	17	17	18	19	20	21	22
23	0	1	2	3	4	5	6	7	8	9	10	11	12	12	13	14	15	16	17	18	19	20	21	22	23
24	0	1	2	3	4	5	6	7	8	9	10	11	12	13	14	15	16	17	18	19	20	21	22	23	24
25	0	1	2	3	4	5	6	7	8	9	10	11	13	14	15	16	17	18	19	20	21	22	23	24	25
26	0	1	2	3	4	5	7	8	9	10	11	12	13	14	15	16	17	18	20	21	22	23	24	25	26
27	0	1	2	3	5	6	7	8	9	10	11	12	14	15	16	17	18	19	20	21	23	24	25	26	27
28	0	1	2	4	5	6	7	8	9	11	12	13	14	15	16	18	19	20	21	22	23	25	26	27	28
29	0	1	2	4	5	6	7	8	10	11	12	13	15	16	17	18	19	21	22	23	24	25	27	28	29
30	0	1	3	4	5	6	8	9	10	11	13	14	15	16	18	19	20	21	23	24	25	26	28	29	30
31	0	1	3	4	5	6	8	9	10	12	13	14	16	17	18	19	21	22	23	25	26	27	28	30	31
32	0	1	3	4	5	7	8	9	11	12	13	15	16	17	19	20	21	23	24	25	27	28	29	31	32
33	0	1	3	4	6	7	8	10	11	12	14	15	17	18	19	21	22	23	25	26	28	29	30	32	33
34	0	1	3	4	6	7	9	10	11	13	14	16	17	18	20	21	23	24	26	27	28	30	31	33	34
35	0	1	3	4	6	7	9	10	12	13	15	16	18	19	20	22	23	25	26	28	29	31	32	34	35
36	0	2	3	5	6	8	9	11	12	14	15	17	18	20	21	23	24	26	27	29	30	32	33	35	36
37	0	2	3	5	6	8	9	11	12	14	15	17	19	20	22	23	25	26	28	29	31	32	34	35	37
38	0	2	3	5	6	8	10	11	13	14	16	17	19	21	22	24	25	27	29	30	32	33	35	36	38
39	0	2	3	5	7	8	10	11	13	15	16	18	20	21	23	24	26	28	29	31	33	34	36	37	39
40	0	2	3	5	7	8	10	12	13	15	17	18	20	22	23	25	27	28	30	32	33	35	37	38	40
41	0	2	3	5	7	9	10	12	14	15	17	19	21	22	24	26	27	29	31	32	34	36	38	39	41
42	0	2	4	5	7	9	11	12	14	16	18	19	21	23	25	26	28	30	32	33	35	37	39	40	42
43	0	2	4	5	7	9	11	13	14	16	18	20	22	23	25	27	29	30	32	34	36	38	39	41	43
44	0	2	4	6	7	9	11	13	15	17	18	20	22	24	26	28	29	31	33	35	37	39	40	42	44
45	0	2	4	6	8	9	11	13	15	17	19	21	23	24	26	28	30	32	34	36	38	39	41	43	45
46	0	2	4	6	8	10	12	13	15	17	19	21	23	25	27	29	31	33	35	36	38	40	42	44	46
47	0	2	4	6	8	10	12	14	16	18	20	22	24	25	27	29	31	33	35	37	39	41	43	45	47
48	0	2	4	6	8	10	12	14	16	18	20	22	24	26	28	30	32	34	36	38	40	42	44	46	48
49	0	2	4	6	8	10	12	14	16	18	20	22	25	27	29	31	33	35	37	39	41	43	45	47	49
50	0	2	4	6	8	10	13	15	17	19	21	23	25	27	29	31	33	35	38	40	42	44	46	48	50
51	0	2	4	6	9	11	13	15	17	19	21	23	26	28	30	32	34	36	38	40	43	45	47	49	51
52	0	2	4	7	9	11	13	15	17	20	22	24	26	28	30	33	35	37	39	41	43	46	48	50	52
53	0	2	4	7	9	11	13	15	18	20	22	24	27	29	31	33	35	38	40	42	44	46	49	51	53
54	0	2	5	7	9	11	14	16	18	20	23	25	27	29	32	34	36	38	41	43	45	47	50	52	54
55	0	2	5	7	9	11	14	16	18	21	23	25	28	30	32	34	37	39	41	44	46	48	50	53	55
56	0	2	5	7	9	12	14	16	19	21	23	26	28	30	33	35	37	40	42	44	47	49	51	54	56
57	0	2	5	7	10	12	14	17	19	21	24	26	29	31	33	36	38	40	43	45	48	50	52	55	57
58	0	2	5	7	10	12	15	17	19	22	24	27	29	31	34	36	39	41	44	46	48	51	53	56	58
59	0	2	5	7	10	12	15	17	20	22	25	27	30	32	34	37	39	42	44	47	49	52	54	57	59
60	0	3	5	8	10	13	15	18	20	23	25	28	30	33	35	38	40	43	45	48	50	53	55	58	60

SUN AND PLANET INTERPOLATION

v/d 60' to 120'

v/d	00	01	02	03	04	05	06	07	08	09	10	11	12	13	14	15	16	17	18	19	20	21	22	23	24	00	10	20	30	40	50	60
						GMT				HOURS																			MINUTES			
60	0	3	5	8	10	13	15	18	20	23	25	28	30	33	35	38	40	43	45	48	50	53	55	58	60	0	0	1	1	2	2	3
61	0	3	5	8	10	13	15	18	20	23	25	28	31	33	36	38	41	43	46	48	51	53	56	58	61	0	0	1	1	2	2	3
62	0	3	5	8	10	13	16	18	21	23	26	28	31	34	36	39	41	44	47	49	52	54	57	59	62	0	0	1	1	2	2	3
63	0	3	5	8	11	13	16	18	21	24	26	29	32	34	37	39	42	45	47	50	53	55	58	60	63	0	0	1	1	2	2	3
64	0	3	5	8	11	13	16	19	21	24	27	29	32	35	37	40	43	45	48	51	53	56	59	61	64	0	0	1	1	2	2	3
65	0	3	5	8	11	14	16	19	22	24	27	30	33	35	38	41	43	46	49	51	54	57	60	62	65	0	0	1	1	2	2	3
66	0	3	6	8	11	14	17	19	22	25	28	30	33	36	39	41	44	47	50	52	55	58	61	63	66	0	0	1	1	2	2	3
67	0	3	6	8	11	14	17	20	22	25	28	31	34	36	39	42	45	47	50	53	56	59	61	64	67	0	0	1	1	2	2	3
68	0	3	6	9	11	14	17	20	23	26	28	31	34	37	40	43	45	48	51	54	57	60	62	65	68	0	0	1	1	2	2	3
69	0	3	6	9	12	14	17	20	23	26	29	32	35	37	40	43	46	49	52	55	58	60	63	66	69	0	0	1	1	2	2	3
70	0	3	6	9	12	15	18	20	23	26	29	32	35	38	41	44	47	50	53	55	58	61	64	67	70	0	0	1	1	2	2	3
71	0	3	6	9	12	15	18	21	24	27	30	33	36	38	41	44	47	50	53	56	59	62	65	68	71	0	0	1	1	2	2	3
72	0	3	6	9	12	15	18	21	24	27	30	33	36	39	42	45	48	51	54	57	60	63	66	69	72	0	1	1	2	2	3	3
73	0	3	6	9	12	15	18	21	24	27	30	33	37	40	43	46	49	52	55	58	61	64	67	70	73	0	1	1	2	2	3	3
74	0	3	6	9	12	15	19	22	25	28	31	34	37	40	43	46	49	52	56	59	62	65	68	71	74	0	1	1	2	2	3	3
75	0	3	6	9	13	16	19	22	25	28	31	34	38	41	44	47	50	53	56	59	63	66	69	72	75	0	1	1	2	2	3	3
76	0	3	6	10	13	16	19	22	25	29	32	35	38	41	44	48	51	54	57	60	63	67	70	73	76	0	1	1	2	2	3	3
77	0	3	6	10	13	16	19	22	26	29	32	35	39	42	45	48	51	55	58	61	64	67	71	74	77	0	1	1	2	2	3	3
78	0	3	7	10	13	16	20	23	26	29	33	36	39	42	46	49	52	55	59	62	65	68	72	75	78	0	1	1	2	2	3	3
79	0	3	7	10	13	16	20	23	26	30	33	36	40	43	46	49	53	56	59	63	66	69	72	76	79	0	1	1	2	2	3	3
80	0	3	7	10	13	17	20	23	27	30	33	37	40	43	47	50	53	57	60	63	67	70	73	77	80	0	1	1	2	2	3	3
81	0	3	7	10	14	17	20	24	27	30	34	37	41	44	47	51	54	57	61	64	68	71	74	78	81	0	1	1	2	2	3	3
82	0	3	7	10	14	17	21	24	27	31	34	38	41	44	48	51	55	58	62	65	68	72	75	79	82	0	1	1	2	2	3	3
83	0	3	7	10	14	17	21	24	28	31	35	38	42	45	48	52	55	59	62	66	69	73	76	80	83	0	1	1	2	2	3	3
84	0	4	7	11	14	18	21	25	28	32	35	39	42	46	49	53	56	60	63	67	70	74	77	81	84	0	1	1	2	2	3	4
85	0	4	7	11	14	18	21	25	28	32	35	39	43	46	50	53	57	60	64	67	71	74	78	81	85	0	1	1	2	2	3	4
86	0	4	7	11	14	18	22	25	29	32	36	39	43	47	50	54	57	61	65	68	72	75	79	82	86	0	1	1	2	2	3	4
87	0	4	7	11	15	18	22	25	29	33	36	40	44	47	51	54	58	62	65	69	73	76	80	83	87	0	1	1	2	2	3	4
88	0	4	7	11	15	18	22	26	29	33	37	40	44	48	51	55	59	62	66	70	73	77	81	84	88	0	1	1	2	2	3	4
89	0	4	7	11	15	19	22	26	30	33	37	41	45	48	52	56	59	63	67	70	74	78	82	85	89	0	1	1	2	2	3	4
90	0	4	8	11	15	19	23	26	30	34	38	41	45	49	53	56	60	64	68	71	75	79	83	86	90	0	1	1	2	3	3	4
91	0	4	8	11	15	19	23	27	30	34	38	42	46	49	53	57	61	64	68	72	76	80	83	87	91	0	1	1	2	3	3	4
92	0	4	8	12	15	19	23	27	31	35	38	42	46	50	54	58	61	65	69	73	77	81	84	88	92	0	1	1	2	3	3	4
93	0	4	8	12	16	19	23	27	31	35	39	43	47	50	54	58	62	66	70	74	78	81	85	89	93	0	1	1	2	3	3	4
94	0	4	8	12	16	20	24	27	31	35	39	43	47	51	55	59	63	67	71	74	78	82	86	90	94	0	1	1	2	3	3	4
95	0	4	8	12	16	20	24	28	32	36	40	44	48	51	55	59	63	67	71	75	79	83	87	91	95	0	1	1	2	3	3	4
96	0	4	8	12	16	20	24	28	32	36	40	44	48	52	56	60	64	68	72	76	80	84	88	92	96	0	1	1	2	3	3	4
97	0	4	8	12	16	20	24	28	32	36	40	44	49	53	57	61	65	69	73	77	81	85	89	93	97	0	1	1	2	3	3	4
98	0	4	8	12	16	20	25	29	33	37	41	45	49	53	57	61	65	69	74	78	82	86	90	94	98	0	1	1	2	3	3	4
99	0	4	8	12	17	21	25	29	33	37	41	45	50	54	58	62	66	70	74	78	83	87	91	95	99	0	1	1	2	3	3	4
100	0	4	8	13	17	21	25	29	33	38	42	46	50	54	58	63	67	71	75	79	83	88	92	96	100	0	1	1	2	3	3	4
101	0	4	8	13	17	21	25	29	34	38	42	46	51	55	59	63	67	72	76	80	84	88	93	97	101	0	1	1	2	3	4	4
102	0	4	9	13	17	21	26	30	34	38	43	47	51	55	60	64	68	72	77	81	85	89	94	98	102	0	1	1	2	3	4	4
103	0	4	9	13	17	21	26	30	34	39	43	47	52	56	60	64	69	73	77	82	86	90	94	99	103	0	1	1	2	3	4	4
104	0	4	9	13	17	22	26	30	35	39	43	48	52	56	61	65	69	74	78	82	87	91	95	100	104	0	1	1	2	3	4	4
105	0	4	9	13	18	22	26	31	35	39	44	48	53	57	61	66	70	74	79	83	88	92	96	101	105	0	1	1	2	3	4	4
106	0	4	9	13	18	22	27	31	35	40	44	49	53	57	62	66	71	75	80	84	88	93	97	102	106	0	1	1	2	3	4	4
107	0	4	9	13	18	22	27	31	36	40	45	49	54	58	62	67	71	76	80	85	89	94	98	103	107	0	1	1	2	3	4	4
108	0	5	9	14	18	23	27	32	36	41	45	50	54	59	63	68	72	77	81	86	90	95	99	104	108	0	1	2	2	3	4	5
109	0	5	9	14	18	23	27	32	36	41	45	50	55	59	64	68	73	77	82	86	91	95	100	104	109	0	1	2	2	3	4	5
110	0	5	9	14	18	23	28	32	37	41	46	50	55	60	64	69	73	78	83	87	92	96	101	105	110	0	1	2	2	3	4	5
111	0	5	9	14	19	23	28	32	37	42	46	51	56	60	65	69	74	79	83	88	93	97	102	106	111	0	1	2	2	3	4	5
112	0	5	9	14	19	23	28	33	37	42	47	51	56	61	65	70	75	79	84	89	93	98	103	107	112	0	1	2	2	3	4	5
113	0	5	9	14	19	24	28	33	38	42	47	52	57	61	66	71	75	80	85	89	94	99	104	108	113	0	1	2	2	3	4	5
114	0	5	10	14	19	24	29	33	38	43	48	52	57	62	67	71	76	81	86	90	95	100	105	109	114	0	1	2	2	3	4	5
115	0	5	10	14	19	24	29	34	38	43	48	53	58	62	67	72	77	81	86	91	96	101	105	110	115	0	1	2	2	3	4	5
116	0	5	10	15	19	24	29	34	39	44	48	53	58	63	68	73	77	82	87	92	97	102	106	111	116	0	1	2	2	3	4	5
117	0	5	10	15	20	24	29	34	39	44	49	54	59	63	68	73	78	83	88	93	98	102	107	112	117	0	1	2	2	3	4	5
118	0	5	10	15	20	25	30	34	39	44	49	54	59	64	69	74	79	84	89	93	98	103	108	113	118	0	1	2	2	3	4	5
119	0	5	10	15	20	25	30	35	40	45	50	55	60	64	69	74	79	84	89	94	99	104	109	114	119	0	1	2	2	3	4	5
120	0	5	10	15	20	25	30	35	40	45	50	55	60	65	70	75	80	85	90	95	100	105	110	115	120	0	1	2	3	3	4	5

MOON AT EVERY 6hrs GMT JANUARY 1999

Day GMT	GHA-GMT v	Dec	d	Day GMT	GHA-GMT v	Dec	d	Day GMT	GHA-GMT v	Dec	d	Day GMT	GHA-GMT v	Dec	d
1 00h	15° 31' -217'	N18° 59'	16'	9 00h	275° 48' -155'	S 1° 00'	60'	17 00h	186° 12' -188'	S19° 16'	13'	25 00h	87° 22' -191'	N 9° 06'	62'
FRI 06	11 54 -217	N19 15	11	SAT 06	273 13 -155	S 2 00	60	SUN 06	183 04 -188	S19 03	17	MON 06	84 11 -192	N10 08	60
HP 12	8 17 -217	N19 26	7	HP 12	270 38 -154	S 3 00	59	HP 12	179 56 -189	S18 46	21	HP 12	80 59 -194	N11 08	58
60' 18	4 40 -215	N19 33	1	55' 18	268 04 -154	S 3 59	58	56' 18	176 47 -189	S18 25	24	59' 18	77 45 -196	N12 06	55
2 00	1 05 -215	N19 34	3	10 00	265 30 -155	S 4 57	57	18 00	173 38 -189	S18 01	28	26 00	74 29 -198	N13 01	53
SAT 06	357 30 -214	N19 31	8	SUN 06	262 55 -155	S 5 54	57	MON 06	170 29 -189	S17 33	32	TUE 06	71 11 -199	N13 54	49
HP 12	353 56 -212	N19 23	13	HP 12	260 20 -155	S 6 51	55	HP 12	167 20 -188	S17 01	35	HP 12	67 52 -201	N14 43	47
59' 18	350 24 -209	N19 10	17	54' 18	257 45 -156	S 7 46	54	57' 18	164 12 -188	S16 26	39	59' 18	64 31 -203	N15 30	42
3 00	346 55 -208	N18 53	22	11 00	255 09 -156	S 8 40	53	19 00	161 04 -188	S15 47	42	27 00	61 08 -204	N16 12	39
SUN 06	343 27 -205	N18 31	26	MON 06	252 33 -157	S 9 33	51	TUE 06	157 56 -187	S15 05	45	WED 06	57 44 -206	N16 51	36
HP 12	340 02 -203	N18 05	29	HP 12	249 56 -159	S10 24	50	HP 12	154 49 -186	S14 20	48	HP 12	54 18 -207	N17 27	31
59' 18	336 39 -200	N17 36	34	54' 18	247 17 -159	S11 14	49	57' 18	151 43 -186	S13 32	51	59' 18	50 51 -208	N17 58	27
4 00	333 19 -197	N17 02	36	12 00	244 38 -161	S12 03	46	20 00	148 37 -185	S12 41	54	28 00	47 23 -209	N18 25	22
MON 06	330 02 -194	N16 26	40	TUE 06	241 57 -162	S12 49	45	WED 06	145 32 -184	S11 47	56	THU 06	43 54 -210	N18 47	18
HP 12	326 48 -191	N15 46	43	HP 12	239 15 -163	S13 34	43	HP 12	142 28 -184	S10 51	58	HP 12	40 24 -210	N19 05	14
58' 18	323 37 -187	N15 03	46	54' 18	236 32 -165	S14 17	40	58' 18	139 24 -183	S 9 53	61	59' 18	36 54 -211	N19 19	8
5 00	320 30 -186	N14 17	48	13 00	233 47 -167	S14 57	38	21 00	136 21 -183	S 8 52	62	29 00	33 23 -210	N19 27	5
TUE 06	317 24 -182	N13 29	50	WED 06	231 00 -168	S15 35	36	THU 06	133 18 -182	S 7 50	64	FRI 06	29 53 -210	N19 32	1
HP 12	314 22 -179	N12 39	52	HP 12	228 12 -170	S16 11	34	HP 12	130 16 -182	S 6 46	66	HP 12	26 23 -209	N19 31	5
57' 18	311 23 -176	N11 47	54	54' 18	225 22 -172	S16 45	30	58' 18	127 14 -182	S 5 40	67	59' 18	22 54 -208	N19 26	9
6 00	308 27 -174	N10 53	56	14 00	222 30 -173	S17 15	28	22 00	124 12 -181	S 4 33	68	30 00	19 26 -207	N19 17	14
WED 06	305 33 -172	N 9 57	56	THU 06	219 37 -175	S17 43	26	FRI 06	121 11 -182	S 3 25	69	SAT 06	15 59 -206	N19 03	19
HP 12	302 41 -169	N 9 01	58	HP 12	216 42 -177	S18 09	22	HP 12	118 09 -182	S 2 16	69	HP 12	12 33 -204	N18 44	22
56' 18	299 52 -167	N 8 03	59	55' 18	213 45 -178	S18 31	19	59' 18	115 07 -181	S 1 07	70	59' 18	9 09 -202	N18 22	27
7 00	297 05 -165	N 7 04	60	15 00	210 47 -180	S18 50	15	23 00	112 06 -183	N 0 03	70	31 00	5 47 -199	N17 55	30
THU 06	294 20 -163	N 6 04	60	FRI 06	207 47 -182	S19 05	13	SAT 06	109 03 -183	N 1 13	69	SUN 06	2 28 -198	N17 25	34
HP 12	291 37 -161	N 5 04	60	HP 12	204 45 -182	S19 18	8	HP 12	106 00 -184	N 2 22	70	HP 12	359 10 -195	N16 51	37
56' 18	288 56 -160	N 4 04	61	55' 18	201 43 -184	S19 26	6	59' 18	102 56 -184	N 3 32	69	58' 18	355 55 -193	N16 14	41
8 00	286 16 -158	N 3 03	61	16 00	198 39 -186	S19 32	1	24 00	99 52 -186	N 4 41	68	32 00	352 42	N15 33	
FRI 06	283 38 -158	N 2 02	61	SAT 06	195 33 -186	S19 31	3	SUN 06	96 46 -186	N 5 49	67				
HP 12	281 00 -156	N 1 01	61	HP 12	192 27 -187	S19 31	5	HP 12	93 40 -188	N 6 56	65		Phases of the Moon		
55' 18	278 24 -156	N 0 00	60	56' 18	189 20 -188	S19 26	10	59' 18	90 32 -190	N 8 01	65		New: 17d First Quarter: 24d		
9 00	275° 48'	S 1° 00'		17 00	186° 12'	S19° 16'		25 00	87° 22'	N 9° 06'			Full: 2d&31d Last Quarter: 9d		

MOON AT EVERY 6hrs GMT FEBRUARY 1999

Day GMT	GHA-GMT v	Dec	d	Day GMT	GHA-GMT v	Dec	d	Day GMT	GHA-GMT v	Dec	d	Day GMT	GHA-GMT v	Dec	d
1 00h	352° 42' -190'	N15° 33'	44'	9 00h	264° 28' -164'	S13° 56'	42'	17 00h	167° 12' -188'	S10° 10'	61'	25 00h	63° 53' -205'	N19° 18'	9'
MON 06	349 32 -188	N14 49	46	TUE 06	261 44 -165	S14 38	39	WED 06	164 04 -188	S 9 09	64	THU 06	60 28 -205	N19 27	4
HP 12	346 24 -185	N14 03	49	HP 12	258 59 -166	S15 17	37	HP 12	160 56 -188	S 8 05	65	HP 12	57 03 -204	N19 31	0
57' 18	343 19 -183	N13 14	51	54' 18	256 13 -168	S15 54	34	59' 18	157 48 -187	S 7 00	67	58' 18	53 39 -204	N19 31	4
2 00	340 16 -180	N12 23	53	10 00	253 25 -170	S16 28	32	18 00	154 41 -187	S 5 53	68	26 00	50 15 -203	N19 27	9
TUE 06	337 16 -177	N11 30	55	WED 06	250 35 -171	S17 00	29	THU 06	151 34 -187	S 4 45	70	FRI 06	46 52 -201	N19 18	13
HP 12	334 19 -175	N10 35	56	HP 12	247 44 -172	S17 29	26	HP 12	148 27 -186	S 3 35	70	HP 12	43 31 -201	N19 05	17
57' 18	331 24 -173	N 9 39	58	55' 18	244 52 -175	S17 55	23	59' 18	145 21 -187	S 2 25	72	58' 18	40 10 -199	N18 48	21
3 00	328 31 -171	N 8 41	59	11 00	241 57 -176	S18 18	20	19 00	142 14 -187	S 1 13	71	27 00	36 51 -197	N18 27	25
WED 06	325 40 -169	N 7 42	59	THU 06	239 01 -178	S18 38	18	FRI 06	139 07 -187	S 0 02	72	SAT 06	33 34 -196	N18 02	28
HP 12	322 51 -167	N 6 43	61	HP 12	236 03 -179	S18 56	14	HP 12	136 00 -187	N 1 10	71	HP 12	30 18 -193	N17 34	33
56' 18	320 04 -165	N 5 42	61	55' 18	233 04 -181	S19 10	10	59' 18	132 52 -187	N 2 21	71	58' 18	27 05 -192	N17 01	35
4 00	317 19 -163	N 4 41	62	12 00	230 03 -182	S19 20	7	20 00	129 45 -189	N 3 32	70	28 00	23 53 -189	N16 26	39
THU 06	314 36 -162	N 3 39	61	FRI 06	227 01 -183	S19 27	4	SAT 06	126 36 -189	N 4 42	69	SUN 06	20 44 -188	N15 47	42
HP 12	311 54 -161	N 2 38	62	HP 12	223 58 -185	S19 31	0	HP 12	123 27 -190	N 5 51	68	HP 12	17 36 -185	N15 05	45
55' 18	309 13 -159	N 1 36	62	56' 18	220 53 -186	S19 31	4	59' 18	120 17 -190	N 6 59	67	57' 18	14 31 -183	N14 20	47
5 00	306 34 -159	N 0 34	61	13 00	217 47 -187	S19 27	8	21 00	117 07 -192	N 8 06	64	29 00	11 28	N13 33	
FRI 06	303 55 -158	S 0 27	61	SAT 06	214 40 -189	S19 19	11	SUN 06	113 55 -193	N 9 10	62				
HP 12	301 17 -157	S 1 28	61	HP 12	211 31 -188	S19 08	15	HP 12	110 42 -194	N10 13	60				
55' 18	298 40 -156	S 2 29	60	56' 18	208 23 -190	S18 53	19	59' 18	107 28 -194	N11 13	58				
6 00	296 04 -157	S 3 29	59	14 00	205 13 -190	S18 34	23	22 00	104 14 -197	N12 11	55				
SAT 06	293 27 -156	S 4 28	58	SUN 06	202 03 -190	S18 11	26	MON 06	100 57 -197	N13 06	52				
HP 12	290 51 -156	S 5 26	58	HP 12	198 53 -191	S17 45	30	HP 12	97 40 -198	N13 58	49				
55' 18	288 15 -156	S 6 24	56	57' 18	195 42 -191	S17 15	34	59' 18	94 22 -200	N14 47	46				
7 00	285 39 -156	S 7 20	55	15 00	192 31 -190	S16 41	38	23 00	91 02 -201	N15 33	42				
SUN 06	283 03 -157	S 8 15	53	MON 06	189 21 -191	S16 03	41	TUE 06	87 41 -202	N16 15	39				
HP 12	280 26 -158	S 9 08	53	HP 12	186 10 -191	S15 22	44	HP 12	84 19 -203	N16 54	34				
54' 18	277 48 -158	S10 01	50	58' 18	182 59 -190	S14 38	48	59' 18	80 56 -203	N17 28	30				
8 00	275 10 -159	S10 51	49	16 00	179 49 -190	S13 50	51	24 00	77 33 -204	N17 58	27				
MON 06	272 31 -160	S11 40	48	TUE 06	176 39 -189	S12 59	53	WED 06	74 09 -205	N18 25	22				
HP 12	269 51 -161	S12 28	45	HP 12	173 30 -189	S12 06	57	HP 12	70 44 -205	N18 47	18		Phases of the Moon		
54' 18	267 10 -162	S13 13	43	58' 18	170 21 -189	S11 09	59	59' 18	67 19 -206	N19 05	13		New: 16d First Quarter: 23d		
9 00	264° 28'	S13° 56'		17 00	167° 12'	S10° 10'		25 00	63° 53'	N19° 18'			Full: No Last Quarter: 8d		

MOON AT EVERY 6hrs GMT MARCH 1999

Day GMT	GHA-GMT	v	Dec	d	Day GMT	GHA-GMT	v	Dec	d	Day GMT	GHA-GMT	v	Dec	d	Day GMT	GHA-GMT	v	Dec	d
1 00h	11° 28'	-181	N13° 33'	49'	9 00h	284° 10'	-166	S15° 44'	35	17 00h	186° 41'	-191	S 7° 39'	68	25 00h	80° 07'	-203	N19° 38'	5
MON 06	8 27	-179	N12 44	52	TUE 06	281 24	-168	S16 19	33	WED 06	183 30	-190	S 6 31	69	THU 06	76 44	-202	N19 33	9
HP 12	5 28	-176	N11 52	54	HP 12	278 36	-169	S16 52	30	HP 12	180 20	-191	S 5 22	71	HP 12	73 22	-200	N19 24	13
57' 18	2 32	-175	N10 58	55	54' 18	275 47	-170	S17 22	27	60' 18	177 09	-192	S 4 11	72	58' 18	70 02	-198	N19 11	18
2 00	359 37	-173	N10 03	57	10 00	272 57	-172	S17 49	24	18 00	173 57	-191	S 2 59	72	26 00	66 44	-197	N18 53	21
TUE 06	356 44	-171	N 9 06	58	WED 06	270 05	-173	S18 13	21	THU 06	170 46	-192	S 1 47	74	FRI 06	63 27	-195	N18 32	25
HP 12	353 53	-169	N 8 08	60	HP 12	267 12	-175	S18 34	19	HP 12	167 34	-193	S 0 33	74	HP 12	60 12	-192	N18 07	29
56' 18	351 04	-167	N 7 08	60	55' 18	264 17	-176	S18 53	15	60' 18	164 21	-193	N 0 41	74	57' 18	57 00	-191	N17 38	32
3 00	348 17	-166	N 6 08	61	11 00	261 21	-177	S19 08	12	19 00	161 08	-193	N 1 55	73	27 00	53 49	-188	N17 06	36
WED 06	345 31	-164	N 5 07	62	THU 06	258 24	-179	S19 20	8	FRI 06	157 55	-195	N 3 08	73	SAT 06	50 41	-187	N16 30	38
HP 12	342 47	-163	N 4 05	62	HP 12	255 25	-180	S19 28	5	HP 12	154 40	-195	N 4 21	73	HP 12	47 34	-184	N15 52	42
56' 18	340 04	-162	N 3 03	62	55' 18	252 25	-181	S19 33	2	60' 18	151 25	-196	N 5 34	70	57' 18	44 30	-182	N15 10	44
4 00	337 22	-161	N 2 01	62	12 00	249 24	-182	S19 35	2	20 00	148 09	-198	N 6 44	70	28 00	41 28	-179	N14 26	47
THU 06	334 41	-160	N 0 59	62	FRI 06	246 22	-184	S19 33	6	SAT 06	144 51	-198	N 7 54	67	SUN 06	38 29	-178	N13 39	49
HP 12	332 01	-159	S 0 03	62	HP 12	243 18	-184	S19 27	9	HP 12	141 33	-199	N 9 01	66	HP 12	35 31	-176	N12 50	51
55' 18	329 22	-158	S 1 05	61	56' 18	240 14	-186	S19 18	13	60' 18	138 14	-200	N10 07	63	56' 18	32 35	-173	N11 59	53
5 00	326 44	-158	S 2 06	61	13 00	237 08	-186	S19 05	16	21 00	134 54	-201	N11 10	60	29 00	29 42	-172	N11 06	55
FRI 06	324 06	-158	S 3 07	60	SAT 06	234 02	-187	S18 49	21	SUN 06	131 33	-202	N12 10	57	MON 06	26 50	-170	N10 11	56
HP 12	321 28	-157	S 4 07	59	HP 12	230 55	-188	S18 28	24	HP 12	128 11	-204	N13 07	54	HP 12	24 00	-168	N 9 15	57
55' 18	318 51	-158	S 5 06	58	56' 18	227 47	-188	S18 04	28	60' 18	124 47	-204	N14 01	51	56' 18	21 12	-167	N 8 18	59
6 00	316 13	-157	S 6 04	57	14 00	224 39	-189	S17 36	31	22 00	121 23	-205	N14 52	47	30 00	18 25	-165	N 7 19	60
SAT 06	313 36	-157	S 7 01	56	SUN 06	221 30	-189	S17 05	35	MON 06	117 58	-205	N15 39	43	TUE 06	15 40	-164	N 6 19	61
HP 12	310 59	-158	S 7 57	55	HP 12	218 21	-189	S16 30	39	HP 12	114 33	-207	N16 22	40	HP 12	12 56	-162	N 5 18	61
54' 18	308 21	-158	S 8 52	53	57' 18	215 12	-190	S15 51	42	60' 18	111 06	-207	N17 02	35	55' 18	10 14	-162	N 4 17	62
7 00	305 43	-159	S 9 45	51	15 00	212 02	-190	S15 09	46	23 00	107 39	-207	N17 37	31	31 00	7 32	-160	N 3 15	62
SUN 06	303 04	-159	S10 36	50	MON 06	208 52	-190	S14 23	49	TUE 06	104 12	-207	N18 08	26	WED 06	4 52	-160	N 2 13	62
HP 12	300 25	-160	S11 26	48	HP 12	205 42	-190	S13 34	52	HP 12	100 45	-208	N18 34	22	HP 12	2 12	-159	N 1 11	62
54' 18	297 45	-161	S12 14	47	58' 18	202 32	-190	S12 42	56	59' 18	97 17	-207	N18 56	17	55' 18	359 33	-158	N 0 09	62
8 00	295 04	-162	S13 01	44	16 00	199 22	-190	S11 46	58	24 00	93 50	-207	N19 13	13	32 00	356 55		S 0 53	
MON 06	292 22	-163	S13 45	42	TUE 06	196 12	-190	S10 48	60	WED 06	90 23	-206	N19 26	9					
HP 12	289 39	-164	S14 27	40	HP 12	193 02	-191	S 9 48	64	HP 12	86 57	-205	N19 35	4		Phases of the Moon			
54' 18	286 55	-165	S15 07	37	59' 18	189 51	-190	S 8 44	65	59' 18	83 32	-205	N19 39	1		New: 17d First Quarter: 24d/31d			
9 00	284° 10'		S15° 44'		17 00	186° 41'		S 7° 39'		25 00	80° 07'		N19° 38'			Full: 2d Last Quarter: 10d			

MOON AT EVERY 6hrs GMT APRIL 1999

Day GMT	GHA-GMT	v	Dec	d	Day GMT	GHA-GMT	v	Dec	d	Day GMT	GHA-GMT	v	Dec	d	Day GMT	GHA-GMT	v	Dec	d
1 00h	356° 55'	-158	S 0° 53'	62	9 00h	268° 22'	-182	S19° 34'	12	17 00h	167° 18'	-205	N 9° 32'	67	25 00h	59° 07'	-172	N12° 05'	54
THU 06	354 17	-157	S 1 55	61	FRI 06	265 20	-182	S19 22	15	SAT 06	163 53	-207	N10 39	65	SUN 06	56 15	-171	N11 11	55
HP 12	351 40	-158	S 2 56	60	HP 12	262 18	-182	S19 07	18	HP 12	160 26	-209	N11 44	61	HP 12	53 24	-168	N10 16	56
55' 18	349 02	-157	S 3 56	60	56' 18	259 16	-183	S18 49	22	61' 18	156 57	-210	N12 45	58	56' 18	50 36	-166	N 9 20	58
2 00	346 25	-157	S 4 56	59	10 00	256 13	-183	S18 27	26	18 00	153 27	-211	N13 43	55	26 00	47 50	-165	N 8 22	59
FRI 06	343 48	-157	S 5 55	58	SAT 06	253 10	-184	S18 01	29	SUN 06	149 56	-212	N14 38	51	MON 06	45 05	-164	N 7 23	60
HP 12	341 11	-158	S 6 53	57	HP 12	250 06	-185	S17 32	33	HP 12	146 24	-213	N15 29	47	HP 12	42 21	-161	N 6 23	60
54' 18	338 33	-157	S 7 50	55	56' 18	247 01	-184	S16 59	36	61' 18	142 51	-215	N16 16	43	55' 18	39 40	-161	N 5 23	61
3 00	335 56	-159	S 8 45	54	11 00	243 57	-185	S16 23	40	19 00	139 16	-214	N16 59	38	27 00	36 59	-160	N 4 22	62
SAT 06	333 17	-159	S 9 39	52	SUN 06	240 52	-186	S15 43	43	MON 06	135 42	-215	N17 37	34	TUE 06	34 19	-158	N 3 20	62
HP 12	330 38	-159	S10 31	51	HP 12	237 46	-185	S15 00	47	HP 12	132 07	-216	N18 11	29	HP 12	31 41	-158	N 2 18	62
54' 18	327 59	-160	S11 22	49	57' 18	234 41	-186	S14 13	49	60' 18	128 31	-215	N18 40	24	55' 18	29 03	-157	N 1 16	63
4 00	325 19	-161	S12 11	47	12 00	231 35	-186	S13 24	53	20 00	124 56	-215	N19 04	19	28 00	26 26	-156	N 0 13	62
SUN 06	322 38	-162	S12 58	45	MON 06	228 29	-187	S12 31	56	TUE 06	121 21	-214	N19 23	14	WED 06	23 50	-156	S 0 49	61
HP 12	319 56	-163	S13 43	43	HP 12	225 22	-186	S11 35	58	HP 12	117 47	-213	N19 37	10	HP 12	21 14	-156	S 1 50	62
54' 18	317 13	-163	S14 26	41	58' 18	222 16	-188	S10 37	61	60' 18	114 14	-212	N19 47	5	55' 18	18 38	-156	S 2 52	60
5 00	314 30	-165	S15 07	38	13 00	219 08	-187	S 9 36	64	21 00	110 42	-211	N19 52	0	29 00	16 02	-156	S 3 52	61
MON 06	311 45	-166	S15 45	36	TUE 06	216 01	-188	S 8 32	66	WED 06	107 11	-209	N19 52	5	THU 06	13 26	-156	S 4 53	59
HP 12	308 59	-167	S16 21	34	HP 12	212 53	-189	S 7 26	68	HP 12	103 42	-207	N19 47	9	HP 12	10 50	-156	S 5 52	58
54' 18	306 12	-168	S16 55	30	59' 18	209 44	-190	S 6 18	70	59' 18	100 15	-205	N19 38	14	54' 18	8 14	-156	S 6 50	57
6 00	303 24	-169	S17 25	28	14 00	206 34	-190	S 5 08	71	22 00	96 50	-202	N19 24	18	30 00	5 38	-157	S 7 47	56
TUE 06	300 35	-171	S17 53	25	WED 06	203 24	-191	S 3 57	73	THU 06	93 28	-200	N19 06	22	FRI 06	3 01	-158	S 8 43	55
HP 12	297 44	-171	S18 18	22	HP 12	200 13	-192	S 2 44	74	HP 12	90 08	-198	N18 44	26	HP 12	0 23	-158	S 9 38	53
54' 18	294 53	-173	S18 40	19	60' 18	197 01	-193	S 1 30	75	58' 18	86 50	-195	N18 18	29	54' 18	357 45	-159	S10 31	52
7 00	292 00	-174	S19 00	15	15 00	193 48	-194	S 0 15	75	23 00	83 35	-193	N17 49	33	31 00	355 06		S11 23	
WED 06	289 06	-175	S19 15	13	THU 06	190 34	-195	N 1 00	75	FRI 06	80 22	-190	N17 16	37					
HP 12	286 11	-176	S19 28	9	HP 12	187 19	-197	N 2 15	76	HP 12	77 12	-187	N16 39	39					
55' 18	283 15	-177	S19 37	7	61' 18	184 02	-198	N 3 31	74	57' 18	74 05	-184	N16 00	42					
8 00	280 18	-177	S19 44	2	16 00	180 44	-199	N 4 45	74	24 00	71 01	-182	N15 18	45					
THU 06	277 21	-179	S19 46	0	FRI 06	177 25	-201	N 5 59	73	SAT 06	67 59	-180	N14 33	47		Phases of the Moon			
HP 12	274 22	-180	S19 46	5	HP 12	174 04	-202	N 7 12	71	HP 12	64 59	-177	N13 46	50		New: 16d First Quarter: 22d			
55' 18	271 22	-180	S19 41	11	61' 18	170 42	-204	N 8 23	69	57' 18	62 02	-175	N12 56	51		Full: 30d Last Quarter: 9d			
9 00	268° 22'		S19° 34'		17 00	167° 18'		N 9° 32'		25 00	59° 07'		N12° 05'						

69

MOON AT EVERY 6hrs GMT MAY 1999

Day GMT	GHA-GMT v	Dec	d	Day GMT	GHA-GMT v	Dec	d	Day GMT	GHA-GMT v	Dec	d	Day GMT	GHA-GMT v	Dec	d
1 00h	355°06' -160	S11°23'	49	9 00h	262°42' -180	S14°45'	47	17 00h	157°51' -222	N18°30'	29	25 00h	55°42' -156	N 1°23'	63
SAT 06	352 26 -161	S12 12	48	SUN 06	259 42 -181	S13 58	50	MON 06	154 09 -223	N18 59	24	TUE 06	53 06 -156	N 0 20	62
HP 12	349 45 -161	S13 00	46	HP 12	256 41 -180	S13 08	54	HP 12	150 26 -222	N19 23	18	HP 12	50 30 -156	S 0 42	62
54' 18	347 04 -163	S13 46	44	57' 18	253 41 -181	S12 14	56	61' 18	146 44 -221	N19 41	13	55' 18	47 54 -155	S 1 44	62
2 00	344 21 -164	S14 30	41	10 00	250 40 -181	S11 18	58	18 00	143 03 -221	N19 54	8	26 00	45 19 -154	S 2 46	61
SUN 06	341 37 -165	S15 11	40	MON 06	247 39 -182	S10 20	61	TUE 06	139 22 -219	N20 02	3	WED 06	42 45 -155	S 3 47	61
HP 12	338 52 -166	S15 51	36	HP 12	244 37 -182	S 9 19	64	HP 12	135 43 -218	N20 05	2	HP 12	40 10 -155	S 4 48	59
54' 18	336 06 -167	S16 27	34	58' 18	241 35 -183	S 8 15	65	60' 18	132 05 -216	N20 03	8	54' 18	37 35 -155	S 5 47	59
3 00	333 19 -168	S17 01	32	11 00	238 32 -183	S 7 10	68	19 00	128 29 -214	N19 55	12	27 00	35 00 -156	S 6 46	57
MON 06	330 31 -169	S17 33	28	TUE 06	235 29 -184	S 6 02	69	WED 06	124 55 -211	N19 43	17	THU 06	32 24 -156	S 7 43	57
HP 12	327 42 -170	S18 01	26	HP 12	232 25 -185	S 4 53	71	HP 12	121 24 -208	N19 26	21	HP 12	29 48 -156	S 8 40	55
54' 18	324 52 -172	S18 27	23	59' 18	229 20 -187	S 3 42	72	59' 18	117 56 -206	N19 05	25	54' 18	27 12 -158	S 9 35	53
4 00	322 00 -172	S18 50	20	12 00	226 13 -187	S 2 30	73	20 00	114 30 -203	N18 40	30	28 00	24 34 -158	S10 28	52
TUE 06	319 08 -174	S19 10	16	WED 06	223 06 -189	S 1 17	74	THU 06	111 07 -199	N18 10	33	FRI 06	21 56 -159	S11 20	51
HP 12	316 14 -174	S19 26	14	HP 12	219 57 -191	S 0 03	75	HP 12	107 48 -196	N17 37	37	HP 12	19 17 -160	S12 11	48
54' 18	313 20 -175	S19 40	10	60' 18	216 46 -192	N 1 12	75	58' 18	104 32 -194	N17 00	40	54' 18	16 37 -162	S12 59	47
5 00	310 25 -176	S19 50	7	13 00	213 34 -194	N 2 27	75	21 00	101 18 -190	N16 20	43	29 00	13 55 -162	S13 46	44
WED 06	307 29 -177	S19 57	3	THU 06	210 20 -195	N 3 42	75	FRI 06	98 08 -187	N15 37	45	SAT 06	11 13 -164	S14 30	42
HP 12	304 32 -177	S20 00	0	HP 12	207 05 -198	N 4 57	74	HP 12	95 01 -184	N14 52	49	HP 12	8 29 -164	S15 12	40
55' 18	301 35 -178	S20 00	3	61' 18	203 47 -200	N 6 11	73	57' 18	91 57 -181	N14 03	50	54' 18	5 45 -166	S15 52	38
6 00	298 37 -178	S19 57	7	14 00	200 27 -202	N 7 24	71	22 00	88 56 -178	N13 13	53	30 00	2 59 -168	S16 30	35
THU 06	295 39 -179	S19 50	11	FRI 06	197 05 -204	N 8 35	70	SAT 06	85 58 -175	N12 20	54	SUN 06	0 11 -168	S17 05	32
HP 12	292 40 -179	S19 39	14	HP 12	193 41 -206	N 9 45	68	HP 12	83 03 -173	N11 26	56	HP 12	357 23 -170	S17 37	29
55' 18	289 41 -179	S19 25	17	61' 18	190 15 -209	N10 53	65	57' 18	80 10 -170	N10 30	58	54' 18	354 33 -170	S18 06	27
7 00	286 42 -180	S19 08	21	15 00	186 46 -210	N11 58	63	23 00	77 20 -169	N 9 32	58	31 00	351 43 -172	S18 33	23
FRI 06	283 42 -180	S18 47	25	SAT 06	183 16 -213	N13 01	59	SUN 06	74 31 -166	N 8 34	60	MON 06	348 51 -173	S18 56	21
HP 12	280 42 -180	S18 22	28	HP 12	179 43 -215	N14 00	55	HP 12	71 45 -164	N 7 34	61	HP 12	345 58 -175	S19 17	17
56' 18	277 42 -180	S17 54	31	61' 18	176 08 -217	N14 55	52	56' 18	69 01 -162	N 6 33	61	54' 18	343 03 -174	S19 34	14
8 00	274 42 -180	S17 23	34	16 00	172 31 -218	N15 47	48	24 00	66 19 -161	N 5 32	62	32 00	340 09	S19 48	
SAT 06	271 42 -180	S16 49	38	SUN 06	168 53 -220	N16 35	43	MON 06	63 38 -160	N 4 30	62				
HP 12	268 42 -180	S16 11	41	HP 12	165 13 -220	N17 18	39	HP 12	60 58 -158	N 3 28	62		Phases of the Moon		
56' 18	265 42 -180	S15 30	45	61' 18	161 33 -222	N17 57	33	55' 18	58 20 -158	N 2 25	62		New: 15d First Quarter: 22d		
9 00	262 42	S14 45		17 00	157 51	N18 30		25 00	55 42	N 1 23			Full: 30d Last Quarter: 8d		

MOON AT EVERY 6hrs GMT JUNE 1999

Day GMT	GHA-GMT v	Dec	d	Day GMT	GHA-GMT v	Dec	d	Day GMT	GHA-GMT v	Dec	d	Day GMT	GHA-GMT v	Dec	d
1 00h	340°09' -176	S19°48'	11	9 00h	245°11' -185	N 0°26'	73	17 00h	133°06' -201	N17°31'	40	25 00h	43°33' -161	S12°51'	47
TUE 06	337 13 -177	S19 59	7	WED 06	242 06 -186	N 1 39	73	THU 06	129 45 -198	N16 51	42	FRI 06	40 52 -162	S13 38	45
HP 12	334 16 -177	S20 06	4	HP 12	239 00 -188	N 2 52	73	HP 12	126 27 -195	N16 09	46	HP 12	38 10 -163	S14 23	43
54' 18	331 19 -178	S20 10	0	60' 18	235 52 -190	N 4 05	73	59' 18	123 12 -192	N15 23	48	54' 18	35 27 -165	S15 06	41
2 00	328 21 -178	S20 10	3	10 00	232 42 -192	N 5 18	72	18 00	120 00 -188	N14 35	51	26 00	32 42 -165	S15 47	38
WED 06	325 23 -179	S20 07	6	THU 06	229 30 -195	N 6 30	72	FRI 06	116 52 -185	N13 44	54	SAT 06	29 57 -168	S16 25	35
HP 12	322 24 -179	S20 01	11	HP 12	226 15 -197	N 7 42	69	HP 12	113 47 -181	N12 50	55	HP 12	27 09 -168	S17 00	33
55' 18	319 25 -178	S19 50	13	60' 18	222 58 -199	N 8 51	69	58' 18	110 46 -179	N11 55	57	54' 18	24 21 -170	S17 33	30
3 00	316 27 -179	S19 37	17	11 00	219 39 -202	N10 00	66	19 00	107 47 -176	N10 58	59	27 00	21 31 -171	S18 03	27
THU 06	313 28 -179	S19 20	21	FRI 06	216 17 -205	N11 06	64	SAT 06	104 51 -173	N 9 59	60	SUN 06	18 40 -172	S18 30	25
HP 12	310 29 -179	S18 59	24	HP 12	212 52 -207	N12 10	62	HP 12	101 58 -171	N 8 59	61	HP 12	15 48 -174	S18 55	21
55' 18	307 30 -179	S18 35	27	61' 18	209 25 -210	N13 12	58	57' 18	99 07 -168	N 7 58	61	54' 18	12 54 -175	S19 16	18
4 00	304 31 -178	S18 08	31	12 00	205 55 -213	N14 10	55	20 00	96 19 -167	N 6 57	63	28 00	9 59 -175	S19 34	14
FRI 06	301 33 -178	S17 37	34	SAT 06	202 22 -214	N15 05	51	SUN 06	93 32 -164	N 5 54	63	MON 06	7 04 -177	S19 48	12
HP 12	298 35 -178	S17 03	37	HP 12	198 48 -218	N15 56	48	HP 12	90 48 -163	N 4 51	64	HP 12	4 07 -178	S20 00	8
56' 18	295 37 -178	S16 26	40	61' 18	195 10 -219	N16 44	43	56' 18	88 05 -161	N 3 47	63	54' 18	1 09 -178	S20 08	4
5 00	292 39 -177	S15 46	44	13 00	191 31 -221	N17 27	38	21 00	85 24 -159	N 2 44	64	29 00	358 11 -180	S20 12	1
SAT 06	289 42 -177	S15 02	46	SUN 06	187 50 -222	N18 05	34	MON 06	82 45 -159	N 1 40	63	TUE 06	355 11 -179	S20 13	2
HP 12	286 45 -177	S14 16	49	HP 12	184 08 -224	N18 39	29	HP 12	80 06 -157	N 0 37	64	HP 12	352 12 -180	S20 11	7
56' 18	283 48 -176	S13 27	52	61' 18	180 24 -224	N19 08	23	55' 18	77 29 -157	S 0 27	63	55' 18	349 12 -181	S20 04	9
6 00	280 52 -177	S12 35	54	14 00	176 40 -225	N19 31	19	22 00	74 52 -156	S 1 30	62	30 00	346 11 -180	S19 55	14
SUN 06	277 55 -176	S11 41	57	MON 06	172 55 -225	N19 50	12	TUE 06	72 16 -156	S 2 32	62	WED 06	343 11 -181	S19 41	16
HP 12	274 59 -177	S10 44	59	HP 12	169 10 -224	N20 02	8	HP 12	69 40 -155	S 3 34	61	HP 12	340 10 -180	S19 25	21
57' 18	272 02 -176	S 9 45	61	61' 18	165 26 -224	N20 10	2	55' 18	67 05 -156	S 4 35	60	55' 18	337 10 -181	S19 04	24
7 00	269 06 -177	S 8 44	64	15 00	161 42 -222	N20 12	3	23 00	64 29 -155	S 5 35	59	31 00	334 09	S18 40	
MON 06	266 09 -177	S 7 40	65	TUE 06	158 00 -221	N20 08	7	WED 06	61 54 -155	S 6 34	58				
HP 12	263 12 -178	S 6 35	67	HP 12	154 19 -219	N20 00	13	HP 12	59 18 -155	S 7 32	57				
58' 18	260 14 -179	S 5 28	69	60' 18	150 40 -216	N19 47	19	54' 18	56 43 -157	S 8 29	56				
8 00	257 15 -179	S 4 19	69	16 00	147 04 -214	N19 28	23	24 00	54 06 -157	S 9 25	54				
TUE 06	254 16 -181	S 3 10	71	WED 06	143 30 -211	N19 05	27	THU 06	51 29 -158	S10 19	52		Phases of the Moon		
HP 12	251 15 -181	S 1 59	72	HP 12	139 59 -208	N18 38	32	HP 12	48 51 -159	S11 11	51		New: 13d First Quarter: 20d		
59' 18	248 14 -183	S 0 47	73	59' 18	136 31 -205	N18 06	35	54' 18	46 12 -159	S12 02	49		Full: 28d Last Quarter: 7d		
9 00	245 11	N 0 26		17 00	133 06	N17 31		25 00	43 33	S12 51					

MOON AT EVERY 6hrs GMT JULY 1999

Day GMT	GHA-GMT v	Dec	d	Day GMT	GHA-GMT v	Dec	d	Day GMT	GHA-GMT v	Dec	d	Day GMT	GHA-GMT v	Dec	d
1 00h	334° 09' -180'	S18° 40'	27'	9 00h	237° 54' -201'	N12° 38'	58'	17 00h	127° 22' -174'	N 8° 34'	63'	25 00h	40° 16' -175'	S19° 09'	19'
THU 06	331 09 -179	S18 13	31	FRI 06	234 33 -205	N13 36	56	SAT 06	124 28 -172	N 7 31	63	SUN 06	37 21 -176	S19 28	16
HP 12	328 10 -180	S17 42	34	HP 12	231 08 -206	N14 32	52	HP 12	121 36 -169	N 6 28	64	HP 12	34 25 -177	S19 44	12
56' 18	325 10 -178	S17 08	37	60' 18	227 42 -210	N15 24	49	57' 18	118 47 -167	N 5 24	65	54' 18	31 28 -178	S19 56	9
2 00	322 12 -178	S16 31	40	10 00	224 12 -211	N16 13	45	18 00	116 00 -166	N 4 19	65	26 00	28 30 -179	S20 05	5
FRI 06	319 14 -178	S15 51	44	SAT 06	220 41 -214	N16 58	40	SUN 06	113 14 -164	N 3 14	65	MON 06	25 31 -180	S20 10	2
HP 12	316 16 -177	S15 07	46	HP 12	217 07 -217	N17 38	37	HP 12	110 30 -162	N 2 09	65	HP 12	22 31 -180	S20 12	2
56' 18	313 19 -177	S14 21	49	61' 18	213 30 -218	N18 15	32	56' 18	107 48 -161	N 1 04	65	55' 18	19 31 -182	S20 10	5
3 00	310 22 -176	S13 32	51	11 00	209 52 -219	N18 47	27	19 00	105 07 -160	S 0 01	64	27 00	16 29 -181	S20 05	9
SAT 06	307 26 -176	S12 41	55	SUN 06	206 13 -221	N19 14	22	MON 06	102 27 -159	S 1 05	64	TUE 06	13 28 -182	S19 56	13
HP 12	304 30 -175	S11 46	56	HP 12	202 32 -222	N19 36	17	HP 12	99 48 -158	S 2 09	63	HP 12	10 26 -183	S19 43	16
57' 18	301 35 -175	S10 50	59	61' 18	198 50 -222	N19 53	12	55' 18	97 10 -158	S 3 12	62	55' 18	7 23 -182	S19 27	20
4 00	298 40 -174	S 9 51	60	12 00	195 08 -222	N20 05	6	20 00	94 32 -157	S 4 14	61	28 00	4 21 -183	S19 07	24
SUN 06	295 46 -175	S 8 51	63	MON 06	191 26 -222	N20 11	1	TUE 06	91 55 -157	S 5 15	60	WED 06	1 18 -182	S18 43	27
HP 12	292 51 -175	S 7 48	64	HP 12	187 44 -221	N20 12	4	HP 12	89 18 -157	S 6 15	59	HP 12	358 16 -182	S18 16	31
57' 18	289 56 -174	S 6 44	66	60' 18	184 03 -221	N20 08	9	55' 18	86 41 -158	S 7 14	58	56' 18	355 14 -182	S17 45	34
5 00	287 02 -176	S 5 38	67	13 00	180 22 -219	N19 59	14	21 00	84 03 -157	S 8 12	56	29 00	352 12 -181	S17 11	37
MON 06	284 06 -175	S 4 31	69	TUE 06	176 43 -217	N19 45	20	WED 06	81 26 -158	S 9 08	55	THU 06	349 11 -181	S16 34	40
HP 12	281 11 -176	S 3 22	69	HP 12	173 06 -214	N19 25	24	HP 12	78 48 -158	S10 03	53	HP 12	346 10 -180	S15 54	44
58' 18	278 15 -177	S 2 13	70	60' 18	169 32 -213	N19 01	28	54' 18	76 10 -159	S10 56	52	56' 18	343 10 -180	S15 10	47
6 00	275 18 -178	S 1 03	71	14 00	165 59 -210	N18 33	33	22 00	73 31 -160	S11 48	49	30 00	340 10 -179	S14 23	49
TUE 06	272 20 -179	N 0 08	71	WED 06	162 29 -207	N18 00	37	THU 06	70 51 -161	S12 37	48	FRI 06	337 11 -179	S13 34	52
HP 12	269 21 -180	N 1 19	72	HP 12	159 02 -204	N17 23	40	HP 12	68 10 -162	S13 25	45	HP 12	334 12 -178	S12 42	55
59' 18	266 21 -181	N 2 31	71	59' 18	155 38 -201	N16 43	45	54' 18	65 28 -163	S14 10	44	57' 18	331 14 -177	S11 47	57
7 00	263 20 -184	N 3 42	71	15 00	152 17 -197	N15 58	47	23 00	62 45 -164	S14 54	41	31 00	328 17 -178	S10 50	59
WED 06	260 16 -185	N 4 53	70	THU 06	149 00 -195	N15 11	50	FRI 06	60 01 -165	S15 35	39	SAT 06	325 19 -176	S 9 51	61
HP 12	257 11 -187	N 6 03	70	HP 12	145 45 -191	N14 21	53	HP 12	57 16 -167	S16 14	36	HP 12	322 23 -176	S 8 50	64
59' 18	254 04 -189	N 7 13	68	59' 18	142 34 -189	N13 28	55	54' 18	54 29 -168	S16 50	33	57' 18	319 27 -177	S 7 46	64
8 00	250 55 -192	N 8 21	67	16 00	139 25 -185	N12 33	57	24 00	51 41 -169	S17 23	31	32 00	316 30	S 6 42	
THU 06	247 43 -194	N 9 28	65	FRI 06	136 20 -182	N11 36	59	SAT 06	48 52 -171	S17 54	28				
HP 12	244 29 -196	N10 33	64	HP 12	133 18 -179	N10 37	61	HP 12	46 01 -172	S18 22	25		Phases of the Moon		
60' 18	241 13 -199	N11 37	61	58' 18	130 19 -177	N 9 36	62	54' 18	43 09 -173	S18 47	22		New: 13d First Quarter: 20d		
9 00	237° 54'	N12° 38'		17 00	127° 22'	N 8° 34'		25 00	40° 16'	S19° 09'			Full: 28d Last Quarter: 6d		

MOON AT EVERY 6hrs GMT AUGUST 1999

Day GMT	GHA-GMT v	Dec	d	Day GMT	GHA-GMT v	Dec	d	Day GMT	GHA-GMT v	Dec	d	Day GMT	GHA-GMT v	Dec	d
1 00h	316° 30' -175'	S 6° 42'	67'	9 00h	212° 52' -216'	N20° 10'	6'	17 00h	114° 33' -159'	S 6° 52'	59'	25 00h	23° 06' -183'	S17° 55'	33'
SUN 06	313 35 -176	S 5 35	67	MON 06	209 16 -215	N20 04	12	TUE 06	111 54 -159	S 7 51	58	WED 06	20 03 -183	S17 22	37
HP 12	310 39 -176	S 4 28	69	HP 12	205 41 -214	N19 52	16	HP 12	109 15 -159	S 8 49	56	HP 12	17 00 -183	S16 45	40
58' 18	307 43 -177	S 3 19	69	60' 18	202 07 -212	N19 36	21	55' 18	106 36 -160	S 9 45	54	56' 18	13 57 -183	S16 05	43
2 00	304 46 -176	S 2 10	71	10 00	198 35 -211	N19 15	25	18 00	103 56 -160	S10 39	53	26 00	10 54 -182	S15 22	47
MON 06	301 50 -178	S 0 59	70	TUE 06	195 04 -209	N18 50	29	WED 06	101 16 -161	S11 32	50	THU 06	7 52 -182	S14 35	49
HP 12	298 52 -178	N 0 11	71	HP 12	191 35 -207	N18 20	34	HP 12	98 35 -161	S12 22	49	HP 12	4 50 -182	S13 46	53
58' 18	295 54 -178	N 1 22	71	59' 18	188 08 -204	N17 46	38	54' 18	95 54 -163	S13 11	46	57' 18	1 48 -181	S12 53	55
3 00	292 56 -180	N 2 33	70	11 00	184 44 -202	N17 08	42	19 00	93 11 -163	S13 57	44	27 00	358 47 -181	S11 58	57
TUE 06	289 56 -181	N 3 43	70	WED 06	181 22 -199	N16 26	45	THU 06	90 28 -164	S14 41	42	FRI 06	355 46 -181	S11 01	60
HP 12	286 55 -183	N 4 53	70	HP 12	178 03 -196	N15 41	48	HP 12	87 44 -165	S15 23	40	HP 12	352 45 -180	S10 01	63
59' 18	283 52 -184	N 6 03	68	59' 18	174 47 -194	N14 53	51	54' 18	84 59 -166	S16 03	37	57' 18	349 45 -180	S 8 58	64
4 00	280 48 -185	N 7 11	67	12 00	171 33 -191	N14 02	54	20 00	82 13 -168	S16 40	34	28 00	346 45 -180	S 7 54	66
WED 06	277 43 -188	N 8 18	66	THU 06	168 22 -188	N13 08	56	FRI 06	79 25 -168	S17 14	32	SAT 06	343 45 -179	S 6 48	68
HP 12	274 35 -189	N 9 24	64	HP 12	165 14 -185	N12 12	59	HP 12	76 37 -170	S17 46	28	HP 12	340 46 -180	S 5 40	68
59' 18	271 26 -191	N10 28	62	58' 18	162 09 -183	N11 13	60	54' 18	73 47 -171	S18 14	26	58' 18	337 46 -180	S 4 32	71
5 00	268 15 -194	N11 30	60	13 00	159 06 -181	N10 13	61	21 00	70 56 -172	S18 40	23	29 00	334 46 -180	S 3 21	71
THU 06	265 01 -195	N12 30	57	FRI 06	156 05 -177	N 9 12	63	SAT 06	68 04 -174	S19 03	20	SUN 06	331 46 -180	S 2 10	71
HP 12	261 46 -198	N13 27	52	HP 12	153 08 -176	N 8 09	64	HP 12	65 10 -175	S19 23	16	HP 12	328 46 -181	S 0 59	72
59' 18	258 28 -200	N14 21	52	57' 18	150 12 -173	N 7 05	65	54' 18	62 15 -176	S19 39	14	58' 18	325 45 -181	N 0 13	72
6 00	255 08 -202	N15 13	48	14 00	147 19 -171	N 6 00	66	22 00	59 19 -177	S19 53	9	30 00	322 44 -182	N 1 25	72
FRI 06	251 46 -205	N16 01	44	SAT 06	144 28 -170	N 4 54	66	SUN 06	56 22 -178	S20 02	7	MON 06	319 42 -183	N 2 37	72
HP 12	248 21 -206	N16 45	41	HP 12	141 38 -167	N 3 48	66	HP 12	53 24 -179	S20 09	3	HP 12	316 39 -184	N 3 49	71
60' 18	244 55 -209	N17 26	37	57' 18	138 51 -166	N 2 42	66	55' 18	50 25 -180	S20 12	1	59' 18	313 35 -185	N 5 00	71
7 00	241 26 -210	N18 03	32	15 00	136 05 -165	N 1 36	66	23 00	47 25 -181	S20 11	4	31 00	310 30 -186	N 6 11	69
SAT 06	237 56 -212	N18 35	28	SUN 06	133 20 -163	N 0 30	65	MON 06	44 24 -181	S20 07	8	TUE 06	307 24 -187	N 7 20	67
HP 12	234 24 -214	N19 03	23	HP 12	130 37 -163	S 0 35	65	HP 12	41 23 -182	S19 59	11	HP 12	304 17 -189	N 8 27	66
60' 18	230 50 -215	N19 26	19	56' 18	127 54 -161	S 1 40	65	55' 18	38 21 -183	S19 48	16	59' 18	301 08 -190	N 9 33	65
8 00	227 15 -215	N19 45	14	16 00	125 13 -161	S 2 45	63	24 00	35 18 -182	S19 32	19	32 00	297 58	N10 38	
SUN 06	223 40 -216	N19 59	8	MON 06	122 32 -160	S 3 48	63	TUE 06	32 16 -183	S19 13	22				
HP 12	220 04 -216	N20 07	4	HP 12	119 52 -159	S 4 51	62	HP 12	29 13 -184	S18 51	26		Phases of the Moon		
60' 18	216 28 -216	N20 11	1	55' 18	117 13 -160	S 5 52	60	56' 18	26 09 -183	S18 25	30		New: 11d First Quarter: 19d		
9 00	212° 52'	N20° 10'		17 00	114° 33'	S 6° 52'		25 00	23° 06'	S17° 55'			Full: 26d Last Quarter: 4d		

MOON AT EVERY 6hrs GMT SEPTEMBER 1999

Day GMT	GHA-GMT	v	Dec	d	Day GMT	GHA-GMT	v	Dec	d	Day GMT	GHA-GMT	v	Dec	d	Day GMT	GHA-GMT	v	Dec	d
1 00h	297° 58'	-192'	N10° 38'	62'	9 00h	190° 29'	-182'	N11° 39'	59'	17 00h	101° 43'	-170'	S18° 12'	27'	25 00h	6° 01'	-183'	S 5° 00'	72'
WED 06	294 46	-194	N11 40	59	THU 06	187 27	-179	N10 40	61	FRI 06	98 53	-172	S18 39	24	SAT 06	2 58	-184	S 3 48	72
HP 12	291 32	-195	N12 39	57	HP 12	184 28	-178	N 9 39	62	HP 12	96 01	-172	S19 03	21	HP 12	359 54	-184	S 2 36	74
59' 18	288 17	-197	N13 36	54	57' 18	181 30	-176	N 8 37	64	54' 18	93 09	-173	S19 24	17	59' 18	356 50	-185	S 1 22	74
2 00	285 00	-199	N14 30	51	10 00	178 34	-173	N 7 33	64	18 00	90 16	-174	S19 41	15	26 00	353 45	-186	S 0 08	74
THU 06	281 41	-200	N15 21	47	FRI 06	175 41	-172	N 6 29	66	SAT 06	87 22	-175	S19 56	10	SUN 06	350 39	-186	N 1 06	75
HP 12	278 21	-203	N16 08	44	HP 12	172 49	-170	N 5 23	66	HP 12	84 27	-177	S20 06	8	HP 12	347 33	-188	N 2 21	74
59' 18	274 58	-203	N16 52	40	57' 18	169 59	-169	N 4 17	66	54' 18	81 30	-177	S20 14	4	59' 18	344 25	-189	N 3 35	74
3 00	271 35	-206	N17 32	36	11 00	167 10	-167	N 3 11	67	19 00	78 33	-177	S20 18	1	27 00	341 16	-190	N 4 49	72
FRI 06	268 09	-206	N18 08	31	SAT 06	164 23	-166	N 2 04	66	SUN 06	75 36	-179	S20 19	3	MON 06	338 06	-191	N 6 01	72
HP 12	264 43	-208	N18 39	28	HP 12	161 37	-165	N 0 58	67	HP 12	72 37	-179	S20 16	6	HP 12	334 55	-192	N 7 13	70
59' 18	261 15	-209	N19 07	23	56' 18	158 52	-164	S 0 09	66	55' 18	69 38	-180	S20 10	11	60' 18	331 43	-194	N 8 23	69
4 00	257 46	-210	N19 30	18	12 00	156 08	-163	S 1 15	65	20 00	66 38	-181	S19 59	13	28 00	328 29	-196	N 9 32	67
SAT 06	254 16	-210	N19 48	13	SUN 06	153 25	-162	S 2 20	65	MON 06	63 37	-180	S19 46	17	TUE 06	325 13	-197	N10 39	64
HP 12	250 46	-211	N20 01	9	HP 12	150 43	-162	S 3 25	63	HP 12	60 37	-182	S19 29	21	HP 12	321 56	-199	N11 43	61
59' 18	247 15	-210	N20 10	4	56' 18	148 01	-161	S 4 28	63	55' 18	57 35	-181	S19 08	25	60' 18	318 37	-200	N12 44	59
5 00	243 45	-211	N20 14	1	13 00	145 20	-161	S 5 31	62	21 00	54 34	-182	S18 43	28	29 00	315 17	-202	N13 43	56
SUN 06	240 14	-210	N20 13	5	MON 06	142 39	-161	S 6 33	60	TUE 06	51 32	-182	S18 15	32	WED 06	311 55	-203	N14 39	52
HP 12	236 44	-209	N20 08	11	HP 12	139 58	-161	S 7 33	59	HP 12	48 30	-182	S17 43	35	HP 12	308 32	-205	N15 31	48
59' 18	233 15	-208	N19 57	15	55' 18	137 17	-161	S 8 32	57	56' 18	45 28	-182	S17 08	38	60' 18	305 07	-206	N16 19	45
6 00	229 47	-208	N19 42	19	14 00	134 36	-161	S 9 29	56	22 00	42 26	-182	S16 30	42	30 00	301 41	-208	N17 04	40
MON 06	226 19	-205	N19 23	24	TUE 06	131 55	-161	S10 25	54	WED 06	39 24	-182	S15 48	46	THU 06	298 13	-208	N17 44	37
HP 12	222 54	-204	N18 59	28	HP 12	129 14	-162	S11 19	51	HP 12	36 22	-182	S15 02	48	HP 12	294 45	-209	N18 21	31
59' 18	219 30	-202	N18 31	32	55' 18	126 32	-162	S12 10	50	57' 18	33 20	-182	S14 14	51	60' 18	291 16	-211	N18 52	28
7 00	216 08	-200	N17 59	37	15 00	123 50	-163	S13 00	48	23 00	30 18	-182	S13 23	55	31 00	287 45		N19 20	
TUE 06	212 48	-198	N17 22	39	WED 06	121 07	-164	S13 48	45	THU 06	27 16	-182	S12 28	57					
HP 12	209 30	-196	N16 43	44	HP 12	118 23	-164	S14 33	43	HP 12	24 14	-182	S11 31	60					
58' 18	206 14	-194	N15 59	46	54' 18	115 39	-166	S15 16	41	57' 18	21 12	-182	S10 31	62					
8 00	203 00	-191	N15 13	50	16 00	112 53	-166	S15 57	38	24 00	18 10	-182	S 9 29	64					
WED 06	199 49	-189	N14 23	52	THU 06	110 07	-167	S16 35	35	FRI 06	15 08	-182	S 8 25	67					
HP 12	196 40	-186	N13 31	55	HP 12	107 20	-168	S17 10	33	HP 12	12 06	-183	S 7 18	68		Phases of the Moon			
58' 18	193 34	-185	N12 36	57	54' 18	104 32	-169	S17 43	29	58' 18	9 03	-182	S 6 10	70	New: 9d			First Quarter: 17d	
9 00	190° 29'		N11° 39'		17 00	101° 43'		S18° 12'		25 00	6° 01'		S 5° 00'		Full: 25d			Last Quarter: 2d	

MOON AT EVERY 6hrs GMT OCTOBER 1999

Day GMT	GHA-GMT	v	Dec	d	Day GMT	GHA-GMT	v	Dec	d	Day GMT	GHA-GMT	v	Dec	d	Day GMT	GHA-GMT	v	Dec	d
1 00h	287° 45'	-210'	N19° 20'	22'	9 00h	186° 37'	-163'	N 0° 09'	66'	17 00h	97° 39'	-177'	S20° 26'	9'	25 00h	0° 36'	-198'	N 7° 46'	73'
FRI 06	284 15	-211	N19 42	18	SAT 06	183 54	-162	S 0 57	66	SUN 06	94 42	-178	S20 17	12	MON 06	357 18	-200	N 8 59	70
HP 12	280 44	-211	N20 00	13	HP 12	181 12	-161	S 2 03	65	HP 12	91 44	-177	S20 05	16	HP 12	353 58	-202	N10 09	68
59' 18	277 13	-211	N20 13	8	56' 18	178 31	-162	S 3 08	65	55' 18	88 47	-178	S19 49	19	61' 18	350 36	-204	N11 17	66
2 00	273 42	-210	N20 21	4	10 00	175 49	-160	S 4 13	63	18 00	85 49	-178	S19 30	22	26 00	347 12	-206	N12 23	62
SAT 06	270 12	-209	N20 25	2	SUN 06	173 09	-161	S 5 16	63	MON 06	82 51	-179	S19 08	26	TUE 06	343 46	-208	N13 25	60
HP 12	266 43	-209	N20 23	6	HP 12	170 28	-161	S 6 19	61	HP 12	79 52	-178	S18 41	29	HP 12	340 18	-210	N14 25	56
59' 18	263 14	-207	N20 17	11	55' 18	167 47	-161	S 7 20	60	55' 18	76 54	-178	S18 12	34	61' 18	336 48	-212	N15 21	52
3 00	259 47	-206	N20 06	15	11 00	165 06	-161	S 8 20	59	19 00	73 56	-179	S17 38	36	27 00	333 16	-213	N16 13	48
SUN 06	256 21	-204	N19 51	20	MON 06	162 25	-161	S 9 19	56	TUE 06	70 57	-178	S17 02	40	WED 06	329 43	-215	N17 01	44
HP 12	252 57	-203	N19 31	24	HP 12	159 44	-162	S10 15	55	HP 12	67 59	-179	S16 22	43	HP 12	326 08	-216	N17 45	39
58' 18	249 34	-200	N19 07	29	55' 18	157 02	-162	S11 10	54	56' 18	65 00	-178	S15 39	46	61' 18	322 32	-217	N18 24	35
4 00	246 14	-199	N18 38	32	12 00	154 20	-163	S12 04	52	20 00	62 02	-179	S14 53	49	28 00	318 55	-217	N18 59	29
MON 06	242 55	-196	N18 06	36	TUE 06	151 37	-164	S12 55	49	WED 06	59 03	-178	S14 04	53	THU 06	315 17	-218	N19 28	25
HP 12	239 39	-194	N17 30	39	HP 12	148 53	-164	S13 44	46	HP 12	56 05	-179	S13 11	55	HP 12	311 40	-218	N19 53	19
58' 18	236 25	-192	N16 51	43	54' 18	146 09	-165	S14 30	44	57' 18	53 06	-179	S12 16	58	60' 18	308 02	-218	N20 12	14
5 00	233 13	-190	N16 08	46	13 00	143 24	-165	S15 14	42	21 00	50 07	-180	S11 18	60	29 00	304 24	-218	N20 26	9
TUE 06	230 03	-187	N15 22	49	WED 06	140 39	-167	S15 56	39	THU 06	47 07	-179	S10 18	63	FRI 06	300 46	-216	N20 35	4
HP 12	226 56	-185	N14 33	51	HP 12	137 52	-167	S16 35	37	HP 12	44 08	-181	S 9 15	65	HP 12	297 10	-215	N20 39	1
58' 18	223 51	-183	N13 42	54	54' 18	135 05	-168	S17 12	34	58' 18	41 07	-180	S 8 10	68	60' 18	293 35	-214	N20 38	6
6 00	220 48	-180	N12 48	56	14 00	132 17	-169	S17 46	31	22 00	38 07	-181	S 7 02	69	30 00	290 01	-212	N20 32	11
WED 06	217 48	-179	N11 52	59	THU 06	129 28	-170	S18 17	27	FRI 06	35 06	-183	S 5 53	71	SAT 06	286 29	-210	N20 21	16
HP 12	214 49	-176	N10 53	60	HP 12	126 38	-170	S18 44	25	HP 12	32 03	-182	S 4 42	73	HP 12	282 59	-208	N20 05	21
57' 18	211 53	-175	N 9 53	61	54' 18	123 48	-172	S19 09	22	59' 18	29 01	-184	S 3 29	73	59' 18	279 31	-205	N19 44	24
7 00	208 58	-172	N 8 52	63	15 00	120 56	-172	S19 31	19	23 00	25 57	-185	S 2 16	75	31 00	276 04	-203	N19 20	29
THU 06	206 06	-171	N 7 49	64	FRI 06	118 04	-173	S19 50	15	SAT 06	22 52	-187	S 1 01	75	SUN 06	272 43	-200	N18 51	33
HP 12	203 15	-170	N 6 45	65	HP 12	115 11	-174	S20 05	12	HP 12	19 45	-187	N 0 15	76	HP 12	269 23	-198	N18 18	37
57' 18	200 25	-168	N 5 40	65	54' 18	112 17	-175	S20 17	9	59' 18	16 38	-189	N 1 31	76	58' 18	266 05	-194	N17 41	40
8 00	197 37	-166	N 4 35	66	16 00	109 22	-175	S20 26	5	24 00	13 29	-191	N 2 47	76	32 00	262 51		N17 01	
FRI 06	194 51	-166	N 3 29	67	SAT 06	106 27	-176	S20 31	2	SUN 06	10 18	-192	N 4 03	75					
HP 12	192 05	-164	N 2 22	66	HP 12	103 31	-176	S20 33	2	HP 12	7 06	-194	N 5 18	75		Phases of the Moon			
56' 18	189 21	-164	N 1 16	67	54' 18	100 35	-176	S20 31	5	60' 18	3 52	-196	N 6 33	73	New: 9d			First Quarter: 17d	
9 00	186° 37'		N 0° 09'		17 00	97° 39'		S20° 26'		25 00	0° 36'		N 7° 46'		Full: 24d&31d			Last Quarter: 2d	

MOON AT EVERY 6hrs GMT NOVEMBER 1999

Day	GMT	GHA-GMT	v	Dec	d	Day	GMT	GHA-GMT	v	Dec	d	Day	GMT	GHA-GMT	v	Dec	d	Day	GMT	GHA-GMT	v	Dec	d
1	00ʰ	262° 51'	-192'	N17° 01'	44'	9	00ʰ	173° 30'	-164'	S14° 29'	46'	17	00ʰ	81° 24'	-173'	S12° 57'	55'	25	00ʰ	337° 10'	-226'	N20° 11'	19'
MON	06	259 39	-190	N16 17	47	TUE	06	170 46	-166	S15 15	42	WED	06	78 31	-174	S12 02	58	THU	06	333 24	-227	N20 30	13
HP	12	256 29	-186	N15 30	49	HP	12	168 00	-166	S15 57	41	HP	12	75 37	-174	S11 04	60	HP	12	329 37	-225	N20 43	7
58'	18	253 23	-184	N14 41	52	54'	18	165 14	-167	S16 38	37	57'	18	72 43	-174	S10 04	63	61'	18	325 52	-225	N20 50	2
2	00	250 19	-181	N13 49	54	10	00	162 27	-169	S17 15	35	18	00	69 49	-175	S 9 01	64	26	00	322 07	-224	N20 52	4
TUE	06	247 18	-179	N12 55	57	WED	06	159 38	-169	S17 50	32	THU	06	66 54	-176	S 7 57	67	FRI	06	318 23	-221	N20 48	9
HP	12	244 19	-177	N11 58	58	HP	12	156 49	-170	S18 22	29	HP	12	63 58	-176	S 6 50	69	HP	12	314 42	-220	N20 39	14
57'	18	241 22	-174	N11 00	60	54'	18	153 59	-171	S18 51	26	58'	18	61 02	-177	S 5 41	70	60'	18	311 02	-217	N20 25	20
3	00	238 28	-172	N10 00	62	11	00	151 08	-171	S19 17	23	19	00	58 05	-178	S 4 31	72	27	00	307 25	-215	N20 05	24
WED	06	235 36	-170	N 8 58	62	THU	06	148 17	-172	S19 40	20	FRI	06	55 07	-180	S 3 19	73	SAT	06	303 50	-211	N19 41	29
HP	12	232 46	-168	N 7 56	64	HP	12	145 25	-173	S20 00	16	HP	12	52 07	-181	S 2 06	74	HP	12	300 19	-209	N19 12	33
56'	18	229 58	-167	N 6 52	65	54'	18	142 32	-174	S20 16	13	59'	18	49 06	-182	S 0 52	75	60'	18	296 50	-205	N18 39	37
4	00	227 11	-165	N 5 47	65	12	00	139 38	-174	S20 29	9	20	00	46 04	-185	N 0 23	76	28	00	293 25	-202	N18 02	41
THU	06	224 26	-164	N 4 42	66	FRI	06	136 44	-175	S20 38	7	SAT	06	42 59	-186	N 1 39	75	SUN	06	290 03	-198	N17 21	44
HP	12	221 42	-163	N 3 36	66	HP	12	133 49	-175	S20 45	2	HP	12	39 53	-188	N 2 54	76	HP	12	286 45	-195	N16 37	48
56'	18	218 59	-162	N 2 30	67	54'	18	130 54	-175	S20 47	0	60'	18	36 45	-190	N 4 10	75	59'	18	283 30	-192	N15 49	51
5	00	216 17	-161	N 1 23	66	13	00	127 59	-175	S20 47	5	21	00	33 35	-193	N 5 26	75	29	00	280 18	-188	N14 58	53
FRI	06	213 36	-160	N 0 17	66	SAT	06	125 04	-176	S20 42	7	SUN	06	30 22	-195	N 6 41	74	MON	06	277 10	-186	N14 05	55
HP	12	210 56	-160	S 0 49	66	HP	12	122 08	-175	S20 35	11	HP	12	27 07	-198	N 7 55	73	HP	12	274 04	-182	N13 10	58
55'	18	208 16	-159	S 1 55	65	54'	18	119 13	-176	S20 24	15	60'	18	23 49	-201	N 9 08	71	58'	18	271 02	-179	N12 12	59
6	00	205 37	-159	S 3 00	65	14	00	116 17	-175	S20 09	18	22	00	20 28	-203	N10 19	69	30	00	268 03	-177	N11 13	61
SAT	06	202 58	-159	S 4 05	63	SUN	06	113 22	-175	S19 51	21	MON	06	17 05	-206	N11 28	66	TUE	06	265 06	-174	N10 12	63
HP	12	200 19	-159	S 5 08	63	HP	12	110 26	-175	S19 29	24	HP	12	13 39	-208	N12 34	64	HP	12	262 12	-171	N 9 09	64
55'	18	197 40	-159	S 6 11	62	55'	18	107 31	-175	S19 05	29	61'	18	10 11	-212	N13 38	61	57'	18	259 21	-170	N 8 05	64
7	00	195 01	-160	S 7 13	60	15	00	104 36	-174	S18 36	31	23	00	6 39	-214	N14 39	57	31	00	256 31		N 7 01	
SUN	06	192 21	-160	S 8 13	59	MON	06	101 42	-175	S18 05	35	TUE	06	3 05	-217	N15 36	53						
HP	12	189 41	-160	S 9 12	58	HP	12	98 47	-174	S17 30	38	HP	12	359 28	-218	N16 29	49						
55'	18	187 01	-161	S10 10	56	55'	18	95 53	-174	S16 52	41	61'	18	355 50	-221	N17 18	45						
8	00	184 20	-161	S11 06	54	16	00	92 59	-174	S16 11	44	24	00	352 09	-223	N18 03	40						
MON	06	181 39	-162	S12 00	52	TUE	06	90 05	-174	S15 27	47	WED	06	348 26	-224	N18 43	34						
HP	12	178 57	-163	S12 52	50	HP	12	87 11	-173	S14 40	50	HP	12	344 42	-226	N19 17	30						
54'	18	176 14	-164	S13 42	47	56'	18	84 18	-174	S13 50	53	61'	18	340 56	-226	N19 47	24						
9	00	173° 30'		S14° 29'		17	00	81° 24'		S12° 57'		25	00	337° 10'		N20° 11'							

Phases of the Moon
New: 8d   First Quarter: 16d
Full: 23d   Last Quarter: 29d

MOON AT EVERY 6hrs GMT DECEMBER 1999

Day	GMT	GHA-GMT	v	Dec	d	Day	GMT	GHA-GMT	v	Dec	d	Day	GMT	GHA-GMT	v	Dec	d	Day	GMT	GHA-GMT	v	Dec	d
1	00ʰ	256° 31'	-167'	N 7° 01'	66'	9	00ʰ	169° 30'	-174'	S20° 21'	14'	17	00ʰ	77° 29'	-175'	S 1° 40'	72'	25	00ʰ	326° 07'	-216'	N19° 10'	35'
WED	06	253 44	-166	N 5 55	66	THU	06	166 36	-174	S20 35	11	FRI	06	74 34	-176	S 0 28	73	SAT	06	322 31	-212	N18 35	40
HP	12	250 58	-164	N 4 49	66	HP	12	163 42	-175	S20 46	6	HP	12	71 38	-178	N 0 45	74	HP	12	318 59	-209	N17 55	44
56'	18	248 14	-162	N 3 43	67	54'	18	160 47	-176	S20 52	2	58'	18	68 40	-179	N 1 59	74	60'	18	315 30	-205	N17 11	47
2	00	245 32	-161	N 2 36	66	10	00	157 51	-175	S20 56	0	18	00	65 41	-182	N 3 13	73	26	00	312 05	-201	N16 24	51
THU	06	242 51	-160	N 1 30	67	FRI	06	154 56	-176	S20 56	4	SAT	06	62 39	-184	N 4 26	74	SUN	06	308 44	-198	N15 33	54
HP	12	240 11	-159	N 0 23	66	HP	12	152 00	-176	S20 52	7	HP	12	59 35	-187	N 5 40	73	HP	12	305 26	-194	N14 39	56
56'	18	237 32	-159	S 0 43	66	54'	18	149 04	-176	S20 45	11	59'	18	56 28	-189	N 6 53	72	59'	18	302 12	-191	N13 43	59
3	00	234 53	-158	S 1 49	66	11	00	146 08	-175	S20 34	14	19	00	53 19	-193	N 8 05	71	27	00	299 01	-187	N12 44	61
FRI	06	232 15	-157	S 2 55	64	SAT	06	143 13	-176	S20 20	20	SUN	06	50 06	-195	N 9 16	69	MON	06	295 54	-185	N11 43	62
HP	12	229 38	-158	S 4 01	64	HP	12	140 17	-174	S20 03	21	HP	12	46 51	-198	N10 25	68	HP	12	292 49	-181	N10 41	64
55'	18	227 00	-157	S 5 03	63	54'	18	137 23	-175	S19 42	24	60'	18	43 33	-201	N11 33	65	58'	18	289 48	-178	N 9 37	66
4	00	224 23	-158	S 6 06	62	12	00	134 28	-174	S19 18	28	20	00	40 12	-205	N12 38	63	28	00	286 50	-175	N 8 31	66
SAT	06	221 45	-157	S 7 08	60	SUN	06	131 34	-173	S18 50	31	MON	06	36 47	-208	N13 41	60	TUE	06	283 55	-173	N 7 25	67
HP	12	219 08	-159	S 8 08	59	HP	12	128 41	-173	S18 19	34	HP	12	33 19	-211	N14 41	57	HP	12	281 02	-170	N 6 18	68
55'	18	216 29	-158	S 9 07	58	55'	18	125 48	-173	S17 45	37	61'	18	29 48	-214	N15 38	53	57'	18	278 12	-168	N 5 10	68
5	00	213 51	-159	S10 05	56	13	00	122 55	-171	S17 08	40	21	00	26 14	-217	N16 31	49	29	00	275 24	-166	N 4 02	68
SUN	06	211 12	-160	S11 01	55	MON	06	120 04	-172	S16 28	43	TUE	06	22 37	-220	N17 20	45	WED	06	272 38	-165	N 2 54	68
HP	12	208 32	-161	S11 56	52	HP	12	117 12	-170	S15 45	46	HP	12	18 57	-223	N18 05	40	HP	12	269 53	-163	N 1 46	68
54'	18	205 51	-162	S12 48	50	55'	18	114 22	-171	S14 59	48	61'	18	15 14	-224	N18 45	36	56'	18	267 10	-162	N 0 38	68
6	00	203 09	-162	S13 38	48	14	00	111 31	-169	S14 11	52	22	00	11 30	-227	N19 21	30	30	00	264 28	-161	S 0 30	67
MON	06	200 27	-164	S14 26	46	TUE	06	108 42	-170	S13 19	53	WED	06	7 43	-229	N19 51	24	THU	06	261 47	-159	S 1 37	66
HP	12	197 43	-165	S15 12	44	HP	12	105 52	-169	S12 26	56	HP	12	3 54	-229	N20 15	19	HP	12	259 08	-159	S 2 43	66
54'	18	194 58	-165	S15 56	41	56'	18	103 03	-169	S11 30	59	61'	18	0 05	-230	N20 34	14	56'	18	256 29	-159	S 3 49	64
7	00	192 13	-167	S16 37	38	15	00	100 14	-169	S10 31	60	23	00	356 15	-231	N20 48	7	31	00	253 50	-158	S 4 53	64
TUE	06	189 26	-168	S17 15	36	WED	06	97 25	-169	S 9 31	62	THU	06	352 24	-230	N20 55	2	FRI	06	251 12	-158	S 5 57	62
HP	12	186 38	-169	S17 51	33	HP	12	94 36	-170	S 8 29	65	HP	12	348 34	-229	N20 57	4	HP	12	248 34	-158	S 6 59	61
54'	18	183 49	-170	S18 24	30	57'	18	91 46	-170	S 7 24	66	61'	18	344 45	-228	N20 53	10	55'	18	245 56	-158	S 8 00	60
8	00	180 59	-171	S18 54	26	16	00	88 56	-170	S 6 18	67	24	00	340 57	-226	N20 43	15	32	00	243 18		S 9 00	
WED	06	178 08	-172	S19 20	24	THU	06	86 06	-172	S 5 11	69	FRI	06	337 11	-224	N20 28	21						
HP	12	175 16	-172	S19 44	20	HP	12	83 14	-172	S 4 02	71	HP	12	333 27	-222	N20 07	26						
54'	18	172 24	-174	S20 04	17	57'	18	80 22	-173	S 2 51	71	61'	18	329 45	-218	N19 41	31						
9	00	169° 30'		S20° 21'		17	00	77° 29'		S 1° 40'		25	00	326° 07'		N19° 10'							

Phases of the Moon
New: 7d   First Quarter: 16d
Full: 22d   Last Quarter: 29d

MOON AT EVERY 6hrs GMT JANUARY 2000

Days 1–8

Day	GMT	GHA-GMT	v	Dec	d
1	00h	243° 18'	-159'	S 9° 00'	58'
SAT	06	240 39	-159	S 9 58	56
HP	12	238 00	-159	S10 54	55
54'	18	235 21	-160	S11 49	52
2	00	232 41	-161	S12 41	51
SUN	06	230 00	-162	S13 32	48
HP	12	227 18	-163	S14 20	47
54'	18	224 35	-164	S15 07	43
3	00	221 51	-165	S15 50	42
MON	06	219 06	-166	S16 32	38
HP	12	216 20	-167	S17 10	37
54'	18	213 33	-168	S17 47	33
4	00	210 45	-169	S18 20	30
TUE	06	207 56	-171	S18 50	27
HP	12	205 05	-171	S19 17	24
54'	18	202 14	-173	S19 41	21
5	00	199 21	-173	S20 02	18
WED	06	196 28	-175	S20 20	14
HP	12	193 33	-175	S20 34	11
54'	18	190 38	-175	S20 45	8
6	00	187 43	-176	S20 53	4
THU	06	184 47	-177	S20 57	0
HP	12	181 50	-177	S20 57	3
54'	18	178 53	-177	S20 54	7
7	00	175 56	-177	S20 47	10
FRI	06	172 59	-176	S20 37	14
HP	12	170 03	-177	S20 23	17
54'	18	167 06	-176	S20 06	21
8	00	164 10	-176	S19 45	24
SAT	06	161 14	-175	S19 21	28
HP	12	158 19	-175	S18 53	31
55'	18	155 24	-174	S18 22	34
9	00	152° 30'		S17° 48'	

Days 9–16

Day	GMT	GHA-GMT	v	Dec	d
9	00h	152° 30'	-173'	S17° 48'	37'
SUN	06	149 37	-173	S17 11	40
HP	12	146 44	-171	S16 31	43
55'	18	143 53	-172	S15 48	46
10	00	141 01	-170	S15 02	48
MON	06	138 11	-169	S14 14	51
HP	12	135 22	-169	S13 23	54
55'	18	132 33	-169	S12 29	55
11	00	129 44	-168	S11 34	58
TUE	06	126 56	-167	S10 36	60
HP	12	124 09	-168	S 9 36	62
56'	18	121 21	-167	S 8 34	63
12	00	118 34	-167	S 7 31	65
WED	06	115 47	-167	S 6 26	67
HP	12	113 00	-168	S 5 19	67
57'	18	110 12	-168	S 4 12	69
13	00	107 24	-169	S 3 03	70
THU	06	104 35	-169	S 1 53	70
HP	12	101 46	-171	S 0 43	71
57'	18	98 55	-172	N 0 28	71
14	00	96 03	-173	N 1 39	72
FRI	06	93 10	-175	N 2 51	71
HP	12	90 15	-177	N 4 02	71
58'	18	87 18	-178	N 5 13	71
15	00	84 20	-181	N 6 24	70
SAT	06	81 19	-184	N 7 34	69
HP	12	78 15	-186	N 8 43	67
59'	18	75 09	-188	N 9 50	66
16	00	72 01	-192	N10 56	65
SUN	06	68 49	-194	N12 01	62
HP	12	65 35	-198	N13 03	59
60'	18	62 17	-201	N14 02	57
17	00	58° 56'		N14° 59'	

Days 17–24

Day	GMT	GHA-GMT	v	Dec	d
17	00h	58° 56'	-204'	N14° 59'	54'
MON	06	55 32	-207	N15 53	51
HP	12	52 05	-210	N16 44	46
60'	18	48 35	-213	N17 30	43
18	00	45 02	-216	N18 13	38
TUE	06	41 26	-219	N18 51	34
HP	12	37 47	-221	N19 25	28
61'	18	34 06	-223	N19 53	24
19	00	30 23	-225	N20 17	18
WED	06	26 38	-227	N20 35	13
HP	12	22 51	-227	N20 48	7
61'	18	19 04	-227	N20 55	2
20	00	15 17	-228	N20 57	5
THU	06	11 29	-227	N20 52	10
HP	12	7 42	-226	N20 42	15
61'	18	3 56	-224	N20 27	21
21	00	0 12	-223	N20 06	26
FRI	06	356 29	-220	N19 40	32
HP	12	352 49	-219	N19 08	36
61'	18	349 10	-215	N18 32	40
22	00	345 35	-212	N17 52	45
SAT	06	342 03	-209	N17 07	49
HP	12	338 34	-206	N16 18	52
60'	18	335 08	-203	N15 26	56
23	00	331 45	-199	N14 30	58
SUN	06	328 26	-196	N13 32	61
HP	12	325 10	-192	N12 31	63
59'	18	321 54	-189	N11 28	65
24	00	318 49	-187	N10 23	67
MON	06	315 42	-183	N 9 16	68
HP	12	312 39	-180	N 8 08	69
58'	18	309 39	-178	N 6 59	69
25	00	306° 41'		N 5° 50'	

Days 25–32

Day	GMT	GHA-GMT	v	Dec	d
25	00h	306° 41'	-176'	N 5° 50'	70'
TUE	06	303 45	-173	N 4 40	71
HP	12	300 52	-171	N 3 29	70
57'	18	298 01	-169	N 2 19	70
26	00	295 12	-167	N 1 09	70
WED	06	292 25	-166	S 0 01	69
HP	12	289 39	-165	S 1 10	68
57'	18	286 54	-164	S 2 18	68
27	00	284 10	-162	S 3 26	66
THU	06	281 28	-162	S 4 32	65
HP	12	278 46	-162	S 5 37	64
56'	18	276 04	-161	S 6 41	63
28	00	273 23	-161	S 7 44	61
FRI	06	270 42	-161	S 8 45	59
HP	12	268 01	-161	S 9 44	58
55'	18	265 20	-161	S10 42	55
29	00	262 39	-162	S11 37	54
SAT	06	259 57	-162	S12 31	51
HP	12	257 15	-162	S13 22	49
55'	18	254 33	-164	S14 11	47
30	00	251 49	-164	S14 58	45
SUN	06	249 05	-165	S15 43	42
HP	12	246 20	-166	S16 25	39
54'	18	243 34	-167	S17 04	36
31	00	240 47	-168	S17 40	34
MON	06	237 59	-170	S18 14	31
HP	12	235 09	-170	S18 45	27
54'	18	232 19	-171	S19 12	25
32	00	229 28		S19 37	

Phases of the Moon
New: 6d   First Quarter: 14
Full: 21d   Last Quarter: 28d

MOON AT EVERY 6hrs GMT FEBRUARY 2000

Days 1–8

Day	GMT	GHA-GMT	v	Dec	d
1	00h	229° 28'	-172'	S19° 37'	21'
TUE	06	226 36	-173	S19 58	19
HP	12	223 43	-174	S20 17	14
54'	18	220 49	-175	S20 31	12
2	00	217 54	-175	S20 43	8
WED	06	214 59	-176	S20 51	4
HP	12	212 03	-177	S20 55	1
54'	18	209 06	-177	S20 56	2
3	00	206 09	-177	S20 54	7
THU	06	203 12	-178	S20 47	9
HP	12	200 14	-177	S20 38	14
54'	18	197 17	-178	S20 24	17
4	00	194 19	-177	S20 07	20
FRI	06	191 22	-177	S19 47	24
HP	12	188 25	-177	S19 23	28
55'	18	185 28	-177	S18 55	30
5	00	182 31	-175	S18 25	34
SAT	06	179 36	-176	S17 51	38
HP	12	176 40	-174	S17 13	40
55'	18	173 46	-174	S16 33	44
6	00	170 52	-174	S15 49	46
SUN	06	167 58	-172	S15 03	49
HP	12	165 06	-172	S14 14	52
56'	18	162 14	-171	S13 22	54
7	00	159 23	-171	S12 28	56
MON	06	156 32	-170	S11 32	59
HP	12	153 42	-170	S10 33	61
56'	18	150 52	-169	S 9 32	62
8	00	148 03	-169	S 8 30	64
TUE	06	145 14	-169	S 7 26	66
HP	12	142 25	-168	S 6 20	67
57'	18	139 37	-169	S 5 13	68
9	00	136° 48'		S 4° 05'	

Days 9–16

Day	GMT	GHA-GMT	v	Dec	d
9	00h	136° 48'	-169'	S 4° 05'	69'
WED	06	133 59	-169	S 2 56	70
HP	12	131 10	-170	S 1 46	71
57'	18	128 20	-170	S 0 35	71
10	00	125 30	-171	N 0 36	71
THU	06	122 39	-172	N 1 47	71
HP	12	119 47	-174	N 2 58	71
58'	18	116 53	-174	N 4 09	70
11	00	113 59	-177	N 5 19	70
FRI	06	111 02	-178	N 6 29	69
HP	12	108 04	-179	N 7 38	67
58'	18	105 05	-182	N 8 45	67
12	00	102 03	-184	N 9 52	64
SAT	06	98 59	-187	N10 56	63
HP	12	95 52	-189	N11 59	61
59'	18	92 43	-191	N13 00	58
13	00	89 32	-194	N13 58	56
SUN	06	86 18	-196	N14 54	52
HP	12	83 02	-200	N15 46	50
59'	18	79 42	-202	N16 36	45
14	00	76 20	-204	N17 21	43
MON	06	72 56	-207	N18 04	38
HP	12	69 29	-210	N18 42	34
60'	18	65 59	-212	N19 16	29
15	00	62 27	-214	N19 45	25
TUE	06	58 53	-215	N20 10	19
HP	12	55 18	-218	N20 29	15
60'	18	51 40	-218	N20 44	9
16	00	48 02	-220	N20 53	5
WED	06	44 22	-219	N20 58	1
HP	12	40 43	-220	N20 57	7
60'	18	37 03	-220	N20 50	12
17	00	33° 23'		N20° 38'	

Days 17–24

Day	GMT	GHA-GMT	v	Dec	d
17	00h	33° 23'	-219'	N20° 38'	17'
THU	06	29 44	-219	N20 21	22
HP	12	26 05	-217	N19 59	27
60'	18	22 28	-215	N19 32	33
18	00	18 53	-213	N18 59	36
FRI	06	15 20	-212	N18 23	42
HP	12	11 48	-209	N17 41	45
60'	18	8 19	-206	N16 56	50
19	00	4 53	-204	N16 06	52
SAT	06	1 29	-201	N15 14	57
HP	12	358 08	-199	N14 17	59
60'	18	354 49	-195	N13 18	62
20	00	351 34	-193	N12 16	64
SUN	06	348 21	-190	N11 12	66
HP	12	345 11	-188	N10 06	68
59'	18	342 03	-185	N 8 58	69
21	00	338 58	-182	N 7 49	70
MON	06	335 56	-181	N 6 39	71
HP	12	332 55	-178	N 5 28	72
58'	18	329 57	-176	N 4 16	72
22	00	327 01	-174	N 3 04	72
TUE	06	324 07	-173	N 1 52	71
HP	12	321 14	-171	N 0 41	72
57'	18	318 23	-169	S 0 31	70
23	00	315 34	-169	S 1 41	70
WED	06	312 45	-167	S 2 51	69
HP	12	309 58	-167	S 4 00	68
57'	18	307 11	-166	S 5 08	66
24	00	304 25	-165	S 6 14	65
THU	06	301 40	-165	S 7 19	63
HP	12	298 55	-165	S 8 22	62
56'	18	296 10	-164	S 9 24	59
25	00	293° 26'		S10° 23'	

Days 25–30

Day	GMT	GHA-GMT	v	Dec	d
25	00h	293° 26'	-165'	S10° 23'	58'
FRI	06	290 41	-165	S11 21	55
HP	12	287 56	-165	S12 16	54
55'	18	285 11	-165	S13 10	50
26	00	282 26	-166	S14 00	49
SAT	06	279 40	-166	S14 49	46
HP	12	276 54	-167	S15 35	43
55'	18	274 07	-168	S16 18	40
27	00	271 19	-168	S16 58	38
SUN	06	268 31	-169	S17 36	35
HP	12	265 42	-170	S18 11	31
54'	18	262 52	-171	S18 42	29
28	00	260 01	-171	S19 11	25
MON	06	257 10	-173	S19 36	23
HP	12	254 17	-173	S19 59	19
54'	18	251 24	-173	S20 18	15
29	00	248 31	-175	S20 33	12
TUE	06	245 36	-175	S20 45	9
HP	12	242 41	-175	S20 54	5
54'	18	239 46	-176	S20 59	2
30	00	236 50		S21 01	

Phases of the Moon
New: 5d   First Quarter: 12d
Full: 19d   Last Quarter: 27d

Day GMT	GHA-GMT v	Dec	d	Day GMT	GHA-GMT v	Dec	d	Day GMT	GHA-GMT v	Dec	d	Day GMT	GHA-GMT v	Dec	d
1 00h	236° 50' -177'	S21° 01'	2'	9 00h	143° 43' -178'	N 4° 17'	72'	17 00h	36° 35' -201'	N17° 18'	47'	25 00h	302° 17' -170'	S16° 12'	42'
WED 06	233 53 -177	S20 59	5	THU 06	140 45 -179	N 5 29	71	FRI 06	33 14 -200	N16 31	51	SAT 06	299 27 -170	S16 54	39
HP 12	230 56 -177	S20 54	9	HP 12	137 46 -181	N 6 40	70	HP 12	29 54 -197	N15 40	54	HP 12	296 37 -171	S17 33	37
54' 18	227 59 -177	S20 45	13	58' 18	134 45 -182	N 7 50	68	59' 18	26 37 -194	N14 46	57	55' 18	293 46 -172	S18 10	33
2 00	225 02 -177	S20 32	16	10 00	131 43 -184	N 8 58	68	18 00	23 23 -192	N13 49	60	26 00	290 54 -172	S18 43	30
THU 06	222 05 -177	S20 16	20	FRI 06	128 39 -186	N10 06	65	SAT 06	20 11 -191	N12 49	62	SUN 06	288 02 -172	S19 13	27
HP 12	219 08 -178	S19 56	23	HP 12	125 33 -187	N11 11	63	HP 12	17 00 -187	N11 47	64	HP 12	285 10 -174	S19 40	24
55' 18	216 10 -176	S19 33	27	59' 18	122 26 -190	N12 14	61	59' 18	13 53 -186	N10 43	67	54' 18	282 16 -173	S20 04	20
3 00	213 14 -177	S19 06	30	11 00	119 16 -192	N13 15	58	19 00	10 47 -183	N 9 36	68	27 00	279 23 -175	S20 24	17
FRI 06	210 17 -177	S18 36	34	SAT 06	116 04 -194	N14 13	55	SUN 06	7 44 -182	N 8 28	70	MON 06	276 28 -174	S20 41	13
HP 12	207 20 -176	S18 02	36	HP 12	112 50 -196	N15 08	53	HP 12	4 42 -180	N 7 18	70	HP 12	273 34 -175	S20 54	10
55' 18	204 24 -175	S17 26	41	59' 18	109 34 -199	N16 01	49	58' 18	1 42 -177	N 6 08	72	54' 18	270 39 -176	S21 04	6
4 00	201 29 -175	S16 45	43	12 00	106 15 -200	N16 50	45	20 00	358 45 -177	N 4 56	72	28 00	267 43 -176	S21 10	3
SAT 06	198 34 -175	S16 02	46	SUN 06	102 55 -203	N17 35	41	MON 06	355 48 -174	N 3 44	72	TUE 06	264 47 -176	S21 13	0
HP 12	195 39 -174	S15 16	49	HP 12	99 32 -205	N18 16	38	HP 12	352 54 -174	N 2 32	72	HP 12	261 51 -176	S21 13	5
56' 18	192 45 -174	S14 27	52	59' 18	96 07 -206	N18 54	33	58' 18	350 00 -172	N 1 20	73	54' 18	258 55 -176	S21 08	8
5 00	189 51 -173	S13 35	55	13 00	92 41 -208	N19 27	28	21 00	347 08 -171	N 0 07	72	29 00	255 59 -176	S21 00	11
SUN 06	186 58 -173	S12 40	57	MON 06	89 13 -210	N19 55	24	TUE 06	344 17 -170	S 1 05	71	WED 06	253 03 -176	S20 49	15
HP 12	184 05 -173	S11 43	59	HP 12	85 43 -211	N20 19	19	HP 12	341 27 -169	S 2 16	70	HP 12	250 07 -176	S20 34	19
56' 18	181 12 -172	S10 44	62	59' 18	82 12 -212	N20 38	15	57' 18	338 38 -169	S 3 26	70	55' 18	247 11 -176	S20 15	22
6 00	178 20 -172	S 9 42	63	14 00	78 40 -212	N20 53	9	22 00	335 49 -168	S 4 36	68	30 00	244 15 -176	S19 53	26
MON 06	175 28 -172	S 8 39	65	TUE 06	75 08 -214	N21 02	4	WED 06	333 01 -167	S 5 44	67	THU 06	241 19 -175	S19 27	29
HP 12	172 36 -172	S 7 34	68	HP 12	71 34 -213	N21 06	1	HP 12	330 14 -167	S 6 51	66	HP 12	238 24 -175	S18 58	32
57' 18	169 44 -171	S 6 26	68	59' 18	68 01 -214	N21 05	6	56' 18	327 27 -168	S 7 57	63	55' 18	235 29 -175	S18 26	36
7 00	166 53 -172	S 5 18	70	15 00	64 27 -213	N20 59	11	23 00	324 39 -167	S 9 00	62	31 00	232 34 -175	S17 50	39
TUE 06	164 01 -173	S 4 08	71	WED 06	60 54 -212	N20 48	16	THU 06	321 52 -167	S10 02	60	FRI 06	229 39 -174	S17 11	42
HP 12	161 08 -172	S 2 57	71	HP 12	57 22 -212	N20 32	21	HP 12	319 05 -167	S11 02	58	HP 12	226 45 -174	S16 29	45
57' 18	158 16 -173	S 1 46	72	59' 18	53 50 -210	N20 11	25	56' 18	316 18 -168	S12 00	55	55' 18	223 51 -173	S15 44	48
8 00	155 23 -174	S 0 34	73	16 00	50 20 -209	N19 46	31	24 00	313 30 -167	S12 55	53	32 00	220 58	S14 56	
WED 06	152 29 -174	N 0 39	73	THU 06	46 51 -207	N19 15	35	FRI 06	310 43 -169	S13 48	51				
HP 12	149 35 -176	N 1 52	72	HP 12	43 24 -206	N18 40	39	HP 12	307 54 -168	S14 39	47				
58' 18	146 39 -176	N 3 04	73	59' 18	39 58 -203	N18 01	43	55' 18	305 06 -169	S15 26	46				
9 00	143° 43'	N 4° 17'		17 00	36° 35'	N17° 18'		25 00	302° 17'	S16° 12'					

Phases of the Moon
New: 6d   First Quarter: 13d
Full: 20d   Last Quarter: 28d

MOON AT EVERY 6hrs GMT APRIL 2000

Day GMT	GHA-GMT v	Dec	d	Day GMT	GHA-GMT v	Dec	d	Day GMT	GHA-GMT v	Dec	d	Day GMT	GHA-GMT v	Dec	d
1 00h	220° 58' -173'	S14° 56'	51'	9 00h	122° 49' -210'	N19° 09'	33'	17 00h	17° 49' -170'	N 1° 43'	72'	25 00h	286° 47' -176'	S21° 26'	7'
SAT 06	218 05 -173	S14 05	54	SUN 06	119 19 -211	N19 42	29	MON 06	14 59 -168	N 0 31	71	TUE 06	283 51 -176	S21 19	10
HP 12	215 12 -173	S13 11	56	HP 12	115 48 -213	N20 11	24	HP 12	12 11 -168	S 0 40	72	HP 12	280 55 -175	S21 09	14
56' 18	212 19 -172	S12 15	59	60' 18	112 15 -213	N20 35	19	57' 18	9 23 -167	S 1 52	71	54' 18	278 00 -175	S20 55	18
2 00	209 27 -173	S11 16	62	10 00	108 42 -214	N20 54	14	18 00	6 36 -167	S 3 03	70	26 00	275 05 -175	S20 37	20
SUN 06	206 34 -172	S10 14	63	MON 06	105 08 -214	N21 08	9	TUE 06	3 49 -166	S 4 13	69	WED 06	272 10 -174	S20 17	25
HP 12	203 42 -173	S 9 11	66	HP 12	101 34 -214	N21 17	4	HP 12	1 03 -167	S 5 22	67	HP 12	269 16 -174	S19 52	27
57' 18	200 49 -173	S 8 05	67	59' 18	98 00 -214	N21 21	2	56' 18	358 16 -166	S 6 29	67	55' 18	266 22 -173	S19 25	31
3 00	197 56 -173	S 6 58	69	11 00	94 26 -213	N21 19	6	19 00	355 30 -166	S 7 36	65	27 00	263 29 -173	S18 54	35
MON 06	195 03 -173	S 5 49	71	TUE 06	90 53 -212	N21 13	11	WED 06	352 44 -167	S 8 41	63	THU 06	260 36 -172	S18 19	37
HP 12	192 10 -174	S 4 38	72	HP 12	87 21 -211	N21 01	17	HP 12	349 57 -167	S 9 44	61	HP 12	257 44 -172	S17 42	41
57' 18	189 16 -175	S 3 26	73	59' 18	83 50 -210	N20 44	21	56' 18	347 10 -167	S10 45	59	55' 18	254 52 -171	S17 01	43
4 00	186 21 -175	S 2 13	74	12 00	80 20 -207	N20 23	26	20 00	344 23 -168	S11 44	58	28 00	252 01 -171	S16 18	47
TUE 06	183 26 -177	S 0 59	74	WED 06	76 53 -206	N19 57	31	THU 06	341 35 -168	S12 42	54	FRI 06	249 10 -170	S15 31	49
HP 12	180 29 -177	N 0 15	75	HP 12	73 27 -204	N19 26	35	HP 12	338 47 -169	S13 36	53	HP 12	246 20 -170	S14 42	52
58' 18	177 32 -179	N 1 30	75	59' 18	70 03 -202	N18 51	39	55' 18	335 58 -169	S14 29	49	56' 18	243 30 -170	S13 50	55
5 00	174 33 -180	N 2 45	75	13 00	66 41 -199	N18 12	43	21 00	333 09 -170	S15 18	48	29 00	240 40 -170	S12 55	58
WED 06	171 33 -182	N 4 00	74	THU 06	63 22 -198	N17 29	46	FRI 06	330 19 -170	S16 06	44	SAT 06	237 50 -170	S11 57	59
HP 12	168 31 -183	N 5 14	74	HP 12	60 04 -194	N16 43	51	HP 12	327 29 -172	S16 50	41	HP 12	235 00 -170	S10 58	63
59' 18	165 28 -184	N 6 28	73	59' 18	56 50 -193	N15 52	53	55' 18	324 37 -172	S17 31	38	56' 18	232 10 -170	S 9 55	64
6 00	162 24 -187	N 7 41	71	14 00	53 37 -190	N14 59	56	22 00	321 45 -172	S18 09	35	30 00	229 20 -170	S 8 51	66
THU 06	159 17 -189	N 8 52	70	FRI 06	50 27 -187	N14 03	59	SAT 06	318 53 -173	S18 44	32	SUN 06	226 30 -171	S 7 45	68
HP 12	156 08 -190	N10 02	68	HP 12	47 20 -186	N13 04	61	HP 12	316 00 -174	S19 16	29	HP 12	223 39 -172	S 6 37	70
59' 18	152 58 -193	N11 10	66	58' 18	44 14 -183	N12 03	64	54' 18	313 06 -174	S19 45	25	57' 18	220 48 -172	S 5 27	71
7 00	149 45 -195	N12 16	63	15 00	41 11 -181	N10 59	65	23 00	310 12 -175	S20 10	22	31 00	217 56	S 4 16	
FRI 06	146 30 -196	N13 19	60	SAT 06	38 10 -180	N 9 54	67	SUN 06	307 17 -175	S20 32	18				
HP 12	143 14 -199	N14 19	58	HP 12	35 10 -177	N 8 47	69	HP 12	304 22 -176	S20 50	15				
59' 18	139 55 -202	N15 17	54	58' 18	32 13 -176	N 7 38	69	54' 18	301 26 -175	S21 05	11				
8 00	136 33 -203	N16 11	50	16 00	29 17 -174	N 6 29	71	24 00	298 31 -176	S21 16	8				
SAT 06	133 10 -205	N17 01	47	SUN 06	26 23 -173	N 5 18	71	MON 06	295 35 -176	S21 24	4				
HP 12	129 45 -207	N17 48	42	HP 12	23 30 -171	N 4 07	72	HP 12	292 39 -176	S21 28	1				
60' 18	126 18 -209	N18 30	39	57' 18	20 39 -170	N 2 55	72	54' 18	289 43 -176	S21 29	3				
9 00	122° 49'	N19° 09'		17 00	17° 49'	N 1° 43'		25 00	286° 47'	S21° 26'					

Phases of the Moon
New: 4d   First Quarter: 11d
Full: 18d   Last Quarter: 26d

MOON AT EVERY 6hrs GMT MAY 2000

Day	GMT	GHA-GMT	v	Dec	d
1	00h	217° 56'	-173'	S 4° 16'	73'
MON	06	215 03	-174	S 3 03	74
HP	12	212 09	-175	S 1 49	75
58'	18	209 14	-177	S 0 34	75
2	00	206 17	-178	N 0 41	76
TUE	06	203 19	-180	N 1 57	76
HP	12	200 19	-181	N 3 13	76
59'	18	197 18	-184	N 4 29	76
3	00	194 14	-186	N 5 45	74
WED	06	191 08	-187	N 6 59	74
HP	12	188 01	-191	N 8 13	73
59'	18	184 50	-193	N 9 26	71
4	00	181 37	-195	N10 37	69
THU	06	178 22	-198	N11 46	67
HP	12	175 04	-201	N12 53	64
60'	18	171 43	-203	N13 57	61
5	00	168 20	-206	N14 58	58
FRI	06	164 54	-208	N15 56	54
HP	12	161 26	-211	N16 50	51
60'	18	157 55	-213	N17 41	46
6	00	154 22	-215	N18 27	41
SAT	06	150 47	-217	N19 08	37
HP	12	147 10	-219	N19 45	31
60'	18	143 31	-219	N20 16	27
7	00	139 52	-221	N20 43	21
SUN	06	136 11	-221	N21 04	16
HP	12	132 30	-221	N21 20	10
60'	18	128 49	-220	N21 30	5
8	00	125 09	-220	N21 35	1
MON	06	121 29	-220	N21 34	7
HP	12	117 49	-217	N21 27	11
60'	18	114 12	-216	N21 16	17
9	00	110° 36'		N20° 59'	

Day	GMT	GHA-GMT	v	Dec	d
9	00h	110° 36'	-215'	N20° 59'	22'
TUE	06	107 01	-211	N20 37	27
HP	12	103 30	-210	N20 10	31
59'	18	100 00	-207	N19 39	36
10	00	96 33	-204	N19 03	40
WED	06	93 09	-201	N18 23	44
HP	12	89 48	-198	N17 39	47
59'	18	86 30	-196	N16 52	51
11	00	83 14	-192	N16 01	54
THU	06	80 02	-190	N15 07	57
HP	12	76 52	-187	N14 10	59
58'	18	73 45	-184	N13 11	62
12	00	70 41	-182	N12 09	63
FRI	06	67 39	-179	N11 06	66
HP	12	64 40	-177	N10 00	67
58'	18	61 43	-175	N 8 53	68
13	00	58 48	-173	N 7 45	70
SAT	06	55 55	-172	N 6 35	70
HP	12	53 03	-170	N 5 25	71
57'	18	50 13	-168	N 4 14	71
14	00	47 25	-167	N 3 03	71
SUN	06	44 38	-166	N 1 52	72
HP	12	41 52	-166	N 0 40	71
57'	18	39 06	-164	S 0 31	71
15	00	36 22	-165	S 1 42	71
MON	06	33 37	-163	S 2 53	69
HP	12	30 54	-164	S 4 02	69
56'	18	28 10	-164	S 5 11	68
16	00	25 26	-163	S 6 19	66
TUE	06	22 43	-164	S 7 25	65
HP	12	19 59	-164	S 8 30	63
56'	18	17 15	-165	S 9 33	62
17	00	14° 30'		S10° 35'	

Day	GMT	GHA-GMT	v	Dec	d
17	00h	14° 30'	-165'	S10° 35'	60'
WED	06	11 45	-166	S11 35	58
HP	12	8 59	-166	S12 33	55
55'	18	6 13	-168	S13 28	53
18	00	3 25	-168	S14 21	51
THU	06	0 37	-169	S15 12	48
HP	12	357 48	-169	S16 00	45
55'	18	354 59	-171	S16 45	43
19	00	352 08	-171	S17 28	39
FRI	06	349 17	-173	S18 07	37
HP	12	346 24	-173	S18 44	33
54'	18	343 31	-173	S19 17	30
20	00	340 38	-175	S19 47	26
SAT	06	337 43	-175	S20 13	24
HP	12	334 48	-175	S20 37	19
54'	18	331 53	-176	S20 56	16
21	00	328 57	-176	S21 12	13
SUN	06	326 01	-177	S21 25	9
HP	12	323 04	-176	S21 34	5
54'	18	320 08	-176	S21 39	2
22	00	317 12	-177	S21 41	2
MON	06	314 15	-176	S21 39	6
HP	12	311 19	-175	S21 33	9
54'	18	308 24	-175	S21 24	13
23	00	305 29	-175	S21 11	16
TUE	06	302 34	-174	S20 55	20
HP	12	299 40	-174	S20 35	23
54'	18	296 46	-172	S20 12	27
24	00	293 54	-172	S19 45	30
WED	06	291 02	-172	S19 15	33
HP	12	288 10	-170	S18 42	36
54'	18	285 20	-170	S18 06	40
25	00	282° 30'		S17° 26'	

Day	GMT	GHA-GMT	v	Dec	d
25	00h	282° 30'	-169'	S17° 26'	42'
THU	06	279 41	-168	S16 44	45
HP	12	276 53	-168	S15 59	48
55'	18	274 05	-167	S15 11	50
26	00	271 18	-167	S14 21	53
FRI	06	268 31	-166	S13 28	56
HP	12	265 45	-166	S12 32	58
55'	18	262 59	-166	S11 34	60
27	00	260 13	-166	S10 34	63
SAT	06	257 27	-166	S 9 31	64
HP	12	254 41	-167	S 8 27	66
56'	18	251 54	-167	S 7 21	68
28	00	249 07	-167	S 6 13	69
SUN	06	246 20	-168	S 5 04	71
HP	12	243 32	-169	S 3 53	72
57'	18	240 43	-171	S 2 41	73
29	00	237 52	-171	S 1 28	74
MON	06	235 01	-174	S 0 14	75
HP	12	232 07	-175	N 1 01	75
58'	18	229 12	-177	N 2 16	76
30	00	226 15	-179	N 3 32	75
TUE	06	223 16	-181	N 4 47	75
HP	12	220 15	-184	N 6 02	75
59'	18	217 11	-187	N 7 17	73
31	00	214 04	-189	N 8 30	73
WED	06	210 55	-193	N 9 43	71
HP	12	207 42	-195	N10 54	69
60'	18	204 27	-199	N12 03	67
32	00	201 08		N13 10	

Phases of the Moon
New: 4d   First Quarter: 10d
Full: 18d   Last Quarter: 26d

MOON AT EVERY 6hrs GMT JUNE 2000

Day	GMT	GHA-GMT	v	Dec	d
1	00h	201° 08'	-202'	N13° 10'	64'
THU	06	197 46	-205	N14 14	61
HP	12	194 21	-208	N15 15	58
60'	18	190 53	-212	N16 13	55
2	00	187 21	-214	N17 08	50
FRI	06	183 47	-218	N17 58	46
HP	12	180 09	-220	N18 44	41
61'	18	176 29	-222	N19 25	37
3	00	172 47	-225	N20 02	31
SAT	06	169 02	-226	N20 33	25
HP	12	165 16	-227	N20 58	20
61'	18	161 29	-228	N21 18	14
4	00	157 41	-229	N21 32	9
SUN	06	153 52	-228	N21 41	2
HP	12	150 04	-227	N21 43	4
61'	18	146 17	-226	N21 39	9
5	00	142 31	-225	N21 32	15
MON	06	138 46	-223	N21 15	20
HP	12	135 03	-221	N20 55	26
61'	18	131 22	-217	N20 29	31
6	00	127 45	-215	N19 58	36
TUE	06	124 10	-212	N19 22	40
HP	12	120 38	-209	N18 42	44
60'	18	117 09	-205	N17 58	48
7	00	113 44	-202	N17 09	51
WED	06	110 22	-198	N16 18	55
HP	12	107 04	-195	N15 23	58
59'	18	103 49	-192	N14 25	61
8	00	100 37	-188	N13 24	63
THU	06	97 29	-185	N12 21	65
HP	12	94 24	-183	N11 16	67
58'	18	91 21	-180	N10 09	68
9	00	88° 21'		N 9° 01'	

Day	GMT	GHA-GMT	v	Dec	d
9	00h	88° 21'	-177'	N 9° 01'	69'
FRI	06	85 24	-175	N 7 52	71
HP	12	82 29	-172	N 6 41	71
58'	18	79 37	-171	N 5 30	71
10	00	76 46	-169	N 4 19	72
SAT	06	73 57	-167	N 3 07	72
HP	12	71 10	-167	N 1 55	72
57'	18	68 23	-164	N 0 43	71
11	00	65 39	-164	S 0 28	72
SUN	06	62 55	-164	S 1 40	70
HP	12	60 11	-162	S 2 50	70
56'	18	57 29	-163	S 4 00	68
12	00	54 46	-162	S 5 08	68
MON	06	52 04	-162	S 6 16	66
HP	12	49 22	-162	S 7 22	65
56'	18	46 40	-162	S 8 27	63
13	00	43 58	-163	S 9 30	62
TUE	06	41 15	-164	S10 32	59
HP	12	38 31	-164	S11 31	58
55'	18	35 47	-164	S12 29	55
14	00	33 03	-166	S13 24	53
WED	06	30 17	-166	S14 17	51
HP	12	27 31	-167	S15 08	48
55'	18	24 44	-168	S15 56	46
15	00	21 56	-170	S16 42	43
THU	06	19 06	-170	S17 25	40
HP	12	16 16	-171	S18 05	37
54'	18	13 25	-172	S18 42	33
16	00	10 33	-173	S19 15	31
FRI	06	7 40	-173	S19 46	27
HP	12	4 47	-175	S20 13	24
54'	18	1 52	-175	S20 37	20
17	00	358° 57'		S20° 57'	

Day	GMT	GHA-GMT	v	Dec	d
17	00h	358° 57'	-175'	S20° 57'	17'
SAT	06	356 02	-176	S21 14	13
HP	12	353 06	-176	S21 27	10
54'	18	350 10	-177	S21 37	6
18	00	347 13	-176	S21 43	2
SUN	06	344 17	-177	S21 45	2
HP	12	341 20	-176	S21 44	5
54'	18	338 24	-176	S21 39	9
19	00	335 28	-175	S21 30	12
MON	06	332 33	-175	S21 18	16
HP	12	329 38	-175	S21 02	19
54'	18	326 43	-173	S20 43	23
20	00	323 50	-173	S20 20	26
TUE	06	320 57	-172	S19 54	29
HP	12	318 05	-171	S19 25	33
54'	18	315 14	-170	S18 52	36
21	00	312 24	-169	S18 16	38
WED	06	309 35	-168	S17 38	42
HP	12	306 47	-167	S16 56	44
54'	18	304 00	-167	S16 12	47
22	00	301 13	-165	S15 25	50
THU	06	298 28	-165	S14 35	52
HP	12	295 43	-164	S13 43	55
55'	18	292 59	-164	S12 48	56
23	00	290 15	-163	S11 52	59
FRI	06	287 32	-163	S10 53	61
HP	12	284 49	-162	S 9 52	63
55'	18	282 07	-163	S 8 49	64
24	00	279 24	-163	S 7 45	66
SAT	06	276 41	-163	S 6 39	68
HP	12	273 58	-163	S 5 31	69
56'	18	271 15	-164	S 4 22	70
25	00	268° 31'		S 3° 12'	

Day	GMT	GHA-GMT	v	Dec	d
25	00h	268° 31'	-165'	S 3° 12'	71'
SUN	06	265 46	-167	S 2 01	72
HP	12	262 59	-167	S 0 49	72
57'	18	260 12	-169	N 0 23	73
26	00	257 23	-170	N 1 36	74
MON	06	254 34	-173	N 2 50	73
HP	12	251 40	-174	N 4 03	74
58'	18	248 46	-177	N 5 17	73
27	00	245 49	-180	N 6 30	72
TUE	06	242 49	-182	N 7 42	72
HP	12	239 47	-185	N 8 54	70
59'	18	236 42	-189	N10 04	69
28	00	233 33	-191	N11 13	67
WED	06	230 22	-195	N12 20	65
HP	12	227 07	-199	N13 25	63
60'	18	223 48	-202	N14 28	60
29	00	220 26	-205	N15 28	57
THU	06	217 01	-210	N16 25	53
HP	12	213 31	-212	N17 18	49
60'	18	209 59	-217	N18 07	45
30	00	206 22	-219	N18 52	40
FRI	06	202 43	-222	N19 32	36
HP	12	199 01	-225	N20 08	30
61'	18	195 16	-227	N20 38	25
31	00	191 29		N21 03	

Phases of the Moon
New: 2d   First Quarter: 9d
Full: 16d   Last Quarter: 25d

MOON AT EVERY 6hrs GMT JULY 2000

Day	GMT	GHA-GMT	v	Dec	d
1	00h	191° 29'	-229'	N21° 03'	19'
SAT	06	187 40	-230	N21 22	14
HP	12	183 50	-231	N21 36	7
61'	18	179 59	-232	N21 43	1
2	00	176 07	-231	N21 44	4
SUN	06	172 16	-231	N21 40	11
HP	12	168 25	-230	N21 29	17
61'	18	164 35	-228	N21 12	22
3	00	160 47	-225	N20 50	28
MON	06	157 02	-224	N20 22	34
HP	12	153 18	-220	N19 48	38
61'	18	149 38	-218	N19 10	43
4	00	146 00	-214	N18 27	48
TUE	06	142 26	-210	N17 39	51
HP	12	138 56	-208	N16 48	55
60'	18	135 28	-203	N15 53	59
5	00	132 05	-200	N14 54	61
WED	06	128 45	-197	N13 53	64
HP	12	125 28	-193	N12 49	67
60'	18	122 15	-190	N11 42	68
6	00	119 05	-186	N10 34	70
THU	06	115 59	-184	N 9 24	71
HP	12	112 55	-181	N 8 13	72
59'	18	109 54	-178	N 7 01	73
7	00	106 56	-176	N 5 48	74
FRI	06	104 00	-173	N 4 34	73
HP	12	101 07	-172	N 3 21	74
58'	18	98 15	-170	N 2 07	73
8	00	95 25	-168	N 0 54	73
SAT	06	92 37	-167	S 0 19	73
HP	12	89 50	-166	S 1 32	71
57'	18	87 04	-165	S 2 43	71
9	00	84° 19'		S 3° 54'	
9	00h	84° 19'	-164'	S 3° 54'	70'
SUN	06	81 35	-164	S 5 04	68
HP	12	78 51	-163	S 6 12	67
56'	18	76 08	-163	S 7 19	65
10	00	73 25	-164	S 8 24	64
MON	06	70 41	-163	S 9 28	61
HP	12	67 58	-163	S10 29	60
55'	18	65 15	-164	S11 29	58
11	00	62 31	-165	S12 27	56
TUE	06	59 46	-165	S13 23	53
HP	12	57 01	-166	S14 16	51
55'	18	54 15	-167	S15 07	48
12	00	51 28	-167	S15 55	45
WED	06	48 41	-169	S16 40	43
HP	12	45 52	-169	S17 23	40
54'	18	43 03	-170	S18 03	37
13	00	40 13	-171	S18 40	33
THU	06	37 22	-172	S19 13	31
HP	12	34 30	-173	S19 44	27
54'	18	31 37	-174	S20 11	24
14	00	28 43	-174	S20 35	21
FRI	06	25 49	-175	S20 56	16
HP	12	22 54	-175	S21 12	14
54'	18	19 58	-175	S21 26	10
15	00	17 03	-177	S21 36	6
SAT	06	14 06	-176	S21 42	2
HP	12	11 10	-176	S21 44	1
54'	18	8 14	-177	S21 43	5
16	00	5 17	-176	S21 38	8
SUN	06	2 21	-176	S21 30	12
HP	12	359 25	-175	S21 18	16
54'	18	356 30	-175	S21 02	19
17	00	353° 35'		S20° 43'	
17	00h	353° 35'	-174'	S20° 43'	22'
MON	06	350 41	-173	S20 21	26
HP	12	347 48	-173	S19 55	30
54'	18	344 55	-171	S19 25	32
18	00	342 04	-171	S18 53	36
TUE	06	339 13	-170	S18 17	39
HP	12	336 23	-168	S17 38	41
54'	18	333 35	-168	S16 57	45
19	00	330 47	-166	S16 12	47
WED	06	328 01	-166	S15 25	50
HP	12	325 15	-165	S14 35	52
55'	18	322 30	-164	S13 43	54
20	00	319 46	-163	S12 49	57
THU	06	317 03	-163	S11 52	58
HP	12	314 20	-162	S10 54	61
55'	18	311 38	-161	S 9 53	62
21	00	308 57	-161	S 8 51	64
FRI	06	306 16	-161	S 7 47	66
HP	12	303 35	-161	S 6 41	66
56'	18	300 54	-162	S 5 35	68
22	00	298 12	-161	S 4 27	69
SAT	06	295 31	-162	S 3 18	70
HP	12	292 49	-163	S 2 08	71
56'	18	290 06	-164	S 0 57	71
23	00	287 22	-164	N 0 14	71
SUN	06	284 38	-166	N 1 25	72
HP	12	281 52	-168	N 2 37	72
57'	18	279 04	-169	N 3 49	71
24	00	276 15	-171	N 5 00	72
MON	06	273 24	-174	N 6 12	70
HP	12	270 30	-175	N 7 22	70
58'	18	267 35	-179	N 8 32	69
25	00	264° 36'		N 9° 41'	
25	00h	264° 36'	-181'	N 9° 41'	67'
TUE	06	261 35	-183	N10 48	66
HP	12	258 32	-187	N11 54	64
58'	18	255 25	-191	N12 58	62
26	00	252 14	-193	N14 00	59
WED	06	249 01	-197	N14 59	56
HP	12	245 44	-201	N15 55	54
59'	18	242 23	-204	N16 49	50
27	00	238 59	-207	N17 39	46
THU	06	235 32	-211	N18 25	42
HP	12	232 01	-214	N19 07	38
60'	18	228 27	-217	N19 45	33
28	00	224 50	-220	N20 18	28
FRI	06	221 10	-223	N20 46	23
HP	12	217 27	-225	N21 09	17
61'	18	213 42	-227	N21 26	12
29	00	209 55	-227	N21 38	6
SAT	06	206 08	-229	N21 44	0
HP	12	202 19	-230	N21 44	6
61'	18	198 29	-229	N21 38	12
30	00	194 40	-228	N21 26	18
SUN	06	190 52	-228	N21 08	24
HP	12	187 04	-226	N20 44	29
61'	18	183 18	-224	N20 15	35
31	00	179 34	-222	N19 40	39
MON	06	175 52	-219	N19 01	45
HP	12	172 13	-217	N18 16	49
61'	18	168 36	-213	N17 27	54
32	00	165 03		N16 33	

Phases of the Moon
New: 1d&31d   First Quarter: 8d
Full: 16d   Last Quarter: 24d

MOON AT EVERY 6hrs GMT AUGUST 2000

Day	GMT	GHA-GMT	v	Dec	d
1	00h	165° 03'	-211'	N16° 33'	57'
TUE	06	161 32	-207	N15 36	61
HP	12	158 05	-204	N14 35	64
60'	18	154 41	-200	N13 31	66
2	00	151 21	-197	N12 25	69
WED	06	148 04	-194	N11 16	71
HP	12	144 50	-191	N10 05	72
60'	18	141 39	-189	N 8 53	74
3	00	138 30	-185	N 7 39	75
THU	06	135 25	-183	N 6 24	76
HP	12	132 22	-180	N 5 08	75
59'	18	129 22	-178	N 3 53	76
4	00	126 24	-176	N 2 37	76
FRI	06	123 28	-174	N 1 21	75
HP	12	120 34	-173	N 0 06	75
58'	18	117 41	-171	S 1 09	74
5	00	114 50	-170	S 2 23	73
SAT	06	112 00	-169	S 3 36	72
HP	12	109 11	-168	S 4 48	70
57'	18	106 23	-168	S 5 58	69
6	00	103 35	-167	S 7 07	67
SUN	06	100 48	-166	S 8 14	65
HP	12	98 02	-167	S 9 19	63
56'	18	95 15	-166	S10 22	61
7	00	92 29	-167	S11 23	59
MON	06	89 42	-166	S12 22	57
HP	12	86 56	-168	S13 19	54
55'	18	84 08	-167	S14 13	51
8	00	81 21	-168	S15 04	49
TUE	06	78 33	-169	S15 53	46
HP	12	75 44	-169	S16 39	43
55'	18	72 55	-170	S17 22	41
9	00	70° 05'		S18° 03'	
9	00h	70° 05'	-171'	S18° 03'	37'
WED	06	67 14	-172	S18 40	34
HP	12	64 22	-172	S19 14	30
54'	18	61 30	-173	S19 44	28
10	00	58 37	-174	S20 12	24
THU	06	55 43	-174	S20 36	20
HP	12	52 49	-175	S20 56	17
54'	18	49 54	-175	S21 13	14
11	00	46 59	-176	S21 27	9
FRI	06	44 03	-176	S21 36	7
HP	12	41 07	-176	S21 43	4
54'	18	38 11	-177	S21 45	1
12	00	35 14	-176	S21 44	5
SAT	06	32 18	-176	S21 39	8
HP	12	29 22	-176	S21 31	12
54'	18	26 26	-176	S21 19	16
13	00	23 30	-175	S21 03	19
SUN	06	20 35	-174	S20 44	22
HP	12	17 41	-174	S20 22	27
54'	18	14 47	-173	S19 55	29
14	00	11 54	-173	S19 26	33
MON	06	9 01	-171	S18 53	36
HP	12	6 10	-171	S18 17	39
54'	18	3 19	-169	S17 38	42
15	00	0 30	-169	S16 56	45
TUE	06	357 41	-168	S16 11	47
HP	12	354 53	-167	S15 24	51
55'	18	352 06	-166	S14 33	52
16	00	349 20	-165	S13 41	55
WED	06	346 35	-165	S12 46	55
HP	12	343 50	-163	S11 48	59
55'	18	341 07	-164	S10 49	61
17	00	338° 23'		S 9° 48'	
17	00h	338° 23'	-162'	S 9° 48'	63'
THU	06	335 41	-162	S 8 45	65
HP	12	332 59	-162	S 7 40	66
55'	18	330 17	-162	S 6 34	67
18	00	327 35	-162	S 5 27	69
FRI	06	324 53	-162	S 4 18	69
HP	12	322 11	-162	S 3 09	71
56'	18	319 29	-163	S 1 58	70
19	00	316 46	-163	S 0 48	72
SAT	06	314 03	-165	N 0 24	71
HP	12	311 18	-165	N 1 35	72
56'	18	308 33	-166	N 2 47	71
20	00	305 47	-168	N 3 58	71
SUN	06	302 59	-169	N 5 09	71
HP	12	300 10	-171	N 6 20	69
57'	18	297 19	-173	N 7 29	69
21	00	294 26	-175	N 8 38	67
MON	06	291 31	-177	N 9 46	66
HP	12	288 34	-180	N10 52	65
58'	18	285 34	-183	N11 57	63
22	00	282 31	-185	N13 00	60
TUE	06	279 26	-188	N14 00	58
HP	12	276 18	-191	N14 58	55
58'	18	273 07	-194	N15 53	53
23	00	269 53	-197	N16 46	49
WED	06	266 36	-200	N17 35	46
HP	12	263 16	-203	N18 21	41
59'	18	259 53	-206	N19 02	38
24	00	256 27	-209	N19 40	33
THU	06	252 58	-211	N20 13	29
HP	12	249 27	-214	N20 42	24
60'	18	245 53	-217	N21 06	18
25	00	242° 16'		N21° 24'	
25	00h	242° 16'	-218'	N21° 24'	14'
FRI	06	238 38	-220	N21 38	8
HP	12	234 58	-221	N21 46	3
60'	18	231 17	-222	N21 49	3
26	00	227 35	-223	N21 46	9
SAT	06	223 52	-222	N21 37	15
HP	12	220 10	-223	N21 22	20
60'	18	216 27	-221	N21 02	25
27	00	212 46	-221	N20 37	31
SUN	06	209 05	-219	N20 06	36
HP	12	205 26	-217	N19 30	41
61'	18	201 49	-216	N18 49	46
28	00	198 13	-213	N18 03	50
MON	06	194 40	-211	N17 13	55
HP	12	191 09	-208	N16 18	58
61'	18	187 41	-205	N15 20	62
29	00	184 16	-203	N14 18	65
TUE	06	180 53	-200	N13 13	68
HP	12	177 33	-197	N12 05	70
60'	18	174 16	-195	N10 55	72
30	00	171 01	-192	N 9 43	74
WED	06	167 49	-190	N 8 29	76
HP	12	164 39	-187	N 7 13	76
60'	18	161 32	-185	N 5 57	78
31	00	158 27	-183	N 4 39	77
THU	06	155 24	-181	N 3 22	78
HP	12	152 23	-179	N 2 04	78
59'	18	149 24	-178	N 0 46	77
32	00	146 26		S 0 31	

Phases of the Moon
New: 29d   First Quarter: 7d
Full: 15d   Last Quarter: 22d

MOON AT EVERY 6hrs GMT SEPTEMBER 2000

Day	GMT	GHA-GMT	v	Dec	d
1	00h	146° 26'	-176	S 0° 31'	76'
FRI	06	143 30	-175	S 1 47	76
HP	12	140 35	-174	S 3 03	74
58'	18	137 41	-173	S 4 17	73
2	00	134 48	-172	S 5 30	72
SAT	06	131 56	-172	S 6 42	70
HP	12	129 04	-171	S 7 52	67
57'	18	126 13	-171	S 8 59	66
3	00	123 22	-170	S10 05	64
SUN	06	120 32	-171	S11 09	61
HP	12	117 41	-171	S12 10	59
56'	18	114 50	-170	S13 09	56
4	00	112 00	-171	S14 05	53
MON	06	109 09	-172	S14 58	51
HP	12	106 17	-171	S15 49	47
55'	18	103 26	-173	S16 36	45
5	00	100 33	-172	S17 21	41
TUE	06	97 41	-173	S18 02	39
HP	12	94 48	-174	S18 41	35
55'	18	91 54	-174	S19 16	31
6	00	89 00	-175	S19 47	28
WED	06	86 05	-175	S20 15	25
HP	12	83 10	-175	S20 40	21
55'	18	80 15	-176	S21 01	18
7	00	77 19	-176	S21 19	14
THU	06	74 23	-176	S21 33	10
HP	12	71 27	-177	S21 43	7
54'	18	68 30	-176	S21 50	3
8	00	65 34	-177	S21 53	1
FRI	06	62 37	-176	S21 52	5
HP	12	59 41	-176	S21 47	8
54'	18	56 45	-176	S21 39	11
9	00	53° 49'		S21° 28'	

Day	GMT	GHA-GMT	v	Dec	d
9	00h	53 49	-176	S21° 28'	16'
SAT	06	50 53	-175	S21 12	19
HP	12	47 58	-174	S20 53	22
54'	18	45 04	-174	S20 31	26
10	00	42 10	-174	S20 05	30
SUN	06	39 16	-172	S19 35	32
HP	12	36 24	-172	S19 03	36
54'	18	33 32	-171	S18 27	39
11	00	30 41	-170	S17 48	42
MON	06	27 51	-170	S17 06	45
HP	12	25 01	-169	S16 21	48
55'	18	22 12	-168	S15 33	51
12	00	19 24	-167	S14 42	53
TUE	06	16 37	-166	S13 49	56
HP	12	13 51	-166	S12 53	58
55'	18	11 05	-165	S11 55	60
13	00	8 20	-165	S10 55	62
WED	06	5 35	-165	S 9 53	64
HP	12	2 50	-164	S 8 49	66
56'	18	0 06	-164	S 7 43	67
14	00	357 22	-164	S 6 36	69
THU	06	354 38	-164	S 5 27	70
HP	12	351 54	-164	S 4 17	71
56'	18	349 10	-164	S 3 06	71
15	00	346 26	-165	S 1 55	73
FRI	06	343 41	-166	S 0 42	72
HP	12	340 55	-166	N 0 30	73
57'	18	338 09	-168	N 1 43	73
16	00	335 21	-168	N 2 56	73
SAT	06	332 33	-170	N 4 09	72
HP	12	329 43	-171	N 5 21	72
57'	18	326 52	-173	N 6 33	71
17	00	323° 59'		N 7° 44'	

Day	GMT	GHA-GMT	v	Dec	d
17	00h	323 59	-175	N 7° 44'	69'
SUN	06	321 04	-176	N 8 53	69
HP	12	318 08	-179	N10 02	67
58'	18	315 09	-180	N11 09	65
18	00	312 09	-183	N12 14	62
MON	06	309 06	-185	N13 16	61
HP	12	306 01	-188	N14 17	58
58'	18	302 53	-190	N15 15	55
19	00	299 43	-193	N16 10	52
TUE	06	296 30	-196	N17 02	48
HP	12	293 14	-198	N17 50	45
58'	18	289 56	-200	N18 35	41
20	00	286 36	-203	N19 16	37
WED	06	283 13	-205	N19 53	33
HP	12	279 48	-208	N20 26	28
59'	18	276 20	-209	N20 54	23
21	00	272 51	-211	N21 17	18
THU	06	269 20	-213	N21 35	14
HP	12	265 47	-214	N21 49	8
59'	18	262 13	-215	N21 57	3
22	00	258 38	-215	N22 00	3
FRI	06	255 03	-216	N21 57	8
HP	12	251 27	-215	N21 49	13
59'	18	247 52	-216	N21 36	18
23	00	244 16	-214	N21 18	24
SAT	06	240 42	-214	N20 54	29
HP	12	237 08	-213	N20 25	34
60'	18	233 35	-211	N19 51	39
24	00	230 04	-209	N19 12	43
SUN	06	226 35	-208	N18 29	48
HP	12	223 07	-205	N17 41	52
60'	18	219 42	-204	N16 49	56
25	00	216° 18'		N15° 53'	

Day	GMT	GHA-GMT	v	Dec	d
25	00h	216 18	-201	N15° 53'	59'
MON	06	212 57	-199	N14 54	63
HP	12	209 38	-197	N13 51	65
60'	18	206 21	-194	N12 46	69
26	00	203 07	-193	N11 37	70
TUE	06	199 54	-190	N10 27	73
HP	12	196 44	-188	N 9 14	75
59'	18	193 36	-186	N 7 59	75
27	00	190 30	-185	N 6 44	77
WED	06	187 25	-183	N 5 27	78
HP	12	184 22	-181	N 4 09	78
59'	18	181 21	-180	N 2 51	79
28	00	178 21	-179	N 1 32	78
THU	06	175 22	-177	N 0 14	78
HP	12	172 25	-177	S 1 04	77
58'	18	169 28	-175	S 2 21	76
29	00	166 33	-175	S 3 37	76
FRI	06	163 38	-175	S 4 53	74
HP	12	160 43	-174	S 6 07	72
58'	18	157 49	-174	S 7 19	70
30	00	154 55	-174	S 8 29	69
SAT	06	152 01	-173	S 9 38	66
HP	12	149 08	-174	S10 44	64
57'	18	146 14	-174	S11 48	62
31	00	143 20		S12 50	

Phases of the Moon
New: 27d   First Quarter: 5d
Full: 13d   Last Quarter: 21d

MOON AT EVERY 6hrs GMT OCTOBER 2000

Day	GMT	GHA-GMT	v	Dec	d
1	00h	143° 20'	-173'	S12° 50'	59'
SUN	06	140 27	-175	S13 49	56
HP	12	137 32	-174	S14 45	53
56'	18	134 38	-175	S15 38	50
2	00	131 43	-175	S16 28	47
MON	06	128 48	-176	S17 15	44
HP	12	125 52	-176	S17 59	41
55'	18	122 56	-176	S18 40	37
3	00	120 00	-177	S19 17	33
TUE	06	117 03	-177	S19 50	30
HP	12	114 06	-178	S20 20	26
55'	18	111 08	-177	S20 46	23
4	00	108 11	-178	S21 09	19
WED	06	105 13	-178	S21 28	15
HP	12	102 15	-178	S21 43	12
55'	18	99 17	-178	S21 55	7
5	00	96 19	-177	S22 02	4
THU	06	93 22	-178	S22 06	1
HP	12	90 24	-177	S22 07	4
54'	18	87 27	-176	S22 03	7
6	00	84 31	-177	S21 56	11
FRI	06	81 34	-175	S21 45	15
HP	12	78 39	-175	S21 30	18
54'	18	75 44	-175	S21 12	22
7	00	72 49	-173	S20 50	25
SAT	06	69 56	-173	S20 25	28
HP	12	67 03	-172	S19 57	32
54'	18	64 11	-172	S19 25	36
8	00	61 19	-170	S18 49	38
SUN	06	58 29	-170	S18 11	41
HP	12	55 39	-169	S17 30	45
55'	18	52 50	-168	S16 45	47
9	00	50° 02'		S15° 58'	

Day	GMT	GHA-GMT	v	Dec	d
9	00h	50 02	-168	S15° 58'	50'
MON	06	47 14	-166	S15 08	53
HP	12	44 28	-167	S14 15	56
55'	18	41 41	-166	S13 19	58
10	00	38 55	-165	S12 21	60
TUE	06	36 10	-165	S11 21	62
HP	12	33 25	-165	S10 19	64
56'	18	30 40	-164	S 9 15	66
11	00	27 56	-165	S 8 09	68
WED	06	25 11	-165	S 7 01	70
HP	12	22 26	-166	S 5 51	70
56'	18	19 41	-166	S 4 41	72
12	00	16 55	-166	S 3 29	73
THU	06	14 09	-167	S 2 16	74
HP	12	11 22	-167	S 1 02	74
57'	18	8 35	-169	N 0 12	75
13	00	5 46	-170	N 1 27	75
FRI	06	2 56	-171	N 2 42	75
HP	12	0 05	-173	N 3 57	75
57'	18	357 12	-174	N 5 12	74
14	00	354 18	-176	N 6 26	73
SAT	06	351 22	-178	N 7 39	72
HP	12	348 24	-180	N 8 51	71
58'	18	345 24	-182	N10 02	69
15	00	342 22	-185	N11 11	67
SUN	06	339 17	-187	N12 18	65
HP	12	336 10	-189	N13 23	62
58'	18	333 01	-192	N14 25	60
16	00	329 49	-194	N15 25	57
MON	06	326 35	-197	N16 22	53
HP	12	323 18	-199	N17 15	50
59'	18	319 59	-202	N18 05	46
17	00	316° 37'		N18° 51'	

Day	GMT	GHA-GMT	v	Dec	d
17	00h	316 37	-203	N18° 51'	42'
TUE	06	313 14	-206	N19 33	37
HP	12	309 48	-208	N20 10	33
59'	18	306 20	-210	N20 43	28
18	00	302 50	-211	N21 11	23
WED	06	299 19	-213	N21 34	18
HP	12	295 46	-213	N21 52	13
59'	18	292 13	-214	N22 05	8
19	00	288 39	-215	N22 13	2
THU	06	285 04	-214	N22 15	3
HP	12	281 30	-214	N22 12	8
59'	18	277 56	-214	N22 04	14
20	00	274 22	-213	N21 50	19
FRI	06	270 49	-211	N21 31	24
HP	12	267 18	-210	N21 07	29
59'	18	263 48	-209	N20 38	34
21	00	260 19	-206	N20 04	38
SAT	06	256 53	-205	N19 26	43
HP	12	253 28	-202	N18 43	47
59'	18	250 06	-201	N17 56	51
22	00	246 45	-198	N17 05	55
SUN	06	243 27	-196	N16 10	58
HP	12	240 11	-193	N15 12	61
59'	18	236 58	-192	N14 11	64
23	00	233 46	-189	N13 07	67
MON	06	230 37	-187	N12 00	69
HP	12	227 30	-186	N10 51	71
59'	18	224 24	-183	N 9 40	73
24	00	221 21	-182	N 8 27	74
TUE	06	218 19	-180	N 7 13	76
HP	12	215 19	-178	N 5 57	76
58'	18	212 21	-177	N 4 41	78
25	00	209° 24'		N 3° 23'	

Day	GMT	GHA-GMT	v	Dec	d
25	00h	209 24	-177	N 3° 23'	77'
WED	06	206 27	-175	N 2 06	78
HP	12	203 32	-174	N 0 48	77
58'	18	200 38	-174	S 0 29	78
26	00	197 44	-173	S 1 47	76
THU	06	194 51	-173	S 3 03	76
HP	12	191 58	-173	S 4 19	75
58'	18	189 05	-172	S 5 34	73
27	00	186 13	-173	S 6 47	72
FRI	06	183 20	-173	S 7 59	70
HP	12	180 27	-173	S 9 09	68
57'	18	177 34	-173	S10 17	66
28	00	174 41	-174	S11 23	63
SAT	06	171 47	-174	S12 26	62
HP	12	168 53	-175	S13 28	58
58'	18	165 58	-175	S14 26	56
29	00	163 03	-176	S15 22	52
SUN	06	160 07	-177	S16 14	50
HP	12	157 10	-177	S17 04	46
56'	18	154 13	-177	S17 50	43
30	00	151 16	-179	S18 33	40
MON	06	148 17	-178	S19 13	36
HP	12	145 19	-179	S19 49	32
55'	18	142 20	-180	S20 21	28
31	00	139 20	-179	S20 49	25
TUE	06	136 21	-180	S21 14	21
HP	12	133 21	-180	S21 35	17
55'	18	130 21	-180	S21 52	14
32	00	127 21		S22 06	

Phases of the Moon
New: 27d   First Quarter: 5d
Full: 13d   Last Quarter: 20d

MOON AT EVERY 6hrs GMT NOVEMBER 2000

Day	GMT	GHA-GMT	v	Dec	d	Day	GMT	GHA-GMT	v	Dec	d	Day	GMT	GHA-GMT	v	Dec	d	Day	GMT	GHA-GMT	v	Dec	d
1	00h	127° 21'	-179'	S22° 06'	9'	9	00h	37° 03'	-168'	S 0° 34'	75'	17	00h	290° 18'	-211'	N20° 50'	35'	25	00h	193° 45'	-173'	S14° 10'	56'
WED	06	124 22	-179	S22 15	6	THU	06	34 15	-169	N 0 41	76	FRI	06	286 47	-209	N20 15	39	SAT	06	190 52	-174	S15 06	54
HP	12	121 23	-179	S22 21	2	HP	12	31 26	-171	N 1 57	76	HP	12	283 18	-206	N19 36	44	HP	12	187 58	-175	S16 00	51
54'	18	118 24	-179	S22 23	3	57'	18	28 35	-172	N 3 13	76	59'	18	279 52	-203	N18 52	47	56'	18	185 03	-176	S16 51	48
2	00	115 25	-178	S22 20	5	10	00	25 43	-175	N 4 29	76	18	00	276 29	-201	N18 05	52	26	00	182 07	-177	S17 39	44
THU	06	112 27	-177	S22 15	10	FRI	06	22 48	-177	N 5 45	75	SAT	06	273 08	-198	N17 13	55	SUN	06	179 10	-177	S18 23	42
HP	12	109 30	-176	S22 05	13	HP	12	19 51	-179	N 7 00	74	HP	12	269 50	-195	N16 18	59	HP	12	176 13	-178	S19 05	37
54'	18	106 34	-175	S21 52	17	58'	18	16 52	-181	N 8 14	73	59'	18	266 35	-192	N15 19	61	55'	18	173 15	-179	S19 42	34
3	00	103 39	-175	S21 35	21	11	00	13 51	-184	N 9 27	72	19	00	263 23	-189	N14 18	65	27	00	170 16	-180	S20 16	31
FRI	06	100 44	-174	S21 14	24	SAT	06	10 47	-187	N10 39	70	SUN	06	260 14	-188	N13 13	66	MON	06	167 16	-180	S20 47	26
HP	12	97 50	-172	S20 50	27	HP	12	7 40	-189	N11 49	68	HP	12	257 06	-184	N12 07	69	HP	12	164 16	-180	S21 13	23
54'	18	94 58	-172	S20 23	31	59'	18	4 31	-193	N12 57	66	59'	18	254 02	-182	N10 58	71	55'	18	161 16	-181	S21 36	19
4	00	92 06	-170	S19 52	34	12	00	1 18	-195	N14 03	63	20	00	251 00	-181	N 9 47	72	28	00	158 15	-180	S21 55	15
SAT	06	89 16	-170	S19 18	37	SUN	06	358 03	-198	N15 06	61	MON	06	247 59	-178	N 8 35	74	TUE	06	155 15	-181	S22 10	12
HP	12	86 26	-168	S18 41	40	HP	12	354 45	-202	N16 07	56	HP	12	245 01	-176	N 7 21	74	HP	12	152 14	-180	S22 22	7
54'	18	83 38	-168	S18 01	44	59'	18	351 23	-204	N17 03	54	58'	18	242 05	-175	N 6 07	76	55'	18	149 14	-180	S22 29	3
5	00	80 50	-167	S17 17	46	13	00	347 59	-207	N17 57	49	21	00	239 10	-173	N 4 51	76	29	00	146 14	-180	S22 32	0
SUN	06	78 03	-166	S16 31	49	MON	06	344 32	-209	N18 46	45	TUE	06	236 17	-173	N 3 35	77	WED	06	143 14	-179	S22 32	5
HP	12	75 17	-165	S15 42	51	HP	12	341 03	-212	N19 31	40	HP	12	233 24	-171	N 2 18	76	HP	12	140 15	-178	S22 27	8
55'	18	72 32	-164	S14 51	54	60'	18	337 31	-214	N20 11	36	58'	18	230 33	-170	N 1 02	77	54'	18	137 17	-177	S22 19	12
6	00	69 48	-164	S13 57	57	14	00	333 57	-216	N20 47	30	22	00	227 43	-170	S 0 15	76	30	00	134 20	-176	S22 07	16
MON	06	67 04	-163	S13 00	59	TUE	06	330 21	-218	N21 17	25	WED	06	224 53	-169	S 1 31	76	THU	06	131 24	-176	S21 51	19
HP	12	64 21	-163	S12 01	61	HP	12	326 43	-219	N21 42	20	HP	12	222 04	-169	S 2 47	75	HP	12	128 28	-174	S21 32	23
55'	18	61 38	-163	S11 00	63	60'	18	323 04	-220	N22 02	15	57'	18	219 15	-169	S 4 02	74	54'	18	125 34	-173	S21 09	26
7	00	58 55	-163	S 9 57	65	15	00	319 24	-221	N22 17	8	23	00	216 26	-168	S 5 16	73	31	00	122 41		S20 43	
TUE	06	56 12	-162	S 8 52	67	WED	06	315 43	-220	N22 25	3	THU	06	213 38	-169	S 6 29	71						
HP	12	53 30	-163	S 7 45	68	HP	12	312 03	-221	N22 28	2	HP	12	210 49	-169	S 7 40	70						
56'	18	50 47	-164	S 6 37	71	60'	18	308 22	-219	N22 26	9	57'	18	208 00	-170	S 8 50	68						
8	00	48 03	-164	S 5 26	71	16	00	304 43	-219	N22 17	14	24	00	205 10	-171	S 9 58	67						
WED	06	45 19	-164	S 4 15	73	THU	06	301 04	-217	N22 03	19	FRI	06	202 20	-171	S11 05	64						
HP	12	42 35	-166	S 3 02	74	HP	12	297 27	-215	N21 44	25	HP	12	199 29	-172	S12 09	62						
56'	18	39 49	-166	S 1 48	74	60'	18	293 52	-214	N21 19	29	56'	18	196 37	-172	S13 11	59						
9	00	37° 03'		S 0° 34'		17	00	290° 18'		N20° 50'		25	00	193° 45'		S14° 10'							

Phases of the Moon
New: 25d   First Quarter: 4d
Full: 11d   Last Quarter: 18d

MOON AT EVERY 6hrs GMT DECEMBER 2000

Day	GMT	GHA-GMT	v	Dec	d	Day	GMT	GHA-GMT	v	Dec	d	Day	GMT	GHA-GMT	v	Dec	d	Day	GMT	GHA-GMT	v	Dec	d
1	00h	122° 41'	-171'	S20° 43'	29'	9	00h	33° 53'	-190'	N12° 03'	68'	17	00h	280° 43'	-186'	N11° 05'	72'	25	00h	188° 37'	-180'	S21° 33'	20'
FRI	06	119 50	-171	S20 14	33	SAT	06	30 43	-193	N13 11	66	SUN	06	277 37	-183	N 9 53	74	MON	06	185 37	-180	S21 53	16
HP	12	116 59	-169	S19 41	36	HP	12	27 30	-197	N14 17	63	HP	12	274 34	-180	N 8 39	75	HP	12	182 37	-180	S22 09	12
54'	18	114 10	-168	S19 05	39	59'	18	24 13	-200	N15 20	61	59'	18	271 34	-178	N 7 24	75	54'	18	179 37	-179	S22 21	9
2	00	111 22	-166	S18 26	42	10	00	20 53	-204	N16 21	57	18	00	268 36	-176	N 6 09	77	26	00	176 38	-180	S22 30	4
SAT	06	108 36	-166	S17 44	45	SUN	06	17 29	-207	N17 18	53	MON	06	265 40	-174	N 4 52	76	TUE	06	173 38	-180	S22 34	0
HP	12	105 50	-164	S16 59	48	HP	12	14 02	-211	N18 11	50	HP	12	262 46	-172	N 3 36	77	HP	12	170 38	-179	S22 34	3
54'	18	103 06	-163	S16 11	50	60'	18	10 31	-214	N19 01	44	58'	18	259 54	-171	N 2 19	77	54'	18	167 39	-178	S22 31	7
3	00	100 23	-163	S15 21	52	11	00	6 57	-217	N19 45	41	19	00	257 03	-170	N 1 02	77	27	00	164 41	-178	S22 24	11
SUN	06	97 40	-161	S14 29	55	MON	06	3 20	-220	N20 26	35	TUE	06	254 13	-168	S 0 15	76	WED	06	161 43	-177	S22 13	15
HP	12	94 59	-161	S13 34	57	HP	12	359 40	-223	N21 01	30	HP	12	251 25	-168	S 1 31	75	HP	12	158 46	-176	S21 58	19
55'	18	92 18	-160	S12 37	60	61'	18	355 57	-225	N21 31	24	57'	18	248 37	-168	S 2 46	75	54'	18	155 50	-174	S21 39	22
4	00	89 38	-159	S11 37	61	12	00	352 12	-226	N21 55	19	20	00	245 49	-167	S 4 01	74	28	00	152 56	-174	S21 17	25
MON	06	86 59	-160	S10 36	63	TUE	06	348 26	-228	N22 14	12	WED	06	243 02	-166	S 5 15	72	THU	06	150 02	-172	S20 52	29
HP	12	84 19	-159	S 9 33	65	HP	12	344 38	-228	N22 26	7	HP	12	240 16	-167	S 6 27	71	HP	12	147 10	-171	S20 23	33
55'	18	81 40	-159	S 8 28	67	61'	18	340 50	-229	N22 33	0	57'	18	237 29	-167	S 7 38	69	54'	18	144 19	-169	S19 50	35
5	00	79 01	-159	S 7 21	68	13	00	337 01	-228	N22 33	5	21	00	234 42	-167	S 8 47	68	29	00	141 30	-168	S19 15	38
TUE	06	76 22	-160	S 6 13	70	WED	06	333 13	-228	N22 28	12	THU	06	231 55	-167	S 9 55	65	FRI	06	138 42	-167	S18 37	42
HP	12	73 42	-160	S 5 03	71	HP	12	329 25	-226	N22 16	17	HP	12	229 08	-168	S11 00	64	HP	12	135 55	-165	S17 55	44
56'	18	71 02	-161	S 3 52	72	61'	18	325 39	-225	N21 59	24	56'	18	226 20	-169	S12 04	61	54'	18	133 10	-164	S17 11	47
6	00	68 21	-162	S 2 40	73	14	00	321 54	-222	N21 35	28	22	00	223 31	-170	S13 05	59	30	00	130 26	-163	S16 24	49
WED	06	65 39	-163	S 1 27	73	THU	06	318 12	-220	N21 07	35	FRI	06	220 41	-170	S14 04	56	SAT	06	127 43	-161	S15 35	52
HP	12	62 56	-165	S 0 14	75	HP	12	314 32	-218	N20 32	39	HP	12	217 51	-171	S15 00	53	HP	12	125 02	-160	S14 43	54
57'	18	60 11	-166	N 1 01	75	61'	18	310 54	-214	N19 53	44	56'	18	215 00	-173	S15 54	51	54'	18	122 22	-160	S13 49	56
7	00	57 25	-168	N 2 16	75	15	00	307 20	-211	N19 09	48	23	00	212 07	-173	S16 45	48	31	00	119 42	-158	S12 53	58
THU	06	54 37	-170	N 3 31	75	FRI	06	303 49	-208	N18 21	53	SAT	06	209 14	-174	S17 33	44	SUN	06	117 04	-157	S11 55	60
HP	12	51 47	-172	N 4 46	75	HP	12	300 21	-205	N17 28	57	HP	12	206 20	-175	S18 17	42	HP	12	114 27	-157	S10 55	62
57'	18	48 55	-175	N 6 01	74	60'	18	296 56	-201	N16 31	59	55'	18	203 25	-176	S18 59	38	55'	18	111 50	-157	S 9 53	64
8	00	46 00	-177	N 7 15	74	16	00	293 35	-198	N15 32	63	24	00	200 29	-177	S19 37	34	32	00	109 13		S 8 49	
FRI	06	43 03	-180	N 8 29	73	SAT	06	290 17	-195	N14 29	66	SUN	06	197 32	-178	S20 11	31						
HP	12	40 03	-184	N 9 42	71	HP	12	287 02	-191	N13 23	68	HP	12	194 34	-178	S20 42	28						
58'	18	36 59	-186	N10 53	70	59'	18	283 51	-188	N12 15	70	55'	18	191 36	-179	S21 10	23						
9	00	33° 53'		N12° 03'		17	00	280° 43'		N11° 05'		25	00	188° 37'		S21° 33'							

Phases of the Moon
New: 25d   First Quarter: 4d
Full: 11d   Last Quarter: 18d

MOON AT EVERY 6hrs GMT JANUARY 2001

Day	GMT	GHA-GMT	v	Dec	d
1	00h	109° 13'	-156'	S 8° 49'	65'
MON	06	106 37	-156	S 7 44	66
HP	12	104 01	-156	S 6 38	68
55'	18	101 25	-156	S 5 30	69
2	00	98 49	-156	S 4 21	70
TUE	06	96 13	-158	S 3 11	71
HP	12	93 35	-157	S 2 00	72
56'	18	90 58	-159	S 0 48	72
3	00	88 19	-161	N 0 24	73
WED	06	85 38	-161	N 1 37	73
HP	12	82 57	-164	N 2 50	73
56'	18	80 13	-165	N 4 03	73
4	00	77 28	-168	N 5 16	72
THU	06	74 40	-170	N 6 28	72
HP	12	71 50	-172	N 7 40	72
57'	18	68 58	-176	N 8 52	70
5	00	66 02	-178	N10 02	70
FRI	06	63 04	-182	N11 12	67
HP	12	60 02	-185	N12 19	66
58'	18	56 57	-189	N13 25	64
6	00	53 48	-193	N14 29	62
SAT	06	50 35	-196	N15 31	58
HP	12	47 19	-200	N16 29	56
59'	18	43 59	-205	N17 25	52
7	00	40 34	-208	N18 17	48
SUN	06	37 06	-212	N19 05	44
HP	12	33 34	-215	N19 49	40
60'	18	29 59	-219	N20 29	35
8	00	26 20	-223	N21 04	29
MON	06	22 37	-225	N21 33	24
HP	12	18 52	-227	N21 57	18
61'	18	15 05	-230	N22 15	13
9	00	11° 15'		N22° 28'	

Day	GMT	GHA-GMT	v	Dec	d
9	00h	11° 15'	-231'	N22° 28'	6'
TUE	06	7 24	-232	N22 34	1
HP	12	3 32	-232	N22 33	6
61'	18	359 40	-233	N22 27	13
10	00	355 47	-231	N22 14	19
WED	06	351 56	-231	N21 55	25
HP	12	348 05	-228	N21 30	31
61'	18	344 17	-227	N20 59	36
11	00	340 30	-224	N20 23	42
THU	06	336 46	-221	N19 41	47
HP	12	333 05	-219	N18 54	52
61'	18	329 26	-215	N18 02	57
12	00	325 51	-211	N17 05	60
FRI	06	322 20	-208	N16 05	64
HP	12	318 52	-204	N15 01	66
61'	18	315 28	-201	N13 55	70
13	00	312 07	-198	N12 45	72
SAT	06	308 49	-194	N11 33	75
HP	12	305 35	-192	N10 18	75
60'	18	302 23	-188	N 9 03	78
14	00	299 15	-185	N 7 45	78
SUN	06	296 10	-183	N 6 27	79
HP	12	293 07	-180	N 5 08	79
59'	18	290 07	-179	N 3 49	79
15	00	287 08	-176	N 2 30	79
MON	06	284 12	-174	N 1 11	79
HP	12	281 18	-174	S 0 08	78
58'	18	278 24	-171	S 1 26	77
16	00	275 33	-171	S 2 43	75
TUE	06	272 42	-170	S 3 59	75
HP	12	269 52	-170	S 5 14	74
57'	18	267 02	-168	S 6 28	71
17	00	264° 14'		S 7° 39'	

Day	GMT	GHA-GMT	v	Dec	d
17	00h	264° 14'	-169'	S 7° 39'	70'
WED	06	261 25	-168	S 8 49	68
HP	12	258 37	-169	S 9 57	66
56'	18	255 48	-169	S11 03	64
18	00	252 59	-169	S12 07	61
THU	06	250 10	-170	S13 08	59
HP	12	247 20	-170	S14 07	56
56'	18	244 30	-171	S15 03	54
19	00	241 39	-171	S15 57	50
FRI	06	238 48	-172	S16 47	48
HP	12	235 56	-174	S17 35	44
55'	18	233 02	-173	S18 19	41
20	00	230 09	-175	S19 00	38
SAT	06	227 14	-176	S19 38	34
HP	12	224 18	-176	S20 12	31
55'	18	221 22	-177	S20 43	27
21	00	218 25	-177	S21 10	23
SUN	06	215 28	-178	S21 33	20
HP	12	212 30	-179	S21 53	16
54'	18	209 31	-178	S22 09	12
22	00	206 33	-179	S22 21	8
MON	06	203 34	-179	S22 29	4
HP	12	200 35	-178	S22 33	1
54'	18	197 37	-178	S22 34	3
23	00	194 39	-178	S22 31	8
TUE	06	191 41	-177	S22 23	10
HP	12	188 44	-177	S22 13	15
54'	18	185 47	-175	S21 58	19
24	00	182 52	-175	S21 39	23
WED	06	179 57	-174	S21 18	26
HP	12	177 03	-172	S20 52	29
54'	18	174 11	-171	S20 23	32
25	00	171° 20'		S19° 51'	

Day	GMT	GHA-GMT	v	Dec	d
25	00h	171° 20'	-170'	S19° 51'	35'
THU	06	168 30	-168	S19 16	39
HP	12	165 42	-167	S18 37	41
54'	18	162 55	-166	S17 56	44
26	00	160 09	-164	S17 12	47
FRI	06	157 25	-163	S16 25	50
HP	12	154 42	-162	S15 35	52
54'	18	152 00	-161	S14 43	54
27	00	149 19	-159	S13 49	56
SAT	06	146 40	-159	S12 53	59
HP	12	144 01	-157	S11 54	60
54'	18	141 24	-156	S10 54	62
28	00	138 48	-156	S 9 52	63
SUN	06	136 12	-156	S 8 49	65
HP	12	133 36	-155	S 7 44	66
55'	18	131 01	-154	S 6 38	68
29	00	128 27	-155	S 5 30	68
MON	06	125 52	-154	S 4 22	69
HP	12	123 18	-155	S 3 13	70
55'	18	120 43	-156	S 2 03	71
30	00	118 07	-156	S 0 52	71
TUE	06	115 31	-157	N 0 19	71
HP	12	112 54	-157	N 1 30	72
56'	18	110 17	-160	N 2 42	72
31	00	107 37	-160	N 3 54	71
WED	06	104 57	-163	N 5 05	71
HP	12	102 14	-164	N 6 16	70
56'	18	99 30	-167	N 7 26	70
32	00	96 43		N 8 36	

Phases of the Moon
New: 24d   First Quarter: 2d
Full: 9d   Last Quarter: 16d

MOON AT EVERY 6hrs GMT FEBRUARY 2001

Day	GMT	GHA-GMT	v	Dec	d
1	00h	96° 43'	-168'	N 8° 36'	68'
THU	06	93 55	-172	N 9 44	68
HP	12	91 03	-174	N10 52	66
57'	18	88 09	-177	N11 58	65
2	00	85 12	-180	N13 03	62
FRI	06	82 12	-184	N14 05	60
HP	12	79 08	-187	N15 05	58
58'	18	76 01	-191	N16 03	56
3	00	72 50	-194	N16 59	52
SAT	06	69 36	-199	N17 51	48
HP	12	66 17	-201	N18 39	46
59'	18	62 56	-206	N19 25	41
4	00	59 30	-209	N20 06	36
SUN	06	56 01	-213	N20 42	33
HP	12	52 28	-216	N21 15	27
60'	18	48 52	-219	N21 42	22
5	00	45 13	-222	N22 04	16
MON	06	41 31	-225	N22 20	11
HP	12	37 46	-226	N22 31	5
61'	18	34 00	-228	N22 36	1
6	00	30 12	-228	N22 35	7
TUE	06	26 24	-230	N22 28	14
HP	12	22 34	-229	N22 14	19
61'	18	18 45	-229	N21 55	26
7	00	14 56	-228	N21 29	32
WED	06	11 08	-227	N20 57	37
HP	12	7 21	-225	N20 20	43
61'	18	3 36	-223	N19 37	48
8	00	359 53	-220	N18 49	53
THU	06	356 13	-218	N17 56	58
HP	12	352 35	-215	N16 58	62
61'	18	349 00	-212	N15 56	66
9	00	345° 28'		N14° 50'	

Day	GMT	GHA-GMT	v	Dec	d
9	00h	345° 28'	-209'	N14° 50'	70'
FRI	06	341 59	-206	N13 40	72
HP	12	338 33	-203	N12 28	75
61'	18	335 10	-199	N11 13	77
10	00	331 51	-197	N 9 56	79
SAT	06	328 34	-194	N 8 37	81
HP	12	325 20	-192	N 7 16	81
60'	18	322 08	-189	N 5 55	82
11	00	318 59	-186	N 4 33	83
SUN	06	315 53	-185	N 3 10	82
HP	12	312 48	-182	N 1 48	82
60'	18	309 46	-181	N 0 26	82
12	00	306 45	-179	S 0 56	81
MON	06	303 46	-178	S 2 17	79
HP	12	300 48	-177	S 3 36	78
59'	18	297 51	-176	S 4 54	77
13	00	294 55	-175	S 6 11	75
TUE	06	292 00	-175	S 7 26	73
HP	12	289 05	-174	S 8 39	70
58'	18	286 11	-173	S 9 49	69
14	00	283 18	-174	S10 58	66
WED	06	280 24	-174	S12 04	63
HP	12	277 30	-173	S13 07	60
57'	18	274 37	-174	S14 07	58
15	00	271 43	-175	S15 05	55
THU	06	268 48	-174	S16 00	51
HP	12	265 54	-175	S16 51	48
56'	18	262 59	-176	S17 39	45
16	00	260 03	-176	S18 24	42
FRI	06	257 07	-176	S19 06	38
HP	12	254 11	-177	S19 44	34
55'	18	251 14	-177	S20 18	31
17	00	248° 17'		S20° 49'	

Day	GMT	GHA-GMT	v	Dec	d
17	00h	248° 17'	-178'	S20° 49'	27'
SAT	06	245 19	-178	S21 16	23
HP	12	242 21	-179	S21 39	20
55'	18	239 22	-178	S21 59	15
18	00	236 24	-179	S22 14	12
SUN	06	233 25	-178	S22 26	8
HP	12	230 27	-179	S22 34	4
54'	18	227 28	-178	S22 38	1
19	00	224 30	-177	S22 39	4
MON	06	221 33	-178	S22 35	8
HP	12	218 35	-176	S22 27	11
54'	18	215 39	-176	S22 16	15
20	00	212 43	-175	S22 01	18
TUE	06	209 48	-175	S21 43	23
HP	12	206 53	-173	S21 20	25
54'	18	204 00	-172	S20 55	29
21	00	201 08	-171	S20 26	33
WED	06	198 17	-169	S19 53	36
HP	12	195 28	-169	S19 17	38
54'	18	192 39	-167	S18 39	42
22	00	189 52	-166	S17 57	45
THU	06	187 06	-165	S17 12	47
HP	12	184 21	-164	S16 25	50
54'	18	181 37	-162	S15 35	53
23	00	178 55	-161	S14 42	55
FRI	06	176 14	-160	S13 47	57
HP	12	173 34	-159	S12 50	59
54'	18	170 55	-159	S11 51	61
24	00	168 16	-157	S10 50	63
SAT	06	165 39	-157	S 9 47	64
HP	12	163 02	-156	S 8 43	66
54'	18	160 26	-156	S 7 37	67
25	00	157° 50'		S 6° 30'	

Day	GMT	GHA-GMT	v	Dec	d
25	00h	157° 50'	-156'	S 6° 30'	68'
SUN	06	155 14	-155	S 5 22	69
HP	12	152 39	-155	S 4 13	70
55'	18	150 04	-156	S 3 03	71
26	00	147 28	-155	S 1 52	72
MON	06	144 53	-157	S 0 40	71
HP	12	142 16	-157	N 0 31	72
55'	18	139 39	-157	N 1 43	72
27	00	137 02	-159	N 2 55	71
TUE	06	134 23	-160	N 4 06	72
HP	12	131 43	-162	N 5 18	71
56'	18	129 01	-163	N 6 29	70
28	00	126 18	-165	N 7 39	69
WED	06	123 33	-166	N 8 48	68
HP	12	120 47	-169	N 9 56	67
56'	18	117 58	-172	N11 03	65
29	00	115 06	-175	N12 08	64
THU	06	112 13	-177	N13 12	61
HP	12	109 40	-179	N14 13	60
57'	18	106 17	-182	N15 13	56
30	00	103 15		N16 09	

Phases of the Moon
New: 23d   First Quarter: 1d
Full: 8d   Last Quarter: 15d

MOON AT EVERY 6hrs GMT MARCH 2001

Day GMT	GHA-GMT	v	Dec	d
1 00h	115° 06'	-173'	N12° 08'	64'
THU 06	112 13	-177	N13 12	61
HP 12	109 16	-179	N14 13	60
57' 18	106 17	-182	N15 13	56
2 00	103 15	-185	N16 09	55
FRI 06	100 10	-189	N17 04	51
HP 12	97 01	-191	N17 55	48
58' 18	93 50	-195	N18 43	44
3 00	90 35	-198	N19 27	41
SAT 06	87 17	-201	N20 08	36
HP 12	83 56	-204	N20 44	32
58' 18	80 32	-207	N21 16	28
4 00	77 05	-210	N21 44	23
SUN 06	73 35	-213	N22 07	17
HP 12	70 02	-214	N22 24	13
59' 18	66 28	-217	N22 37	7
5 00	62 51	-219	N22 44	1
MON 06	59 12	-219	N22 45	4
HP 12	55 33	-221	N22 41	10
60' 18	51 52	-222	N22 31	16
6 00	48 10	-221	N22 15	21
TUE 06	44 29	-222	N21 54	28
HP 12	40 47	-220	N21 26	33
61' 18	37 07	-220	N20 53	38
7 00	33 27	-219	N20 15	44
WED 06	29 48	-217	N19 31	49
HP 12	26 11	-215	N18 42	54
61' 18	22 36	-213	N17 48	58
8 00	19 03	-212	N16 50	63
THU 06	15 31	-208	N15 47	66
HP 12	12 03	-207	N14 41	70
61' 18	8 36	-204	N13 31	74
9 00	5° 12'		N12° 17'	

Day GMT	GHA-GMT	v	Dec	d
9 00h	5° 12'	-202'	N12° 17'	76'
FRI 06	1 50	-199	N11 01	78
HP 12	358 31	-198	N 9 43	80
61' 18	355 13	-195	N 8 23	82
10 00	351 58	-193	N 7 01	83
SAT 06	348 45	-191	N 5 38	84
HP 12	345 34	-189	N 4 14	85
60' 18	342 25	-187	N 2 49	85
11 00	339 18	-186	N 1 24	84
SUN 06	336 12	-185	N 0 00	84
HP 12	333 07	-184	S 1 24	83
60' 18	330 03	-182	S 2 47	82
12 00	327 01	-182	S 4 09	80
MON 06	323 59	-181	S 5 29	79
HP 12	320 58	-181	S 6 48	77
59' 18	317 57	-180	S 8 05	74
13 00	314 57	-179	S 9 19	73
TUE 06	311 58	-180	S10 32	69
HP 12	308 58	-180	S11 41	67
58' 18	305 59	-179	S12 48	64
14 00	302 59	-180	S13 52	61
WED 06	299 59	-180	S14 53	58
HP 12	296 59	-180	S15 51	55
57' 18	293 59	-180	S16 46	51
15 00	290 59	-180	S17 37	47
THU 06	287 59	-181	S18 24	44
HP 12	284 58	-181	S19 08	40
56' 18	281 57	-181	S19 48	36
16 00	278 56	-182	S20 24	32
FRI 06	275 54	-181	S20 56	28
HP 12	272 53	-182	S21 24	25
55' 18	269 51	-181	S21 49	20
17 00	266° 50'		S22° 09'	

Day GMT	GHA-GMT	v	Dec	d
17 00h	266° 50'	-182'	S22° 09'	17'
SAT 06	263 48	-181	S22 26	12
HP 12	260 47	-180	S22 38	8
55' 18	257 47	-181	S22 46	5
18 00	254 46	-179	S22 51	0
SUN 06	251 47	-180	S22 51	3
HP 12	248 48	-178	S22 48	8
54' 18	245 49	-177	S22 40	11
19 00	242 52	-177	S22 29	15
MON 06	239 55	-176	S22 14	19
HP 12	236 59	-174	S21 55	22
54' 18	234 05	-173	S21 33	26
20 00	231 12	-173	S21 07	29
TUE 06	228 19	-171	S20 38	33
HP 12	225 28	-169	S20 05	35
54' 18	222 39	-169	S19 30	39
21 00	219 50	-167	S18 51	42
WED 06	217 03	-166	S18 09	45
HP 12	214 17	-165	S17 24	48
54' 18	211 32	-163	S16 36	50
22 00	208 49	-163	S15 46	53
THU 06	206 06	-161	S14 53	56
HP 12	203 25	-161	S13 57	57
54' 18	200 44	-159	S13 00	60
23 00	198 05	-159	S12 00	62
FRI 06	195 26	-158	S10 58	63
HP 12	192 48	-158	S 9 55	66
55' 18	190 10	-157	S 8 49	66
24 00	187 33	-157	S 7 43	69
SAT 06	184 56	-157	S 6 34	69
HP 12	182 19	-156	S 5 25	71
55' 18	179 43	-157	S 4 14	71
25 00	177° 06'		S 3° 03'	

Day GMT	GHA-GMT	v	Dec	d
25 00h	177° 06'	-157'	S 3° 03'	72'
SUN 06	174 29	-157	S 1 51	73
HP 12	171 52	-158	S 0 38	73
55' 18	169 14	-159	N 0 35	73
26 00	166 35	-160	N 1 48	74
MON 06	163 55	-160	N 3 02	73
HP 12	161 15	-162	N 4 15	73
56' 18	158 33	-164	N 5 28	72
27 00	155 49	-165	N 6 40	71
TUE 06	153 04	-166	N 7 51	71
HP 12	150 18	-169	N 9 02	69
56' 18	147 29	-171	N10 11	68
28 00	144 38	-172	N11 19	66
WED 06	141 46	-176	N12 25	64
HP 12	138 50	-177	N13 29	63
57' 18	135 53	-180	N14 32	59
29 00	132 53	-183	N15 31	57
THU 06	129 50	-186	N16 28	55
HP 12	126 44	-188	N17 23	51
57' 18	123 36	-191	N18 14	47
30 00	120 25	-194	N19 01	44
FRI 06	117 11	-196	N19 45	41
HP 12	113 55	-199	N20 26	35
58' 18	110 36	-202	N21 01	32
31 00	107 14	-204	N21 33	27
SAT 06	103 50	-206	N22 00	22
HP 12	100 24	-208	N22 22	18
58' 18	96 56	-210	N22 40	12
32 00	93 26		N22 52	

Phases of the Moon
New: 25d   First Quarter: 3d
Full: 9d   Last Quarter: 16d

MOON AT EVERY 6hrs GMT APRIL 2001

Day GMT	GHA-GMT	v	Dec	d
1 00h	93° 26'	-212'	N22° 52'	7'
SUN 06	89 54	-213	N22 59	1
HP 12	86 21	-213	N23 00	3
59' 18	82 48	-214	N22 57	10
2 00	79 14	-215	N22 47	15
MON 06	75 39	-214	N22 32	20
HP 12	72 05	-214	N22 12	26
59' 18	68 31	-213	N21 46	31
3 00	64 58	-213	N21 15	36
TUE 06	61 25	-211	N20 39	42
HP 12	57 54	-210	N19 57	46
60' 18	54 24	-208	N19 11	51
4 00	50 56	-206	N18 20	55
WED 06	47 30	-205	N17 25	60
HP 12	44 05	-203	N16 25	63
60' 18	40 42	-201	N15 22	67
5 00	37 21	-199	N14 15	70
THU 06	34 02	-197	N13 05	74
HP 12	30 45	-195	N11 51	76
60' 18	27 30	-193	N10 35	78
6 00	24 17	-192	N 9 17	80
FRI 06	21 05	-190	N 7 57	82
HP 12	17 55	-188	N 6 35	83
60' 18	14 47	-188	N 5 12	84
7 00	11 39	-186	N 3 48	84
SAT 06	8 33	-185	N 2 24	85
HP 12	5 28	-184	N 0 59	84
60' 18	2 24	-183	S 0 25	85
8 00	359 21	-183	S 1 50	83
SUN 06	356 18	-182	S 3 13	83
HP 12	353 16	-183	S 4 36	81
59' 18	350 13	-181	S 5 57	79
9 00	347° 12'		S 7° 16'	

Day GMT	GHA-GMT	v	Dec	d
9 00h	347° 12'	-182'	S 7° 16'	78'
MON 06	344 10	-182	S 8 34	76
HP 12	341 08	-182	S 9 50	73
58' 18	338 06	-183	S11 03	71
10 00	335 03	-182	S12 14	67
TUE 06	332 01	-184	S13 21	65
HP 12	328 57	-183	S14 26	62
58' 18	325 54	-184	S15 28	58
11 00	322 50	-184	S16 26	54
WED 06	319 46	-185	S17 20	51
HP 12	316 41	-185	S18 11	48
57' 18	313 36	-185	S18 59	43
12 00	310 31	-186	S19 42	39
THU 06	307 25	-186	S20 21	35
HP 12	304 19	-186	S20 56	31
56' 18	301 13	-186	S21 27	27
13 00	298 07	-186	S21 54	23
FRI 06	295 01	-185	S22 17	19
HP 12	291 56	-185	S22 36	14
55' 18	288 51	-185	S22 50	10
14 00	285 46	-184	S23 00	6
SAT 06	282 42	-183	S23 06	2
HP 12	279 39	-182	S23 08	2
55' 18	276 37	-181	S23 05	6
15 00	273 36	-181	S22 59	11
SUN 06	270 35	-178	S22 48	14
HP 12	267 37	-178	S22 34	18
54' 18	264 39	-176	S22 16	22
16 00	261 43	-175	S21 54	25
MON 06	258 48	-174	S21 29	29
HP 12	255 54	-172	S21 00	32
54' 18	253 02	-170	S20 28	36
17 00	250° 12'		S19° 52'	

Day GMT	GHA-GMT	v	Dec	d
17 00h	250° 12'	-169'	S19° 52'	38'
TUE 06	247 23	-168	S19 14	42
HP 12	244 35	-166	S18 32	45
54' 18	241 49	-164	S17 47	47
18 00	239 05	-164	S17 00	50
WED 06	236 21	-162	S16 10	53
HP 12	233 39	-162	S15 17	55
54' 18	230 57	-160	S14 22	58
19 00	228 17	-159	S13 24	59
THU 06	225 38	-158	S12 25	62
HP 12	223 00	-158	S11 23	64
55' 18	220 22	-158	S10 19	65
20 00	217 44	-157	S 9 14	67
FRI 06	215 07	-156	S 8 07	68
HP 12	212 31	-157	S 6 59	70
55' 18	209 54	-157	S 5 49	71
21 00	207 17	-157	S 4 38	73
SAT 06	204 40	-157	S 3 25	73
HP 12	202 03	-158	S 2 12	73
55' 18	199 25	-159	S 0 59	75
22 00	196 46	-159	N 0 16	74
SUN 06	194 07	-161	N 1 30	75
HP 12	191 26	-162	N 2 45	75
56' 18	188 44	-164	N 4 00	74
23 00	186 00	-165	N 5 14	74
MON 06	183 15	-167	N 6 28	74
HP 12	180 28	-169	N 7 42	72
57' 18	177 39	-171	N 8 54	71
24 00	174 48	-173	N10 05	70
TUE 06	171 55	-175	N11 15	69
HP 12	169 00	-179	N12 24	66
57' 18	166 01	-180	N13 30	64
25 00	163° 01'		N14° 34'	

Day GMT	GHA-GMT	v	Dec	d
25 00h	163° 01'	-184'	N14° 34'	62'
WED 06	159 57	-186	N15 36	59
HP 12	156 51	-189	N16 35	54
58' 18	153 42	-192	N17 31	52
26 00	150 30	-194	N18 23	50
THU 06	147 16	-198	N19 13	45
HP 12	143 58	-200	N19 58	41
58' 18	140 38	-202	N20 39	37
27 00	137 16	-205	N21 16	32
FRI 06	133 51	-207	N21 48	27
HP 12	130 24	-209	N22 15	23
59' 18	126 55	-210	N22 38	17
28 00	123 25	-212	N22 55	12
SAT 06	119 53	-213	N23 07	7
HP 12	116 20	-213	N23 14	1
59' 18	112 47	-214	N23 15	5
29 00	109 13	-214	N23 10	9
SUN 06	105 39	-213	N23 01	16
HP 12	102 06	-213	N22 45	21
59' 18	98 33	-212	N22 24	26
30 00	95 01	-211	N21 58	31
MON 06	91 30	-209	N21 27	36
HP 12	88 01	-208	N20 51	41
59' 18	84 33	-206	N20 10	46
31 00	81 07		N19 24	

Phases of the Moon
New: 23d   First Quarter: 1d&30d
Full: 8d   Last Quarter: 15d

MOON AT EVERY 6hrs GMT MAY 2001

Day GMT	GHA-GMT	v	Dec	d	Day GMT	GHA-GMT	v	Dec	d	Day GMT	GHA-GMT	v	Dec	d	Day GMT	GHA-GMT	v	Dec	d
1 00h	81° 07'	-203'	N19° 24'	51'	9 00h	342° 17'	-186'	S18° 41'	46'	17 00h	248° 11'	-156'	S10° 53'	65'	25 00h	154° 23'	-216'	N22° 41'	19'
TUE 06	77 44	-202	N18 33	54	WED 06	339 11	-187	S19 27	42	THU 06	245 35	-156	S 9 48	66	FRI 06	150 47	-218	N23 00	13
HP 12	74 22	-200	N17 39	58	HP 12	336 04	-188	S20 09	39	HP 12	242 59	-156	S 8 42	68	HP 12	147 09	-218	N23 13	8
59' 18	71 02	-197	N16 41	63	56' 18	332 56	-188	S20 48	34	55' 18	240 23	-155	S 7 34	69	59' 18	143 31	-219	N23 21	2
2 00	67 45	-196	N15 38	65	10 00	329 48	-189	S21 22	30	18 00	237 48	-155	S 6 25	71	26 00	139 52	-219	N23 23	4
WED 06	64 29	-193	N14 33	69	THU 06	326 39	-188	S21 52	25	FRI 06	235 13	-156	S 5 14	71	SAT 06	136 13	-220	N23 19	9
HP 12	61 16	-191	N13 24	71	HP 12	323 31	-188	S22 17	24	HP 12	232 37	-156	S 4 03	73	HP 12	132 33	-218	N23 10	16
59' 18	58 05	-190	N12 13	74	56' 18	320 23	-188	S22 38	17	55' 18	230 01	-156	S 2 50	73	60' 18	128 55	-217	N22 54	21
3 00	54 55	-187	N10 59	76	11 00	317 15	-188	S22 55	13	19 00	227 25	-157	S 1 37	75	27 00	125 18	-217	N22 33	26
THU 06	51 48	-186	N 9 43	78	FRI 06	314 07	-187	S23 08	8	SAT 06	224 48	-159	S 0 22	74	SUN 06	121 41	-214	N22 07	32
HP 12	48 42	-185	N 8 25	80	HP 12	311 00	-186	S23 16	4	HP 12	222 09	-159	N 0 52	75	HP 12	118 07	-213	N21 35	37
59' 18	45 37	-183	N 7 05	81	55' 18	307 54	-186	S23 20	1	56' 18	219 30	-161	N 2 07	75	60' 18	114 34	-210	N20 58	42
4 00	42 34	-182	N 5 44	82	12 00	304 48	-184	S23 19	4	20 00	216 49	-162	N 3 22	76	28 00	111 04	-208	N20 16	47
FRI 06	39 32	-180	N 4 22	83	SAT 06	301 44	-183	S23 15	9	SUN 06	214 07	-165	N 4 38	75	MON06	107 36	-205	N19 29	51
HP 12	36 32	-180	N 2 59	83	HP 12	298 41	-182	S23 06	13	HP 12	211 22	-166	N 5 53	74	HP 12	104 11	-203	N18 38	55
59' 18	33 32	-180	N 1 36	84	55' 18	295 39	-180	S22 53	17	57' 18	208 36	-168	N 7 07	74	59' 18	100 48	-200	N17 43	59
5 00	30 32	-179	N 0 12	83	13 00	292 39	-179	S22 36	20	21 00	205 48	-171	N 8 21	73	29 00	97 28	-198	N16 44	63
SAT 06	27 33	-178	S 1 11	83	SUN 06	289 40	-177	S22 16	24	MON06	202 57	-174	N 9 34	71	TUE 06	94 10	-195	N15 41	65
HP 12	24 35	-178	S 2 34	82	HP 12	286 43	-176	S21 52	28	HP 12	200 03	-176	N10 45	70	HP 12	90 55	-192	N14 36	69
59' 18	21 37	-179	S 3 56	81	54' 18	283 47	-173	S21 24	32	57' 18	197 07	-178	N11 55	69	59' 18	87 43	-190	N13 27	72
6 00	18 38	-178	S 5 17	80	14 00	280 54	-172	S20 52	34	22 00	194 09	-182	N13 04	66	30 00	84 33	-188	N12 15	73
SUN 06	15 40	-179	S 6 37	78	MON06	278 02	-171	S20 18	38	TUE 06	191 07	-185	N14 10	64	WED 06	81 25	-185	N11 02	76
HP 12	12 41	-179	S 7 55	76	HP 12	275 11	-168	S19 40	41	HP 12	188 02	-188	N15 14	62	HP 12	78 20	-183	N 9 46	78
58' 18	9 42	-180	S 9 11	75	54' 18	272 23	-167	S18 59	44	58' 18	184 54	-192	N16 16	58	59' 18	75 17	-182	N 8 28	79
7 00	6 42	-180	S10 26	72	15 00	269 36	-165	S18 15	47	23 00	181 42	-194	N17 14	56	31 00	72 15	-180	N 7 09	80
MON 06	3 42	-181	S11 38	70	TUE 06	266 51	-164	S17 28	49	WED 06	178 28	-198	N18 10	52	THU 06	69 15	-178	N 5 49	81
HP 12	0 41	-182	S12 48	67	HP 12	264 07	-162	S16 39	52	HP 12	175 10	-201	N19 02	48	HP 12	66 17	-177	N 4 28	82
58' 18	357 39	-183	S13 55	64	54' 18	261 25	-161	S15 47	55	59' 18	171 49	-204	N19 50	43	59' 18	63 20	-177	N 3 06	82
8 00	354 36	-183	S14 59	60	16 00	258 44	-160	S14 52	56	24 00	168 25	-207	N20 33	40	32 00	60 23		N 1 44	
TUE 06	351 33	-185	S15 59	58	WED 06	256 04	-159	S13 56	59	THU 06	164 58	-209	N21 13	34					
HP 12	348 28	-185	S16 57	54	HP 12	253 25	-157	S12 57	61	HP 12	161 29	-212	N21 47	30					
57' 18	345 23	-186	S17 51	50	54' 18	250 48	-157	S11 56	63	59' 18	157 57	-214	N22 17	24					
9 00	342° 17'		S18° 41'		17 00	248° 11'		S10° 53'		25 00	154° 23'		N22° 41'						

Phases of the Moon
New: 23d   First Quarter: 29d
Full: 7d   Last Quarter: 15d

MOON AT EVERY 6hrs GMT JUNE 2001

Day GMT	GHA-GMT	v	Dec	d	Day GMT	GHA-GMT	v	Dec	d	Day GMT	GHA-GMT	v	Dec	d	Day GMT	GHA-GMT	v	Dec	d
1 00h	60° 23'	-175'	N 1° 44'	82'	9 00h	323° 37'	-182'	S23° 04'	16'	17 00h	237° 00'	-164'	N 6° 24'	73'	25 00h	128° 03'	-206'	N17° 53'	60'
FRI 06	57 28	-175	N 0 22	82	SAT 06	320 35	-180	S22 48	19	SUN 06	234 16	-168	N 7 37	73	MON06	124 37	-204	N16 53	64
HP 12	54 33	-174	S 1 00	81	HP 12	317 35	-179	S22 28	23	HP 12	231 28	-170	N 8 50	72	HP 12	121 13	-200	N15 49	67
58' 18	51 39	-174	S 2 21	81	55' 18	314 36	-177	S22 06	26	57' 18	228 38	-172	N10 02	71	60' 18	117 53	-197	N14 42	70
2 00	48 45	-174	S 3 42	80	10 00	311 39	-175	S21 40	31	18 00	225 46	-176	N11 13	69	26 00	114 36	-194	N13 32	73
SAT 06	45 51	-174	S 5 02	79	SUN 06	308 44	-174	S21 09	33	MON06	222 50	-179	N12 22	67	TUE 06	111 22	-192	N12 19	76
HP 12	42 57	-174	S 6 21	77	HP 12	305 50	-171	S20 36	37	HP 12	219 51	-182	N13 29	66	HP 12	108 10	-188	N11 03	77
58' 18	40 03	-175	S 7 38	76	54' 18	302 59	-170	S19 59	40	58' 18	216 49	-186	N14 35	63	60' 18	105 02	-187	N 9 46	79
3 00	37 08	-176	S 8 54	73	11 00	300 09	-168	S19 19	43	19 00	213 43	-189	N15 38	61	27 00	101 55	-183	N 8 27	80
SUN 06	34 12	-176	S10 07	72	MON06	297 21	-166	S18 36	46	TUE 06	210 34	-193	N16 39	57	WED 06	98 52	-182	N 7 07	81
HP 12	31 16	-177	S11 19	69	HP 12	294 35	-164	S17 50	49	HP 12	207 21	-196	N17 36	55	HP 12	95 50	-180	N 5 46	82
57' 18	28 19	-178	S12 28	67	54' 18	291 51	-163	S17 01	51	58' 18	204 05	-201	N18 31	51	59' 18	92 50	-178	N 4 24	82
4 00	25 21	-179	S13 35	65	12 00	289 08	-161	S16 10	53	20 00	200 44	-204	N19 22	46	28 00	89 52	-177	N 3 02	82
MON06	22 22	-180	S14 40	61	TUE 06	286 27	-159	S15 17	56	WED 06	197 20	-207	N20 08	43	THU 06	86 55	-176	N 1 40	83
HP 12	19 22	-181	S15 41	58	HP 12	283 48	-159	S14 21	58	HP 12	193 53	-211	N20 51	38	HP 12	83 59	-174	N 0 17	82
57' 18	16 21	-182	S16 39	55	54' 18	281 09	-157	S13 23	60	59' 18	190 22	-214	N21 29	33	58' 18	81 05	-174	S 1 05	81
5 00	13 19	-184	S17 34	51	13 00	278 32	-156	S12 23	62	21 00	186 48	-216	N22 02	28	29 00	78 11	-173	S 2 26	80
TUE 06	10 15	-184	S18 25	47	WED 06	275 56	-155	S11 21	64	THU 06	183 12	-220	N22 30	22	FRI 06	75 18	-173	S 3 46	80
HP 12	7 11	-185	S19 12	44	HP 12	273 21	-154	S10 17	65	HP 12	179 32	-221	N22 52	17	HP 12	72 25	-172	S 5 06	78
56' 18	4 06	-186	S19 56	40	54' 18	270 47	-154	S 9 12	67	60' 18	175 51	-223	N23 09	11	58' 18	69 33	-173	S 6 24	77
6 00	1 00	-187	S20 36	36	14 00	268 13	-153	S 8 05	68	22 00	172 08	-225	N23 20	5	30 00	66 40	-173	S 7 41	75
WED 06	357 53	-188	S21 12	32	THU 06	265 40	-153	S 6 57	69	FRI 06	168 23	-225	N23 25	1	SAT 06	63 47	-173	S 8 56	73
HP 12	354 45	-187	S21 44	27	HP 12	263 07	-153	S 5 48	71	HP 12	164 38	-225	N23 24	8	HP 12	60 54	-174	S10 09	70
56' 18	351 38	-189	S22 11	23	55' 18	260 34	-154	S 4 37	71	60' 18	160 53	-226	N23 16	13	57' 18	58 00	-174	S11 19	69
7 00	348 29	-188	S22 34	19	15 00	258 00	-153	S 3 26	72	23 00	157 07	-224	N23 03	20	31 00	55 06		S12 28	
THU 06	345 21	-188	S22 53	14	FRI 06	255 27	-155	S 2 14	73	SAT 06	153 23	-224	N22 43	25					
HP 12	342 13	-188	S23 08	10	HP 12	252 52	-155	S 1 01	73	HP 12	149 39	-222	N22 18	31					
55' 18	339 05	-187	S23 18	5	55' 18	250 17	-156	N 0 13	74	60' 18	145 57	-220	N21 47	37					
8 00	335 58	-187	S23 23	2	16 00	247 41	-158	N 1 27	74	24 00	142 17	-217	N21 10	42					
FRI 06	332 51	-185	S23 25	3	SAT 06	245 03	-159	N 2 41	75	SUN 06	138 40	-215	N20 28	47					
HP 12	329 46	-185	S23 22	7	HP 12	242 24	-161	N 3 56	74	HP 12	135 05	-213	N19 41	52					
55' 18	326 41	-184	S23 15	11	56' 18	239 43	-163	N 5 10	74	60' 18	131 32	-209	N18 49	56					
9 00	323° 37'		S23° 04'		17 00	237° 00'		N 6° 24'		25 00	128° 03'		N17° 53'						

Phases of the Moon
New: 21d   First Quarter: 28d
Full: 6d   Last Quarter: 14d

MOON AT EVERY 6hrs GMT JULY 2001

Day	GMT	GHA-GMT	v	Dec	d
1	00h	55° 06'	-176	S12° 28'	66'
SUN	06	52 10	-176	S13 34	63
HP	12	49 14	-177	S14 37	61
57'	18	46 17	-178	S15 38	57
2	00	43 19	-179	S16 35	54
MON	06	40 20	-180	S17 29	51
HP	12	37 20	-182	S18 20	48
56'	18	34 18	-182	S19 08	43
3	00	31 16	-183	S19 51	40
TUE	06	28 13	-185	S20 31	36
HP	12	25 08	-184	S21 07	32
56'	18	22 04	-186	S21 39	28
4	00	18 58	-186	S22 07	24
WED	06	15 52	-186	S22 31	19
HP	12	12 46	-187	S22 50	15
55'	18	9 39	-186	S23 05	11
5	00	6 33	-186	S23 16	6
THU	06	3 27	-186	S23 22	3
HP	12	0 21	-185	S23 25	2
55'	18	357 16	-184	S23 23	6
6	00	354 12	-183	S23 17	11
FRI	06	351 09	-182	S23 06	14
HP	12	348 07	-181	S22 52	18
55'	18	345 06	-179	S22 34	23
7	00	342 07	-177	S22 11	25
SAT	06	339 10	-176	S21 46	30
HP	12	336 14	-174	S21 16	33
54'	18	333 20	-172	S20 43	36
8	00	330 28	-171	S20 07	40
SUN	06	327 37	-168	S19 27	42
HP	12	324 49	-167	S18 45	46
54'	18	322 02	-164	S17 59	48
9	00	319° 18'	-163	S17° 11'	50'
MON	06	316 35	-161	S16 21	53
HP	12	313 54	-160	S15 28	56
54'	18	311 14	-158	S14 32	57
10	00	308 36	-157	S13 35	60
TUE	06	305 59	-155	S12 35	61
HP	12	303 24	-155	S11 34	63
54'	18	300 49	-153	S10 31	65
11	00	298 16	-153	S 9 26	66
WED	06	295 43	-152	S 8 20	67
HP	12	293 11	-151	S 7 13	68
54'	18	290 40	-152	S 6 05	70
12	00	288 08	-151	S 4 55	70
THU	06	285 37	-151	S 3 45	71
HP	12	283 06	-152	S 2 34	72
55'	18	280 34	-152	S 1 22	72
13	00	278 02	-153	S 0 10	73
FRI	06	275 29	-154	N 1 03	73
HP	12	272 55	-155	N 2 16	73
55'	18	270 40	-156	N 3 29	73
14	00	267 44	-159	N 4 42	72
SAT	06	265 05	-160	N 5 54	72
HP	12	262 25	-162	N 7 06	72
56'	18	259 43	-165	N 8 18	71
15	00	256 58	-167	N 9 29	69
SUN	06	254 11	-170	N10 38	69
HP	12	251 21	-173	N11 47	67
57'	18	248 28	-176	N12 54	65
16	00	245 32	-180	N13 59	63
MON	06	242 32	-183	N15 02	61
HP	12	239 29	-187	N16 03	59
58'	18	236 22	-191	N17 02	55
17	00h	233° 11'	-194	N17° 57'	53'
TUE	06	229 57	-199	N18 50	48
HP	12	226 38	-202	N19 38	45
59'	18	223 16	-206	N20 23	41
18	00	219 50	-210	N21 04	36
WED	06	216 20	-214	N21 40	31
HP	12	212 46	-216	N22 11	26
59'	18	209 10	-220	N22 37	21
19	00	205 30	-222	N22 58	15
THU	06	201 48	-224	N23 13	9
HP	12	198 04	-227	N23 22	3
60'	18	194 17	-227	N23 25	3
20	00	190 30	-228	N23 22	10
FRI	06	186 42	-229	N23 12	16
HP	12	182 53	-228	N22 56	22
61'	18	179 05	-227	N22 34	28
21	00	175 18	-226	N22 06	34
SAT	06	171 32	-225	N21 32	40
HP	12	167 47	-222	N20 52	45
61'	18	164 05	-220	N20 07	51
22	00	160 25	-217	N19 16	55
SUN	06	156 48	-215	N18 21	61
HP	12	153 13	-211	N17 20	64
61'	18	149 42	-208	N16 16	68
23	00	146 14	-206	N15 08	72
MON	06	142 48	-202	N13 56	74
HP	12	139 26	-199	N12 42	77
61'	18	136 07	-196	N11 25	80
24	00	132 51	-193	N10 05	81
TUE	06	129 38	-191	N 8 44	82
HP	12	126 27	-188	N 7 22	84
60'	18	123 19	-186	N 5 58	84
25	00h	120° 13'	-184	N 4° 34'	85'
WED	06	117 09	-182	N 3 09	84
HP	12	114 07	-181	N 1 45	85
59'	18	111 06	-179	N 0 20	84
26	00	108 07	-178	S 1 04	83
THU	06	105 09	-177	S 2 27	82
HP	12	102 12	-176	S 3 49	81
59'	18	99 16	-176	S 5 10	80
27	00	96 20	-175	S 6 30	77
FRI	06	93 25	-175	S 7 47	76
HP	12	90 30	-175	S 9 03	74
58'	18	87 35	-176	S10 17	71
28	00	84 39	-175	S11 28	69
SAT	06	81 44	-176	S12 37	66
HP	12	78 48	-177	S13 43	63
57'	18	75 51	-177	S14 46	60
29	00	72 54	-178	S15 46	57
SUN	06	69 56	-179	S16 43	54
HP	12	66 57	-180	S17 37	50
56'	18	63 57	-180	S18 27	47
30	00	60 57	-182	S19 14	43
MON	06	57 55	-182	S19 57	39
HP	12	54 53	-183	S20 36	35
56'	18	51 50	-183	S21 11	32
31	00	48 47	-184	S21 43	27
TUE	06	45 43	-184	S22 10	23
HP	12	42 39	-185	S22 33	19
55'	18	39 34	-185	S22 52	15
32	00	36 29		S23 07	

Phases of the Moon
New: 20d   First Quarter: 27d
Full: 5d   Last Quarter: 13d

MOON AT EVERY 6hrs GMT AUGUST 2001

Day	GMT	GHA-GMT	v	Dec	d
1	00h	36° 29'	-184	S23° 07'	10'
WED	06	33 25	-185	S23 17	7
HP	12	30 20	-184	S23 24	2
55'	18	27 16	-183	S23 26	1
2	00	24 13	-183	S23 24	7
THU	06	21 10	-182	S23 17	10
HP	12	18 08	-181	S23 07	14
54'	18	15 07	-179	S22 53	19
3	00	12 08	-178	S22 34	22
FRI	06	9 10	-177	S22 12	26
HP	12	6 13	-175	S21 46	29
54'	18	3 18	-174	S21 17	33
4	00	0 24	-172	S20 44	36
SAT	06	357 32	-170	S20 08	40
HP	12	354 42	-168	S19 28	42
54'	18	351 54	-166	S18 46	46
5	00	349 08	-165	S18 00	48
SUN	06	346 23	-163	S17 12	51
HP	12	343 40	-161	S16 21	53
54'	18	340 59	-160	S15 28	56
6	00	338 19	-158	S14 32	57
MON	06	335 41	-157	S13 35	60
HP	12	333 04	-155	S12 35	61
54'	18	330 29	-155	S11 34	63
7	00	327 54	-153	S10 31	65
TUE	06	325 21	-152	S 9 26	66
HP	12	322 49	-152	S 8 20	67
54'	18	320 17	-151	S 7 13	69
8	00	317 46	-150	S 6 04	69
WED	06	315 16	-150	S 4 55	70
HP	12	312 46	-151	S 3 45	71
54'	18	310 15	-150	S 2 34	71
9	00h	307° 45'	-150	S 1° 23'	72'
THU	06	305 15	-151	S 0 11	72
HP	12	302 44	-152	N 1 01	72
55'	18	300 12	-153	N 2 13	72
10	00	297 39	-154	N 3 25	72
FRI	06	295 05	-155	N 4 37	72
HP	12	292 30	-157	N 5 49	71
55'	18	289 53	-158	N 7 00	70
11	00	287 15	-160	N 8 10	70
SAT	06	284 35	-163	N 9 20	68
HP	12	281 52	-165	N10 28	68
56'	18	279 07	-168	N11 36	66
12	00	276 19	-170	N12 42	64
SUN	06	273 29	-174	N13 46	62
HP	12	270 35	-176	N14 48	60
57'	18	267 39	-180	N15 48	58
13	00	264 39	-184	N16 46	55
MON	06	261 35	-187	N17 41	52
HP	12	258 28	-191	N18 33	49
58'	18	255 17	-194	N19 22	45
14	00	252 03	-198	N20 07	42
TUE	06	248 45	-202	N20 49	37
HP	12	245 23	-206	N21 26	33
58'	18	241 57	-209	N21 59	29
15	00	238 28	-212	N22 28	23
WED	06	234 56	-216	N22 51	18
HP	12	231 20	-218	N23 09	12
59'	18	227 42	-220	N23 21	7
16	00	224 02	-223	N23 28	1
THU	06	220 19	-224	N23 29	5
HP	12	216 35	-225	N23 24	12
60'	18	212 50	-226	N23 12	17
17	00h	209° 04'	-226	N22° 55'	24'
FRI	06	205 18	-226	N22 31	30
HP	12	201 32	-225	N22 01	36
61'	18	197 47	-224	N21 25	42
18	00	194 03	-223	N20 43	47
SAT	06	190 20	-220	N19 56	53
HP	12	186 40	-219	N19 03	57
61'	18	183 01	-216	N18 06	63
19	00	179 25	-214	N17 03	67
SUN	06	175 51	-211	N15 56	71
HP	12	172 20	-208	N14 45	74
61'	18	168 52	-206	N13 31	77
20	00	165 26	-203	N12 14	81
MON	06	162 03	-201	N10 53	82
HP	12	158 42	-198	N 9 31	85
61'	18	155 24	-195	N 8 06	86
21	00	152 09	-193	N 6 40	87
TUE	06	148 56	-192	N 5 13	87
HP	12	145 44	-189	N 3 46	88
61'	18	142 35	-187	N 2 18	88
22	00	139 28	-187	N 0 50	86
WED	06	136 21	-184	S 0 38	86
HP	12	133 17	-184	S 2 04	86
60'	18	130 13	-183	S 3 30	84
23	00	127 10	-181	S 4 54	83
THU	06	124 09	-182	S 6 17	81
HP	12	121 07	-181	S 7 38	78
59'	18	118 06	-180	S 8 56	77
24	00	115 06	-181	S10 13	74
FRI	06	112 05	-181	S11 27	71
HP	12	109 04	-181	S12 38	68
58'	18	106 03	-181	S13 46	65
25	00h	103° 02'	-181	S14° 51'	61'
SAT	06	100 01	-182	S15 52	59
HP	12	96 59	-182	S16 51	54
57'	18	93 57	-183	S17 45	52
26	00	90 54	-183	S18 37	47
SUN	06	87 51	-184	S19 24	43
HP	12	84 47	-184	S20 07	40
56'	18	81 43	-185	S20 47	35
27	00	78 38	-185	S21 22	31
MON	06	75 33	-185	S21 53	27
HP	12	72 28	-185	S22 20	23
56'	18	69 23	-185	S22 43	18
28	00	66 18	-185	S23 01	15
TUE	06	63 13	-185	S23 16	10
HP	12	60 08	-184	S23 26	5
55'	18	57 04	-184	S23 31	2
29	00	54 00	-183	S23 33	3
WED	06	50 57	-182	S23 30	7
HP	12	47 55	-182	S23 23	11
55'	18	44 53	-180	S23 12	15
30	00	41 53	-178	S22 57	18
THU	06	38 55	-178	S22 39	23
HP	12	35 57	-176	S22 16	26
54'	18	33 01	-174	S21 50	30
31	00	30 07	-173	S21 20	34
FRI	06	27 14	-171	S20 46	36
HP	12	24 23	-169	S20 10	40
54'	18	21 34	-168	S19 30	43
32	00	18 46		S18 47	

Phases of the Moon
New: 19d   First Quarter: 25d
Full: 4d   Last Quarter: 12d

MOON AT EVERY 6hrs GMT SEPTEMBER 2001

Day GMT	GHA-GMT	v	Dec	d	Day GMT	GHA-GMT	v	Dec	d	Day GMT	GHA-GMT	v	Dec	d	Day GMT	GHA-GMT	v	Dec	d
1 00h	18° 46'	-166	S18° 47'	46'	9 00h	294° 50'	-176	N15° 56'	57'	17 00h	185° 09'	-199	N 9° 13'	86'	25 00h	84° 12'	-186	S23° 45'	2'
SAT 06	16 00	-165	S18 01	49	SUN 06	291 54	-179	N16 53	55	MON 06	181 50	-196	N 7 47	88	TUE 06	81 06	-185	S23 47	3
HP 12	13 15	-162	S17 12	51	HP 12	288 55	-182	N17 48	51	HP 12	178 34	-195	N 6 19	89	HP 12	78 01	-184	S23 44	7
54' 18	10 33	-161	S16 21	54	57' 18	285 55	-186	N18 39	48	61' 18	175 19	-193	N 4 50	90	55' 18	74 57	-183	S23 37	11
2 00	7 52	-160	S15 27	56	10 00	282 47	-188	N19 27	45	18 00	172 05	-192	N 3 20	90	26 00	71 54	-181	S23 26	15
SUN 06	5 12	-158	S14 31	58	MON 06	279 39	-192	N20 12	41	TUE 06	168 54	-191	N 1 50	90	WED 06	68 53	-180	S23 11	19
HP 12	2 34	-157	S13 33	60	HP 12	276 27	-195	N20 53	38	HP 12	165 43	-190	N 0 20	90	HP 12	65 53	-178	S22 52	23
54' 18	359 57	-156	S12 33	62	57' 18	273 12	-198	N21 31	33	61' 18	162 33	-188	S 1 10	89	55' 18	62 55	-176	S22 29	27
3 00	357 21	-154	S11 31	64	11 00	269 54	-202	N22 04	28	19 00	159 25	-189	S 2 39	88	27 00	59 59	-175	S22 02	30
MON 06	354 47	-154	S10 27	66	TUE 06	266 32	-204	N22 32	24	WED 06	156 16	-187	S 4 07	87	THU 06	57 04	-173	S21 32	34
HP 12	352 13	-152	S 9 21	66	HP 12	263 08	-207	N22 56	19	HP 12	153 09	-187	S 5 34	85	HP 12	54 11	-171	S20 58	37
54' 18	349 41	-152	S 8 15	68	58' 18	259 41	-210	N23 15	14	60' 18	150 02	-187	S 6 59	83	54' 18	51 20	-169	S20 21	41
4 00	347 09	-151	S 7 07	69	12 00	256 11	-212	N23 29	9	20 00	146 55	-186	S 8 22	80	28 00	48 31	-168	S19 40	43
TUE 06	344 38	-151	S 5 58	71	WED 06	252 39	-215	N23 38	3	THU 06	143 49	-187	S 9 42	78	FRI 06	45 43	-166	S18 57	46
HP 12	342 07	-151	S 4 47	70	HP 12	249 04	-216	N23 41	3	HP 12	140 42	-187	S11 00	75	HP 12	42 57	-164	S18 11	50
54' 18	339 36	-150	S 3 37	72	59' 18	245 28	-217	N23 38	3	59' 18	137 35	-187	S12 15	73	54' 18	40 13	-163	S17 21	51
5 00	337 06	-150	S 2 25	72	13 00	241 51	-218	N23 30	15	21 00	134 28	-187	S13 28	69	29 00	37 30	-160	S16 30	55
WED 06	334 36	-151	S 1 13	72	THU 06	238 13	-219	N23 15	20	FRI 06	131 21	-187	S14 37	65	SAT 06	34 50	-160	S15 35	56
HP 12	332 05	-151	S 0 01	73	HP 12	234 34	-220	N22 55	26	HP 12	128 14	-188	S15 42	62	HP 12	32 10	-158	S14 39	59
55' 18	329 34	-152	N 1 12	72	60' 18	230 54	-219	N22 29	32	58' 18	125 06	-188	S16 44	58	54' 18	29 32	-157	S13 40	61
6 00	327 02	-152	N 2 24	73	14 00	227 15	-219	N21 57	37	22 00	121 58	-188	S17 42	54	30 00	26 55	-155	S12 39	63
THU 06	324 30	-153	N 3 37	72	FRI 06	223 36	-217	N21 20	43	SAT 06	118 50	-189	S18 36	50	SUN 06	24 20	-155	S11 36	64
HP 12	321 57	-155	N 4 49	72	HP 12	219 59	-217	N20 37	49	HP 12	115 41	-189	S19 26	45	HP 12	21 45	-153	S10 32	66
55' 18	319 22	-156	N 6 01	71	61' 18	216 22	-216	N19 48	54	57' 18	112 32	-190	S20 11	42	54' 18	19 12	-153	S 9 26	68
7 00	316 46	-157	N 7 12	70	15 00	212 46	-214	N18 54	58	23 00	109 22	-189	S20 53	37	31 00	16 39		S 8 18	
FRI 06	314 09	-159	N 8 22	69	SAT 06	209 12	-212	N17 56	64	SUN 06	106 13	-190	S21 30	33					
HP 12	311 30	-161	N 9 31	69	HP 12	205 40	-210	N16 52	68	HP 12	103 03	-189	S22 03	28					
55' 18	308 49	-163	N10 40	66	61' 18	202 10	-209	N15 44	71	56' 18	99 54	-189	S22 31	24					
8 00	306 06	-165	N11 46	66	16 00	198 41	-206	N14 33	76	24 00	96 45	-189	S22 55	19					
SAT 06	303 21	-168	N12 52	63	SUN 06	195 15	-204	N13 17	79	MON 06	93 36	-189	S23 14	15					
HP 12	300 33	-170	N13 55	62	HP 12	191 51	-202	N11 58	81	HP 12	90 27	-188	S23 29	10					
56' 18	297 43	-173	N14 57	59	61' 18	188 29	-200	N10 37	84	56' 18	87 19	-187	S23 39	6					
9 00	294° 50'		N15° 56'		17 00	185° 09'		N 9° 13'		25 00	84° 12'		S23° 45'						

Phases of the Moon
New: 17d   First Quarter: 24d
Full: 2d   Last Quarter: 10d

MOON AT EVERY 6hrs GMT OCTOBER 2001

Day GMT	GHA-GMT	v	Dec	d	Day GMT	GHA-GMT	v	Dec	d	Day GMT	GHA-GMT	v	Dec	d	Day GMT	GHA-GMT	v	Dec	d
1 00h	16° 39'	-152	S 8° 18'	69'	9 00h	286° 39'	-205	N23° 30'	14'	17 00h	179° 31'	-188	S 5° 58'	85'	25 00h	78° 44'	-171	S20° 42'	40'
MON 06	14 07	-152	S 7 09	70	TUE 06	283 14	-207	N23 44	9	WED 06	176 23	-188	S 7 23	84	THU 06	75 53	-169	S20 02	44
HP 12	11 35	-151	S 5 59	71	HP 12	279 47	-208	N23 53	3	HP 12	173 15	-189	S 8 47	82	HP 12	73 04	-167	S19 18	46
54' 18	9 04	-152	S 4 48	72	58' 18	276 19	-210	N23 56	2	60' 18	170 06	-189	S10 09	79	54' 18	70 17	-164	S18 32	49
2 00	6 32	-151	S 3 36	72	10 00	272 49	-211	N23 54	7	18 00	166 57	-190	S11 28	77	26 00	67 33	-163	S17 43	52
TUE 06	4 01	-151	S 2 24	73	WED 06	269 18	-211	N23 47	14	THU 06	163 47	-191	S12 45	73	FRI 06	64 50	-161	S16 51	54
HP 12	1 30	-152	S 1 11	74	HP 12	265 47	-212	N23 33	18	HP 12	160 36	-191	S13 58	70	HP 12	62 09	-160	S15 57	57
55' 18	358 58	-152	N 0 03	74	59' 18	262 15	-212	N23 15	24	59' 18	157 25	-192	S15 08	66	54' 18	59 29	-158	S15 00	59
3 00	356 26	-152	N 1 17	74	11 00	258 43	-212	N22 51	30	19 00	154 13	-192	S16 14	63	27 00	56 51	-157	S14 01	61
WED 06	353 54	-154	N 2 31	73	THU 06	255 11	-211	N22 21	35	FRI 06	151 01	-193	S17 17	58	SAT 06	54 14	-155	S13 00	63
HP 12	351 20	-154	N 3 44	74	HP 12	251 40	-210	N21 46	41	HP 12	147 48	-194	S18 15	54	HP 12	51 39	-154	S11 57	64
55' 18	348 46	-156	N 4 58	73	59' 18	248 10	-210	N21 05	45	58' 18	144 34	-194	S19 09	50	54' 18	49 05	-154	S10 53	67
4 00	346 10	-157	N 6 11	72	12 00	244 40	-208	N20 20	51	20 00	141 20	-195	S19 59	46	28 00	46 31	-152	S 9 46	68
THU 06	343 33	-159	N 7 23	71	FRI 06	241 12	-207	N19 29	55	SAT 06	138 05	-195	S20 45	40	SUN 06	43 59	-152	S 8 38	69
HP 12	340 54	-160	N 8 34	72	HP 12	237 45	-205	N18 34	60	HP 12	134 50	-195	S21 25	37	HP 12	41 27	-152	S 7 29	70
55' 18	338 14	-162	N 9 45	69	60' 18	234 20	-204	N17 34	64	57' 18	131 35	-195	S22 02	31	54' 18	38 55	-151	S 6 19	72
5 00	335 32	-164	N10 54	68	13 00	230 56	-202	N16 30	68	21 00	128 20	-194	S22 33	27	29 00	36 24	-151	S 5 07	72
FRI 06	332 48	-166	N12 02	66	SAT 06	227 34	-201	N15 22	72	SUN 06	125 05	-194	S23 00	22	MON 06	33 53	-152	S 3 55	73
HP 12	330 02	-169	N13 08	64	HP 12	224 13	-199	N14 10	76	HP 12	121 51	-194	S23 22	17	HP 12	31 21	-151	S 2 41	74
56' 18	327 13	-171	N14 12	62	60' 18	220 54	-197	N12 54	78	56' 18	118 37	-193	S23 39	13	55' 18	28 50	-152	S 1 27	74
6 00	324 22	-173	N15 14	60	14 00	217 37	-196	N11 36	82	22 00	115 24	-192	S23 52	7	30 00	26 18	-152	S 0 13	75
SAT 06	321 29	-176	N16 14	57	SUN 06	214 21	-195	N10 14	83	MON 06	112 12	-191	S23 59	3	TUE 06	23 46	-154	N 1 02	75
HP 12	318 33	-179	N17 11	54	HP 12	211 06	-193	N 8 51	86	HP 12	109 01	-190	S24 02	1	HP 12	21 12	-154	N 2 17	75
56' 18	315 34	-182	N18 05	52	61' 18	207 53	-192	N 7 25	87	56' 18	105 51	-188	S24 01	6	55' 18	18 38	-156	N 3 32	74
7 00	312 32	-184	N18 57	48	15 00	204 41	-191	N 5 58	89	23 00	102 43	-187	S23 55	10	31 00	16 02	-156	N 4 46	75
SUN 06	309 28	-188	N19 45	44	MON 06	201 30	-190	N 4 29	90	TUE 06	99 36	-185	S23 45	15	WED 06	13 26	-159	N 6 01	73
HP 12	306 20	-190	N20 29	41	HP 12	198 20	-189	N 2 59	90	HP 12	96 31	-183	S23 30	18	HP 12	10 47	-160	N 7 14	74
57' 18	303 10	-193	N21 10	37	61' 18	195 11	-188	N 1 29	90	55' 18	93 28	-181	S23 12	23	55' 18	8 07	-162	N 8 28	72
8 00	299 57	-195	N21 47	33	16 00	192 03	-189	S 0 01	91	24 00	90 27	-179	S22 49	26	32 00	5 25		N 9 40	
MON 06	296 42	-199	N22 20	28	TUE 06	188 54	-187	S 1 32	89	WED 06	87 28	-177	S22 23	30					
HP 12	293 23	-201	N22 48	24	HP 12	185 47	-188	S 3 01	89	HP 12	84 31	-175	S21 53	34					
57' 18	290 02	-203	N23 12	18	60' 18	182 39	-188	S 4 30	88	55' 18	81 36	-172	S21 19	37					
9 00	286° 39'		N23° 30'		17 00	179° 31'		S 5° 58'		25 00	78° 44'		S20° 42'						

Phases of the Moon
New: 16d   First Quarter: 24d
Full: 2d   Last Quarter: 10d

84

MOON AT EVERY 6hrs GMT NOVEMBER 2001

Day	GMT	GHA-GMT	v	Dec	d
1	00h	5° 25'	-163	N 9° 40'	70'
THU	06	2 42	-167	N10 50	70
HP	12	359 55	-168	N12 02	68
56'	18	357 07	-171	N13 08	66
2	00	354 16	-173	N14 14	63
FRI	06	351 23	-176	N15 17	62
HP	12	348 27	-179	N16 19	58
56'	18	345 28	-182	N17 17	56
3	00	342 26	-185	N18 13	53
SAT	06	339 21	-187	N19 06	49
HP	12	336 14	-190	N19 55	46
57'	18	333 04	-193	N20 41	42
4	00	329 51	-196	N21 23	37
SUN	06	326 35	-198	N22 00	33
HP	12	323 17	-201	N22 33	29
57'	18	319 56	-202	N23 02	24
5	00	316 34	-205	N23 26	18
MON	06	313 09	-206	N23 44	14
HP	12	309 43	-208	N23 58	8
58'	18	306 15	-209	N24 06	3
6	00	302 46	-209	N24 09	2
TUE	06	299 17	-210	N24 07	8
HP	12	295 47	-211	N23 59	14
58'	18	292 16	-209	N23 45	19
7	00	288 47	-210	N23 26	24
WED	06	285 17	-208	N23 02	29
HP	12	281 49	-208	N22 33	35
59'	18	278 21	-206	N21 58	40
8	00	274 55	-205	N21 18	45
THU	06	271 30	-203	N20 33	50
HP	12	268 07	-202	N19 43	54
59'	18	264 45	-200	N18 49	58
9	00	261° 25'		N17° 51'	
9	00h	261° 25'	-197	N17° 51'	62'
FRI	06	258 08	-197	N16 49	66
HP	12	254 51	-194	N15 43	70
59'	18	251 37	-192	N14 33	73
10	00	248 25	-191	N13 20	76
SAT	06	245 14	-189	N12 04	78
HP	12	242 05	-188	N10 46	81
60'	18	238 57	-187	N 9 25	83
11	00	235 50	-185	N 8 02	85
SUN	06	232 45	-185	N 6 37	86
HP	12	229 40	-183	N 5 11	87
60'	18	226 37	-183	N 3 44	88
12	00	223 34	-183	N 2 16	88
MON	06	220 31	-183	N 0 48	89
HP	12	217 28	-182	S 0 41	88
60'	18	214 26	-183	S 2 09	88
13	00	211 23	-183	S 3 37	87
TUE	06	208 20	-184	S 5 04	86
HP	12	205 16	-184	S 6 30	84
59'	18	202 12	-185	S 7 54	83
14	00	199 07	-186	S 9 17	80
WED	06	196 01	-187	S10 37	78
HP	12	192 54	-188	S11 55	76
59'	18	189 46	-189	S13 11	72
15	00	186 37	-191	S14 23	69
THU	06	183 26	-192	S15 32	66
HP	12	180 40	-193	S16 38	62
59'	18	177 01	-194	S17 40	58
16	00	173 47	-195	S18 38	54
FRI	06	170 32	-196	S19 32	49
HP	12	167 16	-197	S20 21	45
58'	18	163 59	-197	S21 06	40
17	00	160° 42'		S21° 46'	
17	00h	160° 42'	-198	S21° 46'	36'
SAT	06	157 24	-198	S22 22	30
HP	12	154 06	-199	S22 52	26
57'	18	150 47	-198	S23 18	21
18	00	147 29	-197	S23 39	15
SUN	06	144 12	-197	S23 54	11
HP	12	140 55	-195	S24 05	6
56'	18	137 40	-195	S24 11	2
19	00	134 25	-193	S24 13	4
MON	06	131 12	-191	S24 09	8
HP	12	128 01	-189	S24 01	13
56'	18	124 52	-188	S23 48	17
20	00	121 44	-185	S23 31	21
TUE	06	118 39	-183	S23 10	25
HP	12	115 36	-181	S22 45	29
55'	18	112 35	-178	S22 16	33
21	00	109 37	-176	S21 43	36
WED	06	106 41	-174	S21 07	40
HP	12	103 47	-171	S20 27	42
55'	18	100 56	-169	S19 45	46
22	00	98 07	-167	S18 59	49
THU	06	95 20	-164	S18 10	51
HP	12	92 36	-163	S17 19	54
54'	18	89 53	-160	S16 25	56
23	00	87 13	-159	S15 29	59
FRI	06	84 34	-157	S14 30	60
HP	12	81 57	-155	S13 30	63
54'	18	79 21	-154	S12 27	64
24	00	76 47	-153	S11 23	66
SAT	06	74 14	-152	S10 17	67
HP	12	71 42	-151	S 9 10	69
54'	18	69 11	-151	S 8 01	70
25	00	66° 40'		S 6° 51'	
25	00h	66° 40'	-150	S 6° 51'	71'
SUN	06	64 10	-151	S 5 40	72
HP	12	61 39	-150	S 4 28	73
55'	18	59 09	-150	S 3 15	74
26	00	56 39	-151	S 2 01	74
MON	06	54 08	-151	S 0 47	75
HP	12	51 37	-152	N 0 28	75
55'	18	49 05	-153	N 1 43	75
27	00	46 32	-155	N 2 58	75
TUE	06	43 57	-156	N 4 13	75
HP	12	41 21	-157	N 5 28	74
55'	18	38 44	-159	N 6 42	74
28	00	36 05	-162	N 7 56	73
WED	06	33 23	-163	N 9 09	72
HP	12	30 40	-166	N10 21	71
56'	18	27 54	-169	N11 32	69
29	00	25 05	-171	N12 41	68
THU	06	22 14	-175	N13 49	66
HP	12	19 19	-177	N14 55	63
57'	18	16 22	-180	N15 58	61
30	00	13 22	-184	N16 59	58
FRI	06	10 18	-187	N17 57	55
HP	12	7 11	-190	N18 52	52
57'	18	4 01	-193	N19 44	48
31	00	0 48		N20 32	

Phases of the Moon
New: 15d First Quarter: 22d
Full: 1d&30d Last Quarter: 8d

MOON AT EVERY 6hrs GMT DECEMBER 2001

Day	GMT	GHA-GMT	v	Dec	d
1	00h	0° 48'	-197	N20° 32'	44'
SAT	06	357 31	-199	N21 16	39
HP	12	354 12	-203	N21 55	35
58'	18	350 49	-205	N22 30	31
2	00	347 24	-207	N23 01	25
SUN	06	343 57	-210	N23 26	21
HP	12	340 27	-211	N23 47	15
58'	18	336 56	-213	N24 02	9
3	00	333 23	-214	N24 11	4
MON	06	329 49	-215	N24 15	2
HP	12	326 14	-214	N24 13	8
59'	18	322 40	-215	N24 05	14
4	00	319 05	-215	N23 51	19
TUE	06	315 30	-213	N23 32	24
HP	12	311 57	-212	N23 08	31
59'	18	308 25	-211	N22 37	35
5	00	304 54	-209	N22 02	41
WED	06	301 25	-207	N21 21	45
HP	12	297 59	-205	N20 36	51
59'	18	294 34	-203	N19 45	55
6	00	291 11	-200	N18 50	58
THU	06	287 51	-197	N17 52	63
HP	12	284 34	-196	N16 49	67
59'	18	281 18	-193	N15 42	69
7	00	278 05	-190	N14 33	73
FRI	06	274 55	-189	N13 20	75
HP	12	271 46	-186	N12 05	78
59'	18	268 40	-185	N10 47	80
8	00	265 35	-183	N 9 27	82
SAT	06	262 32	-182	N 8 05	83
HP	12	259 30	-180	N 6 42	84
59'	18	256 30	-179	N 5 18	86
9	00	253° 31'		N 3° 52'	
9	00h	253° 31'	-178	N 3° 52'	86'
SUN	06	250 33	-178	N 2 26	86
HP	12	247 35	-177	N 1 00	87
59'	18	244 38	-177	S 0 27	86
10	00	241 41	-177	S 1 53	86
MON	06	238 44	-178	S 3 19	85
HP	12	235 46	-178	S 4 44	84
59'	18	232 48	-178	S 6 08	82
11	00	229 50	-179	S 7 30	82
TUE	06	226 51	-180	S 8 52	79
HP	12	223 51	-182	S10 11	77
59'	18	220 49	-182	S11 28	75
12	00	217 47	-184	S12 43	72
WED	06	214 43	-186	S13 55	69
HP	12	211 37	-186	S15 04	66
58'	18	208 31	-189	S16 10	63
13	00	205 22	-189	S17 13	59
THU	06	202 13	-192	S18 12	55
HP	12	199 01	-192	S19 07	51
58'	18	195 49	-194	S19 58	47
14	00	192 35	-195	S20 45	42
FRI	06	189 20	-196	S21 27	38
HP	12	186 04	-197	S22 05	33
57'	18	182 47	-197	S22 38	28
15	00	179 30	-198	S23 06	24
SAT	06	176 12	-197	S23 30	19
HP	12	172 55	-198	S23 49	13
57'	18	169 37	-197	S24 02	9
16	00	166 20	-196	S24 15	1
SUN	06	163 04	-195	S24 14	6
HP	12	159 49	-193	S24 08	10
56'	18	156 36	-192	S24 08	10
17	00	153° 24'		S23° 58'	
17	00h	153° 24'	-191	S23° 58'	15'
MON	06	150 13	-188	S23 43	19
HP	12	147 05	-186	S23 24	24
55'	18	143 59	-184	S23 00	27
18	00	140 55	-182	S22 33	31
TUE	06	137 53	-179	S22 02	35
HP	12	134 54	-176	S21 27	39
55'	18	131 58	-174	S20 48	42
19	00	129 04	-172	S20 06	45
WED	06	126 12	-169	S19 21	48
HP	12	123 23	-167	S18 33	50
55'	18	120 36	-164	S17 43	54
20	00	117 52	-162	S16 49	55
THU	06	115 10	-161	S15 54	58
HP	12	112 29	-158	S14 56	60
54'	18	109 51	-156	S13 56	62
21	00	107 15	-155	S12 54	64
FRI	06	104 40	-153	S11 50	65
HP	12	102 07	-152	S10 45	67
54'	18	99 35	-151	S 9 38	68
22	00	97 04	-150	S 8 30	69
SAT	06	94 34	-150	S 7 21	70
HP	12	92 04	-148	S 6 11	72
54'	18	89 36	-149	S 4 59	72
23	00	87 07	-149	S 3 47	72
SUN	06	84 38	-148	S 2 35	74
HP	12	82 10	-149	S 1 21	73
55'	18	79 41	-150	S 0 08	74
24	00	77 11	-150	N 1 06	75
MON	06	74 41	-152	N 2 21	74
HP	12	72 09	-153	N 3 35	74
55'	18	69 36	-154	N 4 49	74
25	00	67° 02'		N 6° 03'	
25	00h	67° 02'	-156	N 6° 03'	73'
TUE	06	64 26	-158	N 7 16	73
HP	12	61 48	-160	N 8 29	71
56'	18	59 08	-163	N 9 40	71
26	00	56 25	-165	N10 51	70
WED	06	53 40	-168	N12 01	68
HP	12	50 52	-171	N13 09	66
56'	18	48 01	-174	N14 15	65
27	00	45 07	-178	N15 20	62
THU	06	42 09	-181	N16 22	60
HP	12	39 08	-184	N17 22	57
57'	18	36 04	-189	N18 19	53
28	00	32 55	-192	N19 12	51
FRI	06	29 43	-195	N20 03	46
HP	12	26 28	-199	N20 49	43
58'	18	23 09	-203	N21 32	38
29	00	19 46	-206	N22 10	34
SAT	06	16 20	-209	N22 44	29
HP	12	12 51	-212	N23 13	23
59'	18	9 19	-215	N23 36	18
30	00	5 44	-217	N23 54	13
SUN	06	2 07	-218	N24 07	6
HP	12	358 29	-220	N24 13	1
59'	18	354 49	-221	N24 14	5
31	00	351 08	-221	N24 09	12
MON	06	347 27	-221	N23 57	17
HP	12	343 46	-221	N23 40	24
60'	18	340 05	-219	N23 16	29
32	00	336 26		N22 47	

Phases of the Moon
New: 14d First Quarter: 22d
Full: 30d Last Quarter: 7d

MOON AT EVERY 6hrs GMT JANUARY 2002

Day	GMT	GHA-GMT	v	Dec	d
1	00h	336° 26'	-218'	N22° 47'	35'
TUE	06	332 48	-217	N22 12	41
HP	12	329 11	-214	N21 31	46
60'	18	325 37	-212	N20 45	51
2	00	322 05	-210	N19 54	55
WED	06	318 35	-206	N18 59	61
HP	12	315 09	-205	N17 58	64
60'	18	311 44	-201	N16 54	68
3	00	308 23	-198	N15 46	71
THU	06	305 05	-196	N14 35	75
HP	12	301 49	-193	N13 20	77
60'	18	298 36	-191	N12 03	79
4	00	295 25	-188	N10 44	82
FRI	06	292 17	-186	N 9 22	83
HP	12	289 11	-184	N 7 59	84
60'	18	286 07	-182	N 6 35	86
5	00	283 05	-181	N 5 09	86
SAT	06	280 04	-179	N 3 43	87
HP	12	277 05	-178	N 2 16	86
59'	18	274 07	-178	N 0 50	87
6	00	271 09	-177	S 0 37	86
SUN	06	268 12	-176	S 2 03	85
HP	12	265 16	-176	S 3 28	85
59'	18	262 20	-176	S 4 53	83
7	00	259 24	-177	S 6 16	82
MON	06	256 27	-176	S 7 38	80
HP	12	253 31	-178	S 8 58	78
58'	18	250 33	-178	S 10 16	75
8	00	247 35	-179	S11 31	74
TUE	06	244 36	-181	S12 45	71
HP	12	241 35	-181	S13 56	67
58'	18	238 34	-183	S15 03	65
9	00	235° 31'		S16° 08'	

Day	GMT	GHA-GMT	v	Dec	d
9	00h	235° 31'	-184'	S16° 08'	62'
WED	06	232 27	-186	S17 10	58
HP	12	229 21	-186	S18 08	54
57'	18	226 15	-189	S19 02	50
10	00	223 06	-189	S19 52	47
THU	06	219 57	-191	S20 39	42
HP	12	216 46	-192	S21 21	38
57'	18	213 34	-192	S21 59	33
11	00	210 22	-194	S22 32	29
FRI	06	207 08	-194	S23 01	24
HP	12	203 54	-194	S23 25	19
56'	18	200 40	-195	S23 44	15
12	00	197 25	-194	S23 59	10
SAT	06	194 11	-194	S24 09	5
HP	12	190 57	-193	S24 14	0
56'	18	187 44	-193	S24 14	4
13	00	184 31	-191	S24 10	9
SUN	06	181 20	-189	S24 01	14
HP	12	178 11	-188	S23 47	18
55'	18	175 03	-187	S23 29	22
14	00	171 56	-184	S23 07	26
MON	06	168 52	-182	S22 41	31
HP	12	165 50	-180	S22 10	34
55'	18	162 50	-177	S21 36	37
15	00	159 53	-176	S20 59	41
TUE	06	156 57	-172	S20 18	45
HP	12	154 05	-171	S19 33	47
55'	18	151 14	-168	S18 46	50
16	00	148 26	-166	S17 56	53
WED	06	145 40	-163	S17 03	55
HP	12	142 57	-161	S16 08	58
54'	18	140 16	-160	S15 10	60
17	00	137° 36'		S14° 10'	

Day	GMT	GHA-GMT	v	Dec	d
17	00h	137° 36'	-157'	S14° 10'	61'
THU	06	134 59	-156	S13 09	64
HP	12	132 23	-154	S12 05	65
54'	18	129 49	-152	S11 00	66
18	00	127 17	-151	S 9 54	68
FRI	06	124 46	-150	S 8 46	69
HP	12	122 16	-149	S 7 37	70
54'	18	119 47	-148	S 6 27	71
19	00	117 19	-148	S 5 16	71
SAT	06	114 51	-147	S 4 05	73
HP	12	112 24	-148	S 2 52	72
54'	18	109 56	-147	S 1 40	73
20	00	107 29	-148	S 0 27	73
SUN	06	105 01	-148	N 0 46	74
HP	12	102 33	-148	N 2 00	73
54'	18	100 05	-150	N 3 13	73
21	00	97 35	-151	N 4 26	73
MON	06	95 04	-152	N 5 39	72
HP	12	92 32	-154	N 6 51	72
55'	18	89 58	-156	N 8 03	70
22	00	87 22	-158	N 9 13	70
TUE	06	84 44	-160	N10 23	69
HP	12	82 04	-163	N11 32	67
55'	18	79 21	-165	N12 39	66
23	00	76 36	-168	N13 45	64
WED	06	73 48	-172	N14 49	62
HP	12	70 56	-175	N15 51	60
56'	18	68 01	-178	N16 51	57
24	00	65 03	-182	N17 48	55
THU	06	62 01	-185	N18 43	51
HP	12	58 56	-190	N19 34	48
57'	18	55 46	-193	N20 22	45
25	00	52° 33'		N21° 07'	

Day	GMT	GHA-GMT	v	Dec	d
25	00h	52° 33'	-197'	N21° 07'	40'
FRI	06	49 16	-201	N21 47	36
HP	12	45 55	-204	N22 23	32
58'	18	42 31	-208	N22 55	27
26	00	39 03	-211	N23 22	22
SAT	06	35 32	-214	N23 44	16
HP	12	31 58	-217	N24 00	11
59'	18	28 21	-218	N24 11	5
27	00	24 43	-221	N24 16	1
SUN	06	21 02	-222	N24 15	8
HP	12	17 20	-224	N24 07	13
60'	18	13 36	-223	N23 54	20
28	00	9 53	-224	N23 34	25
MON	06	6 09	-223	N23 09	32
HP	12	2 26	-222	N22 37	38
60'	18	358 44	-220	N21 59	44
29	00	355 04	-220	N21 15	49
TUE	06	351 24	-217	N20 26	55
HP	12	347 47	-214	N19 31	60
61'	18	344 13	-213	N18 31	64
30	00	340 40	-209	N17 27	69
WED	06	337 11	-207	N16 18	72
HP	12	333 44	-205	N15 06	76
61'	18	330 19	-201	N13 50	79
31	00	326 58	-199	N12 31	82
THU	06	323 39	-197	N11 09	84
HP	12	320 22	-194	N 9 45	86
61'	18	317 08	-192	N 8 19	88
32	00	313 56		N 6 51	

Phases of the Moon

New: 13d   First Quarter: 21d

Full: 28d   Last Quarter: 6d

MOON AT EVERY 6hrs GMT FEBRUARY 2002

Day	GMT	GHA-GMT	v	Dec	d
1	00h	313° 56'	-189'	N 6° 51'	88'
FRI	06	310 47	-188	N 5 23	90
HP	12	307 39	-186	N 3 53	90
60'	18	304 33	-185	N 2 23	89
2	00	301 28	-184	N 0 54	90
SAT	06	298 24	-182	S 0 36	89
HP	12	295 22	-182	S 2 05	88
60'	18	292 20	-181	S 3 33	87
3	00	289 19	-180	S 5 00	85
SUN	06	286 19	-181	S 6 25	83
HP	12	283 18	-180	S 7 48	82
59'	18	280 18	-181	S 9 10	79
4	00	277 17	-181	S10 29	77
MON	06	274 16	-182	S11 46	74
HP	12	271 14	-182	S13 00	71
58'	18	268 12	-183	S14 11	68
5	00	265 09	-184	S15 19	64
TUE	06	262 05	-185	S16 23	61
HP	12	259 00	-185	S17 24	58
58'	18	255 55	-187	S18 22	53
6	00	252 48	-188	S19 15	50
WED	06	249 40	-189	S20 05	45
HP	12	246 32	-190	S20 50	41
57'	18	243 22	-190	S21 31	37
7	00	240 12	-191	S22 08	33
THU	06	237 01	-191	S22 41	27
HP	12	233 50	-192	S23 08	24
56'	18	230 38	-192	S23 32	18
8	00	227 26	-192	S23 50	14
FRI	06	224 14	-192	S24 04	9
HP	12	221 02	-191	S24 13	5
56'	18	217 51	-190	S24 18	0
9	00	214° 41'		S24° 18'	

Day	GMT	GHA-GMT	v	Dec	d
9	00h	214° 41'	-190'	S24° 18'	5'
SAT	06	211 31	-189	S24 13	9
HP	12	208 22	-187	S24 04	14
55'	18	205 15	-186	S23 50	18
10	00	202 09	-184	S23 32	22
SUN	06	199 05	-182	S23 10	26
HP	12	196 03	-181	S22 44	30
55'	18	193 02	-178	S22 14	34
11	00	190 04	-176	S21 40	37
MON	06	187 08	-174	S21 03	41
HP	12	184 14	-172	S20 22	44
55'	18	181 22	-170	S19 38	48
12	00	178 32	-168	S18 50	50
TUE	06	175 44	-165	S18 00	53
HP	12	172 59	-163	S17 07	55
54'	18	170 16	-161	S16 12	58
13	00	167 35	-160	S15 14	60
WED	06	164 55	-157	S14 14	61
HP	12	162 21	-156	S13 13	64
54'	18	159 42	-154	S12 09	65
14	00	157 08	-152	S11 04	67
THU	06	154 36	-152	S 9 57	68
HP	12	152 04	-150	S 8 49	70
54'	18	149 34	-149	S 7 39	70
15	00	147 05	-148	S 6 29	71
FRI	06	144 37	-148	S 5 18	72
HP	12	142 09	-147	S 4 06	72
54'	18	139 42	-147	S 2 54	73
16	00	137 15	-147	S 1 41	73
SAT	06	134 48	-146	S 0 28	74
HP	12	132 22	-147	N 0 46	73
54'	18	129 55	-148	N 1 59	73
17	00	127° 27'		N 3° 12'	

Day	GMT	GHA-GMT	v	Dec	d
17	00h	127° 27'	-148'	N 3° 12'	73'
SUN	06	124 59	-149	N 4 25	72
HP	12	122 30	-151	N 5 37	72
54'	18	119 59	-151	N 6 49	71
18	00	117 28	-153	N 8 00	70
MON	06	114 55	-155	N 9 10	70
HP	12	112 20	-157	N10 20	68
55'	18	109 43	-158	N11 28	66
19	00	107 05	-161	N12 34	65
TUE	06	104 24	-164	N13 39	63
HP	12	101 40	-166	N14 42	62
55'	18	98 54	-170	N15 44	59
20	00	96 04	-172	N16 43	56
WED	06	93 12	-175	N17 39	55
HP	12	90 17	-179	N18 34	51
56'	18	87 18	-182	N19 25	48
21	00	84 16	-186	N20 13	45
THU	06	81 10	-189	N20 58	41
HP	12	78 01	-193	N21 39	37
57'	18	74 48	-196	N22 16	33
22	00	71 32	-199	N22 49	29
FRI	06	68 13	-203	N23 18	23
HP	12	64 50	-206	N23 41	19
58'	18	61 24	-209	N24 00	14
23	00	57 55	-212	N24 14	8
SAT	06	54 23	-214	N24 22	3
HP	12	50 49	-215	N24 25	3
59'	18	47 14	-218	N24 22	9
24	00	43 36	-219	N24 13	15
SUN	06	39 57	-219	N23 58	21
HP	12	36 18	-220	N23 37	27
60'	18	32 38	-220	N23 10	34
25	00	28° 58'		N22° 36'	

Day	GMT	GHA-GMT	v	Dec	d
25	00h	28° 58'	-220'	N22° 36'	39'
MON	06	25 18	-219	N21 57	45
HP	12	21 39	-218	N21 12	51
61'	18	18 01	-216	N20 21	56
26	00	14 25	-215	N19 25	61
TUE	06	10 50	-213	N18 24	66
HP	12	7 17	-212	N17 18	71
61'	18	3 45	-209	N16 07	75
27	00	0 16	-207	N14 52	78
WED	06	356 49	-204	N13 34	82
HP	12	353 25	-203	N12 12	85
61'	18	350 02	-201	N10 47	87
28	00	346 41	-198	N 9 20	90
THU	06	343 23	-197	N 7 50	91
HP	12	340 06	-195	N 6 19	93
61'	18	336 51	-194	N 4 46	93
29	00	333 37	-192	N 3 13	93
FRI	06	330 25	-191	N 1 40	94
HP	12	327 14	-191	N 0 06	93
61'	18	324 03	-189	S 1 27	93
30	00	320 54		S 3 00	

Phases of the Moon

New: 12d   First Quarter: 20d

Full: 27d   Last Quarter: 4d

Day	GMT	GHA-GMT	v	Dec	d
1	00h	333° 37'	-192'	N 3° 13'	93'
FRI	06	330 25	-191	N 1 40	94
HP	12	327 14	-191	N 0 06	93
61'	18	324 03	-189	S 1 27	93
2	00	320 54	-188	S 3 00	91
SAT	06	317 46	-189	S 4 31	90
HP	12	314 37	-188	S 6 01	88
60'	18	311 29	-188	S 7 29	85
3	00	308 21	-188	S 8 54	84
SUN	06	305 13	-188	S10 18	80
HP	12	302 05	-188	S11 38	78
59'	18	298 57	-189	S12 56	75
4	00	295 48	-190	S14 11	71
MON	06	292 38	-190	S15 22	67
HP	12	289 28	-190	S16 29	63
59'	18	286 18	-192	S17 32	60
5	00	283 06	-192	S18 32	55
TUE	06	279 54	-192	S19 27	51
HP	12	276 42	-193	S20 18	46
58'	18	273 29	-194	S21 04	42
6	00	270 15	-194	S21 46	37
WED	06	267 01	-194	S22 23	33
HP	12	263 47	-194	S22 56	28
57'	18	260 33	-194	S23 24	23
7	00	257 19	-194	S23 47	18
THU	06	254 05	-193	S24 05	13
HP	12	250 52	-193	S24 18	9
56'	18	247 39	-192	S24 27	3
8	00	244 27	-191	S24 30	1
FRI	06	241 16	-189	S24 29	5
HP	12	238 07	-188	S24 24	10
55'	18	234 59	-187	S24 14	14
9	00	231° 52'		S24° 00'	
9	00h	231° 52'	-185'	S24° 00'	19'
SAT	06	228 47	-183	S23 41	23
HP	12	225 44	-181	S23 18	27
55'	18	222 43	-179	S22 51	31
10	00	219 44	-177	S22 20	34
SUN	06	216 47	-175	S21 46	38
HP	12	213 52	-173	S21 08	41
55'	18	210 59	-170	S20 27	45
11	00	208 09	-169	S19 42	48
MON	06	205 20	-166	S18 54	50
HP	12	202 34	-164	S18 04	54
54'	18	199 50	-162	S17 10	55
12	00	197 08	-160	S16 15	58
TUE	06	194 28	-159	S15 17	61
HP	12	191 49	-156	S14 16	62
54'	18	189 13	-155	S13 14	64
13	00	186 38	-154	S12 10	66
WED	06	184 04	-152	S11 04	67
HP	12	181 32	-151	S 9 57	69
54'	18	179 01	-150	S 8 48	70
14	00	176 31	-148	S 7 38	71
THU	06	174 03	-149	S 6 27	72
HP	12	171 34	-147	S 5 15	73
54'	18	169 07	-147	S 4 02	73
15	00	166 40	-147	S 2 49	74
FRI	06	164 13	-147	S 1 35	73
HP	12	161 46	-147	S 0 22	74
54'	18	159 19	-147	N 0 52	75
16	00	156 52	-148	N 2 07	73
SAT	06	154 24	-148	N 3 20	74
HP	12	151 56	-149	N 4 34	73
54'	18	149 27	-151	N 5 47	72
17	00	146° 56'		N 6° 59'	
17	00h	146° 56'	-151'	N 6° 59'	72'
SUN	06	144 25	-153	N 8 11	71
HP	12	141 52	-154	N 9 22	69
54'	18	139 18	-156	N10 31	68
18	00	136 42	-158	N11 39	67
MON	06	134 04	-159	N12 46	65
HP	12	131 25	-163	N13 51	63
55'	18	128 42	-164	N14 54	61
19	00	125 58	-167	N15 55	59
TUE	06	123 11	-170	N16 54	57
HP	12	120 21	-172	N17 51	53
55'	18	117 29	-176	N18 44	51
20	00	114 33	-178	N19 35	48
WED	06	111 35	-181	N20 23	45
HP	12	108 34	-185	N21 08	40
56'	18	105 29	-187	N21 48	37
21	00	102 22	-190	N22 25	33
THU	06	99 12	-194	N22 58	29
HP	12	95 58	-196	N23 27	25
57'	18	92 42	-199	N23 52	19
22	00	89 23	-201	N24 11	15
FRI	06	86 02	-204	N24 26	10
HP	12	82 38	-206	N24 36	4
58'	18	79 12	-208	N24 40	1
23	00	75 44	-209	N24 39	7
SAT	06	72 15	-211	N24 32	12
HP	12	68 44	-211	N24 20	18
59'	18	65 13	-212	N24 02	23
24	00	61 41	-213	N23 39	30
SUN	06	58 08	-212	N23 09	35
HP	12	54 36	-212	N22 34	40
59'	18	51 04	-212	N21 54	47
25	00	47° 32'		N21° 07'	
25	00h	47° 32'	-211'	N21° 07'	51'
MON	06	44 01	-210	N20 16	57
HP	12	40 31	-208	N19 19	62
60'	18	37 03	-208	N18 17	66
26	00	33 35	-206	N17 11	71
TUE	06	30 09	-204	N16 00	75
HP	12	26 45	-203	N14 45	79
61'	18	23 22	-202	N13 26	82
27	00	20 00	-200	N12 04	86
WED	06	16 40	-198	N10 38	88
HP	12	13 22	-198	N 9 10	90
61'	18	10 04	-196	N 7 40	93
28	00	6 48	-195	N 6 07	93
THU	06	3 33	-195	N 4 34	95
HP	12	0 18	-194	N 2 59	96
61'	18	357 04	-193	N 1 23	95
29	00	353 51	-193	S 0 12	96
FRI	06	350 38	-192	S 1 48	95
HP	12	347 26	-193	S 3 23	93
61'	18	344 13	-192	S 4 56	93
30	00	341 01	-193	S 6 29	90
SAT	06	337 48	-194	S 7 59	89
HP	12	334 34	-194	S 9 28	86
61'	18	331 20	-194	S10 54	82
31	00	328 06	-196	S12 16	80
SUN	06	324 50	-196	S13 36	76
HP	12	321 34	-197	S14 52	73
60'	18	318 17	-197	S16 05	68
32	00	315 00		S17 13	

Phases of the Moon
New: 14d   First Quarter: 22d
Full: 28d   Last Quarter: 6d

Day	GMT	GHA-GMT	v	Dec	d
1	00h	315° 00'	-199'	S17° 13'	64'
MON	06	311 41	-199	S18 17	60
HP	12	308 22	-200	S19 17	55
59'	18	305 02	-200	S20 12	50
2	00	301 42	-201	S21 02	46
TUE	06	298 21	-201	S21 48	40
HP	12	295 00	-201	S22 28	35
58'	18	291 39	-201	S23 03	30
3	00	288 18	-200	S23 33	25
WED	06	284 58	-200	S23 58	18
HP	12	281 38	-199	S24 18	14
57'	18	278 19	-199	S24 32	10
4	00	275 00	-197	S24 42	4
THU	06	271 43	-195	S24 46	1
HP	12	268 28	-194	S24 45	5
56'	18	265 14	-192	S24 40	10
5	00	262 02	-190	S24 30	15
FRI	06	258 52	-188	S24 15	19
HP	12	255 44	-185	S23 56	23
55'	18	252 39	-183	S23 33	28
6	00	249 36	-181	S23 05	31
SAT	06	246 35	-178	S22 34	35
HP	12	243 37	-176	S21 59	39
55'	18	240 41	-174	S21 20	42
7	00	237 47	-170	S20 38	45
SUN	06	234 57	-169	S19 53	48
HP	12	232 08	-166	S19 05	51
54'	18	229 22	-164	S18 14	54
8	00	226 38	-162	S17 20	56
MON	06	223 56	-159	S16 24	59
HP	12	221 17	-158	S15 25	61
54'	18	218 39	-156	S14 24	63
9	00	216° 03'		S13° 21'	
9	00h	216° 03'	-155'	S13° 21'	64'
TUE	06	213 28	-153	S12 17	67
HP	12	210 55	-151	S11 10	68
54'	18	208 24	-151	S10 02	69
10	00	205 53	-149	S 8 53	70
WED	06	203 24	-148	S 7 43	72
HP	12	200 56	-148	S 6 31	72
54'	18	198 28	-148	S 5 19	74
11	00	196 00	-147	S 4 05	74
THU	06	193 33	-147	S 2 51	74
HP	12	191 06	-146	S 1 37	75
54'	18	188 40	-148	S 0 22	75
12	00	186 12	-147	N 0 53	75
FRI	06	183 45	-148	N 2 08	74
HP	12	181 17	-149	N 3 22	75
54'	18	178 48	-150	N 4 37	74
13	00	176 18	-150	N 5 51	73
SAT	06	173 48	-153	N 7 04	73
HP	12	171 15	-153	N 8 17	72
54'	18	168 42	-155	N 9 29	70
14	00	166 07	-157	N10 39	69
SUN	06	163 30	-159	N11 48	68
HP	12	160 51	-161	N12 56	66
55'	18	158 10	-163	N14 02	64
15	00	155 27	-165	N15 06	62
MON	06	152 42	-168	N16 08	59
HP	12	149 54	-171	N17 07	57
55'	18	147 03	-173	N18 04	54
16	00	144 10	-176	N18 59	51
TUE	06	141 14	-178	N19 50	48
HP	12	138 16	-181	N20 38	44
56'	18	135 15	-184	N21 22	41
17	00	132° 11'		N22° 03'	
17	00h	132° 11'	-187'	N22° 03'	37'
WED	06	129 04	-190	N22 40	33
HP	12	125 54	-192	N23 13	29
56'	18	122 42	-194	N23 42	24
18	00	119 28	-197	N24 06	20
THU	06	116 11	-198	N24 26	14
HP	12	112 53	-201	N24 40	10
57'	18	109 32	-202	N24 50	4
19	00	106 10	-203	N24 54	1
FRI	06	102 47	-205	N24 53	6
HP	12	99 22	-205	N24 47	11
58'	18	95 57	-206	N24 36	17
20	00	92 31	-206	N24 19	22
SAT	06	89 05	-206	N23 57	28
HP	12	85 39	-206	N23 29	33
58'	18	82 13	-205	N22 56	39
21	00	78 48	-205	N22 17	43
SUN	06	75 23	-203	N21 34	49
HP	12	72 00	-203	N20 45	54
59'	18	68 37	-201	N19 51	58
22	00	65 16	-200	N18 53	63
MON	06	61 56	-199	N17 50	67
HP	12	58 37	-197	N16 43	71
60'	18	55 20	-197	N15 32	75
23	00	52 03	-195	N14 17	79
TUE	06	48 48	-193	N12 58	81
HP	12	45 35	-193	N11 37	85
60'	18	42 22	-192	N10 12	87
24	00	39 10	-191	N 8 45	89
WED	06	35 59	-190	N 7 16	92
HP	12	32 49	-190	N 5 44	92
61'	18	29 39	-189	N 4 12	94
25	00	26° 30'		N 2° 38'	
25	00h	26° 30'	-190'	N 2° 38'	95'
THU	06	23 20	-189	N 1 03	94
HP	12	20 11	-190	S 0 31	95
61'	18	17 01	-190	S 2 06	95
26	00	13 51	-190	S 3 41	93
FRI	06	10 40	-191	S 5 14	93
HP	12	7 29	-193	S 6 47	91
61'	18	4 16	-193	S 8 18	88
27	00	1 03	-195	S 9 46	87
SAT	06	357 48	-196	S11 13	83
HP	12	354 32	-197	S12 36	81
60'	18	351 15	-199	S13 57	77
28	00	347 56	-200	S15 14	73
SUN	06	344 36	-201	S16 27	70
HP	12	341 15	-203	S17 37	65
60'	18	337 52	-204	S18 42	60
29	00	334 28	-205	S19 42	55
MON	06	331 03	-206	S20 37	51
HP	12	327 37	-206	S21 28	45
59'	18	324 11	-207	S22 13	40
30	00	320 44	-208	S22 53	34
TUE	06	317 16	-207	S23 27	29
HP	12	313 49	-207	S23 56	23
58'	18	310 22	-206	S24 19	18
31	00	306 56		S24 37	

Phases of the Moon
New: 12d   First Quarter: 20d
Full: 27d   Last Quarter: 4d

MOON AT EVERY 6hrs GMT MAY 2002

Day	GMT	GHA-GMT	v	Dec	d
1	00h	306° 56'	-205	S24° 37'	13'
WED	06	303 31	-204	S24 50	7
HP	12	300 07	-202	S24 57	2
57'	18	296 45	-201	S24 59	4
2	00	293 24	-198	S24 55	8
THU	06	290 06	-196	S24 47	14
HP	12	286 50	-194	S24 33	18
56'	18	283 36	-191	S24 15	23
3	00	280 25	-189	S23 52	27
FRI	06	277 16	-185	S23 25	31
HP	12	274 11	-183	S22 54	35
56'	18	271 08	-180	S22 19	39
4	00	268 08	-177	S21 40	42
SAT	06	265 11	-174	S20 58	45
HP	12	262 17	-171	S20 13	49
55'	18	259 26	-168	S19 24	51
5	00	256 38	-166	S18 33	55
SUN	06	253 52	-164	S17 38	56
HP	12	251 08	-161	S16 42	59
55'	18	248 27	-159	S15 43	61
6	00	245 48	-157	S14 42	64
MON	06	243 11	-155	S13 38	65
HP	12	240 36	-153	S12 33	66
54'	18	238 03	-152	S11 27	69
7	00	235 31	-150	S10 18	69
TUE	06	233 01	-150	S 9 09	71
HP	12	230 31	-148	S 7 58	72
54'	18	228 03	-148	S 6 46	73
8	00	225 35	-147	S 5 33	73
WED	06	223 08	-147	S 4 20	74
HP	12	220 41	-146	S 3 06	75
54'	18	218 15	-147	S 1 51	75
9	00	215° 48'		S 0° 36'	

Day	GMT	GHA-GMT	v	Dec	d
9	00h	215° 48'	-147	S 0° 36'	76
THU	06	213 21	-147	N 0 40	75
HP	12	210 54	-148	N 1 55	76
54'	18	208 26	-149	N 3 11	75
10	00	205 57	-150	N 4 26	75
FRI	06	203 27	-151	N 5 41	74
HP	12	200 56	-153	N 6 55	73
55'	18	198 23	-154	N 8 08	73
11	00	195 49	-155	N 9 21	72
SAT	06	193 14	-158	N10 33	70
HP	12	190 36	-160	N11 43	69
55'	18	187 56	-162	N12 52	67
12	00	185 14	-164	N13 59	65
SUN	06	182 30	-167	N15 04	63
HP	12	179 43	-170	N16 07	61
55'	18	176 53	-172	N17 08	58
13	00	174 01	-175	N18 06	55
MON	06	171 06	-178	N19 01	52
HP	12	168 08	-181	N19 53	49
56'	18	165 07	-184	N20 42	46
14	00	162 03	-186	N21 28	42
TUE	06	158 57	-189	N22 10	37
HP	12	155 48	-192	N22 47	34
56'	18	152 36	-194	N23 21	29
15	00	149 22	-197	N23 50	24
WED	06	146 05	-198	N24 14	20
HP	12	142 47	-201	N24 34	14
57'	18	139 26	-202	N24 48	10
16	00	136 04	-203	N24 58	4
THU	06	132 41	-204	N25 02	1
HP	12	129 17	-205	N25 01	6
57'	18	125 52	-206	N24 55	12
17	00	122° 26'		N24° 43'	

Day	GMT	GHA-GMT	v	Dec	d
17	00h	122° 26'	-205	N24° 43'	18
FRI	06	119 01	-205	N24 25	22
HP	12	115 36	-205	N24 03	28
58'	18	112 11	-204	N23 35	33
18	00	108 47	-203	N23 02	39
SAT	06	105 24	-201	N22 23	43
HP	12	102 03	-200	N21 40	48
58'	18	98 43	-199	N20 52	53
19	00	95 24	-197	N19 59	57
SUN	06	92 07	-196	N19 02	62
HP	12	88 51	-194	N18 00	65
59'	18	85 37	-192	N16 55	70
20	00	82 25	-191	N15 45	72
MON	06	79 14	-189	N14 33	77
HP	12	76 05	-187	N13 16	79
59'	18	72 58	-187	N11 57	81
21	00	69 51	-185	N10 36	85
TUE	06	66 46	-185	N 9 11	86
HP	12	63 41	-184	N 7 45	88
60'	18	60 37	-183	N 6 17	90
22	00	57 34	-183	N 4 47	90
WED	06	54 31	-182	N 3 17	92
HP	12	51 29	-183	N 1 45	92
60'	18	48 26	-183	N 0 13	93
23	00	45 23	-184	S 1 20	92
THU	06	42 19	-184	S 2 52	92
HP	12	39 15	-186	S 4 24	91
60'	18	36 09	-186	S 5 55	90
24	00	33 03	-188	S 7 25	88
FRI	06	29 55	-189	S 8 53	86
HP	12	26 46	-191	S10 19	85
60'	18	23 35	-193	S11 44	81
25	00	20° 22'		S13° 05'	

Day	GMT	GHA-GMT	v	Dec	d
25	00h	20° 22'	-195	S13° 05'	79
SAT	06	17 07	-196	S14 24	75
HP	12	13 51	-198	S15 39	72
60'	18	10 33	-200	S16 51	67
26	00	7 13	-202	S17 58	64
SUN	06	3 51	-204	S19 02	59
HP	12	0 27	-205	S20 01	54
59'	18	357 02	-207	S20 55	50
27	00	353 35	-208	S21 45	44
MON	06	350 07	-208	S22 29	38
HP	12	346 39	-210	S23 07	34
59'	18	343 09	-209	S23 41	27
28	00	339 40	-210	S24 08	22
TUE	06	336 10	-209	S24 30	17
HP	12	332 41	-208	S24 47	11
58'	18	329 13	-207	S24 58	5
29	00	325 46	-206	S25 03	0
WED	06	322 20	-204	S25 03	6
HP	12	318 56	-202	S24 57	11
57'	18	315 34	-199	S24 46	16
30	00	312 15	-197	S24 30	20
THU	06	308 58	-194	S24 10	26
HP	12	305 44	-191	S23 44	29
56'	18	302 33	-188	S23 15	34
31	00	299 25	-185	S22 41	38
FRI	06	296 20	-182	S22 03	42
HP	12	293 18	-179	S21 21	45
56'	18	290 19	-175	S20 36	48
32	00	287 24		S19 48	

Phases of the Moon
New: 12d   First Quarter: 19d
Full: 26d   Last Quarter: 4d

MOON AT EVERY 6hrs GMT JUNE 2002

Day	GMT	GHA-GMT	v	Dec	d
1	00h	287° 24'	-173	S19° 48'	52'
SAT	06	284 31	-170	S18 56	54
HP	12	281 41	-166	S18 02	56
55'	18	278 55	-165	S17 06	60
2	00	276 10	-161	S16 06	61
SUN	06	273 29	-159	S15 05	63
HP	12	270 50	-157	S14 02	65
55'	18	268 13	-155	S12 57	67
3	00	265 38	-154	S11 50	69
MON	06	263 04	-151	S10 41	69
HP	12	260 33	-151	S 9 32	71
54'	18	258 02	-149	S 8 21	72
4	00	255 33	-148	S 7 09	73
TUE	06	253 05	-147	S 5 56	74
HP	12	250 38	-147	S 4 42	74
54'	18	248 11	-146	S 3 28	75
5	00	245 45	-147	S 2 13	75
WED	06	243 18	-146	S 0 58	75
HP	12	240 52	-147	N 0 17	76
54'	18	238 25	-148	N 1 33	75
6	00	235 57	-148	N 2 48	75
THU	06	233 29	-149	N 4 03	75
HP	12	231 00	-150	N 5 18	75
55'	18	228 30	-152	N 6 33	75
7	00	225 58	-153	N 7 47	73
FRI	06	223 25	-155	N 9 00	72
HP	12	220 50	-158	N10 12	70
55'	18	218 12	-159	N11 22	70
8	00	215 33	-162	N12 32	68
SAT	06	212 51	-164	N13 40	66
HP	12	210 07	-167	N14 46	64
55'	18	207 20	-170	N15 50	62
9	00	204° 30'		N16° 52'	

Day	GMT	GHA-GMT	v	Dec	d
9	00h	204° 30'	-173	N16° 52'	59'
SUN	06	201 37	-175	N17 51	57
HP	12	198 42	-179	N18 48	53
56'	18	195 43	-182	N19 41	51
10	00	192 41	-186	N20 32	47
MON	06	189 35	-188	N21 19	43
HP	12	186 27	-191	N22 02	39
56'	18	183 16	-194	N22 41	35
11	00	180 02	-197	N23 16	30
TUE	06	176 45	-200	N23 46	26
HP	12	173 25	-202	N24 12	20
57'	18	170 03	-204	N24 32	16
12	00	166 39	-206	N24 48	10
WED	06	163 13	-207	N24 58	5
HP	12	159 46	-208	N25 03	1
58'	18	156 18	-209	N25 02	5
13	00	152 49	-209	N24 56	12
THU	06	149 20	-209	N24 44	17
HP	12	145 51	-209	N24 27	23
58'	18	142 22	-208	N24 04	29
14	00	138 54	-207	N23 35	34
FRI	06	135 27	-205	N23 01	39
HP	12	132 02	-204	N22 22	44
58'	18	128 38	-202	N21 38	49
15	00	125 16	-201	N20 49	54
SAT	06	121 55	-198	N19 55	58
HP	12	118 37	-196	N18 57	62
59'	18	115 21	-194	N17 55	66
16	00	112 07	-192	N16 49	70
SUN	06	108 55	-190	N15 39	73
HP	12	105 45	-188	N14 26	76
59'	18	102 37	-186	N13 10	79
17	00	99° 31'		N11° 51'	

Day	GMT	GHA-GMT	v	Dec	d
17	00h	99° 31'	-185	N11° 51'	81
MON	06	96 26	-183	N10 30	83
HP	12	93 23	-182	N 9 07	86
59'	18	90 21	-180	N 7 41	86
18	00	87 21	-180	N 6 15	89
TUE	06	84 21	-179	N 4 46	89
HP	12	81 22	-179	N 3 17	90
59'	18	78 23	-178	N 1 47	90
19	00	75 25	-179	N 0 17	90
WED	06	72 26	-178	S 1 13	90
HP	12	69 28	-180	S 2 43	90
59'	18	66 28	-180	S 4 13	89
20	00	63 28	-181	S 5 42	87
THU	06	60 27	-182	S 7 09	87
HP	12	57 25	-183	S 8 36	84
59'	18	54 22	-185	S10 00	83
21	00	51 17	-187	S11 23	80
FRI	06	48 10	-188	S12 43	77
HP	12	45 02	-190	S14 00	75
59'	18	41 52	-193	S15 15	71
22	00	38 39	-194	S16 26	67
SAT	06	35 25	-197	S17 33	64
HP	12	32 08	-198	S18 37	60
59'	18	28 50	-201	S19 37	55
23	00	25 29	-202	S20 32	51
SUN	06	22 07	-203	S21 23	45
HP	12	18 44	-206	S22 08	41
58'	18	15 18	-206	S22 49	36
24	00	11 52	-207	S23 25	30
MON	06	8 25	-208	S23 55	24
HP	12	4 57	-208	S24 19	20
58'	18	1 29	-207	S24 39	13
25	00	358° 02'		S24° 52'	

Day	GMT	GHA-GMT	v	Dec	d
25	00h	358° 02'	-208	S24° 52'	8'
TUE	06	354 34	-206	S25 00	3
HP	12	351 08	-205	S25 03	3
57'	18	347 43	-203	S25 00	8
26	00	344 20	-202	S24 52	14
WED	06	340 58	-199	S24 38	18
HP	12	337 39	-197	S24 20	23
57'	18	334 22	-195	S23 57	28
27	00	331 07	-191	S23 29	32
THU	06	327 56	-188	S22 57	37
HP	12	324 48	-186	S22 20	40
56'	18	321 42	-182	S21 40	44
28	00	318 40	-179	S20 56	47
FRI	06	315 41	-176	S20 09	51
HP	12	312 45	-173	S19 18	54
55'	18	309 52	-171	S18 24	56
29	00	307 01	-167	S17 28	59
SAT	06	304 14	-164	S16 29	61
HP	12	301 30	-162	S15 28	64
55'	18	298 48	-160	S14 24	65
30	00	296 08	-157	S13 19	67
SUN	06	293 31	-155	S12 12	68
HP	12	290 56	-154	S11 04	70
55'	18	288 22	-151	S 9 54	71
31	00	285 51		S 8 43	

Phases of the Moon
New: 10d   First Quarter: 18d
Full: 24d   Last Quarter: 3d

Day GMT	GHA-GMT	v	Dec	d	Day GMT	GHA-GMT	v	Dec	d	Day GMT	GHA-GMT	v	Dec	d	Day GMT	GHA-GMT	v	Dec	d
1 00h	285° 51'	-150'	S 8° 43'	72'	9 00h	198° 21'	-205'	N24° 25'	17'	17 00h	93° 03'	-179'	S 4° 27'	88'	25 00h	349° 45'	-183'	S21° 52'	43'
MON 06	283 21	-149	S 7 31	73	TUE 06	194 56	-208	N24 42	13	WED 06	90 04	-180	S 5 55	87	THU 06	346 42	-180	S21 09	47
HP 12	280 52	-148	S 6 18	74	HP 12	191 28	-210	N24 55	6	HP 12	87 04	-180	S 7 22	85	HP 12	343 42	-177	S20 22	50
54' 18	278 24	-148	S 5 04	74	58' 18	187 58	-211	N25 01	1	59' 18	84 04	-181	S 8 47	84	55' 18	340 45	-174	S19 32	53
2 00	275 56	-146	S 3 50	75	10 00	184 27	-212	N25 02	4	18 00	81 03	-183	S10 11	81	26 00	337 51	-172	S18 39	56
TUE 06	273 30	-147	S 2 35	75	WED 06	180 55	-213	N24 58	11	THU 06	78 00	-184	S11 32	79	FRI 06	334 59	-168	S17 43	59
HP 12	271 03	-146	S 1 20	75	HP 12	177 22	-214	N24 47	16	HP 12	74 56	-185	S12 51	76	HP 12	332 11	-166	S16 44	61
54' 18	268 37	-146	S 0 05	75	58' 18	173 48	-213	N24 31	23	59' 18	71 51	-187	S14 07	73	55' 18	329 25	-164	S15 43	63
3 00	266 11	-147	N 1 10	75	11 00	170 15	-213	N24 08	27	19 00	68 44	-189	S15 20	69	27 00	326 41	-161	S14 40	65
WED 06	263 44	-147	N 2 25	75	THU 06	166 42	-212	N23 41	34	FRI 06	65 35	-190	S16 29	67	SAT 06	324 00	-158	S13 35	67
HP 12	261 17	-148	N 3 40	75	HP 12	163 10	-211	N23 07	39	HP 12	62 25	-192	S17 36	62	HP 12	321 22	-157	S12 28	69
54' 18	258 49	-149	N 4 55	74	59' 18	159 39	-209	N22 28	45	58' 18	59 13	-195	S18 38	59	55' 18	318 45	-154	S11 19	70
4 00	256 20	-150	N 6 09	74	12 00	156 10	-208	N21 43	49	20 00	55 58	-195	S19 37	54	28 00	316 11	-153	S10 09	71
THU 06	253 50	-151	N 7 23	72	FRI 06	152 42	-206	N20 54	55	SAT 06	52 43	-198	S20 31	50	SUN 06	313 38	-151	S 8 58	72
HP 12	251 19	-154	N 8 35	72	HP 12	149 16	-203	N19 59	59	HP 12	49 25	-199	S21 21	45	HP 12	311 07	-150	S 7 46	73
55' 18	248 45	-155	N 9 47	71	59' 18	145 53	-201	N19 00	63	58' 18	46 06	-201	S22 06	40	54' 18	308 37	-149	S 6 33	74
5 00	246 10	-157	N10 58	70	13 00	142 32	-199	N17 57	68	21 00	42 45	-201	S22 46	35	29 00	306 08	-148	S 5 19	74
FRI 06	243 33	-160	N12 08	67	SAT 06	139 13	-197	N16 49	71	SUN 06	39 24	-203	S23 21	31	MON 06	303 40	-147	S 4 05	75
HP 12	240 53	-162	N13 15	67	HP 12	135 56	-194	N15 38	75	HP 12	36 01	-204	S23 52	25	HP 12	301 13	-146	S 2 50	75
55' 18	238 11	-165	N14 22	64	60' 18	132 42	-192	N14 23	77	58' 18	32 37	-204	S24 17	19	54' 18	298 47	-146	S 1 35	76
6 00	235 26	-167	N15 26	63	14 00	129 30	-190	N13 06	81	22 00	29 13	-204	S24 36	15	30 00	296 21	-146	S 0 19	75
SAT 06	232 39	-171	N16 29	60	SUN 06	126 20	-188	N11 45	83	MON 06	25 49	-204	S24 51	8	TUE 06	293 55	-146	N 0 56	75
HP 12	229 48	-174	N17 29	57	HP 12	123 12	-186	N10 22	85	HP 12	22 25	-203	S24 59	4	HP 12	291 29	-146	N 2 11	75
56' 18	226 54	-177	N18 26	55	60' 18	120 06	-184	N 8 57	86	57' 18	19 02	-202	S25 03	2	54' 18	289 03	-147	N 3 26	74
7 00	223 57	-180	N19 21	51	15 00	117 02	-181	N 7 31	89	23 00	15 40	-202	S25 01	6	31 00	286 36	-148	N 4 40	74
SUN 06	220 57	-184	N20 12	49	MON 06	113 59	-181	N 6 02	89	TUE 06	12 18	-199	S24 55	13	WED 06	284 08	-148	N 5 54	74
HP 12	217 53	-188	N21 01	44	HP 12	110 58	-181	N 4 33	90	HP 12	8 59	-198	S24 42	17	HP 12	281 40	-150	N 7 08	72
56' 18	214 45	-190	N21 45	41	60' 18	107 57	-179	N 3 03	90	57' 18	5 41	-196	S24 25	21	54' 18	279 10	-151	N 8 20	72
8 00	211 35	-194	N22 26	37	16 00	104 58	-179	N 1 33	91	24 00	2 25	-194	S24 04	27	32 00	276 39		N 9 32	
MON 06	208 21	-197	N23 03	32	TUE 06	101 59	-179	N 0 02	90	WED 06	359 11	-191	S23 37	31					
HP 12	205 04	-200	N23 35	27	HP 12	99 00	-179	S 1 28	90	HP 12	356 00	-189	S23 06	35		Phases of the Moon			
57' 18	201 44	-203	N24 02	23	59' 18	96 01	-178	S 2 58	89	56' 18	352 51	-186	S22 31	39		New: 10d	First Quarter: 17d		
9 00	198° 21'		N24° 25'		17 00	93° 03'		S 4° 27'		25 00	349° 45'		S21° 52'			Full: 24d	Last Quarter: 2d		

MOON AT EVERY 6hrs GMT AUGUST 2002

Day GMT	GHA-GMT	v	Dec	d	Day GMT	GHA-GMT	v	Dec	d	Day GMT	GHA-GMT	v	Dec	d	Day GMT	GHA-GMT	v	Dec	d
1 00h	276° 39'	-153'	N 9° 32'	70'	9 00h	174° 27'	-207'	N19° 25'	63'	17 00h	72° 41'	-199'	S22° 19'	40'	25 00h	336° 03'	-149'	S 6° 39'	74'
THU 06	274 06	-155	N10 42	69	FRI 06	171 00	-204	N18 22	68	SAT 06	69 22	-200	S22 59	34	SUN 06	333 34	-147	S 5 25	75
HP 12	271 31	-156	N11 51	68	HP 12	167 36	-203	N17 14	72	HP 12	66 02	-201	S23 33	29	HP 12	331 07	-147	S 4 10	75
55' 18	268 55	-159	N12 59	66	60' 18	164 13	-200	N16 02	76	57' 18	62 41	-201	S24 02	24	54' 18	328 40	-147	S 2 55	76
2 00	266 16	-162	N14 05	64	10 00	160 53	-199	N14 46	79	18 00	59 20	-201	S24 26	19	26 00	326 13	-146	S 1 39	75
FRI 06	263 34	-164	N15 09	62	SAT 06	157 34	-196	N13 27	83	SUN 06	55 59	-201	S24 45	13	MON 06	323 47	-145	S 0 24	76
HP 12	260 50	-167	N16 11	60	HP 12	154 18	-194	N12 04	85	HP 12	52 38	-201	S24 58	9	HP 12	321 22	-146	N 0 52	75
55' 18	258 03	-170	N17 11	58	60' 18	151 04	-192	N10 39	87	57' 18	49 17	-201	S25 07	3	54' 18	318 56	-146	N 2 07	76
3 00	255 13	-173	N18 09	55	11 00	147 52	-191	N 9 12	90	19 00	45 56	-199	S25 10	2	27 00	316 30	-146	N 3 23	74
SAT 06	252 20	-176	N19 04	52	SUN 06	144 41	-188	N 7 42	90	MON 06	42 37	-198	S25 08	8	TUE 06	314 04	-147	N 4 37	75
HP 12	249 24	-180	N19 56	49	HP 12	141 33	-188	N 6 12	92	HP 12	39 19	-197	S25 00	12	HP 12	311 37	-148	N 5 52	73
56' 18	246 24	-183	N20 45	46	60' 18	138 25	-186	N 4 40	93	56' 18	36 02	-195	S24 48	17	54' 18	309 09	-149	N 7 05	73
4 00	243 21	-186	N21 31	42	12 00	135 19	-184	N 3 07	94	20 00	32 47	-194	S24 31	22	28 00	306 40	-149	N 8 18	71
SUN 06	240 15	-190	N22 13	38	MON 06	132 15	-185	N 1 33	93	TUE 06	29 33	-191	S24 09	26	WED 06	304 11	-152	N 9 29	71
HP 12	237 05	-193	N22 51	33	HP 12	129 10	-183	N 0 00	93	HP 12	26 22	-188	S23 43	31	HP 12	301 39	-152	N10 40	69
57' 18	233 52	-197	N23 24	30	60' 18	126 07	-183	S 1 33	92	56' 18	23 14	-187	S23 12	35	54' 18	299 07	-155	N11 49	67
5 00	230 35	-199	N23 54	25	13 00	123 04	-183	S 3 05	92	21 00	20 07	-184	S22 37	39	29 00	296 32	-156	N12 56	66
MON 06	227 16	-203	N24 19	19	TUE 06	120 01	-183	S 4 37	90	WED 06	17 03	-181	S21 58	43	THU 06	293 56	-159	N14 02	64
HP 12	223 53	-205	N24 38	15	HP 12	116 58	-183	S 6 07	89	HP 12	14 02	-178	S21 15	46	HP 12	291 17	-161	N15 06	62
57' 18	220 28	-208	N24 53	9	60' 18	113 55	-184	S 7 36	86	55' 18	11 04	-176	S20 29	48	55' 18	288 36	-163	N16 08	60
6 00	217 00	-210	N25 02	4	14 00	110 51	-185	S 9 02	85	22 00	8 08	-173	S19 39	52	30 00	285 52	-166	N17 08	58
TUE 06	213 30	-212	N25 06	2	WED 06	107 46	-185	S10 27	82	THU 06	5 15	-171	S18 47	56	FRI 06	283 06	-169	N18 06	54
HP 12	209 58	-213	N25 04	8	HP 12	104 41	-186	S11 49	79	HP 12	2 24	-168	S17 51	59	HP 12	280 17	-172	N19 00	52
58' 18	206 25	-214	N24 56	13	59' 18	101 35	-187	S13 08	77	55' 18	359 36	-165	S16 52	61	55' 18	277 25	-174	N19 52	50
7 00	202 51	-215	N24 43	20	15 00	98 28	-189	S14 25	73	23 00	356 51	-163	S15 51	63	31 00	274 31	-178	N20 42	45
WED 06	199 16	-215	N24 23	25	THU 06	95 19	-190	S15 38	70	FRI 06	354 08	-161	S14 48	65	SAT 06	271 33	-182	N21 27	43
HP 12	195 41	-215	N23 58	32	HP 12	92 09	-191	S16 48	65	HP 12	351 27	-158	S13 43	67	HP 12	268 31	-184	N22 10	38
59' 18	192 06	-214	N23 26	37	59' 18	88 58	-193	S17 53	62	55' 18	348 49	-157	S12 36	69	56' 18	265 27	-187	N22 48	35
8 00	188 32	-213	N22 49	43	16 00	85 45	-194	S18 55	58	24 00	346 12	-154	S11 27	70	32 00	262 20		N23 23	
THU 06	184 59	-212	N22 06	48	FRI 06	82 31	-195	S19 53	53	SAT 06	343 38	-153	S10 17	71					
HP 12	181 27	-211	N21 18	54	HP 12	79 16	-197	S20 46	48	HP 12	341 05	-152	S 9 06	73		Phases of the Moon			
60' 18	177 56	-209	N20 24	59	58' 18	75 59	-198	S21 35	44	54' 18	338 33	-150	S 7 53	74		New: 8d	First Quarter: 15d		
9 00	174° 27'		N19° 25'		17 00	72° 41'		S22° 19'		25 00	336° 03'		S 6° 39'			Full: 22d	Last Quarter: 1d&31d		

MOON AT EVERY 6hrs GMT SEPTEMBER 2002

Day GMT	GHA-GMT	v	Dec	d	Day GMT	GHA-GMT	v	Dec	d	Day GMT	GHA-GMT	v	Dec	d	Day GMT	GHA-GMT	v	Dec	d
1 00h	262° 20'	-191	N23° 23'	31'	9 00h	154° 32'	-190	S 1° 00'	96	17 00h	49° 52'	-185	S23° 19'	35	25 00h	326° 14'	-154	N11° 55'	68
SUN 06	259 09	-194	N23 54	26	MON 06	151 22	-189	S 2 36	96	TUE 06	46 47	-182	S22 44	40	WED 06	323 40	-156	N13 03	66
HP 12	255 55	-196	N24 20	21	HP 12	148 13	-189	S 4 12	94	HP 12	43 45	-180	S22 04	43	HP 12	321 04	-158	N14 09	65
56' 18	252 39	-200	N24 41	17	61' 18	145 04	-190	S 5 46	93	55' 18	40 45	-176	S21 21	46	54' 18	318 26	-160	N15 14	62
2 00	249 19	-202	N24 58	12	10 00	141 54	-190	S 7 19	91	18 00	37 49	-174	S20 35	50	26 00	315 46	-162	N16 16	60
MON 06	245 57	-204	N25 10	6	TUE 06	138 44	-191	S 8 50	88	WED 06	34 55	-171	S19 45	53	THU 06	313 04	-164	N17 16	58
HP 12	242 33	-207	N25 16	1	HP 12	135 33	-192	S10 18	86	HP 12	32 04	-169	S18 52	56	HP 12	310 20	-167	N18 14	55
57' 18	239 06	-208	N25 17	5	60' 18	132 21	-192	S11 44	83	55' 18	29 15	-166	S17 56	59	55' 18	307 33	-169	N19 09	52
3 00	235 38	-210	N25 12	10	11 00	129 09	-193	S13 07	80	19 00	26 29	-164	S16 57	61	27 00	304 44	-172	N20 01	49
TUE 06	232 08	-211	N25 02	16	WED 06	125 56	-195	S14 27	76	THU 06	23 45	-162	S15 56	63	FRI 06	301 52	-175	N20 50	46
HP 12	228 37	-211	N24 46	22	HP 12	122 41	-195	S15 43	72	HP 12	21 03	-159	S14 53	66	HP 12	298 57	-178	N21 36	42
58' 18	225 06	-212	N24 24	28	60' 18	119 26	-197	S16 55	68	55' 18	18 24	-157	S13 47	67	55' 18	295 59	-181	N22 18	39
4 00	221 34	-212	N23 56	34	12 00	116 09	-198	S18 03	64	20 00	15 47	-156	S12 40	69	28 00	292 58	-183	N22 57	35
WED 06	218 02	-212	N23 22	39	THU 06	112 51	-199	S19 07	60	FRI 06	13 11	-153	S11 31	71	SAT 06	289 55	-186	N23 32	31
HP 12	214 30	-212	N22 43	45	HP 12	109 32	-200	S20 07	54	HP 12	10 38	-152	S10 20	71	HP 12	286 49	-188	N24 03	26
59' 18	210 58	-210	N21 58	51	59' 18	106 12	-201	S21 01	50	54' 18	8 06	-151	S 9 09	73	56' 18	283 41	-192	N24 29	22
5 00	207 28	-210	N21 07	55	13 00	102 51	-202	S21 51	45	21 00	5 35	-149	S 7 56	74	29 00	280 29	-193	N24 51	18
THU 06	203 58	-208	N20 12	61	FRI 06	99 29	-203	S22 36	39	SAT 06	3 06	-148	S 6 42	75	SUN 06	277 16	-196	N25 09	13
HP 12	200 30	-207	N19 11	66	HP 12	96 06	-203	S23 15	34	HP 12	0 38	-148	S 5 27	75	HP 12	274 00	-198	N25 22	7
60' 18	197 03	-205	N18 05	71	58' 18	92 43	-203	S23 49	29	54' 18	358 10	-146	S 4 12	76	56' 18	270 42	-200	N25 29	3
6 00	193 38	-203	N16 54	75	14 00	89 20	-203	S24 18	24	22 00	355 44	-146	S 2 56	76	30 00	267 22	-202	N25 32	3
FRI 06	190 15	-202	N15 39	78	SAT 06	85 57	-203	S24 42	18	SUN 06	353 18	-146	S 1 40	77	MON 06	264 00	-203	N25 29	8
HP 12	186 53	-201	N14 21	83	HP 12	82 34	-203	S25 00	13	HP 12	350 52	-146	S 0 23	76	HP 12	260 37	-204	N25 21	13
61' 18	183 32	-198	N12 58	85	57' 18	79 11	-202	S25 13	8	54' 18	348 26	-145	N 0 53	76	57' 18	257 13	-205	N25 08	19
7 00	180 14	-197	N11 33	88	15 00	75 49	-201	S25 21	2	23 00	346 01	-146	N 2 09	76	31 00	253 48		N24 49	
SAT 06	176 57	-195	N10 05	91	SUN 06	72 28	-199	S25 23	3	MON 06	343 35	-146	N 3 25	76					
HP 12	173 42	-195	N 8 34	93	HP 12	69 09	-198	S25 20	8	HP 12	341 09	-147	N 4 41	75					
61' 18	170 27	-192	N 7 01	95	57' 18	65 51	-196	S25 12	13	54' 18	338 42	-147	N 5 56	74					
8 00	167 15	-192	N 5 26	95	16 00	62 35	-195	S24 59	18	24 00	336 15	-149	N 7 10	73					
SUN 06	164 03	-191	N 3 51	97	MON 06	59 20	-192	S24 41	23	TUE 06	333 46	-149	N 8 23	72					
HP 12	160 52	-190	N 2 14	97	HP 12	56 08	-189	S24 18	27	HP 12	331 17	-151	N 9 35	71	Phases of the Moon				
61' 18	157 42	-190	N 0 37	97	56' 18	52 59	-187	S23 51	32	54' 18	328 46	-152	N10 46	69	New: 7d First Quarter: 13d				
9 00	154° 32'		S 1° 00'		17 00	49° 52'		S23° 19'		25 00	326° 14'		N11° 55'		Full: 21d Last Quarter: 29d				

MOON AT EVERY 6hrs GMT OCTOBER 2002

Day GMT	GHA-GMT	v	Dec	d	Day GMT	GHA-GMT	v	Dec	d	Day GMT	GHA-GMT	v	Dec	d	Day GMT	GHA-GMT	v	Dec	d
1 00h	253° 48'	-205	N24° 49'	25'	9 00h	148° 09'	-203	S16° 29'	73'	17 00h	45° 08'	-156	S13° 53'	68'	25 00h	322° 48'	-180	N22° 29'	39'
TUE 06	250 23	-206	N24 24	30	WED 06	144 46	-205	S17 42	69	THU 06	42 32	-154	S12 45	69	FRI 06	319 48	-183	N23 08	35
HP 12	246 57	-205	N23 54	35	HP 12	141 21	-206	S18 51	64	HP 12	39 58	-153	S11 36	71	HP 12	316 45	-185	N23 43	31
58' 18	243 32	-206	N23 19	41	60' 18	137 55	-208	S19 55	59	54' 18	37 25	-151	S10 25	72	55' 18	313 40	-187	N24 14	26
2 00	240 06	-205	N22 38	47	10 00	134 27	-208	S20 54	54	18 00	34 54	-150	S 9 13	73	26 00	310 33	-189	N24 40	23
WED 06	236 41	-204	N21 51	51	THU 06	130 59	-209	S21 48	48	FRI 06	32 24	-148	S 8 00	74	SAT 06	307 24	-191	N25 03	17
HP 12	233 17	-204	N21 00	57	HP 12	127 30	-210	S22 36	43	HP 12	29 56	-148	S 6 46	75	HP 12	304 13	-194	N25 20	13
59' 18	229 53	-202	N20 03	62	59' 18	124 00	-210	S23 19	37	54' 18	27 28	-146	S 5 31	76	56' 18	300 59	-195	N25 33	8
3 00	226 31	-202	N19 01	66	11 00	120 30	-211	S23 56	31	19 00	25 02	-146	S 4 15	76	27 00	297 44	-196	N25 41	3
THU 06	223 09	-200	N17 55	71	FRI 06	116 59	-210	S24 27	26	SAT 06	22 36	-146	S 2 59	77	SUN 06	294 28	-197	N25 44	2
HP 12	219 49	-200	N16 44	76	HP 12	113 29	-210	S24 53	20	HP 12	20 10	-145	S 1 42	77	HP 12	291 11	-199	N25 42	7
60' 18	216 29	-198	N15 28	79	58' 18	109 59	-208	S25 13	14	54' 18	17 45	-145	S 0 25	77	56' 18	287 52	-199	N25 35	13
4 00	213 11	-197	N14 09	83	12 00	106 31	-208	S25 27	8	20 00	15 20	-146	N 0 52	76	28 00	284 33	-199	N25 22	18
FRI 06	209 54	-195	N12 46	86	SAT 06	103 03	-206	S25 35	3	SUN 06	12 54	-145	N 2 08	76	MON 06	281 14	-200	N25 04	23
HP 12	206 39	-195	N11 20	89	HP 12	99 37	-204	S25 38	3	HP 12	10 29	-146	N 3 25	76	HP 12	277 54	-199	N24 41	28
61' 18	203 24	-194	N 9 51	92	57' 18	96 13	-203	S25 35	8	54' 18	8 03	-147	N 4 41	76	57' 18	274 35	-200	N24 13	33
5 00	200 10	-194	N 8 19	94	13 00	92 50	-200	S25 27	14	21 00	5 36	-148	N 5 57	75	29 00	271 15	-199	N23 40	39
SAT 06	196 56	-193	N 6 45	96	SUN 06	89 30	-197	S25 13	18	MON 06	3 08	-148	N 7 12	74	TUE 06	267 56	-198	N23 01	43
HP 12	193 43	-192	N 5 09	97	HP 12	86 13	-195	S24 55	23	HP 12	0 40	-150	N 8 26	72	HP 12	264 38	-197	N22 18	49
61' 18	190 31	-192	N 3 32	98	57' 18	82 58	-192	S24 32	28	54' 18	358 10	-151	N 9 38	72	58' 18	261 21	-197	N21 29	53
6 00	187 19	-192	N 1 54	99	14 00	79 46	-190	S24 04	32	22 00	355 39	-153	N10 50	70	30 00	258 04	-195	N20 36	59
SUN 06	184 07	-192	N 0 15	99	MON 06	76 36	-186	S23 32	37	TUE 06	353 06	-155	N12 00	69	WED 06	254 49	-195	N19 37	62
HP 12	180 55	-193	S 1 24	99	HP 12	73 30	-183	S22 55	40	HP 12	350 31	-156	N13 09	67	HP 12	251 34	-193	N18 35	67
61' 18	177 42	-193	S 3 03	98	56' 18	70 27	-180	S22 15	44	54' 18	347 55	-158	N14 16	65	59' 18	248 21	-192	N17 28	71
7 00	174 29	-193	S 4 41	96	15 00	67 27	-177	S21 31	47	23 00	345 17	-160	N15 21	63	31 00	245 09	-192	N16 17	75
MON 06	171 16	-195	S 6 17	96	TUE 06	64 30	-174	S20 44	51	WED 06	342 37	-163	N16 24	61	THU 06	241 57	-190	N15 02	79
HP 12	168 01	-195	S 7 53	93	HP 12	61 36	-171	S19 53	53	HP 12	339 54	-165	N17 25	58	HP 12	238 47	-190	N13 43	81
61' 18	164 46	-197	S 9 26	91	55' 18	58 45	-169	S19 00	57	54' 18	337 09	-167	N18 23	55	60' 18	235 37	-188	N12 22	85
8 00	161 29	-198	S10 57	88	16 00	55 56	-165	S18 03	59	24 00	334 22	-170	N19 18	53	32 00	232 29		N10 57	
TUE 06	158 11	-199	S12 25	85	WED 06	53 11	-163	S17 04	62	THU 06	331 32	-172	N20 11	49					
HP 12	154 52	-201	S13 50	82	HP 12	50 28	-161	S16 02	63	HP 12	328 40	-175	N21 00	46	Phases of the Moon				
61' 18	151 31	-202	S15 12	77	55' 18	47 47	-159	S14 59	66	55' 18	325 45	-177	N21 46	43	New: 6d First Quarter: 13d				
9 00	148° 09'		S16° 29'		17 00	45° 08'		S13° 53'		25 00	322° 48'		N22° 29'		Full: 21d Last Quarter: 29d				

MOON AT EVERY 6hrs GMT NOVEMBER 2002

Day	GMT	GHA-GMT	v	Dec	d	Day	GMT	GHA-GMT	v	Dec	d	Day	GMT	GHA-GMT	v	Dec	d	Day	GMT	GHA-GMT	v	Dec	d
1	00h	232° 29'	-188'	N10° 57'	88'	9	00h	124° 36'	-211'	S25° 46'	6'	17	00h	35° 05'	-146'	N 4° 32'	76'	25	00h	301° 13'	-198'	N24° 17'	34'
FRI	06	229 21	-188	N 9 29	91	SAT	06	121 05	-207	S25 40	12	SUN	06	32 39	-148	N 5 48	76	MON	06	297 55	-196	N23 43	38
HP	12	226 13	-187	N 7 58	92	HP	12	117 38	-206	S25 28	17	HP	12	30 11	-148	N 7 04	74	HP	12	294 39	-195	N23 05	43
60'	18	223 06	-187	N 6 26	95	58'	18	114 12	-202	S25 11	22	54'	18	27 43	-150	N 8 18	74	57'	18	291 24	-194	N22 22	48
2	00	219 59	-188	N 4 51	96	10	00	110 50	-198	S24 49	27	18	00	25 13	-152	N 9 32	72	26	00	288 10	-192	N21 34	53
SAT	06	216 51	-187	N 3 15	97	SUN	06	107 32	-196	S24 22	32	MON	06	22 41	-153	N10 44	71	TUE	06	284 58	-192	N20 41	56
HP	12	213 44	-188	N 1 38	97	HP	12	104 16	-192	S23 50	36	HP	12	20 08	-154	N11 55	69	HP	12	281 46	-189	N19 45	61
61'	18	210 36	-189	N 0 01	98	57'	18	101 04	-188	S23 14	41	54'	18	17 34	-157	N13 04	68	58'	18	278 37	-188	N18 44	65
3	00	207 27	-190	S 1 37	99	11	00	97 56	-185	S22 33	44	19	00	14 57	-159	N14 12	66	27	00	275 29	-187	N17 39	69
SUN	06	204 17	-191	S 3 16	97	MON	06	94 51	-181	S21 49	48	TUE	06	12 18	-162	N15 18	64	WED	06	272 22	-186	N16 30	72
HP	12	201 06	-192	S 4 53	97	HP	12	91 50	-178	S21 01	51	HP	12	9 36	-163	N16 22	61	HP	12	269 16	-184	N15 18	76
61'	18	197 54	-194	S 6 30	95	56'	18	88 52	-175	S20 10	54	54'	18	6 53	-166	N17 23	59	58'	18	266 12	-183	N14 02	79
4	00	194 40	-195	S 8 05	94	12	00	85 57	-171	S19 16	57	20	00	4 07	-169	N18 22	57	28	00	263 09	-182	N12 43	82
MON	06	191 25	-198	S 9 39	92	TUE	06	83 06	-168	S18 19	60	WED	06	1 18	-171	N19 19	53	THU	06	260 07	-181	N11 21	84
HP	12	188 07	-199	S11 11	88	HP	12	80 18	-165	S17 19	62	HP	12	358 27	-174	N20 12	50	HP	12	257 06	-180	N 9 57	87
61'	18	184 48	-201	S12 39	86	55'	18	77 33	-163	S16 17	65	55'	18	355 33	-177	N21 02	47	59'	18	254 06	-180	N 8 30	88
5	00	181 27	-204	S14 05	83	13	00	74 50	-159	S15 12	66	21	00	352 36	-179	N21 49	43	29	00	251 06	-180	N 7 02	91
TUE	06	178 03	-205	S15 28	78	WED	06	72 11	-158	S14 06	68	THU	06	349 37	-182	N22 32	40	FRI	06	248 06	-180	N 5 31	92
HP	12	174 38	-208	S16 46	75	HP	12	69 33	-155	S12 58	70	HP	12	346 35	-184	N23 12	35	HP	12	245 06	-180	N 3 59	93
61'	18	171 10	-209	S18 01	70	55'	18	66 58	-153	S11 48	71	55'	18	343 31	-187	N23 47	31	60'	18	242 06	-180	N 2 26	94
6	00	167 41	-212	S19 11	64	14	00	64 25	-151	S10 37	72	22	00	340 24	-189	N24 18	27	30	00	239 06	-182	N 0 52	95
WED	06	164 09	-213	S20 15	60	THU	06	61 54	-150	S 9 25	74	FRI	06	337 15	-191	N24 45	23	SAT	06	236 04	-182	S 0 43	95
HP	12	160 36	-215	S21 15	54	HP	12	59 24	-148	S 8 11	75	HP	12	334 04	-193	N25 08	17	HP	12	233 02	-183	S 2 18	95
60'	18	157 01	-216	S22 09	49	54'	18	56 56	-148	S 6 56	75	56'	18	330 51	-195	N25 25	13	60'	18	229 59	-185	S 3 53	94
7	00	153 25	-217	S22 58	42	15	00	54 28	-146	S 5 41	76	23	00	327 36	-196	N25 38	3	31	00	226 54		S 5 27	
THU	06	149 48	-217	S23 40	37	FRI	06	52 02	-146	S 4 25	76	SAT	06	324 20	-197	N25 46	3						
HP	12	146 11	-218	S24 17	30	HP	12	49 36	-145	S 3 09	77	HP	12	321 03	-198	N25 49	3						
60'	18	142 33	-218	S24 47	24	54'	18	47 11	-145	S 1 52	77	56'	18	317 45	-198	N25 46	7						
8	00	138 55	-216	S25 11	18	16	00	44 46	-145	S 0 35	77	24	00	314 27	-199	N25 39	13						
FRI	06	135 19	-216	S25 29	12	SAT	06	42 21	-145	N 0 42	77	SUN	06	311 08	-199	N25 26	18						
HP	12	131 43	-215	S25 41	5	HP	12	39 56	-145	N 1 59	77	HP	12	307 49	-198	N25 08	23						
59'	18	128 08	-212	S25 46	0	54'	18	37 31	-146	N 3 16	76	57'	18	304 31	-198	N24 45	28						
9	00	124° 36'		S25° 46'		17	00	35° 05'		N 4° 32'		25	00	301° 13'		N24° 17'							

Phases of the Moon
New: 4d   First Quarter: 11d
Full: 20d   Last Quarter: 27d

MOON AT EVERY 6hrs GMT DECEMBER 2002

Day	GMT	GHA-GMT	v	Dec	d	Day	GMT	GHA-GMT	v	Dec	d	Day	GMT	GHA-GMT	v	Dec	d	Day	GMT	GHA-GMT	v	Dec	d
1	00h	226° 54'	-186'	S 5° 27'	94'	9	00h	117° 08'	-181'	S20° 35'	55'	17	00h	34° 25'	-167'	N17° 09'	60'	25	00h	292° 46'	-181'	N13° 51'	78'
SUN	06	223 48	-188	S 7 01	93	MON	06	114 07	-177	S19 40	57	TUE	06	31 38	-168	N18 09	57	WED	06	289 45	-180	N12 33	81
HP	12	220 40	-191	S 8 34	90	HP	12	111 10	-173	S18 43	60	HP	12	28 50	-172	N19 06	55	HP	12	286 45	-179	N11 12	84
60'	18	217 29	-192	S10 04	89	56'	18	108 17	-170	S17 43	63	55'	18	25 58	-175	N20 01	51	59'	18	283 46	-178	N 9 48	85
2	00	214 17	-195	S11 33	87	10	00	105 27	-167	S16 40	65	18	00	23 03	-177	N20 52	48	26	00	280 48	-176	N 8 23	88
MON	06	211 02	-198	S13 00	83	TUE	06	102 40	-164	S15 35	67	WED	06	20 06	-181	N21 40	44	THU	06	277 52	-176	N 6 55	89
HP	12	207 44	-200	S14 23	81	HP	12	99 56	-161	S14 28	68	HP	12	17 05	-183	N22 24	40	HP	12	274 56	-176	N 5 26	90
61'	18	204 24	-203	S15 44	77	55'	18	97 15	-158	S13 20	71	55'	18	14 02	-186	N23 04	37	59'	18	272 00	-176	N 3 56	91
3	00	201 01	-206	S17 01	73	11	00	94 37	-156	S12 09	72	19	00	10 56	-189	N23 41	32	27	00	269 04	-175	N 2 25	92
TUE	06	197 35	-208	S18 14	68	WED	06	92 01	-154	S10 57	73	THU	06	7 47	-191	N24 13	28	FRI	06	266 09	-176	N 0 53	92
HP	12	194 07	-210	S19 22	64	HP	12	89 27	-152	S 9 44	74	HP	12	4 36	-194	N24 41	23	HP	12	263 13	-176	S 0 39	92
60'	18	190 37	-214	S20 26	59	55'	18	86 55	-150	S 8 30	75	56'	18	1 22	-195	N25 04	19	59'	18	260 17	-178	S 2 11	92
4	00	187 03	-215	S21 25	53	12	00	84 25	-148	S 7 15	75	20	00	358 07	-198	N25 23	13	28	00	257 19	-178	S 3 43	92
WED	06	183 28	-217	S22 18	48	THU	06	81 57	-148	S 6 00	77	FRI	06	354 49	-199	N25 36	8	SAT	06	254 21	-180	S 5 15	90
HP	12	179 51	-219	S23 06	42	HP	12	79 29	-146	S 4 43	77	HP	12	351 30	-201	N25 44	3	HP	12	251 21	-181	S 6 45	90
60'	18	176 12	-219	S23 48	36	54'	18	77 03	-146	S 3 26	77	56'	18	348 09	-201	N25 47	2	59'	18	248 20	-183	S 8 15	88
5	00	172 33	-221	S24 24	30	13	00	74 37	-145	S 2 09	77	21	00	344 48	-202	N25 45	7	29	00	245 17	-185	S 9 43	86
THU	06	168 52	-221	S24 54	23	FRI	06	72 12	-145	S 0 52	77	SAT	06	341 26	-203	N25 38	13	SUN	06	242 12	-187	S11 09	85
HP	12	165 11	-220	S25 17	17	HP	12	69 47	-145	N 0 25	77	HP	12	338 03	-202	N25 25	19	HP	12	239 05	-190	S12 34	82
59'	18	161 31	-220	S25 34	10	54'	18	67 22	-145	N 1 42	77	57'	18	334 41	-202	N25 06	23	60'	18	235 55	-192	S13 56	78
6	00	157 51	-219	S25 44	4	14	00	64 57	-146	N 2 59	76	22	00	331 19	-201	N24 43	29	30	00	232 43	-195	S15 14	76
FRI	06	154 12	-217	S25 48	1	SAT	06	62 31	-146	N 4 15	76	SUN	06	327 58	-200	N24 14	34	MON	06	229 28	-198	S16 30	73
HP	12	150 35	-215	S25 47	8	HP	12	60 05	-147	N 5 31	76	HP	12	324 38	-199	N23 40	40	HP	12	226 10	-200	S17 43	68
59'	18	147 00	-213	S25 39	14	54'	18	57 38	-148	N 6 47	74	57'	18	321 19	-197	N23 00	44	60'	18	222 50	-203	S18 51	64
7	00	143 27	-209	S25 25	20	15	00	55 10	-149	N 8 01	74	23	00	318 02	-196	N22 16	49	31	00	219 27	-206	S19 55	60
SAT	06	139 58	-207	S25 05	24	SUN	06	52 41	-151	N 9 15	72	MON	06	314 46	-194	N21 27	53	TUE	06	216 01	-209	S20 55	55
HP	12	136 31	-203	S24 41	30	HP	12	50 10	-152	N10 27	72	HP	12	311 32	-192	N20 34	58	HP	12	212 32	-210	S21 50	49
58'	18	133 08	-200	S24 11	35	54'	18	47 38	-154	N11 39	69	58'	18	308 20	-191	N19 36	61	59'	18	209 02	-213	S22 39	44
8	00	129 48	-196	S23 36	39	16	00	45 04	-157	N12 48	69	24	00	305 09	-188	N18 35	66	32	00	205 29		S23 23	
SUN	06	126 32	-192	S22 57	44	MON	06	42 27	-158	N13 57	66	TUE	06	302 01	-187	N17 29	69						
HP	12	123 20	-188	S22 13	47	HP	12	39 49	-161	N15 03	64	HP	12	298 54	-185	N16 20	73						
57'	18	120 12	-184	S21 26	51	55'	18	37 08	-163	N16 07	62	58'	18	295 49	-183	N15 07	76						
9	00	117° 08'		S20° 35'		17	00	34° 25'		N17° 09'		25	00	292° 46'		N13° 51'							

Phases of the Moon
New: 4d   First Quarter: 11d
Full: 19d   Last Quarter: 27d

MOON AT EVERY 6hrs GMT JANUARY 2003

Day GMT	GHA-GMT v	Dec	d	Day GMT	GHA-GMT v	Dec	d	Day GMT	GHA-GMT v	Dec	d	Day GMT	GHA-GMT v	Dec	d
1 00h	205° 29' -215'	S23° 23'	39'	9 00h	104° 58' -148'	S 3° 48'	77'	17 00h	16° 23' -203'	N25° 47'	1'	25 00h	274° 58' -181'	S 8° 34'	87'
WED 06	201 54 -217	S24 02	33	THU 06	102 30 -146	S 2 31	78	FRI 06	13 00 -205	N25 46	6	SAT 06	271 57 -183	S10 01	85
HP 12	198 17 -217	S24 35	27	HP 12	100 04 -146	S 1 13	78	HP 12	9 35 -206	N25 40	12	HP 12	268 54 -185	S11 26	82
59' 18	194 40 -218	S25 02	20	54' 18	97 38 -146	N 0 05	77	57' 18	6 09 -205	N25 28	17	59' 18	265 49 -186	S12 48	80
2 00	191 02 -219	S25 22	15	10 00	95 12 -146	N 1 22	78	18 00	2 44 -206	N25 11	23	26 00	262 43 -188	S14 08	78
THU 06	187 23 -218	S25 37	8	FRI 06	92 46 -145	N 2 40	76	SAT 06	359 18 -205	N24 48	28	SUN 06	259 35 -191	S15 26	73
HP 12	183 45 -217	S25 45	2	HP 12	90 21 -146	N 3 56	77	HP 12	355 53 -205	N24 20	34	HP 12	256 24 -193	S16 39	71
59' 18	180 08 -216	S25 47	4	54' 18	87 55 -147	N 5 13	75	58' 18	352 28 -204	N23 46	39	59' 18	253 11 -196	S17 50	67
3 00	176 32 -215	S25 43	10	11 00	85 28 -147	N 6 28	75	19 00	349 04 -202	N23 07	45	27 00	249 55 -198	S18 57	62
FRI 06	172 57 -212	S25 33	16	SAT 06	83 01 -149	N 7 43	74	SUN 06	345 42 -201	N22 22	49	MON 06	246 37 -200	S19 59	58
HP 12	169 25 -210	S25 17	22	HP 12	80 32 -149	N 8 57	72	HP 12	342 21 -200	N21 33	55	HP 12	243 17 -202	S20 57	54
58' 18	165 55 -207	S24 55	27	54' 18	78 03 -151	N10 09	71	58' 18	339 01 -197	N20 38	58	59' 18	239 55 -205	S21 51	48
4 00	162 28 -204	S24 28	32	12 00	75 32 -153	N11 20	70	20 00	335 44 -195	N19 40	63	28 00	236 30 -207	S22 39	44
SAT 06	159 04 -201	S23 56	37	SUN 06	72 59 -155	N12 30	68	MON 06	332 29 -194	N18 37	68	TUE 06	233 03 -208	S23 23	38
HP 12	155 43 -197	S23 19	41	HP 12	70 24 -157	N13 38	67	HP 12	329 15 -191	N17 29	71	HP 12	229 35 -210	S24 01	33
57' 18	152 26 -193	S22 38	46	54' 18	67 47 -159	N14 45	64	59' 18	326 04 -190	N16 18	74	59' 18	226 05 -212	S24 34	27
5 00	149 13 -190	S21 52	50	13 00	65 08 -161	N15 49	63	21 00	322 54 -187	N15 04	78	29 00	222 33 -212	S25 01	21
SUN 06	146 03 -186	S21 02	53	MON 06	62 27 -164	N16 52	60	TUE 06	319 47 -186	N13 46	81	WED 06	219 01 -212	S25 22	15
HP 12	142 57 -183	S20 09	57	HP 12	59 43 -167	N17 52	57	HP 12	316 41 -183	N12 25	83	HP 12	215 29 -213	S25 37	9
57' 18	139 54 -178	S19 12	60	55' 18	56 56 -170	N18 49	55	59' 18	313 38 -183	N11 02	85	58' 18	211 56 -213	S25 46	4
6 00	136 56 -175	S18 12	63	14 00	54 06 -172	N19 44	52	22 00	310 35 -180	N 9 37	88	30 00	208 23 -212	S25 50	3
MON 06	134 01 -172	S17 09	65	TUE 06	51 14 -176	N20 36	49	WED 06	307 35 -180	N 8 09	89	THU 06	204 51 -210	S25 47	8
HP 12	131 09 -169	S16 04	67	HP 12	48 18 -179	N21 25	45	HP 12	304 35 -179	N 6 40	90	HP 12	201 21 -209	S25 39	14
56' 18	128 20 -165	S14 57	70	55' 18	45 19 -182	N22 10	42	59' 18	301 36 -177	N 5 10	92	58' 18	197 52 -208	S25 25	19
7 00	125 35 -163	S13 47	71	15 00	42 17 -185	N22 52	38	23 00	298 39 -177	N 3 38	92	31 00	194 24 -205	S25 06	25
TUE 06	122 52 -159	S12 36	72	WED 06	39 12 -188	N23 30	33	THU 06	295 42 -177	N 2 06	92	FRI 06	190 59 -202	S24 41	30
HP 12	120 13 -158	S11 24	74	HP 12	36 04 -190	N24 03	30	HP 12	292 45 -177	N 0 34	93	HP 12	187 37 -200	S24 11	35
55' 18	117 35 -155	S10 10	75	56' 18	32 54 -194	N24 33	24	59' 18	289 48 -177	S 0 59	93	57' 18	184 17 -197	S23 36	40
8 00	115 00 -153	S 8 55	76	16 00	29 40 -196	N24 57	20	24 00	286 51 -177	S 2 32	92	32 00	181 00	S22 56	
WED 06	112 27 -151	S 7 39	76	THU 06	26 24 -198	N25 17	16	FRI 06	283 54 -178	S 4 04	91				
HP 12	109 56 -150	S 6 23	77	HP 12	23 06 -201	N25 33	9	HP 12	280 56 -178	S 5 35	90		Phases of the Moon		
55' 18	107 26 -148	S 5 06	78	56' 18	19 45 -202	N25 43	4	59' 18	277 58 -180	S 7 05	89		New: 2d First Quarter: 10d		
9 00	104° 58'	S 3° 48'		17 00	16° 23'	N25° 47'		25 00	274° 58'	S 8° 34'			Full: 18d Last Quarter: 25d		

MOON AT EVERY 6hrs GMT FEBRUARY 2003

Day GMT	GHA-GMT v	Dec	d	Day GMT	GHA-GMT v	Dec	d	Day GMT	GHA-GMT v	Dec	d	Day GMT	GHA-GMT v	Dec	d
1 00h	181° 00' -193'	S22° 56'	44'	9 00h	95° 50' -157'	N14° 33'	65'	17 00h	354° 37' -195'	N16° 50'	75'	25 00h	252° 39' -209'	S24° 50'	25'
SAT 06	177 47 -190	S22 12	48	SUN 06	93 13 -159	N15 38	63	MON 06	351 22 -193	N15 35	79	TUE 06	249 10 -210	S25 15	20
HP 12	174 37 -187	S21 24	53	HP 12	90 34 -162	N16 41	60	HP 12	348 09 -191	N14 16	83	HP 12	245 40 -209	S25 35	15
57' 18	171 30 -184	S20 31	55	54' 18	87 52 -164	N17 41	58	60' 18	344 58 -190	N12 53	85	58' 18	242 11 -210	S25 50	8
2 00	168 26 -180	S19 36	59	10 00	85 08 -166	N18 39	55	18 00	341 48 -188	N11 28	88	26 00	238 41 -209	S25 58	3
SUN 06	165 26 -177	S18 37	62	MON 06	82 22 -170	N19 34	52	TUE 06	338 40 -187	N10 00	90	WED 06	235 12 -207	S26 01	3
HP 12	162 29 -174	S17 35	65	HP 12	79 32 -172	N20 26	50	HP 12	335 33 -186	N 8 30	92	HP 12	231 45 -207	S25 58	9
56' 18	159 35 -171	S16 30	67	55' 18	76 40 -175	N21 16	46	60' 18	332 27 -184	N 6 58	94	57' 18	228 28 -205	S25 49	14
3 00	156 44 -167	S15 23	69	11 00	73 45 -178	N22 02	42	19 00	329 23 -184	N 5 24	94	27 00	224 53 -203	S25 35	20
MON 06	153 57 -165	S14 14	71	TUE 06	70 47 -181	N22 44	39	WED 06	326 19 -183	N 3 50	96	THU 06	221 30 -201	S25 15	24
HP 12	151 12 -162	S13 03	73	HP 12	67 46 -184	N23 23	35	HP 12	323 16 -183	N 2 14	96	HP 12	218 09 -199	S24 51	30
56' 18	148 30 -160	S11 50	75	55' 18	64 42 -187	N23 58	31	60' 18	320 13 -182	N 0 38	96	57' 18	214 50 -196	S24 21	35
4 00	145 50 -157	S10 35	75	12 00	61 35 -189	N24 29	27	20 00	317 11 -182	S 0 58	96	28 00	211 34 -193	S23 46	39
TUE 06	143 13 -156	S 9 20	77	WED 06	58 26 -193	N24 55	22	THU 06	314 09 -183	S 2 34	95	FRI 06	208 23 -190	S23 07	43
HP 12	140 37 -153	S 8 03	77	HP 12	55 13 -195	N25 17	17	HP 12	311 06 -183	S 4 09	94	HP 12	205 11 -188	S22 24	48
55' 18	138 04 -152	S 6 46	78	56' 18	51 58 -197	N25 34	12	60' 18	308 03 -183	S 5 43	93	56' 18	202 03 -184	S21 36	51
5 00	135 32 -150	S 5 28	78	13 00	48 41 -200	N25 46	8	21 00	305 00 -185	S 7 16	91	29 00	198 59 -181	S20 45	55
WED 06	133 02 -150	S 4 10	79	THU 06	45 21 -201	N25 54	1	FRI 06	301 55 -186	S 8 47	90	SAT 06	195 58 -178	S19 50	59
HP 12	130 32 -148	S 2 52	79	HP 12	42 00 -203	N25 52	5	HP 12	298 49 -186	S10 17	86	HP 12	193 00 -175	S18 51	61
55' 18	128 04 -147	S 1 32	78	57' 18	38 37 -204	N25 52	9	60' 18	295 43 -189	S11 43	85	56' 18	190 05 -172	S17 50	64
6 00	125 37 -147	S 0 14	79	14 00	35 13 -205	N25 43	15	22 00	292 34 -189	S13 08	81	30 00	187 13	S16 46	
THU 06	123 10 -146	N 1 05	78	FRI 06	31 48 -206	N25 28	20	SAT 06	289 25 -192	S14 29	78				
HP 12	120 44 -147	N 2 23	78	HP 12	28 22 -206	N25 08	26	HP 12	286 13 -193	S15 47	75				
54' 18	118 17 -146	N 3 41	77	58' 18	24 56 -206	N24 42	32	59' 18	283 00 -195	S17 02	70				
7 00	115 51 -147	N 4 58	76	15 00	21 30 -206	N24 10	37	23 00	279 45 -198	S18 12	67				
FRI 06	113 24 -147	N 6 14	75	SAT 06	18 04 -205	N23 33	43	SUN 06	276 27 -199	S19 19	62				
HP 12	110 57 -148	N 7 29	74	HP 12	14 39 -203	N22 50	48	HP 12	273 08 -201	S20 21	58				
54' 18	108 29 -149	N 8 43	73	58' 18	11 16 -203	N22 02	53	59' 18	269 47 -202	S21 19	52				
8 00	106 00 -151	N 9 56	72	16 00	7 53 -202	N21 09	58	24 00	266 25 -205	S22 11	48				
SAT 06	103 29 -151	N11 08	70	SUN 06	4 31 -199	N20 11	62	MON 06	263 00 -206	S22 59	42		Phases of the Moon		
HP 12	100 58 -153	N12 18	68	HP 12	1 12 -199	N19 09	67	HP 12	259 34 -207	S23 41	37		New: 1d First Quarter: 9d		
54' 18	98 25 -154	N13 26	67	59' 18	357 53 -196	N18 01	71	58' 18	256 07 -208	S24 18	32		Full: 16d Last Quarter: 23d		
9 00	95° 50'	N14° 33'		17 00	354° 37'	N16° 50'		25 00	252° 39'	S24° 50'					

MOON AT EVERY 6hrs GMT MARCH 2003

Day	GMT	GHA-GMT	v	Dec	d
1	00h	198°59'	-181	S20°45'	55'
SAT	06	195 58	-178	S19 50	59
HP	12	193 00	-175	S18 51	61
56'	18	190 05	-172	S17 50	64
2	00	187 13	-169	S16 46	67
SUN	06	184 24	-167	S15 39	68
HP	12	181 37	-164	S14 31	71
55'	18	178 53	-161	S13 20	73
3	00	176 12	-159	S12 07	74
MON	06	173 33	-157	S10 53	76
HP	12	170 56	-156	S 9 37	77
55'	18	168 20	-153	S 8 20	77
4	00	165 47	-152	S 7 03	79
TUE	06	163 15	-150	S 5 44	79
HP	12	160 45	-150	S 4 25	79
55'	18	158 15	-148	S 3 06	80
5	00	155 47	-148	S 1 46	79
WED	06	153 19	-147	S 0 27	78
HP	12	150 52	-147	N 0 53	79
54'	18	148 25	-147	N 2 12	78
6	00	145 58	-146	N 3 30	78
THU	06	143 32	-147	N 4 48	77
HP	12	141 05	-148	N 6 05	76
54'	18	138 37	-148	N 7 21	75
7	00	136 09	-149	N 8 36	74
FRI	06	133 40	-150	N 9 50	73
HP	12	131 10	-151	N11 03	70
54'	18	128 39	-152	N12 13	70
8	00	126 07	-154	N13 23	67
SAT	06	123 33	-156	N14 30	65
HP	12	120 57	-158	N15 35	64
54'	18	118 19	-160	N16 39	60
9	00	115°39'		N17°39'	
9	00h	115°39'	-162	N17°39'	59'
SUN	06	112 57	-164	N18 38	55
HP	12	110 13	-167	N19 33	53
54'	18	107 26	-169	N20 26	50
10	00	104 37	-172	N21 16	47
MON	06	101 45	-174	N22 03	43
HP	12	98 51	-177	N22 46	39
55'	18	95 54	-180	N23 25	36
11	00	92 54	-182	N24 01	32
TUE	06	89 52	-185	N24 33	27
HP	12	86 47	-188	N25 00	24
55'	18	83 39	-190	N25 24	18
12	00	80 29	-192	N25 42	14
WED	06	77 17	-194	N25 56	9
HP	12	74 03	-196	N26 05	4
56'	18	70 47	-198	N26 09	1
13	00	67 29	-199	N26 08	6
THU	06	64 10	-201	N26 02	12
HP	12	60 49	-201	N25 50	17
57'	18	57 28	-201	N25 33	23
14	00	54 07	-202	N25 10	28
FRI	06	50 45	-202	N24 42	33
HP	12	47 23	-202	N24 09	39
58'	18	44 01	-202	N23 30	44
15	00	40 39	-201	N22 46	50
SAT	06	37 18	-200	N21 56	55
HP	12	33 58	-199	N21 01	59
59'	18	30 39	-198	N20 02	65
16	00	27 21	-196	N18 57	69
SUN	06	24 05	-196	N17 48	73
HP	12	20 49	-194	N16 35	77
59'	18	17 35	-193	N15 18	81
17	00	14 22		N13 57	
17	00h	14°22'	-192	N13°57'	85'
MON	06	11 10	-191	N12 32	87
HP	12	7 59	-190	N11 05	91
60'	18	4 49	-189	N 9 34	93
18	00	1 40	-189	N 8 01	95
TUE	06	358 31	-188	N 6 26	97
HP	12	355 23	-187	N 4 49	98
61'	18	352 16	-188	N 3 11	99
19	00	349 08	-187	N 1 32	99
WED	06	346 01	-188	S 0 07	##
HP	12	342 53	-188	S 1 47	99
61'	18	339 45	-189	S 3 26	99
20	00	336 36	-189	S 5 05	97
THU	06	333 27	-191	S 6 42	96
HP	12	330 16	-192	S 8 18	94
61'	18	327 04	-194	S 9 52	92
21	00	323 50	-195	S11 24	89
FRI	06	320 35	-196	S12 53	86
HP	12	317 19	-199	S14 19	82
61'	18	314 00	-200	S15 41	78
22	00	310 40	-202	S16 59	75
SAT	06	307 18	-204	S18 14	69
HP	12	303 54	-206	S19 23	66
60'	18	300 28	-207	S20 29	60
23	00	297 01	-209	S21 29	54
SUN	06	293 32	-210	S22 23	50
HP	12	290 02	-212	S23 13	43
59'	18	286 30	-212	S23 56	38
24	00	282 58	-213	S24 34	32
MON	06	279 25	-214	S25 06	26
HP	12	275 51	-213	S25 32	20
59'	18	272 18	-213	S25 52	14
25	00	268°45'		S26°06'	
25	00h	268°45'	-212	S26°06'	8'
TUE	06	265 13	-211	S26 14	1
HP	12	261 42	-209	S26 15	4
58'	18	258 13	-208	S26 11	9
26	00	254 45	-205	S26 02	15
WED	06	251 20	-203	S25 47	21
HP	12	247 57	-201	S25 26	26
57'	18	244 36	-197	S25 00	30
27	00	241 19	-195	S24 30	36
THU	06	238 04	-192	S23 54	39
HP	12	234 52	-188	S23 15	44
61'	18	231 44	-185	S22 31	48
28	00	228 39	-182	S21 43	52
FRI	06	225 37	-179	S20 51	55
HP	12	222 38	-175	S19 56	59
56'	18	219 43	-173	S18 57	61
29	00	216 50	-169	S17 56	64
SAT	06	214 01	-167	S16 52	66
HP	12	211 14	-164	S15 46	69
55'	18	208 30	-162	S14 37	71
30	00	205 48	-159	S13 26	72
SUN	06	203 09	-157	S12 14	74
HP	12	200 32	-156	S11 00	76
55'	18	197 56	-153	S 9 44	77
31	00	195 23	-152	S 8 27	77
MON	06	192 51	-150	S 7 10	79
HP	12	190 21	-149	S 5 51	79
55'	18	187 52	-148	S 4 32	79
32	00	185 24		S 3 13	

Phases of the Moon
New: 3d   First Quarter: 11d
Full: 18d   Last Quarter: 25d

MOON AT EVERY 6hrs GMT APRIL 2003

Day	GMT	GHA-GMT	v	Dec	d
1	00h	185°24'	-148	S 3°13'	80'
TUE	06	182 56	-147	S 1 53	79
HP	12	180 29	-146	S 0 34	80
54'	18	178 03	-146	N 0 46	80
2	00	175 37	-146	N 2 06	79
WED	06	173 11	-146	N 3 25	78
HP	12	170 45	-147	N 4 43	78
54'	18	168 18	-147	N 6 01	77
3	00	165 51	-148	N 7 18	76
THU	06	163 23	-149	N 8 34	74
HP	12	160 54	-149	N 9 48	73
54'	18	158 25	-151	N11 01	72
4	00	155 54	-153	N12 13	70
FRI	06	153 21	-154	N13 23	68
HP	12	150 47	-155	N14 31	66
54'	18	148 12	-158	N15 37	64
5	00	145 34	-159	N16 41	62
SAT	06	142 55	-161	N17 43	59
HP	12	140 14	-164	N18 42	56
54'	18	137 30	-166	N19 38	53
6	00	134 44	-168	N20 31	50
SUN	06	131 56	-170	N21 21	47
HP	12	129 06	-173	N22 08	44
54'	18	126 13	-176	N22 52	40
7	00	123 17	-177	N23 32	36
MON	06	120 20	-180	N24 08	33
HP	12	117 20	-182	N24 41	28
55'	18	114 18	-185	N25 09	24
8	00	111 13	-186	N25 33	19
TUE	06	108 07	-188	N25 52	15
HP	12	104 59	-190	N26 07	10
55'	18	101 49	-192	N26 17	5
9	00	98°37'		N26°22'	
9	00h	98°37'	-193	N26°22'	1'
WED	06	95 24	-194	N26 23	5
HP	12	92 10	-195	N26 18	10
56'	18	88 55	-195	N26 08	15
10	00	85 40	-196	N25 53	20
THU	06	82 24	-197	N25 33	25
HP	12	79 07	-196	N25 08	31
57'	18	75 51	-196	N24 37	36
11	00	72 35	-196	N24 01	40
FRI	06	69 19	-195	N23 21	46
HP	12	66 04	-194	N22 35	51
58'	18	62 50	-194	N21 44	56
12	00	59 36	-192	N20 48	60
SAT	06	56 24	-192	N19 48	65
HP	12	53 12	-191	N18 43	69
58'	18	50 01	-190	N17 34	73
13	00	46 51	-189	N16 21	77
SUN	06	43 42	-189	N15 04	81
HP	12	40 33	-187	N13 43	85
59'	18	37 26	-187	N12 18	87
14	00	34 19	-187	N10 51	91
MON	06	31 12	-186	N 9 20	93
HP	12	28 06	-186	N 7 47	95
60'	18	25 00	-186	N 6 12	97
15	00	21 54	-187	N 4 35	99
TUE	06	18 47	-187	N 2 56	99
HP	12	15 40	-187	N 1 17	##
61'	18	12 33	-189	S 0 24	##
16	00	9 24	-189	S 2 04	##
WED	06	6 15	-191	S 3 45	##
HP	12	3 04	-193	S 5 25	##
61'	18	359 51	-194	S 7 05	97
17	00	356°37'		S 8°42'	
17	00h	356°37'	-196	S 8°42'	96'
THU	06	353 21	-198	S10 18	94
HP	12	350 03	-201	S11 52	91
61'	18	346 42	-203	S13 23	88
18	00	343 19	-205	S14 51	84
FRI	06	339 54	-207	S16 15	80
HP	12	336 27	-210	S17 35	75
61'	18	332 57	-212	S18 50	71
19	00	329 25	-215	S20 01	65
SAT	06	325 50	-216	S21 06	60
HP	12	322 14	-218	S22 06	55
61'	18	318 36	-219	S23 01	48
20	00	314 57	-221	S23 49	42
SUN	06	311 16	-222	S24 31	35
HP	12	307 34	-221	S25 06	29
60'	18	303 53	-222	S25 35	23
21	00	300 11	-221	S25 58	16
MON	06	296 30	-220	S26 14	9
HP	12	292 50	-218	S26 23	4
59'	18	289 12	-217	S26 27	4
22	00	285 35	-214	S26 23	9
TUE	06	282 01	-212	S26 14	15
HP	12	278 29	-209	S25 59	21
58'	18	275 00	-205	S25 38	26
23	00	271 35	-203	S25 12	31
WED	06	268 12	-198	S24 41	36
HP	12	264 54	-195	S24 05	41
57'	18	261 39	-191	S23 24	45
24	00	258 28	-188	S22 39	49
THU	06	255 20	-183	S21 50	52
HP	12	252 17	-180	S20 58	56
56'	18	249 17	-177	S20 02	60
25	00	246°20'		S19°02'	
25	00h	246°20'	-173	S19°02'	62'
FRI	06	243 27	-170	S18 00	64
HP	12	240 37	-167	S16 56	67
56'	18	237 50	-163	S15 49	69
26	00	235 07	-161	S14 40	72
SAT	06	232 26	-159	S13 28	72
HP	12	229 47	-156	S12 16	75
55'	18	227 11	-154	S11 01	75
27	00	224 37	-153	S 9 46	77
SUN	06	222 04	-150	S 8 29	77
HP	12	219 34	-149	S 7 12	79
55'	18	217 05	-148	S 5 53	79
28	00	214 37	-147	S 4 34	79
MON	06	212 10	-147	S 3 15	80
HP	12	209 43	-145	S 1 55	80
54'	18	207 18	-146	S 0 35	79
29	00	204 52	-145	N 0 44	80
TUE	06	202 27	-145	N 2 04	79
HP	12	200 02	-145	N 3 23	78
54'	18	197 37	-146	N 4 41	78
30	00	195 11	-146	N 5 59	77
WED	06	192 45	-148	N 7 16	76
HP	12	190 17	-148	N 8 32	75
54'	18	187 49	-149	N 9 47	74
31	00	185 20		N11 01	

Phases of the Moon
New: 1d   First Quarter: 9d
Full: 16d   Last Quarter: 23d

MOON AT EVERY 6hrs GMT MAY 2003

Day	GMT	GHA-GMT	v	Dec	d
1	00h	185°20'	-151'	N11°01'	72'
THU	06	182 49	-152	N12 13	70
HP	12	180 17	-154	N13 23	69
54'	18	177 43	-156	N14 32	66
2	00	175 07	-157	N15 38	65
FRI	06	172 30	-160	N16 43	62
HP	12	169 50	-162	N17 45	59
54'	18	167 08	-164	N18 44	57
3	00	164 24	-166	N19 41	54
SAT	06	161 38	-168	N20 35	50
HP	12	158 50	-171	N21 25	48
54'	18	155 59	-173	N22 13	44
4	00	153 06	-176	N22 57	40
SUN	06	150 10	-177	N23 37	37
HP	12	147 13	-180	N24 14	32
54'	18	144 13	-182	N24 46	28
5	00	141 11	-184	N25 14	24
MON	06	138 07	-186	N25 38	20
HP	12	135 01	-187	N25 58	15
55'	18	131 54	-189	N26 13	10
6	00	128 45	-190	N26 23	6
TUE	06	125 35	-191	N26 29	0
HP	12	122 24	-192	N26 29	4
55'	18	119 12	-192	N26 25	9
7	00	116 00	-192	N26 16	15
WED	06	112 48	-193	N26 01	19
HP	12	109 35	-192	N25 42	24
56'	18	106 23	-193	N25 18	30
8	00	103 10	-191	N24 48	34
THU	06	99 59	-191	N24 14	39
HP	12	96 48	-190	N23 35	44
57'	18	93 38	-189	N22 51	48
9	00	90 29'		N22°03'	
9	00h	90°29'	-188'	N22°03'	53'
FRI	06	87 21	-187	N21 10	58
HP	12	84 14	-186	N20 12	61
57'	18	81 08	-185	N19 11	66
10	00	78 03	-184	N18 05	70
SAT	06	74 59	-183	N16 55	73
HP	12	71 56	-182	N15 42	77
58'	18	68 54	-181	N14 25	80
11	00	65 53	-181	N13 05	84
SUN	06	62 52	-180	N11 41	86
HP	12	59 52	-180	N10 15	89
59'	18	56 52	-180	N 8 46	91
12	00	53 52	-180	N 7 15	94
MON	06	50 52	-180	N 5 41	95
HP	12	47 52	-181	N 4 06	96
60'	18	44 51	-182	N 2 30	98
13	00	41 49	-183	N 0 52	99
TUE	06	38 46	-184	S 0 47	99
HP	12	35 42	-186	S 2 26	99
61'	18	32 36	-188	S 4 05	99
14	00	29 28	-189	S 5 44	97
WED	06	26 19	-192	S 7 21	97
HP	12	23 07	-195	S 8 58	95
61'	18	19 52	-197	S10 33	94
15	00	16 35	-201	S12 07	90
THU	06	13 14	-203	S13 37	88
HP	12	9 51	-206	S15 05	84
61'	18	6 25	-209	S16 29	80
16	00	2 56	-213	S17 49	75
FRI	06	359 23	-215	S19 04	71
HP	12	355 48	-219	S20 15	66
61'	18	352 09	-221	S21 21	60
17	00	348 28'		S22°21'	
17	00h	348°28'	-223'	S22°21'	54'
SAT	06	344 45	-225	S23 15	48
HP	12	341 00	-227	S24 03	42
61'	18	337 13	-228	S24 45	34
18	00	333 25	-229	S25 19	28
SUN	06	329 36	-228	S25 47	21
HP	12	325 48	-228	S26 08	14
60'	18	322 00	-227	S26 22	7
19	00	318 13	-226	S26 29	1
MON	06	314 27	-223	S26 30	7
HP	12	310 44	-221	S26 23	12
59'	18	307 03	-218	S26 11	19
20	00	303 25	-214	S25 52	25
TUE	06	299 51	-211	S25 27	30
HP	12	296 20	-206	S24 57	36
58'	18	292 54	-203	S24 21	41
21	00	289 31	-199	S23 40	45
WED	06	286 12	-194	S22 55	49
HP	12	282 58	-190	S22 06	53
57'	18	279 48	-185	S21 13	57
22	00	276 43	-182	S20 16	60
THU	06	273 41	-178	S19 16	63
HP	12	270 43	-174	S18 13	66
56'	18	267 49	-170	S17 07	68
23	00	264 59	-167	S15 59	70
FRI	06	262 12	-164	S14 49	73
HP	12	259 28	-161	S13 36	73
56'	18	256 47	-158	S12 23	75
24	00	254 09	-156	S11 08	77
SAT	06	251 33	-154	S 9 51	77
HP	12	248 59	-151	S 8 34	78
55'	18	246 28	-150	S 7 16	79
25	00	243 58'		S 5°57'	
25	00h	243°58'	-149'	S 5°57'	80'
SUN	06	241 29	-147	S 4 37	79
HP	12	239 02	-147	S 3 18	80
55'	18	236 35	-145	S 1 58	80
26	00	234 10	-146	S 0 38	80
MON	06	231 44	-145	N 0 42	79
HP	12	229 20	-145	N 2 01	79
54'	18	226 55	-145	N 3 20	79
27	00	224 30	-146	N 4 39	78
TUE	06	222 04	-146	N 5 57	77
HP	12	219 38	-147	N 7 14	76
54'	18	217 11	-148	N 8 30	75
28	00	214 43	-149	N 9 45	73
WED	06	212 14	-151	N10 58	72
HP	12	209 43	-152	N12 10	71
54'	18	207 11	-153	N13 21	68
29	00	204 38	-156	N14 29	67
THU	06	202 02	-158	N15 36	65
HP	12	199 24	-159	N16 41	62
54'	18	196 45	-162	N17 43	60
30	00	194 03	-165	N18 43	57
FRI	06	191 18	-166	N19 40	54
HP	12	188 32	-170	N20 34	51
54'	18	185 42	-171	N21 25	47
31	00	182 51	-174	N22 12	45
SAT	06	179 57	-177	N22 57	40
HP	12	177 00	-178	N23 37	37
54'	18	174 02	-181	N24 14	32
32	00	171 01		N24 46	

Phases of the Moon
New: 1d&31d   First Quarter: 9d
Full: 16d   Last Quarter: 23d

MOON AT EVERY 6hrs GMT JUNE 2003

Day	GMT	GHA-GMT	v	Dec	d
1	00h	171°01'	-184'	N24°46'	29'
SUN	06	167 57	-185	N25 15	24
HP	12	164 52	-187	N25 39	19
55'	18	161 45	-188	N25 58	15
2	00	158 37	-190	N26 13	10
MON	06	155 27	-191	N26 23	6
HP	12	152 16	-192	N26 29	0
55'	18	149 04	-193	N26 29	5
3	00	145 51	-192	N26 24	9
TUE	06	142 39	-193	N26 15	15
HP	12	139 26	-193	N26 00	20
56'	18	136 13	-192	N25 40	24
4	00	133 01	-191	N25 16	30
WED	06	129 50	-191	N24 46	34
HP	12	126 39	-190	N24 12	40
56'	18	123 29	-188	N23 32	43
5	00	120 21	-187	N22 49	49
THU	06	117 14	-186	N22 00	52
HP	12	114 08	-184	N21 08	56
57'	18	111 04	-183	N20 11	61
6	00	108 01	-181	N19 10	64
FRI	06	105 00	-180	N18 06	69
HP	12	102 00	-179	N16 57	71
57'	18	99 01	-177	N15 46	75
7	00	96 04	-177	N14 33	78
SAT	06	93 07	-175	N13 13	81
HP	12	90 12	-175	N11 52	84
58'	18	87 17	-174	N10 28	86
8	00	84 23	-174	N 9 02	88
SUN	06	81 29	-174	N 7 34	90
HP	12	78 35	-174	N 6 04	91
59'	18	75 41	-174	N 4 33	93
9	00	72 47'		N 3°00'	
9	00h	72°47'	-175'	N 3°00'	94'
MON	06	69 52	-176	N 1 26	95
HP	12	66 56	-177	S 0 09	96
59'	18	63 59	-179	S 1 45	96
10	00	61 00	-180	S 3 21	95
TUE	06	58 00	-182	S 4 56	94
HP	12	54 58	-185	S 6 32	94
60'	18	51 53	-187	S 8 06	93
11	00	48 46	-190	S 9 39	92
WED	06	45 36	-193	S11 11	90
HP	12	42 23	-195	S12 41	87
61'	18	39 08	-200	S14 08	84
12	00	35 48	-202	S15 32	81
THU	06	32 26	-206	S16 53	78
HP	12	29 00	-210	S18 11	73
61'	18	25 30	-213	S19 24	68
13	00	21 57	-217	S20 32	64
FRI	06	18 20	-219	S21 36	58
HP	12	14 41	-223	S22 34	52
61'	18	10 58	-225	S23 26	46
14	00	7 13	-227	S24 12	40
SAT	06	3 26	-229	S24 52	33
HP	12	359 37	-230	S25 25	26
60'	18	355 47	-231	S25 51	20
15	00	351 56	-230	S26 11	12
SUN	06	348 06	-230	S26 23	5
HP	12	344 16	-229	S26 28	1
60'	18	340 27	-227	S26 27	9
16	00	336 40	-224	S26 18	15
MON	06	332 56	-222	S26 03	21
HP	12	329 14	-218	S25 42	28
59'	18	325 36	-214	S25 14	33
17	00	322 02'		S24°41'	
17	00h	322°02'	-211'	S24°41'	39'
TUE	06	318 31	-206	S24 02	44
HP	12	315 05	-202	S23 18	48
58'	18	311 43	-198	S22 30	53
18	00	308 25	-193	S21 37	57
WED	06	305 12	-189	S20 40	64
HP	12	302 03	-185	S19 40	64
57'	18	298 58	-180	S18 36	66
19	00	295 58	-177	S17 30	69
THU	06	293 01	-173	S16 21	71
HP	12	290 08	-169	S15 10	74
57'	18	287 19	-166	S13 56	75
20	00	284 33	-162	S12 41	76
FRI	06	281 51	-160	S11 25	78
HP	12	279 11	-158	S10 07	78
56'	18	276 33	-155	S 8 49	80
21	00	273 58	-153	S 7 29	80
SAT	06	271 25	-151	S 6 09	80
HP	12	268 54	-150	S 4 49	81
55'	18	266 24	-148	S 3 28	81
22	00	263 56	-148	S 2 07	80
SUN	06	261 28	-147	S 0 47	81
HP	12	259 01	-146	N 0 34	80
55'	18	256 35	-147	N 1 54	80
23	00	254 09	-146	N 3 14	78
MON	06	251 43	-146	N 4 33	78
HP	12	249 17	-146	N 5 51	77
54'	18	246 51	-148	N 7 08	76
24	00	244 23	-148	N 8 24	75
TUE	06	241 55	-149	N 9 39	74
HP	12	239 26	-151	N10 53	72
54'	18	236 55	-152	N12 05	71
25	00	234 23'		N13°16'	
25	00h	234°23'	-153'	N13°16'	68'
WED	06	231 50	-156	N14 24	67
HP	12	229 14	-157	N15 31	65
54'	18	226 37	-160	N16 36	62
26	00	223 57	-162	N17 38	60
THU	06	221 15	-164	N18 38	57
HP	12	218 31	-167	N19 35	54
54'	18	215 44	-169	N20 29	51
27	00	212 55	-172	N21 20	48
FRI	06	210 03	-174	N22 08	45
HP	12	207 09	-177	N22 53	41
54'	18	204 12	-180	N23 34	37
28	00	201 12	-181	N24 11	33
SAT	06	198 11	-185	N24 44	28
HP	12	195 06	-186	N25 12	24
55'	18	192 00	-188	N25 36	20
29	00	188 52	-190	N25 56	15
SUN	06	185 42	-192	N26 11	10
HP	12	182 30	-193	N26 21	6
55'	18	179 17	-194	N26 27	0
30	00	176 03	-195	N26 27	5
MON	06	172 48	-194	N26 22	10
HP	12	169 34	-195	N26 12	15
56'	18	166 19	-195	N25 57	21
31	00	163 04		N25 36	

Phases of the Moon
New: 29d   First Quarter: 7d
Full: 14d   Last Quarter: 21d

MOON AT EVERY 6hrs GMT JULY 2003

Day GMT	GHA-GMT	v	Dec	d	Day GMT	GHA-GMT	v	Dec	d	Day GMT	GHA-GMT	v	Dec	d	Day GMT	GHA-GMT	v	Dec	d
1 00h	163°04'	-195	N25°36'	25'	9 00h	67°00'	-192	S13°50'	83'	17 00h	315°49'	-170	S14°27'	76'	25 00h	231°54'	-179	N23°30'	38'
TUE 06	159 49	-193	N25 11	30	WED 06	63 48	-195	S15 13	79	THU 06	312 59	-168	S13 11	78	FRI 06	228 55	-181	N24 08	33
HP 12	156 36	-193	N24 41	36	HP 12	60 33	-198	S16 32	76	HP 12	310 11	-165	S11 53	79	HP 12	225 54	-184	N24 41	30
56' 18	153 23	-191	N24 05	40	60' 18	57 15	-202	S17 48	72	56' 18	307 26	-161	S10 34	80	55' 18	222 50	-186	N25 11	25
2 00	150 12	-190	N23 25	44	10 00	53 53	-205	S19 00	68	18 00	304 45	-159	S 9 14	80	26 00	219 44	-189	N25 36	20
WED 06	147 02	-189	N22 41	49	THU 06	50 28	-209	S20 08	64	FRI 06	302 06	-157	S 7 54	82	SAT 06	216 35	-190	N25 56	16
HP 12	143 53	-187	N21 52	54	HP 12	46 59	-212	S21 12	59	HP 12	299 29	-155	S 6 32	82	HP 12	213 25	-192	N26 12	11
57' 18	140 46	-185	N20 58	58	60' 18	43 27	-215	S22 11	53	56' 18	296 54	-153	S 5 10	82	55' 18	210 13	-194	N26 23	5
3 00	137 41	-184	N20 00	61	11 00	39 52	-219	S23 04	48	19 00	294 21	-152	S 3 48	82	27 00	206 59	-195	N26 28	1
THU 06	134 37	-181	N18 59	66	FRI 06	36 13	-220	S23 52	41	SAT 06	291 49	-150	S 2 26	82	SUN 06	203 44	-195	N26 29	4
HP 12	131 36	-180	N17 53	69	HP 12	32 33	-224	S24 33	36	HP 12	289 19	-149	S 1 04	82	HP 12	200 29	-197	N26 25	10
57' 18	128 36	-179	N16 44	72	60' 18	28 49	-225	S25 09	29	55' 18	286 50	-149	N 0 18	81	56' 18	197 12	-197	N26 15	14
4 00	125 37	-177	N15 32	75	12 00	25 04	-226	S25 38	23	20 00	284 21	-148	N 1 39	81	28 00	193 55	-197	N26 01	20
FRI 06	122 40	-176	N14 17	79	SAT 06	21 18	-227	S26 01	16	SUN 06	281 53	-148	N 3 00	80	MON 06	190 38	-196	N25 41	26
HP 12	119 44	-174	N12 58	80	HP 12	17 31	-228	S26 17	9	HP 12	279 25	-147	N 4 20	79	HP 12	187 22	-196	N25 15	30
58' 18	116 50	-173	N11 38	84	60' 18	13 43	-227	S26 26	2	55' 18	276 58	-148	N 5 39	79	56' 18	184 06	-196	N24 45	35
5 00	113 57	-173	N10 14	85	13 00	9 56	-226	S26 28	5	21 00	274 30	-149	N 6 58	77	29 00	180 50	-194	N24 10	41
SAT 06	111 04	-172	N 8 49	87	SUN 06	6 10	-225	S26 23	11	MON 06	272 01	-149	N 8 15	75	TUE 06	177 36	-193	N23 29	45
HP 12	108 12	-171	N 7 22	89	HP 12	2 25	-223	S26 12	18	HP 12	269 32	-149	N 9 30	75	HP 12	174 23	-192	N22 44	50
58' 18	105 21	-171	N 5 53	91	59' 18	358 42	-220	S25 54	24	54' 18	267 03	-151	N10 45	72	57' 18	171 11	-190	N21 54	55
6 00	102 30	-171	N 4 22	91	14 00	355 02	-217	S25 30	30	22 00	264 32	-152	N11 57	71	30 00	168 01	-189	N20 59	59
SUN 06	99 39	-171	N 2 51	93	MON 06	351 25	-214	S25 00	36	TUE 06	262 00	-154	N13 08	70	WED 06	164 52	-187	N20 00	63
HP 12	96 48	-172	N 1 18	93	HP 12	347 51	-210	S24 24	41	HP 12	259 26	-156	N14 18	67	HP 12	161 45	-185	N18 57	66
59' 18	93 56	-173	S 0 15	93	59' 18	344 21	-207	S23 43	47	54' 18	256 50	-157	N15 25	65	57' 18	158 40	-183	N17 51	71
7 00	91 03	-174	S 1 48	93	15 00	340 54	-202	S22 56	51	23 00	254 13	-159	N16 30	62	31 00	155 37	-182	N16 40	74
MON 06	88 09	-175	S 3 21	93	TUE 06	337 32	-199	S22 05	55	WED 06	251 34	-161	N17 32	60	THU 06	152 35	-180	N15 26	77
HP 12	85 14	-177	S 4 54	93	HP 12	334 13	-194	S21 10	59	HP 12	248 53	-164	N18 32	58	HP 12	149 35	-178	N14 09	80
59' 18	82 17	-178	S 6 27	92	58' 18	330 59	-190	S20 11	63	54' 18	246 09	-166	N19 30	54	58' 18	146 37	-177	N12 49	83
8 00	79 19	-181	S 7 59	90	16 00	327 49	-185	S19 08	67	24 00	243 23	-168	N20 24	52	32 00	143 40		N11 26	
TUE 06	76 18	-183	S 9 29	89	WED 06	324 44	-182	S18 01	69	THU 06	240 35	-171	N21 16	48					
HP 12	73 15	-186	S10 58	87	HP 12	321 42	-178	S16 52	71	HP 12	237 44	-174	N22 04	45		Phases of the Moon			
60' 18	70 09	-189	S12 25	85	57' 18	318 44	-175	S15 41	74	54' 18	234 50	-176	N22 49	41		New: 29d First Quarter: 7d			
9 00	67°00'		S13°50'		17 00	315°49'		S14°27'		25 00	231°54'		N23°30'			Full: 13d Last Quarter: 21d			

MOON AT EVERY 6hrs GMT AUGUST 2003

Day GMT	GHA-GMT	v	Dec	d	Day GMT	GHA-GMT	v	Dec	d	Day GMT	GHA-GMT	v	Dec	d	Day GMT	GHA-GMT	v	Dec	d
1 00h	143°40'	-176'	N11°26'	85'	9 00h	41°51'	-222	S26°30'	3'	17 00h	304°55'	-149	N 5°23'	80'	25 00h	212°25'	-196	N25°04'	34'
FRI 06	140 44	-175	N10 01	87	SAT 06	38 09	-221	S26 33	3	SUN 06	302 26	-150	N 6 43	78	MON 06	209 09	-196	N24 30	40
HP 12	137 49	-174	N 8 34	89	HP 12	34 28	-220	S26 30	9	HP 12	299 56	-150	N 8 01	77	HP 12	205 53	-194	N23 50	44
58' 18	134 55	-173	N 7 05	90	59' 18	30 48	-219	S26 21	16	55' 18	297 26	-151	N 9 18	75	57' 18	202 39	-194	N23 06	49
2 00	132 02	-172	N 5 35	91	10 00	27 09	-217	S26 05	21	18 00	294 55	-151	N10 33	74	26 00	199 25	-192	N22 17	54
SAT 06	129 10	-173	N 4 04	93	SUN 06	23 32	-214	S25 44	28	MON 06	292 24	-153	N11 47	72	TUE 06	196 13	-191	N21 23	59
HP 12	126 17	-172	N 2 31	93	HP 12	19 58	-212	S25 16	34	HP 12	289 51	-154	N12 59	70	HP 12	193 02	-190	N20 24	63
59' 18	123 25	-173	N 0 58	94	59' 18	16 26	-209	S24 42	39	54' 18	287 17	-155	N14 09	69	58' 18	189 52	-188	N19 21	67
3 00	120 32	-173	S 0 36	94	11 00	12 57	-205	S24 03	44	19 00	284 42	-157	N15 18	65	27 00	186 44	-187	N18 14	71
SUN 06	117 39	-173	S 2 10	93	MON 06	9 32	-202	S23 19	49	TUE 06	282 05	-159	N16 23	64	WED 06	183 37	-185	N17 03	75
HP 12	114 46	-175	S 3 43	93	HP 12	6 10	-198	S22 30	54	HP 12	279 26	-161	N17 27	61	HP 12	180 32	-184	N15 48	78
59' 18	111 51	-176	S 5 16	92	58' 18	2 52	-195	S21 36	58	54' 18	276 45	-162	N18 28	58	58' 18	177 28	-182	N14 30	81
4 00	108 55	-178	S 6 48	91	12 00	359 37	-191	S20 38	61	20 00	274 03	-165	N19 26	55	28 00	174 26	-181	N13 09	85
MON 06	105 57	-179	S 8 19	90	TUE 06	356 26	-187	S19 37	65	WED 06	271 18	-168	N20 21	52	THU 06	171 25	-180	N11 44	87
HP 12	102 58	-182	S 9 49	88	HP 12	353 19	-183	S18 32	69	HP 12	268 30	-169	N21 13	49	HP 12	168 25	-179	N10 17	89
59' 18	99 56	-183	S11 17	86	57' 18	350 16	-180	S17 23	71	54' 18	265 41	-172	N22 02	46	59' 18	165 26	-178	N 8 48	91
5 00	96 53	-186	S12 43	83	13 00	347 16	-176	S16 12	73	21 00	262 49	-175	N22 48	42	29 00	162 28	-177	N 7 17	93
TUE 06	93 47	-189	S14 06	81	WED 06	344 20	-173	S14 59	76	THU 06	259 54	-179	N23 30	38	FRI 06	159 31	-177	N 5 44	94
HP 12	90 38	-191	S15 27	78	HP 12	341 27	-170	S13 43	78	HP 12	256 57	-179	N24 08	35	HP 12	156 34	-177	N 4 10	96
59' 18	87 27	-195	S16 45	74	57' 18	338 37	-167	S12 25	79	55' 18	253 58	-182	N24 43	30	59' 18	153 37	-176	N 2 34	96
6 00	84 12	-197	S17 59	71	14 00	335 50	-164	S11 06	81	22 00	250 56	-184	N25 13	26	30 00	150 41	-177	N 0 58	96
WED 06	80 55	-200	S19 10	66	THU 06	333 06	-162	S 9 45	82	FRI 06	247 52	-187	N25 39	21	SAT 06	147 44	-177	S 0 38	97
HP 12	77 35	-204	S20 16	62	HP 12	330 24	-159	S 8 23	82	HP 12	244 45	-188	N26 00	17	HP 12	144 47	-178	S 2 15	96
59' 18	74 11	-206	S21 18	57	56' 18	327 45	-158	S 7 01	83	55' 18	241 37	-190	N26 17	12	60' 18	141 49	-179	S 3 51	95
7 00	70 45	-209	S22 15	52	15 00	325 07	-155	S 5 38	83	23 00	238 27	-192	N26 29	2	31 00	138 50	-180	S 5 26	93
THU 06	67 16	-212	S23 07	47	FRI 06	322 32	-154	S 4 15	84	SAT 06	235 15	-194	N26 37	2	SUN 06	135 50	-181	S 7 01	93
HP 12	63 44	-215	S23 54	41	HP 12	319 58	-152	S 2 51	84	HP 12	232 01	-194	N26 39	3	HP 12	132 49	-183	S 8 34	92
59' 18	60 09	-217	S24 35	36	56' 18	317 26	-152	S 1 27	83	55' 18	228 47	-196	N26 36	8	60' 18	129 46	-184	S10 06	89
8 00	56 32	-218	S25 11	29	16 00	314 54	-150	S 0 04	83	24 00	225 31	-196	N26 28	13	32 00	126 42		S11 35	
FRI 06	52 54	-220	S25 40	23	SAT 06	312 24	-150	N 1 19	82	SUN 06	222 15	-196	N26 16	18					
HP 12	49 14	-221	S26 03	17	HP 12	309 54	-150	N 2 41	81	HP 12	218 58	-196	N25 57	24		Phases of the Moon			
59' 18	45 33	-222	S26 20	10	55' 18	307 24	-149	N 4 02	81	56' 18	215 42	-197	N25 33	29		New: 27d First Quarter: 5d			
9 00	41°51'		S26°30'		17 00	304°55'		N 5°23'		25 00	212°25'		N25°04'			Full: 12d Last Quarter: 20d			

MOON AT EVERY 6hrs GMT SEPTEMBER 2003

Day GMT	GHA-GMT	v	Dec	d
1 00h	126° 42'	-187'	S11° 35'	87'
MON 06	123 35	-189	S13 02	85
HP 12	120 26	-191	S14 27	82
60' 18	117 15	-193	S15 49	78
2 00	114 02	-196	S17 07	74
TUE 06	110 46	-199	S18 21	71
HP 12	107 27	-201	S19 32	66
59' 18	104 06	-204	S20 38	61
3 00	100 42	-206	S21 39	56
WED 06	97 16	-209	S22 35	52
HP 12	93 47	-211	S23 27	46
59' 18	90 16	-212	S24 13	40
4 00	86 44	-215	S24 53	34
THU 06	83 09	-216	S25 27	28
HP 12	79 33	-217	S25 55	22
59' 18	75 56	-218	S26 17	16
5 00	72 18	-218	S26 33	9
FRI 06	68 40	-217	S26 42	3
HP 12	65 03	-217	S26 45	3
58' 18	61 26	-216	S26 42	10
6 00	57 50	-214	S26 32	16
SAT 06	54 16	-213	S26 16	21
HP 12	50 43	-209	S25 55	27
58' 18	47 14	-208	S25 28	33
7 00	43 46	-204	S24 55	39
SUN 06	40 22	-202	S24 16	43
HP 12	37 00	-198	S23 33	48
58' 18	33 42	-195	S22 45	52
8 00	30 27	-191	S21 53	57
MON 06	27 16	-188	S20 56	60
HP 12	24 08	-185	S19 56	64
57' 18	21 03	-181	S18 52	67
9 00	18° 02'		S17° 45'	

Day GMT	GHA-GMT	v	Dec	d
9 00h	18° 02'	-177'	S17° 45'	71'
TUE 06	15 05	-175	S16 34	72
HP 12	12 10	-172	S15 22	75
57' 18	9 18	-168	S14 07	77
10 00	6 30	-167	S12 50	79
WED 06	3 43	-163	S11 31	81
HP 12	1 00	-161	S10 10	81
56' 18	358 19	-159	S 8 49	83
11 00	355 40	-158	S 7 26	83
THU 06	353 02	-155	S 6 03	84
HP 12	350 27	-154	S 4 39	84
56' 18	347 53	-153	S 3 15	84
12 00	345 20	-152	S 1 51	84
FRI 06	342 48	-151	S 0 27	84
HP 12	340 17	-151	N 0 57	84
55' 18	337 46	-150	N 2 21	82
13 00	335 16	-149	N 3 43	82
SAT 06	332 47	-150	N 5 05	81
HP 12	330 17	-151	N 6 26	80
55' 18	327 46	-150	N 7 46	78
14 00	325 16	-151	N 9 04	77
SUN 06	322 45	-152	N10 21	75
HP 12	320 13	-153	N11 36	73
54' 18	317 40	-154	N12 49	71
15 00	315 06	-156	N14 00	70
MON 06	312 30	-157	N15 10	67
HP 12	309 53	-158	N16 17	64
54' 18	307 15	-160	N17 21	62
16 00	304 35	-163	N18 23	59
TUE 06	301 52	-164	N19 22	57
HP 12	299 08	-166	N20 19	53
54' 18	296 22	-168	N21 12	50
17 00	293° 34'		N22° 02'	

Day GMT	GHA-GMT	v	Dec	d
17 00h	293° 34'	-171'	N22° 02'	46'
WED 06	290 43	-173	N22 48	43
HP 12	287 50	-175	N23 31	40
54' 18	284 55	-177	N24 11	35
18 00	281 58	-180	N24 46	31
THU 06	278 58	-181	N25 17	28
HP 12	275 57	-184	N25 45	22
55' 18	272 53	-185	N26 07	19
19 00	269 48	-187	N26 26	13
FRI 06	266 41	-189	N26 39	9
HP 12	263 32	-190	N26 48	4
55' 18	260 22	-192	N26 52	1
20 00	257 10	-192	N26 51	6
SAT 06	253 58	-193	N26 45	11
HP 12	250 45	-193	N26 34	16
56' 18	247 32	-194	N26 18	21
21 00	244 18	-194	N25 57	26
SUN 06	241 04	-193	N25 31	32
HP 12	237 51	-194	N24 59	37
56' 18	234 37	-192	N24 22	41
22 00	231 25	-192	N23 41	47
MON 06	228 13	-191	N22 54	51
HP 12	225 02	-190	N22 03	56
57' 18	221 52	-189	N21 07	61
23 00	218 43	-188	N20 06	65
TUE 06	215 35	-187	N19 01	69
HP 12	212 28	-185	N17 52	73
58' 18	209 23	-185	N16 39	77
24 00	206 18	-183	N15 22	81
WED 06	203 15	-183	N14 01	84
HP 12	200 12	-182	N12 37	87
59' 18	197 10	-181	N11 10	89
25 00	194° 09'		N 9° 41'	

Day GMT	GHA-GMT	v	Dec	d
25 00h	194° 09'	-180'	N 9° 41'	92'
THU 06	191 09	-180	N 8 09	94
HP 12	188 09	-180	N 6 35	96
60' 18	185 09	-180	N 4 59	97
26 00	182 09	-180	N 3 22	99
FRI 06	179 09	-181	N 1 43	99
HP 12	176 08	-181	N 0 04	##
60' 18	173 07	-183	S 1 36	99
27 00	170 04	-183	S 3 15	99
SAT 06	167 01	-185	S 4 54	99
HP 12	163 56	-186	S 6 33	97
60' 18	160 50	-188	S 8 10	95
28 00	157 42	-190	S 9 45	94
SUN 06	154 32	-192	S11 19	91
HP 12	151 20	-194	S12 50	88
60' 18	148 06	-197	S14 18	86
29 00	144 49	-199	S15 44	81
MON 06	141 30	-202	S17 05	78
HP 12	138 08	-204	S18 23	73
60' 18	134 44	-207	S19 36	69
30 00	131 17	-210	S20 45	64
TUE 06	127 47	-212	S21 49	58
HP 12	124 15	-213	S22 47	53
60' 18	120 42	-216	S23 40	46
31 00	117 06		S24 26	

Phases of the Moon
New: 26d   First Quarter: 3d
Full: 10d   Last Quarter: 18d

MOON AT EVERY 6hrs GMT OCTOBER 2003

Day GMT	GHA-GMT	v	Dec	d
1 00h	117° 06'	-218'	S24° 26'	41'
WED 06	113 28	-219	S25 07	35
HP 12	109 49	-219	S25 42	28
59' 18	106 10	-220	S26 10	22
2 00	102 30	-221	S26 32	15
THU 06	98 49	-220	S26 47	9
HP 12	95 09	-219	S26 56	2
59' 18	91 30	-217	S26 58	4
3 00	87 53	-216	S26 54	11
FRI 06	84 17	-214	S26 43	16
HP 12	80 43	-212	S26 27	23
58' 18	77 11	-209	S26 04	28
4 00	73 42	-205	S25 36	34
SAT 06	70 17	-203	S25 02	38
HP 12	66 54	-199	S24 24	44
58' 18	63 35	-196	S23 40	48
5 00	60 19	-192	S22 52	53
SUN 06	57 07	-188	S21 59	56
HP 12	53 59	-185	S21 03	60
57' 18	50 54	-182	S20 03	64
6 00	47 52	-178	S18 59	67
MON 06	44 54	-174	S17 52	69
HP 12	42 00	-172	S16 43	72
56' 18	39 08	-169	S15 31	75
7 00	36 19	-166	S14 16	76
TUE 06	33 33	-163	S13 00	78
HP 12	30 50	-161	S11 42	80
56' 18	28 09	-159	S10 22	81
8 00	25 30	-157	S 9 01	82
WED 06	22 53	-155	S 7 39	82
HP 12	20 18	-154	S 6 17	84
55' 18	17 44	-152	S 4 53	84
9 00	15° 12'		S 3° 29'	

Day GMT	GHA-GMT	v	Dec	d
9 00h	15° 12'	-152'	S 3° 29'	84'
THU 06	12 40	-150	S 2 05	84
HP 12	10 10	-150	S 0 41	84
55' 18	7 40	-149	N 0 43	83
10 00	5 11	-150	N 2 06	83
FRI 06	2 41	-149	N 3 29	82
HP 12	0 12	-149	N 4 51	82
55' 18	357 43	-149	N 6 13	80
11 00	355 14	-150	N 7 33	79
SAT 06	352 44	-151	N 8 52	77
HP 12	350 13	-152	N10 09	76
54' 18	347 41	-153	N11 25	75
12 00	345 08	-154	N12 40	72
SUN 06	342 34	-155	N13 52	70
HP 12	339 59	-157	N15 02	68
54' 18	337 22	-158	N16 10	66
13 00	334 44	-160	N17 16	63
MON 06	332 04	-162	N18 19	60
HP 12	329 22	-164	N19 19	57
54' 18	326 38	-166	N20 16	54
14 00	323 52	-168	N21 10	51
TUE 06	321 04	-170	N22 01	48
HP 12	318 14	-172	N22 49	43
54' 18	315 22	-174	N23 32	41
15 00	312 28	-176	N24 13	36
WED 06	309 32	-178	N24 49	32
HP 12	306 34	-180	N25 21	28
54' 18	303 34	-181	N25 49	24
16 00	300 33	-184	N26 13	19
THU 06	297 29	-184	N26 32	15
HP 12	294 25	-186	N26 47	10
54' 18	291 19	-187	N26 57	5
17 00	288° 12'		N27° 02'	

Day GMT	GHA-GMT	v	Dec	d
17 00h	288° 12'	-188'	N27° 02'	1'
FRI 06	285 04	-189	N27 03	4
HP 12	281 55	-189	N26 59	10
55' 18	278 46	-190	N26 49	14
18 00	275 36	-189	N26 35	19
SAT 06	272 27	-190	N26 16	24
HP 12	269 17	-189	N25 52	29
55' 18	266 08	-189	N25 23	34
19 00	262 59	-188	N24 49	39
SUN 06	259 51	-187	N24 10	43
HP 12	256 44	-187	N23 27	48
56' 18	253 37	-185	N22 39	53
20 00	250 32	-185	N21 46	57
MON 06	247 27	-184	N20 49	61
HP 12	244 23	-182	N19 48	66
57' 18	241 21	-182	N18 42	69
21 00	238 19	-181	N17 33	74
TUE 06	235 18	-180	N16 19	77
HP 12	232 18	-179	N15 02	80
58' 18	229 19	-179	N13 42	84
22 00	226 20	-178	N12 18	87
WED 06	223 22	-179	N10 51	89
HP 12	220 23	-178	N 9 22	92
59' 18	217 25	-178	N 7 50	94
23 00	214 27	-178	N 6 16	96
THU 06	211 29	-179	N 4 40	98
HP 12	208 30	-180	N 3 02	99
60' 18	205 30	-181	N 1 23	##
24 00	202 29	-182	S 0 17	##
FRI 06	199 27	-183	S 1 57	##
HP 12	196 24	-186	S 3 38	##
61' 18	193 18	-187	S 5 19	99
25 00	190° 11'		S 6° 58'	

Day GMT	GHA-GMT	v	Dec	d
25 00h	190° 11'	-190'	S 6° 58'	99'
SAT 06	187 01	-192	S 8 37	97
HP 12	183 49	-194	S10 14	96
61' 18	180 35	-198	S11 50	93
26 00	177 17	-200	S13 23	90
SUN 06	173 57	-204	S14 53	86
HP 12	170 33	-206	S16 19	83
61' 18	167 07	-210	S17 42	79
27 00	163 37	-213	S19 01	74
MON 06	160 04	-216	S20 15	69
HP 12	156 28	-218	S21 24	63
61' 18	152 50	-221	S22 27	58
28 00	149 09	-224	S23 25	51
TUE 06	145 25	-225	S24 16	45
HP 12	141 40	-227	S25 01	38
61' 18	137 53	-228	S25 39	31
29 00	134 05	-229	S26 10	24
WED 06	130 16	-228	S26 34	18
HP 12	126 28	-228	S26 52	10
60' 18	122 40	-226	S27 02	4
30 00	118 54	-225	S27 06	4
THU 06	115 09	-223	S27 02	10
HP 12	111 26	-220	S26 52	16
59' 18	107 46	-217	S26 36	23
31 00	104 09	-214	S26 10	29
FRI 06	100 35	-210	S25 44	34
HP 12	97 05	-206	S25 10	40
58' 18	93 39	-203	S24 30	44
32 00	90 16		S23 46	

Phases of the Moon
New: 25d   First Quarter: 2d
Full: 10d   Last Quarter: 18d

Day	GMT	GHA-GMT	v	Dec	d
1	00h	90°16'	-198'	S23°46'	49'
SAT	06	86 58	-194	S22 57	54
HP	12	83 44	-189	S22 03	57
58'	18	80 35	-186	S21 06	61
2	00	77 29	-182	S20 05	65
SUN	06	74 27	-178	S19 00	67
HP	12	71 29	-175	S17 53	70
57'	18	68 34	-171	S16 43	72
3	00	65 43	-168	S15 31	75
MON	06	62 55	-165	S14 16	76
HP	12	60 10	-162	S13 00	78
56'	18	57 28	-160	S11 42	80
4	00	54 48	-157	S10 22	80
TUE	06	52 11	-155	S 9 02	82
HP	12	49 36	-154	S 7 40	82
55'	18	47 02	-152	S 6 18	83
5	00	44 30	-150	S 4 55	84
WED	06	42 00	-150	S 3 31	83
HP	12	39 30	-149	S 2 08	84
55'	18	37 01	-148	S 0 44	83
6	00	34 33	-148	N 0 39	83
THU	06	32 05	-147	N 2 02	82
HP	12	29 38	-148	N 3 24	82
55'	18	27 10	-148	N 4 46	81
7	00	24 42	-148	N 6 07	80
FRI	06	22 14	-149	N 7 27	79
HP	12	19 45	-150	N 8 46	78
54'	18	17 15	-150	N10 04	76
8	00	14 45	-152	N11 20	74
SAT	06	12 13	-153	N12 34	72
HP	12	9 40	-155	N13 46	71
54'	18	7 05	-156	N14 57	68
9	00	4°29'		N16°05'	
9	00h	4°29'	-159'	N16°05'	66'
SUN	06	1 50	-159	N17 11	64
HP	12	359 11	-162	N18 15	60
54'	18	356 29	-164	N19 15	58
10	00	353 45	-166	N20 13	55
MON	06	350 59	-168	N21 08	51
HP	12	348 11	-170	N21 59	48
54'	18	345 21	-172	N22 47	44
11	00	342 29	-174	N23 31	41
TUE	06	339 35	-176	N24 12	37
HP	12	336 39	-178	N24 49	32
54'	18	333 41	-180	N25 21	29
12	00	330 41	-181	N25 50	24
WED	06	327 40	-183	N26 14	20
HP	12	324 37	-184	N26 34	15
54'	18	321 33	-186	N26 49	10
13	00	318 27	-186	N26 59	6
THU	06	315 21	-186	N27 05	1
HP	12	312 15	-188	N27 06	4
54'	18	309 07	-187	N27 02	8
14	00	306 00	-187	N26 54	14
FRI	06	302 53	-187	N26 40	18
HP	12	299 46	-187	N26 22	23
55'	18	296 39	-186	N25 59	28
15	00	293 33	-185	N25 31	32
SAT	06	290 28	-184	N24 59	37
HP	12	287 24	-184	N24 22	42
55'	18	284 20	-182	N23 40	46
16	00	281 18	-181	N22 54	50
SUN	06	278 17	-179	N22 04	54
HP	12	275 18	-179	N21 10	59
56'	18	272 19	-177	N20 11	62
17	00	269°22'		N19°09'	
17	00h	269°22'	-177'	N19°09'	66'
MON	06	266 25	-175	N18 03	70
HP	12	263 30	-174	N16 53	73
57'	18	260 36	-174	N15 40	77
18	00	257 42	-172	N14 23	80
TUE	06	254 50	-173	N13 03	82
HP	12	251 57	-172	N11 41	85
58'	18	249 05	-171	N10 16	88
19	00	246 14	-172	N 8 48	90
WED	06	243 22	-173	N 7 18	92
HP	12	240 29	-173	N 5 46	94
59'	18	237 36	-173	N 4 12	96
20	00	234 43	-175	N 2 36	96
THU	06	231 48	-176	N 1 00	98
HP	12	228 52	-178	S 0 38	98
60'	18	225 54	-180	S 2 16	99
21	00	222 54	-182	S 3 55	99
FRI	06	219 52	-184	S 5 34	98
HP	12	216 48	-187	S 7 12	97
61'	18	213 41	-191	S 8 49	97
22	00	210 30	-193	S10 26	94
SAT	06	207 17	-197	S12 00	92
HP	12	204 00	-201	S13 32	90
61'	18	200 39	-204	S15 02	87
23	00	197 15	-208	S16 29	83
SUN	06	193 47	-212	S17 52	79
HP	12	190 15	-216	S19 11	74
61'	18	186 39	-220	S20 25	69
24	00	182 59	-223	S21 34	63
MON	06	179 16	-227	S22 37	58
HP	12	175 29	-229	S23 35	51
61'	18	171 40	-232	S24 26	45
25	00	167°48'		S25°11'	
25	00h	167°48'	-234'	S25°11'	37'
TUE	06	163 54	-236	S25 48	30
HP	12	159 58	-236	S26 18	23
61'	18	156 02	-237	S26 41	16
26	00	152 05	-236	S26 57	7
WED	06	148 09	-235	S27 04	1
HP	12	144 14	-232	S27 05	7
60'	18	140 22	-231	S26 58	14
27	00	136 31	-227	S26 44	20
THU	06	132 44	-224	S26 24	27
HP	12	129 00	-220	S25 57	34
60'	18	125 20	-215	S25 23	39
28	00	121 45	-211	S24 44	44
FRI	06	118 14	-207	S24 00	50
HP	12	114 47	-202	S23 10	54
59'	18	111 25	-197	S22 16	59
29	00	108 08	-192	S21 17	62
SAT	06	104 56	-188	S20 15	65
HP	12	101 48	-184	S19 10	69
58'	18	98 44	-179	S18 01	71
30	00	95 45	-176	S16 50	74
SUN	06	92 49	-171	S15 36	76
HP	12	89 58	-168	S14 20	78
57'	18	87 10	-165	S13 02	79
31	00	84 25		S11 43	

Phases of the Moon
New: 23d   First Quarter: 1d&30d
Full: 9d   Last Quarter: 17d

MOON AT EVERY 6hrs GMT DECEMBER 2003

Day	GMT	GHA-GMT	v	Dec	d
1	00h	84°25'	-162'	S11°43'	80'
MON	06	81 43	-159	S10 23	82
HP	12	79 04	-157	S 9 01	82
56'	18	76 27	-155	S 7 39	83
2	00	73 52	-152	S 6 16	83
TUE	06	71 20	-152	S 4 53	84
HP	12	68 48	-149	S 3 29	84
55'	18	66 19	-149	S 2 05	83
3	00	63 50	-148	S 0 42	84
WED	06	61 22	-148	N 0 42	82
HP	12	58 54	-147	N 2 04	83
55'	18	56 27	-147	N 3 27	81
4	00	54 00	-147	N 4 48	81
THU	06	51 33	-148	N 6 09	79
HP	12	49 05	-148	N 7 28	79
54'	18	46 37	-149	N 8 47	77
5	00	44 08	-150	N10 04	76
FRI	06	41 38	-151	N11 20	74
HP	12	39 07	-153	N12 34	72
54'	18	36 34	-154	N13 46	70
6	00	34 00	-156	N14 56	68
SAT	06	31 24	-157	N16 04	65
HP	12	28 47	-160	N17 09	64
54'	18	26 07	-161	N18 13	60
7	00	23 26	-164	N19 13	58
SUN	06	20 42	-165	N20 11	54
HP	12	17 57	-168	N21 05	52
54'	18	15 09	-171	N21 57	48
8	00	12 18	-172	N22 45	44
MON	06	9 26	-175	N23 29	41
HP	12	6 31	-176	N24 10	37
54'	18	3 35	-179	N24 47	32
9	00	0°36'		N25°19'	
9	00h	0°36'	-180'	N25°19'	29'
TUE	06	357 36	-183	N25 48	24
HP	12	354 33	-183	N26 12	19
54'	18	351 30	-185	N26 31	16
10	00	348 25	-186	N26 47	10
WED	06	345 19	-187	N26 57	5
HP	12	342 12	-188	N27 02	4
54'	18	339 04	-188	N27 03	4
11	00	335 56	-188	N26 59	9
THU	06	332 48	-187	N26 50	13
HP	12	329 41	-188	N26 37	19
55'	18	326 33	-186	N26 18	23
12	00	323 27	-186	N25 55	28
FRI	06	320 21	-185	N25 27	33
HP	12	317 16	-183	N24 54	37
55'	18	314 13	-182	N24 17	42
13	00	311 11	-181	N23 35	46
SAT	06	308 10	-179	N22 49	50
HP	12	305 11	-178	N21 59	54
55'	18	302 13	-176	N21 05	57
14	00	299 17	-174	N20 08	62
SUN	06	296 23	-173	N19 06	65
HP	12	293 30	-172	N18 01	68
56'	18	290 38	-171	N16 53	72
15	00	287 47	-169	N15 41	74
MON	06	284 58	-168	N14 27	78
HP	12	282 10	-167	N13 09	80
57'	18	279 23	-167	N11 49	82
16	00	276 36	-166	N10 27	85
TUE	06	273 50	-166	N 9 02	86
HP	12	271 04	-166	N 7 36	89
58'	18	268 18	-167	N 6 07	90
17	00	265°31'		N 4°37'	
17	00h	265°31'	-166'	N 4°37'	92'
WED	06	262 45	-168	N 3 05	92
HP	12	259 57	-169	N 1 33	94
58'	18	257 08	-170	S 0 01	94
18	00	254 18	-172	S 1 35	95
THU	06	251 26	-173	S 3 10	95
HP	12	248 33	-176	S 4 45	95
59'	18	245 37	-179	S 6 20	94
19	00	242 38	-181	S 7 54	94
FRI	06	239 37	-185	S 9 28	92
HP	12	236 32	-188	S11 00	91
60'	18	233 24	-191	S12 31	88
20	00	230 13	-196	S13 59	86
SAT	06	226 57	-199	S15 25	84
HP	12	223 38	-204	S16 49	80
61'	18	220 14	-208	S18 09	76
21	00	216 46	-212	S19 25	71
SUN	06	213 14	-217	S20 36	67
HP	12	209 37	-220	S21 43	62
61'	18	205 57	-225	S22 45	56
22	00	202 12	-228	S23 41	50
MON	06	198 24	-232	S24 31	43
HP	12	194 32	-234	S25 14	36
61'	18	190 38	-237	S25 50	29
23	00	186 41	-238	S26 19	22
TUE	06	182 43	-239	S26 41	14
HP	12	178 44	-238	S26 55	7
61'	18	174 46	-239	S27 02	1
24	00	170 47	-237	S27 01	8
WED	06	166 50	-235	S26 53	16
HP	12	162 55	-232	S26 37	23
61'	18	159 03	-229	S26 14	30
25	00	155°14'		S25°44'	
25	00h	155°14'	-225'	S25°44'	36'
THU	06	151 29	-221	S25 08	42
HP	12	147 48	-216	S24 26	48
60'	18	144 12	-212	S23 38	53
26	00	140 40	-207	S22 45	58
FRI	06	137 13	-202	S21 47	62
HP	12	133 51	-197	S20 45	66
59'	18	130 34	-193	S19 39	69
27	00	127 21	-188	S18 30	73
SAT	06	124 13	-183	S17 17	75
HP	12	121 10	-180	S16 02	78
58'	18	118 10	-175	S14 44	80
28	00	115 15	-171	S13 24	81
SUN	06	112 24	-168	S12 03	82
HP	12	109 36	-165	S10 41	84
57'	18	106 51	-162	S 9 17	84
29	00	104 09	-160	S 7 53	85
MON	06	101 29	-157	S 6 28	85
HP	12	98 52	-155	S 5 03	86
56'	18	96 17	-153	S 3 37	85
30	00	93 44	-152	S 2 12	85
TUE	06	91 12	-151	S 0 47	85
HP	12	88 41	-150	N 0 38	84
55'	18	86 11	-149	N 2 02	83
31	00	83 42	-149	N 3 25	82
WED	06	81 13	-149	N 4 47	81
HP	12	78 44	-149	N 6 09	80
55'	18	76 15	-149	N 7 29	79
32	00	73 46		N 8 48	

Phases of the Moon
New: 23d   First Quarter: 30d
Full: 8d   Last Quarter: 16d

MOON INTERPOLATION: DECLINATION

d 0' to 60'

d	00/06/12/18	01/07/13/19	02/08/14/20	03/09/15/21	04/10/16/22	05/11/17/23	00	10	20	30	40	50	60
0	0	0	0	0	0	0	0	0	0	0	0	0	0
1	0	0	0	1	1	1	0	0	0	0	0	0	0
2	0	0	1	1	1	2	0	0	0	0	0	0	0
3	0	1	1	2	2	3	0	0	0	0	0	0	1
4	0	1	1	2	3	3	0	0	0	0	0	1	1
5	0	1	2	3	3	4	0	0	0	0	1	1	1
6	0	1	2	3	4	5	0	0	0	1	1	1	1
7	0	1	2	4	5	6	0	0	0	1	1	1	1
8	0	1	3	4	5	7	0	0	0	1	1	1	1
9	0	2	3	5	6	8	0	0	1	1	1	1	2
10	0	2	3	5	7	8	0	0	1	1	1	1	2
11	0	2	4	6	7	9	0	0	1	1	1	2	2
12	0	2	4	6	8	10	0	0	1	1	1	2	2
13	0	2	4	7	9	11	0	0	1	1	1	2	2
14	0	2	5	7	9	12	0	0	1	1	2	2	2
15	0	3	5	8	10	13	0	0	1	1	2	2	3
16	0	3	5	8	11	13	0	0	1	1	2	2	3
17	0	3	6	9	11	14	0	0	1	1	2	2	3
18	0	3	6	9	12	15	0	1	1	2	2	3	3
19	0	3	6	10	13	16	0	1	1	2	2	3	3
20	0	3	7	10	13	17	0	1	1	2	2	3	3
21	0	4	7	11	14	18	0	1	1	2	2	3	4
22	0	4	7	11	15	18	0	1	1	2	2	3	4
23	0	4	8	12	15	19	0	1	1	2	3	3	4
24	0	4	8	12	16	20	0	1	1	2	3	3	4
25	0	4	8	13	17	21	0	1	1	2	3	3	4
26	0	4	9	13	17	22	0	1	1	2	3	4	4
27	0	5	9	14	18	23	0	1	2	2	3	4	5
28	0	5	9	14	19	23	0	1	2	2	3	4	5
29	0	5	10	15	19	24	0	1	2	2	3	4	5
30	0	5	10	15	20	25	0	1	2	3	3	4	5
31	0	5	10	16	21	26	0	1	2	3	3	4	5
32	0	5	11	16	21	27	0	1	2	3	4	4	5
33	0	6	11	17	22	28	0	1	2	3	4	5	6
34	0	6	11	17	23	28	0	1	2	3	4	5	6
35	0	6	12	18	23	29	0	1	2	3	4	5	6
36	0	6	12	18	24	30	0	1	2	3	4	5	6
37	0	6	12	19	25	31	0	1	2	3	4	5	6
38	0	6	13	19	25	32	0	1	2	3	4	5	6
39	0	7	13	20	26	33	0	1	2	3	4	5	7
40	0	7	13	20	27	33	0	1	2	3	4	6	7
41	0	7	14	21	27	34	0	1	2	3	5	6	7
42	0	7	14	21	28	35	0	1	2	4	5	6	7
43	0	7	14	22	29	36	0	1	2	4	5	6	7
44	0	7	15	22	29	37	0	1	2	4	5	6	7
45	0	8	15	23	30	38	0	1	3	4	5	6	8
46	0	8	15	23	31	38	0	1	3	4	5	6	8
47	0	8	16	24	31	39	0	1	3	4	5	7	8
48	0	8	16	24	32	40	0	1	3	4	5	7	8
49	0	8	16	25	33	41	0	1	3	4	5	7	8
50	0	8	17	25	33	42	0	1	3	4	6	7	8
51	0	9	17	26	34	43	0	1	3	4	6	7	9
52	0	9	17	26	35	43	0	1	3	4	6	7	9
53	0	9	18	27	35	44	0	1	3	4	6	7	9
54	0	9	18	27	36	45	0	2	3	5	6	8	9
55	0	9	18	28	37	46	0	2	3	5	6	8	9
56	0	9	19	28	37	47	0	2	3	5	6	8	9
57	0	10	19	29	38	48	0	2	3	5	6	8	10
58	0	10	19	29	39	48	0	2	3	5	6	8	10
59	0	10	20	30	39	49	0	2	3	5	7	8	10
60	0	10	20	30	40	50	0	2	3	5	7	8	10

d 60' to 120'

d	00/06/12/18	01/07/13/19	02/08/14/20	03/09/15/21	04/10/16/22	05/11/17/23	00	05	10	15	20	25	30	35	40	45	50	55	60
60	0	10	20	30	40	50	0	1	2	3	3	4	5	6	7	8	8	9	10
61	0	10	20	31	41	51	0	1	2	3	3	4	5	6	7	8	8	9	10
62	0	10	21	31	41	52	0	1	2	3	3	4	5	6	7	8	9	9	10
63	0	11	21	32	42	53	0	1	2	3	4	4	5	6	7	8	9	10	11
64	0	11	21	32	43	53	0	1	2	3	4	4	5	6	7	8	9	10	11
65	0	11	22	33	43	54	0	1	2	3	4	5	5	6	7	8	9	10	11
66	0	11	22	33	44	55	0	1	2	3	4	5	6	6	7	8	9	10	11
67	0	11	22	34	45	56	0	1	2	3	4	5	6	7	7	8	9	10	11
68	0	11	23	34	45	57	0	1	2	3	4	5	6	7	8	9	9	10	11
69	0	12	23	35	46	58	0	1	2	3	4	5	6	7	8	9	10	11	12
70	0	12	23	35	47	58	0	1	2	3	4	5	6	7	8	9	10	11	12
71	0	12	24	36	47	59	0	1	2	3	4	5	6	7	8	9	10	11	12
72	0	12	24	36	48	60	0	1	2	3	4	5	6	7	8	9	10	11	12
73	0	12	24	37	49	61	0	1	2	3	4	5	6	7	8	9	10	11	12
74	0	12	25	37	49	62	0	1	2	3	4	5	6	7	8	9	10	11	12
75	0	13	25	38	50	63	0	1	2	3	4	5	6	7	8	9	10	11	13
76	0	13	25	38	51	63	0	1	2	3	4	5	6	7	8	10	11	12	13
77	0	13	26	39	51	64	0	1	2	3	4	5	6	7	9	10	11	12	13
78	0	13	26	39	52	65	0	1	2	3	4	5	7	8	9	10	11	12	13
79	0	13	26	40	53	66	0	1	2	3	4	5	7	8	9	10	11	12	13
80	0	13	27	40	53	67	0	1	2	3	4	6	7	8	9	10	11	12	13
81	0	14	27	41	54	68	0	1	2	3	5	6	7	8	9	10	11	12	14
82	0	14	27	41	55	68	0	1	2	3	5	6	7	8	9	10	11	13	14
83	0	14	28	42	55	69	0	1	2	3	5	6	7	8	9	10	12	13	14
84	0	14	28	42	56	70	0	1	2	4	5	6	7	8	9	11	12	13	14
85	0	14	28	43	57	71	0	1	2	4	5	6	7	8	9	11	12	13	14
86	0	14	29	43	57	72	0	1	2	4	5	6	7	8	10	11	12	13	14
87	0	15	29	44	58	73	0	1	2	4	5	6	7	8	10	11	12	13	15
88	0	15	29	44	59	73	0	1	2	4	5	6	7	9	10	11	12	13	15
89	0	15	30	45	59	74	0	1	2	4	5	6	7	9	10	11	12	14	15
90	0	15	30	45	60	75	0	1	3	4	5	6	8	9	10	11	13	14	15
91	0	15	30	46	61	76	0	1	3	4	5	6	8	9	10	11	13	14	15
92	0	15	31	46	61	77	0	1	3	4	5	6	8	9	10	12	13	14	15
93	0	16	31	47	62	78	0	1	3	4	5	6	8	9	10	12	13	14	16
94	0	16	31	47	63	78	0	1	3	4	5	7	8	9	10	12	13	14	16
95	0	16	32	48	63	79	0	1	3	4	5	7	8	9	11	12	13	15	16
96	0	16	32	48	64	80	0	1	3	4	5	7	8	9	11	12	13	15	16
97	0	16	32	49	65	81	0	1	3	4	5	7	8	9	11	12	13	15	16
98	0	16	33	49	65	82	0	1	3	4	5	7	8	10	11	12	14	15	16
99	0	17	33	50	66	83	0	1	3	4	6	7	8	10	11	12	14	15	17
100	0	17	33	50	67	83	0	1	3	4	6	7	8	10	11	13	14	15	17
101	0	17	34	51	67	84	0	1	3	4	6	7	8	10	11	13	14	15	17
102	0	17	34	51	68	85	0	1	3	4	6	7	9	10	11	13	14	16	17
103	0	17	34	52	69	86	0	1	3	4	6	7	9	10	11	13	14	16	17
104	0	17	35	52	69	87	0	1	3	4	6	7	9	10	12	13	14	16	17
105	0	18	35	53	70	88	0	1	3	4	6	7	9	10	12	13	15	16	18
106	0	18	35	53	71	88	0	1	3	4	6	7	9	10	12	13	15	16	18
107	0	18	36	54	71	89	0	1	3	4	6	7	9	10	12	13	15	16	18
108	0	18	36	54	72	90	0	2	3	5	6	8	9	11	12	14	15	17	18
109	0	18	36	55	73	91	0	2	3	5	6	8	9	11	12	14	15	17	18
110	0	18	37	55	73	92	0	2	3	5	6	8	9	11	12	14	15	17	18
111	0	19	37	56	74	93	0	2	3	5	6	8	9	11	12	14	15	17	19
112	0	19	37	56	75	93	0	2	3	5	6	8	9	11	12	14	16	17	19
113	0	19	38	57	75	94	0	2	3	5	6	8	9	11	13	14	16	17	19
114	0	19	38	57	76	95	0	2	3	5	6	8	10	11	13	14	16	17	19
115	0	19	38	58	77	96	0	2	3	5	6	8	10	11	13	14	16	18	19
116	0	19	39	58	77	97	0	2	3	5	6	8	10	11	13	15	16	18	19
117	0	20	39	59	78	98	0	2	3	5	7	8	10	11	13	15	16	18	20
118	0	20	39	59	79	98	0	2	3	5	7	8	10	11	13	15	16	18	20
119	0	20	40	60	79	99	0	2	3	5	7	8	10	12	13	15	17	18	20
120	0	20	40	60	80	100	0	2	3	5	7	8	10	12	13	15	17	18	20

MOON INTERPOLATION: GHA–GMT

v 130' to 190'

GMT HOURS column groups:
00 01 02 03 04 05 / 06 07 08 09 10 11 / 12 13 14 15 16 17 / 18 19 20 21 22 23

MINUTES

v	00	01	02	03	04	05	00	02	04	06	08	10	12	14	16	18	20	22	24	26	28	30	32	34	36	38	40	42	44	46	48	50	52	54	56	58	60
130	0	22	43	65	87	108	0	1	1	2	3	4	4	5	6	7	7	8	9	9	10	11	12	12	13	14	14	15	16	17	17	18	19	20	20	21	22
131	0	22	44	66	87	109	0	1	1	2	3	4	4	5	6	7	7	8	9	9	10	11	12	12	13	14	15	15	16	17	17	18	19	20	20	21	22
132	0	22	44	66	88	110	0	1	1	2	3	4	4	5	6	7	7	8	9	10	10	11	12	12	13	14	15	15	16	17	18	18	19	20	21	21	22
133	0	22	44	67	89	111	0	1	1	2	3	4	4	5	6	7	7	8	9	10	10	11	12	13	13	14	15	16	16	17	18	18	19	20	21	21	22
134	0	22	45	67	89	112	0	1	1	2	3	4	4	5	6	7	7	8	9	10	10	11	12	13	13	14	15	16	16	17	18	19	19	20	21	22	22
135	0	23	45	68	90	113	0	1	2	2	3	4	5	5	6	7	8	8	9	10	11	11	12	13	14	14	15	16	17	17	18	19	20	20	21	22	23
136	0	23	45	68	91	113	0	1	2	2	3	4	5	5	6	7	8	8	9	10	11	11	12	13	14	14	15	16	17	17	18	19	20	20	21	22	23
137	0	23	46	69	91	114	0	1	2	2	3	4	5	5	6	7	8	8	9	10	11	11	12	13	14	14	15	16	17	18	18	19	20	21	21	22	23
138	0	23	46	69	92	115	0	1	2	2	3	4	5	5	6	7	8	8	9	10	11	12	12	13	14	15	15	16	17	18	18	19	20	21	21	22	23
139	0	23	46	70	93	116	0	1	2	2	3	4	5	5	6	7	8	8	9	10	11	12	12	13	14	15	15	16	17	18	19	19	20	21	22	22	23
140	0	23	47	70	93	117	0	1	2	2	3	4	5	5	6	7	8	9	9	10	11	12	12	13	14	15	16	16	17	18	19	19	20	21	22	23	23
141	0	24	47	71	94	118	0	1	2	2	3	4	5	5	6	7	8	9	9	10	11	12	13	13	14	15	16	16	17	18	19	20	20	21	22	23	24
142	0	24	47	71	95	118	0	1	2	2	3	4	5	6	6	7	8	9	9	10	11	12	13	13	14	15	16	17	17	18	19	20	21	21	22	23	24
143	0	24	48	72	95	119	0	1	2	2	3	4	5	6	6	7	8	9	10	10	11	12	13	14	14	15	16	17	17	18	19	20	21	21	22	23	24
144	0	24	48	72	96	120	0	1	2	2	3	4	5	6	6	7	8	9	10	10	11	12	13	14	14	15	16	17	18	18	19	20	21	22	22	23	24
145	0	24	48	73	97	121	0	1	2	2	3	4	5	6	6	7	8	9	10	10	11	12	13	14	15	15	16	17	18	19	19	20	21	22	23	23	24
146	0	24	49	73	97	122	0	1	2	2	3	4	5	6	6	7	8	9	10	11	11	12	13	14	15	15	16	17	18	19	19	20	21	22	23	24	24
147	0	25	49	74	98	123	0	1	2	2	3	4	5	6	7	7	8	9	10	11	11	12	13	14	15	16	16	17	18	19	20	20	21	22	23	24	25
148	0	25	49	74	99	123	0	1	2	2	3	4	5	6	7	7	8	9	10	11	12	12	13	14	15	16	16	17	18	19	20	21	21	22	23	24	25
149	0	25	50	75	99	124	0	1	2	2	3	4	5	6	7	7	8	9	10	11	12	12	13	14	15	16	17	17	18	19	20	21	22	22	23	24	25
150	0	25	50	75	100	125	0	1	2	3	3	4	5	6	7	8	8	9	10	11	12	13	13	14	15	16	17	18	18	19	20	21	22	23	23	24	25
151	0	25	50	76	101	126	0	1	2	3	3	4	5	6	7	8	8	9	10	11	12	13	13	14	15	16	17	18	18	19	20	21	22	23	23	24	25
152	0	25	51	76	101	127	0	1	2	3	3	4	5	6	7	8	8	9	10	11	12	13	14	14	15	16	17	18	19	19	20	21	22	23	24	24	25
153	0	26	51	77	102	128	0	1	2	3	3	4	5	6	7	8	9	9	10	11	12	13	14	14	15	16	17	18	19	20	20	21	22	23	24	25	26
154	0	26	51	77	103	128	0	1	2	3	3	4	5	6	7	8	9	9	10	11	12	13	14	15	15	16	17	18	19	20	21	21	22	23	24	25	26
155	0	26	52	78	103	129	0	1	2	3	3	4	5	6	7	8	9	9	10	11	12	13	14	15	16	16	17	18	19	20	21	22	22	23	24	25	26
156	0	26	52	78	104	130	0	1	2	3	3	4	5	6	7	8	9	10	10	11	12	13	14	15	16	16	17	18	19	20	21	22	23	23	24	25	26
157	0	26	52	79	105	131	0	1	2	3	3	4	5	6	7	8	9	10	10	11	12	13	14	15	16	17	17	18	19	20	21	22	23	24	24	25	26
158	0	26	53	79	105	132	0	1	2	3	4	4	5	6	7	8	9	10	11	11	12	13	14	15	16	17	18	18	19	20	21	22	23	24	25	25	26
159	0	27	53	80	106	133	0	1	2	3	4	4	5	6	7	8	9	10	11	11	12	13	14	15	16	17	18	19	19	20	21	22	23	24	25	26	27
160	0	27	53	80	107	133	0	1	2	3	4	4	5	6	7	8	9	10	11	12	12	13	14	15	16	17	18	19	20	20	21	22	23	24	25	26	27
161	0	27	54	81	107	134	0	1	2	3	4	4	5	6	7	8	9	10	11	12	13	13	14	15	16	17	18	19	20	21	21	22	23	24	25	26	27
162	0	27	54	81	108	135	0	1	2	3	4	5	5	6	7	8	9	10	11	12	13	14	14	15	16	17	18	19	20	21	22	22	23	24	25	26	27
163	0	27	54	82	109	136	0	1	2	3	4	5	5	6	7	8	9	10	11	12	13	14	14	15	16	17	18	19	20	21	22	23	24	24	25	26	27
164	0	27	55	82	109	137	0	1	2	3	4	5	5	6	7	8	9	10	11	12	13	14	15	15	16	17	18	19	20	21	22	23	24	25	26	26	27
165	0	28	55	83	110	138	0	1	2	3	4	5	6	6	7	8	9	10	11	12	13	14	15	16	17	17	18	19	20	21	22	23	24	25	26	27	28
166	0	28	55	83	111	138	0	1	2	3	4	5	6	6	7	8	9	10	11	12	13	14	15	16	17	18	18	19	20	21	22	23	24	25	26	27	28
167	0	28	56	84	111	139	0	1	2	3	4	5	6	6	7	8	9	10	11	12	13	14	15	16	17	18	19	19	20	21	22	23	24	25	26	27	28
168	0	28	56	84	112	140	0	1	2	3	4	5	6	7	7	8	9	10	11	12	13	14	15	16	17	18	19	20	21	21	22	23	24	25	26	27	28
169	0	28	56	85	113	141	0	1	2	3	4	5	6	7	8	8	9	10	11	12	13	14	15	16	17	18	19	20	21	22	23	23	24	25	26	27	28
170	0	28	57	85	113	142	0	1	2	3	4	5	6	7	8	9	9	10	11	12	13	14	15	16	17	18	19	20	21	22	23	24	25	26	26	27	28
171	0	29	57	86	114	143	0	1	2	3	4	5	6	7	8	9	10	10	11	12	13	14	15	16	17	18	19	20	21	22	23	24	25	26	27	28	29
172	0	29	57	86	115	143	0	1	2	3	4	5	6	7	8	9	10	11	11	12	13	14	15	16	17	18	19	20	21	22	23	24	25	26	27	28	29
173	0	29	58	87	115	144	0	1	2	3	4	5	6	7	8	9	10	11	12	12	13	14	15	16	17	18	19	20	21	22	23	24	25	26	27	28	29
174	0	29	58	87	116	145	0	1	2	3	4	5	6	7	8	9	10	11	12	13	14	15	15	16	17	18	19	20	21	22	23	24	25	26	27	28	29
175	0	29	58	88	117	146	0	1	2	3	4	5	6	7	8	9	10	11	12	13	14	15	16	17	18	18	19	20	21	22	23	24	25	26	27	28	29
176	0	29	59	88	117	147	0	1	2	3	4	5	6	7	8	9	10	11	12	13	14	15	16	17	18	19	20	21	22	22	23	24	25	26	27	28	29
177	0	30	59	89	118	148	0	1	2	3	4	5	6	7	8	9	10	11	12	13	14	15	16	17	18	19	20	21	22	23	24	25	26	27	28	29	30
178	0	30	59	89	119	148	0	1	2	3	4	5	6	7	8	9	10	11	12	13	14	15	16	17	18	19	20	21	22	23	24	25	26	27	28	29	30
179	0	30	60	90	119	149	0	1	2	3	4	5	6	7	8	9	10	11	12	13	14	15	16	17	18	19	20	21	22	23	24	25	26	27	28	29	30
180	0	30	60	90	120	150	0	1	2	3	4	5	6	7	8	9	10	11	12	13	14	15	16	17	18	19	20	21	22	23	24	25	26	27	28	29	30
181	0	30	60	91	121	151	0	1	2	3	4	5	6	7	8	9	10	11	12	13	14	15	16	17	18	19	20	21	22	23	24	25	26	27	28	29	30
182	0	30	61	91	121	152	0	1	2	3	4	5	6	7	8	9	10	11	12	13	14	15	16	17	18	19	20	21	22	23	24	25	26	27	28	29	30
183	0	31	61	92	122	153	0	1	2	3	4	5	6	7	8	9	10	11	12	13	14	15	16	17	18	19	20	21	22	23	24	25	26	27	28	29	31
184	0	31	61	92	123	153	0	1	2	3	4	5	6	7	8	9	10	11	12	13	14	15	16	17	18	19	20	21	22	24	25	26	27	28	29	30	31
185	0	31	62	93	123	154	0	1	2	3	4	5	6	7	8	9	10	11	12	13	14	15	16	17	19	20	21	22	23	24	25	26	27	28	29	30	31
186	0	31	62	93	124	155	0	1	2	3	4	5	6	7	8	9	10	11	12	13	14	16	17	18	19	20	21	22	23	24	25	26	27	28	29	30	31
187	0	31	62	94	125	156	0	1	2	3	4	5	6	7	8	9	10	11	12	14	15	16	17	18	19	20	21	22	23	24	25	26	27	28	29	30	31
188	0	31	63	94	125	157	0	1	2	3	4	5	6	7	8	9	10	11	13	14	15	16	17	18	19	20	21	22	23	24	25	26	27	28	29	30	31
189	0	32	63	95	126	158	0	1	2	3	4	5	6	7	8	9	11	12	13	14	15	16	17	18	19	20	21	22	23	24	25	26	27	28	29	30	32
190	0	32	63	95	127	158	0	1	2	3	4	5	6	7	8	10	11	12	13	14	15	16	17	18	19	20	21	22	23	24	25	26	27	29	30	31	32

MOON INTERPOLATION: GHA–GMT

v 190' to 250'

MINUTES

v	00 06 12 18	01 07 13 19	02 08 14 20	03 09 15 21	04 10 16 22	05 11 17 23	00	02	04	06	08	10	12	14	16	18	20	22	24	26	28	30	32	34	36	38	40	42	44	46	48	50	52	54	56	58	60
190	0	32	63	95	127	158	0	1	2	3	4	5	6	7	8	10	11	12	13	14	15	16	17	18	19	20	21	22	23	24	25	26	27	29	30	31	32
191	0	32	64	96	127	159	0	1	2	3	4	5	6	7	8	10	11	12	13	14	15	16	17	18	19	20	21	22	23	24	25	27	28	29	30	31	32
192	0	32	64	96	128	160	0	1	2	3	4	5	6	7	9	10	11	12	13	14	15	16	17	18	19	20	21	22	23	25	26	27	28	29	30	31	32
193	0	32	64	97	129	161	0	1	2	3	4	5	6	8	9	10	11	12	13	14	15	16	17	18	19	20	21	23	24	25	26	27	28	29	30	31	32
194	0	32	65	97	129	162	0	1	2	3	4	5	6	8	9	10	11	12	13	14	15	16	17	18	20	21	22	23	24	25	26	27	28	29	30	31	33
195	0	33	65	98	130	163	0	1	2	3	4	5	7	8	9	10	11	12	13	14	15	16	17	19	20	21	22	23	24	25	26	27	28	29	30	32	33
196	0	33	65	98	131	163	0	1	2	3	4	5	7	8	9	10	11	12	13	14	15	16	18	19	20	21	22	23	24	25	26	27	28	30	31	32	33
197	0	33	66	99	131	164	0	1	2	3	4	5	7	8	9	10	11	12	13	14	15	16	18	19	20	21	22	23	24	25	26	27	28	30	31	32	33
198	0	33	66	99	132	165	0	1	2	3	4	6	7	8	9	10	11	12	13	14	15	17	18	19	20	21	22	23	24	25	26	28	29	30	31	32	33
199	0	33	66	100	133	166	0	1	2	3	4	6	7	8	9	10	11	12	13	14	15	17	18	19	20	21	22	23	24	25	27	28	29	30	31	32	33
200	0	33	67	100	133	167	0	1	2	3	4	6	7	8	9	10	11	12	13	14	16	17	18	19	20	21	22	23	24	26	27	28	29	30	31	32	33
201	0	34	67	101	134	168	0	1	2	3	4	6	7	8	9	10	11	12	13	15	16	17	18	19	20	21	22	23	25	26	27	28	29	30	31	32	34
202	0	34	67	101	135	168	0	1	2	3	4	6	7	8	9	10	11	12	13	15	16	17	18	19	20	21	23	24	25	26	27	28	29	30	31	33	34
203	0	34	68	102	135	169	0	1	2	3	5	6	7	8	9	10	11	12	14	15	16	17	18	19	20	22	23	24	25	26	27	28	29	31	32	33	34
204	0	34	68	102	136	170	0	1	2	3	5	6	7	8	9	10	11	12	14	15	16	17	18	19	21	22	23	24	25	26	27	28	30	31	32	33	34
205	0	34	68	103	137	171	0	1	2	3	5	6	7	8	9	10	11	13	14	15	16	17	18	19	21	22	23	24	25	26	27	29	30	31	32	33	34
206	0	34	69	103	137	172	0	1	2	3	5	6	7	8	9	10	11	13	14	15	16	17	18	19	21	22	23	24	25	26	28	29	30	31	32	33	34
207	0	35	69	104	138	173	0	1	2	3	5	6	7	8	9	10	12	13	14	15	16	17	18	20	21	22	23	24	25	26	28	29	30	31	32	33	35
208	0	35	69	104	139	173	0	1	2	3	5	6	7	8	9	10	12	13	14	15	16	17	18	20	21	22	23	24	25	27	28	29	30	31	32	34	35
209	0	35	70	105	139	174	0	1	2	3	5	6	7	8	9	10	12	13	14	15	16	17	19	20	21	22	23	24	26	27	28	29	30	31	33	34	35
210	0	35	70	105	140	175	0	1	2	4	5	6	7	8	9	11	12	13	14	15	16	18	19	20	21	22	23	25	26	27	28	29	30	32	33	34	35
211	0	35	70	106	141	176	0	1	2	4	5	6	7	8	9	11	12	13	14	15	16	18	19	20	21	22	23	25	26	27	28	29	30	32	33	34	35
212	0	35	71	106	141	177	0	1	2	4	5	6	7	8	9	11	12	13	14	15	16	18	19	20	21	22	24	25	26	27	28	29	31	32	33	34	35
213	0	36	71	107	142	178	0	1	2	4	5	6	7	8	9	11	12	13	14	15	17	18	19	20	21	23	24	25	26	27	29	30	31	32	33	34	36
214	0	36	71	107	143	178	0	1	2	4	5	6	7	8	10	11	12	13	14	15	17	18	19	20	21	23	24	25	26	27	29	30	31	32	33	34	36
215	0	36	72	108	143	179	0	1	2	4	5	6	7	8	10	11	12	13	14	16	17	18	19	20	22	23	24	25	26	27	29	30	31	32	33	35	36
216	0	36	72	108	144	180	0	1	2	4	5	6	7	8	10	11	12	13	14	16	17	18	19	20	22	23	24	25	26	28	29	30	31	32	34	35	36
217	0	36	72	109	145	181	0	1	2	4	5	6	7	8	10	11	12	13	14	16	17	18	19	20	22	23	24	25	27	28	29	30	31	33	34	35	36
218	0	36	73	109	145	182	0	1	2	4	5	6	7	8	10	11	12	13	15	16	17	18	19	21	22	23	24	25	27	28	29	30	31	33	34	35	36
219	0	37	73	110	146	183	0	1	2	4	5	6	7	9	10	11	12	13	15	16	17	18	19	21	22	23	24	26	27	28	29	30	32	33	34	35	37
220	0	37	73	110	147	183	0	1	2	4	5	6	7	9	10	11	12	13	15	16	17	18	20	21	22	23	24	26	27	28	29	31	32	33	34	35	37
221	0	37	74	111	147	184	0	1	2	4	5	6	7	9	10	11	12	14	15	16	17	18	20	21	22	23	25	26	27	28	29	31	32	33	34	36	37
222	0	37	74	111	148	185	0	1	2	4	5	6	7	9	10	11	12	14	15	16	17	19	20	21	22	23	25	26	27	28	30	31	32	33	35	36	37
223	0	37	74	112	149	186	0	1	2	4	5	6	7	9	10	11	12	14	15	16	17	19	20	21	22	24	25	26	27	28	30	31	32	33	35	36	37
224	0	37	75	112	149	187	0	1	2	4	5	6	7	9	10	11	12	14	15	16	17	19	20	21	22	24	25	26	27	29	30	31	32	34	35	36	37
225	0	38	75	113	150	188	0	1	3	4	5	6	8	9	10	11	13	14	15	16	18	19	20	21	23	24	25	26	28	29	30	31	33	34	35	36	38
226	0	38	75	113	151	188	0	1	3	4	5	6	8	9	10	11	13	14	15	16	18	19	20	21	23	24	25	26	28	29	30	31	33	34	35	36	38
227	0	38	76	114	151	189	0	1	3	4	5	6	8	9	10	11	13	14	15	16	18	19	20	22	23	24	25	26	28	29	30	32	33	34	35	37	38
228	0	38	76	114	152	190	0	1	3	4	5	6	8	9	10	11	13	14	15	17	18	19	20	22	23	24	25	27	28	29	31	32	33	34	36	37	38
229	0	38	76	115	153	191	0	1	3	4	5	6	8	9	10	11	13	14	15	17	18	19	20	22	23	24	26	27	28	29	31	32	33	34	36	37	38
230	0	38	77	115	153	192	0	1	3	4	5	6	8	9	10	12	13	14	15	17	18	19	20	22	23	24	26	27	28	30	31	32	33	35	36	37	39
231	0	39	77	116	154	193	0	1	3	4	5	6	8	9	10	12	13	14	15	17	18	19	21	22	23	24	26	27	28	30	31	32	34	35	36	37	39
232	0	39	77	116	155	193	0	1	3	4	5	6	8	9	10	12	13	14	15	17	18	19	21	22	23	24	26	27	28	30	31	32	34	35	36	37	39
233	0	39	78	117	155	194	0	1	3	4	5	6	8	9	10	12	13	14	16	17	18	19	21	22	23	25	26	27	28	30	31	32	34	35	36	38	39
234	0	39	78	117	156	195	0	1	3	4	5	7	8	9	10	12	13	14	16	17	18	20	21	22	23	25	26	27	29	30	31	33	34	35	36	38	39
235	0	39	78	118	157	196	0	1	3	4	5	7	8	9	10	12	13	14	16	17	18	20	21	22	24	25	26	27	29	30	31	33	34	35	37	38	39
236	0	39	79	118	157	197	0	1	3	4	5	7	8	9	10	12	13	14	16	17	18	20	21	22	24	25	26	28	29	30	31	33	34	35	37	38	39
237	0	40	79	119	158	198	0	1	3	4	5	7	8	9	11	12	13	14	16	17	18	20	21	22	24	25	26	28	29	30	32	33	34	36	37	38	40
238	0	40	79	119	159	198	0	1	3	4	5	7	8	9	11	12	13	15	16	17	19	20	21	22	24	25	27	28	29	30	32	33	34	36	37	38	40
239	0	40	80	120	159	199	0	1	3	4	5	7	8	9	11	12	13	15	16	17	19	20	21	23	24	25	27	28	29	31	32	33	35	36	37	39	40
240	0	40	80	120	160	200	0	1	3	4	5	7	8	9	11	12	13	15	16	17	19	20	21	23	24	25	27	28	29	31	32	33	35	36	37	39	40
241	0	40	80	121	161	201	0	1	3	4	5	7	8	9	11	12	13	15	16	17	19	20	21	23	24	25	27	28	30	31	32	34	35	36	37	39	40
242	0	40	81	121	161	202	0	1	3	4	5	7	8	9	11	12	13	15	16	17	19	20	22	23	24	26	27	28	30	31	32	34	35	36	38	39	40
243	0	41	81	122	162	203	0	1	3	4	5	7	8	9	11	12	14	15	16	18	19	20	22	23	24	26	27	28	30	31	32	34	35	36	38	39	41
244	0	41	81	122	163	203	0	1	3	4	5	7	8	9	11	12	14	15	16	18	19	20	22	23	24	26	27	28	30	31	33	34	35	37	38	39	41
245	0	41	82	123	163	204	0	1	3	4	5	7	8	10	11	12	14	15	16	18	19	20	22	23	25	26	27	29	30	31	33	34	35	37	38	39	41
246	0	41	82	123	164	205	0	1	3	4	5	7	8	10	11	12	14	15	16	18	19	21	22	23	25	26	27	29	30	31	33	34	36	37	38	40	41
247	0	41	82	124	165	206	0	1	3	4	5	7	8	10	11	12	14	15	16	18	19	21	22	23	25	26	27	29	30	32	33	34	36	37	38	40	41
248	0	41	83	124	165	207	0	1	3	4	6	7	8	10	11	12	14	15	17	18	19	21	22	23	25	26	28	29	30	32	33	34	36	37	39	40	41
249	0	42	83	125	166	208	0	1	3	4	6	7	8	10	11	12	14	15	17	18	19	21	22	24	25	26	28	29	30	32	33	35	36	37	39	40	42
250	0	42	83	125	167	208	0	1	3	4	6	7	8	10	11	13	14	15	17	18	19	21	22	24	25	26	28	29	31	32	33	35	36	38	39	40	42

MOON ALTITUDE CORRECTIONS–UPPER LIMB

DIP Corrn

m	Corrn	ft
0.0	0'	0
	-1	
0.7		2
	-2	
2.0		6
	-3	
3.9		13
	-4	
6.5		21
	-5	
9.7		32
	-6	
13.6		44
	-7	
18.1		59
	-8	
23.3		76
	-9	
29.1		95
	-10	

HP = 54'

Corrn	Alt
-14'	89°
-13	88
-12	87
-11	86
-10	85
-9	84
-8	83
-7	82
-6	81
-5	79
-4	78
-3	77
-2	76
-1	75
0	74
+1	73
+2	72
+3	70

Alt	Corrn	Alt
0° 02'	+4	69
0 07	+5	68
0 12	+6	67
0 17	+7	66
0 23	+8	65
0 29	+9	63
0 35	+10	62
0 41	+11	61
0 48	+12	60
0 55	+13	58
1 03	+14	57
1 11	+15	56
1 20	+16	54
1 30	+17	53
1 40	+18	52
1 52	+19	50
2 04	+20	49
2 18	+21	47
2 33	+22	46
2 50	+23	44
3 10	+24	42
3 32	+25	41
3 59	+26	39
4 30	+27	37
5 07	+28	35
5 54	+29	33
6 56	+30	30
8 25	+31	28
11 05	+32	25
	+33	20
	+34	

HP = 55'

Corrn	Alt
-14'	89°
-13	88
-12	87
-11	86
-10	85
-9	84
-8	83
-7	81
-6	80
-5	79
-4	78
-3	77
-2	76
-1	75
0	74
+1	73
+2	72
+3	71
+4	69
+5	68

Alt	Corrn	Alt
0° 04'	+6	67
0 08	+7	66
0 14	+8	65
0 19	+9	64
0 24	+10	62
0 30	+11	61
0 37	+12	60
0 43	+13	59
0 50	+14	57
0 57	+15	56
1 05	+16	55
1 14	+17	53
1 23	+18	52
1 33	+19	51
1 43	+20	49
1 55	+21	48
2 08	+22	46
2 22	+23	45
2 38	+24	43
2 56	+25	41
3 16	+26	40
3 39	+27	38
4 07	+28	36
4 39	+29	34
5 19	+30	32
6 10	+31	29
7 18	+32	27
8 59	+33	23
12 46	+34	18
	+35	

HP = 56'

Corrn	Alt
-14'	89°
-13	88
-12	87
-11	86
-10	85
-9	83
-8	82
-7	81
-6	80
-5	79
-4	78
-3	77
-2	76
-1	75
0	74
+1	73
+2	72
+3	71
+4	69
+5	68
+6	67

Alt	Corrn	Alt
0° 05'	+7	66
0 10	+8	65
0 15	+9	64
0 20	+10	63
0 26	+11	61
0 32	+12	60
0 38	+13	59
0 45	+14	58
0 52	+15	56
0 59	+16	55
1 07	+17	54
1 16	+18	53
1 25	+19	51
1 35	+20	50
1 46	+21	48
1 58	+22	47
2 11	+23	45
2 26	+24	44
2 42	+25	42
3 01	+26	41
3 22	+27	39
3 46	+28	37
4 15	+29	35
4 49	+30	33
5 32	+31	31
6 27	+32	28
7 42	+33	25
9 41	+34	22
	+35	

HP = 57'

Corrn	Alt
-15'	89°
-14	88
-13	87
-12	86
-11	85
-10	84
-9	83
-8	82
-7	81
-6	80
-5	79
-4	78
-3	77
-2	76
-1	75
0	74
+1	73
+2	72
+3	71
+4	70
+5	68
+6	67

Alt	Corrn	Alt
0° 01'	+7	66
0 06	+8	65
0 11	+9	64
0 16	+10	63
0 22	+11	62
0 28	+12	60
0 34	+13	59
0 40	+14	58
0 47	+15	57
0 54	+16	56
1 02	+17	54
1 10	+18	53
1 19	+19	52
1 28	+20	50
1 38	+21	49
1 49	+22	47
2 02	+23	46
2 15	+24	45
2 30	+25	43
2 47	+26	41
3 06	+27	40
3 28	+28	38
3 54	+29	36
4 24	+30	34
5 00	+31	32
5 46	+32	29
6 45	+33	27
8 09	+34	24
10 34	+35	20
	+36	

HP = 58'

Corrn	Alt
-15'	89°
-14	88
-13	87
-12	86
-11	85
-10	84
-9	83
-8	82
-7	81
-6	80
-5	79
-4	78
-3	77
-2	76
-1	75
0	74
+1	73
+2	72
+3	71
+4	70
+5	69
+6	67
+7	66

Alt	Corrn	Alt
0° 03'	+8	65
0 08	+9	64
0 13	+10	63
0 18	+11	62
0 23	+12	61
0 29	+13	60
0 35	+14	58
0 42	+15	57
0 49	+16	56
0 56	+17	55
1 04	+18	54
1 12	+19	52
1 21	+20	51
1 31	+21	49
1 41	+22	48
1 53	+23	47
2 05	+24	45
2 19	+25	44
2 35	+26	42
2 52	+27	41
3 12	+28	39
3 35	+29	37
4 01	+30	35
4 33	+31	33
5 12	+32	31
6 00	+33	29
7 05	+34	26
8 41	+35	23
11 56	+36	18
	+37	

HP = 59'

Corrn	Alt
-15'	89°
-14	88
-13	87
-12	86
-11	85
-10	84
-9	83
-8	82
-7	81
-6	80
-5	79
-4	78
-3	77
-2	76
-1	75
0	74
+1	73
+2	72
+3	71
+4	70
+5	69
+6	68
+7	66

Alt	Corrn	Alt
0° 03'	+8	65
0 08	+9	64
0 13	+10	63
0 19	+11	62
0 25	+12	61
0 31	+13	60
0 37	+14	58
0 44	+15	57
0 51	+16	56
0 58	+17	55
1 06	+18	53
1 14	+19	52
1 24	+20	51
1 33	+21	49
1 44	+22	48
1 56	+23	46
2 09	+24	44
2 23	+25	43
2 39	+26	41
2 57	+27	39
3 18	+28	38
3 42	+29	36
4 10	+30	34
4 43	+31	32
5 24	+32	29
6 16	+33	28
7 28	+34	25
9 19	+35	22
	+36	
	+37	

HP = 60'

Corrn	Alt
-15'	89°
-14	88
-13	87
-12	86
-11	85
-10	84
-9	83
-8	82
-7	81
-6	80
-5	79
-4	78
-3	77
-2	76
-1	75
0	74
+1	73
+2	72
+3	71
+4	70
+5	69
+6	68
+7	67
+8	66

Alt	Corrn	Alt
0° 01'	+9	65
0 05	+10	63
0 10	+11	62
0 15	+12	61
0 21	+13	60
0 27	+14	59
0 33	+15	58
0 39	+16	57
0 46	+17	55
0 53	+18	54
1 00	+19	53
1 08	+20	52
1 17	+21	50
1 26	+22	49
1 36	+23	48
1 47	+24	46
1 59	+25	45
2 13	+26	44
2 27	+27	42
2 44	+28	41
3 03	+29	39
3 24	+30	37
3 49	+31	35
4 18	+32	34
4 53	+33	32
5 37	+34	29
6 34	+35	28
7 54	+36	24
10 07	+37	20
	+38	

HP = 61'

Corrn	Alt
-15'	89°
-14	88
-13	87
-12	86
-11	85
-10	84
-9	83
-8	82
-7	81
-6	80
-5	79
-4	78
-3	77
-2	76
-1	75
0	74
+1	73
+2	72
+3	71
+4	70
+5	69
+6	68
+7	67
+8	66
+9	65

Alt	Corrn	Alt
0° 02'	+10	64
0 07	+11	63
0 12	+12	61
0 17	+13	60
0 22	+14	59
0 28	+15	58
0 34	+16	57
0 41	+17	56
0 47	+18	55
0 55	+19	53
1 02	+20	52
1 11	+21	51
1 19	+22	50
1 29	+23	48
1 39	+24	47
1 51	+25	46
2 03	+26	44
2 17	+27	43
2 32	+28	41
2 49	+29	40
3 08	+30	38
3 31	+31	35
3 56	+32	35
4 27	+33	33
5 05	+34	31
5 51	+35	28
6 53	+36	26
8 23	+37	23
11 15	+38	18
	+39	

MOON ALTITUDE CORRECTIONS–LOWER LIMB

DIP Corrn

m	Corrn 0′	ft
0.0	0′	0
0.7	-1	2
2.0	-2	6
3.9	-3	13
6.5	-4	21
9.7	-5	32
13.6	-6	44
18.1	-7	59
23.3	-8	76
29.1	-9	95
	-10	

HP = 54′

Alt	Corrn	Alt
	+16′	89°
	+17	87
	+18	86
	+19	85
	+20	84
	+21	83
	+22	82
	+23	81
	+24	80
	+25	79
	+26	78
	+27	77
	+28	75
	+29	74
	+30	73
	+31	72
	+32	71
	+33	70
	+34	69
0° 05′	+35	67
0 10	+36	66
0 15	+37	65
0 21	+38	64
0 26	+39	63
0 32	+40	61
0 38	+41	60
0 45	+42	59
0 52	+43	58
1 00	+44	56
1 08	+45	55
1 16	+46	54
1 26	+47	52
1 36	+48	51
1 47	+49	49
1 59	+50	48
2 12	+51	46
2 26	+52	45
2 43	+53	43
3 01	+54	41
3 22	+55	40
3 47	+56	38
4 16	+57	36
4 50	+58	34
5 33	+59	31
6 27	+60	29
7 42	+61	26
9 40	+62	22
	+63	

HP = 55′

Alt	Corrn	Alt
	+16′	89°
	+17	88
	+18	87
	+19	86
	+20	85
	+21	84
	+22	83
	+23	81
	+24	80
	+25	79
	+26	78
	+27	77
	+28	76
	+29	75
	+30	74
	+31	73
	+32	72
	+33	70
	+34	69
	+35	68
	+36	67
0° 04′	+37	66
0 09	+38	65
0 14	+39	64
0 19	+40	62
0 25	+41	61
0 30	+42	60
0 37	+43	59
0 43	+44	57
0 50	+45	56
0 58	+46	55
1 05	+47	53
1 14	+48	52
1 23	+49	51
1 33	+50	49
1 43	+51	48
1 55	+52	46
2 08	+53	45
2 22	+54	43
2 38	+55	41
2 56	+56	40
3 16	+57	38
3 40	+58	36
4 07	+59	34
4 40	+60	32
5 20	+61	29
6 11	+62	26
7 20	+63	23
9 03	+64	17
13 00	+65	

HP = 56′

Alt	Corrn	Alt
	+16′	89°
	+17	88
	+18	87
	+19	86
	+20	85
	+21	84
	+22	83
	+23	82
	+24	81
	+25	80
	+26	79
	+27	78
	+28	77
	+29	76
	+30	74
	+31	73
	+32	72
	+33	71
	+34	70
	+35	69
	+36	68
0° 02′	+37	67
0 07	+38	66
0 12	+39	64
0 18	+40	63
0 23	+41	62
0 29	+42	61
0 35	+43	60
0 41	+44	58
0 48	+45	57
0 55	+46	56
1 03	+47	55
1 12	+48	53
1 20	+49	52
1 30	+50	50
1 40	+51	49
1 52	+52	48
2 04	+53	46
2 18	+54	45
2 34	+55	43
2 51	+56	41
3 11	+57	40
3 33	+58	38
3 59	+59	36
4 31	+60	34
5 09	+61	32
5 56	+62	30
6 59	+63	27
8 30	+64	24
11 21	+65	19
	+66	

HP = 57′

Alt	Corrn	Alt
	+17′	88°
	+18	87
	+19	86
	+20	85
	+21	84
	+22	83
	+23	82
	+24	81
	+25	80
	+26	79
	+27	78
	+28	77
	+29	76
	+30	75
	+31	74
	+32	73
	+33	72
	+34	71
	+35	70
	+36	69
	+37	67
0° 01′	+38	66
0 06	+39	65
0 11	+40	64
0 16	+41	63
0 22	+42	62
0 27	+43	61
0 33	+44	59
0 40	+45	58
0 46	+46	57
0 53	+47	56
1 01	+48	54
1 09	+49	53
1 18	+50	52
1 27	+51	50
1 38	+52	49
1 49	+53	48
2 01	+54	46
2 14	+55	45
2 29	+56	43
2 46	+57	41
3 05	+58	40
3 27	+59	38
3 52	+60	36
4 22	+61	35
4 58	+62	32
5 42	+63	30
6 41	+64	27
8 02	+65	24
10 21	+66	21
	+67	

HP = 58′

Alt	Corrn	Alt
	+17′	89°
	+18	88
	+19	87
	+20	86
	+21	85
	+22	84
	+23	82
	+24	82
	+25	81
	+26	80
	+27	79
	+28	78
	+29	77
	+30	76
	+31	75
	+32	73
	+33	72
	+34	71
	+35	70
	+36	69
	+37	68
	+38	67
0° 05′	+39	66
0 10	+40	65
0 15	+41	64
0 20	+42	63
0 26	+43	62
0 32	+44	60
0 38	+45	59
0 44	+46	58
0 51	+47	57
0 59	+48	55
1 07	+49	54
1 15	+50	53
1 25	+51	52
1 35	+52	50
1 46	+53	49
1 57	+54	48
2 11	+55	46
2 25	+56	45
2 46	+57	43
3 00	+58	42
3 21	+59	40
3 45	+60	38
4 13	+61	36
4 47	+62	35
5 29	+63	33
6 23	+64	30
7 37	+65	28
9 35	+66	25
	+67	21
	+68	

HP = 59′

Alt	Corrn	Alt
	+17′	89°
	+18	88
	+19	87
	+20	86
	+21	85
	+22	84
	+23	83
	+24	82
	+25	81
	+26	80
	+27	79
	+28	78
	+29	77
	+30	76
	+31	75
	+32	74
	+33	73
	+34	72
	+35	71
	+36	70
	+37	69
	+38	68
	+39	67
0° 03′	+40	66
0 08	+41	65
0 13	+42	63
0 19	+43	62
0 24	+44	61
0 30	+45	60
0 36	+46	59
0 43	+47	57
0 50	+48	56
0 57	+49	55
1 05	+50	54
1 13	+51	53
1 22	+52	51
1 32	+53	50
1 43	+54	49
1 54	+55	47
2 07	+56	46
2 21	+57	45
2 37	+58	43
2 54	+59	42
3 15	+60	40
3 38	+61	38
4 05	+62	37
4 37	+63	35
5 17	+64	33
6 07	+65	31
7 15	+66	28
8 57	+67	26
	+68	22
	+69	

HP = 60′

Alt	Corrn	Alt
	+18′	89°
	+19	88
	+20	87
	+21	86
	+22	85
	+23	84
	+24	83
	+25	82
	+26	81
	+27	80
	+28	79
	+29	78
	+30	77
	+31	76
	+32	75
	+33	74
	+34	73
	+35	72
	+36	71
	+37	70
	+38	68
	+39	67
	+40	66
	+41	65
0° 02′	+42	64
0 07	+43	63
0 12	+44	62
0 17	+45	61
0 23	+46	60
0 28	+47	59
0 34	+48	57
0 41	+49	56
0 48	+50	55
0 55	+51	54
1 03	+52	53
1 11	+53	51
1 20	+54	50
1 29	+55	49
1 40	+56	47
1 51	+57	46
2 03	+58	45
2 17	+59	43
2 32	+60	42
2 49	+61	40
3 09	+62	38
3 31	+63	37
3 57	+64	35
4 28	+65	33
5 06	+66	31
5 53	+67	29
6 55	+68	26
8 25	+69	23
11 17	+70	19
	+71	

HP = 61′

Alt	Corrn	Alt
	+18′	89°
	+19	88
	+20	87
	+21	86
	+22	85
	+23	84
	+24	83
	+25	82
	+26	81
	+27	80
	+28	79
	+29	78
	+30	77
	+31	76
	+32	75
	+33	74
	+34	73
	+35	72
	+36	71
	+37	70
	+38	69
	+39	68
	+40	67
	+41	66
	+42	65
0° 01′	+43	64
0 05	+44	63
0 10	+45	62
0 16	+46	61
0 21	+47	60
0 27	+48	58
0 33	+49	57
0 39	+50	56
0 46	+51	55
0 53	+52	54
1 00	+53	52
1 08	+54	51
1 17	+55	50
1 26	+56	49
1 37	+57	47
1 48	+58	46
2 00	+59	45
2 13	+60	43
2 28	+61	42
2 45	+62	40
3 03	+63	39
3 25	+64	37
3 50	+65	35
4 19	+66	33
4 55	+67	31
5 39	+68	29
6 36	+69	27
7 57	+70	24
10 15	+71	20
	+72	

SEXTANT ALTITUDE OBSERVATIONS

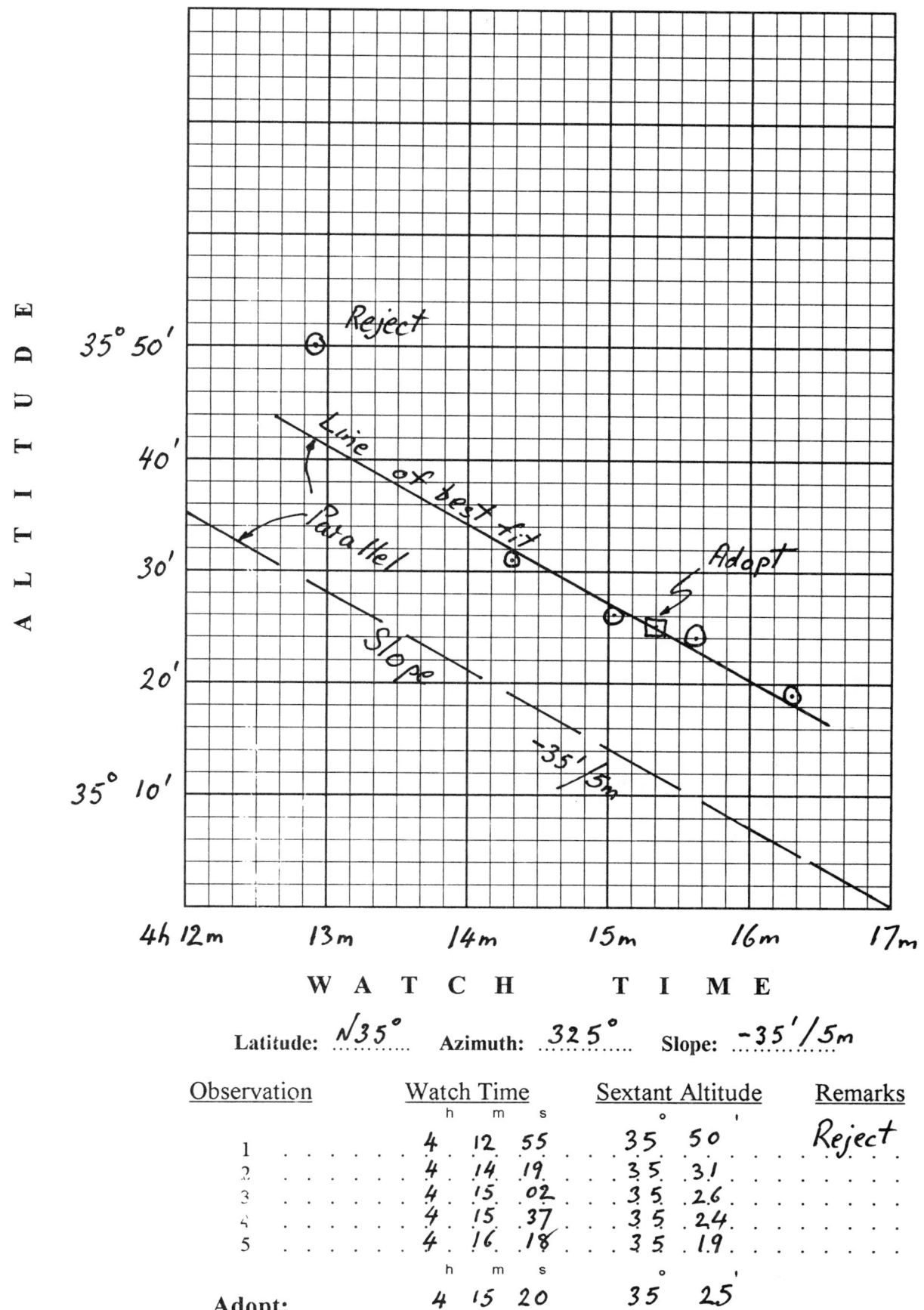

Latitude: N35° Azimuth: 32.5° Slope: -35'/5m

Observation	Watch Time			Sextant Altitude		Remarks
	h	m	s	°	'	
1	4	12	55	35	50	Reject
2	4	14	19	35	31	
3	4	15	02	35	26	
4	4	15	37	35	24	
5	4	16	18	35	19	
	h	m	s	°	'	
Adopt:	4	15	20	35	25	

Latitude N60° | Latitude N60°

STARS — Local Hour Angle Aries

Name	Mag	0° Alt Az	10° Alt Az	20° Alt Az	30° Alt Az	40° Alt Az	50° Alt Az	60° Alt Az	70° Alt Az	80° Alt Az	90° Alt Az	100° Alt Az	110° Alt Az	120° Alt Az	130° Alt Az	140° Alt Az	150° Alt Az	160° Alt Az	170° Alt Az	180° Alt Az
		° °	° °	° °	° °	° °	° °	° °	° °	° °	° °	° °	° °	° °	° °	° °	° °	° °	° °	° °
Alpheratz	2.2	59 176	59 193	57 209	54 224	50 237	46 248	41 258	36 267	31 276	26 284	21 292	17 300	13 308	9 316	6 324	3 332	1 341	# ####	# ####
Ankaa	2.4	# ####	# ####	# ####	# ####	# ####	# ####	# ####	# ####	# ####	# ####	# ####	# ####	# ####	# ####	# ####	# ####	# ####	# ####	# ####
Schedah	2.5	84 119	87 179	84 241	79 260	74 271	69 278	64 285	59 290	55 296	50 302	46 307	42 313	39 318	36 324	33 330	31 336	29 342	28 348	27 354
Diphda	2.2	12 169	12 179	12 189	10 198	9 208	6 217	3 226	# ####	# ####	# ####	# ####	# ####	# ####	# ####	# ####	# ####	# ####	# ####	# ####
Achernar	0.6	# ####	# ####	# ####	# ####	# ####	# ####	# ####	# ####	# ####	# ####	# ####	# ####	# ####	# ####	# ####	# ####	# ####	# ####	# ####
Hamal	2.2	47 135	50 148	53 162	53 177	53 193	51 207	49 221	45 233	41 244	36 254	31 264	26 272	21 281	16 289	12 297	7 305	4 314	0 322	# ####
Polaris	2.1	61 001	61 001	61 000	61 000	61 000	61 000	61 359	61 359	61 359	60 359	60 359	60 359	60 359	60 359	60 359	60 359	60 359	59 359	59 359
Acamar	3.1	# ####	# ####	# ####	# ####	# ####	# ####	# ####	# ####	# ####	# ####	# ####	# ####	# ####	# ####	# ####	# ####	# ####	# ####	# ####
Menkar	2.8	24 129	28 139	31 150	33 161	34 173	34 185	33 197	31 209	28 220	25 230	21 240	16 249	11 258	6 267	1 276	# ####	# ####	# ####	# ####
Mirfak	1.9	60 086	65 095	70 106	74 121	78 143	80 176	79 211	75 235	71 251	66 263	61 272	56 280	51 287	46 293	42 300	38 306	34 313	30 319	27 326
Aldebaran	1.1	25 100	30 109	34 119	38 130	42 142	44 154	46 168	47 181	46 195	44 209	41 221	37 232	33 243	29 253	24 262	19 271	14 279	9 288	4 296
Rigel	0.3	# ####	3 113	8 121	12 131	15 140	18 150	20 160	21 171	22 181	21 192	20 203	17 213	14 222	11 232	7 241	2 250	# ####	# ####	# ####
Capella	0.2	43 070	48 077	53 085	58 094	63 104	68 116	72 132	75 155	76 182	75 209	71 231	67 246	62 258	57 268	52 276	47 284	43 291	38 298	34 305
Bellatrix	1.7	10 094	15 103	20 112	24 122	28 132	31 143	34 154	36 166	36 178	36 191	35 203	32 214	29 225	25 236	21 245	16 254	11 263	6 272	1 281
Elnath	1.8	29 082	34 090	39 099	43 109	48 119	52 132	55 145	58 161	59 177	58 194	56 210	53 224	49 237	45 248	40 258	35 267	30 276	25 284	21 292
Alnilam	1.8	2 096	7 105	12 114	16 123	20 132	23 143	26 153	28 164	29 176	29 187	28 198	25 209	23 220	19 230	15 239	11 248	6 257	1 266	# ####
Betelgeuse	*	7 087	12 096	17 105	22 114	26 124	30 134	33 145	36 157	37 169	37 182	37 194	35 206	32 217	29 228	25 239	21 248	16 257	11 266	6 275
Canopus	-0.9	# ####	# ####	# ####	# ####	# ####	# ####	# ####	# ####	# ####	# ####	# ####	# ####	# ####	# ####	# ####	# ####	# ####	# ####	# ####
Sirius	-1.6	# ####	# ####	# ####	# ####	# ####	3 132	6 141	9 150	11 159	13 169	13 179	13 189	12 198	10 208	7 217	4 226	# ####	# ####	# ####
Adhara	1.6	# ####	# ####	# ####	# ####	# ####	# ####	# ####	# ####	# ####	0 167	1 176	1 185	0 193	# ####	# ####	# ####	# ####	# ####	# ####
Procyon	0.5	# ####	# ####	2 083	7 092	12 101	17 110	21 119	26 129	29 139	32 150	34 162	35 174	35 186	34 198	32 210	29 221	25 231	21 241	17 251
Pollux	1.2	12 054	16 062	21 070	26 078	31 086	36 095	41 104	45 115	50 126	53 139	56 154	58 170	58 186	57 202	54 217	51 231	47 242	42 253	37 263
Avior	1.7	# ####	# ####	# ####	# ####	# ####	# ####	# ####	# ####	# ####	# ####	# ####	# ####	# ####	# ####	# ####	# ####	# ####	# ####	# ####
Suhail	2.2	# ####	# ####	# ####	# ####	# ####	# ####	# ####	# ####	# ####	# ####	# ####	# ####	# ####	# ####	# ####	# ####	# ####	# ####	# ####
Miaplacidus	1.8	# ####	# ####	# ####	# ####	# ####	# ####	# ####	# ####	# ####	# ####	# ####	# ####	# ####	# ####	# ####	# ####	# ####	# ####	# ####
Alphard	2.2	# ####	# ####	# ####	# ####	# ####	# ####	# ####	1 110	6 119	10 128	14 137	17 147	19 157	21 167	21 178	21 189	20 199	18 209	15 219
Regulus	1.3	# ####	# ####	# ####	# ####	# ####	4 074	9 082	14 091	19 100	24 109	29 118	33 129	36 140	39 152	41 164	42 177	42 190	40 203	38 215
Dubhe	2.0	32 008	33 013	35 019	36 024	39 029	41 034	44 039	48 044	51 049	55 053	59 058	64 062	68 065	73 069	77 071	82 070	87 056	87 313	83 290
Denebola	2.2	# ####	# ####	# ####	# ####	# ####	# ####	# ####	4 068	9 076	14 085	19 094	24 103	29 112	33 122	37 133	40 144	43 157	44 170	45 184
Gienah	2.8	# ####	# ####	# ####	# ####	# ####	# ####	# ####	# ####	# ####	# ####	# ####	# ####	# ####	1 130	5 138	8 147	10 157	12 166	12 176
Acrux	1.1	# ####	# ####	# ####	# ####	# ####	# ####	# ####	# ####	# ####	# ####	# ####	# ####	# ####	# ####	# ####	# ####	# ####	# ####	# ####
Gacrux	1.6	# ####	# ####	# ####	# ####	# ####	# ####	# ####	# ####	# ####	# ####	# ####	# ####	# ####	# ####	# ####	# ####	# ####	# ####	# ####
Alioth	1.7	26 352	26 358	26 004	27 010	28 016	30 022	32 028	34 034	37 040	41 046	44 052	49 057	53 063	57 068	62 074	67 081	72 088	77 098	82 114
Spica	1.2	# ####	# ####	# ####	# ####	# ####	# ####	# ####	# ####	# ####	# ####	# ####	# ####	# ####	# ####	4 120	8 129	12 139	15 148	17 158
Alkaid	1.9	21 342	20 348	19 355	19 002	20 009	21 016	23 023	25 029	27 036	31 043	34 049	38 055	42 062	47 068	52 075	57 083	62 091	67 100	71 113
Hadar	0.9	# ####	# ####	# ####	# ####	# ####	# ####	# ####	# ####	# ####	# ####	# ####	# ####	# ####	# ####	# ####	# ####	# ####	# ####	# ####
Menkent	2.3	# ####	# ####	# ####	# ####	# ####	# ####	# ####	# ####	# ####	# ####	# ####	# ####	# ####	# ####	# ####	# ####	# ####	# ####	# ####
Arcturus	0.2	# ####	# ####	# ####	# ####	# ####	# ####	# ####	# ####	# ####	1 052	5 060	10 069	15 077	20 085	25 094	29 103	34 113	39 123	43 134
Rigil Kent.	0.1	# ####	# ####	# ####	# ####	# ####	# ####	# ####	# ####	# ####	# ####	# ####	# ####	# ####	# ####	# ####	# ####	# ####	# ####	# ####
Zuben'ubi	2.9	# ####	# ####	# ####	# ####	# ####	# ####	# ####	# ####	# ####	# ####	# ####	# ####	# ####	# ####	# ####	# ####	# ####	3 130	7 139
Kochab	2.2	47 344	46 348	45 351	44 355	44 359	44 003	45 007	45 010	46 014	48 017	49 021	51 024	53 027	56 029	58 031	61 032	64 033	66 033	69 031
Alphecca	2.3	7 314	4 322	1 330	# ####	# ####	# ####	# ####	# ####	# ####	2 032	5 040	8 049	12 057	16 065	21 073	26 081	31 090	36 098	41 108
Antares	1.2	# ####	# ####	# ####	# ####	# ####	# ####	# ####	# ####	# ####	# ####	# ####	# ####	# ####	# ####	# ####	# ####	# ####	# ####	# ####
Atria	1.9	# ####	# ####	# ####	# ####	# ####	# ####	# ####	# ####	# ####	# ####	# ####	# ####	# ####	# ####	# ####	# ####	# ####	# ####	# ####
Sabik	2.6	# ####	# ####	# ####	# ####	# ####	# ####	# ####	# ####	# ####	# ####	# ####	# ####	# ####	# ####	# ####	# ####	# ####	# ####	# ####
Shaula	1.7	# ####	# ####	# ####	# ####	# ####	# ####	# ####	# ####	# ####	# ####	# ####	# ####	# ####	# ####	# ####	# ####	# ####	# ####	# ####
Rasalhague	2.1	8 282	3 290	# ####	# ####	# ####	# ####	# ####	# ####	# ####	# ####	# ####	# ####	# ####	# ####	# ####	# ####	4 072	9 080	14 089
Eltanin	2.4	42 303	38 309	35 315	31 321	28 328	26 334	24 341	23 347	22 354	21 001	22 007	23 014	24 020	26 027	29 033	32 040	35 046	39 052	43 058
Kaus Aust.	2.0	# ####	# ####	# ####	# ####	# ####	# ####	# ####	# ####	# ####	# ####	# ####	# ####	# ####	# ####	# ####	# ####	# ####	# ####	# ####
Vega	0.1	37 285	33 292	28 300	24 307	20 315	17 322	14 329	12 337	10 345	9 353	9 001	9 008	10 016	12 024	14 032	17 039	21 047	24 054	29 061
Nunki	2.1	# ####	# ####	# ####	# ####	# ####	# ####	# ####	# ####	# ####	# ####	# ####	# ####	# ####	# ####	# ####	# ####	# ####	# ####	# ####
Altair	0.9	21 250	16 259	12 268	7 276	2 285	# ####	# ####	# ####	# ####	# ####	# ####	# ####	# ####	# ####	# ####	# ####	# ####	# ####	# ####
Peacock	2.1	# ####	# ####	# ####	# ####	# ####	# ####	# ####	# ####	# ####	# ####	# ####	# ####	# ####	# ####	# ####	# ####	# ####	# ####	# ####
Deneb	1.3	57 266	52 274	48 282	43 290	38 297	34 303	30 310	26 317	23 324	20 331	18 338	17 345	16 352	15 000	16 007	16 014	18 021	20 029	23 036
Enif	2.5	34 222	30 232	26 242	21 252	16 261	12 270	7 278	2 287	# ####	# ####	# ####	# ####	# ####	# ####	# ####	# ####	# ####	# ####	# ####
Al Na'ir	2.2	# ####	# ####	# ####	# ####	# ####	# ####	# ####	# ####	# ####	# ####	# ####	# ####	# ####	# ####	# ####	# ####	# ####	# ####	# ####
Fomalhaut	1.3	# ####	# ####	# ####	# ####	# ####	# ####	# ####	# ####	# ####	# ####	# ####	# ####	# ####	# ####	# ####	# ####	# ####	# ####	# ####
Markab	2.6	44 199	42 212	39 224	35 235	31 245	26 255	21 264	16 272	11 281	6 289	2 298	# ####	# ####	# ####	# ####	# ####	# ####	# ####	# ####

* Variable 0.1 - 1.2

SUN MOON PLANETS — Local Hour Angle Body

	0° Alt Az	10° Alt Az	20° Alt Az	30° Alt Az	40° Alt Az	50° Alt Az	60° Alt Az	70° Alt Az	80° Alt Az	90° Alt Az	100° Alt Az	110° Alt Az	120° Alt Az	130° Alt Az	140° Alt Az	150° Alt Az	160° Alt Az	170° Alt Az	180° Alt Az
	° °	° °	° °	° °	° °	° °	° °	° °	° °	° °	° °	° °	° °	° °	° °	° °	° °	° °	° °
Decl'n N30°	60 180	59 197	57 213	54 227	50 240	45 251	41 261	36 270	31 278	26 286	21 294	17 302	13 310	9 318	6 326	3 334	1 343	0 351	# ####
Decl'n N25°	55 180	54 196	52 210	49 224	45 236	41 247	36 257	31 266	26 275	21 283	17 291	12 299	8 308	4 316	1 324	# ####	# ####	# ####	# ####
Decl'n N20°	50 180	49 195	48 208	45 221	41 233	37 244	32 254	27 263	22 272	17 280	12 289	8 297	4 305	# ####	# ####	# ####	# ####	# ####	# ####
Decl'n N15°	45 180	44 194	43 207	40 219	36 231	32 241	28 251	23 260	18 269	13 278	8 286	3 295	# ####	# ####	# ####	# ####	# ####	# ####	# ####
Decl'n N10°	40 180	39 193	38 205	35 217	32 228	28 239	23 248	19 258	14 266	9 275	4 284	# ####	# ####	# ####	# ####	# ####	# ####	# ####	# ####
Decl'n N5°	35 180	34 192	33 204	30 215	27 226	23 236	19 246	14 255	9 264	4 273	# ####	# ####	# ####	# ####	# ####	# ####	# ####	# ####	# ####
Decl'n 0°	30 180	29 192	28 203	26 214	23 224	19 234	14 243	10 253	5 261	0 270	# ####	# ####	# ####	# ####	# ####	# ####	# ####	# ####	# ####
Decl'n S5°	25 180	25 191	23 202	21 212	18 222	14 232	10 241	5 250	1 259	# ####	# ####	# ####	# ####	# ####	# ####	# ####	# ####	# ####	# ####
Decl'n S10°	20 180	20 190	18 201	16 211	13 221	10 230	5 239	1 248	# ####	# ####	# ####	# ####	# ####	# ####	# ####	# ####	# ####	# ####	# ####
Decl'n S15°	15 180	15 190	13 200	11 209	8 219	5 228	1 237	# ####	# ####	# ####	# ####	# ####	# ####	# ####	# ####	# ####	# ####	# ####	# ####
Decl'n S20°	10 180	10 190	8 199	6 208	4 217	0 226	# ####	# ####	# ####	# ####	# ####	# ####	# ####	# ####	# ####	# ####	# ####	# ####	# ####
Decl'n S25°	5 180	5 189	3 198	2 207	# ####	# ####	# ####	# ####	# ####	# ####	# ####	# ####	# ####	# ####	# ####	# ####	# ####	# ####	# ####
Decl'n S30°	0 180	# ####	# ####	# ####	# ####	# ####	# ####	# ####	# ####	# ####	# ####	# ####	# ####	# ####	# ####	# ####	# ####	# ####	# ####

Latitude N60°

Latitude N60°

STARS — Local Hour Angle Aries (Alt ° Az °)

Name	Mag	180° Alt Az	190° Alt Az	200° Alt Az	210° Alt Az	220° Alt Az	230° Alt Az	240° Alt Az	250° Alt Az	260° Alt Az	270° Alt Az	280° Alt Az	290° Alt Az	300° Alt Az	310° Alt Az	320° Alt Az	330° Alt Az	340° Alt Az	350° Alt Az	360° Alt Az
Alpheratz	2.2	# ####	# ####	0 016	2 024	4 033	7 041	11 049	15 057	19 065	24 073	29 081	34 089	39 098	44 108	48 119	52 131	56 144	58 160	59 176
Ankaa	2.4	# ####	# ####	# ####	# ####	# ####	# ####	# ####	# ####	# ####	# ####	# ####	# ####	# ####	# ####	# ####	# ####	# ####	# ####	# ####
Schedah	2.5	27 354	27 000	27 006	28 012	29 018	31 024	33 030	36 036	39 042	42 047	46 053	50 058	55 064	59 069	64 075	69 082	74 089	79 099	84 119
Diphda	2.2	# ####	# ####	# ####	# ####	# ####	# ####	# ####	# ####	# ####	# ####	# ####	# ####	# ####	# ####	2 132	5 141	8 150	10 160	12 169
Achernar	0.6	# ####	# ####	# ####	# ####	# ####	# ####	# ####	# ####	# ####	# ####	# ####	# ####	# ####	# ####	# ####	# ####	# ####	# ####	# ####
Hamal	2.2	# ####	# ####	# ####	# ####	# ####	# ####	# ####	# ####	2 043	6 052	10 060	15 068	19 076	24 085	29 093	34 102	39 112	43 123	47 135
Polaris	2.1	59 359	59 359	59 000	59 000	59 000	59 000	59 001	59 001	59 001	60 001	60 001	60 001	60 001	60 001	60 001	60 001	60 001	60 001	61 001
Acamar	3.1	# ####	# ####	# ####	# ####	# ####	# ####	# ####	# ####	# ####	# ####	# ####	# ####	# ####	# ####	# ####	# ####	# ####	# ####	# ####
Menkar	2.8	# ####	# ####	# ####	# ####	# ####	# ####	# ####	# ####	# ####	# ####	# ####	# ####	# ####	1 083	6 092	11 101	16 110	20 119	24 129
Mirfak	1.9	27 326	25 332	23 339	21 346	20 352	20 359	20 006	21 013	22 020	24 026	27 033	30 039	33 046	37 052	41 059	45 065	50 072	55 079	60 086
Aldebaran	1.1	4 296	# ####	# ####	# ####	# ####	# ####	# ####	# ####	# ####	# ####	# ####	# ####	# ####	1 057	5 066	10 074	15 082	20 091	25 100
Rigel	0.3	# ####	# ####	# ####	# ####	# ####	# ####	# ####	# ####	# ####	# ####	# ####	# ####	# ####	# ####	# ####	# ####	# ####	# ####	# ####
Capella	0.2	34 305	30 311	26 318	23 325	21 332	19 339	17 346	16 353	16 001	16 008	17 015	19 022	21 029	24 036	27 043	31 050	35 056	39 063	43 070
Bellatrix	1.7	1 281	# ####	# ####	# ####	# ####	# ####	# ####	# ####	# ####	# ####	# ####	# ####	# ####	# ####	# ####	# ####	# ####	5 086	10 094
Elnath	1.8	21 292	16 300	12 308	8 316	5 324	2 333	0 341	# ####	# ####	# ####	# ####	2 025	4 033	7 041	11 050	15 058	19 066	24 073	29 082
Alnilam	1.8	# ####	# ####	# ####	# ####	# ####	# ####	# ####	# ####	# ####	# ####	# ####	# ####	# ####	# ####	# ####	# ####	# ####	# ####	2 096
Betelgeuse	*	6 275	1 283	# ####	# ####	# ####	# ####	# ####	# ####	# ####	# ####	# ####	# ####	# ####	# ####	# ####	# ####	# ####	2 079	7 087
Canopus	-0.9	# ####	# ####	# ####	# ####	# ####	# ####	# ####	# ####	# ####	# ####	# ####	# ####	# ####	# ####	# ####	# ####	# ####	# ####	# ####
Sirius	-1.6	# ####	# ####	# ####	# ####	# ####	# ####	# ####	# ####	# ####	# ####	# ####	# ####	# ####	# ####	# ####	# ####	# ####	# ####	# ####
Adhara	1.6	# ####	# ####	# ####	# ####	# ####	# ####	# ####	# ####	# ####	# ####	# ####	# ####	# ####	# ####	# ####	# ####	# ####	# ####	# ####
Procyon	0.5	17 251	12 260	7 268	2 277	# ####	# ####	# ####	# ####	# ####	# ####	# ####	# ####	# ####	# ####	# ####	# ####	# ####	# ####	# ####
Pollux	1.2	37 263	32 271	27 280	22 288	18 296	13 304	9 312	6 320	3 328	1 337	# ####	# ####	# ####	# ####	0 021	2 029	5 038	8 046	12 054
Avior	1.7	# ####	# ####	# ####	# ####	# ####	# ####	# ####	# ####	# ####	# ####	# ####	# ####	# ####	# ####	# ####	# ####	# ####	# ####	# ####
Suhail	2.2	# ####	# ####	# ####	# ####	# ####	# ####	# ####	# ####	# ####	# ####	# ####	# ####	# ####	# ####	# ####	# ####	# ####	# ####	# ####
Miaplacidus	1.8	# ####	# ####	# ####	# ####	# ####	# ####	# ####	# ####	# ####	# ####	# ####	# ####	# ####	# ####	# ####	# ####	# ####	# ####	# ####
Alphard	2.2	15 219	12 229	8 238	3 247	# ####	# ####	# ####	# ####	# ####	# ####	# ####	# ####	# ####	# ####	# ####	# ####	# ####	# ####	# ####
Regulus	1.3	38 215	34 227	30 237	26 247	21 257	16 266	11 274	6 283	2 291	# ####	# ####	# ####	# ####	# ####	# ####	# ####	# ####	# ####	# ####
Dubhe	2.0	83 290	78 289	74 291	69 294	64 298	60 302	56 306	52 310	48 315	45 320	42 325	39 330	37 335	35 340	33 346	32 351	32 357	32 002	32 008
Denebola	2.2	45 184	44 197	42 210	39 222	35 233	31 244	26 253	21 262	16 271	11 280	6 288	2 297	# ####	# ####	# ####	# ####	# ####	# ####	# ####
Gienah	2.8	12 176	12 186	11 196	10 205	7 214	4 223	0 232	# ####	# ####	# ####	# ####	# ####	# ####	# ####	# ####	# ####	# ####	# ####	# ####
Acrux	1.1	# ####	# ####	# ####	# ####	# ####	# ####	# ####	# ####	# ####	# ####	# ####	# ####	# ####	# ####	# ####	# ####	# ####	# ####	# ####
Gacrux	1.6	# ####	# ####	# ####	# ####	# ####	# ####	# ####	# ####	# ####	# ####	# ####	# ####	# ####	# ####	# ####	# ####	# ####	# ####	# ####
Alioth	1.7	82 114	86 154	85 223	80 252	75 266	71 274	66 281	61 287	56 293	52 299	47 305	43 310	40 316	36 322	33 327	31 333	29 339	27 345	26 352
Spica	1.2	17 158	18 168	19 179	18 189	17 199	15 209	12 219	9 228	5 237	1 246	# ####	# ####	# ####	# ####	# ####	# ####	# ####	# ####	# ####
Alkaid	1.9	71 113	76 130	79 157	79 191	77 221	73 241	68 255	63 266	58 274	54 282	49 289	44 296	40 302	36 309	32 315	29 322	26 328	23 335	21 342
Hadar	0.9	# ####	# ####	# ####	# ####	# ####	# ####	# ####	# ####	# ####	# ####	# ####	# ####	# ####	# ####	# ####	# ####	# ####	# ####	# ####
Menkent	2.3	# ####	# ####	# ####	# ####	# ####	# ####	# ####	# ####	# ####	# ####	# ####	# ####	# ####	# ####	# ####	# ####	# ####	# ####	# ####
Arcturus	0.2	43 134	46 147	48 160	49 174	49 189	48 203	45 216	42 228	38 239	33 250	28 259	23 268	18 277	14 285	9 293	4 302	0 310	# ####	# ####
Rigil Kent.	0.1	# ####	# ####	# ####	# ####	# ####	# ####	# ####	# ####	# ####	# ####	# ####	# ####	# ####	# ####	# ####	# ####	# ####	# ####	# ####
Zuben'ubi	2.9	7 139	9 148	12 158	13 167	14 177	14 187	13 197	11 207	8 216	5 225	1 234	# ####	# ####	# ####	# ####	# ####	# ####	# ####	# ####
Kochab	2.2	69 031	71 028	74 022	75 013	76 003	76 352	74 342	73 335	70 331	68 328	65 327	62 327	60 328	57 330	55 332	52 335	50 338	49 341	47 344
Alphecca	2.3	41 108	45 118	50 130	53 143	55 158	57 174	56 190	55 206	52 220	49 233	44 244	40 255	35 264	30 273	25 281	20 289	15 297	11 305	7 314
Antares	1.2	# ####	# ####	# ####	# ####	1 156	2 164	3 173	4 182	3 191	2 200	# ####	# ####	# ####	# ####	# ####	# ####	# ####	# ####	# ####
Atria	1.9	# ####	# ####	# ####	# ####	# ####	# ####	# ####	# ####	# ####	# ####	# ####	# ####	# ####	# ####	# ####	# ####	# ####	# ####	# ####
Sabik	2.6	# ####	# ####	1 126	5 134	8 144	11 153	13 163	14 172	14 182	14 192	12 202	10 212	7 221	3 230	# ####	# ####	# ####	# ####	# ####
Shaula	1.7	# ####	# ####	# ####	# ####	# ####	# ####	# ####	# ####	# ####	# ####	# ####	# ####	# ####	# ####	# ####	# ####	# ####	# ####	# ####
Rasalhague	2.1	14 089	19 098	24 107	28 116	33 127	36 138	39 149	41 162	42 175	42 188	41 201	39 214	36 225	32 236	27 246	23 255	18 264	13 273	8 282
Eltanin	2.4	43 058	47 065	52 071	57 078	62 085	67 094	72 105	76 120	80 145	81 184	80 220	76 243	71 257	66 268	61 276	56 283	51 290	47 296	42 303
Kaus Aust.	2.0	# ####	# ####	# ####	# ####	# ####	# ####	# ####	# ####	# ####	# ####	# ####	# ####	# ####	# ####	# ####	# ####	# ####	# ####	# ####
Vega	0.1	29 061	33 069	38 076	43 084	48 093	53 102	58 113	62 126	66 142	68 160	69 182	68 203	65 221	61 236	57 249	52 259	47 269	42 277	37 285
Nunki	2.1	# ####	# ####	# ####	# ####	# ####	# ####	# ####	# ####	2 159	3 168	4 177	4 186	3 194	1 203	# ####	# ####	# ####	# ####	# ####
Altair	0.9	# ####	# ####	4 079	9 088	14 096	19 105	23 114	28 124	32 135	35 146	37 158	39 170	39 183	38 195	36 208	33 219	30 230	26 240	21 250
Peacock	2.1	# ####	# ####	# ####	# ####	# ####	# ####	# ####	# ####	# ####	# ####	# ####	# ####	# ####	# ####	# ####	# ####	# ####	# ####	# ####
Deneb	1.3	23 036	26 042	30 049	34 056	38 063	42 070	47 077	52 085	57 094	62 103	67 116	71 131	74 153	75 179	74 206	71 227	67 243	62 256	57 266
Enif	2.5	# ####	# ####	# ####	# ####	1 071	6 080	11 088	16 097	20 106	25 116	29 126	33 136	36 148	38 160	40 172	40 185	39 198	37 210	34 222
Al Na'ir	2.2	# ####	# ####	# ####	# ####	# ####	# ####	# ####	# ####	# ####	# ####	# ####	# ####	# ####	# ####	# ####	# ####	# ####	# ####	# ####
Fomalhaut	1.3	# ####	# ####	# ####	# ####	# ####	# ####	# ####	# ####	# ####	# ####	# ####	# ####	# ####	# ####	# ####	# ####	0 176	0 185	# ####
Markab	2.6	# ####	# ####	# ####	# ####	# ####	1 060	5 069	10 077	15 086	20 094	25 103	30 113	34 123	38 134	41 145	44 158	45 172	45 185	44 199

* Variable 0.1 - 1.2

SUN MOON PLANETS — Local Hour Angle Body (Alt ° Az °)

Decl'n	180° Alt Az	190° Alt Az	200° Alt Az	210° Alt Az	220° Alt Az	230° Alt Az	240° Alt Az	250° Alt Az	260° Alt Az	270° Alt Az	280° Alt Az	290° Alt Az	300° Alt Az	310° Alt Az	320° Alt Az	330° Alt Az	340° Alt Az	350° Alt Az	360° Alt Az
Decl'n N30°	# ####	0 009	1 017	3 026	6 034	9 042	13 050	17 058	21 066	26 074	31 082	36 090	41 099	45 109	50 120	54 133	57 147	59 163	60 180
Decl'n N25°	# ####	# ####	# ####	# ####	1 036	4 044	8 052	12 061	17 069	21 077	26 085	31 094	36 103	41 113	45 124	49 136	52 150	54 164	55 180
Decl'n N20°	# ####	# ####	# ####	# ####	# ####	# ####	4 055	8 063	12 071	17 080	22 088	27 097	32 106	37 116	41 127	45 139	48 152	49 165	50 180
Decl'n N15°	# ####	# ####	# ####	# ####	# ####	# ####	# ####	3 065	8 074	13 082	18 091	23 100	28 109	32 119	36 129	40 141	43 153	44 166	45 180
Decl'n N10°	# ####	# ####	# ####	# ####	# ####	# ####	# ####	# ####	4 076	9 085	14 094	19 102	23 112	28 121	32 132	35 143	38 155	39 167	40 180
Decl'n N5°	# ####	# ####	# ####	# ####	# ####	# ####	# ####	# ####	# ####	4 087	9 096	14 105	19 114	23 124	27 134	30 145	33 156	34 168	35 180
Decl'n 0°	# ####	# ####	# ####	# ####	# ####	# ####	# ####	# ####	# ####	# ####	5 099	10 107	14 117	19 126	23 136	26 146	28 157	29 168	30 180
Decl'n S5°	# ####	# ####	# ####	# ####	# ####	# ####	# ####	# ####	# ####	# ####	1 101	5 110	10 119	14 128	18 138	21 148	23 158	25 169	25 180
Decl'n S10°	# ####	# ####	# ####	# ####	# ####	# ####	# ####	# ####	# ####	# ####	# ####	1 112	5 121	10 130	13 139	16 149	18 159	20 170	20 180
Decl'n S15°	# ####	# ####	# ####	# ####	# ####	# ####	# ####	# ####	# ####	# ####	# ####	# ####	1 123	5 132	8 141	11 151	13 160	15 170	15 180
Decl'n S20°	# ####	# ####	# ####	# ####	# ####	# ####	# ####	# ####	# ####	# ####	# ####	# ####	# ####	0 134	4 143	6 152	8 161	10 170	10 180
Decl'n S25°	# ####	# ####	# ####	# ####	# ####	# ####	# ####	# ####	# ####	# ####	# ####	# ####	# ####	# ####	# ####	2 153	3 162	5 171	5 180
Decl'n S30°	# ####	# ####	# ####	# ####	# ####	# ####	# ####	# ####	# ####	# ####	# ####	# ####	# ####	# ####	# ####	# ####	# ####	# ####	0 180

PREDICTION & IDENTIFICATION

Latitude N50° Latitude N50°

STARS — Local Hour Angle Aries

Name	Mag	0° Alt Az	10° Alt Az	20° Alt Az	30° Alt Az	40° Alt Az	50° Alt Az	60° Alt Az	70° Alt Az	80° Alt Az	90° Alt Az	100° Alt Az	110° Alt Az	120° Alt Az	130° Alt Az	140° Alt Az	150° Alt Az	160° Alt Az	170° Alt Az	180° Alt Az
		° °	° °	° °	° °	° °	° °	° °	° °	° °	° °	° °	° °	° °	° °	° °	° °	° °	° °	° °
Alpheratz	2.2	69 175	68 199	65 220	60 236	55 248	49 258	42 267	36 274	29 281	23 288	17 295	12 302	6 309	2 316	# ####	# ####	# ####	# ####	# ####
Ankaa	2.4	# ####	# ####	# ####	# ####	# ####	# ####	# ####	# ####	# ####	# ####	# ####	# ####	# ####	# ####	# ####	# ####	# ####	# ####	# ####
Schedah	2.5	81 039	83 001	81 322	77 307	71 302	66 301	60 302	55 304	50 307	45 310	40 314	35 318	31 323	28 327	24 332	22 338	19 343	18 349	17 354
Diphda	2.2	21 169	22 179	22 189	20 199	17 209	14 218	9 227	4 235	# ####	# ####	# ####	# ####	# ####	# ####	# ####	# ####	# ####	# ####	# ####
Achernar	0.6	# ####	# ####	# ####	# ####	# ####	# ####	# ####	# ####	# ####	# ####	# ####	# ####	# ####	# ####	# ####	# ####	# ####	# ####	# ####
Hamal	2.2	54 125	58 139	62 157	63 176	63 197	60 215	56 230	50 242	44 253	38 262	32 270	25 277	19 284	13 291	7 299	2 306	# ####	# ####	# ####
Polaris	2.1	51 001	51 001	51 000	51 000	51 000	51 000	51 000	51 359	51 359	50 359	50 359	50 359	50 359	50 359	50 359	50 359	50 359	50 359	49 359
Acamar	3.1	# ####	# ####	# ####	# ####	# ####	# ####	# ####	# ####	# ####	# ####	# ####	# ####	# ####	# ####	# ####	# ####	# ####	# ####	# ####
Menkar	2.8	30 124	35 135	39 146	42 159	44 172	44 186	42 200	40 212	36 224	31 234	25 244	19 252	13 261	7 268	0 276	# ####	# ####	# ####	# ####
Mirfak	1.9	58 070	64 074	70 078	76 082	83 087	89 101	84 272	78 277	71 281	65 285	59 289	53 293	47 298	42 302	36 307	31 312	27 317	23 322	19 328
Aldebaran	1.1	26 095	32 103	38 112	44 123	49 135	53 149	56 165	56 182	55 199	52 214	48 228	43 239	37 249	31 258	25 266	18 274	12 282	6 289	# ####
Rigel	0.3	1 104	7 112	13 120	18 129	23 138	27 148	30 159	31 170	32 182	31 193	29 204	26 215	22 225	17 234	11 242	5 250	# ####	# ####	# ####
Capella	0.2	39 062	45 067	51 072	57 078	64 084	70 090	77 100	83 120	86 188	82 245	76 262	69 271	63 277	56 283	50 289	44 294	38 299	33 304	28 309
Bellatrix	1.7	10 093	17 100	23 109	29 118	34 127	39 138	43 151	45 164	46 178	46 192	44 206	40 219	36 230	30 240	25 249	18 258	12 265	6 273	# ####
Elnath	1.8	27 076	33 083	39 091	46 099	52 109	58 120	63 135	67 153	69 176	68 200	64 220	60 236	54 248	48 258	41 267	35 274	29 281	22 288	17 295
Alnilam	1.8	3 095	9 103	15 111	21 120	27 129	31 139	35 150	37 162	39 175	39 188	37 200	34 212	30 223	25 233	20 242	14 251	8 259	2 266	# ####
Betelgeuse	*	6 086	13 094	19 102	25 110	31 119	37 129	41 141	45 153	47 167	47 182	46 196	44 210	40 222	35 233	30 243	24 252	18 260	11 268	5 276
Canopus	-0.9	# ####	# ####	# ####	# ####	# ####	# ####	# ####	# ####	# ####	# ####	# ####	# ####	# ####	# ####	# ####	# ####	# ####	# ####	# ####
Sirius	-1.6	# ####	# ####	# ####	# ####	4 123	9 131	14 139	18 149	21 158	23 168	23 179	23 189	21 199	19 209	15 218	11 227	6 235	0 243	# ####
Adhara	1.6	# ####	# ####	# ####	# ####	# ####	# ####	2 142	5 150	8 158	10 167	11 176	11 185	10 194	8 202	5 211	1 219	# ####	# ####	# ####
Procyon	0.5	# ####	# ####	1 083	7 091	14 098	20 106	26 115	32 125	37 135	41 147	44 159	45 173	45 187	43 201	40 214	36 225	31 236	26 245	20 254
Pollux	1.2	6 053	12 060	17 067	23 074	30 081	36 088	42 096	49 104	55 115	60 128	65 144	68 165	68 189	66 210	62 228	56 242	50 253	44 262	38 270
Avior	1.7	# ####	# ####	# ####	# ####	# ####	# ####	# ####	# ####	# ####	# ####	# ####	# ####	# ####	# ####	# ####	# ####	# ####	# ####	# ####
Suhail	2.2	# ####	# ####	# ####	# ####	# ####	# ####	# ####	# ####	# ####	# ####	# ####	# ####	# ####	# ####	# ####	# ####	# ####	# ####	# ####
Miaplacidus	1.8	# ####	# ####	# ####	# ####	# ####	# ####	# ####	# ####	# ####	# ####	# ####	# ####	# ####	# ####	# ####	# ####	# ####	# ####	# ####
Alphard	2.2	# ####	# ####	# ####	# ####	# ####	# ####	# ####	5 109	11 117	16 126	21 135	25 145	28 155	30 166	31 178	31 189	29 201	26 211	23 221
Regulus	1.3	# ####	# ####	# ####	# ####	# ####	2 073	8 081	14 088	21 096	27 104	33 113	39 123	44 134	48 147	51 161	52 177	51 192	49 207	46 221
Dubhe	2.0	22 007	23 012	25 017	27 022	30 026	33 030	36 034	40 038	44 041	48 044	53 046	58 047	62 047	67 046	72 041	75 031	78 013	78 351	76 332
Denebola	2.2	# ####	# ####	# ####	# ####	# ####	# ####	# ####	0 068	7 075	13 083	19 090	26 098	32 106	38 116	43 126	48 138	52 152	54 168	55 185
Gienah	2.8	# ####	# ####	# ####	# ####	# ####	# ####	# ####	# ####	# ####	# ####	# ####	# ####	2 121	7 129	12 137	16 146	19 156	21 166	22 176
Acrux	1.1	# ####	# ####	# ####	# ####	# ####	# ####	# ####	# ####	# ####	# ####	# ####	# ####	# ####	# ####	# ####	# ####	# ####	# ####	# ####
Gacrux	1.6	# ####	# ####	# ####	# ####	# ####	# ####	# ####	# ####	# ####	# ####	# ####	# ####	# ####	# ####	# ####	# ####	# ####	# ####	# ####
Alioth	1.7	17 352	16 358	16 004	17 010	18 015	20 021	23 026	26 031	29 036	33 041	38 045	42 049	47 053	53 056	58 058	64 060	69 060	75 058	80 048
Spica	1.2	# ####	# ####	# ####	# ####	# ####	# ####	# ####	# ####	# ####	# ####	# ####	# ####	# ####	3 111	9 119	14 128	19 137	23 146	26 157
Alkaid	1.9	12 342	10 349	9 355	9 002	10 009	11 015	13 021	16 028	19 034	23 039	27 045	32 050	37 055	43 059	48 064	54 069	60 073	66 077	73 082
Hadar	0.9	# ####	# ####	# ####	# ####	# ####	# ####	# ####	# ####	# ####	# ####	# ####	# ####	# ####	# ####	# ####	# ####	# ####	# ####	# ####
Menkent	2.3	# ####	# ####	# ####	# ####	# ####	# ####	# ####	# ####	# ####	# ####	# ####	# ####	# ####	# ####	# ####	# ####	# ####	# ####	# ####
Arcturus	0.2	# ####	# ####	# ####	# ####	# ####	# ####	# ####	# ####	# ####	# ####	0 060	6 067	12 075	18 082	25 089	31 097	38 106	44 115	49 126
Rigil Kent.	0.1	# ####	# ####	# ####	# ####	# ####	# ####	# ####	# ####	# ####	# ####	# ####	# ####	# ####	# ####	# ####	# ####	# ####	# ####	# ####
Zuben'ubi	2.9	# ####	# ####	# ####	# ####	# ####	# ####	# ####	# ####	# ####	# ####	# ####	# ####	# ####	# ####	# ####	# ####	4 121	9 129	14 138
Kochab	2.2	37 347	36 349	35 353	34 356	34 359	34 002	35 006	36 009	37 012	38 015	40 017	42 020	44 022	47 023	49 025	52 025	55 025	57 024	60 022
Alphecca	2.3	0 314	# ####	# ####	# ####	# ####	# ####	# ####	# ####	# ####	# ####	# ####	1 048	7 055	12 063	18 070	24 076	30 084	37 091	43 099
Antares	1.2	# ####	# ####	# ####	# ####	# ####	# ####	# ####	# ####	# ####	# ####	# ####	# ####	# ####	# ####	# ####	# ####	# ####	# ####	# ####
Atria	1.9	# ####	# ####	# ####	# ####	# ####	# ####	# ####	# ####	# ####	# ####	# ####	# ####	# ####	# ####	# ####	# ####	# ####	# ####	# ####
Sabik	2.6	# ####	# ####	# ####	# ####	# ####	# ####	# ####	# ####	# ####	# ####	# ####	# ####	# ####	# ####	# ####	# ####	# ####	# ####	# ####
Shaula	1.7	# ####	# ####	# ####	# ####	# ####	# ####	# ####	# ####	# ####	# ####	# ####	# ####	# ####	# ####	# ####	# ####	# ####	# ####	# ####
Rasalhague	2.1	6 283	# ####	# ####	# ####	# ####	# ####	# ####	# ####	# ####	# ####	# ####	# ####	# ####	# ####	# ####	# ####	1 071	7 079	14 087
Eltanin	2.4	36 309	32 314	27 319	23 324	20 330	17 336	14 342	13 348	12 354	11 001	12 007	13 013	15 019	17 025	20 031	24 036	28 042	32 047	37 051
Kaus Aust.	2.0	# ####	# ####	# ####	# ####	# ####	# ####	# ####	# ####	# ####	# ####	# ####	# ####	# ####	# ####	# ####	# ####	# ####	# ####	# ####
Vega	0.1	34 292	28 298	23 304	18 310	13 317	9 323	5 330	2 338	0 345	# ####	# ####	# ####	1 016	3 024	6 031	9 038	14 044	18 051	24 057
Nunki	2.1	# ####	# ####	# ####	# ####	# ####	# ####	# ####	# ####	# ####	# ####	# ####	# ####	# ####	# ####	# ####	# ####	# ####	# ####	# ####
Altair	0.9	24 254	18 262	12 270	5 277	# ####	# ####	# ####	# ####	# ####	# ####	# ####	# ####	# ####	# ####	# ####	# ####	# ####	# ####	# ####
Peacock	2.1	# ####	# ####	# ####	# ####	# ####	# ####	# ####	# ####	# ####	# ####	# ####	# ####	# ####	# ####	# ####	# ####	# ####	# ####	# ####
Deneb	1.3	57 281	51 287	45 292	39 297	33 303	28 308	23 314	19 320	15 326	12 332	9 339	7 346	6 353	5 000	6 007	7 014	9 021	11 027	15 034
Enif	2.5	41 227	36 238	30 247	24 256	18 264	11 272	5 279	# ####	# ####	# ####	# ####	# ####	# ####	# ####	# ####	# ####	# ####	# ####	# ####
Al Na'ir	2.2	# ####	# ####	# ####	# ####	# ####	# ####	# ####	# ####	# ####	# ####	# ####	# ####	# ####	# ####	# ####	# ####	# ####	# ####	# ####
Fomalhaut	1.3	9 194	7 202	4 210	1 218	# ####	# ####	# ####	# ####	# ####	# ####	# ####	# ####	# ####	# ####	# ####	# ####	# ####	# ####	# ####
Markab	2.6	53 203	50 217	46 230	40 241	35 251	28 260	22 268	16 275	9 283	3 290	# ####	# ####	# ####	# ####	# ####	# ####	# ####	# ####	# ####

* Variable 0.1 - 1.2

SUN MOON PLANETS — Local Hour Angle Body

	0° Alt Az	10° Alt Az	20° Alt Az	30° Alt Az	40° Alt Az	50° Alt Az	60° Alt Az	70° Alt Az	80° Alt Az	90° Alt Az	100° Alt Az	110° Alt Az	120° Alt Az	130° Alt Az	140° Alt Az	150° Alt Az	160° Alt Az	170° Alt Az	180° Alt Az
	° °	° °	° °	° °	° °	° °	° °	° °	° °	° °	° °	° °	° °	° °	° °	° °	° °	° °	° °
Decl'n N30°	70 180	69 204	65 224	60 240	54 251	48 261	41 269	35 277	29 284	23 290	17 297	11 304	6 311	1 318	# ####	# ####	# ####	# ####	# ####
Decl'n N25°	65 180	64 201	61 219	56 234	50 246	44 256	38 265	32 272	25 280	19 287	13 294	7 301	2 308	# ####	# ####	# ####	# ####	# ####	# ####
Decl'n N20°	60 180	59 198	56 215	52 229	46 241	41 251	34 260	28 268	22 276	15 283	9 290	3 298	# ####	# ####	# ####	# ####	# ####	# ####	# ####
Decl'n N15°	55 180	54 197	51 212	47 226	42 237	37 247	31 256	24 265	18 272	11 280	5 287	# ####	# ####	# ####	# ####	# ####	# ####	# ####	# ####
Decl'n N10°	50 180	49 195	47 209	43 222	38 234	33 244	27 253	20 261	14 269	8 276	1 284	# ####	# ####	# ####	# ####	# ####	# ####	# ####	# ####
Decl'n N5°	45 180	44 194	42 207	38 219	34 230	29 240	23 249	17 258	10 266	4 273	# ####	# ####	# ####	# ####	# ####	# ####	# ####	# ####	# ####
Decl'n 0°	40 180	39 193	37 205	34 217	29 228	24 237	19 246	13 254	6 262	0 270	# ####	# ####	# ####	# ####	# ####	# ####	# ####	# ####	# ####
Decl'n S5°	35 180	34 192	32 204	29 215	25 225	20 234	15 243	9 251	3 259	# ####	# ####	# ####	# ####	# ####	# ####	# ####	# ####	# ####	# ####
Decl'n S10°	30 180	29 191	28 202	25 213	21 223	16 232	11 240	5 248	# ####	# ####	# ####	# ####	# ####	# ####	# ####	# ####	# ####	# ####	# ####
Decl'n S15°	25 180	24 191	23 201	20 211	16 220	12 229	6 237	1 245	# ####	# ####	# ####	# ####	# ####	# ####	# ####	# ####	# ####	# ####	# ####
Decl'n S20°	20 180	19 190	18 200	15 209	12 218	7 227	2 235	# ####	# ####	# ####	# ####	# ####	# ####	# ####	# ####	# ####	# ####	# ####	# ####
Decl'n S25°	15 180	14 189	13 199	10 207	7 216	3 224	# ####	# ####	# ####	# ####	# ####	# ####	# ####	# ####	# ####	# ####	# ####	# ####	# ####
Decl'n S30°	10 180	10 189	8 197	6 206	2 214	# ####	# ####	# ####	# ####	# ####	# ####	# ####	# ####	# ####	# ####	# ####	# ####	# ####	# ####

PREDICTION & IDENTIFICATION

Latitude N50° Latitude N50°

STARS — Local Hour Angle Aries

Name	Mag	180° Alt Az	190° Alt Az	200° Alt Az	210° Alt Az	220° Alt Az	230° Alt Az	240° Alt Az	250° Alt Az	260° Alt Az	270° Alt Az	280° Alt Az	290° Alt Az	300° Alt Az	310° Alt Az	320° Alt Az	330° Alt Az	340° Alt Az	350° Alt Az	360° Alt Az
		° °	° °	° °	° °	° °	° °	° °	° °	° °	° °	° °	° °	° °	° °	° °	° °	° °	° °	° °
Alpheratz	2.2	# ####	# ####	# ####	# ####	# ####	# ####	4 048	9 055	15 062	21 069	27 076	33 083	39 090	46 098	52 107	58 119	63 133	67 152	69 175
Ankaa	2.4	# ####	# ####	# ####	# ####	# ####	# ####	# ####	# ####	# ####	# ####	# ####	# ####	# ####	# ####	# ####	# ####	# ####	# ####	# ####
Schedah	2.5	17 354	17 000	17 006	18 011	19 017	22 022	24 028	27 033	31 037	35 042	40 046	44 050	49 053	55 056	60 058	66 059	71 058	76 054	81 039
Diphda	2.2	# ####	# ####	# ####	# ####	# ####	# ####	# ####	# ####	# ####	# ####	# ####	# ####	# ####	3 124	9 132	13 140	17 149	20 159	21 169
Achernar	0.6	# ####	# ####	# ####	# ####	# ####	# ####	# ####	# ####	# ####	# ####	# ####	# ####	# ####	# ####	# ####	# ####	# ####	# ####	# ####
Hamal	2.2	# ####	# ####	# ####	# ####	# ####	# ####	# ####	# ####	# ####	# ####	5 059	11 066	17 073	23 080	29 088	36 095	42 104	48 114	54 125
Polaris	2.1	49 359	49 359	49 000	49 000	49 000	49 000	49 000	49 001	49 001	50 001	50 001	50 001	50 001	50 001	50 001	50 001	50 001	50 001	51 001
Acamar	3.1	# ####	# ####	# ####	# ####	# ####	# ####	# ####	# ####	# ####	# ####	# ####	# ####	# ####	# ####	# ####	# ####	# ####	# ####	# ####
Menkar	2.8	# ####	# ####	# ####	# ####	# ####	# ####	# ####	# ####	# ####	# ####	# ####	# ####	# ####	# ####	6 091	12 099	19 107	25 115	30 124
Mirfak	1.9	19 328	16 334	13 340	11 346	10 353	10 359	10 006	11 012	13 019	15 025	18 031	22 036	26 042	30 047	35 052	41 057	46 061	52 066	58 070
Aldebaran	1.1	# ####	# ####	# ####	# ####	# ####	# ####	# ####	# ####	# ####	# ####	# ####	# ####	# ####	# ####	1 065	7 073	13 080	20 087	26 095
Rigel	0.3	# ####	# ####	# ####	# ####	# ####	# ####	# ####	# ####	# ####	# ####	# ####	# ####	# ####	# ####	# ####	# ####	# ####	# ####	1 104
Capella	0.2	28 309	23 315	19 321	15 327	12 333	9 340	7 347	6 354	6 001	6 008	8 014	10 021	12 028	16 034	19 040	24 046	29 051	34 057	39 062
Bellatrix	1.7	# ####	# ####	# ####	# ####	# ####	# ####	# ####	# ####	# ####	# ####	# ####	# ####	# ####	# ####	# ####	# ####	# ####	4 085	10 093
Elnath	1.8	17 295	11 302	6 309	1 317	# ####	# ####	# ####	# ####	# ####	# ####	# ####	# ####	# ####	# ####	4 049	9 056	15 063	21 070	27 076
Alnilam	1.8	# ####	# ####	# ####	# ####	# ####	# ####	# ####	# ####	# ####	# ####	# ####	# ####	# ####	# ####	# ####	# ####	# ####	# ####	3 095
Betelgeuse	*	5 276	# ####	# ####	# ####	# ####	# ####	# ####	# ####	# ####	# ####	# ####	# ####	# ####	# ####	# ####	# ####	# ####	0 079	6 086
Canopus	-0.9	# ####	# ####	# ####	# ####	# ####	# ####	# ####	# ####	# ####	# ####	# ####	# ####	# ####	# ####	# ####	# ####	# ####	# ####	# ####
Sirius	-1.6	# ####	# ####	# ####	# ####	# ####	# ####	# ####	# ####	# ####	# ####	# ####	# ####	# ####	# ####	# ####	# ####	# ####	# ####	# ####
Adhara	1.6	# ####	# ####	# ####	# ####	# ####	# ####	# ####	# ####	# ####	# ####	# ####	# ####	# ####	# ####	# ####	# ####	# ####	# ####	# ####
Procyon	0.5	20 254	14 262	7 270	1 277	# ####	# ####	# ####	# ####	# ####	# ####	# ####	# ####	# ####	# ####	# ####	# ####	# ####	# ####	# ####
Pollux	1.2	38 270	31 278	25 285	19 291	13 298	8 305	3 313	# ####	# ####	# ####	# ####	# ####	# ####	# ####	# ####	# ####	# ####	1 045	6 053
Avior	1.7	# ####	# ####	# ####	# ####	# ####	# ####	# ####	# ####	# ####	# ####	# ####	# ####	# ####	# ####	# ####	# ####	# ####	# ####	# ####
Suhail	2.2	# ####	# ####	# ####	# ####	# ####	# ####	# ####	# ####	# ####	# ####	# ####	# ####	# ####	# ####	# ####	# ####	# ####	# ####	# ####
Miaplacidus	1.8	# ####	# ####	# ####	# ####	# ####	# ####	# ####	# ####	# ####	# ####	# ####	# ####	# ####	# ####	# ####	# ####	# ####	# ####	# ####
Alphard	2.2	23 221	18 231	13 239	7 248	1 255	# ####	# ####	# ####	# ####	# ####	# ####	# ####	# ####	# ####	# ####	# ####	# ####	# ####	# ####
Regulus	1.3	46 221	41 233	35 243	30 252	23 261	17 269	10 276	4 284	# ####	# ####	# ####	# ####	# ####	# ####	# ####	# ####	# ####	# ####	# ####
Dubhe	2.0	76 332	72 321	68 315	63 313	59 313	54 314	49 316	45 318	41 321	37 325	33 329	30 333	28 337	25 342	24 347	22 352	22 357	22 002	22 007
Denebola	2.2	55 185	53 201	50 216	46 229	41 240	35 250	29 258	22 266	16 274	9 282	3 289	# ####	# ####	# ####	# ####	# ####	# ####	# ####	# ####
Gienah	2.8	22 176	22 186	21 196	19 206	15 216	11 224	6 233	1 241	# ####	# ####	# ####	# ####	# ####	# ####	# ####	# ####	# ####	# ####	# ####
Acrux	1.1	# ####	# ####	# ####	# ####	# ####	# ####	# ####	# ####	# ####	# ####	# ####	# ####	# ####	# ####	# ####	# ####	# ####	# ####	# ####
Gacrux	1.6	# ####	# ####	# ####	# ####	# ####	# ####	# ####	# ####	# ####	# ####	# ####	# ####	# ####	# ####	# ####	# ####	# ####	# ####	# ####
Alioth	1.7	80 048	84 018	83 329	78 307	73 301	68 299	62 300	56 302	51 305	46 308	41 312	36 316	32 321	28 325	25 330	22 335	20 341	18 346	17 352
Spica	1.2	26 157	28 167	29 179	28 190	27 201	24 211	20 221	16 230	10 238	5 246	# ####	# ####	# ####	# ####	# ####	# ####	# ####	# ####	# ####
Alkaid	1.9	73 082	79 087	85 096	88 252	81 270	75 276	69 281	62 285	56 290	50 294	45 299	39 303	34 308	29 313	25 319	21 324	17 330	14 336	12 342
Hadar	0.9	# ####	# ####	# ####	# ####	# ####	# ####	# ####	# ####	# ####	# ####	# ####	# ####	# ####	# ####	# ####	# ####	# ####	# ####	# ####
Menkent	2.3	# ####	2 163	3 171	4 179	3 187	2 195	0 202	# ####	# ####	# ####	# ####	# ####	# ####	# ####	# ####	# ####	# ####	# ####	# ####
Arcturus	0.2	49 126	54 140	57 155	59 173	59 191	57 208	53 223	48 236	42 247	36 256	30 265	23 272	17 280	11 287	5 294	# ####	# ####	# ####	# ####
Rigil Kent.	0.1	# ####	# ####	# ####	# ####	# ####	# ####	# ####	# ####	# ####	# ####	# ####	# ####	# ####	# ####	# ####	# ####	# ####	# ####	# ####
Zuben'ubi	2.9	14 138	18 147	21 157	23 167	24 177	24 188	22 198	20 208	16 217	12 226	7 235	2 242	# ####	# ####	# ####	# ####	# ####	# ####	# ####
Kochab	2.2	60 022	62 018	64 014	65 008	66 002	66 355	65 349	63 344	61 340	59 337	56 336	54 335	51 335	48 336	46 337	43 339	41 341	39 344	37 347
Alphecca	2.3	43 099	49 108	55 120	60 133	64 151	67 172	66 194	64 214	59 231	54 244	48 254	42 263	35 271	29 278	22 285	16 292	11 299	5 306	0 314
Antares	1.2	# ####	# ####	3 139	7 147	10 155	12 164	13 173	14 182	13 192	11 201	8 209	5 217	0 225	# ####	# ####	# ####	# ####	# ####	# ####
Atria	1.9	# ####	# ####	# ####	# ####	# ####	# ####	# ####	# ####	# ####	# ####	# ####	# ####	# ####	# ####	# ####	# ####	# ####	# ####	# ####
Sabik	2.6	# ####	2 117	7 125	12 133	16 142	20 152	22 162	24 172	24 183	23 193	21 203	18 213	14 222	10 231	5 239	# ####	# ####	# ####	# ####
Shaula	1.7	# ####	# ####	# ####	# ####	# ####	# ####	0 162	2 169	3 177	3 185	2 193	# ####	# ####	# ####	# ####	# ####	# ####	# ####	# ####
Rasalhague	2.1	14 087	20 094	26 102	33 111	38 121	43 132	48 144	51 158	52 174	52 190	50 205	47 219	42 231	37 242	31 251	25 260	18 268	12 275	6 283
Eltanin	2.4	37 051	42 056	48 060	54 064	59 068	65 071	72 074	78 076	84 072	88 341	83 286	77 284	71 286	64 289	58 293	53 296	47 300	42 305	36 309
Kaus Aust.	2.0	# ####	# ####	# ####	# ####	# ####	# ####	# ####	3 159	4 167	5 175	6 183	5 192	3 200	0 207	# ####	# ####	# ####	# ####	# ####
Vega	0.1	24 057	29 063	35 069	41 075	47 082	54 089	60 097	66 107	72 122	77 146	79 183	76 218	72 241	66 255	59 264	53 272	46 279	40 286	34 292
Nunki	2.1	# ####	# ####	# ####	# ####	# ####	0 134	4 141	8 150	11 158	13 167	14 176	14 186	12 195	10 204	7 212	3 220	# ####	# ####	# ####
Altair	0.9	# ####	# ####	2 078	8 086	15 094	21 102	27 110	33 119	38 130	43 141	46 154	48 168	49 183	48 198	45 212	41 224	36 235	30 245	24 254
Peacock	2.1	# ####	# ####	# ####	# ####	# ####	# ####	# ####	# ####	# ####	# ####	# ####	# ####	# ####	# ####	# ####	# ####	# ####	# ####	# ####
Deneb	1.3	15 034	18 040	23 046	28 051	33 057	38 062	44 067	50 073	56 078	63 084	69 091	76 101	82 120	85 177	82 238	76 258	70 268	63 275	57 281
Enif	2.5	# ####	# ####	# ####	# ####	# ####	4 079	10 087	17 094	23 102	29 111	35 120	40 131	44 143	48 156	50 171	50 186	48 201	45 215	41 227
Al Na'ir	2.2	# ####	# ####	# ####	# ####	# ####	# ####	# ####	# ####	# ####	# ####	# ####	# ####	# ####	# ####	# ####	# ####	# ####	# ####	# ####
Fomalhaut	1.3	# ####	# ####	# ####	# ####	# ####	# ####	# ####	# ####	# ####	# ####	# ####	# ####	1 143	5 150	7 159	9 167	10 176	10 185	9 194
Markab	2.6	# ####	# ####	# ####	# ####	# ####	# ####	2 068	8 075	14 083	20 090	27 098	33 107	39 116	45 127	49 139	53 154	55 170	55 186	53 203

* Variable 0.1 - 1.2

SUN MOON PLANETS — Local Hour Angle Body

	180° Alt Az	190° Alt Az	200° Alt Az	210° Alt Az	220° Alt Az	230° Alt Az	240° Alt Az	250° Alt Az	260° Alt Az	270° Alt Az	280° Alt Az	290° Alt Az	300° Alt Az	310° Alt Az	320° Alt Az	330° Alt Az	340° Alt Az	350° Alt Az	360° Alt Az
	° °	° °	° °	° °	° °	° °	° °	° °	° °	° °	° °	° °	° °	° °	° °	° °	° °	° °	° °
Decl'n N30°	# ####	# ####	# ####	# ####	# ####	1 042	6 049	11 056	17 063	23 070	29 076	35 083	41 091	48 099	54 109	60 120	65 136	69 156	70 180
Decl'n N25°	# ####	# ####	# ####	# ####	# ####	# ####	2 052	7 059	13 066	19 073	25 080	32 088	38 095	44 104	50 114	56 126	61 141	64 159	65 180
Decl'n N20°	# ####	# ####	# ####	# ####	# ####	# ####	# ####	3 062	9 070	15 077	22 084	28 092	34 100	41 109	46 119	52 131	56 145	59 162	60 180
Decl'n N15°	# ####	# ####	# ####	# ####	# ####	# ####	# ####	# ####	5 073	11 080	18 088	24 095	31 104	37 113	42 123	47 134	51 148	54 163	55 180
Decl'n N10°	# ####	# ####	# ####	# ####	# ####	# ####	# ####	# ####	1 076	8 084	14 091	20 099	27 107	33 116	38 126	43 138	47 151	49 165	50 180
Decl'n N5°	# ####	# ####	# ####	# ####	# ####	# ####	# ####	# ####	# ####	4 087	10 094	17 102	23 111	29 120	34 130	38 141	42 153	44 166	45 180
Decl'n 0°	# ####	# ####	# ####	# ####	# ####	# ####	# ####	# ####	# ####	# ####	6 098	13 106	19 114	24 123	29 132	34 143	37 155	39 167	40 180
Decl'n S5°	# ####	# ####	# ####	# ####	# ####	# ####	# ####	# ####	# ####	# ####	3 101	9 109	15 117	20 126	25 135	29 145	32 156	34 168	35 180
Decl'n S10°	# ####	# ####	# ####	# ####	# ####	# ####	# ####	# ####	# ####	# ####	# ####	5 112	11 120	16 128	21 137	25 147	28 158	29 169	30 180
Decl'n S15°	# ####	# ####	# ####	# ####	# ####	# ####	# ####	# ####	# ####	# ####	# ####	1 115	6 123	12 131	16 140	20 149	23 159	24 169	25 180
Decl'n S20°	# ####	# ####	# ####	# ####	# ####	# ####	# ####	# ####	# ####	# ####	# ####	# ####	2 125	7 133	12 142	15 151	18 160	19 170	20 180
Decl'n S25°	# ####	# ####	# ####	# ####	# ####	# ####	# ####	# ####	# ####	# ####	# ####	# ####	# ####	3 136	7 144	10 153	13 161	14 171	15 180
Decl'n S30°	# ####	# ####	# ####	# ####	# ####	# ####	# ####	# ####	# ####	# ####	# ####	# ####	# ####	# ####	2 146	6 154	8 163	10 171	10 180

PREDICTION & IDENTIFICATION

Latitude N40° Latitude N40°

STARS — Local Hour Angle Aries

Name	Mag	0° Alt Az	10° Alt Az	20° Alt Az	30° Alt Az	40° Alt Az	50° Alt Az	60° Alt Az	70° Alt Az	80° Alt Az	90° Alt Az	100° Alt Az	110° Alt Az	120° Alt Az	130° Alt Az	140° Alt Az	150° Alt Az	160° Alt Az	170° Alt Az	180° Alt Az
		° °	° °	° °	° °	° °	° °	° °	° °	° °	° °	° °	° °	° °	° °	° °	° °	° °	° °	° °
Alpheratz	2.2	79 170	77 213	72 239	65 253	57 262	50 270	42 276	34 281	27 287	20 292	13 297	6 303	# ####	# ####	# ####	# ####	# ####	# ####	# ####
Ankaa	2.4	7 175	8 183	7 190	5 197	2 204	# ####	# ####	# ####	# ####	# ####	# ####	# ####	# ####	# ####	# ####	# ####	# ####	# ####	# ####
Schedah	2.5	72 018	73 000	72 342	69 328	64 320	59 316	54 314	48 314	43 315	38 317	32 319	28 322	23 326	19 330	15 334	12 339	10 344	8 349	7 354
Diphda	2.2	31 168	32 179	31 190	29 201	26 211	22 220	16 228	10 236	4 243	# ####	# ####	# ####	# ####	# ####	# ####	# ####	# ####	# ####	# ####
Achernar	0.6	# ####	# ####	# ####	# ####	# ####	# ####	# ####	# ####	# ####	# ####	# ####	# ####	# ####	# ####	# ####	# ####	# ####	# ####	# ####
Hamal	2.2	59 112	65 125	71 145	73 174	72 205	67 228	61 244	54 254	46 263	39 270	31 276	24 282	16 287	9 293	2 299	# ####	# ####	# ####	# ####
Polaris	2.1	41 001	41 000	41 000	41 000	41 000	41 000	41 000	41 359	41 359	40 359	40 359	40 359	40 359	40 359	40 359	40 359	40 359	40 359	39 359
Acamar	3.1	0 148	4 154	7 161	9 169	10 176	10 184	8 192	6 199	3 206	# ####	# ####	# ####	# ####	# ####	# ####	# ####	# ####	# ####	# ####
Menkar	2.8	36 119	42 129	47 141	51 155	54 171	54 188	52 204	48 218	43 230	36 240	29 249	22 256	15 263	7 270	# ####	# ####	# ####	# ####	# ####
Mirfak	1.9	53 057	60 057	66 055	72 049	77 035	80 004	78 330	73 313	67 306	61 303	55 303	48 304	42 306	36 309	30 312	25 316	19 320	15 324	10 329
Aldebaran	1.1	26 090	34 097	42 104	49 113	56 125	61 140	65 159	66 182	65 205	60 224	54 238	47 249	40 257	33 264	25 271	17 277	10 283	2 290	# ####
Rigel	0.3	3 104	11 110	18 118	24 125	30 134	35 145	39 156	41 169	42 182	41 195	38 207	34 218	29 228	22 237	16 245	9 252	1 258	# ####	# ####
Capella	0.2	34 056	41 059	47 062	54 064	61 065	68 065	75 060	81 045	84 354	80 311	74 298	67 295	60 295	53 297	46 299	40 302	33 305	27 309	21 313
Bellatrix	1.7	11 091	18 097	26 104	33 112	40 121	46 132	51 145	55 160	56 178	55 195	52 212	48 225	42 236	35 246	28 254	20 261	13 268	5 274	# ####
Elnath	1.8	24 072	31 077	39 083	47 089	54 095	62 104	69 116	75 137	79 173	77 214	71 239	64 253	57 262	49 269	41 275	34 281	26 286	19 292	12 297
Alnilam	1.8	4 095	11 101	19 108	26 116	33 125	38 135	43 146	47 159	49 174	48 189	46 204	42 217	37 228	31 237	24 246	17 253	10 260	2 267	# ####
Betelgeuse	*	6 085	13 091	21 098	28 105	36 113	42 123	48 134	53 148	56 164	57 182	56 200	52 216	47 229	41 240	34 249	27 257	19 264	11 270	4 276
Canopus	-0.9	# ####	# ####	# ####	# ####	# ####	# ####	# ####	# ####	# ####	# ####	# ####	# ####	# ####	# ####	# ####	# ####	# ####	# ####	# ####
Sirius	-1.6	# ####	# ####	# ####	3 115	10 122	16 129	21 137	26 146	30 156	32 167	33 179	33 190	31 201	27 211	23 221	17 229	11 237	5 244	# ####
Adhara	1.6	# ####	# ####	# ####	# ####	# ####	4 134	10 141	14 149	17 158	20 166	21 176	21 185	20 194	17 203	14 211	9 219	4 226	# ####	# ####
Procyon	0.5	# ####	# ####	# ####	7 089	15 096	23 103	30 110	37 119	43 129	49 141	53 155	55 172	55 189	53 205	48 220	43 232	37 242	30 250	22 258
Pollux	1.2	0 052	6 058	13 064	20 070	28 075	35 081	43 086	50 093	58 101	65 111	72 127	77 155	78 195	74 227	67 246	60 257	52 265	45 272	37 278
Avior	1.7	# ####	# ####	# ####	# ####	# ####	# ####	# ####	# ####	# ####	# ####	# ####	# ####	# ####	# ####	# ####	# ####	# ####	# ####	# ####
Suhail	2.2	# ####	# ####	# ####	# ####	# ####	# ####	# ####	# ####	# ####	# ####	0 154	3 161	5 168	6 175	7 182	6 189	4 197	1 203	# ####
Miaplacidus	1.8	# ####	# ####	# ####	# ####	# ####	# ####	# ####	# ####	# ####	# ####	# ####	# ####	# ####	# ####	# ####	# ####	# ####	# ####	# ####
Alphard	2.2	# ####	# ####	# ####	# ####	# ####	# ####	1 102	8 108	15 115	22 123	28 132	33 141	37 152	40 165	41 178	41 191	39 203	35 215	30 225
Regulus	1.3	# ####	# ####	# ####	# ####	# ####	# ####	6 079	14 086	21 092	29 099	36 106	44 115	50 126	56 139	60 156	62 176	61 196	58 214	53 229
Dubhe	2.0	12 007	14 011	15 016	18 020	21 024	24 028	28 031	32 034	36 036	41 037	46 038	50 038	55 036	59 033	63 027	66 019	68 007	68 355	67 343
Denebola	2.2	# ####	# ####	# ####	# ####	# ####	# ####	# ####	# ####	4 074	11 080	19 087	27 093	34 100	42 108	49 117	55 129	60 144	64 164	64 186
Gienah	2.8	# ####	# ####	# ####	# ####	# ####	# ####	# ####	# ####	# ####	# ####	# ####	0 114	7 120	14 128	19 135	24 144	28 154	31 164	32 176
Acrux	1.1	# ####	# ####	# ####	# ####	# ####	# ####	# ####	# ####	# ####	# ####	# ####	# ####	# ####	# ####	# ####	# ####	# ####	# ####	# ####
Gacrux	1.6	# ####	# ####	# ####	# ####	# ####	# ####	# ####	# ####	# ####	# ####	# ####	# ####	# ####	# ####	# ####	# ####	# ####	# ####	# ####
Alioth	1.7	7 352	6 358	6 004	7 009	9 015	11 020	14 025	17 029	21 033	26 037	30 040	36 043	41 045	46 047	52 047	58 046	63 043	68 036	72 025
Spica	1.2	# ####	# ####	# ####	# ####	# ####	# ####	# ####	# ####	# ####	# ####	# ####	# ####	# ####	7 111	14 118	20 125	26 134	31 143	35 154
Alkaid	1.9	2 343	1 349	# ####	# ####	0 009	2 015	4 021	7 027	11 032	15 037	20 042	25 046	31 049	37 053	43 055	49 057	56 058	62 058	69 055
Hadar	0.9	# ####	# ####	# ####	# ####	# ####	# ####	# ####	# ####	# ####	# ####	# ####	# ####	# ####	# ####	# ####	# ####	# ####	# ####	# ####
Menkent	2.3	# ####	# ####	# ####	# ####	# ####	# ####	# ####	# ####	# ####	# ####	# ####	# ####	# ####	# ####	# ####	# ####	0 141	5 148	8 155
Arcturus	0.2	# ####	# ####	# ####	# ####	# ####	# ####	# ####	# ####	# ####	# ####	# ####	2 067	9 073	17 079	24 085	32 091	40 098	47 106	54 116
Rigil Kent.	0.1	# ####	# ####	# ####	# ####	# ####	# ####	# ####	# ####	# ####	# ####	# ####	# ####	# ####	# ####	# ####	# ####	# ####	# ####	# ####
Zuben'ubi	2.9	# ####	# ####	# ####	# ####	# ####	# ####	# ####	# ####	# ####	# ####	# ####	# ####	# ####	# ####	# ####	2 113	9 120	16 127	21 136
Kochab	2.2	28 348	26 351	25 353	24 356	24 359	24 002	25 005	26 008	27 011	28 013	30 015	33 017	35 019	37 020	40 021	43 021	46 020	48 019	51 017
Alphecca	2.3	# ####	# ####	# ####	# ####	# ####	# ####	# ####	# ####	# ####	# ####	# ####	# ####	1 055	7 061	14 067	21 072	29 078	36 084	44 090
Antares	1.2	# ####	# ####	# ####	# ####	# ####	# ####	# ####	# ####	# ####	# ####	# ####	# ####	# ####	# ####	# ####	# ####	# ####	# ####	# ####
Atria	1.9	# ####	# ####	# ####	# ####	# ####	# ####	# ####	# ####	# ####	# ####	# ####	# ####	# ####	# ####	# ####	# ####	# ####	# ####	# ####
Sabik	2.6	# ####	# ####	# ####	# ####	# ####	# ####	# ####	# ####	# ####	# ####	# ####	# ####	# ####	# ####	# ####	# ####	# ####	# ####	# ####
Shaula	1.7	# ####	# ####	# ####	# ####	# ####	# ####	# ####	# ####	# ####	# ####	# ####	# ####	# ####	# ####	# ####	# ####	# ####	# ####	# ####
Rasalhague	2.1	3 284	# ####	# ####	# ####	# ####	# ####	# ####	# ####	# ####	# ####	# ####	# ####	# ####	# ####	# ####	# ####	# ####	5 078	13 084
Eltanin	2.4	30 314	24 318	19 322	15 326	11 331	8 337	5 342	3 348	2 354	1 001	2 007	3 013	5 019	8 024	12 030	16 034	20 039	25 043	31 046
Kaus Aust.	2.0	# ####	# ####	# ####	# ####	# ####	# ####	# ####	# ####	# ####	# ####	# ####	# ####	# ####	# ####	# ####	# ####	# ####	# ####	# ####
Vega	0.1	30 297	23 302	17 307	11 312	6 318	1 324	# ####	# ####	# ####	# ####	# ####	# ####	# ####	# ####	# ####	1 037	6 043	12 049	18 054
Nunki	2.1	# ####	# ####	# ####	# ####	# ####	# ####	# ####	# ####	# ####	# ####	# ####	# ####	# ####	# ####	# ####	# ####	# ####	# ####	# ####
Altair	0.9	27 259	19 265	12 272	4 278	# ####	# ####	# ####	# ####	# ####	# ####	# ####	# ####	# ####	# ####	# ####	# ####	# ####	# ####	# ####
Peacock	2.1	# ####	# ####	# ####	# ####	# ####	# ####	# ####	# ####	# ####	# ####	# ####	# ####	# ####	# ####	# ####	# ####	# ####	# ####	# ####
Deneb	1.3	54 295	47 297	40 300	34 304	27 308	22 312	16 316	11 321	6 327	3 333	# ####	# ####	# ####	# ####	# ####	# ####	# ####	2 027	6 033
Enif	2.5	47 234	41 245	34 253	26 261	19 267	11 274	3 280	# ####	# ####	# ####	# ####	# ####	# ####	# ####	# ####	# ####	# ####	# ####	# ####
Al Na'ir	2.2	# ####	# ####	# ####	# ####	# ####	# ####	# ####	# ####	# ####	# ####	# ####	# ####	# ####	# ####	# ####	# ####	# ####	# ####	# ####
Fomalhaut	1.3	19 194	16 203	13 211	9 219	3 226	# ####	# ####	# ####	# ####	# ####	# ####	# ####	# ####	# ####	# ####	# ####	# ####	# ####	# ####
Markab	2.6	62 210	58 227	52 240	45 250	37 258	30 265	22 272	14 278	7 284	# ####	# ####	# ####	# ####	# ####	# ####	# ####	# ####	# ####	# ####

* Variable 0.1 - 1.2

SUN MOON PLANETS — Local Hour Angle Body

	0° Alt Az	10° Alt Az	20° Alt Az	30° Alt Az	40° Alt Az	50° Alt Az	60° Alt Az	70° Alt Az	80° Alt Az	90° Alt Az	100° Alt Az	110° Alt Az	120° Alt Az	130° Alt Az	140° Alt Az	150° Alt Az	160° Alt Az	170° Alt Az	180° Alt Az
	° °	° °	° °	° °	° °	° °	° °	° °	° °	° °	° °	° °	° °	° °	° °	° °	° °	° °	° °
Decl'n N30°	80 180	77 222	71 245	64 257	56 266	48 272	41 278	33 283	26 289	19 294	12 299	5 305	# ####	# ####	# ####	# ####	# ####	# ####	# ####
Decl'n N25°	75 180	73 212	68 234	61 248	53 258	46 266	38 272	31 278	23 284	16 290	9 295	2 302	# ####	# ####	# ####	# ####	# ####	# ####	# ####
Decl'n N20°	70 180	68 206	64 226	57 241	50 252	43 260	35 267	28 274	20 280	13 286	5 292	# ####	# ####	# ####	# ####	# ####	# ####	# ####	# ####
Decl'n N15°	65 180	64 202	60 221	54 235	47 246	40 255	32 262	25 269	17 275	10 282	2 288	# ####	# ####	# ####	# ####	# ####	# ####	# ####	# ####
Decl'n N10°	60 180	59 199	55 216	50 230	44 241	37 250	29 258	22 265	14 271	6 278	# ####	# ####	# ####	# ####	# ####	# ####	# ####	# ####	# ####
Decl'n N5°	55 180	54 197	51 212	46 226	40 237	33 246	26 254	18 261	11 267	3 274	# ####	# ####	# ####	# ####	# ####	# ####	# ####	# ####	# ####
Decl'n 0°	50 180	49 195	46 210	42 222	36 233	29 242	23 250	15 257	8 264	0 270	# ####	# ####	# ####	# ####	# ####	# ####	# ####	# ####	# ####
Decl'n S5°	45 180	44 194	41 207	37 219	32 229	26 238	19 246	12 253	4 260	# ####	# ####	# ####	# ####	# ####	# ####	# ####	# ####	# ####	# ####
Decl'n S10°	40 180	39 193	37 205	33 216	28 226	22 234	15 242	8 249	1 256	# ####	# ####	# ####	# ####	# ####	# ####	# ####	# ####	# ####	# ####
Decl'n S15°	35 180	34 192	32 203	28 213	24 223	18 231	12 239	5 246	# ####	# ####	# ####	# ####	# ####	# ####	# ####	# ####	# ####	# ####	# ####
Decl'n S20°	30 180	29 191	27 201	24 211	19 220	14 228	8 235	2 242	# ####	# ####	# ####	# ####	# ####	# ####	# ####	# ####	# ####	# ####	# ####
Decl'n S25°	25 180	24 190	22 200	19 209	15 217	10 225	4 232	# ####	# ####	# ####	# ####	# ####	# ####	# ####	# ####	# ####	# ####	# ####	# ####
Decl'n S30°	20 180	19 189	18 198	15 207	11 215	6 222	1 229	# ####	# ####	# ####	# ####	# ####	# ####	# ####	# ####	# ####	# ####	# ####	# ####

Latitude N40° Latitude N40°

STARS — Local Hour Angle Aries

Name	Mag	180° Alt Az	190° Alt Az	200° Alt Az	210° Alt Az	220° Alt Az	230° Alt Az	240° Alt Az	250° Alt Az	260° Alt Az	270° Alt Az	280° Alt Az	290° Alt Az	300° Alt Az	310° Alt Az	320° Alt Az	330° Alt Az	340° Alt Az	350° Alt Az	360° Alt Az
		° °	° °	° °	° °	° °	° °	° °	° °	° °	° °	° °	° °	° °	° °	° °	° °	° °	° °	° °
Alpheratz	2.2	# ####	# ####	# ####	# ####	# ####	# ####	# ####	3 054	10 060	17 066	24 071	31 076	39 082	46 088	54 094	62 103	69 114	75 134	79 170
Ankaa	2.4	# ####	# ####	# ####	# ####	# ####	# ####	# ####	# ####	# ####	# ####	# ####	# ####	# ####	# ####	# ####	1 154	4 161	6 168	7 175
Schedah	2.5	7 354	7 000	7 005	8 011	10 016	12 021	15 026	19 030	23 034	28 038	32 041	37 043	43 045	48 046	54 046	59 044	64 040	69 032	72 018
Diphda	2.2	# ####	# ####	# ####	# ####	# ####	# ####	# ####	# ####	# ####	# ####	# ####	# ####	2 116	9 123	15 130	21 138	25 147	29 157	31 168
Achernar	0.6	# ####	# ####	# ####	# ####	# ####	# ####	# ####	# ####	# ####	# ####	# ####	# ####	# ####	# ####	# ####	# ####	# ####	# ####	# ####
Hamal	2.2	# ####	# ####	# ####	# ####	# ####	# ####	# ####	# ####	# ####	# ####	# ####	6 065	14 071	21 076	28 082	36 088	44 095	51 102	59 112
Polaris	2.1	39 359	39 000	39 000	39 000	39 000	39 000	39 000	39 001	39 001	40 001	40 001	40 001	40 001	40 001	40 001	40 001	40 001	40 001	41 001
Acamar	3.1	# ####	# ####	# ####	# ####	# ####	# ####	# ####	# ####	# ####	# ####	# ####	# ####	# ####	# ####	# ####	# ####	# ####	# ####	0 148
Menkar	2.8	# ####	# ####	# ####	# ####	# ####	# ####	# ####	# ####	# ####	# ####	# ####	# ####	# ####	# ####	6 090	14 096	21 103	29 111	36 119
Mirfak	1.9	10 329	7 335	4 341	2 347	0 353	# ####	0 006	1 012	3 018	6 024	10 030	14 035	18 039	23 044	29 047	35 051	41 054	47 056	53 057
Aldebaran	1.1	# ####	# ####	# ####	# ####	# ####	# ####	# ####	# ####	# ####	# ####	# ####	# ####	# ####	# ####	# ####	4 072	11 078	19 084	26 090
Rigel	0.3	# ####	# ####	# ####	# ####	# ####	# ####	# ####	# ####	# ####	# ####	# ####	# ####	# ####	# ####	# ####	# ####	# ####	# ####	3 104
Capella	0.2	21 313	16 318	11 323	7 328	3 334	# ####	# ####	# ####	# ####	# ####	# ####	0 021	3 027	7 033	12 038	17 043	22 048	28 052	34 056
Bellatrix	1.7	# ####	# ####	# ####	# ####	# ####	# ####	# ####	# ####	# ####	# ####	# ####	# ####	# ####	# ####	# ####	# ####	# ####	3 084	11 091
Elnath	1.8	12 297	5 303	# ####	# ####	# ####	# ####	# ####	# ####	# ####	# ####	# ####	# ####	# ####	# ####	# ####	3 055	10 061	17 066	24 072
Alnilam	1.8	# ####	# ####	# ####	# ####	# ####	# ####	# ####	# ####	# ####	# ####	# ####	# ####	# ####	# ####	# ####	# ####	# ####	# ####	4 095
Betelgeuse	*	4 276	# ####	# ####	# ####	# ####	# ####	# ####	# ####	# ####	# ####	# ####	# ####	# ####	# ####	# ####	# ####	# ####	# ####	6 085
Canopus	-0.9	# ####	# ####	# ####	# ####	# ####	# ####	# ####	# ####	# ####	# ####	# ####	# ####	# ####	# ####	# ####	# ####	# ####	# ####	# ####
Sirius	-1.6	# ####	# ####	# ####	# ####	# ####	# ####	# ####	# ####	# ####	# ####	# ####	# ####	# ####	# ####	# ####	# ####	# ####	# ####	# ####
Adhara	1.6	# ####	# ####	# ####	# ####	# ####	# ####	# ####	# ####	# ####	# ####	# ####	# ####	# ####	# ####	# ####	# ####	# ####	# ####	# ####
Procyon	0.5	22 258	15 264	7 271	# ####	# ####	# ####	# ####	# ####	# ####	# ####	# ####	# ####	# ####	# ####	# ####	# ####	# ####	# ####	# ####
Pollux	1.2	37 278	29 283	22 289	15 294	8 300	2 306	# ####	# ####	# ####	# ####	# ####	# ####	# ####	# ####	# ####	# ####	# ####	# ####	0 052
Avior	1.7	# ####	# ####	# ####	# ####	# ####	# ####	# ####	# ####	# ####	# ####	# ####	# ####	# ####	# ####	# ####	# ####	# ####	# ####	# ####
Suhail	2.2	# ####	# ####	# ####	# ####	# ####	# ####	# ####	# ####	# ####	# ####	# ####	# ####	# ####	# ####	# ####	# ####	# ####	# ####	# ####
Miaplacidus	1.8	# ####	# ####	# ####	# ####	# ####	# ####	# ####	# ####	# ####	# ####	# ####	# ####	# ####	# ####	# ####	# ####	# ####	# ####	# ####
Alphard	2.2	30 225	24 234	18 242	11 249	3 256	# ####	# ####	# ####	# ####	# ####	# ####	# ####	# ####	# ####	# ####	# ####	# ####	# ####	# ####
Regulus	1.3	53 229	46 241	39 250	32 258	25 265	17 272	9 278	2 284	# ####	# ####	# ####	# ####	# ####	# ####	# ####	# ####	# ####	# ####	# ####
Dubhe	2.0	67 343	64 334	60 328	56 324	51 322	46 322	42 322	37 324	33 326	29 328	25 332	21 335	18 339	16 343	14 348	13 352	12 357	12 002	12 007
Denebola	2.2	64 186	62 207	58 224	52 238	45 248	38 257	30 264	22 271	15 277	7 283	# ####	# ####	# ####	# ####	# ####	# ####	# ####	# ####	# ####
Gienah	2.8	32 176	32 187	31 198	28 208	23 218	18 226	12 234	6 241	# ####	# ####	# ####	# ####	# ####	# ####	# ####	# ####	# ####	# ####	# ####
Acrux	1.1	# ####	# ####	# ####	# ####	# ####	# ####	# ####	# ####	# ####	# ####	# ####	# ####	# ####	# ####	# ####	# ####	# ####	# ####	# ####
Gacrux	1.6	# ####	# ####	# ####	# ####	# ####	# ####	# ####	# ####	# ####	# ####	# ####	# ####	# ####	# ####	# ####	# ####	# ####	# ####	# ####
Alioth	1.7	72 025	74 007	73 347	71 331	66 321	61 316	56 314	50 313	45 314	39 315	34 318	29 321	24 324	20 328	16 332	13 337	10 342	8 347	7 352
Spica	1.2	35 154	38 166	39 178	38 191	36 203	32 214	28 224	22 233	15 240	9 248	1 254	# ####	# ####	# ####	# ####	# ####	# ####	# ####	# ####
Alkaid	1.9	69 055	75 046	79 025	80 348	77 319	71 307	65 303	58 302	52 302	46 304	39 306	33 309	27 313	22 317	17 321	12 326	8 331	5 337	2 343
Hadar	0.9	# ####	# ####	# ####	# ####	# ####	# ####	# ####	# ####	# ####	# ####	# ####	# ####	# ####	# ####	# ####	# ####	# ####	# ####	# ####
Menkent	2.3	8 155	11 162	13 170	14 179	13 187	12 195	9 203	6 210	2 217	# ####	# ####	# ####	# ####	# ####	# ####	# ####	# ####	# ####	# ####
Arcturus	0.2	54 116	61 128	66 146	69 170	69 196	65 218	59 235	53 247	45 256	38 264	30 270	23 277	15 283	8 289	1 295	# ####	# ####	# ####	# ####
Rigil Kent.	0.1	# ####	# ####	# ####	# ####	# ####	# ####	# ####	# ####	# ####	# ####	# ####	# ####	# ####	# ####	# ####	# ####	# ####	# ####	# ####
Zuben'ubi	2.9	21 136	26 145	30 155	33 165	34 177	34 188	32 200	28 210	24 220	19 228	13 236	6 243	# ####	# ####	# ####	# ####	# ####	# ####	# ####
Kochab	2.2	51 017	53 014	54 010	55 006	56 001	56 356	55 352	54 348	52 345	49 342	47 340	44 339	42 339	39 339	36 340	34 342	31 343	29 346	28 348
Alphecca	2.3	44 090	52 097	59 105	66 117	73 135	76 166	76 203	71 231	64 247	57 257	50 265	42 272	34 278	27 284	19 289	12 295	6 301	# ####	# ####
Antares	1.2	# ####	5 131	10 138	15 146	19 154	22 163	23 173	24 183	23 192	20 202	17 210	13 218	7 226	2 233	# ####	# ####	# ####	# ####	# ####
Atria	1.9	# ####	# ####	# ####	# ####	# ####	# ####	# ####	# ####	# ####	# ####	# ####	# ####	# ####	# ####	# ####	# ####	# ####	# ####	# ####
Sabik	2.6	# ####	6 116	13 124	19 131	24 140	29 149	32 160	34 171	34 183	33 194	31 205	27 215	22 224	16 233	10 240	3 247	# ####	# ####	# ####
Shaula	1.7	# ####	# ####	# ####	# ####	3 147	7 154	10 161	12 169	13 177	13 185	11 193	9 201	6 209	2 215	# ####	# ####	# ####	# ####	# ####
Rasalhague	2.1	13 084	20 091	28 097	36 105	43 113	50 123	56 136	60 152	62 172	62 193	59 212	54 227	48 240	41 249	34 257	26 265	19 271	11 277	3 284
Eltanin	2.4	31 046	36 049	42 052	48 054	55 054	61 054	67 051	72 043	77 026	78 357	76 330	72 315	66 309	60 306	54 306	47 307	41 309	35 311	30 314
Kaus Aust.	2.0	# ####	# ####	# ####	# ####	# ####	4 143	9 151	12 158	14 166	15 175	16 183	15 192	12 200	9 208	5 215	1 222	# ####	# ####	# ####
Vega	0.1	18 054	24 059	31 063	38 067	45 072	52 075	60 079	67 084	75 088	83 097	89 206	82 265	74 272	66 277	59 281	51 285	44 289	37 293	30 297
Nunki	2.1	# ####	# ####	# ####	# ####	1 126	7 133	12 141	17 149	20 157	22 167	24 176	23 186	22 196	19 205	16 213	11 221	6 228	# ####	# ####
Altair	0.9	# ####	# ####	# ####	7 085	15 091	23 098	30 105	37 113	44 122	50 134	55 148	58 165	59 184	57 203	53 219	48 232	41 242	34 251	27 259
Peacock	2.1	# ####	# ####	# ####	# ####	# ####	# ####	# ####	# ####	# ####	# ####	# ####	# ####	# ####	# ####	# ####	# ####	# ####	# ####	# ####
Deneb	1.3	6 033	11 038	16 043	21 048	27 052	33 056	40 059	46 062	53 065	60 066	67 067	74 064	81 052	85 003	81 310	75 297	68 293	61 294	54 295
Enif	2.5	# ####	# ####	# ####	# ####	# ####	2 079	9 085	17 091	25 098	32 105	39 114	46 123	52 135	57 150	59 168	60 188	57 206	53 222	47 234
Al Na'ir	2.2	# ####	# ####	# ####	# ####	# ####	# ####	# ####	# ####	# ####	# ####	# ####	# ####	# ####	1 165	2 172	3 179	3 185	2 192	# ####
Fomalhaut	1.3	# ####	# ####	# ####	# ####	# ####	# ####	# ####	# ####	# ####	# ####	# ####	4 135	9 142	13 150	17 158	19 167	20 176	20 185	19 194
Markab	2.6	# ####	# ####	# ####	# ####	# ####	# ####	# ####	5 074	13 081	20 087	28 093	35 100	43 108	50 118	56 130	61 146	65 166	65 189	62 210

* Variable 0.1 - 1.2

SUN MOON PLANETS — Local Hour Angle Body

	180° Alt Az	190° Alt Az	200° Alt Az	210° Alt Az	220° Alt Az	230° Alt Az	240° Alt Az	250° Alt Az	260° Alt Az	270° Alt Az	280° Alt Az	290° Alt Az	300° Alt Az	310° Alt Az	320° Alt Az	330° Alt Az	340° Alt Az	350° Alt Az	360° Alt Az
	° °	° °	° °	° °	° °	° °	° °	° °	° °	° °	° °	° °	° °	° °	° °	° °	° °	° °	° °
Decl'n N30°	# ####	# ####	# ####	# ####	# ####	# ####	# ####	5 055	12 061	19 066	26 071	33 077	41 082	48 088	56 094	64 103	71 115	77 138	80 180
Decl'n N25°	# ####	# ####	# ####	# ####	# ####	# ####	# ####	2 058	9 065	16 070	23 076	31 082	38 088	46 094	53 102	61 112	68 126	73 148	75 180
Decl'n N20°	# ####	# ####	# ####	# ####	# ####	# ####	# ####	# ####	5 068	13 074	20 080	28 086	35 093	43 100	50 108	57 119	64 134	68 154	70 180
Decl'n N15°	# ####	# ####	# ####	# ####	# ####	# ####	# ####	# ####	2 072	10 078	17 085	25 091	32 098	40 105	47 114	54 125	60 139	64 158	65 180
Decl'n N10°	# ####	# ####	# ####	# ####	# ####	# ####	# ####	# ####	# ####	6 082	14 089	22 095	29 102	37 110	44 119	50 130	55 144	59 161	60 180
Decl'n N5°	# ####	# ####	# ####	# ####	# ####	# ####	# ####	# ####	# ####	3 086	11 093	18 099	26 106	33 114	40 123	46 134	51 148	54 163	55 180
Decl'n 0°	# ####	# ####	# ####	# ####	# ####	# ####	# ####	# ####	# ####	# ####	8 096	15 103	23 110	29 118	36 127	42 138	46 150	49 165	50 180
Decl'n S5°	# ####	# ####	# ####	# ####	# ####	# ####	# ####	# ####	# ####	# ####	4 100	12 107	19 114	26 122	32 131	37 141	41 153	44 166	45 180
Decl'n S10°	# ####	# ####	# ####	# ####	# ####	# ####	# ####	# ####	# ####	# ####	1 104	8 111	15 118	22 126	28 134	33 144	37 155	39 167	40 180
Decl'n S15°	# ####	# ####	# ####	# ####	# ####	# ####	# ####	# ####	# ####	# ####	# ####	5 114	12 121	18 129	24 137	28 147	32 157	34 168	35 180
Decl'n S20°	# ####	# ####	# ####	# ####	# ####	# ####	# ####	# ####	# ####	# ####	# ####	2 118	8 125	14 132	19 140	24 149	27 159	29 169	30 180
Decl'n S25°	# ####	# ####	# ####	# ####	# ####	# ####	# ####	# ####	# ####	# ####	# ####	# ####	4 128	10 135	15 143	19 151	22 160	24 170	25 180
Decl'n S30°	# ####	# ####	# ####	# ####	# ####	# ####	# ####	# ####	# ####	# ####	# ####	# ####	1 131	6 138	11 145	15 153	18 162	19 171	20 180

Latitude N30° Latitude N30°

STARS — Local Hour Angle Aries

Name	Mag	0°	10°	20°	30°	40°	50°	60°	70°	80°	90°	100°	110°	120°	130°	140°	150°	160°	170°	180°
		Alt Az	Alt Az	Alt Az	Alt Az	Alt Az	Alt Az	Alt Az	Alt Az	Alt Az	Alt Az	Alt Az	Alt Az	Alt Az	Alt Az	Alt Az	Alt Az	Alt Az	Alt Az	Alt Az
		° °	° °	° °	° °	° °	° °	° °	° °	° °	° °	° °	° °	° °	° °	° °	° °	° °	° °	° °
Alpheratz	2.2	88 116	83 264	74 271	66 275	57 278	49 281	40 284	32 288	24 291	16 295	8 299	1 304	# ####	# ####	# ####	# ####	# ####	# ####	# ####
Ankaa	2.4	17 175	18 183	17 190	15 198	11 205	7 211	3 216	# ####	# ####	# ####	# ####	# ####	# ####	# ####	# ####	# ####	# ####	# ####	# ####
Schedah	2.5	63 012	63 000	63 348	60 338	56 330	52 325	46 322	41 321	36 320	30 321	25 323	20 325	15 328	10 331	6 335	3 339	0 344	# ####	# ####
Diphda	2.2	41 166	42 179	41 192	39 203	34 214	29 223	23 231	16 238	8 244	0 249	# ####	# ####	# ####	# ####	# ####	# ####	# ####	# ####	# ####
Achernar	0.6	0 167	2 172	3 178	3 183	2 188	0 194	# ####	# ####	# ####	# ####	# ####	# ####	# ####	# ####	# ####	# ####	# ####	# ####	# ####
Hamal	2.2	61 095	70 103	78 119	83 166	80 230	73 252	64 262	55 268	47 273	38 278	30 282	21 286	13 290	5 294	# ####	# ####	# ####	# ####	# ####
Polaris	2.1	31 001	31 000	31 000	31 000	31 000	31 000	31 000	31 000	31 359	30 359	30 359	30 359	30 359	30 359	30 359	30 359	30 359	30 359	29 359
Acamar	3.1	8 147	13 154	16 161	18 168	20 176	20 184	18 192	16 200	12 207	8 213	3 219	# ####	# ####	# ####	# ####	# ####	# ####	# ####	# ####
Menkar	2.8	40 112	48 121	55 132	60 147	64 167	64 190	61 211	55 226	48 238	41 247	33 254	24 260	16 266	7 271	# ####	# ####	# ####	# ####	# ####
Mirfak	1.9	47 048	53 045	59 041	65 033	68 020	70 002	69 344	66 330	61 321	55 315	49 313	42 312	36 312	29 313	23 316	17 318	12 321	6 325	2 330
Aldebaran	1.1	26 085	35 090	43 095	52 102	60 110	68 124	74 147	76 184	73 219	67 240	59 252	50 260	42 266	33 271	24 276	16 280	7 285	# ####	# ####
Rigel	0.3	6 103	14 108	22 114	30 121	37 130	43 140	48 152	51 166	52 182	50 198	47 212	41 223	35 233	28 241	20 247	12 253	3 259	# ####	# ####
Capella	0.2	28 051	35 052	42 053	49 053	56 051	62 047	68 038	72 022	74 358	72 335	67 320	61 312	55 308	48 307	41 307	34 308	27 310	21 312	14 315
Bellatrix	1.7	11 089	19 094	28 099	36 106	45 113	52 123	59 136	64 154	66 177	65 201	61 220	54 235	47 245	39 253	30 259	22 265	13 270	4 275	# ####
Elnath	1.8	21 068	29 072	37 075	45 078	54 082	63 085	71 089	80 095	88 135	83 261	74 270	65 274	57 277	48 281	40 284	31 287	23 291	15 295	7 299
Alnilam	1.8	5 094	13 099	22 105	30 111	38 119	45 128	51 140	56 155	59 173	58 192	55 209	50 223	44 234	36 243	28 250	20 256	11 262	3 267	# ####
Betelgeuse	*	5 084	13 089	22 094	31 100	39 106	47 114	55 124	61 138	66 158	67 183	65 207	60 226	53 239	45 248	37 256	29 262	20 267	11 272	3 277
Canopus	-0.9	# ####	# ####	# ####	# ####	# ####	# ####	2 159	4 165	6 170	7 176	7 182	6 188	5 194	2 200	# ####	# ####	# ####	# ####	# ####
Sirius	-1.6	# ####	# ####	# ####	7 114	15 120	22 126	29 134	34 143	39 153	42 165	43 178	43 191	40 204	36 215	30 224	24 232	17 239	9 245	1 250
Adhara	1.6	# ####	# ####	# ####	# ####	5 128	11 133	17 140	22 147	27 156	29 165	31 175	31 185	29 195	26 205	22 213	17 221	11 227	4 233	# ####
Procyon	0.5	# ####	# ####	# ####	7 088	16 093	24 098	33 104	41 111	49 120	56 132	62 148	65 169	65 192	61 213	56 229	49 240	41 249	33 256	24 262
Pollux	1.2	# ####	1 058	9 063	16 067	25 071	33 074	41 078	50 081	58 084	67 088	76 094	84 108	86 239	78 264	69 270	61 275	52 278	43 282	35 285
Avior	1.7	# ####	# ####	# ####	# ####	# ####	# ####	# ####	# ####	# ####	# ####	# ####	# ####	0 177	0 182	# ####	# ####	# ####	# ####	# ####
Suhail	2.2	# ####	# ####	# ####	# ####	# ####	# ####	# ####	# ####	# ####	5 148	9 154	13 160	15 167	16 175	17 182	16 190	14 197	11 204	7 210
Miaplacidus	1.8	# ####	# ####	# ####	# ####	# ####	# ####	# ####	# ####	# ####	# ####	# ####	# ####	# ####	# ####	# ####	# ####	# ####	# ####	# ####
Alphard	2.2	# ####	# ####	# ####	# ####	# ####	# ####	3 102	11 107	19 113	27 119	34 127	41 136	46 148	50 162	51 177	51 193	48 207	43 219	37 230
Regulus	1.3	# ####	# ####	# ####	# ####	# ####	# ####	4 079	13 083	21 088	30 093	39 099	47 106	55 114	63 127	69 146	72 173	71 204	65 226	58 241
Dubhe	2.0	2 007	4 011	6 015	8 019	12 023	15 026	19 029	23 031	28 032	33 033	37 033	42 032	47 030	51 026	54 021	57 014	58 005	58 356	57 348
Denebola	2.2	# ####	# ####	# ####	# ####	# ####	# ####	# ####	# ####	1 074	10 079	18 083	27 088	35 093	44 099	52 106	61 116	68 130	73 155	74 190
Gienah	2.8	# ####	# ####	# ####	# ####	# ####	# ####	# ####	# ####	# ####	# ####	# ####	4 113	12 119	20 125	26 132	32 141	37 151	41 162	42 175
Acrux	1.1	# ####	# ####	# ####	# ####	# ####	# ####	# ####	# ####	# ####	# ####	# ####	# ####	# ####	# ####	# ####	# ####	# ####	# ####	# ####
Gacrux	1.6	# ####	# ####	# ####	# ####	# ####	# ####	# ####	# ####	# ####	# ####	# ####	# ####	# ####	# ####	# ####	# ####	# ####	2 170	3 176
Alioth	1.7	# ####	# ####	# ####	# ####	# ####	1 019	5 024	8 028	13 032	18 035	23 037	28 039	34 040	39 040	45 039	50 037	55 033	59 026	62 016
Spica	1.2	# ####	# ####	# ####	# ####	# ####	# ####	# ####	# ####	# ####	# ####	# ####	# ####	2 104	10 109	18 115	26 122	33 130	39 139	44 150
Alkaid	1.9	# ####	# ####	# ####	# ####	# ####	# ####	# ####	# ####	2 031	7 036	12 040	18 043	24 046	30 047	37 049	43 049	50 048	56 045	62 039
Hadar	0.9	# ####	# ####	# ####	# ####	# ####	# ####	# ####	# ####	# ####	# ####	# ####	# ####	# ####	# ####	# ####	# ####	# ####	# ####	# ####
Menkent	2.3	# ####	# ####	# ####	# ####	# ####	# ####	# ####	# ####	# ####	# ####	# ####	# ####	# ####	# ####	# ####	2 135	8 140	13 147	17 154
Arcturus	0.2	# ####	# ####	# ####	# ####	# ####	# ####	# ####	# ####	# ####	# ####	# ####	# ####	6 071	15 076	23 080	32 085	40 090	49 095	57 102
Rigil Kent.	0.1	# ####	# ####	# ####	# ####	# ####	# ####	# ####	# ####	# ####	# ####	# ####	# ####	# ####	# ####	# ####	# ####	# ####	# ####	# ####
Zuben'ubi	2.9	# ####	# ####	# ####	# ####	# ####	# ####	# ####	# ####	# ####	# ####	# ####	# ####	# ####	# ####	# ####	6 113	14 118	21 125	28 132
Kochab	2.2	18 349	16 351	15 354	15 356	14 359	14 002	15 005	16 007	17 010	19 012	21 014	23 016	25 017	28 018	31 018	33 018	36 017	39 016	41 014
Alphecca	2.3	# ####	# ####	# ####	# ####	# ####	# ####	# ####	# ####	# ####	# ####	# ####	# ####	# ####	2 060	10 065	18 069	26 073	35 077	43 080
Antares	1.2	# ####	# ####	# ####	# ####	# ####	# ####	# ####	# ####	# ####	# ####	# ####	# ####	# ####	# ####	# ####	# ####	# ####	# ####	4 124
Atria	1.9	# ####	# ####	# ####	# ####	# ####	# ####	# ####	# ####	# ####	# ####	# ####	# ####	# ####	# ####	# ####	# ####	# ####	# ####	# ####
Sabik	2.6	# ####	# ####	# ####	# ####	# ####	# ####	# ####	# ####	# ####	# ####	# ####	# ####	# ####	# ####	# ####	# ####	# ####	# ####	2 110
Shaula	1.7	# ####	# ####	# ####	# ####	# ####	# ####	# ####	# ####	# ####	# ####	# ####	# ####	# ####	# ####	# ####	# ####	# ####	# ####	# ####
Rasalhague	2.1	1 284	# ####	# ####	# ####	# ####	# ####	# ####	# ####	# ####	# ####	# ####	# ####	# ####	# ####	# ####	# ####	# ####	3 077	12 082
Eltanin	2.4	23 318	17 320	12 324	7 327	2 332	# ####	# ####	# ####	# ####	# ####	# ####	# ####	# ####	# ####	3 029	7 033	12 037	18 040	24 043
Kaus Aust.	2.0	# ####	# ####	# ####	# ####	# ####	# ####	# ####	# ####	# ####	# ####	# ####	# ####	# ####	# ####	# ####	# ####	# ####	# ####	# ####
Vega	0.1	25 302	18 305	11 309	4 313	# ####	# ####	# ####	# ####	# ####	# ####	# ####	# ####	# ####	# ####	# ####	# ####	# ####	5 048	12 052
Nunki	2.1	# ####	# ####	# ####	# ####	# ####	# ####	# ####	# ####	# ####	# ####	# ####	# ####	# ####	# ####	# ####	# ####	# ####	# ####	# ####
Altair	0.9	28 264	20 269	11 274	2 279	# ####	# ####	# ####	# ####	# ####	# ####	# ####	# ####	# ####	# ####	# ####	# ####	# ####	# ####	# ####
Peacock	2.1	# ####	# ####	# ####	# ####	# ####	# ####	# ####	# ####	# ####	# ####	# ####	# ####	# ####	# ####	# ####	# ####	# ####	# ####	# ####
Deneb	1.3	49 306	42 306	35 307	28 309	21 311	15 314	9 318	3 322	# ####	# ####	# ####	# ####	# ####	# ####	# ####	# ####	# ####	# ####	# ####
Enif	2.5	52 245	44 253	36 260	27 266	19 271	10 276	1 281	# ####	# ####	# ####	# ####	# ####	# ####	# ####	# ####	# ####	# ####	# ####	# ####
Al Na'ir	2.2	9 199	6 205	2 210	# ####	# ####	# ####	# ####	# ####	# ####	# ####	# ####	# ####	# ####	# ####	# ####	# ####	# ####	# ####	# ####
Fomalhaut	1.3	29 195	26 205	21 213	16 220	10 227	4 232	# ####	# ####	# ####	# ####	# ####	# ####	# ####	# ####	# ####	# ####	# ####	# ####	# ####
Markab	2.6	71 224	64 241	56 252	47 260	39 266	30 271	21 276	13 280	4 285	# ####	# ####	# ####	# ####	# ####	# ####	# ####	# ####	# ####	# ####

* Variable 0.1 - 1.2

SUN MOON PLANETS — Local Hour Angle Body

	0°	10°	20°	30°	40°	50°	60°	70°	80°	90°	100°	110°	120°	130°	140°	150°	160°	170°	180°
	Alt Az	Alt Az	Alt Az	Alt Az	Alt Az	Alt Az	Alt Az	Alt Az	Alt Az	Alt Az	Alt Az	Alt Az	Alt Az	Alt Az	Alt Az	Alt Az	Alt Az	Alt Az	Alt Az
	° °	° °	° °	° °	° °	° °	° °	° °	° °	° °	° °	° °	° °	° °	° °	° °	° °	° °	° °
Decl'n N30°	90 000	81 273	73 275	64 278	56 280	47 283	39 286	30 289	22 293	14 297	7 301	# ####	# ####	# ####	# ####	# ####	# ####	# ####	# ####
Decl'n N25°	85 180	80 243	72 259	63 267	54 272	46 276	37 280	29 284	20 288	12 292	4 296	# ####	# ####	# ####	# ####	# ####	# ####	# ####	# ####
Decl'n N20°	80 180	77 224	69 246	61 257	53 264	44 270	35 274	27 279	18 283	10 287	2 292	# ####	# ####	# ####	# ####	# ####	# ####	# ####	# ####
Decl'n N15°	75 180	72 214	66 235	59 248	50 257	42 263	33 269	25 274	16 278	7 283	# ####	# ####	# ####	# ####	# ####	# ####	# ####	# ####	# ####
Decl'n N10°	70 180	68 207	63 227	56 241	48 250	39 258	31 264	22 269	14 274	5 279	# ####	# ####	# ####	# ####	# ####	# ####	# ####	# ####	# ####
Decl'n N5°	65 180	63 203	59 221	52 234	45 244	37 252	28 259	20 264	11 269	2 274	# ####	# ####	# ####	# ####	# ####	# ####	# ####	# ####	# ####
Decl'n 0°	60 180	59 199	54 216	49 229	42 239	34 247	26 254	17 260	9 265	0 270	# ####	# ####	# ####	# ####	# ####	# ####	# ####	# ####	# ####
Decl'n S5°	55 180	54 197	50 212	45 225	38 234	31 243	23 249	15 255	6 261	# ####	# ####	# ####	# ####	# ####	# ####	# ####	# ####	# ####	# ####
Decl'n S10°	50 180	49 195	46 209	41 220	35 230	27 238	20 245	12 251	4 256	# ####	# ####	# ####	# ####	# ####	# ####	# ####	# ####	# ####	# ####
Decl'n S15°	45 180	44 193	41 206	37 217	31 226	24 234	17 241	9 247	1 252	# ####	# ####	# ####	# ####	# ####	# ####	# ####	# ####	# ####	# ####
Decl'n S20°	40 180	39 192	36 204	32 214	27 223	21 230	14 237	6 243	# ####	# ####	# ####	# ####	# ####	# ####	# ####	# ####	# ####	# ####	# ####
Decl'n S25°	35 180	34 191	32 201	28 211	23 219	17 227	10 233	3 239	# ####	# ####	# ####	# ####	# ####	# ####	# ####	# ####	# ####	# ####	# ####
Decl'n S30°	30 180	29 190	27 199	24 208	19 216	13 223	7 229	0 234	# ####	# ####	# ####	# ####	# ####	# ####	# ####	# ####	# ####	# ####	# ####

Latitude N30° Latitude N30°

STARS		Local Hour Angle Aries																		
Name	Mag	180° Alt Az	190° Alt Az	200° Alt Az	210° Alt Az	220° Alt Az	230° Alt Az	240° Alt Az	250° Alt Az	260° Alt Az	270° Alt Az	280° Alt Az	290° Alt Az	300° Alt Az	310° Alt Az	320° Alt Az	330° Alt Az	340° Alt Az	350° Alt Az	360° Alt Az
		° °	° °	° °	° °	° °	° °	° °	° °	° °	° °	° °	° °	° °	° °	° °	° °	° °	° °	° °
Alpheratz	2.2	# ###	# ###	# ###	# ###	# ###	# ###	# ###	# ###	5 059	12 063	20 067	28 071	37 074	45 078	54 081	62 084	71 087	79 092	88 116
Ankaa	2.4	# ###	# ###	# ###	# ###	# ###	# ###	# ###	# ###	# ###	# ###	# ###	# ###	# ###	1 142	6 147	10 153	14 160	16 167	17 175
Schedah	2.5	# ###	# ###	# ###	# ###	0 016	3 021	6 025	10 029	15 032	19 035	25 037	30 039	35 040	41 039	46 038	51 035	56 030	60 022	63 012
Diphda	2.2	# ###	# ###	# ###	# ###	# ###	# ###	# ###	# ###	# ###	# ###	# ###	# ###	7 115	14 121	21 128	28 135	34 144	38 155	41 166
Achernar	0.6	# ###	# ###	# ###	# ###	# ###	# ###	# ###	# ###	# ###	# ###	# ###	# ###	# ###	# ###	# ###	# ###	# ###	# ###	0 167
Hamal	2.2	# ###	# ###	# ###	# ###	# ###	# ###	# ###	# ###	# ###	# ###	# ###	2 064	10 069	18 073	27 077	35 081	44 085	52 090	61 095
Polaris	2.1	29 359	29 000	29 000	29 000	29 000	29 000	29 000	29 000	29 001	30 001	30 001	30 001	30 001	30 001	30 001	30 001	30 001	30 001	31 001
Acamar	3.1	# ###	# ###	# ###	# ###	# ###	# ###	# ###	# ###	# ###	# ###	# ###	# ###	# ###	# ###	# ###	# ###	# ###	3 142	8 147
Menkar	2.8	# ###	# ###	# ###	# ###	# ###	# ###	# ###	# ###	# ###	# ###	# ###	# ###	# ###	# ###	6 089	15 094	23 099	32 105	40 112
Mirfak	1.9	2 330	# ###	# ###	# ###	# ###	# ###	# ###	# ###	# ###	# ###	1 029	5 034	10 038	16 041	22 044	28 046	34 048	41 048	47 048
Aldebaran	1.1	# ###	# ###	# ###	# ###	# ###	# ###	# ###	# ###	# ###	# ###	# ###	# ###	# ###	# ###	# ###	1 071	9 076	18 081	26 085
Rigel	0.3	# ###	# ###	# ###	# ###	# ###	# ###	# ###	# ###	# ###	# ###	# ###	# ###	# ###	# ###	# ###	# ###	# ###	# ###	6 103
Capella	0.2	14 315	8 319	3 323	# ###	# ###	# ###	# ###	# ###	# ###	# ###	# ###	# ###	# ###	# ###	4 037	9 042	15 045	22 048	28 051
Bellatrix	1.7	# ###	# ###	# ###	# ###	# ###	# ###	# ###	# ###	# ###	# ###	# ###	# ###	# ###	# ###	# ###	# ###	# ###	2 084	11 089
Elnath	1.8	7 299	# ###	# ###	# ###	# ###	# ###	# ###	# ###	# ###	# ###	# ###	# ###	# ###	# ###	# ###	# ###	5 060	13 064	21 068
Alnilam	1.8	# ###	# ###	# ###	# ###	# ###	# ###	# ###	# ###	# ###	# ###	# ###	# ###	# ###	# ###	# ###	# ###	# ###	# ###	5 094
Betelgeuse	*	3 277	# ###	# ###	# ###	# ###	# ###	# ###	# ###	# ###	# ###	# ###	# ###	# ###	# ###	# ###	# ###	# ###	# ###	5 084
Canopus	-0.9	# ###	# ###	# ###	# ###	# ###	# ###	# ###	# ###	# ###	# ###	# ###	# ###	# ###	# ###	# ###	# ###	# ###	# ###	# ###
Sirius	-1.6	1 250	# ###	# ###	# ###	# ###	# ###	# ###	# ###	# ###	# ###	# ###	# ###	# ###	# ###	# ###	# ###	# ###	# ###	# ###
Adhara	1.6	# ###	# ###	# ###	# ###	# ###	# ###	# ###	# ###	# ###	# ###	# ###	# ###	# ###	# ###	# ###	# ###	# ###	# ###	# ###
Procyon	0.5	24 262	15 267	7 272	# ###	# ###	# ###	# ###	# ###	# ###	# ###	# ###	# ###	# ###	# ###	# ###	# ###	# ###	# ###	# ###
Pollux	1.2	35 285	27 288	19 292	11 296	3 301	# ###	# ###	# ###	# ###	# ###	# ###	# ###	# ###	# ###	# ###	# ###	# ###	# ###	# ###
Avior	1.7	# ###	# ###	# ###	# ###	# ###	# ###	# ###	# ###	# ###	# ###	# ###	# ###	# ###	# ###	# ###	# ###	# ###	# ###	# ###
Suhail	2.2	7 210	2 215	# ###	# ###	# ###	# ###	# ###	# ###	# ###	# ###	# ###	# ###	# ###	# ###	# ###	# ###	# ###	# ###	# ###
Miaplacidus	1.8	# ###	# ###	# ###	# ###	# ###	# ###	# ###	# ###	# ###	# ###	# ###	# ###	# ###	# ###	# ###	# ###	# ###	# ###	# ###
Alphard	2.2	37 230	30 238	22 245	14 251	6 256	# ###	# ###	# ###	# ###	# ###	# ###	# ###	# ###	# ###	# ###	# ###	# ###	# ###	# ###
Regulus	1.3	58 241	51 251	42 258	34 264	25 270	16 275	8 279	# ###	# ###	# ###	# ###	# ###	# ###	# ###	# ###	# ###	# ###	# ###	# ###
Dubhe	2.0	57 348	55 341	51 335	47 331	43 328	38 327	34 327	29 327	24 329	20 331	16 333	12 336	9 340	6 344	4 348	3 353	2 357	2 002	2 007
Denebola	2.2	74 190	71 220	64 239	56 250	48 258	39 264	31 270	22 275	13 279	5 284	# ###	# ###	# ###	# ###	# ###	# ###	# ###	# ###	# ###
Gienah	2.8	42 175	42 188	40 200	36 211	31 221	25 229	18 236	11 242	3 248	# ###	# ###	# ###	# ###	# ###	# ###	# ###	# ###	# ###	# ###
Acrux	1.1	# ###	# ###	# ###	# ###	# ###	# ###	# ###	# ###	# ###	# ###	# ###	# ###	# ###	# ###	# ###	# ###	# ###	# ###	# ###
Gacrux	1.6	3 176	3 181	2 187	1 192	# ###	# ###	# ###	# ###	# ###	# ###	# ###	# ###	# ###	# ###	# ###	# ###	# ###	# ###	# ###
Alioth	1.7	62 016	64 004	64 352	62 341	58 332	54 326	48 322	43 320	37 320	32 320	26 321	21 323	16 326	11 329	7 333	4 337	1 342	# ###	# ###
Spica	1.2	44 150	47 163	49 178	48 193	45 206	40 218	34 228	28 236	20 243	12 249	4 255	# ###	# ###	# ###	# ###	# ###	# ###	# ###	# ###
Alkaid	1.9	62 039	67 029	70 013	71 354	68 336	64 324	58 317	52 313	46 311	39 311	33 312	27 314	20 316	15 319	9 323	4 327	# ###	# ###	# ###
Hadar	0.9	# ###	# ###	# ###	# ###	# ###	# ###	# ###	# ###	# ###	# ###	# ###	# ###	# ###	# ###	# ###	# ###	# ###	# ###	# ###
Menkent	2.3	17 154	21 161	23 170	24 179	23 187	21 196	18 204	15 211	10 218	4 223	# ###	# ###	# ###	# ###	# ###	# ###	# ###	# ###	# ###
Arcturus	0.2	57 102	66 111	73 127	79 161	78 208	72 237	64 251	56 260	47 266	38 272	30 276	21 281	13 285	4 290	# ###	# ###	# ###	# ###	# ###
Rigil Kent.	0.1	# ###	# ###	# ###	# ###	# ###	# ###	# ###	# ###	# ###	# ###	# ###	# ###	# ###	# ###	# ###	# ###	# ###	# ###	# ###
Zuben'ubi	2.9	28 132	34 141	39 151	42 163	44 176	43 190	41 202	37 213	32 223	25 231	18 238	11 244	3 250	# ###	# ###	# ###	# ###	# ###	# ###
Kochab	2.2	41 014	43 012	44 008	45 005	46 001	46 357	45 353	44 350	42 347	40 345	37 343	35 342	32 342	29 342	27 342	24 343	22 345	20 347	18 349
Alphecca	2.3	43 080	52 084	60 088	69 093	78 102	85 135	84 241	75 261	67 268	58 273	49 277	41 281	32 284	24 288	16 292	8 296	0 301	# ###	# ###
Antares	1.2	4 124	11 130	18 136	23 144	28 152	31 162	33 172	34 183	32 193	30 203	25 212	20 220	14 227	8 233	1 239	# ###	# ###	# ###	# ###
Atria	1.9	# ###	# ###	# ###	# ###	# ###	# ###	# ###	# ###	# ###	# ###	# ###	# ###	# ###	# ###	# ###	# ###	# ###	# ###	# ###
Sabik	2.6	2 110	10 115	18 121	25 128	32 136	37 146	41 157	44 170	44 183	43 196	39 208	35 219	29 228	22 235	15 242	7 247	# ###	# ###	# ###
Shaula	1.7	# ###	# ###	0 135	6 140	12 146	16 153	19 160	22 169	23 177	23 186	21 194	18 202	15 209	10 216	5 222	# ###	# ###	# ###	# ###
Rasalhague	2.1	12 082	20 087	29 092	37 097	46 104	54 112	62 123	68 141	72 168	72 200	67 224	60 240	52 250	44 258	35 264	27 269	18 274	9 279	1 284
Eltanin	2.4	24 043	30 045	36 046	42 046	48 045	54 042	60 037	64 028	67 015	68 359	67 343	64 330	59 322	53 317	47 315	41 314	35 314	28 316	23 318
Kaus Aust.	2.0	# ###	# ###	# ###	0 131	7 136	12 143	17 149	21 157	24 166	25 174	26 184	24 193	22 201	18 209	13 216	8 222	2 228	# ###	# ###
Vega	0.1	12 052	19 055	26 058	34 061	41 063	49 064	57 064	64 062	72 056	78 038	81 356	78 318	71 303	63 298	56 296	48 296	40 297	32 299	25 302
Nunki	2.1	# ###	# ###	# ###	# ###	7 126	14 132	20 139	25 147	29 155	32 165	34 176	33 187	32 197	28 207	24 215	18 223	12 230	5 235	# ###
Altair	0.9	# ###	# ###	# ###	6 083	15 088	24 093	32 099	41 105	49 113	57 123	63 138	68 160	69 186	66 211	60 229	53 242	45 251	37 258	28 264
Peacock	2.1	# ###	# ###	# ###	# ###	# ###	# ###	# ###	# ###	# ###	# ###	0 166	2 171	3 176	3 182	3 187	1 193	# ###	# ###	# ###
Deneb	1.3	# ###	3 037	8 042	14 046	21 049	27 051	34 053	41 054	48 054	55 053	62 049	68 041	73 025	75 001	73 336	68 320	62 312	56 308	49 306
Enif	2.5	# ###	# ###	# ###	# ###	# ###	# ###	8 083	17 088	26 093	34 099	43 105	51 113	58 124	65 140	69 163	70 191	66 216	60 233	52 245
Al Na'ir	2.2	# ###	# ###	# ###	# ###	# ###	# ###	# ###	# ###	# ###	# ###	# ###	4 153	8 159	11 165	12 172	13 179	13 186	11 192	9 199
Fomalhaut	1.3	# ###	# ###	# ###	# ###	# ###	# ###	# ###	# ###	# ###	# ###	4 128	11 134	17 141	22 148	26 156	29 166	30 176	30 186	29 195
Markab	2.6	# ###	# ###	# ###	# ###	# ###	# ###	# ###	2 074	11 079	19 083	28 088	37 093	45 099	54 106	62 116	69 131	74 158	75 194	71 224

* Variable 0.1 - 1.2

SUN MOON PLANETS	Local Hour Angle Body																		
	180° Alt Az	190° Alt Az	200° Alt Az	210° Alt Az	220° Alt Az	230° Alt Az	240° Alt Az	250° Alt Az	260° Alt Az	270° Alt Az	280° Alt Az	290° Alt Az	300° Alt Az	310° Alt Az	320° Alt Az	330° Alt Az	340° Alt Az	350° Alt Az	360° Alt Az
	° °	° °	° °	° °	° °	° °	° °	° °	° °	° °	° °	° °	° °	° °	° °	° °	° °	° °	° °
Decl'n N30°	# ###	# ###	# ###	# ###	# ###	# ###	# ###	# ###	7 059	14 063	22 067	30 071	39 074	47 077	56 080	64 082	73 085	81 087	90 077
Decl'n N25°	# ###	# ###	# ###	# ###	# ###	# ###	# ###	# ###	4 064	12 068	20 072	29 076	37 080	46 084	54 088	63 093	72 101	80 117	85 180
Decl'n N20°	# ###	# ###	# ###	# ###	# ###	# ###	# ###	# ###	2 068	10 073	18 077	27 081	35 086	44 090	53 096	61 103	69 114	77 136	80 180
Decl'n N15°	# ###	# ###	# ###	# ###	# ###	# ###	# ###	# ###	# ###	7 077	16 082	25 086	33 091	42 097	50 103	59 112	66 125	72 146	75 180
Decl'n N10°	# ###	# ###	# ###	# ###	# ###	# ###	# ###	# ###	# ###	5 081	14 086	22 091	31 096	39 102	48 110	56 119	63 133	68 153	70 180
Decl'n N5°	# ###	# ###	# ###	# ###	# ###	# ###	# ###	# ###	# ###	2 086	11 091	20 096	28 101	37 108	45 116	52 126	59 139	63 157	65 180
Decl'n 0°	# ###	# ###	# ###	# ###	# ###	# ###	# ###	# ###	# ###	# ###	9 095	17 100	26 106	34 113	42 121	49 131	54 144	59 161	60 180
Decl'n S5°	# ###	# ###	# ###	# ###	# ###	# ###	# ###	# ###	# ###	# ###	6 099	15 105	23 111	31 117	38 126	45 135	50 148	54 163	55 180
Decl'n S10°	# ###	# ###	# ###	# ###	# ###	# ###	# ###	# ###	# ###	# ###	4 104	12 109	20 115	27 122	35 130	41 140	46 151	49 165	50 180
Decl'n S15°	# ###	# ###	# ###	# ###	# ###	# ###	# ###	# ###	# ###	# ###	1 108	9 113	17 119	24 126	31 134	37 143	41 154	44 167	45 180
Decl'n S20°	# ###	# ###	# ###	# ###	# ###	# ###	# ###	# ###	# ###	# ###	# ###	6 117	14 123	21 130	27 137	32 146	36 156	39 168	40 180
Decl'n S25°	# ###	# ###	# ###	# ###	# ###	# ###	# ###	# ###	# ###	# ###	# ###	3 121	10 127	17 133	23 141	28 149	32 159	34 169	35 180
Decl'n S30°	# ###	# ###	# ###	# ###	# ###	# ###	# ###	# ###	# ###	# ###	# ###	0 126	7 131	13 137	19 144	24 152	27 161	29 170	30 180

Latitude N20° Latitude N20°

STARS — Local Hour Angle Aries

Name	Mag	0° Alt Az	10° Alt Az	20° Alt Az	30° Alt Az	40° Alt Az	50° Alt Az	60° Alt Az	70° Alt Az	80° Alt Az	90° Alt Az	100° Alt Az	110° Alt Az	120° Alt Az	130° Alt Az	140° Alt Az	150° Alt Az	160° Alt Az	170° Alt Az	180° Alt Az
		° °	° °	° °	° °	° °	° °	° °	° °	° °	° °	° °	° °	° °	° °	° °	° °	° °	° °	° °
Alpheratz	2.2	81 011	78 323	71 303	63 295	55 292	46 292	37 292	28 293	20 295	11 297	3 300	# ###	# ###	# ###	# ###	# ###	# ###	# ###	# ###
Ankaa	2.4	27 175	28 183	26 191	24 199	20 206	16 212	11 217	5 222	# ###	# ###	# ###	# ###	# ###	# ###	# ###	# ###	# ###	# ###	# ###
Schedah	2.5	53 009	53 000	53 351	51 343	47 336	43 331	38 328	33 325	28 324	22 324	17 325	11 326	6 329	2 331	# ###	# ###	# ###	# ###	# ###
Diphda	2.2	51 164	52 179	51 194	48 208	42 219	36 228	29 235	21 241	12 245	4 249	# ###	# ###	# ###	# ###	# ###	# ###	# ###	# ###	# ###
Achernar	0.6	10 167	12 172	13 178	13 183	12 189	10 194	7 199	4 203	# ###	# ###	# ###	# ###	# ###	# ###	# ###	# ###	# ###	# ###	# ###
Hamal	2.2	60 077	69 076	79 070	86 025	82 296	73 285	64 283	54 283	45 284	36 285	27 287	18 289	9 292	1 295	# ###	# ###	# ###	# ###	# ###
Polaris	2.1	21 000	21 000	21 000	21 000	21 000	21 000	21 000	21 000	21 359	20 359	20 359	20 359	20 359	20 359	20 359	20 359	20 359	20 359	19 000
Acamar	3.1	17 146	22 152	26 159	28 167	30 176	29 185	28 193	25 201	21 208	16 214	11 220	4 224	# ###	# ###	# ###	# ###	# ###	# ###	# ###
Menkar	2.8	43 104	52 110	60 119	68 134	73 160	74 196	69 223	61 239	53 249	44 256	35 261	25 265	16 269	7 272	# ###	# ###	# ###	# ###	# ###
Mirfak	1.9	40 041	46 037	51 032	56 024	59 014	60 001	59 349	57 338	52 329	47 323	41 320	35 318	29 317	22 317	16 318	10 320	4 322	# ###	# ###
Aldebaran	1.1	25 081	34 083	44 086	53 089	62 092	72 098	81 111	86 196	79 253	70 264	60 268	51 272	42 275	32 277	23 280	14 283	5 286	# ###	# ###
Rigel	0.3	8 102	17 106	26 110	34 116	43 123	50 132	56 145	61 162	62 183	60 203	55 219	48 231	40 239	32 246	23 251	14 256	5 259	# ###	# ###
Capella	0.2	22 047	29 048	35 047	42 045	49 042	55 036	60 027	63 014	64 359	63 344	59 331	54 323	48 318	41 314	34 313	27 312	20 313	14 314	7 317
Bellatrix	1.7	10 087	20 090	29 094	38 098	48 103	57 110	65 121	72 140	76 175	74 213	67 236	59 248	50 255	41 261	32 265	22 269	13 272	3 276	# ###
Elnath	1.8	17 065	25 067	34 068	43 069	51 069	60 067	69 062	76 049	81 009	78 320	71 301	63 294	54 291	45 291	37 291	28 293	19 294	11 297	2 300
Alnilam	1.8	5 093	15 097	24 101	33 105	42 111	51 119	58 129	65 146	68 169	68 197	64 219	57 233	49 243	40 250	31 256	22 260	13 264	3 268	# ###
Betelgeuse	*	4 083	13 087	22 090	32 094	41 098	50 103	59 110	68 122	75 145	77 185	73 222	66 241	57 252	48 258	39 263	30 267	20 271	11 274	1 277
Canopus	-0.9	# ###	# ###	# ###	# ###	3 150	7 154	11 159	14 164	16 170	17 176	17 183	16 189	14 195	12 200	8 205	4 209	# ###	# ###	# ###
Sirius	-1.6	# ###	# ###	2 109	11 112	20 117	28 122	35 129	42 138	48 149	52 162	53 178	52 194	49 208	44 220	37 229	30 236	22 242	13 246	4 250
Adhara	1.6	# ###	# ###	# ###	3 122	11 126	18 131	25 137	31 145	36 153	39 163	41 175	41 186	39 197	35 207	30 216	24 223	18 229	10 234	2 238
Procyon	0.5	# ###	# ###	# ###	7 087	16 090	25 094	35 098	44 103	53 109	62 118	69 134	74 162	74 200	69 227	61 242	53 251	44 258	34 262	25 266
Pollux	1.2	# ###	# ###	4 062	12 064	21 067	30 068	38 070	47 070	56 069	65 066	73 059	80 035	81 338	75 305	67 295	58 291	50 290	41 290	32 291
Avior	1.7	# ###	# ###	# ###	# ###	# ###	# ###	# ###	# ###	2 159	5 163	8 167	9 172	10 177	10 182	10 187	8 192	6 197	3 201	# ###
Suhail	2.2	# ###	# ###	# ###	# ###	# ###	# ###	# ###	2 138	8 142	13 147	18 153	22 159	25 166	26 174	27 182	25 190	23 198	20 205	15 211
Miaplacidus	1.8	# ###	# ###	# ###	# ###	# ###	# ###	# ###	# ###	# ###	# ###	# ###	# ###	# ###	0 177	0 181	# ###	# ###	# ###	# ###
Alphard	2.2	# ###	# ###	# ###	# ###	# ###	# ###	5 101	14 105	23 109	31 114	40 121	47 129	54 141	59 157	61 176	60 196	56 214	50 227	43 236
Regulus	1.3	# ###	# ###	# ###	# ###	# ###	# ###	2 078	11 081	21 084	30 087	39 091	49 095	58 100	67 107	76 123	82 166	79 225	71 248	62 258
Dubhe	2.0	# ###	# ###	# ###	# ###	2 023	6 025	10 028	15 029	19 030	24 030	29 030	33 028	38 025	41 022	45 017	47 011	48 004	48 357	47 350
Denebola	2.2	# ###	# ###	# ###	# ###	# ###	# ###	# ###	# ###	# ###	7 077	17 080	26 083	35 086	45 089	54 093	63 097	73 106	81 127	84 206
Gienah	2.8	# ###	# ###	# ###	# ###	# ###	# ###	# ###	# ###	# ###	# ###	# ###	8 112	17 116	25 122	33 128	40 136	46 146	50 159	52 174
Acrux	1.1	# ###	# ###	# ###	# ###	# ###	# ###	# ###	# ###	# ###	# ###	# ###	# ###	# ###	# ###	# ###	2 164	4 168	6 173	7 177
Gacrux	1.6	# ###	# ###	# ###	# ###	# ###	# ###	# ###	# ###	# ###	# ###	# ###	# ###	# ###	# ###	3 156	7 160	9 165	11 170	13 176
Alioth	1.7	# ###	# ###	# ###	# ###	# ###	# ###	# ###	# ###	4 031	9 033	15 035	20 036	26 037	31 036	37 034	42 031	46 027	50 020	53 012
Spica	1.2	# ###	# ###	# ###	# ###	# ###	# ###	# ###	# ###	# ###	# ###	# ###	# ###	4 103	13 107	22 112	31 117	39 124	46 133	52 144
Alkaid	1.9	# ###	# ###	# ###	# ###	# ###	# ###	# ###	# ###	# ###	# ###	5 039	11 041	17 043	23 044	30 044	36 043	43 040	49 036	54 030
Hadar	0.9	# ###	# ###	# ###	# ###	# ###	# ###	# ###	# ###	# ###	# ###	# ###	# ###	# ###	# ###	# ###	# ###	# ###	3 161	6 165
Menkent	2.3	# ###	# ###	# ###	# ###	# ###	# ###	# ###	# ###	# ###	# ###	# ###	# ###	# ###	# ###	2 130	9 134	15 139	21 145	26 152
Arcturus	0.2	# ###	# ###	# ###	# ###	# ###	# ###	# ###	# ###	# ###	# ###	# ###	# ###	3 071	12 074	21 076	30 079	39 081	49 083	58 086
Rigil Kent.	0.1	# ###	# ###	# ###	# ###	# ###	# ###	# ###	# ###	# ###	# ###	# ###	# ###	# ###	# ###	# ###	# ###	# ###	# ###	3 162
Zuben'ubi	2.9	# ###	# ###	# ###	# ###	# ###	# ###	# ###	# ###	# ###	# ###	# ###	# ###	# ###	# ###	1 108	10 111	19 116	27 121	35 128
Kochab	2.2	8 349	6 351	5 354	5 357	4 359	4 002	5 005	6 007	7 010	9 012	11 014	13 015	16 016	18 017	21 017	24 017	27 016	29 014	31 012
Alphecca	2.3	# ###	# ###	# ###	# ###	# ###	# ###	# ###	# ###	# ###	# ###	# ###	# ###	# ###	# ###	6 064	14 066	23 069	32 070	41 071
Antares	1.2	# ###	# ###	# ###	# ###	# ###	# ###	# ###	# ###	# ###	# ###	# ###	# ###	# ###	# ###	# ###	# ###	# ###	2 119	10 123
Atria	1.9	# ###	# ###	# ###	# ###	# ###	# ###	# ###	# ###	# ###	# ###	# ###	# ###	# ###	# ###	# ###	# ###	# ###	# ###	# ###
Sabik	2.6	# ###	# ###	# ###	# ###	# ###	# ###	# ###	# ###	# ###	# ###	# ###	# ###	# ###	# ###	# ###	# ###	# ###	# ###	6 109
Shaula	1.7	# ###	# ###	# ###	# ###	# ###	# ###	# ###	# ###	# ###	# ###	# ###	# ###	# ###	# ###	# ###	# ###	# ###	# ###	# ###
Rasalhague	2.1	# ###	# ###	# ###	# ###	# ###	# ###	# ###	# ###	# ###	# ###	# ###	# ###	# ###	# ###	# ###	# ###	# ###	1 077	10 080
Eltanin	2.4	15 320	9 322	3 324	# ###	# ###	# ###	# ###	# ###	# ###	# ###	# ###	# ###	# ###	# ###	# ###	# ###	4 036	10 039	16 040
Kaus Aust.	2.0	# ###	# ###	# ###	# ###	# ###	# ###	# ###	# ###	# ###	# ###	# ###	# ###	# ###	# ###	# ###	# ###	# ###	# ###	# ###
Vega	0.1	19 305	12 307	4 310	# ###	# ###	# ###	# ###	# ###	# ###	# ###	# ###	# ###	# ###	# ###	# ###	# ###	# ###	# ###	6 051
Nunki	2.1	3 241	# ###	# ###	# ###	# ###	# ###	# ###	# ###	# ###	# ###	# ###	# ###	# ###	# ###	# ###	# ###	# ###	# ###	# ###
Altair	0.9	29 269	20 273	10 276	1 279	# ###	# ###	# ###	# ###	# ###	# ###	# ###	# ###	# ###	# ###	# ###	# ###	# ###	# ###	# ###
Peacock	2.1	1 206	# ###	# ###	# ###	# ###	# ###	# ###	# ###	# ###	# ###	# ###	# ###	# ###	# ###	# ###	# ###	# ###	# ###	# ###
Deneb	1.3	42 314	35 312	28 312	21 312	14 313	8 316	1 318	# ###	# ###	# ###	# ###	# ###	# ###	# ###	# ###	# ###	# ###	# ###	# ###
Enif	2.5	56 258	46 263	37 267	28 271	18 274	9 277	# ###	# ###	# ###	# ###	# ###	# ###	# ###	# ###	# ###	# ###	# ###	# ###	# ###
Al Na'ir	2.2	18 200	15 206	10 211	5 216	# ###	# ###	# ###	# ###	# ###	# ###	# ###	# ###	# ###	# ###	# ###	# ###	# ###	# ###	# ###
Fomalhaut	1.3	38 197	35 207	30 216	24 223	17 229	10 233	2 237	# ###	# ###	# ###	# ###	# ###	# ###	# ###	# ###	# ###	# ###	# ###	# ###
Markab	2.6	76 252	67 262	57 267	48 271	39 274	29 277	20 279	11 282	2 286	# ###	# ###	# ###	# ###	# ###	# ###	# ###	# ###	# ###	# ###

* Variable 0.1 - 1.2

SUN MOON PLANETS — Local Hour Angle Body

	0° Alt Az	10° Alt Az	20° Alt Az	30° Alt Az	40° Alt Az	50° Alt Az	60° Alt Az	70° Alt Az	80° Alt Az	90° Alt Az	100° Alt Az	110° Alt Az	120° Alt Az	130° Alt Az	140° Alt Az	150° Alt Az	160° Alt Az	170° Alt Az	180° Alt Az
	° °	° °	° °	° °	° °	° °	° °	° °	° °	° °	° °	° °	° °	° °	° °	° °	° °	° °	° °
Decl'n N30°	80 000	77 320	69 303	61 296	53 294	44 293	35 293	27 294	18 296	10 298	2 301	# ###	# ###	# ###	# ###	# ###	# ###	# ###	# ###
Decl'n N25°	85 000	80 300	71 289	62 286	53 285	44 286	35 287	26 289	17 291	8 294	# ###	# ###	# ###	# ###	# ###	# ###	# ###	# ###	# ###
Decl'n N20°	90 ###	81 272	71 273	62 275	53 277	43 279	34 281	25 283	16 286	7 289	# ###	# ###	# ###	# ###	# ###	# ###	# ###	# ###	# ###
Decl'n N15°	85 180	79 244	70 258	61 265	52 269	42 272	33 275	24 278	14 281	5 284	# ###	# ###	# ###	# ###	# ###	# ###	# ###	# ###	# ###
Decl'n N10°	80 180	76 225	68 246	59 255	50 261	41 266	31 270	22 273	13 276	3 279	# ###	# ###	# ###	# ###	# ###	# ###	# ###	# ###	# ###
Decl'n N5°	75 180	72 214	65 235	57 247	48 254	39 260	30 264	20 268	11 271	2 275	# ###	# ###	# ###	# ###	# ###	# ###	# ###	# ###	# ###
Decl'n 0°	70 180	68 207	62 227	54 239	46 248	37 254	28 259	19 263	9 267	0 270	# ###	# ###	# ###	# ###	# ###	# ###	# ###	# ###	# ###
Decl'n S5°	65 180	63 203	58 220	51 233	43 242	35 248	26 254	17 258	8 262	# ###	# ###	# ###	# ###	# ###	# ###	# ###	# ###	# ###	# ###
Decl'n S10°	60 180	58 199	54 215	48 227	41 236	32 243	24 249	15 253	6 257	# ###	# ###	# ###	# ###	# ###	# ###	# ###	# ###	# ###	# ###
Decl'n S15°	55 180	54 196	50 211	44 222	37 231	30 238	21 244	13 249	4 252	# ###	# ###	# ###	# ###	# ###	# ###	# ###	# ###	# ###	# ###
Decl'n S20°	50 180	49 194	45 207	40 218	34 227	27 234	19 239	11 244	2 248	# ###	# ###	# ###	# ###	# ###	# ###	# ###	# ###	# ###	# ###
Decl'n S25°	45 180	44 193	41 204	36 214	31 223	24 229	16 235	8 239	0 243	# ###	# ###	# ###	# ###	# ###	# ###	# ###	# ###	# ###	# ###
Decl'n S30°	40 180	39 191	36 202	32 211	27 219	21 225	14 231	6 235	# ###	# ###	# ###	# ###	# ###	# ###	# ###	# ###	# ###	# ###	# ###

Latitude N20°

STARS		Local Hour Angle Aries																		
		180°	190°	200°	210°	220°	230°	240°	250°	260°	270°	280°	290°	300°	310°	320°	330°	340°	350°	360°
Name	Mag	Alt Az	Alt Az	Alt Az	Alt Az	Alt Az	Alt Az	Alt Az	Alt Az	Alt Az	Alt Az	Alt Az	Alt Az	Alt Az	Alt Az	Alt Az	Alt Az	Alt Az	Alt Az	Alt Az
Alpheratz	2.2	# ###	# ###	# ###	# ###	# ###	# ###	# ###	# ###	# ###	8 062	16 064	25 066	33 068	42 068	51 068	60 066	68 061	76 048	81 011
Ankaa	2.4	# ###	# ###	# ###	# ###	# ###	# ###	# ###	# ###	# ###	# ###	# ###	# ###	3 137	9 141	14 146	19 152	23 159	26 166	27 175
Schedah	2.5	# ###	# ###	# ###	# ###	# ###	# ###	# ###	1 028	6 031	11 034	17 035	22 036	27 036	33 035	38 033	43 029	47 024	51 017	53 009
Diphda	2.2	# ###	# ###	# ###	# ###	# ###	# ###	# ###	# ###	# ###	# ###	# ###	2 110	11 114	19 118	27 124	35 131	41 139	47 150	51 164
Achernar	0.6	# ###	# ###	# ###	# ###	# ###	# ###	# ###	# ###	# ###	# ###	# ###	# ###	# ###	# ###	# ###	0 154	4 158	8 162	10 167
Hamal	2.2	# ###	# ###	# ###	# ###	# ###	# ###	# ###	# ###	# ###	# ###	# ###	# ###	6 067	15 070	24 072	33 074	42 076	51 077	60 077
Polaris	2.1	19 000	19 000	19 000	19 000	19 000	19 000	19 000	19 000	19 001	20 001	20 001	20 001	20 001	20 001	20 001	20 001	20 001	20 001	21 000
Acamar	3.1	# ###	# ###	# ###	# ###	# ###	# ###	# ###	# ###	# ###	# ###	# ###	# ###	# ###	# ###	# ###	# ###	5 136	11 141	17 146
Menkar	2.8	# ###	# ###	# ###	# ###	# ###	# ###	# ###	# ###	# ###	# ###	# ###	# ###	# ###	# ###	6 088	15 091	24 095	34 099	43 104
Mirfak	1.9	# ###	# ###	# ###	# ###	# ###	# ###	# ###	# ###	# ###	# ###	# ###	# ###	2 037	8 040	14 042	21 043	27 043	34 043	40 041
Aldebaran	1.1	# ###	# ###	# ###	# ###	# ###	# ###	# ###	# ###	# ###	# ###	# ###	# ###	# ###	# ###	# ###	# ###	7 075	16 078	25 081
Rigel	0.3	# ###	# ###	# ###	# ###	# ###	# ###	# ###	# ###	# ###	# ###	# ###	# ###	# ###	# ###	# ###	# ###	# ###	# ###	8 102
Capella	0.2	7 317	1 320	# ###	# ###	# ###	# ###	# ###	# ###	# ###	# ###	# ###	# ###	# ###	# ###	# ###	2 041	8 044	15 046	22 047
Bellatrix	1.7	# ###	# ###	# ###	# ###	# ###	# ###	# ###	# ###	# ###	# ###	# ###	# ###	# ###	# ###	# ###	# ###	# ###	1 084	10 087
Elnath	1.8	2 300	# ###	# ###	# ###	# ###	# ###	# ###	# ###	# ###	# ###	# ###	# ###	# ###	# ###	# ###	# ###	# ###	8 062	17 065
Alnilam	1.8	# ###	# ###	# ###	# ###	# ###	# ###	# ###	# ###	# ###	# ###	# ###	# ###	# ###	# ###	# ###	# ###	# ###	# ###	5 093
Betelgeuse	*	1 277	# ###	# ###	# ###	# ###	# ###	# ###	# ###	# ###	# ###	# ###	# ###	# ###	# ###	# ###	# ###	# ###	# ###	4 083
Canopus	-0.9	# ###	# ###	# ###	# ###	# ###	# ###	# ###	# ###	# ###	# ###	# ###	# ###	# ###	# ###	# ###	# ###	# ###	# ###	# ###
Sirius	-1.6	4 250	# ###	# ###	# ###	# ###	# ###	# ###	# ###	# ###	# ###	# ###	# ###	# ###	# ###	# ###	# ###	# ###	# ###	# ###
Adhara	1.6	2 238	# ###	# ###	# ###	# ###	# ###	# ###	# ###	# ###	# ###	# ###	# ###	# ###	# ###	# ###	# ###	# ###	# ###	# ###
Procyon	0.5	25 266	16 270	6 273	# ###	# ###	# ###	# ###	# ###	# ###	# ###	# ###	# ###	# ###	# ###	# ###	# ###	# ###	# ###	# ###
Pollux	1.2	32 291	23 293	15 295	6 298	# ###	# ###	# ###	# ###	# ###	# ###	# ###	# ###	# ###	# ###	# ###	# ###	# ###	# ###	# ###
Avior	1.7	# ###	# ###	# ###	# ###	# ###	# ###	# ###	# ###	# ###	# ###	# ###	# ###	# ###	# ###	# ###	# ###	# ###	# ###	# ###
Suhail	2.2	15 211	10 216	4 220	# ###	# ###	# ###	# ###	# ###	# ###	# ###	# ###	# ###	# ###	# ###	# ###	# ###	# ###	# ###	# ###
Miaplacidus	1.8	# ###	# ###	# ###	# ###	# ###	# ###	# ###	# ###	# ###	# ###	# ###	# ###	# ###	# ###	# ###	# ###	# ###	# ###	# ###
Alphard	2.2	43 236	35 243	26 249	17 254	8 258	# ###	# ###	# ###	# ###	# ###	# ###	# ###	# ###	# ###	# ###	# ###	# ###	# ###	# ###
Regulus	1.3	62 258	53 263	43 268	34 271	25 274	15 277	6 281	# ###	# ###	# ###	# ###	# ###	# ###	# ###	# ###	# ###	# ###	# ###	# ###
Dubhe	2.0	47 350	45 344	42 339	38 335	34 332	30 331	25 330	20 330	16 331	11 332	7 334	3 337	# ###	# ###	# ###	# ###	# ###	# ###	# ###
Denebola	2.2	84 206	77 248	68 260	58 265	49 269	40 273	30 276	21 279	12 281	2 285	# ###	# ###	# ###	# ###	# ###	# ###	# ###	# ###	# ###
Gienah	2.8	52 174	52 189	49 204	45 216	38 226	31 233	23 240	15 244	6 249	# ###	# ###	# ###	# ###	# ###	# ###	# ###	# ###	# ###	# ###
Acrux	1.1	7 177	7 182	6 186	5 190	3 194	0 198	# ###	# ###	# ###	# ###	# ###	# ###	# ###	# ###	# ###	# ###	# ###	# ###	# ###
Gacrux	1.6	13 176	13 181	12 187	11 192	8 197	5 201	1 205	# ###	# ###	# ###	# ###	# ###	# ###	# ###	# ###	# ###	# ###	# ###	# ###
Alioth	1.7	53 012	54 003	54 354	52 345	49 338	45 332	40 328	35 325	30 324	24 323	18 324	13 325	8 327	3 330	# ###	# ###	# ###	# ###	# ###
Spica	1.2	52 144	57 159	59 178	58 196	54 212	48 225	41 234	33 241	24 247	16 252	7 256	# ###	# ###	# ###	# ###	# ###	# ###	# ###	# ###
Alkaid	1.9	54 030	58 021	60 009	61 356	59 343	55 333	51 326	45 321	39 318	32 316	26 316	19 317	13 318	7 320	1 323	# ###	# ###	# ###	# ###
Hadar	0.9	6 165	8 170	9 175	10 180	9 185	8 189	6 194	4 198	0 202	# ###	# ###	# ###	# ###	# ###	# ###	# ###	# ###	# ###	# ###
Menkent	2.3	26 152	30 160	33 169	34 178	33 188	31 197	28 206	23 213	17 219	11 224	4 229	# ###	# ###	# ###	# ###	# ###	# ###	# ###	# ###
Arcturus	0.2	58 086	67 088	77 091	86 102	84 263	75 270	65 273	56 275	47 277	37 279	28 282	19 284	10 287	1 290	# ###	# ###	# ###	# ###	# ###
Rigil Kent.	0.1	3 162	6 166	8 170	9 175	9 180	9 185	8 190	6 194	3 198	# ###	# ###	# ###	# ###	# ###	# ###	# ###	# ###	# ###	# ###
Zuben'ubi	2.9	35 128	42 136	48 147	52 160	54 176	53 192	50 206	45 219	39 228	31 236	23 242	15 246	6 250	# ###	# ###	# ###	# ###	# ###	# ###
Kochab	2.2	31 012	33 010	34 007	35 004	36 001	36 358	35 354	34 351	32 349	30 347	28 345	25 344	23 343	20 343	17 344	15 344	12 346	10 347	8 349
Alphecca	2.3	41 071	50 072	58 071	67 068	76 059	82 026	81 320	74 297	65 291	56 288	47 288	38 289	29 290	21 292	12 294	4 297	# ###	# ###	# ###
Antares	1.2	10 123	18 128	25 134	31 141	37 149	41 159	43 171	43 183	42 195	39 206	34 216	28 223	21 230	14 235	6 239	# ###	# ###	# ###	# ###
Atria	1.9	# ###	# ###	# ###	# ###	# ###	# ###	1 176	1 179	1 183	0 186	# ###	# ###	# ###	# ###	# ###	# ###	# ###	# ###	# ###
Sabik	2.6	6 109	15 113	23 118	31 124	39 131	45 141	50 153	54 168	54 184	52 200	48 213	42 224	35 233	27 239	19 244	10 249	2 253	# ###	# ###
Shaula	1.7	# ###	0 130	7 134	14 139	20 144	25 151	29 159	32 167	33 177	33 186	31 195	28 204	23 211	18 218	12 223	5 227	# ###	# ###	# ###
Rasalhague	2.1	10 080	19 083	29 086	38 089	47 093	57 098	66 104	75 117	82 154	80 220	73 247	64 258	54 264	45 268	36 271	26 274	17 278	8 281	# ###
Eltanin	2.4	16 040	22 041	28 041	35 040	41 038	46 035	51 029	55 021	58 011	59 359	57 347	55 338	50 330	45 325	40 321	34 319	27 319	21 319	15 320
Kaus Aust.	2.0	# ###	# ###	# ###	7 131	14 135	20 141	26 147	30 155	34 164	35 174	35 184	34 194	31 203	27 211	21 218	15 224	8 229	1 232	# ###
Vega	0.1	6 051	13 053	21 055	28 056	36 056	44 055	51 052	59 047	65 037	70 021	71 358	69 336	64 321	58 312	50 307	43 305	35 304	27 304	19 305
Nunki	2.1	# ###	# ###	# ###	5 120	13 124	20 130	27 136	33 143	38 153	42 163	44 175	43 188	41 199	37 210	32 219	26 226	19 232	11 237	3 241
Altair	0.9	# ###	# ###	# ###	5 082	15 086	24 089	33 092	43 096	52 101	61 109	70 121	77 145	79 192	74 229	66 246	57 255	48 261	38 265	29 269
Peacock	2.1	# ###	# ###	# ###	# ###	# ###	# ###	# ###	# ###	4 157	7 161	10 166	12 171	13 176	13 182	12 188	11 193	8 198	5 202	1 206
Deneb	1.3	# ###	# ###	1 041	7 044	14 046	21 048	28 048	35 048	42 047	48 043	54 038	60 029	63 016	65 001	63 345	60 332	55 323	49 317	42 314
Enif	2.5	# ###	# ###	# ###	# ###	# ###	# ###	7 082	16 085	26 088	35 092	45 096	54 101	63 108	72 121	78 149	79 201	73 235	65 250	56 258
Al Na'ir	2.2	# ###	# ###	# ###	# ###	# ###	# ###	# ###	# ###	# ###	3 143	8 147	13 152	17 158	20 164	22 171	23 178	23 186	21 193	18 200
Fomalhaut	1.3	# ###	# ###	# ###	# ###	# ###	# ###	# ###	# ###	# ###	3 123	11 127	18 132	24 138	30 145	35 154	38 164	40 175	40 186	38 197
Markab	2.6	# ###	# ###	# ###	# ###	# ###	# ###	# ###	# ###	9 077	18 080	27 083	36 086	46 089	55 092	65 097	74 105	82 128	84 218	76 252

* Variable 0.1 - 1.2

SUN MOON PLANETS	Local Hour Angle Body																		
	180°	190°	200°	210°	220°	230°	240°	250°	260°	270°	280°	290°	300°	310°	320°	330°	340°	350°	360°
	Alt Az	Alt Az	Alt Az	Alt Az	Alt Az	Alt Az	Alt Az	Alt Az	Alt Az	Alt Az	Alt Az	Alt Az	Alt Az	Alt Az	Alt Az	Alt Az	Alt Az	Alt Az	Alt Az
Decl'n N30°	# ###	# ###	# ###	# ###	# ###	# ###	# ###	# ###	2 059	10 062	18 064	27 066	35 067	44 067	53 066	61 064	69 057	77 040	80 000
Decl'n N25°	# ###	# ###	# ###	# ###	# ###	# ###	# ###	# ###	# ###	8 066	17 069	26 071	35 073	44 074	53 075	62 074	71 071	80 060	85 000
Decl'n N20°	# ###	# ###	# ###	# ###	# ###	# ###	# ###	# ###	# ###	7 071	16 074	25 077	34 079	43 081	53 083	62 085	71 087	81 088	90 090
Decl'n N15°	# ###	# ###	# ###	# ###	# ###	# ###	# ###	# ###	# ###	5 076	14 079	24 082	33 085	42 088	52 091	61 095	70 102	79 116	85 180
Decl'n N10°	# ###	# ###	# ###	# ###	# ###	# ###	# ###	# ###	# ###	3 081	13 084	22 087	31 090	41 094	50 099	59 105	68 114	76 135	80 180
Decl'n N5°	# ###	# ###	# ###	# ###	# ###	# ###	# ###	# ###	# ###	2 085	11 089	20 092	30 096	39 100	48 106	57 113	65 125	72 146	75 180
Decl'n 0°	# ###	# ###	# ###	# ###	# ###	# ###	# ###	# ###	# ###	# ###	9 093	19 097	28 101	37 106	46 112	54 121	62 133	68 153	70 180
Decl'n S5°	# ###	# ###	# ###	# ###	# ###	# ###	# ###	# ###	# ###	# ###	8 098	17 102	26 106	35 112	43 118	51 127	58 140	63 157	65 180
Decl'n S10°	# ###	# ###	# ###	# ###	# ###	# ###	# ###	# ###	# ###	# ###	6 103	15 107	24 111	32 117	41 124	48 133	54 145	58 161	60 180
Decl'n S15°	# ###	# ###	# ###	# ###	# ###	# ###	# ###	# ###	# ###	# ###	4 108	13 111	21 116	30 122	37 129	44 138	50 149	54 164	55 180
Decl'n S20°	# ###	# ###	# ###	# ###	# ###	# ###	# ###	# ###	# ###	# ###	2 112	11 116	19 121	27 126	34 133	40 142	45 153	49 166	50 180
Decl'n S25°	# ###	# ###	# ###	# ###	# ###	# ###	# ###	# ###	# ###	# ###	0 117	8 121	16 125	24 131	31 137	36 146	41 156	44 167	45 180
Decl'n S30°	# ###	# ###	# ###	# ###	# ###	# ###	# ###	# ###	# ###	# ###	# ###	6 125	14 129	21 135	27 141	32 149	36 158	39 169	40 180

PREDICTION & IDENTIFICATION

Latitude N10°

Latitude N10°

STARS — Local Hour Angle Aries

Name	Mag	0° Alt Az	10° Alt Az	20° Alt Az	30° Alt Az	40° Alt Az	50° Alt Az	60° Alt Az	70° Alt Az	80° Alt Az	90° Alt Az	100° Alt Az	110° Alt Az	120° Alt Az	130° Alt Az	140° Alt Az	150° Alt Az	160° Alt Az	170° Alt Az	180° Alt Az
		° °	° °	° °	° °	° °	° °	° °	° °	° °	° °	° °	° °	° °	° °	° °	° °	° °	° °	° °
Alpheratz	2.2	71 006	70 340	65 321	58 310	50 304	41 300	33 298	24 298	15 298	7 298	# ####	# ####	# ####	# ####	# ####	# ####	# ####	# ####	# ####
Ankaa	2.4	37 174	38 183	36 192	33 201	29 208	24 214	18 219	12 223	5 225	# ####	# ####	# ####	# ####	# ####	# ####	# ####	# ####	# ####	# ####
Schedah	2.5	43 008	43 000	43 353	41 346	38 340	34 335	30 331	25 328	19 327	14 326	8 326	3 327	# ####	# ####	# ####	# ####	# ####	# ####	# ####
Diphda	2.2	60 159	62 178	61 198	56 214	50 226	42 234	34 240	25 245	16 248	7 250	# ####	# ####	# ####	# ####	# ####	# ####	# ####	# ####	# ####
Achernar	0.6	20 166	22 172	23 177	23 183	22 189	20 194	17 199	13 203	9 207	4 210	# ####	# ####	# ####	# ####	# ####	# ####	# ####	# ####	# ####
Hamal	2.2	57 062	65 054	72 038	76 007	74 331	68 310	60 300	51 295	42 293	33 292	24 291	15 292	6 293	# ####	# ####	# ####	# ####	# ####	# ####
Polaris	2.1	11 000	11 000	11 000	11 000	11 000	11 000	11 000	11 000	11 359	10 359	10 359	10 359	10 359	10 359	10 359	10 359	10 359	10 359	9 000
Acamar	3.1	25 144	30 150	35 157	38 166	40 175	39 185	38 195	34 203	30 211	24 217	18 221	12 225	4 228	# ####	# ####	# ####	# ####	# ####	# ####
Menkar	2.8	44 094	54 097	64 101	73 110	82 137	83 217	75 249	65 258	55 263	46 266	36 268	26 270	16 271	6 273	# ####	# ####	# ####	# ####	# ####
Mirfak	1.9	32 036	38 032	43 027	46 020	49 011	50 001	49 351	47 342	44 335	39 329	33 324	27 322	21 320	15 319	8 319	2 320	# ####	# ####	# ####
Aldebaran	1.1	23 076	32 077	42 077	52 076	61 074	70 069	79 052	83 351	77 302	69 290	59 286	50 284	40 283	30 283	21 284	11 285	2 286	# ####	# ####
Rigel	0.3	10 100	19 102	29 105	38 109	47 114	56 122	64 134	70 154	72 184	69 212	62 230	54 241	45 248	36 252	26 256	17 258	7 260	# ####	# ####
Capella	0.2	15 045	22 044	28 043	35 040	41 036	46 029	50 021	53 011	54 359	53 348	50 337	45 330	40 324	34 320	27 317	20 316	14 315	7 316	# ####
Bellatrix	1.7	10 085	19 087	29 088	39 090	49 092	59 094	69 098	78 107	86 161	81 248	71 260	61 265	52 268	42 270	32 271	22 273	12 274	2 276	# ####
Elnath	1.8	12 063	21 063	30 063	38 061	47 058	55 053	63 044	68 029	71 004	70 338	65 320	58 309	50 303	41 299	32 298	24 297	15 297	6 298	# ####
Alnilam	1.8	6 092	16 094	25 096	35 099	45 102	54 106	64 114	72 128	78 161	77 209	70 236	62 248	52 255	43 259	33 262	23 264	13 266	4 268	# ####
Betelgeuse	*	2 083	12 085	22 086	32 087	42 089	52 091	61 093	71 096	81 106	87 205	79 258	69 265	59 268	49 270	39 271	30 273	20 274	10 276	0 278
Canopus	-0.9	# ####	# ####	0 144	6 146	11 149	16 153	20 158	23 163	26 169	27 176	27 183	26 189	24 196	21 201	17 206	12 210	7 213	2 216	# ####
Sirius	-1.6	# ####	# ####	5 108	15 110	24 113	33 117	41 123	49 131	56 142	61 157	63 177	62 198	57 215	51 227	43 235	35 241	26 246	17 249	8 251
Adhara	1.6	# ####	# ####	# ####	8 122	17 124	24 128	32 134	39 140	44 149	49 160	51 174	51 187	48 200	44 211	38 220	31 227	24 232	16 236	8 239
Procyon	0.5	# ####	# ####	# ####	6 086	16 087	26 089	36 091	45 093	55 095	65 099	75 107	83 135	83 227	74 254	65 261	55 265	45 267	35 269	25 271
Pollux	1.2	# ####	# ####	# ####	8 063	17 064	26 064	34 063	43 061	51 057	59 050	66 038	71 017	72 350	68 326	61 312	54 304	45 300	37 298	28 297
Avior	1.7	# ####	# ####	# ####	# ####	# ####	# ####	3 152	8 155	12 158	15 162	18 167	19 172	20 177	20 182	20 188	18 193	15 197	12 201	8 205
Suhail	2.2	# ####	# ####	# ####	# ####	# ####	# ####	2 135	9 137	16 141	22 145	27 151	31 157	34 165	36 174	36 183	35 192	33 200	29 207	24 213
Miaplacidus	1.8	# ####	# ####	# ####	# ####	# ####	# ####	# ####	# ####	1 163	4 165	6 168	8 170	9 174	10 177	10 181	10 184	9 187	7 191	5 193
Alphard	2.2	# ####	# ####	# ####	# ####	# ####	# ####	6 100	16 102	26 105	35 108	44 113	53 119	61 130	68 147	71 174	70 204	64 225	56 237	48 245
Regulus	1.3	# ####	# ####	# ####	# ####	# ####	# ####	0 078	10 079	19 081	29 082	39 083	49 083	58 083	68 083	78 079	87 046	82 285	72 278	63 277
Dubhe	2.0	# ####	# ####	# ####	# ####	# ####	# ####	1 027	6 028	11 029	15 028	20 027	24 026	28 023	32 019	35 015	37 009	38 004	38 358	37 352
Denebola	2.2	# ####	# ####	# ####	# ####	# ####	# ####	# ####	# ####	# ####	5 076	15 077	24 078	34 079	44 079	53 079	63 077	73 073	82 056	85 330
Gienah	2.8	# ####	# ####	# ####	# ####	# ####	# ####	# ####	# ####	# ####	# ####	3 108	12 111	21 113	30 117	39 122	47 129	54 139	59 153	62 172
Acrux	1.1	# ####	# ####	# ####	# ####	# ####	# ####	# ####	# ####	# ####	# ####	# ####	# ####	1 155	5 158	9 161	12 164	14 168	16 172	17 177
Gacrux	1.6	# ####	# ####	# ####	# ####	# ####	# ####	# ####	# ####	# ####	# ####	# ####	# ####	3 150	8 152	12 156	16 160	19 164	21 170	23 175
Alioth	1.7	# ####	# ####	# ####	# ####	# ####	# ####	# ####	# ####	# ####	1 033	6 034	12 035	17 034	23 033	28 031	33 027	37 023	40 017	43 010
Spica	1.2	# ####	# ####	# ####	# ####	# ####	# ####	# ####	# ####	# ####	# ####	# ####	# ####	6 103	16 105	25 108	35 111	44 116	52 123	60 134
Alkaid	1.9	# ####	# ####	# ####	# ####	# ####	# ####	# ####	# ####	# ####	# ####	# ####	3 040	10 041	16 041	23 040	29 039	35 035	40 031	45 025
Hadar	0.9	# ####	# ####	# ####	# ####	# ####	# ####	# ####	# ####	# ####	# ####	# ####	# ####	# ####	# ####	0 152	5 154	9 157	13 161	15 165
Menkent	2.3	# ####	# ####	# ####	# ####	# ####	# ####	# ####	# ####	# ####	# ####	# ####	# ####	# ####	1 127	8 129	16 133	23 137	29 142	35 149
Arcturus	0.2	# ####	# ####	# ####	# ####	# ####	# ####	# ####	# ####	# ####	# ####	# ####	# ####	# ####	9 072	18 073	28 073	37 073	47 073	56 070
Rigil Kent.	0.1	# ####	# ####	# ####	# ####	# ####	# ####	# ####	# ####	# ####	# ####	# ####	# ####	# ####	# ####	# ####	1 153	5 155	9 158	12 161
Zuben'ubi	2.9	# ####	# ####	# ####	# ####	# ####	# ####	# ####	# ####	# ####	# ####	# ####	# ####	# ####	# ####	4 107	13 109	23 112	32 116	40 121
Kochab	2.2	# ####	# ####	# ####	# ####	# ####	# ####	# ####	# ####	# ####	# ####	1 013	4 015	6 016	9 016	12 016	14 016	17 015	19 013	21 011
Alphecca	2.3	# ####	# ####	# ####	# ####	# ####	# ####	# ####	# ####	# ####	# ####	# ####	# ####	# ####	# ####	1 063	10 064	19 065	28 065	37 064
Antares	1.2	# ####	# ####	# ####	# ####	# ####	# ####	# ####	# ####	# ####	# ####	# ####	# ####	# ####	# ####	# ####	# ####	# ####	7 118	15 121
Atria	1.9	# ####	# ####	# ####	# ####	# ####	# ####	# ####	# ####	# ####	# ####	# ####	# ####	# ####	# ####	# ####	# ####	# ####	# ####	# ####
Sabik	2.6	# ####	# ####	# ####	# ####	# ####	# ####	# ####	# ####	# ####	# ####	# ####	# ####	# ####	# ####	# ####	# ####	# ####	# ####	9 108
Shaula	1.7	# ####	# ####	# ####	# ####	# ####	# ####	# ####	# ####	# ####	# ####	# ####	# ####	# ####	# ####	# ####	# ####	# ####	# ####	# ####
Rasalhague	2.1	# ####	# ####	# ####	# ####	# ####	# ####	# ####	# ####	# ####	# ####	# ####	# ####	# ####	# ####	# ####	# ####	# ####	# ####	# ####
Eltanin	2.4	7 321	1 322	# ####	# ####	# ####	# ####	# ####	# ####	# ####	# ####	# ####	# ####	# ####	# ####	# ####	# ####	# ####	# ####	8 079
Kaus Aust.	2.0	# ####	# ####	# ####	# ####	# ####	# ####	# ####	# ####	# ####	# ####	# ####	# ####	# ####	# ####	# ####	# ####	# ####	2 038	8 039
Vega	0.1	13 308	6 308	# ####	# ####	# ####	# ####	# ####	# ####	# ####	# ####	# ####	# ####	# ####	# ####	# ####	# ####	# ####	# ####	# ####
Nunki	2.1	8 241	# ####	# ####	# ####	# ####	# ####	# ####	# ####	# ####	# ####	# ####	# ####	# ####	# ####	# ####	# ####	# ####	# ####	# ####
Altair	0.9	29 275	19 276	9 277	# ####	# ####	# ####	# ####	# ####	# ####	# ####	# ####	# ####	# ####	# ####	# ####	# ####	# ####	# ####	# ####
Peacock	2.1	10 207	5 210	0 212	# ####	# ####	# ####	# ####	# ####	# ####	# ####	# ####	# ####	# ####	# ####	# ####	# ####	# ####	# ####	# ####
Deneb	1.3	35 319	28 316	21 315	14 314	7 315	0 316	# ####	# ####	# ####	# ####	# ####	# ####	# ####	# ####	# ####	# ####	# ####	# ####	# ####
Enif	2.5	57 273	47 274	37 275	27 276	17 277	8 279	# ####	# ####	# ####	# ####	# ####	# ####	# ####	# ####	# ####	# ####	# ####	# ####	# ####
Al Na'ir	2.2	28 201	24 207	19 212	13 216	7 220	1 222	# ####	# ####	# ####	# ####	# ####	# ####	# ####	# ####	# ####	# ####	# ####	# ####	# ####
Fomalhaut	1.3	48 200	43 211	38 220	31 226	23 231	16 235	7 238	# ####	# ####	# ####	# ####	# ####	# ####	# ####	# ####	# ####	# ####	# ####	# ####
Markab	2.6	76 293	66 285	57 283	47 282	37 282	28 282	18 283	9 284	# ####	# ####	# ####	# ####	# ####	# ####	# ####	# ####	# ####	# ####	# ####

* Variable 0.1 - 1.2

SUN MOON PLANETS — Local Hour Angle Body

	0° Alt Az	10° Alt Az	20° Alt Az	30° Alt Az	40° Alt Az	50° Alt Az	60° Alt Az	70° Alt Az	80° Alt Az	90° Alt Az	100° Alt Az	110° Alt Az	120° Alt Az	130° Alt Az	140° Alt Az	150° Alt Az	160° Alt Az	170° Alt Az	180° Alt Az
	° °	° °	° °	° °	° °	° °	° °	° °	° °	° °	° °	° °	° °	° °	° °	° °	° °	° °	° °
Decl'n N30°	70 000	68 336	63 320	56 310	48 304	39 301	31 299	22 298	14 299	5 300	# ####	# ####	# ####	# ####	# ####	# ####	# ####	# ####	# ####
Decl'n N25°	75 000	72 329	66 311	58 302	49 297	40 294	31 293	22 293	13 294	4 295	# ####	# ####	# ####	# ####	# ####	# ####	# ####	# ####	# ####
Decl'n N20°	80 000	76 317	68 300	59 293	50 289	41 288	31 287	22 288	13 288	3 290	# ####	# ####	# ####	# ####	# ####	# ####	# ####	# ####	# ####
Decl'n N15°	85 000	79 298	70 286	60 283	51 282	41 281	31 282	22 282	12 283	3 285	# ####	# ####	# ####	# ####	# ####	# ####	# ####	# ####	# ####
Decl'n N10°	90 ####	80 271	70 272	60 273	51 274	41 275	31 276	21 277	11 278	2 280	# ####	# ####	# ####	# ####	# ####	# ####	# ####	# ####	# ####
Decl'n N5°	85 180	79 244	70 257	60 263	50 266	40 268	30 270	21 272	11 273	1 275	# ####	# ####	# ####	# ####	# ####	# ####	# ####	# ####	# ####
Decl'n 0°	80 180	76 225	68 244	59 253	49 258	39 262	29 264	20 266	10 268	0 270	# ####	# ####	# ####	# ####	# ####	# ####	# ####	# ####	# ####
Decl'n S5°	75 180	72 214	65 234	57 245	47 251	38 256	28 259	19 261	9 263	# ####	# ####	# ####	# ####	# ####	# ####	# ####	# ####	# ####	# ####
Decl'n S10°	70 180	68 207	62 225	54 237	45 244	36 250	27 253	18 256	8 258	# ####	# ####	# ####	# ####	# ####	# ####	# ####	# ####	# ####	# ####
Decl'n S15°	65 180	63 202	58 219	51 230	43 238	35 244	26 248	16 251	7 253	# ####	# ####	# ####	# ####	# ####	# ####	# ####	# ####	# ####	# ####
Decl'n S20°	60 180	58 198	54 213	48 224	41 233	32 238	24 243	15 246	6 248	# ####	# ####	# ####	# ####	# ####	# ####	# ####	# ####	# ####	# ####
Decl'n S25°	55 180	54 195	50 209	44 219	38 227	30 233	22 238	13 241	5 244	# ####	# ####	# ####	# ####	# ####	# ####	# ####	# ####	# ####	# ####
Decl'n S30°	50 180	49 193	46 205	41 215	35 222	27 228	20 233	12 236	4 239	# ####	# ####	# ####	# ####	# ####	# ####	# ####	# ####	# ####	# ####

Latitude N10°

Latitude N10°

STARS — Local Hour Angle Aries

Name	Mag	180° Alt Az	190° Alt Az	200° Alt Az	210° Alt Az	220° Alt Az	230° Alt Az	240° Alt Az	250° Alt Az	260° Alt Az	270° Alt Az	280° Alt Az	290° Alt Az	300° Alt Az	310° Alt Az	320° Alt Az	330° Alt Az	340° Alt Az	350° Alt Az	360° Alt Az
		° °	° °	° °	° °	° °	° °	° °	° °	° °	° °	° °	° °	° °	° °	° °	° °	° °	° °	° °
Alpheratz	2.2	# ###	# ###	# ###	# ###	# ###	# ###	# ###	# ###	# ###	3 061	12 062	20 063	29 062	38 061	46 058	54 053	62 044	68 029	71 006
Ankaa	2.4	# ###	# ###	# ###	# ###	# ###	# ###	# ###	# ###	# ###	# ###	# ###	3 134	10 136	17 140	23 144	28 150	32 157	36 165	37 174
Schedah	2.5	# ###	# ###	# ###	# ###	# ###	# ###	# ###	# ###	# ###	3 033	8 034	14 034	19 033	25 032	30 029	34 025	38 021	41 015	43 008
Diphda	2.2	# ###	# ###	# ###	# ###	# ###	# ###	# ###	# ###	# ###	# ###	# ###	5 109	15 112	24 115	32 119	41 125	49 132	55 143	60 159
Achernar	0.6	# ###	# ###	# ###	# ###	# ###	# ###	# ###	# ###	# ###	# ###	# ###	# ###	# ###	# ###	5 151	9 153	14 157	17 161	20 166
Hamal	2.2	# ###	# ###	# ###	# ###	# ###	# ###	# ###	# ###	# ###	# ###	# ###	# ###	2 067	11 068	21 069	30 069	39 068	48 066	57 062
Polaris	2.1	9 000	9 000	9 000	9 000	9 000	9 000	9 000	9 000	9 001	10 001	10 001	10 001	10 001	10 001	10 001	10 001	10 001	10 001	11 000
Acamar	3.1	# ###	# ###	# ###	# ###	# ###	# ###	# ###	# ###	# ###	# ###	# ###	# ###	# ###	# ###	# ###	5 132	12 135	19 139	25 144
Menkar	2.8	# ###	# ###	# ###	# ###	# ###	# ###	# ###	# ###	# ###	# ###	# ###	# ###	# ###	# ###	5 087	15 088	25 090	35 092	44 094
Mirfak	1.9	# ###	# ###	# ###	# ###	# ###	# ###	# ###	# ###	# ###	# ###	# ###	# ###	# ###	1 039	7 040	13 041	20 040	26 039	32 036
Aldebaran	1.1	# ###	# ###	# ###	# ###	# ###	# ###	# ###	# ###	# ###	# ###	# ###	# ###	# ###	# ###	# ###	# ###	4 074	13 075	23 076
Rigel	0.3	# ###	# ###	# ###	# ###	# ###	# ###	# ###	# ###	# ###	# ###	# ###	# ###	# ###	# ###	# ###	# ###	# ###	# ###	10 100
Capella	0.2	# ###	# ###	# ###	# ###	# ###	# ###	# ###	# ###	# ###	# ###	# ###	# ###	# ###	# ###	# ###	# ###	1 043	8 045	15 045
Bellatrix	1.7	# ###	# ###	# ###	# ###	# ###	# ###	# ###	# ###	# ###	# ###	# ###	# ###	# ###	# ###	# ###	# ###	# ###	# ###	10 085
Elnath	1.8	# ###	# ###	# ###	# ###	# ###	# ###	# ###	# ###	# ###	# ###	# ###	# ###	# ###	# ###	# ###	# ###	# ###	3 062	12 063
Alnilam	1.8	# ###	# ###	# ###	# ###	# ###	# ###	# ###	# ###	# ###	# ###	# ###	# ###	# ###	# ###	# ###	# ###	# ###	# ###	6 092
Betelgeuse	*	0 278	# ###	# ###	# ###	# ###	# ###	# ###	# ###	# ###	# ###	# ###	# ###	# ###	# ###	# ###	# ###	# ###	# ###	2 083
Canopus	-0.9	# ###	# ###	# ###	# ###	# ###	# ###	# ###	# ###	# ###	# ###	# ###	# ###	# ###	# ###	# ###	# ###	# ###	# ###	# ###
Sirius	-1.6	8 251	# ###	# ###	# ###	# ###	# ###	# ###	# ###	# ###	# ###	# ###	# ###	# ###	# ###	# ###	# ###	# ###	# ###	# ###
Adhara	1.6	8 239	# ###	# ###	# ###	# ###	# ###	# ###	# ###	# ###	# ###	# ###	# ###	# ###	# ###	# ###	# ###	# ###	# ###	# ###
Procyon	0.5	25 271	15 273	6 274	# ###	# ###	# ###	# ###	# ###	# ###	# ###	# ###	# ###	# ###	# ###	# ###	# ###	# ###	# ###	# ###
Pollux	1.2	28 297	19 296	10 297	1 298	# ###	# ###	# ###	# ###	# ###	# ###	# ###	# ###	# ###	# ###	# ###	# ###	# ###	# ###	# ###
Avior	1.7	8 205	4 207	# ###	# ###	# ###	# ###	# ###	# ###	# ###	# ###	# ###	# ###	# ###	# ###	# ###	# ###	# ###	# ###	# ###
Suhail	2.2	24 213	18 218	12 221	5 224	# ###	# ###	# ###	# ###	# ###	# ###	# ###	# ###	# ###	# ###	# ###	# ###	# ###	# ###	# ###
Miaplacidus	1.8	5 193	3 196	# ###	# ###	# ###	# ###	# ###	# ###	# ###	# ###	# ###	# ###	# ###	# ###	# ###	# ###	# ###	# ###	# ###
Alphard	2.2	48 245	39 250	29 254	20 257	10 259	0 261	# ###	# ###	# ###	# ###	# ###	# ###	# ###	# ###	# ###	# ###	# ###	# ###	# ###
Regulus	1.3	63 277	53 277	43 277	33 278	23 279	14 280	4 281	# ###	# ###	# ###	# ###	# ###	# ###	# ###	# ###	# ###	# ###	# ###	# ###
Dubhe	2.0	37 352	35 346	33 342	29 338	25 335	21 333	16 332	12 331	7 332	2 333	# ###	# ###	# ###	# ###	# ###	# ###	# ###	# ###	# ###
Denebola	2.2	85 330	77 291	67 284	58 281	48 281	38 281	29 281	19 282	9 283	# ###	# ###	# ###	# ###	# ###	# ###	# ###	# ###	# ###	# ###
Gienah	2.8	62 172	62 192	58 210	52 223	45 232	37 239	28 244	19 247	10 250	1 252	# ###	# ###	# ###	# ###	# ###	# ###	# ###	# ###	# ###
Acrux	1.1	17 177	17 182	16 186	15 191	13 195	10 198	6 201	3 204	# ###	# ###	# ###	# ###	# ###	# ###	# ###	# ###	# ###	# ###	# ###
Gacrux	1.6	23 175	23 181	22 187	20 193	18 198	14 202	10 206	6 209	1 211	# ###	# ###	# ###	# ###	# ###	# ###	# ###	# ###	# ###	# ###
Alioth	1.7	43 010	44 003	44 355	42 348	40 341	36 336	32 332	27 329	21 327	16 326	10 325	5 326	# ###	# ###	# ###	# ###	# ###	# ###	# ###
Spica	1.2	60 134	66 152	69 176	67 202	62 222	54 234	46 242	37 248	28 252	19 255	9 257	# ###	# ###	# ###	# ###	# ###	# ###	# ###	# ###
Alkaid	1.9	45 025	48 017	50 007	51 357	49 347	46 338	42 331	37 326	31 322	25 320	19 319	12 319	6 319	# ###	# ###	# ###	# ###	# ###	# ###
Hadar	0.9	15 165	18 169	19 174	20 179	19 185	18 190	16 194	13 199	10 202	6 205	1 207	# ###	# ###	# ###	# ###	# ###	# ###	# ###	# ###
Menkent	2.3	35 149	39 157	42 167	44 178	43 189	41 199	37 208	31 216	25 222	18 226	11 230	3 232	# ###	# ###	# ###	# ###	# ###	# ###	# ###
Arcturus	0.2	56 070	65 066	74 054	80 022	79 328	72 302	63 293	54 289	45 287	35 286	26 287	16 287	7 288	# ###	# ###	# ###	# ###	# ###	# ###
Rigil Kent.	0.1	12 161	15 165	17 170	19 175	19 180	19 185	17 190	15 195	12 199	9 202	5 205	1 207	# ###	# ###	# ###	# ###	# ###	# ###	# ###
Zuben'ubi	2.9	40 121	48 128	56 139	61 154	64 174	63 196	59 213	52 226	45 235	36 241	28 246	19 249	9 252	# ###	# ###	# ###	# ###	# ###	# ###
Kochab	2.2	21 011	23 009	25 007	25 004	26 001	26 358	25 355	24 352	22 350	20 348	18 346	16 345	13 344	10 344	8 344	5 345	3 346	0 347	# ###
Alphecca	2.3	37 064	46 062	54 058	62 050	69 036	73 011	72 341	67 319	60 307	52 301	43 297	34 296	26 295	17 295	8 296	# ###	# ###	# ###	# ###
Antares	1.2	15 121	23 125	31 130	39 136	45 144	50 156	53 169	53 184	52 198	47 211	42 220	35 228	27 233	19 237	11 240	2 243	# ###	# ###	# ###
Atria	1.9	# ###	0 162	3 164	6 166	8 169	9 172	11 176	11 179	11 183	10 186	9 190	7 193	4 195	1 198	# ###	# ###	# ###	# ###	# ###
Sabik	2.6	9 108	18 110	27 114	36 118	45 124	52 133	59 146	63 164	64 185	61 206	56 221	49 232	41 239	32 244	23 248	14 251	4 253	# ###	# ###
Shaula	1.7	# ###	7 130	14 133	21 137	28 142	33 148	38 156	41 166	43 176	42 187	40 197	37 206	32 214	26 220	19 225	12 228	4 231	# ###	# ###
Rasalhague	2.1	8 079	18 080	28 081	37 082	47 082	57 082	67 081	76 078	86 055	83 293	74 281	64 278	54 278	45 278	35 278	25 279	15 280	6 282	# ###
Eltanin	2.4	8 039	15 039	21 038	27 037	32 034	38 030	42 024	46 017	48 008	49 359	48 350	45 342	41 335	37 329	32 325	26 323	20 321	14 321	7 321
Kaus Aust.	2.0	# ###	# ###	6 126	13 129	21 133	28 138	34 144	39 152	43 162	45 173	45 185	44 196	40 206	35 214	29 221	22 226	15 230	7 233	# ###
Vega	0.1	# ###	7 052	15 052	22 052	30 051	38 048	45 044	51 037	56 028	60 015	61 359	60 343	56 331	50 321	44 315	36 311	29 309	21 308	13 308
Nunki	2.1	# ###	# ###	1 117	10 119	18 122	26 126	34 131	41 139	47 148	51 160	54 174	53 189	50 203	46 214	39 223	32 230	24 235	16 239	8 241
Altair	0.9	# ###	# ###	# ###	4 082	14 083	23 085	33 086	43 087	53 088	63 090	73 092	82 098	87 244	78 266	68 269	58 271	48 272	38 273	29 275
Peacock	2.1	# ###	# ###	# ###	# ###	# ###	# ###	4 150	9 152	13 156	17 160	20 165	22 170	23 176	23 182	22 188	20 194	18 199	14 203	10 207
Deneb	1.3	# ###	# ###	# ###	# ###	7 045	14 046	21 045	28 044	34 041	41 037	46 031	51 023	54 012	55 000	54 349	51 338	47 330	41 323	35 319
Enif	2.5	# ###	# ###	# ###	# ###	# ###	# ###	6 081	15 082	25 084	35 085	45 086	55 087	64 088	74 089	84 091	86 268	76 271	66 272	57 273
Al Na'ir	2.2	# ###	# ###	# ###	# ###	# ###	# ###	# ###	# ###	5 139	11 142	17 146	22 150	26 156	30 163	32 170	33 178	33 186	31 194	28 201
Fomalhaut	1.3	# ###	# ###	# ###	# ###	# ###	# ###	# ###	# ###	# ###	8 122	16 125	24 129	32 134	38 141	44 150	48 161	50 174	50 188	48 200
Markab	2.6	# ###	# ###	# ###	# ###	# ###	# ###	# ###	# ###	6 076	16 077	25 078	35 078	45 078	54 078	64 076	73 070	82 049	84 325	76 293

* Variable 0.1 - 1.2

SUN MOON PLANETS — Local Hour Angle Body

	180° Alt Az	190° Alt Az	200° Alt Az	210° Alt Az	220° Alt Az	230° Alt Az	240° Alt Az	250° Alt Az	260° Alt Az	270° Alt Az	280° Alt Az	290° Alt Az	300° Alt Az	310° Alt Az	320° Alt Az	330° Alt Az	340° Alt Az	350° Alt Az	360° Alt Az
	° °	° °	° °	° °	° °	° °	° °	° °	° °	° °	° °	° °	° °	° °	° °	° °	° °	° °	° °
Decl'n N30°	# ###	# ###	# ###	# ###	# ###	# ###	# ###	# ###	# ###	5 060	14 061	22 062	31 061	39 059	48 056	56 050	63 040	68 024	70 000
Decl'n N25°	# ###	# ###	# ###	# ###	# ###	# ###	# ###	# ###	# ###	4 065	13 066	22 067	31 067	40 066	49 063	58 058	66 049	72 031	75 000
Decl'n N20°	# ###	# ###	# ###	# ###	# ###	# ###	# ###	# ###	# ###	3 070	13 072	22 072	31 073	41 072	50 071	59 067	68 060	76 043	80 000
Decl'n N15°	# ###	# ###	# ###	# ###	# ###	# ###	# ###	# ###	# ###	3 075	12 077	22 078	31 078	41 079	51 078	60 077	70 074	79 062	85 000
Decl'n N10°	# ###	# ###	# ###	# ###	# ###	# ###	# ###	# ###	# ###	2 080	11 082	21 083	31 084	41 085	51 086	60 087	70 088	80 089	90 090
Decl'n N5°	# ###	# ###	# ###	# ###	# ###	# ###	# ###	# ###	# ###	1 085	11 087	21 088	30 090	40 092	50 094	60 097	70 103	79 116	85 180
Decl'n 0°	# ###	# ###	# ###	# ###	# ###	# ###	# ###	# ###	# ###	# ###	10 092	20 094	29 096	39 098	49 102	59 107	68 116	76 135	80 180
Decl'n S5°	# ###	# ###	# ###	# ###	# ###	# ###	# ###	# ###	# ###	# ###	9 097	19 099	28 101	38 104	47 109	57 115	65 126	72 146	75 180
Decl'n S10°	# ###	# ###	# ###	# ###	# ###	# ###	# ###	# ###	# ###	# ###	8 102	18 104	27 107	36 110	45 116	54 123	62 135	68 153	70 180
Decl'n S15°	# ###	# ###	# ###	# ###	# ###	# ###	# ###	# ###	# ###	# ###	7 107	16 109	26 112	35 116	43 122	51 130	58 141	63 158	65 180
Decl'n S20°	# ###	# ###	# ###	# ###	# ###	# ###	# ###	# ###	# ###	# ###	6 112	15 114	24 117	32 122	41 127	48 136	54 147	58 162	60 180
Decl'n S25°	# ###	# ###	# ###	# ###	# ###	# ###	# ###	# ###	# ###	# ###	5 116	13 119	22 122	30 127	38 133	44 141	50 151	54 165	55 180
Decl'n S30°	# ###	# ###	# ###	# ###	# ###	# ###	# ###	# ###	# ###	# ###	4 121	12 124	20 127	27 132	35 138	41 145	46 155	49 167	50 180

PREDICTION & IDENTIFICATION

Latitude 0°

Latitude 0°

STARS		Local Hour Angle Aries																		
		0°	10°	20°	30°	40°	50°	60°	70°	80°	90°	100°	110°	120°	130°	140°	150°	160°	170°	180°
Name	Mag	Alt Az	Alt Az	Alt Az	Alt Az	Alt Az	Alt Az	Alt Az	Alt Az	Alt Az	Alt Az	Alt Az	Alt Az	Alt Az	Alt Az	Alt Az	Alt Az	Alt Az	Alt Az	Alt Az
		° °	° °	° °	° °	° °	° °	° °	° °	° °	° °	° °	° °	° °	° °	° °	° °	° °	° °	° °
Alpheratz	2.2	61 **004**	60 **346**	56 **331**	51 **320**	44 **312**	36 **307**	28 **303**	19 **301**	11 **300**	2 **299**	# ####	# ####	# ####	# ####	# ####	# ####	# ####	# ####	# ####
Ankaa	2.4	47 **173**	48 **184**	46 **194**	43 **204**	38 **211**	32 **217**	26 **221**	19 **225**	12 **226**	5 **228**	# ####	# ####	# ####	# ####	# ####	# ####	# ####	# ####	# ####
Schedah	2.5	33 **007**	33 **000**	33 **354**	31 **347**	29 **342**	25 **337**	21 **333**	16 **330**	11 **328**	6 **327**	0 **327**	# ####	# ####	# ####	# ####	# ####	# ####	# ####	# ####
Diphda	2.2	69 **150**	72 **177**	70 **206**	64 **225**	56 **236**	48 **243**	39 **247**	29 **249**	20 **251**	10 **252**	1 **252**	# ####	# ####	# ####	# ####	# ####	# ####	# ####	# ####
Achernar	0.6	30 **165**	32 **171**	33 **177**	33 **184**	31 **190**	29 **196**	26 **201**	22 **205**	18 **208**	13 **210**	8 **212**	2 **213**	# ####	# ####	# ####	# ####	# ####	# ####	# ####
Hamal	2.2	51 **051**	58 **041**	64 **025**	66 **004**	65 **342**	61 **324**	54 **313**	46 **305**	38 **300**	29 **297**	20 **295**	11 **294**	2 **293**	# ####	# ####	# ####	# ####	# ####	# ####
Polaris	2.1	1 **000**	1 **000**	1 **000**	1 **000**	1 **000**	1 **000**	1 **000**	1 **000**	1 **000**	0 **359**	0 **359**	0 **359**	0 **359**	# ####	# ####	# ####	# ####	# ####	# ####
Acamar	3.1	33 **140**	39 **146**	44 **154**	48 **163**	49 **175**	49 **186**	47 **197**	44 **207**	38 **214**	32 **220**	26 **224**	18 **227**	11 **229**	3 **230**	# ####	# ####	# ####	# ####	# ####
Menkar	2.8	44 **084**	54 **083**	64 **081**	74 **075**	83 **054**	84 **313**	75 **286**	65 **280**	55 **277**	45 **276**	35 **275**	25 **275**	16 **274**	6 **274**	# ####	# ####	# ####	# ####	# ####
Mirfak	1.9	24 **033**	29 **029**	34 **024**	37 **017**	39 **009**	40 **001**	40 **353**	38 **345**	34 **338**	30 **332**	25 **328**	19 **324**	13 **322**	7 **320**	1 **320**	# ####	# ####	# ####	# ####
Aldebaran	1.1	20 **072**	30 **071**	39 **069**	48 **065**	57 **059**	65 **048**	71 **028**	73 **357**	70 **327**	64 **310**	55 **300**	46 **294**	37 **291**	28 **289**	18 **287**	9 **287**	# ####	# ####	# ####
Rigel	0.3	11 **098**	21 **099**	31 **100**	41 **101**	51 **103**	60 **107**	70 **114**	78 **134**	82 **189**	76 **234**	67 **248**	58 **255**	48 **258**	38 **260**	28 **261**	18 **261**	9 **262**	# ####	# ####
Capella	0.2	8 **043**	14 **042**	21 **040**	27 **036**	33 **031**	37 **025**	41 **018**	43 **009**	44 **359**	43 **350**	40 **341**	37 **334**	32 **328**	26 **323**	20 **320**	13 **318**	6 **316**	# ####	# ####
Bellatrix	1.7	9 **084**	19 **083**	29 **083**	38 **082**	48 **080**	58 **078**	68 **073**	77 **060**	84 **011**	79 **306**	70 **289**	61 **283**	51 **280**	41 **278**	31 **277**	21 **277**	11 **276**	1 **276**	# ####
Elnath	1.8	7 **061**	16 **060**	25 **058**	33 **055**	41 **051**	48 **044**	55 **034**	59 **020**	61 **003**	60 **345**	56 **330**	51 **319**	43 **311**	36 **306**	27 **303**	19 **300**	10 **299**	1 **299**	# ####
Alnilam	1.8	6 **091**	16 **091**	26 **091**	36 **091**	46 **092**	56 **092**	66 **093**	76 **095**	86 **107**	84 **259**	74 **266**	64 **267**	54 **268**	44 **268**	34 **269**	24 **269**	14 **269**	4 **269**	# ####
Betelgeuse	*	1 **083**	11 **082**	21 **082**	31 **081**	41 **080**	51 **078**	60 **075**	70 **068**	79 **050**	82 **351**	77 **304**	68 **290**	58 **284**	48 **281**	38 **279**	29 **278**	19 **278**	9 **277**	# ####
Canopus	-0.9	# ####	2 **143**	8 **144**	14 **145**	20 **148**	25 **151**	29 **156**	33 **162**	36 **168**	37 **175**	37 **183**	36 **190**	34 **197**	30 **203**	26 **208**	21 **212**	15 **214**	10 **216**	4 **217**
Sirius	-1.6	# ####	# ####	8 **107**	18 **108**	27 **109**	37 **111**	46 **114**	55 **120**	63 **130**	70 **147**	73 **176**	71 **207**	65 **227**	57 **238**	48 **244**	39 **248**	30 **251**	20 **252**	11 **253**
Adhara	1.6	# ####	# ####	5 **119**	13 **120**	22 **121**	30 **124**	38 **128**	46 **134**	53 **143**	58 **155**	61 **172**	61 **190**	58 **206**	52 **218**	46 **226**	38 **232**	30 **236**	21 **239**	13 **240**
Procyon	0.5	# ####	# ####	# ####	5 **085**	15 **085**	25 **084**	35 **084**	45 **083**	55 **081**	65 **078**	74 **070**	83 **043**	83 **315**	74 **289**	64 **282**	54 **279**	45 **277**	35 **276**	25 **276**
Pollux	1.2	# ####	# ####	# ####	3 **062**	12 **061**	21 **060**	29 **057**	38 **054**	45 **048**	52 **040**	58 **028**	61 **012**	62 **353**	59 **336**	54 **323**	47 **314**	40 **308**	32 **303**	23 **301**
Avior	1.7	# ####	# ####	# ####	# ####	2 **150**	7 **150**	12 **152**	17 **154**	21 **157**	24 **161**	27 **166**	29 **171**	30 **177**	30 **183**	29 **188**	28 **194**	25 **198**	21 **202**	17 **206**
Suhail	2.2	# ####	# ####	# ####	# ####	# ####	2 **133**	9 **134**	16 **136**	23 **138**	30 **142**	35 **148**	40 **154**	44 **163**	46 **173**	46 **183**	45 **193**	42 **202**	38 **210**	32 **216**
Miaplacidus	1.8	# ####	# ####	# ####	# ####	# ####	1 **160**	4 **160**	7 **161**	10 **163**	13 **165**	16 **167**	18 **170**	19 **173**	20 **177**	20 **181**	20 **184**	19 **188**	17 **191**	15 **194**
Alphard	2.2	# ####	# ####	# ####	# ####	# ####	# ####	8 **099**	18 **099**	28 **100**	38 **101**	47 **103**	57 **106**	67 **112**	75 **126**	81 **168**	78 **223**	70 **244**	61 **252**	51 **256**
Regulus	1.3	# ####	# ####	# ####	# ####	# ####	# ####	# ####	8 **078**	18 **077**	27 **077**	37 **075**	47 **072**	56 **068**	65 **061**	73 **045**	78 **010**	76 **327**	69 **305**	60 **294**
Dubhe	2.0	# ####	# ####	# ####	# ####	# ####	# ####	# ####	# ####	2 **028**	7 **028**	11 **026**	15 **024**	19 **021**	23 **017**	25 **013**	27 **008**	28 **003**	28 **358**	27 **353**
Denebola	2.2	# ####	# ####	# ####	# ####	# ####	# ####	# ####	# ####	# ####	3 **075**	12 **075**	22 **074**	32 **073**	41 **071**	50 **067**	59 **060**	68 **049**	74 **026**	75 **350**
Gienah	2.8	# ####	# ####	# ####	# ####	# ####	# ####	# ####	# ####	# ####	# ####	6 **108**	15 **108**	25 **109**	34 **111**	43 **114**	52 **120**	61 **128**	68 **143**	72 **168**
Acrux	1.1	# ####	# ####	# ####	# ####	# ####	# ####	# ####	# ####	# ####	# ####	2 **153**	6 **154**	10 **155**	14 **157**	18 **160**	21 **163**	24 **167**	26 **172**	27 **177**
Gacrux	1.6	# ####	# ####	# ####	# ####	# ####	# ####	# ####	# ####	# ####	# ####	1 **147**	7 **148**	12 **149**	17 **151**	21 **154**	25 **158**	29 **163**	31 **169**	33 **175**
Alioth	1.7	# ####	# ####	# ####	# ####	# ####	# ####	# ####	# ####	# ####	# ####	# ####	4 **034**	9 **033**	14 **031**	19 **029**	24 **025**	28 **020**	31 **015**	33 **009**
Spica	1.2	# ####	# ####	# ####	# ####	# ####	# ####	# ####	# ####	# ####	# ####	# ####	# ####	9 **101**	18 **102**	28 **103**	38 **104**	47 **107**	57 **111**	66 **119**
Alkaid	1.9	# ####	# ####	# ####	# ####	# ####	# ####	# ####	# ####	# ####	# ####	# ####	# ####	2 **041**	9 **040**	15 **038**	21 **036**	26 **032**	31 **027**	36 **021**
Hadar	0.9	# ####	# ####	# ####	# ####	# ####	# ####	# ####	# ####	# ####	# ####	# ####	# ####	# ####	4 **151**	9 **152**	14 **154**	18 **156**	22 **160**	25 **164**
Menkent	2.3	# ####	# ####	# ####	# ####	# ####	# ####	# ####	# ####	# ####	# ####	# ####	# ####	# ####	7 **127**	15 **128**	22 **130**	30 **133**	37 **138**	43 **145**
Arcturus	0.2	# ####	# ####	# ####	# ####	# ####	# ####	# ####	# ####	# ####	# ####	# ####	# ####	# ####	6 **071**	15 **070**	25 **069**	34 **067**	43 **063**	52 **058**
Rigil Kent.	0.1	# ####	# ####	# ####	# ####	# ####	# ####	# ####	# ####	# ####	# ####	# ####	# ####	# ####	0 **151**	5 **151**	10 **152**	14 **154**	18 **157**	22 **160**
Zuben'ubi	2.9	# ####	# ####	# ####	# ####	# ####	# ####	# ####	# ####	# ####	# ####	# ####	# ####	# ####	# ####	7 **106**	17 **107**	26 **108**	36 **110**	45 **113**
Kochab	2.2	# ####	# ####	# ####	# ####	# ####	# ####	# ####	# ####	# ####	# ####	# ####	# ####	# ####	# ####	2 **016**	5 **015**	7 **014**	10 **013**	12 **011**
Alphecca	2.3	# ####	# ####	# ####	# ####	# ####	# ####	# ####	# ####	# ####	# ####	# ####	# ####	# ####	# ####	# ####	6 **063**	15 **062**	23 **061**	32 **058**
Antares	1.2	# ####	# ####	# ####	# ####	# ####	# ####	# ####	# ####	# ####	# ####	# ####	# ####	# ####	# ####	# ####	# ####	2 **116**	11 **117**	20 **118**
Atria	1.9	# ####	# ####	# ####	# ####	# ####	# ####	# ####	# ####	# ####	# ####	# ####	# ####	# ####	# ####	# ####	# ####	# ####	3 **159**	6 **160**
Sabik	2.6	# ####	# ####	# ####	# ####	# ####	# ####	# ####	# ####	# ####	# ####	# ####	# ####	# ####	# ####	# ####	# ####	# ####	2 **106**	12 **106**
Shaula	1.7	# ####	# ####	# ####	# ####	# ####	# ####	# ####	# ####	# ####	# ####	# ####	# ####	# ####	# ####	# ####	# ####	# ####	# ####	5 **127**
Rasalhague	2.1	# ####	# ####	# ####	# ####	# ####	# ####	# ####	# ####	# ####	# ####	# ####	# ####	# ####	# ####	# ####	# ####	# ####	# ####	6 **077**
Eltanin	2.4	# ####	# ####	# ####	# ####	# ####	# ####	# ####	# ####	# ####	# ####	# ####	# ####	# ####	# ####	# ####	# ####	# ####	# ####	1 **039**
Kaus Aust.	2.0	5 **235**	# ####	# ####	# ####	# ####	# ####	# ####	# ####	# ####	# ####	# ####	# ####	# ####	# ####	# ####	# ####	# ####	# ####	# ####
Vega	0.1	7 **309**	# ####	# ####	# ####	# ####	# ####	# ####	# ####	# ####	# ####	# ####	# ####	# ####	# ####	# ####	# ####	# ####	# ####	# ####
Nunki	2.1	12 **243**	3 **244**	# ####	# ####	# ####	# ####	# ####	# ####	# ####	# ####	# ####	# ####	# ####	# ####	# ####	# ####	# ####	# ####	# ####
Altair	0.9	27 **280**	17 **279**	8 **279**	# ####	# ####	# ####	# ####	# ####	# ####	# ####	# ####	# ####	# ####	# ####	# ####	# ####	# ####	# ####	# ####
Peacock	2.1	19 **208**	14 **210**	9 **212**	4 **213**	# ####	# ####	# ####	# ####	# ####	# ####	# ####	# ####	# ####	# ####	# ####	# ####	# ####	# ####	# ####
Deneb	1.3	27 **323**	21 **319**	14 **317**	7 **316**	0 **315**	# ####	# ####	# ####	# ####	# ####	# ####	# ####	# ####	# ####	# ####	# ####	# ####	# ####	# ####
Enif	2.5	55 **287**	45 **284**	35 **282**	26 **281**	16 **280**	6 **280**	# ####	# ####	# ####	# ####	# ####	# ####	# ####	# ####	# ####	# ####	# ####	# ####	# ####
Al Na'ir	2.2	37 **204**	33 **210**	27 **215**	21 **218**	15 **221**	8 **222**	1 **223**	# ####	# ####	# ####	# ####	# ####	# ####	# ####	# ####	# ####	# ####	# ####	# ####
Fomalhaut	1.3	57 **205**	52 **217**	45 **226**	37 **231**	29 **235**	21 **238**	13 **240**	4 **240**	# ####	# ####	# ####	# ####	# ####	# ####	# ####	# ####	# ####	# ####	# ####
Markab	2.6	70 **319**	62 **304**	53 **296**	44 **291**	35 **289**	25 **287**	16 **286**	6 **285**	# ####	# ####	# ####	# ####	# ####	# ####	# ####	# ####	# ####	# ####	# ####

* Variable 0.1 - 1.2

SUN MOON PLANETS	Local Hour Angle Body																		
	0°	10°	20°	30°	40°	50°	60°	70°	80°	90°	100°	110°	120°	130°	140°	150°	160°	170°	180°
	Alt Az	Alt Az	Alt Az	Alt Az	Alt Az	Alt Az	Alt Az	Alt Az	Alt Az	Alt Az	Alt Az	Alt Az	Alt Az	Alt Az	Alt Az	Alt Az	Alt Az	Alt Az	Alt Az
	° °	° °	° °	° °	° °	° °	° °	° °	° °	° °	° °	° °	° °	° °	° °	° °	° °	° °	° °
Decl'n N30°	60 **000**	59 **343**	54 **329**	49 **319**	42 **312**	34 **307**	26 **304**	17 **302**	9 **300**	0 **300**	# ####	# ####	# ####	# ####	# ####	# ####	# ####	# ####	# ####
Decl'n N25°	65 **000**	63 **340**	58 **324**	52 **313**	44 **306**	36 **301**	27 **298**	18 **296**	9 **295**	0 **295**	# ####	# ####	# ####	# ####	# ####	# ####	# ####	# ####	# ####
Decl'n N20°	70 **000**	68 **334**	62 **317**	54 **306**	46 **300**	37 **295**	28 **293**	19 **291**	9 **290**	0 **290**	# ####	# ####	# ####	# ####	# ####	# ####	# ####	# ####	# ####
Decl'n N15°	75 **000**	72 **327**	65 **308**	57 **298**	48 **293**	38 **289**	29 **287**	19 **286**	10 **285**	0 **285**	# ####	# ####	# ####	# ####	# ####	# ####	# ####	# ####	# ####
Decl'n N10°	80 **000**	76 **315**	68 **297**	59 **289**	49 **285**	39 **283**	29 **282**	20 **281**	10 **280**	0 **280**	# ####	# ####	# ####	# ####	# ####	# ####	# ####	# ####	# ####
Decl'n N5°	85 **000**	79 **297**	69 **284**	60 **280**	50 **278**	40 **277**	30 **276**	20 **275**	10 **275**	0 **275**	# ####	# ####	# ####	# ####	# ####	# ####	# ####	# ####	# ####
Decl'n 0°	90 **####**	80 **270**	70 **270**	60 **270**	50 **270**	40 **270**	30 **270**	20 **270**	10 **270**	0 **270**	# ####	# ####	# ####	# ####	# ####	# ####	# ####	# ####	# ####
Decl'n S5°	85 **180**	79 **243**	69 **256**	60 **260**	50 **262**	40 **263**	30 **264**	20 **265**	10 **265**	0 **265**	# ####	# ####	# ####	# ####	# ####	# ####	# ####	# ####	# ####
Decl'n S10°	80 **180**	76 **225**	68 **243**	59 **251**	49 **255**	39 **257**	29 **258**	20 **259**	10 **260**	0 **260**	# ####	# ####	# ####	# ####	# ####	# ####	# ####	# ####	# ####
Decl'n S15°	75 **180**	72 **213**	65 **232**	57 **242**	48 **247**	38 **251**	29 **253**	19 **254**	10 **255**	0 **255**	# ####	# ####	# ####	# ####	# ####	# ####	# ####	# ####	# ####
Decl'n S20°	70 **180**	68 **206**	62 **223**	54 **234**	46 **240**	37 **245**	28 **247**	19 **249**	9 **250**	0 **250**	# ####	# ####	# ####	# ####	# ####	# ####	# ####	# ####	# ####
Decl'n S25°	65 **180**	63 **200**	58 **216**	52 **227**	44 **234**	36 **239**	27 **242**	18 **244**	9 **245**	0 **245**	# ####	# ####	# ####	# ####	# ####	# ####	# ####	# ####	# ####
Decl'n S30°	60 **180**	59 **197**	54 **211**	49 **221**	42 **228**	34 **233**	26 **236**	17 **238**	9 **240**	0 **240**	# ####	# ####	# ####	# ####	# ####	# ####	# ####	# ####	# ####

PREDICTION & IDENTIFICATION

Latitude 0°

Latitude 0°

STARS		Local Hour Angle Aries																		
		180°	190°	200°	210°	220°	230°	240°	250°	260°	270°	280°	290°	300°	310°	320°	330°	340°	350°	360°
Name	Mag	Alt Az	Alt Az	Alt Az	Alt Az	Alt Az	Alt Az	Alt Az	Alt Az	Alt Az	Alt Az	Alt Az	Alt Az	Alt Az	Alt Az	Alt Az	Alt Az	Alt Az	Alt Az	Alt Az
		° °	° °	° °	° °	° °	° °	° °	° °	° °	° °	° °	° °	° °	° °	° °	° °	° °	° °	° °
Alpheratz	2.2	# ####	# ####	# ####	# ####	# ####	# ####	# ####	# ####	# ####	# ####	7 061	16 060	24 058	32 055	40 050	48 044	54 034	59 021	61 004
Ankaa	2.4	# ####	# ####	# ####	# ####	# ####	# ####	# ####	# ####	# ####	# ####	3 132	10 133	17 135	24 137	31 141	36 147	41 154	45 163	47 173
Schedah	2.5	# ####	# ####	# ####	# ####	# ####	# ####	# ####	# ####	# ####	# ####	# ####	5 033	11 032	16 030	21 027	25 023	28 018	31 013	33 007
Diphda	2.2	# ####	# ####	# ####	# ####	# ####	# ####	# ####	# ####	# ####	# ####	# ####	9 108	18 109	28 110	37 113	46 116	55 122	63 132	69 150
Achernar	0.6	# ####	# ####	# ####	# ####	# ####	# ####	# ####	# ####	# ####	# ####	# ####	# ####	3 147	8 148	14 150	18 152	23 156	27 160	30 165
Hamal	2.2	# ####	# ####	# ####	# ####	# ####	# ####	# ####	# ####	# ####	# ####	# ####	# ####	# ####	8 066	17 065	26 064	35 061	43 057	51 051
Polaris	2.1	# ####	# ####	# ####	# ####	# ####	# ####	# ####	# ####	# ####	# ####	# ####	# ####	# ####	0 001	0 001	0 001	0 001	0 001	1 000
Acamar	3.1	# ####	# ####	# ####	# ####	# ####	# ####	# ####	# ####	# ####	# ####	# ####	# ####	# ####	# ####	4 130	12 131	19 133	26 136	33 140
Menkar	2.8	# ####	# ####	# ####	# ####	# ####	# ####	# ####	# ####	# ####	# ####	# ####	# ####	# ####	# ####	4 086	14 086	24 086	34 085	44 084
Mirfak	1.9	# ####	# ####	# ####	# ####	# ####	# ####	# ####	# ####	# ####	# ####	# ####	# ####	# ####	# ####	# ####	6 040	12 039	18 036	24 033
Aldebaran	1.1	# ####	# ####	# ####	# ####	# ####	# ####	# ####	# ####	# ####	# ####	# ####	# ####	# ####	# ####	# ####	# ####	1 073	11 073	20 072
Rigel	0.3	# ####	# ####	# ####	# ####	# ####	# ####	# ####	# ####	# ####	# ####	# ####	# ####	# ####	# ####	# ####	# ####	# ####	1 098	11 098
Capella	0.2	# ####	# ####	# ####	# ####	# ####	# ####	# ####	# ####	# ####	# ####	# ####	# ####	# ####	# ####	# ####	# ####	# ####	1 044	8 043
Bellatrix	1.7	# ####	# ####	# ####	# ####	# ####	# ####	# ####	# ####	# ####	# ####	# ####	# ####	# ####	# ####	# ####	# ####	# ####	# ####	9 084
Elnath	1.8	# ####	# ####	# ####	# ####	# ####	# ####	# ####	# ####	# ####	# ####	# ####	# ####	# ####	# ####	# ####	# ####	# ####	# ####	7 061
Alnilam	1.8	# ####	# ####	# ####	# ####	# ####	# ####	# ####	# ####	# ####	# ####	# ####	# ####	# ####	# ####	# ####	# ####	# ####	# ####	6 091
Betelgeuse	*	# ####	# ####	# ####	# ####	# ####	# ####	# ####	# ####	# ####	# ####	# ####	# ####	# ####	# ####	# ####	# ####	# ####	# ####	1 083
Canopus	-0.9	4 217	# ####	# ####	# ####	# ####	# ####	# ####	# ####	# ####	# ####	# ####	# ####	# ####	# ####	# ####	# ####	# ####	# ####	# ####
Sirius	-1.6	11 253	1 253	# ####	# ####	# ####	# ####	# ####	# ####	# ####	# ####	# ####	# ####	# ####	# ####	# ####	# ####	# ####	# ####	# ####
Adhara	1.6	13 240	4 241	# ####	# ####	# ####	# ####	# ####	# ####	# ####	# ####	# ####	# ####	# ####	# ####	# ####	# ####	# ####	# ####	# ####
Procyon	0.5	25 276	15 275	5 275	# ####	# ####	# ####	# ####	# ####	# ####	# ####	# ####	# ####	# ####	# ####	# ####	# ####	# ####	# ####	# ####
Pollux	1.2	23 301	14 299	6 298	# ####	# ####	# ####	# ####	# ####	# ####	# ####	# ####	# ####	# ####	# ####	# ####	# ####	# ####	# ####	# ####
Avior	1.7	17 206	13 208	8 210	3 210	# ####	# ####	# ####	# ####	# ####	# ####	# ####	# ####	# ####	# ####	# ####	# ####	# ####	# ####	# ####
Suhail	2.2	32 216	26 220	19 223	12 225	5 226	# ####	# ####	# ####	# ####	# ####	# ####	# ####	# ####	# ####	# ####	# ####	# ####	# ####	# ####
Miaplacidus	1.8	15 194	12 196	9 198	6 199	3 200	# ####	# ####	# ####	# ####	# ####	# ####	# ####	# ####	# ####	# ####	# ####	# ####	# ####	# ####
Alphard	2.2	51 256	41 258	31 260	22 261	12 261	2 261	# ####	# ####	# ####	# ####	# ####	# ####	# ####	# ####	# ####	# ####	# ####	# ####	# ####
Regulus	1.3	60 294	51 289	41 286	31 284	22 283	12 282	2 282	# ####	# ####	# ####	# ####	# ####	# ####	# ####	# ####	# ####	# ####	# ####	# ####
Dubhe	2.0	27 353	26 348	23 343	20 340	16 336	12 334	7 333	3 332	# ####	# ####	# ####	# ####	# ####	# ####	# ####	# ####	# ####	# ####	# ####
Denebola	2.2	75 350	71 320	63 304	55 296	45 291	36 288	26 286	17 285	7 285	# ####	# ####	# ####	# ####	# ####	# ####	# ####	# ####	# ####	# ####
Gienah	2.8	72 168	71 198	66 221	59 234	50 242	41 246	32 249	23 251	13 252	4 252	# ####	# ####	# ####	# ####	# ####	# ####	# ####	# ####	# ####
Acrux	1.1	27 177	27 182	26 187	25 191	22 196	19 199	16 202	12 204	7 206	3 207	# ####	# ####	# ####	# ####	# ####	# ####	# ####	# ####	# ####
Gacrux	1.6	33 175	33 181	32 188	30 194	27 199	24 203	19 207	15 210	10 212	4 213	# ####	# ####	# ####	# ####	# ####	# ####	# ####	# ####	# ####
Alioth	1.7	33 009	34 002	34 356	32 349	30 343	27 338	23 334	18 331	13 328	8 327	2 326	# ####	# ####	# ####	# ####	# ####	# ####	# ####	# ####
Spica	1.2	66 119	74 135	79 173	76 217	68 238	59 248	50 252	40 255	31 257	21 258	11 259	1 259	# ####	# ####	# ####	# ####	# ####	# ####	# ####
Alkaid	1.9	36 021	39 014	40 006	41 357	39 349	37 341	33 335	28 330	23 325	17 323	11 321	4 320	# ####	# ####	# ####	# ####	# ####	# ####	# ####
Hadar	0.9	25 164	27 169	29 174	30 179	29 185	28 191	26 195	23 200	19 203	15 206	10 208	5 209	0 210	# ####	# ####	# ####	# ####	# ####	# ####
Menkent	2.3	43 145	48 153	52 165	54 178	53 191	50 203	45 213	39 220	32 225	25 229	17 232	9 233	1 234	# ####	# ####	# ####	# ####	# ####	# ####
Arcturus	0.2	52 058	60 049	66 035	70 011	70 343	65 321	58 308	50 301	41 296	32 293	23 291	13 290	4 289	# ####	# ####	# ####	# ####	# ####	# ####
Rigil Kent.	0.1	22 160	25 164	27 169	29 175	29 180	29 186	27 191	25 196	22 200	18 203	14 206	10 208	5 209	# ####	# ####	# ####	# ####	# ####	# ####
Zuben'ubi	2.9	45 113	54 118	62 127	70 143	74 171	72 204	67 226	59 238	50 245	41 249	31 251	22 253	12 254	3 254	# ####	# ####	# ####	# ####	# ####
Kochab	2.2	12 011	13 009	15 006	15 004	16 001	16 358	15 355	14 353	13 350	11 348	8 347	6 345	3 345	1 344	# ####	# ####	# ####	# ####	# ####
Alphecca	2.3	32 058	40 054	48 048	55 039	60 025	63 007	63 348	59 331	53 319	46 310	38 305	30 301	21 299	12 297	3 297	# ####	# ####	# ####	# ####
Antares	1.2	20 118	29 121	37 124	45 129	53 137	59 149	63 166	63 185	61 204	56 218	49 227	41 234	33 238	24 241	15 242	7 243	# ####	# ####	# ####
Atria	1.9	6 160	10 161	13 163	15 166	18 168	19 172	20 175	21 179	21 183	20 187	18 190	16 193	14 196	11 198	8 200	4 201	1 201	# ####	# ####
Sabik	2.6	12 106	22 107	31 108	40 111	50 115	59 121	67 133	73 155	74 188	70 217	63 234	54 242	45 247	36 250	26 252	17 254	7 254	# ####	# ####
Shaula	1.7	5 127	13 128	21 130	28 133	35 138	42 144	47 152	51 163	53 176	52 189	50 201	45 211	40 218	33 224	26 228	18 231	11 232	3 233	# ####
Rasalhague	2.1	6 077	16 077	26 076	35 075	45 072	54 068	63 061	71 047	77 016	76 334	70 309	61 297	52 291	42 287	33 285	23 284	13 283	4 283	# ####
Eltanin	2.4	1 039	7 038	13 037	19 034	24 031	29 027	33 021	36 015	38 007	39 359	38 351	36 344	32 338	28 333	23 328	18 325	12 323	6 322	# ####
Kaus Aust.	2.0	# ####	3 124	11 125	20 127	27 130	35 134	42 139	48 147	52 158	55 171	55 186	53 199	49 211	43 219	36 225	29 230	21 233	13 235	5 235
Vega	0.1	# ####	1 051	8 051	16 049	23 047	31 043	37 038	43 031	47 022	50 011	51 359	50 347	47 336	42 328	36 321	30 316	22 313	15 310	7 309
Nunki	2.1	# ####	# ####	6 116	14 117	23 119	32 121	40 126	48 132	55 141	61 154	63 172	63 192	59 209	54 222	46 230	38 236	30 239	21 242	12 243
Altair	0.9	# ####	# ####	# ####	2 081	12 081	22 080	32 080	42 078	51 076	61 071	70 063	78 041	81 346	75 306	66 292	57 286	47 283	37 281	27 280
Peacock	2.1	# ####	# ####	# ####	# ####	2 147	7 147	13 149	18 151	22 155	26 159	29 164	32 169	33 176	33 182	32 189	30 195	27 200	23 204	19 208
Deneb	1.3	# ####	# ####	# ####	# ####	# ####	7 044	14 043	20 041	27 037	32 033	37 027	41 019	44 010	45 000	44 351	42 342	38 334	33 328	27 323
Enif	2.5	# ####	# ####	# ####	# ####	# ####	# ####	4 080	14 080	24 079	33 078	43 076	53 074	62 068	71 058	78 031	79 338	73 306	64 293	55 287
Al Na'ir	2.2	# ####	# ####	# ####	# ####	# ####	# ####	# ####	5 137	12 138	19 140	25 144	30 148	35 154	39 161	42 169	43 178	43 187	40 196	37 204
Fomalhaut	1.3	# ####	# ####	# ####	# ####	# ####	# ####	# ####	# ####	5 120	14 121	22 122	30 125	38 129	46 135	52 144	57 156	60 172	60 190	57 205
Markab	2.6	# ####	# ####	# ####	# ####	# ####	# ####	# ####	# ####	4 075	13 074	23 073	32 072	42 069	51 065	60 058	68 046	74 022	74 346	70 319

* Variable 0.1 - 1.2

SUN MOON PLANETS	Local Hour Angle Body																		
	180°	190°	200°	210°	220°	230°	240°	250°	260°	270°	280°	290°	300°	310°	320°	330°	340°	350°	360°
	Alt Az	Alt Az	Alt Az	Alt Az	Alt Az	Alt Az	Alt Az	Alt Az	Alt Az	Alt Az	Alt Az	Alt Az	Alt Az	Alt Az	Alt Az	Alt Az	Alt Az	Alt Az	Alt Az
	° °	° °	° °	° °	° °	° °	° °	° °	° °	° °	° °	° °	° °	° °	° °	° °	° °	° °	° °
Decl'n N30°	# ####	# ####	# ####	# ####	# ####	# ####	# ####	# ####	# ####	# ####	9 060	17 058	26 056	34 053	42 048	49 041	54 031	59 017	60 000
Decl'n N25°	# ####	# ####	# ####	# ####	# ####	# ####	# ####	# ####	# ####	# ####	9 065	18 064	27 062	36 059	44 054	52 047	58 036	63 020	65 000
Decl'n N20°	# ####	# ####	# ####	# ####	# ####	# ####	# ####	# ####	# ####	# ####	9 070	19 069	28 067	37 065	46 060	54 054	62 043	68 026	70 000
Decl'n N15°	# ####	# ####	# ####	# ####	# ####	# ####	# ####	# ####	# ####	# ####	10 075	19 074	29 073	38 071	48 067	57 062	65 052	72 033	75 000
Decl'n N10°	# ####	# ####	# ####	# ####	# ####	# ####	# ####	# ####	# ####	# ####	10 080	20 079	29 078	39 077	49 075	59 071	68 063	76 045	80 000
Decl'n N5°	# ####	# ####	# ####	# ####	# ####	# ####	# ####	# ####	# ####	# ####	10 085	20 085	30 084	40 083	50 082	60 080	69 076	79 063	85 000
Decl'n 0°	# ####	# ####	# ####	# ####	# ####	# ####	# ####	# ####	# ####	# ####	10 090	20 090	30 090	40 090	50 090	60 090	70 090	80 090	90 090
Decl'n S5°	# ####	# ####	# ####	# ####	# ####	# ####	# ####	# ####	# ####	# ####	10 095	20 095	30 096	40 097	50 098	60 100	69 104	79 117	85 180
Decl'n S10°	# ####	# ####	# ####	# ####	# ####	# ####	# ####	# ####	# ####	# ####	10 100	20 101	29 102	39 103	49 105	59 109	68 117	76 135	80 180
Decl'n S15°	# ####	# ####	# ####	# ####	# ####	# ####	# ####	# ####	# ####	# ####	10 105	19 106	29 107	38 109	48 113	57 118	65 128	72 147	75 180
Decl'n S20°	# ####	# ####	# ####	# ####	# ####	# ####	# ####	# ####	# ####	# ####	9 110	19 111	28 113	37 115	46 120	54 126	62 137	68 154	70 180
Decl'n S25°	# ####	# ####	# ####	# ####	# ####	# ####	# ####	# ####	# ####	# ####	9 115	18 116	27 118	36 121	44 126	52 133	58 144	63 160	65 180
Decl'n S30°	# ####	# ####	# ####	# ####	# ####	# ####	# ####	# ####	# ####	# ####	9 120	17 122	26 124	34 127	42 132	49 139	54 149	59 163	60 180

Latitude S10° | Latitude S10°

STARS — Local Hour Angle Aries

Name	Mag	0° Alt Az	10° Alt Az	20° Alt Az	30° Alt Az	40° Alt Az	50° Alt Az	60° Alt Az	70° Alt Az	80° Alt Az	90° Alt Az	100° Alt Az	110° Alt Az	120° Alt Az	130° Alt Az	140° Alt Az	150° Alt Az	160° Alt Az	170° Alt Az	180° Alt Az
		o o	o o	o o	o o	o o	o o	o o	o o	o o	o o	o o	o o	o o	o o	o o	o o	o o	o o	o o
Alpheratz	2.2	51 003	50 349	47 337	43 326	36 318	30 312	22 307	14 303	6 301	# ###	# ###	# ###	# ###	# ###	# ###	# ###	# ###	# ###	# ###
Ankaa	2.4	57 171	58 185	56 198	52 208	46 216	40 222	33 225	26 228	19 229	12 229	4 228	# ###	# ###	# ###	# ###	# ###	# ###	# ###	# ###
Schedah	2.5	23 006	23 000	23 354	21 348	19 343	16 338	12 334	7 331	2 329	# ###	# ###	# ###	# ###	# ###	# ###	# ###	# ###	# ###	# ###
Diphda	2.2	77 128	82 174	78 227	70 245	61 251	51 254	42 255	32 255	23 255	13 254	4 252	# ###	# ###	# ###	# ###	# ###	# ###	# ###	# ###
Achernar	0.6	39 163	41 170	43 177	43 184	41 191	39 197	35 203	31 207	27 210	21 212	16 213	11 213	5 213	0 211	# ###	# ###	# ###	# ###	# ###
Hamal	2.2	44 042	50 032	55 019	56 003	56 347	52 332	47 321	40 312	32 306	24 301	15 298	7 295	# ###	# ###	# ###	# ###	# ###	# ###	# ###
Polaris	2.1	# ###	# ###	# ###	# ###	# ###	# ###	# ###	# ###	# ###	# ###	# ###	# ###	# ###	# ###	# ###	# ###	# ###	# ###	# ###
Acamar	3.1	40 135	47 141	53 148	57 159	59 173	59 188	57 202	52 212	46 220	40 225	33 228	25 230	18 231	10 231	2 229	# ###	# ###	# ###	# ###
Menkar	2.8	42 075	52 070	61 062	69 048	75 022	75 342	70 314	62 299	53 291	44 286	34 282	24 279	15 277	5 275	# ###	# ###	# ###	# ###	# ###
Mirfak	1.9	15 031	20 027	24 021	27 015	29 008	30 001	30 353	28 346	25 340	21 334	17 330	11 326	5 323	# ###	# ###	# ###	# ###	# ###	# ###
Aldebaran	1.1	17 069	26 066	35 062	43 056	51 048	58 035	62 019	63 358	61 338	56 322	49 311	42 303	33 297	24 293	15 290	6 288	# ###	# ###	# ###
Rigel	0.3	13 096	22 095	32 093	42 092	52 091	62 089	72 086	81 079	88 323	79 278	69 273	59 271	49 269	39 268	29 266	20 265	10 263	0 262	# ###
Capella	0.2	0 043	7 041	13 038	19 034	24 029	28 023	31 016	33 008	34 359	33 351	31 343	28 336	23 330	18 326	12 322	6 319	# ###	# ###	# ###
Bellatrix	1.7	7 082	17 080	27 078	36 074	46 070	55 064	63 053	70 035	74 005	71 332	65 310	57 299	48 291	39 287	29 283	20 280	10 278	0 276	# ###
Elnath	1.8	2 060	11 058	19 055	27 051	34 045	41 037	46 028	50 016	51 002	51 348	47 336	43 325	36 317	29 311	22 306	14 303	5 300	# ###	# ###
Alnilam	1.8	6 090	16 088	26 086	36 084	46 081	55 078	65 071	74 058	80 024	79 325	72 298	63 287	53 281	43 278	34 275	24 273	14 271	4 269	# ###
Betelgeuse	*	# ###	10 081	19 078	29 076	38 072	48 067	56 060	64 048	71 027	73 356	69 327	63 309	54 298	45 291	36 287	27 284	17 281	7 279	# ###
Canopus	-0.9	4 143	10 142	16 142	22 143	28 145	34 148	38 153	42 159	45 166	47 175	47 184	46 192	43 200	39 206	35 211	29 214	24 216	18 218	12 218
Sirius	-1.6	# ###	2 107	11 105	21 104	30 104	40 103	49 104	59 106	68 110	77 123	83 170	79 231	71 248	61 253	52 256	42 256	33 256	23 256	14 255
Adhara	1.6	# ###	1 119	9 118	18 117	27 118	36 119	44 121	52 125	60 133	67 146	71 168	70 194	66 215	60 228	52 235	44 239	35 242	26 243	18 243
Procyon	0.5	# ###	# ###	# ###	4 084	14 082	24 080	33 077	43 073	52 068	61 059	69 045	74 018	74 341	69 315	61 300	52 292	42 287	33 283	23 280
Pollux	1.2	# ###	# ###	# ###	# ###	7 060	16 057	24 053	31 048	38 042	44 033	49 022	51 009	52 355	50 341	46 330	40 320	33 313	26 308	18 304
Avior	1.7	# ###	# ###	1 151	6 150	11 149	16 149	21 150	26 152	30 155	34 159	37 164	39 170	40 176	40 183	39 189	37 195	34 200	30 204	26 207
Suhail	2.2	# ###	# ###	# ###	# ###	2 134	9 133	16 133	24 133	31 135	37 138	44 143	49 150	53 159	56 171	56 184	55 196	51 207	46 215	40 220
Miaplacidus	1.8	# ###	# ###	0 162	3 161	7 160	10 159	13 160	17 160	20 162	23 164	26 166	28 169	29 173	30 177	30 181	30 185	29 188	27 192	25 195
Alphard	2.2	# ###	# ###	# ###	# ###	# ###	# ###	9 097	19 096	29 094	39 093	49 092	59 090	68 088	78 084	88 055	82 279	72 273	62 270	52 269
Regulus	1.3	# ###	# ###	# ###	# ###	# ###	# ###	# ###	6 077	15 075	25 072	34 068	43 063	51 056	59 045	65 029	68 005	67 340	62 321	55 308
Dubhe	2.0	# ###	# ###	# ###	# ###	# ###	# ###	# ###	# ###	# ###	# ###	2 026	6 023	10 020	13 017	15 012	17 008	18 003	18 358	17 353
Denebola	2.2	# ###	# ###	# ###	# ###	# ###	# ###	# ###	# ###	# ###	0 075	10 073	19 071	28 067	37 063	46 057	53 048	60 035	64 016	65 354
Gienah	2.8	# ###	# ###	# ###	# ###	# ###	# ###	# ###	# ###	# ###	# ###	9 106	18 105	28 105	37 105	47 105	56 107	66 111	75 121	82 153
Acrux	1.1	# ###	# ###	# ###	# ###	# ###	# ###	# ###	# ###	2 154	6 153	10 153	15 153	19 154	24 156	27 158	31 162	34 166	36 171	37 176
Gacrux	1.6	# ###	# ###	# ###	# ###	# ###	# ###	# ###	# ###	# ###	4 147	10 147	15 147	20 148	26 149	30 152	35 156	38 161	41 167	42 174
Alioth	1.7	# ###	# ###	# ###	# ###	# ###	# ###	# ###	# ###	# ###	# ###	# ###	# ###	1 032	6 030	11 027	15 023	18 019	21 014	23 008
Spica	1.2	# ###	# ###	# ###	# ###	# ###	# ###	# ###	# ###	# ###	# ###	# ###	1 101	10 100	20 098	30 097	40 096	49 096	59 095	69 095
Alkaid	1.9	# ###	# ###	# ###	# ###	# ###	# ###	# ###	# ###	# ###	# ###	# ###	# ###	# ###	1 039	7 037	13 034	18 030	22 025	26 019
Hadar	0.9	# ###	# ###	# ###	# ###	# ###	# ###	# ###	# ###	# ###	# ###	# ###	3 151	8 150	13 150	18 151	23 152	27 154	31 158	35 162
Menkent	2.3	# ###	# ###	# ###	# ###	# ###	# ###	# ###	# ###	# ###	# ###	# ###	# ###	5 126	13 125	21 125	29 126	36 128	44 132	51 138
Arcturus	0.2	# ###	# ###	# ###	# ###	# ###	# ###	# ###	# ###	# ###	# ###	# ###	# ###	# ###	2 070	12 068	21 065	29 061	38 056	46 049
Rigil Kent.	0.1	# ###	# ###	# ###	# ###	# ###	# ###	# ###	# ###	# ###	# ###	# ###	# ###	4 151	9 150	14 150	18 151	23 153	27 155	31 159
Zuben'ubi	2.9	# ###	# ###	# ###	# ###	# ###	# ###	# ###	# ###	# ###	# ###	# ###	# ###	# ###	0 106	10 105	19 104	29 103	38 103	48 103
Kochab	2.2	# ###	# ###	# ###	# ###	# ###	# ###	# ###	# ###	# ###	# ###	# ###	# ###	# ###	# ###	# ###	# ###	# ###	# ###	2 011
Alphecca	2.3	# ###	# ###	# ###	# ###	# ###	# ###	# ###	# ###	# ###	# ###	# ###	# ###	# ###	# ###	# ###	1 063	10 060	18 057	26 053
Antares	1.2	# ###	# ###	# ###	# ###	# ###	# ###	# ###	# ###	# ###	# ###	# ###	# ###	# ###	# ###	# ###	# ###	7 116	16 115	25 115
Atria	1.9	3 200	# ###	# ###	# ###	# ###	# ###	# ###	# ###	# ###	# ###	# ###	# ###	# ###	# ###	2 161	5 159	9 159	12 159	16 159
Sabik	2.6	# ###	# ###	# ###	# ###	# ###	# ###	# ###	# ###	# ###	# ###	# ###	# ###	# ###	# ###	# ###	# ###	# ###	5 105	15 104
Shaula	1.7	1 232	# ###	# ###	# ###	# ###	# ###	# ###	# ###	# ###	# ###	# ###	# ###	# ###	# ###	# ###	# ###	# ###	3 127	11 126
Rasalhague	2.1	# ###	# ###	# ###	# ###	# ###	# ###	# ###	# ###	# ###	# ###	# ###	# ###	# ###	# ###	# ###	# ###	# ###	# ###	4 077
Eltanin	2.4	# ###	# ###	# ###	# ###	# ###	# ###	# ###	# ###	# ###	# ###	# ###	# ###	# ###	# ###	# ###	# ###	# ###	# ###	# ###
Kaus Aust.	2.0	11 237	2 235	# ###	# ###	# ###	# ###	# ###	# ###	# ###	# ###	# ###	# ###	# ###	# ###	# ###	# ###	# ###	# ###	1 125
Vega	0.1	1 310	# ###	# ###	# ###	# ###	# ###	# ###	# ###	# ###	# ###	# ###	# ###	# ###	# ###	# ###	# ###	# ###	# ###	# ###
Nunki	2.1	17 245	8 245	# ###	# ###	# ###	# ###	# ###	# ###	# ###	# ###	# ###	# ###	# ###	# ###	# ###	# ###	# ###	# ###	# ###
Altair	0.9	25 285	16 282	6 280	# ###	# ###	# ###	# ###	# ###	# ###	# ###	# ###	# ###	# ###	# ###	# ###	# ###	# ###	# ###	# ###
Peacock	2.1	28 210	23 212	17 213	12 214	6 213	1 212	# ###	# ###	# ###	# ###	# ###	# ###	# ###	# ###	# ###	# ###	# ###	# ###	# ###
Deneb	1.3	19 325	13 321	7 318	0 316	# ###	# ###	# ###	# ###	# ###	# ###	# ###	# ###	# ###	# ###	# ###	# ###	# ###	# ###	# ###
Enif	2.5	51 299	42 293	33 289	23 285	14 283	4 281	# ###	# ###	# ###	# ###	# ###	# ###	# ###	# ###	# ###	# ###	# ###	# ###	# ###
Al Na'ir	2.2	46 207	41 214	35 218	29 221	22 223	16 224	9 224	2 223	# ###	# ###	# ###	# ###	# ###	# ###	# ###	# ###	# ###	# ###	# ###
Fomalhaut	1.3	66 214	59 227	51 234	43 238	35 241	26 242	17 242	9 241	0 240	# ###	# ###	# ###	# ###	# ###	# ###	# ###	# ###	# ###	# ###
Markab	2.6	61 331	55 317	48 307	40 300	31 295	22 291	13 288	3 286	# ###	# ###	# ###	# ###	# ###	# ###	# ###	# ###	# ###	# ###	# ###

* Variable 0.1 - 1.2

SUN MOON PLANETS — Local Hour Angle Body

	0° Alt Az	10° Alt Az	20° Alt Az	30° Alt Az	40° Alt Az	50° Alt Az	60° Alt Az	70° Alt Az	80° Alt Az	90° Alt Az	100° Alt Az	110° Alt Az	120° Alt Az	130° Alt Az	140° Alt Az	150° Alt Az	160° Alt Az	170° Alt Az	180° Alt Az
	o o	o o	o o	o o	o o	o o	o o	o o	o o	o o	o o	o o	o o	o o	o o	o o	o o	o o	o o
Decl'n N30°	50 000	49 347	46 335	41 325	35 318	27 312	20 307	12 304	4 301	# ###	# ###	# ###	# ###	# ###	# ###	# ###	# ###	# ###	# ###
Decl'n N25°	55 000	54 345	50 331	44 321	38 313	30 307	22 302	13 299	5 296	# ###	# ###	# ###	# ###	# ###	# ###	# ###	# ###	# ###	# ###
Decl'n N20°	60 000	58 342	54 327	48 316	41 307	32 302	24 297	15 294	6 292	# ###	# ###	# ###	# ###	# ###	# ###	# ###	# ###	# ###	# ###
Decl'n N15°	65 000	63 338	58 321	51 310	43 302	35 296	26 292	16 289	7 287	# ###	# ###	# ###	# ###	# ###	# ###	# ###	# ###	# ###	# ###
Decl'n N10°	70 000	68 333	62 315	54 303	45 296	36 290	27 287	18 284	8 282	# ###	# ###	# ###	# ###	# ###	# ###	# ###	# ###	# ###	# ###
Decl'n N5°	75 000	72 326	65 306	57 295	47 289	38 284	28 281	19 279	9 277	# ###	# ###	# ###	# ###	# ###	# ###	# ###	# ###	# ###	# ###
Decl'n 0°	80 000	76 315	68 296	59 287	49 282	39 278	29 276	20 274	10 272	0 270	# ###	# ###	# ###	# ###	# ###	# ###	# ###	# ###	# ###
Decl'n S5°	85 000	79 296	70 283	60 277	50 274	40 272	30 270	21 268	11 267	1 265	# ###	# ###	# ###	# ###	# ###	# ###	# ###	# ###	# ###
Decl'n S10°	90 ###	80 269	70 268	60 267	51 266	41 265	31 264	21 263	11 262	2 260	# ###	# ###	# ###	# ###	# ###	# ###	# ###	# ###	# ###
Decl'n S15°	85 180	79 242	70 254	60 257	51 258	41 259	31 258	22 258	12 257	3 255	# ###	# ###	# ###	# ###	# ###	# ###	# ###	# ###	# ###
Decl'n S20°	80 180	76 223	68 240	59 247	50 251	41 252	31 253	22 252	13 252	3 250	# ###	# ###	# ###	# ###	# ###	# ###	# ###	# ###	# ###
Decl'n S25°	75 180	72 211	66 229	58 238	49 243	40 246	31 247	22 247	13 246	4 245	# ###	# ###	# ###	# ###	# ###	# ###	# ###	# ###	# ###
Decl'n S30°	70 180	68 204	63 220	56 230	48 236	39 239	31 241	22 242	14 241	5 240	# ###	# ###	# ###	# ###	# ###	# ###	# ###	# ###	# ###

PREDICTION & IDENTIFICATION

Latitude S10° | Latitude S10°

STARS — Local Hour Angle Aries

Name	Mag	180°	190°	200°	210°	220°	230°	240°	250°	260°	270°	280°	290°	300°	310°	320°	330°	340°	350°	360°
		Alt Az	Alt Az	Alt Az	Alt Az	Alt Az	Alt Az	Alt Az	Alt Az	Alt Az	Alt Az	Alt Az	Alt Az	Alt Az	Alt Az	Alt Az	Alt Az	Alt Az	Alt Az	Alt Az
		° °	° °	° °	° °	° °	° °	° °	° °	° °	° °	° °	° °	° °	° °	° °	° °	° °	° °	° °
Alpheratz	2.2	# ####	# ####	# ####	# ####	# ####	# ####	# ####	# ####	# ####	# ####	2 060	10 058	19 055	26 050	34 045	40 037	45 028	49 016	51 003
Ankaa	2.4	# ####	# ####	# ####	# ####	# ####	# ####	# ####	# ####	# ####	2 133	9 132	17 131	24 132	31 134	38 137	45 142	50 149	55 159	57 171
Schedah	2.5	# ####	# ####	# ####	# ####	# ####	# ####	# ####	# ####	# ####	# ####	# ####	# ####	2 031	7 029	12 026	16 022	19 017	21 012	23 006
Diphda	2.2	# ####	# ####	# ####	# ####	# ####	# ####	# ####	# ####	# ####	# ####	2 108	12 106	21 106	31 105	40 105	50 106	59 108	68 114	77 128
Achernar	0.6	# ####	# ####	# ####	# ####	# ####	# ####	# ####	# ####	# ####	# ####	1 148	6 147	11 147	17 147	22 148	27 150	32 154	36 158	39 163
Hamal	2.2	# ####	# ####	# ####	# ####	# ####	# ####	# ####	# ####	# ####	# ####	# ####	# ####	# ####	3 065	12 063	21 060	29 056	37 050	44 042
Polaris	2.1	# ####	# ####	# ####	# ####	# ####	# ####	# ####	# ####	# ####	# ####	# ####	# ####	# ####	# ####	# ####	# ####	# ####	# ####	# ####
Acamar	3.1	# ####	# ####	# ####	# ####	# ####	# ####	# ####	# ####	# ####	# ####	# ####	# ####	# ####	3 130	11 129	18 129	26 130	33 132	40 135
Menkar	2.8	# ####	# ####	# ####	# ####	# ####	# ####	# ####	# ####	# ####	# ####	# ####	# ####	# ####	# ####	4 085	13 083	23 081	33 078	42 075
Mirfak	1.9	# ####	# ####	# ####	# ####	# ####	# ####	# ####	# ####	# ####	# ####	# ####	# ####	# ####	# ####	# ####	# ####	4 038	10 035	15 031
Aldebaran	1.1	# ####	# ####	# ####	# ####	# ####	# ####	# ####	# ####	# ####	# ####	# ####	# ####	# ####	# ####	# ####	# ####	# ####	8 072	17 069
Rigel	0.3	# ####	# ####	# ####	# ####	# ####	# ####	# ####	# ####	# ####	# ####	# ####	# ####	# ####	# ####	# ####	# ####	# ####	3 098	13 096
Capella	0.2	# ####	# ####	# ####	# ####	# ####	# ####	# ####	# ####	# ####	# ####	# ####	# ####	# ####	# ####	# ####	# ####	# ####	# ####	0 043
Bellatrix	1.7	# ####	# ####	# ####	# ####	# ####	# ####	# ####	# ####	# ####	# ####	# ####	# ####	# ####	# ####	# ####	# ####	# ####	# ####	7 082
Elnath	1.8	# ####	# ####	# ####	# ####	# ####	# ####	# ####	# ####	# ####	# ####	# ####	# ####	# ####	# ####	# ####	# ####	# ####	# ####	2 060
Alnilam	1.8	# ####	# ####	# ####	# ####	# ####	# ####	# ####	# ####	# ####	# ####	# ####	# ####	# ####	# ####	# ####	# ####	# ####	# ####	6 090
Betelgeuse	*	# ####	# ####	# ####	# ####	# ####	# ####	# ####	# ####	# ####	# ####	# ####	# ####	# ####	# ####	# ####	# ####	# ####	# ####	# ####
Canopus	-0.9	12 218	6 217	# ####	# ####	# ####	# ####	# ####	# ####	# ####	# ####	# ####	# ####	# ####	# ####	# ####	# ####	# ####	# ####	4 143
Sirius	-1.6	14 255	4 254	# ####	# ####	# ####	# ####	# ####	# ####	# ####	# ####	# ####	# ####	# ####	# ####	# ####	# ####	# ####	# ####	# ####
Adhara	1.6	18 243	9 242	0 241	# ####	# ####	# ####	# ####	# ####	# ####	# ####	# ####	# ####	# ####	# ####	# ####	# ####	# ####	# ####	# ####
Procyon	0.5	23 280	14 278	4 276	# ####	# ####	# ####	# ####	# ####	# ####	# ####	# ####	# ####	# ####	# ####	# ####	# ####	# ####	# ####	# ####
Pollux	1.2	18 304	9 301	1 299	# ####	# ####	# ####	# ####	# ####	# ####	# ####	# ####	# ####	# ####	# ####	# ####	# ####	# ####	# ####	# ####
Avior	1.7	26 207	21 209	17 211	11 211	6 211	1 209	# ####	# ####	# ####	# ####	# ####	# ####	# ####	# ####	# ####	# ####	# ####	# ####	# ####
Suhail	2.2	40 220	33 224	26 226	19 227	12 227	5 227	# ####	# ####	# ####	# ####	# ####	# ####	# ####	# ####	# ####	# ####	# ####	# ####	# ####
Miaplacidus	1.8	25 195	22 197	19 199	16 200	12 201	9 201	5 200	2 199	# ####	# ####	# ####	# ####	# ####	# ####	# ####	# ####	# ####	# ####	# ####
Alphard	2.2	52 269	43 267	33 266	23 265	13 263	3 262	# ####	# ####	# ####	# ####	# ####	# ####	# ####	# ####	# ####	# ####	# ####	# ####	# ####
Regulus	1.3	55 308	46 299	38 294	28 290	19 286	10 284	# ####	# ####	# ####	# ####	# ####	# ####	# ####	# ####	# ####	# ####	# ####	# ####	# ####
Dubhe	2.0	17 353	16 348	13 344	10 340	7 337	3 335	# ####	# ####	# ####	# ####	# ####	# ####	# ####	# ####	# ####	# ####	# ####	# ####	# ####
Denebola	2.2	65 354	62 333	57 317	49 307	41 299	32 294	23 291	14 288	4 286	# ####	# ####	# ####	# ####	# ####	# ####	# ####	# ####	# ####	# ####
Gienah	2.8	82 153	80 217	73 242	64 251	54 254	45 255	35 256	26 255	16 254	7 253	# ####	# ####	# ####	# ####	# ####	# ####	# ####	# ####	# ####
Acrux	1.1	37 176	37 182	36 187	34 193	32 197	29 201	25 204	21 206	16 207	12 207	7 207	3 206	# ####	# ####	# ####	# ####	# ####	# ####	# ####
Gacrux	1.6	42 174	43 182	42 189	40 196	37 201	33 206	28 209	23 212	18 213	13 213	7 213	2 212	# ####	# ####	# ####	# ####	# ####	# ####	# ####
Alioth	1.7	23 008	24 002	24 356	23 350	20 345	17 340	14 335	9 332	4 329	# ####	# ####	# ####	# ####	# ####	# ####	# ####	# ####	# ####	# ####
Spica	1.2	69 095	79 097	88 132	81 261	72 265	62 265	52 265	42 264	32 263	23 262	13 261	3 259	# ####	# ####	# ####	# ####	# ####	# ####	# ####
Alkaid	1.9	26 019	29 012	30 005	31 358	30 350	27 343	24 337	20 332	15 327	9 324	3 321	# ####	# ####	# ####	# ####	# ####	# ####	# ####	# ####
Hadar	0.9	35 162	37 167	39 173	40 179	39 186	38 192	35 197	32 202	28 205	24 208	19 209	14 210	9 210	4 209	# ####	# ####	# ####	# ####	# ####
Menkent	2.3	51 138	57 147	62 160	64 177	63 195	59 209	53 220	46 226	39 231	31 233	23 235	15 235	7 234	# ####	# ####	# ####	# ####	# ####	# ####
Arcturus	0.2	46 049	52 039	58 025	61 008	60 348	57 331	51 319	44 309	36 303	28 298	19 294	10 292	0 290	# ####	# ####	# ####	# ####	# ####	# ####
Rigil Kent.	0.1	31 159	35 163	37 168	39 174	39 180	39 186	37 192	35 197	31 202	27 205	23 207	18 209	14 210	9 210	4 209	# ####	# ####	# ####	# ####
Zuben'ubi	2.9	48 103	58 104	67 108	76 117	83 157	81 229	72 248	63 254	53 257	44 257	34 257	24 257	15 256	5 255	# ####	# ####	# ####	# ####	# ####
Kochab	2.2	2 011	3 008	5 006	5 003	6 001	6 358	5 355	4 353	3 350	1 348	# ####	# ####	# ####	# ####	# ####	# ####	# ####	# ####	# ####
Alphecca	2.3	26 053	34 048	41 041	47 032	51 020	53 005	53 351	50 337	45 326	39 317	32 310	24 305	16 302	7 299	# ####	# ####	# ####	# ####	# ####
Antares	1.2	25 115	34 115	42 117	51 120	59 126	67 137	72 158	73 188	70 214	63 229	55 238	47 242	38 244	29 245	20 245	11 245	2 244	# ####	# ####
Atria	1.9	16 159	19 160	22 162	25 165	27 168	29 171	30 175	31 179	31 183	30 187	28 191	26 194	24 197	20 199	17 200	14 201	10 201	7 201	3 200
Sabik	2.6	15 104	24 103	34 102	43 102	53 103	63 105	72 110	81 128	84 202	77 243	67 253	58 256	48 258	39 258	29 257	19 257	10 256	0 254	# ####
Shaula	1.7	11 126	19 126	27 127	35 129	42 132	49 137	56 146	60 158	63 174	62 191	59 206	54 217	47 225	40 229	32 232	25 234	17 234	9 234	1 232
Rasalhague	2.1	4 077	13 074	23 072	32 068	41 063	50 057	57 047	64 031	67 009	67 344	62 324	56 310	48 301	39 295	30 291	20 288	11 285	1 283	# ####
Eltanin	2.4	# ####	# ####	5 036	10 033	15 029	20 025	24 019	26 013	28 006	29 359	28 352	26 346	23 340	19 334	15 330	9 327	4 324	# ####	# ####
Kaus Aust.	2.0	1 125	9 124	17 123	25 123	33 125	41 128	49 132	56 140	62 151	65 168	65 188	62 205	57 218	51 227	43 232	35 235	27 236	19 237	11 237
Vega	0.1	# ####	# ####	2 050	9 048	16 044	23 040	29 034	34 027	38 019	40 009	41 359	40 349	38 340	33 331	28 325	22 319	15 315	8 312	1 310
Nunki	2.1	# ####	1 117	10 115	19 115	28 115	37 115	46 118	54 122	62 129	69 143	73 168	73 199	68 221	60 233	52 240	43 243	35 245	26 246	17 245
Altair	0.9	# ####	# ####	# ####	1 081	10 079	20 077	30 074	39 070	48 065	57 057	64 044	70 022	71 353	68 327	61 310	53 299	44 293	35 288	25 285
Peacock	2.1	# ####	# ####	# ####	5 147	10 146	16 146	21 147	26 149	31 152	35 156	39 162	42 168	43 175	43 183	42 190	40 197	37 202	32 207	28 210
Deneb	1.3	# ####	# ####	# ####	# ####	# ####	# ####	6 042	13 039	19 035	24 030	28 024	32 017	34 009	35 000	34 352	32 344	29 337	24 331	19 325
Enif	2.5	# ####	# ####	# ####	# ####	# ####	# ####	2 080	12 078	21 075	31 072	40 068	49 062	57 053	65 039	69 017	70 349	66 325	59 309	51 299
Al Na'ir	2.2	# ####	# ####	# ####	# ####	# ####	# ####	6 137	13 136	20 136	26 138	33 140	39 144	44 150	49 157	52 167	53 178	52 189	50 199	46 207
Fomalhaut	1.3	# ####	# ####	# ####	# ####	# ####	# ####	# ####	1 120	10 119	18 118	27 118	36 119	44 122	52 126	60 134	66 148	70 169	70 194	66 214
Markab	2.6	# ####	# ####	# ####	# ####	# ####	# ####	# ####	# ####	1 074	10 072	20 070	29 066	38 062	46 055	54 046	60 033	64 014	65 351	61 331

* Variable 0.1 - 1.2

SUN MOON PLANETS — Local Hour Angle Body

	180°	190°	200°	210°	220°	230°	240°	250°	260°	270°	280°	290°	300°	310°	320°	330°	340°	350°	360°
	Alt Az	Alt Az	Alt Az	Alt Az	Alt Az	Alt Az	Alt Az	Alt Az	Alt Az	Alt Az	Alt Az	Alt Az	Alt Az	Alt Az	Alt Az	Alt Az	Alt Az	Alt Az	Alt Az
	° °	° °	° °	° °	° °	° °	° °	° °	° °	° °	° °	° °	° °	° °	° °	° °	° °	° °	° °
Decl'n N30°	# ####	# ####	# ####	# ####	# ####	# ####	# ####	# ####	# ####	# ####	4 059	12 056	20 053	27 048	35 042	41 035	46 025	49 013	50 000
Decl'n N25°	# ####	# ####	# ####	# ####	# ####	# ####	# ####	# ####	# ####	# ####	5 064	13 061	22 058	30 053	38 047	44 039	50 029	54 015	55 000
Decl'n N20°	# ####	# ####	# ####	# ####	# ####	# ####	# ####	# ####	# ####	# ####	6 068	15 066	24 063	32 058	41 053	48 044	54 033	58 018	60 000
Decl'n N15°	# ####	# ####	# ####	# ####	# ####	# ####	# ####	# ####	# ####	# ####	7 073	16 071	26 068	35 064	43 058	51 050	58 039	63 022	65 000
Decl'n N10°	# ####	# ####	# ####	# ####	# ####	# ####	# ####	# ####	# ####	# ####	8 078	18 076	27 073	36 070	45 064	54 057	62 045	68 027	70 000
Decl'n N5°	# ####	# ####	# ####	# ####	# ####	# ####	# ####	# ####	# ####	# ####	9 083	19 081	28 079	38 076	47 071	57 065	65 054	72 034	75 000
Decl'n 0°	# ####	# ####	# ####	# ####	# ####	# ####	# ####	# ####	# ####	# ####	10 088	20 086	29 084	39 082	49 078	59 073	68 064	76 045	80 000
Decl'n S5°	# ####	# ####	# ####	# ####	# ####	# ####	# ####	# ####	# ####	1 095	11 093	21 092	30 090	40 088	50 086	60 083	70 077	79 064	85 000
Decl'n S10°	# ####	# ####	# ####	# ####	# ####	# ####	# ####	# ####	# ####	2 100	11 098	21 097	31 096	41 095	51 094	60 093	70 092	80 091	90 090
Decl'n S15°	# ####	# ####	# ####	# ####	# ####	# ####	# ####	# ####	# ####	3 105	12 103	22 102	31 102	41 101	51 102	60 103	70 106	79 118	85 180
Decl'n S20°	# ####	# ####	# ####	# ####	# ####	# ####	# ####	# ####	# ####	3 110	13 108	22 108	31 107	41 108	50 109	59 113	68 120	76 137	80 180
Decl'n S25°	# ####	# ####	# ####	# ####	# ####	# ####	# ####	# ####	# ####	4 115	13 114	22 113	31 113	40 114	49 117	58 122	66 131	72 149	75 180
Decl'n S30°	# ####	# ####	# ####	# ####	# ####	# ####	# ####	# ####	# ####	5 120	14 119	22 118	31 119	39 121	48 124	56 130	63 140	68 156	70 180

Latitude S20° | Latitude S20°

STARS		Local Hour Angle Aries																		
Name	Mag	0° Alt Az	10° Alt Az	20° Alt Az	30° Alt Az	40° Alt Az	50° Alt Az	60° Alt Az	70° Alt Az	80° Alt Az	90° Alt Az	100° Alt Az	110° Alt Az	120° Alt Az	130° Alt Az	140° Alt Az	150° Alt Az	160° Alt Az	170° Alt Az	180° Alt Az
Alpheratz	2.2	41 002	40 351	38 340	34 330	29 322	23 315	16 310	8 305	0 301	# ###	# ###	# ###	# ###	# ###	# ###	# ###	# ###	# ###	# ###
Ankaa	2.4	67 167	68 187	65 204	60 216	54 224	47 229	40 231	33 232	25 232	18 231	11 229	4 226	# ###	# ###	# ###	# ###	# ###	# ###	# ###
Schedah	2.5	13 006	13 000	13 354	12 349	9 344	6 339	3 335	# ###	# ###	# ###	# ###	# ###	# ###	# ###	# ###	# ###	# ###	# ###	# ###
Diphda	2.2	80 081	88 023	81 282	72 273	62 269	53 266	44 264	34 261	25 259	16 256	7 253	# ###	# ###	# ###	# ###	# ###	# ###	# ###	# ###
Achernar	0.6	49 160	51 168	53 176	53 185	51 193	48 201	45 206	40 210	35 213	30 215	24 215	19 215	14 214	9 212	4 209	# ###	# ###	# ###	# ###
Hamal	2.2	37 037	42 027	45 015	47 002	46 349	43 337	39 326	33 318	26 310	19 305	11 300	2 296	# ###	# ###	# ###	# ###	# ###	# ###	# ###
Polaris	2.1	# ###	# ###	# ###	# ###	# ###	# ###	# ###	# ###	# ###	# ###	# ###	# ###	# ###	# ###	# ###	# ###	# ###	# ###	# ###
Acamar	3.1	47 128	54 132	61 139	66 152	69 170	69 192	66 210	60 221	54 228	46 232	39 234	31 234	24 234	16 232	9 230	2 227	# ###	# ###	# ###
Menkar	2.8	39 067	48 059	55 049	61 034	65 013	66 349	62 328	56 312	48 302	40 294	31 288	22 283	13 279	4 276	# ###	# ###	# ###	# ###	# ###
Mirfak	1.9	7 030	11 026	15 020	18 014	19 008	20 001	20 354	18 347	16 341	12 336	8 331	3 326	# ###	# ###	# ###	# ###	# ###	# ###	# ###
Aldebaran	1.1	13 067	22 062	30 056	37 049	44 040	49 028	52 014	53 358	52 343	48 329	42 318	36 309	28 302	20 297	11 292	2 289	# ###	# ###	# ###
Rigel	0.3	13 094	23 091	32 087	42 083	51 078	60 071	68 059	76 037	78 353	74 315	66 297	57 287	48 280	39 276	30 272	20 268	11 265	2 262	# ###
Capella	0.2	# ###	# ###	5 037	10 032	15 027	19 021	22 014	23 007	24 359	23 352	21 345	18 338	14 332	10 327	4 323	# ###	# ###	# ###	# ###
Bellatrix	1.7	6 081	15 077	24 073	33 068	42 061	49 053	56 041	61 024	64 003	62 341	58 323	51 310	44 301	35 294	27 288	18 284	8 280	# ###	# ###
Elnath	1.8	# ###	6 057	13 052	20 047	27 041	33 033	37 024	40 013	41 002	41 350	38 339	34 330	29 321	23 315	16 309	8 304	0 301	# ###	# ###
Alnilam	1.8	6 089	16 086	25 082	34 077	43 072	52 065	60 054	67 038	71 012	70 342	65 318	58 303	50 294	41 287	32 282	23 277	13 274	4 270	# ###
Betelgeuse	*	# ###	8 079	17 075	26 071	35 065	43 058	51 049	57 036	61 018	63 357	60 337	56 321	49 309	41 300	33 293	24 288	15 284	6 280	# ###
Canopus	-0.9	12 142	18 140	24 140	30 140	36 142	42 144	47 148	52 155	55 163	57 173	57 184	56 195	52 204	48 210	43 215	37 218	31 220	25 220	19 220
Sirius	-1.6	# ###	4 106	14 103	23 100	32 098	41 095	51 092	60 089	70 084	79 075	86 021	81 290	72 277	63 272	53 269	44 266	34 263	25 260	16 258
Adhara	1.6	# ###	6 119	14 116	23 114	31 112	40 112	49 112	57 113	66 117	74 127	80 156	80 207	73 234	65 244	57 247	48 249	39 248	31 247	22 246
Procyon	0.5	# ###	# ###	# ###	3 083	12 080	22 076	31 071	39 065	47 057	55 047	61 032	64 011	64 348	61 328	55 313	47 302	39 295	30 289	21 284
Pollux	1.2	# ###	# ###	# ###	# ###	2 059	10 055	17 050	24 044	31 037	36 029	39 019	42 007	42 356	40 344	37 334	32 325	26 317	19 311	12 306
Avior	1.7	1 156	5 153	10 150	14 149	19 148	24 147	29 148	34 150	39 152	43 156	46 161	49 168	50 176	50 183	49 191	47 198	43 203	39 207	35 210
Suhail	2.2	# ###	# ###	# ###	2 136	9 133	16 131	23 130	30 129	37 130	44 132	51 136	57 142	63 153	66 168	66 185	64 202	60 214	54 222	47 227
Miaplacidus	1.8	4 167	7 164	10 162	13 160	16 159	19 158	23 158	26 159	29 160	33 162	35 165	37 168	39 172	40 176	40 181	40 185	39 189	37 193	34 196
Alphard	2.2	# ###	# ###	# ###	# ###	# ###	1 099	11 095	20 092	29 089	39 085	48 081	57 074	66 065	74 047	79 009	76 324	69 300	61 289	51 282
Regulus	1.3	# ###	# ###	# ###	# ###	# ###	# ###	# ###	3 076	12 072	21 068	30 063	38 056	45 047	51 036	56 021	58 004	57 346	53 330	48 317
Dubhe	2.0	# ###	# ###	# ###	# ###	# ###	# ###	# ###	# ###	# ###	# ###	# ###	# ###	0 020	3 016	6 012	7 008	8 003	8 358	7 353
Denebola	2.2	# ###	# ###	# ###	# ###	# ###	# ###	# ###	# ###	# ###	# ###	7 072	15 068	24 063	32 057	40 050	46 040	51 027	55 012	55 355
Gienah	2.8	# ###	# ###	# ###	# ###	# ###	# ###	# ###	# ###	# ###	2 108	11 105	21 102	30 099	39 097	48 094	58 091	67 088	77 082	86 057
Acrux	1.1	# ###	# ###	# ###	# ###	# ###	# ###	3 159	7 156	11 154	15 152	19 151	24 151	28 152	33 153	37 156	40 159	43 164	45 169	47 176
Gacrux	1.6	# ###	# ###	# ###	# ###	# ###	# ###	# ###	3 151	8 149	13 147	18 145	23 145	29 145	34 146	39 149	44 153	48 158	51 165	52 173
Alioth	1.7	# ###	# ###	# ###	# ###	# ###	# ###	# ###	# ###	# ###	# ###	# ###	# ###	# ###	# ###	2 027	6 023	9 018	11 013	13 008
Spica	1.2	# ###	# ###	# ###	# ###	# ###	# ###	# ###	# ###	# ###	# ###	# ###	3 101	12 098	21 095	31 091	40 088	49 084	59 078	68 070
Alkaid	1.9	# ###	# ###	# ###	# ###	# ###	# ###	# ###	# ###	# ###	# ###	# ###	# ###	# ###	# ###	# ###	4 033	9 029	13 024	17 018
Hadar	0.9	# ###	# ###	# ###	# ###	# ###	# ###	# ###	# ###	# ###	3 155	8 152	12 150	17 149	22 148	27 148	32 150	36 152	40 155	44 159
Menkent	2.3	# ###	# ###	# ###	# ###	# ###	# ###	# ###	# ###	# ###	# ###	# ###	3 128	10 125	18 123	26 122	34 121	42 121	50 123	58 127
Arcturus	0.2	# ###	# ###	# ###	# ###	# ###	# ###	# ###	# ###	# ###	# ###	# ###	# ###	# ###	# ###	8 066	16 062	24 057	32 050	39 042
Rigil Kent.	0.1	# ###	# ###	# ###	# ###	# ###	# ###	# ###	# ###	# ###	0 158	4 155	8 152	13 151	17 149	22 149	27 149	32 150	36 152	41 156
Zuben'ubi	2.9	# ###	# ###	# ###	# ###	# ###	# ###	# ###	# ###	# ###	# ###	# ###	# ###	# ###	3 106	12 103	21 100	31 097	40 095	49 092
Kochab	2.2	# ###	# ###	# ###	# ###	# ###	# ###	# ###	# ###	# ###	# ###	# ###	# ###	# ###	# ###	# ###	# ###	# ###	# ###	# ###
Alphecca	2.3	# ###	# ###	# ###	# ###	# ###	# ###	# ###	# ###	# ###	# ###	# ###	# ###	# ###	# ###	# ###	# ###	5 059	13 055	20 050
Antares	1.2	# ###	# ###	# ###	# ###	# ###	# ###	# ###	# ###	# ###	# ###	# ###	# ###	# ###	# ###	# ###	3 117	11 114	20 112	28 110
Atria	1.9	13 200	9 199	6 197	4 194	2 191	0 188	# ###	# ###	# ###	# ###	1 170	3 167	5 165	8 162	11 160	14 159	18 158	21 158	25 158
Sabik	2.6	# ###	# ###	# ###	# ###	# ###	# ###	# ###	# ###	# ###	# ###	# ###	# ###	# ###	# ###	# ###	# ###	# ###	8 104	17 101
Shaula	1.7	7 233	# ###	# ###	# ###	# ###	# ###	# ###	# ###	# ###	# ###	# ###	# ###	# ###	# ###	# ###	# ###	2 129	9 126	17 124
Rasalhague	2.1	# ###	# ###	# ###	# ###	# ###	# ###	# ###	# ###	# ###	# ###	# ###	# ###	# ###	# ###	# ###	# ###	# ###	# ###	1 076
Eltanin	2.4	# ###	# ###	# ###	# ###	# ###	# ###	# ###	# ###	# ###	# ###	# ###	# ###	# ###	# ###	# ###	# ###	# ###	# ###	# ###
Kaus Aust.	2.0	16 239	8 236	0 233	# ###	# ###	# ###	# ###	# ###	# ###	# ###	# ###	# ###	# ###	# ###	# ###	# ###	# ###	# ###	6 124
Vega	0.1	# ###	# ###	# ###	# ###	# ###	# ###	# ###	# ###	# ###	# ###	# ###	# ###	# ###	# ###	# ###	# ###	# ###	# ###	# ###
Nunki	2.1	21 248	12 246	3 243	# ###	# ###	# ###	# ###	# ###	# ###	# ###	# ###	# ###	# ###	# ###	# ###	# ###	# ###	# ###	# ###
Altair	0.9	22 289	13 285	4 281	# ###	# ###	# ###	# ###	# ###	# ###	# ###	# ###	# ###	# ###	# ###	# ###	# ###	# ###	# ###	# ###
Peacock	2.1	36 213	31 215	26 216	20 215	15 214	9 213	5 210	0 207	# ###	# ###	# ###	# ###	# ###	# ###	# ###	# ###	# ###	# ###	# ###
Deneb	1.3	11 327	5 322	# ###	# ###	# ###	# ###	# ###	# ###	# ###	# ###	# ###	# ###	# ###	# ###	# ###	# ###	# ###	# ###	# ###
Enif	2.5	45 309	37 300	29 294	20 289	11 285	2 281	# ###	# ###	# ###	# ###	# ###	# ###	# ###	# ###	# ###	# ###	# ###	# ###	# ###
Al Na'ir	2.2	55 214	49 220	43 224	36 226	29 227	23 226	16 225	9 223	3 221	# ###	# ###	# ###	# ###	# ###	# ###	# ###	# ###	# ###	# ###
Fomalhaut	1.3	73 233	65 242	56 246	48 248	39 248	30 247	22 245	13 243	5 240	# ###	# ###	# ###	# ###	# ###	# ###	# ###	# ###	# ###	# ###
Markab	2.6	52 338	48 325	42 314	34 306	26 300	18 294	9 290	0 286	# ###	# ###	# ###	# ###	# ###	# ###	# ###	# ###	# ###	# ###	# ###

* Variable 0.1 - 1.2

SUN MOON PLANETS	Local Hour Angle Body																	
	0° Alt Az	10° Alt Az	20° Alt Az	30° Alt Az	40° Alt Az	50° Alt Az	60° Alt Az	70° Alt Az	80° Alt Az	90° Alt Az	100° Alt Az	110° Alt Az	120° Alt Az	130° Alt Az	140° Alt Az	150° Alt Az	160° Alt Az	170° Alt Az	180° Alt Az
Decl'n N30°	40 000	39 349	36 338	32 329	27 321	21 315	14 309	6 305	# ###	# ###	# ###	# ###	# ###	# ###	# ###	# ###	# ###	# ###	# ###
Decl'n N25°	45 000	44 347	41 336	36 326	31 317	24 311	16 305	8 301	0 297	# ###	# ###	# ###	# ###	# ###	# ###	# ###	# ###	# ###	# ###
Decl'n N20°	50 000	49 346	45 333	40 322	34 313	27 306	19 301	11 296	2 292	# ###	# ###	# ###	# ###	# ###	# ###	# ###	# ###	# ###	# ###
Decl'n N15°	55 000	54 344	50 329	44 318	37 309	30 302	21 296	13 291	4 288	# ###	# ###	# ###	# ###	# ###	# ###	# ###	# ###	# ###	# ###
Decl'n N10°	60 000	58 341	54 325	48 313	41 304	32 297	24 291	15 287	6 283	# ###	# ###	# ###	# ###	# ###	# ###	# ###	# ###	# ###	# ###
Decl'n N5°	65 000	63 337	58 320	51 307	43 298	35 292	26 286	17 282	8 278	# ###	# ###	# ###	# ###	# ###	# ###	# ###	# ###	# ###	# ###
Decl'n 0°	70 000	68 333	62 313	54 301	46 292	37 286	28 281	19 277	9 273	0 270	# ###	# ###	# ###	# ###	# ###	# ###	# ###	# ###	# ###
Decl'n S5°	75 000	72 326	65 305	57 293	48 286	39 280	30 276	20 272	11 269	2 265	# ###	# ###	# ###	# ###	# ###	# ###	# ###	# ###	# ###
Decl'n S10°	80 000	76 315	68 294	59 285	50 279	41 274	31 270	22 267	13 264	3 261	# ###	# ###	# ###	# ###	# ###	# ###	# ###	# ###	# ###
Decl'n S15°	85 000	79 296	70 282	61 275	52 271	42 268	33 265	24 262	14 259	5 256	# ###	# ###	# ###	# ###	# ###	# ###	# ###	# ###	# ###
Decl'n S20°	90 ###	81 268	71 267	62 265	53 263	43 261	34 259	25 257	16 254	7 251	# ###	# ###	# ###	# ###	# ###	# ###	# ###	# ###	# ###
Decl'n S25°	85 180	80 240	71 251	62 254	53 255	44 254	35 253	26 251	17 249	8 246	# ###	# ###	# ###	# ###	# ###	# ###	# ###	# ###	# ###
Decl'n S30°	80 180	77 220	69 237	61 244	53 246	44 247	35 247	27 246	18 244	10 242	2 239	# ###	# ###	# ###	# ###	# ###	# ###	# ###	# ###

PREDICTION & IDENTIFICATION

Latitude S20° Latitude S20°

STARS — Local Hour Angle Aries

Name	Mag	180° Alt Az	190° Alt Az	200° Alt Az	210° Alt Az	220° Alt Az	230° Alt Az	240° Alt Az	250° Alt Az	260° Alt Az	270° Alt Az	280° Alt Az	290° Alt Az	300° Alt Az	310° Alt Az	320° Alt Az	330° Alt Az	340° Alt Az	350° Alt Az	360° Alt Az
		° °	° °	° °	° °	° °	° °	° °	° °	° °	° °	° °	° °	° °	° °	° °	° °	° °	° °	° °
Alpheratz	2.2	# ####	# ####	# ####	# ####	# ####	# ####	# ####	# ####	# ####	# ####	# ####	5 057	13 052	20 047	26 041	32 033	36 024	40 014	41 002
Ankaa	2.4	# ####	# ####	# ####	# ####	# ####	# ####	# ####	# ####	2 135	9 132	16 130	23 129	30 128	38 129	45 130	52 134	58 141	64 152	67 167
Schedah	2.5	# ####	# ####	# ####	# ####	# ####	# ####	# ####	# ####	# ####	# ####	# ####	# ####	# ####	# ####	3 025	6 021	9 016	12 011	13 006
Diphda	2.2	# ####	# ####	# ####	# ####	# ####	# ####	# ####	# ####	# ####	# ####	5 107	14 104	23 102	33 099	42 097	51 094	61 091	70 088	80 081
Achernar	0.6	# ####	# ####	# ####	# ####	# ####	# ####	# ####	# ####	0 153	4 150	9 148	14 146	20 145	25 145	30 145	36 147	41 150	45 154	49 160
Hamal	2.2	# ####	# ####	# ####	# ####	# ####	# ####	# ####	# ####	# ####	# ####	# ####	# ####	# ####	# ####	8 062	16 057	23 052	30 045	37 037
Polaris	2.1	# ####	# ####	# ####	# ####	# ####	# ####	# ####	# ####	# ####	# ####	# ####	# ####	# ####	# ####	# ####	# ####	# ####	# ####	# ####
Acamar	3.1	# ####	# ####	# ####	# ####	# ####	# ####	# ####	# ####	# ####	# ####	# ####	# ####	2 132	9 130	17 128	24 126	32 126	40 126	47 128
Menkar	2.8	# ####	# ####	# ####	# ####	# ####	# ####	# ####	# ####	# ####	# ####	# ####	# ####	# ####	# ####	3 085	12 081	21 077	30 072	39 067
Mirfak	1.9	# ####	# ####	# ####	# ####	# ####	# ####	# ####	# ####	# ####	# ####	# ####	# ####	# ####	# ####	# ####	# ####	# ####	2 034	7 030
Aldebaran	1.1	# ####	# ####	# ####	# ####	# ####	# ####	# ####	# ####	# ####	# ####	# ####	# ####	# ####	# ####	# ####	# ####	# ####	4 071	13 067
Rigel	0.3	# ####	# ####	# ####	# ####	# ####	# ####	# ####	# ####	# ####	# ####	# ####	# ####	# ####	# ####	# ####	# ####	# ####	4 097	13 094
Capella	0.2	# ####	# ####	# ####	# ####	# ####	# ####	# ####	# ####	# ####	# ####	# ####	# ####	# ####	# ####	# ####	# ####	# ####	# ####	# ####
Bellatrix	1.7	# ####	# ####	# ####	# ####	# ####	# ####	# ####	# ####	# ####	# ####	# ####	# ####	# ####	# ####	# ####	# ####	# ####	# ####	6 081
Elnath	1.8	# ####	# ####	# ####	# ####	# ####	# ####	# ####	# ####	# ####	# ####	# ####	# ####	# ####	# ####	# ####	# ####	# ####	# ####	# ####
Alnilam	1.8	# ####	# ####	# ####	# ####	# ####	# ####	# ####	# ####	# ####	# ####	# ####	# ####	# ####	# ####	# ####	# ####	# ####	# ####	6 089
Betelgeuse	*	# ####	# ####	# ####	# ####	# ####	# ####	# ####	# ####	# ####	# ####	# ####	# ####	# ####	# ####	# ####	# ####	# ####	# ####	# ####
Canopus	-0.9	19 220	13 218	8 216	2 214	# ####	# ####	# ####	# ####	# ####	# ####	# ####	# ####	# ####	# ####	# ####	# ####	1 147	7 144	12 142
Sirius	-1.6	16 258	7 255	# ####	# ####	# ####	# ####	# ####	# ####	# ####	# ####	# ####	# ####	# ####	# ####	# ####	# ####	# ####	# ####	# ####
Adhara	1.6	22 246	13 244	5 241	# ####	# ####	# ####	# ####	# ####	# ####	# ####	# ####	# ####	# ####	# ####	# ####	# ####	# ####	# ####	# ####
Procyon	0.5	21 284	12 280	3 277	# ####	# ####	# ####	# ####	# ####	# ####	# ####	# ####	# ####	# ####	# ####	# ####	# ####	# ####	# ####	# ####
Pollux	1.2	12 306	4 302	# ####	# ####	# ####	# ####	# ####	# ####	# ####	# ####	# ####	# ####	# ####	# ####	# ####	# ####	# ####	# ####	# ####
Avior	1.7	35 210	30 212	25 213	20 212	15 212	10 210	6 208	1 205	# ####	# ####	# ####	# ####	# ####	# ####	# ####	# ####	# ####	# ####	1 156
Suhail	2.2	47 227	40 229	33 231	26 230	19 229	12 228	5 225	# ####	# ####	# ####	# ####	# ####	# ####	# ####	# ####	# ####	# ####	# ####	# ####
Miaplacidus	1.8	34 196	32 199	28 200	25 201	22 202	18 201	15 201	12 199	9 197	6 195	4 192	2 189	1 186	# ####	# ####	0 176	1 173	3 169	4 167
Alphard	2.2	51 282	42 277	33 273	23 269	14 266	5 262	# ####	# ####	# ####	# ####	# ####	# ####	# ####	# ####	# ####	# ####	# ####	# ####	# ####
Regulus	1.3	48 317	41 307	33 300	25 294	16 289	7 285	# ####	# ####	# ####	# ####	# ####	# ####	# ####	# ####	# ####	# ####	# ####	# ####	# ####
Dubhe	2.0	7 353	6 349	4 345	1 341	# ####	# ####	# ####	# ####	# ####	# ####	# ####	# ####	# ####	# ####	# ####	# ####	# ####	# ####	# ####
Denebola	2.2	55 355	53 339	49 325	43 315	36 306	28 300	19 294	11 290	2 286	# ####	# ####	# ####	# ####	# ####	# ####	# ####	# ####	# ####	# ####
Gienah	2.8	86 057	84 292	75 277	65 271	56 268	46 265	37 263	28 260	19 258	9 255	0 251	# ####	# ####	# ####	# ####	# ####	# ####	# ####	# ####
Acrux	1.1	47 176	47 182	46 189	44 194	41 199	38 203	34 206	30 208	25 209	21 209	16 208	12 207	8 205	4 202	1 199	# ####	# ####	# ####	# ####
Gacrux	1.6	52 173	53 182	52 191	49 198	46 205	42 209	37 212	32 214	26 215	21 215	16 214	10 213	5 210	1 207	# ####	# ####	# ####	# ####	# ####
Alioth	1.7	13 008	14 002	14 356	13 351	11 345	8 340	5 336	0 332	# ####	# ####	# ####	# ####	# ####	# ####	# ####	# ####	# ####	# ####	# ####
Spica	1.2	68 070	76 053	81 008	78 315	70 293	61 283	52 277	42 273	33 269	24 266	14 263	5 260	# ####	# ####	# ####	# ####	# ####	# ####	# ####
Alkaid	1.9	17 018	19 012	20 005	21 358	20 351	18 344	15 338	11 333	6 328	1 324	# ####	# ####	# ####	# ####	# ####	# ####	# ####	# ####	# ####
Hadar	0.9	44 159	47 165	49 172	50 179	49 187	47 194	45 200	41 204	37 208	32 210	28 211	23 212	18 211	13 210	8 208	4 206	0 203	# ####	# ####
Menkent	2.3	58 127	65 135	71 150	74 175	72 202	67 221	60 231	53 236	45 238	37 239	29 239	21 238	13 236	5 233	# ####	# ####	# ####	# ####	# ####
Arcturus	0.2	39 042	44 032	49 020	51 006	50 351	48 337	43 325	37 316	30 308	23 302	14 297	6 293	# ####	# ####	# ####	# ####	# ####	# ####	# ####
Rigil Kent.	0.1	41 156	44 160	47 166	49 173	49 180	49 187	47 194	44 200	40 204	36 208	32 210	27 211	22 211	17 211	13 209	8 208	4 205	0 202	# ####
Zuben'ubi	2.9	49 092	59 088	68 083	77 074	85 034	82 299	73 281	64 274	54 270	45 267	36 264	26 261	17 259	8 256	# ####	# ####	# ####	# ####	# ####
Kochab	2.2	# ####	# ####	# ####	# ####	# ####	# ####	# ####	# ####	# ####	# ####	# ####	# ####	# ####	# ####	# ####	# ####	# ####	# ####	# ####
Alphecca	2.3	20 050	27 044	33 036	38 027	41 016	43 005	43 352	41 341	37 330	32 322	25 314	18 309	11 304	3 300	# ####	# ####	# ####	# ####	# ####
Antares	1.2	28 110	37 109	46 108	55 108	64 110	73 115	81 135	83 200	77 239	68 249	59 252	50 252	42 252	33 251	24 249	15 247	7 244	# ####	# ####
Atria	1.9	25 158	28 159	32 161	35 163	37 166	39 170	40 174	41 179	41 184	40 188	38 192	36 196	33 198	30 200	27 202	23 202	19 202	16 202	13 200
Sabik	2.6	17 101	26 098	35 096	45 093	54 089	63 085	73 079	82 061	85 332	77 288	68 278	59 273	50 269	40 266	31 263	21 260	12 258	3 254	# ####
Shaula	1.7	17 124	25 123	33 122	41 122	49 124	56 128	63 135	69 148	73 171	72 197	68 217	61 228	54 234	46 237	38 238	30 238	22 237	15 235	7 233
Rasalhague	2.1	1 076	11 072	19 068	28 063	36 057	43 048	50 038	55 024	57 007	57 349	54 332	48 319	42 309	34 302	26 296	17 291	8 287	# ####	# ####
Eltanin	2.4	# ####	# ####	# ####	2 032	7 028	11 024	14 018	17 012	18 006	19 359	18 353	16 347	14 341	10 336	6 331	1 327	# ####	# ####	# ####
Kaus Aust.	2.0	6 124	14 122	22 120	31 119	39 119	47 119	55 122	63 127	70 139	75 161	75 193	71 218	64 231	57 237	49 240	41 241	32 241	24 240	16 239
Vega	0.1	# ####	# ####	# ####	3 047	9 043	15 038	21 032	25 025	29 017	31 008	31 359	30 350	28 342	25 334	20 327	14 321	8 317	2 313	# ####
Nunki	2.1	# ####	5 116	14 113	23 111	32 109	40 108	49 107	58 108	67 111	76 119	83 152	82 221	74 244	65 250	56 252	47 252	38 252	29 250	21 248
Altair	0.9	# ####	# ####	# ####	# ####	8 077	17 073	26 069	35 063	43 056	50 046	56 033	60 015	61 355	59 336	54 321	47 309	39 301	31 294	22 289
Peacock	2.1	# ####	3 151	8 148	13 146	19 145	24 144	29 145	35 146	40 149	44 153	48 158	51 166	53 174	53 183	52 192	49 200	46 206	41 210	36 213
Deneb	1.3	# ####	# ####	# ####	# ####	# ####	# ####	# ####	5 038	10 033	15 028	19 022	22 015	24 008	25 000	24 353	22 345	19 338	15 332	11 327
Enif	2.5	# ####	# ####	# ####	# ####	# ####	# ####	0 079	10 076	19 072	27 067	36 061	44 053	51 043	56 029	60 012	60 352	57 334	52 319	45 309
Al Na'ir	2.2	# ####	# ####	# ####	# ####	1 141	7 138	13 136	20 134	27 133	33 134	40 135	47 138	53 143	58 151	61 163	63 177	62 192	59 204	55 214
Fomalhaut	1.3	# ####	# ####	# ####	# ####	# ####	# ####	# ####	6 119	14 117	23 115	31 113	40 112	49 113	57 114	66 118	74 129	80 158	79 207	73 233
Markab	2.6	# ####	# ####	# ####	# ####	# ####	# ####	# ####	# ####	# ####	7 071	16 067	25 062	33 056	40 048	46 038	51 026	54 010	55 354	52 338

* Variable 0.1 - 1.2

SUN MOON PLANETS — Local Hour Angle Body

	180° Alt Az	190° Alt Az	200° Alt Az	210° Alt Az	220° Alt Az	230° Alt Az	240° Alt Az	250° Alt Az	260° Alt Az	270° Alt Az	280° Alt Az	290° Alt Az	300° Alt Az	310° Alt Az	320° Alt Az	330° Alt Az	340° Alt Az	350° Alt Az	360° Alt Az
	° °	° °	° °	° °	° °	° °	° °	° °	° °	° °	° °	° °	° °	° °	° °	° °	° °	° °	° °
Decl'n N30°	# ####	# ####	# ####	# ####	# ####	# ####	# ####	# ####	# ####	# ####	# ####	6 055	14 051	21 045	27 039	32 031	36 022	39 011	40 000
Decl'n N25°	# ####	# ####	# ####	# ####	# ####	# ####	# ####	# ####	# ####	# ####	0 063	8 059	16 055	24 049	31 043	36 034	41 024	44 013	45 000
Decl'n N20°	# ####	# ####	# ####	# ####	# ####	# ####	# ####	# ####	# ####	# ####	2 068	11 064	19 059	27 054	34 047	40 038	45 027	49 014	50 000
Decl'n N15°	# ####	# ####	# ####	# ####	# ####	# ####	# ####	# ####	# ####	# ####	4 072	13 069	21 064	30 058	37 051	44 042	50 031	54 016	55 000
Decl'n N10°	# ####	# ####	# ####	# ####	# ####	# ####	# ####	# ####	# ####	# ####	6 077	15 073	24 069	32 063	41 056	48 047	54 035	58 019	60 000
Decl'n N5°	# ####	# ####	# ####	# ####	# ####	# ####	# ####	# ####	# ####	# ####	8 082	17 078	26 074	35 068	43 062	51 053	58 040	63 023	65 000
Decl'n 0°	# ####	# ####	# ####	# ####	# ####	# ####	# ####	# ####	# ####	# ####	9 087	19 083	28 079	37 074	46 068	54 059	62 047	68 027	70 000
Decl'n S5°	# ####	# ####	# ####	# ####	# ####	# ####	# ####	# ####	# ####	2 095	11 091	20 088	30 084	39 080	48 074	57 067	65 055	72 034	75 000
Decl'n S10°	# ####	# ####	# ####	# ####	# ####	# ####	# ####	# ####	# ####	3 099	13 096	22 093	31 090	41 086	50 081	59 075	68 066	76 045	80 000
Decl'n S15°	# ####	# ####	# ####	# ####	# ####	# ####	# ####	# ####	# ####	5 104	14 101	24 098	33 095	42 092	52 089	61 085	70 078	79 064	85 000
Decl'n S20°	# ####	# ####	# ####	# ####	# ####	# ####	# ####	# ####	# ####	7 109	16 106	25 103	34 101	43 099	53 097	62 095	71 093	81 092	90 090
Decl'n S25°	# ####	# ####	# ####	# ####	# ####	# ####	# ####	# ####	# ####	8 114	17 111	26 109	35 107	44 106	53 105	62 106	71 109	80 120	85 180
Decl'n S30°	# ####	# ####	# ####	# ####	# ####	# ####	# ####	# ####	2 121	10 118	18 116	27 114	35 113	44 113	53 114	61 116	69 123	77 140	80 180

Latitude S30° Latitude S30°

STARS		Local Hour Angle Aries																		
Name	Mag	0° Alt Az	10° Alt Az	20° Alt Az	30° Alt Az	40° Alt Az	50° Alt Az	60° Alt Az	70° Alt Az	80° Alt Az	90° Alt Az	100° Alt Az	110° Alt Az	120° Alt Az	130° Alt Az	140° Alt Az	150° Alt Az	160° Alt Az	170° Alt Az	180° Alt Az
		o o	o o	o o	o o	o o	o o	o o	o o	o o	o o	o o	o o	o o	o o	o o	o o	o o	o o	o o
Alpheratz	2.2	31 002	30 352	28 342	25 333	21 325	15 318	9 311	2 306	# ###	# ###	# ###	# ###	# ###	# ###	# ###	# ###	# ###	# ###	# ###
Ankaa	2.4	77 159	77 192	74 218	68 230	61 236	53 238	46 239	39 238	31 236	24 234	17 231	11 227	5 223	# ###	# ###	# ###	# ###	# ###	# ###
Schedah	2.5	3 006	3 000	3 355	2 349	# ###	# ###	# ###	# ###	# ###	# ###	# ###	# ###	# ###	# ###	# ###	# ###	# ###	# ###	# ###
Diphda	2.2	74 042	78 004	75 323	69 300	61 288	53 280	44 274	35 268	27 264	18 259	10 255	1 250	# ###	# ###	# ###	# ###	# ###	# ###	# ###
Achernar	0.6	58 155	61 164	63 175	62 187	61 197	57 206	53 212	48 216	43 218	38 219	32 218	27 217	22 216	17 213	13 210	8 206	5 202	2 198	# ###
Hamal	2.2	28 033	33 024	35 013	37 002	36 351	34 340	30 330	25 321	19 314	13 307	6 301	# ###	# ###	# ###	# ###	# ###	# ###	# ###	# ###
Polaris	2.1	# ###	# ###	# ###	# ###	# ###	# ###	# ###	# ###	# ###	# ###	# ###	# ###	# ###	# ###	# ###	# ###	# ###	# ###	# ###
Acamar	3.1	53 118	60 120	68 124	74 135	79 161	79 202	74 227	67 237	59 241	52 242	44 241	37 240	29 238	22 235	15 232	8 228	2 224	# ###	# ###
Menkar	2.8	35 060	42 051	48 040	53 026	55 010	56 352	53 335	49 321	43 310	36 301	28 293	20 287	11 282	3 276	# ###	# ###	# ###	# ###	# ###
Mirfak	1.9	# ###	2 025	6 020	8 014	10 007	10 001	10 354	8 348	6 342	3 336	# ###	# ###	# ###	# ###	# ###	# ###	# ###	# ###	# ###
Aldebaran	1.1	9 065	17 059	24 052	30 044	36 035	40 024	43 012	43 359	42 346	39 334	35 323	29 314	22 306	15 300	7 294	# ###	# ###	# ###	# ###
Rigel	0.3	14 092	23 086	31 081	40 075	48 067	55 057	62 042	67 022	68 356	66 332	60 313	53 300	46 291	37 283	29 277	20 272	12 267	3 262	# ###
Capella	0.2	# ###	# ###	# ###	2 032	6 026	10 020	12 013	14 007	14 359	13 352	12 345	9 339	5 333	1 327	# ###	# ###	# ###	# ###	# ###
Bellatrix	1.7	4 080	13 075	21 069	29 062	36 054	43 045	48 033	52 018	54 002	53 346	49 331	44 318	38 308	31 300	23 293	15 287	6 281	# ###	# ###
Elnath	1.8	# ###	0 056	7 051	13 045	19 038	24 030	28 021	30 012	31 002	31 351	29 342	25 332	21 324	15 317	9 311	2 305	# ###	# ###	# ###
Alnilam	1.8	6 088	15 083	23 077	31 071	39 064	47 055	53 043	58 027	61 008	61 347	57 329	52 314	45 303	38 294	30 287	21 281	13 276	4 271	# ###
Betelgeuse	*	# ###	6 078	14 073	22 067	30 060	37 051	43 041	48 029	52 014	53 358	51 342	47 328	42 316	36 307	28 299	20 292	12 286	4 281	# ###
Canopus	-0.9	20 140	26 138	32 136	38 136	44 136	50 138	55 141	60 147	64 157	67 171	67 186	65 200	61 211	56 218	51 222	45 224	39 224	33 224	27 223
Sirius	-1.6	# ###	7 105	16 101	24 096	33 091	41 086	50 080	59 072	66 060	73 040	77 005	75 327	68 304	61 290	52 282	44 275	35 270	26 265	18 261
Adhara	1.6	3 122	10 118	18 113	26 110	35 106	43 103	51 100	60 097	69 093	77 089	86 077	85 281	77 271	68 266	59 263	51 260	42 257	34 253	26 250
Procyon	0.5	# ###	# ###	# ###	2 083	10 078	19 072	27 066	34 058	41 049	47 038	52 024	54 008	54 351	52 335	47 321	41 310	34 301	27 294	18 288
Pollux	1.2	# ###	# ###	# ###	# ###	# ###	4 054	11 048	17 042	22 034	27 026	30 017	32 007	32 356	31 346	28 336	24 328	19 320	13 313	6 307
Avior	1.7	10 155	14 152	18 149	23 147	28 145	33 144	38 144	43 145	48 147	52 151	56 157	59 165	60 174	60 184	59 194	56 202	53 208	48 212	43 215
Suhail	2.2	# ###	# ###	3 140	9 135	15 132	22 128	29 126	36 124	43 123	51 123	58 125	65 130	71 139	75 159	76 189	73 214	67 227	61 234	53 236
Miaplacidus	1.8	14 166	16 164	19 161	22 159	25 158	29 157	32 156	35 157	39 158	42 160	45 162	47 166	49 170	50 176	50 181	50 186	48 191	46 195	44 199
Alphard	2.2	# ###	# ###	# ###	# ###	# ###	3 098	11 094	20 089	29 083	37 077	45 070	53 061	60 048	66 030	69 005	67 339	63 318	56 303	49 293
Regulus	1.3	# ###	# ###	# ###	# ###	# ###	# ###	# ###	1 076	9 070	17 065	25 058	32 050	38 041	43 030	46 017	48 003	47 349	45 335	40 323
Dubhe	2.0	# ###	# ###	# ###	# ###	# ###	# ###	# ###	# ###	# ###	# ###	# ###	# ###	# ###	# ###	# ###	# ###	# ###	# ###	# ###
Denebola	2.2	# ###	# ###	# ###	# ###	# ###	# ###	# ###	# ###	# ###	# ###	3 071	11 066	19 059	26 052	33 044	38 034	42 023	45 010	45 356
Gienah	2.8	# ###	# ###	# ###	# ###	# ###	# ###	# ###	# ###	# ###	5 107	14 103	22 098	31 093	40 089	48 083	57 076	65 066	72 049	77 017
Acrux	1.1	3 183	3 178	4 174	5 170	7 165	9 162	12 158	16 155	19 153	24 151	28 149	32 149	37 149	41 150	46 152	49 155	53 160	55 167	57 175
Gacrux	1.6	# ###	# ###	# ###	# ###	1 163	4 159	8 154	12 151	16 147	21 145	26 143	31 142	37 141	42 142	47 144	52 147	57 153	60 161	62 171
Alioth	1.7	# ###	# ###	# ###	# ###	# ###	# ###	# ###	# ###	# ###	# ###	# ###	# ###	# ###	# ###	# ###	# ###	# ###	2 013	3 008
Spica	1.2	# ###	# ###	# ###	# ###	# ###	# ###	# ###	# ###	# ###	# ###	# ###	4 100	13 096	22 091	30 085	39 080	47 073	55 064	63 051
Alkaid	1.9	# ###	# ###	# ###	# ###	# ###	# ###	# ###	# ###	# ###	# ###	# ###	# ###	# ###	# ###	# ###	# ###	0 028	4 023	7 017
Hadar	0.9	4 195	2 190	1 185	0 180	1 176	2 171	3 166	6 162	9 158	12 154	16 151	21 149	25 147	30 146	35 145	40 146	45 147	49 150	53 155
Menkent	2.3	# ###	# ###	# ###	# ###	# ###	# ###	# ###	# ###	# ###	# ###	2 132	9 127	16 123	23 120	31 117	39 114	47 113	55 112	63 112
Arcturus	0.2	# ###	# ###	# ###	# ###	# ###	# ###	# ###	# ###	# ###	# ###	# ###	# ###	# ###	# ###	4 065	11 060	19 054	25 046	31 038
Rigil Kent.	0.1	6 198	4 194	2 190	1 185	1 180	1 175	2 170	4 166	7 162	10 158	13 154	17 151	21 149	26 147	31 146	36 146	40 146	45 148	49 151
Zuben'ubi	2.9	# ###	# ###	# ###	# ###	# ###	# ###	# ###	# ###	# ###	# ###	# ###	# ###	# ###	6 105	14 101	23 096	31 091	40 086	49 080
Kochab	2.2	# ###	# ###	# ###	# ###	# ###	# ###	# ###	# ###	# ###	# ###	# ###	# ###	# ###	# ###	# ###	# ###	# ###	# ###	# ###
Alphecca	2.3	# ###	# ###	# ###	# ###	# ###	# ###	# ###	# ###	# ###	# ###	# ###	# ###	# ###	# ###	# ###	# ###	# ###	7 054	13 048
Antares	1.2	# ###	# ###	# ###	# ###	# ###	# ###	# ###	# ###	# ###	# ###	# ###	# ###	# ###	# ###	# ###	7 117	15 112	23 108	31 104
Atria	1.9	22 202	19 200	16 197	14 194	12 191	10 188	9 184	9 181	9 177	10 174	11 170	13 167	15 164	18 161	20 159	24 158	27 156	31 156	34 156
Sabik	2.6	# ###	# ###	# ###	# ###	# ###	# ###	# ###	# ###	# ###	# ###	# ###	# ###	# ###	# ###	# ###	# ###	1 107	10 103	18 098
Shaula	1.7	13 234	6 230	# ###	# ###	# ###	# ###	# ###	# ###	# ###	# ###	# ###	# ###	# ###	# ###	# ###	2 133	8 128	15 124	22 121
Rasalhague	2.1	# ###	# ###	# ###	# ###	# ###	# ###	# ###	# ###	# ###	# ###	# ###	# ###	# ###	# ###	# ###	# ###	# ###	# ###	# ###
Eltanin	2.4	# ###	# ###	# ###	# ###	# ###	# ###	# ###	# ###	# ###	# ###	# ###	# ###	# ###	# ###	# ###	# ###	# ###	# ###	# ###
Kaus Aust.	2.0	21 242	13 238	6 234	# ###	# ###	# ###	# ###	# ###	# ###	# ###	# ###	# ###	# ###	# ###	# ###	# ###	# ###	5 127	12 123
Vega	0.1	# ###	# ###	# ###	# ###	# ###	# ###	# ###	# ###	# ###	# ###	# ###	# ###	# ###	# ###	# ###	# ###	# ###	# ###	# ###
Nunki	2.1	24 252	16 248	8 244	0 239	# ###	# ###	# ###	# ###	# ###	# ###	# ###	# ###	# ###	# ###	# ###	# ###	# ###	# ###	2 119
Altair	0.9	19 293	11 287	2 282	# ###	# ###	# ###	# ###	# ###	# ###	# ###	# ###	# ###	# ###	# ###	# ###	# ###	# ###	# ###	# ###
Peacock	2.1	44 218	39 219	34 219	28 218	23 216	18 214	13 211	9 208	5 204	2 199	# ###	# ###	# ###	# ###	# ###	# ###	1 162	4 158	8 154
Deneb	1.3	2 328	# ###	# ###	# ###	# ###	# ###	# ###	# ###	# ###	# ###	# ###	# ###	# ###	# ###	# ###	# ###	# ###	# ###	# ###
Enif	2.5	38 315	32 306	25 299	17 292	9 287	0 282	# ###	# ###	# ###	# ###	# ###	# ###	# ###	# ###	# ###	# ###	# ###	# ###	# ###
Al Na'ir	2.2	63 224	56 229	50 231	43 232	36 231	29 230	23 228	16 225	11 221	5 217	0 213	# ###	# ###	# ###	# ###	# ###	# ###	# ###	# ###
Fomalhaut	1.3	76 268	68 265	59 262	51 259	42 256	34 253	26 249	18 246	10 241	3 237	# ###	# ###	# ###	# ###	# ###	# ###	# ###	# ###	# ###
Markab	2.6	43 342	39 330	34 319	28 311	21 303	14 297	6 291	# ###	# ###	# ###	# ###	# ###	# ###	# ###	# ###	# ###	# ###	# ###	# ###

* Variable 0.1 - 1.2

SUN MOON PLANETS	Local Hour Angle Body																		
	0° Alt Az	10° Alt Az	20° Alt Az	30° Alt Az	40° Alt Az	50° Alt Az	60° Alt Az	70° Alt Az	80° Alt Az	90° Alt Az	100° Alt Az	110° Alt Az	120° Alt Az	130° Alt Az	140° Alt Az	150° Alt Az	160° Alt Az	170° Alt Az	180° Alt Az
	o o	o o	o o	o o	o o	o o	o o	o o	o o	o o	o o	o o	o o	o o	o o	o o	o o	o o	o o
Decl'n N30°	30 000	29 350	27 341	24 332	19 324	13 317	7 311	0 306	# ###	# ###	# ###	# ###	# ###	# ###	# ###	# ###	# ###	# ###	# ###
Decl'n N25°	35 000	34 349	32 339	28 329	23 321	17 313	10 307	3 301	# ###	# ###	# ###	# ###	# ###	# ###	# ###	# ###	# ###	# ###	# ###
Decl'n N20°	40 000	39 348	36 336	32 326	27 317	21 310	14 303	6 297	# ###	# ###	# ###	# ###	# ###	# ###	# ###	# ###	# ###	# ###	# ###
Decl'n N15°	45 000	44 347	41 334	37 323	31 314	24 306	17 299	9 293	1 288	# ###	# ###	# ###	# ###	# ###	# ###	# ###	# ###	# ###	# ###
Decl'n N10°	50 000	49 345	46 331	41 320	35 310	27 302	20 295	12 289	4 284	# ###	# ###	# ###	# ###	# ###	# ###	# ###	# ###	# ###	# ###
Decl'n N5°	55 000	54 343	50 328	45 315	38 306	31 297	23 291	15 285	6 279	# ###	# ###	# ###	# ###	# ###	# ###	# ###	# ###	# ###	# ###
Decl'n 0°	60 000	59 341	54 324	49 311	42 301	34 293	26 286	17 280	9 275	0 270	# ###	# ###	# ###	# ###	# ###	# ###	# ###	# ###	# ###
Decl'n S5°	65 000	63 337	59 319	52 306	45 296	37 288	28 281	20 276	11 271	2 266	# ###	# ###	# ###	# ###	# ###	# ###	# ###	# ###	# ###
Decl'n S10°	70 000	68 333	63 313	56 299	48 290	39 282	31 276	22 271	14 266	5 261	# ###	# ###	# ###	# ###	# ###	# ###	# ###	# ###	# ###
Decl'n S15°	75 000	72 326	66 305	59 292	50 283	42 277	33 271	25 266	16 262	7 257	# ###	# ###	# ###	# ###	# ###	# ###	# ###	# ###	# ###
Decl'n S20°	80 000	77 316	69 294	61 283	53 276	44 270	35 266	27 261	18 257	10 253	2 248	# ###	# ###	# ###	# ###	# ###	# ###	# ###	# ###
Decl'n S25°	85 000	80 297	72 281	63 273	54 268	46 264	37 260	29 256	20 252	12 248	4 244	# ###	# ###	# ###	# ###	# ###	# ###	# ###	# ###
Decl'n S30°	90 180	81 267	73 265	64 262	56 260	47 257	39 254	30 251	22 247	14 243	7 239	# ###	# ###	# ###	# ###	# ###	# ###	# ###	# ###

Latitude S30° Latitude S30°

STARS		Local Hour Angle Aries																		
		180°	190°	200°	210°	220°	230°	240°	250°	260°	270°	280°	290°	300°	310°	320°	330°	340°	350°	360°
Name	Mag	Alt° Az°	Alt° Az°	Alt° Az°	Alt° Az°	Alt° Az°	Alt° Az°	Alt° Az°	Alt° Az°	Alt° Az°	Alt° Az°	Alt° Az°	Alt° Az°	Alt° Az°	Alt° Az°	Alt° Az°	Alt° Az°	Alt° Az°	Alt° Az°	Alt° Az°
Alpheratz	2.2	# ####	# ####	# ####	# ####	# ####	# ####	# ####	# ####	# ####	# ####	# ####	# ####	6 051	13 045	19 038	23 030	27 022	30 012	31 002
Ankaa	2.4	# ####	# ####	# ####	# ####	# ####	# ####	# ####	3 139	9 134	15 130	22 127	29 125	36 123	44 122	51 121	58 123	65 127	72 137	77 159
Schedah	2.5	# ####	# ####	# ####	# ####	# ####	# ####	# ####	# ####	# ####	# ####	# ####	# ####	# ####	# ####	# ####	# ####	# ####	2 011	3 006
Diphda	2.2	# ####	# ####	# ####	# ####	# ####	# ####	# ####	# ####	# ####	# ####	8 106	17 102	25 097	34 092	42 087	51 082	59 074	68 062	74 042
Achernar	0.6	# ####	# ####	# ####	# ####	# ####	# ####	2 162	5 157	9 153	13 150	18 147	23 144	28 142	33 142	39 141	44 142	49 145	54 149	58 155
Hamal	2.2	# ####	# ####	# ####	# ####	# ####	# ####	# ####	# ####	# ####	# ####	# ####	# ####	# ####	# ####	3 061	10 055	17 049	23 042	28 033
Polaris	2.1	# ####	# ####	# ####	# ####	# ####	# ####	# ####	# ####	# ####	# ####	# ####	# ####	# ####	# ####	# ####	# ####	# ####	# ####	# ####
Acamar	3.1	# ####	# ####	# ####	# ####	# ####	# ####	# ####	# ####	# ####	# ####	# ####	3 136	9 132	16 128	23 125	30 122	37 120	45 119	53 118
Menkar	2.8	# ####	# ####	# ####	# ####	# ####	# ####	# ####	# ####	# ####	# ####	# ####	# ####	# ####	# ####	2 084	10 079	19 074	27 067	35 060
Mirfak	1.9	# ####	# ####	# ####	# ####	# ####	# ####	# ####	# ####	# ####	# ####	# ####	# ####	# ####	# ####	# ####	# ####	# ####	# ####	# ####
Aldebaran	1.1	# ####	# ####	# ####	# ####	# ####	# ####	# ####	# ####	# ####	# ####	# ####	# ####	# ####	# ####	# ####	# ####	# ####	1 070	9 065
Rigel	0.3	# ####	# ####	# ####	# ####	# ####	# ####	# ####	# ####	# ####	# ####	# ####	# ####	# ####	# ####	# ####	# ####	# ####	5 096	14 092
Capella	0.2	# ####	# ####	# ####	# ####	# ####	# ####	# ####	# ####	# ####	# ####	# ####	# ####	# ####	# ####	# ####	# ####	# ####	# ####	# ####
Bellatrix	1.7	# ####	# ####	# ####	# ####	# ####	# ####	# ####	# ####	# ####	# ####	# ####	# ####	# ####	# ####	# ####	# ####	# ####	# ####	4 080
Elnath	1.8	# ####	# ####	# ####	# ####	# ####	# ####	# ####	# ####	# ####	# ####	# ####	# ####	# ####	# ####	# ####	# ####	# ####	# ####	# ####
Alnilam	1.8	# ####	# ####	# ####	# ####	# ####	# ####	# ####	# ####	# ####	# ####	# ####	# ####	# ####	# ####	# ####	# ####	# ####	# ####	6 088
Betelgeuse	*	# ####	# ####	# ####	# ####	# ####	# ####	# ####	# ####	# ####	# ####	# ####	# ####	# ####	# ####	# ####	# ####	# ####	# ####	# ####
Canopus	-0.9	27 223	21 220	16 218	11 214	6 210	2 206	# ####	# ####	# ####	# ####	# ####	# ####	# ####	# ####	1 155	5 151	10 146	15 143	20 140
Sirius	-1.6	18 261	9 256	1 251	# ####	# ####	# ####	# ####	# ####	# ####	# ####	# ####	# ####	# ####	# ####	# ####	# ####	# ####	# ####	# ####
Adhara	1.6	26 250	18 246	10 242	2 238	# ####	# ####	# ####	# ####	# ####	# ####	# ####	# ####	# ####	# ####	# ####	# ####	# ####	# ####	3 122
Procyon	0.5	18 288	10 282	2 277	# ####	# ####	# ####	# ####	# ####	# ####	# ####	# ####	# ####	# ####	# ####	# ####	# ####	# ####	# ####	# ####
Pollux	1.2	6 307	# ####	# ####	# ####	# ####	# ####	# ####	# ####	# ####	# ####	# ####	# ####	# ####	# ####	# ####	# ####	# ####	# ####	# ####
Avior	1.7	43 215	38 216	33 216	28 215	23 213	19 211	14 209	11 205	7 201	4 197	2 193	0 188	# ####	# ####	0 173	2 168	4 163	7 159	10 155
Suhail	2.2	53 236	46 237	39 236	32 235	25 233	18 230	12 226	6 222	0 218	# ####	# ####	# ####	# ####	# ####	# ####	# ####	# ####	# ####	# ####
Miaplacidus	1.8	44 199	41 201	38 203	34 203	31 204	27 203	24 202	21 200	18 198	16 196	13 193	12 190	11 186	10 183	10 179	10 176	11 172	12 169	14 166
Alphard	2.2	49 293	40 285	32 279	23 273	15 268	6 263	# ####	# ####	# ####	# ####	# ####	# ####	# ####	# ####	# ####	# ####	# ####	# ####	# ####
Regulus	1.3	40 323	34 313	28 305	20 298	12 292	4 286	# ####	# ####	# ####	# ####	# ####	# ####	# ####	# ####	# ####	# ####	# ####	# ####	# ####
Dubhe	2.0	# ####	# ####	# ####	# ####	# ####	# ####	# ####	# ####	# ####	# ####	# ####	# ####	# ####	# ####	# ####	# ####	# ####	# ####	# ####
Denebola	2.2	45 356	44 343	40 331	35 320	29 311	22 304	15 297	7 291	# ####	# ####	# ####	# ####	# ####	# ####	# ####	# ####	# ####	# ####	# ####
Gienah	2.8	77 017	76 335	71 307	63 292	55 283	46 276	38 270	29 266	20 261	12 257	4 252	# ####	# ####	# ####	# ####	# ####	# ####	# ####	# ####
Acrux	1.1	57 175	57 183	56 191	54 198	51 203	47 207	43 210	38 211	34 211	29 211	25 210	21 208	17 206	13 203	10 200	8 196	5 192	4 187	3 183
Gacrux	1.6	62 171	63 183	62 194	59 203	55 210	50 215	45 217	40 219	34 219	29 218	24 216	19 214	14 211	10 208	6 204	3 199	0 195	# ####	# ####
Alioth	1.7	3 008	4 002	4 356	3 351	1 346	# ####	# ####	# ####	# ####	# ####	# ####	# ####	# ####	# ####	# ####	# ####	# ####	# ####	# ####
Spica	1.2	63 051	68 032	71 004	69 335	64 313	57 299	49 289	41 282	33 276	24 271	15 266	7 261	# ####	# ####	# ####	# ####	# ####	# ####	# ####
Alkaid	1.9	7 017	9 011	10 005	11 358	10 351	8 345	5 339	2 334	# ####	# ####	# ####	# ####	# ####	# ####	# ####	# ####	# ####	# ####	# ####
Hadar	0.9	53 155	57 161	59 170	60 179	59 189	57 197	54 204	50 209	46 212	41 214	36 215	31 215	26 213	22 212	17 209	13 206	10 203	6 199	4 195
Menkent	2.3	63 112	71 115	78 126	83 168	81 225	73 243	66 247	58 248	49 248	42 246	34 244	26 241	18 238	11 234	4 230	# ####	# ####	# ####	# ####
Arcturus	0.2	31 038	36 028	39 017	41 005	40 352	38 340	35 330	30 320	24 312	17 305	10 299	2 293	# ####	# ####	# ####	# ####	# ####	# ####	# ####
Rigil Kent.	0.1	49 151	53 156	56 163	58 171	59 180	58 189	56 198	53 204	49 209	45 212	40 214	35 214	31 214	26 213	21 211	17 209	13 206	9 202	6 198
Zuben'ubi	2.9	49 080	57 072	65 061	72 043	76 011	75 333	69 308	61 293	53 284	45 277	36 271	27 267	19 262	10 257	2 253	# ####	# ####	# ####	# ####
Kochab	2.2	# ####	# ####	# ####	# ####	# ####	# ####	# ####	# ####	# ####	# ####	# ####	# ####	# ####	# ####	# ####	# ####	# ####	# ####	# ####
Alphecca	2.3	13 048	20 041	25 033	29 024	32 014	33 004	33 353	31 343	28 333	23 325	18 317	12 311	5 305	# ####	# ####	# ####	# ####	# ####	# ####
Antares	1.2	31 104	40 101	48 097	57 093	66 088	74 081	83 063	86 326	78 285	70 275	61 269	52 265	44 261	35 257	27 254	19 250	11 246	3 241	# ####
Atria	1.9	34 156	38 156	41 158	44 160	47 164	49 168	50 173	51 179	51 184	50 190	48 194	45 198	42 201	39 203	36 204	32 204	29 204	25 203	22 202
Sabik	2.6	18 098	27 093	36 088	44 083	53 076	61 067	68 052	74 028	76 351	72 319	65 300	57 288	49 281	40 274	31 269	23 264	14 260	6 255	# ####
Shaula	1.7	22 121	30 118	38 116	46 114	53 113	61 113	69 116	77 126	82 159	81 216	74 238	67 245	59 247	51 247	43 246	35 244	28 241	20 238	13 234
Rasalhague	2.1	# ####	7 071	15 065	23 059	30 051	36 042	42 032	45 019	47 005	47 351	45 337	40 325	35 315	28 307	21 300	13 293	5 288	# ####	# ####
Eltanin	2.4	# ####	# ####	# ####	# ####	# ####	2 023	5 018	7 012	8 006	9 359	8 353	6 347	4 341	1 336	# ####	# ####	# ####	# ####	# ####
Kaus Aust.	2.0	12 123	19 119	27 116	35 113	43 111	51 109	59 108	68 108	76 112	83 132	84 216	77 246	69 252	61 252	53 251	45 250	37 247	29 245	21 242
Vega	0.1	# ####	# ####	# ####	# ####	2 042	7 037	12 030	16 023	19 016	21 008	21 359	20 351	19 343	15 336	11 329	7 323	1 317	# ####	# ####
Nunki	2.1	2 119	10 115	18 111	26 107	34 103	43 099	51 096	60 091	69 086	77 076	85 043	83 303	75 281	67 273	58 268	49 264	41 260	32 256	24 252
Altair	0.9	# ####	# ####	# ####	# ####	6 076	14 071	22 065	30 057	37 049	43 039	48 026	50 012	51 356	49 341	46 328	40 316	34 307	27 299	19 293
Peacock	2.1	8 154	12 150	16 147	21 144	27 142	32 141	37 141	43 141	48 143	53 147	58 153	61 161	63 172	63 184	62 196	59 205	54 211	50 216	44 218
Deneb	1.3	# ####	# ####	# ####	# ####	# ####	# ####	# ####	# ####	2 033	6 027	10 021	12 015	14 008	15 000	14 353	13 346	10 339	7 333	2 328
Enif	2.5	# ####	# ####	# ####	# ####	# ####	# ####	# ####	7 074	15 069	23 063	30 055	37 047	43 036	47 024	50 009	50 354	48 339	44 326	38 315
Al Na'ir	2.2	# ####	# ####	# ####	3 145	8 140	14 137	20 133	27 131	33 129	40 128	47 128	54 130	60 133	66 141	71 155	73 175	72 198	68 214	63 224
Fomalhaut	1.3	# ####	# ####	# ####	# ####	# ####	# ####	3 122	11 118	19 114	27 110	35 107	43 104	52 101	60 098	69 095	77 092	86 085	85 273	76 268
Markab	2.6	# ####	# ####	# ####	# ####	# ####	# ####	# ####	# ####	# ####	4 070	12 064	20 058	27 051	33 043	38 033	42 021	44 008	45 355	43 342

* Variable 0.1 - 1.2

SUN MOON PLANETS	Local Hour Angle Body																		
	180°	190°	200°	210°	220°	230°	240°	250°	260°	270°	280°	290°	300°	310°	320°	330°	340°	350°	360°
	Alt° Az°	Alt° Az°	Alt° Az°	Alt° Az°	Alt° Az°	Alt° Az°	Alt° Az°	Alt° Az°	Alt° Az°	Alt° Az°	Alt° Az°	Alt° Az°	Alt° Az°	Alt° Az°	Alt° Az°	Alt° Az°	Alt° Az°	Alt° Az°	Alt° Az°
Decl'n N30°	# ####	# ####	# ####	# ####	# ####	# ####	# ####	# ####	# ####	# ####	# ####	0 054	7 049	13 043	19 036	24 028	27 019	29 010	30 000
Decl'n N25°	# ####	# ####	# ####	# ####	# ####	# ####	# ####	# ####	# ####	# ####	# ####	3 059	10 053	17 047	23 039	28 031	32 021	34 011	35 000
Decl'n N20°	# ####	# ####	# ####	# ####	# ####	# ####	# ####	# ####	# ####	# ####	# ####	6 063	14 057	21 050	27 043	32 034	36 024	39 012	40 000
Decl'n N15°	# ####	# ####	# ####	# ####	# ####	# ####	# ####	# ####	# ####	# ####	1 072	9 067	17 061	24 054	31 046	37 037	41 026	44 013	45 000
Decl'n N10°	# ####	# ####	# ####	# ####	# ####	# ####	# ####	# ####	# ####	# ####	4 076	12 071	20 065	27 058	35 050	41 040	46 029	49 015	50 000
Decl'n N5°	# ####	# ####	# ####	# ####	# ####	# ####	# ####	# ####	# ####	# ####	6 081	15 075	23 069	31 063	38 054	45 045	50 032	54 017	55 000
Decl'n 0°	# ####	# ####	# ####	# ####	# ####	# ####	# ####	# ####	# ####	# ####	9 085	17 080	26 074	34 067	42 059	49 049	54 036	59 019	60 000
Decl'n S5°	# ####	# ####	# ####	# ####	# ####	# ####	# ####	# ####	# ####	2 094	11 089	20 084	28 079	37 072	45 064	52 054	59 041	63 023	65 000
Decl'n S10°	# ####	# ####	# ####	# ####	# ####	# ####	# ####	# ####	# ####	5 099	14 094	22 089	31 084	39 078	48 070	56 061	63 047	68 027	70 000
Decl'n S15°	# ####	# ####	# ####	# ####	# ####	# ####	# ####	# ####	# ####	7 103	16 098	25 094	33 089	42 083	50 077	59 068	66 055	72 034	75 000
Decl'n S20°	# ####	# ####	# ####	# ####	# ####	# ####	# ####	# ####	2 112	10 107	18 103	27 099	35 094	44 090	53 084	61 077	69 066	77 044	80 000
Decl'n S25°	# ####	# ####	# ####	# ####	# ####	# ####	# ####	# ####	4 116	12 112	20 108	29 104	37 100	46 096	54 092	63 087	72 079	80 063	85 000
Decl'n S30°	# ####	# ####	# ####	# ####	# ####	# ####	# ####	# ####	7 121	14 117	22 113	30 109	39 106	47 103	56 100	64 098	73 095	81 093	90 103

PREDICTION & IDENTIFICATION

Latitude S40° Latitude S40°

STARS — Local Hour Angle Aries

Name	Mag	0°	10°	20°	30°	40°	50°	60°	70°	80°	90°	100°	110°	120°	130°	140°	150°	160°	170°	180°
		Alt Az	Alt Az	Alt Az	Alt Az	Alt Az	Alt Az	Alt Az	Alt Az	Alt Az	Alt Az	Alt Az	Alt Az	Alt Az	Alt Az	Alt Az	Alt Az	Alt Az	Alt Az	Alt Az
		o o	o o	o o	o o	o o	o o	o o	o o	o o	o o	o o	o o	o o	o o	o o	o o	o o	o o	o o
Alpheratz	2.2	21 002	21 353	19 344	16 335	12 327	8 319	2 312	# ###	# ###	# ###	# ###	# ###	# ###	# ###	# ###	# ###	# ###	# ###	# ###
Ankaa	2.4	85 117	87 227	80 253	72 255	65 254	58 251	50 249	43 245	36 242	30 238	23 234	18 229	12 224	7 218	2 213	# ###	# ###	# ###	# ###
Schedah	2.5	# ###	# ###	# ###	# ###	# ###	# ###	# ###	# ###	# ###	# ###	# ###	# ###	# ###	# ###	# ###	# ###	# ###	# ###	# ###
Diphda	2.2	66 026	68 002	67 338	62 318	57 303	50 292	42 283	35 275	27 269	20 263	12 257	5 250	# ###	# ###	# ###	# ###	# ###	# ###	# ###
Achernar	0.6	67 146	70 156	73 172	72 190	70 205	66 215	61 221	56 224	51 225	45 225	40 223	35 221	30 218	25 215	21 212	17 207	14 203	11 198	9 193
Hamal	2.2	20 031	23 022	26 012	27 002	26 352	24 342	21 332	17 324	12 316	7 308	0 302	# ###	# ###	# ###	# ###	# ###	# ###	# ###	# ###
Polaris	2.1	# ###	# ###	# ###	# ###	# ###	# ###	# ###	# ###	# ###	# ###	# ###	# ###	# ###	# ###	# ###	# ###	# ###	# ###	# ###
Acamar	3.1	56 105	64 102	71 099	79 096	87 096	86 264	78 264	71 261	63 258	56 254	48 251	41 247	34 243	28 239	21 234	15 230	9 224	4 219	# ###
Menkar	2.8	29 055	35 045	40 034	44 022	46 008	46 354	44 340	41 327	36 316	30 306	23 298	16 290	9 283	2 277	# ###	# ###	# ###	# ###	# ###
Mirfak	1.9	# ###	# ###	# ###	# ###	# ###	0 001	# ###	# ###	# ###	# ###	# ###	# ###	# ###	# ###	# ###	# ###	# ###	# ###	# ###
Aldebaran	1.1	5 064	11 057	17 049	23 041	27 032	31 021	33 010	33 359	33 347	30 337	27 326	22 317	16 309	10 302	3 295	# ###	# ###	# ###	# ###
Rigel	0.3	14 089	22 082	29 075	36 067	43 058	49 047	54 033	57 016	58 357	57 339	53 323	48 310	41 299	34 290	27 283	20 276	12 269	4 263	# ###
Capella	0.2	# ###	# ###	# ###	# ###	# ###	0 020	2 013	4 006	4 359	3 352	2 346	# ###	# ###	# ###	# ###	# ###	# ###	# ###	# ###
Bellatrix	1.7	3 080	10 073	17 066	24 058	30 049	35 039	40 028	42 015	44 002	43 348	41 335	37 323	32 313	26 304	19 296	12 289	4 282	# ###	# ###
Elnath	1.8	# ###	# ###	1 051	6 044	11 036	15 028	19 020	21 011	21 001	21 352	19 343	16 334	13 326	8 318	3 312	# ###	# ###	# ###	# ###
Alnilam	1.8	5 087	13 080	21 073	28 066	34 057	41 047	46 035	49 022	51 006	51 350	49 335	45 322	39 310	33 301	26 292	19 285	11 278	4 272	# ###
Betelgeuse	*	# ###	4 077	11 070	18 063	25 055	31 046	36 036	40 024	42 012	43 358	41 345	39 333	35 321	29 312	23 303	16 295	9 288	2 281	# ###
Canopus	-0.9	28 137	33 134	39 131	44 129	50 128	57 128	62 130	68 134	73 145	77 164	77 191	74 212	69 224	64 230	58 232	52 232	46 231	40 229	34 227
Sirius	-1.6	2 110	10 104	17 098	25 091	33 085	40 078	47 069	54 058	60 045	65 026	67 003	66 339	62 320	56 305	49 293	42 284	34 277	27 270	19 264
Adhara	1.6	8 121	15 116	22 110	29 105	37 099	44 094	52 087	60 080	67 069	74 052	78 021	78 337	73 306	66 290	59 280	51 272	44 266	36 260	29 255
Procyon	0.5	# ###	# ###	# ###	1 083	8 076	15 069	22 062	29 053	35 044	39 033	43 020	45 007	45 353	43 339	39 327	34 316	29 306	22 298	15 291
Pollux	1.2	# ###	# ###	# ###	# ###	# ###	# ###	4 047	9 040	14 033	18 024	20 015	22 006	22 357	21 347	18 338	15 330	11 322	6 314	# ###
Avior	1.7	19 154	23 150	27 147	31 144	36 141	41 140	46 139	51 139	56 140	60 143	65 149	68 158	70 172	70 187	68 200	65 210	61 216	56 220	51 221
Suhail	2.2	2 150	6 144	11 139	16 134	22 129	28 125	35 121	41 117	48 114	55 111	62 109	70 109	77 111	84 126	86 212	80 246	73 251	65 251	58 249
Miaplacidus	1.8	24 165	26 162	28 160	31 157	34 155	38 154	41 153	45 153	48 154	51 156	54 158	57 163	59 168	60 174	60 181	60 188	58 194	56 199	53 203
Alphard	2.2	# ###	# ###	# ###	# ###	# ###	4 098	12 092	19 085	27 078	34 070	41 062	48 051	53 038	57 022	59 004	58 345	55 328	50 314	44 302
Regulus	1.3	# ###	# ###	# ###	# ###	# ###	# ###	# ###	# ###	6 069	13 062	19 055	25 046	30 037	34 026	37 015	38 003	38 350	35 338	32 327
Dubhe	2.0	# ###	# ###	# ###	# ###	# ###	# ###	# ###	# ###	# ###	# ###	# ###	# ###	# ###	# ###	# ###	# ###	# ###	# ###	# ###
Denebola	2.2	# ###	# ###	# ###	# ###	# ###	# ###	# ###	# ###	# ###	# ###	0 071	7 064	14 057	20 049	25 040	30 031	33 020	35 009	35 357
Gienah	2.8	# ###	# ###	# ###	# ###	# ###	# ###	# ###	# ###	1 112	8 106	16 100	23 094	31 087	39 080	46 072	53 062	59 050	65 032	67 010
Acrux	1.1	13 183	13 178	14 174	15 169	16 165	19 161	21 157	25 154	28 151	32 148	36 146	41 144	45 144	50 144	54 146	58 149	62 154	65 162	67 172
Gacrux	1.6	7 184	7 179	8 173	9 168	11 163	13 158	17 153	20 149	24 145	29 142	34 139	39 137	44 135	50 135	55 135	60 138	65 143	69 152	72 166
Alioth	1.7	# ###	# ###	# ###	# ###	# ###	# ###	# ###	# ###	# ###	# ###	# ###	# ###	# ###	# ###	# ###	# ###	# ###	# ###	# ###
Spica	1.2	# ###	# ###	# ###	# ###	# ###	# ###	# ###	# ###	# ###	# ###	# ###	6 099	14 093	21 087	29 080	36 072	44 063	50 053	56 039
Alkaid	1.9	# ###	# ###	# ###	# ###	# ###	# ###	# ###	# ###	# ###	# ###	# ###	# ###	# ###	# ###	# ###	# ###	# ###	# ###	# ###
Hadar	0.9	14 195	12 190	11 185	10 180	11 175	12 171	13 166	15 161	18 157	21 153	25 149	29 146	34 144	38 142	43 140	48 140	53 141	58 143	62 147
Menkent	2.3	# ###	# ###	# ###	# ###	# ###	# ###	# ###	# ###	# ###	3 137	9 131	15 125	21 120	28 115	35 111	42 106	50 102	57 097	65 092
Arcturus	0.2	# ###	# ###	# ###	# ###	# ###	# ###	# ###	# ###	# ###	# ###	# ###	# ###	# ###	# ###	# ###	6 059	12 051	18 044	23 035
Rigil Kent.	0.1	16 199	14 194	12 190	11 185	11 180	11 175	12 170	14 165	16 161	19 157	22 153	26 149	30 146	34 144	39 142	44 141	48 141	53 141	58 144
Zuben'ubi	2.9	# ###	# ###	# ###	# ###	# ###	# ###	# ###	# ###	# ###	# ###	# ###	# ###	1 110	8 104	16 098	23 092	31 085	39 078	46 070
Kochab	2.2	# ###	# ###	# ###	# ###	# ###	# ###	# ###	# ###	# ###	# ###	# ###	# ###	# ###	# ###	# ###	# ###	# ###	# ###	# ###
Alphecca	2.3	# ###	# ###	# ###	# ###	# ###	# ###	# ###	# ###	# ###	# ###	# ###	# ###	# ###	# ###	# ###	# ###	# ###	1 053	7 046
Antares	1.2	1 236	# ###	# ###	# ###	# ###	# ###	# ###	# ###	# ###	# ###	# ###	# ###	# ###	# ###	5 121	11 115	19 109	26 104	33 098
Atria	1.9	31 203	28 201	26 198	23 195	22 192	20 188	19 185	19 181	19 177	20 173	21 170	23 166	25 163	27 160	30 158	33 155	36 154	40 153	43 152
Sabik	2.6	1 250	# ###	# ###	# ###	# ###	# ###	# ###	# ###	# ###	# ###	# ###	# ###	# ###	# ###	# ###	# ###	4 107	12 101	19 095
Shaula	1.7	19 237	12 231	7 226	1 220	# ###	# ###	# ###	# ###	# ###	# ###	# ###	# ###	# ###	# ###	3 138	8 132	14 127	21 122	27 117
Rasalhague	2.1	# ###	# ###	# ###	# ###	# ###	# ###	# ###	# ###	# ###	# ###	# ###	# ###	# ###	# ###	# ###	# ###	# ###	# ###	# ###
Eltanin	2.4	# ###	# ###	# ###	# ###	# ###	# ###	# ###	# ###	# ###	# ###	# ###	# ###	# ###	# ###	# ###	# ###	# ###	# ###	# ###
Kaus Aust.	2.0	25 245	19 240	12 235	6 229	1 223	# ###	# ###	# ###	# ###	# ###	# ###	# ###	# ###	# ###	# ###	# ###	5 132	11 126	17 121
Vega	0.1	# ###	# ###	# ###	# ###	# ###	# ###	# ###	# ###	# ###	# ###	# ###	# ###	# ###	# ###	# ###	# ###	# ###	# ###	# ###
Nunki	2.1	27 257	19 251	12 246	5 240	# ###	# ###	# ###	# ###	# ###	# ###	# ###	# ###	# ###	# ###	# ###	# ###	# ###	# ###	# ###
Altair	0.9	15 295	8 288	0 282	# ###	# ###	# ###	# ###	# ###	# ###	# ###	# ###	# ###	# ###	# ###	# ###	# ###	# ###	0 125	7 119
Peacock	2.1	52 226	46 225	41 224	36 222	31 220	26 216	22 213	18 209	14 204	11 199	9 194	8 189	7 184	7 178	7 173	9 167	11 162	13 157	17 153
Deneb	1.3	# ###	# ###	# ###	# ###	# ###	# ###	# ###	# ###	# ###	# ###	# ###	# ###	# ###	# ###	# ###	# ###	# ###	# ###	# ###
Enif	2.5	31 320	26 311	19 302	13 295	6 288	# ###	# ###	# ###	# ###	# ###	# ###	# ###	# ###	# ###	# ###	# ###	# ###	# ###	# ###
Al Na'ir	2.2	69 242	62 243	55 242	48 241	42 238	35 235	29 231	23 227	18 223	13 218	9 213	5 207	2 201	# ###	# ###	# ###	# ###	# ###	0 161
Fomalhaut	1.3	74 304	67 288	59 279	52 271	44 265	36 259	29 254	22 249	15 243	8 238	2 232	# ###	# ###	# ###	# ###	# ###	# ###	# ###	# ###
Markab	2.6	33 344	31 333	26 323	21 314	16 306	9 299	2 292	# ###	# ###	# ###	# ###	# ###	# ###	# ###	# ###	# ###	# ###	# ###	# ###

* Variable 0.1 - 1.2

SUN MOON PLANETS — Local Hour Angle Body

	0°	10°	20°	30°	40°	50°	60°	70°	80°	90°	100°	110°	120°	130°	140°	150°	160°	170°	180°
	Alt Az	Alt Az	Alt Az	Alt Az	Alt Az	Alt Az	Alt Az	Alt Az	Alt Az	Alt Az	Alt Az	Alt Az	Alt Az	Alt Az	Alt Az	Alt Az	Alt Az	Alt Az	Alt Az
	o o	o o	o o	o o	o o	o o	o o	o o	o o	o o	o o	o o	o o	o o	o o	o o	o o	o o	o o
Decl'n N30°	20 000	19 351	18 342	15 333	11 325	6 318	1 311	# ###	# ###	# ###	# ###	# ###	# ###	# ###	# ###	# ###	# ###	# ###	# ###
Decl'n N25°	25 000	24 350	22 340	19 331	15 323	10 315	4 308	# ###	# ###	# ###	# ###	# ###	# ###	# ###	# ###	# ###	# ###	# ###	# ###
Decl'n N20°	30 000	29 349	27 339	24 329	19 320	14 312	8 305	2 298	# ###	# ###	# ###	# ###	# ###	# ###	# ###	# ###	# ###	# ###	# ###
Decl'n N15°	35 000	34 348	32 337	28 327	24 317	18 309	12 301	5 294	# ###	# ###	# ###	# ###	# ###	# ###	# ###	# ###	# ###	# ###	# ###
Decl'n N10°	40 000	39 347	37 335	33 324	28 314	22 306	15 298	8 291	1 284	# ###	# ###	# ###	# ###	# ###	# ###	# ###	# ###	# ###	# ###
Decl'n N5°	45 000	44 346	41 333	37 321	32 311	26 302	19 294	12 287	4 280	# ###	# ###	# ###	# ###	# ###	# ###	# ###	# ###	# ###	# ###
Decl'n 0°	50 000	49 345	46 330	42 318	36 307	29 298	23 290	15 283	8 276	0 270	# ###	# ###	# ###	# ###	# ###	# ###	# ###	# ###	# ###
Decl'n S5°	55 000	54 343	51 328	46 314	40 303	33 294	26 286	18 279	11 273	3 266	# ###	# ###	# ###	# ###	# ###	# ###	# ###	# ###	# ###
Decl'n S10°	60 000	59 341	55 324	50 310	44 299	37 290	29 282	22 275	14 269	6 262	# ###	# ###	# ###	# ###	# ###	# ###	# ###	# ###	# ###
Decl'n S15°	65 000	64 338	60 319	54 305	47 294	40 285	32 278	25 271	17 265	10 258	2 252	# ###	# ###	# ###	# ###	# ###	# ###	# ###	# ###
Decl'n S20°	70 000	68 334	64 314	57 299	50 288	43 280	35 273	28 266	20 260	13 254	5 248	# ###	# ###	# ###	# ###	# ###	# ###	# ###	# ###
Decl'n S25°	75 000	73 328	68 306	61 292	53 282	46 274	38 268	31 262	23 256	16 250	9 245	2 238	# ###	# ###	# ###	# ###	# ###	# ###	# ###
Decl'n S30°	80 000	77 318	71 295	64 283	56 274	48 268	41 262	33 257	26 251	19 246	12 241	5 235	# ###	# ###	# ###	# ###	# ###	# ###	# ###

PREDICTION & IDENTIFICATION

Latitude S40°

Latitude S40°

STARS		Local Hour Angle Aries																		
		180°	190°	200°	210°	220°	230°	240°	250°	260°	270°	280°	290°	300°	310°	320°	330°	340°	350°	360°
Name	Mag	Alt Az	Alt Az	Alt Az	Alt Az	Alt Az	Alt Az	Alt Az	Alt Az	Alt Az	Alt Az	Alt Az	Alt Az	Alt Az	Alt Az	Alt Az	Alt Az	Alt Az	Alt Az	Alt Az
		° °	° °	° °	° °	° °	° °	° °	° °	° °	° °	° °	° °	° °	° °	° °	° °	° °	° °	° °
Alpheratz	2.2	# ####	# ####	# ####	# ####	# ####	# ####	# ####	# ####	# ####	# ####	# ####	# ####	0 **051**	6 **044**	11 **037**	15 **029**	18 **020**	20 **011**	21 **002**
Ankaa	2.4	# ####	# ####	# ####	# ####	# ####	1 **149**	5 **143**	10 **138**	16 **133**	22 **128**	28 **123**	34 **119**	41 **116**	48 **112**	55 **109**	63 **107**	70 **105**	77 **106**	85 **117**
Schedah	2.5	# ####	# ####	# ####	# ####	# ####	# ####	# ####	# ####	# ####	# ####	# ####	# ####	# ####	# ####	# ####	# ####	# ####	# ####	# ####
Diphda	2.2	# ####	# ####	# ####	# ####	# ####	# ####	# ####	# ####	# ####	3 **111**	11 **105**	18 **098**	26 **092**	34 **086**	41 **079**	49 **070**	55 **059**	62 **045**	66 **026**
Achernar	0.6	9 **193**	8 **188**	7 **182**	7 **177**	8 **172**	10 **166**	12 **161**	14 **156**	18 **152**	22 **148**	26 **144**	31 **141**	36 **139**	41 **137**	46 **135**	51 **135**	57 **136**	62 **139**	67 **146**
Hamal	2.2	# ####	# ####	# ####	# ####	# ####	# ####	# ####	# ####	# ####	# ####	# ####	# ####	# ####	# ####	# ####	4 **054**	10 **047**	16 **039**	20 **031**
Polaris	2.1	# ####	# ####	# ####	# ####	# ####	# ####	# ####	# ####	# ####	# ####	# ####	# ####	# ####	# ####	# ####	# ####	# ####	# ####	# ####
Acamar	3.1	# ####	# ####	# ####	# ####	# ####	# ####	# ####	# ####	# ####	0 **147**	5 **141**	10 **135**	16 **130**	22 **125**	28 **121**	35 **116**	42 **112**	49 **109**	56 **105**
Menkar	2.8	# ####	# ####	# ####	# ####	# ####	# ####	# ####	# ####	# ####	# ####	# ####	# ####	# ####	# ####	1 **084**	8 **077**	16 **071**	23 **063**	29 **055**
Mirfak	1.9	# ####	# ####	# ####	# ####	# ####	# ####	# ####	# ####	# ####	# ####	# ####	# ####	# ####	# ####	# ####	# ####	# ####	# ####	# ####
Aldebaran	1.1	# ####	# ####	# ####	# ####	# ####	# ####	# ####	# ####	# ####	# ####	# ####	# ####	# ####	# ####	# ####	# ####	# ####	# ####	5 **064**
Rigel	0.3	# ####	# ####	# ####	# ####	# ####	# ####	# ####	# ####	# ####	# ####	# ####	# ####	# ####	# ####	# ####	# ####	# ####	6 **095**	14 **089**
Capella	0.2	# ####	# ####	# ####	# ####	# ####	# ####	# ####	# ####	# ####	# ####	# ####	# ####	# ####	# ####	# ####	# ####	# ####	# ####	# ####
Bellatrix	1.7	# ####	# ####	# ####	# ####	# ####	# ####	# ####	# ####	# ####	# ####	# ####	# ####	# ####	# ####	# ####	# ####	# ####	# ####	3 **080**
Elnath	1.8	# ####	# ####	# ####	# ####	# ####	# ####	# ####	# ####	# ####	# ####	# ####	# ####	# ####	# ####	# ####	# ####	# ####	# ####	# ####
Alnilam	1.8	# ####	# ####	# ####	# ####	# ####	# ####	# ####	# ####	# ####	# ####	# ####	# ####	# ####	# ####	# ####	# ####	# ####	# ####	5 **087**
Betelgeuse	*	# ####	# ####	# ####	# ####	# ####	# ####	# ####	# ####	# ####	# ####	# ####	# ####	# ####	# ####	# ####	# ####	# ####	# ####	# ####
Canopus	-0.9	34 **227**	29 **224**	24 **220**	19 **216**	15 **211**	11 **206**	8 **201**	5 **195**	4 **190**	3 **184**	3 **178**	3 **172**	5 **166**	7 **160**	10 **155**	14 **150**	18 **145**	23 **141**	28 **137**
Sirius	-1.6	19 **264**	12 **258**	4 **252**	# ####	# ####	# ####	# ####	# ####	# ####	# ####	# ####	# ####	# ####	# ####	# ####	# ####	# ####	# ####	2 **110**
Adhara	1.6	29 **255**	21 **250**	14 **244**	8 **238**	1 **232**	# ####	# ####	# ####	# ####	# ####	# ####	# ####	# ####	# ####	# ####	# ####	# ####	2 **127**	8 **121**
Procyon	0.5	15 **291**	8 **284**	0 **277**	# ####	# ####	# ####	# ####	# ####	# ####	# ####	# ####	# ####	# ####	# ####	# ####	# ####	# ####	# ####	# ####
Pollux	1.2	# ####	# ####	# ####	# ####	# ####	# ####	# ####	# ####	# ####	# ####	# ####	# ####	# ####	# ####	# ####	# ####	# ####	# ####	# ####
Avior	1.7	51 **221**	46 **221**	41 **220**	36 **219**	32 **216**	27 **214**	23 **210**	20 **206**	16 **202**	14 **198**	12 **193**	10 **188**	10 **183**	10 **178**	10 **173**	12 **168**	13 **163**	16 **158**	19 **154**
Suhail	2.2	58 **249**	51 **247**	44 **244**	37 **241**	31 **237**	24 **233**	18 **228**	13 **223**	8 **218**	4 **212**	# ####	# ####	# ####	# ####	# ####	# ####	# ####	# ####	2 **150**
Miaplacidus	1.8	53 **203**	50 **205**	47 **206**	43 **207**	40 **207**	37 **206**	33 **204**	30 **202**	28 **199**	25 **197**	23 **194**	22 **190**	21 **187**	20 **183**	20 **179**	20 **176**	21 **172**	22 **169**	24 **165**
Alphard	2.2	44 **302**	37 **293**	30 **285**	22 **278**	15 **271**	7 **265**	# ####	# ####	# ####	# ####	# ####	# ####	# ####	# ####	# ####	# ####	# ####	# ####	# ####
Regulus	1.3	32 **327**	27 **317**	22 **309**	15 **301**	9 **294**	1 **287**	# ####	# ####	# ####	# ####	# ####	# ####	# ####	# ####	# ####	# ####	# ####	# ####	# ####
Dubhe	2.0	# ####	# ####	# ####	# ####	# ####	# ####	# ####	# ####	# ####	# ####	# ####	# ####	# ####	# ####	# ####	# ####	# ####	# ####	# ####
Denebola	2.2	35 **357**	34 **345**	31 **334**	28 **324**	23 **315**	17 **306**	10 **299**	3 **292**	# ####	# ####	# ####	# ####	# ####	# ####	# ####	# ####	# ####	# ####	# ####
Gienah	2.8	67 **010**	67 **345**	64 **324**	58 **307**	52 **295**	44 **286**	37 **278**	29 **271**	22 **265**	14 **259**	7 **253**	# ####	# ####	# ####	# ####	# ####	# ####	# ####	# ####
Acrux	1.1	67 **172**	67 **184**	66 **195**	63 **203**	60 **209**	56 **213**	51 **215**	47 **216**	42 **216**	38 **215**	34 **213**	30 **210**	26 **207**	23 **204**	20 **200**	17 **196**	15 **192**	14 **188**	13 **183**
Gacrux	1.6	72 **166**	73 **184**	71 **201**	68 **213**	63 **220**	58 **223**	53 **225**	47 **225**	42 **224**	37 **222**	32 **220**	27 **217**	22 **213**	19 **209**	15 **205**	12 **200**	10 **195**	8 **190**	7 **184**
Alioth	1.7	# ####	# ####	# ####	# ####	# ####	# ####	# ####	# ####	# ####	# ####	# ####	# ####	# ####	# ####	# ####	# ####	# ####	# ####	# ####
Spica	1.2	56 **039**	59 **022**	61 **003**	60 **343**	57 **325**	52 **311**	45 **299**	38 **290**	31 **282**	23 **275**	16 **269**	8 **262**	1 **256**	# ####	# ####	# ####	# ####	# ####	# ####
Alkaid	1.9	# ####	# ####	0 **004**	1 **358**	# ####	# ####	# ####	# ####	# ####	# ####	# ####	# ####	# ####	# ####	# ####	# ####	# ####	# ####	# ####
Hadar	0.9	62 **147**	66 **154**	69 **165**	70 **179**	69 **192**	66 **204**	63 **212**	59 **217**	54 **219**	49 **220**	44 **220**	39 **219**	34 **217**	30 **214**	26 **211**	22 **208**	19 **204**	16 **200**	14 **195**
Menkent	2.3	65 **092**	73 **085**	80 **072**	86 **020**	83 **296**	75 **278**	68 **270**	60 **264**	52 **260**	45 **255**	38 **251**	30 **246**	24 **241**	17 **236**	11 **231**	5 **225**	# ####	# ####	# ####
Arcturus	0.2	23 **035**	27 **025**	29 **015**	31 **004**	31 **353**	29 **343**	26 **332**	22 **323**	17 **315**	11 **307**	5 **300**	# ####	# ####	# ####	# ####	# ####	# ####	# ####	# ####
Rigil Kent.	0.1	58 **144**	62 **149**	66 **156**	68 **167**	69 **180**	68 **193**	66 **204**	62 **212**	58 **216**	53 **219**	48 **219**	44 **219**	39 **218**	34 **216**	30 **214**	26 **211**	22 **207**	19 **203**	16 **199**
Zuben'ubi	2.9	46 **070**	53 **059**	59 **046**	64 **028**	66 **006**	65 **343**	62 **323**	56 **307**	50 **296**	43 **286**	35 **279**	28 **272**	20 **265**	12 **259**	5 **253**	# ####	# ####	# ####	# ####
Kochab	2.2	# ####	# ####	# ####	# ####	# ####	# ####	# ####	# ####	# ####	# ####	# ####	# ####	# ####	# ####	# ####	# ####	# ####	# ####	# ####
Alphecca	2.3	7 **046**	12 **039**	16 **031**	20 **022**	22 **013**	23 **004**	23 **354**	22 **344**	19 **335**	15 **327**	11 **319**	5 **312**	# ####	# ####	# ####	# ####	# ####	# ####	# ####
Antares	1.2	33 **098**	41 **092**	49 **086**	56 **078**	64 **068**	70 **052**	75 **027**	76 **350**	73 **318**	67 **299**	60 **287**	52 **278**	45 **271**	37 **265**	29 **259**	22 **253**	15 **248**	8 **242**	1 **236**
Atria	1.9	43 **152**	47 **152**	50 **154**	53 **156**	56 **160**	59 **165**	60 **171**	61 **178**	61 **186**	59 **192**	57 **198**	55 **202**	52 **205**	48 **207**	45 **208**	41 **208**	38 **207**	34 **205**	31 **203**
Sabik	2.6	19 **095**	27 **088**	35 **081**	42 **074**	49 **064**	56 **053**	61 **037**	65 **017**	66 **354**	63 **332**	59 **315**	53 **301**	46 **291**	39 **283**	31 **275**	23 **269**	16 **262**	8 **256**	1 **250**
Shaula	1.7	27 **117**	34 **112**	41 **108**	49 **104**	56 **099**	64 **094**	72 **088**	79 **079**	86 **044**	84 **297**	77 **277**	69 **269**	61 **264**	54 **259**	46 **255**	39 **251**	32 **246**	25 **242**	19 **237**
Rasalhague	2.1	# ####	4 **070**	11 **063**	18 **056**	24 **047**	29 **038**	33 **028**	36 **017**	37 **005**	37 **352**	35 **340**	32 **329**	28 **319**	22 **310**	16 **302**	9 **295**	2 **288**	# ####	# ####
Eltanin	2.4	# ####	# ####	# ####	# ####	# ####	# ####	# ####	# ####	# ####	# ####	# ####	# ####	# ####	# ####	# ####	# ####	# ####	# ####	# ####
Kaus Aust.	2.0	17 **121**	24 **116**	31 **111**	38 **106**	46 **101**	53 **096**	61 **090**	69 **083**	76 **071**	83 **043**	84 **330**	78 **292**	70 **279**	63 **271**	55 **265**	47 **260**	40 **255**	33 **250**	25 **245**
Vega	0.1	# ####	# ####	# ####	# ####	# ####	# ####	3 **030**	7 **023**	9 **015**	11 **007**	11 **359**	11 **351**	9 **344**	6 **336**	3 **329**	# ####	# ####	# ####	# ####
Nunki	2.1	7 **119**	14 **113**	21 **107**	28 **102**	36 **096**	44 **090**	51 **083**	59 **074**	66 **063**	72 **044**	76 **014**	75 **338**	71 **311**	64 **294**	57 **283**	49 **275**	42 **269**	34 **263**	27 **257**
Altair	0.9	# ####	# ####	# ####	# ####	4 **075**	11 **069**	18 **061**	24 **053**	30 **044**	35 **034**	38 **023**	41 **010**	41 **357**	40 **344**	37 **332**	33 **321**	27 **311**	21 **303**	15 **295**
Peacock	2.1	17 **153**	21 **148**	25 **145**	29 **141**	34 **138**	40 **136**	45 **135**	50 **134**	56 **135**	61 **138**	66 **143**	70 **153**	73 **168**	73 **187**	71 **203**	67 **215**	63 **221**	57 **224**	52 **226**
Deneb	1.3	# ####	# ####	# ####	# ####	# ####	# ####	# ####	# ####	# ####	# ####	0 **021**	3 **014**	4 **007**	5 **000**	4 **353**	3 **346**	1 **340**	# ####	# ####
Enif	2.5	# ####	# ####	# ####	# ####	# ####	# ####	# ####	4 **073**	11 **067**	18 **059**	24 **051**	30 **042**	35 **032**	38 **020**	40 **008**	40 **355**	38 **342**	35 **331**	31 **320**
Al Na'ir	2.2	0 **161**	3 **155**	7 **149**	11 **144**	16 **139**	21 **134**	27 **130**	33 **126**	39 **123**	46 **120**	52 **118**	59 **117**	66 **117**	73 **121**	79 **133**	83 **169**	81 **217**	75 **236**	69 **242**
Fomalhaut	1.3	# ####	# ####	# ####	# ####	# ####	2 **128**	9 **122**	15 **116**	22 **111**	30 **105**	37 **100**	45 **094**	52 **088**	60 **080**	68 **070**	74 **053**	79 **021**	79 **335**	74 **304**
Markab	2.6	# ####	# ####	# ####	# ####	# ####	# ####	# ####	# ####	# ####	0 **070**	7 **063**	14 **056**	20 **048**	25 **039**	30 **029**	33 **019**	34 **007**	35 **356**	33 **344**

* Variable 0.1 - 1.2

SUN MOON PLANETS	Local Hour Angle Body																		
	180°	190°	200°	210°	220°	230°	240°	250°	260°	270°	280°	290°	300°	310°	320°	330°	340°	350°	360°
	Alt Az	Alt Az	Alt Az	Alt Az	Alt Az	Alt Az	Alt Az	Alt Az	Alt Az	Alt Az	Alt Az	Alt Az	Alt Az	Alt Az	Alt Az	Alt Az	Alt Az	Alt Az	Alt Az
	° °	° °	° °	° °	° °	° °	° °	° °	° °	° °	° °	° °	° °	° °	° °	° °	° °	° °	° °
Decl'n N30°	# ####	# ####	# ####	# ####	# ####	# ####	# ####	# ####	# ####	# ####	# ####	# ####	1 **049**	6 **042**	11 **035**	15 **027**	18 **018**	19 **009**	20 **000**
Decl'n N25°	# ####	# ####	# ####	# ####	# ####	# ####	# ####	# ####	# ####	# ####	# ####	# ####	4 **052**	10 **045**	15 **037**	19 **029**	22 **020**	24 **010**	25 **000**
Decl'n N20°	# ####	# ####	# ####	# ####	# ####	# ####	# ####	# ####	# ####	# ####	# ####	2 **062**	8 **055**	14 **048**	19 **040**	24 **031**	27 **021**	29 **011**	30 **000**
Decl'n N15°	# ####	# ####	# ####	# ####	# ####	# ####	# ####	# ####	# ####	# ####	# ####	5 **066**	12 **059**	18 **051**	24 **043**	28 **033**	32 **023**	34 **012**	35 **000**
Decl'n N10°	# ####	# ####	# ####	# ####	# ####	# ####	# ####	# ####	# ####	# ####	1 **076**	8 **069**	15 **062**	22 **054**	28 **046**	33 **036**	37 **025**	39 **013**	40 **000**
Decl'n N5°	# ####	# ####	# ####	# ####	# ####	# ####	# ####	# ####	# ####	# ####	4 **080**	12 **073**	19 **066**	26 **058**	32 **049**	37 **039**	41 **027**	44 **014**	45 **000**
Decl'n 0°	# ####	# ####	# ####	# ####	# ####	# ####	# ####	# ####	# ####	# ####	8 **084**	15 **077**	23 **070**	29 **062**	36 **053**	42 **042**	46 **030**	49 **015**	50 **000**
Decl'n S5°	# ####	# ####	# ####	# ####	# ####	# ####	# ####	# ####	# ####	3 **094**	11 **087**	18 **081**	26 **074**	33 **066**	40 **057**	46 **046**	51 **032**	54 **017**	55 **000**
Decl'n S10°	# ####	# ####	# ####	# ####	# ####	# ####	# ####	# ####	# ####	6 **098**	14 **091**	22 **085**	29 **078**	37 **070**	44 **061**	50 **050**	55 **036**	59 **019**	60 **000**
Decl'n S15°	# ####	# ####	# ####	# ####	# ####	# ####	# ####	# ####	2 **108**	10 **102**	17 **095**	25 **089**	32 **082**	40 **075**	47 **066**	54 **055**	60 **041**	64 **022**	65 **000**
Decl'n S20°	# ####	# ####	# ####	# ####	# ####	# ####	# ####	# ####	5 **112**	13 **106**	20 **100**	28 **094**	35 **087**	43 **080**	50 **072**	57 **061**	64 **046**	68 **026**	70 **000**
Decl'n S25°	# ####	# ####	# ####	# ####	# ####	# ####	# ####	2 **122**	9 **115**	16 **110**	23 **104**	31 **098**	38 **092**	46 **086**	53 **078**	61 **068**	68 **054**	73 **032**	75 **000**
Decl'n S30°	# ####	# ####	# ####	# ####	# ####	# ####	# ####	5 **125**	12 **119**	19 **114**	26 **109**	33 **103**	41 **098**	48 **092**	56 **086**	64 **077**	71 **065**	77 **042**	80 **000**

Latitude S50°

STARS		Local				Hour					Angle					Aries				
		0°	10°	20°	30°	40°	50°	60°	70°	80°	90°	100°	110°	120°	130°	140°	150°	160°	170°	180°
Name	Mag	Alt Az	Alt Az	Alt Az	Alt Az	Alt Az	Alt Az	Alt Az	Alt Az	Alt Az	Alt Az	Alt Az	Alt Az	Alt Az	Alt Az	Alt Az	Alt Az	Alt Az	Alt Az	Alt Az
		° °	° °	° °	° °	° °	° °	° °	° °	° °	° °	° °	° °	° °	° °	° °	° °	° °	° °	° °
Alpheratz	2.2	11 002	11 353	9 344	7 336	4 327	0 320	# ###	# ###	# ###	# ###	# ###	# ###	# ###	# ###	# ###	# ###	# ###	# ###	# ###
Ankaa	2.4	81 033	82 342	78 305	72 287	66 276	59 268	53 261	47 255	41 249	35 243	29 238	24 232	19 226	15 220	11 213	8 206	5 199	3 192	2 185
Schedah	2.5	# ###	# ###	# ###	# ###	# ###	# ###	# ###	# ###	# ###	# ###	# ###	# ###	# ###	# ###	# ###	# ###	# ###	# ###	# ###
Diphda	2.2	57 019	58 002	57 344	55 328	50 313	45 301	40 291	33 282	27 274	21 266	14 259	8 252	2 244	# ###	# ###	# ###	# ###	# ###	# ###
Achernar	0.6	74 126	79 136	82 162	82 202	78 226	73 235	68 237	63 237	57 236	52 233	47 230	42 227	38 223	33 219	30 214	26 209	23 204	21 199	19 194
Hamal	2.2	11 030	14 021	16 011	17 002	16 352	15 343	12 334	9 325	5 317	0 309	# ###	# ###	# ###	# ###	# ###	# ###	# ###	# ###	# ###
Polaris	2.1	# ###	# ###	# ###	# ###	# ###	# ###	# ###	# ###	# ###	# ###	# ###	# ###	# ###	# ###	# ###	# ###	# ###	# ###	# ###
Acamar	3.1	58 090	64 081	70 070	76 052	80 020	80 336	75 306	70 289	63 278	57 269	51 262	44 256	38 250	32 244	27 238	21 232	17 226	12 219	8 213
Menkar	2.8	23 051	28 041	32 030	34 019	36 007	36 355	34 342	32 331	28 320	24 310	19 301	13 293	7 285	0 277	# ###	# ###	# ###	# ###	# ###
Mirfak	1.9	# ###	# ###	# ###	# ###	# ###	# ###	# ###	# ###	# ###	# ###	# ###	# ###	# ###	# ###	# ###	# ###	# ###	# ###	# ###
Aldebaran	1.1	0 064	6 056	11 047	15 039	19 029	21 020	23 009	23 359	23 349	21 338	18 329	14 319	10 311	5 303	# ###	# ###	# ###	# ###	# ###
Rigel	0.3	14 087	20 079	26 070	32 061	37 051	42 040	45 027	48 013	48 358	47 343	45 330	41 317	36 306	30 296	24 287	18 279	12 271	5 264	# ###
Capella	0.2	# ###	# ###	# ###	# ###	# ###	# ###	# ###	# ###	# ###	# ###	# ###	# ###	# ###	# ###	# ###	# ###	# ###	# ###	# ###
Bellatrix	1.7	1 079	7 071	13 063	18 055	23 046	27 036	31 025	33 013	34 002	33 350	31 338	28 327	24 317	20 308	14 299	8 291	2 283	# ###	# ###
Elnath	1.8	# ###	# ###	# ###	# ###	3 036	7 028	9 019	11 010	11 001	11 352	10 344	7 335	4 327	0 319	# ###	# ###	# ###	# ###	# ###
Alnilam	1.8	5 086	11 078	17 070	23 062	29 052	33 042	37 031	40 018	41 005	41 352	39 339	36 327	32 316	27 306	22 296	16 288	10 280	3 272	# ###
Betelgeuse	*	# ###	1 077	8 069	13 061	19 052	23 043	27 033	30 022	32 010	33 359	32 347	30 336	27 325	22 315	17 306	12 297	6 289	# ###	# ###
Canopus	-0.9	35 133	40 128	45 124	50 120	56 117	62 113	68 111	74 109	80 111	85 128	86 221	81 247	75 251	69 250	63 247	57 244	51 241	46 237	41 232
Sirius	-1.6	6 109	12 102	18 094	25 087	31 079	37 070	43 060	48 048	53 035	55 019	57 002	56 345	53 329	49 315	44 303	39 293	33 283	26 275	20 267
Adhara	1.6	13 120	19 113	25 106	31 099	38 092	44 084	50 075	56 064	62 051	66 033	69 011	69 347	66 325	62 308	56 295	50 284	44 276	37 268	31 260
Procyon	0.5	# ###	# ###	# ###	# ###	6 075	12 067	17 059	23 049	27 040	31 029	33 018	35 006	35 354	33 342	31 331	27 320	22 310	17 301	11 293
Pollux	1.2	# ###	# ###	# ###	# ###	# ###	# ###	# ###	2 040	6 032	9 023	11 015	12 006	12 357	11 348	9 339	6 330	3 322	# ###	# ###
Avior	1.7	28 152	31 148	35 143	39 140	43 136	48 133	53 130	58 129	63 128	68 129	73 133	77 143	80 163	80 193	77 215	73 226	68 231	63 232	58 232
Suhail	2.2	11 150	14 143	18 137	23 131	28 125	33 120	39 114	45 109	51 103	58 097	64 090	70 081	77 067	82 039	83 341	79 301	73 284	67 274	60 266
Miaplacidus	1.8	34 164	35 160	38 157	40 154	43 152	46 150	50 148	53 147	57 148	60 149	63 151	66 156	68 163	70 172	70 182	70 192	68 200	65 206	62 210
Alphard	2.2	# ###	# ###	# ###	# ###	# ###	5 097	12 089	18 082	25 073	30 065	36 055	41 044	45 031	47 018	49 003	48 348	46 334	43 321	38 309
Regulus	1.3	# ###	# ###	# ###	# ###	# ###	# ###	# ###	# ###	2 069	8 061	13 052	18 044	22 034	25 024	27 013	28 002	28 351	26 340	23 330
Dubhe	2.0	# ###	# ###	# ###	# ###	# ###	# ###	# ###	# ###	# ###	# ###	# ###	# ###	# ###	# ###	# ###	# ###	# ###	# ###	# ###
Denebola	2.2	# ###	# ###	# ###	# ###	# ###	# ###	# ###	# ###	# ###	# ###	# ###	3 063	8 055	13 047	18 038	21 028	24 018	25 008	25 357
Gienah	2.8	# ###	# ###	# ###	# ###	# ###	# ###	# ###	# ###	5 112	11 104	17 097	24 089	30 082	36 073	42 063	48 052	52 039	56 024	57 007
Acrux	1.1	23 183	23 178	24 173	25 169	26 164	28 159	31 155	34 151	37 147	41 144	44 141	49 138	53 136	57 135	62 136	66 138	71 142	74 152	76 167
Gacrux	1.6	17 184	17 179	18 173	19 167	20 162	23 157	25 152	29 147	32 142	37 138	41 134	46 130	51 127	56 125	61 123	67 122	72 124	77 131	82 150
Alioth	1.7	# ###	# ###	# ###	# ###	# ###	# ###	# ###	# ###	# ###	# ###	# ###	# ###	# ###	# ###	# ###	# ###	# ###	# ###	# ###
Spica	1.2	# ###	# ###	# ###	# ###	# ###	# ###	# ###	# ###	# ###	# ###	1 106	8 098	14 091	21 083	27 075	33 066	38 056	43 045	47 032
Alkaid	1.9	# ###	# ###	# ###	# ###	# ###	# ###	# ###	# ###	# ###	# ###	# ###	# ###	# ###	# ###	# ###	# ###	# ###	# ###	# ###
Hadar	0.9	23 196	22 191	21 186	20 181	21 175	21 170	23 165	25 160	27 155	30 151	34 146	37 142	41 139	46 136	50 133	55 131	60 130	65 130	70 133
Menkent	2.3	1 205	# ###	# ###	# ###	# ###	# ###	# ###	3 150	6 143	11 136	15 129	20 123	26 116	32 110	38 104	44 097	51 090	57 082	63 071
Arcturus	0.2	# ###	# ###	# ###	# ###	# ###	# ###	# ###	# ###	# ###	# ###	# ###	# ###	# ###	# ###	# ###	1 058	6 050	11 042	15 033
Rigil Kent.	0.1	25 200	23 195	22 190	21 185	21 180	21 175	22 170	23 165	25 160	28 155	31 151	34 146	38 143	42 139	46 136	51 133	56 132	61 131	65 131
Zuben'ubi	2.9	# ###	# ###	# ###	# ###	# ###	# ###	# ###	# ###	# ###	# ###	# ###	# ###	4 110	11 102	17 095	23 087	30 079	36 071	42 061
Kochab	2.2	# ###	# ###	# ###	# ###	# ###	# ###	# ###	# ###	# ###	# ###	# ###	# ###	# ###	# ###	# ###	# ###	# ###	# ###	# ###
Alphecca	2.3	# ###	# ###	# ###	# ###	# ###	# ###	# ###	# ###	# ###	# ###	# ###	# ###	# ###	# ###	# ###	# ###	# ###	# ###	# ###
Antares	1.2	7 236	2 229	# ###	# ###	# ###	# ###	# ###	# ###	# ###	# ###	# ###	# ###	# ###	4 127	10 120	16 113	22 106	28 099	34 092
Atria	1.9	40 206	37 203	35 200	33 197	31 193	30 189	29 185	29 181	29 177	30 173	31 169	32 165	34 161	36 158	39 155	42 152	45 150	48 148	52 147
Sabik	2.6	4 251	# ###	# ###	# ###	# ###	# ###	# ###	# ###	# ###	# ###	# ###	# ###	# ###	# ###	# ###	1 113	7 106	14 098	20 091
Shaula	1.7	24 240	18 234	13 227	9 220	5 213	2 206	# ###	# ###	# ###	# ###	# ###	0 159	3 152	6 144	10 137	15 131	20 124	26 118	31 112
Rasalhague	2.1	# ###	# ###	# ###	# ###	# ###	# ###	# ###	# ###	# ###	# ###	# ###	# ###	# ###	# ###	# ###	# ###	# ###	# ###	# ###
Eltanin	2.4	# ###	# ###	# ###	# ###	# ###	# ###	# ###	# ###	# ###	# ###	# ###	# ###	# ###	# ###	# ###	# ###	# ###	# ###	# ###
Kaus Aust.	2.0	29 250	23 244	18 237	13 231	8 224	4 217	0 209	# ###	# ###	# ###	# ###	# ###	# ###	# ###	3 145	7 138	12 131	17 124	22 118
Vega	0.1	# ###	# ###	# ###	# ###	# ###	# ###	# ###	# ###	# ###	# ###	# ###	# ###	# ###	# ###	# ###	# ###	# ###	# ###	# ###
Nunki	2.1	28 262	22 255	16 248	10 241	5 234	# ###	# ###	# ###	# ###	# ###	# ###	# ###	# ###	# ###	# ###	# ###	1 132	6 124	12 117
Altair	0.9	10 297	4 289	# ###	# ###	# ###	# ###	# ###	# ###	# ###	# ###	# ###	# ###	# ###	# ###	# ###	# ###	# ###	# ###	# ###
Peacock	2.1	58 237	53 234	48 231	43 228	38 224	34 220	30 215	26 211	23 206	21 200	19 195	18 189	17 184	17 178	17 172	19 167	20 161	23 156	26 151
Deneb	1.3	# ###	# ###	# ###	# ###	# ###	# ###	# ###	# ###	# ###	# ###	# ###	# ###	# ###	# ###	# ###	# ###	# ###	# ###	# ###
Enif	2.5	23 323	19 314	14 305	8 296	2 289	# ###	# ###	# ###	# ###	# ###	# ###	# ###	# ###	# ###	# ###	# ###	# ###	# ###	# ###
Al Na'ir	2.2	71 269	65 262	59 257	52 252	46 247	41 242	35 237	30 231	25 226	21 220	17 214	14 208	11 202	9 195	8 188	7 181	7 175	8 168	10 161
Fomalhaut	1.3	66 324	62 307	56 294	50 283	44 275	38 267	31 260	25 253	19 246	13 239	8 232	3 225	# ###	# ###	# ###	# ###	# ###	# ###	# ###
Markab	2.6	24 345	22 335	18 326	14 316	10 308	4 300	# ###	# ###	# ###	# ###	# ###	# ###	# ###	# ###	# ###	# ###	# ###	# ###	# ###

* Variable 0.1 - 1.2

SUN MOON PLANETS	Local				Hour					Angle					Body				
	0°	10°	20°	30°	40°	50°	60°	70°	80°	90°	100°	110°	120°	130°	140°	150°	160°	170°	180°
	Alt Az	Alt Az	Alt Az	Alt Az	Alt Az	Alt Az	Alt Az	Alt Az	Alt Az	Alt Az	Alt Az	Alt Az	Alt Az	Alt Az	Alt Az	Alt Az	Alt Az	Alt Az	Alt Az
	° °	° °	° °	° °	° °	° °	° °	° °	° °	° °	° °	° °	° °	° °	° °	° °	° °	° °	° °
Decl'n N30°	10 000	10 351	8 343	6 334	2 326	# ###	# ###	# ###	# ###	# ###	# ###	# ###	# ###	# ###	# ###	# ###	# ###	# ###	# ###
Decl'n N25°	15 000	14 351	13 341	10 333	7 324	3 316	# ###	# ###	# ###	# ###	# ###	# ###	# ###	# ###	# ###	# ###	# ###	# ###	# ###
Decl'n N20°	20 000	19 350	18 340	15 331	12 322	7 313	2 305	# ###	# ###	# ###	# ###	# ###	# ###	# ###	# ###	# ###	# ###	# ###	# ###
Decl'n N15°	25 000	24 349	23 339	20 329	16 320	12 311	6 303	1 295	# ###	# ###	# ###	# ###	# ###	# ###	# ###	# ###	# ###	# ###	# ###
Decl'n N10°	30 000	29 349	28 338	25 327	21 317	16 308	11 300	5 292	# ###	# ###	# ###	# ###	# ###	# ###	# ###	# ###	# ###	# ###	# ###
Decl'n N5°	35 000	34 348	32 336	29 325	25 315	20 306	15 297	9 289	3 281	# ###	# ###	# ###	# ###	# ###	# ###	# ###	# ###	# ###	# ###
Decl'n 0°	40 000	39 347	37 335	34 323	29 312	24 303	19 294	13 286	6 278	0 270	# ###	# ###	# ###	# ###	# ###	# ###	# ###	# ###	# ###
Decl'n S5°	45 000	44 346	42 333	38 321	34 310	29 300	23 291	17 282	10 274	4 267	# ###	# ###	# ###	# ###	# ###	# ###	# ###	# ###	# ###
Decl'n S10°	50 000	49 345	47 331	43 318	38 306	33 296	27 287	20 279	14 271	8 264	1 256	# ###	# ###	# ###	# ###	# ###	# ###	# ###	# ###
Decl'n S15°	55 000	54 343	51 328	47 314	42 303	37 293	31 284	24 275	18 268	11 260	5 253	# ###	# ###	# ###	# ###	# ###	# ###	# ###	# ###
Decl'n S20°	60 000	59 342	56 325	52 311	46 299	41 289	34 280	28 272	22 264	15 257	9 250	3 242	# ###	# ###	# ###	# ###	# ###	# ###	# ###
Decl'n S25°	65 000	64 339	61 321	56 306	50 294	44 284	38 275	32 268	25 260	19 253	13 246	7 239	2 232	# ###	# ###	# ###	# ###	# ###	# ###
Decl'n S30°	70 000	69 336	65 316	60 300	54 289	48 279	41 271	35 263	29 256	23 250	17 243	11 236	6 229	1 222	# ###	# ###	# ###	# ###	# ###

PREDICTION & IDENTIFICATION

Latitude S50°

STARS		Local Hour Angle Aries																		
Name	Mag	180° Alt Az	190° Alt Az	200° Alt Az	210° Alt Az	220° Alt Az	230° Alt Az	240° Alt Az	250° Alt Az	260° Alt Az	270° Alt Az	280° Alt Az	290° Alt Az	300° Alt Az	310° Alt Az	320° Alt Az	330° Alt Az	340° Alt Az	350° Alt Az	360° Alt Az
		° °	° °	° °	° °	° °	° °	° °	° °	° °	° °	° °	° °	° °	° °	° °	° °	° °	° °	° °
Alpheratz	2.2	# ####	# ####	# ####	# ####	# ####	# ####	# ####	# ####	# ####	# ####	# ####	# ####	# ####	# ####	3 036	6 028	9 019	10 011	11 002
Ankaa	2.4	2 185	2 177	3 170	5 163	7 156	10 149	13 142	18 136	22 130	27 124	33 118	39 113	45 107	51 101	57 095	64 087	70 077	76 062	81 033
Schedah	2.5	# ####	# ####	# ####	# ####	# ####	# ####	# ####	# ####	# ####	# ####	# ####	# ####	# ####	# ####	# ####	# ####	# ####	# ####	# ####
Diphda	2.2	# ####	# ####	# ####	# ####	# ####	# ####	# ####	# ####	1 117	7 110	13 102	19 095	26 087	32 079	38 071	44 061	50 049	54 035	57 019
Achernar	0.6	19 194	18 188	17 183	17 177	18 171	19 166	21 160	24 155	27 150	30 145	34 141	38 137	43 133	48 129	53 127	58 124	63 123	69 123	74 126
Hamal	2.2	# ####	# ####	# ####	# ####	# ####	# ####	# ####	# ####	# ####	# ####	# ####	# ####	# ####	# ####	# ####	# ####	3 046	8 038	11 030
Polaris	2.1	# ####	# ####	# ####	# ####	# ####	# ####	# ####	# ####	# ####	# ####	# ####	# ####	# ####	# ####	# ####	# ####	# ####	# ####	# ####
Acamar	3.1	8 213	5 206	3 199	1 191	0 183	0 176	1 168	3 161	6 154	9 147	13 140	17 134	22 127	27 121	33 115	39 109	45 103	51 097	58 090
Menkar	2.8	# ####	# ####	# ####	# ####	# ####	# ####	# ####	# ####	# ####	# ####	# ####	# ####	# ####	# ####	# ####	6 076	12 068	18 060	23 051
Mirfak	1.9	# ####	# ####	# ####	# ####	# ####	# ####	# ####	# ####	# ####	# ####	# ####	# ####	# ####	# ####	# ####	# ####	# ####	# ####	# ####
Aldebaran	1.1	# ####	# ####	# ####	# ####	# ####	# ####	# ####	# ####	# ####	# ####	# ####	# ####	# ####	# ####	# ####	# ####	# ####	# ####	0 064
Rigel	0.3	# ####	# ####	# ####	# ####	# ####	# ####	# ####	# ####	# ####	# ####	# ####	# ####	# ####	# ####	# ####	# ####	1 102	7 094	14 087
Capella	0.2	# ####	# ####	# ####	# ####	# ####	# ####	# ####	# ####	# ####	# ####	# ####	# ####	# ####	# ####	# ####	# ####	# ####	# ####	# ####
Bellatrix	1.7	# ####	# ####	# ####	# ####	# ####	# ####	# ####	# ####	# ####	# ####	# ####	# ####	# ####	# ####	# ####	# ####	# ####	# ####	1 079
Elnath	1.8	# ####	# ####	# ####	# ####	# ####	# ####	# ####	# ####	# ####	# ####	# ####	# ####	# ####	# ####	# ####	# ####	# ####	# ####	# ####
Alnilam	1.8	# ####	# ####	# ####	# ####	# ####	# ####	# ####	# ####	# ####	# ####	# ####	# ####	# ####	# ####	# ####	# ####	# ####	# ####	5 086
Betelgeuse	*	# ####	# ####	# ####	# ####	# ####	# ####	# ####	# ####	# ####	# ####	# ####	# ####	# ####	# ####	# ####	# ####	# ####	# ####	# ####
Canopus	-0.9	41 232	36 228	31 223	27 218	23 213	20 208	17 202	15 196	14 190	13 184	13 178	13 171	15 165	17 159	19 154	22 148	26 143	30 138	35 133
Sirius	-1.6	20 267	14 260	7 253	1 245	# ####	# ####	# ####	# ####	# ####	# ####	# ####	# ####	# ####	# ####	# ####	# ####	# ####	# ####	6 109
Adhara	1.6	31 260	25 254	19 247	13 240	7 233	3 226	# ####	# ####	# ####	# ####	# ####	# ####	# ####	# ####	# ####	# ####	3 134	8 127	13 120
Procyon	0.5	11 293	5 285	# ####	# ####	# ####	# ####	# ####	# ####	# ####	# ####	# ####	# ####	# ####	# ####	# ####	# ####	# ####	# ####	# ####
Pollux	1.2	# ####	# ####	# ####	# ####	# ####	# ####	# ####	# ####	# ####	# ####	# ####	# ####	# ####	# ####	# ####	# ####	# ####	# ####	# ####
Avior	1.7	58 232	53 230	48 227	44 224	39 221	35 217	32 213	28 208	26 204	23 199	21 194	20 188	20 183	20 178	20 172	21 167	23 162	25 157	28 152
Suhail	2.2	60 266	54 260	48 254	42 248	36 243	30 237	25 231	20 225	16 219	12 213	9 206	6 199	5 192	4 185	3 178	4 171	6 163	8 156	11 150
Miaplacidus	1.8	62 210	59 212	56 213	52 212	49 211	45 210	42 207	40 205	37 202	35 198	33 195	31 191	30 187	30 183	30 179	30 175	31 171	32 168	34 164
Alphard	2.2	38 309	33 299	27 290	21 281	14 274	8 266	1 258	# ####	# ####	# ####	# ####	# ####	# ####	# ####	# ####	# ####	# ####	# ####	# ####
Regulus	1.3	23 330	20 320	15 311	10 303	4 295	# ####	# ####	# ####	# ####	# ####	# ####	# ####	# ####	# ####	# ####	# ####	# ####	# ####	# ####
Dubhe	2.0	# ####	# ####	# ####	# ####	# ####	# ####	# ####	# ####	# ####	# ####	# ####	# ####	# ####	# ####	# ####	# ####	# ####	# ####	# ####
Denebola	2.2	25 357	24 346	22 336	19 326	15 317	11 308	5 300	# ####	# ####	# ####	# ####	# ####	# ####	# ####	# ####	# ####	# ####	# ####	# ####
Gienah	2.8	57 007	57 349	55 333	51 318	47 305	41 295	35 285	29 277	22 269	16 261	10 254	4 247	# ####	# ####	# ####	# ####	# ####	# ####	# ####
Acrux	1.1	76 167	77 187	75 204	72 215	68 221	63 224	59 225	54 224	50 222	46 220	42 217	38 214	35 210	32 206	29 202	27 198	25 193	24 188	23 183
Gacrux	1.6	82 150	83 190	80 221	75 233	70 237	64 238	59 236	54 234	49 231	44 228	39 224	35 220	31 216	27 211	24 206	22 201	20 196	18 190	17 184
Alioth	1.7	# ####	# ####	# ####	# ####	# ####	# ####	# ####	# ####	# ####	# ####	# ####	# ####	# ####	# ####	# ####	# ####	# ####	# ####	# ####
Spica	1.2	47 032	50 017	51 002	51 347	48 332	45 319	40 307	34 297	28 288	22 279	16 271	9 264	3 256	# ####	# ####	# ####	# ####	# ####	# ####
Alkaid	1.9	# ####	# ####	# ####	# ####	# ####	# ####	# ####	# ####	# ####	# ####	# ####	# ####	# ####	# ####	# ####	# ####	# ####	# ####	# ####
Hadar	0.9	70 133	74 139	78 153	80 177	78 203	75 219	71 226	66 230	61 230	56 229	51 227	47 225	42 222	38 218	34 214	31 210	28 206	25 201	23 196
Menkent	2.3	63 071	69 057	74 036	76 006	75 333	71 309	65 293	59 282	53 273	47 265	40 258	34 252	28 246	22 239	17 233	12 226	8 220	4 212	1 205
Arcturus	0.2	15 033	18 024	20 014	21 004	21 354	19 344	17 334	14 325	10 316	5 308	# ####	# ####	# ####	# ####	# ####	# ####	# ####	# ####	# ####
Rigil Kent.	0.1	65 131	70 134	74 142	78 157	79 180	78 204	74 218	70 226	65 229	60 229	56 228	51 227	46 224	42 221	38 217	34 214	31 209	28 205	25 200
Zuben'ubi	2.9	42 061	47 050	51 037	55 021	56 005	56 348	53 331	50 317	45 305	39 295	33 285	27 277	20 269	14 262	8 254	2 247	# ####	# ####	# ####
Kochab	2.2	# ####	# ####	# ####	# ####	# ####	# ####	# ####	# ####	# ####	# ####	# ####	# ####	# ####	# ####	# ####	# ####	# ####	# ####	# ####
Alphecca	2.3	# ####	4 038	8 030	10 021	12 012	13 003	13 354	12 345	10 336	7 328	3 320	# ####	# ####	# ####	# ####	# ####	# ####	# ####	# ####
Antares	1.2	34 092	41 084	47 075	53 065	58 052	63 036	66 016	66 354	65 333	61 315	56 301	50 290	44 280	37 272	31 265	25 257	18 250	12 243	7 236
Atria	1.9	52 147	55 146	59 147	62 149	66 153	68 159	70 167	71 178	71 188	69 198	67 205	64 210	60 213	57 214	53 214	50 213	46 211	43 209	40 206
Sabik	2.6	20 091	26 083	33 075	39 066	44 055	49 043	53 029	55 013	56 356	54 339	51 324	47 311	42 300	36 290	30 281	23 273	17 265	10 258	4 251
Shaula	1.7	31 112	37 106	44 099	50 092	57 084	63 074	69 061	74 042	77 012	76 337	72 311	67 294	61 282	55 273	48 266	42 259	36 252	30 246	24 240
Rasalhague	2.1	# ####	1 070	6 062	12 054	17 045	21 035	24 025	26 015	27 004	27 353	26 342	23 332	20 322	15 313	10 304	5 296	# ####	# ####	# ####
Eltanin	2.4	# ####	# ####	# ####	# ####	# ####	# ####	# ####	# ####	# ####	# ####	# ####	# ####	# ####	# ####	# ####	# ####	# ####	# ####	# ####
Kaus Aust.	2.0	22 118	28 111	34 105	40 098	47 091	53 083	59 073	65 061	70 043	74 018	74 348	71 322	67 303	61 289	55 279	48 271	42 263	35 257	29 250
Vega	0.1	# ####	# ####	# ####	# ####	# ####	# ####	# ####	# ####	# ####	1 007	1 359	1 352	# ####	# ####	# ####	# ####	# ####	# ####	# ####
Nunki	2.1	12 117	18 110	24 103	30 096	36 089	43 081	49 071	55 060	60 047	64 029	66 008	66 346	63 326	59 310	54 297	48 286	41 277	35 269	28 262
Altair	0.9	# ####	# ####	# ####	# ####	1 075	7 067	13 059	18 050	23 041	26 031	29 020	31 009	31 357	30 346	28 335	25 324	21 315	16 306	10 297
Peacock	2.1	26 151	29 146	33 141	37 137	41 133	46 129	51 126	57 124	62 122	68 121	73 123	78 131	82 153	83 196	79 225	75 235	69 238	64 238	58 237
Deneb	1.3	# ####	# ####	# ####	# ####	# ####	# ####	# ####	# ####	# ####	# ####	# ####	# ####	# ####	# ####	# ####	# ####	# ####	# ####	# ####
Enif	2.5	# ####	# ####	# ####	# ####	# ####	# ####	# ####	1 073	7 065	13 057	18 048	22 039	26 029	29 018	30 007	30 355	29 344	27 333	23 323
Al Na'ir	2.2	10 161	12 155	15 148	19 142	23 136	28 131	33 126	38 120	44 115	50 110	56 105	62 100	69 094	75 087	81 074	87 025	84 297	78 278	71 269
Fomalhaut	1.3	# ####	# ####	# ####	# ####	4 134	8 127	14 120	20 113	26 106	32 099	38 092	45 084	51 075	57 065	63 051	67 033	69 011	69 346	66 324
Markab	2.6	# ####	# ####	# ####	# ####	# ####	# ####	# ####	# ####	# ####	# ####	3 062	8 054	13 046	17 037	21 027	23 017	25 007	25 356	24 345

* Variable 0.1 - 1.2

SUN MOON PLANETS	Local Hour Angle Body																		
	180° Alt Az	190° Alt Az	200° Alt Az	210° Alt Az	220° Alt Az	230° Alt Az	240° Alt Az	250° Alt Az	260° Alt Az	270° Alt Az	280° Alt Az	290° Alt Az	300° Alt Az	310° Alt Az	320° Alt Az	330° Alt Az	340° Alt Az	350° Alt Az	360° Alt Az
	° °	° °	° °	° °	° °	° °	° °	° °	° °	° °	° °	° °	° °	° °	° °	° °	° °	° °	° °
Decl'n N30°	# ####	# ####	# ####	# ####	# ####	# ####	# ####	# ####	# ####	# ####	# ####	# ####	# ####	# ####	2 034	6 026	8 017	10 009	10 000
Decl'n N25°	# ####	# ####	# ####	# ####	# ####	# ####	# ####	# ####	# ####	# ####	# ####	# ####	# ####	3 044	7 036	10 027	13 019	14 009	15 000
Decl'n N20°	# ####	# ####	# ####	# ####	# ####	# ####	# ####	# ####	# ####	# ####	# ####	# ####	2 055	7 047	12 038	15 029	18 020	19 010	20 000
Decl'n N15°	# ####	# ####	# ####	# ####	# ####	# ####	# ####	# ####	# ####	# ####	# ####	1 065	6 057	12 049	16 040	20 031	23 021	24 011	25 000
Decl'n N10°	# ####	# ####	# ####	# ####	# ####	# ####	# ####	# ####	# ####	# ####	# ####	5 068	11 060	16 052	21 043	25 033	28 022	29 011	30 000
Decl'n N5°	# ####	# ####	# ####	# ####	# ####	# ####	# ####	# ####	# ####	# ####	3 079	9 071	15 063	20 054	25 045	29 035	32 024	34 012	35 000
Decl'n 0°	# ####	# ####	# ####	# ####	# ####	# ####	# ####	# ####	# ####	# ####	6 082	13 074	19 066	24 057	29 048	34 037	37 025	39 013	40 000
Decl'n S5°	# ####	# ####	# ####	# ####	# ####	# ####	# ####	# ####	# ####	4 093	10 086	17 078	23 069	29 060	34 050	38 039	42 027	44 014	45 000
Decl'n S10°	# ####	# ####	# ####	# ####	# ####	# ####	# ####	# ####	1 104	8 096	14 089	20 081	27 073	33 064	38 054	43 042	47 029	49 015	50 000
Decl'n S15°	# ####	# ####	# ####	# ####	# ####	# ####	# ####	5 107	11 100	18 092	24 085	31 076	37 067	42 057	47 046	51 032	54 017	55 000	
Decl'n S20°	# ####	# ####	# ####	# ####	# ####	# ####	# ####	3 118	9 110	15 103	22 096	28 088	34 080	41 071	46 061	52 049	56 035	59 018	60 000
Decl'n S25°	# ####	# ####	# ####	# ####	# ####	# ####	2 128	7 121	13 114	19 107	25 100	32 092	38 085	44 076	50 066	56 054	61 039	64 021	65 000
Decl'n S30°	# ####	# ####	# ####	# ####	# ####	1 138	6 131	11 124	17 117	23 110	29 104	35 097	41 089	48 081	54 071	60 060	65 044	69 024	70 000

Latitude S60° Latitude S60°

STARS — Local Hour Angle Aries

Name	Mag	0° Alt Az	10° Alt Az	20° Alt Az	30° Alt Az	40° Alt Az	50° Alt Az	60° Alt Az	70° Alt Az	80° Alt Az	90° Alt Az	100° Alt Az	110° Alt Az	120° Alt Az	130° Alt Az	140° Alt Az	150° Alt Az	160° Alt Az	170° Alt Az	180° Alt Az
Alpheratz	2.2	1 002	1 353	# ###	# ###	# ###	# ###	# ###	# ###	# ###	# ###	# ###	# ###	# ###	# ###	# ###	# ###	# ###	# ###	# ###
Ankaa	2.4	72 016	72 352	70 329	67 311	63 296	58 284	53 274	48 266	43 258	39 250	34 243	30 236	26 229	22 222	19 215	17 207	15 200	13 193	12 185
Schedah	2.5	# ###	# ###	# ###	# ###	# ###	# ###	# ###	# ###	# ###	# ###	# ###	# ###	# ###	# ###	# ###	# ###	# ###	# ###	# ###
Diphda	2.2	47 015	48 001	47 347	46 333	43 321	40 309	35 298	31 288	26 279	21 270	16 262	11 253	6 245	2 236	# ###	# ###	# ###	# ###	# ###
Achernar	0.6	77 088	82 076	86 042	86 311	81 282	76 271	72 263	67 257	62 251	57 245	53 240	49 235	45 229	41 224	38 218	35 212	32 207	30 201	29 195
Hamal	2.2	3 029	5 020	6 011	7 002	6 352	5 343	3 334	1 325	# ###	# ###	# ###	# ###	# ###	# ###	# ###	# ###	# ###	# ###	# ###
Polaris	2.1	# ###	# ###	# ###	# ###	# ###	# ###	# ###	# ###	# ###	# ###	# ###	# ###	# ###	# ###	# ###	# ###	# ###	# ###	# ###
Acamar	3.1	56 075	61 063	65 049	68 031	70 010	70 348	68 327	65 310	61 296	56 284	51 275	46 266	41 258	36 250	32 243	27 236	23 229	20 221	17 214
Menkar	2.8	17 048	20 038	23 028	25 017	26 006	26 355	25 344	23 333	20 323	17 313	13 304	9 294	4 286	# ###	# ###	# ###	# ###	# ###	# ###
Mirfak	1.9	# ###	# ###	# ###	# ###	# ###	# ###	# ###	# ###	# ###	# ###	# ###	# ###	# ###	# ###	# ###	# ###	# ###	# ###	# ###
Aldebaran	1.1	# ###	0 055	4 046	7 037	10 028	12 019	13 009	13 359	13 349	12 339	9 330	7 321	3 312	# ###	# ###	# ###	# ###	# ###	# ###
Rigel	0.3	13 084	18 075	22 066	27 056	31 046	34 035	36 023	38 011	38 358	37 346	36 334	33 322	30 311	26 301	21 291	16 282	11 273	6 265	1 256
Capella	0.2	# ###	# ###	# ###	# ###	# ###	# ###	# ###	# ###	# ###	# ###	# ###	# ###	# ###	# ###	# ###	# ###	# ###	# ###	# ###
Bellatrix	1.7	# ###	4 071	8 062	12 053	16 043	19 033	22 023	23 012	24 001	23 351	22 340	20 329	17 319	13 310	9 301	5 292	0 283	# ###	# ###
Elnath	1.8	# ###	# ###	# ###	# ###	# ###	# ###	# ###	1 010	1 001	1 353	0 344	# ###	# ###	# ###	# ###	# ###	# ###	# ###	# ###
Alnilam	1.8	4 085	9 077	14 068	18 058	22 048	26 038	28 027	30 016	31 005	31 353	30 341	28 330	25 319	21 309	17 300	13 290	8 281	3 273	# ###
Betelgeuse	*	# ###	# ###	4 068	8 059	12 050	16 040	19 030	21 020	22 009	23 359	22 348	21 337	18 327	15 317	11 308	7 299	3 290	# ###	# ###
Canopus	-0.9	41 127	45 121	50 115	54 108	59 102	64 094	69 086	74 074	79 057	82 027	82 341	79 307	75 288	70 276	65 267	60 260	55 253	51 247	46 240
Sirius	-1.6	9 108	14 100	19 091	24 082	29 073	33 063	38 053	41 041	44 029	46 016	47 002	46 348	45 334	42 322	39 310	34 299	30 289	25 280	20 271
Adhara	1.6	18 117	23 109	27 101	32 093	37 084	42 075	47 064	51 053	55 039	57 024	59 008	59 351	57 335	55 320	51 307	47 295	42 285	37 275	32 267
Procyon	0.5	# ###	# ###	# ###	# ###	3 074	8 065	12 056	16 047	19 037	22 027	24 016	25 005	25 354	24 343	22 333	19 323	16 313	12 303	7 294
Pollux	1.2	# ###	# ###	# ###	# ###	# ###	# ###	# ###	# ###	# ###	# ###	1 014	2 006	2 357	1 348	# ###	# ###	# ###	# ###	# ###
Avior	1.7	37 149	40 144	43 138	46 133	50 128	54 123	58 118	63 114	67 109	72 104	77 099	82 093	87 083	88 281	83 268	78 262	73 257	68 252	63 247
Suhail	2.2	19 148	22 141	26 134	29 127	33 120	38 113	43 106	48 098	52 090	57 081	62 070	67 057	71 039	73 018	73 352	72 329	68 310	64 295	59 283
Miaplacidus	1.8	43 162	45 157	47 153	49 150	52 146	55 143	58 140	61 138	65 137	68 136	72 137	75 141	78 149	80 164	80 184	79 202	77 214	74 220	70 223
Alphard	2.2	# ###	# ###	# ###	# ###	2 105	7 096	12 087	16 079	21 069	26 060	30 050	33 039	36 027	38 015	39 002	38 350	37 337	35 326	31 314
Regulus	1.3	# ###	# ###	# ###	# ###	# ###	# ###	# ###	# ###	# ###	3 060	7 051	11 042	14 032	16 022	17 012	18 002	18 352	17 342	15 332
Dubhe	2.0	# ###	# ###	# ###	# ###	# ###	# ###	# ###	# ###	# ###	# ###	# ###	# ###	# ###	# ###	# ###	# ###	# ###	# ###	# ###
Denebola	2.2	# ###	# ###	# ###	# ###	# ###	# ###	# ###	# ###	# ###	# ###	# ###	# ###	3 055	6 046	10 036	12 027	14 017	15 007	15 357
Gienah	2.8	# ###	# ###	# ###	# ###	# ###	# ###	# ###	4 119	8 111	13 102	18 094	23 085	28 076	33 067	37 056	41 045	44 033	46 019	47 006
Acrux	1.1	33 184	33 178	34 173	34 167	36 162	37 157	40 152	42 147	45 142	48 138	52 133	56 129	60 125	64 121	68 118	73 116	77 115	82 119	86 137
Gacrux	1.6	27 185	27 179	28 173	28 167	30 161	32 155	34 149	37 143	40 137	44 132	48 127	52 121	56 116	61 110	65 105	70 098	75 091	80 080	85 058
Alioth	1.7	# ###	# ###	# ###	# ###	# ###	# ###	# ###	# ###	# ###	# ###	# ###	# ###	# ###	# ###	# ###	# ###	# ###	# ###	# ###
Spica	1.2	# ###	# ###	# ###	# ###	# ###	# ###	# ###	# ###	# ###	# ###	4 105	9 097	14 088	19 079	24 070	28 060	32 050	36 039	39 027
Alkaid	1.9	# ###	# ###	# ###	# ###	# ###	# ###	# ###	# ###	# ###	# ###	# ###	# ###	# ###	# ###	# ###	# ###	# ###	# ###	# ###
Hadar	0.9	33 198	31 192	31 186	30 181	31 175	31 169	32 163	34 158	36 152	39 147	42 142	45 137	48 132	52 127	56 122	61 118	65 113	70 109	75 105
Menkent	2.3	10 205	8 197	7 189	6 181	7 173	8 165	9 157	11 149	14 142	18 134	21 127	26 119	30 111	35 104	40 096	45 087	50 078	55 067	59 055
Arcturus	0.2	# ###	# ###	# ###	# ###	# ###	# ###	# ###	# ###	# ###	# ###	# ###	# ###	# ###	# ###	# ###	# ###	# ###	3 041	6 032
Rigil Kent.	0.1	35 202	33 197	32 191	31 186	31 180	31 174	32 169	33 163	35 158	37 152	39 147	42 142	46 137	49 132	53 127	57 123	61 118	66 114	71 110
Zuben'ubi	2.9	# ###	# ###	# ###	# ###	# ###	# ###	# ###	# ###	# ###	# ###	# ###	3 117	8 109	13 100	17 092	22 083	27 074	32 064	36 054
Kochab	2.2	# ###	# ###	# ###	# ###	# ###	# ###	# ###	# ###	# ###	# ###	# ###	# ###	# ###	# ###	# ###	# ###	# ###	# ###	# ###
Alphecca	2.3	# ###	# ###	# ###	# ###	# ###	# ###	# ###	# ###	# ###	# ###	# ###	# ###	# ###	# ###	# ###	# ###	# ###	# ###	# ###
Antares	1.2	12 238	8 230	5 221	2 213	# ###	# ###	# ###	# ###	# ###	# ###	0 151	3 143	7 134	10 126	15 118	19 110	24 102	29 093	34 085
Atria	1.9	49 211	46 207	44 203	43 199	41 195	40 190	39 186	39 181	39 176	40 172	41 167	42 163	44 159	46 154	48 150	50 147	53 143	56 140	60 138
Sabik	2.6	8 252	3 243	# ###	# ###	# ###	# ###	# ###	# ###	# ###	# ###	# ###	# ###	# ###	# ###	1 121	5 113	10 104	15 096	20 087
Shaula	1.7	28 244	24 237	20 229	17 222	13 214	11 207	9 199	8 191	7 183	7 175	8 167	10 159	12 151	14 143	18 136	21 128	25 121	30 113	35 106
Rasalhague	2.1	# ###	# ###	# ###	# ###	# ###	# ###	# ###	# ###	# ###	# ###	# ###	# ###	# ###	# ###	# ###	# ###	# ###	# ###	# ###
Eltanin	2.4	# ###	# ###	# ###	# ###	# ###	# ###	# ###	# ###	# ###	# ###	# ###	# ###	# ###	# ###	# ###	# ###	# ###	# ###	# ###
Kaus Aust.	2.0	32 256	27 248	23 240	19 233	15 225	12 217	9 209	7 201	5 193	5 185	4 177	5 168	6 160	8 152	11 144	14 136	18 129	22 121	26 114
Vega	0.1	# ###	# ###	# ###	# ###	# ###	# ###	# ###	# ###	# ###	# ###	# ###	# ###	# ###	# ###	# ###	# ###	# ###	# ###	# ###
Nunki	2.1	29 268	24 259	20 251	15 243	11 235	7 227	3 218	1 210	# ###	# ###	# ###	# ###	# ###	# ###	1 148	4 140	8 131	12 123	16 115
Altair	0.9	6 298	1 290	# ###	# ###	# ###	# ###	# ###	# ###	# ###	# ###	# ###	# ###	# ###	# ###	# ###	# ###	# ###	# ###	# ###
Peacock	2.1	62 253	58 247	53 242	49 236	45 231	41 225	38 220	35 214	32 208	30 202	29 196	27 190	27 184	27 178	27 172	28 166	30 160	32 154	34 148
Deneb	1.3	# ###	# ###	# ###	# ###	# ###	# ###	# ###	# ###	# ###	# ###	# ###	# ###	# ###	# ###	# ###	# ###	# ###	# ###	# ###
Enif	2.5	15 325	12 316	8 306	4 297	# ###	# ###	# ###	# ###	# ###	# ###	# ###	# ###	# ###	# ###	# ###	# ###	# ###	# ###	# ###
Al Na'ir	2.2	69 296	64 284	59 273	54 265	50 257	45 250	40 243	36 237	32 230	28 223	25 216	22 210	20 203	18 196	17 189	17 181	17 174	18 167	19 160
Fomalhaut	1.3	58 334	55 319	51 306	47 294	42 284	37 275	32 266	27 258	23 250	18 242	14 234	10 226	7 218	4 210	2 201	0 193	# ###	# ###	1 166
Markab	2.6	14 346	12 336	10 327	7 318	3 309	# ###	# ###	# ###	# ###	# ###	# ###	# ###	# ###	# ###	# ###	# ###	# ###	# ###	# ###

* Variable 0.1 - 1.2

SUN MOON PLANETS — Local Hour Angle Body

	0° Alt Az	10° Alt Az	20° Alt Az	30° Alt Az	40° Alt Az	50° Alt Az	60° Alt Az	70° Alt Az	80° Alt Az	90° Alt Az	100° Alt Az	110° Alt Az	120° Alt Az	130° Alt Az	140° Alt Az	150° Alt Az	160° Alt Az	170° Alt Az	180° Alt Az
Decl'n N30°	0 000	# ###	# ###	# ###	# ###	# ###	# ###	# ###	# ###	# ###	# ###	# ###	# ###	# ###	# ###	# ###	# ###	# ###	# ###
Decl'n N25°	5 000	5 351	3 342	2 333	# ###	# ###	# ###	# ###	# ###	# ###	# ###	# ###	# ###	# ###	# ###	# ###	# ###	# ###	# ###
Decl'n N20°	10 000	10 350	8 341	6 332	4 323	0 314	# ###	# ###	# ###	# ###	# ###	# ###	# ###	# ###	# ###	# ###	# ###	# ###	# ###
Decl'n N15°	15 000	15 350	13 340	11 331	8 321	5 312	1 303	# ###	# ###	# ###	# ###	# ###	# ###	# ###	# ###	# ###	# ###	# ###	# ###
Decl'n N10°	20 000	20 350	18 339	16 329	13 319	10 310	5 301	1 292	# ###	# ###	# ###	# ###	# ###	# ###	# ###	# ###	# ###	# ###	# ###
Decl'n N5°	25 000	25 349	23 338	21 328	18 318	14 308	10 299	5 290	1 281	# ###	# ###	# ###	# ###	# ###	# ###	# ###	# ###	# ###	# ###
Decl'n 0°	30 000	29 348	28 337	26 326	23 316	19 306	14 297	10 287	5 279	0 270	# ###	# ###	# ###	# ###	# ###	# ###	# ###	# ###	# ###
Decl'n S5°	35 000	34 348	33 336	30 325	27 314	23 304	19 294	14 285	9 276	4 267	# ###	# ###	# ###	# ###	# ###	# ###	# ###	# ###	# ###
Decl'n S10°	40 000	39 347	38 335	35 323	32 312	28 301	23 292	19 282	14 274	9 265	4 256	# ###	# ###	# ###	# ###	# ###	# ###	# ###	# ###
Decl'n S15°	45 000	44 346	43 333	40 321	36 309	32 299	28 289	23 280	18 271	13 262	8 254	3 245	# ###	# ###	# ###	# ###	# ###	# ###	# ###
Decl'n S20°	50 000	49 345	48 332	45 319	41 307	37 296	32 286	27 277	22 268	17 260	12 251	8 243	4 235	# ###	# ###	# ###	# ###	# ###	# ###
Decl'n S25°	55 000	54 344	52 330	49 316	45 304	41 293	36 283	31 274	26 265	21 257	17 249	12 241	8 232	4 224	1 216	# ###	# ###	# ###	# ###
Decl'n S30°	60 000	59 343	57 327	54 313	50 300	45 289	41 279	36 270	31 262	26 254	21 246	17 238	13 230	9 222	6 214	3 206	1 197	0 189	# ###

Latitude S60°

STARS — Local Hour Angle Aries

Name	Mag	180° Alt Az	190° Alt Az	200° Alt Az	210° Alt Az	220° Alt Az	230° Alt Az	240° Alt Az	250° Alt Az	260° Alt Az	270° Alt Az	280° Alt Az	290° Alt Az	300° Alt Az	310° Alt Az	320° Alt Az	330° Alt Az	340° Alt Az	350° Alt Az	360° Alt Az
		° °	° °	° °	° °	° °	° °	° °	° °	° °	° °	° °	° °	° °	° °	° °	° °	° °	° °	° °
Alpheratz	2.2	# ####	# ####	# ####	# ####	# ####	# ####	# ####	# ####	# ####	# ####	# ####	# ####	# ####	# ####	# ####	# ####	# ####	0 011	1 002
Ankaa	2.4	12 185	12 177	13 170	14 162	16 155	18 148	21 140	25 133	29 126	33 119	37 112	42 105	47 097	52 088	57 079	62 068	66 054	70 037	72 016
Schedah	2.5	# ####	# ####	# ####	# ####	# ####	# ####	# ####	# ####	# ####	# ####	# ####	# ####	# ####	# ####	# ####	# ####	# ####	# ####	# ####
Diphda	2.2	# ####	# ####	# ####	# ####	# ####	# ####	# ####	1 125	6 117	10 108	15 100	20 091	25 083	30 073	35 064	39 053	42 041	45 029	47 015
Achernar	0.6	29 195	28 189	27 183	27 177	28 171	29 165	31 159	33 153	35 147	38 141	41 136	45 130	49 125	53 119	58 114	62 109	67 103	72 096	77 088
Hamal	2.2	# ####	# ####	# ####	# ####	# ####	# ####	# ####	# ####	# ####	# ####	# ####	# ####	# ####	# ####	# ####	# ####	# ####	# ####	3 029
Polaris	2.1	# ####	# ####	# ####	# ####	# ####	# ####	# ####	# ####	# ####	# ####	# ####	# ####	# ####	# ####	# ####	# ####	# ####	# ####	# ####
Acamar	3.1	17 214	14 207	12 199	11 191	10 184	10 176	11 168	12 160	14 153	17 145	20 138	24 131	28 124	32 116	37 109	41 101	46 093	51 085	56 075
Menkar	2.8	# ####	# ####	# ####	# ####	# ####	# ####	# ####	# ####	# ####	# ####	# ####	# ####	# ####	# ####	# ####	4 075	8 067	13 058	17 048
Mirfak	1.9	# ####	# ####	# ####	# ####	# ####	# ####	# ####	# ####	# ####	# ####	# ####	# ####	# ####	# ####	# ####	# ####	# ####	# ####	# ####
Aldebaran	1.1	# ####	# ####	# ####	# ####	# ####	# ####	# ####	# ####	# ####	# ####	# ####	# ####	# ####	# ####	# ####	# ####	3 102	8 093	13 084
Rigel	0.3	1 256	# ####	# ####	# ####	# ####	# ####	# ####	# ####	# ####	# ####	# ####	# ####	# ####	# ####	# ####	# ####	# ####	# ####	# ####
Capella	0.2	# ####	# ####	# ####	# ####	# ####	# ####	# ####	# ####	# ####	# ####	# ####	# ####	# ####	# ####	# ####	# ####	# ####	# ####	# ####
Bellatrix	1.7	# ####	# ####	# ####	# ####	# ####	# ####	# ####	# ####	# ####	# ####	# ####	# ####	# ####	# ####	# ####	# ####	# ####	# ####	# ####
Elnath	1.8	# ####	# ####	# ####	# ####	# ####	# ####	# ####	# ####	# ####	# ####	# ####	# ####	# ####	# ####	# ####	# ####	# ####	# ####	# ####
Alnilam	1.8	# ####	# ####	# ####	# ####	# ####	# ####	# ####	# ####	# ####	# ####	# ####	# ####	# ####	# ####	# ####	# ####	# ####	# ####	4 085
Betelgeuse	*	# ####	# ####	# ####	# ####	# ####	# ####	# ####	# ####	# ####	# ####	# ####	# ####	# ####	# ####	# ####	# ####	# ####	# ####	# ####
Canopus	-0.9	46 240	42 234	38 228	34 222	31 216	29 210	26 203	25 197	23 190	23 184	23 177	23 171	24 164	26 158	28 151	31 145	34 139	37 133	41 127
Sirius	-1.6	20 271	15 263	10 254	5 246	1 237	# ####	# ####	# ####	# ####	# ####	# ####	# ####	# ####	# ####	# ####	# ####	0 125	4 116	9 108
Adhara	1.6	32 267	27 258	22 250	18 242	13 234	10 226	6 218	3 210	1 201	# ####	# ####	# ####	# ####	1 158	4 150	6 141	10 133	14 125	18 117
Procyon	0.5	7 294	3 285	# ####	# ####	# ####	# ####	# ####	# ####	# ####	# ####	# ####	# ####	# ####	# ####	# ####	# ####	# ####	# ####	# ####
Pollux	1.2	# ####	# ####	# ####	# ####	# ####	# ####	# ####	# ####	# ####	# ####	# ####	# ####	# ####	# ####	# ####	# ####	# ####	# ####	# ####
Avior	1.7	63 247	59 242	55 237	50 232	47 227	43 222	40 217	37 212	35 206	33 201	31 195	30 189	30 183	30 177	30 172	31 166	32 160	34 155	37 149
Suhail	2.2	59 283	54 273	49 265	45 257	40 250	35 243	31 236	27 229	23 222	20 214	18 207	16 200	14 193	14 185	13 178	14 170	15 163	17 156	19 148
Miaplacidus	1.8	70 223	67 224	63 223	60 221	57 219	54 216	51 213	48 209	46 205	44 201	43 197	41 193	40 188	40 184	40 179	40 175	41 170	42 166	43 162
Alphard	2.2	31 314	27 304	23 294	18 285	13 276	8 267	3 259	# ####	# ####	# ####	# ####	# ####	# ####	# ####	# ####	# ####	# ####	# ####	# ####
Regulus	1.3	15 332	12 322	9 313	5 304	0 295	# ####	# ####	# ####	# ####	# ####	# ####	# ####	# ####	# ####	# ####	# ####	# ####	# ####	# ####
Dubhe	2.0	# ####	# ####	# ####	# ####	# ####	# ####	# ####	# ####	# ####	# ####	# ####	# ####	# ####	# ####	# ####	# ####	# ####	# ####	# ####
Denebola	2.2	15 357	15 347	13 337	11 328	8 318	4 309	0 301	# ####	# ####	# ####	# ####	# ####	# ####	# ####	# ####	# ####	# ####	# ####	# ####
Gienah	2.8	47 006	47 351	46 338	44 325	40 313	36 302	32 291	27 282	22 273	17 264	12 256	7 248	3 239	# ####	# ####	# ####	# ####	# ####	# ####
Acrux	1.1	86 137	87 206	83 238	79 244	74 244	70 243	65 240	61 236	57 232	53 228	49 224	46 219	43 215	40 210	38 205	36 200	35 194	34 189	33 184
Gacrux	1.6	85 058	87 337	83 289	78 274	73 266	68 259	63 253	59 247	54 242	50 236	46 231	42 226	39 220	36 214	33 209	31 203	29 197	28 191	27 185
Alioth	1.7	# ####	# ####	# ####	# ####	# ####	# ####	# ####	# ####	# ####	# ####	# ####	# ####	# ####	# ####	# ####	# ####	# ####	# ####	# ####
Spica	1.2	39 027	40 015	41 002	41 349	39 336	37 324	33 313	29 302	25 292	20 283	15 274	10 265	5 257	1 248	# ####	# ####	# ####	# ####	# ####
Alkaid	1.9	# ####	# ####	# ####	# ####	# ####	# ####	# ####	# ####	# ####	# ####	# ####	# ####	# ####	# ####	# ####	# ####	# ####	# ####	# ####
Hadar	0.9	75 105	80 101	85 099	89 129	85 261	81 259	76 256	71 252	66 248	62 243	57 239	53 234	49 229	46 224	42 219	39 214	37 209	34 203	33 198
Menkent	2.3	59 055	63 040	65 023	66 003	66 343	64 325	60 310	56 297	51 286	46 276	41 267	37 259	32 251	27 243	23 236	19 228	15 221	12 213	10 205
Arcturus	0.2	6 032	8 023	10 013	11 004	11 354	10 345	8 335	6 326	2 317	# ####	# ####	# ####	# ####	# ####	# ####	# ####	# ####	# ####	# ####
Rigil Kent.	0.1	71 110	75 106	80 104	85 104	89 183	85 256	80 256	75 254	71 250	66 246	61 242	57 237	53 233	49 228	46 223	42 218	39 213	37 208	35 202
Zuben'ubi	2.9	36 054	40 043	43 031	45 017	46 004	46 350	44 337	42 324	38 312	34 301	30 291	25 282	20 273	15 264	10 256	6 247	1 239	# ####	# ####
Kochab	2.2	# ####	# ####	# ####	# ####	# ####	# ####	# ####	# ####	# ####	# ####	# ####	# ####	# ####	# ####	# ####	# ####	# ####	# ####	# ####
Alphecca	2.3	# ####	# ####	# ####	1 021	3 012	3 003	3 354	2 345	1 337	# ####	# ####	# ####	# ####	# ####	# ####	# ####	# ####	# ####	# ####
Antares	1.2	34 085	39 075	44 065	48 054	52 041	54 027	56 012	56 356	55 340	53 325	50 312	46 300	41 289	36 280	31 271	26 262	21 254	17 246	12 238
Atria	1.9	60 138	63 136	67 134	70 135	74 137	77 143	80 155	81 175	80 197	78 213	75 221	72 225	68 226	65 225	61 223	58 221	55 218	52 215	49 211
Sabik	2.6	20 087	25 078	30 069	34 059	38 048	41 036	44 024	45 010	46 357	45 343	43 330	40 318	36 306	32 296	27 286	22 277	17 268	12 260	8 252
Shaula	1.7	35 106	40 098	45 089	49 080	54 070	59 058	63 044	66 027	67 007	67 347	65 328	62 312	57 298	53 287	48 277	43 268	38 260	33 252	28 244
Rasalhague	2.1	# ####	# ####	2 061	6 052	9 043	13 034	15 024	17 014	17 004	17 354	16 343	14 334	12 324	9 315	5 305	0 297	# ####	# ####	# ####
Eltanin	2.4	# ####	# ####	# ####	# ####	# ####	# ####	# ####	# ####	# ####	# ####	# ####	# ####	# ####	# ####	# ####	# ####	# ####	# ####	# ####
Kaus Aust.	2.0	26 114	31 106	36 098	41 089	46 080	51 070	55 059	59 045	62 029	64 011	64 352	63 334	60 318	56 304	52 292	47 282	42 272	37 264	32 256
Vega	0.1	# ####	# ####	# ####	# ####	# ####	# ####	# ####	# ####	# ####	# ####	# ####	# ####	# ####	# ####	# ####	# ####	# ####	# ####	# ####
Nunki	2.1	16 115	21 107	26 099	31 090	36 081	40 072	45 061	49 050	53 037	55 022	56 006	56 350	55 335	52 320	48 307	44 296	39 286	34 276	29 268
Altair	0.9	# ####	# ####	# ####	# ####	# ####	3 066	7 057	11 048	15 039	18 029	20 019	21 008	21 358	20 347	19 337	17 327	13 317	10 308	6 298
Peacock	2.1	34 148	37 142	40 136	44 131	48 125	52 120	56 114	61 109	66 103	71 096	76 088	81 076	85 049	86 329	82 289	77 275	72 266	67 259	62 253
Deneb	1.3	# ####	# ####	# ####	# ####	# ####	# ####	# ####	# ####	# ####	# ####	# ####	# ####	# ####	# ####	# ####	# ####	# ####	# ####	# ####
Enif	2.5	# ####	# ####	# ####	# ####	# ####	# ####	# ####	# ####	3 064	7 055	11 046	15 037	17 027	19 017	20 006	20 356	19 345	18 335	15 325
Al Na'ir	2.2	19 160	21 153	24 146	27 140	30 133	34 126	38 120	43 113	48 106	52 098	57 090	62 081	67 069	72 055	75 034	77 006	76 337	73 313	69 296
Fomalhaut	1.3	1 166	2 158	4 150	7 141	11 133	14 125	19 117	23 109	28 101	33 093	38 084	43 075	48 064	52 053	55 039	58 024	59 008	59 350	58 334
Markab	2.6	# ####	# ####	# ####	# ####	# ####	# ####	# ####	# ####	# ####	# ####	# ####	2 053	6 044	9 035	12 026	14 016	15 006	15 356	14 346

* Variable 0.1 - 1.2

SUN MOON PLANETS — Local Hour Angle Body

		180° Alt Az	190° Alt Az	200° Alt Az	210° Alt Az	220° Alt Az	230° Alt Az	240° Alt Az	250° Alt Az	260° Alt Az	270° Alt Az	280° Alt Az	290° Alt Az	300° Alt Az	310° Alt Az	320° Alt Az	330° Alt Az	340° Alt Az	350° Alt Az	360° Alt Az
		° °	° °	° °	° °	° °	° °	° °	° °	° °	° °	° °	° °	° °	° °	° °	° °	° °	° °	° °
Decl'n	N30°	# ####	# ####	# ####	# ####	# ####	# ####	# ####	# ####	# ####	# ####	# ####	# ####	# ####	# ####	# ####	# ####	# ####	# ####	0 000
Decl'n	N25°	# ####	# ####	# ####	# ####	# ####	# ####	# ####	# ####	# ####	# ####	# ####	# ####	# ####	# ####	# ####	2 027	3 018	5 009	5 000
Decl'n	N20°	# ####	# ####	# ####	# ####	# ####	# ####	# ####	# ####	# ####	# ####	# ####	# ####	# ####	0 046	4 037	6 028	8 019	10 010	10 000
Decl'n	N15°	# ####	# ####	# ####	# ####	# ####	# ####	# ####	# ####	# ####	# ####	# ####	# ####	1 057	5 048	8 039	11 029	13 020	15 010	15 000
Decl'n	N10°	# ####	# ####	# ####	# ####	# ####	# ####	# ####	# ####	# ####	# ####	# ####	1 068	5 059	10 050	13 041	16 031	18 021	20 010	20 000
Decl'n	N5°	# ####	# ####	# ####	# ####	# ####	# ####	# ####	# ####	# ####	# ####	1 079	5 070	10 061	14 052	18 042	21 032	23 022	25 011	25 000
Decl'n	0°	# ####	# ####	# ####	# ####	# ####	# ####	# ####	# ####	# ####	# ####	5 081	10 073	14 063	19 054	23 044	26 034	28 023	29 012	30 000
Decl'n	S5°	# ####	# ####	# ####	# ####	# ####	# ####	# ####	# ####	# ####	4 093	9 084	14 075	19 066	23 056	27 046	30 035	33 024	34 012	35 000
Decl'n	S10°	# ####	# ####	# ####	# ####	# ####	# ####	# ####	# ####	4 104	9 095	14 086	19 078	23 068	28 059	32 048	35 037	38 025	39 013	40 000
Decl'n	S15°	# ####	# ####	# ####	# ####	# ####	# ####	# ####	3 115	8 106	13 098	18 089	23 080	28 071	32 061	36 051	40 039	43 027	44 014	45 000
Decl'n	S20°	# ####	# ####	# ####	# ####	# ####	# ####	4 125	8 117	12 109	17 100	22 092	27 083	32 074	37 064	41 053	45 041	48 028	49 015	50 000
Decl'n	S25°	# ####	# ####	# ####	# ####	1 144	4 136	8 128	12 119	17 111	21 103	26 095	31 086	36 077	41 067	45 056	49 044	52 030	54 016	55 000
Decl'n	S30°	# ####	0 171	1 163	3 154	6 146	9 138	13 130	17 122	21 114	26 106	31 098	36 090	41 081	45 071	50 060	54 047	57 033	59 017	60 000

LAT OF SUNRISE & SUNSET

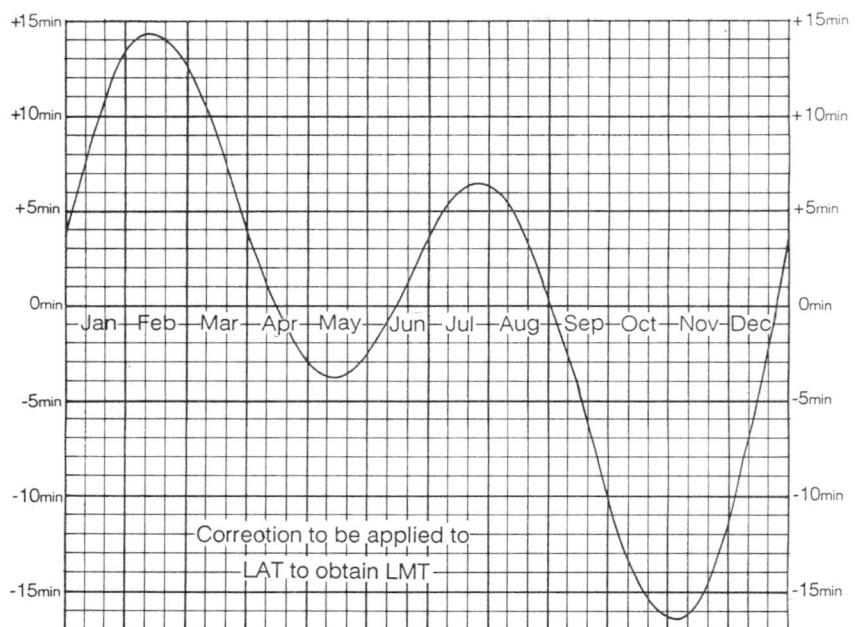

LAT of Sunrise & Sunset

(1) Enter the lower diagram with the date, follow horizontally and interpolate the required latitude.(If it is not possible to interpolate the latitude, refer to Special Cases of Rising and Setting in Section 5.5.) From this point move vertically up or down to obtain the LAT of Sunrise or Sunset respectively.
(2) Enter the left-hand diagram with the date and read off from the graph the correction which is then applied to the LAT found previously to obtain the LMT of the phenomenon.

LAT OF SUNRISE

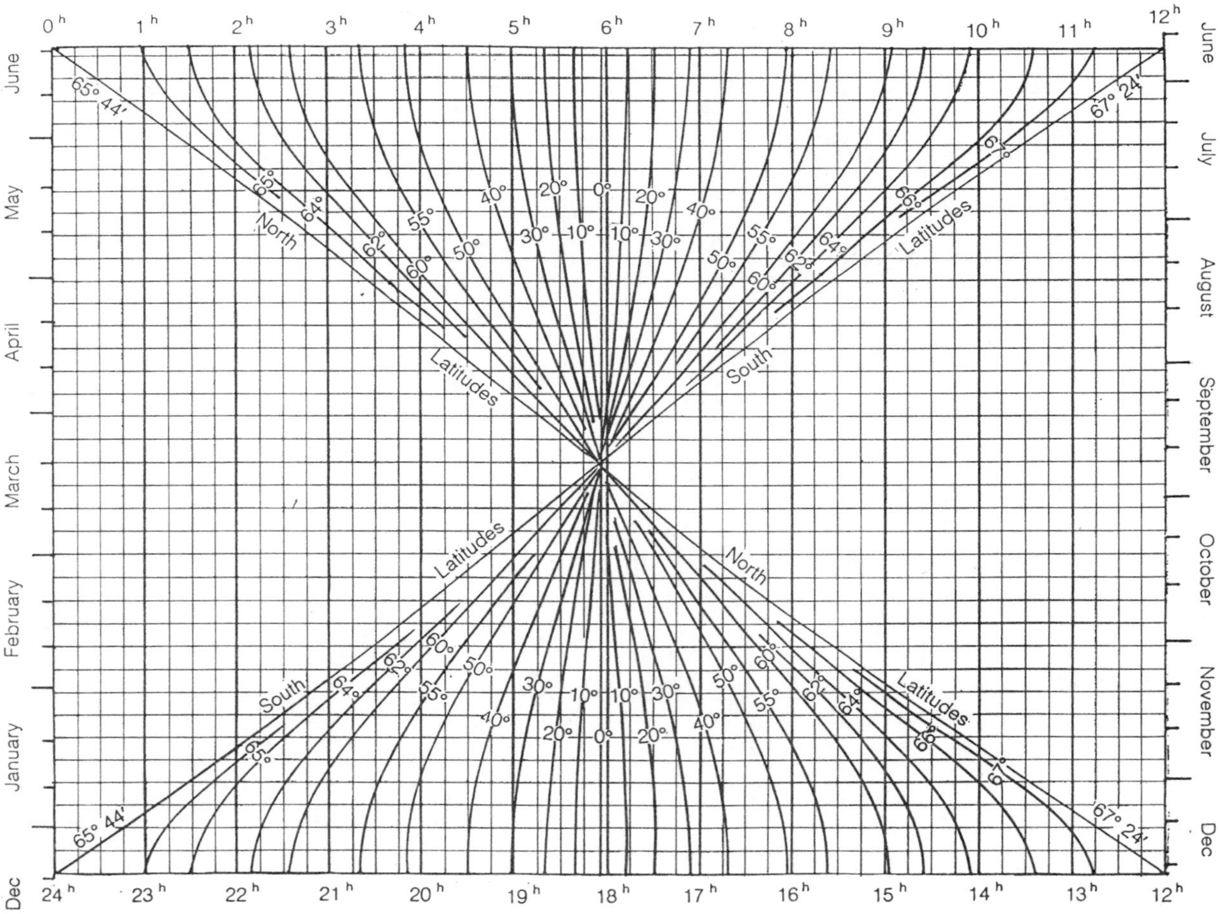

LAT OF SUNSET

LAT OF MORNING & EVENING CIVIL TWILIGHT

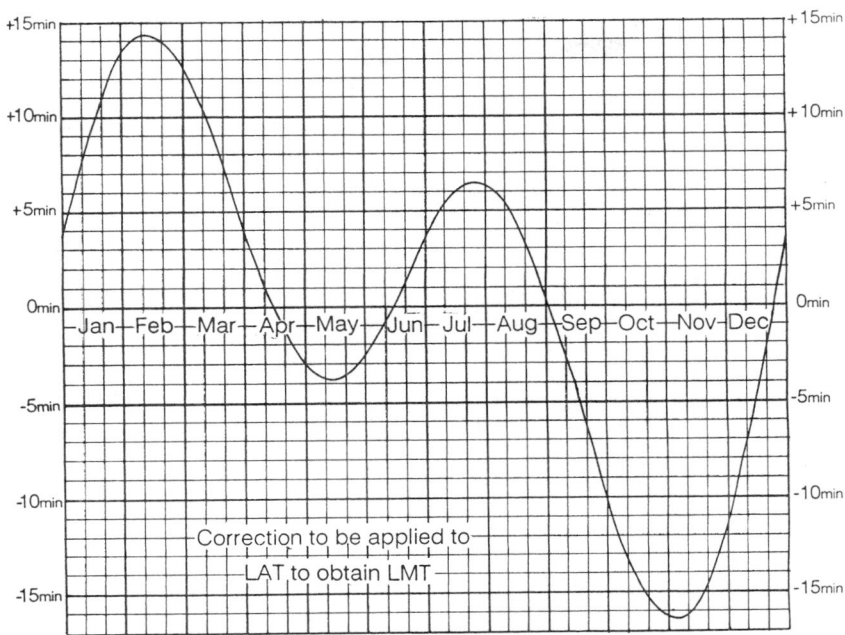

LAT of Morning & Evening Civil Twilight

(1) Enter the lower diagram with the date, follow horizontally and interpolate the required latitude. (If it is not possible to interpolate the latitude, refer to Special Cases of Rising and Setting in Section 5.5.) From this point move vertically up or down to obtain the LAT of Morning or Evening Twilight respectively.

(2) Enter the left-hand diagram with the date and read off from the graph the correction which is then applied to the LAT found previously to obtain the LMT of the phenomenon.

LAT OF MORNING CIVIL TWILIGHT

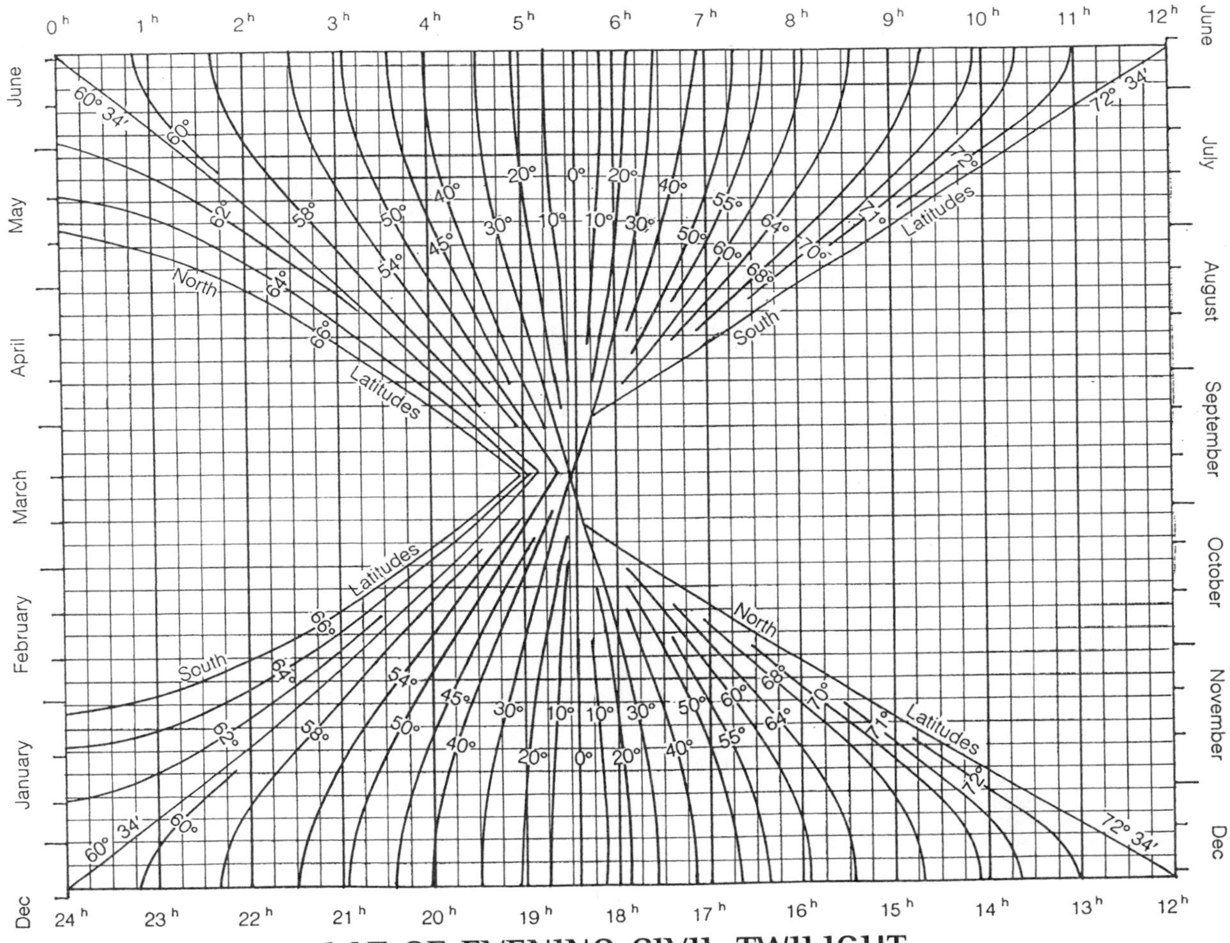

LAT OF EVENING CIVIL TWILIGHT

SIGHT REDUCTION

	0°			1°			2°			3°			4°			5°			
	LAT	LHA	L~D	LAT	LHA	L~D	LAT	LHA	L~D	LAT	LHA	L~D	LAT	LHA	L~D	LAT	LHA	L~D	
	DEC	SUM	RES	DEC	SUM	RES	DEC	SUM	RES	DEC	SUM	RES	DEC	SUM	RES	DEC	SUM	RES	
00'	0	######	0	1	53661	15	3	45817	61	8	41229	137	14	37974	244	22	35450	381	60'
01	0	99999	0	1	53474	16	4	45723	62	8	41166	139	14	37927	246	22	35412	383	59
02	0	92154	0	1	53290	16	4	45630	63	8	41104	140	14	37880	248	22	35374	386	58
03	0	87565	0	1	53109	17	4	45537	64	8	41042	142	14	37833	250	22	35337	388	57
04	0	84309	0	1	52931	17	4	45446	65	8	40980	143	14	37787	252	22	35300	391	56
05	0	81784	0	1	52755	18	4	45355	66	8	40919	145	14	37740	254	22	35263	393	55
06	0	79721	0	1	52582	18	4	45265	67	8	40858	146	15	37694	256	22	35226	396	54
07	0	77976	0	1	52412	19	4	45175	68	8	40797	148	15	37648	258	23	35189	398	53
08	0	76465	0	1	52245	20	4	45086	69	8	40737	149	15	37603	260	23	35152	401	52
09	0	75132	0	1	52079	20	4	44998	70	9	40677	151	15	37557	262	23	35115	404	51
10	0	73939	0	1	51916	21	4	44911	71	9	40617	153	15	37512	264	23	35079	406	50
11	0	72861	1	1	51756	21	4	44824	73	9	40557	154	15	37467	266	23	35042	409	49
12	0	71876	1	1	51598	22	4	44738	74	9	40498	156	15	37422	269	23	35006	412	48
13	0	70970	1	1	51442	23	4	44653	75	9	40440	158	15	37377	271	23	34970	414	47
14	0	70131	1	1	51288	23	4	44568	76	9	40381	159	15	37332	273	24	34934	417	46
15	0	69350	1	1	51136	24	4	44484	77	9	40323	161	16	37288	275	24	34898	420	45
16	0	68620	1	1	50986	24	4	44400	78	9	40265	162	16	37244	277	24	34862	422	44
17	0	67934	1	1	50838	25	4	44317	79	9	40207	164	16	37199	279	24	34826	425	43
18	0	67287	1	1	50692	26	5	44235	81	9	40150	166	16	37156	281	24	34791	428	42
19	0	66675	2	1	50548	26	5	44153	82	9	40093	167	16	37112	284	24	34755	430	41
20	0	66095	2	2	50405	27	5	44072	83	10	40036	169	16	37068	286	25	34720	433	40
21	0	65542	2	2	50265	28	5	43992	84	10	39980	171	16	37025	288	25	34684	436	39
22	0	65016	2	2	50126	28	5	43912	85	10	39924	173	16	36982	290	25	34649	438	38
23	0	64513	2	2	49989	29	5	43832	87	10	39868	174	17	36938	292	25	34614	441	37
24	0	64031	2	2	49853	30	5	43754	88	10	39812	176	17	36896	295	25	34579	444	36
25	0	63569	3	2	49719	31	5	43675	89	10	39757	178	17	36853	297	25	34544	447	35
26	0	63125	3	2	49587	31	5	43597	90	10	39702	179	17	36810	299	25	34510	449	34
27	0	62698	3	2	49456	32	5	43520	91	10	39647	181	17	36768	301	26	34475	452	33
28	0	62287	3	2	49327	33	5	43443	93	10	39593	183	17	36725	304	26	34440	455	32
29	0	61889	4	2	49199	34	5	43367	94	10	39538	185	17	36683	306	26	34406	458	31
30	0	61506	4	2	49072	34	5	43292	95	11	39484	187	17	36641	308	26	34372	460	30
31	0	61135	4	2	48947	35	5	43216	96	11	39431	188	18	36599	311	26	34337	463	29
32	0	60775	4	2	48824	36	6	43142	98	11	39377	190	18	36558	313	26	34303	466	28
33	0	60427	5	2	48701	37	6	43068	99	11	39324	192	18	36516	315	27	34269	469	27
34	0	60089	5	2	48580	37	6	42994	100	11	39271	194	18	36475	317	27	34235	472	26
35	0	59761	5	2	48460	38	6	42921	102	11	39218	196	18	36434	320	27	34202	474	25
36	0	59442	5	2	48342	39	6	42848	103	11	39166	197	18	36393	322	27	34168	477	24
37	0	59132	6	2	48225	40	6	42775	104	11	39113	199	18	36352	324	27	34134	480	23
38	0	58830	6	2	48109	41	6	42704	106	11	39061	201	19	36311	327	27	34101	483	22
39	0	58536	6	2	47994	41	6	42632	107	11	39010	203	19	36270	329	28	34067	486	21
40	0	58250	7	2	47880	42	6	42561	108	12	38958	205	19	36230	332	28	34034	489	20
41	0	57970	7	2	47767	43	6	42491	110	12	38907	207	19	36190	334	28	34001	492	19
42	0	57698	7	2	47656	44	6	42421	111	12	38856	208	19	36149	336	28	33968	494	18
43	0	57431	8	3	47545	45	6	42351	112	12	38805	210	19	36109	339	28	33935	497	17
44	0	57171	8	3	47436	46	6	42282	114	12	38754	212	19	36069	341	28	33902	500	16
45	0	56917	9	3	47328	47	7	42213	115	12	38704	214	19	36030	343	29	33869	503	15
46	1	56668	9	3	47221	48	7	42145	117	12	38654	216	20	35990	346	29	33836	506	14
47	1	56425	9	3	47114	48	7	42077	118	12	38604	218	20	35951	348	29	33804	509	13
48	1	56186	10	3	47009	49	7	42009	119	12	38554	220	20	35911	351	29	33771	512	12
49	1	55953	10	3	46905	50	7	41942	121	13	38504	222	20	35872	353	29	33739	515	11
50	1	55724	11	3	46801	51	7	41875	122	13	38455	224	20	35833	356	29	33706	518	10
51	1	55500	11	3	46699	52	7	41809	124	13	38406	226	20	35794	358	30	33674	521	09
52	1	55281	11	3	46597	53	7	41743	125	13	38357	228	20	35755	361	30	33642	524	08
53	1	55065	12	3	46497	54	7	41677	127	13	38309	230	21	35717	363	30	33610	527	07
54	1	54853	12	3	46397	55	7	41612	128	13	38260	232	21	35678	365	30	33578	530	06
55	1	54646	13	3	46298	56	7	41547	130	13	38212	234	21	35640	368	30	33546	533	05
56	1	54442	13	3	46200	57	7	41483	131	13	38164	236	21	35601	370	30	33514	536	04
57	1	54242	14	3	46103	58	8	41419	133	13	38116	238	21	35563	373	31	33482	539	03
58	1	54045	14	3	46007	59	8	41355	134	14	38068	240	21	35525	375	31	33451	542	02
59	1	53851	15	3	45911	60	8	41292	136	14	38021	242	21	35487	378	31	33419	545	01
60	1	53661	15	3	45817	61	8	41229	137	14	37974	244	22	35450	381	31	33388	548	00
	89°			**88°**			**87°**			**86°**			**85°**			**84°**			
	LHA	ALT		LHA	ALT		LHA	ALT		LHA	ALT		LHA	ALT		LHA	ALT		
	359°			358°			357°			356°			355°			354°			

SIGHT REDUCTION

	6° LAT/DEC	6° LHA/SUM	6° L~D/RES	7° LAT/DEC	7° LHA/SUM	7° L~D/RES	8° LAT/DEC	8° LHA/SUM	8° L~D/RES	9° LAT/DEC	9° LHA/SUM	9° L~D/RES	10° LAT/DEC	10° LHA/SUM	10° L~D/RES	11° LAT/DEC	11° LHA/SUM	11° L~D/RES	
00'	31	33388	548	42	31645	745	55	30136	973	70	28805	1231	87	27616	1519	105	26540	1837	60'
01	31	33356	551	43	31618	749	56	30112	977	70	28784	1236	87	27597	1524	105	26523	1843	59
02	31	33325	554	43	31591	752	56	30089	981	71	28764	1240	87	27578	1529	106	26506	1848	58
03	32	33294	557	43	31564	756	56	30065	985	71	28743	1245	88	27559	1534	106	26489	1854	57
04	32	33263	560	43	31538	760	56	30042	989	71	28722	1249	88	27541	1539	106	26472	1860	56
05	32	33232	563	43	31511	763	57	30019	994	71	28701	1254	88	27522	1545	107	26455	1865	55
06	32	33201	566	44	31485	767	57	29995	998	72	28680	1259	88	27503	1550	107	26438	1871	54
07	32	33170	569	44	31458	770	57	29972	1002	72	28660	1263	89	27485	1555	107	26421	1876	53
08	32	33139	572	44	31432	774	57	29949	1006	72	28639	1268	89	27466	1560	108	26404	1882	52
09	33	33108	576	44	31405	778	57	29926	1010	72	28619	1272	89	27448	1565	108	26387	1888	51
10	33	33078	579	44	31379	781	58	29903	1014	73	28598	1277	90	27429	1570	108	26370	1893	50
11	33	33047	582	45	31353	785	58	29880	1018	73	28578	1282	90	27410	1575	108	26353	1899	49
12	33	33017	585	45	31327	789	58	29857	1022	73	28557	1286	90	27392	1580	109	26337	1904	48
13	33	32987	588	45	31300	792	58	29834	1027	74	28537	1291	90	27374	1586	109	26320	1910	47
14	34	32956	591	45	31274	796	59	29811	1031	74	28516	1296	91	27355	1591	109	26303	1916	46
15	34	32926	594	45	31248	799	59	29788	1035	74	28496	1300	91	27337	1596	110	26286	1921	45
16	34	32896	598	46	31222	803	59	29765	1039	74	28476	1305	91	27318	1601	110	26270	1927	44
17	34	32866	601	46	31196	807	59	29743	1043	75	28455	1310	92	27300	1606	110	26253	1933	43
18	34	32836	604	46	31171	811	60	29720	1047	75	28435	1314	92	27282	1611	111	26236	1939	42
19	34	32806	607	46	31145	814	60	29697	1052	75	28415	1319	92	27264	1617	111	26220	1944	41
20	35	32776	610	46	31119	818	60	29675	1056	75	28395	1324	93	27245	1622	111	26203	1950	40
21	35	32747	614	47	31093	822	60	29652	1060	76	28374	1329	93	27227	1627	112	26187	1956	39
22	35	32717	617	47	31068	825	61	29630	1064	76	28354	1333	93	27209	1632	112	26170	1961	38
23	35	32687	620	47	31042	829	61	29607	1069	76	28334	1338	93	27191	1638	112	26153	1967	37
24	35	32658	623	47	31017	833	61	29585	1073	77	28314	1343	94	27173	1643	113	26137	1973	36
25	36	32629	626	48	30991	837	61	29562	1077	77	28294	1348	94	27155	1648	113	26120	1979	35
26	36	32599	630	48	30966	840	62	29540	1081	77	28274	1352	94	27137	1653	113	26104	1984	34
27	36	32570	633	48	30941	844	62	29518	1086	77	28254	1357	95	27119	1659	114	26088	1990	33
28	36	32541	636	48	30915	848	62	29495	1090	78	28234	1362	95	27101	1664	114	26071	1996	32
29	36	32512	640	48	30890	852	62	29473	1094	78	28215	1367	95	27083	1669	114	26055	2002	31
30	36	32483	643	49	30865	856	63	29451	1098	78	28195	1371	96	27065	1674	115	26038	2008	30
31	37	32454	646	49	30840	859	63	29429	1103	78	28175	1376	96	27047	1680	115	26022	2013	29
32	37	32425	649	49	30815	863	63	29407	1107	79	28155	1381	96	27029	1685	115	26006	2019	28
33	37	32396	653	49	30790	867	63	29385	1111	79	28135	1386	96	27011	1690	116	25990	2025	27
34	37	32367	656	49	30765	871	63	29363	1116	79	28116	1391	97	26993	1696	116	25973	2031	26
35	37	32339	659	50	30740	875	64	29341	1120	80	28096	1396	97	26976	1701	116	25957	2037	25
36	38	32310	663	50	30715	878	64	29319	1124	80	28076	1400	97	26958	1706	117	25941	2042	24
37	38	32282	666	50	30691	882	64	29297	1129	80	28057	1405	98	26940	1712	117	25925	2048	23
38	38	32253	669	50	30666	886	64	29275	1133	80	28037	1410	98	26922	1717	117	25908	2054	22
39	38	32225	673	51	30641	890	65	29253	1137	81	28018	1415	98	26905	1723	118	25892	2060	21
40	38	32196	676	51	30617	894	65	29232	1142	81	27998	1420	99	26887	1728	118	25876	2066	20
41	39	32168	680	51	30592	898	65	29210	1146	81	27979	1425	99	26870	1733	118	25860	2072	19
42	39	32140	683	51	30568	902	65	29188	1151	81	27959	1430	99	26852	1739	119	25844	2078	18
43	39	32112	686	51	30543	906	66	29167	1155	82	27940	1435	100	26834	1744	119	25828	2084	17
44	39	32084	690	52	30519	909	66	29145	1159	82	27921	1439	100	26817	1750	119	25812	2090	16
45	39	32056	693	52	30495	913	66	29123	1164	82	27901	1444	100	26799	1755	120	25796	2095	15
46	40	32028	697	52	30470	917	66	29102	1168	83	27882	1449	101	26782	1760	120	25780	2101	14
47	40	32000	700	52	30446	921	67	29081	1173	83	27863	1454	101	26764	1766	121	25764	2107	13
48	40	31973	703	53	30422	925	67	29059	1177	83	27844	1459	101	26747	1771	121	25748	2113	12
49	40	31945	707	53	30398	929	67	29038	1182	83	27824	1464	101	26730	1777	121	25732	2119	11
50	40	31917	710	53	30374	933	68	29016	1186	84	27805	1469	102	26712	1782	122	25716	2125	10
51	41	31890	714	53	30350	937	68	28995	1191	84	27786	1474	102	26695	1788	122	25700	2131	09
52	41	31862	717	54	30326	941	68	28974	1195	84	27767	1479	102	26678	1793	122	25684	2137	08
53	41	31835	721	54	30302	945	68	28953	1200	85	27748	1484	103	26660	1799	123	25669	2143	07
54	41	31808	724	54	30278	949	69	28931	1204	85	27729	1489	103	26643	1804	123	25653	2149	06
55	41	31780	728	54	30254	953	69	28910	1209	85	27710	1494	103	26626	1810	123	25637	2155	05
56	42	31753	731	54	30230	957	69	28889	1213	85	27691	1499	104	26608	1815	124	25621	2161	04
57	42	31726	735	55	30207	961	69	28868	1218	86	27672	1504	104	26591	1821	124	25606	2167	03
58	42	31699	738	55	30183	965	70	28847	1222	86	27653	1509	104	26574	1826	124	25590	2173	02
59	42	31672	742	55	30159	969	70	28826	1227	86	27634	1514	105	26557	1832	125	25574	2179	01
60	42	31645	745	55	30136	973	70	28805	1231	87	27616	1519	105	26540	1837	125	25558	2185	00

83°			82°			81°			80°			79°			78°			
LHA ALT			LHA ALT			LHA ALT			LHA ALT			LHA ALT			LHA ALT			
353°			352°			351°			350°			349°			348°			

133

SIGHT REDUCTION

	12° LAT DEC	12° LHA SUM	12° L~D RES	13° LAT DEC	13° LHA SUM	13° L~D RES	14° LAT DEC	14° LHA SUM	14° L~D RES	15° LAT DEC	15° LHA SUM	15° L~D RES	16° LAT DEC	16° LHA SUM	16° L~D RES	17° LAT DEC	17° LHA SUM	17° L~D RES	
00'	125	25558	2185	147	24656	2563	171	23821	2970	196	23045	3407	224	22319	3874	253	21637	4369	60'
01	125	25543	2191	147	24642	2570	171	23808	2977	197	23032	3415	224	22307	3882	253	21626	4378	59
02	126	25527	2197	148	24627	2576	171	23795	2984	197	23020	3422	225	22295	3890	254	21615	4387	58
03	126	25512	2203	148	24613	2583	172	23781	2992	198	23007	3430	225	22284	3898	254	21604	4395	57
04	126	25496	2209	148	24599	2589	172	23768	2999	198	22995	3438	225	22272	3906	255	21593	4404	56
05	127	25480	2216	149	24584	2596	173	23754	3006	198	22982	3445	226	22260	3914	255	21582	4412	55
06	127	25465	2222	149	24570	2602	173	23741	3013	199	22970	3453	226	22249	3922	256	21571	4421	54
07	127	25449	2228	150	24555	2609	174	23728	3020	199	22957	3460	227	22237	3930	256	21560	4429	53
08	128	25434	2234	150	24541	2616	174	23715	3027	200	22945	3468	227	22225	3938	257	21550	4438	52
09	128	25418	2240	150	24527	2622	174	23701	3034	200	22933	3475	228	22214	3946	257	21539	4446	51
10	129	25403	2246	151	24513	2629	175	23688	3041	201	22920	3483	228	22202	3954	258	21528	4455	50
11	129	25387	2252	151	24498	2635	175	23675	3048	201	22908	3491	229	22191	3962	258	21517	4464	49
12	129	25372	2258	152	24484	2642	176	23662	3055	202	22896	3498	229	22179	3971	259	21506	4472	48
13	130	25357	2265	152	24470	2649	176	23648	3063	202	22883	3506	230	22167	3979	259	21495	4481	47
14	130	25341	2271	152	24456	2655	176	23635	3070	202	22871	3514	230	22156	3987	260	21484	4489	46
15	130	25326	2277	153	24442	2662	177	23622	3077	203	22859	3521	231	22144	3995	260	21473	4498	45
16	131	25311	2283	153	24427	2669	177	23609	3084	203	22846	3529	231	22133	4003	261	21462	4507	44
17	131	25295	2289	153	24413	2675	178	23596	3091	204	22834	3537	232	22121	4011	261	21452	4515	43
18	131	25280	2295	154	24399	2682	178	23583	3098	204	22822	3544	232	22110	4019	262	21441	4524	42
19	132	25265	2302	154	24385	2689	179	23569	3106	205	22810	3552	233	22098	4028	262	21430	4533	41
20	132	25250	2308	155	24371	2695	179	23556	3113	205	22797	3560	233	22087	4036	263	21419	4541	40
21	132	25234	2314	155	24357	2702	179	23543	3120	206	22785	3567	234	22075	4044	264	21408	4550	39
22	133	25219	2320	155	24343	2709	180	23530	3127	206	22773	3575	234	22064	4052	264	21398	4559	38
23	133	25204	2327	156	24329	2716	180	23517	3134	206	22761	3583	235	22053	4060	265	21387	4567	37
24	134	25189	2333	156	24315	2722	181	23504	3142	207	22749	3590	235	22041	4069	265	21376	4576	36
25	134	25174	2339	157	24301	2729	181	23491	3149	207	22736	3598	236	22030	4077	266	21365	4585	35
26	134	25158	2345	157	24287	2736	181	23478	3156	208	22724	3606	236	22018	4085	266	21355	4593	34
27	135	25143	2352	157	24273	2743	182	23465	3163	208	22712	3614	237	22007	4093	267	21344	4602	33
28	135	25128	2358	158	24259	2749	182	23452	3171	209	22700	3621	237	21995	4101	267	21333	4611	32
29	135	25113	2364	158	24245	2756	183	23439	3178	209	22688	3629	237	21984	4110	268	21322	4620	31
30	136	25098	2370	159	24231	2763	183	23426	3185	210	22676	3637	238	21973	4118	268	21312	4628	30
31	136	25083	2377	159	24217	2770	184	23413	3192	210	22664	3645	238	21961	4126	269	21301	4637	29
32	136	25068	2383	159	24203	2777	184	23400	3200	211	22652	3652	239	21950	4135	269	21290	4646	28
33	137	25053	2389	160	24189	2783	184	23387	3207	211	22640	3660	239	21939	4143	270	21280	4655	27
34	137	25038	2396	160	24175	2790	185	23375	3214	211	22627	3668	240	21927	4151	270	21269	4663	26
35	138	25023	2402	161	24162	2797	185	23362	3222	212	22615	3676	240	21916	4159	271	21258	4672	25
36	138	25008	2408	161	24148	2804	186	23349	3229	212	22603	3684	241	21905	4168	271	21248	4681	24
37	138	24993	2415	161	24134	2811	186	23336	3236	213	22591	3692	241	21894	4176	272	21237	4690	23
38	139	24979	2421	162	24120	2818	187	23323	3244	213	22579	3699	242	21882	4184	272	21227	4698	22
39	139	24964	2427	162	24106	2824	187	23310	3251	214	22567	3707	242	21871	4193	273	21216	4707	21
40	139	24949	2434	163	24093	2831	187	23298	3258	214	22555	3715	243	21860	4201	273	21205	4716	20
41	140	24934	2440	163	24079	2838	188	23285	3266	215	22543	3723	243	21849	4209	274	21195	4725	19
42	140	24919	2447	163	24065	2845	188	23272	3273	215	22532	3731	244	21837	4218	274	21184	4734	18
43	141	24905	2453	164	24052	2852	189	23259	3281	216	22520	3739	244	21826	4226	275	21174	4743	17
44	141	24890	2459	164	24038	2859	189	23247	3288	216	22508	3747	245	21815	4234	275	21163	4752	16
45	141	24875	2466	165	24024	2866	190	23234	3295	217	22496	3754	245	21804	4243	276	21152	4760	15
46	142	24860	2472	165	24011	2873	190	23221	3303	217	22484	3762	246	21793	4251	277	21142	4769	14
47	142	24846	2479	165	23997	2880	190	23208	3310	217	22472	3770	246	21781	4260	277	21131	4778	13
48	142	24831	2485	166	23983	2887	191	23196	3318	218	22460	3778	247	21770	4268	278	21121	4787	12
49	143	24816	2491	166	23970	2893	191	23183	3325	218	22448	3786	247	21759	4276	278	21110	4796	11
50	143	24802	2498	167	23956	2900	192	23170	3333	219	22436	3794	248	21748	4285	279	21100	4805	10
51	144	24787	2504	167	23943	2907	192	23158	3340	219	22425	3802	248	21737	4293	279	21089	4814	09
52	144	24772	2511	167	23929	2914	193	23145	3347	220	22413	3810	249	21726	4302	280	21079	4823	08
53	144	24758	2517	168	23916	2921	193	23133	3355	220	22401	3818	249	21715	4310	280	21068	4832	07
54	145	24743	2524	168	23902	2928	194	23120	3362	221	22389	3826	250	21704	4319	281	21058	4841	06
55	145	24729	2530	169	23889	2935	194	23107	3370	221	22377	3834	250	21693	4327	281	21048	4849	05
56	145	24714	2537	169	23875	2942	194	23095	3377	222	22366	3842	251	21681	4336	282	21037	4858	04
57	146	24700	2543	169	23862	2949	195	23082	3385	222	22354	3850	251	21670	4344	282	21027	4867	03
58	146	24685	2550	170	23848	2956	195	23070	3392	223	22342	3858	252	21659	4352	283	21016	4876	02
59	147	24671	2556	170	23835	2963	196	23057	3400	223	22330	3866	252	21648	4361	283	21006	4885	01
60	147	24656	2563	171	23821	2970	196	23045	3407	224	22319	3874	253	21637	4369	284	20995	4894	00

77° LHA ALT 347°	76° LHA ALT 346°	75° LHA ALT 345°	74° LHA ALT 344°	73° LHA ALT 343°	72° LHA ALT 342°

SIGHT REDUCTION

	18° LAT / DEC	LHA / SUM	L~D / RES	19° LAT / DEC	LHA / SUM	L~D / RES	20° LAT / DEC	LHA / SUM	L~D / RES	21° LAT / DEC	LHA / SUM	L~D / RES	22° LAT / DEC	LHA / SUM	L~D / RES	23° LAT / DEC	LHA / SUM	L~D / RES	
00'	284	20995	4894	317	20389	5448	352	19814	6031	389	19268	6642	428	18747	7282	469	18251	7949	60'
01	285	20985	4903	318	20379	5458	353	19805	6041	390	19259	6652	428	18739	7292	469	18243	7961	59
02	285	20975	4912	318	20369	5467	353	19795	6051	390	19250	6663	429	18730	7303	470	18235	7972	58
03	286	20964	4921	319	20359	5477	354	19786	6061	391	19241	6673	430	18722	7314	471	18227	7984	57
04	286	20954	4930	319	20350	5486	354	19777	6071	391	19232	6684	430	18714	7325	472	18218	7995	56
05	287	20944	4939	320	20340	5496	355	19767	6081	392	19223	6694	431	18705	7336	472	18210	8006	55
06	287	20933	4948	320	20330	5505	356	19758	6091	393	19215	6705	432	18697	7347	473	18202	8018	54
07	288	20923	4957	321	20320	5515	356	19749	6101	393	19206	6715	432	18688	7358	474	18194	8029	53
08	288	20913	4966	322	20310	5524	357	19740	6111	394	19197	6726	433	18680	7369	474	18186	8041	52
09	289	20902	4976	322	20301	5534	357	19730	6121	395	19188	6736	434	18671	7380	475	18178	8052	51
10	289	20892	4985	323	20291	5543	358	19721	6131	395	19179	6747	435	18663	7391	476	18170	8063	50
11	290	20882	4994	323	20281	5553	359	19712	6141	396	19170	6757	435	18655	7402	476	18162	8075	49
12	290	20871	5003	324	20271	5562	359	19703	6151	397	19162	6768	436	18646	7413	477	18154	8086	48
13	291	20861	5012	324	20262	5572	360	19693	6161	397	19153	6778	437	18638	7424	478	18146	8098	47
14	292	20851	5021	325	20252	5581	360	19684	6171	398	19144	6789	437	18629	7435	479	18138	8109	46
15	292	20841	5030	326	20242	5591	361	19675	6181	398	19135	6799	438	18621	7446	479	18130	8121	45
16	293	20830	5039	326	20233	5601	362	19666	6191	399	19126	6810	439	18613	7457	480	18122	8132	44
17	293	20820	5048	327	20223	5610	362	19656	6201	400	19118	6820	439	18604	7468	481	18114	8144	43
18	294	20810	5057	327	20213	5620	363	19647	6211	400	19109	6831	440	18596	7479	481	18106	8155	42
19	294	20800	5067	328	20204	5629	363	19638	6221	401	19100	6841	441	18588	7490	482	18098	8167	41
20	295	20790	5076	328	20194	5639	364	19629	6231	402	19091	6852	441	18579	7501	483	18090	8178	40
21	295	20779	5085	329	20184	5649	365	19620	6241	402	19083	6863	442	18571	7512	484	18082	8190	39
22	296	20769	5094	330	20175	5658	365	19610	6251	403	19074	6873	443	18563	7523	484	18074	8201	38
23	296	20759	5103	330	20165	5668	366	19601	6262	404	19065	6884	443	18554	7534	485	18066	8213	37
24	297	20749	5112	331	20155	5678	367	19592	6272	404	19057	6894	444	18546	7545	486	18058	8224	36
25	298	20739	5122	331	20146	5687	367	19583	6282	405	19048	6905	445	18538	7556	486	18050	8236	35
26	298	20728	5131	332	20136	5697	368	19574	6292	406	19039	6916	445	18529	7568	487	18042	8248	34
27	299	20718	5140	333	20126	5707	368	19565	6302	406	19030	6926	446	18521	7579	488	18034	8259	33
28	299	20708	5149	333	20117	5716	369	19556	6312	407	19022	6937	447	18513	7590	489	18027	8271	32
29	300	20698	5158	334	20107	5726	370	19547	6323	407	19013	6948	447	18505	7601	489	18019	8282	31
30	300	20688	5168	334	20098	5736	370	19537	6333	408	19004	6958	448	18496	7612	490	18011	8294	30
31	301	20678	5177	335	20088	5746	371	19528	6343	409	18996	6969	449	18488	7623	491	18003	8306	29
32	301	20668	5186	335	20079	5755	371	19519	6353	409	18987	6980	449	18480	7634	491	17995	8317	28
33	302	20658	5195	336	20069	5765	372	19510	6363	410	18978	6990	450	18471	7645	492	17987	8329	27
34	302	20648	5205	337	20059	5775	373	19501	6374	411	18970	7001	451	18463	7657	493	17979	8340	26
35	303	20638	5214	337	20050	5784	373	19492	6384	411	18961	7012	451	18455	7668	494	17971	8352	25
36	304	20628	5223	338	20040	5794	374	19483	6394	412	18953	7022	452	18447	7679	494	17963	8364	24
37	304	20617	5232	338	20031	5804	375	19474	6404	413	18944	7033	453	18438	7690	495	17955	8375	23
38	305	20607	5242	339	20021	5814	375	19465	6414	413	18935	7044	453	18430	7701	496	17948	8387	22
39	305	20597	5251	340	20012	5824	376	19456	6425	414	18927	7054	454	18422	7712	496	17940	8399	21
40	306	20587	5260	340	20002	5833	376	19447	6435	415	18918	7065	455	18414	7724	497	17932	8410	20
41	306	20577	5270	341	19993	5843	377	19438	6445	415	18909	7076	456	18406	7735	498	17924	8422	19
42	307	20567	5279	341	19983	5853	378	19429	6456	416	18901	7087	456	18397	7746	499	17916	8434	18
43	307	20557	5288	342	19974	5863	378	19420	6466	417	18892	7097	457	18389	7757	499	17908	8445	17
44	308	20547	5298	342	19964	5873	379	19411	6476	417	18884	7108	458	18381	7769	500	17900	8457	16
45	309	20537	5307	343	19955	5882	380	19402	6486	418	18875	7119	458	18373	7780	501	17893	8469	15
46	309	20527	5316	344	19945	5892	380	19393	6497	419	18867	7130	459	18365	7791	501	17885	8480	14
47	310	20517	5326	344	19936	5902	381	19384	6507	419	18858	7141	460	18356	7802	502	17877	8492	13
48	310	20508	5335	345	19927	5912	381	19375	6517	420	18849	7151	460	18348	7814	503	17869	8504	12
49	311	20498	5344	345	19917	5922	382	19366	6528	421	18841	7162	461	18340	7825	504	17861	8516	11
50	311	20488	5354	346	19908	5932	383	19357	6538	421	18832	7173	462	18332	7836	504	17854	8527	10
51	312	20478	5363	347	19898	5941	383	19348	6548	422	18824	7184	462	18324	7847	505	17846	8539	09
52	312	20468	5373	347	19889	5951	384	19339	6559	423	18815	7195	463	18316	7859	506	17838	8551	08
53	313	20458	5382	348	19880	5961	385	19330	6569	423	18807	7205	464	18308	7870	507	17830	8563	07
54	314	20448	5391	348	19870	5971	385	19321	6579	424	18798	7216	465	18299	7881	507	17822	8575	06
55	314	20438	5401	349	19861	5981	386	19312	6590	425	18790	7227	465	18291	7893	508	17815	8586	05
56	315	20428	5410	350	19851	5991	386	19303	6600	425	18781	7238	466	18283	7904	509	17807	8598	04
57	315	20418	5420	350	19842	6001	387	19294	6611	426	18773	7249	467	18275	7915	509	17799	8610	03
58	316	20409	5429	351	19833	6011	388	19285	6621	426	18764	7260	467	18267	7927	510	17791	8622	02
59	316	20399	5439	351	19823	6021	388	19277	6631	427	18756	7271	468	18259	7938	511	17784	8634	01
60	317	20389	5448	352	19814	6031	389	19268	6642	428	18747	7282	469	18251	7949	512	17776	8645	00

71° LHA ALT 341°	70° LHA ALT 340°	69° LHA ALT 339°	68° LHA ALT 338°	67° LHA ALT 337°	66° LHA ALT 336°

SIGHT REDUCTION

	24° LAT/DEC	24° LHA/SUM	24° L~D/RES	25° LAT/DEC	25° LHA/SUM	25° L~D/RES	26° LAT/DEC	26° LHA/SUM	26° L~D/RES	27° LAT/DEC	27° LHA/SUM	27° L~D/RES	28° LAT/DEC	28° LHA/SUM	28° L~D/RES	29° LAT/DEC	29° LHA/SUM	29° L~D/RES	
00'	512	17776	8645	557	17321	9369	604	16884	10120	653	16465	10899	704	16061	11705	758	15672	12538	60'
01	512	17768	8657	557	17314	9381	605	16877	10133	654	16458	10912	705	16055	11719	759	15666	12552	59
02	513	17760	8669	558	17306	9394	605	16870	10146	655	16451	10926	706	16048	11732	760	15660	12566	58
03	514	17753	8681	559	17299	9406	606	16863	10159	656	16444	10939	707	16041	11746	761	15653	12580	57
04	515	17745	8693	560	17291	9418	607	16856	10172	656	16438	10952	708	16035	11760	762	15647	12594	56
05	515	17737	8705	561	17284	9431	608	16849	10184	657	16431	10965	709	16028	11773	763	15641	12609	55
06	516	17730	8716	561	17276	9443	609	16842	10197	658	16424	10979	710	16022	11787	764	15634	12623	54
07	517	17722	8728	562	17269	9455	609	16835	10210	659	16417	10992	711	16015	11801	764	15628	12637	53
08	518	17714	8740	563	17262	9468	610	16828	10223	660	16410	11005	711	16009	11815	765	15622	12651	52
09	518	17706	8752	564	17254	9480	611	16820	10236	661	16403	11018	712	16002	11828	766	15615	12665	51
10	519	17699	8764	564	17247	9492	612	16813	10248	661	16397	11032	713	15995	11842	767	15609	12679	50
11	520	17691	8776	565	17240	9505	613	16806	10261	662	16390	11045	714	15989	11856	768	15603	12693	49
12	521	17683	8788	566	17232	9517	613	16799	10274	663	16383	11058	715	15982	11870	769	15596	12708	48
13	521	17676	8800	567	17225	9530	614	16792	10287	664	16376	11072	716	15976	11883	770	15590	12722	47
14	522	17668	8812	567	17217	9542	615	16785	10300	665	16369	11085	717	15969	11897	771	15584	12736	46
15	523	17660	8824	568	17210	9554	616	16778	10313	666	16363	11098	718	15963	11911	772	15577	12750	45
16	523	17653	8836	569	17203	9567	617	16771	10325	667	16356	11111	719	15956	11925	773	15571	12764	44
17	524	17645	8848	570	17195	9579	618	16764	10338	667	16349	11125	719	15950	11938	774	15565	12779	43
18	525	17637	8860	571	17188	9592	618	16757	10351	668	16342	11138	720	15943	11952	775	15558	12793	42
19	526	17630	8872	571	17181	9604	619	16750	10364	669	16335	11152	721	15937	11966	776	15552	12807	41
20	526	17622	8884	572	17173	9617	620	16743	10377	670	16329	11165	722	15930	11980	776	15546	12821	40
21	527	17614	8896	573	17166	9629	621	16736	10390	671	16322	11178	723	15923	11994	777	15539	12836	39
22	528	17607	8908	574	17159	9641	622	16729	10403	672	16315	11192	724	15917	12007	778	15533	12850	38
23	529	17599	8920	574	17151	9654	622	16722	10416	672	16308	11205	725	15910	12021	779	15527	12864	37
24	529	17592	8932	575	17144	9666	623	16715	10429	673	16302	11218	726	15904	12035	780	15521	12878	36
25	530	17584	8944	576	17137	9679	624	16708	10442	674	16295	11232	727	15897	12049	781	15514	12893	35
26	531	17576	8956	577	17130	9691	625	16701	10455	675	16288	11245	727	15891	12063	782	15508	12907	34
27	532	17569	8968	578	17122	9704	626	16694	10468	676	16281	11259	728	15884	12077	783	15502	12921	33
28	532	17561	8980	578	17115	9716	627	16687	10481	677	16275	11272	729	15878	12090	784	15496	12936	32
29	533	17554	8992	579	17108	9729	627	16680	10493	678	16268	11285	730	15871	12104	785	15489	12950	31
30	534	17546	9004	580	17100	9741	628	16673	10506	678	16261	11299	731	15865	12118	786	15483	12964	30
31	535	17538	9016	581	17093	9754	629	16666	10519	679	16254	11312	732	15859	12132	787	15477	12979	29
32	535	17531	9028	582	17086	9766	630	16659	10532	680	16248	11326	733	15852	12146	788	15471	12993	28
33	536	17523	9040	582	17079	9779	631	16652	10545	681	16241	11339	734	15846	12160	789	15464	13007	27
34	537	17516	9052	583	17071	9792	631	16645	10558	682	16234	11353	735	15839	12174	789	15458	13022	26
35	538	17508	9064	584	17064	9804	632	16638	10571	683	16228	11366	735	15833	12188	790	15452	13036	25
36	538	17501	9076	585	17057	9817	633	16631	10584	684	16221	11380	736	15826	12202	791	15446	13050	24
37	539	17493	9088	585	17050	9829	634	16624	10597	684	16214	11393	737	15820	12216	792	15439	13065	23
38	540	17486	9101	586	17042	9842	635	16617	10611	685	16207	11406	738	15813	12229	793	15433	13079	22
39	541	17478	9113	587	17035	9854	636	16610	10624	686	16201	11420	739	15807	12243	794	15427	13094	21
40	541	17470	9125	588	17028	9867	636	16603	10637	687	16194	11433	740	15800	12257	795	15421	13108	20
41	542	17463	9137	589	17021	9880	637	16596	10650	688	16187	11447	741	15794	12271	796	15415	13122	19
42	543	17455	9149	589	17014	9892	638	16589	10663	689	16181	11461	742	15788	12285	797	15408	13137	18
43	544	17448	9161	590	17006	9905	639	16582	10676	690	16174	11474	743	15781	12299	798	15402	13151	17
44	544	17440	9173	591	16999	9917	640	16575	10689	691	16167	11488	744	15775	12313	799	15396	13166	16
45	545	17433	9186	592	16992	9930	641	16568	10702	691	16161	11501	744	15768	12327	800	15390	13180	15
46	546	17425	9198	593	16985	9943	641	16561	10715	692	16154	11515	745	15762	12341	801	15384	13194	14
47	547	17418	9210	593	16977	9955	642	16554	10728	693	16147	11528	746	15755	12355	802	15377	13209	13
48	548	17410	9222	594	16970	9968	643	16547	10741	694	16141	11542	747	15749	12369	803	15371	13223	12
49	548	17403	9234	595	16963	9981	644	16541	10754	695	16134	11555	748	15743	12383	804	15365	13238	11
50	549	17395	9247	596	16956	9993	645	16534	10768	696	16127	11569	749	15736	12397	804	15359	13252	10
51	550	17388	9259	597	16949	10006	646	16527	10781	697	16121	11583	750	15730	12411	805	15353	13267	09
52	551	17380	9271	597	16942	10019	646	16520	10794	697	16114	11596	751	15723	12425	806	15346	13281	08
53	551	17373	9283	598	16934	10031	647	16513	10807	698	16108	11610	752	15717	12439	807	15340	13296	07
54	552	17366	9296	599	16927	10044	648	16506	10820	699	16101	11623	753	15711	12453	808	15334	13310	06
55	553	17358	9308	600	16920	10057	649	16499	10833	700	16094	11637	754	15704	12467	809	15328	13325	05
56	554	17351	9320	601	16913	10070	650	16492	10846	701	16088	11651	754	15698	12482	810	15322	13339	04
57	554	17343	9332	601	16906	10082	651	16485	10860	702	16081	11664	755	15691	12496	811	15316	13354	03
58	555	17336	9345	602	16899	10095	651	16479	10873	703	16074	11678	756	15685	12510	812	15309	13368	02
59	556	17328	9357	603	16892	10108	652	16472	10886	704	16068	11691	757	15679	12524	813	15303	13383	01
60	557	17321	9369	604	16884	10120	653	16465	10899	704	16061	11705	758	15672	12538	814	15297	13397	00

65° LHA ALT 335°	64° LHA ALT 334°	63° LHA ALT 333°	62° LHA ALT 332°	61° LHA ALT 331°	60° LHA ALT 330°

SIGHT REDUCTION

DEC	30° LAT LHA L~D DEC SUM RES			31° LAT LHA L~D DEC SUM RES			32° LAT LHA L~D DEC SUM RES			33° LAT LHA L~D DEC SUM RES			34° LAT LHA L~D DEC SUM RES			35° LAT LHA L~D DEC SUM RES			
00'	814	15297	13397	872	14935	14283	933	14585	15195	996	14246	16133	1061	13918	17096	1129	13599	18085	60'
01	815	15291	13412	873	14929	14298	934	14579	15210	997	14240	16149	1062	13912	17112	1130	13594	18101	59
02	816	15285	13426	874	14923	14313	935	14573	15226	998	14235	16164	1063	13907	17129	1131	13589	18118	58
03	817	15279	13441	875	14917	14328	936	14567	15241	999	14229	16180	1064	13901	17145	1132	13584	18135	57
04	818	15273	13456	876	14911	14343	937	14562	15257	1000	14224	16196	1065	13896	17161	1133	13579	18151	56
05	819	15266	13470	877	14905	14358	938	14556	15272	1001	14218	16212	1067	13891	17177	1135	13573	18168	55
06	820	15260	13485	878	14899	14373	939	14550	15288	1002	14212	16228	1068	13885	17194	1136	13568	18185	54
07	821	15254	13499	879	14893	14388	940	14545	15303	1003	14207	16244	1069	13880	17210	1137	13563	18202	53
08	822	15248	13514	880	14887	14403	941	14539	15319	1004	14201	16260	1070	13875	17226	1138	13558	18218	52
09	823	15242	13529	881	14882	14418	942	14533	15334	1005	14196	16276	1071	13869	17243	1139	13553	18235	51
10	824	15236	13543	882	14876	14433	943	14527	15350	1006	14190	16292	1072	13864	17259	1140	13547	18252	50
11	824	15230	13558	883	14870	14448	944	14522	15365	1007	14185	16307	1073	13859	17275	1142	13542	18269	49
12	825	15224	13572	884	14864	14463	945	14516	15381	1008	14179	16323	1074	13853	17292	1143	13537	18285	48
13	826	15218	13587	885	14858	14479	946	14510	15396	1010	14174	16339	1075	13848	17308	1144	13532	18302	47
14	827	15211	13602	886	14852	14494	947	14505	15412	1011	14168	16355	1077	13842	17324	1145	13527	18319	46
15	828	15205	13616	887	14846	14509	948	14499	15427	1012	14163	16371	1078	13837	17341	1146	13521	18336	45
16	829	15199	13631	888	14840	14524	949	14493	15443	1013	14157	16387	1079	13832	17357	1147	13516	18352	44
17	830	15193	13646	889	14834	14539	950	14487	15458	1014	14152	16403	1080	13826	17374	1149	13511	18369	43
18	831	15187	13660	890	14829	14554	951	14482	15474	1015	14146	16419	1081	13821	17390	1150	13506	18386	42
19	832	15181	13675	891	14823	14569	952	14476	15489	1016	14141	16435	1082	13816	17406	1151	13501	18403	41
20	833	15175	13690	892	14817	14584	953	14470	15505	1017	14135	16451	1083	13810	17423	1152	13496	18420	40
21	834	15169	13704	893	14811	14599	954	14465	15520	1018	14130	16467	1084	13805	17439	1153	13490	18437	39
22	835	15163	13719	894	14805	14614	955	14459	15536	1019	14124	16483	1086	13800	17456	1154	13485	18453	38
23	836	15157	13734	895	14799	14630	957	14453	15551	1020	14119	16499	1087	13794	17472	1156	13480	18470	37
24	837	15151	13748	896	14793	14645	958	14448	15567	1021	14113	16515	1088	13789	17488	1157	13475	18487	36
25	838	15145	13763	897	14787	14660	959	14442	15583	1023	14108	16531	1089	13784	17505	1158	13470	18504	35
26	839	15139	13778	898	14782	14675	960	14436	15598	1024	14102	16547	1090	13779	17521	1159	13465	18521	34
27	840	15133	13793	899	14776	14690	961	14431	15614	1025	14097	16563	1091	13773	17538	1160	13459	18538	33
28	841	15127	13807	900	14770	14705	962	14425	15629	1026	14091	16579	1092	13768	17554	1161	13454	18554	32
29	842	15120	13822	901	14764	14721	963	14419	15645	1027	14086	16595	1093	13763	17571	1163	13449	18571	31
30	843	15114	13837	902	14758	14736	964	14414	15661	1028	14080	16611	1095	13757	17587	1164	13444	18588	30
31	844	15108	13852	903	14752	14751	965	14408	15676	1029	14075	16627	1096	13752	17604	1165	13439	18605	29
32	845	15102	13866	904	14747	14766	966	14403	15692	1030	14069	16643	1097	13747	17620	1166	13434	18622	28
33	846	15096	13881	905	14741	14781	967	14397	15708	1031	14064	16659	1098	13741	17637	1167	13429	18639	27
34	847	15090	13896	906	14735	14797	968	14391	15723	1032	14059	16676	1099	13736	17653	1168	13423	18656	26
35	848	15084	13911	907	14729	14812	969	14386	15739	1033	14053	16692	1100	13731	17670	1170	13418	18673	25
36	849	15078	13926	908	14723	14827	970	14380	15755	1035	14048	16708	1101	13726	17686	1171	13413	18690	24
37	850	15072	13940	909	14717	14842	971	14374	15770	1036	14042	16724	1103	13720	17703	1172	13408	18707	23
38	851	15066	13955	910	14712	14858	972	14369	15786	1037	14037	16740	1104	13715	17719	1173	13403	18724	22
39	852	15060	13970	911	14706	14873	973	14363	15802	1038	14031	16756	1105	13710	17736	1174	13398	18741	21
40	852	15054	13985	912	14700	14888	974	14357	15817	1039	14026	16772	1106	13704	17752	1176	13393	18758	20
41	853	15048	14000	913	14694	14903	975	14352	15833	1040	14020	16788	1107	13699	17769	1177	13388	18774	19
42	854	15042	14015	914	14688	14919	976	14346	15849	1041	14015	16804	1108	13694	17785	1178	13383	18791	18
43	855	15036	14029	915	14683	14934	978	14341	15864	1042	14010	16821	1109	13689	17802	1179	13377	18808	17
44	856	15030	14044	916	14677	14949	979	14335	15880	1043	14004	16837	1110	13683	17819	1180	13372	18825	16
45	857	15024	14059	917	14671	14965	980	14329	15896	1044	13999	16853	1112	13678	17835	1181	13367	18842	15
46	858	15018	14074	918	14665	14980	981	14324	15912	1045	13993	16869	1113	13673	17852	1183	13362	18859	14
47	859	15012	14089	919	14660	14995	982	14318	15927	1047	13988	16885	1114	13668	17868	1184	13357	18876	13
48	860	15006	14104	920	14654	15011	983	14313	15943	1048	13982	16901	1115	13662	17885	1185	13352	18893	12
49	861	15000	14119	921	14648	15026	984	14307	15959	1049	13977	16918	1116	13657	17902	1186	13347	18910	11
50	862	14994	14134	922	14642	15041	985	14301	15975	1050	13972	16934	1117	13652	17918	1187	13342	18927	10
51	863	14988	14149	923	14636	15057	986	14296	15990	1051	13966	16950	1119	13647	17935	1189	13337	18945	09
52	864	14982	14164	924	14631	15072	987	14290	16006	1052	13961	16966	1120	13641	17951	1190	13332	18962	08
53	865	14976	14178	925	14625	15087	988	14285	16022	1053	13955	16982	1121	13636	17968	1191	13326	18979	07
54	866	14971	14193	927	14619	15103	989	14279	16038	1054	13950	16999	1122	13631	17985	1192	13321	18996	06
55	867	14965	14208	928	14613	15118	990	14274	16054	1055	13945	17015	1123	13626	18001	1193	13316	19013	05
56	868	14959	14223	929	14608	15133	991	14268	16069	1057	13939	17031	1124	13620	18018	1195	13311	19030	04
57	869	14953	14238	930	14602	15149	992	14262	16085	1058	13934	17047	1125	13615	18035	1196	13306	19047	03
58	870	14947	14253	931	14596	15164	993	14257	16101	1059	13928	17064	1127	13610	18051	1197	13301	19064	02
59	871	14941	14268	932	14590	15180	995	14251	16117	1060	13923	17080	1128	13605	18068	1198	13296	19081	01
60	872	14935	14283	933	14585	15195	996	14246	16133	1061	13918	17096	1129	13599	18085	1199	13291	19098	00

59°	58°	57°	56°	55°	54°
LHA ALT	LHA ALT	LHA ALT	LHA ALT	LHA ALT	LHA ALT
329°	328°	327°	326°	325°	324°

SIGHT REDUCTION

	36°			37°			38°			39°			40°			41°		
	LAT / DEC	LHA / SUM	L~D / RES	LAT / DEC	LHA / SUM	L~D / RES	LAT / DEC	LHA / SUM	L~D / RES	LAT / DEC	LHA / SUM	L~D / RES	LAT / DEC	LHA / SUM	L~D / RES	LAT / DEC	LHA / SUM	L~D / RES	
00'	1199	13291	19098	1272	12991	20136	1348	12700	21199	1427	12418	22285	1508	12142	23395	1593	11875	24529	60'
01	1200	13286	19115	1274	12986	20154	1349	12696	21217	1428	12413	22303	1510	12138	23414	1594	11870	24548	59
02	1202	13281	19132	1275	12982	20171	1351	12691	21235	1429	12408	22322	1511	12133	23433	1595	11866	24567	58
03	1203	13276	19149	1276	12977	20189	1352	12686	21252	1431	12404	22340	1512	12129	23451	1597	11862	24586	57
04	1204	13271	19167	1277	12972	20206	1353	12681	21270	1432	12399	22358	1514	12124	23470	1598	11857	24605	56
05	1205	13266	19184	1279	12967	20224	1355	12677	21288	1433	12394	22377	1515	12120	23489	1600	11853	24624	55
06	1206	13261	19201	1280	12962	20241	1356	12672	21306	1435	12390	22395	1516	12115	23508	1601	11848	24643	54
07	1208	13256	19218	1281	12957	20259	1357	12667	21324	1436	12385	22413	1518	12111	23526	1603	11844	24663	53
08	1209	13250	19235	1282	12952	20277	1358	12662	21342	1437	12380	22432	1519	12106	23545	1604	11840	24682	52
09	1210	13245	19252	1284	12947	20294	1360	12657	21360	1439	12376	22450	1521	12102	23564	1605	11835	24701	51
10	1211	13240	19269	1285	12942	20312	1361	12653	21378	1440	12371	22469	1522	12097	23583	1607	11831	24720	50
11	1212	13235	19287	1286	12937	20329	1362	12648	21396	1441	12367	22487	1523	12093	23601	1608	11826	24739	49
12	1214	13230	19304	1287	12933	20347	1364	12643	21414	1443	12362	22505	1525	12088	23620	1610	11822	24758	48
13	1215	13225	19321	1289	12928	20364	1365	12638	21432	1444	12357	22524	1526	12084	23639	1611	11818	24777	47
14	1216	13220	19338	1290	12923	20382	1366	12634	21450	1445	12353	22542	1528	12079	23658	1613	11813	24797	46
15	1217	13215	19355	1291	12918	20400	1368	12629	21468	1447	12348	22561	1529	12075	23677	1614	11809	24816	45
16	1219	13210	19373	1292	12913	20417	1369	12624	21486	1448	12343	22579	1530	12070	23695	1616	11805	24835	44
17	1220	13205	19390	1294	12908	20435	1370	12619	21504	1450	12339	22597	1532	12066	23714	1617	11800	24854	43
18	1221	13200	19407	1295	12903	20452	1371	12615	21522	1451	12334	22616	1533	12061	23733	1618	11796	24873	42
19	1222	13195	19424	1296	12898	20470	1373	12610	21540	1452	12330	22634	1535	12057	23752	1620	11791	24893	41
20	1223	13190	19441	1297	12893	20488	1374	12605	21558	1454	12325	22653	1536	12052	23771	1621	11787	24912	40
21	1225	13185	19459	1299	12889	20505	1375	12601	21576	1455	12320	22671	1537	12048	23789	1623	11783	24931	39
22	1226	13180	19476	1300	12884	20523	1377	12596	21594	1456	12316	22690	1539	12043	23808	1624	11778	24950	38
23	1227	13175	19493	1301	12879	20541	1378	12591	21612	1458	12311	22708	1540	12039	23827	1626	11774	24969	37
24	1228	13170	19510	1302	12874	20558	1379	12586	21630	1459	12307	22726	1542	12035	23846	1627	11770	24989	36
25	1229	13165	19528	1304	12869	20576	1381	12582	21649	1460	12302	22745	1543	12030	23865	1629	11765	25008	35
26	1231	13160	19545	1305	12864	20594	1382	12577	21667	1462	12297	22763	1544	12026	23884	1630	11761	25027	34
27	1232	13155	19562	1306	12859	20611	1383	12572	21685	1463	12293	22782	1546	12021	23903	1631	11757	25046	33
28	1233	13150	19580	1307	12855	20629	1384	12567	21703	1464	12288	22800	1547	12017	23921	1633	11752	25066	32
29	1234	13145	19597	1309	12850	20647	1386	12563	21721	1466	12284	22819	1549	12012	23940	1634	11748	25085	31
30	1236	13140	19614	1310	12845	20664	1387	12558	21739	1467	12279	22837	1550	12008	23959	1636	11744	25104	30
31	1237	13135	19631	1311	12840	20682	1388	12553	21757	1468	12274	22856	1551	12003	23978	1637	11739	25123	29
32	1238	13130	19649	1312	12835	20700	1390	12549	21775	1470	12270	22874	1553	11999	23997	1639	11735	25143	28
33	1239	13125	19666	1314	12830	20718	1391	12544	21793	1471	12265	22893	1554	11994	24016	1640	11731	25162	27
34	1240	13120	19683	1315	12825	20735	1392	12539	21811	1473	12261	22911	1556	11990	24035	1642	11726	25181	26
35	1242	13115	19701	1316	12821	20753	1394	12534	21830	1474	12256	22930	1557	11985	24054	1643	11722	25201	25
36	1243	13110	19718	1318	12816	20771	1395	12530	21848	1475	12252	22948	1558	11981	24073	1645	11718	25220	24
37	1244	13105	19735	1319	12811	20789	1396	12525	21866	1477	12247	22967	1560	11977	24092	1646	11713	25239	23
38	1245	13100	19753	1320	12806	20806	1398	12520	21884	1478	12242	22986	1561	11972	24111	1647	11709	25259	22
39	1246	13095	19770	1321	12801	20824	1399	12516	21902	1479	12238	23004	1563	11968	24129	1649	11705	25278	21
40	1248	13090	19787	1323	12796	20842	1400	12511	21920	1481	12233	23023	1564	11963	24148	1650	11700	25297	20
41	1249	13085	19805	1324	12792	20860	1402	12506	21939	1482	12229	23041	1565	11959	24167	1652	11696	25317	19
42	1250	13080	19822	1325	12787	20877	1403	12502	21957	1483	12224	23060	1567	11954	24186	1653	11692	25336	18
43	1251	13075	19840	1326	12782	20895	1404	12497	21975	1485	12220	23078	1568	11950	24205	1655	11687	25355	17
44	1253	13070	19857	1328	12777	20913	1406	12492	21993	1486	12215	23097	1570	11945	24224	1656	11683	25375	16
45	1254	13065	19874	1329	12772	20931	1407	12488	22011	1488	12211	23116	1571	11941	24243	1658	11679	25394	15
46	1255	13060	19892	1330	12768	20949	1408	12483	22030	1489	12206	23134	1573	11937	24262	1659	11674	25413	14
47	1256	13056	19909	1332	12763	20966	1409	12478	22048	1490	12201	23153	1574	11932	24281	1661	11670	25433	13
48	1258	13051	19927	1333	12758	20984	1411	12474	22066	1492	12197	23171	1575	11928	24300	1662	11666	25452	12
49	1259	13046	19944	1334	12753	21002	1412	12469	22084	1493	12192	23190	1577	11923	24319	1664	11661	25472	11
50	1260	13041	19962	1335	12748	21020	1413	12464	22102	1494	12188	23209	1578	11919	24338	1665	11657	25491	10
51	1261	13036	19979	1337	12744	21038	1415	12459	22121	1496	12183	23227	1580	11914	24357	1667	11653	25510	09
52	1262	13031	19996	1338	12739	21056	1416	12455	22139	1497	12179	23246	1581	11910	24376	1668	11648	25530	08
53	1264	13026	20014	1339	12734	21074	1417	12450	22157	1499	12174	23265	1583	11906	24395	1670	11644	25549	07
54	1265	13021	20031	1340	12729	21091	1419	12446	22175	1500	12170	23283	1584	11901	24414	1671	11640	25569	06
55	1266	13016	20049	1342	12724	21109	1420	12441	22194	1501	12165	23302	1585	11897	24433	1672	11636	25588	05
56	1267	13011	20066	1343	12720	21127	1421	12436	22212	1503	12161	23321	1587	11892	24453	1674	11631	25607	04
57	1269	13006	20084	1344	12715	21145	1423	12432	22230	1504	12156	23339	1588	11888	24472	1675	11627	25627	03
58	1270	13001	20101	1346	12710	21163	1424	12427	22249	1505	12152	23358	1590	11884	24491	1677	11623	25646	02
59	1271	12996	20119	1347	12705	21181	1425	12422	22267	1507	12147	23377	1591	11879	24510	1678	11618	25666	01
60	1272	12991	20136	1348	12700	21199	1427	12418	22285	1508	12142	23395	1593	11875	24529	1680	11614	25685	00
	53°			52°			51°			50°			49°			48°			
	LHA ALT 323°			LHA ALT 322°			LHA ALT 321°			LHA ALT 320°			LHA ALT 319°			LHA ALT 318°			

SIGHT REDUCTION

DEC	42° LAT	42° LHA SUM	42° L~D RES	43° LAT	43° LHA SUM	43° L~D RES	44° LAT	44° LHA SUM	44° L~D RES	45° LAT	45° LHA SUM	45° L~D RES	46° LAT	46° LHA SUM	46° L~D RES	47° LAT	47° LHA SUM	47° L~D RES	
00'	1680	11614	25685	1770	11360	26864	1864	11112	28066	1961	10871	29289	2062	10636	30534	2166	10406	31800	60'
01	1681	11610	25705	1772	11356	26884	1866	11108	28086	1963	10867	29310	2063	10632	30555	2168	10402	31821	59
02	1683	11605	25724	1773	11352	26904	1867	11104	28106	1964	10863	29330	2065	10628	30576	2169	10398	31842	58
03	1684	11601	25744	1775	11348	26924	1869	11100	28126	1966	10859	29351	2067	10624	30597	2171	10394	31864	57
04	1686	11597	25763	1777	11343	26944	1870	11096	28147	1968	10855	29371	2069	10620	30618	2173	10391	31885	56
05	1687	11593	25783	1778	11339	26964	1872	11092	28167	1969	10851	29392	2070	10616	30639	2175	10387	31906	55
06	1689	11588	25802	1780	11335	26984	1874	11088	28187	1971	10847	29413	2072	10612	30660	2176	10383	31928	54
07	1690	11584	25822	1781	11331	27003	1875	11084	28207	1973	10843	29433	2074	10608	30680	2178	10379	31949	53
08	1692	11580	25841	1783	11327	27023	1877	11080	28228	1974	10839	29454	2075	10605	30701	2180	10375	31970	52
09	1693	11576	25861	1784	11323	27043	1878	11076	28248	1976	10835	29474	2077	10601	30722	2182	10372	31992	51
10	1695	11571	25880	1786	11318	27063	1880	11072	28268	1978	10831	29495	2079	10597	30743	2183	10368	32013	50
11	1696	11567	25900	1787	11314	27083	1882	11068	28288	1979	10827	29516	2081	10593	30764	2185	10364	32034	49
12	1698	11563	25919	1789	11310	27103	1883	11064	28309	1981	10824	29536	2082	10589	30785	2187	10360	32056	48
13	1699	11558	25939	1790	11306	27123	1885	11060	28329	1983	10820	29557	2084	10585	30806	2189	10357	32077	47
14	1701	11554	25958	1792	11302	27143	1886	11056	28349	1984	10816	29578	2086	10581	30827	2191	10353	32098	46
15	1702	11550	25978	1794	11298	27163	1888	11052	28370	1986	10812	29598	2087	10578	30848	2192	10349	32120	45
16	1704	11546	25997	1795	11293	27183	1890	11048	28390	1988	10808	29619	2089	10574	30869	2194	10345	32141	44
17	1705	11541	26017	1797	11289	27203	1891	11043	28410	1989	10804	29640	2091	10570	30890	2196	10342	32162	43
18	1707	11537	26037	1798	11285	27222	1893	11039	28430	1991	10800	29660	2093	10566	30911	2198	10338	32184	42
19	1708	11533	26056	1800	11281	27242	1894	11035	28451	1993	10796	29681	2094	10562	30932	2200	10334	32205	41
20	1710	11529	26076	1801	11277	27262	1896	11031	28471	1994	10792	29702	2096	10558	30954	2201	10330	32226	40
21	1711	11524	26095	1803	11273	27282	1898	11027	28491	1996	10788	29722	2098	10554	30975	2203	10326	32248	39
22	1713	11520	26115	1804	11269	27302	1899	11023	28512	1998	10784	29743	2099	10551	30996	2205	10323	32269	38
23	1714	11516	26135	1806	11264	27322	1901	11019	28532	1999	10780	29764	2101	10547	31017	2207	10319	32291	37
24	1716	11512	26154	1807	11260	27342	1903	11015	28552	2001	10776	29784	2103	10543	31038	2208	10315	32312	36
25	1717	11507	26174	1809	11256	27362	1904	11011	28573	2003	10772	29805	2105	10539	31059	2210	10311	32333	35
26	1719	11503	26193	1811	11252	27382	1906	11007	28593	2004	10768	29826	2106	10535	31080	2212	10308	32355	34
27	1720	11499	26213	1812	11248	27402	1907	11003	28614	2006	10764	29847	2108	10531	31101	2214	10304	32376	33
28	1722	11495	26233	1814	11244	27422	1909	10999	28634	2008	10760	29867	2110	10528	31122	2216	10300	32398	32
29	1723	11490	26252	1815	11240	27442	1911	10995	28654	2009	10757	29888	2112	10524	31143	2217	10296	32419	31
30	1725	11486	26272	1817	11235	27462	1912	10991	28675	2011	10753	29909	2113	10520	31164	2219	10293	32441	30
31	1726	11482	26292	1818	11231	27482	1914	10987	28695	2013	10749	29930	2115	10516	31185	2221	10289	32462	29
32	1728	11478	26311	1820	11227	27502	1915	10983	28715	2014	10745	29950	2117	10512	31206	2223	10285	32484	28
33	1729	11474	26331	1822	11223	27522	1917	10979	28736	2016	10741	29971	2118	10508	31228	2225	10282	32505	27
34	1731	11469	26351	1823	11219	27542	1919	10975	28756	2018	10737	29992	2120	10505	31249	2226	10278	32526	26
35	1732	11465	26370	1825	11215	27562	1920	10971	28777	2019	10733	30013	2122	10501	31270	2228	10274	32548	25
36	1734	11461	26390	1826	11211	27583	1922	10967	28797	2021	10729	30033	2124	10497	31291	2230	10270	32569	24
37	1735	11457	26410	1828	11207	27603	1924	10963	28818	2023	10725	30054	2125	10493	31312	2232	10267	32591	23
38	1737	11452	26429	1829	11203	27623	1925	10959	28838	2024	10721	30075	2127	10489	31333	2234	10263	32612	22
39	1738	11448	26449	1831	11198	27643	1927	10955	28858	2026	10717	30096	2129	10485	31354	2235	10259	32634	21
40	1740	11444	26469	1833	11194	27663	1928	10951	28879	2028	10713	30117	2131	10482	31376	2237	10255	32655	20
41	1741	11440	26489	1834	11190	27683	1930	10947	28899	2029	10710	30137	2132	10478	31397	2239	10252	32677	19
42	1743	11436	26508	1836	11186	27703	1932	10943	28920	2031	10706	30158	2134	10474	31418	2241	10248	32698	18
43	1744	11431	26528	1837	11182	27723	1933	10939	28940	2033	10702	30179	2136	10470	31439	2243	10244	32720	17
44	1746	11427	26548	1839	11178	27743	1935	10935	28961	2035	10698	30200	2138	10466	31460	2244	10241	32741	16
45	1747	11423	26567	1840	11174	27763	1937	10931	28981	2036	10694	30221	2139	10463	31481	2246	10237	32763	15
46	1749	11419	26587	1842	11170	27783	1938	10927	29002	2038	10690	30241	2141	10459	31503	2248	10233	32785	14
47	1751	11415	26607	1844	11166	27804	1940	10923	29022	2040	10686	30262	2143	10455	31524	2250	10229	32806	13
48	1752	11410	26627	1845	11162	27824	1942	10919	29043	2041	10682	30283	2145	10451	31545	2252	10226	32828	12
49	1754	11406	26647	1847	11157	27844	1943	10915	29063	2043	10678	30304	2146	10447	31566	2254	10222	32849	11
50	1755	11402	26666	1848	11153	27864	1945	10911	29084	2045	10674	30325	2148	10444	31587	2255	10218	32871	10
51	1757	11398	26686	1850	11149	27884	1946	10907	29104	2046	10671	30346	2150	10440	31609	2257	10215	32892	09
52	1758	11394	26706	1851	11145	27904	1948	10903	29125	2048	10667	30367	2152	10436	31630	2259	10211	32914	08
53	1760	11389	26726	1853	11141	27924	1950	10899	29145	2050	10663	30388	2153	10432	31651	2261	10207	32935	07
54	1761	11385	26745	1855	11137	27945	1951	10895	29166	2051	10659	30408	2155	10428	31672	2263	10203	32957	06
55	1763	11381	26765	1856	11133	27965	1953	10891	29186	2053	10655	30429	2157	10425	31694	2264	10200	32979	05
56	1764	11377	26785	1858	11129	27985	1955	10887	29207	2055	10651	30450	2159	10421	31715	2266	10196	33000	04
57	1766	11373	26805	1859	11125	28005	1956	10883	29227	2057	10647	30471	2160	10417	31736	2268	10192	33022	03
58	1767	11368	26825	1861	11121	28025	1958	10879	29248	2058	10643	30492	2162	10413	31757	2270	10189	33043	02
59	1769	11364	26845	1863	11117	28046	1960	10875	29268	2060	10639	30513	2164	10409	31779	2272	10185	33065	01
60	1770	11360	26864	1864	11112	28066	1961	10871	29289	2062	10636	30534	2166	10406	31800	2274	10181	33087	00

47° LHA ALT 317°	46° LHA ALT 316°	45° LHA ALT 315°	44° LHA ALT 314°	43° LHA ALT 313°	42° LHA ALT 312°

SIGHT REDUCTION

	48° LAT DEC	48° LHA SUM	48° L~D RES	49° LAT DEC	49° LHA SUM	49° L~D RES	50° LAT DEC	50° LHA SUM	50° L~D RES	51° LAT DEC	51° LHA SUM	51° L~D RES	52° LAT DEC	52° LHA SUM	52° L~D RES	53° LAT DEC	53° LHA SUM	53° L~D RES	
00'	2274	10181	33087	2385	9962	34394	2501	9748	35721	2621	9538	37068	2745	9333	38433	2874	9133	39818	60'
01	2275	10177	33108	2387	9958	34416	2503	9744	35743	2623	9535	37090	2747	9330	38456	2876	9130	39841	59
02	2277	10174	33130	2389	9955	34438	2505	9741	35765	2625	9531	37113	2749	9327	38479	2878	9127	39865	58
03	2279	10170	33151	2391	9951	34460	2507	9737	35788	2627	9528	37135	2751	9323	38502	2880	9123	39888	57
04	2281	10166	33173	2393	9947	34482	2509	9734	35810	2629	9524	37158	2753	9320	38525	2882	9120	39911	56
05	2283	10163	33195	2395	9944	34504	2511	9730	35832	2631	9521	37181	2755	9317	38548	2885	9117	39934	55
06	2285	10159	33216	2397	9940	34526	2513	9727	35855	2633	9518	37203	2758	9313	38571	2887	9113	39958	54
07	2286	10155	33238	2398	9937	34548	2515	9723	35877	2635	9514	37226	2760	9310	38594	2889	9110	39981	53
08	2288	10152	33260	2400	9933	34570	2517	9719	35899	2637	9511	37249	2762	9307	38617	2891	9107	40004	52
09	2290	10148	33281	2402	9929	34592	2519	9716	35922	2639	9507	37271	2764	9303	38640	2893	9104	40027	51
10	2292	10144	33303	2404	9926	34614	2521	9712	35944	2641	9504	37294	2766	9300	38663	2895	9100	40051	50
11	2294	10141	33325	2406	9922	34636	2523	9709	35966	2643	9500	37317	2768	9296	38686	2898	9097	40074	49
12	2296	10137	33346	2408	9919	34658	2524	9705	35989	2645	9497	37339	2770	9293	38709	2900	9094	40097	48
13	2297	10133	33368	2410	9915	34680	2526	9702	36011	2647	9494	37362	2772	9290	38732	2902	9090	40121	47
14	2299	10130	33390	2412	9911	34702	2528	9698	36033	2649	9490	37385	2774	9286	38755	2904	9087	40144	46
15	2301	10126	33411	2414	9908	34724	2530	9695	36056	2651	9487	37407	2777	9283	38778	2906	9084	40167	45
16	2303	10122	33433	2416	9904	34746	2532	9691	36078	2653	9483	37430	2779	9280	38801	2909	9081	40190	44
17	2305	10119	33455	2418	9901	34768	2534	9688	36100	2655	9480	37453	2781	9276	38824	2911	9077	40214	43
18	2307	10115	33477	2419	9897	34790	2536	9684	36123	2657	9476	37475	2783	9273	38847	2913	9074	40237	42
19	2308	10111	33498	2421	9894	34812	2538	9681	36145	2660	9473	37498	2785	9270	38870	2915	9071	40260	41
20	2310	10108	33520	2423	9890	34834	2540	9677	36168	2662	9469	37521	2787	9266	38893	2918	9067	40284	40
21	2312	10104	33542	2425	9886	34856	2542	9674	36190	2664	9466	37543	2789	9263	38916	2920	9064	40307	39
22	2314	10100	33564	2427	9883	34878	2544	9670	36212	2666	9463	37566	2792	9260	38939	2922	9061	40330	38
23	2316	10097	33585	2429	9879	34900	2546	9667	36235	2668	9459	37589	2794	9256	38962	2924	9058	40354	37
24	2318	10093	33607	2431	9876	34922	2548	9663	36257	2670	9456	37612	2796	9253	38985	2926	9054	40377	36
25	2320	10089	33629	2433	9872	34944	2550	9660	36280	2672	9452	37634	2798	9250	39008	2929	9051	40400	35
26	2321	10086	33651	2435	9868	34966	2552	9656	36302	2674	9449	37657	2800	9246	39031	2931	9048	40424	34
27	2323	10082	33672	2437	9865	34988	2554	9653	36325	2676	9446	37680	2802	9243	39054	2933	9045	40447	33
28	2325	10078	33694	2439	9861	35011	2556	9649	36347	2678	9442	37703	2804	9239	39077	2935	9041	40471	32
29	2327	10075	33716	2441	9858	35033	2558	9646	36369	2680	9439	37725	2806	9236	39100	2937	9038	40494	31
30	2329	10071	33738	2443	9854	35055	2560	9642	36392	2682	9435	37748	2809	9233	39123	2940	9035	40517	30
31	2331	10067	33759	2444	9851	35077	2562	9639	36414	2684	9432	37771	2811	9229	39147	2942	9031	40541	29
32	2333	10064	33781	2446	9847	35099	2564	9635	36437	2686	9428	37794	2813	9226	39170	2944	9028	40564	28
33	2334	10060	33803	2448	9843	35121	2566	9632	36459	2688	9425	37816	2815	9223	39193	2946	9025	40587	27
34	2336	10056	33825	2450	9840	35143	2568	9628	36482	2690	9422	37839	2817	9219	39216	2949	9022	40611	26
35	2338	10053	33847	2452	9836	35166	2570	9625	36504	2693	9418	37862	2819	9216	39239	2951	9018	40634	25
36	2340	10049	33868	2454	9833	35188	2572	9621	36527	2695	9415	37885	2822	9213	39262	2953	9015	40658	24
37	2342	10045	33890	2456	9829	35210	2574	9618	36549	2697	9411	37908	2824	9209	39285	2955	9012	40681	23
38	2344	10042	33912	2458	9826	35232	2576	9614	36572	2699	9408	37930	2826	9206	39308	2958	9009	40705	22
39	2346	10038	33934	2460	9822	35254	2578	9611	36594	2701	9405	37953	2828	9203	39331	2960	9005	40728	21
40	2348	10034	33956	2462	9819	35276	2580	9608	36617	2703	9401	37976	2830	9199	39354	2962	9002	40751	20
41	2349	10031	33978	2464	9815	35298	2582	9604	36639	2705	9398	37999	2832	9196	39378	2964	8999	40775	19
42	2351	10027	33999	2466	9811	35321	2584	9601	36662	2707	9394	38022	2834	9193	39401	2966	8996	40798	18
43	2353	10024	34021	2468	9808	35343	2586	9597	36684	2709	9391	38045	2837	9190	39424	2969	8992	40822	17
44	2355	10020	34043	2470	9804	35365	2588	9594	36707	2711	9388	38067	2839	9186	39447	2971	8989	40845	16
45	2357	10016	34065	2472	9801	35387	2590	9590	36729	2713	9384	38090	2841	9183	39470	2973	8986	40869	15
46	2359	10013	34087	2474	9797	35409	2592	9587	36752	2715	9381	38113	2843	9180	39493	2975	8983	40892	14
47	2361	10009	34109	2475	9794	35432	2594	9583	36774	2718	9377	38136	2845	9176	39517	2978	8979	40916	13
48	2363	10005	34131	2477	9790	35454	2596	9580	36797	2720	9374	38159	2847	9173	39540	2980	8976	40939	12
49	2364	10002	34153	2479	9787	35476	2598	9576	36819	2722	9371	38182	2850	9170	39563	2982	8973	40962	11
50	2366	9998	34174	2481	9783	35498	2600	9573	36842	2724	9367	38205	2852	9166	39586	2984	8970	40986	10
51	2368	9994	34196	2483	9780	35521	2602	9569	36864	2726	9364	38227	2854	9163	39609	2987	8966	41009	09
52	2370	9991	34218	2485	9776	35543	2604	9566	36887	2728	9361	38250	2856	9160	39632	2989	8963	41033	08
53	2372	9987	34240	2487	9772	35565	2606	9562	36909	2730	9357	38273	2858	9156	39656	2991	8960	41056	07
54	2374	9984	34262	2489	9769	35587	2608	9559	36932	2732	9354	38296	2860	9153	39679	2993	8957	41080	06
55	2376	9980	34284	2491	9765	35610	2611	9556	36955	2734	9350	38319	2863	9150	39702	2996	8953	41103	05
56	2378	9976	34306	2493	9762	35632	2613	9552	36977	2736	9347	38342	2865	9146	39725	2998	8950	41127	04
57	2380	9973	34328	2495	9758	35654	2615	9549	37000	2739	9344	38365	2867	9143	39748	3000	8947	41150	03
58	2381	9969	34350	2497	9755	35676	2617	9545	37022	2741	9340	38388	2869	9140	39772	3003	8944	41174	02
59	2383	9966	34372	2499	9751	35699	2619	9542	37045	2743	9337	38411	2871	9137	39795	3005	8940	41198	01
60	2385	9962	34394	2501	9748	35721	2621	9538	37068	2745	9333	38433	2874	9133	39818	3007	8937	41221	00

| | 41° LHA ALT 311° | | | 40° LHA ALT 310° | | | 39° LHA ALT 309° | | | 38° LHA ALT 308° | | | 37° LHA ALT 307° | | | 36° LHA ALT 306° | | | |

SIGHT REDUCTION

DEC	54° LAT/DEC	54° LHA/SUM	54° L~D/RES	55° LAT/DEC	55° LHA/SUM	55° L~D/RES	56° LAT/DEC	56° LHA/SUM	56° L~D/RES	57° LAT/DEC	57° LHA/SUM	57° L~D/RES	58° LAT/DEC	58° LHA/SUM	58° L~D/RES	59° LAT/DEC	59° LHA/SUM	59° L~D/RES	
00'	3007	8937	41221	3146	8745	42642	3289	8558	44080	3438	8374	45536	3594	8194	47008	3755	8018	48496	60'
01	3009	8934	41245	3148	8742	42666	3292	8555	44104	3441	8371	45560	3596	8191	47032	3757	8015	48521	59
02	3012	8931	41268	3150	8739	42690	3294	8552	44129	3444	8368	45584	3599	8188	47057	3760	8012	48546	58
03	3014	8928	41292	3153	8736	42713	3297	8548	44153	3446	8365	45609	3601	8185	47082	3763	8009	48571	57
04	3016	8924	41315	3155	8733	42737	3299	8545	44177	3449	8362	45633	3604	8182	47106	3766	8006	48595	56
05	3018	8921	41339	3157	8730	42761	3301	8542	44201	3451	8359	45658	3607	8179	47131	3768	8003	48620	55
06	3021	8918	41362	3160	8727	42785	3304	8539	44225	3454	8356	45682	3609	8176	47156	3771	8000	48645	54
07	3023	8915	41386	3162	8723	42809	3306	8536	44249	3456	8353	45707	3612	8173	47180	3774	7997	48670	53
08	3025	8911	41409	3164	8720	42833	3309	8533	44273	3459	8350	45731	3615	8170	47205	3777	7994	48695	52
09	3027	8908	41433	3167	8717	42857	3311	8530	44297	3461	8347	45755	3617	8167	47230	3779	7991	48720	51
10	3030	8905	41457	3169	8714	42880	3314	8527	44322	3464	8344	45780	3620	8164	47255	3782	7989	48745	50
11	3032	8902	41480	3171	8711	42904	3316	8524	44346	3466	8341	45804	3623	8161	47279	3785	7986	48770	49
12	3034	8899	41504	3174	8708	42928	3319	8521	44370	3469	8338	45829	3625	8158	47304	3788	7983	48795	48
13	3037	8895	41527	3176	8704	42952	3321	8518	44394	3472	8335	45853	3628	8155	47329	3790	7980	48820	47
14	3039	8892	41551	3179	8701	42976	3324	8515	44418	3474	8332	45878	3631	8152	47353	3793	7977	48845	46
15	3041	8889	41575	3181	8698	43000	3326	8511	44443	3477	8329	45902	3633	8149	47378	3796	7974	48870	45
16	3043	8886	41598	3183	8695	43024	3328	8508	44467	3479	8326	45927	3636	8147	47403	3799	7971	48895	44
17	3046	8883	41622	3186	8692	43048	3331	8505	44491	3482	8323	45951	3639	8144	47428	3802	7968	48920	43
18	3048	8879	41645	3188	8689	43072	3333	8502	44515	3484	8320	45976	3641	8141	47452	3804	7965	48945	42
19	3050	8876	41669	3190	8686	43096	3336	8499	44539	3487	8317	46000	3644	8138	47477	3807	7962	48970	41
20	3053	8873	41693	3193	8682	43119	3338	8496	44564	3489	8314	46024	3647	8135	47502	3810	7960	48995	40
21	3055	8870	41716	3195	8679	43143	3341	8493	44588	3492	8311	46049	3649	8132	47527	3813	7957	49020	39
22	3057	8866	41740	3198	8676	43167	3343	8490	44612	3495	8308	46073	3652	8129	47551	3815	7954	49045	38
23	3060	8863	41764	3200	8673	43191	3346	8487	44636	3497	8304	46098	3655	8126	47576	3818	7951	49070	37
24	3062	8860	41787	3202	8670	43215	3348	8484	44660	3500	8301	46122	3657	8123	47601	3821	7948	49095	36
25	3064	8857	41811	3205	8667	43239	3351	8481	44685	3502	8298	46147	3660	8120	47626	3824	7945	49120	35
26	3066	8854	41835	3207	8664	43263	3353	8478	44709	3505	8295	46171	3663	8117	47650	3827	7942	49145	34
27	3069	8850	41858	3210	8661	43287	3356	8475	44733	3507	8292	46196	3665	8114	47675	3829	7939	49171	33
28	3071	8847	41882	3212	8657	43311	3358	8472	44757	3510	8289	46221	3668	8111	47700	3832	7936	49196	32
29	3073	8844	41906	3214	8654	43335	3361	8468	44782	3513	8286	46245	3671	8108	47725	3835	7934	49221	31
30	3076	8841	41929	3217	8651	43359	3363	8465	44806	3515	8283	46270	3673	8105	47750	3838	7931	49246	30
31	3078	8838	41953	3219	8648	43383	3366	8462	44830	3518	8280	46294	3676	8102	47774	3840	7928	49271	29
32	3080	8834	41977	3221	8645	43407	3368	8459	44854	3520	8277	46319	3679	8099	47799	3843	7925	49296	28
33	3083	8831	42000	3224	8642	43431	3371	8456	44879	3523	8274	46343	3681	8096	47824	3846	7922	49321	27
34	3085	8828	42024	3226	8639	43455	3373	8453	44903	3526	8271	46368	3684	8094	47849	3849	7919	49346	26
35	3087	8825	42048	3229	8636	43479	3376	8450	44927	3528	8268	46392	3687	8091	47874	3852	7916	49371	25
36	3090	8822	42071	3231	8632	43503	3378	8447	44951	3531	8265	46417	3689	8088	47899	3854	7913	49396	24
37	3092	8819	42095	3234	8629	43527	3381	8444	44976	3533	8262	46441	3692	8085	47923	3857	7911	49421	23
38	3094	8815	42119	3236	8626	43551	3383	8441	45000	3536	8259	46466	3695	8082	47948	3860	7908	49446	22
39	3096	8812	42143	3238	8623	43575	3386	8438	45024	3539	8257	46491	3698	8079	47973	3863	7905	49471	21
40	3099	8809	42166	3241	8620	43599	3388	8435	45049	3541	8254	46515	3700	8076	47998	3866	7902	49497	20
41	3101	8806	42190	3243	8617	43623	3391	8432	45073	3544	8251	46540	3703	8073	48023	3869	7899	49522	19
42	3103	8803	42214	3246	8614	43647	3393	8429	45097	3546	8248	46564	3706	8070	48048	3871	7896	49547	18
43	3106	8799	42238	3248	8611	43671	3396	8426	45122	3549	8245	46589	3708	8067	48072	3874	7893	49572	17
44	3108	8796	42261	3250	8607	43695	3398	8423	45146	3552	8242	46613	3711	8064	48097	3877	7890	49597	16
45	3110	8793	42285	3253	8604	43719	3401	8420	45170	3554	8239	46638	3714	8061	48122	3880	7888	49622	15
46	3113	8790	42309	3255	8601	43743	3403	8416	45195	3557	8236	46663	3717	8058	48147	3883	7885	49647	14
47	3115	8787	42333	3258	8598	43767	3406	8413	45219	3559	8233	46687	3719	8055	48172	3885	7882	49672	13
48	3117	8784	42356	3260	8595	43791	3408	8410	45243	3562	8230	46712	3722	8053	48197	3888	7879	49698	12
49	3120	8780	42380	3262	8592	43815	3411	8407	45268	3565	8227	46737	3725	8050	48222	3891	7876	49723	11
50	3122	8777	42404	3265	8589	43839	3413	8404	45292	3567	8224	46761	3727	8047	48247	3894	7873	49748	10
51	3124	8774	42428	3267	8586	43863	3416	8401	45316	3570	8221	46786	3730	8044	48271	3897	7870	49773	09
52	3127	8771	42451	3270	8583	43887	3418	8398	45341	3572	8218	46810	3733	8041	48296	3900	7868	49798	08
53	3129	8768	42475	3272	8579	43912	3421	8395	45365	3575	8215	46835	3736	8038	48321	3902	7865	49823	07
54	3131	8764	42499	3275	8576	43936	3423	8392	45389	3578	8212	46860	3738	8035	48346	3905	7862	49848	06
55	3134	8761	42523	3277	8573	43960	3426	8389	45414	3580	8209	46884	3741	8032	48371	3908	7859	49874	05
56	3136	8758	42547	3279	8570	43984	3428	8386	45438	3583	8206	46909	3744	8029	48396	3911	7856	49899	04
57	3138	8755	42570	3282	8567	44008	3431	8383	45462	3586	8203	46934	3746	8026	48421	3914	7853	49924	03
58	3141	8752	42594	3284	8564	44032	3433	8380	45487	3588	8200	46958	3749	8023	48446	3917	7850	49949	02
59	3143	8749	42618	3287	8561	44056	3436	8377	45511	3591	8197	46983	3752	8020	48471	3920	7848	49974	01
60	3146	8745	42642	3289	8558	44080	3438	8374	45536	3594	8194	47008	3755	8018	48496	3922	7845	50000	00

35°	34°	33°	32°	31°	30°
LHA ALT	LHA ALT	LHA ALT	LHA ALT	LHA ALT	LHA ALT
305°	304°	303°	302°	301°	300°

SIGHT REDUCTION

	60°			61°			62°			63°			64°			65°			
	LAT	LHA	L~D	LAT	LHA	L~D	LAT	LHA	L~D	LAT	LHA	L~D	LAT	LHA	L~D	LAT	LHA	L~D	
	DEC	SUM	RES	DEC	SUM	RES	DEC	SUM	RES	DEC	SUM	RES	DEC	SUM	RES	DEC	SUM	RES	
00'	3922	7845	50000	4097	7675	51519	4279	7509	53052	4469	7347	54600	4667	7187	56162	4874	7030	57738	60'
01	3925	7842	50025	4100	7673	51544	4282	7507	53078	4472	7344	54626	4670	7184	56188	4877	7028	57764	59
02	3928	7839	50050	4103	7670	51569	4285	7504	53104	4475	7341	54652	4674	7182	56215	4881	7025	57790	58
03	3931	7836	50075	4106	7667	51595	4288	7501	53129	4478	7339	54678	4677	7179	56241	4884	7023	57817	57
04	3934	7833	50100	4112	7664	51620	4291	7498	53155	4482	7336	54704	4680	7176	56267	4888	7020	57843	56
05	3937	7831	50126	4112	7661	51646	4294	7496	53181	4485	7333	54730	4684	7174	56293	4892	7018	57869	55
06	3940	7828	50151	4115	7659	51671	4297	7493	53206	4488	7331	54756	4687	7171	56319	4895	7015	57896	54
07	3942	7825	50176	4118	7656	51697	4301	7490	53232	4491	7328	54782	4690	7169	56345	4899	7012	57922	53
08	3945	7822	50201	4121	7653	51722	4304	7487	53258	4495	7325	54808	4694	7166	56372	4902	7010	57949	52
09	3948	7819	50226	4124	7650	51748	4307	7485	53284	4498	7322	54834	4697	7163	56398	4906	7007	57975	51
10	3951	7816	50252	4127	7647	51773	4310	7482	53309	4501	7320	54860	4701	7161	56424	4909	7005	58001	50
11	3954	7813	50277	4130	7645	51799	4313	7479	53335	4504	7317	54886	4704	7158	56450	4913	7002	58028	49
12	3957	7811	50302	4133	7642	51824	4316	7477	53361	4508	7314	54912	4707	7155	56476	4916	7000	58054	48
13	3960	7808	50327	4136	7639	51850	4319	7474	53387	4511	7312	54938	4711	7153	56503	4920	6997	58081	47
14	3962	7805	50353	4139	7636	51875	4322	7471	53412	4514	7309	54964	4714	7150	56529	4924	6994	58107	46
15	3965	7802	50378	4142	7634	51901	4326	7468	53438	4517	7306	54990	4718	7148	56555	4927	6992	58133	45
16	3968	7799	50403	4145	7631	51926	4329	7466	53464	4521	7304	55016	4721	7145	56581	4931	6989	58160	44
17	3971	7796	50428	4148	7628	51952	4332	7463	53490	4524	7301	55042	4724	7142	56607	4934	6987	58186	43
18	3974	7794	50454	4151	7625	51977	4335	7460	53515	4527	7298	55068	4728	7140	56634	4938	6984	58213	42
19	3977	7791	50479	4154	7622	52003	4338	7457	53541	4530	7296	55094	4731	7137	56660	4941	6982	58239	41
20	3980	7788	50504	4157	7620	52028	4341	7455	53567	4534	7293	55120	4735	7134	56686	4945	6979	58266	40
21	3983	7785	50529	4160	7617	52054	4344	7452	53593	4537	7290	55146	4738	7132	56712	4949	6976	58292	39
22	3986	7782	50555	4163	7614	52079	4348	7449	53618	4540	7288	55172	4742	7129	56738	4952	6974	58318	38
23	3988	7779	50580	4166	7611	52105	4351	7447	53644	4544	7285	55198	4745	7127	56765	4956	6971	58345	37
24	3991	7777	50605	4169	7609	52130	4354	7444	53670	4547	7282	55224	4748	7124	56791	4959	6969	58371	36
25	3994	7774	50631	4172	7606	52156	4357	7441	53696	4550	7280	55250	4752	7121	56817	4963	6966	58398	35
26	3997	7771	50656	4175	7603	52181	4360	7438	53721	4553	7277	55276	4755	7119	56843	4967	6964	58424	34
27	4000	7768	50681	4178	7600	52207	4363	7436	53747	4557	7274	55302	4759	7116	56870	4970	6961	58451	33
28	4003	7765	50707	4181	7598	52232	4366	7433	53773	4560	7272	55328	4762	7114	56896	4974	6958	58477	32
29	4006	7762	50732	4184	7595	52258	4370	7430	53799	4563	7269	55354	4766	7111	56922	4977	6956	58504	31
30	4009	7760	50757	4187	7592	52284	4373	7428	53825	4567	7266	55380	4769	7108	56948	4981	6953	58530	30
31	4012	7757	50782	4190	7589	52309	4376	7425	53850	4570	7264	55406	4773	7106	56975	4985	6951	58557	29
32	4015	7754	50808	4193	7586	52335	4379	7422	53876	4573	7261	55432	4776	7103	57001	4988	6948	58583	28
33	4018	7751	50833	4196	7584	52360	4382	7419	53902	4577	7258	55458	4779	7101	57027	4992	6946	58610	27
34	4020	7748	50858	4199	7581	52386	4385	7417	53928	4580	7256	55484	4783	7098	57053	4995	6943	58636	26
35	4023	7746	50884	4202	7578	52411	4389	7414	53954	4583	7253	55510	4786	7095	57080	4999	6941	58662	25
36	4026	7743	50909	4205	7575	52437	4392	7411	53979	4586	7250	55536	4790	7093	57106	5003	6938	58689	24
37	4029	7740	50934	4208	7573	52463	4395	7409	54005	4590	7248	55562	4793	7090	57132	5006	6935	58715	23
38	4032	7737	50960	4211	7570	52488	4398	7406	54031	4593	7245	55588	4797	7088	57158	5010	6933	58742	22
39	4035	7734	50985	4214	7567	52514	4401	7403	54057	4596	7243	55614	4800	7085	57185	5014	6930	58768	21
40	4038	7731	51011	4217	7564	52539	4404	7401	54083	4600	7240	55640	4804	7082	57211	5017	6928	58795	20
41	4041	7729	51036	4220	7562	52565	4408	7398	54109	4603	7237	55666	4807	7080	57237	5021	6925	58821	19
42	4044	7726	51061	4224	7559	52591	4411	7395	54135	4606	7235	55692	4811	7077	57264	5025	6923	58848	18
43	4047	7723	51087	4227	7556	52616	4414	7392	54160	4610	7232	55718	4814	7075	57290	5028	6920	58874	17
44	4050	7720	51112	4230	7553	52642	4417	7390	54186	4613	7229	55744	4818	7072	57316	5032	6918	58901	16
45	4053	7717	51137	4233	7551	52668	4420	7387	54212	4616	7227	55771	4821	7069	57343	5035	6915	58928	15
46	4056	7715	51163	4236	7548	52693	4424	7384	54238	4620	7224	55797	4825	7067	57369	5039	6912	58954	14
47	4059	7712	51188	4239	7545	52719	4427	7382	54264	4623	7221	55823	4828	7064	57395	5043	6910	58981	13
48	4061	7709	51214	4242	7542	52744	4430	7379	54290	4626	7219	55849	4832	7062	57421	5046	6907	59007	12
49	4064	7706	51239	4245	7540	52770	4433	7376	54316	4630	7216	55875	4835	7059	57448	5050	6905	59034	11
50	4067	7703	51264	4248	7537	52796	4436	7374	54341	4633	7213	55901	4839	7056	57474	5054	6902	59060	10
51	4070	7701	51290	4251	7534	52821	4440	7371	54367	4636	7211	55927	4842	7054	57500	5057	6900	59087	09
52	4073	7698	51315	4254	7531	52847	4443	7368	54393	4640	7208	55953	4846	7051	57527	5061	6897	59113	08
53	4076	7695	51341	4257	7529	52873	4446	7365	54419	4643	7205	55979	4849	7049	57553	5065	6895	59140	07
54	4079	7692	51366	4260	7526	52898	4449	7363	54445	4647	7203	56006	4853	7046	57579	5068	6892	59166	06
55	4082	7689	51391	4263	7523	52924	4453	7360	54471	4650	7200	56032	4856	7043	57606	5072	6890	59193	05
56	4085	7687	51417	4267	7520	52950	4456	7357	54497	4653	7198	56058	4860	7041	57632	5076	6887	59219	04
57	4088	7684	51442	4270	7518	52975	4459	7355	54523	4657	7195	56084	4863	7038	57659	5080	6885	59246	03
58	4091	7681	51468	4273	7515	53001	4462	7352	54549	4660	7192	56110	4867	7036	57685	5083	6882	59273	02
59	4094	7678	51493	4276	7512	53027	4465	7349	54574	4663	7190	56136	4870	7033	57711	5087	6879	59299	01
60	4097	7675	51519	4279	7509	53052	4469	7347	54600	4667	7187	56162	4874	7030	57738	5091	6877	59326	00
			29°			28°			27°			26°			25°			24°	
		LHA	ALT		LHA	ALT		LHA	ALT		LHA	ALT		LHA	ALT		LHA	ALT	
		299°			298°			297°			296°			295°			294°		

SIGHT REDUCTION

	66°			67°			68°			69°			70°			71°		
LAT DEC	**LHA SUM**	**L ~ D RES**	**LAT DEC**	**LHA SUM**	**L ~ D RES**	**LAT DEC**	**LHA SUM**	**L ~ D RES**	**LAT DEC**	**LHA SUM**	**L ~ D RES**	**LAT DEC**	**LHA SUM**	**L ~ D RES**	**LAT DEC**	**LHA SUM**	**L ~ D RES**	
00'	5091	6877	59326	5318	6726	60926	5556	6578	62539	5807	6433	64163	6071	6291	65797	6350	6151	67443	60'
01	5094	6874	59352	5322	6724	60953	5560	6576	62566	5811	6431	64190	6076	6289	65825	6355	6149	67470	59
02	5098	6872	59379	5326	6721	60980	5564	6574	62593	5816	6429	64217	6080	6286	65852	6360	6147	67498	58
03	5102	6869	59405	5329	6719	61007	5568	6571	62620	5820	6426	64244	6085	6284	65879	6365	6144	67525	57
04	5105	6867	59432	5333	6716	61033	5573	6569	62647	5824	6424	64271	6089	6282	65907	6369	6142	67553	56
05	5109	6864	59459	5337	6714	61060	5577	6566	62674	5829	6421	64298	6094	6279	65934	6374	6140	67580	55
06	5113	6862	59485	5341	6711	61087	5581	6564	62701	5833	6419	64326	6098	6277	65961	6379	6137	67608	54
07	5117	6859	59512	5345	6709	61114	5585	6561	62728	5837	6417	64353	6103	6275	65989	6384	6135	67635	53
08	5120	6857	59538	5349	6706	61141	5589	6559	62755	5841	6414	64380	6108	6272	66016	6389	6133	67663	52
09	5124	6854	59565	5353	6704	61167	5593	6557	62782	5846	6412	64407	6112	6270	66043	6393	6131	67690	51
10	5128	6852	59592	5357	6701	61194	5597	6554	62809	5850	6409	64434	6117	6268	66071	6398	6128	67718	50
11	5131	6849	59618	5361	6699	61221	5601	6552	62836	5854	6407	64461	6121	6265	66098	6403	6126	67745	49
12	5135	6847	59645	5365	6696	61248	5605	6549	62863	5859	6405	64489	6126	6263	66126	6408	6124	67773	48
13	5139	6844	59671	5368	6694	61275	5610	6547	62890	5863	6402	64516	6130	6261	66153	6413	6121	67800	47
14	5143	6842	59698	5372	6692	61301	5614	6544	62917	5867	6400	64543	6135	6258	66180	6418	6119	67828	46
15	5146	6839	59725	5376	6689	61328	5618	6542	62944	5872	6398	64570	6140	6256	66208	6422	6117	67855	45
16	5150	6836	59751	5380	6687	61355	5622	6540	62971	5876	6395	64597	6144	6254	66235	6427	6114	67883	44
17	5154	6834	59778	5384	6684	61382	5626	6537	62998	5880	6393	64625	6149	6251	66262	6432	6112	67910	43
18	5158	6831	59805	5388	6682	61409	5630	6535	63025	5885	6390	64652	6153	6249	66290	6437	6110	67938	42
19	5161	6829	59831	5392	6679	61436	5634	6532	63052	5889	6388	64679	6158	6247	66317	6442	6108	67966	41
20	5165	6826	59858	5396	6677	61462	5638	6530	63079	5894	6386	64706	6163	6244	66345	6447	6105	67993	40
21	5169	6824	59885	5400	6674	61489	5643	6527	63106	5898	6383	64734	6167	6242	66372	6452	6103	68021	39
22	5173	6821	59911	5404	6672	61516	5647	6525	63133	5902	6381	64761	6172	6239	66399	6456	6101	68048	38
23	5176	6819	59938	5408	6669	61543	5651	6523	63160	5907	6379	64788	6176	6237	66427	6461	6098	68076	37
24	5180	6816	59964	5412	6667	61570	5655	6520	63187	5911	6376	64815	6181	6235	66454	6466	6096	68103	36
25	5184	6814	59991	5416	6664	61597	5659	6518	63214	5915	6374	64842	6186	6232	66482	6471	6094	68131	35
26	5188	6811	60018	5420	6662	61624	5663	6515	63241	5920	6371	64870	6190	6230	66509	6476	6092	68159	34
27	5191	6809	60044	5424	6659	61650	5668	6513	63268	5924	6369	64897	6195	6228	66536	6481	6089	68186	33
28	5195	6806	60071	5428	6657	61677	5672	6510	63295	5929	6367	64924	6199	6225	66564	6486	6087	68214	32
29	5199	6804	60098	5432	6654	61704	5676	6508	63322	5933	6364	64951	6204	6223	66591	6491	6085	68241	31
30	5203	6801	60124	5436	6652	61731	5680	6506	63349	5937	6362	64979	6209	6221	66619	6496	6082	68269	30
31	5207	6799	60151	5440	6650	61758	5684	6503	63376	5942	6360	65006	6213	6219	66646	6501	6080	68296	29
32	5210	6796	60178	5443	6647	61785	5688	6501	63403	5946	6357	65033	6218	6216	66673	6506	6078	68324	28
33	5214	6794	60205	5447	6645	61812	5693	6498	63430	5951	6355	65060	6223	6214	66701	6510	6076	68352	27
34	5218	6791	60231	5451	6642	61839	5697	6496	63458	5955	6352	65088	6227	6212	66728	6515	6073	68379	26
35	5222	6789	60258	5455	6640	61865	5701	6494	63485	5959	6350	65115	6232	6209	66756	6520	6071	68407	25
36	5226	6786	60285	5459	6637	61892	5705	6491	63512	5964	6348	65142	6237	6207	66783	6525	6069	68434	24
37	5229	6784	60311	5463	6635	61919	5709	6489	63539	5968	6345	65169	6241	6205	66811	6530	6066	68462	23
38	5233	6781	60338	5467	6632	61946	5714	6486	63566	5973	6343	65197	6246	6202	66838	6535	6064	68490	22
39	5237	6779	60365	5471	6630	61973	5718	6484	63593	5977	6341	65224	6251	6200	66866	6540	6062	68517	21
40	5241	6776	60391	5475	6627	62000	5722	6481	63620	5982	6338	65251	6255	6198	66893	6545	6060	68545	20
41	5245	6774	60418	5479	6625	62027	5726	6479	63647	5986	6336	65279	6260	6195	66920	6550	6057	68572	19
42	5248	6771	60445	5483	6623	62054	5730	6477	63674	5990	6333	65306	6265	6193	66948	6555	6055	68600	18
43	5252	6769	60472	5487	6620	62081	5735	6474	63701	5995	6331	65333	6270	6191	66975	6560	6053	68628	17
44	5256	6766	60498	5491	6618	62108	5739	6472	63728	5999	6329	65360	6274	6188	67003	6565	6050	68655	16
45	5260	6764	60525	5496	6615	62135	5743	6469	63756	6004	6326	65388	6279	6186	67030	6570	6048	68683	15
46	5264	6761	60552	5500	6613	62161	5747	6467	63783	6008	6324	65415	6284	6184	67058	6575	6046	68711	14
47	5268	6759	60578	5504	6610	62188	5752	6465	63810	6013	6322	65442	6288	6181	67085	6580	6044	68738	13
48	5271	6756	60605	5508	6608	62215	5756	6462	63837	6017	6319	65470	6293	6179	67113	6585	6041	68766	12
49	5275	6754	60632	5512	6605	62242	5760	6460	63864	6022	6317	65497	6298	6177	67140	6590	6039	68793	11
50	5279	6751	60659	5516	6603	62269	5764	6457	63891	6026	6315	65524	6303	6174	67168	6595	6037	68821	10
51	5283	6749	60685	5520	6600	62296	5769	6455	63918	6031	6312	65551	6307	6172	67195	6600	6035	68849	09
52	5287	6746	60712	5524	6598	62323	5773	6453	63945	6035	6310	65579	6312	6170	67223	6605	6032	68876	08
53	5291	6744	60739	5528	6596	62350	5777	6450	63973	6040	6308	65606	6317	6167	67250	6610	6030	68904	07
54	5295	6741	60766	5532	6593	62377	5781	6448	64000	6044	6305	65633	6322	6165	67278	6615	6028	68932	06
55	5298	6739	60792	5536	6591	62404	5786	6445	64027	6049	6303	65661	6326	6163	67305	6620	6025	68959	05
56	5302	6736	60819	5540	6588	62431	5790	6443	64054	6053	6300	65688	6331	6161	67333	6625	6023	68987	04
57	5306	6734	60846	5544	6586	62458	5794	6441	64081	6058	6298	65715	6336	6158	67360	6630	6021	69015	03
58	5310	6731	60873	5548	6583	62485	5798	6438	64108	6062	6296	65743	6341	6156	67388	6635	6019	69042	02
59	5314	6729	60900	5552	6581	62512	5803	6436	64135	6067	6293	65770	6345	6154	67415	6640	6016	69070	01
60	5318	6726	60926	5556	6578	62539	5807	6433	64163	6071	6291	65797	6350	6151	67443	6645	6014	69098	00
			23°			**22°**			**21°**			**20°**			**19°**			**18°**	
		LHA ALT			**LHA ALT**			**LHA ALT**			**LHA ALT**			**LHA ALT**			**LHA ALT**		
		293°			**292°**			**291°**			**290°**			**289°**			**288°**		

SIGHT REDUCTION

	72° LAT DEC	72° LHA SUM	72° L~D RES	73° LAT DEC	73° LHA SUM	73° L~D RES	74° LAT DEC	74° LHA SUM	74° L~D RES	75° LAT DEC	75° LHA SUM	75° L~D RES	76° LAT DEC	76° LHA SUM	76° L~D RES	77° LAT DEC	77° LHA SUM	77° L~D RES	
00'	6645	6014	69098	6959	5879	70762	7292	5747	72436	7649	5617	74117	8031	5490	75807	8442	5364	77504	60'
01	6651	6012	69125	6964	5877	70790	7298	5745	72464	7655	5615	74145	8037	5488	75835	8449	5362	77532	59
02	6656	6010	69153	6970	5875	70818	7304	5743	72491	7661	5613	74174	8044	5485	75864	8456	5360	77561	58
03	6661	6007	69181	6975	5873	70846	7310	5741	72519	7667	5611	74202	8050	5483	75892	8464	5358	77589	57
04	6666	6005	69208	6980	5870	70873	7315	5738	72547	7673	5609	74230	8057	5481	75920	8471	5356	77618	56
05	6671	6003	69236	6986	5868	70901	7321	5736	72575	7679	5607	74258	8064	5479	75948	8478	5354	77646	55
06	6676	6001	69264	6991	5866	70929	7327	5734	72603	7686	5604	74286	8070	5477	75976	8485	5352	77674	54
07	6681	5998	69291	6997	5864	70957	7333	5732	72631	7692	5602	74314	8077	5475	76005	8492	5350	77703	53
08	6686	5996	69319	7002	5862	70985	7338	5730	72659	7698	5600	74342	8084	5473	76033	8500	5348	77731	52
09	6691	5994	69347	7007	5859	71013	7344	5727	72687	7704	5598	74370	8090	5471	76061	8507	5346	77759	51
10	6696	5991	69374	7013	5857	71040	7350	5725	72715	7710	5596	74398	8097	5469	76089	8514	5344	77788	50
11	6701	5989	69402	7018	5855	71068	7356	5723	72743	7717	5594	74427	8104	5467	76118	8521	5342	77816	49
12	6707	5987	69430	7024	5853	71096	7362	5721	72771	7723	5592	74455	8110	5464	76146	8528	5340	77844	48
13	6712	5985	69457	7029	5851	71124	7367	5719	72799	7729	5589	74483	8117	5462	76174	8536	5338	77873	47
14	6717	5982	69485	7035	5848	71152	7373	5717	72827	7735	5587	74511	8124	5460	76202	8543	5335	77901	46
15	6722	5980	69513	7040	5846	71180	7379	5714	72855	7742	5585	74539	8131	5458	76231	8550	5333	77929	45
16	6727	5978	69541	7046	5844	71208	7385	5712	72883	7748	5583	74567	8137	5456	76259	8558	5331	77958	44
17	6732	5976	69568	7051	5842	71235	7391	5710	72911	7754	5581	74595	8144	5454	76287	8565	5329	77986	43
18	6737	5973	69596	7057	5839	71263	7397	5708	72939	7760	5579	74623	8151	5452	76315	8572	5327	78015	42
19	6743	5971	69624	7062	5837	71291	7403	5706	72967	7767	5577	74652	8158	5450	76344	8579	5325	78043	41
20	6748	5969	69651	7068	5835	71319	7408	5704	72995	7773	5574	74680	8164	5448	76372	8587	5323	78071	40
21	6753	5967	69679	7073	5833	71347	7414	5701	73023	7779	5572	74708	8171	5446	76400	8594	5321	78100	39
22	6758	5964	69707	7079	5831	71375	7420	5699	73051	7785	5570	74736	8178	5443	76428	8601	5319	78128	38
23	6763	5962	69735	7084	5828	71403	7426	5697	73079	7792	5568	74764	8185	5441	76457	8609	5317	78157	37
24	6769	5960	69762	7090	5826	71430	7432	5695	73107	7798	5566	74792	8191	5439	76485	8616	5315	78185	36
25	6774	5958	69790	7095	5824	71458	7438	5693	73135	7804	5564	74820	8198	5437	76513	8623	5313	78213	35
26	6779	5955	69818	7101	5822	71486	7444	5691	73163	7811	5562	74849	8205	5435	76542	8631	5311	78242	34
27	6784	5953	69846	7106	5820	71514	7450	5688	73191	7817	5560	74877	8212	5433	76570	8638	5309	78270	33
28	6789	5951	69873	7112	5817	71542	7456	5686	73219	7823	5557	74905	8219	5431	76598	8646	5307	78298	32
29	6795	5949	69901	7117	5815	71570	7461	5684	73247	7830	5555	74933	8226	5429	76626	8653	5305	78327	31
30	6800	5946	69929	7123	5813	71598	7467	5682	73275	7836	5553	74961	8232	5427	76655	8660	5303	78355	30
31	6805	5944	69956	7128	5811	71626	7473	5680	73303	7843	5551	74989	8239	5425	76683	8668	5301	78384	29
32	6810	5942	69984	7134	5809	71654	7479	5678	73331	7849	5549	75018	8246	5423	76711	8675	5298	78412	28
33	6815	5940	70012	7140	5806	71681	7485	5675	73360	7855	5547	75046	8253	5421	76740	8683	5296	78440	27
34	6821	5937	70040	7145	5804	71709	7491	5673	73388	7862	5545	75074	8260	5418	76768	8690	5294	78469	26
35	6826	5935	70067	7151	5802	71737	7497	5671	73416	7868	5543	75102	8267	5416	76796	8698	5292	78497	25
36	6831	5933	70095	7156	5800	71765	7503	5669	73444	7874	5540	75130	8274	5414	76824	8705	5290	78526	24
37	6836	5931	70123	7162	5798	71793	7509	5667	73472	7881	5538	75158	8281	5412	76853	8713	5288	78554	23
38	6842	5928	70151	7168	5795	71821	7515	5665	73500	7887	5536	75187	8288	5410	76881	8720	5286	78583	22
39	6847	5926	70179	7173	5793	71849	7521	5662	73528	7894	5534	75215	8295	5408	76909	8728	5284	78611	21
40	6852	5924	70206	7179	5791	71877	7527	5660	73556	7900	5532	75243	8301	5406	76938	8735	5282	78639	20
41	6857	5922	70234	7184	5789	71905	7533	5658	73584	7907	5530	75271	8308	5404	76966	8743	5280	78668	19
42	6863	5920	70262	7190	5787	71933	7539	5656	73612	7913	5528	75299	8315	5402	76994	8750	5278	78696	18
43	6868	5917	70290	7196	5784	71961	7545	5654	73640	7920	5526	75328	8322	5400	77023	8758	5276	78725	17
44	6873	5915	70317	7201	5782	71988	7551	5652	73668	7926	5523	75356	8329	5398	77051	8765	5274	78753	16
45	6879	5913	70345	7207	5780	72016	7557	5649	73696	7933	5521	75384	8336	5396	77079	8773	5272	78781	15
46	6884	5911	70373	7213	5778	72044	7563	5647	73724	7939	5519	75412	8343	5393	77108	8781	5270	78810	14
47	6889	5908	70401	7218	5776	72072	7569	5645	73752	7945	5517	75440	8350	5391	77136	8788	5268	78838	13
48	6895	5906	70428	7224	5773	72100	7575	5643	73780	7952	5515	75469	8357	5389	77164	8796	5266	78867	12
49	6900	5904	70456	7230	5771	72128	7581	5641	73808	7958	5513	75497	8364	5387	77192	8803	5264	78895	11
50	6905	5902	70484	7235	5769	72156	7587	5639	73836	7965	5511	75525	8371	5385	77221	8811	5262	78924	10
51	6911	5899	70512	7241	5767	72184	7594	5637	73865	7972	5509	75553	8378	5383	77249	8819	5260	78952	09
52	6916	5897	70540	7247	5765	72212	7600	5634	73893	7978	5507	75581	8385	5381	77277	8826	5258	78980	08
53	6921	5895	70567	7252	5762	72240	7606	5632	73921	7985	5504	75610	8393	5379	77306	8834	5256	79009	07
54	6927	5893	70595	7258	5760	72268	7612	5630	73949	7991	5502	75638	8400	5377	77334	8842	5254	79037	06
55	6932	5891	70623	7264	5758	72296	7618	5628	73977	7998	5500	75666	8407	5375	77362	8849	5252	79066	05
56	6937	5888	70651	7269	5756	72324	7624	5626	74005	8004	5498	75694	8414	5373	77391	8857	5249	79094	04
57	6943	5886	70679	7275	5754	72352	7630	5624	74033	8011	5496	75722	8421	5371	77419	8865	5247	79123	03
58	6948	5884	70706	7281	5751	72380	7636	5622	74061	8017	5494	75751	8428	5369	77447	8872	5245	79151	02
59	6953	5882	70734	7287	5749	72408	7642	5619	74089	8024	5492	75779	8435	5366	77476	8880	5243	79180	01
60	6959	5879	70762	7292	5747	72436	7649	5617	74117	8031	5490	75807	8442	5364	77504	8888	5241	79208	00

17° LHA ALT 287°	16° LHA ALT 286°	15° LHA ALT 285°	14° LHA ALT 284°	13° LHA ALT 283°	12° LHA ALT 282°

SIGHT REDUCTION

	78°			79°			80°			81°			82°			83°		
	LAT DEC	LHA SUM	L~D RES	LAT DEC	LHA SUM	L~D RES	LAT DEC	LHA SUM	L~D RES	LAT DEC	LHA SUM	L~D RES	LAT DEC	LHA SUM	L~D RES	LAT DEC	LHA SUM	L~D RES	
00'	8888	5241	79208	9374	5120	80918	9907	5002	82634	10498	4885	84356	11159	4770	86082	11911	4658	87812	60'
01	8896	5239	79236	9382	5118	80947	9916	5000	82663	10508	4883	84384	11171	4769	86111	11924	4656	87841	59
02	8903	5237	79265	9391	5116	80975	9926	4998	82692	10519	4881	84413	11183	4767	86139	11938	4654	87870	58
03	8911	5235	79293	9399	5114	81004	9935	4996	82720	10529	4879	84442	11195	4765	86168	11951	4652	87899	57
04	8919	5233	79322	9408	5112	81033	9944	4994	82749	10539	4877	84471	11206	4763	86197	11965	4650	87928	56
05	8927	5231	79350	9416	5110	81061	9954	4992	82778	10550	4875	84499	11218	4761	86226	11978	4648	87957	55
06	8935	5229	79379	9425	5108	81090	9963	4990	82806	10560	4873	84528	11230	4759	86255	11992	4647	87985	54
07	8942	5227	79407	9433	5106	81118	9973	4988	82835	10571	4872	84557	11242	4757	86283	12005	4645	88014	53
08	8950	5225	79436	9442	5105	81147	9982	4986	82864	10582	4870	84586	11254	4755	86312	12019	4643	88043	52
09	8958	5223	79464	9450	5103	81175	9992	4984	82892	10592	4868	84614	11266	4753	86341	12033	4641	88072	51
10	8966	5221	79493	9459	5101	81204	10001	4982	82921	10603	4866	84643	11278	4752	86370	12046	4639	88101	50
11	8974	5219	79521	9468	5099	81232	10011	4980	82950	10613	4864	84672	11290	4750	86399	12060	4637	88130	49
12	8982	5217	79550	9476	5097	81261	10020	4978	82978	10624	4862	84701	11302	4748	86428	12074	4636	88159	48
13	8990	5215	79578	9485	5095	81290	10030	4976	83007	10635	4860	84729	11314	4746	86456	12088	4634	88188	47
14	8997	5213	79607	9494	5093	81318	10039	4974	83036	10645	4858	84758	11326	4744	86485	12102	4632	88216	46
15	9005	5211	79635	9502	5091	81347	10049	4972	83064	10656	4856	84787	11338	4742	86514	12115	4630	88245	45
16	9013	5209	79664	9511	5089	81375	10058	4970	83093	10667	4854	84816	11350	4740	86543	12129	4628	88274	44
17	9021	5207	79692	9520	5087	81404	10068	4968	83122	10677	4852	84844	11362	4738	86572	12143	4626	88303	43
18	9029	5205	79720	9528	5085	81433	10078	4966	83150	10688	4850	84873	11374	4736	86601	12157	4624	88332	42
19	9037	5203	79749	9537	5083	81461	10087	4965	83179	10699	4849	84902	11386	4735	86629	12171	4623	88361	41
20	9045	5201	79777	9546	5081	81490	10097	4963	83208	10710	4847	84931	11399	4733	86658	12185	4621	88390	40
21	9053	5199	79806	9554	5079	81518	10107	4961	83236	10720	4845	84959	11411	4731	86687	12200	4619	88419	39
22	9061	5197	79834	9563	5077	81547	10116	4959	83265	10731	4843	84988	11423	4729	86716	12214	4617	88448	38
23	9069	5195	79863	9572	5075	81575	10126	4957	83294	10742	4841	85017	11435	4727	86745	12228	4615	88477	37
24	9077	5193	79891	9581	5073	81604	10136	4955	83322	10753	4839	85046	11448	4725	86773	12242	4613	88505	36
25	9085	5191	79920	9590	5071	81633	10145	4953	83351	10764	4837	85074	11460	4723	86802	12256	4611	88534	35
26	9093	5189	79948	9598	5069	81661	10155	4951	83380	10775	4835	85103	11473	4721	86831	12271	4610	88563	34
27	9101	5187	79977	9607	5067	81690	10165	4949	83408	10786	4833	85132	11485	4719	86860	12285	4608	88592	33
28	9109	5185	80005	9616	5065	81718	10175	4947	83437	10797	4831	85161	11497	4718	86889	12299	4606	88621	32
29	9117	5183	80034	9625	5063	81747	10185	4945	83466	10808	4829	85189	11510	4716	86918	12314	4604	88650	31
30	9125	5181	80062	9634	5061	81776	10194	4943	83494	10819	4827	85218	11522	4714	86947	12328	4602	88679	30
31	9133	5179	80091	9643	5059	81804	10204	4941	83523	10830	4826	85247	11535	4712	86975	12343	4600	88708	29
32	9142	5177	80119	9652	5057	81833	10214	4939	83552	10841	4824	85276	11547	4710	87004	12357	4599	88737	28
33	9150	5175	80148	9661	5055	81861	10224	4937	83580	10852	4822	85305	11560	4708	87033	12372	4597	88766	27
34	9158	5173	80176	9669	5053	81890	10234	4935	83609	10863	4820	85333	11573	4706	87062	12386	4595	88794	26
35	9166	5171	80205	9678	5051	81919	10244	4933	83638	10874	4818	85362	11585	4704	87091	12401	4593	88823	25
36	9174	5169	80233	9687	5049	81947	10254	4931	83667	10885	4816	85391	11598	4703	87120	12415	4591	88852	24
37	9182	5167	80262	9696	5047	81976	10264	4930	83695	10896	4814	85420	11611	4701	87148	12430	4589	88881	23
38	9191	5165	80290	9705	5045	82004	10274	4928	83724	10907	4812	85448	11623	4699	87177	12445	4587	88910	22
39	9199	5163	80319	9714	5043	82033	10284	4926	83753	10919	4810	85477	11636	4697	87206	12460	4586	88939	21
40	9207	5161	80348	9723	5041	82062	10294	4924	83781	10930	4808	85506	11649	4695	87235	12474	4584	88968	20
41	9215	5159	80376	9732	5039	82090	10304	4922	83810	10941	4806	85535	11662	4693	87264	12489	4582	88997	19
42	9223	5156	80405	9741	5037	82119	10314	4920	83839	10952	4805	85564	11674	4691	87293	12504	4580	89026	18
43	9232	5154	80433	9751	5035	82148	10324	4918	83867	10964	4803	85592	11687	4690	87322	12519	4578	89055	17
44	9240	5152	80462	9760	5033	82176	10334	4916	83896	10975	4801	85621	11700	4688	87350	12534	4576	89084	16
45	9248	5150	80490	9769	5031	82205	10344	4914	83925	10986	4799	85650	11713	4686	87379	12549	4575	89112	15
46	9256	5148	80519	9778	5029	82233	10354	4912	83954	10998	4797	85679	11726	4684	87408	12564	4573	89141	14
47	9265	5146	80547	9787	5027	82262	10364	4910	83982	11009	4795	85707	11739	4682	87437	12579	4571	89170	13
48	9273	5144	80576	9796	5025	82291	10374	4908	84011	11021	4793	85736	11752	4680	87466	12594	4569	89199	12
49	9281	5142	80604	9805	5023	82319	10385	4906	84040	11032	4791	85765	11765	4678	87495	12610	4567	89228	11
50	9290	5140	80633	9814	5021	82348	10395	4904	84068	11043	4789	85794	11778	4676	87524	12625	4565	89257	10
51	9298	5138	80661	9824	5019	82377	10405	4902	84097	11055	4787	85823	11791	4675	87552	12640	4564	89286	09
52	9306	5136	80690	9833	5017	82405	10415	4900	84126	11066	4786	85851	11804	4673	87581	12655	4562	89315	08
53	9315	5134	80718	9842	5015	82434	10425	4899	84155	11078	4784	85880	11818	4671	87610	12671	4560	89344	07
54	9323	5132	80747	9851	5013	82463	10436	4897	84183	11090	4782	85909	11831	4669	87639	12686	4558	89373	06
55	9332	5130	80776	9861	5012	82491	10446	4895	84212	11101	4780	85938	11844	4667	87668	12701	4556	89402	05
56	9340	5128	80804	9870	5010	82520	10456	4893	84241	11113	4778	85967	11857	4665	87697	12717	4554	89431	04
57	9348	5126	80833	9879	5008	82548	10467	4891	84270	11124	4776	85995	11871	4663	87726	12732	4553	89459	03
58	9357	5124	80861	9888	5006	82577	10477	4889	84298	11136	4774	86024	11884	4662	87754	12748	4551	89488	02
59	9365	5122	80890	9898	5004	82606	10487	4887	84327	11148	4772	86053	11897	4660	87783	12764	4549	89517	01
60	9374	5120	80918	9907	5002	82634	10498	4885	84356	11159	4770	86082	11911	4658	87812	12779	4547	89546	00

	11°			10°			9°			8°			7°			6°	
	LHA ALT 281°			LHA ALT 280°			LHA ALT 279°			LHA ALT 278°			LHA ALT 277°			LHA ALT 276°	

SIGHT REDUCTION

	84° DEC	84° SUM	84° RES	85° DEC	85° SUM	85° RES	86° DEC	86° SUM	86° RES	87° DEC	87° SUM	87° RES	88° DEC	88° SUM	88° RES	89° DEC	89° SUM	89° RES	
	LAT	LHA	L~D	LAT	LHA	L~D	LAT	LHA	L~D	LAT	LHA	L~D	LAT	LHA	L~D	LAT	LHA	L~D	
00'	12779	4547	89546	13808	4438	91284	15068	4332	93023	16694	4227	94765	18987	4123	96509	22908	4022	98254	60'
01	12795	4545	89575	13827	4437	91312	15092	4330	93052	16725	4225	94795	19034	4122	96538	23003	4020	98283	59
02	12811	4543	89604	13846	4435	91341	15115	4328	93081	16757	4223	94824	19082	4120	96567	23100	4019	98312	58
03	12826	4542	89633	13865	4433	91370	15139	4326	93110	16789	4221	94853	19130	4118	96596	23199	4017	98341	57
04	12842	4540	89662	13884	4431	91399	15163	4325	93139	16821	4220	94882	19179	4117	96625	23299	4015	98370	56
05	12858	4538	89691	13903	4429	91428	15187	4323	93169	16853	4218	94911	19228	4115	96654	23401	4014	98399	55
06	12874	4536	89720	13922	4428	91457	15211	4321	93198	16886	4216	94940	19277	4113	96684	23505	4012	98428	54
07	12890	4534	89749	13941	4426	91486	15235	4319	93227	16918	4214	94969	19327	4111	96713	23610	4010	98457	53
08	12906	4533	89778	13960	4424	91515	15259	4317	93256	16951	4213	94998	19377	4110	96742	23718	4009	98486	52
09	12922	4531	89807	13980	4422	91544	15284	4316	93285	16984	4211	95027	19428	4108	96771	23828	4007	98516	51
10	12938	4529	89836	13999	4420	91573	15308	4314	93314	17017	4209	95056	19479	4106	96800	23940	4005	98545	50
11	12954	4527	89865	14019	4419	91602	15333	4312	93343	17050	4208	95085	19531	4105	96829	24054	4004	98574	49
12	12970	4525	89893	14038	4417	91631	15358	4310	93372	17084	4206	95114	19583	4103	96858	24171	4002	98603	48
13	12987	4523	89922	14058	4415	91660	15383	4309	93401	17118	4204	95143	19635	4101	96887	24290	4000	98632	47
14	13003	4522	89951	14078	4413	91689	15408	4307	93430	17152	4202	95172	19689	4100	96916	24412	3999	98661	46
15	13019	4520	89980	14097	4412	91718	15433	4305	93459	17186	4201	95201	19742	4098	96945	24536	3997	98690	45
16	13036	4518	90009	14117	4410	91747	15458	4303	93488	17220	4199	95230	19796	4096	96974	24663	3995	98719	44
17	13052	4516	90038	14137	4408	91776	15483	4302	93517	17255	4197	95259	19851	4094	97003	24793	3994	98748	43
18	13068	4514	90067	14157	4406	91805	15508	4300	93546	17290	4195	95288	19906	4093	97032	24927	3992	98777	42
19	13085	4512	90096	14177	4404	91834	15534	4298	93575	17325	4194	95317	19962	4091	97061	25063	3990	98806	41
20	13102	4511	90125	14197	4403	91863	15560	4296	93604	17360	4192	95347	20018	4089	97091	25203	3989	98835	40
21	13118	4509	90154	14217	4401	91892	15585	4295	93633	17395	4190	95376	20075	4088	97120	25346	3987	98865	39
22	13135	4507	90183	14238	4399	91921	15611	4293	93662	17431	4189	95405	20133	4086	97149	25493	3985	98894	38
23	13152	4505	90212	14258	4397	91950	15637	4291	93691	17467	4187	95434	20191	4084	97178	25644	3984	98923	37
24	13168	4503	90241	14279	4395	91979	15663	4289	93720	17503	4185	95463	20249	4083	97207	25799	3982	98952	36
25	13185	4502	90270	14299	4394	92008	15689	4288	93749	17539	4183	95492	20308	4081	97236	25958	3980	98981	35
26	13202	4500	90299	14320	4392	92037	15716	4286	93778	17576	4182	95521	20368	4079	97265	26122	3979	99010	34
27	13219	4498	90328	14340	4390	92066	15742	4284	93807	17613	4180	95550	20429	4078	97294	26291	3977	99039	33
28	13236	4496	90357	14361	4388	92095	15769	4282	93836	17650	4178	95579	20490	4076	97323	26465	3975	99068	32
29	13253	4494	90386	14382	4387	92124	15796	4281	93865	17687	4176	95608	20552	4074	97352	26645	3974	99097	31
30	13270	4493	90415	14403	4385	92153	15822	4279	93894	17725	4175	95637	20614	4072	97381	26831	3972	99126	30
31	13287	4491	90443	14424	4383	92182	15849	4277	93923	17763	4173	95666	20677	4071	97410	27022	3970	99155	29
32	13304	4489	90472	14445	4381	92211	15877	4275	93952	17801	4171	95695	20741	4069	97439	27221	3969	99185	28
33	13321	4487	90501	14466	4379	92240	15904	4274	93981	17839	4170	95724	20806	4067	97469	27427	3967	99214	27
34	13339	4485	90530	14487	4378	92269	15931	4272	94010	17878	4168	95753	20871	4066	97498	27640	3965	99243	26
35	13356	4483	90559	14508	4376	92298	15959	4270	94039	17916	4166	95782	20938	4064	97527	27862	3964	99272	25
36	13373	4482	90588	14530	4374	92327	15986	4268	94068	17956	4164	95811	21005	4062	97556	28093	3962	99301	24
37	13391	4480	90617	14551	4372	92356	16014	4267	94097	17995	4163	95841	21072	4061	97585	28334	3960	99330	23
38	13408	4478	90646	14572	4371	92385	16042	4265	94126	18035	4161	95870	21141	4059	97614	28586	3959	99359	22
39	13426	4476	90675	14594	4369	92414	16070	4263	94156	18075	4159	95899	21210	4057	97643	28849	3957	99388	21
40	13444	4474	90704	14616	4367	92443	16098	4261	94185	18115	4158	95928	21281	4056	97672	29125	3955	99417	20
41	13461	4473	90733	14638	4365	92472	16127	4260	94214	18156	4156	95957	21352	4054	97701	29415	3954	99446	19
42	13479	4471	90762	14659	4363	92501	16155	4258	94243	18196	4154	95986	21424	4052	97730	29721	3952	99475	18
43	13497	4469	90791	14681	4362	92530	16184	4256	94272	18237	4152	96015	21497	4051	97759	30045	3950	99504	17
44	13515	4467	90820	14703	4360	92559	16212	4254	94301	18279	4151	96044	21571	4049	97788	30388	3949	99534	16
45	13532	4465	90849	14725	4358	92588	16241	4253	94330	18321	4149	96073	21646	4047	97818	30753	3947	99563	15
46	13550	4464	90878	14748	4356	92617	16270	4251	94359	18363	4147	96102	21722	4046	97847	31143	3945	99592	14
47	13568	4462	90907	14770	4355	92646	16300	4249	94388	18405	4146	96131	21799	4044	97876	31563	3944	99621	13
48	13586	4460	90936	14792	4353	92675	16329	4247	94417	18448	4144	96160	21877	4042	97905	32016	3942	99650	12
49	13605	4458	90965	14815	4351	92704	16359	4246	94446	18491	4142	96189	21956	4040	97934	32508	3941	99679	11
50	13623	4456	90994	14837	4349	92733	16388	4244	94475	18534	4140	96218	22036	4039	97963	33047	3939	99708	10
51	13641	4455	91023	14860	4347	92762	16418	4242	94504	18578	4139	96247	22118	4037	97992	33643	3937	99737	09
52	13659	4453	91052	14883	4346	92791	16448	4240	94533	18622	4137	96277	22200	4035	98021	34310	3936	99766	08
53	13678	4451	91081	14906	4344	92820	16478	4239	94562	18666	4135	96306	22284	4034	98050	35066	3934	99795	07
54	13696	4449	91110	14928	4342	92849	16508	4237	94591	18711	4134	96335	22369	4032	98079	35938	3932	99824	06
55	13714	4447	91139	14951	4340	92878	16539	4235	94620	18756	4132	96364	22455	4030	98108	36970	3931	99854	05
56	13733	4446	91168	14975	4339	92907	16570	4234	94649	18801	4130	96393	22543	4029	98137	38232	3929	99883	04
57	13752	4444	91197	14998	4337	92936	16600	4232	94678	18847	4129	96422	22632	4027	98167	39860	3927	99912	03
58	13770	4442	91226	15021	4335	92965	16631	4230	94707	18893	4127	96451	22723	4025	98196	42155	3926	99941	02
59	13789	4440	91255	15044	4333	92994	16663	4228	94736	18940	4125	96480	22815	4024	98225	46077	3924	99970	01
60	13808	4438	91284	15068	4332	93023	16694	4227	94765	18987	4123	96509	22908	4022	98254	211251	3922	99999	00

	5°			4°			3°			2°			1°			0°		
	LHA	ALT		LHA	ALT		LHA	ALT		LHA	ALT		LHA	ALT		LHA	ALT	
	275°			274°			273°			272°			271°			270°		

SIGHT REDUCTION

	90° LHA	91° LHA	92° LHA	93° LHA	94° LHA	95° LHA	96° LHA	97° LHA	98° LHA	99° LHA	100° LHA	101° LHA	102° LHA	103° LHA	104° LHA	105° LHA	106° LHA	107° LHA	
00'	3922	3824	3728	3634	3541	3449	3360	3272	3185	3100	3016	2934	2853	2774	2696	2620	2545	2471	60'
01	3921	3823	3727	3632	3539	3448	3358	3270	3184	3099	3015	2933	2852	2773	2695	2619	2544	2470	59
02	3919	3821	3725	3631	3538	3446	3357	3269	3182	3097	3014	2931	2851	2772	2694	2617	2542	2469	58
03	3917	3820	3723	3629	3536	3445	3355	3267	3181	3096	3012	2930	2849	2770	2692	2616	2541	2467	57
04	3916	3818	3722	3627	3535	3443	3354	3266	3179	3094	3011	2929	2848	2769	2691	2615	2540	2466	56
05	3914	3816	3720	3626	3533	3442	3352	3264	3178	3093	3009	2927	2847	2768	2690	2614	2539	2465	55
06	3913	3815	3719	3624	3532	3440	3351	3263	3176	3091	3008	2926	2845	2766	2689	2612	2537	2464	54
07	3911	3813	3717	3623	3530	3439	3349	3261	3175	3090	3007	2925	2844	2765	2687	2611	2536	2462	53
08	3909	3812	3716	3621	3529	3437	3348	3260	3174	3089	3005	2923	2843	2764	2686	2610	2535	2461	52
09	3908	3810	3714	3620	3527	3436	3346	3259	3172	3087	3004	2922	2841	2762	2685	2609	2534	2460	51
10	3906	3808	3712	3618	3525	3434	3345	3257	3171	3086	3003	2921	2840	2761	2684	2607	2532	2459	50
11	3904	3807	3711	3617	3524	3433	3344	3256	3169	3084	3001	2919	2839	2760	2682	2606	2531	2458	49
12	3903	3805	3709	3615	3522	3431	3342	3254	3168	3083	3000	2918	2838	2759	2681	2605	2530	2456	48
13	3901	3803	3708	3613	3521	3430	3341	3253	3166	3082	2998	2917	2836	2757	2680	2603	2529	2455	47
14	3899	3802	3706	3612	3519	3428	3339	3251	3165	3080	2997	2915	2835	2756	2678	2602	2527	2454	46
15	3898	3800	3704	3610	3518	3427	3338	3250	3164	3079	2996	2914	2834	2755	2677	2601	2526	2453	45
16	3896	3799	3703	3609	3516	3425	3336	3248	3162	3077	2994	2913	2832	2753	2676	2600	2525	2452	44
17	3894	3797	3701	3607	3515	3424	3335	3247	3161	3076	2993	2911	2831	2752	2675	2598	2524	2450	43
18	3893	3795	3700	3606	3513	3422	3333	3245	3159	3075	2992	2910	2830	2751	2673	2597	2522	2449	42
19	3891	3794	3698	3604	3512	3421	3332	3244	3158	3073	2990	2908	2828	2749	2672	2596	2521	2448	41
20	3890	3792	3697	3603	3510	3419	3330	3243	3156	3072	2989	2907	2827	2748	2671	2595	2520	2447	40
21	3888	3791	3695	3601	3509	3418	3329	3241	3155	3070	2987	2906	2826	2747	2669	2593	2519	2446	39
22	3886	3789	3693	3599	3507	3416	3327	3240	3154	3069	2986	2904	2824	2745	2668	2592	2518	2444	38
23	3885	3787	3692	3598	3506	3415	3326	3238	3152	3068	2985	2903	2823	2744	2667	2591	2516	2443	37
24	3883	3786	3690	3596	3504	3413	3324	3237	3151	3066	2983	2902	2822	2743	2666	2590	2515	2442	36
25	3881	3784	3689	3595	3503	3412	3323	3235	3149	3065	2982	2900	2820	2742	2664	2588	2514	2441	35
26	3880	3783	3687	3593	3501	3410	3321	3234	3148	3064	2981	2899	2819	2740	2663	2587	2513	2439	34
27	3878	3781	3686	3592	3500	3409	3320	3232	3147	3062	2979	2898	2818	2739	2662	2586	2511	2438	33
28	3876	3779	3684	3590	3498	3407	3318	3231	3145	3061	2978	2896	2816	2738	2660	2585	2510	2437	32
29	3875	3778	3682	3589	3496	3406	3317	3230	3144	3059	2976	2895	2815	2736	2659	2583	2509	2436	31
30	3873	3776	3681	3587	3495	3404	3316	3228	3142	3058	2975	2894	2814	2735	2658	2582	2508	2435	30
31	3872	3775	3679	3586	3493	3403	3314	3227	3141	3057	2974	2892	2812	2734	2657	2581	2506	2433	29
32	3870	3773	3678	3584	3492	3401	3313	3225	3139	3055	2972	2891	2811	2733	2655	2580	2505	2432	28
33	3868	3771	3676	3582	3490	3400	3311	3224	3138	3054	2971	2890	2810	2731	2654	2578	2504	2431	27
34	3867	3770	3674	3581	3489	3398	3310	3222	3137	3052	2970	2888	2808	2730	2653	2577	2503	2430	26
35	3865	3768	3673	3579	3487	3397	3308	3221	3135	3051	2968	2887	2807	2729	2652	2576	2502	2429	25
36	3863	3767	3671	3578	3486	3395	3307	3219	3134	3050	2967	2886	2806	2727	2650	2575	2500	2427	24
37	3862	3765	3670	3576	3484	3394	3305	3218	3132	3048	2965	2884	2804	2726	2649	2573	2499	2426	23
38	3860	3763	3668	3575	3483	3392	3304	3217	3131	3047	2964	2883	2803	2725	2648	2572	2498	2425	22
39	3859	3762	3667	3573	3481	3391	3302	3215	3130	3045	2963	2882	2802	2723	2646	2571	2497	2424	21
40	3857	3760	3665	3572	3480	3390	3301	3214	3128	3044	2961	2880	2800	2722	2645	2570	2495	2423	20
41	3855	3759	3663	3570	3478	3388	3299	3212	3127	3043	2960	2879	2799	2721	2644	2568	2494	2421	19
42	3854	3757	3662	3569	3477	3387	3298	3211	3125	3041	2959	2878	2798	2720	2643	2567	2493	2420	18
43	3852	3755	3660	3567	3475	3385	3296	3209	3124	3040	2957	2876	2797	2718	2641	2566	2492	2419	17
44	3850	3754	3659	3565	3474	3384	3295	3208	3122	3038	2956	2875	2795	2717	2640	2565	2491	2418	16
45	3849	3752	3657	3564	3472	3382	3294	3207	3121	3037	2955	2874	2794	2716	2639	2563	2489	2417	15
46	3847	3751	3656	3562	3471	3381	3292	3205	3120	3036	2953	2872	2793	2714	2638	2562	2488	2415	14
47	3846	3749	3654	3561	3469	3379	3291	3204	3118	3034	2952	2871	2791	2713	2636	2561	2487	2414	13
48	3844	3747	3652	3559	3468	3378	3289	3202	3117	3033	2950	2869	2790	2712	2635	2560	2486	2413	12
49	3842	3746	3651	3558	3466	3376	3288	3201	3115	3032	2949	2868	2789	2711	2634	2558	2484	2412	11
50	3841	3744	3649	3556	3465	3375	3286	3199	3114	3030	2948	2867	2787	2709	2633	2557	2483	2411	10
51	3839	3743	3648	3555	3463	3373	3285	3198	3113	3029	2946	2865	2786	2708	2631	2556	2482	2409	09
52	3837	3741	3646	3553	3462	3372	3283	3196	3111	3027	2945	2864	2785	2707	2630	2555	2481	2408	08
53	3836	3739	3645	3552	3460	3370	3282	3195	3110	3026	2944	2863	2783	2705	2629	2553	2480	2407	07
54	3834	3738	3643	3550	3459	3369	3280	3194	3108	3025	2942	2861	2782	2704	2627	2552	2478	2406	06
55	3833	3736	3642	3548	3457	3367	3279	3192	3107	3023	2941	2860	2781	2703	2626	2551	2477	2405	05
56	3831	3735	3640	3547	3456	3366	3277	3191	3106	3022	2940	2859	2779	2701	2625	2550	2476	2403	04
57	3829	3733	3638	3545	3454	3364	3276	3189	3104	3020	2938	2857	2778	2700	2624	2548	2475	2402	03
58	3828	3731	3637	3544	3453	3363	3275	3188	3103	3019	2937	2856	2777	2699	2622	2547	2473	2401	02
59	3826	3730	3635	3542	3451	3361	3273	3186	3101	3018	2936	2855	2776	2698	2621	2546	2472	2400	01
60	3824	3728	3634	3541	3449	3360	3272	3185	3100	3016	2934	2853	2774	2696	2620	2545	2471	2399	00
	LHA 269°	LHA 268°	LHA 267°	LHA 266°	LHA 265°	LHA 264°	LHA 263°	LHA 262°	LHA 261°	LHA 260°	LHA 259°	LHA 258°	LHA 257°	LHA 256°	LHA 255°	LHA 254°	LHA 253°	LHA 252°	

SIGHT REDUCTION

	108° LHA	109° LHA	110° LHA	111° LHA	112° LHA	113° LHA	114° LHA	115° LHA	116° LHA	117° LHA	118° LHA	119° LHA	120° LHA	121° LHA	122° LHA	123° LHA	124° LHA	125° LHA	
00'	2399	2327	2258	2189	2122	2056	1991	1928	1865	1804	1744	1686	1628	1571	1516	1462	1409	1357	60'
01	2397	2326	2257	2188	2121	2055	1990	1927	1864	1803	1743	1685	1627	1571	1515	1461	1408	1356	59
02	2396	2325	2255	2187	2120	2054	1989	1926	1863	1802	1742	1684	1626	1570	1514	1460	1407	1355	58
03	2395	2324	2254	2186	2119	2053	1988	1925	1862	1801	1741	1683	1625	1569	1513	1459	1406	1354	57
04	2394	2323	2253	2185	2117	2052	1987	1923	1861	1800	1740	1682	1624	1568	1513	1458	1405	1354	56
05	2393	2322	2252	2184	2116	2050	1986	1922	1860	1799	1739	1681	1623	1567	1512	1458	1405	1353	55
06	2391	2320	2251	2182	2115	2049	1985	1921	1859	1798	1738	1680	1622	1566	1511	1457	1404	1352	54
07	2390	2319	2250	2181	2114	2048	1984	1920	1858	1797	1737	1679	1621	1565	1510	1456	1403	1351	53
08	2389	2318	2248	2180	2113	2047	1983	1919	1857	1796	1736	1678	1620	1564	1509	1455	1402	1350	52
09	2388	2317	2247	2179	2112	2046	1982	1918	1856	1795	1735	1677	1619	1563	1508	1454	1401	1349	51
10	2387	2316	2246	2178	2111	2045	1981	1917	1855	1794	1734	1676	1618	1562	1507	1453	1400	1348	50
11	2385	2315	2245	2177	2110	2044	1979	1916	1854	1793	1733	1675	1617	1561	1506	1452	1399	1348	49
12	2384	2313	2244	2176	2109	2043	1978	1915	1853	1792	1732	1674	1617	1560	1505	1451	1398	1347	48
13	2383	2312	2243	2175	2108	2042	1977	1914	1852	1791	1731	1673	1616	1559	1504	1450	1398	1346	47
14	2382	2311	2242	2173	2106	2041	1976	1913	1851	1790	1730	1672	1614	1558	1503	1450	1397	1345	46
15	2381	2310	2240	2172	2105	2040	1975	1912	1850	1789	1729	1671	1613	1558	1502	1449	1396	1344	45
16	2380	2309	2239	2171	2104	2039	1974	1911	1849	1788	1729	1670	1612	1557	1501	1448	1395	1343	44
17	2378	2308	2238	2170	2103	2037	1973	1910	1848	1787	1728	1669	1611	1556	1500	1447	1394	1342	43
18	2377	2306	2237	2169	2102	2036	1972	1909	1847	1786	1727	1668	1611	1555	1500	1446	1393	1342	42
19	2376	2305	2236	2168	2101	2035	1971	1908	1846	1785	1726	1667	1610	1554	1499	1445	1392	1341	41
20	2375	2304	2235	2167	2100	2034	1970	1907	1845	1784	1725	1666	1609	1553	1498	1444	1391	1340	40
21	2374	2303	2234	2165	2099	2033	1969	1906	1844	1783	1724	1665	1608	1552	1497	1443	1391	1339	39
22	2372	2302	2232	2164	2098	2032	1968	1905	1843	1782	1723	1664	1607	1551	1496	1442	1390	1338	38
23	2371	2301	2231	2163	2096	2031	1967	1904	1842	1781	1722	1663	1606	1550	1495	1442	1389	1337	37
24	2370	2299	2230	2162	2095	2030	1966	1903	1841	1780	1721	1662	1605	1549	1494	1441	1388	1336	36
25	2369	2298	2229	2161	2094	2029	1965	1902	1840	1779	1720	1661	1604	1548	1493	1440	1387	1336	35
26	2368	2297	2228	2160	2093	2028	1964	1901	1839	1778	1719	1660	1603	1547	1493	1439	1386	1335	34
27	2366	2296	2227	2159	2092	2027	1962	1899	1838	1777	1718	1659	1602	1546	1492	1438	1385	1334	33
28	2365	2295	2226	2158	2091	2026	1961	1898	1837	1776	1717	1659	1601	1546	1491	1437	1385	1333	32
29	2364	2294	2224	2157	2090	2024	1960	1897	1836	1775	1716	1658	1601	1545	1490	1436	1384	1332	31
30	2363	2292	2223	2155	2089	2023	1959	1896	1835	1774	1715	1657	1600	1544	1489	1435	1383	1331	30
31	2362	2291	2222	2154	2088	2022	1958	1895	1834	1773	1714	1656	1599	1543	1488	1434	1382	1331	29
32	2361	2290	2221	2153	2087	2021	1957	1894	1833	1772	1713	1655	1598	1542	1487	1434	1381	1330	28
33	2359	2289	2220	2152	2085	2020	1956	1893	1832	1771	1712	1654	1597	1541	1486	1433	1380	1329	27
34	2358	2288	2219	2151	2084	2019	1955	1892	1831	1770	1711	1653	1596	1540	1485	1432	1379	1328	26
35	2357	2287	2218	2150	2083	2018	1954	1891	1830	1769	1710	1652	1595	1539	1484	1431	1378	1327	25
36	2356	2285	2216	2149	2082	2017	1953	1890	1829	1768	1709	1651	1594	1538	1484	1430	1378	1326	24
37	2355	2284	2215	2148	2081	2016	1952	1889	1828	1767	1708	1650	1593	1537	1483	1429	1377	1325	23
38	2353	2283	2214	2146	2080	2015	1951	1888	1826	1766	1707	1649	1592	1536	1482	1428	1376	1325	22
39	2352	2282	2213	2145	2079	2014	1950	1887	1825	1765	1706	1648	1591	1535	1481	1427	1375	1324	21
40	2351	2281	2212	2144	2078	2013	1949	1886	1824	1764	1705	1647	1590	1534	1480	1426	1374	1323	20
41	2350	2280	2211	2143	2077	2012	1948	1885	1823	1763	1704	1646	1589	1534	1479	1426	1373	1322	19
42	2349	2278	2210	2142	2076	2010	1947	1884	1822	1762	1703	1645	1588	1533	1478	1425	1372	1321	18
43	2348	2277	2208	2141	2075	2009	1946	1883	1821	1761	1702	1644	1587	1532	1477	1424	1372	1320	17
44	2346	2276	2207	2140	2073	2008	1944	1882	1820	1760	1701	1643	1586	1531	1476	1423	1371	1320	16
45	2345	2275	2206	2139	2072	2007	1943	1881	1819	1759	1700	1642	1585	1530	1475	1422	1370	1319	15
46	2344	2274	2205	2138	2071	2006	1942	1880	1818	1758	1699	1641	1585	1529	1475	1421	1369	1318	14
47	2343	2273	2204	2136	2070	2005	1941	1879	1817	1757	1698	1640	1584	1528	1474	1420	1368	1317	13
48	2342	2272	2203	2135	2069	2004	1940	1878	1816	1756	1697	1639	1583	1527	1473	1419	1367	1316	12
49	2340	2270	2202	2134	2068	2003	1939	1877	1815	1755	1696	1638	1582	1526	1472	1419	1366	1315	11
50	2339	2269	2201	2133	2067	2002	1938	1876	1814	1754	1695	1637	1581	1525	1471	1418	1366	1314	10
51	2338	2268	2199	2132	2066	2001	1937	1875	1813	1753	1694	1636	1580	1524	1470	1417	1365	1314	09
52	2337	2267	2198	2131	2065	2000	1936	1874	1812	1752	1693	1636	1579	1523	1469	1416	1364	1313	08
53	2336	2266	2197	2130	2064	1999	1935	1873	1811	1751	1692	1635	1578	1523	1468	1415	1363	1312	07
54	2335	2265	2196	2129	2062	1998	1934	1872	1810	1750	1691	1634	1577	1522	1467	1414	1362	1311	06
55	2333	2263	2195	2127	2061	1997	1933	1870	1809	1749	1690	1633	1576	1521	1466	1413	1361	1310	05
56	2332	2262	2194	2126	2060	1995	1932	1869	1808	1748	1689	1632	1575	1520	1466	1412	1360	1309	04
57	2331	2261	2193	2125	2059	1994	1931	1868	1807	1747	1688	1631	1574	1519	1465	1412	1360	1309	03
58	2330	2260	2191	2124	2058	1993	1930	1867	1806	1746	1687	1630	1573	1518	1464	1411	1359	1308	02
59	2329	2259	2190	2123	2057	1992	1929	1866	1805	1745	1687	1629	1572	1517	1463	1410	1358	1307	01
60	2327	2258	2189	2122	2056	1991	1928	1865	1804	1744	1686	1628	1571	1516	1462	1409	1357	1306	00
	LHA 251°	LHA 250°	LHA 249°	LHA 248°	LHA 247°	LHA 246°	LHA 245°	LHA 244°	LHA 243°	LHA 242°	LHA 241°	LHA 240°	LHA 239°	LHA 238°	LHA 237°	LHA 236°	LHA 235°	LHA 234°	

SIGHT REDUCTION

	126° LHA	127° LHA	128° LHA	129° LHA	130° LHA	131° LHA	132° LHA	133° LHA	134° LHA	135° LHA	136° LHA	137° LHA	138° LHA	139° LHA	140° LHA	141° LHA	142° LHA	143° LHA	
00'	1306	1256	1208	1160	1113	1068	1023	980	937	896	856	816	778	740	704	669	634	601	60'
01	1305	1255	1207	1159	1113	1067	1023	979	937	895	855	816	777	740	703	668	633	600	59
02	1304	1255	1206	1158	1112	1066	1022	978	936	895	854	815	777	739	703	667	633	599	58
03	1304	1254	1205	1158	1111	1066	1021	978	935	894	854	814	776	739	702	667	632	599	57
04	1303	1253	1204	1157	1110	1065	1020	977	935	893	853	814	775	738	702	666	632	598	56
05	1302	1252	1204	1156	1110	1064	1020	976	934	893	852	813	775	737	701	666	631	598	55
06	1301	1251	1203	1155	1109	1063	1019	976	933	892	852	812	774	737	700	665	631	597	54
07	1300	1251	1202	1154	1108	1063	1018	975	933	891	851	812	773	736	700	664	630	597	53
08	1299	1250	1201	1154	1107	1062	1018	974	932	891	850	811	773	736	699	664	630	596	52
09	1299	1249	1200	1153	1106	1061	1017	973	931	890	850	810	772	735	699	663	629	596	51
10	1298	1248	1200	1152	1106	1060	1016	973	930	889	849	810	772	734	698	663	628	595	50
11	1297	1247	1199	1151	1105	1060	1015	972	930	889	848	809	771	734	697	662	628	594	49
12	1296	1246	1198	1151	1104	1059	1015	971	929	888	848	808	770	733	697	662	627	594	48
13	1295	1246	1197	1150	1103	1058	1014	971	928	887	847	808	770	732	696	661	627	593	47
14	1294	1245	1196	1149	1103	1057	1013	970	928	887	846	807	769	732	696	660	626	593	46
15	1294	1244	1196	1148	1102	1057	1012	969	927	886	846	807	768	731	695	660	626	592	45
16	1293	1243	1195	1147	1101	1056	1012	968	926	885	845	806	768	731	694	659	625	592	44
17	1292	1242	1194	1147	1100	1055	1011	968	926	885	844	805	767	730	694	659	624	591	43
18	1291	1242	1193	1146	1100	1054	1010	967	925	884	844	805	767	729	693	658	624	591	42
19	1290	1241	1192	1145	1099	1054	1009	966	924	883	843	804	766	729	693	657	623	590	41
20	1289	1240	1192	1144	1098	1053	1009	966	924	882	842	803	765	728	692	657	623	590	40
21	1289	1239	1191	1144	1097	1052	1008	965	923	882	842	803	765	728	691	656	622	589	39
22	1288	1238	1190	1143	1097	1051	1007	964	922	881	841	802	764	727	691	656	622	588	38
23	1287	1238	1189	1142	1096	1051	1007	964	921	880	840	801	763	726	690	655	621	588	37
24	1286	1237	1188	1141	1095	1050	1006	963	921	880	840	801	763	726	690	655	621	587	36
25	1285	1236	1188	1140	1094	1049	1005	962	920	879	839	800	762	725	689	654	620	587	35
26	1284	1235	1187	1140	1094	1048	1004	961	919	878	838	799	762	725	688	653	619	586	34
27	1284	1234	1186	1139	1093	1048	1004	961	919	878	838	799	761	724	688	653	619	586	33
28	1283	1233	1185	1138	1092	1047	1003	960	918	877	837	798	760	723	687	652	618	585	32
29	1282	1233	1184	1137	1091	1046	1002	959	917	876	836	798	760	723	687	652	618	585	31
30	1281	1232	1184	1137	1090	1045	1002	959	917	876	836	797	759	722	686	651	617	584	30
31	1280	1231	1183	1136	1090	1045	1001	958	916	875	835	796	758	721	686	651	617	584	29
32	1279	1230	1182	1135	1089	1044	1000	957	915	874	835	796	758	721	685	650	616	583	28
33	1279	1229	1181	1134	1088	1043	999	956	915	874	834	795	757	720	684	649	615	582	27
34	1278	1229	1180	1133	1087	1043	999	956	914	873	833	794	757	720	684	649	615	582	26
35	1277	1228	1180	1133	1087	1042	998	955	913	872	833	794	756	719	683	648	614	581	25
36	1276	1227	1179	1132	1086	1041	997	954	912	872	832	793	755	718	683	648	614	581	24
37	1275	1226	1178	1131	1085	1040	996	954	912	871	831	792	755	718	682	647	613	580	23
38	1274	1225	1177	1130	1084	1040	996	953	911	870	831	792	754	717	681	647	613	580	22
39	1274	1225	1177	1130	1084	1039	995	952	910	870	830	791	753	717	681	646	612	579	21
40	1273	1224	1176	1129	1083	1038	994	952	910	869	829	791	753	716	680	645	612	579	20
41	1272	1223	1175	1128	1082	1037	994	951	909	868	829	790	752	715	680	645	611	578	19
42	1271	1222	1174	1127	1081	1037	993	950	908	868	828	789	752	715	679	644	610	578	18
43	1270	1221	1173	1126	1081	1036	992	949	908	867	827	789	751	714	678	644	610	577	17
44	1269	1220	1173	1126	1080	1035	991	949	907	866	827	788	750	714	678	643	609	577	16
45	1269	1220	1172	1125	1079	1034	991	948	906	866	826	787	750	713	677	643	609	576	15
46	1268	1219	1171	1124	1078	1034	990	947	906	865	825	787	749	712	677	642	608	575	14
47	1267	1218	1170	1123	1078	1033	989	947	905	864	825	786	748	712	676	641	608	575	13
48	1266	1217	1169	1123	1077	1032	989	946	904	864	824	785	748	711	676	641	607	574	12
49	1265	1216	1169	1122	1076	1031	988	945	904	863	823	785	747	711	675	640	607	574	11
50	1265	1216	1168	1121	1075	1031	987	944	903	862	823	784	747	710	674	640	606	573	10
51	1264	1215	1167	1120	1075	1030	986	944	902	862	822	784	746	709	674	639	605	573	09
52	1263	1214	1166	1120	1074	1029	986	943	902	861	821	783	745	709	673	639	605	572	08
53	1262	1213	1165	1119	1073	1028	985	942	901	860	821	782	745	708	673	638	604	572	07
54	1261	1212	1165	1118	1072	1028	984	942	900	860	820	782	744	708	672	637	604	571	06
55	1260	1212	1164	1117	1072	1027	983	941	899	859	819	781	743	707	671	637	603	571	05
56	1260	1211	1163	1116	1071	1026	983	940	899	858	819	780	743	706	671	636	603	570	04
57	1259	1210	1162	1116	1070	1026	982	940	898	858	818	780	742	706	670	636	602	570	03
58	1258	1209	1162	1115	1069	1025	981	939	897	857	818	779	742	705	670	635	602	569	02
59	1257	1208	1161	1114	1069	1024	981	938	897	856	817	778	741	705	669	635	601	568	01
60	1256	1208	1160	1113	1068	1023	980	937	896	856	816	778	740	704	669	634	601	568	00
	LHA 233°	LHA 232°	LHA 231°	LHA 230°	LHA 229°	LHA 228°	LHA 227°	LHA 226°	LHA 225°	LHA 224°	LHA 223°	LHA 222°	LHA 221°	LHA 220°	LHA 219°	LHA 218°	LHA 217°	LHA 216°	

SIGHT REDUCTION

	144° LHA	145° LHA	146° LHA	147° LHA	148° LHA	149° LHA	150° LHA	151° LHA	152° LHA	153° LHA	154° LHA	155° LHA	156° LHA	157° LHA	158° LHA	159° LHA	160° LHA	161° LHA	
00'	568	536	506	476	447	419	392	366	341	317	294	272	250	230	210	191	173	156	60'
01	567	536	505	475	447	419	392	366	341	317	293	271	250	229	210	191	173	156	59
02	567	535	505	475	446	418	391	366	340	316	293	271	249	229	209	191	173	156	58
03	566	535	504	474	446	418	391	365	340	316	293	270	249	229	209	190	172	155	57
04	566	534	504	474	445	417	391	365	340	316	292	270	249	228	209	190	172	155	56
05	565	534	503	473	445	417	390	364	339	315	292	270	248	228	208	190	172	155	55
06	565	533	503	473	444	417	390	364	339	315	292	269	248	228	208	189	172	155	54
07	564	533	502	473	444	416	389	363	338	314	291	269	248	227	208	189	171	154	53
08	564	532	502	472	443	416	389	363	338	314	291	269	247	227	207	189	171	154	52
09	563	532	501	472	443	415	388	363	338	314	290	268	247	227	207	188	171	154	51
10	563	531	501	471	442	415	388	362	337	313	290	268	247	226	207	188	170	154	50
11	562	531	500	471	442	414	388	362	337	313	290	268	246	226	206	188	170	153	49
12	562	530	500	470	441	414	387	361	336	312	289	267	246	226	206	187	170	153	48
13	561	530	499	470	441	413	387	361	336	312	289	267	246	225	206	187	170	153	47
14	560	529	499	469	441	413	386	360	336	312	289	266	245	225	205	187	169	152	46
15	560	529	498	469	440	412	386	360	335	311	288	266	245	225	205	187	169	152	45
16	559	528	498	468	440	412	385	360	335	311	288	266	244	224	205	186	169	152	44
17	559	528	497	468	439	412	385	359	334	310	287	265	244	224	204	186	168	152	43
18	558	527	497	467	439	411	384	359	334	310	287	265	244	224	204	186	168	151	42
19	558	527	496	467	438	411	384	358	334	310	287	265	243	223	204	185	168	151	41
20	557	526	496	466	438	410	384	358	333	309	286	264	243	223	204	185	168	151	40
21	557	525	495	466	437	410	383	357	333	309	286	264	243	223	203	185	167	151	39
22	556	525	495	465	437	409	383	357	332	308	286	264	242	222	203	184	167	150	38
23	556	524	494	465	436	409	382	357	332	308	285	263	242	222	203	184	167	150	37
24	555	524	494	464	436	408	382	356	331	308	285	263	242	222	202	184	166	150	36
25	555	523	493	464	435	408	381	356	331	307	284	262	241	221	202	184	166	149	35
26	554	523	493	463	435	408	381	355	331	307	284	262	241	221	202	183	166	149	34
27	554	522	492	463	434	407	381	355	330	307	284	262	241	221	201	183	166	149	33
28	553	522	492	462	434	407	380	355	330	306	283	261	240	220	201	183	165	149	32
29	553	521	491	462	434	406	380	354	329	306	283	261	240	220	201	182	165	148	31
30	552	521	491	461	433	406	379	354	329	305	283	261	240	220	200	182	165	148	30
31	551	520	490	461	433	405	379	353	329	305	282	260	239	219	200	182	164	148	29
32	551	520	490	460	432	405	378	353	328	305	282	260	239	219	200	181	164	148	28
33	550	519	489	460	432	404	378	352	328	304	281	260	239	219	199	181	164	147	27
34	550	519	489	460	431	404	378	352	327	304	281	259	238	218	199	181	164	147	26
35	549	518	488	459	431	403	377	352	327	303	281	259	238	218	199	181	163	147	25
36	549	518	488	459	430	403	377	351	327	303	280	259	238	218	199	180	163	147	24
37	548	517	487	458	430	403	376	351	326	303	280	258	237	217	198	180	163	146	23
38	548	517	487	458	429	402	376	350	326	302	280	258	237	217	198	180	162	146	22
39	547	516	486	457	429	402	375	350	325	302	279	257	237	217	198	179	162	146	21
40	547	516	486	457	428	401	375	350	325	302	279	257	236	216	197	179	162	145	20
41	546	515	485	456	428	401	374	349	325	301	278	257	236	216	197	179	162	145	19
42	546	515	485	456	428	400	374	349	324	301	278	256	236	216	197	179	161	145	18
43	545	514	484	455	427	400	374	348	324	300	278	256	235	215	196	178	161	145	17
44	545	514	484	455	427	399	373	348	323	300	277	256	235	215	196	178	161	144	16
45	544	513	483	454	426	399	373	347	323	300	277	255	235	215	196	178	160	144	15
46	544	513	483	454	426	399	372	347	323	299	277	255	234	214	195	177	160	144	14
47	543	512	482	453	425	398	372	347	322	299	276	255	234	214	195	177	160	144	13
48	543	512	482	453	425	398	371	346	322	298	276	254	234	214	195	177	160	143	12
49	542	511	481	452	424	397	371	346	321	298	276	254	233	213	194	176	159	143	11
50	542	511	481	452	424	397	371	345	321	298	275	254	233	213	194	176	159	143	10
51	541	510	480	451	423	396	370	345	321	297	275	253	233	213	194	176	159	143	09
52	540	510	480	451	423	396	370	345	320	297	274	253	232	212	194	176	158	142	08
53	540	509	479	450	422	395	369	344	320	297	274	253	232	212	193	175	158	142	07
54	539	509	479	450	422	395	369	344	319	296	274	252	232	212	193	175	158	142	06
55	539	508	478	450	422	395	368	343	319	296	273	252	231	211	193	175	158	142	05
56	538	508	478	449	421	394	368	343	319	295	273	251	231	211	192	174	157	141	04
57	538	507	477	449	421	394	368	343	318	295	273	251	231	211	192	174	157	141	03
58	537	507	477	448	420	393	367	342	318	295	272	251	230	211	192	174	157	141	02
59	537	506	476	448	420	393	367	342	318	294	272	250	230	210	191	174	157	140	01
60	536	506	476	447	419	392	366	341	317	294	272	250	230	210	191	173	156	140	00
	215° LHA	214° LHA	213° LHA	212° LHA	211° LHA	210° LHA	209° LHA	208° LHA	207° LHA	206° LHA	205° LHA	204° LHA	203° LHA	202° LHA	201° LHA	200° LHA	199° LHA	198° LHA	

SIGHT REDUCTION

	162° LHA	163° LHA	164° LHA	165° LHA	166° LHA	167° LHA	168° LHA	169° LHA	170° LHA	171° LHA	172° LHA	173° LHA	174° LHA	175° LHA	176° LHA	177° LHA	178° LHA	179° LHA	
00'	140	125	111	97	85	73	62	52	43	35	28	21	16	11	7	4	2	0	60'
01	140	125	110	97	84	73	62	52	43	35	27	21	15	11	7	4	2	0	59
02	140	125	110	97	84	73	62	52	43	35	27	21	15	11	7	4	2	0	58
03	139	124	110	97	84	72	62	52	43	35	27	21	15	11	7	4	2	0	57
04	139	124	110	96	84	72	61	52	43	34	27	21	15	10	7	4	2	0	56
05	139	124	110	96	84	72	61	51	42	34	27	21	15	10	7	4	2	0	55
06	139	124	109	96	83	72	61	51	42	34	27	21	15	10	7	4	2	0	54
07	138	123	109	96	83	72	61	51	42	34	27	20	15	10	6	4	2	0	53
08	138	123	109	96	83	71	61	51	42	34	27	20	15	10	6	4	2	0	52
09	138	123	109	95	83	71	61	51	42	34	27	20	15	10	6	4	1	0	51
10	138	123	108	95	83	71	60	51	42	34	26	20	15	10	6	3	1	0	50
11	137	122	108	95	82	71	60	50	42	34	26	20	15	10	6	3	1	0	49
12	137	122	108	95	82	71	60	50	41	33	26	20	15	10	6	3	1	0	48
13	137	122	108	94	82	71	60	50	41	33	26	20	14	10	6	3	1	0	47
14	137	122	107	94	82	70	60	50	41	33	26	20	14	10	6	3	1	0	46
15	136	121	107	94	82	70	60	50	41	33	26	20	14	10	6	3	1	0	45
16	136	121	107	94	81	70	59	50	41	33	26	20	14	10	6	3	1	0	44
17	136	121	107	94	81	70	59	50	41	33	26	19	14	10	6	3	1	0	43
18	136	121	107	93	81	70	59	49	41	33	26	19	14	10	6	3	1	0	42
19	135	120	106	93	81	69	59	49	40	33	25	19	14	9	6	3	1	0	41
20	135	120	106	93	81	69	59	49	40	32	25	19	14	9	6	3	1	0	40
21	135	120	106	93	80	69	59	49	40	32	25	19	14	9	6	3	1	0	39
22	135	120	106	93	80	69	58	49	40	32	25	19	14	9	6	3	1	0	38
23	134	119	105	92	80	69	58	49	40	32	25	19	14	9	6	3	1	0	37
24	134	119	105	92	80	69	58	48	40	32	25	19	14	9	6	3	1	0	36
25	134	119	105	92	80	68	58	48	40	32	25	19	13	9	6	3	1	0	35
26	134	119	105	92	80	68	58	48	39	32	25	19	13	9	5	3	1	0	34
27	133	118	105	91	79	68	58	48	39	32	25	18	13	9	5	3	1	0	33
28	133	118	104	91	79	68	57	48	39	31	24	18	13	9	5	3	1	0	32
29	133	118	104	91	79	68	57	48	39	31	24	18	13	9	5	3	1	0	31
30	132	118	104	91	79	67	57	48	39	31	24	18	13	9	5	3	1	0	30
31	132	117	104	91	79	67	57	47	39	31	24	18	13	9	5	3	1	0	29
32	132	117	103	90	78	67	57	47	39	31	24	18	13	9	5	3	1	0	28
33	132	117	103	90	78	67	57	47	39	31	24	18	13	9	5	3	1	0	27
34	131	117	103	90	78	67	56	47	38	31	24	18	13	8	5	3	1	0	26
35	131	117	103	90	78	67	56	47	38	31	24	18	13	8	5	3	1	0	25
36	131	116	103	90	78	66	56	47	38	30	24	18	13	8	5	2	1	0	24
37	131	116	102	89	77	66	56	47	38	30	24	18	12	8	5	2	1	0	23
38	130	116	102	89	77	66	56	46	38	30	23	17	12	8	5	2	1	0	22
39	130	116	102	89	77	66	56	46	38	30	23	17	12	8	5	2	1	0	21
40	130	115	102	89	77	66	55	46	38	30	23	17	12	8	5	2	1	0	20
41	130	115	101	89	77	66	55	46	37	30	23	17	12	8	5	2	1	0	19
42	129	115	101	88	76	65	55	46	37	30	23	17	12	8	5	2	1	0	18
43	129	115	101	88	76	65	55	46	37	30	23	17	12	8	5	2	1	0	17
44	129	114	101	88	76	65	55	45	37	29	23	17	12	8	5	2	1	0	16
45	129	114	101	88	76	65	55	45	37	29	23	17	12	8	5	2	1	0	15
46	128	114	100	88	76	65	54	45	37	29	23	17	12	8	5	2	1	0	14
47	128	114	100	87	75	64	54	45	37	29	22	17	12	8	4	2	1	0	13
48	128	113	100	87	75	64	54	45	37	29	22	17	12	8	4	2	1	0	12
49	128	113	100	87	75	64	54	45	36	29	22	16	12	8	4	2	1	0	11
50	127	113	99	87	75	64	54	45	36	29	22	16	12	7	4	2	1	0	10
51	127	113	99	87	75	64	54	44	36	29	22	16	11	7	4	2	1	0	09
52	127	113	99	86	74	64	53	44	36	29	22	16	11	7	4	2	1	0	08
53	127	112	99	86	74	63	53	44	36	28	22	16	11	7	4	2	1	0	07
54	126	112	99	86	74	63	53	44	36	28	22	16	11	7	4	2	1	0	06
55	126	112	98	86	74	63	53	44	36	28	22	16	11	7	4	2	1	0	05
56	126	112	98	85	74	63	53	44	35	28	22	16	11	7	4	2	0	0	04
57	126	111	98	85	74	63	53	44	35	28	21	16	11	7	4	2	0	0	03
58	125	111	98	85	73	63	53	43	35	28	21	16	11	7	4	2	0	0	02
59	125	111	97	85	73	62	52	43	35	28	21	16	11	7	4	2	0	0	01
60	125	111	97	85	73	62	52	43	35	28	21	16	11	7	4	2	0	0	00
	LHA 197°	LHA 196°	LHA 195°	LHA 194°	LHA 193°	LHA 192°	LHA 191°	LHA 190°	LHA 189°	LHA 188°	LHA 187°	LHA 186°	LHA 185°	LHA 184°	LHA 183°	LHA 182°	LHA 181°	LHA 180°	

AZIMUTH

AZIMUTH SOLUTION

Declination or Altitude

LATITUDE

LHA/AZ		0°	1°	2°	3°	4°	5°	6°	7°	8°	9°	10°	11°	12°	13°	14°	15°	16°	17°	18°	19°	20°	21°	22°	LHA/AZ	
0°	**180°**	0	0	0	0	0	0	0	0	0	0	0	0	0	0	0	0	0	0	0	0	0	0	0	**180°**	**360°**
1	**179**	17	17	17	17	17	17	17	17	17	17	17	17	17	17	17	17	17	17	17	16	16	16	16	**181**	**359**
2	**178**	35	35	35	35	35	35	35	35	35	34	34	34	34	34	34	34	34	33	33	33	33	33	32	**182**	**358**
3	**177**	52	52	52	52	52	52	52	52	52	52	51	51	51	51	51	51	50	50	50	49	49	49	48	**183**	**357**
4	**176**	70	70	70	70	70	69	69	69	69	69	69	68	68	68	68	67	67	67	66	66	65	65	65	**184**	**356**
5	**175**	87	87	87	87	87	87	87	86	86	86	86	85	85	85	84	84	84	83	83	82	82	81	81	**185**	**355**
6	**174**	104	104	104	104	104	104	104	104	103	103	103	103	102	102	101	101	100	100	99	99	98	97	97	**186**	**354**
7	**173**	122	122	122	122	121	121	121	121	121	120	120	120	119	119	118	118	117	116	116	115	114	114	113	**187**	**353**
8	**172**	139	139	139	139	139	139	138	138	138	137	137	136	136	135	135	134	134	133	132	131	131	130	129	**188**	**352**
9	**171**	156	156	156	156	156	156	155	155	155	154	154	153	153	152	152	151	150	149	149	148	147	146	145	**189**	**351**
10	**170**	173	173	173	173	173	173	173	172	172	171	171	170	170	169	168	168	167	166	165	164	163	162	161	**190**	**350**
11	**169**	191	191	191	190	190	190	190	189	189	188	188	187	186	186	185	184	183	182	181	180	179	178	177	**191**	**349**
12	**168**	208	208	208	207	207	207	207	206	206	205	205	204	203	202	202	201	200	199	198	196	195	194	193	**192**	**348**
13	**167**	225	225	225	224	224	224	223	223	223	222	221	221	220	219	218	217	216	215	214	212	211	210	208	**193**	**347**
14	**166**	242	242	242	241	241	241	240	240	239	239	238	237	236	235	235	233	232	231	230	229	227	226	224	**194**	**346**
15	**165**	259	259	258	258	258	258	257	257	256	255	255	254	253	252	251	250	249	247	246	244	243	241	240	**195**	**345**
16	**164**	275	275	275	275	275	274	274	273	273	272	271	270	269	268	267	266	265	263	262	260	259	257	255	**196**	**344**
17	**163**	292	292	292	292	291	291	290	290	289	288	288	287	286	285	283	282	281	279	278	276	274	273	271	**197**	**343**
18	**162**	309	309	309	308	308	308	307	306	306	305	304	303	302	301	300	298	297	295	294	292	290	288	286	**198**	**342**
19	**161**	325	325	325	325	324	324	323	323	322	321	320	319	318	317	316	314	313	311	309	308	306	304	302	**199**	**341**
20	**160**	342	342	341	341	341	340	340	339	338	337	336	335	334	333	332	330	328	327	325	323	321	319	317	**200**	**340**
21	**159**	358	358	358	358	357	357	356	355	355	354	353	351	350	349	347	346	344	342	340	339	336	334	332	**201**	**339**
22	**158**	374	374	374	374	373	373	372	371	371	370	369	367	366	365	363	361	360	358	356	354	352	349	347	**202**	**338**
23	**157**	390	390	390	390	389	389	388	387	387	386	384	383	382	380	379	377	375	373	371	369	367	364	362	**203**	**337**
24	**156**	406	406	406	406	405	405	404	403	402	401	400	399	397	396	394	392	391	389	386	384	382	379	377	**204**	**336**
25	**155**	422	422	422	422	421	421	420	419	418	417	416	414	413	411	410	408	406	404	402	399	397	394	391	**205**	**335**
26	**154**	438	438	438	437	437	436	436	435	434	433	431	430	428	427	425	423	421	419	416	414	412	409	406	**206**	**334**
27	**153**	454	453	453	453	452	452	451	450	449	448	447	445	444	442	440	438	436	434	431	429	426	423	421	**207**	**333**
28	**152**	469	469	469	468	468	467	466	466	464	463	462	460	459	457	455	453	451	449	446	443	441	438	435	**208**	**332**
29	**151**	484	484	484	484	483	482	482	481	480	478	477	475	474	472	470	468	466	463	461	458	455	452	449	**209**	**331**
30	**150**	500	499	499	499	498	498	497	496	495	493	492	490	489	487	485	482	480	478	475	472	469	466	463	**210**	**330**
31	**149**	515	514	514	514	513	513	512	511	510	508	507	505	503	501	499	497	495	492	489	486	483	480	477	**211**	**329**
32	**148**	529	529	529	529	528	527	526	525	524	523	521	520	518	516	514	511	509	506	503	501	497	494	491	**212**	**328**
33	**147**	544	544	544	543	543	542	541	540	539	537	536	534	532	530	528	526	523	520	517	514	511	508	504	**213**	**327**
34	**146**	559	559	558	558	557	557	556	554	553	552	550	548	546	544	542	540	537	534	531	528	525	522	518	**214**	**326**
35	**145**	573	573	573	572	572	571	570	569	567	566	564	562	560	558	556	553	551	548	545	542	538	535	531	**215**	**325**
36	**144**	587	587	587	586	586	585	584	583	581	580	578	576	574	572	570	567	564	562	558	555	552	548	544	**216**	**324**
37	**143**	601	601	601	600	600	599	598	597	595	594	592	590	588	586	583	581	578	575	572	568	565	561	557	**217**	**323**
38	**142**	615	615	615	614	614	613	612	610	609	607	606	604	602	599	597	594	591	588	585	582	578	574	570	**218**	**322**
39	**141**	629	629	628	628	627	626	625	624	623	621	619	617	615	613	610	607	604	601	598	594	591	587	583	**219**	**321**
40	**140**	642	642	642	641	641	640	639	637	636	634	632	630	628	626	623	620	617	614	611	607	603	599	595	**220**	**320**
41	**139**	655	655	655	655	654	653	652	651	649	647	645	643	641	639	636	633	630	627	623	620	616	612	608	**221**	**319**
42	**138**	668	668	668	668	667	666	665	663	662	660	658	656	654	651	649	646	643	639	636	632	628	624	620	**222**	**318**
43	**137**	681	681	681	680	680	679	678	676	675	673	671	669	666	664	661	658	655	652	648	644	640	636	632	**223**	**317**
44	**136**	694	694	694	693	692	691	690	689	687	685	683	681	679	676	673	670	667	664	660	656	652	648	643	**224**	**316**
45	**135**	706	706	706	705	705	704	703	701	700	698	696	693	691	688	685	682	679	676	672	668	664	659	655	**225**	**315**
46	**134**	719	719	718	718	717	716	715	713	712	710	708	705	703	700	697	694	691	687	683	679	675	671	666	**226**	**314**
47	**133**	731	731	730	730	729	728	727	725	724	722	720	717	715	712	709	706	702	699	695	691	687	682	677	**227**	**313**
48	**132**	742	742	742	741	741	740	738	737	735	733	731	729	726	723	720	717	714	710	706	702	698	693	688	**228**	**312**
49	**131**	754	754	753	753	752	751	750	748	747	745	743	740	737	735	732	728	725	721	717	713	708	704	699	**229**	**311**
50	**130**	765	765	765	764	763	762	761	760	758	756	754	751	749	746	743	739	736	732	728	724	719	714	710	**230**	**310**
51	**129**	776	776	776	775	774	773	772	771	769	767	765	762	759	756	753	750	746	742	738	734	730	725	720	**231**	**309**
52	**128**	787	787	787	786	785	784	783	781	780	778	775	773	770	767	764	760	757	753	749	744	740	735	730	**232**	**308**
53	**127**	798	798	797	797	796	795	793	792	790	788	786	783	780	777	774	771	767	763	759	754	750	745	740	**233**	**307**
54	**126**	808	808	808	807	806	805	804	802	800	798	796	793	791	787	784	781	777	773	769	764	759	755	749	**234**	**306**
55	**125**	818	818	818	817	816	815	814	812	810	808	806	803	800	797	794	790	787	783	778	774	769	764	759	**235**	**305**
56	**124**	828	828	828	827	826	825	824	822	820	818	816	813	810	807	804	800	796	792	788	783	778	773	768	**236**	**304**
57	**123**	838	838	837	837	836	835	833	832	830	828	825	822	820	816	813	809	805	801	797	792	787	782	777	**237**	**303**
58	**122**	847	847	847	846	845	844	843	841	839	837	834	832	829	825	822	818	814	810	806	801	796	791	786	**238**	**302**
59	**121**	856	856	856	855	854	853	852	850	848	846	843	841	838	834	831	827	823	819	814	810	805	799	794	**239**	**301**
60	**120**	865	865	865	864	863	862	860	859	857	855	852	849	846	843	839	836	832	827	823	818	813	808	802	**240**	**300**
61	**119**	874	874	873	873	872	870	869	867	865	863	860	858	855	851	848	844	840	836	831	826	821	816	810	**241**	**299**
62	**118**	882	882	882	881	880	879	877	875	873	871	869	866	863	859	856	852	848	844	839	834	829	823	818	**242**	**298**
63	**117**	890	890	890	889	888	887	885	883	881	879	877	874	871	867	864	860	856	851	847	842	836	831	825	**243**	**297**
64	**116**	898	898	897	897	896	894	893	891	889	887	884	881	878	875	871	867	863	859	854	849	844	838	833	**244**	**296**
65	**115**	905	905	905	904	903	902	900	899	897	894	892	889	886	882	879	875	870	866	861	856	851	845	839	**245**	**295**
66	**114**	913	912	912	911	910	909	908	906	904	901	899	896	893	889	886	882	877	873	868	863	858	852	846	**246**	**294**
67	**113**	920	919	919	918	917	916	915	913	911	908	906	903	899	896	892	888	884	879	875	869	864	859	853	**247**	**293**
68	**112**	926	926	926	925	924	923	921	919	917	915	912	909	906	903	899	895	890	886	881	876	870	865	859	**248**	**292**
69	**111**	933	933	932	931	930	929	928	926	924	921	918	916	912	909	905	901	897	892	887	882	876	871	865	**249**	**291**
70	**110**	939	939	938	937	936	935	934	932	930	927	924	922	918	915	911	907	902	898	893	888	882	876	870	**250**	**290**
71	**109**	945	944	944	943	942	941	939	938	935	933	930	927	924	920	917	912	908	903	898	893	888	882	876	**251**	**289**
72	**108**	950	950	950	949	948	946	945	943	941	938	936	933	929	926	922	918	913	909	904	898	893	887	881	**252**	**288**
73	**107**	955	955	955	954	953	952	950	948	946	944	941	938	934	931	927	923	918	914	909	903	898	892	886	**253**	**287**
74	**106**	960	960	960	959	958	957	955	953	951	948	946	943	939	936	932	928	923	918	913	908	902	897	890	**254**	**286**
75	**105**	965	965	964	964	963	961	960	958	956	953	950	947	944	940	936	932	928	923	918	912	907	901	895	**255**	**285**
76	**104**	969	969	969	968	967	966	964	962	960	957	955	952	948	944	941	936	932	927	922	917	911	905	899	**256**	**284**
77	**103**	973	973	973	972	971	970	968	966	964	961	959	956	952	948	944	940	936	931	926	920	915	909	903	**257**	**283**
78	**102**	977	977	977	976	975	973	972	970	968	965	962	959	956	952	948	944	939	934	929	924	918	912	906	**258**	**282**
79	**101**	981	980	980	979	978	977	975	973	971	969	966	963	959	956	952	947	943	938	933	927	922	916	909	**259**	**281**
80	**100**	984	984	983	982	981	980	978	976	974	972	969	966	962	959	955	950	946	941	936	930	924	918	912	**260**	**280**
81	**99**	987	987	986	985	984	983	981	979	977	975	972	969	965	961	957	953	948	944	938	933	927	921	915	**261**	**279**
82	**98**	989	989	989	988	987	986	984	982	980	977	974	971	968	964	960	956	951	946	941	935	930	924	917	**262**	**278**
83	**97**	992	991	991	990	989	988	986	984	982	979	976	973	970	966	962	958	953	948	943	938	932	926	919	**263**	**277**
84	**96**	994	993	993	992	991	990	988	986	984	981	978	975	972	968	964	960	955	950	945	939	934	928	921	**264**	**276**
85	**95**	995	995	995	994	993	991	990	988	986	983	980	977	973	970	966	961	957	952	946	941	935	929	923	**265**	**275**
86	**94**	997	996	996	995	994	993	991	989	987	984	981	978	975	971	967	963	958	953	948	942	936	930	924	**266**	**274**
87	**93**	998	997	997	996	995	994	992	990	988	985	982	979	976	972	968	964	959	954	949	943	937	931	925	**267**	**273**
88	**92**	998	998	998	997	996	995	993	991	989	986	983	980	977	973	969	964	960	955	950	944	938	932	926	**268**	**272**
89	**91**	999	999	998	997	996	995	993	991	989	987	984	980	977	973	969	965	960	955	950	944	939	933	926	**269**	**271**
90	**90**	999	999	998	998	997	995	994	992	989	987	984	981	977	973	969	965	960	955	950	945	939	933	926	**270**	**270**
LHA/AZ		**90°**	**89°**	**88°**	**87°**	**86°**	**85°**	**84°**	**83°**	**82°**	**81°**	**80°**	**79°**	**78°**	**77°**	**76°**	**75°**	**74°**	**73°**	**72°**	**71°**	**70°**	**69°**	**68°**	**LHA/AZ**	

Declination or Altitude

QUADRANT SOLUTION

AZIMUTH SOLUTION

Declination or Altitude

LATITUDE

LHA/AZ		22°	23°	24°	25°	26°	27°	28°	29°	30°	31°	32°	33°	34°	35°	36°	37°	38°	39°	40°	41°	42°	43°	44°	45°	LHA/AZ	
0°	180°	0	0	0	0	0	0	0	0	0	0	0	0	0	0	0	0	0	0	0	0	0	0	0	0	180°	360°
1	179	16	16	16	16	16	16	15	15	15	15	15	15	14	14	14	14	14	14	13	13	13	13	13	12	181	359
2	178	32	32	32	32	31	31	31	30	30	30	30	29	29	29	28	28	27	27	27	26	26	25	25	25	182	358
3	177	48	48	48	47	47	47	46	46	45	45	44	44	43	43	42	42	41	41	40	39	39	38	38	37	183	357
4	176	65	64	64	63	63	62	62	61	60	60	59	58	58	57	56	56	55	54	53	53	52	51	50	49	184	356
5	175	81	80	80	79	78	78	77	76	75	75	74	73	72	71	70	70	69	68	67	66	65	64	63	62	185	355
6	174	97	96	95	95	94	93	92	91	90	90	89	88	87	86	84	83	82	81	80	79	78	76	75	74	186	354
7	173	113	112	111	110	109	108	107	106	105	104	103	102	101	100	98	97	96	95	93	92	90	89	88	86	187	353
8	172	129	128	127	126	125	124	123	122	120	119	118	117	115	114	112	111	110	108	107	105	103	102	100	98	188	352
9	171	145	144	143	142	140	139	138	137	135	134	133	131	130	128	126	125	123	121	120	118	116	114	112	111	189	351
10	170	161	160	158	157	156	155	153	152	150	149	147	145	144	142	140	139	137	135	133	131	129	127	125	123	190	350
11	169	177	175	174	173	171	170	168	167	165	163	162	160	158	156	154	152	150	148	146	144	142	139	137	135	191	349
12	168	193	191	190	188	187	185	183	182	180	178	176	174	172	170	168	166	164	161	159	157	154	152	149	147	192	348
13	167	208	207	205	204	202	200	198	197	195	193	191	188	186	184	182	179	177	175	172	170	167	164	162	159	193	347
14	166	224	222	221	219	217	215	213	211	209	207	205	203	200	198	196	193	190	188	185	182	180	177	174	171	194	346
15	165	240	238	236	234	232	230	228	226	224	222	219	217	214	212	209	206	204	201	198	195	192	189	186	183	195	345
16	164	255	253	252	250	247	245	243	241	238	236	234	231	228	226	223	220	217	214	211	208	205	201	198	195	196	344
17	163	271	269	267	265	263	260	258	255	253	250	248	245	242	239	236	233	230	227	224	220	217	214	210	207	197	343
18	162	286	284	282	280	277	275	273	270	267	265	262	259	256	253	250	247	243	240	236	233	229	226	222	218	198	342
19	161	302	299	297	295	292	290	287	284	282	279	276	273	270	266	263	260	256	253	249	245	242	238	234	230	199	341
20	160	317	315	312	310	307	304	302	299	296	293	290	287	283	280	276	273	269	266	262	258	254	250	246	242	200	340
21	159	332	330	327	324	322	319	316	313	310	307	304	300	297	293	290	286	282	278	274	270	266	262	258	253	201	339
22	158	347	344	342	339	336	333	330	327	324	321	317	314	310	307	303	299	295	291	287	282	278	274	269	265	202	338
23	157	362	359	357	354	351	348	345	341	338	335	331	327	324	320	316	312	308	303	299	295	290	285	281	276	203	337
24	156	377	374	371	368	365	362	359	355	352	348	345	341	337	333	329	325	320	316	311	307	302	297	292	287	204	336
25	155	391	389	386	383	379	376	373	369	366	362	358	354	350	346	342	337	333	328	323	319	314	309	304	299	205	335
26	154	406	403	400	397	394	390	387	383	379	375	371	367	363	359	354	350	345	340	335	331	325	320	315	310	206	334
27	153	421	417	414	411	408	404	400	397	393	389	385	380	376	372	367	362	357	352	347	342	337	332	326	321	207	333
28	152	435	432	428	425	422	418	414	410	406	402	398	393	389	384	379	375	370	364	359	354	349	343	337	332	208	332
29	151	449	446	442	439	435	432	428	424	419	415	411	406	402	397	392	387	382	376	371	366	360	354	348	342	209	331
30	150	463	460	456	453	449	445	441	437	433	428	424	419	414	409	404	399	394	388	383	377	371	365	359	353	210	330
31	149	477	474	470	466	462	458	454	450	446	441	436	432	427	421	416	411	405	400	394	388	382	376	370	364	211	329
32	148	491	487	484	480	476	472	467	463	458	454	449	444	439	434	428	423	417	411	406	400	393	387	381	374	212	328
33	147	504	501	497	493	489	485	480	476	471	466	461	456	451	446	440	435	429	423	417	411	404	398	391	385	213	327
34	146	518	514	510	506	502	498	493	489	484	479	474	469	463	458	452	446	440	434	428	422	415	409	402	395	214	326
35	145	531	527	523	519	515	511	506	501	496	491	486	481	475	469	464	458	452	445	439	432	426	419	412	405	215	325
36	144	544	541	536	532	528	523	518	514	509	503	498	492	487	481	475	469	463	456	450	443	436	429	422	415	216	324
37	143	557	553	549	545	540	536	531	526	521	515	510	504	498	492	486	480	474	467	461	454	447	440	432	425	217	323
38	142	570	566	562	557	553	548	543	538	533	527	522	516	510	504	498	491	485	478	471	464	457	450	442	435	218	322
39	141	583	579	574	570	565	560	555	550	544	539	533	527	521	515	509	502	495	489	482	474	467	460	452	445	219	321
40	140	595	591	587	582	577	572	567	562	556	550	545	539	532	526	520	513	506	499	492	485	477	470	462	454	220	320
41	139	608	603	599	594	589	584	579	573	568	562	556	550	543	537	530	523	516	509	502	495	487	479	471	463	221	319
42	138	620	615	611	606	601	596	590	585	579	573	567	561	554	548	541	534	527	519	512	504	497	489	481	473	222	318
43	137	632	627	622	617	612	607	602	596	590	584	578	571	565	558	551	544	537	529	522	514	506	498	490	482	223	317
44	136	643	639	634	629	624	618	613	607	601	595	589	582	575	568	561	554	547	539	532	524	516	508	499	491	224	316
45	135	655	650	645	640	635	629	624	618	612	606	599	592	586	579	571	564	557	549	541	533	525	517	508	500	225	315
46	134	666	661	656	651	646	640	635	629	622	616	609	603	596	589	581	574	566	558	550	542	534	526	517	508	226	314
47	133	677	673	667	662	657	651	645	639	633	626	620	613	606	598	591	584	576	568	560	551	543	534	526	517	227	313
48	132	688	683	678	673	667	661	656	649	643	636	630	623	615	608	601	593	585	577	569	560	552	543	534	525	228	312
49	131	699	694	689	683	678	672	666	659	653	646	639	632	625	618	610	602	594	586	578	569	560	551	542	533	229	311
50	130	710	704	699	694	688	682	676	669	663	656	649	642	634	627	619	611	603	595	586	578	569	560	550	541	230	310
51	129	720	715	709	704	698	692	685	679	672	665	658	651	644	636	628	620	612	603	595	586	577	568	558	549	231	309
52	128	730	725	719	713	708	701	695	689	682	675	668	660	653	645	637	629	620	612	603	594	585	576	566	557	232	308
53	127	740	734	729	723	717	711	704	698	691	684	677	669	661	654	645	637	629	620	611	602	593	584	574	564	233	307
54	126	749	744	738	732	726	720	714	707	700	693	685	678	670	662	654	645	637	628	619	610	601	591	581	571	234	306
55	125	759	753	748	742	736	729	723	716	709	701	694	686	678	670	662	654	645	636	627	618	608	598	589	579	235	305
56	124	768	762	757	751	744	738	731	724	717	710	702	695	687	678	670	661	653	644	634	625	615	606	596	586	236	304
57	123	777	771	765	759	753	747	740	733	726	718	711	703	695	686	678	669	660	651	642	632	623	613	603	592	237	303
58	122	786	780	774	768	761	755	748	741	734	726	718	711	702	694	685	677	668	658	649	639	630	620	609	599	238	302
59	121	794	788	782	776	770	763	756	749	742	734	726	718	710	701	693	684	675	665	656	646	636	626	616	606	239	301
60	120	802	796	790	784	778	771	764	757	749	742	734	726	717	709	700	691	682	672	663	653	643	633	622	612	240	300
61	119	810	804	798	792	785	779	771	764	757	749	741	733	724	716	707	698	689	679	669	659	649	639	629	618	241	299
62	118	818	812	806	799	793	786	779	771	764	756	748	740	731	723	714	704	695	685	676	666	656	645	635	624	242	298
63	117	825	819	813	807	800	793	786	779	771	763	755	747	738	729	720	711	701	692	682	672	661	651	640	629	243	297
64	116	833	827	820	814	807	800	793	785	778	770	761	753	744	736	726	717	708	698	688	678	667	657	646	635	244	296
65	115	839	833	827	821	814	807	799	792	784	776	768	759	751	742	732	723	713	704	694	683	673	662	651	640	245	295
66	114	846	840	834	827	820	813	806	798	790	782	774	765	757	748	738	729	719	709	699	689	678	667	656	645	246	294
67	113	853	846	840	833	827	819	812	804	796	788	780	771	762	753	744	734	725	715	704	694	683	673	661	650	247	293
68	112	859	853	846	839	833	825	818	810	802	794	786	777	768	759	749	740	730	720	710	699	688	677	666	655	248	292
69	111	865	859	852	845	838	831	823	816	808	799	791	782	773	764	755	745	735	725	714	704	693	682	671	659	249	291
70	110	870	864	858	851	844	836	829	821	813	805	796	787	778	769	759	750	740	730	719	708	698	687	675	664	250	290
71	109	876	869	863	856	849	842	834	826	818	810	801	792	783	774	764	754	744	734	724	713	702	691	679	668	251	289
72	108	881	875	868	861	854	847	839	831	823	814	806	797	788	778	769	759	749	738	728	717	706	695	683	672	252	288
73	107	886	879	873	866	859	851	844	836	827	819	810	801	792	783	773	763	753	742	732	721	710	699	687	676	253	287
74	106	890	884	877	870	863	856	848	840	832	823	814	805	796	787	777	767	757	746	736	725	714	702	691	679	254	286
75	105	895	888	882	875	867	860	852	844	836	827	818	809	800	790	781	771	760	750	739	728	717	706	694	682	255	285
76	104	899	892	886	879	871	864	856	848	839	831	822	813	804	794	784	774	764	753	743	732	720	709	697	685	256	284
77	103	903	896	889	882	875	867	859	851	843	834	825	816	807	797	787	777	767	756	746	735	723	712	700	688	257	283
78	102	906	899	893	886	878	871	863	855	846	838	829	820	810	800	791	780	770	759	749	737	726	715	703	691	258	282
79	101	909	903	896	889	881	874	866	858	849	841	832	822	813	803	793	783	773	762	751	740	729	717	705	693	259	281
80	100	912	906	899	892	884	877	869	860	852	843	834	825	816	806	796	786	775	765	754	743	731	720	708	696	260	280
81	99	915	908	901	894	887	879	871	863	855	846	837	828	818	808	798	788	778	767	756	745	733	722	710	698	261	279
82	98	917	911	904	897	889	881	873	865	857	848	839	830	820	810	800	790	780	769	758	747	735	724	712	700	262	278
83	97	919	913	906	899	891	883	875	867	859	850	841	832	822	812	802	792	781	771	760	748	737	725	713	701	263	277
84	96	921	915	908	900	893	885	877	869	860	852	843	833	824	814	804	793	783	772	761	750	738	727	715	703	264	276
85	95	923	916	909	902	894	887	879	870	862	853	844	835	825	815	805	795	784	773	762	751	740	728	716	704	265	275
86	94	924	917	910	903	896	888	880	872	863	854	845	836	826	816	806	796	785	774	763	752	741	729	717	705	266	274
87	93	925	918	911	904	897	889	881	873	864	855	846	837	827	817	807	797	786	775	764	753	741	730	718	705	267	273
88	92	926	919	912	905	897	890	882	873	865	856	847	837	828	818	808	797	787	776	765	753	742	730	718	706	268	272
89	91	926	919	912	905	898	890	882	874	865	856	847	838	828	818	808	798	787	776	765	754	742	731	719	706	269	271
90	90	926	920	913	905	898	890	882	874	865	856	847	838	828	818	808	798	787	776	765	754	742	731	719	706	270	270
LHA/AZ		68°	67°	66°	65°	64°	63°	62°	61°	60°	59°	58°	57°	56°	55°	54°	53°	52°	51°	50°	49°	48°	47°	46°	45°	LHA/AZ	

Declination or Altitude

QUADRANT SOLUTION

AZIMUTH

AZIMUTH SOLUTION

Declination or Altitude

LATITUDE

LHA/AZ		45°	46°	47°	48°	49°	50°	51°	52°	53°	54°	55°	56°	57°	58°	59°	60°	61°	62°	63°	64°	65°	66°	67°	LHA/AZ	
0°	180°	0	0	0	0	0	0	0	0	0	0	0	0	0	0	0	0	0	0	0	0	0	0	0	180°	360°
1	179	12	12	12	12	11	11	11	11	10	10	10	10	9	9	9	9	8	8	8	8	7	7	7	181	359
2	178	25	24	24	23	23	22	22	21	21	20	20	19	19	18	18	17	17	16	16	15	15	14	14	182	358
3	177	37	36	36	35	34	34	33	32	31	31	30	29	28	28	27	26	25	25	24	23	22	21	20	183	357
4	176	49	48	48	47	46	45	44	43	42	41	40	39	38	37	36	35	34	33	32	31	29	28	27	184	356
5	175	62	60	59	58	57	56	55	54	52	51	50	49	47	46	45	44	42	41	40	38	37	35	34	185	355
6	174	74	73	71	70	69	67	66	64	63	61	60	58	57	55	54	52	51	49	47	46	44	42	41	186	354
7	173	86	85	83	81	80	78	77	75	73	72	70	68	66	65	63	61	59	57	55	53	51	50	48	187	353
8	172	98	97	95	93	91	89	87	86	84	82	80	78	76	74	72	70	67	65	63	61	59	57	54	188	352
9	171	111	109	107	105	103	100	98	96	94	92	90	87	85	83	80	78	76	73	71	69	66	64	61	189	351
10	170	123	121	118	116	114	112	109	107	104	102	100	97	94	92	89	87	84	81	79	76	73	71	68	190	350
11	169	135	132	130	128	125	123	120	117	115	112	109	107	104	101	98	95	92	89	87	84	81	78	74	191	349
12	168	147	144	142	139	136	134	131	128	125	122	119	116	113	110	107	104	101	98	94	91	88	84	81	192	348
13	167	159	156	153	150	147	144	141	138	135	132	129	126	122	119	116	112	109	106	102	99	95	91	88	193	347
14	166	171	168	165	162	159	155	152	149	145	142	139	135	132	128	124	121	117	113	110	106	102	98	94	194	346
15	165	183	180	176	173	170	166	163	159	156	152	148	145	141	137	133	129	125	121	117	113	109	105	101	195	345
16	164	195	191	188	184	181	177	173	170	166	162	158	154	150	146	142	138	133	129	125	121	116	112	108	196	344
17	163	207	203	199	195	192	188	184	180	176	172	168	163	159	155	150	146	142	137	133	128	123	119	114	197	343
18	162	218	214	211	207	203	198	194	190	186	181	177	173	168	164	159	154	150	145	140	135	130	126	121	198	342
19	161	230	226	222	218	213	209	205	200	196	191	187	182	177	172	168	163	158	153	148	143	137	132	127	199	341
20	160	242	237	233	229	224	220	215	210	206	201	196	191	186	181	176	171	166	160	155	150	144	139	134	200	340
21	159	253	249	244	240	235	230	225	220	215	210	205	200	195	190	184	179	174	168	163	157	151	146	140	201	339
22	158	265	260	255	250	246	241	236	230	225	220	215	209	204	198	193	187	181	176	170	164	158	152	146	202	338
23	157	276	271	266	261	256	251	246	240	235	229	224	218	213	207	201	195	189	183	177	171	165	159	153	203	337
24	156	287	282	277	272	267	261	256	250	245	239	233	227	221	215	209	203	197	191	184	178	172	165	159	204	336
25	155	299	293	288	283	277	271	266	260	254	248	242	236	230	224	217	211	205	198	192	185	178	172	165	205	335
26	154	310	304	299	293	287	281	276	270	264	257	251	245	239	232	226	219	212	206	199	192	185	178	171	206	334
27	153	321	315	309	303	298	292	285	279	273	267	260	254	247	240	234	227	220	213	206	199	192	184	177	207	333
28	152	332	326	320	314	308	301	295	289	282	276	269	262	255	249	242	235	227	220	213	206	198	191	183	208	332
29	151	342	336	330	324	318	311	305	298	291	285	278	271	264	257	249	242	235	227	220	212	205	197	189	209	331
30	150	353	347	341	334	328	321	314	308	301	294	287	279	272	265	257	250	242	235	227	219	211	203	195	210	330
31	149	364	357	351	344	338	331	324	317	310	302	295	288	280	273	265	257	249	242	234	226	217	209	201	211	329
32	148	374	368	361	354	347	340	333	326	319	311	304	296	288	281	273	265	257	249	240	232	224	215	207	212	328
33	147	385	378	371	364	357	350	342	335	327	320	312	304	296	288	280	272	264	255	247	239	230	221	213	213	327
34	146	395	388	381	374	366	359	352	344	336	328	320	312	304	296	288	279	271	262	254	245	236	227	218	214	326
35	145	405	398	391	383	376	368	361	353	345	337	329	320	312	304	295	287	278	269	260	251	242	233	224	215	325
36	144	415	408	400	393	385	377	370	362	353	345	337	328	320	311	302	294	285	276	267	257	248	239	229	216	324
37	143	425	418	410	402	394	386	378	370	362	353	345	336	327	319	310	301	291	282	273	264	254	245	235	217	323
38	142	435	427	419	412	404	395	387	379	370	362	353	344	335	326	317	308	298	289	279	270	260	250	240	218	322
39	141	445	437	429	421	412	404	396	387	378	370	361	352	342	333	324	314	305	295	285	276	266	256	246	219	321
40	140	454	446	438	430	421	413	404	395	386	377	368	359	350	340	331	321	311	301	292	281	271	261	251	220	320
41	139	463	455	447	439	430	421	412	404	394	385	376	366	357	347	338	328	318	308	298	287	277	267	256	221	319
42	138	473	464	456	447	439	430	421	412	402	393	383	374	364	354	344	334	324	314	303	293	283	272	261	222	318
43	137	482	473	465	456	447	438	429	419	410	400	391	381	371	361	351	341	330	320	309	299	288	277	266	223	317
44	136	491	482	473	464	455	446	437	427	418	408	398	388	378	368	357	347	336	326	315	304	293	282	271	224	316
45	135	500	491	482	473	463	454	445	435	425	415	405	395	385	374	364	353	342	332	321	310	299	287	276	225	315
46	134	508	499	490	481	471	462	452	442	432	422	412	402	391	381	370	359	348	337	326	315	304	292	281	226	314
47	133	517	508	498	489	479	470	460	450	440	429	419	409	398	387	376	365	354	343	332	320	309	297	285	227	313
48	132	525	516	506	497	487	477	467	457	447	436	426	415	404	393	382	371	360	349	337	325	314	302	290	228	312
49	131	533	524	514	504	495	485	474	464	454	443	432	422	411	400	388	377	366	354	342	331	319	307	295	229	311
50	130	541	532	522	512	502	492	482	471	461	450	439	428	417	406	394	383	371	359	347	335	323	311	299	230	310
51	129	549	539	529	519	509	499	489	478	467	456	445	434	423	411	400	388	376	364	352	340	328	316	303	231	309
52	128	557	547	537	527	516	506	495	485	474	463	452	440	429	417	405	394	382	370	357	345	333	320	308	232	308
53	127	564	554	544	534	523	513	502	491	480	469	458	446	435	423	411	399	387	375	362	350	337	325	312	233	307
54	126	571	561	551	541	530	520	509	498	486	475	464	452	440	428	416	404	392	379	367	354	342	329	316	234	306
55	125	579	568	558	548	537	526	515	504	492	481	469	458	446	434	421	409	397	384	372	359	346	333	320	235	305
56	124	586	575	565	554	543	532	521	510	498	487	475	463	451	439	427	414	402	389	376	363	350	337	324	236	304
57	123	592	582	571	561	550	539	527	516	504	492	481	469	456	444	432	419	406	393	380	367	354	341	327	237	303
58	122	599	589	578	567	556	545	533	522	510	498	486	474	461	449	436	424	411	398	385	371	358	345	331	238	302
59	121	606	595	584	573	562	550	539	527	515	503	491	479	466	454	441	428	415	402	389	375	362	348	335	239	301
60	120	612	601	590	579	568	556	544	533	521	509	496	484	471	458	446	433	419	406	393	379	366	352	338	240	300
61	119	618	607	596	585	573	562	550	538	526	514	501	489	476	463	450	437	424	410	397	383	369	355	341	241	299
62	118	624	613	602	590	579	567	555	543	531	518	506	493	480	467	454	441	428	414	400	387	373	359	345	242	298
63	117	629	618	607	596	584	572	560	548	536	523	511	498	485	472	458	445	432	418	404	390	376	362	348	243	297
64	116	635	624	612	601	589	577	565	553	540	528	515	502	489	476	462	449	435	422	408	394	379	365	351	244	296
65	115	640	629	617	606	594	582	570	557	545	532	519	506	493	480	466	453	439	425	411	397	383	368	354	245	295
66	114	645	634	622	611	599	587	574	562	549	536	523	510	497	484	470	456	442	428	414	400	386	371	357	246	294
67	113	650	639	627	615	603	591	579	566	553	541	527	514	501	487	474	460	446	432	417	403	389	374	359	247	293
68	112	655	643	632	620	608	595	583	570	557	544	531	518	504	491	477	463	449	435	421	406	391	377	362	248	292
69	111	659	648	636	624	612	599	587	574	561	548	535	522	508	494	480	466	452	438	423	409	394	379	364	249	291
70	110	664	652	640	628	616	603	591	578	565	552	538	525	511	497	483	469	455	441	426	412	397	382	367	250	290
71	109	668	656	644	632	620	607	594	582	568	555	542	528	514	501	486	472	458	443	429	414	399	384	369	251	289
72	108	672	660	648	636	623	611	598	585	572	558	545	531	517	503	489	475	461	446	431	416	402	386	371	252	288
73	107	676	664	652	639	627	614	601	588	575	562	548	534	520	506	492	478	463	449	434	419	404	389	373	253	287
74	106	679	667	655	643	630	617	604	591	578	564	551	537	523	509	495	480	466	451	436	421	406	391	375	254	286
75	105	682	670	658	646	633	620	607	594	581	567	553	540	526	511	497	482	468	453	438	423	408	392	377	255	285
76	104	685	673	661	649	636	623	610	597	583	570	556	542	528	514	499	485	470	455	440	425	410	394	379	256	284
77	103	688	676	664	651	639	626	613	599	586	572	558	544	530	516	501	487	472	457	442	427	411	396	380	257	283
78	102	691	679	666	654	641	628	615	602	588	574	560	546	532	518	503	489	474	459	444	428	413	397	382	258	282
79	101	693	681	669	656	643	630	617	604	590	576	562	548	534	520	505	490	475	460	445	430	414	399	383	259	281
80	100	696	683	671	658	645	632	619	606	592	578	564	550	536	521	507	492	477	462	447	431	416	400	384	260	280
81	99	698	685	673	660	647	634	621	607	594	580	566	552	537	523	508	493	478	463	448	433	417	401	386	261	279
82	98	700	687	675	662	649	636	623	609	595	581	567	553	539	524	510	495	480	464	449	434	418	402	387	262	278
83	97	701	689	676	663	651	637	624	610	597	583	569	554	540	525	511	496	481	466	450	435	419	403	387	263	277
84	96	703	690	678	665	652	639	625	612	598	584	570	556	541	526	512	497	482	466	451	436	420	404	388	264	276
85	95	704	691	679	666	653	640	626	613	599	585	571	557	542	527	513	498	482	467	452	436	421	405	389	265	275
86	94	705	692	680	667	654	641	627	614	600	586	572	557	543	528	513	498	483	468	452	437	421	405	389	266	274
87	93	705	693	680	668	655	641	628	614	600	586	572	558	543	529	514	499	484	468	453	437	422	406	390	267	273
88	92	706	694	681	668	655	642	628	615	601	587	573	558	544	529	514	499	484	469	453	438	422	406	390	268	272
89	91	706	694	681	668	655	642	629	615	601	587	573	559	544	529	514	499	484	469	453	438	422	406	390	269	271
90	90	706	694	681	668	655	642	629	615	601	587	573	559	544	529	515	500	484	469	454	438	422	406	390	270	270
LHA/AZ		45°	44°	43°	42°	41°	40°	39°	38°	37°	36°	35°	34°	33°	32°	31°	30°	29°	28°	27°	26°	25°	24°	23°	LHA/AZ	

Declination or Altitude

QUADRANT SOLUTION

AZIMUTH SOLUTION

Declination or Altitude

LATITUDE

LHA/AZ	67°	68°	69°	70°	71°	72°	73°	74°	75°	76°	77°	78°	79°	80°	81°	82°	83°	84°	85°	86°	87°	88	89°	90°	LHA/AZ
0° 180°	0	0	0	0	0	0	0	0	0	0	0	0	0	0	0	0	0	0	0	0	0	0	0	0	180° 360°
1 179	7	7	6	6	6	5	5	5	5	4	4	4	3	3	3	2	2	2	2	1	1	1	0	0	181 359
2 178	14	13	12	12	11	11	10	10	9	8	8	7	7	6	5	5	4	4	3	2	2	1	1	0	182 358
3 177	20	20	19	18	17	16	15	14	14	13	12	11	10	9	8	7	6	5	5	4	3	2	1	0	183 357
4 176	27	26	25	24	23	22	20	19	18	17	16	14	13	12	11	10	8	7	6	5	4	2	1	0	184 356
5 175	34	33	31	30	28	27	25	24	23	21	20	18	17	15	14	12	11	9	8	6	5	3	2	0	185 355
6 174	41	39	37	36	34	32	31	29	27	25	23	22	20	18	16	15	13	11	9	7	5	4	2	0	186 354
7 173	48	46	44	42	40	38	36	34	32	29	27	25	23	21	19	17	15	13	11	8	6	4	2	0	187 353
8 172	54	52	50	48	45	43	41	38	36	34	31	29	27	24	22	19	17	15	12	10	7	5	2	0	188 352
9 171	61	59	56	53	51	48	46	43	40	38	35	32	30	27	24	22	19	16	14	11	8	5	3	0	189 351
10 170	68	65	62	59	56	54	51	48	45	42	39	36	33	30	27	24	21	18	15	12	9	6	3	0	190 350
11 169	74	71	68	65	62	59	56	53	49	46	43	40	36	33	30	27	23	20	17	13	10	7	3	0	191 349
12 168	81	78	74	71	68	64	61	57	54	50	47	43	40	36	32	29	25	22	18	14	11	7	4	0	192 348
13 167	88	84	81	77	73	69	66	62	58	54	51	47	43	39	35	31	27	23	20	16	12	8	4	0	193 347
14 166	94	91	87	83	79	75	71	67	63	58	54	50	46	42	38	34	29	25	21	17	13	8	4	0	194 346
15 165	101	97	93	88	84	80	76	71	67	63	58	54	49	45	40	36	32	27	23	18	14	9	5	0	195 345
16 164	108	103	99	94	90	85	81	76	71	67	62	57	53	48	43	38	34	29	24	19	14	10	5	0	196 344
17 163	114	109	105	100	95	90	85	81	76	71	66	61	56	51	46	41	36	31	25	20	15	10	5	0	197 343
18 162	121	116	111	106	101	95	90	85	80	75	69	64	59	54	48	43	38	32	27	22	16	11	5	0	198 342
19 161	127	122	117	111	106	101	95	90	84	79	73	68	62	56	51	45	40	34	28	23	17	11	6	0	199 341
20 160	134	128	122	117	111	106	100	94	88	83	77	71	65	59	53	48	42	36	30	24	18	12	6	0	200 340
21 159	140	134	128	122	117	111	105	99	93	87	81	74	68	62	56	50	44	37	31	25	19	12	6	0	201 339
22 158	146	140	134	128	122	116	109	103	97	91	84	78	71	65	59	52	46	39	33	26	20	13	7	0	202 338
23 157	153	146	140	134	127	121	114	108	101	94	88	81	74	68	61	54	48	41	34	27	20	14	7	0	203 337
24 156	159	152	146	139	132	126	119	112	105	98	91	84	78	71	64	57	50	42	35	28	21	14	7	0	204 336
25 155	165	158	151	144	137	130	123	116	109	102	95	88	81	73	66	59	51	44	37	29	22	15	7	0	205 335
26 154	171	164	157	150	143	135	128	121	113	106	99	91	84	76	69	61	53	46	38	31	23	15	8	0	206 334
27 153	177	170	163	155	148	140	133	125	117	110	102	94	87	79	71	63	55	47	40	32	24	16	8	0	207 333
28 152	183	176	168	160	153	145	137	129	121	113	106	98	89	81	73	65	57	49	41	33	25	16	8	0	208 332
29 151	189	181	174	166	158	150	142	133	125	117	109	101	92	84	76	67	59	51	42	34	25	17	8	0	209 331
30 150	195	187	179	171	163	154	146	138	129	121	112	104	95	87	78	70	61	52	44	35	26	17	9	0	210 330
31 149	201	193	184	176	168	159	150	142	133	124	116	107	98	89	80	72	63	54	45	36	27	18	9	0	211 329
32 148	207	198	190	181	172	164	155	146	137	128	119	110	101	92	83	74	65	55	46	37	28	18	9	0	212 328
33 147	213	204	195	186	177	168	159	150	141	132	122	113	104	94	85	76	66	57	47	38	28	19	9	0	213 327
34 146	218	209	200	191	182	173	163	154	145	135	126	116	107	97	87	78	68	58	49	39	29	19	10	0	214 326
35 145	224	215	205	196	187	177	168	158	148	139	129	119	109	100	90	80	70	60	50	40	30	20	10	0	215 325
36 144	229	220	210	201	191	181	172	162	152	142	132	122	112	102	92	82	72	61	51	41	31	20	10	0	216 324
37 143	235	225	215	206	196	186	176	166	156	145	135	125	115	104	94	84	73	63	52	42	31	21	10	0	217 323
38 142	240	230	220	210	200	190	180	170	159	149	138	128	117	107	96	86	75	64	54	43	32	21	11	0	218 322
39 141	246	236	225	215	205	194	184	173	163	152	141	131	120	109	98	87	77	66	55	44	33	22	11	0	219 321
40 140	251	241	230	220	209	198	188	177	166	155	144	134	123	112	100	89	78	67	56	45	34	22	11	0	220 320
41 139	256	246	235	224	213	203	192	181	170	159	147	136	125	114	103	91	80	69	57	46	34	23	11	0	221 319
42 138	261	250	240	229	218	207	195	184	173	162	150	139	128	116	105	93	81	70	58	47	35	23	12	0	222 318
43 137	266	255	244	233	222	211	199	188	176	165	153	142	130	118	107	95	83	71	59	48	36	24	12	0	223 317
44 136	271	260	249	237	226	214	203	191	180	168	156	144	132	121	109	97	85	73	60	48	36	24	12	0	224 316
45 135	276	265	253	242	230	218	207	195	183	171	159	147	135	123	111	98	86	74	62	49	37	25	12	0	225 315
46 134	281	269	258	246	234	222	210	198	186	174	162	149	137	125	112	100	88	75	63	50	38	25	13	0	226 314
47 133	285	274	262	250	238	226	214	201	189	177	164	152	139	127	114	102	89	76	64	51	38	25	13	0	227 313
48 132	290	278	266	254	242	229	217	205	192	180	167	154	142	129	116	103	90	78	65	52	39	26	13	0	228 312
49 131	295	282	270	258	245	233	220	208	195	182	170	157	144	131	118	105	92	79	66	53	39	26	13	0	229 311
50 130	299	287	274	262	249	236	224	211	198	185	172	159	146	133	120	107	93	80	67	53	40	27	13	0	230 310
51 129	303	291	278	266	253	240	227	214	201	188	175	161	148	135	121	108	95	81	68	54	41	27	14	0	231 309
52 128	308	295	282	269	256	243	230	217	204	190	177	164	150	137	123	110	96	82	69	55	41	27	14	0	232 308
53 127	312	299	286	273	260	247	233	220	206	193	179	166	152	139	125	111	97	83	70	56	42	28	14	0	233 307
54 126	316	303	290	276	263	250	236	223	209	196	182	168	154	140	126	112	98	84	70	56	42	28	14	0	234 306
55 125	320	307	293	280	266	253	239	226	212	198	184	170	156	142	128	114	100	86	71	57	43	29	14	0	235 305
56 124	324	310	297	283	270	256	242	228	214	200	186	172	158	144	130	115	101	87	72	58	43	29	14	0	236 304
57 123	327	314	300	287	273	259	245	231	217	203	188	174	160	145	131	117	102	88	73	58	44	29	15	0	237 303
58 122	331	317	304	290	276	262	248	234	219	205	191	176	162	147	133	118	103	89	74	59	44	30	15	0	238 302
59 121	335	321	307	293	279	265	250	236	222	207	193	178	163	149	134	119	104	90	75	60	45	30	15	0	239 301
60 120	338	324	310	296	282	267	253	238	224	209	195	180	165	150	135	120	105	90	75	60	45	30	15	0	240 300
61 119	341	327	313	299	284	270	255	241	226	211	197	182	167	152	137	122	106	91	76	61	46	30	15	0	241 299
62 118	345	330	316	302	287	273	258	243	228	213	198	183	168	153	138	123	107	92	77	62	46	31	15	0	242 298
63 117	348	333	319	304	290	275	260	245	230	215	200	185	170	155	139	124	108	93	78	62	47	31	16	0	243 297
64 116	351	336	322	307	292	277	263	247	232	217	202	187	171	156	140	125	109	94	78	63	47	31	16	0	244 296
65 115	354	339	324	310	295	280	265	250	234	219	204	188	173	157	142	126	110	95	79	63	47	32	16	0	245 295
66 114	357	342	327	312	297	282	267	252	236	221	205	190	174	158	143	127	111	95	80	64	48	32	16	0	246 294
67 113	359	344	330	315	299	284	269	253	238	222	207	191	175	160	144	128	112	96	80	64	48	32	16	0	247 293
68 112	362	347	332	317	302	286	271	255	240	224	208	193	177	161	145	129	113	97	81	65	48	32	16	0	248 292
69 111	364	349	334	319	304	288	273	257	241	226	210	194	178	162	146	130	114	97	81	65	49	33	16	0	249 291
70 110	367	352	336	321	306	290	274	259	243	227	211	195	179	163	147	131	114	98	82	65	49	33	16	0	250 290
71 109	369	354	339	323	308	292	276	260	244	229	212	196	180	164	148	131	115	99	82	66	49	33	16	0	251 289
72 108	371	356	340	325	309	294	278	262	246	230	214	198	181	165	149	132	116	99	83	66	50	33	17	0	252 288
73 107	373	358	342	327	311	295	279	263	247	231	215	199	182	166	149	133	116	100	83	67	50	33	17	0	253 287
74 106	375	360	344	328	313	297	281	265	249	232	216	200	183	167	150	134	117	100	84	67	50	34	17	0	254 286
75 105	377	361	346	330	314	298	282	266	250	233	217	201	184	168	151	134	118	101	84	67	51	34	17	0	255 285
76 104	379	363	347	332	316	300	283	267	251	235	218	202	185	168	152	135	118	101	84	68	51	34	17	0	256 284
77 103	380	365	349	333	317	301	285	268	252	235	219	202	186	169	152	135	119	102	85	68	51	34	17	0	257 283
78 102	382	366	350	334	318	302	286	269	253	236	220	203	186	170	153	136	119	102	85	68	51	34	17	0	258 282
79 101	383	367	351	335	319	303	287	270	254	237	221	204	187	170	153	136	120	103	85	68	51	34	17	0	259 281
80 100	384	369	353	336	320	304	288	271	255	238	221	205	188	171	154	137	120	103	86	69	51	34	17	0	260 280
81 99	386	370	354	337	321	305	288	272	255	239	222	205	188	171	154	137	120	103	86	69	52	34	17	0	261 279
82 98	387	371	355	338	322	306	289	273	256	239	223	206	189	172	155	138	121	103	86	69	52	35	17	0	262 278
83 97	387	371	355	339	323	306	290	273	257	240	223	206	189	172	155	138	121	104	86	69	52	35	17	0	263 277
84 96	388	372	356	340	323	307	290	274	257	240	223	207	190	173	155	138	121	104	87	69	52	35	17	0	264 276
85 95	389	373	357	340	324	308	291	274	258	241	224	207	190	173	156	139	121	104	87	69	52	35	17	0	265 275
86 94	389	373	357	341	324	308	291	275	258	241	224	207	190	173	156	139	121	104	87	70	52	35	17	0	266 274
87 93	390	374	358	341	325	308	292	275	258	241	224	207	190	173	156	139	122	104	87	70	52	35	17	0	267 273
88 92	390	374	358	341	325	309	292	275	258	242	225	208	191	173	156	139	122	104	87	70	52	35	17	0	268 272
89 91	390	374	358	342	325	309	292	275	259	242	225	208	191	173	156	139	122	104	87	70	52	35	17	0	269 271
90 90	390	374	358	342	325	309	292	275	259	242	225	208	191	173	156	139	122	104	87	70	52	35	17	0	270 270
LHA/AZ	23°	22°	21°	20°	19°	18°	17°	16°	15°	14°	13°	12°	11°	10°	9°	8°	7°	6°	5°	4°	3°	2°	1°	0°	LHA/AZ

Declination or Altitude

QUADRANT SOLUTION

AZIMUTH DIAGRAM NORTH LATITUDES

LHA 0° - 180°(WEST)

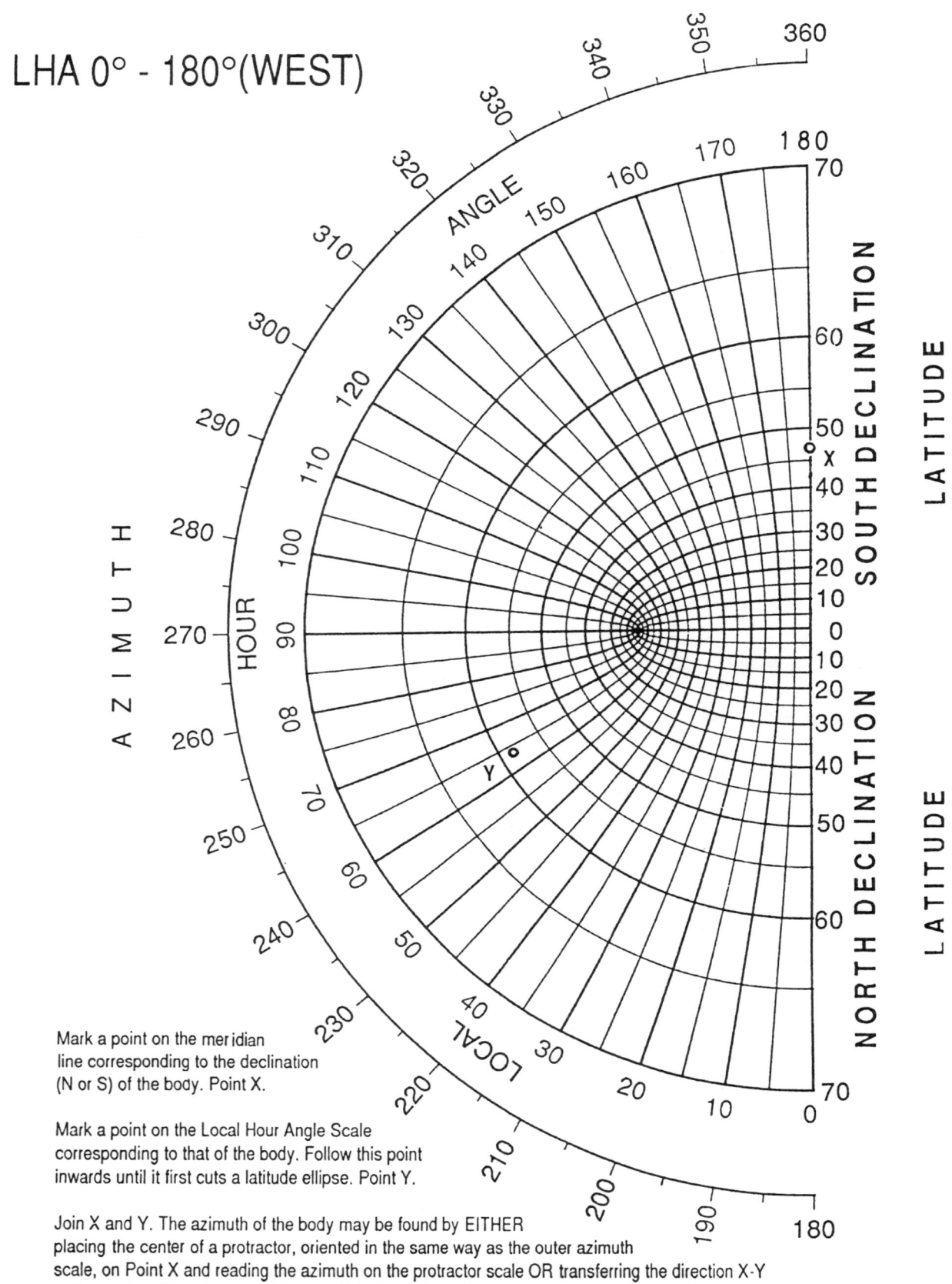

Mark a point on the meridian line corresponding to the declination (N or S) of the body. Point X.

Mark a point on the Local Hour Angle Scale corresponding to that of the body. Follow this point inwards until it first cuts a latitude ellipse. Point Y.

Join X and Y. The azimuth of the body may be found by EITHER placing the center of a protractor, oriented in the same way as the outer azimuth scale, on Point X and reading the azimuth on the protractor scale OR transferring the direction X-Y to the center of the diagram with a parallel ruler and reading the azimuth off the outer azimuth scale.

AZIMUTH DIAGRAM NORTH LATITUDES

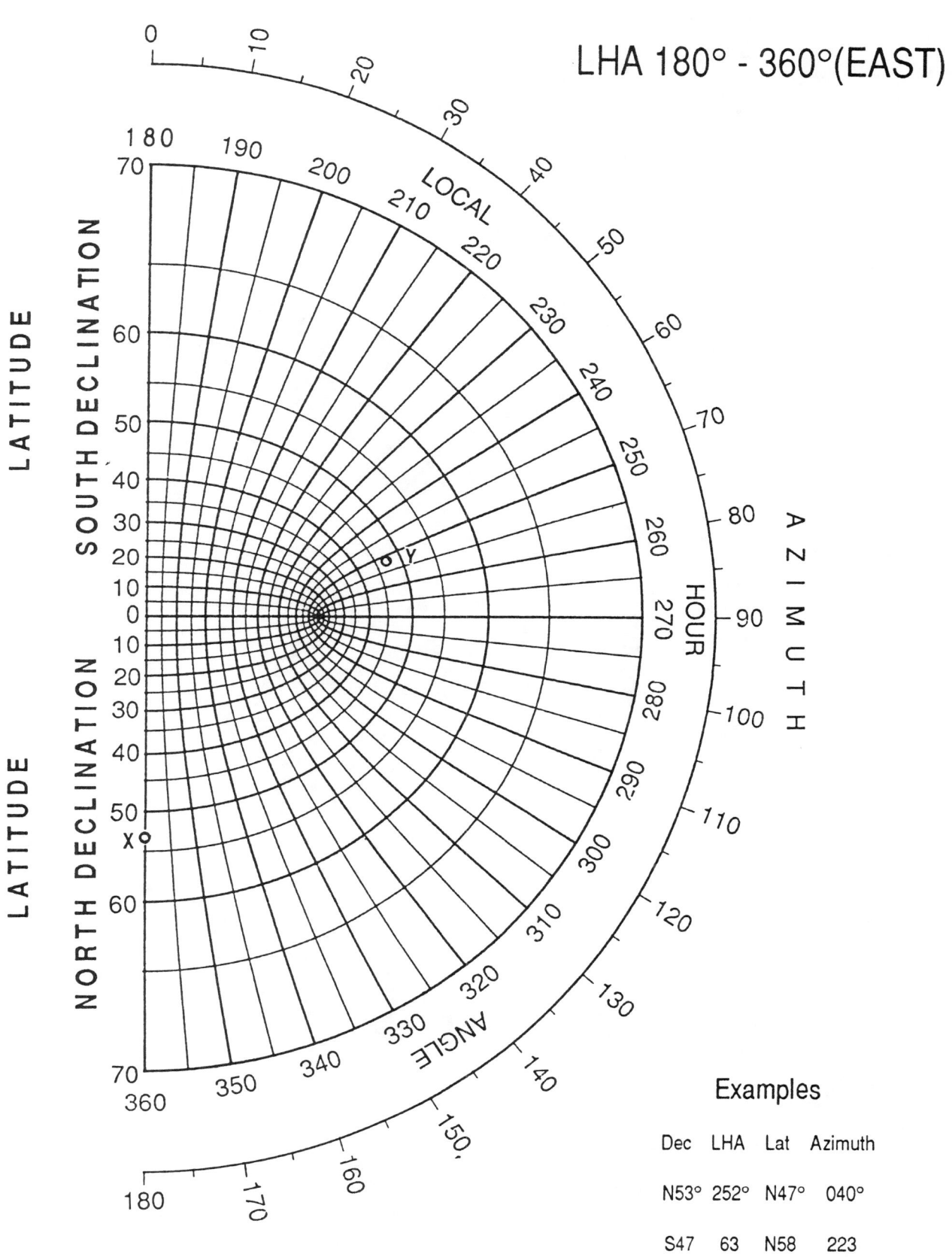

LHA 180° - 360°(EAST)

LOCAL HOUR ANGLE

SOUTH DECLINATION

NORTH DECLINATION

LATITUDE

AZIMUTH

Examples

Dec	LHA	Lat	Azimuth
N53°	252°	N47°	040°
S47	63	N58	223

AZIMUTH DIAGRAM SOUTH LATITUDES

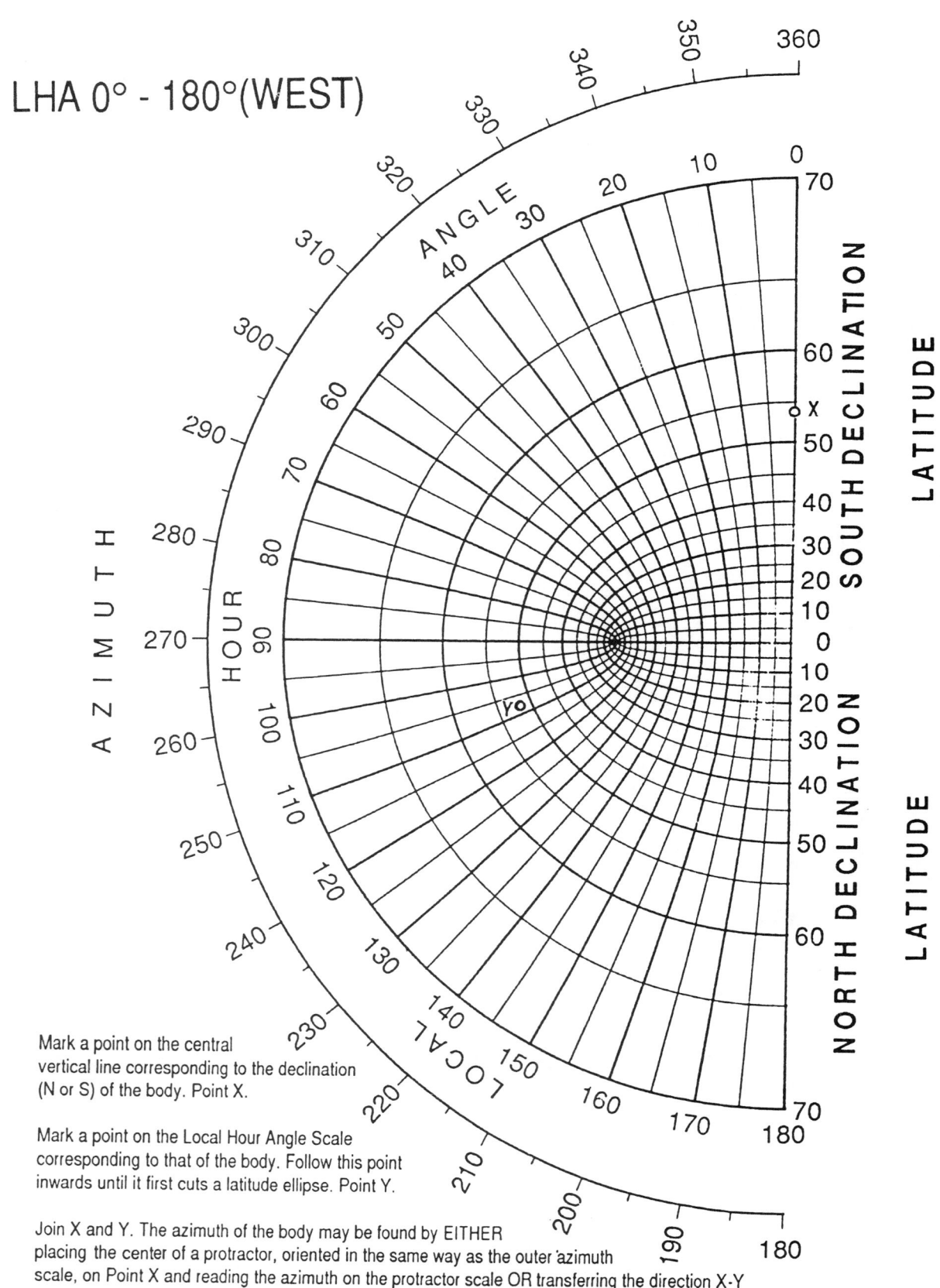

LHA 0° - 180°(WEST)

Mark a point on the central
vertical line corresponding to the declination
(N or S) of the body. Point X.

Mark a point on the Local Hour Angle Scale
corresponding to that of the body. Follow this point
inwards until it first cuts a latitude ellipse. Point Y.

Join X and Y. The azimuth of the body may be found by EITHER
placing the center of a protractor, oriented in the same way as the outer azimuth
scale, on Point X and reading the azimuth on the protractor scale OR transferring the direction X-Y
to the center of the diagram with a parallel ruler and reading the azimuth off the outer azimuth scale.

AZIMUTH DIAGRAM SOUTH LATITUDES

LHA 180° - 360°(EAST)

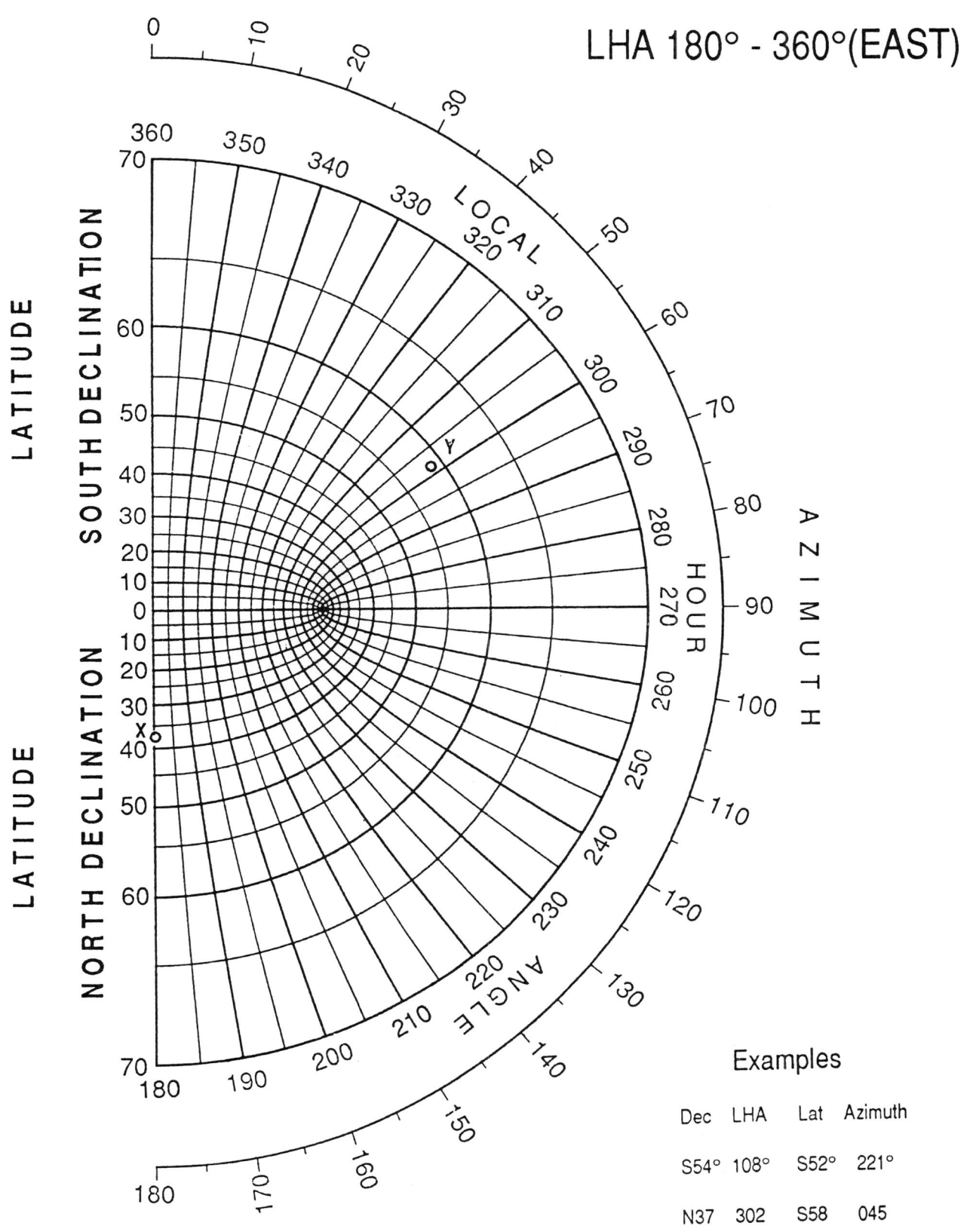

Examples

Dec	LHA	Lat	Azimuth
S54°	108°	S52°	221°
N37	302	S58	045

AZIMUTH AND LATITUDE FROM POLARIS

AZIMUTH OF POLARIS

LAT	LOCAL HOUR ANGLE OF ARIES										LAT
	0°	20°	40°	60°	80°	100°	120°	140°	160°	180°	
0°	000.5°	000.2°	000.0°	359.7°	359.5°	359.4°	359.3°	359.3°	359.4°	359.5°	0°
30	000.5	000.3	000.0	359.7	359.4	359.3	359.2	359.2	359.3	359.5	30
40	000.6	000.3	000.0	359.6	359.4	359.2	359.1	359.1	359.2	359.4	40
50	000.7	000.4	000.0	359.6	359.2	359.0	358.9	358.9	359.0	359.3	50
55	000.8	000.4	000.0	359.5	359.2	358.9	358.7	358.8	358.9	359.2	55
60	000.9	000.5	000.0	359.5	359.0	358.7	358.6	358.6	358.8	359.1	60

LAT	LOCAL HOUR ANGLE OF ARIES										LAT
	180°	200°	220°	240°	260°	280°	300°	320°	340°	360°	
0°	359.5°	359.8°	000.0°	000.3°	000.5°	000.6°	000.7°	000.7°	000.6°	000.5°	0°
30	359.5	359.7	000.0	000.3	000.6	000.7	000.8	000.8	000.7	000.5	30
40	359.4	359.7	000.0	000.4	000.6	000.8	000.9	000.9	000.8	000.6	40
50	359.3	359.6	000.0	000.4	000.8	001.0	001.1	001.1	001.0	000.7	50
55	359.2	359.6	000.0	000.5	000.8	001.1	001.3	001.2	001.1	000.8	55
60	359.1	359.5	000.0	000.5	001.0	001.3	001.4	001.4	001.2	000.9	60

DIP Corrn

	Corrn	
m	0'	ft
0.0	0	0
0.7	-1	2
2.0	-2	6
3.9	-3	13
6.5	-4	21
9.7	-5	32
13.6	-6	44
18.1	-7	59
23.3	-8	76
29.1	-9	95
	-10	

REFN Corrn

Alt	Corrn
0° 05'	-34'
0 10	-33
0 15	-32
0 20	-31
0 26	-30
0 32	-29
0 38	-28
0 45	-27
0 52	-26
0 59	-25
1 07	-24
1 16	-23
1 25	-22
1 35	-21
1 46	-20
1 58	-19
2 11	-18
2 25	-17
2 41	-16
2 58	-15
3 18	-14
3 41	-13
4 07	-12
4 38	-11
5 14	-10
5 59	-9
6 54	-8
8 06	-7
9 41	-6
11 56	-5
15 21	-4
21 10	-3
32 54	-2
62 22	-1
	0

ALTITUDE CORRECTION

LHA Aries	Corrn	LHA Aries	LHA Aries	Corrn	LHA Aries
129°05'	0'	307°47'	127°47'	0'	309°05'
130 23	+1	306 29	126 29	-1	310 23
131 41	+2	305 11	125 11	-2	311 41
133 00	+3	303 52	123 52	-3	313 00
134 19	+4	302 34	122 34	-4	314 19
135 37	+5	301 15	121 15	-5	315 37
136 56	+6	299 56	119 56	-6	316 56
138 16	+7	298 36	118 36	-7	318 16
139 35	+8	297 17	117 17	-8	319 35
140 55	+9	295 57	115 57	-9	320 55
142 16	+10	294 36	114 36	-10	322 16
143 37	+11	293 15	113 15	-11	323 37
144 58	+12	291 54	111 54	-12	324 58
146 20	+13	290 32	110 32	-13	326 20
147 43	+14	289 09	109 09	-14	327 43
149 06	+15	287 46	107 46	-15	329 06
150 30	+16	286 22	106 22	-16	330 30
151 55	+17	284 57	104 57	-17	331 55
153 21	+18	283 31	103 31	-18	333 21
154 48	+19	282 04	102 04	-19	334 48
156 16	+20	280 36	100 36	-20	336 16
157 45	+21	279 07	99 07	-21	337 45
159 16	+22	277 37	97 37	-22	339 16
160 47	+23	276 05	96 05	-23	340 47
162 21	+24	274 31	94 31	-24	342 21
163 56	+25	272 56	92 56	-25	343 56
165 33	+26	271 19	91 19	-26	345 33
167 13	+27	269 39	89 39	-27	347 13
168 54	+28	267 58	87 58	-28	348 54
170 39	+29	266 13	86 13	-29	350 39
172 26	+30	264 26	84 26	-30	352 26
174 17	+31	262 35	82 35	-31	354 17
176 11	+32	260 41	80 41	-32	356 11
178 10	+33	258 42	78 42	-33	358 10
180 14	+34	256 38	76 38	-34	0 14
182 23	+35	254 29	74 29	-35	2 23
184 40	+36	252 12	72 12	-36	4 40
187 06	+37	249 46	69 46	-37	7 06
189 43	+38	247 10	67 10	-38	9 43
192 33	+39	244 19	64 19	-39	12 33
195 44	+40	241 08	61 08	-40	15 44
199 24	+41	237 29	57 29	-41	19 24
203 55	+42	232 57	52 57	-42	23 55
210 41	+43	226 11	46 11	-43	30 41
	+44			-44	

CHANGE OF ALTITUDE IN 5 MINUTES OF TIME

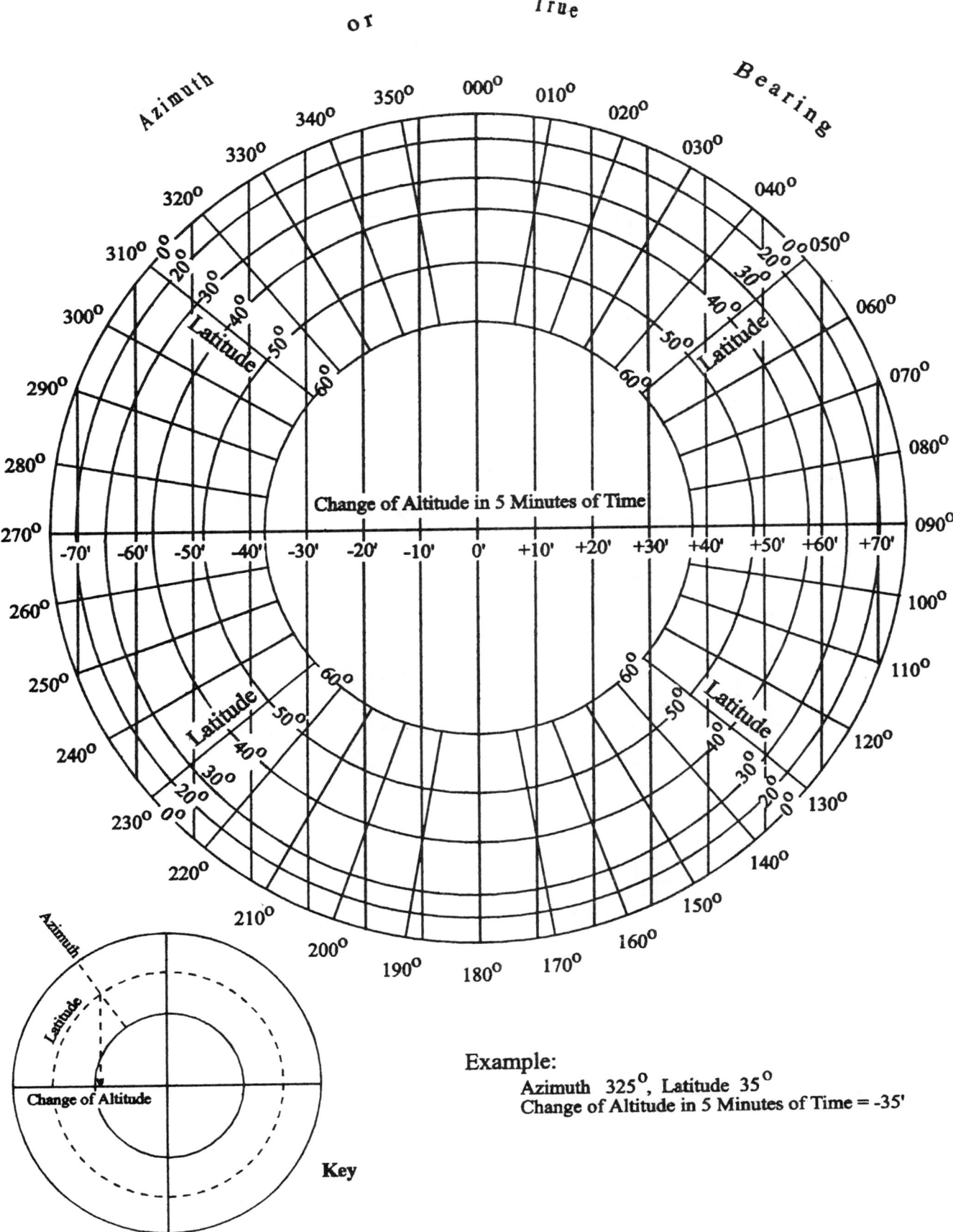

Example:
Azimuth 325°, Latitude 35°
Change of Altitude in 5 Minutes of Time = -35'

Key

SIGHT REDUCTION FORM

	Vega	Fomalhaut	Jupiter	Moon LL
1 Day and Date (Local)	Sunday 30th May	1999		
2 Body	Vega	Fomalhaut	Jupiter	Moon LL
3 Observed Watch Time	5^h 15^m 35^s	5^h 16^m 20^s	5^h 17^m 18^s	5^h 18^m 52^s
4 Watch Correction (+Slow, –Fast)	–15	–15	–15	–15
5 Standard Time	5 15 20	5 16 05	5 17 03	5 18 37
6 Time Zone (+West, –East)	+9	+9	+9	+9
7 GMT (h m s)	14 15 20	14 16 05	14 17 03	14 18 37
8 GMT (Degrees & Minutes)	213° 50' {247°04'}	214° 01' {247°04'}	214° 16' {223° 52'}	214° 39' {357° 23'}
9 GHA or (GHA – GMT) of body*	247 39 {+35}	247 39 {+35}	224 21 {v+48' Corrn +29'}	356 17 {v –170' Corrn –66'}
10 SHA of Star	80 46	15 36		
11 GHA Sum	542 15	477 16	438 37	570 56
12 DR Longitude (+East, –West)	–135 50	–135 50	–135 50	–135 50
13 Local Hour Angle (LHA)	46 25 10539	341 26 20648	302 47 8335 {N8°28'}	75 06 5604 {S17°57'}
14 DR Latitude (North or South)	N10 30 96	N10 30 96	N10 30 96 {d+4'}	N10 30 96 {d+29'}
15 Declination (North or South)	N38 47 1409	S29 37 792	N8 30 63 {Corrn 2'}	S17 49 278 {Corrn+12'}
16 Sum / Res	Sum 12044 Res 23808	Sum 21536 Res 4446	Sum 8494 Res 44564	Sum 5978 Res 6954
17 Latitude ~ Declination	28 17 11938	40 07	2 00 61	28 19
18 Computed Altitude	39 59 357 46	46 05 27972	33 37 44615	10 39 815 07
19 Sextant Altitude	39° 57'	45° 50'	33° 56'	9° 10'
20 Dip 2m	–2	–2	–2	–2
21 Sextant Correction (– On, + Off Arc)	+5	+5	+5	+5
22 Apparent Altitude	40 00	45 53	33 59	9 13 HP 54'
23 Altitude Correction	–1	–1	–1	+1 02
24 Observed Altitude	39 59	45 52	33 58	10 15
25 Intercept (Difference lines 18&24)**	0	13 A	21 T	24 A
26 Azimuth	312°	157°	087°	249°

* Interpolate from Tables: **Star:** GHA Aries, **Sun or Planet:** GHA, **Moon:** (GHA–GMT) at nearest preceding 6h of GMT.

** If the Observed Altitude is Greater than the Computed Altitude the Intercept is 'Toward', otherwise 'Away'.

UNIVERSAL PLOTTING SHEET

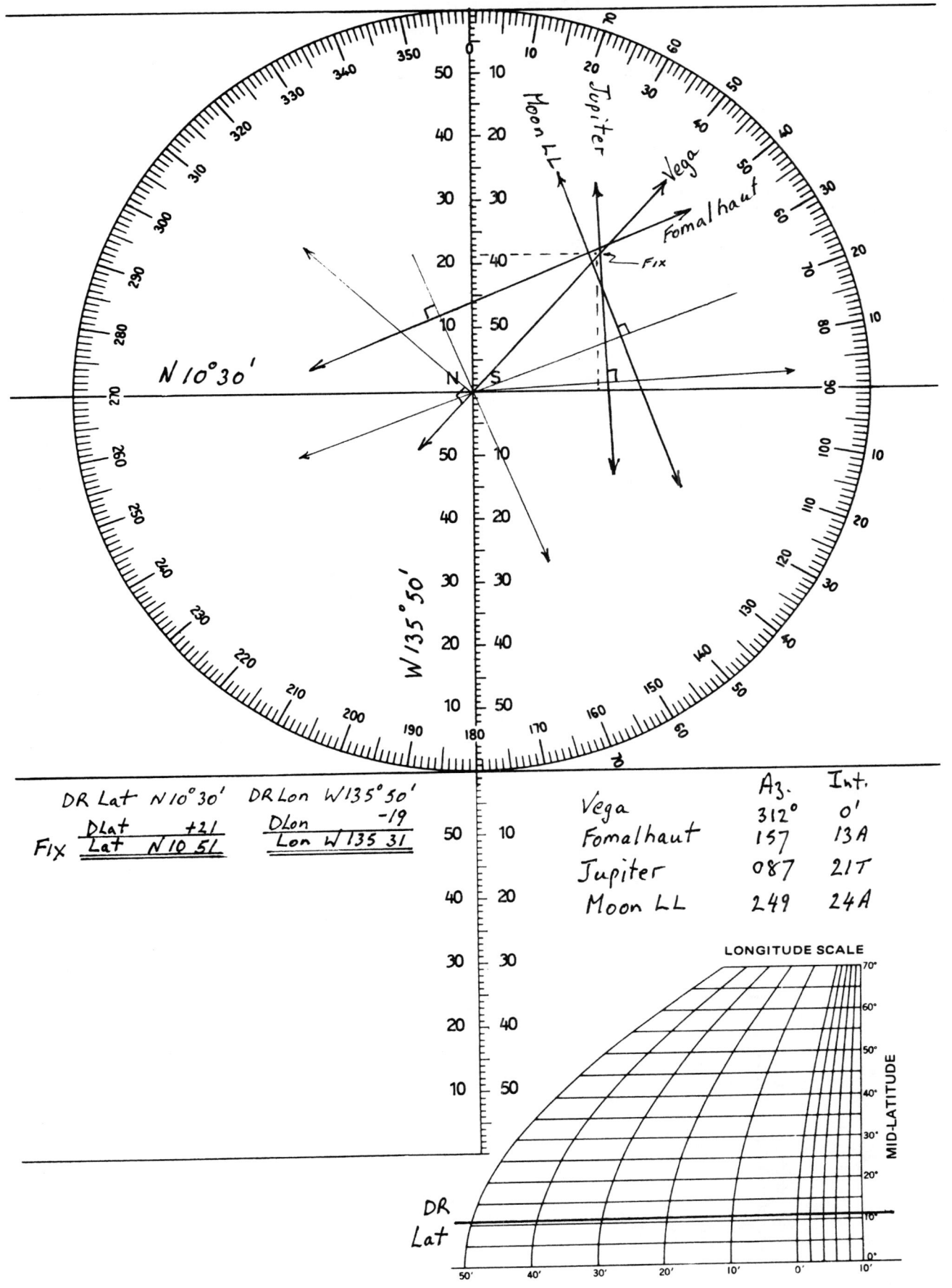

N 10°30'

W 135°50'

DR Lat N 10°30'   DR Lon W135°50'

Fix   DLat   +21   DLon   -19
       Lat   N 10 51   Lon   W 135 31

	Az.	Int.
Vega	312°	0'
Fomalhaut	157	13A
Jupiter	087	21T
Moon LL	249	24A

LONGITUDE SCALE

MID-LATITUDE

DR Lat

SIGHT REDUCTION FORM

#	Item	Units			
1	Day and Date (Local)		Thursday 15th July 1999		
2	Body		Sun LL	Sun LL	Sun LL
3	Observed Watch Time	h m s	8h 08m 30s	12h 14m 47s	15h 57m 14s
4	Watch Correction (+Slow, – Fast)		+1 10	+1 10	+1 10
5	Standard Time		8 09 40	12 15 57	15 58 24
6	Time Zone (+ West, – East)		–10	–10	–10
7	GMT (h m s)		22 09 40 (14th)	2 15 57	5 58 24
8	GMT (Degrees & Minutes)	° '	332° 25' { 178°34' v –2' Corrn –2' }	33° 59' { 178°32' v –1 Corrn 0' }	89° 36' { 178°32' v –1 Corrn 0' }
9	GHA or (GHA – GMT) of body*		178 32	178 32	178 32
10	SHA of Star				
11	GHA Sum		510 57	212 31	268 08
12	DR Longitude (+ East, – West)		+155 24	+155 41	+156 03
13	Local Hour Angle (LHA)		306 21 900 5 { N21°47' d –9' Corrn –8' }	8 12 29857 { N21°38' d –10' Corrn –1' }	64 11 715 8 { N21°38' d –10' Corrn –3' }
14	DR Latitude (North or South)		S33 15 1012	S33 04 1000	S32 52 987
15	Declination (North or South)		N21 39 414	N21 37 413	N21 35 411
16			Sum 10431 Res 31651	Sum 31270 Res 796	Sum 8556 Res 44104
17	Latitude ~ Declination		54 54 / 424 99	54 41 / 42190	54 27 / 41858
18	Computed Altitude		14 59 / 741 50	34 46 / 42986	8 04 / 8 59 62
19	Sextant Altitude	° '	14° 34'	34° 30'	8° 11'
20	Dip		–3	–3	–3
21	Sextant Correction (– On, + Off Arc)		–2	–2	–2
22	Apparent Altitude		14 29	34 25	8 06
23	Altitude Correction		+12	+15	+10
24	Observed Altitude		14 41	34 40	8 16
25	Intercept (Difference lines 18&24)**	° '	18 A	6 A	12 T
26	Azimuth	°	051°	351°	302°

* Interpolate from Tables: **Star**: GHA Aries, **Sun or Planet**: GHA, **Moon**: (GHA-GMT) at nearest preceding 6h of GMT.

** If the Observed Altitude is Greater than the Computed Altitude the Intercept is 'Toward', otherwise 'Away'.

UNIVERSAL PLOTTING SHEET

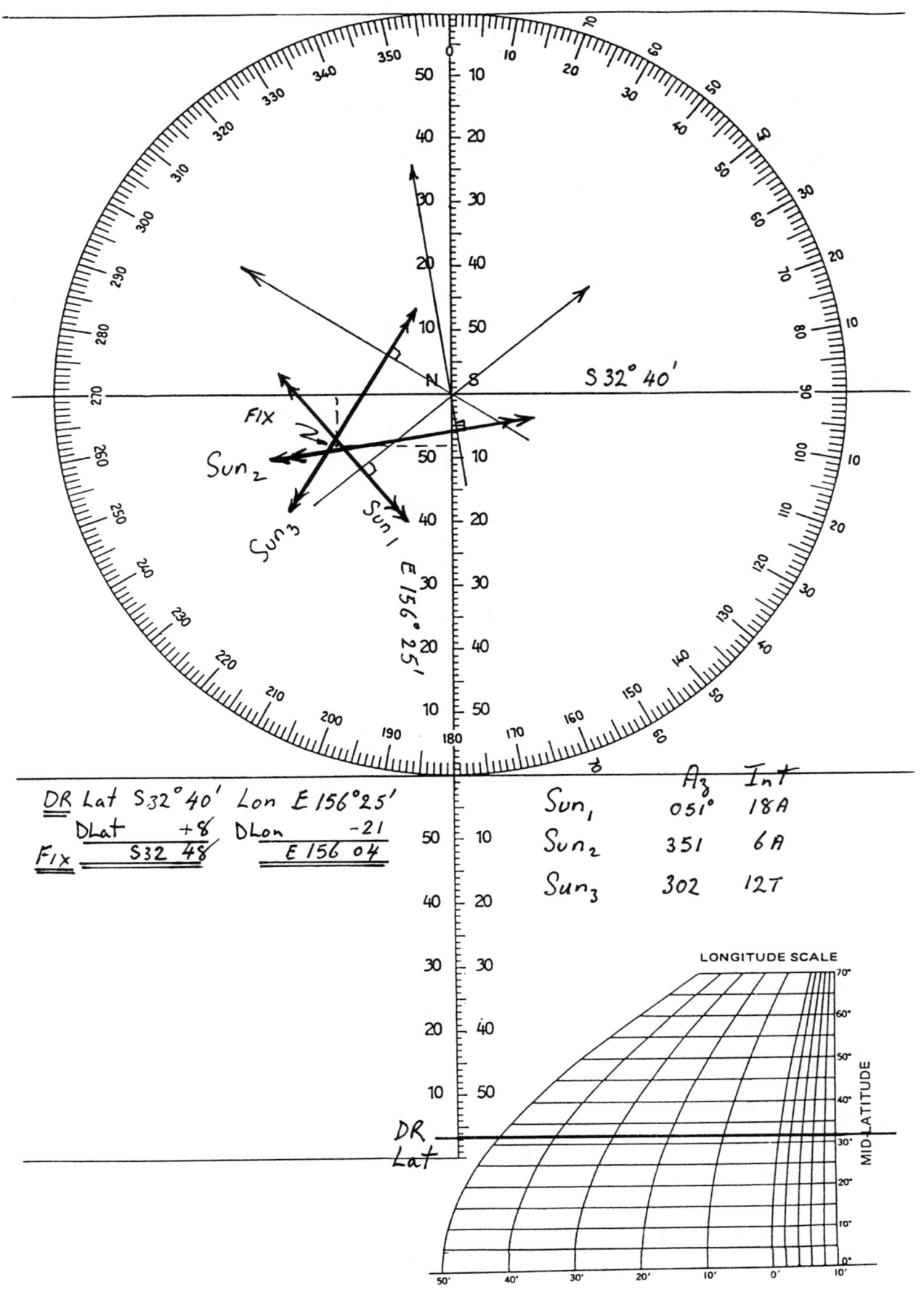

S 32° 40'

FIX

Sun₂

Sun₃

Sun 1   E 156° 25'

DR Lat S 32° 40' Lon E 156° 25'

DLat   +8   DLon   -21

FIX   S 32 48   E 156 04

	Az	Int
Sun₁	051°	18A
Sun₂	351	6A
Sun₃	302	12T

LONGITUDE SCALE

MID-LATITUDE

DR Lat

CALCULATOR INTERPOLATION

MOON INTERPOLATION

SUN AND PLANET INTERPOLATION

0ʰ - 12ʰ			12ʰ - 24ʰ		
h	m	F	h	m	F
0	00	0.00	12	00	0.50
0	15	0.00	12	15	0.51
0	30	0.00	12	30	0.52
0	45	0.00	12	45	0.53
1	00	0.04	13	00	0.54
1	15	0.05	13	15	0.55
1	30	0.06	13	30	0.56
1	45	0.07	13	45	0.57
2	00	0.08	14	00	0.58
2	15	0.09	14	15	0.59
2	30	0.10	14	30	0.60
2	45	0.11	14	45	0.61
3	00	0.13	15	00	0.63
3	15	0.14	15	15	0.64
3	30	0.15	15	30	0.65
3	45	0.16	15	45	0.66
4	00	0.17	16	00	0.67
4	15	0.18	16	15	0.68
4	30	0.19	16	30	0.69
4	45	0.20	16	45	0.70
5	00	0.21	17	00	0.71
5	15	0.22	17	15	0.72
5	30	0.23	17	30	0.73
5	45	0.24	17	45	0.74
6	00	0.25	18	00	0.75
6	15	0.26	18	15	0.76
6	30	0.27	18	30	0.77
6	45	0.28	18	45	0.78
7	00	0.29	19	00	0.79
7	15	0.30	19	15	0.80
7	30	0.31	19	30	0.81
7	45	0.32	19	45	0.82
8	00	0.33	20	00	0.83
8	15	0.34	20	15	0.84
8	30	0.35	20	30	0.85
8	45	0.36	20	45	0.86
9	00	0.38	21	00	0.88
9	15	0.39	21	15	0.89
9	30	0.40	21	30	0.90
9	45	0.41	21	45	0.91
10	00	0.42	22	00	0.92
10	15	0.43	22	15	0.93
10	30	0.44	22	30	0.94
10	45	0.45	22	45	0.95
11	00	0.46	23	00	0.96
11	15	0.47	23	15	0.97
11	30	0.48	23	30	0.98
11	45	0.49	23	45	0.99
12	00	0.50	24	00	1.00
h	m	F	h	m	F
0ʰ - 12ʰ			12ʰ - 24ʰ		

GMT or GMT- 6h or GMT - 12h or GMT -18h

0ʰ - 1ʰ			1ʰ - 2ʰ			2ʰ - 3ʰ			3ʰ - 4ʰ			4ʰ - 5ʰ			5ʰ - 6ʰ		
h	m	F	h	m	F	h	m	F	h	m	F	h	m	F	h	m	F
0	00	0.000	1	00	0.167	2	00	0.333	3	00	0.500	4	00	0.667	5	00	0.833
0	01	0.003	1	01	0.169	2	01	0.336	3	01	0.503	4	01	0.669	5	01	0.836
0	02	0.006	1	02	0.172	2	02	0.339	3	02	0.506	4	02	0.672	5	02	0.839
0	03	0.008	1	03	0.175	2	03	0.342	3	03	0.508	4	03	0.675	5	03	0.842
0	04	0.011	1	04	0.178	2	04	0.344	3	04	0.511	4	04	0.678	5	04	0.844
0	05	0.014	1	05	0.181	2	05	0.347	3	05	0.514	4	05	0.681	5	05	0.847
0	06	0.017	1	06	0.183	2	06	0.350	3	06	0.517	4	06	0.683	5	06	0.850
0	07	0.019	1	07	0.186	2	07	0.353	3	07	0.519	4	07	0.686	5	07	0.853
0	08	0.022	1	08	0.189	2	08	0.356	3	08	0.522	4	08	0.689	5	08	0.856
0	09	0.025	1	09	0.192	2	09	0.358	3	09	0.525	4	09	0.692	5	09	0.858
0	10	0.028	1	10	0.194	2	10	0.361	3	10	0.528	4	10	0.694	5	10	0.861
0	11	0.031	1	11	0.197	2	11	0.364	3	11	0.531	4	11	0.697	5	11	0.864
0	12	0.033	1	12	0.200	2	12	0.367	3	12	0.533	4	12	0.700	5	12	0.867
0	13	0.036	1	13	0.203	2	13	0.369	3	13	0.536	4	13	0.703	5	13	0.869
0	14	0.039	1	14	0.206	2	14	0.372	3	14	0.539	4	14	0.706	5	14	0.872
0	15	0.042	1	15	0.208	2	15	0.375	3	15	0.542	4	15	0.708	5	15	0.875
0	16	0.044	1	16	0.211	2	16	0.378	3	16	0.544	4	16	0.711	5	16	0.878
0	17	0.047	1	17	0.214	2	17	0.381	3	17	0.547	4	17	0.714	5	17	0.881
0	18	0.050	1	18	0.217	2	18	0.383	3	18	0.550	4	18	0.717	5	18	0.883
0	19	0.053	1	19	0.219	2	19	0.386	3	19	0.553	4	19	0.719	5	19	0.886
0	20	0.056	1	20	0.222	2	20	0.389	3	20	0.556	4	20	0.722	5	20	0.889
0	21	0.058	1	21	0.225	2	21	0.392	3	21	0.558	4	21	0.725	5	21	0.892
0	22	0.061	1	22	0.228	2	22	0.394	3	22	0.561	4	22	0.728	5	22	0.894
0	23	0.064	1	23	0.231	2	23	0.397	3	23	0.564	4	23	0.731	5	23	0.897
0	24	0.067	1	24	0.233	2	24	0.400	3	24	0.567	4	24	0.733	5	24	0.900
0	25	0.069	1	25	0.236	2	25	0.403	3	25	0.569	4	25	0.736	5	25	0.903
0	26	0.072	1	26	0.239	2	26	0.406	3	26	0.572	4	26	0.739	5	26	0.906
0	27	0.075	1	27	0.242	2	27	0.408	3	27	0.575	4	27	0.742	5	27	0.908
0	28	0.078	1	28	0.244	2	28	0.411	3	28	0.578	4	28	0.744	5	28	0.911
0	29	0.081	1	29	0.247	2	29	0.414	3	29	0.581	4	29	0.747	5	29	0.914
0	30	0.083	1	30	0.250	2	30	0.417	3	30	0.583	4	30	0.750	5	30	0.917
0	31	0.086	1	31	0.253	2	31	0.419	3	31	0.586	4	31	0.753	5	31	0.919
0	32	0.089	1	32	0.256	2	32	0.422	3	32	0.589	4	32	0.756	5	32	0.922
0	33	0.092	1	33	0.258	2	33	0.425	3	33	0.592	4	33	0.758	5	33	0.925
0	34	0.094	1	34	0.261	2	34	0.428	3	34	0.594	4	34	0.761	5	34	0.928
0	35	0.097	1	35	0.264	2	35	0.431	3	35	0.597	4	35	0.764	5	35	0.931
0	36	0.100	1	36	0.267	2	36	0.433	3	36	0.600	4	36	0.767	5	36	0.933
0	37	0.103	1	37	0.269	2	37	0.436	3	37	0.603	4	37	0.769	5	37	0.936
0	38	0.106	1	38	0.272	2	38	0.439	3	38	0.606	4	38	0.772	5	38	0.939
0	39	0.108	1	39	0.275	2	39	0.442	3	39	0.608	4	39	0.775	5	39	0.942
0	40	0.111	1	40	0.278	2	40	0.444	3	40	0.611	4	40	0.778	5	40	0.944
0	41	0.114	1	41	0.281	2	41	0.447	3	41	0.614	4	41	0.781	5	41	0.947
0	42	0.117	1	42	0.283	2	42	0.450	3	42	0.617	4	42	0.783	5	42	0.950
0	43	0.119	1	43	0.286	2	43	0.453	3	43	0.619	4	43	0.786	5	43	0.953
0	44	0.122	1	44	0.289	2	44	0.456	3	44	0.622	4	44	0.789	5	44	0.956
0	45	0.125	1	45	0.292	2	45	0.458	3	45	0.625	4	45	0.792	5	45	0.958
0	46	0.128	1	46	0.294	2	46	0.461	3	46	0.628	4	46	0.794	5	46	0.961
0	47	0.131	1	47	0.297	2	47	0.464	3	47	0.631	4	47	0.797	5	47	0.964
0	48	0.133	1	48	0.300	2	48	0.467	3	48	0.633	4	48	0.800	5	48	0.967
0	49	0.136	1	49	0.303	2	49	0.469	3	49	0.636	4	49	0.803	5	49	0.969
0	50	0.139	1	50	0.306	2	50	0.472	3	50	0.639	4	50	0.806	5	50	0.972
0	51	0.142	1	51	0.308	2	51	0.475	3	51	0.642	4	51	0.808	5	51	0.975
0	52	0.144	1	52	0.311	2	52	0.478	3	52	0.644	4	52	0.811	5	52	0.978
0	53	0.147	1	53	0.314	2	53	0.481	3	53	0.647	4	53	0.814	5	53	0.981
0	54	0.150	1	54	0.317	2	54	0.483	3	54	0.650	4	54	0.817	5	54	0.983
0	55	0.153	1	55	0.319	2	55	0.486	3	55	0.653	4	55	0.819	5	55	0.986
0	56	0.156	1	56	0.322	2	56	0.489	3	56	0.656	4	56	0.822	5	56	0.989
0	57	0.158	1	57	0.325	2	57	0.492	3	57	0.658	4	57	0.825	5	57	0.992
0	58	0.161	1	58	0.328	2	58	0.494	3	58	0.661	4	58	0.828	5	58	0.994
0	59	0.164	1	59	0.331	2	59	0.497	3	59	0.664	4	59	0.831	5	59	0.997
1	00	0.167	2	00	0.333	3	00	0.500	4	00	0.667	5	00	0.833	6	00	1.000
h	m	F	h	m	F	h	m	F	h	m	F	h	m	F	h	m	F
0ʰ - 1ʰ			1ʰ - 2ʰ			2ʰ - 3ʰ			3ʰ - 4ʰ			4ʰ - 5ʰ			5ʰ - 6ʰ		

SEXTANT ALTITUDE OBSERVATIONS

A L T I T U D E

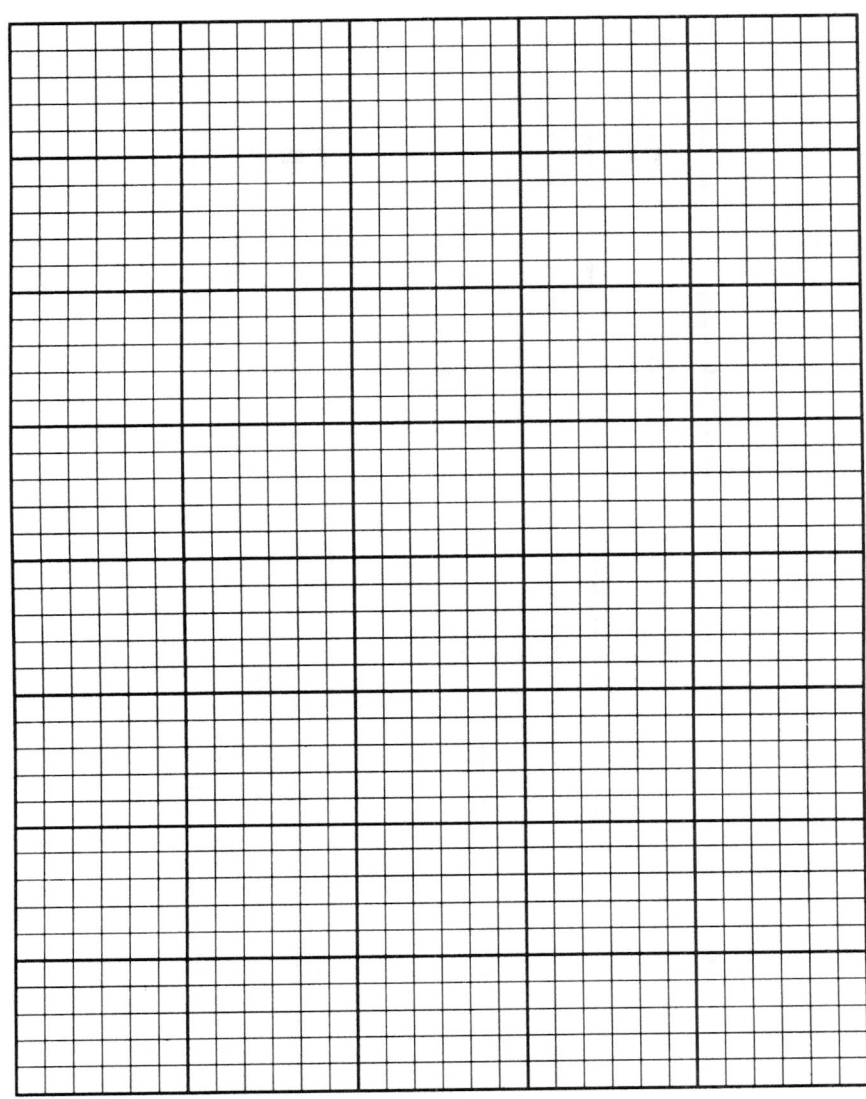

W A T C H   T I M E

Latitude: ....   **Azimuth:** ....   **Slope:** ....

Observation	Watch Time			Sextant Altitude		Remarks
	h	m	s	o	'	
1						
2						
3						
4						
5						
	h	m	s		o	'

Adopt: _____   _____

SIGHT REDUCTION FORM

#		
1	Day and Date (Local)	
2	Body	
3	Observed Watch Time	h m s
4	Watch Correction (+Slow, - Fast)	
5	Standard Time	
6	Time Zone (+ West, - East)	
7	GMT (h m s)	
8	GMT (Degrees & Minutes)	° '
9	GHA or (GHA - GMT) of body*	
10	SHA of Star	
11	GHA	Sum
12	DR Longitude (+ East, - West)	
13	Local Hour Angle (LHA)	
14	DR Latitude (North or South)	
15	Declination (North or South)	
16		Sum Res
17	Latitude ~ Declination	
18	Computed Altitude	
19	Sextant Altitude	° '
20	Dip	
21	Sextant Correction (- On, + Off Arc)	
22	Apparent Altitude	
23	Altitude Correction	
24	Observed Altitude	
25	Intercept (Difference lines 18&24)**	
26	Azimuth	°

* Interpolate from Tables: **Star**: GHA Aries, **Sun or Planet**: GHA, **Moon**: (GHA-GMT) at nearest preceding 6h of GMT.
** If the Observed Altitude is Greater than the Computed Altitude the Intercept is 'Toward', otherwise 'Away'.

UNIVERSAL PLOTTING SHEET

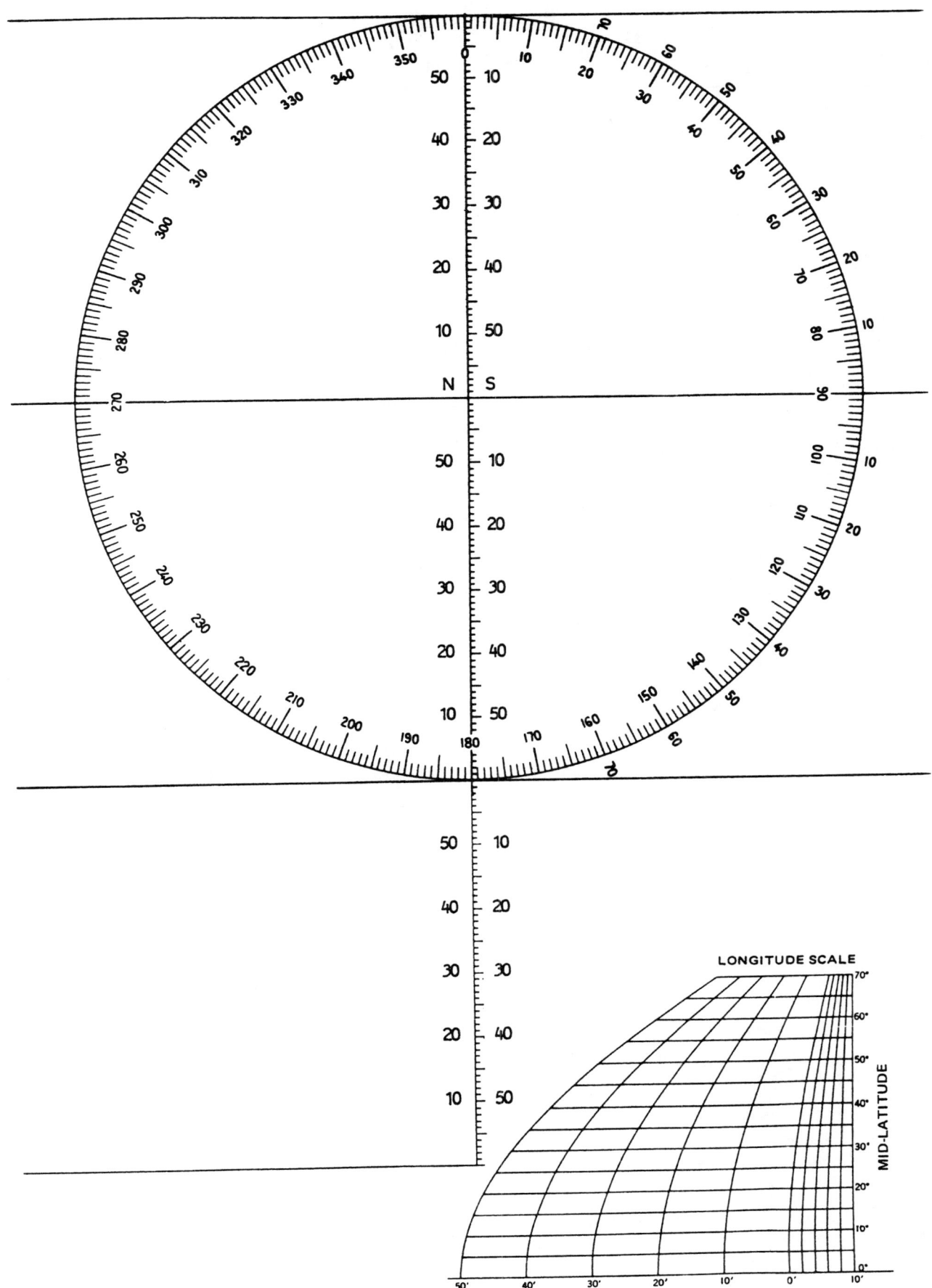

LONGITUDE SCALE

MID-LATITUDE

THE NAVIGATIONAL STARS

The following list contains basic information on 58 stars used for navigation during morning and evening twilight—that is, when it is dark enough to see the stars but light enough to see the horizon. Information includes the constellation in which the star is found, whether it is in the northern or southern sky, and its position relative to other stars.

Acamar One of two navigational stars in Eridanus (southern sky), Acamar is situated well to the west of Adhara, and lies halfway between Sirius (CMa) and Diphda (Cet).

Achernar One of two navigational stars in Eridanus (southern sky), Achernar lies about 70° west of Canopus (Car) about halfway between Canopus and Fomalhaut (PsA).

Acrux Acrux is the brightest and most southerly star in the Southern Cross, a constellation visible only south of latitude 20°N.

Adhara The second-brightest star in Canis Major (southern equatorial zone), Adhara lies about 10° south of Sirius, the Dog Star.

Aldebaran Lying at one end of a conspicuous "V" pattern in Taurus (northern equatorial zone), just below the cluster of stars known as the Pleiades, Aldebaran can be found by tracing a line northward from the three stars of Orion's Belt.

Alioth Part of Ursa Major (northern sky), Alioth is the innermost star of the Big Dipper's handle—the one closest to the actual dipper.

Alkaid The second-magnitude star in Ursa Major (northern sky), Alkaid is the outermost star in the handle of the Big Dipper.

Alnilam The middle of the three bright stars in Orion's belt (equatorial zone), Alnilam lies almost directly over the equator.

Al Na'ir A second magnitude star in Grus—the Crane (southern sky)—Al Na'ir lies about halfway between Fomalhaut (PsA) and Peacock (Pav).

Alphard With a name meaning the lonely one, Alphard is the brightest star in Hydra (equatorial zone). It lies just below the equator about midway between Gienah (Cor) and Procyon (CMi).

Alphecca The brightest star in Corona Borealis (the Northern Crown). Alphecca is located at the southern end of a line drawn from Polaris and Kochab [UMi].

Alpheratz The brightest star in Pegasus (northern equatorial zone), Alpheratz lies about halfway between Markab (Peg) and Hamal (Ari). It is one of four bright stars (with Markab, Algenib, and Scheat) that form the Square of Pegasus.

Altair The brightest star in Aquila (northern equatorial zone), Altair is the southern apex of the "summer triangle" formed with Deneb (Cyg) and Vega (Lyr), prominent in the northern sky in summer.

Ankaa A second-magnitude star in Phoenix (southern sky), Ankaa lies just south of a line between Acamar (Eri) and Fomalhaut (PsA).

Antares The brightest star in Scorpius (southern equatorial zone), Antares lies on a line extending from Acrux (Southern Cross) and Hadar (Cen).

Arcturus The second-brightest star in the northern sky, Arcturus is located in Boötes and can be found at the end of a long curve starting at the Big Dipper's handle (including Alioth and Alkaid). "Follow the arc to Arcturus."

Atria Atria is the brightest of the three stars at the southeast apex of the Triangulum Australis (Southern Triangle), which lies between Rigil Kentaurus (Cen) and Peacock (Pav).

Avior One of three navigational stars in Carina (southern sky), it lies north of a line between Miaplacidus and Canopus.

Bellatrix One of four navigational stars in Orion (equatorial zone), Bellatrix lies in the northern sky slightly south of Betelgeuse, or about "10 o'clock" relative to the axis of Orion's Belt.

Betelgeuse The northernmost and brightest of the stars in Orion (equatorial zone), Betelgeuse is at about "9 o'clock" relative to the axis of Orion's Belt.

Canopus The second-brightest star in the night sky, Canopus is one of three navigational stars in Carina (southern sky), with Avior and Miaplacidus. It lies about 36° south of Sirius—the Dog Star—the brightest star.

Capella A bright star in Auriga (northern sky), Capella is at the end of a line drawn from Bellatrix through Elnath.

Deneb The brightest star in the constellation Cygnus (the Swan; northern sky), Deneb is one of three stars comprising the "Summer Triangle"; the others are Vega (Lyr) and Altair (Aql).

Denebola The second brightest star in Leo (northern equatorial zone), Denebola lies just south of a line between Regulus (Leo) and Arcturus (Boö).

Diphda One of two navigational stars in Cetus (equatorial zone), Diphda lies below the equator on a line between Menkar (at the northern end of Cetus) and Fomalhaut (PsA).

Dubhe The brighter and northernmost of the Big Dipper's two pointer stars showing the way to Polaris (UMi), Dubhe is at the far edge of the Big Dipper.

Elnath The second brightest star in Taurus (northern equatorial zone) after Aldebaran, Elnath lies about halfway between Bellatrix (Ori) and Capella (Aur).

Eltanin The brightest star in Draco (northern sky), Eltanin lies about one-third the distance from Vega (Lyr) and Kochab (UMi).

Enif One of two navigational stars in Pegasus (northern equatorial zone), Enif is located just below the midway point of a line halfway between Altair (Aql) and Markab (Peg).

Fomalhaut Found in relative isolation in Piscis Austrinus (southern equatorial zone), Fomalhaut is at one corner of a trapezoid formed by Al Na'ir (Gru), Ankaa (Pho), and Diphda (Cet).

Gacrux The dimmer of two navigational stars in the Crux (the Southern Cross), Gacrux is found opposite Acrux at the northern end of the cross.

Gienah The brightest star in Corvus (southern equatorial zone), Gienah is at the end of a curve that runs from Arcturus (Boö) and Spica (Vir).

Hadar One of three navigational stars in Centaurus (southern sky), Hadar lies near Rigil Kentaurus between that star and the Southern Cross.

Hamal Located in Aries (northern equatorial zone), Hamal lies halfway between Aldebaran (Tau) and Alpheratz (Peg).

Kaus Australis One of two navigational stars in Sagittarius (southern equatorial zone), Kaus Australis lies just south of a line from Nunki (Sag) to Shaula (Sco).

Kochab The brightest star in the Little Dipper (northern sky), Kochab is the nearest bright star to Polaris.

Markab One of two navigational stars in Pegasus (northern equatorial zone), Markab lies south of a line between Enif (Peg) and Alpheratz (Peg) and is in the southwest corner of the "Square of Pegasus" opposite Alpheratz (Peg).

Menkar One of two navigational stars in Cetus (equatorial zone), Menkar lies north of the equator at the end of a line drawn from Procyon (CMi) and Aldebaran (Tau).

Menkent One of three navigational stars in Centaurus (southern sky), Menkent lies well north of Hadar and Rigil Kentaurus.

Miaplacidus The southernmost of the three navigational stars (with Canopus and Avior) in Carina (southern sky), Miaplacidus lies about halfway between Canopus and Rigil Kentaurus (Cen).

Mirfak The brightest star in Perseus, Mirfak lies near the intersection of lines between Menkar (Cet) and Polaris (UMi), and Aldebaran (Tau) and Schedar (Cas).

Nunki The dimmer of the two navigational stars in Sagittarius (southern equatorial zone), Nunki lies north of Kaus Australis on a line between Antares (Sco) and Fomalhaut (PsA).

Peacock The brightest star in Pavo (the Peacock; southern sky), Peacock lies between Al Na'ir (Gru) and Atria (TriA).

Polaris The Pole Star, Polaris is at the end of the handle of the little dipper (Ursa Minor). It is easily found by tracing a line through the Big Dipper's pointer stars Merak and Dubhe (UMa). The altitude of Polaris is within one degree of the observer's latitude.

Pollux The brighter of the Gemini twins in the northern equatorial zone (the other is Castor), Pollux lies nearly halfway between the Big Dipper (UMa) and Orion.

Procyon Known as the Little Dog Star from its position in Canis Minor (northern equatorial zone), Procyon is located about halfway between Sirius—the Dog Star, in Canis Major—and Castor and Pollux (Gem).

Rasalhague The brightest star in Ophiuchus (the Serpent Bearer, northern equatorial zone), Rasalhague lies across the Milky Way from Altair (Aql).

Regulus The brighter of the two navigational stars in Leo (northern equatorial zone), Regulus lies between Denebola (Leo) and Procyon (CMi).

Rigel The most southerly of the four navigational stars in Orion (equatorial zone), Rigel lies diagonally across the belt from Betelgeuse.

Rigil Kentaurus One of three navigational stars (with Hadar and Menkent) in Centaurus, Rigil Kentaurus is the third-brightest star in the night sky. Rigil Kentaurus and Hadar are Southern Cross pointer stars.

Sabik One of two navigational stars in Ophiuchus (equatorial zone), Sabik lies in the southern sky on a line between Antares (Sco) and Rasalhague (Oph).

Schedar The brightest star in Cassiopeia (northern sky), Schedar lies on the far side of a line drawn from Alioth (UMa) and Polaris (UMi).

Shaula One of two navigational stars in Scorpius (southern sky), Shaula lies south of a line between Antares (Sco) and Kaus Australis (Sag).

Sirius Sirius—the Dog Star—is the brightest in the night sky. The three stars in Orion's belt point down to Sirius.

Spica The brightest star in Virgo (southern equatorial zone), Spica can be found by following the arc from the handle of the Big Dipper down through Arcturus (Boö).

Suhail The brightest star in Vela (southern sky), Suhail lies at the end of an arc drawn from Orion's Belt through Sirius (CMa).

Vega The brightest and most beautiful star in the northern summer sky, Vega (one of the stars in Lyra) forms the summer triangle with Altair (Aql) and Deneb (Cyg).

Zubenelgenubi The brightest star in Libra (southern equatorial zone), Zubenelgenubi lies on a line between Spica (Vir) and Antares (Sco).

INDEX

INDEX

CONVERSION OF TIME TO ARC

0ʰ - 4ʰ		4ʰ - 8ʰ		8ʰ - 12ʰ		12ʰ - 16ʰ		16ʰ - 20ʰ		20ʰ - 24ʰ		0ᵐ - 4ᵐ	
0ʰ00ᵐ	0°	4ʰ00ᵐ	60°	8ʰ00ᵐ	120°	12ʰ00ᵐ	180°	16ʰ00ᵐ	240°	20ʰ00ᵐ	300°	0ᵐ00ˢ	0'
0 04	1	4 04	61	8 04	121	12 04	181	16 04	241	20 04	301	0 04	1
0 08	2	4 08	62	8 08	122	12 08	182	16 08	242	20 08	302	0 08	2
0 12	3	4 12	63	8 12	123	12 12	183	16 12	243	20 12	303	0 12	3
0 16	4	4 16	64	8 16	124	12 16	184	16 16	244	20 16	304	0 16	4
0 20	5	4 20	65	8 20	125	12 20	185	16 20	245	20 20	305	0 20	5
0 24	6	4 24	66	8 24	126	12 24	186	16 24	246	20 24	306	0 24	6
0 28	7	4 28	67	8 28	127	12 28	187	16 28	247	20 28	307	0 28	7
0 32	8	4 32	68	8 32	128	12 32	188	16 32	248	20 32	308	0 32	8
0 36	9	4 36	69	8 36	129	12 36	189	16 36	249	20 36	309	0 36	9
0 40	10	4 40	70	8 40	130	12 40	190	16 40	250	20 40	310	0 40	10
0 44	11	4 44	71	8 44	131	12 44	191	16 44	251	20 44	311	0 44	11
0 48	12	4 48	72	8 48	132	12 48	192	16 48	252	20 48	312	0 48	12
0 52	13	4 52	73	8 52	133	12 52	193	16 52	253	20 52	313	0 52	13
0 56	14	4 56	74	8 56	134	12 56	194	16 56	254	20 56	314	0 56	14
1 00	15	5 00	75	9 00	135	13 00	195	17 00	255	21 00	315	1 00	15
1 04	16	5 04	76	9 04	136	13 04	196	17 04	256	21 04	316	1 04	16
1 08	17	5 08	77	9 08	137	13 08	197	17 08	257	21 08	317	1 08	17
1 12	18	5 12	78	9 12	138	13 12	198	17 12	258	21 12	318	1 12	18
1 16	19	5 16	79	9 16	139	13 16	199	17 16	259	21 16	319	1 16	19
1 20	20	5 20	80	9 20	140	13 20	200	17 20	260	21 20	320	1 20	20
1 24	21	5 24	81	9 24	141	13 24	201	17 24	261	21 24	321	1 24	21
1 28	22	5 28	82	9 28	142	13 28	202	17 28	262	21 28	322	1 28	22
1 32	23	5 32	83	9 32	143	13 32	203	17 32	263	21 32	323	1 32	23
1 36	24	5 36	84	9 36	144	13 36	204	17 36	264	21 36	324	1 36	24
1 40	25	5 40	85	9 40	145	13 40	205	17 40	265	21 40	325	1 40	25
1 44	26	5 44	86	9 44	146	13 44	206	17 44	266	21 44	326	1 44	26
1 48	27	5 48	87	9 48	147	13 48	207	17 48	267	21 48	327	1 48	27
1 52	28	5 52	88	9 52	148	13 52	208	17 52	268	21 52	328	1 52	28
1 56	29	5 56	89	9 56	149	13 56	209	17 56	269	21 56	329	1 56	29
2 00	30	6 00	90	10 00	150	14 00	210	18 00	270	22 00	330	2 00	30
2 04	31	6 04	91	10 04	151	14 04	211	18 04	271	22 04	331	2 04	31
2 08	32	6 08	92	10 08	152	14 08	212	18 08	272	22 08	332	2 08	32
2 12	33	6 12	93	10 12	153	14 12	213	18 12	273	22 12	333	2 12	33
2 16	34	6 16	94	10 16	154	14 16	214	18 16	274	22 16	334	2 16	34
2 20	35	6 20	95	10 20	155	14 20	215	18 20	275	22 20	335	2 20	35
2 24	36	6 24	96	10 24	156	14 24	216	18 24	276	22 24	336	2 24	36
2 28	37	6 28	97	10 28	157	14 28	217	18 28	277	22 28	337	2 28	37
2 32	38	6 32	98	10 32	158	14 32	218	18 32	278	22 32	338	2 32	38
2 36	39	6 36	99	10 36	159	14 36	219	18 36	279	22 36	339	2 36	39
2 40	40	6 40	100	10 40	160	14 40	220	18 40	280	22 40	340	2 40	40
2 44	41	6 44	101	10 44	161	14 44	221	18 44	281	22 44	341	2 44	41
2 48	42	6 48	102	10 48	162	14 48	222	18 48	282	22 48	342	2 48	42
2 52	43	6 52	103	10 52	163	14 52	223	18 52	283	22 52	343	2 52	43
2 56	44	6 56	104	10 56	164	14 56	224	18 56	284	22 56	344	2 56	44
3 00	45	7 00	105	11 00	165	15 00	225	19 00	285	23 00	345	3 00	45
3 04	46	7 04	106	11 04	166	15 04	226	19 04	286	23 04	346	3 04	46
3 08	47	7 08	107	11 08	167	15 08	227	19 08	287	23 08	347	3 08	47
3 12	48	7 12	108	11 12	168	15 12	228	19 12	288	23 12	348	3 12	48
3 16	49	7 16	109	11 16	169	15 16	229	19 16	289	23 16	349	3 16	49
3 20	50	7 20	110	11 20	170	15 20	230	19 20	290	23 20	350	3 20	50
3 24	51	7 24	111	11 24	171	15 24	231	19 24	291	23 24	351	3 24	51
3 28	52	7 28	112	11 28	172	15 28	232	19 28	292	23 28	352	3 28	52
3 32	53	7 32	113	11 32	173	15 32	233	19 32	293	23 32	353	3 32	53
3 36	54	7 36	114	11 36	174	15 36	234	19 36	294	23 36	354	3 36	54
3 40	55	7 40	115	11 40	175	15 40	235	19 40	295	23 40	355	3 40	55
3 44	56	7 44	116	11 44	176	15 44	236	19 44	296	23 44	356	3 44	56
3 48	57	7 48	117	11 48	177	15 48	237	19 48	297	23 48	357	3 48	57
3 52	58	7 52	118	11 52	178	15 52	238	19 52	298	23 52	358	3 52	58
3 56	59	7 56	119	11 56	179	15 56	239	19 56	299	23 56	359	3 56	59
4 00	60	8 00	120	12 00	180	16 00	240	20 00	300	24 00	360	4 00	60
0ʰ - 4ʰ		4ʰ - 8ʰ		8ʰ - 12ʰ		12ʰ - 16ʰ		16ʰ - 20ʰ		20ʰ - 24ʰ		0ᵐ - 4ᵐ	